INTERNATIONAL LAW
AND REPARATIONS
The Inter-American System

INTERNATIONAL LAW AND REPARATIONS

The Inter-American System

Claudio Grossman

Agustina del Campo

Mina A. Trudeau

CLARITY PRESS

© 2018 Claudio Grossman, Agustine del Campo, Mina A. Trudeau
ISBN: 9780997896572
EBOOK ISBN: 9780997896589

In-house editor: Diana G. Collier
Cover: R. Jordan P. Santos

Library of Congress Cataloging-in-Publication Data

Names: Grossman, Claudio, author. | Campo, Agustina del, author. | Trudeau,
  Mina A., author.
Title: International law and reparations : the Inter-American system / By
  Claudio Grossman, Agustina del Campo, Mina A. Trudeau.
Description: Atlanta, GA : Clarity Press, Inc., 2018. | Includes
  bibliographical references and index.
Identifiers: LCCN 2017022409 (print) | LCCN 2017022525 (ebook) | ISBN
  9780997896589 | ISBN 9780997896572 (alk. paper)
Subjects: LCSH: Inter-American Court of Human Rights. | Reparation (Criminal
  justice)--America--Cases. | War reparations--America--Cases. | American
  Convention on Human Rights (1969 November 22) | War victims--Legal status,
  laws, etc.--America--Cases. | LCGFT: Casebooks.
Classification: LCC KDZ579.I5 (ebook) | LCC KDZ579.I5 G76 2017 (print) | DDC
  341.6/6--dc23
LC record available at https://lccn.loc.gov/2017022409

Clarity Press, Inc.
2625 Piedmont Rd. NE, Ste. 56
Atlanta, GA. 30324 , USA
http://www.claritypress.com

TABLE OF CONTENTS

CHAPTER TWO
COMPENSATION FOR DAMAGES

CHAPTER THREE
BEYOND COMPENSATION: RESTITUTIO IN INTEGRUM

CHAPTER FOUR
ENSURING EFFECTIVENSS: ORDERING PROVISIONAL MEASURES AND MONITORING COMPLIANCE

PREFACE

This book encompasses the Inter-American Court of Human Rights' jurisprudential developments concerning full reparation, in accordance with Article 63 of the American Convention on Human Rights (Pact of San José, Costa Rica). Article 63 states that, "[if] the Court finds that there has been a violation of a right or freedom protected by this Convention, the Court shall rule that the injured party be ensured the enjoyment of his right or freedom that was violated. It shall also rule, if appropriate, that the consequences of the measure or situation that constituted the breach of such right or freedom be remedied and that fair compensation be paid to the injured party." What does fair remedy mean? Who are the injured parties? Is it possible to achieve *restitutio in integrum* in all human rights violations? A simple reading of this text makes apparent the need for interpretation of its terms. The Inter-American Court, through its decisions, has made a rich contribution in developing Article 63.

These contributions in the area of reparations of the Inter-American system are widely recognized and influential in international law. The latest example is evidenced in the adoption of General Comment No. 3 of the Committee against Torture of the United Nations. However, the contributions of the Inter-American System, including the original documents, have not been fully presented in a systematic way. As a result, it is difficult for all stakeholders, including States, non-governmental organizations, and individuals, to understand the full scope of the different topics covered under Article 63.

Further, while the need to simply present the jurisprudence is a great one, it is also crucial to understand that it cannot remain static and that new circumstances and different sets of facts could lead the Inter-American Court's jurisprudence to develop in directions that have not yet been addressed or even imagined. Accordingly, this book is structured not simply by presenting the status of the law and the original documents essential for legal reasoning, but also by raising questions and presenting problems. These questions could prove useful not only for practical purposes, but also for theoretical purposes by striving to achieve coherence in the application of international legal standards.

In this matter, it is important to consider that international human rights treaties have a special humanitarian purpose, unlike that of classic treaties that present a system of reciprocal rights and obligations. In classic international law, when there is doubt about the intended scope of the treaty, the Courts preferred the interpretation that less impedes national sovereignty, assuming that the State parties did not have the intention to limit their sovereignty unless that could be demonstrated. On the other hand, human rights treaties do not establish a system of reciprocal rights and obligations among states, but have a humanitarian purpose. Accordingly, courts, including the Inter-American Court, have concluded that such an object and purpose leads to the conclusion that, in cases of justifiable doubts concerning the application of the treaty, the preferred interpretation was that which protected more human rights."

To achieve its goals, this book is organized in the following fashion: Chapter 1 defines victims, beneficiaries, and the right of action; Chapter 2 covers compensation for damages; Chapter 3 examines reparations beyond compensations: *resitutio in integrum*; finally, Chapter 4 explores provisional measures and monitoring compliance with judgments.

All of the chapters follow a common methodology. After an introduction presenting the topic, the chapters include a normative framework of valid sources of international law. This is followed by the jurisprudence of the court, specifically leading cases, and later an analysis section with questions raised by the Court's jurisprudence. In every chapter, a detailed table of contents is provided.

Finally, my recognitions go to Agustina del Campo and Mina

A. Trudeau who worked tirelessly with me in achieving this final result. I would also like to recognize Pablo Saavedra, Diego Rodriguez-Pinzon, and Viviana Krsticevic who each provided valuable case suggestions. In addition, I want to extend my appreciation to Michael Miller, Cleopatra Mawaro, Mathew Solis, Cecilia Mullan, Pablo Saavedra, Diego Rodriguez-Pinzon and Viviana Krsticevic. Finally, my recognitions are extended to the Dean's Fellows at American University Washington College of Law who participated in completing this manuscript: Maria Victoria Gama, Stefania Butoi Varga, Daniel Cappelletti, and all other students and interns who over the years have contributed to this project. Without them this work would not have been possible.

Claudio Grossman
Professor of Law and Dean Emeritus
R. Geraldson Scholar for International and
Humanitarian Law
American University Washington College of Law

Chapter One

DEFINING VICTIM, BENEFICIARY, AND THE RIGHT OF ACTION

I. INTRODUCTION

While the concept of "victim" often may seem self-evident, throughout its jurisprudence, the Inter-American Court of Human Rights has developed nuanced definitions of "injured party" for the purposes of compensation and other reparations in cases involving violations of rights and freedoms guaranteed by the American Convention on Human Rights. As demonstrated through case excerpts in this chapter, the Court has detailed and made modifications as to who may be considered the "next of kin" or beneficiary of a victim, when their suffering may be presumed, and when such potential beneficiaries bear the burden of proof. The Court has also considered cases in which the identification of victims and beneficiaries may be difficult, including cases involving indigenous communities and local customary law. Additional case excerpts demonstrate the Court's consideration of the impact of violations upon society as a whole. Finally, this chapter reviews the Court's efforts to improve financial accessibility to the Inter-American human rights system through creation of the Victims' Legal Assistance Fund.

II. NORMATIVE FRAMEWORK

A. AMERICAN CONVENTION ON HUMAN RIGHTS
      ARTICLE 1
      1.   The States Parties to this Convention undertake to respect the rights and freedoms recognized herein and to ensure to all persons

subject to their jurisdiction the free and full exercise of those rights and freedoms, without any discrimination for reasons of race, color, sex, language, religion, political or other opinion, national or social origin, economic status, birth, or any other social condition.

2.   For the purposes of this Convention, "person" means every human being.

ARTICLE 63

1.   If the Court finds that there has been a violation of a right or freedom protected by this Convention, the Court shall rule that the injured party be ensured the enjoyment of his right or freedom that was violated. It shall also rule, if appropriate, that the consequences of the measure or situation that constituted the breach of such right or freedom be remedied and that fair compensation be paid to the injured party.

B. RULES OF PROCEDURE OF THE INTER-AMERICAN COURT OF HUMAN RIGHTS [1]

ARTICLE 2. DEFINITIONS

16.   The expression "next-of-kin" refers to the immediate family, that is, the direct ascendants and descendants, siblings, spouses or permanent companions, or those determined by the Court, if applicable.

27.   The term "alleged victim" refers to the person whose rights under the American Convention have allegedly been violated.

33.   The term "victim" refers to a person whose rights have been violated, according to a judgment emitted by the Court.

ARTICLE 50. CONVOCATION OF ALLEGED VICTIMS, WITNESSES, AND EXPERT WITNESSES

2.   A party offering testimonial or expert evidence shall bear the costs of the appearance of alleged victims, witnesses, or expert witnesses before the Tribunal.

C. RULES OF PROCEDURE OF THE INTER-AMERICAN COMMIS-SION ON HUMAN RIGHTS [2]

ARTICLE 23. PRESENTATION OF PETITIONS

Any person or group of persons or nongovernmental entity legally recognized in one or more of the Member States of the OAS may submit petitions to the Commission, on their behalf or on behalf of third persons, concerning alleged violations of a human right recognized in, as the case may be, the American Declaration of the Rights and Duties of Man, the American Convention on Human Rights "Pact of San José, Costa Rica", the Additional Protocol to the American Convention on Human Rights in the Area of Economic, Social and Cultural Rights "Protocol of San Salvador", the Protocol to the American Convention on Human Rights to Abolish the Death Penalty, the Inter-American Convention to

Prevent and Punish Torture, the Inter-American Convention on Forced Disappearance of Persons, and/or the Inter-American Convention on the Prevention, Punishment and Eradication of Violence Against Women "Convention of Belém do Pará", in accordance with their respective provisions, the Statute of the Commission, and these Rules of Procedure. The petitioner may designate an attorney or other person to represent him or her before the Commission, either in the petition itself or in a separate document.

D. BASIC PRINCIPLES AND GUIDELINES ON THE RIGHT TO A REMEDY AND REPARATION FOR VICTIMS OF GROSS VIOLATIONS OF INTERNATIONAL HUMAN RIGHTS LAW AND SERIOUS VIOLATIONS OF INTERNATIONAL HUMANITARIAN LAW [3]

8. [V]ictims are persons who individually or collectively suffered harm, including physical or mental injury, emotional suffering, economic loss or substantial impairment of their fundamental rights, through acts of omissions that constitute gross violations of international human rights law, or serious violations of international humanitarian law. Where appropriate, and in accordance with domestic law, the term "victim" also includes the immediate family or dependents of the direct victim and persons who have suffered harm in intervening to assist victims in distress or to prevent victimization.

9. A person shall be considered a victim regardless of whether the perpetrator of the violation is identified, apprehended, prosecuted, or convicted and regardless of the familial relationship between the perpetrator and the victim.

10. Victims should be treated with humanity and respect for their dignity and human rights, and appropriate measures should be taken to ensure their safety, physical and psychological well-being and privacy, as well as those of their families. The State should ensure that its domestic laws, to the extent possible, provide that a victim who has suffered violence or trauma should benefit from special consideration and care to avoid his or her re-traumatization in the course of legal and administrative procedures designed to provide justice and reparation.

11. Remedies for gross violations of international human rights law and serious violations of international humanitarian law include the victim's right to the following as provided for under international law:

(a) Equal and effective access to justice;

(b) Adequate, effective and prompt reparation for harm suffered;

(c) Access to relevant information concerning violations and reparation mechanisms.

III. DEFINING VICTIMS AND OTHER INJURED PARTIES

The definitions of victim and injured party are central to the concept of seeking reparations. These definitions determine who may seek and receive compensation and other measures of reparation for violations of rights and freedoms guaranteed by the American Convention on Human Rights. The American Convention, along with the Rules of Procedure of the Inter-American Court of Human Rights and the Inter-American Commission on Human Rights, provide fundamental guides as to who is considered a victim or alleged victim or injured party within the Inter-American human rights system. The Court's jurisprudence has augmented these definitions as demonstrated by the following case excerpts.

Blake v. Guatemala
24-Jan-1998
Series C No. 36—*Merits*

1.   The Commission submitted this case for the Court to decide whether the State had violated the following articles of the Convention: 4 (Right to Life), 7 (Right to Personal Liberty), 8 (Right to a Fair Trial), 13 (Freedom of Thought and Expression), 22 (Right of Movement and Residence), and 25 (Right to Judicial Protection), all these in relation to Article 1(1) of the Convention, for the alleged abduction and murder of Mr. Nicholas Chapman Blake (hereinafter "Nicholas Blake") by agents of the Guatemalan State on March 28, 1985, and his disappearance, which lasted over seven years until June 14, 1992. The Commission also asked the Court to find that the State had violated Article 51(2) of the Convention by its refusal to "implement the recommendations made by the Commission."

22-Jan-99
Series C No. 48—*Reparations and Costs*

32.   The obligation to make reparation established by international courts is governed, as has been universally accepted, by international law in all its aspects: scope, nature, forms, and determination of beneficiaries, none of which the respondent State may alter by invoking its domestic law.

35.   As regards the beneficiaries of the reparations, in their March 27, 1998 brief, the parents and brothers of Mr. Nicholas Blake asserted that they had been directly injured by the violations of the fundamental rights of their son and brother.

37.   The State maintains that the relatives of Mr. Nicholas Blake may not receive reparations in their own right, since the parents and brothers of the victim have not demonstrated that they had a relationship of dependence on him.

38.   This Court already recognized, in operative paragraphs 1 and 2 of the January 24, 1998 Judgment, that violations of Articles 8(1) and 5 of the Convention, in conjunction with Article 1(1), were to the detriment of the relatives of Nicholas Blake. Therefore, for the purpose of reparations, the Court determines that these relatives constitute the injured party within the meaning of Article 63(1) of the American Convention. The Court determines that Richard Blake, Mary Blake, Richard Blake Jr., and Samuel Blake may receive reparations in their own right as the injured party in the present case.

Bamaca Velasquez v. Guatemala
25-Nov-2000
Series C No. 70—*Merits*

2.   The Commission stated that the purpose of the application was for the Court to decide whether the State had violated the following rights of Efraín Bámaca Velásquez:

> Article 3 (Right to Juridical Personality), Article 4 (Right to Life), Article 5 (Right to Humane Treatment), Article 7 (Right to Personal Liberty), Article 8 (Right to a Fair Trial), Article 13 (Freedom of Thought and Expression), Article 25 (Right to Judicial Protection), and Article 1 (Obligation to Respect Rights), all of the American Convention, and also Articles 1, 2 and 6 of the Inter-American Convention to Prevent and Punish Torture and Article 3 common to the Geneva Conventions.

18.   The Court summarizes the facts set out in the application as follows:

(a)   Efraín Bámaca Velásquez, known as "Comandante Everardo," formed part of the Revolutionary Organization of the People in Arms (hereinafter "ORPA"), one of the guerrilla groups that made up the URNG; Bámaca Velásquez led this group's Luis Ixmatá Front.

(b)   Efraín Bámaca Velásquez disappeared on March 12, 1992, after an encounter between the Army and the guerrilla in the village of Montúfar, near Nuevo San Carlos, Retalhuleu, in the western part of Guatemala.

(c)   Bámaca Velásquez was alive when the Guatemalan armed forces took him prisoner, and "they imprisoned him secretly in several military installations, where they tortured and eventually executed him."

22-Feb.-02
Series C No. 91—*Reparations and Costs*

29. With the aim of determining the appropriate measures of reparation in the instant case, the Court will base itself on the facts admitted as proven in the November 25, 2000 Judgment. During the current stage of the proceedings, the parties have also contributed new evidence with the aim of proving the existence of supplementary facts that are relevant to the aforementioned measures. The Court has examined the evidence and the respective arguments of the parties on the declarations and, as a result of this examination, declares that the following facts have been proven.

B) with respect to the next of kin of Efraín Bámaca Velásquez:

    a)   that José León Bámaca Hernández is his father, and his sisters are Egidia Gebia and Josefina Bámaca Velásquez and Alberta Velásquez, and that they as well as their father are members of the Mayan culture, Mam ethnic group. His wife was Jennifer Harbury;

30.   The court will now determine the person or persons who in the instant case are the "injured party," pursuant to Article 63(1) of the American Convention. In view of the fact that the violations of the American Convention determined by the Court in its November 25, 2000 Judgment were committed against Efraín Bámaca Velásquez, Jennifer Harbury, José León Bámaca Hernández, Egidia Gebia Bámaca Velásquez, and Josefina Bámaca Velásquez, all of them—as victims— must be included in that category and be entitled to the reparations decided by the Court, both in connection with pecuniary damages, when appropriate, and in connection with non-pecuniary damages.

31.   In the case of Mrs. Jennifer Harbury, the State has objected to her being entitled to possible reparations, both in her own right and through inheritance, as a consequence of her own statement that this reparation will be delivered, in full, to the relatives of Bámaca Velásquez, and it is therefore the opinion of the State that this is "an explicit waiver of the right declared in her favor by the Court, one that constitutes full evidence because it was made during the contentious phase of the case before the Court." The Court does not share the interpretation of the State regarding that statement, as it does not issue from the terms of that statement that such was Mrs. Harbury's intention, and for these reasons the Court believes that a determination of the compensation due to her is in order, and she can freely dispose of it.

Juvenile Reeducation Institute v. Paraguay
2-Sep-2004
Series C No. 112—*Preliminary Objections, Merits, Reparations, and Costs*
2.   The Commission filed the application pursuant to Article 61 of the American Convention, seeking a judgment from the Court as to whether the State had violated, in relation to its obligation under Article 1(1) (Obligation to Respect Rights) of the Convention, Article 4 (Right to Life) of that instrument by virtue of the deaths of inmates Elvio Epifanio Acosta Ocampos, Marco Antonio Giménez, Diego Walter Valdez, Sergio Daniel Vega Figueredo, Sergio David Poletti Domínguez, Mario Álvarez Pérez, Juan Alcides Román Barrios, Antonio Damián Escobar Morinigo, and Carlos Raúl de la Cruz, all of whom perished as a result of a fire at the *Instituto de Reeducación del Menor "Coronel Panchito López"* ("Colonel Panchito López" Juvenile Reeducation Institute, hereinafter "the Center" or "the 'Panchito López' Center") and by virtue of the death of Benito Augusto Adorno, who died of a bullet wound sustained at the Center. The Commission also asked the Court to decide whether the State had violated Article 5 (Right to Humane Treatment) of the American Convention, in relation to its obligation under Article 1(1) thereof, by virtue of the injuries and smoke inhalation that minors Abel Achar Acuña, José Milicades Cañete, Ever Ramón Molinas Zárate, Arsenio Joel Barrios Báez, Alfredo Duarte Ramos, Sergio Vincent Navarro Moraez, Raúl Esteban Portillo, Ismael Méndez Aranda, Pedro Iván Peña, Osvaldo Daniel Sosa, Walter Javier Riveros Rojas, Osmar López Verón, Miguel Coronel, César Ojeda, Heriberto Zarate, Francisco Noé Andrada, Jorge Daniel Toledo, Pablo Emmanuel Rojas, Sixto Gonzáles Franco, Francisco Ramón Adorno, Antonio Delgado, Claudio Coronel Quiroga, Clemente Luis Escobar González, Julio César García, José Amado Jara Fernando, Alberto David Martínez, Miguel Ángel Martínez, Osvaldo Espinola Mora, Hugo Antonio Quintana Vera, Juan Carlos Viveros Zarza, Eduardo Vera, Ulises Zelaya Flores,Hugo Olmedo, Rafael Aquino Acuña, Nelson Rodríguez, Demetrio Silguero, Aristides Ramón Ortiz B., and Carlos Raúl Romero Giacomo sustained in three fires at the Center.[4]
3.   The Commission also petitioned the Court to find that the respondent State had violated Articles 5 (Right to Humane Treatment), 7 (Right to Personal Liberty), 19 (Rights of the Child), 8 (Right to a Fair Trial), and 25 (Judicial Protection) of the American Convention, all in relation to Article 1(1) thereof, to the detriment of all juveniles incarcerated at the Center at any time in the period between August 14, 1996, and July 25, 2001, and those juvenile inmates subsequently remanded to the country's adult prisons.
4.   The Commission's contention was that the "Panchito López Center" embodied a system that was the antithesis of every international standard pertaining to the incarceration of juveniles, given the allegedly grossly inadequate conditions under which the children were interned. Specifically, those conditions

involved a combination of: overpopulation, overcrowding, lack of sanitation, inadequate infrastructure, and a prison guard staff that was both too small and poorly trained.

271.   The Court will now proceed to determine which persons are to be regarded as an "injured party," in the terms of Article 63(1) of the American Convention, and who shall be entitled to the reparations that the Court orders, both for pecuniary and, where appropriate, non-pecuniary damages.

272.   To begin with, the injured parties are the deceased inmates, as victims of the violation of the right recognized in Article 4(1) of the American Convention, in relation to Article 1(1) thereof, and also in relation to Article 19 when the victims are children; all those inmates at the Center between August 14, 1996 and July 25, 2001, as victims of the violation of the rights protected in Articles 4(1), 5(1), 5(2), and 5(6) of the American Convention, in relation to Article 1(1) thereof, and also in relation to Article 19 of the Convention, when the victims in question are children; the children injured in the fires, as victims of the violation of the rights upheld in Articles 5(1) and 5(2) of the American Convention, in relation to Articles 1(1) and 19 thereof; the identified next of kin of the deceased and injured inmates, as victims of violation of the right protected in Article 5(1) of the American Convention, in relation to Article 1(1) thereof; all the children interned at the Center between August 14, 1996 and July 25, 2001, as victims of the violation of the rights recognized in Articles 2 and 8(1) of the American Convention, in relation to Articles 1(1) and 19 thereof; and the 239 inmates named in the writ of generic habeas corpus, as victims of the violation of the right recognized in Article 25 of the American Convention, in relation to Article 1(1) thereof. All these persons shall be entitled to the reparations set by the Court for pecuniary and non-pecuniary damages.

273.   This Court observes that when a contentious case is being litigated before the Court, the interested party must decide who the beneficiary or beneficiaries will be. Therefore, the Court is not prepared to order compensation for any potential next of kin of the inmates who were victims of human rights violations but were not identified.

Moiwana Community v. Suriname

15-Jun-2005

Series C No. 124—*Preliminary Objections, Merits, Reparations, and Costs*

2.   The Commission submitted the application for the Court to decide whether the State has violated Articles 25 (Right to Judicial Protection), 8 (Right to a Fair Trial), and 1(1) (Obligation to Respect Rights) of the Convention, to the

detriment of certain former residents of Moiwana Village. . . Furthermore, the Commission requested that the Court order the State to adopt several monetary and non-monetary reparations measures, as well as to pay the legal costs and fees incurred during both the domestic and international proceedings of the instant case.

3.   According to the Commission, on November 29, 1986, members of the armed forces of Suriname attacked the N'djuka Maroon village of Moiwana. State agents allegedly massacred over 40 men, women, and children, and razed the village to the ground. Those who escaped the attack supposedly fled into the surrounding forest, and then into exile or internal displacement. Furthermore, as of the date of the application, there allegedly had not been an adequate investigation of the massacre, no one had been prosecuted or punished and the survivors remained displaced from their lands; in consequence, they have been supposedly unable to return to their traditional way of life. Thus, the Commission stated that, while the attack itself predated Suriname's ratification of the American Convention and its recognition of the Court's jurisdiction, the alleged denial of justice and displacement of the Moiwana community occurring subsequent to the attack comprise the subject matter of the application.

177.   It is necessary to recall that within the context of the contentious process, the identities of the beneficiaries must be properly communicated to the Court. [99] [5] Thus, this Tribunal cannot grant the request that additional victims, which to date have not been individualized before the Court, be named for compensation purposes subsequent to the instant judgment. Such a decision is consistent with the case of *Plan de Sanchez Massacre*, as in that case no additional victims were permitted to be identified, following the judgment on reparations, in order to receive monetary awards. [100] [6]

178.   Following precedent, [101] [7] this Court considers as properly identified those victims who are referred to in an official document, such as a birth certificate or "family book," submitted before the Tribunal. Regarding the other victims individualized in the application who have not been suitably identified, the Court holds that the compensation that corresponds to each one shall be awarded in the same manner as those properly identified by State documents— as long as they appear before the appropriate State officials within 24 months following the notification of the instant judgment and provide sufficient means of identification. [102] [8]   Adequate identification shall entail either: a) an official document attesting to the person's identity, or b) a statement before a competent state official by a recognized leader of the Moiwana community members, as well as the declarations of two additional persons, all of which clearly attest to the individual's identity. The Court notes that it is granting more latitude in this case with respect to acceptable means of proving identity, in light of the statements by

the Commission and the representatives that many Maroons do not possess formal identity documents and were never inscribed in the national registry.

The Ituango Massacres v. Colombia
1-Jul-2006
Series C No. 148—*Preliminary Objections, Merits, Reparations, and Costs*

1.   On July 30, 2004, in accordance with the provisions of Articles 50 and 61 of the American Convention, the Inter-American Commission on Human Rights (hereinafter "the Commission" or "the Inter-American Commission") lodged before the Court an application against the State of Colombia (hereinafter "the State" or "Colombia"), which originated from petitions No. 12,050 (La Granja) and 12,266 (El Aro), with regard to the Municipality of Ituango, received by the Secretariat of the Commission on July 14, 1998, and March 3, 2000, respectively. On March 11, 2004, the Commission decided to joinder the cases.

2.   In its application, the Commission referred to events that occurred in June 1996 and October 1997 in the municipal districts (*corregimientos*) of La Granja and El Aro, respectively, both of them located in the Municipality of Ituango, Department of Antioquia, Colombia. The Commission alleged that "the State's responsibility . . . arose from the [alleged] acts of omission, acquiescence, and collaboration by members of law enforcement bodies based in the Municipality of Ituango with paramilitary groups belonging to the United Self-Defense Forces of Colombia (AUC), which [allegedly] perpetrated successive armed raids in this Municipality, assassinating defenseless civilians, robbing others of their property, and causing terror and displacement." The Commission also stated that "eight years after the raid in the municipal district of La Granja and more than six years after the armed incursion in the municipal district of El Aro, the Colombian State ha[d] still not complied significantly with its obligation to clarify the facts, prosecute all those responsible effectively, and provide adequate reparation to the [alleged] victims and their next of kin."

3.   The Commission presented the application for the Court to decide whether the State is responsible for the alleged violation of the following rights established in the following articles of the American Convention, in relation to Article 1(1) thereof:

  (a) 4 (Right to Life), to the detriment of the following nineteen
       (19) persons: William Villa García, Graciela Arboleda, Héctor
       Hernán Correa García, Jairo Sepúlveda, Arnulfo Sánchez, José
       Darío Martínez, Olcris Fail Díaz, Wilmar de Jesús Restrepo
       Torres, Omar de Jesús Ortiz Carmona, Fabio Antonio Zuleta
       Zabala, Otoniel de Jesús Tejada Jaramillo, Omar Iván Gutiérrez

Nohavá, Guillermo Andrés Mendoza Posso, Nelson de Jesús Palacio Cárdenas, Luis Modesto Múnera, Dora Luz Areiza, Alberto Correa, Marco Aurelio Areiza Osorio, and Rosa Areiza Barrera;

(b) 19 (Rights of the Child), to the detriment of the minor, Wilmar de Jesús Restrepo Torres;

(c) 7 (Right to Personal Liberty), to the detriment of the following three (3) persons: Jairo Sepúlveda, Marco Aurelio Areiza Osorio, and Rosa Areiza Barrera;

(d) 5 (Right to Humane Treatment), to the detriment of the following two (2) persons: Marco Aurelio Areiza and Rosa Areiza Barrera;

(e) 21 (Right to Property), to the detriment of the following six (6) persons: Luis Humberto Mendoza, Libardo Mendoza, Francisco Osvaldo Pino Posada, Omar Alfredo Torres Jaramillo, Ricardo Alfredo Builes Echeverry, and Bernardo María Jiménez Lopera; and

(f) 8 (Right to a Fair Trial) and 25 (Right to Judicial Protection), to the detriment "of all the [alleged] victims and their next of kin."

4. Lastly, the Commission requested the Court to order the State to adopt a series of measures of pecuniary and non-pecuniary reparation, and also to pay the costs and expenses arising from processing the case in the domestic jurisdiction and before the inter-American system for the protection of human rights.

90. The Court will now determine, pursuant to the Rules of Procedure and its case law, and bearing in mind the characteristics of this specific case, which of the people who were not included by the State's acknowledgement of responsibility will be considered alleged victims in this case.

91. The Court has developed extensive case law on the determination of alleged victims in the cases it hears using criteria applicable to the circumstances of this case. According to Article 50 of the Convention, the alleged victims must be indicated in the application and in the Commission's report. However, owing to the particularities of each case, this has not always been so, and the Court has therefore considered as alleged victims persons who were not alleged as such in the application, provided that the right to defense of the parties has been respected and that the alleged victims have some connection with the facts described in the application and the evidence provided to the Court.[129]

92. Particularly in cases of massacres or of multiple victims, the Court has been flexible in the identification of alleged victims, even when they have been alleged in the Commission's application as "the survivors" of the massacre and "their next of kin," or when the parties have submitted additional information on the identification of the alleged victims in briefs submitted subsequent to the application.[13 10] In other cases involving massacres, the Court has considered as

alleged victims, "the persons identified by the Commission in its application . . . and those who may be identified subsequently, since the complexities and difficulties in individualizing them, suggest that there are still other victims to be determined."[14] [11]

93.   In some cases, the Court has emphasized that the right to defense of the parties is the determining criteria.[15] [12] Nevertheless, even in the presence of objections by the State, the Court has considered that such alleged new victims should be included.[16] [13]

94.   Based on its jurisdictional function and pursuant to Article 62 of the Convention, which indicates that the Court has jurisdiction to hear "all cases concerning the interpretation and application of the provisions of [the] Convention" in cases with multiple alleged victims, the Court has considered several ways to overcome "shortcomings in the identification or individualization of some of the alleged victims" in the application,[17] [14] whose names are to be found in the briefs where other alleged victims appear. For example, the Court has requested the Commission to remedy such flaws by presenting lists of alleged victims identified following the application.[18] [15] Also, in cases where the alleged victims "have or have not been identified or individualized" in the application,[19] [16] the Court has ordered the State to "individualize and identify the victims . . . and their next of kin," for the effects of reparations.[20] [17] Finally, the Court has taken the initiative to overcome the shortcomings in the identification of alleged victims in the application, by its own examination of the evidence presented by the parties, even when the parties have admitted that some people "by error, were not included in the list of alleged victims."[21] [18] Likewise, the Court has declared individuals who were identified in the evidence provided by the parties as "possible victims," even when these people were not identified in the Commission's application.[22] [19]

95.   The foregoing makes it clear that, although the identification of alleged victims in a case is governed by the parameters established in the Convention and in the Rules of Procedure, the Court, based on its jurisdictional function and in accordance with Article 62 of the Convention, may take decisions in this respect that take into account the particularities of each case and the rights regarding which a violation has been alleged, provided that the right to defense of the parties is respected and that the alleged victims have some connection with the facts described in the application and the evidence provided to the Court.

96.   In keeping with these criteria, the Court will examine the determination of the alleged victims in this case who were not included in the State's acknowledgement of responsibility in the chapters on the merits of each alleged violation.

97.   The Court deems it pertinent to indicate its concern regarding the discrepancy between the persons indicated by the Commission in its report based

on Article 50 of the Convention as alleged victims of Article 21 thereof, versus the persons that its application alleges are victims of this article. Neither the number nor names of the individuals listed in these two documents coincide. The Court also notes that the persons alleged by the representatives in their requests and arguments brief are totally different from those indicated in the said Article 50 report.

98.   This Court has had to make a laborious examination of the evidence provided by the parties in order to extract the elements required to make a precise identification of the victims, since the Commission's application did not include complete information in this regard. The Court observes that the Commission's application contained general references to the victims in relation to some groups of them, such as "17 herdsmen" or "victims of displacement," without providing the necessary details for the appropriate identification of individual alleged victims. The Court considers that, in accordance with Article 33(1) of the Rules of Procedure of the Court, it falls to the Commission, and not to the Court, to identify precisely the alleged victims in a case before the Court.

Miguel Castro Castro Prison v. Peru
25-Nov-2006
Series C No. 160—*Merits, Reparations, and Costs*

2.   The Commission submitted the petition for the Court to decide if the State is responsible for the violation of the rights enshrined in Articles 4 (Right to Life) and 5 (Right to Humane Treatment) of the American Convention, in relation to the obligation established in Article 1(1) (Obligation to Respect Rights) of the same, in detriment of "at least 42" inmates that died; the violation of Article 5 (Right to Humane Treatment) of the Convention, in relation to the obligation established in Article 1(1) (Obligation to Respect Rights) of the Convention, to the detriment of "at least 175" inmates that were injured and of 322 inmates "that were [allegedly] uninjured were submitted to a cruel, inhuman, and degrading treatment;" and for the violation of Articles 8(1) (Right to a Fair Trial) and 25 (Right to Judicial Protection) of the Convention, in relation to the obligation established in Article 1(1) of the same, to the detriment of "the [alleged] victims and their next of kin."

3.   The facts presented by the Commission in the application occurred as of May 6, 1992,and they refer to the execution of "Operative Transfer 1" within the Miguel Castro Castro Prison, during which the State, allegedly, caused the death of at least 42 inmates, injured 175 inmates, and submitted another 322 inmates to a cruel, inhuman, and degrading treatment. The facts also refer to the alleged cruel, inhuman, and degrading treatment experienced by the alleged victims after "Operative Transfer 1."

418.   The Court has determined that the facts of the present case constituted a violation of Article 4 of the American Convention, in relation to Article 1(1) of the same, to the detriment of the 41 deceased inmates identified in Appendix 1 of victims of this Judgment; of Article 5 of the American Convention, in relation to Article 1(1) of the same, and in connection to Articles 1, 6, and 8 of the Inter-American Convention to Prevent and Punish Torture, to the detriment of the 41 deceased inmates identified and of the inmates who survived; of Article 5 of the American Convention, in relation to Article 1(1) of the same, in detriment of the next of kin of the inmates determined in paragraphs 336, 337, 340, and 341 of the chapter on the violation to the right to humane treatment and identified in Appendix 2 of victims of this Judgment; and of Articles 8(1) and 25 of the American Convention, in relation to Article 1(1) of the same, in connection to Articles 7(b) of the Inter-American Convention to Prevent, Punish, and Eradicate Violence Against Women and 1, 6, and 8 of the Inter- American Convention to Prevent and Punish Torture, to the detriment of the next of kin of the 41 dead inmates, of the surviving inmates, and of the next of kin of the inmates determined in paragraphs 336, 337, 340, and 341 of the chapter on the violation to the right to humane treatment and identified in Appendix 2 of victims of this Judgment. These people are entitled to the reparations set by the Tribunal, as victims of the mentioned violations.

420.   According to the evidence presented, the Court has identified some of the mentioned next of kin, whose names are listed in Appendix 3 of the present Judgment In that appendix only those people are listed with regard to whom there is evidence that allows the Court to determine that they were alive at the time of the facts. In relation to the other next of kin of the 41 deceased victims identified that have not been individualized in these proceedings, the Court states that the compensation that corresponds to them be delivered to them directly, in the same way provided regarding those who have been individualized, after they present themselves before the competent State authorities within the eight months following the notification of this Judgment, and they prove, through a sufficient means of identification,[217][20] their relationship or kinship with the victim and that they were alive at the time of the facts.

The Saramaka People v. Suriname

28-Nov-2007

Series C No. 172—*Preliminary Objections, Merits, Reparations, and Costs*

2.   The application submits to the Court's jurisdiction alleged violations committed by the State against the members of the Saramaka people, an allegedly

tribal community living in the Upper Suriname River region. The Commission alleged that the State has not adopted effective measures to recognize their right to the use and enjoyment of the territory they have traditionally occupied and used, that the State has allegedly violated the right to judicial protection to the detriment of such people by not providing them effective access to justice for the protection of their fundamental rights, particularly the right to own property in accordance with their communal traditions, and that the State has allegedly failed to adopt domestic legal provisions in order to ensure and guarantee such rights to the Saramakas.

3.   The Commission asked the Court to determine the international responsibility of the State for the violation of Articles 21 (Right to Property) and 25 (Right to Judicial Protection), in conjunction with Articles 1(1) and 2 of the American Convention. Furthermore, the Commission requested that the Court order the State to adopt several monetary and nonmonetary reparation measures.

4.   The representatives of the alleged victims, namely, Mr. Fergus MacKay, of the Forest Peoples Programme, Mr. David Padilla, and the Association of Saramaka Authorities (hereinafter "the representatives"), submitted their written brief containing pleadings, motions and evidence (hereinafter "representatives' brief"), in accordance with Article 23 of the Rules of Procedure. The representatives asked the Court to declare that the State had violated the same rights alleged by the Commission, and additionally alleged that the State had violated Article 3 (Right to Juridical Personality) of the Convention by "failing to recognize the legal personality of the Saramaka people." Moreover, the representatives submitted additional facts and arguments regarding the alleged ongoing and continuous effects associated with the construction of a hydroelectric dam in the 1960s that allegedly flooded traditional Saramaka territory. Additionally, they requested certain measures of reparation and the reimbursement of the costs and expenses incurred in processing the case at the national level and before the international proceedings.

188.   The Tribunal has previously held that in a contentious case before the Court, the Commission must individually name the beneficiaries of possible reparations.[208] [21]   However, given the size and geographic diversity of the Saramaka people[209] [22] and, particularly, the collective nature of reparations to be ordered in the present case, the Court does not find it necessary in the instant case to individually name the members of the Saramaka people in order to recognize them as the injured party. Nevertheless, the Court observes that the members of the Saramaka people are identifiable in accordance with Saramaka customary law, given that each Saramaka individual belongs to only one of the twelve matrilineal *lös* in which the community is organized.

189.   Thus, in accordance with the Court's jurisprudence regarding indigenous and tribal peoples,[210] [23] the Court considers the members of the Saramaka people

as the "injured party" in the present case who, due to their status as victims of the violations established in the present Judgment, are the beneficiaries of the collective forms of reparations ordered by the Court.

Ticona Estrada et al. v. Bolivia
27-Nov-2008
Series C No 191—*Merits, Reparations, and Costs*

2.   The application refers to the alleged forced disappearance of Renato Ticona Estrada (hereinafter, "Renato Ticona," "Mr. Ticona Estrada," or the "victim") as of July 22, 1980, date on which he and his brother, Hugo Ticona Estrada (hereinafter, "Hugo Ticona" or "Hugo"), were detained by an Army patrol in the vicinity of the control gate of Cala-Cala in Oruro, Bolivia; the application also relates to the alleged impunity that surrounded the case for more than 27 years since the occurrence of such event, as well as the long denial of justice experienced by the next-of-kin of Renato Ticona and the alleged lack of reparation of said next-of-kin for the damages caused as a consequence of the loss of a loved one. Moreover, the Commission stated that, given the fact that the Court has no jurisdiction *ratione temporis* to hear the illegal and arbitrary detention and the tortures suffered by Hugo Ticona in the year 1980, it did not include the allegation of these violations in the application. Nevertheless, the Commission did include the alleged denial of justice of which Hugo Ticona was an alleged victim as of the date on which the State acknowledged the competence of the Court to hear such violations.

3.   In the application, the Commission requested that this Tribunal decide that the State violated the rights of Renato Ticona as enshrined in Articles 3 (Right to Juridical Personality), 4 (Right to Life), 5 (Right to Humane Treatment), 7 (Right to Personal Liberty), 8 (Right to a Fair Trial), and 25 (Right to Judicial Protection) of the American Convention, as well as Articles I, III, and XI of the Inter-American Convention on Forced Disappearance of Persons (hereinafter, "IACFDP"). In addition, the Commission requested the Court to declare that Bolivia has violated the rights contained in Articles 5 (Right to Humane Treatment), 8 (Right to a Fair Trial), and 25 (Right to Judicial Protection) of the American Convention, to the detriment of the next-of-kin of Renato Ticona; in particular, his parents, María Honoria Estrada Figueroa de Ticona (hereinafter, "Honoria Estrada de Ticona") and César Ticona Olivares, as well as his brothers Hugo Ticona and Rodo Ticona Estrada (hereinafter, "Rodo Ticona") and his sister, Betzy Ticona Estrada (hereinafter, "Betzy Ticona"). The foregoing is in relation to the general obligations to respect and ensure the rights contained

in Article 1(1) (Obligation to Respect Rights). Furthermore, the Commission considered that the State failed to comply with the duty to adopt domestic legal provisions according to the provisions of Article 2 (Domestic Legal Effects) of the American Convention, in relation to Articles I and III of the IACFDP. Finally, the Commission requested the Court to order certain measures of reparations.

108.   The Tribunal recalls that an injured party is considered to be the victim of a violation of some of the rights enshrined in the Convention. In this sense, the Court considers that Renato Ticona Estrada, Honoria Estrada de Ticona, César Ticona Olivares, Hugo Ticona, Rodo Ticona, and Betzy Ticona are the "injured parties" in their capacity of victims of the violations declared in the previous chapters, and therefore, they shall be entitled to the reparations ordered by the Tribunal as pecuniary and non-pecuniary damage.

Valle Jaramillo et al. v. Colombia
27-Nov-2008
Series C No. 192—*Merits, Reparations, and Costs*

1.   On February 13, 2007, the Inter-American Commission on Human Rights (hereinafter "the Commission" or "the Inter-American Commission") submitted to the Court, in accordance with the provisions of Articles 50 and 61 of the American Convention, an application against the Republic of Colombia (hereinafter "the State" or "Colombia"). This application originated from petition No. 12,415, forwarded to the Secretariat of the Commission on August 2, 2001, by the *Grupo Interdisciplinario por los Derechos Humanos* (Interdisciplinary Group for Human Rights, hereinafter "GIDH"). On February 20, 2003, the Commission approved Admissibility Report No. 5/03 and, on October 16, 2006, it approved Merits Report No. 75/06 in the terms of Article 50 of the Convention,[2][24] which contained various recommendations to the State. Taking into consideration the "State's report on the implementation of the recommendations included in the Report on the merits, and the lack of substantive progress in compliance with them," the Commission decided to submit the instant case to the jurisdiction of the Court on February 13, 2007. The Commission appointed Víctor Abramovich, Commissioner, and Santiago A. Canton, Executive Secretary, as delegates, and Ariel E. Dulitzky, Elizabeth Abi-Mershed, Juan Pablo Albán A., Verónica Gómez, Andrea Repetto, and Karin Mansel as legal advisers.

2.   In its application, the Commission alleged that:
> On February 27, 1998, . . . two armed men entered Jesús María Valle Jaramillo's office in . . . Medellín [where Carlos Fernando Jaramillo Correa and] Nelly Valle [Jaramillo], Jesús María

Valle's sister, were also present . . . . [Subsequently, a woman entered and, together with two armed men, proceeded to] tie up and immobilize the hostages . . . . Jesús María Valle was murdered with two shots to his head, [and] died instantly. . . . Following the extrajudicial execution, Mrs. Valle and Mr. Jaramillo Correa were dragged to the lobby, [where] they were threatened with guns . . . . [T]he perpetrators [then] left the office. . . . Carlos Fernando Jaramillo . . . had to go into exile because of his fears owing to the threats he had received. . . . The available evidence indicates that the motive for the murder was to silence the reports of the human rights defender Jesús María Valle about the crimes perpetrated in the municipality of Ituango by members of paramilitary forces in connivance with members of the Army. . . . [A]lmost nine years have passed, . . . three civilians have been convicted in absentia, and there are no judicial investigations underway to determine whether State agents bear any responsibility.

3. Based on the above, the Commission alleged that the State is responsible for:

The [alleged] extrajudicial execution of the human rights defender Jesús María Valle Jaramillo; the [alleged] detention and cruel, inhuman, and degrading treatment that preceded it, to the detriment of Mr. Valle Jaramillo, Nelly Valle Jaramillo, his sister, and Carlos Fernando Jaramillo Correa . . . ; the [alleged] lack of investigation and punishment of those responsible for these acts; the [alleged] lack of adequate reparation in favor of the [presumed] victims and their next of kin; and the [alleged] forced displacement that Mr. Jaramillo Correa suffered following the facts.

4. The Commission asked the Court to declare the international responsibility of the State for the violation of:

   (a) Articles 4 (Right to Life), 5 (Right to Humane Treatment) and 7 (Right to Personal Liberty) of the American Convention, in relation to Article 1(1) (Obligation to Respect Rights) thereof, to the detriment of Jesús María Valle Jaramillo;

   (b) Articles 5 (Right to Humane Treatment) and 7 (Right to Personal Liberty) of the American Convention, in relation to Article 1(1) (Obligation to Respect Rights) thereof, to the detriment of Nelly Valle Jaramillo Jaramillo (hereinafter "María Nelly Valle Jaramillo" or "Nelly Valle Jaramillo") and Carlos Fernando Jaramillo Correa;

(c) Article 22 (Freedom of Movement and Residence) of the American Convention, in relation to Article 1(1) (Obligation to Respect Rights) thereof, to the detriment of Carlos Fernando Jaramillo Correa "and his next of kin"; and

(d) Articles 8(1) (Right to a Fair Trial) and 25 (Right to Judicial Protection) of the American Convention, in relation to Article 1(1) (Obligation to Respect Rights) thereof, to the detriment of Nelly Valle Jaramillo, Carlos Fernando Jaramillo Correa, and "the next of kin" of Jesús María Valle Jaramillo.

Finally, the Commission asked the Court to order the State to adopt various measures of pecuniary and non-pecuniary reparation.

5.   On May 9, 2007, the GIDH, represented by María Victoria Fallon Morales, Patricia Fuenmayor Gómez, and John Arturo Cárdenas Mesa, and the *Comisión Colombiana de Juristas* (Colombian Commission of Jurists, hereinafter "CCJ"), represented by Gustavo Gallón Giraldo and Luz Marina Monzón Cifuentes, as representatives of the alleged victims and their next of kin (hereinafter "the representatives"), presented their brief with pleadings, motions, and evidence (hereinafter "brief with pleadings and motions" or "the representatives' brief"), in the terms of Article 23 of the Rules of Procedure. The representatives asked the Court to declare that the State had violated the same rights as those alleged by the Commission and, in addition, they alleged that the State was responsible for the violation of:

(a) Article 5(1) (Right to Humane Treatment) of the Convention, in relation to Article 1(1) (Obligation to Respect Rights) thereof, to the detriment of "the next of kin of Jesús María Valle Jaramillo and Nelly Valle Jaramillo";

(b) Article 13 (Freedom of Thought and Expression) of the Convention, in relation to Article 1(1) (Obligation to Respect Rights) thereof, to the detriment of Jesús María Valle Jaramillo;

(c) Article 22 (1) (Freedom of Movement and Residence) of the Convention, in relation to Article 1(1) (Obligation to Respect Rights) thereof, to the detriment of the following next of kin of Carlos Fernando Jaramillo Correa: Gloria Lucía Correa García, Carlos Enrique Jaramillo Correa, Carolina Jaramillo Correa, and María Lucía Jaramillo Correa;

(d) Articles 8(1) (Right to a Fair Trial) and 25 (Right to Judicial Protection) of the Convention, in relation to Article 1(1) (Obligation to Respect Rights) thereof, to the detriment of "all the [alleged] victims and their next of kin";

(e) Article 11(1) and (2) (Right to Privacy) of the Convention, in relation to Article 1(1) (Obligation to Respect Rights) thereof, to the detriment of Jesús María Valle Jaramillo, Carlos Fernando Jaramillo Correa, "and their/his next of kin";

(f) Articles 5(1) (Right to Humane Treatment), 13 (Freedom of Thought and Expression), and 16 (Freedom of Association) of the Convention, in relation to Article 1(1) (Obligation to Respect Rights) thereof, to the detriment of "the indirect victims, [namely,] the human rights defenders"; and

(g) Article 17 (Rights of the Family) of the Convention, to the detriment of "the next of kin of the victims."

Additionally, the representatives requested the adoption of certain measures of reparation and the reimbursement of the expenses incurred during the proceedings before the Court.

119. In this regard, the Court finds it pertinent to clarify some aspects of its case law concerning the determination of violations of the personal integrity of the next of kin of victims of certain human rights violations,[77][25] or other persons with close ties to such victims. For instance, the Court considers that a violation of the right to mental and moral integrity of the direct next of kin of victims of certain human rights violations can be declared, applying a presumption *iuris tantum* with regard to mothers and fathers, daughters and sons, husbands and wives, permanent companions (hereinafter "direct next of kin"), provided this responds to the specific circumstances of a case, as has happened, for example, in the cases of various massacres,[78][26] forced disappearance of persons,[79][27] and extrajudicial executions.[80][28] With regard to these direct next of kin, it is for the State to disprove their claim. In other cases, the Court must analyze if the evidence in the case file proves a violation of the right to personal integrity of the alleged victim, whether he/she is a next of kin of another victim in the case or not. In relation to those persons regarding whom the Court does not presume that the right to personal integrity has been harmed, because they are not direct next of kin, the Court must assess, for example, whether there is a particularly close tie between them and the victims in the case that would allow the Court to declare a violation of their right to personal integrity. The Court can also assess whether the alleged victims have been involved in seeking justice in the specific case[81][29] or whether they have endured special suffering as a result of the facts of the case or of subsequent acts or omissions of the State authorities in relation to the facts.[82][30]

Radilla-Pacheco v. Mexico

23-Nov-2009

Series C No. 209—*Preliminary Objections, Merits, Reparations, and Costs*

2. The facts of the present case refer to the alleged forced disappearance of

Mr. Rosendo Radilla-Pacheco, which supposedly occurred since August 25, 1974, in the hands of members of the Army in the State of Guerrero, Mexico. According to the Inter-American Commission, the alleged violations derived from this fact "continue to exist up to this date, since the State of Mexico has not established the whereabouts of the [alleged] victim, nor have his remains been found." According to that argued by the Commission, "more than 33 years after the occurrence of the facts, there is complete impunity since the State has not criminally punished those responsible, nor has it guaranteed the next of kin an adequate reparation."

3.   Based on the aforementioned, the Commission requested that the Court declare the international responsibility of the State for the alleged violation of the rights enshrined in Articles 3 (Right to Juridical Personality), 4 (Right to Life), 5 (Right to Humane Treatment), 7 (Right to Personal Liberty), 8 (Right to a Fair Trial), and 25 (Judicial Protection) of the American Convention, in relation to Article 1(1) of the same treaty to the detriment of Rosendo Radilla-Pacheco. Likewise, it requested that the Court declare the international responsibility of the State for the alleged violation of Articles 5 (Right to Humane Treatment), 8 (Right to a Fair Trial), and 25 (Judicial Protection) of the American Convention, to the detriment of the following next of kin of Mr. Radilla-Pacheco: Victoria Martínez Nerí (deceased), Tita, Andrea, Rosendo, Romana, Evelina, Rosa, Agustina, Ana María, Carmen, Pilar, Victoria, and Judith, all with the surnames Radilla Martínez. On the other hand, it requested that the Court declare the State's failure to comply with Article 2 of the American Convention (Domestic Legal Effects). Finally, the Commission requested that the Court order that the State adopt certain measures of reparation, both pecuniary and non-pecuniary.

4.   On June 19, 2008 Messrs. Mario Solórzano Betancourt, Humberto Guerrero Rosales, and María Sirvent Bravo-Ahuja, of the Mexican Commission for the Defense and Promotion of Human Rights, and Mrs. Tita Radilla Martínez and Mr. Julio Mata Montiel, of the Association of Relatives of Disappeared Detainees and Victims of Violations of Human Rights in Mexico, representatives of the alleged victims, filed their brief of pleadings, motions, and evidence (hereinafter "brief of pleadings and motions"), in the terms of Article 24 of the Rules of Procedure. In that brief they agreed with that argued by the Inter-American Commission in the application and they also argued the alleged violation of other rights enshrined in the American Convention and the Inter-American Convention on Forced Disappearance of Persons (hereinafter, "the Inter-American Convention on Forced Disappearance" or "CIDFP").

5.   The representatives requested that the Court declare the State responsible for the violation of the rights enshrined in Articles 4 (Right to Life), 5 (Right to Humane Treatment), and 7 (Right to Personal Liberty) of the American Convention, in relation to Article 1(1) of the same treaty and Articles II and XI of

the CIDFP, in detriment of Mr. Rosendo Radilla. Likewise, they argued that the State is responsible for the violation of Article 5 (Right to Humane Treatment) of the American Convention in relation to Article 1(1) of the same instrument, to the detriment of the following next of kin of Mr. Radilla-Pacheco: Victoria Martínez Neri and Tita, Andrea, Romana, Evelina, Rosa, Ana, Agustina, María del Carmen, María del Pilar, Judith, Victoria, and Rosendo, all of them with the surnames Radilla Martínez, as well as of the "community to which Mr. Rosendo Radilla-Pacheco belonged." On the other hand, they requested that the State be declared responsible for the violation of Articles 8 (Right to a Fair Trial) and 25 (Judicial Protection) of the American Convention, in relation to Article 1(1) of said treaty and Articles I, subparagraph (b), and IX of the CIDFP, to the detriment of Mr. Rosendo Radilla and "his next of kin." Additionally, they requested that the Tribunal declare the violation of Article 13 (Freedom of Thought and Expression) in relation to Articles 8 (Right to a Fair Trial), 25 (Judicial Protection), and 1(1) (Obligation to Respect Rights), all of the American Convention, in consistence with Article I, subparagraphs (a) and (b), of the CIDFP, in relation to the "right to the truth" to the detriment of "the next of kin" of Mr. Rosendo Radilla-Pacheco and the Mexican society as a whole. Finally, they requested that the Court declare that "[t]he State of Mexico is responsible for not adopting the legislative measures or that of any other nature necessary for the obtainment of justice and truth, thus violating Article 2 of the American Convention, in consistence with Article III of the [CIDFP]," and that "the reservation filed by the State of Mexico to Article IX of the [CIDFP] be declared null for going against [its] object and purpose."

104.   Before ruling on the merits of the present matter, this Court considers it necessary to specify, in the present chapter, the next of kin of the alleged victim, Mr. Rosendo Radilla-Pacheco, regarding whom it will analyze the existence of possible violations to their human rights.

105.   In the application, the Inter-American Commission indicated that "[t]he next of kin of Rosendo Radilla-Pacheco are his spouse, Mrs. Victoria Martínez Neri (deceased) and his twelve children Tita, Andrea, Rosendo, Romana, Evelina, Rosa, Agustina, Ana María, Carmen, Pilar, Victoria, and Judith, all of surnames Radilla Martínez." The representatives agreed with the list of the alleged victims presented by the Commission.

106.   In its response to the application, the State indicated that "[i]n good faith, it acknowledge[d] the family relationship of Messrs. Tita, Andrea, and Rosendo, all of surnames Radilla Martínez," with Mr. Rosendo Radilla-Pacheco. However, it asked the Court "[n]ot to consider Victoria Martínez Neri, or Romana, Evelina, Rosa, Agustina, Ana María, Carmen, Pilar, Victoria or Judith, all of surnames Radilla Martínez, [alleged] victims in the present case, since they were not presented as such by the Commission at the correct procedural moment." In this

regard, it stated that in "the Report [on Merits] No. 60/07 of July 27, 2007, the Commission only mentioned Mr. Rosendo Radilla-Pacheco as an [alleged] victim and made brief references to three of his next of kin: Tita Radilla, Andrea Radilla, and Rosendo Radilla Martínez, but it never referred to them as [alleged] victims." According to the State, in that report the Commission did not mention "Victoria Martínez Neri or Romana, Evelina, Rosa, Agustina, Ana María, Carmen, Pilar, Victoria, and Judith, all of surnames Radilla Martínez, as injured parties, which it does do so in its application."

107.   In response to that requested by the State, in their final written arguments the representatives stated that the alleged victims in the present case have been "[d]uly identified with their voter credentials and acknowledged as victims in the [Commission's] application in its paragraph 75." The Inter-American Commission did not make any comments in this regard.

108.   The Court has established that the alleged victims must be established in the application and in the Commission's report according to Article 50 of the Convention. Additionally, pursuant to Article 34(1) of the Rules of Procedure, the Commission, and not this Tribunal, shall identify with precision and at due procedural time the alleged victims in a case before this Court.[71][31]

109.   In this regard, the Tribunal warns that the Report on Merits adopted by the Commission in this case mentioned Mr. "[R]osendo Radilla-Pacheco and his next of kin, Tita Radilla Martínez, Andrea Radilla Martínez, and Rosendo Radilla Martínez" as victims of the rights enshrined, *inter alia*, in Articles 8 and 25 of the American Convention.[72][32] At the same time, said report recommends that the State "[a]dequately repair the next of kin of Mr. Rosendo Radilla-Pacheco, Tita Radilla Martínez, Andrea Radilla Martínez, and Rosendo Radilla Martínez, for the violations of human rights established in the . . . report . . . ."[73][33] In the rest of the document there are no specific references to any other of the next of kin of the alleged victim, only generic mentions to the same.[74][34] An expanded list with the names of thirteen of Mr. Radilla-Pacheco's next of kin is presented before the Inter-American Commission after the adoption of that report, on September 18, 2007, through a brief in which the representatives stated their position on the submission of the case to this Tribunal.[75][35] Thus, in the application filed by the Commission before the Court, thirteen of Mr. Radilla-Pacheco's next of kin, that is, his 12 children and deceased wife, are identified as alleged victims.

110.   Pursuant to the jurisprudence of this Tribunal, the determination made by the Commission in its application regarding who should be considered next of kin of the alleged disappeared victim shall correspond to that decided by it in the Report on Merits. Legal certainty demands, as a general rule, that all the alleged victims be duly identified in both briefs, not making it possible to add new alleged victims in the application, without this resulting in a detriment to the

right to defense of the accused State. In this case the Commission has not argued difficulties in the timely determination of all the next of kin of Mr. Rosendo Radilla as alleged victims. Likewise, it cannot be concluded from the case file that this is one of those cases in which, due to its characteristics, the determination of the same is a complex task, which would make other considerations by this Tribunal necessary.

111. Based on the aforementioned and taking into consideration the acknowledgment made by the State, it decides to only consider Mrs. Tita and Andrea and Mr. Rosendo, all of them with the surnames Radilla Martínez, as alleged victims. The Court regrets that, due to procedural reasons, this Tribunal cannot consider the other next of kin of Mr. Rosendo Radilla-Pacheco, whom it presumes suffered in equal conditions, as alleged victims. However, it points out that the non-determination of violations in their detriment by this international instance does not prevent or discard the possibility that the State, in good faith, adopt reparation measures in their favor.

ANALYSIS AND QUESTIONS RAISED BY THE COURT'S JURISPRUDENCE

Through its jurisprudence, the Inter-American Court of Human Rights has reaffirmed that victims of violations of the American Convention are considered injured parties. These injured parties also include the direct next of kin of the victim and, generally, must be individually identified. In certain cases, however, the Court has recognized the difficulty of identifying injured parties, as in cases involving massacres or multiple murders. Moreover, in some cases, the Court has declared that injured parties need not be individually identified, especially when reparations are to be awarded collectively, as in certain cases involving indigenous communities.

- In *Valle Jaramillo et al.*, the Court stated that "direct next of kin" (e.g., parents, children and spouses or permanent partners of victims) are presumed to be injured parties, such that the burden of proof is on the State to disprove that such direct of next of kin are injured parties. Should all direct next of kin be considered to be injured parties? Should others be presumed to be injured parties?

- Also in *Valle Jaramillo et al.*, the Court stated that when persons cannot be presumed to be injured parties based on a direct next of kin status, the Court can assess whether they have a "particularly close tie" or have "endured special suffering" in relation to the victim and the facts of the case. What constitutes a "particularly close tie" or enduring "special suffering"?

- In some cases, when injured parties were not identified at the correct procedural moment, the Court excluded them from the reparations award, citing respect for the right to defense of all parties. If violations are proven, is it equitable for such injured parties to be excluded?
- Are there circumstances other than those of collective reparations to indigenous communities where individual identifications may be unnecessary?
- The Court has recognized that the circumstances of certain cases, such as those involving massacres and multiple murders, make the identification of all victims and injured parties difficult. What other circumstances could make the identification of victims and injured parties difficult? How should the Court address identifications which are subsequent to the Court's judgment or those that are anticipated, but not confirmed, at the time of the Court's judgment?

IV. IDENTIFICATION OF BENEFICIARIES ENTITLED TO REPARATIONS

Closely linked to the definitions of victim and other injured party is the identification of beneficiaries who are entitled to reparations ordered by the Inter-American Court of Human Rights. As demonstrated by the following case excerpts, beneficiaries frequently are victims or other injured parties in cases before the Court; however, in some cases the Court has drawn distinctions between these categories.

Velasquez Rodriguez v. Honduras
29-Jul-1988
Series C No. 4—*Merits*

2.   In submitting the case, the Commission invoked Articles 50 and 51 of the American Convention on Human Rights (hereinafter "the Convention" or "the American Convention") and requested that the Court determine whether the State in question had violated Articles 4 (Right to Life), 5 (Right to Humane Treatment), and 7 (Right to Personal Liberty) of the Convention in the case of Angel Manfredo Velásquez Rodríguez (also known as Manfredo Velásquez). In addition, the Commission asked the Court to rule that "the consequences of the situation that constituted the breach of such right or freedom be remedied and that fair compensation be paid to the injured party or parties."

3.   According to the petition filed with the Commission, and the supplementary information received subsequently, Manfredo Velásquez, a student at the National Autonomous University of Honduras, "was violently detained without a warrant for his arrest by members of the National Office of Investigations (DNI) and G-2 of the Armed Forces of Honduras." The detention took place in Tegucigalpa on the afternoon of September 12, 1981. According to the petitioners, several eyewitnesses reported that Manfredo Velásquez and others were detained and taken to the cells of Public Security Forces Station No. 2 located in the Barrio El Manchén of Tegucigalpa, where he was "accused of alleged political crimes and subjected to harsh interrogation and cruel torture." The petition added that on September 17, 1981, Manfredo Velásquez was moved to the First Infantry Battalion, where the interrogation continued, but that the police and security forces denied that he had been detained.

53.   With regard to entitlement to receive the compensation, the representative of the Government and of the Commission, in the document they signed on January 23, 1989, recognized as the sole beneficiaries of that compensation the wife of Manfredo Velásquez, Mrs. Emma Guzmán Urbina, and the children of that marriage, Héctor Ricardo, Nadia Waleska and Herling Lizzett Velásquez Guzmán. They added that their right could only be enforced once they had fulfilled the requirements of Honduran law to be recognized as heirs of the victim.

54.   As previously stated, the obligation to indemnify is not derived from internal law, but from violation of the American Convention. It is the result of an international obligation. To demand indemnification, the family members of Manfredo Velásquez need only show their family relationship. They are not required to follow the procedure of Honduran inheritance law.

55.   At the hearing of October 2, 1987, Zenaida Velásquez Rodríguez, referred to four children of her brother, Manfredo Velásquez, but in the document signed by the Commission and the Government on January 23, 1989, only three children are mentioned. Nor was any proof of the existence of a fourth child found in the Government's reply to point 5 of the request made by the Secretariat of the Court on April 3, 1989. Should there be a fourth child, he would be entitled to a proportionate share of the indemnity the Court has awarded to the children of the victim.

Aloeboetoe et al. v. Suriname
10-Sep-1993
Series C No. 15—*Reparations and Costs*

1.   The instant case was brought to the Inter-American Court of Human

Rights (hereinafter "the Court") by the Commission on August 27, 1990, by a note transmitting its Report 03/90. It originated in Petition N° 10.150 of January 15, 1988, against Suriname.

In its communication, the Commission asserted that "the Government of Suriname violated Articles 1, 2, 4(1), 5(1), 5(2), 7(1), 7(2), 7(3), 25(1), and 25(2) of the American Convention on Human Rights" (hereinafter "the Convention" or "the American Convention"). On those grounds, the Commission asked the Court "to adjudicate this case in accordance with the terms of the Convention, to fix responsibility for the violation described herein, and to award just compensation to the victims' next of kin."

2.   The Commission submitted its memorial on April 1, 1991.

The events that gave rise to the petition apparently occurred on December 31, 1987, in Atjoni (village of Pokigron, District of Sipaliwini) and in Tjongalangapassi, District of Brokopondo. In Atjoni, more than 20 male, unarmed Bushnegroes (Maroons) had been attacked, abused, and beaten with riflebutts by a group of soldiers. A number of them had been wounded with bayonets and knives and were detained on suspicion of belonging to the Jungle Commando, a subversive group. Some 50 persons witnessed these occurrences.

4.   The petition asserts that the soldiers allowed some of the Maroons to continue on their way, but that seven of them, including a 15-year old boy, were dragged, blindfolded, into a military vehicle and taken through Tjongalangapassi in the direction of Paramaribo. The names of the persons taken by the soldiers, their place, and date of birth, insofar as is known, are as follows: Daison Aloeboetoe, of Gujaba, born June 7, 1960; Dedemanu Aloeboetoe, of Gujaba; Mikuwendje Aloeboetoe, of Gujaba, born February 4, 1973; John Amoida, of Asindonhopo (resident of Gujaba); Richenel Voola, alias Aside or Ameikanbuka, of Grantatai (found alive); Martin Indisie Banai, of Gujaba, born June 3, 1955; and, Beri Tiopo, of Gujaba.

5.   The petition goes on to state that the vehicle stopped when it came to Kilometer 30. The soldiers ordered the victims to get out or forcibly dragged them out of the vehicle. They were given a spade and ordered to start digging. Aside was injured while trying to escape, but was not followed. The other six Maroons were killed.

17.   With regard to the persons who would be entitled to compensation for actual damages, the Commission explains that it is necessary to take into account the family structure of the Maroons, of which the Saramakas (the tribe to which the victims belonged) are a part. It is essentially a matriarchal[36] structure, where polygamy is common. In Suriname, marriages must be registered in order to be recognized by the State. Due to the dearth of registry offices in the interior of the country, however, that requirement is generally not met. The Commission

is of the opinion that this should not affect the right to compensation of the relatives or spouses of unregistered marriages. It is argued that the care of family members is entrusted to a communal group organized along maternal lines; this is something that should be borne in mind in determining which of the relatives should be compensated. The direct, personal damages of a monetary nature that give rise to compensatory rights should be measured principally by the degree of financial dependence that existed between the claimant and the deceased. The list of aggrieved parties entitled to compensation was drawn up by the Commission partly on the basis of sworn statements by the next of kin of the victims.

54.   The damages suffered by the victims up to the time of their death entitle them to compensation. That right to compensation is transmitted to their heirs by succession.

The damages payable for causing loss of life represent an inherent right that belongs to the injured parties. It is for this reason that national jurisprudence generally accepts that the right to apply for compensation for the death of a person passes to the survivors affected by that death. In that jurisprudence a distinction is made between successors and injured third parties. With respect to the former, it is assumed that the death of the victim has caused them actual and moral damages and the burden of proof is on the other party to show that such damages do not exist. Claimants who are not successors, however, must provide specific proof justifying their right to damages, as explained below (cf. infra, para. 68).

67.   The obligation to make reparation for damages caused is sometimes, and within the limits imposed by the legal system, extended to cover persons who, though not successors of the victims, have suffered some consequence of the unlawful act. This issue has been the subject of numerous judgments by domestic courts. Case law nevertheless establishes certain conditions that must be met for a claim of compensatory damages filed by a third party to be admitted.

68.   First, the payment sought must be based on payments actually made by the victim to the claimant, regardless of whether or not they constituted a legal obligation to pay support. Such payments cannot be simply a series of sporadic contributions; they must be regular, periodic payments either in cash, in kind, or in services. What is important here is the effectiveness and regularity of the contributions.

Second, the nature of the relationship between the victim and the claimant should be such that it provides some basis for the assumption that the payments would have continued had the victim not been killed.

Lastly, the claimant must have experienced a financial need that was periodically met by the contributions made by the victim. This does not necessarily mean that the person should be indigent, but only that it be somebody for whom the payment represented a benefit that, had it not been for the victim's attitude, it would not have been able to obtain on his or her own.

83. In its brief, the Commission explains that, in traditional Maroon society, a person is a member not only of his or her own family group, but also of his or her own village community and tribal group. According to the Commission, the villagers make up a family in the broad sense. This is why damages caused to one of its members also represent damages to the community, which would have to be indemnified.

As for the argument linking the claim for moral damages to the unique social structure of the Saramakas who were generally harmed by the killings, the Court believes that all persons, in addition to being members of their own families and citizens of a State, also generally belong to intermediate communities. In practice, the obligation to pay moral compensation does not extend to such communities, nor to the State in which the victim participated; these are redressed by the enforcement of the system of laws. If in some exceptional case such compensation has ever been granted, it would have been to a community that suffered direct damages.

Loayza Tamayo v. Peru
17-Nov-1998
Series C No. 33—*Merits*

1. The Commission submitted this case for a ruling on whether the following articles of the Convention were violated: 7 (Right to Personal Liberty), 5 (Right to Humane Treatment), 8 (Right to a Fair Trial), and 25 (Right to Judicial Protection), all these in relation to Article 1(1) of the Convention for the alleged "unlawful deprivation of liberty, torture, cruel, inhuman or degrading treatment, violation of the judicial guarantees, and double jeopardy to María Elena Loayza-Tamayo for the same cause, in violation of the Convention," and of Article 51(2) of the Convention for refusing "to comply with the recommendations formulated by the Commission." It also asked the Court to declare that Peru "must pay full compensation to María Elena Loayza-Tamayo for the grave damage—material and moral—she has suffered and, consequently, [to] instruct the Peruvian State to order her immediate release and make her appropriate reparation" and to pay the costs incurred in processing the Case.

3. The facts set out in the application are summarized in the following paragraphs:

   (a) On February 6, 1993, Ms. María Elena Loayza-Tamayo, a Peruvian citizen and a professor at the Universidad San Martín de Porres, was arrested together with a relative, Mr. Ladislao Alberto Huamán-Loayza, by officers of the National Counter-

Terrorism Bureau (hereinafter "DINCOTE") of the Peruvian National Police Force, at a property on Mitobamba Street, Block D, Lot 18, Los Naranjos Estate, Los Olivos District, Lima, Peru. Under the Ley de Arrepentimiento (Repentance Law) enacted through Decree-Law N°. 25.499, Angélica Torres-García, alias "Mirtha," captured on February 5, 1993, denounced Ms. María Elena Loayza-Tamayo. The application also indicates that the Peruvian State, failing to observe the verification procedure required by that law and its regulations, arrested Ms. Loayza-Tamayo the following day without an arrest warrant issued by the competent judicial authority, as an alleged collaborator of the subversive group "Shining Path."

(b) Ms. María Elena Loayza-Tamayo was detained by DINCOTE from February 6 to 26, 1993, and was not taken before the Special Naval Court, in violation of Article 12(c) of Decree-Law N° 25.475 (crime of terrorism). She was held incommunicado in the DINCOTE offices for ten days and subjected to torture, cruel and degrading treatment, and unlawful pressure, for example, "torture, . . . threats of drowning on the beach at night, and rape to [which] she was subjected by members of DINCOTE," in an effort to force her to incriminate herself and admit that she was a member of the Peruvian Communist Party—Shining Path (hereinafter "PCP-SL"). However, Ms. María Elena Loayza-Tamayo claimed that she was innocent, denied membership in the PCP-SL, and, in fact, "criticized its methods: the violence and the human rights violations committed by that subversive group."

(c) During the ten days in which she was held incommunicado, Ms. Loayza-Tamayo was allowed no contact with her family or attorney, nor were they informed of her arrest. Her family learned of her arrest through an anonymous telephone call on February 8, 1993. No protective remedy could be filed on her behalf because Decree-Law N° 25.659 (Treason) prohibited the filing of "a petition of habeas corpus when the acts in question concern the crime of terrorism."

(d) On February 26, 1993, Ms. María Elena Loayza-Tamayo was exhibited to the press in "prison stripes," and accused of the crime of treason. She was then taken to the former Army Veterinary Hospital—later converted into a "holding-station"—where she remained until March 3 of that year when she was transferred to the Chorrillos Women's Maximum Security Prison.

(e) María Elena Loayza-Tamayo was prosecuted before the military jurisdiction on the charge of treason. Police Report N° 049-DIVICOTE 3-DINCOTE was established, charging her with that crime on February 25, 1993. She was later brought before the Special Naval Court for trial. The Special Naval Court, composed of faceless military judges, acquitted her in its judgment of March 5, 1993. She was subsequently convicted by the Special Naval Court Martial in its judgment of April 2, 1993. The Special Tribunal of the Supreme Council of Military Justice, in its judgment of August 11, 1993, rejected a petition seeking nullification of the sentence, acquitted her of treason and ordered the case file to be remitted to the civil courts so that she could be tried for the crime of terrorism. The Assistant Special Attorney General filed with the Full Chamber of the Special Supreme Military Tribunal a petition for special review of that sentence, which culminated in a judgment upholding her acquittal on September 24, 1993.

(f) Ms. María Elena Loayza-Tamayo continued in detention for the period between the judgment of the Special Tribunal of the Supreme Council of Military Justice issued on August 11, 1993, and the detention order issued by the civil courts on October 8, 1993, although during that period "her judicial position was that of an acquitted detainee who had been neither tried nor convicted."

(g) Ms. María Elena Loayza-Tamayo was tried in various instances of the civil courts for the crime of terrorism: the Forty-third Criminal Court of Lima bound her over for trial on October 8, 1993. Ms. Loayza filed a *res judicata* objection based on the principle of *non bis in idem*. On October 10, 1994, the "faceless special tribunal of the civil courts" dismissed her objection and sentenced her to 20 years' imprisonment on the basis of the same cause.

(h) Subsequent to the filing of its application, the Commission informed the Court that a writ seeking nullification of that judgment was filed with the Supreme Court of Justice and was dismissed on October 6, 1995. Ms. María Elena Loayza-Tamayo remained in prison throughout the proceedings in both the military and the civil courts.

27-Nov-98
Series C No. 42—*Reparations and Costs*

88.   It is obvious that in the instant Case the victim is Ms. María Elena Loayza-Tamayo. In its Judgment of September 17, 1997, the Court found that the State had violated, to her detriment, a number of rights upheld in the Convention. Hence, she is entitled to the payment of the compensation ordered by the Court in her favor.

89.   In keeping with the language used in the Judgment on the merits and in Article 63 of the Convention, it is also up to the Court to determine which of the victim's "next of kin" are, in the instant case, "injured parties."

92.   The Court considers that the expression "next of kin" of the victim should be interpreted in a broad sense to include all persons related by close kinship. Hence, the victim's children, Gisselle Elena and Paul Abelardo Zambrano-Loayza; her parents, Julio Loayza-Sudario and Adelina Tamayo-Trujillo de Loayza, and her siblings, Delia Haydée, Carolina Maida, Julio William, Olga Adelina, Rubén Edilberto and Giovanna Elizabeth, all by the surname of Loayza-Tamayo, are considered her next of kin. As such, they could be entitled to receive compensation if they meet the tests established in the jurisprudence of this Court.

103.   Although the injured parties' direct participation in the reparations stage is important for the Court, their nonappearance, as in the instant Case, does not relieve either the Commission or the Court of their duty as organs of the inter-American system for the protection of human rights. That duty is to ensure that those rights are effectively protected, which includes matters related to the duty to make reparations.

104.   Inasmuch as the Court has held that reparations for the victim's next of kin are in order, it must now determine their nature and amount. Lacking claims or allegations from certain family members, the Court will act on the basis of the information at hand.

105.   For the reasons explained and contrary to what the State alleged, the fact that the victim's next of kin did not appear before the Court does not prevent the latter from ordering reparations on their behalf.

Cantoral Benavides v. Peru
18-Aug-2000
Series C No. 69—*Merits*

1.   The Inter-American Commission on Human Rights (hereinafter "the Commission" or "the Inter-American Commission"), in filing the application,

invoked Articles 50 and 51 of the American Convention on Human Rights (hereinafter "the American Convention" or "the Convention") and Article 26 et seq. of the Rules of Procedure then in force.[137] In filing said application, the Commission asked the Court to decide whether the State of Peru (hereinafter "the State" or "Peru") had violated the following Articles of the Convention: 1(1) (Obligation to Respect Rights), 2 (Domestic Legal Effects), 7(1) to 7(6) (Right to Personal Liberty), 5 (Right to Humane Treatment), 8(1), 8(2), 8(2)d, 8(2)f, 8.2.g), 8(3), and 8(4) (Right to a Fair Trial) and 25 (Right to Judicial Protection), and Articles 2 and 8 of the Inter-American Convention to Prevent and Punish Torture (hereinafter "Inter-American Convention Against Torture"). According to the application, these violations were suffered by Mr. Luis Alberto Cantoral-Benavides due to the unlawful deprivation of his liberty, following his arbitrary detention and incarceration: cruel, inhuman, and degrading treatment; violation of the judicial guarantees; and double jeopardy based on the same facts. In its final written brief, the Commission added the alleged violation of Articles 8(2)(c), 8(5), and 9 of the American Convention, and 6 of the Inter-American Convention Against Torture.

Therefore,

THE COURT,

1. declares that the State violated, to the detriment of Luis Alberto Cantoral-Benavides, Article 5(1) and 5(2) of the American Convention on Human Rights.

2. declares that the State violated, to the detriment of Luis Alberto Cantoral-Benavides, Article 7(1), 7(2), 7(3), 7(4) and 7(5) of the American Convention on Human Rights.

3. declares that the State violated, to the detriment of Luis Alberto Cantoral-Benavides, Article 8(1) of the American Convention on Human Rights.

4. declares that the State violated, to the detriment of Luis Alberto Cantoral-Benavides, Article 8(2) of the American Convention on Human Rights.

5. declares that the State violated, to the detriment of Luis Alberto Cantoral-Benavides, Article 8(2)(c), 8(2)d and 8(2)f of the American Convention on Human Rights.

6. declares that the State violated, to the detriment of Luis Alberto Cantoral-Benavides, Article 8(2)(g), 8(3) of the American Convention on Human Rights.

7. declares that the State violated, to the detriment of Luis Alberto Cantoral-Benavides, Article 8(5) of the American Convention on Human Rights.

8. declares that the State violated, to the detriment of Luis Alberto Cantoral-Benavides, Article 9 of the American Convention on Human Rights.

9. declares that the State violated, to the detriment of Luis Alberto Cantoral-Benavides, Articles 7(6) and 25(1) of the American Convention on Human Rights.

3-Dec-01

Series C No. 88—*Reparations and Costs*

36.   Inasmuch as the Convention violations that the Court established in its judgment of August 18, 2000, were committed to the detriment of Luis Alberto Cantoral Benavides, he must be regarded as an "injured party" and as such is entitled to the reparations established by the Court in the present case.

37.   That Gladys Benavides López and Luis Fernando, Isaac Alonso and José Antonio Cantoral Benavides are beneficiaries is not in dispute. Mrs. Benavides López must be regarded as a beneficiary inasmuch as she is the victim's mother. The *jurisprudence constante* of this Court[25][38] has been that a victim's parents' suffering can be presumed and must be compensated. Luis Fernando, Isaac Alonso, and José Antonio Cantoral Benavides are Luis Alberto Cantoral Benavides' brothers and as such were not indifferent to his sufferings.[26][39]

38.   The Court also notes that in the instant case, there is proof that the events that befell Luis Alberto Cantoral Benavides caused his mother and his three brother's damages of various kinds and to varying degrees of intensity, thus making them *titulaires* of the right to compensation.

61.

    a)   In the case of Mrs. Gladys Benavides López, the Court's *jurisprudence constante* is that in the case of a victim's parents, moral damages need not be shown.[48][40] Moreover, in the instant case it is clear that the victim's mother personally undertook the responsibility of securing the release of her son Luis Alberto. Aware as she was of the conditions of her son's incarceration, her mental torment can be presumed. She suffered physical ailments as well. She was humiliated, harassed, and intimidated. She was forced to endure vaginal inspections on some of the visits she made to her son's prison. During those visits, she was denied any affectionate physical contact with her son. Often the visits to the detention and incarceration centers were restricted. Her family broke apart: her sons Luis Alberto, Luis Fernando, and José Antonio had to leave the country because of the situation in Peru at the time and the circumstances they had experienced. She also suffered from a variety of health problems caused by the events in this case.

    b)   In the case of Luis Fernando Cantoral Benavides, the victim's twin brother who went with him when he was detained and was also detained and incarcerated for similar reasons and experienced his brother's suffering firsthand: asa consequence of the events in this case, he too had to leave the country and [now] lives apart from his family. Given these facts, the Court reiterates that in the case of siblings, the intensity of the bond and affective relationship between them has to be considered.[49] [41] Hence, given the circumstances of the case, Luis Fernando Cantoral Benavides must also be compensated for non-pecuniary damages.

   c) Isaac Alonso Cantoral Benavides was being followed and constantly harassed by unknown persons. As his mother testified at the public hearing, Isaac Alonso has had psychological problems because he was alone when his brothers were exhibited to the press:

> He took it hard. He left that night. He was walking around alone. When family went to see him, he didn't want to talk, he was crying. He [was] traumatize[d] and did not want to continue his studies. He [had] to be put into psychotherapy. Little by little he recovered and is now back to his studies.

His family environment changed and his family was torn apart. The trauma that Isaac Alonso experienced clearly demonstrates the affective bond that exists between him and his brother Luis Alberto, and how the situation affected him. Given the foregoing, he too must be compensated for non-pecuniary damages.

d) José Antonio Cantoral Benavides was also affected by the difficulty his family was experiencing and by the incarceration of his brothers, felt a sense of insecurity, and was afraid that he too would be taken into custody. He left the country and now lives in Bolivia. While there is no reliable evidence proving the non-pecuniary damages he suffered, it is reasonable to presume that he, like his mother and other brothers, could not be indifferent to what happened to his brother and to his family and therefore must be compensated for non-pecuniary damages.[50] [42]

Bamaca Velasquez v. Guatemala
22-Feb-2002
Series C No. 91—*Reparations and Costs*

33.   Likewise, claims can be made regarding the damage caused by the death of a victim to his next of kin or to third parties, based on a right of their own.[38] [43] However, the Court has pointed out that there must be certain circumstances, such as that of a relationship of effective and regular dependence having existed between the claimant and the victim, so that it can be reasonably assumed that the

benefits received by the former would have continued if the victim had not died and that the claimant had an economic need that was covered on a regular basis by the assistance provided by the victim.[39][44]

34.   As regards these claimants, the *onus probandi* rests on the next of kin of the victim,[40][45] the term "next of kin" being understood in accordance with Article 2(15) of the Rules of Procedure[41][46] of the Court (adopted in its November 24, 2000 Order, [which] entered into force on July 1, 2001) as a broad concept that covers all persons having close kinship, including children, parents, and siblings, who may be considered as next of kin and have the right to receive compensation, insofar as they fulfill the requirements set forth in case law by this Court.[42][47]

Myrna Mack Chang v. Guatemala
25-Nov-2003
Series C No. 101—*Merits, Reparations, and Costs*

2.   The Commission filed the application on the basis of Article 51 of the American Convention, for the Court to decide whether the State violated Articles 4 (Right to Life), 8 (Right to Fair Trial), and 25 (Judicial Protection), in combination with Article 1(1) (Obligation to Respect Rights) of the American Convention, to the detriment of Myrna Elizabeth Mack Chang (hereinafter "Myrna Mack Chang") and her next of kin, "due to the extra-legal execution of Myrna Mack Chang [that took place] on September 11, 1990, in Guatemala City."

4.   According to the Commission, Guatemala is responsible for the arbitrary deprivation of the right to life of Myrna Mack Chang because the murder of the victim, committed on September 11, 1990, was the consequence of a military intelligence operation, springing from a prior plan and carefully prepared by the high command of the Presidential General Staff. Said plan involved, first, selecting the victim in a precise manner due to her professional activity; second, brutally murdering Myrna Mack Chang; and third, covering up the direct perpetrators and accessories of the murder, obstructing the judicial investigation, and, insofar as possible, ensuring that impunity prevailed with respect to the murder. The Commission added that the State has not resorted to all the means available to it with the aim of conducting a serious and effective investigation that could be the basis for complete elucidation of the facts [and] prosecution, trial, and punishment of those responsible—both direct perpetrators and accessories—within a reasonable term. This situation has been made worse by the existence of de facto and legal mechanisms, tolerated by the Guatemalan State, that obstruct adequate administration of justice.

243.   The provision of Article 2(15) of the Rules of Procedure[278][48] should be

underlined, as regards the necessary breadth of the concept of "next of kin of the victim." Said concept includes all persons linked by close kinship, including the parents, children, and siblings, who might have the right to compensation, insofar as they fulfill the requirements set forth in the case law of this Court. Regarding this point, we must highlight the criterion followed by the Court of assuming that the death of an individual causes non-pecuniary damage to the closest members of the family, especially those who were in close emotional contact with the victim,[279][49] a situation that will be determined in the respective chapter.

244.   It has also been proven that Ronald Chang Apuy, first cousin of the victim, was raised by the Mack Chang family since he was a small child and is considered one more member of the family. Therefore, the Court deems that Ronald Chang Apuy will be assimilated to the status of sibling and it assumes that he could not be indifferent to what happened to Myrna Mack Chang, for which reason the acts in violation of the Convention set forth in this Judgment also affected him and he must be considered a beneficiary of the reparations.

245.   With respect to Vivian Mack Chang, this Court deems that, even though she has not participated in the instant proceeding, personally or through a representative, it has been proven that she is a sister of the victim. Therefore, the Court assumes that she has undergone the same suffering as the rest of the family, for which reason she must also be a beneficiary of reparations.

Mapiripán Massacre v. Colombia
15-Sep-2005
Series C No. 134—*Merits, Reparations, and Costs*

1.   On September 5, 2003, in accordance with the provisions of Articles 50 and 61 of the American Convention, the Inter-American Commission on Human Rights (hereinafter "the Commission" or "the Inter-American Commission") filed before the Court the application in this case against the State of Colombia (hereinafter "the State" or "Colombia"), which originated in complaint No. 12.250 [was] received at the Secretariat of the Commission on October 6, 1999.

2.   The Commission filed the application in this case for the Court to decide whether the State breached Articles 4 (Right to Life), 5 (Right to Humane Treatment), and 7 (Right to Personal Liberty) of the American Convention, to the detriment of the alleged victims of the alleged massacre carried out in Mapiripán [who were] stated in the application. The Commission also asked the Court to decide whether the State breached Articles 8.1 (Right to Fair Trial) and 25 (Right to Judicial Protection) of the Convention, in combination with Article 1(1) (Obligation to Respect Rights) of said treaty, to the detriment of the alleged victims

of the alleged massacre and their next of kin. When it filed the application, the Commission pointed out that "between July 15 and 20, 1997, . . . approximately one hundred members of the Autodefensas Unidas de Colombia, . . . with the collaboration and acquiescence of agents of the . . . State, deprived of their liberty, tortured, and murdered at least 49 civilians, after which they destroyed their bodies and threw their remains into the Guaviare River, in the Municipality of Mapiripán, Department of Meta." The Commission also pointed out that the alleged victims were "approximately 49 individuals," of whom it identified ten individuals and some of their next of kin.

3.   The Commission also asked the Court, in accordance with Article 63(1) of the Convention, to order the State to carry out several measures of pecuniary and non-pecuniary reparation, such as payment of costs and expenses incurred by the next of kin of the alleged victims under both domestic and international venues.

257.   The next of kin of the victims will be entitled to the reparations set by the Court, as victims themselves of the violations found regarding the Convention, as well as of those set by the Court as injured parties due to the violations committed against the approximately 49 victims recognized by the State. In this regard:

a)   in accordance with its jurisprudence,[279][50] this Court deems that the next of kin of the victims referred to in a document issued by a competent authority—a birth certificate, death certificate, or identification card—or those recognized as such in domestic proceedings, have been identified; and

b)   with regard to the other next of kin who have not been adequately identified or at least individually listed in this proceeding, the Court deems that the compensation due to each must be granted in the same manner set forth with regard to those who have been duly identified, in the understanding that they must appear before the official mechanisms that will be established for this purpose, in accordance with the instant Judgment, within 24 months of when it was notified, and they must prove their relationship or kinship with the victim through sufficient means of identification or by means of two attesting witnesses, as the case may be.[230][51]

Chaparro Álvarez and Lapo Íñiguez v. Ecuador

21-Nov-2007

Series C No. 170—*Preliminary Objections, Merits, Reparations, and Costs*

1.   On June 23, 2006, in accordance with the provisions of Articles 51 and

61 of the Inter-American Convention, the Inter-American Commission on Human Rights (hereinafter "the Commission" or "the Inter-American Commission") lodged before the Court an application against the Republic of Ecuador (hereinafter "the State" or "Ecuador"), arising from petitions Nos. 12,091 and 172/99, forwarded, respectively, by Juan Carlos Chaparro Álvarez on September 8, 1998, and by Freddy Hernán Lapo Iñiguez on April 14, 1999. On October 22, 2003, the Commission adopted Report No. 77/03 in which it decided to joinder the petitions of Mr. Chaparro and Mr. Lapo in a single case and to declare them admissible. Subsequently, on February 28, 2006, the Commission adopted Report on Merits No. 6/06 in the terms of Article 50 of the Convention, which included specific recommendations for the State. The State was notified of this report on March 23, 2006. On June 16, 2006, the Commission decided to submit the instant case to the jurisdiction of the Court[1 52] in view of the lack of response from the State.

2.   The Commission indicated that, at the time of the facts, Mr. Chaparro, a Chilean national, was the owner of the Aislantes Plumavit Compañía Limitada factory (hereinafter "the factory" or "the Plumavit factor"), which manufactured ice chests for transporting and exporting different products, while Mr. Lapo, an Ecuadorean national, was the manager of the factory. According to the application, as a result of the "Rivera anti-narcotics operation," on November 14, 1997, anti-narcotics police officials seized a shipment of fish belonging to the company *"Mariscos Oreana Maror"* in Guayaquil's Simón Bolívar Airport that was going to be sent to Miami, United States of America. The Commission stated that, in this shipment, some thermal insulated boxes or ice chests were found in which the presence of heroin and cocaine hydrochloride was discovered. According to the application, Mr. Chaparro was deemed to belong to an "international criminal organization" dedicated to international drug trafficking, because his factory produced ice chests similar to those seized. For this reason, the Guayas Twelfth Criminal Judge ordered a search of the Plumavit factory and the detention of Mr. Chaparro for investigative purposes. According to the Commission, at the time of Mr. Chaparro's detention, the State authorities did not advise him of the respective reasons or justification, or of his right to request consular assistance from the country of which he was a national. The Commission advised that, during the search of the said factory, Mr. Lapo and other employees of the Plumavit factory were detained. The detention of Mr. Lapo was allegedly not made *in flagrante delicto*, and it was not preceded by a written order by a judge; moreover, he also was not advised of the reasons and justification for his detention. The two alleged victims were allegedly transferred to a police station and remained incommunicado for five days. Supposedly, Mr. Chaparro did not have a lawyer present when he made his pre-trial statement, and Mr. Lapo's public defender was unsatisfactory.

According to the Commission, the detention of the alleged victims exceeded the legal maximum allowed by domestic law, and they were not taken before a judge promptly.

3.   The Commission added that, even though several expert appraisals were conducted that concluded that it was not possible that the seized ice chests had been made in the Plumavit factory and that there was no evidence at all to incriminate Mr. Chaparro and Mr. Lapo for the crime of illegal drug-trafficking, the alleged victims were remanded in custody for over a year. According to the application, Messrs. Chaparro and Lapo filed the recourses available to them requesting a review of the grounds for the preventive detention measure, but these recourses were unsuccessful. The Commission stated that the Plumavit factory was "seized" on November 15, 1997, following the search and, even though no drugs had been found, it was only returned to its owner almost five years after it had been confiscated. Mr. Lapo's vehicle has not yet been returned. Also, it appears that there are still public records and records in private institutions that include the criminal records of the alleged victims in relation to the facts of the instant case.

4.   The Commission asked the Court to establish the international responsibility of the State for the violation, to the detriment of the two alleged victims, of the rights embodied in Articles 5 (Right to Humane Treatment), 7 (Right to Personal Liberty), 8 (Right to a Fair Trial), 21 (Right to Property), and 25 (Right to Judicial Protection) of the Inter-American Convention, in relation to Article 1(1) (Obligation to Respect Rights) thereof. Lastly, the Commission asked the Court to declare that the State had failed to comply with the obligation contained in Article 2 (Domestic Legal Effects) of the Convention to the detriment of Mr. Lapo.

5.   On October 9, 2006, Xavier Flores Aguirre and Pablo Cevallos Palomeque, representatives of the alleged victims (hereinafter "the representatives"), presented their written brief containing requests, arguments, and evidence (hereinafter "requests and arguments brief") pursuant to Article 23 of the Court's Rules of Procedure (hereinafter "the Rules of Procedure"). They stated that they "endorsed all aspects of the legal principles and facts set out by the Commission . . . in its application."

223.   Regarding the next of kin of Messrs. Chaparro and Lapo, the Court observes that the Commission did not declare them victims of any violation of the Convention in its Report on merits No. 06/06 (*supra* para. 1); that, when preparing its application, the Commission requested the representatives to provide "essential information in order to determine the beneficiaries of reparations";[153 53] that, in response to this, the representatives presented testimonial statements by Mr. Chaparro's wife and children[154 54] describing alleged changes in their lives; that, despite this, in the application it lodged before the Court, the Commission did not

request that the next of kin of Messrs. Chaparro and Lapo be considered victims; that the representatives did not submit allegations to this effect when presenting their requests and arguments brief (*supra* para. 5); that the representatives waited until their final written arguments to identify the next of kin of the victims and to request compensation for them; that the Commission, in its final written arguments, only included a general allegation that the State should repair the "damage caused to the next of kin of the victims," without identifying them and without requesting the Court to declare the violation of any provision of the Convention against them.

224.   The Court reiterates that it considers the injured party to be those persons who have been declared victims of violations of a right embodied in the Convention. The Court's case law has stated that the alleged victims must be mentioned in the application and in the Commission's report under Article 50 [of the] Convention. Consequently, according to Article 33(1) of the Court's Rules of Procedure, it is the Commission, and not this Court, that must identify the alleged victims in a case before the Court precisely and at the appropriate procedural opportunity.[155 55]

225.   This has not occurred in the instant case and, accordingly, the Court has not declared any violation to the detriment of the next of kin of Messrs. Chaparro and Lapo; hence, they cannot be considered to be an injured party.

Uson Ramirez v. Venezuela
20-Nov-2009
Ser. C No. 207—*Preliminary Objections, Merits, Reparations, and Costs*

1.   On July 25, 2008 pursuant to Articles 51 and 61 of the American Convention, the Inter-American Commission on Human Rights (hereinafter "the Inter-American Commission" or "the Commission") submitted an application to the Court against the Bolivarian Republic of Venezuela (hereinafter "the State" or "Venezuela"). The application was based on the petition presented on May 23, 2005 before the Inter-American Commission by Mr. Héctor Faúndez Ledesma, then joined to the Impact Litigation Project of Washington College of Law (WCL) of the American University (hereinafter "the representatives").[3 56] On March 15, 2006, the Commission declared the application was admissible in Report No. 36/06, and on March 14, 2008, it approved Merit Report No. 24/08, according to Article 50 of the Convention. Such report included certain recommendations for the State.[4 57] Considering that the term granted to the State to comply with such recommendations had elapsed without the State presenting information showing satisfactory compliance with such recommendation, the Commission decided to submit the case to the Court's jurisdiction, pursuant to Articles 51(1) of the

Convention and 44 of the Commission's Rules of Procedure. The Commission appointed Messrs. Paulo Sergio Pinheiro, Commissioner, and Santiago A. Canton, Executive Secretary, and as legal consultants Mrs. Elizabeth Abi-Mershed, Assistant Executive Secretary, and Mrs. Verónica Gómez, Débora Benchoam, and Lilly Ching, as specialists of the Commission's Executive Secretariat.

2.   As indicated by the Commission, the application refers to the alleged "filing of a criminal action before the military court due to the crime of *Slander against the National Armed Forces*, to the detriment of Retired General Francisco Usón Ramírez . . . and the subsequent judgment of deprivation of liberty for five years and six months as a consequence of certain [alleged] statements that Mr. Usón made in a television interview about some facts that [allegedly] were the subject of controversy and public debate at that time."

3.   In the application the Commission requested the Court declare that the State had violated the rights set forth in Articles 13 (Freedom of Thought and Expression), 7 (Right to Personal Liberty), 8 (Right to a Fair Trial), and 25 (Right to Judicial Protection) of the American Convention, in connection with Articles 1(1) (Obligation to Respect Rights) and 2 (Domestic Legal Affects) of the same, to the detriment of Mr. Francisco Usón Ramírez. Consequently, the Commission requested the Court order the State to adopt certain measures of reparation pursuant to Article 63(1) of the American Convention.

A) Injured Party

206.   The Commission and the representatives agreed that the "injured party" was Mr. Usón Ramírez, his spouse, María Eugenia Borges de Usón, and his daughter, María José Usón Borges.

207.   To that end, the Tribunal reiterates that an injured party is any person who has been declared a victim of violations of any right under the Convention.[155][58] The only person who has been declared a victim in this judgment has been Mr. Usón Ramírez. Therefore, this Tribunal considers that the only "injured party" is Mr. Francisco Usón Ramírez, as a victim of the violations that were declared against him, so Mr. Usón Ramírez shall receive the reparation measures ordered by the Tribunal.

208.   On the other hand, although evidence was submitted in this case regarding the alleged injuries suffered by Mrs. María Eugenia Borges de Usón as a consequence of the declared violations,[156][59] neither the Commission nor the representatives alleged that she or her daughter were victims of any violation of the rights under the American Convention. Due to the above, and taking into account the Tribunal's jurisprudence,[157][60] the Court does not consider that Mrs. María Eugenia Borges de Usón and Mrs. María José Usón Borges are "injured parties."

The Massacres of El Mozote and Nearby Places v. El Salvador
25-Oct-2012
Series C No. 252—*Merits, reparations and costs*
2.   The case relates to the alleged successive massacres committed between December 11 and 13, 1981, in the context of a military operation by the Atlacatl Battalion, together with other military units, in seven places in the northern part of the department of Morazán, Republic of El Salvador, during which approximately 1,000 people were killed, "including an alarming number of children," as well as to the alleged investigation that was opened into these events and the "decision of September 27, 1993, to halt it based on the Law of General Amnesty for the Consolidation of Peace, which is still in force in El Salvador" and, finally, to the alleged exhumations performed over the following years, without leading to the reactivation of the investigations, "despite reiterated requests to the corresponding authorities."
3.   According to the Commission, the alleged massacres of the instant case occurred during the ruthless period of the so-called "counterinsurgency" operations, deployed against civilians on a massive scale by the Salvadoran army during the armed conflict. It was the systematic and generalized nature of this type of action, designed to terrorize the population, which allows it to be concluded that the alleged massacres of the instant case constituted "one of the most heinous manifestations of the crimes against humanity committed at the time by the Salvadoran military." However, owing to the alleged validity of the Law of General Amnesty for the Consolidation of Peace, as well as reiterated omissions by the State, these grave events remain unpunished.
4.   In its merits report, the Commission reached the conclusion that the State of El Salvador was internationally responsible for violating:
    a)   The rights to life, to personal integrity and to personal liberty established in Articles 4, 5, and 7 of the American Convention in relation to Article 1(1) thereof, to the detriment of the victims who were extrajudicially executed;
    b)   The special obligations with regard to children, established in Article 19 of the American Convention, in relation to Article 1(1) of this instrument, to the detriment of the children who were extrajudicially executed;
    c)   The rights to personal integrity and to privacy established in Articles 5 and 11 of the American Convention, to the detriment of the women who were raped in the village of El Mozote;
    d)   The right to property established in Article 21 of the American Convention in relation to Article 1(1) of this instrument, to the detriment of the executed victims who were stripped of

their possessions, as well as of the survivors whose homes were destroyed or whose means of subsistence were seized or eliminated;

e) The right to personal integrity set forth in Article 5 of the American Convention in relation to Article 1(1) thereof, to the detriment of the survivors and next of kin of the executed victims;

f) The right to freedom of movement and residence set forth in Article 22 of the American Convention, in relation to Article 1(1) of this instrument, to the detriment of those who were forcibly displaced, and

g) The rights to judicial guarantees and judicial protection established in Articles 8 and 25 of the American Convention, in relation to the obligations established in Articles 1(1) and 2 of this instrument; Articles 1, 6, and 8 of the Inter-American Convention to Prevent and Punish Torture; and Article 7 of the Inter-American Convention for the Prevention, Punishment, and Eradication of Violence against Women or "Convention of Belém do Pará," to the detriment of the survivors and next of kin of the executed victims.

5.   The Commission submitted to the Inter-American Court[2][61] the State's acts and omissions that occurred after June 6, 1995, the date on which El Salvador accepted the compulsory jurisdiction of the Court. These include: the application of the Law of General Amnesty for the Consolidation of Peace; the failure to reopen the investigations; the absence of continued and sustained efforts to exhume as many mortal remains as possible; the lack of judicial follow-up on the exhumations performed and on the information obtained from them; the lack of response to the requests to re-open the investigations; the effects of the massacres and their impunity on the surviving next of kin; the failure to make reparation to them, and the situation of displacement of some presumed victims. The foregoing, without prejudice to the State of El Salvador accepting the Court's competence to hear this case in full, under the provisions of Article 62(2) of the American Convention. Consequently, the Commission asked that the State be ordered to adopt certain measures of reparation.

Reparations (Application of Article 63(1) of the American Convention)

A) Injured Party

306.   The Court reiterates that, in the terms of Article 63(1) of the Convention, the injured party is the party that has been declared a victim of the violation of any right recognized in the Convention. Therefore, the Court considers as "injured

parties" those persons included in the lists of: (i) victims who were executed; (ii) the surviving victims; (iii) the next of kin of the victims who were executed, and (iv) the victims forcibly displaced, that are included as Annexes identified in the Appendixes "A", "B", "C" and "D" to this Judgment. As victims of the violations declared in Chapters VII and VIII, they will be beneficiaries and recipients of the measures that the Court establishes in this chapter.

307.   In addition, the Commission asked the Court to require the State to establish a mechanism that allows, insofar as possible, the complete identification of the victims executed in the massacres of El Mozote and nearby places. It also indicated that this mechanism should facilitate the complete identification of the next of kin of the executed victims, so that they can become beneficiaries of the reparations that are established. The foregoing in coordination and as a complement to the measures already taken by the representatives.

308.   The representatives considered that the State should endeavor to determine the identities of all those persons who were murdered, as well as all of the next of kin of the deceased victims and of the victims who survived the massacres. Consequently, it requested that the State be granted a maximum of six months to identify all those persons who should be considered entitled to the right to reparation and who are not included on the lists of victims, so that they may be included in the reparations established by this Court. In addition, they asked that all those murdered in the massacres should be added to the lists of victims already provided, even in the eventuality that their remains are not found. According to the representatives, this measure would entail drawing up a list of murdered victims, that also contained the basic characteristics of each of them, including age and gender, and this should be published in the same terms as the Court's judgment. To implement all the above, they considered it essential that the State coordinate with the victims and ensure the provision of all necessary technical and financial resources, as well as trained personnel. However, they also considered it essential that compliance with the other measures of reparation established by the Court should not be dependent on compliance with this measure.

309.   The State indicated that the creation of a list of victims "is a process that the State of El Salvador has already undertaken and is underway," and "it will be the basis to identify not only the individuals but also the geographic areas and the population to which many of the measures of a social nature will be addressed." In this regard, it explained that, in principle, the creation of the "Single List of Victims and Next of Kin of Victims of Grave Human Rights Violations during the Massacre of El Mozote" responds to the representatives' request for the preparation of a list of murdered victims that also contains the basic characteristics of each one, including age and gender and, in addition, includes all the next of kin of the deceased victims and the surviving victims of the massacre. However,

"this list will also allow the future administration of the exercise of human rights arising from the application of the different measures of reparation that have been accepted by the State." [495 62]

310.   The Court observes that, owing to the particular characteristics of the case, and for the reasons already indicated in this Judgment (*supra* paras. 59 and 51), it has not been possible to identify and individualize all the victims. Consequently, the Court considers that, in the instant case, there is a reasonable justification to apply the exception established in Article 35(2) of the Court's Rules of Procedure in order to include other persons as victims even when they have not been identified and individualized previously by this Court, by the Inter-American Commission or by the representatives (*supra* para. 57). To this end, the Court assesses positively the State's initiative to create the "Single List of the Victims and Next of Kin of the Victims of Grave Human Rights Violations during the Massacre of El Mozote." Accordingly, this Court establishes that the State must continue with the full implementation of the "Single List of the Victims and Next of Kin of the Victims of Grave Human Rights Violations during the Massacre of El Mozote"; to this end, it must adopt the necessary measures to ensure its sustainability and the budgetary allocation to guarantee its effective operation. In addition, the Court considers it pertinent that, within one year of notification of this Judgment, the State present the results of the identification of the victims who were executed, the surviving victims, the next of kin of the executed victims, and the victims forcibly displaced of the massacres of El Mozote and nearby places, conducted within the framework of the "Single List of the Victims and Next of Kin of the Victims of Grave Human Rights Violations during the Massacre of El Mozote," so that these persons may request and receive the corresponding reparation in the terms of this Judgment.

311.   The foregoing does not impede or exclude the possibility that, when the one-year time frame has expired, the process of identifying the victims continue, and that any new victims be added to the "Single List of the Victims and Next of Kin of the Victims of Grave Human Rights Violations during the Massacre of El Mozote," and be considered beneficiaries of the reparations established in this Judgment to be made by the State, when they submit this request to the Salvadoran authorities, outside the established time frame. The State must provide information to the Court about the persons who have requested reparations in the context of the said mechanism. To this end, the Court will make the pertinent assessment in the exercise of its authority to monitor this Judgment.

Atala Riffo and Daughters v. Chile
24-Feb-2012
Series C No. 239—*Merits, reparations and costs*

1.	On September 17, 2010, the Inter-American Commission on Human Rights (hereinafter, the "Inter-American Commission" or "the Commission") filed a claim against the Republic of Chile (hereinafter, the "State" or "Chile") in relation to case 12.5023. The initial petition was lodged before the Inter-American Commission on November 24, 2004 by Ms. Karen Atala Riffo, (hereinafter "Ms. Atala") represented by attorneys of the *Asociación Gremial Libertades Públicas, Clínica de Acciones de Interés Público of Diego Portales University and Fundación Ideas.* [463]

2.	On July 23, 2008, the Commission approved Report on Admissibility No. 42/08 and on December 18, 2009, it approved the Report on Merits No. 139/09, according to Article 50 of the American Convention[5]. On September 17, 2010, the Inter-American Commission considered that the State had not complied with the recommendations made in the Merits Report, for which reason it decided to submit the instant case to the jurisdiction of the Inter-American Court. The Inter-American Commission appointed Commissioner Luz Patricia Mejía, and Executive Secretary Santiago A. Canton as its delegates in this case. Assistant Executive Secretary Elizabeth Abi-Mershed and attorneys Silvia Serrano Guzmán, Rosa Celorio and María Claudia Pulido, Specialists of the Executive Secretariat of the Commission, were designated to act as legal advisors.

3.	According to the Commission, the present case concerns the alleged international responsibility of the State for discriminatory treatment and arbitrary interference in the private and family life suffered by Ms. Atala due to her sexual orientation, in the legal process that resulted in the loss of care and custody of her daughters M., V and R. The case also concerns the alleged failure to take into account the best interests of the girls, whose custody and care were determined without having regard to their rights, and on the basis of alleged discriminatory prejudices. The Commission requested the Court to declare the violation of Articles 11 (Right to Privacy), 17(1) and 17(4) (Rights of the Family), 19 (Rights of the Child), 24 (Right to Equal Protection) and 25 (Right to Judicial Protection) of the Convention, in relation to article 1(1) thereof. Likewise, the Commission requested the Court to order the State to adopt reparation measures.

**V.	Right to Equality and Non-Discrimination, Right to Private Life, Right to Family Life, Rights of the Child, Right to a Fair Trial and to Judicial Protection in Relation to the Obligation to Respect and Guarantee regarding the Custody Proceedings**

   B) Prior Considerations
   2. Prior consideration on the participation of the girls M., V. and R.

67.	In the Decision of November 29, 2011 (*supra* para 12) the Court noted that the file contained no specific statements by the daughters M., V. and R. as to whether or not they agreed with the representation exercised by either of their parents or whether they wished to be considered as alleged victims in this case. The Court pointed out that although there were two briefs in which both the mother and the father stated that they were acting on behalf of the three girls before this Court, the position of the mother and the father did not necessarily represent the girls' best interests.

68.   Furthermore, in its Decision, the Court stated that children exercise their rights progressively, as they develop a greater degree of independence, and for this reason during early childhood their relatives act on their behalf. Clearly, the level of physical and intellectual development, experience and information varies widely among children. Therefore, when the hearing was held in accordance with the aforementioned Decision (*supra* para. 13), it was taken into account that the three girls were then aged 12, 13 and 17 years of age and that there might be differences in their views and in the level of personal independence for each of the girls to exercise her rights. In the instant case, the Court heard two of the girls on February 8, 2012. (*supra* para. 13).

69.   During the hearing, the Secretariat staff was accompanied by the psychiatrist María Alicia Espinoza. [80][64] Prior to commencing the proceeding, the delegation of the Secretariat of the Court held a prior meeting with the psychiatrist, consisting of an exchange of ideas, in order to ensure that the information provided was accessible and appropriate for the girls. Taking into account the international standards on a child's right to be heard (infra paras. 196 to 200), the girls M. and R. were, in the first place, informed jointly by the staff of the Secretariat of their right to be heard, the effects or consequences that their opinions might have in the dispute in this case, and the position and arguments of the parties in the present case. They were also asked whether they wished to continue participating in the proceeding. Subsequently, instead of conducting a unilateral examination, a conversation was held with each girl separately, in order to provide the girls with an appropriate environment of trust. During the proceeding neither of the parents and neither of the parties before the Commission (Chile and Ms. Atala) were present. Furthermore, the proceeding conducted with the girls was private, due to the request, both by the Commission and by the representatives in this case, that the identity of the girls remain confidential (*supra* note 3), and to the need to protect the girls' best interest and their right to privacy. In addition, the girls expressly requested that everything said by them during the meeting be kept in the strictest confidence.

70.   During the proceeding of February 8, 2012, the girls M. and R. said they were aware of and understood the matters related to the three alleged violations in which they were presented as alleged victims in the present case (infra paras.

150, 176, 178 and 201). From the statements made by the two girls and bearing in mind the progressive nature of children's rights, the Court noted that the two girls had expressed freely and independently their own views and judgments regarding the facts of the case that concern them, as well as some of their expectations and interests in the resolution of this case. Therefore, the Court shall consider them as alleged victims in the case at hand (infra paras. 150, 176, 178 and 208).

71.   As mentioned previously, the girl V. did not participate in the hearing for reasons of *force majeure* (*supra* para. 13). Based on the preceding considerations, the Court finds no grounds to consider that the girl V. is not in the same situation as her sisters (infra paras. 150, 176, 178 and 208). However, for the purposes of reparations, the competent national authority for children must privately confirm the girl V's free opinion regarding whether she wishes to be considered as an injured party.

Santo Domingo Massacre v. Colombia
30-Nov-2012
Series C No. 239—Preliminary Objections, *Merits and reparations*

1.   In a brief of July 8, 2011 (hereinafter "submission brief"), the Inter-American Commission on Human Rights (hereinafter "the Inter-American Commission" or "the Commission") submitted to the Court's jurisdiction, in accordance with Articles 51 and 61 of the Convention, case 12,416 against the Republic of Colombia (hereinafter also "the State" or "Colombia").

3.   According to the Commission, the case refers to an alleged bombardment perpetrated by the Colombian Air Force on the village of Santo Domingo, municipality of Tame, department of Arauca, on December 13, 1998. In its Merits Report, the Commission considered that, on December 13, 1998, at 10.02 a.m., the crew of a helicopter of the Colombian Air Force (FAC) launched a cluster device, composed of six fragmentation bombs, on the urban area of the village of Santo Domingo, resulting in the death of 17 civilians, including four boys and two girls, and 27 injured civilians, including five girls and four boys. The Commission noted that the members of the Armed Forces who formed the crew of the aircraft were aware that these persons were civilians. In addition, it considered probable that, following the explosion, the survivors and injured were machine-gunned from a helicopter when they tried to assist the injured and to flee the village. It considered that the foregoing resulted in the displacement of the population of Santo Domingo, after which the empty homes were sacked or pillaged. Furthermore, the case refers to the alleged lack of judicial protection and failure to observe judicial guarantees.

4.   Based on the above, the Commission asked the Court to declare that the State was internationally responsible for the violation of the following rights, in relation to Article 1(1) of the Convention:

(a) The right to life, contained in Article 4(1) of the American Convention, to the detriment of Levis Hernando Martinez Carreiio, Teresa Mojica Herniindez de Galvis, Edilma Leal Pacheco, Salom6n Neite, Maria Yolanda Rangel, Pablo Suiirez Daza, Carmen Antonio Diaz Cobo, Nancy Avila Castillo (or Abaunza), Arnulfo Arciniegas Velandia (or Calvo), Luis Enrique Parada Ropero and Rodolfo Carrillo;

(b) The right to life, in relation also to Article 19 of the Convention, to the detriment of the boys Jaime Castro Bello, Luis Carlos Neite Mendez, Oscar Esneider Vanegas Tulibila and Geovani Hern~ndez Becerra, and the girls Egna Margarita Bello and Katherine (or Catherine) Cardenas Tilano;

(c) The rights to life and to personal integrity contained in Articles 4(1) and 5(1) of the American Convention, to the detriment of Alba Yaneth Garcia, Fernando Vanegas, Milciades Bonilla Ostos, Ludwing Vanegas, Xiomara Garcfa Guevara, Mario Galvis, Fredy Monoga Villamizar (or Fredy Villamizar Monoga), M6nica Bello Tilano, Maribel Daza, Amalia Neite Gonz~lez, Marian Arevalo, Jose Agudelo Tamayo, Maria Panqueva, Pedro Uriel Duarte Lagos, Ludo Vanegas, Adela Carrillo, Alcides Bonilla and Fredy Mora;

(d) The rights to life and to personal integrity, to the detriment of the boys Marcos Neite (5), Erinson Olimpo Cardenas (9) and Ricardo Ramirez (11), and the girls Hilda Yuraime Barranco (14), Lida Barranca (8), Yeimi Viviana Contreras (17), Maryori Agudelo Florez (17), Rosmira Daza Rojas (17) and Neftali Neite (17);

(e) The right to property established in Article 21(1) and 21(2) of the Convention, to the detriment of the victims who were stripped of their possessions, as well as of the survivors who lived in the village of Santo Domingo and whose homes and belongings were destroyed or looted;

(f) The right to freedom of movement and residence established in Article 22(1) of the Convention, to the detriment of the persons who were displaced from the village of Santo Domingo; [4 65]

(g) The rights to judicial guarantees and judicial protection, established in Articles 8(1) and 25 of the American Convention,

to the detriment of the victims who were injured and the next of
kin of the victims indicated in annex 1 to the Report, and

(h) The right to personal integrity, to the detriment of the next of kin
of the victims indicated in annex 1 of the Merits Report.

VIII. Reparations (Application of Article 63(1) of the American Convention)
A) *Injured party*

294.   The Court considers as "injured party," in keeping with Article 63(1) of
the American Convention, the persons indicated in paragraphs 247, 268 and 282
and in annexes I, II and III of this Judgment, as victims of the violations declared
herein, so that they will be considered beneficiaries of the reparations ordered
by the Court. [425 66] Similarly, the Court has stated that the presumed victims
must be indicated in the merits report of the Inter-American Commission,[426 67]
and observes that 24 individuals named by the representatives as next of kin of
the victims, are not included in the merits report issued by the Commission in
this case. Nevertheless, of these 24 individuals, six family members of two of
the deceased victims received reparation under the contentious-administrative
jurisdiction; [426 68] thus it can be understood that the State acknowledged them as
victims. Consequently, the Court finds that it is not appropriate to consider as
victims or as injured party 18 of the persons presented as next of kin of victims by
the representatives, [426 69] without prejudice to the reparations that may correspond
to them at the domestic level.

ANALYSIS AND QUESTIONS RAISED BY THE COURT'S JURISPRUDENCE

Early in its jurisprudence, the Court affirmed that "the obligation to
make reparation established by international courts is governed, as has been
universally accepted, by international law in all its aspects, [including] the
determination of beneficiaries, none of which the respondent State may alter by
invoking its domestic law . . . ."[70] Thus, the Court has asserted its competence
and jurisdiction as it interprets and applies the American Convention on
Human Rights and relevant Rules of Procedure to the definitions of victim and
beneficiary.

Article 63(1) of the American Convention on Human Rights refers to
the violation of right or freedom of the injured party. The terms alleged victim,
victim, next of kin, and beneficiary appear only in the Rules of Procedure of the
Inter-American Commission on Human Rights and the Inter-American Court of
Human Rights. The Court has further expanded the use and understandings of
these terms in its jurisprudence.

As former Inter-American Court Judge Sergio Garcia Ramirez has explained:

> Two concepts have been forged: first, natural and necessary, traditional and preferred: the direct victim of a violation, in other words, the person whose legal interests have been affected by an act or omission of a State official or another person for whose conduct the State is responsible. But it doesn't end here. There's also the indirect victim, a more recent—although established—concept, as well as the potential victim.

The indirect victim suffers damages on their property or rights, as a consequence of that damage that is inflicted upon the direct victim. The violation is directed to one person but transcends to another. We should stay on this path, which reflects the concern and the *pro-homine* principle that rules our subject matter, while remaining mindful of potential abuse that could trivialize it and eventually compromise its future.[71]

Many of the Court's judgments reflect the understanding that violations of rights and freedoms guaranteed by the American Convention result in harm to the direct victim, as well as indirect victims. As the case excerpts above demonstrate, however, the determination of who is an indirect victim or beneficiary has varied throughout the Court's jurisprudence. These questions arise:

- Do all of the above case excerpts tend to support the *pro homine* principle that "a law must be interpreted in the manner most advantageous to the human being," as defined by the Inter-American Commission on Human Rights? What reasons might the Court have for a more restrictive interpretation?

- In some cases where all the victims and beneficiaries have not been identified at the time of the Court's judgment, as in the case of the *Massacres of El Mozote*, or in certain cases involving large numbers of people or an entire community, such as an indigenous community, the Court has established a time period following its judgment during which victims and beneficiaries may continue to be identified and individualized. Should these post-judgment identification periods be subject to the Court's discretion depending on the particular circumstances of the case, or are there particular types of cases that should warrant subsequent identification periods? Similarly, should the time periods permitted by the Court for such identifications also be subject to the Court's discretion depending on the particular circumstances of each case, or would pre-determined time periods be appropriate?

- In other cases, the Court has excluded specific beneficiaries from reparations because their identifications were not made at the correct procedural moment. Are such exclusions equitable because the beneficiaries were known and could have been identified earlier? Might there be other reasons for the Court's decisions regarding such exclusions?

- In *Aloeboetoe*, the Court rejected the argument that the village and tribal communities to which the victims belonged were also due reparations on the basis that all persons belong to "intermediate communities." The Court allowed that there may be "some exceptional case" where reparations might be awarded to a community that suffered direct damages. What might constitute an "exceptional case" of direct damages to an entire community?

- In *Loayza Tamayo*, the Court declared that "[a]lthough the injured parties' direct participation in the reparations stage is important for the Court, their nonappearance, as in the instant Case, does not relieve either the Commission or the Court of their duty as organs of the inter-American system for the protection of human rights. That duty is to ensure that those rights are effectively protected, which includes matters related to the duty to make reparations." The Court concluded that the injured parties' nonappearance "[did] not prevent the [Court] from ordering reparations on their behalf." What factors may have accounted for the Court's decision to award these beneficiaries despite their nonappearance? Does the Court's declaration in *Loayza Tamayo* regarding its duty to protect human rights and make reparations provide a foundation for advocates in other cases where beneficiaries may not be able to participate in the proceedings?

- In *Cantoral Benavides*, the Court declared that the suffering of parents and siblings could be presumed and need not be proven. Subsequently, in *Myrna Mack Chang*, the Court stated that beneficiaries have "close kinship" or "close emotional contact" with the victim. In *Bamaca Velasquez*, the Court added that next of kin and third parties had the burden to prove that a "relationship of effective and regular dependence having existed between the claimant and the victim" to claim damages based on a right of their own. What should constitute "close emotional contact" or a "relationship of effective and regular dependence"? When should suffering and damages to next of kin be presumed and when should they bear the burden of proof? What distinctions can be drawn between these cases?

- Is there a clear trajectory in the Court's requirements for identification of victims and beneficiaries, or are such identifications dependent upon the particular circumstances of each case? Should there be objective requirements, or do cases involving violations of human rights and freedoms require case-specific determinations?

V.   SUCCESSORS AND HEIRS

The Inter-American Court of Human Rights has also addressed case circumstances in which a victim's successors and heirs must be identified. The following case excerpts expand upon the Court's jurisprudence regarding beneficiaries of reparations.

Aloeboetoe et al. v. Suriname
10-Sep-1993
Series C No. 15—*Reparations and Costs*

54.   The damages suffered by the victims up to the time of their death entitle them to compensation. That right to compensation is transmitted to their heirs by succession. The damages payable for causing loss of life represent an inherent right that belongs to the injured parties. It is for this reason that national jurisprudence generally accepts that the right to apply for compensation for the death of a person passes to the survivors affected by that death. In that jurisprudence a distinction is made between successors and injured third parties. With respect to the former, it is assumed that the death of the victim has caused them actual and moral damages and the burden of proof is on the other party to show that such damages do not exist. Claimants who are not successors, however, must provide specific proof justifying their right to damages, as explained below.

55.   In the instant case, there is some difference of opinion between the parties as to who the successors of the victims are. The Commission urges that this decision be made with reference to the customs of the Saramaka tribe, whereas Suriname requests that its civil law be applied. The Court earlier stated that the obligation to make reparation provided in Article 63(1) of the American Convention is governed by international law, which also applies to the determination of the manner of compensation and the beneficiaries thereof. Nevertheless, it is useful to refer to the national family law in force, for certain aspects of it may be relevant.

58.   The Commission has pointed out that it does not seek to portray the Saramakas as a community that currently enjoys international juridical status; rather, the autonomy it claims for the tribe is one governed by domestic public law. The Court does not deem it necessary to determine whether the Saramakas

enjoy legislative and jurisdictional autonomy within the region they occupy. The only question of importance here is whether the laws of Suriname in the area of family law apply to the Saramaka tribe. On this issue, the evidence offered leads to the conclusion that Surinamese family law is not effective insofar as the Saramakas are concerned. The members of the tribe are unaware of it and adhere to their own rules. The State for its part does not provide the facilities necessary for the registration of births, marriages, and deaths, an essential requirement for the enforcement of Surinamese law. Furthermore, the Saramakas do not bring the conflicts that arise over such matters before the State's tribunals, whose role in these areas is practically non-existent with respect to the Saramakas. It should be pointed out that, in the instant case, Suriname recognized the existence of a Saramaka customary law. The only evidence produced to the contrary is the statement made by Mr. Ramón de Freitas. However, the manner in which that witness testified, his attitude during the hearing and the personality he revealed led the Court to develop an opinion of the witness that persuaded it to reject his testimony.

59.   The Commission has produced information on the social structure of the Saramakas indicating that the tribe displays a strongly matriarchal[72] familial configuration where polygamy occurs frequently. The principal group of relatives appears to be the "bêè," composed of all the descendants of one single woman. This group assumes responsibility for the actions of any of its members who, in theory, are each in turn responsible to the group as a whole. This means that the compensation payable to one person would be given to the "bêè," whose representative would distribute it among its members.

60.   The Commission also requests compensation for the injured parties and the distribution of such compensation among them. On examining the Commission's brief, it is evident that the identification of the beneficiaries of such compensation has not been carried out in accordance with Saramaka custom, at least not as the Commission has described it before the Court. It is impossible to determine what legal norm the Commission applied for this purpose. It would appear that the Commission simply took a pragmatic approach. Likewise, on the matter of the amount of compensation and its distribution, the Commission's brief asserts that it resorted to an "equilibrium system" which took the following factors into account: the age of the victim, his actual and potential income, the number of his dependents and the customs and petitions of the Bushnegroes.

61.   The I.L.O. Convention N° 169 concerning Indigenous and Tribal Peoples in Independent Countries (1989) has not been accepted by Suriname. Furthermore, under international law there is no conventional or customary rule that would indicate who the successors of a person are. Consequently, the Court has no alternative but to apply general principles of law (Art. 38(1)(c) of the Statute of the International Court of Justice).

62.   It is a norm common to most legal systems that a person's successors are his or her children. It is also generally accepted that the spouse has a share in the assets acquired during a marriage; some legal systems also grant the spouse inheritance rights along with the children. If there is no spouse or children, private common law recognizes the ascendants as heirs. It is the Court's opinion that these rules, generally accepted by the community of nations, should be applied in the instant case, in order to determine the victims' successors for purposes of compensation. These general legal principles refer to "children," "spouse," and "ascendants." Such terms shall be interpreted according to local law. As already stated (*supra*, para. 58), here local law is not Surinamese law, for the latter is not effective in the region insofar as family law is concerned. It is necessary, then, to take Saramaka custom into account. That custom will be the basis for the interpretation of those terms, to the degree that it does not contradict the American Convention. Hence, in referring to "ascendants," the Court shall make no distinction as to sex, even if that might be contrary to Saramaka custom.

63.   It has proved extremely difficult to identify the children, spouses, and, in some cases, the ascendants of the victims in this case. These are all members of a tribe that lives in the jungle, in the interior of Suriname, and speaks only its own native tongue. Marriages and births have in many cases not been registered. In those cases where they have, sufficient data have not been provided to fully document the relationship between persons. The matter of identification becomes even more complex in a community that practices polygamy.

64.   In its observations, Suriname has presented a general critique of the Commission's brief as regards the evidence it presents. The Government asserts the following: "We need to know, based on rational and certainly verifiable data, specifics on all the victims, insofar as the family members left unprotected are concerned . . . ." It is true that a person's identity must, as a general rule, be proved by means of relevant documentation. However, the situation in which the Saramaka find themselves is due in great measure to the fact that the State does not provide sufficient registry offices in the region; consequently, it is unable to issue documentation to all its inhabitants on the basis of the data contained therein. Suriname cannot, therefore, demand proof of the relationship and identity of persons through means that are not available to all of its inhabitants in that region. In addition, Suriname has not here offered to make up for its inaction by providing additional proof as to the identity and relationship of the victims and their successors. In order to clarify the information available on the successors, the Court requested the Commission to provide complementary data about them. Considering the circumstances surrounding the instant case, the Court believes that the evidence supplied is credible and can be admitted.

Bulacio v. Argentina
18-Sep-2003
Series C No. 100—*Merits, Reparations, and Costs*
3.   The submissions by the Commission and by the Center for Justice
and International Law (hereinafter "CEJIL"), the Centro de Estudios Legales y
Sociales (hereinafter "CELS") and the Coordinadora Contra la Represión Policial
e Institucional (hereinafter "CORREPI"), who also act as representatives of the
next of kin of the alleged victim (hereinafter the "representatives of the alleged
victim"), show the following facts:
  (a) On April 19, 1991, the Argentine Federal Police conducted a massive
       detention or "razzia" of "more than eighty persons" in the city of Buenos
       Aires, near the stadium Club Obras Sanitarias de la Nación, where a rock
       music concert was to be held. One of the detainees was Walter David
       Bulacio, a seventeen-year-old, who after his detention was taken to the
       35th Police Station, specifically to its "juvenile detention room." At this
       place, police agents beat him. The detainees were gradually set free
       without any criminal charges being filed against them, and the reason
       for their detention is unknown. In the case of the minors, the Juvenile
       Correctional Judge on duty did not receive notice, as required by law No.
       10,903, and in the specific case of Walter David Bulacio, his next of kin
       were not informed either. During their detention, the minors were held
       under inadequate detention conditions.
  (b) On April 20, 1991, after having vomited in the morning, youth Walter
       David Bulacio was taken to the Pirovano Municipal Hospital in an
       ambulance without informing his parents or the Juvenile Judge. The
       physician who examined him at the hospital pointed out that the youth
       showed injuries and he diagnosed a "cranial traumatism." That same
       afternoon, the alleged victim was taken to the Fernández Municipal
       Hospital for an x-ray study and was taken back to the Pirovano Municipal
       Hospital. Walter David Bulacio told the physician who examined him
       that he had been beaten by the police, and that night he was visited at this
       hospital by his parents, who had shortly before heard from a neighbor
       what had happened to their son.
  (c) On April 21, 1991, minor Walter David Bulacio was transferred to the
       Mitre Sanatorium. The physician on duty reported to the 7th Police
       Station that "a minor with injuries" had been admitted and, therefore,
       that Police Station opened a police investigation for criminal injuries.
  (d) On April 23, 1991, the 9th National Juvenile Criminal Trial Court
       (hereinafter "the 9th Court") took cognizance of the injuries suffered by
       Walter David Bulacio.

(e) On April 26, minor Walter David Bulacio died. On April 30, 1991, the aforementioned Court declared that it did not have jurisdiction and it forwarded the case "against NN for injuries inflicted on Walter [David] Bulacio, followed by death" to the 5th National Criminal Trial Court (hereinafter "the 5th Court"), which heard crimes committed by adults. The parents of the alleged victims appeared as applicants before the 9th Court on May 3 in the case regarding the circumstances under which the detentions took place and the other crimes committed against Walter David Bulacio and other persons. The case was divided and the 5th Court retained the investigation regarding the injuries and death of Walter David Bulacio.

85.   With respect to inheritance of the right to compensation in favor of Walter David Bulacio, this Court has developed applicable criteria to the effect that the children, spouses and parents must receive the compensation.[57 73] This Court points out that in the instant case, the victim was an adolescent and had neither children nor spouse; therefore, the compensation must be given to his parents. It has been proven before this Court that Víctor David Bulacio, the victim's father, has died, and therefore compensation must be paid in full to the mother of the victim, Graciela Rosa Scavone, since pursuant to the criteria set forth by this Court, "[i]f one of the parents has died, his or her part will accrue to that of the other."[58 74]

86.   The criteria set forth regarding the beneficiaries of compensation for pecuniary damage in the previous paragraph will also be applied to distribution of compensation for non-pecuniary damage.

Mapiripán Massacre v. Colombia
15-Sep-2005
Series C No. 134 —*Merits, Reparations, and Costs*

259.   Distribution of compensation amongst the next of kin of the victims who were executed or made to disappear, for pecuniary and non-pecuniary damages, will be as follows:[281 75]

(a) Fifty percent (50%) of the compensation will be divided in equal parts among the victims' children. The stepdaughters and stepson of Gustavo Caicedo Rodríguez, that is, Yur Mary Herrera Contreras, Zuli Herrera Contreras and Rusbel Asdrúbal Martínez Contreras, and the stepdaughter of Sinaí Blanco Santamaría, Carmen Johanna Jaramillo Giraldo, who lived or had lived under the same roof as their stepfathers and had close, affectionate relations with them, will be treated as their daughters and son for purposes of their participation in the distribution of the compensation.

260. If the next of kin of the victims, entitled to the compensation ordered in the instant Judgment, are deceased, and they died before they received the respective compensation, or if they are identified afterwards, the same criteria for distribution of the compensation stated in the previous paragraph will apply.

Supreme Court of Justice (Quintana Coello *et al.*) v. Ecuador
23-Aug-2013
Series C No. 266 —*Preliminary Objections, Merits, Reparations, and Costs*

On August 2, 2011, in accordance with Articles 51 and 61 of the American Convention, the Inter-American Commission on Human rights (hereinafter "the Inter-American Commission" or "the Commission") submitted to the jurisdiction of the Inter-American Court the case of "Quintana Coello et al." (hereinafter "brief submitting the case") against the Republic of Ecuador (hereinafter "the State " or "Ecuador"), concerning "the [alleged] arbitrary removal of 27 judges of the Supreme Court of Justice of Ecuador through a parliamentary resolution on December 8, 2004, in the [alleged] absence of a clear legal framework regulating the grounds and proceedings for their removal from office, and [allegedly] disregarding the constitutional norms under which they were appointed with respect to the indefinite nature of their appointment and the cooptation system as a means of filling possible vacancies." According to the Commission, "[t]he victims were denied even minimal guarantees of due process, were not granted a hearing, and had no opportunity to defend themselves" and "[n]or was there any effective judicial remedy available to them to oppose the arbitrary action of the National Congress."

IX.   Reparations
A) Injured Party

203.   The Court reiterates that, under the terms of Article 63(1) of the American Convention, injured parties are those who have been declared victims of the violation of a right recognized therein. Therefore, this Court considers the following persons as "injured party": Alfonso Ernesto Albán Gómez, Jorge Aurelio Andrade Lara, José Santiago Andrade Ubidia, José Julio Benítez Astudillo, Armando Bermeo Castillo, Eduardo Enrique Brito Mieles, Nicolás Castro Patiño, Lucio Teodoro Coello Vázquez, Alfredo Roberto Contreras Villavicencio, Arturo Javier Donoso Castellón, Galo Miguel Galarza Paz, Luis Alberto Heredia Moreno, Estuardo Agustín Hurtado Larrea, Ángel Ignacio Lescano Fiallo, Teófilo Milton Moreno Aguirre, Galo Alonso Pico Mantilla, Hernán Gonzalo Quevedo Terán, Hugo Eduardo Quintana Coello, Jorge Enrique Ramírez Álvarez, Carlos

Javier Riofrío Corral, Naum Clotary Salinas Montaño, Armando José Ramón Serrano Puig, Ignacio José Vicente Troya Jaramillo, Alberto Rodrigo Varea Avilés, Jaime Gonzalo Velasco Dávila, Miguel Elías Villacís Gómez and Gonzalo Augusto Zambrano Palacios, who as such shall be considered beneficiaries of the reparations ordered by this Court.

204.   Furthermore, the Court notes that the representatives of the victims requested that, given the deaths of two former judges at the time when the contentious case was brought before the Court, their successors be considered as injured party. Specifically, they mentioned the case of Milton Moreno Aguirre and requested that his wife, María Ruth Silva Alava, and his daughters, María Ruth Moreno Silva and Ana Isabel Moreno Silva, be considered as injured party. [241][76] In the case of Estuardo Agustín Hurtado Larrea, they requested that his wife, Letty Mariana Vásquez Grijalva, and his daughters and son, Tulia María Ximena Hurtado Vásquez, Letty Alexandra Hurtado Vásquez and Diego Estuardo Hurtado Vásquez, also be included. [242][77] The Court recalls that only those persons who have been declared victims can be considered as injured party, for which reason the Court must deny the representatives' request. Notwithstanding the foregoing, the reparations ordered in this Judgment to the successors of Messrs. Moreno Aguirre and Hurtado Larrea shall be made as specified in the chapter concerning the method of compliance (*infra* para. 277).

F) Method of compliance with the payments ordered

277.   The State shall make payment of the compensation for pecuniary and non-pecuniary damages and the reimbursement of costs and expenses established in this Judgment directly to the individuals indicated therein, within one year as of notification of this Judgment, under the terms of the following paragraphs. The foregoing, without prejudice to the payment, in three installments, established for the compensation for pecuniary damage. Should the beneficiaries die before payment of the respective compensation is paid to them, such amounts shall be paid directly to their successors, in accordance with the applicable domestic legislation.

ANALYSIS AND QUESTIONS RAISED BY THE COURT'S JURISPRUDENCE

Through its jurisprudence, the Inter-American Court of Human Rights has affirmed that the right to compensation is transmitted to victims' heirs and successors. The victim's children, spouses, and parents inherit the right to compensation and stepchildren are treated as children for the purposes of this inheritance right. In *Aloeboetoe et al.*, the Court also affirmed the necessity of determining the applicable law (e.g., customary law of a tribal community) when identifying successors in tribal and indigenous communities, and applying it without contradiction to the rights and freedoms enshrined by the American Convention (e.g., without gender-based distinctions in inheritance rights).

- In *Bulacio*, the Court further confirmed that parents inherit when the victim has no children or spouse, and that if one parent is since deceased the surviving parent inherits the right to compensation. Does the Court's reasoning support inheritance by other surviving successors?

- Are there other groups or circumstances, in addition to indigenous communities, for which the Court's application of local customary law would be applicable?

VI.   SOCIETY AS VICTIM

Through its Advisory Opinions, as well as its case law, the Inter-American Court of Human Rights has recognized the impact on society of particular violations of rights and freedoms. As the following excerpts emphasize, violations which have a broader societal impact include the rights to free thought and expression and political participation.

Compulsory Membership in an Association Prescribed by Law for the Practice of Journalism (Arts. 13 and 29 American Convention on Human Rights)
13-Nov-1985
Series A 5/85—*Advisory Opinion*

31.   In its individual dimension, freedom of expression goes further than the theoretical recognition of the right to speak or to write. It also includes and cannot be separated from the right to use whatever medium is deemed appropriate to impart ideas and to have them reach as wide an audience as possible. When the Convention proclaims that freedom of thought and expression includes the right to impart information and ideas through "any... medium," it emphasizes the fact that the expression and dissemination of ideas and information are indivisible concepts. This means that restrictions that are imposed on dissemination represent, in equal measure, a direct limitation on the right to express oneself freely. The importance of the legal rules applicable to the press and to the status of those who dedicate themselves professionally to it derives from this concept.

32.   In its social dimension, freedom of expression is a means for the interchange of ideas and information among human beings and for mass

communication. It includes the right of each person to seek to communicate his own views to others, as well as the right to receive opinions and news from others. For the average citizen it is just as important to know the opinions of others or to have access to information generally as is the very right to impart his own opinions.

33.   The two dimensions mentioned of the right to freedom of expression must be guaranteed simultaneously. One cannot legitimately rely on the right of a society to be honestly informed in order to put in place a regime of prior censorship for the alleged purpose of eliminating information deemed to be untrue in the eyes of the censor. It is equally true that the right to impart information and ideas cannot be invoked to justify the establishment of private or public monopolies of the communications media designed to mold public opinion by giving expression to only one point of view.

The Last Temptation of Christ (Olmedo Bustos et al) v. Chile
5-Feb-2001
Series C No. 73—*Merits, Reparations, and Costs*

66.   Regarding the second dimension of the right embodied in Article 13 of the Convention, the social element, it is necessary to indicate that freedom of expression is a way of exchanging ideas and information between persons; it includes the right to try and communicate one's point of view to others, but it also implies everyone's right to know opinions, reports, and news. For the ordinary citizen, the knowledge of other people's opinions and information is as important as the right to impart their own.

67.   The Court considers that both dimensions are of equal importance and should be guaranteed simultaneously in order to give total effect to the right to freedom of thought and expression in the terms of Article 13 of the Convention.

68.   As the cornerstone of a democratic society, freedom of expression is an essential condition for society to be sufficiently informed.

69.   The European Court of Human Rights has indicated that:

> [The] supervisory function [of the Court] signifies that [it] must pay great attention to the principles inherent in a 'democratic society'. Freedom of expression constitutes one of the essential bases of such a society, one of the primordial conditions for its progress and for the development of man. Article 10(2) [of the European Convention on Human Rights][17 78] is valid not only for the information or ideas that are favorably received or considered inoffensive or indifferent, but also for those that shock, concern, or offend the State or any sector of the

population. Such are the requirements of pluralism, tolerance and the spirit of openness, without which no 'democratic society' can exist. This means that any formality, condition, restriction or sanction imposed in that respect, should be proportionate to the legitimate end sought.

Also, those who exercise their freedom of expression assume 'obligations and responsibilities,' the scope of which depends on the context and the technical procedure used.[18 79]

97.   With regard to Article 13 of the Convention, the Court considers that the State must modify its legal system in order to eliminate prior censorship and allow the cinematographic exhibition and publicity of the film "The Last Temptation of Christ" because it is obliged to respect the right to freedom of expression and to guarantee its free and full exercise to all persons subject to its jurisdiction.

YATAMA v. Nicaragua

23-Jun-2005

Series C No. 127—*Preliminary Objections, Merits, Reparations, and Costs*

1.   On June 17, 2003, in accordance with the provisions of Articles 50 and 61 of the American Convention, the Inter-American Commission on Human Rights (hereinafter "the Commission" or "the Inter-American Commission") submitted to the Court an application against the State of Nicaragua (hereinafter "the State" or "Nicaragua"), originating from petition No. 12,388 [and] received by the Secretariat of the Commission on April 26, 2001.

2.   The Commission presented the application for the Court to decide whether the State had violated Articles 8 (Right to a Fair Trial), 23 (Right to Participate in Government), and 25 (Judicial Protection) of the American Convention, all of them in relation to Articles 1(1) (Obligation to Respect Rights) and 2 (Domestic Legal Effects) thereof, to the detriment of the candidates for mayors, deputy mayors, and councilors presented by the indigenous regional political party, Yapti Tasba Masraka Nanih Asla Takanka (hereinafter "YATAMA"). The Commission alleged that these candidates were excluded from participating in the municipal elections held on November 5, 2000, in the North Atlantic and the South Atlantic Autonomous Regions (hereinafter "RAAN" and "RAAS") as a result of a decision issued on August 15, 2000, by the Supreme Electoral Council. The application stated that the alleged victims filed several recourses against this decision and, finally, on October 25, 2000, the Supreme Court of Justice of Nicaragua declared that the application for *amparo* that they had filed was inadmissible. The Commission indicated that the State had not provided a

recourse that would have protected the right of these candidates to participate and to be elected in the municipal elections of November 5, 2000, and it had not adopted the legislative or other measures necessary to make these rights effective; above all, it had not provided for "norms in the electoral law that would facilitate the political participation of the indigenous organizations in the electoral processes of the Atlantic Coast Autonomous Region of Nicaragua, in accordance with the customary law, values, practices, and customs of the indigenous people who reside there."

197. The exercise of the rights to be elected and to vote, which are closely related to each other, is the expression of the individual and social dimension of political participation.

198. Citizens have the right to take part in the management of public affairs through freely elected representatives. The right to vote is an essential element for the existence of democracy and one of the ways in which citizens exercise the right to political participation. This right implies that the citizens may freely elect those who will represent them in conditions of equality.

199. Participation through the exercise of the right to be elected assumes that citizens can stand as candidates in conditions of equality and can occupy elected public office if they obtain the necessary number of votes.

200. The right to have access to public office, under general conditions of equality, protects access to a direct form of participation in the design, implementation, development, and execution of the State's political policies through public office. It is understood that these general conditions of equality refer to access to public office by popular election and by appointment or designation.

226. The violations of the rights of the candidates proposed by YATAMA are particularly serious because, as mentioned above, there is a close relationship between the right to be elected and the right to vote to elect representatives (*supra* para. 197). The Court finds it necessary to observe that the voters were affected as a result of the violation of the right to be elected of the YATAMA candidates. In the instant case, this exclusion meant that the candidates proposed by YATAMA were not included among the options available to the voters, which represented a direct limitation to the exercise of the vote and affected negatively the broadest and freest expression of the will of the electorate, which implies grave consequences for democracy. This harm to the electors constituted non-compliance by the State with the general obligation to guarantee the exercise of the right to vote embodied in Article 1(1) of the Convention.

227. To assess the scope of this harm, it should be recalled that YATAMA contributes to the consolidation and preservation of the cultural identity of the members of the indigenous and ethnic communities of the Atlantic Coast.

Its structure and purposes are related to the practices, customs, and forms of organization of these communities. Consequently, the exclusion of the participation of the YATAMA candidates particularly affected the members of the indigenous and ethnic communities that were represented by this organization in the municipal elections of November 2000 by placing them in a situation of inequality as regards the options among which they could choose to vote, since those persons who, in principle, deserved their confidence because they had been chosen directly in assemblies (according to the practices and customs of these communities) to represent the interests of their members had been excluded from participating as candidates. This exclusion resulted in a lack of representation of the needs of the members of the said communities in the regional bodies responsible for adopting policies and programs that could affect their development.

228.   This harm to the voters was reflected in the 2000 municipal elections; for example, there was an abstention rate of approximately 80% in the RAAN, due to the fact that part of the electorate did not consider they were adequately represented by the participating parties and five political parties requested the Supreme Electoral Council to "[d]eclare the nullity of the elections in the RAAN . . . [and o]rganize new municipal elections . . . with the inclusion of the YATAMA Indigenous Party." Also, the expert witness, Carlos Antonio Hurtado Cabrera, emphasized that YATAMA "is the principal indigenous political organization in the country."

Canese v. Paraguay
31-Aug-2004
Series C No. 111—*Merits, Reparations, and Costs*

82.   In its Advisory Opinion OC-5/85, the Inter-American Court referred to the close relationship that exists between democracy and freedom of expression when it stated that:

> Freedom of expression is a cornerstone upon which the very existence of a democratic society rests. It is indispensable for the formation of public opinion. It is also a *conditio sine qua non* for the development of political parties, trade unions, scientific and cultural societies, and, in general, those who wish to influence the public. It represents, in short, the means that enable the community, when exercising its options, to be sufficiently informed. Consequently, it can be said that a society that is not well informed is not a society that is truly free.[119 80]

85.   In this respect, it is worth underscoring that the Heads of State and

Government of the Americas adopted the Inter-American Democratic Charter on September 11, 2001, in which, *inter alia,* they stated that:

> Transparency in government activities, probity, responsible public administration on the part of Governments, respect for social rights, and freedoms of expression and of the press are essential components of the exercise of democracy.[123][81]

86.   Thus, the different regional systems for the protection of human rights and the universal system agree on the essential role played by freedom of expression in the consolidation and dynamics of a democratic society. Without effective freedom of expression, exercised in all its forms, democracy is enervated, pluralism and tolerance start to deteriorate, the mechanisms for control and complaint by the individual become ineffectual, and, above all, a fertile ground is created for authoritarian systems to take root in society.[124][82]

87.   The Court observes that the statements for which Mr. Canese was sued took place during the debates of the electoral campaign for the presidency of the Republic, in the context of the transition to democracy, because, for 35 years and until 1989, the country had been ruled by a dictatorship. In other words, the presidential elections in which Mr. Canese took part and during which he made his statements formed part of an important process of democratization in Paraguay.

88.   The Court considers it important to emphasize that, within the framework of an electoral campaign, the two dimensions of freedom of thought and expression are the cornerstone for the debate during the electoral process, since they become an essential instrument for the formation of public opinion among the electorate, strengthen the political contest between the different candidates and parties taking part in the elections, and are an authentic mechanism for analyzing the political platforms proposed by the different candidates. This leads to greater transparency and better control over the future authorities and their administration.90.

The Court considers it essential that the exercise of freedom of expression should be protected and guaranteed in the political debate that precedes the election of State authorities that will govern a State. The formation of the collective will through the exercise of individual suffrage is nourished by the different options presented by the political parties through the candidates that represent them. Democratic debate implies that the free circulation of ideas and information on the candidates and their political parties is permitted through the media, the candidates themselves, and any individual who wishes to express his opinion and provide information. Everyone must be allowed to question and investigate the competence and suitability of the candidates, and also to disagree with and compare proposals, ideas, and opinions, so that the electorate may form its opinion in order to vote. In this respect, the exercise of political rights and freedom of thought and expression are closely related and reinforce one another.

THE COURT,
DECLARES:
Unanimously, that:
1.   The State violated the right to freedom of thought and expression embodied in Article 13 of the American Convention on Human Rights, in relation to Article 1(1) thereof, to the detriment of Ricardo Nicolás Canese Krivoshein, in the terms of paragraphs 96 to 108 of this judgment.

Claude Reyes v. Chile
19-Sep-2006
Series C No. 151—*Merits, Reparations, and Costs*

65.   In light of the proven facts in this case, the Court must determine whether the failure to hand over part of the information requested from the Foreign Investment Committee in 1998 constituted a violation of the right to freedom of thought and expression of Marcel Claude Reyes, Sebastián Cox Urrejola, and Arturo Longton Guerrero and, consequently, a violation of Article 13 of the American Convention.

66.   With regard to the specific issues in this case, it has been proved that a request was made for information held by the Foreign Investment Committee and that this Committee is a public-law juridical person. Also, that the requested information related to a foreign investment contract signed originally between the State and two foreign companies and a Chilean company (which would receive the investment) in order to develop a forestry exploitation project that caused considerable public debate owing to its potential environmental impact.

77.   In relation to the facts of the instant case, the Court finds that, by expressly stipulating the right to "seek" and "receive" "information," Article 13 of the Convention protects the right of all individuals to request access to State-held information, with the exceptions permitted by the restrictions established in the Convention. Consequently, this article protects the right of the individual to receive such information and the positive obligation of the State to provide it, so that the individual may have access to such information or receive an answer that includes a justification when, for any reason permitted by the Convention, the State is allowed to restrict access to the information in a specific case. The information should be provided without the need to prove direct interest or personal involvement in order to obtain it, except in cases in which a legitimate restriction is applied. The delivery of information to an individual can, in turn, permit it to circulate in society so that the latter can become acquainted with it,

have access to it, and assess it. In this way, the right to freedom of thought and expression includes the protection of the right of access to State-held information, which also clearly includes the two dimensions, individual and social, of the right to freedom of thought and expression that must be guaranteed simultaneously by the State.[74][83]

86.   In this regard, the State's actions should be governed by the principles of disclosure and transparency in public administration that enable all persons subject to its jurisdiction to exercise the democratic control of those actions so that they can question, investigate, and consider whether public functions are being performed adequately. Access to State-held information of public interest can permit participation in public administration through the social control that can be exercised through such access.

87.   Democratic control by society, through public opinion, fosters transparency in State activities and promotes the accountability of State officials in relation to their public activities.[89][84] Hence, for the individual to be able to exercise democratic control, the State must guarantee access to the information of public interest that it holds. By permitting the exercise of this democratic control, the State encourages greater participation by the individual in the interests of society.103.   Based on the above, the Court finds that the State violated the right to freedom of thought and expression embodied in Article 13 of the American Convention to the detriment of Marcel Claude Reyes and Arturo Longton Guerrero and failed to comply with the general obligation to respect and ensure the rights and freedoms established in Article 1(1) thereof. In addition, by not having adopted the measures that were necessary and compatible with the Convention to make effective the right of access to State-held information, Chile failed to comply with the general obligation to adopt domestic legal provisions arising from Article 2 of the Convention.

Palamara Iribarne v. Chile
22-Nov-2005
Series C No. 135—*Merits, Reparations, and Costs*

68.   As asserted by this Court on earlier occasions, a violation of Article 13 of the Convention may take different forms depending on whether the violation results in the denial of the freedom of expression or whether it entails a restriction beyond permissible limits.[172][85] Not every breach of Article 13 of the Convention entails an outright denial of the right to freedom of expression, which occurs when government power is used to establish means to prevent the free flow of information, ideas, opinions, or news. Examples of this type of violation are prior

censorship, seizure or banning of publications, and, in general, any measures that subject expression or dissemination of information to State control. In such case, there is a gross violation not only of the right of each individual to express their views, but also of the right of each person to be well informed, thus affecting one of the fundamental bases of a democratic society.[173][86]

72.   As asserted by this Court, "the expression and the dissemination of ideas are indivisible";[176][87] therefore, in order to ensure the effective exercise of freedom of thought and expression, the State may not unduly restrict the right to disseminate ideas and opinions.

73.   In the instant case, in order to ensure the effective exercise of Mr. Palamara-Iribarne's right to freedom of thought and expression, it was not enough for the State to allow him to write his ideas and opinions. The protection of such right implied the duty of the State not to restrict their dissemination, enabling him to distribute his book by any appropriate means to make his ideas and opinions reach the maximum number of people and, in turn, allowing these people to receive this information.[177][88]

Afro-Descendant Communities Displaced from the Cacarica River Basin (Operation Genesis) v. Colombia

20-Nov-2013

Series C No. 270—*Preliminary Objections, Merits, Reparations, and Costs*

1. On July 25, 2011, the Inter-American Commission on Human Rights (hereinafter "the Inter-American Commission" or "the Commission") submitted to the jurisdiction of the Court, pursuant to the provisions of Articles 51 and 61 of the American Convention, the case of Marino López et al. (Operation Genesis) v. the Republic of Colombia (hereinafter "the State" or "Colombia"). The Commission submitted all the facts contained in its Merits Report. The case refers to the State's responsibility for alleged human rights violations committed in relation to the so-called "Operation Genesis" conducted from February 24 to 27, 1997, in the general area of the Salaquí River and the Truandó River, a zone near the territories of the Afro-descendant communities of the Cacarica River basin, in the department of El Chocó, which resulted in the death of Marino López Mena and the forced displacement of hundreds of persons, many of whom were members of the Afro-descendant communities that lived on the banks of the Cacarica River. In addition, it was alleged that the right to collective property of these communities had been violated in relation to the territories that they had ancestrally owned and which the State had recognized to them, owing to both

the displacements and the illegal exploitation of natural resources carried out by companies with the State's permission and tolerance. The failure to investigate the facts and to punish those responsible was also alleged, as well as the lack of judicial protection in relation to these events.

X. Reparations (Application of Article 63(1) of the American Convention)

A) Injured Party

415. Bearing in mind that, in Chapter VI, it was decided that Article 35(2) of the Court's Rules of Procedure would be applied in this case and that, consequently, the revised list of victims for the establishment of reparations is the one that includes 531 persons and that was presented by the representatives as an annex to their motions and arguments brief, the Court will proceed to determine the factual issues that, with regard to the victims in this case, have given rise to discussions within these proceedings between the Commission, the representatives and the State, as indicated previously.

A.1. Arguments of the Commission and of the parties

416. The State considered, first, that the community as such could not be considered a victim because it did not comply with the respective requirements. [663][89] Second, it advised that on an individual and general basis, there were gaps[664][90] in the information of the persons who appear on the representatives' list and indicated the importance of establishing a limit to the descendants of the victims who were legally entitled to receive reparations. Third, it had cross-checked the names of the victims indicated in the motions and arguments brief with other national lists and registries with the following results:

(a) Inter-institutional Information System of the Justice and Peace Law (SIJYP): only 28 of them appear in this system; [665][91]

(b) CAVIDA members presented by the representatives in 2006 for the request for precautionary measures: this list includes 581 names and only 111 have the same name, surname and identification as those on the list of 531; [666][92]

(c) National Civil Registry: [667][93] this only includes records of 472[668][94] of whom 16 are deceased and 78 are "non-existent"; [669][95] thus there are only 378 current records in the national archives, and

(d) Central Registry for the Displaced Population (RUPD), [670][96]which is being incorporated into the Central Registry for Victims (RUV): there are two problems:

(i) only 158 names appear in this registry – in other words 373 are not registered, and

(ii) of these 158, 143 stated that they had displaced on February 28,

1997,[671][97] and of those only 14 indicated Chocó as the place they were displaced from;[672][98] of these 14, five stated that they had displaced collectively,[673][99] and nine individually.[674][100]

417.   Lastly, despite acknowledging that the status of displaced persons is obtained *de facto,* the State affirmed that the 373 victims who do not appear on the RUPD disregarded the internal system, leaving to one side the principles of subsidiarity and complementarity of the inter-American system. Based on the foregoing, the State asked the Court to abstain from recognizing as victims those who appear on the list with the representatives' brief, because this was inexact. Furthermore, it asked that, in general, the Court only consider as victims those who prove the causal nexus between Operation Genesis and the harm and, specifically, that "the Court declare that only the 12 persons who stated that they had been displaced from the municipality of Riosucio in February 1997, be considered as presumed victims of the displacement from the Cacarica river basin."

418.   The Commission asked the Court to take into consideration the aspects inherent in the complexity of the case,[675][101] and affirmed that the evidence presented by the State to deny the status of victims was based on records of State entities such as the Central Registry for the Displaced Population (RUPD) and the Prosecutor General's Office, which "do not have evidence to disprove the existence and identity of the victims established in the representatives' list; rather, to the contrary, they merely reveal the difficulties that exist to determine the victims in the case of a phenomenon of massive dimensions such as the displacement that occurred in this case." Lastly, it stated that, as indicated by Colombian Constitutional Court itself, the effect of the RUPD is not to establish the status of victim, because the "status of internally displaced is not something that can depend in any way on an administrative decision of the State."

419.   The representatives reiterated the difficulties they had faced to identify the victims, but indicated that the group of 531 persons presented with the motions and arguments brief was the definitive list. They indicated that the list declares the status of displaced, but does not establish this[676][102] and that, prior to this, there were other lists and, in this regard, it attached a series of statements by public officials confirming the existence of such lists. They had crosschecked the list attached to the motions and arguments brief with (a) a census conducted by the Social Solidarity Network (RSS), an entity attached to the Administrative Department of the Presidency of the Republic of Colombia, between 1998 and 1999,[677][103] and (b) another census conducted by the RSS and the Agrarian Institute (a financial entity entitled Agrarian Credit Institute with the mandate of granting credits to Colombian farmers) in the context of the *"Vivir Mejor"* rural housing program.[678][104] Based on the said crosschecks, they concluded that "there is no doubt that the 531 victims represented by the *Comisión Intereclesial de Justicia*

y Paz before the inter-American system of human rights, has been fully identified by State entities at the time of the forced displacement and subsequently.

A.2. Considerations of the Court[SEP]

A.2.1.   The victims of the forced displacement

420.   Based on the list of 531 presumed victims presented by the representatives with the motions and arguments brief (hereinafter "the list of victims") (*supra* para. 38), the Court will proceed to determine who will be considered victims in this specific case.

421.   First, the Court notes that, apparently by an involuntary omission of the representatives, the victim Jhon James Oviedo Granada – listed as No. 29 in the report of the Commission and currently on the list of victims – was not excluded, even though the representatives had identified him as one of the persons who "owing to the passage of time and the rigor of the armed conflict, had abandoned the community many years ago and the *Comisión Intereclesial de Justicia y Paz* had been unable to locate him and contact him." [679] [105] Therefore, the Court will not take into account the name of Jhon James Oviedo Granada on the list of victims in this case.

422.   Also, the State indicated that only 28 of the persons on the list of victims were registered in the Justice and Peace Inter-institutional Information System. In this regard, the Court indicates that the fact that a person does not appear on the said list in no way affects the status as victim of a person in the instant case, because although it is true that this is a national list with which the Justice and Peace jurisdiction in Colombian operates, the fact that a person has not appeared as a victim in the Justice and Peace proceedings bears no relationship to the proceedings before the inter-American system. Therefore, the Court finds that this argument by the State is not relevant to determine the list of victims in the instant case.

423.   The Court will not make a detailed analysis in relation to the crosscheck made between the list of presumed victims in this case and the list of 581 persons presented by the representatives in 2006 in their request for precautionary measures, because the objectives of the two proceedings are not the same. In particular, it is clear that a request for protection filed before the Commission refers to a potential situation of actual risk that could be affecting a person or a group of persons, while a contentious proceeding before this Court is related to an alleged violation of human rights of a persons or group of persons that occurred in the past. Therefore, there is no justified reason why the beneficiaries of precautionary measures decided by the Commission should be the same person as the presumed victims of a contentious case being considered by the Court. Consequently, the Court finds that this argument of the State is not relevant to determine the list of victims in this case

424.   Regarding the crosscheck with the National Civil Registry, two clarifications are required. First, the Court notes that the fact that a person does not appear in the Registry cannot lead to the conclusion that they do not exist. In particular, the State did not indicate whether the birth of all those born in Colombia is registered and/or they have a citizenship card. In addition, the Court notes that several names of presumed victims appear written in different ways in the documents that were submitted to this Court; thus it is possible that the Registry may contain names written differently, which would lead to erroneous results as regards whether or not certain presumed victims "exist." Second, the 16 persons whose identity cards appear to have been cancelled due to their decease will not be excluded either, because the State has not proved that they died before February 28, 1997, so that, if compensation is declared in their favor, those who are considered their heirs under domestic law would be legitimized to reclaim this, unless it is proved that the decedent died before the facts. Consequently, the Court finds that this argument of the State is not relevant to determine the list of victims in the case.

425.   Regarding the persons who were born after the return to the Peace Communities in the Cacarica River basin, although it may be presumed that they could be affected because they were born in a situation of displacement of their parents or owing to the living conditions that they have faced, it is also true that they were not victims of the forced displacement caused by the paramilitary incursions, or of the conditions of displacement in Turbo, Bocas de Atrato or Panama. Accordingly, the 12 persons who were born during the return are excluded from the list of victims forwarded by the representatives.

426.   The Court also notes that, according to the State, only 158 persons appear in the Central Registry for the Displaced Population (RUPD), and not the others included on the list of victims. However, as the Court has indicated in other cases, and as the Colombian Constitutional Court has acknowledged, "[s] ince forced displacement is a *de facto* situation, there is no need to be declared a displaced person by any public or private entity as an essential requirement to acquire that status. The fact that the Government has established a procedure to include those displaced on a national Registry for the Displaced Population, which regulates access to the assistance that has been established (immediate aid, emergency humanitarian aid, and programs for return, resettlement or relocation), is a different matter; but this mechanism is not intended to unduly determine a *de facto* situation."[680][106]

427.   Regarding the foregoing, as noted in a recent order on monitoring compliance with the judgment delivered by this Court in the case of the *Ituango Massacres v. Colombia*,[681][107] the Colombian Constitutional Court, in its Judgment T-367 of May 11, 2010, considered that certain State entities had violated the

fundamental rights to a decent life and to justice, by requiring the victims of the Ituango massacres to be registered in the Information System for the Displaced Population (SIPOD) as a requirement prior to acceding to some of the measures of reparation (above all, housing, security, and medical services) ordered by the Court in their favor. The high constitutional court of Colombia considered that, in that case, the said Unified List had become "an insurmountable obstacle that [perpetuated] the violation of the fundamental rights of those affected," who are part of the population displaced by the violence, which has been recognized "as the subject of special protection owing to the extreme vulnerability in which it finds itself," so that its rights to prompt redress and reparation of the violated rights must be diligently guaranteed by the competent authorities.

428.   As the Court has established in other cases, a list of those displaced is an instrument that declares that a person is displaced, but does not make that person displaced and, consequently, it is not appropriate to exclude the 360 persons who do not appear on the RUPD from the list of victims. As Juan Pablo Franco, expert witness proposed by the State, indicated, "it is evident that a person is considered an internally displaced person at the time of the events based on which he was forced to migrate within national territory, abandoning his usual place of residence or economic activities." [682] [108]

429.   Regarding the 158 persons who appear on the RUPD and the RUV, the Court indicates that the temporal and spatial circumstances of the events that are the subject of this case are limited to those that occurred in the municipality of Riosucio in the Chocó department in 1997, so that the persons who were displaced from other places and on other dates cannot be considered victims of the events analyzed in this case. This takes into account that, although it is true that the record does not constitute the status of displaced persons, the statements made by these persons in which, presuming they told the truth, they stated that they had been displaced from different places and at different times to the events of the case *sub judice* cannot be disregarded.

430.   The State's obligation to make reparation arises as a result of its responsibility for the facts of the case and the victims affected by these facts. Consequently, the Court cannot order the State to make reparation to individuals who, although they are victims of other situations, have not been declared victims in this specific case. In addition, the representatives have not contested the State's arguments in this regard, or made any observations on the appropriateness of the lists that were provided for these purposes. Thus, without prejudice to the reparations that they may have the right to claim at the domestic level, the following will not be considered victims in the instant case: (a) the 11 persons who declared before the Central Registry for the Displaced Population that they had been displaced at a time other than the weeks following the implementation of

Operation Cacarica and the paramilitary incursions (of these, five were not from Riosucio), and (b) the 135 persons who declared before the Registry that they were displaced from a place other than the municipality of Riosucio. Therefore, regarding the 158 persons included in the RUPD and the RUV, the Court will consider only 12 of these persons as victims of this case. [683] [109]

431.   Therefore, based on the above considerations, of the original list of 531 victims presented by the representatives, the Court will consider 372 persons as victims in this case, because 341 persons had to be displaced owing to the facts of this case (Annex I), of whom 203 were minors at the time of the displacement (Annex II), while 31 children were born in conditions of forced displacement following the events of February 1997 (Annex III).

A.2.2.   The next of kin of Marino López

432.   With regard to the next of kin of Marino López, the initial list of 446 persons with Report No. 64/11 presented by the Commission made no reference to them. However, in the list of 497 persons that the representatives submitted to the Commission and that was provided to the Court in September 2011, without any pertinent clarification, five family members of Marino López were included, [684] [110] and they became part of Family 1 on List No. 2. Subsequently, the list that the representatives submitted to the Commission in November 2011, and that the latter forwarded to the Court in January 2012, [685] [111] included 14 [686] [112] family members of Mr. López. Lastly, in their motions and arguments brief, the representatives excluded Leonardo Lopez Garcia without giving any reason and, thus, the final list included 13 next of kin of Marino López.

433.   The State indicated that the list submitted by the representatives with the motions and arguments brief "included 13 persons who presumably were next of kin of Marino López, but regarding whom no further information was provided"; that only with regard to those who appear as Nos. 4 and 5 (Yenesid Gamboa Palacio and Jhon Freddy Palacio Palacio), it was said that they were "foster children," but "no evidence was provided that certified this relationship. Of the 11 remaining persons, the list does not indicate their relationship to Marino López, or provide any evidence authenticating this." Accordingly, the State asked "that the Court declare that only the two persons who have been recognized as next of kin of Marino López in the criminal proceedings underway for his murder be considered as presumed victims of his death."

434.   Regarding the persons who should be recognized as next of kin of Marino López, the Court finds that it only has a list presented by the representatives, which is not supported by any evidence that would authenticate a relationship to Mr. López, and for this reason the Court cannot recognize them as "next of kin." This was noted and contested on several occasions by the State, without the representatives presenting arguments or evidence in this regard. Therefore, taking

into account that only Emedelia Palacio has been accredited and recognized by the State as his permanent companion, and that the representatives have not provided further information on the persons that they consider family members, this Court considers that, based on what the Eighth Criminal Court of the Bogota Special Circuit recognized, [687][113] it can only recognize Emedelia Palacios as next of kin of Marino López.

435.   Nevertheless, since there is information that would allow it to be concluded that Marino López had other next of kin, the Court establishes, as it has in other cases, that the compensation ordered in this Judgment (*infra* para. 476) must be delivered to the immediate family members who come forward, provided that they appear before the competent authorities of the State between the moment of notification of this Judgment and up until one year after the date of their public summons by the State. The next of kin must provide the necessary information to identify themselves and prove their relationship. [688][114] To this end, the State must make announcements by radio stations, with local and national coverage, at least once a month for six months as of publication of this Judgment, at peak listening hours, summoning the members of the immediate family of Marino López to come forward with the necessary information and advising them of the procedure they should follow in this regard.

ANALYSIS AND QUESTIONS RAISED BY THE COURT'S JURISPRUDENCE

In its jurisprudence, the Inter-American Court of Human Rights has affirmed the rights of individual persons as well as recognizing the consequent impact on society when those rights are upheld or violated. Specifically in the above excerpted cases, the Court has affirmed that the right to free thought and expression involves more than self-expression, but the interchange of ideas. The Court states that free and full exercise of this right must be guaranteed to all persons subject to a State's jurisdiction and that this is a basic condition for society to be informed.

The Court further asserts that free thought and expression provide the foundation for democratic debate and the electoral process. Additionally, the Court recognizes that the right to vote correlates with the right to be elected, and that the guarantee of such individual rights impacts society. The Court also confirms that free thought and expression include the right to access State-held information. And, finally, the Court recognizes that free thought and expression involve the corollary of dissemination of ideas and opinions without prior censorship or State control of expression and publication. Through such jurisprudence, the Court plainly links the violations of the rights of persons to detrimental impacts on society, and the upholding of individual rights to the upholding of the needs of society as a whole.

- The procedural rules of the Inter-American human rights system permit "[a]ny person or group of persons or nongovernmental entity legally recognized in one or more of the Member States of the OAS" to submit a petition on behalf of themselves or third persons to the Inter-American Commission on Human Rights. Would this procedural rule, coupled with the Court's analysis of the impact of violations upon society, potentially allow a case to be successfully brought on behalf of society where no individual victim was identified? What would be the implications of such a case?

- Do the Court's findings that society is impacted by violations of rights and freedoms further uphold these rights and freedoms for individual persons?

VII. THE VICTIMS' LEGAL ASSISTANCE FUND

In Article 50(2) of its Rules of Procedure, the Inter-American Court of Human Rights stipulates that "[a] party offering testimonial or expert evidence shall bear the costs of the appearance of alleged victims, witnesses, or expert witnesses before the Tribunal." However, over time, the Court recognized that lack of financial resources presented a barrier to litigation for some victims. The following excerpts detail the Court's creation and implementation of the Victims' Legal Assistance Fund.

The Kichwa Indigenous People of Sarayaku v. Ecuador
03-Mar-2011
Order of the President of the Inter-American Court of Human Rights

CONSIDERING THAT:

2.   In 2008, the General Assembly of the Organization of American States (hereinafter the "OAS") created the Legal Assistance Fund of the Inter-American Human Rights System (hereinafter "the Inter-American System's Assistance Fund") and commissioned the OAS Permanent Council to draft the Fund's rules of procedure; [2][115] the latter adopted the corresponding rules of procedure in November 2009. [3][116] The Assistance Fund was created "to facilitate access to the inter-American human rights system by persons who currently lack the resources needed to bring their cases before the system." [4][117] According to the

Rules of Procedure adopted by the Permanent Council, the Inter-American System's Assistance Fund has two separate accounts: one corresponding to the Inter-American Commission and the other to the Inter-American Court. As regards the financing of the Inter-American System's Assistance Fund, currently this depends on "voluntary capital contributions from the Members States of the OAS, the Permanent Observer States, and other States and donors that may wish to collaborate with the Fund." [5][118] In addition, according to Article 4 of the Rules of Procedure approved by the Permanent Council, it corresponded to the Court to establish the formal requirements for eligibility to request assistance, and also the approval procedure.

3.　　　　Consequently, on February 4, 2010, the Court adopted its Rules of Procedure for the Assistance Fund, which came into force on June 1, 2010, "whose purpose is to regulate the operation of, and access to, the [...] Assistance Fund for the litigation of cases before it." [6][119] As established therein, in order to use this Fund a presumed victim must fulfill three requirements:

  (a) request this in the brief with pleadings, motions and evidence;
  (b) prove, by means of a sworn affidavit and other appropriate evidence that satisfies the Court, that they lack sufficient financial resources to cover the costs of litigation before the Inter-American Court, and
  (c) indicate precisely which aspects of their defense in the proceedings require the use of the resources of the Assistance Fund.

4.　　　　Article 3 of the Rules of Procedure of the Assistance Fund stipulates that, on receiving a request to use the said Fund, the Court's Secretariat must conduct a preliminary review and will require the applicant to forward any additional background information required for the request to be submitted to the consideration of the President of the Court. Then, the Secretariat will submit the request to the consideration of the President, who will assess the petition and take the pertinent decision within three months of receiving all the necessary information.

5.　　　　In their response to the request for additional information (*supra* having seen paragraph 4), the representatives indicated that the Kichwa Indigenous People of Sarayaku have a subsistence economy and, therefore, do not carry out any remunerated activities. Previously, they had indicated that "the only activity for which the Kichwa People of Sarayaku [...] receive any type of financial income is the community tourism project," which brings in less than three thousand dollars a year. In this regard, they attached a notarized statement by the Sarayaku President concerning the People's lack of resources to pay the expenses arising from these proceedings, together with an income tax return and the 2009 account statements, indicating that the financial situation of Sarayaku was negative and, consequently, that the amount of tax to be paid by the Indigenous People was zero dollars.

6.   Furthermore, the representatives indicated that they, as a non-governmental organization, "did not have a specific budgetary item for paying expenses such as those that the victims – through [them] – requested be covered by the Assistance Fund." They underlined that "it is the victims who must cover the expenses and costs of the proceedings," so that they should benefit from the Legal Assistance Fund if they prove a lack of resources. Nevertheless, they added that, at this stage of the proceedings, they would be willing to cover certain costs that, in consequence, the presumed victims had not included in the request for assistance, such as the travel expenses and professional honoraria of the lawyers, and the logistic expenses during the preparation and holding of the hearing, in the understanding that these expenses should be taken into account by the Court when determining the expenses and costs to be reimbursed by the State, if appropriate.

7.   The representatives indicated that the presumed victims requested help from the Assistance Fund to cover:

(a) travel expenses for the victims, witnesses and experts that the Court summons to testify, pursuant to Article 50 of the Court's Rules of Procedure;

(b) notary expenses arising from preparing the affidavits that the Court finds it pertinent to receive, and

(c) travel expenses in order to conduct the expert appraisals included in the pleadings and motions brief in those cases in which the experts need to travel to Ecuador to make their appraisals."

They emphasized that, at this stage of the proceedings, they were unable to determine whether the Court would admit all the witnesses and experts proposed in their pleadings and motions brief; likewise, they did not know whether the Court would decide to convene a hearing in this case, so that "the travel expenses could vary considerably." In view of the foregoing, they asked the Court to consider their request "based on the testimonies and expert opinions that it decides to admit in its order under Article 50 of the Rules of Procedure" and that, if the request was partially accepted, the Court indicate the number of expert opinions and testimonies that would be covered by the Fund. Lastly, the representatives forwarded the estimated expenses to present the evidence at a hearing, if this was held at the seat of the Court, clarifying that, if it was held elsewhere, the expenses could increase significantly. In addition, they forwarded the average cost to "notarize" the testimony of a witness or an expert opinion in Ecuador, indicating that, in this case, the members of the Sarayaku would have to travel to a city by plane.

8.   First, the President confirms that the request to use the Assistance Fund was made opportunely in the pleadings and motions brief (*supra* having seen paragraph 2), on behalf of the Kichwa People of Sarayaku. The President

appreciates that the said request should be understood to have been made on behalf of the presumed victims, exclusively, because as the representatives have already indicated in their brief of November 23, 2010, it is they who should benefit from the Fund (*supra* considering paragraph 6). In addition, the President takes note of the lack of financial resources alleged by the presumed victims and admits the sworn statement of the representative of the Kichwa People of Sarayaku and the Community's income tax return as evidence of this (*supra* considering paragraph 5).

9.   Furthermore, the President observes that the presumed victims have requested assistance from the said Fund to pay expenses related to the production of evidence before the Court, specifically for the presentation of witness statements and expert opinions, whether at a hearing or by affidavit. In addition, he takes note of the representatives' observations that, at this procedural stage before the Court, they were unable to determine exactly the expenses that this would represent.

10.   The President recalls that the Assistance Fund is made up of voluntary contributions from cooperating sources (*supra* second considering paragraph), and that these limited resources are insufficient to cover all the expenses relating to the appearance and eventual presentation of evidence before the Court by the presumed victims. Consequently, in each specific case, the President must assess the request for assistance in relation to the available funds, taking into account the needs for assistance that could arise in other cases before the Court, in order to ensure the proper administration and fair distribution of the Fund's limited resource.

11.   The President takes note that, at the current stage of the proceedings, it is not possible to determine which of the testimonies offered by the representatives will be received by the Court, or in what form they will be received. In accordance with Article 50(1) of the Court's Rules of Procedure, this determination corresponds to the Court or its President, when the parties have forwarded the final lists of their proposed deponents and the right to defense has been ensured, in the terms of Articles 45 to 49 of the Court's Rules of Procedure.

12.   Based on the foregoing considerations, the President finds admissible the presumed victims' request to use the Legal Assistance Fund, in the understanding that this will be to cover the expenses relating to an adequate appearance of deponents and presentation of testimony before the Court. In this regard, based on the resources currently available in the Assistance Fund, the presumed victims will be awarded the necessary financial assistance for the presentation, charged to the Fund, of a maximum of four testimonies, either by affidavit or at the public hearing. In addition, he finds it appropriate to postpone the determination of the specific amount, purpose and object of the financial assistance that will be provided to the presumed victims until such time as this President, or the Court,

rules on the admissibility and relevance of the testimonial and expert evidence offered and, as appropriate, on the opening of the oral proceedings, in accordance with Article 50(1) of the Court's Rules of Procedure, in order to be certain which testimonies will be received by the Court, and also the way in which they will be presented (*supra* eleventh considering paragraph).

THEREFORE:

THE PRESIDENT OF THE INTER-AMERICAN COURT OF HUMAN RIGHTS

in exercise of his authority in relation to the Victims' Legal Assistance Fund and in accordance with Article 31 of the Court's Rules of Procedure and Article 3 of the Rules of Procedure of the Legal Assistance Fund,

DECIDES:

1. To declare admissible the request submitted by the presumed victims, through their representatives, to use the Victims' Legal Assistance Fund of the Inter-American Court of Human Rights, so that the necessary financial assistance will be granted for the presentation of a maximum of four testimonies, and that the specific amount, purpose and object of this assistance will be defined when deciding on the presentation of testimonial and expert evidence and, as appropriate, on the opening of the oral proceedings, in accordance with Article 50 of the Court's Rules of Procedure, as established in the twelfth considering paragraph of this order.

2. To require the Secretariat of the Court to notify this order to the representatives of the presumed victims, the State of Ecuador, and the Inter-American Commission on Human Rights.

The Massacres of El Mozote and Surrounding Areas v. El Salvador
01-Dec-2011
Victims' Legal Assistance Fund

5.　　The President notes that, with regard to the request for resources from the Court's Assistance Fund, the representatives based their application on the fact that the surviving alleged victims and relatives of the alleged victims of the Massacres of El Mozote "do not have the financial resources to cover the costs of this process." To support their application, the representatives included the sworn statement rendered by María Dorila Márquez de Márquez, the testimonies rendered before the Archdiocese's Human Rights Office (*Tutela Legal*) in San Salvador by José Gervacio Díaz, Juan Bautista Márquez, Lucinda Hernández, María Ángel Díaz and María del Rosario López Sánchez, together with documents justifying the estimated expenses.

6.   The President confirms that the representatives submitted, as attachments to the brief of pleadings and motions, the sworn statement of María Dorila Márquez de Márquez, in which she stated that she knew a large number of alleged victims, including survivors and relatives of alleged victims murdered in the Massacres of El Mozote and surrounding areas, who are "people with very few financial resources," and therefore "these people would not have the necessary financial resources to cover these expenses." She also stated that "until now, the costs of obtaining justice in this case ha[d] been assumed by the Archdiocese's Human Rights Office (*Tutela Legal*) of San Salvador and that without the intervention of this organization, it would not have been possible [...] to proceed with this process to the stage that it has reached now." Likewise, the representatives submitted the testimonies rendered before the Archdiocese's Human Rights Office (*Tutela Legal*) by José Gervacio Díaz, Lucinda Hernández and María del Rosario López Sánchez,[1208] in which they describe, among other matters, their current means of subsistence and the decrease in their incomes. Finally, the representatives included the following approximate estimates of expenses:

(a)   round trip airline tickets from San Salvador to San José and from Buenos Aires to San Jose, based on a quote obtained in March 2012,

(b)   hotel costs,

(c)   notarial services, and

(d)   psychosocial report.

7.   At the same time, the representatives pointed out that "[a]lthough Tutela Legal has, until now, covered the expenses of both the domestic and the international proceedings, the processing of this case before the [...] Court implies additional expenses, which Tutela Legal is not in a position to cover alone." They added that CEJIL and Tutela Legal "would be in a position to assume a number of expenses incurred by the proceeding before this [...] Court, and therefore the [alleged] victims have not included [these] in their application for assistance from the Fund. This, on the understanding that those amounts [would be] reimbursed by the [...] State of El Salvador, if the Court so orders in its judgment in this case." Finally, the representatives requested that the State be required to reimburse said expenses to the Legal Assistance Fund, according to Article 5 of the Rules of the Fund. This, without prejudice to the amounts for expenses and costs that the Court may determine for the alleged victims and their representatives, and for which they should be directly reimbursed.

8.   The representatives explained that the alleged victims were requesting assistance from the Fund to cover:

(a)   travel expenses, including the "fares, hotel and *per diem* expenses" of the alleged victims, witnesses and expert witnesses that the Court may summon to testify at a hearing;

(b) notarial expenses for the formalization of the affidavits that the Court may consider admissible, and

(c) expenses and travel costs incurred in preparing the expert reports, "for those cases in which the expert witnesses need to travel to El Salvador or travel internally within that country."

The representatives emphasized that, at this stage of the proceedings, they were not in a position to determine whether all the witnesses and expert witnesses proposed in their brief of pleadings and motions would be admitted by the Court or, if admitted, whether they would be summoned to testify in person before it or before a notary public. Likewise they pointed out that they did not know where the Court might decide to hold the future hearing in this case, for which reason "the travel expenses could vary considerably." In view of the foregoing, they requested that, should Court approve this request, to do so bearing in mind "the testimonies and expert reports that it may decide to admit in its Decision."

9. Finally, the representatives presented an estimate of the expenses to be covered by the Fund for the appearance of the deponents at a future public hearing and for the production of evidence, including sworn statements and the expert reports offered. For the first item, the representatives estimated a total of fifteen declarants, including eleven alleged victims and witnesses, as well as four expert witnesses, for a total of approximately US$ 21,875.00 (twenty-one thousand, eight hundred and seventy-five dollars of the United States of America). For the second item, the representatives calculated US$100.00 (one hundred United States dollars) for each "notarization" and, given that the majority of the relatives of the alleged victims live outside of San Salvador, they added US$60.00 (sixty United States dollars) for the transfer of two lawyers of Tutela Legal to the locations where they would be found. Finally, the representatives specified a cost of US$ 3,060.00 (three thousand and sixty United States dollars) for the preparation of a psychosocial expert report. This would include at least 12 visits to the hamlet of El Mozote to hold group workshops as well as two workshops in the Canton of Lourdes, which would imply travel and food expenses.

10. First of all, the President confirms that the request for access to the Court's Assistance Fund had been submitted at the appropriate time, in the brief of pleadings and motions (*supra* having seen paragraph 2). Likewise, he notes that the representatives made the request to access the Legal Assistance Fund on behalf of the alleged victims. Indeed, the President reiterates that the alleged victims are the ones who should benefit from the Assistance Fund.[1219] In this regard, the President takes cognizance of the fact that this case involves numerous alleged victims, although at this stage of the proceeding there is no requirement to make a pronouncement on the identification of the alleged victims in the case before the Court.

11.   In this regard, the President takes cognizance of the lack of financial resources claimed by the alleged victims through their representatives and considers that the sworn statement rendered before a notary public, together with other probative evidence submitted, provide sufficient evidence thereof, pursuant to Article 2 of the Rules of the Assistance Fund.

12.   The President also notes that the alleged victims have requested assistance from the Fund to cover expenses related to the production of evidence before the Court, and specifically to cover the presentation of testimonies, either at a hearing or by means of affidavits, as well as the preparation of one expert report (*supra* considering paragraphs 8 and 9). Likewise, the President takes note of the representatives' comments regarding the fact that they are not in a position to precisely determine the expenses that would be incurred at this stage of the proceeding before the Court, even though they have submitted an estimate.

13.   The President recalls that the Assistance Fund of the Court is comprised of voluntary contributions from donor sources (*supra* considering paragraph 2), and that these limited resources are insufficient to cover all the expenses related to the possible appearance and presentation of evidence before the Court by the alleged victims. Therefore, in each specific case, the Presidency must consider a request for financial assistance on the basis of the resources available and bearing in mind the need for assistance that might arise in other cases before the Court, in order to ensure the correct administration and fair distribution of the Fund's limited resources.

14.   The President notes that, at the present stage of the proceedings, it has not been determined which of the testimonies offered by the representatives shall be received by the Court, or the means by which these shall be obtained. In accordance with Article 50.1 of the Court's Rules of Procedure, that decision is taken by the Court or its President, once the parties have submitted the definitive lists of proposed declarants and the right to defense has been guaranteed, under the terms of Articles 45 to 49 of the Court's Rules of Procedure.

15.   Based on the foregoing considerations, the President considers valid the request of the alleged victims to have recourse to the Court's Legal Assistance Fund. Accordingly, having regard to the resources currently available in the Fund, the alleged victims are to be granted the necessary financial assistance for the presentation of a maximum of four testimonies, either by means of affidavits or at a public hearing. Likewise, the President considers it appropriate to defer a decision on the specific recipients and purpose of the financial assistance to be provided to the alleged victims, until such time as the Presidency, or the Court, rules on the validity and relevance of the testimonial and expert evidence and, if applicable, on the opening of the oral proceedings, under the terms of Article 50.1 of the Rules of Procedure of the Court, in order to have certainty regarding which of the testimonies shall be received by the Court, and the means by which these shall be obtained. (*supra* considering paragraph 14).

22-Mar-2012
Victims' Legal Assistance Fund

e) Application of the Victims' Legal Assistance Fund
32.   The Order adopted by this Presidency on December 1, 2011 (*supra* having seen 4), declared admissible the request submitted by the alleged victims, through their representatives, to have recourse to the Victims' Legal Assistance Fund of the Inter-American Court of Human Rights, so that the necessary financial assistance would be granted for the presentation of a maximum of four testimonies, either by affidavit or at a hearing.
33.   Having determined that the statements offered by the representatives shall be received by the Court and the means by which these shall be obtained, it is now appropriate to determine the specific amount, recipients and purpose of said assistance. As stated in the aforementioned Order of the President, in this case, the financial assistance necessary shall be granted for the presentation of a maximum of four testimonies.
34.   Accordingly, the President orders that financial assistance be granted to cover the travel and accommodation expenses of Mrs. Dorila Márquez de Márquez, María del Rosario López Sánchez, María Margarita Chicas Márquez and María Sol Yáñez de la Cruz so that they may appear before the Court and render their testimonies at the public hearing to be held in the city of Guayaquil, Republic of the Ecuador. As to the four persons appearing at the public hearing, the Court shall take the appropriate and necessary steps to cover the costs of travel, board and lodging for these declarants with resources from the Victims' Assistance Fund.

25-Oct-2012
Series C No. 252—*Merits, reparations and costs*

F. Reimbursement of the disbursements from the Victims' Legal Assistance Fund
394.   In 2008, the General Assembly of the Organization of American States created the Legal Assistance Fund of the Inter-American Human Rights System, the purpose of which "is to facilitate access to the inter-American human rights system by persons who currently lack the resources needed to bring their case before the system." [540] [122] In the instant case, the financial assistance needed for the appearance of María Dorila Márquez de Márquez, María del Rosario López Sánchez, María Margarita Chicas Márquez and María Sol Yáñez De la Cruz at the public hearing held in Guayaquil, Republic of Ecuador, was granted from this Fund (*supra* paras. 12 and 13).

395.   The State had the opportunity to present its observations on the disbursements made in this case, which amounted to US$6,034.36 (six thousand and thirty-four United States dollars and thirty-six cents). El Salvador indicated that the details of the expenses in relation to the items covered is in keeping with the Order of the President of the Court that granted the financial assistance; therefore it had no observations to make on them. In addition, it asked the Court, when evaluating whether it is appropriate to order the reimbursement of these disbursements, to "take into consideration the good will manifested during the [...] proceedings before the [...] Court." Consequently, it corresponds to the Court, in application of Article 5 of the Rules of the Fund, to evaluate whether it is appropriate to order the respondent State to reimburse the disbursements made from the Legal Assistance Fund.

396.   Based on the violations declared in this Judgment, the Court orders the State to reimburse this Fund the sum of US$6,034.36 (six thousand and thirty-four United States dollars and thirty-six cents) for the expenditure incurred for the appearance of the deponents at the public hearing in this case. This amount must be reimbursed within 90 days of notification of this Judgment.

Furlan and Family v. Argentina
23- Nov-2011

Victims' Legal Assistance Fund

5.   Article 37 (Inter-American Defender) of the Court's Rules of Procedure states that "[i]n cases where alleged victims are acting without duly accredited legal representation, the Court may, on its own motion, appoint an inter-American defender to represent them during the processing of the case." As established in the introductory remarks to the Rules of the Court, the implementation of the position of the inter-American defender "guarantees that any alleged victim has access to lawyer to represent his or her interests before the Court and ensures that financial reasons do not impede such access to legal representation." Thus, the position of the inter-American defender enables alleged victims who lack financial resources, or legal representation, to obtain assistance in proceedings before the Inter-American Court.

6.   The Inter-American Court signed an Agreement with the Inter-American Association of Public Defender Offices (hereinafter "AIDEF") [7] [123] whereby defenders belonging to said Association would undertake the legal representation of the alleged victims before the Court in the context of the application of Article 37 of the Court's Rules of Procedure. Said agreement regulates the procedure to be followed for the appointment of the representative and other relevant aspects.

7.   Article 4 of the aforementioned Agreement regulates the use of the Victim's Legal Assistance Fund when an inter-American defender intervenes as follows: Legal representation before the Inter-American Court by the person appointed by the Inter-American Association of Public Defender Offices is free of charge and he or she shall only charge for expenses arising from the defense. The Inter-American Court of Human Rights shall, to the extent possible, and through the Victims' Legal Assistance Fund, cover reasonable and necessary expenses incurred by the designated inter-American defender. The designated inter-American defender shall present to the Court all the necessary receipts accounting for the expenses incurred in the course of processing the case before it.

8.   Bearing in mind the provisions of the aforementioned Article 4, the President emphasizes that, unlike other cases before the Court in which it has been stated that alleged victims are the ones who may make use of the Assistance Fund,[8] [124] the present decision must consider the expenses required both by the alleged victims and by the inter-American defenders. This, in acknowledgement of the fact that this case concerns alleged victims who do not have a legal representative in the proceedings before the Inter-American Court and whose representation shall be undertaken by an inter-American defender, pursuant to Article 37 of the Rules of the Inter-American Court, and therefore assistance shall be granted to cover, to the extent possible, reasonable and necessary expenses arising from legal representation in the litigation of the case.

9.   The President notes that, with regard to the request for resources from the Court's Assistance Fund, the inter-American defenders based their request "on the fact that [their] clients lack the resources to cover the costs of litigation before the Inter-American Court." In this regard, they submitted three "socio-environmental reports" as attachments to the brief of pleadings and motions. One of these reports describes "the precarious housing and working conditions of the alleged victims, the meager income that [Mr. Sebastián Furlan] earns as a street vendor and obtains from social security benefits." Another report refers to "the precarious conditions" in Mr. Claudio Furlan's home, as well as his work and family situation. Finally, another report describes the "state of vulnerability" in which Danilo Furlan finds himself. In addition, the inter-American defenders submitted a sworn statement signed by Mr. Claudio Erwin Furlan regarding "the limited nature of his income and the constant financial assistance that he provides to his family of origin." In his statement he pointed out that he does "not have the resources to cover costs related to travel, transfers, accommodation and *per diem* expenses for his intervention as a witness" in the present case.

10.   Specifically, the inter-American defenders requested the use of the Victims' Fund for: i) attendance of witnesses and experts at the hearing before the Court, and ii) reimbursement of necessary expenses and of the estimated expenses of the inter-American defenders.

11.   Regarding the first item, the inter-American defenders explained that the alleged victims were requesting assistance from the Fund to cover:
  (a) the expenses of Mr. Claudio Furlan, brother of Sebastián Furlan, for travel, transfers, accommodation and *per diem* expenses;
  (b) estimated expenses incurred in a possible rendering of testimonies though affidavits by Danilo Furlan, Teresa Grossi and Violeta Florinda, and
  (c) costs of travel, transfers, accommodation and *per diem* expenses related to the expert testimonies offered through Gustavo Moreno, Pablo Rosales, Estela Rodríguez and Laura Subies or, should the case arise, the payment for receiving their testimonies through affidavits, as determined at the procedural stage referred to in Article 46 of the Court's Rules of Procedure.

12.   As to the second item, the representatives requested reimbursement for the following "necessary expenses and estimated expenses" of the inter-American defenders:
  (a) the cognitive evaluation carried out at the "*Centro de Estudios de la Memoria y la Conducta* INECO" to assess the current health status of Mr. Sebastián Furlan, at an appraised cost of US$ 116.00 (one hundred and sixteen United States dollars);
  (b) expenditures made prior to submitting the brief of pleadings and motions, specifically the cost of receiving the *pen drive* containing the computerized case files, for the sum of US$ 23.89 (twenty-three United States dollars and eighty-nine cents);
  (c) estimated future expenses, such the cost of sending the original document plus two copies of the brief of pleadings and motions and its attachments via *courier* service, at a cost that has yet to be determined, and
  (d) the intervention of the inter-American defenders during the hearings: travel expenses, transfers, accommodation and *per diem* expenses during their stay in the city of San Jose, Costa Rica, to attend the hearing envisaged in this case.

13.   Bearing in mind the foregoing points, the President first confirms that the request for access to the Court's Assistance Fund was submitted in a timely manner in the brief of pleadings and motions (*supra* having seen paragraph 2).

14.   Likewise, the President takes cognizance of the lack of financial resources claimed by the alleged victims and accepts the relevant socio-environmental reports and the sworn statement by Mr. Claudio Erwin Furlan as evidence thereof (*supra* considering paragraph 9).

15.   Likewise, the President reiterates that the reasonable and necessary expenses incurred by the designated defenders shall be covered, to the extent possible, through the Assistance Fund. The President reminds the defenders that

they should submit to the Court all the receipts accounting for expenses incurred during the processing of this case. In this regard, he takes note of the receipts submitted for expenses related to the cognitive assessment of Sebastián Furlan and the receipt for the *pen drive* containing the brief submitting the case and its attachments. The President also notes that an invoice is pending for the sending by *courier* of some attachments to the brief of pleadings and motions.

16. Furthermore, the President confirms that the inter-American defenders have requested assistance from the Fund to cover expenses related to the production of evidence before the Court, specifically for the presentation of testimonies, either at a hearing or through affidavits (*supra* considering paragraph 11), and to the preparation of expert reports.

17. The President recalls that the Court's Legal Assistance Fund is comprised of voluntary contributions from donor sources (*supra* considering paragraph 2), and that these limited resources are insufficient to cover all the expenses related to a possible appearance and presentation of evidence before the Court by the alleged victims. Therefore, in each specific case, the Presidency must consider a request for financial assistance on the basis of the resources available and bearing in mind the need for assistance that might arise in other cases before the Court, in order to ensure the correct administration and fair distribution of the Fund's limited resources.

18. The President notes that, at the present stage of the proceedings, it has not been determined which of the testimonies offered by the inter-American defenders shall be admitted by the Court, or the means by which these shall be obtained. In accordance with Article 50(1) of the Court's Rules of Procedure, that decision is taken by the Court or by its President, once the parties have submitted the definitive lists of proposed declarants and the right to defense has been guaranteed, under the terms of Articles 45 to 49 of the Court's Rules of Procedure. Likewise, it is possible that various scenarios could arise that could increase the item of expenses incurred by the inter-American defenders.

19. Based on the foregoing considerations, the President considers valid the request submitted by the alleged victims to have recourse to the Court's Legal Assistance Fund, and considers valid the request by the inter-American defenders to have access to that same Fund, on the understanding that the funds would be used to cover reasonable and necessary expenses incurred by the defenders in order to process the case before this Court. Likewise, the President considers it appropriate to defer a decision on the specific amount, recipients and purpose of the financial assistance to be provided to the alleged victims, until such time as the Presidency, or the Court, rules on the validity and relevance of the evidence offered by experts and witnesses and on the opening of the oral proceedings, in accordance with Article 50.1 of the Court's Rules of Procedure, in order to have

certainty regarding which of the testimonies shall be admitted by the Court, and the means by which these shall be obtained. (*supra* Considering paragraph 18).

THEREFORE:

THE PRESIDENT OF THE INTER-AMERICAN COURT OF HUMAN RIGHTS, in the exercise of his authority in relation to the Victims' Legal Assistance Fund of this Court, and in accordance with Article 31 of the Court's Rules of Procedure and Article 3 of the Rules of the Court's Legal Assistance Fund and Article 4 of the Agreement of Understanding between the Inter-American Court of Human Rights and the Inter-American Association of Public Defender Offices,

DECIDES:

1. To declare admissible the request submitted by the alleged victims and their inter-American defenders to have recourse to the Victims' Legal Assistance Fund of the Inter-American Court of Human Rights, and to grant the financial assistance necessary to cover reasonable and necessary expenses that have been duly accounted for, and that shall be accounted for, by the defenders for the purpose of processing the case before this Court. The specific amount, recipient and purpose of this assistance shall be determined when a decision is made on the production of the testimonial and expert evidence and, if applicable, on the opening of the oral proceedings under the terms of Article 50 of the Court's Rules of Procedure, and in accordance with preambular paragraphs 15 to 19 of this Decision.

ANALYSIS AND QUESTIONS RAISED BY THE COURT'S JURISPRUDENCE

The Court's creation of the Victims' Legal Assistance Fund helps to address the financial barriers that exist for some victims in accessing the Inter-American human rights system. However, the Fund is composed of "voluntary capital contributions from the Members States of the OAS, the Permanent Observer States, and other States and donors that may wish to collaborate with the Fund" and may not have sufficient resources to address all the existing financial needs.

- As a relatively new creation of the Court, the procedures and decision-making regarding the Fund may continue to be developed. What priorities should the Court utilize in making decisions regarding the Fund and its expenditures?
- Should the Court develop predetermined expense guidelines for fact and expert witnesses, the appointment of legal representatives, and

other expenditures, or should the Court review each request and provide support so long as funding is available?

- Given the Court's recognition that it probably cannot provide funding to meet the entire financial need of requesting parties, should the Court determine how the available funding should be spent, or should the requesting party make that decision?
- Should the Court require States to routinely reimburse the Fund if the State is subsequently found to have violated the Convention in the associated case?

ENDNOTES

[1] Approved by the Court during its XLIX Ordinary Period of Sessions, held from November 16 to 25, 2000, and partially amended by the Court during its LXXXII Ordinary Period of Sessions, held from January 19 to 31, 2009, available at http://www.corteidh.or.cr/sitios/reglamento/ene_2009_ing.pdf.

[2] Approved by the Commission at its 137th Regular Period of Sessions, held from October 28 to November 13, 2009, and modified on September 2nd, 2011 and during the 147th Regular Period of Sessions, held from 8 to 22 March 2013, for entry into force on August 1st, 2013.

[3] United Nations General Assembly, A/RES/60/147, adopted at the 64th plenary meeting on 16 December 2005.

[4] [Footnotes 2 – 22 from para. 2 of the Court's judgment, which provided additional details of each minor's name, are omitted here.]

[5 99] *Cf.* case of *Plan de Sánchez Massacre. Reparations,* [(Art. 63.1 American Convention on Human Rights). Judgment of November 19, 2004. Series C No. 116], para. 62; and case of *the "Juvenile Reeducation Institute,"* [Judgment of September 2, 2004. Series C No. 112], para. 273.

[6 100] *Cf.* case of *Plan de Sánchez Massacre. Reparations, supra* note [99], para. 62.

[7 101] *Cf.* case of *Plan de Sánchez Massacre. Reparations, supra* note [99], para. 63.

[8 102] *Cf.* case of *Plan de Sánchez Massacre. Reparations, supra* note [99], para. 67.

[9 12] *Cf.* case of *Acevedo Jaramillo et al.* Judgment of February 7, 2006. Series C No. 144, para. 227; case of the *"Mapiripán Massacre".* [Judgment of September 15, 2005. Series C No. 134], para. 183; case of the *Moiwana Community.* Judgment of June 15, 2005. Series C No. 124, para. 74; case of the *"Juvenile Reeducation Institute".* Judgment September 2, 2004. Series C No. 112, para. 111; and case of the *Plan de Sánchez Massacre.* Judgment of April 29, 2004. Series C No. 105, para. 48.

[10 13] *Cf.* case of the *Moiwana Community, supra* note 12, para. 74; and case of the *"Juvenile Reeducation Institute," supra* note 12, para. 111.

[11 14] *Cf.* case of the *Plan de Sánchez Massacre, supra* note 12, para. 48. *Cf.* likewise, case of the *"Mapiripán Massacre," supra* note [12], paras. 183 and 305.

[12 15] *Cf.* case of the *Moiwana Community, supra* note 12, para. 74; and case of the *"Juvenile Reeducation Institute," supra* note 12, para. 111.

[13 16] *Cf.* case of the *Moiwana Community, supra* note 12, para. 71.

[14 17] *Cf.* case of the *"Juvenile Reeducation Institute," supra* note 12, paras. 107 and 111.

[15 18] *Cf.* case of the *"Juvenile Reeducation Institute," supra* note 12, paras. 107 and 111.

[16 19] *Cf.* case of the *"Mapiripán Massacre," supra* note [12], paras. 247 and 252.

17 20   *Cf.* case of the *"Mapiripán Massacre," supra* note [12], paras. 305 and 306

18 21   *Cf.* case of *Acevedo Jaramillo et al., supra* note 12, para. 227.

19 22   *Cf.* case of the *"Mapiripán Massacre," supra* note [12], paras. 255 and 258.

20 217 *Cfr.* case of the *Ituango Massacres,* [Judgment of July 1, 2006. Series C No. 148], para. 94; case of the *Moiwana Community,* [Judgment of June 15, 2005. Series C No. 124], para. 178; and case of the *Plan de Sánchez Massacre.* Reparations (Art. 63(1) American Convention on Human Rights). Judgment of November 19, 2004. Series C No. 116, para. 67.

21 208 *Cf.* case of the *Ituango Massacres v. Colombia. Preliminary Objection, Merits, Reparations and Costs.* Judgment of July 1, 2006. Series C No. 148, para. 98, and case of *Goiburú et al. [v. Paraguay* Judgment of September 22, 2006. Series C No. 153], para. 29. *Cf.* also case of *The Mayagna (Sumo) Awas Tingni Community [v. Nicaragua. Merits, Reparations and Costs.* Judgment of August 31, 2001. Series C No. 79], paras. 162-167.

22 209 The Saramaka population is comprised of approximately 30,000 people. Given the dearth of accurate census information on the Saramaka community, estimates broadly range from 25,000 to 34,482 members. The Saramaka people are also dispersed throughout the Upper Suriname River, Brokopondo District, and other areas of Suriname, including Paramaribo.

23 210 *Cf.* case of *The Mayagna (Sumo) Awas Tingni Community, supra* note [208], para. 164; case of the *Indigenous Community Yakye Axa,* [*v. Paraguay. Merits, Reparations and Costs.* Judgment of June 17, 2005 Series C No. 125],,para. 189, and case of the *Indigenous Community Sawhoyamaxa* [*v. Paraguay. Merits, Reparations and Costs.* Judgment of March 29, 2006. Series C No. 146], para. 204.

24 2   In the Report on merits, the Commission concluded that the State was responsible for the violation of the rights to life, humane treatment, personal liberty, and judicial protection embodied in Articles 4(1), 5, 7, 8(1), and 25 of the American Convention, as well as the general obligation to respect and ensure rights found in Article 1(1) thereof, to the detriment of Jesús María Valle Jaramillo and his next of kin. The Commission also found that Colombia was responsible for the violation of Articles 5 and 7 of the American Convention, to the detriment of Nelly Valle Jaramillo. Regarding Carlos Fernando Jaramillo, the Commission concluded that the State was responsible for the violation of Articles 5, 7, and 22 of the Convention (file of attachments to the application, appendix 1, folios 1 to 36).

25 77   *Cf. Blake v. Guatemala. Merits.* Judgment of January 24, 1998. Series C No. 36, para. 114; case of *Heliodoro Portugal* [*v. Panama. Preliminary objections, merits, reparations and costs.* Judgment of August 12, 2008. Series C No. 186],,para. 163[;] and case of *Cantoral Huamaní and García Santa Cruz* [*v. Peru. Preliminary objection, merits, reparations and costs.* Judgment of July 10, 2007. Series C No. 167], para. 112.

26 78   *Cf.* case of the *"Mapiripán Massacre,"* [*v. Colombia. Preliminary objections.* Judgment of March 7, 2005. Series C No. 122], para. 146, and case of the *Ituango Massacres* [*v. Colombia. Preliminary objection, merits, reparations and costs.* Judgment of July 1, 2006. Series C No. 148], para. 262.

27 79   *Cf.* case of *Blake, supra* note 7[7], para. 114; case of *Heliodoro Portugal, supra* note [77], paras. 174 and 175, and *Goiburú et al. v. Paraguay. Merits, reparations and costs.* Judgment of September 22, 2006. Series C No. 153, paras. 96 and 97.

80   *Cf. La Cantuta v. Peru. Merits, reparations and costs.* Judgment of November 29, 2006. Series C No. 162, para. 218.

28 80   *Cf. La Cantuta v. Peru. Merits, reparations and costs.* Judgment of November 29, 2006. Series C No. 162, para. 218.

29 81   *Cf. Bámaca Velásquez v. Guatemala. Merits.* Judgment of November 25, 2000. Series C No. 70, para. 163; case of *Heliodoro Portugal, supra* note [77], para. 163, and case of *Albán Cornejo et al.* [*v. Ecuador.* Merits, reparations and costs. Judgment of November

22, 2007. Series C No. 171], para. 46.

³⁰ ⁸² *Cf.* case of *Blake, supra* note 76, para. 114; case of *Heliodoro Portugal, supra* note 13, para. 163, and case of *Albán Cornejo et al., supra* note 5, para. 46.

³¹ ⁷¹ Cf. case of the Ituango Massacres v. Colombia. Preliminary Objection, Merits, Reparations, and Costs. Judgment of July 1, 2006. Series C No. 148, para. 98; case of Perozo et al. v. Venezuela, [Preliminary Objections, Merits, Reparations, and Costs, Judgment of January 28, 2009, Series C No. 195], para. 50, and case of Garibaldi v. Brazil, [Preliminary Objections, Merits, Reparations, and Costs. Judgment of September 23, 2009. Series C No. 203], para. 24.

³² ⁷² Cf. Report on Merits No. 60/07, adopted by the Inter-American Commission of Human Rights on July 27, 2007 (dossier of appendixes of the application, appendix 1, folio 41).

³³ ⁷³ Cf. Report on Merits No. 60/07, adopted by the Inter-American Commission of Human Rights on July 27, 2007 (dossier of appendixes of the application, appendix 1, folio 45).

³⁴ ⁷⁴ Cf. Report on Merits No. 60/07, adopted by the Inter-American Commission of Human Rights on July 27, 2007 (dossier of appendixes of the application, appendix 1, folios 21 through 23).

³⁵ ⁷⁵ Cf. Brief of the representatives addressed to the Inter-American Commission, of September 18, 2007 (dossier of appendixes to the application, appendix 1(32), folios 594 through 595).

³⁶ Probably a more precise anthropological term would be matrilineal.

³⁷ ¹ Rules of Procedure approved by the Court at its Twenty-third Regular Session, held January 9–18, 1991; amended on January 25, 1993; July 16, 1993; and December 2, 1995.

³⁸ ²⁵ *Cf. The "Street Children" Case (Villagrán Morales et al.). Reparations* [(Art. 63(1) American Convention on Human Rights). Judgment of May 26, 2001. Series C No. 77], paragraph 66; *The "White Van" Case (Paniagua Morales et al.). Reparations,* [(Art. 63(1) American Convention on Human Rights). Judgment of May 25, 2001. Series C No. 76], paragraph 108; and *Castillo Páez Case. Reparations (Art. 63(1) American Convention on Human Rights).* Judgment of November 27, 1998. Series C No. 43, paragraph 88.

³⁹ ²⁶ *Cf. The "Street Children" Case (Villagrán Morales et al.). Reparations, supra* note 2[5], paragraph 68; and *The "White Van" Case (Paniagua Morales et al.). Reparations, supra* note 2[5], paragraph 110.

⁴⁰ ⁴⁸ *Cf. The "Street Children" Case (Villagrán Morales et al.). Reparations, supra* note 2[5], paragraph 66; *"White Van" Case (Paniagua Morales et al.). Reparations, supra* note 2[5], paragraph 108, and *Castillo Páez Case. Reparations, supra* note 25, paragraph 88.

⁴¹ ⁴⁹ *Cf. The "White Van" Case (Paniagua Morales et al.). Reparations, supra* note 2[5], paragraph 109.

⁴² ⁵⁰ *Cf. The "Street Children" Case. Reparations, supra* note 2, paragraph 68; *The "White Van" Case (Paniagua Morales et al.). Reparations, supra* note 2[5], paragraph 110; and the *Loayza Tamayo Case. Reparations,* [(Art. 63(1) American Convention on Human Rights).* Judgment of November 27, 1998. Series C No. 42], paragraph 142.

⁴³ ³⁸ See *Villagrán Morales et al. Case, Reparations,* [(Art. 63(1) American Convention on Human Rights).* May 26, 2001 Judgment. C Series No. 77], para. 68; *Paniagua Morales et al. Case, Reparations,* [(Art. 63(1) American Convention on Human Rights).* May 25, 2001 Judgment. C Series No. 76], para. 85; and *Castillo Páez Case, Reparations,* [(Art. 63(1) American Convention on Human Rights).* November 27, 1998 Judgment. C Series No. 43], para. 59

⁴⁴ ³⁹ See *Villagrán Morales et al. Case, Reparations, supra* note [38], para. 68; *Paniagua Morales et al. Case, Reparations, supra* note [38], para. 85; and *Aloeboetoe et al. Case. Reparations (Art. 63(1) American Convention on Human Rights).* September 10, 1993 Judgment. C Series No. 15, para. 67 and 68.

⁴⁵ ⁴⁰ See *Villagrán Morales et al. Case, Reparations, supra* note [38], para. 68; *Paniagua*

Morales et al. Case, Reparations, supra note [38], para. 86; and *Aloeboetoe et al. Case, Reparations, supra* note [39], para. 71.

46 41   Pursuant to Article 2 of the Rules of Procedure, the term "next of kin" means "the immediate family, that is, the direct ascendants and descendants, siblings, spouses or permanent companions, or those determined by the Court, if applicable."

47 42   See *Loayza Tamayo Case, Reparations,* [(*Art. 63(1) American Convention on Human Rights).* November 27, 1998 Judgment. C Series No. 42], para. 92, and in this same regard, *Villagrán Morales et al. Case. Reparations, supra* note [38], para. 68; *Paniagua Morales et al. Case, Reparations, supra* note [38], para. 86.

48 278   Pursuant to Article 2 of the Rules of Procedure, the term "next of kin" means "the immediate family, that is, the direct ascendants and descendants, siblings, spouses, or permanent companions, or those determined by the Court, if applicable."

49 279   *Cf. Bulacio Case,* [Judgment of September 18, 2003. Series C No. 100], para. 78; *Juan Humberto Sánchez Case,* [Judgment of June 7, 2003. Series C No. 99], para. 156; *Las Palmeras Case. Reparations,* [*Reparations* (Art. 63(1) American Convention on Human Rights). Judgment of November 26, 2002. Series C No. 96], para. 54 and 55.

50 279   See case of the *Moiwana Community,* [Judgment of July 15, 2005. Series C No. 124], para. 178, and case of the *Plan de Sánchez Massacre. Reparations* (Art. 63(1) American Convention on Human Rights). Judgment of November 19, 2004. Series C No. 116, para. 63.

51 230   See case of the *Moiwana Community, supra* note [279], para. 178, and case of the *Plan de Sánchez Massacre. Reparations, supra* note 279, para. 67.

52 1   The Commission appointed Evelio Fernández Arévalos, Commissioner, and Santiago A. Canton, Executive Secretary, as delegates, and the lawyers Ariel E. Dulitzky, Mario López Garelli, Víctor H. Madrigal Borloz, and Lilly Ching Soto as legal advisers.

53 153   *Cf.* Note of the Inter-American Commission on Human Rights of March 23, 2006 (file of appendixes to the application, appendix 3, volume II, folios 517 to 519).

54 154   Brief of the representatives of April 25, 2006, which included the testimonies of the next of kin of Mr. Chaparro: Cecilia Aguirre Mollet de Chaparro (wife), José Pedro Chaparrro de Aguirre (son), Gabriela Chaparro Aguirre (daughter), Christián Chaparro Canales (son), Carolina Chaparro Canales (daughter), Juan Pablo Chaparro Canales (son), and Hortensia Álvarez Pineda de Chaparro (mother) (file of appendixes to the application, appendix 3, volume II, folios 573 to 580).

55 155 [IACtHR, Chaparro Alvarez et al vs. Ecuador, Series C 170 citing] *Cf.* case of the *Ituango Massacres v. Colombia. Preliminary objection, merits, reparations, and costs.* Judgment of July 1, 2006 Series C No. 148, para. 98, and case of *Goiburú et al. v. Paraguay. Merits, reparations, and costs.* Judgment of September 22, 2006. Series C No. 153, para. 29.

56 3   On January 23, 2007, the Impact Litigation Project of the Washington College of Law (WCL) of American University submitted a brief, wherein it requested the Commission allow them to be co-petitioners in the present case

57 4   In the report on the merits No. 24/08, the Commission concluded that "the State of Venezuela violated the rights to freedom of expression, personal liberty, and right to a fair trial (included in Articles 13, 7, 8, and 25 of the American Convention on Human Rights), in connection with Articles 1(1) and 2 of the same, to the detriment of [Mr. Francisco Uson Ramirez]." As such, the Commission recommended that the State "1) . . . adopt all the judicial, administrative, and other measures necessary to leave without effect . . . all military criminal proceedings . . . against [Mr. Uson Ramirez] and his judgments, including omitting the criminal charges from the registrar and their implications to all extents; 2) . . . order a reparation for Mr. Francisco Uson Ramirez for the violation of his rights; 3) . . . take all the measures necessary so that Mr. Francisco Uson Ramirez is granted his personal liberty indefinitely without any conditions, and 4) . . . to order their domestic legislation so it is in conformance with Articles 13, 7, and 8 of the American Convention,

58 155   in accordance with what has been established in the . . . report."

Cf. case of the *"White Van" (Paniagua-Morales et al) v. Guatemala. Reparations, and Costs.* Judgment May 25, 2001. Series C No. 76, para. 82; case of *DaCosta Cadogan* [v. Barbados. Preliminary Objections, Merits, Reparations, and Costs. Judgment of September 24, 2009. Series C No. 204], para. 97, and case of *Garibaldi* [v. Brazil. Preliminary Objections, Merits, Reparations, and Costs. Judgment of September 23, 2009. Series C No. 203], para. 152.

59 156   Medical Report of Dr. Jairo Fernández dated October 20, 2008 (case file of attachments [to the] written brief containing pleadings, motions, and evidence, attachment 10, fs. 4932 to 4934).

60 157   IACtHR, citing *Cf.* case of the *"White Van" (Paniagua-Morales et al), supra* note 155, para. 82; case of *DaCosta Cadogan, supra* note [155], para. 97, and case of *Garibaldi, supra* note 155], para. 152.

61 2   According to Article 35(3) of the Court's Rules of Procedure, "[t]he Commission shall indicate which facts contained in the report to which Article 50 of the Convention refers it is submitting to the consideration of the Court."

62 495   In this regard, the State explained that the process of identifying the victims had been designed in four stages: (a) determination of the scope of the list; (b) pre-registration procedure; (c) registration procedure, and (d) delivery of the list. Each of these stages had been defined technically during a process of permanent dialogue with victims and their representatives. Regarding the registration procedure, the process had begun on site on May 21, 2012, and covered the municipalities of Arambala, Meanguera, Jocoaitique, Chilanga and Cacaopera, all in the department of Morazán, as well as the municipalities of Lourdes, Gotera, San Miguel and others, where the displaced population was located. The registration of victims is being carried out in two stages simultaneously; the first consisting in registration on demand, and the second on visits to each house. According to the State, the data gathering process would take 15 consecutive days and the process to revise the list would take 20 working days more, so that it was anticipated that the list would be ready – prior to the administration stage – in six weeks. The first procedure was being prepared by personnel of the General Directorate of Statistics and Censuses (DIGESTYC) of the Ministry of Economy, and the second procedure by a Government technical team (the Technical Secretariat of the Presidency, the Ministry of Foreign Affairs, and the General Directorate of Statistics and Censuses). Both procedures would be guided by the victims' association. In addition, the State indicated that, as part of the comprehensive reparation policy, a mechanism was being developed that would allow the permanent administration of the said list; in other words, it was "not preparing a single physical list; it is a preliminary list that will allow the incorporation of other victims that were not included in these procedures, as necessary."

63 4   In the initial petition, Ms. Atala indicated that Fundación Ideas was represented by Francisco Estévez Valencia and she appointed Verónica Undurraga Valdés, Claudio Moraga Klenner, Felipe González Morales and Domingo Lovera Parmo as her representatives before the Inter-American Commission (File of appendices to the petition, volume III, pages 1533 and 1572).

64 80   In its brief of February 3, 2012 the State presented its observations concerning the participation of the psychiatrist Espinoza in the proceeding. On February 6, 2012, following the instructions of the President of the Court, the parties were informed that psychiatrist Espinoza had been designated to accompany the delegation of the Secretariat, if necessary. Likewise, the record sent to the parties indicated that although the support of psychiatrist Espinoza had been contemplated in this case, this was not necessary.

65 4   The Commission stated, with regard to the identification of the presumed victims of the alleged violations of thedetriment of the persons who were displaced from the village of Santo Domingo; rights to freedom of movement and residence, and to property, that

"owing to the nature of the facts of the case, the Commission could not obtain precise information that would allow it to individualize all the victims of these violations. Letter of July 8, 2011, submitting case No. 12,416 (merits file, tome 1, folio 4).

66 425   The Court places on record that 23 of the 27 injured persons were recognized as such by the domestic courts, and four in the military criminal investigation (not by the judges), based on information obtained from a town meeting. In addition, two people mentioned in the decision of the Military Criminal Investigation Unit, specifically Ludo Vanegas and Alcides Bonilla, are the same age, have no known next of kin, and also have a very similar name to two of the victims identified in the other proceedings, namely: Ludwing Vanegas and Milciades Bonilla, so that they could be the same people.

67 426   *Cf. case of the Ituango Massacres v. Colombia*, para. 98, and case of *Barbani Duarte et al. v. Uruguay. Merits reparations and costs.* Judgment of October 13, 2011. Series C No. 234, para. 42. See also, case of *Uzcategui et al. v. Venezuela*, para. 243.

68 427   Namely, Oscar Andrey Galvis Mojica (son of Teresa Mojica Hernandez and Mario Galvis Gelves), Albeiro GalvisMojica (son of Teresa Mojica Hernandez and Mario Galvis Gelves), Norberto Arciniegas Calvo (brother of Arnulfo Arciniegas), Argemiro Arciniegas Calvo (brother of Arnulfo Arciniegas), Orlando Arciniegas Calvo (brother of Arnulfo Arciniegas) and Erlinda Arciniegas Calvo (sister of Arnulfo Arciniegas).

69 428   Luis Felipe Durtin Mora, Luz Dary Tellez Durtin, Yamile Tellez Durtin, Wilmer Tellez Durtin, Emilse Herntindez Duran, Milena Duran, Yeimi Sulai Hernandez Mora, Mary Molina Panqueva, Moises Molina Panqueva, Genny Carolina Molina Restrepo, Wilson Garcia Reatiga, Wilson Enrique Garcia Guevara, Marfa Antonia Rojas, Elizabeth Daza Rojas, Jose Antonio Daza Rojas, Wilson Daza Rojas, Javier Daza Rojas and Frady Alexi Leal Pacheco (the latter, even though he had recourse to the contentious-administrative proceedings, did not receive compensation because he had not proved that he was the brother of a victim, or a victim himself) (evidence file, tome 2, folios 787 and 792).

70   *See, e.g., Blake v. Guatemala, Reparations and Costs*, Judgment of January 22, 1999, Series C No. 48, para. 32.

71   SERGIO GARCÍA RAMÍREZ, THE VICTIM'S ACCESS TO INTERNATIONAL JURISDICTION OF HUMAN RIGHTS (El acceso de la victima a la jurisdicción internacional sobre derechos humanos, Edición del Instituto de Investigaciones Jurídicas UNAM, 2002, available at: http://www. iidh.ed.cr/Documentos/HerrPed/Fichas/Acceso_victima.htm) The following is the quote provided above in the original Spanish:

Se ha forjado un doble concepto: el primero, natural y necesario, tradicional y preferente: la victima directa de la infracción cometida, o en otros términos, el titular del bien jurídico lesionado o menoscabado por la conducta, comisiva u omisiva, de un agente del Estado u otra persona por la que deba responder este. Pero no termina aquí el elenco. Sigue la victima indirecta, un concepto más reciente — con todo, ya maduro — y se habla asimismo de una víctima potencial.

La indirecta es quien resiente un daño en sus propios bienes o derechos como efecto, reflejo o consecuencia del que se inflige a la víctima directa. El golpe se dirige a una persona, pero trasciende hasta otra. Conviene seguir en esa ruta, que refleja la preocupación y el designio *pro homine* de la materia, aunque debamos hacerlo sin excesos que trivialicen y a la postre comprometan su futuro."

72   Probably a more precise anthropological term would be matrilineal.

73 57   *Cf., Juan Humberto Sánchez Case*, [June 7, 2003 Judgment. Series C No. 99], para. 164; and *El Caracazo Case, Reparations*, [(Art. 63(1) American Convention on Human Rights). August 29, 2002 Judgment. Series C No. 95], para. 91.

74 58   *Cf., El Caracazo Case, Reparations, supra* note 5[7], para. 91.c).

75 281   See case of the *19 Tradesmen*, [Judgment of July 5, 2004. Series C No. 109], para. 230, and case of the *Caracazo.* Judgment of November 11, 1999. Series C No. 58, para. 91.

76 241   *Cf.* "Special power of attorney granted by Mrs. María Ruth Silva Alava, widow of More-

no, and the engineers Ana Isabel Moreno Silva and María Ruth Moreno Silva to Doctor Hugo Quintana Coello", Twelfth Notary of the Canton of Guayaquil issued on October 4, 2011 (File of attachments to the brief of pleadings and motions, volume II, pages 3087 to 3090).

77 242   *Cf.* "Special power of attorney granted by Letty Mariana Vásquez Grijalva, Letty Alexandra Hurtado Vásquez, Tulia María Ximena Hurtado Vásquez and Diego Estuardo Hurtado Vásquez", Thirty-ninth Notary of the Canton of Quito issued on October 5, 2011 (File of attachments to the brief of pleadings and motions, volume II, pages 2963 to 2967).

78 17   This article establishes that: 2. The exercise of these freedoms, which entail rights and responsibilities, may be subject to certain formalities, conditions, restrictions, or sanctions, established by law, which constitute necessary measures, in a democratic society, for national security, territorial integrity, or public security, defense of order and prevention of crime, protection of health or morals, protection of the reputation or the rights of third parties, in order to prevent the dissemination of confidential information or to guarantee the authority and impartiality of the Judiciary.

79 18   *Cf. Eur. Court H.R., Handyside case, judgment of 7 December 1976, Series A No. 24,* para. 49; *Eur. Court H.R., The Sunday Times case, judgment of 26 April 1979, Series A no. 30,* paras. 59 and 65; *Eur. Court H.R., Barthold judgment of 25 March 1985, Series A no. 90,* para. 55; *Eur. Court H.R., Lingens judgment of 8 July 1986, Series A no. 103,* para. 41; *Eur. Court H.R Müller and Others judgment of 24 May 1988, Series A no. 133,* para. 33; and *Eur. Court HR, Otto-Preminger-Institut v. Austria judgment of 20 September 1994, Series A no. 295-A,* para. 49.

80 119   *Cf.* case of *Herrera-Ulloa,* [Judgment of July 2, 2004. Series C No. 107], para. 112; and *Compulsory Membership in an Association prescribed by Law for the Practice of Journalism,* [(Arts. 13 and 29 American Convention on Human Rights). Advisory Opinion OC-5/85 of November 13, 1985. Series A No. 5], para. 70

81 123   Inter-American Democratic Charter, adopted at the plenary session of the OAS General Assembly held on September 11, 2001, Article 4.

82 124   *Cf.* case of *Herrera Ulloa, supra* note [119], para. 116.

83 74   *Cf.* case of *López Álvarez,* [Judgment of February 1, 2006. Series C No. 141], para. 163; case of *Ricardo Canese,* [Judgment of August 31, 2004. Series C No. 111], para. 80; and case of *Herrera Ulloa,* [Judgment of July 2, 2004. Series C No. 107], paras. 108-111.

84 89   *Cf.* case of *Palamara Iribarne,* [Judgment of November 22, 2005. Series C No. 135], para. 83; case of *Ricardo Canese,* [Judgment of August 31, 2004. Series C No. 111], para. 97; and case of *Herrera Ulloa,* [Judgment of July 2, 2004. Series C No. 107], para. 127. Likewise, *cf.* Feldek v. Slovakia, no. 29032/95, § 83, ECHR 2001-VIII; and Surek and Ozdemir v. Turkey, nos. 23927/94 and 24277/94, § 60, ECHR Judgment of 8 July, 1999.

85 172   *Cf.* case of *Ricardo Canese.* Judgment of August 31, 2004. Series C No. 111, para. 77; and *Compulsory Membership in an Association Prescribed by Law for the Practice of Journalism (Articles 13 and 29 of the American Convention on Human Rights).* Advisory Opinion OC-5/85 of November 13, 1985. Series A No. 5, paras. 53 and 54.

86 173   *Cf.* case of *Ivcher-Bronstein.* Judgment of February 6, 2001. Series C No. 74, para. 152; and *Compulsory Membership in an Association Prescribed by Law for the Practice of Journalism, supra* note 172, para. 54.

87 176   *Cf.* case of *Ricardo Canese, supra* note 172, para. 78; case of *Herrera-Ulloa,* [Judgment of July 2, 2004. Series C No. 107], para. 109; and *Compulsory Membership in an Association Prescribed by Law for the Practice of Journalism.* Advisory Opinion OC-5/85, *supra* note 172, para. 36.

88 177   *Cf.* case of *Ricardo Canese, supra* note 172, para. 78; case of *Herrera-Ulloa, supra* note 17[6], para. 108; and case of *Ivcher-Bronstein, supra* note 173, para. 146.

89 663   The State argued that, for the community to be considered a victim, it was necessary to prove: their ethno-cultural characteristics, their relationship with the land, and all those

socio-cultural characteristics that allow a group of persons to be considered and to be part of the said community both objectively and subjectively.

90 664 The State indicated the following gaps: 55 persons are not identified, in the cases of 60 persons their identity documents have irregularities; the names of others are incomplete, some have not proved their connection to the events or their relationships and, lastly, some did not give a power of attorney to their representatives. In the case of the family of Marino López, of the 13 persons named, it was mentioned that two were "foster children" without providing any evidence in this regard.

91 665 Cf. Crosscheck between the final list and the Justice and Peace Information System of the Prosecutor General's Office (evidence file, folio 16941).

92 666 Cf. List of supposed victims beneficiaries of the precautionary measures (evidence file, folios 16943 to 16957).

93 667 Cf. Crosscheck between the victims and the National Civil Registry (evidence file, folios 16922 to 16939).

94 668 The State advised that when crosschecking the names of the victims included in the motions and arguments brief, 52 did not have an identity card number (leaving 479) and 7 were minors (subsequently it was proved that two of these had already attained their majority), for a total of 472.

95 669 The State explained that, by "non-existent" it is understood that, when the National Identification Archive was consulted, no one appears registered due to either an error or misrepresentation. It also indicated that, during a subsequent search for information on these 78 names, several homonyms had appeared.

96 670 Cf. Final written arguments of the Colombian State, Annex No. 7, case No. 12,573 Marino Lopez et al. v. Colombia, April 8, 2013 (merits file, folio 16894).

97 671 The State indicated that the 15 remaining victims of the 158 who appear in the brief of the representatives and on the RUPD state that they had been displaced between 1999 and 2011.

98 672 The State advised that, on the RUPD, it appears that the remaining 129 persons who did not indicate Chocó as the place of expulsion stated that they had been displaced from San Juan de Urabá. In addition, these 129 include the two witnesses who testified during the public hearing before the Court: Bernardo Vivas Mosquera and Ana Sofía Roa Ramirez.

99 673 The State indicated that the victims who were displaced collectively received "payments from the bank for a total of" US$767, "and payment for housing for a total of" US $117,000.

100 674 The State indicated that the victims who were displaced individually received "payments from the bank of between" US$734 and US$294.

101 675 According to the Commission the complex aspects of this case are: (a) the situation arose in the context of the generalized violence derived from the Colombian armed conflict; (b) the massive displacement caused by Operation Genesis; (c) the accentuated vulnerability of the victims in the case, and (d) the passage of time that has resulted in changes in the situation of the victims.

102 676 During the public hearing, the representatives affirmed that there were factual grounds that reveal the status of victims of the facts of this case, because they have maintained direct contact with the State, and are part of an association with which the previous Presidents (Ernesto Samper Pizano and Andrés Pastrana Arango) signed agreements, a situation that was verified by the Public Prosecution Service.

103 677 The representatives advised that, on crosschecking this census, known as "Presidency of the Republic-Social Solidarity Network b, d, e and f. Families returned to Cacarica, including the settlements of Esperanza en Dios and Nueva Vida, census taken and forwarded by the Urabá Territorial Unit," against the list of the motions and arguments brief, 425 persons appeared in the census; thus, there is a difference of 106 of the 531 persons.

104 678 The representatives advised that crosschecking the 531 victims in the motions and argu-

ments brief against the census conducted by the RSS and the Agrarian Institute revealed that 47 of the victims appear on that census. Regarding the remaining persons, three of them had relocated temporarily to Bogota until very recently, and 24 were displaced in other parts of the country.

105 679   Motions and arguments brief (merits file, folio 356). Also, List of victims (evidence file, folio 8215).

106 680   *Cf.* Colombian Constitutional Court, Judgment T-327 of 2001. See also: Colombian Constitutional Court, Judgment T-468-06; Colombian Constitutional Court, Judgment T-211/10; Colombian Constitutional Court, Judgment T- 367/10 (mentioned in the case of the *Ituango Massacres v. Colombia, Monitoring compliance with judgment,* Order of May 21, 2013), and Colombian Constitutional Court, Judgments T-582/11 and T-1000/12.

107 681   *Cf.* case of the *Massacres of Ituango v. Colombia. Monitoring compliance with judgment.* Order of May 21, *2013,* considering paragraphs 28 to 31.

108 682   *Cf.* Expert opinion provided by Juan Pablo Franco by affidavit dated January 31, 2013 (evidence file, folio 15350).

109 683   In order to reach the final list of 372 persons, the Court: (a) took the 158 who appear on the RUPD and subtracted the 129 who were expelled from the department of Antioquia, thereby obtaining a total of 29 victims: 28 who were expelled from the department of Chocó and one who had indicated as department and municipality of expulsion "country," but was included, giving him the benefit of the doubt. Of the 29 victims, six were excluded who had indicated that their municipality of expulsion was Cármen del Darién, Nuuquí, Quibdo, Alto Baudó and Belén Bajirá, thus leaving only 23 victims: 22 from Riosucio and the one from "country." Finally, from the 23 who were left, 11 were subtracted who had not been displaced in 1997, and thus a final list of 12 persons was obtained; and (b) to these 12 persons, were added the 360 persons who do not appear on any RUPD and RUV lists.

110 684   The five members of the family of Marino Lopez included on the list were: 1) Emedelia Palacios Palacios, 2) Erlenson Palacio Palacio, 3) Libia Luz Palacio Palacio, 4) Yenesid Gamboa Palacio and 5) Jhon Freddy Palacio Palacio.

111 685   *Cf.* List of victims. case of Marino López *et al.* (Operation Genesis), forwarded by the Commission to the Court and received by the latter on February 10, 2012 (merits file, folio 179; evidence file, folio 51408 and *ff.*).

112 686   Emedelia Palacios Palacios, Erlenson Palacio Palacio, Libia Luz Palacio Palacio, Yenesid Gamboa Palacio, Jhon Freddy Palacio Palacio, Maria Bonifacia Mosquera Peñaloza, Luis Aristarco Hinestroza, Yulis Maria Hinestroza Mosquera, Alberto Hinestroza Mosquera, Arinson Hinestroza Mosquera, Aristarco Hinestroza Mosquera, Aurelina Hinestroza Mosquera, Alirson Hinestroza Mosquera and Leonardo Lopez Garcia.

113 687   *Cf.* Eighth Criminal Court of the Bogota Special Circuit, file 2009-063, defendant Rito Alejo del Río, judgment of August 23, 2012 (evidence file, folios 14791 to 14823).

114 688   Cf. case of the Pueblo Bello Massacre v. Colombia, para. 237; case of the Moiwana Community v. Suriname, para. 178; case of the Plan de Sánchez Massacre v. Guatemala. Reparations. Judgment of November 19, 2004. Series C No. 116, para. 67, and case of the Ituango Massacres v. Colombia, paras. 358 and 359.

115 2   AG/RES. 2426 (XXXVIII-O/08) Resolution adopted by the thirty-eighth OAS General Assembly, at the fourth plenary session, held on June 3, 2008, *"Establishment of the Legal Assistance Fund of the Inter-American Human Rights System,"* operative paragraph 2(b).

116 3   CP/RES. 963 (1728/09), Resolution adopted on November 11, 2009, by the OAS Permanent Council, *"Rules of Procedure for the Operation of the Legal Assistance Fund of the Inter-American Human Rights System."*

117 4   AG/RES. 2426 (XXXVIII-O/08), *supra* note 2, *operative paragraph 2(a),* and Resolution CP/RES. 963 (1728/09), *supra* note 2, article 1(1).

118 5   Article 2(1) of the Rules of Procedure of the Inter-American System's Assistance Fund, *supra* note 3.

119 6   Rules of Procedure of the Inter-American Court of Human Rights for the Operation of the Victims' Legal Assistance Fund approved by the Court on February 4, 2010, Article 1.

120 8   The President notes that the testimonies of Juan Bautista Márquez and María Ángel Díaz are not included in Appendix 3 to the brief of pleadings and motions of the representatives.

121 9   *Cf. Case González Medina et al. v. the Dominican Republic.* Decision of the President of the Inter-American Court of Human Rights of February 23, 2011, Considering paragraph 8, and *Case Fornerón and daughter v. Argentina.* Decision of the President of the Inter-American Court of Human Rights of May 31, 2011, Considering paragraph 7.

122 540 AG/RES. 2426 (XXXVIII-O/08), resolution adopted by the thirty-eighth OAS General Assembly during the fourth plenary session held on June 3, 2008, "*Establishment of the Legal Assistance Fund of the inter-American human rights system,*" Operative paragraph *2(a),* and CP/RES. 963 (1728/09), resolution adopted on November 11, 2009, by the OAS Permanent Council, "*Rules of Procedure for the Operation of the Legal Assistance Fund of the inter-American human rights system,*" Article 1(1).

123 7   AIDEF is "a not-for-profit civil institution, which is apolitical, non-religious and is socially and culturally comprised of state institutions of Public Defender Offices and Associations of Public Defenders of America that undertake the representation, legal counsel and technical defense at the trials of persons according to laws, constitutions and international treaties. Its objectives, *inter alia,* are to uphold the effective application of the human rights and guarantees enshrined in international agreements and conventions, national constitutions and domestic laws, in the sphere of public defense; and to promote the necessary legal assistance and representation of persons and of justiciable rights, facilitating an effective defense and access to justice with due quality and experience." Agreement of Understanding between the Inter-American Court of Human Rights and the Inter-American Association of Public Defender Offices signed on September 25, 2009 and entered into force on January 1, 2010.

124 8   *Cf.* case of *Contreras et al. v. El Salvador.* Petition submitted by the Alleged Victims. Decision of the President of the Inter-American Court of Human Rights, March 4, 2011, considering paragraph 9.

Chapter Two

COMPENSATION FOR DAMAGES

I.   INTRODUCTION

Compensation is a customary form of reparation ordered to victims when human rights violations result in financially quantifiable damages and also when other forms of reparation are not feasible. In Article 63, the American Convention on Human Rights explicitly establishes the competence of the Inter-American Court of Human Rights to order fair compensation for the violation of a right or freedom protected by the Convention and codifies customary domestic and international norms regarding compensation for such violations. Article 63 of the Convention and the Inter-American Court's jurisprudence on compensation as a form of reparation also reflect the norms articulated in Article 20 of the Basic Principles and Guidelines on the Right to a Remedy and Reparation for Victims of Gross Violations of International Human Rights Law and Serious Violations of International Humanitarian Law, as adopted in 2005 by the United Nations General Assembly.

Throughout its jurisprudence, the Inter-American Court of Human Rights has reaffirmed that "[r]eparations, as their name suggests, are measures that tend to make the effects of violations that were committed disappear. Their nature and amount depend on the damage caused both on a pecuniary and on a non-pecuniary level. Reparations cannot involve enrichment or impoverishment of the victim or [their] successors."[1] However, since the first case in which the Court ordered compensation to be paid, its 1989 decision in *Velásquez Rodríguez v. Honduras*, the Court has honed its analysis and considerations in determining equitable compensation for violations of rights and freedoms.

The Inter-American Court may order compensation for pecuniary damages, which include loss of income (*lucrum cessans*), other direct and consequential damages resulting from the violation (*dannum emergens*), and damage to the victim's life plan ("*proyecto de vida*"), as well as for non-pecuniary or moral damages, also referred to as pain and suffering.

Additionally, the Court may order compensation to reimburse victims for the costs and expenses associated with litigating their case. In some cases, the Court has placed conditions upon the terms of payment of compensation and has also considered the question of punitive damages. This chapter highlights the trajectory of the Court's judgments, including its reasoning and considerations, in cases involving pecuniary and non-pecuniary damages, as well as other compensatory claims.

II.   NORMATIVE FRAMEWORK

A.   AMERICAN CONVENTION ON HUMAN RIGHTS[2]
ARTICLE 10.   RIGHT TO COMPENSATION
Every person has the right to be compensated in accordance with the law in the event he has been sentenced by a final judgment through a miscarriage of justice.
ARTICLE 21.   RIGHT TO PROPERTY
1. Everyone has the right to the use and enjoyment of his property. The law may subordinate such use and enjoyment to the interest of society.
2. No one shall be deprived of his property except upon payment of just compensation, for reasons of public utility or social interest, and in the cases and according to the forms established by law.
[Inter-American Court of Human Rights, Jurisdiction and Functions]
ARTICLE 63.
1. If the Court finds that there has been a violation of a right or freedom protected by this Convention, the Court shall rule that the injured party be ensured the enjoyment of his right or freedom that was violated. It shall also rule, if appropriate, that the consequences of the measure or situation that constituted the breach of such right or freedom be remedied and that fair compensation be paid to the injured party.

B.   BASIC PRINCIPLES AND GUIDELINES ON THE RIGHT TO A REMEDY AND REPARATION FOR VICTIMS OF GROSS VIOLATIONS OF INTERNATIONAL HUMAN RIGHTS

LAW AND SERIOUS VIOLATIONS OF INTERNATIONAL HUMANITARIAN LAW[3]

20. *Compensation* should be provided for any economically assessable damage, as appropriate and proportional to the gravity of the violation and the circumstances of each case, resulting from gross violations of international human rights law and serious violations of international humanitarian law, such as:

(a) Physical or mental harm;

(b) Lost opportunities, including employment, education, and social benefits;

(c) Material damages and loss of earnings, including loss of earning potential;

(d) Moral damage;

(e) Costs required for legal or expert assistance, medicine and medical services, and psychological and social services.

III. PECUNIARY DAMAGES

Pecuniary damages include *lucrum cessans* (loss of earnings resulting from the violation) and *dannum emergens* (direct and consequential damages resulting from the violation, such as medical and funeral expenses). In some cases, the Court has also ordered compensation for damage to the victim's life plan ("proyecto de vida"), i.e., compensation for the loss of an individual's range of options. As reflected in the Court's jurisprudence, advocates and scholars have debated whether life plan damages are quantifiable and whether such damages are implicit in *lucrum cessans* and *dannum emergens* considerations. Through its extensive jurisprudence, the Court has developed criteria to guide its decisions and aid in determination of compensation orders. The following excerpts demonstrate developments in the Court's case law regarding pecuniary damages as well as the complexity involved in quantifying certain pecuniary damages.

A. LOSS OF EARNINGS (*LUCRUM CESSANS*)
1. GENERAL

Velásquez Rodríguez v. Honduras
21-Jul-1989
Series C No. 7—*Reparations and Costs*

8.   As required by the Resolution of January 20, 1989, the Commission submitted its opinion on March 1, 1989. It asserted that the just compensation to be paid by Honduras to the family of Manfredo Velásquez should include the following:

  (a) The granting to the wife and children of Manfredo Velásquez of the following benefits:

  (i) Payment to the wife of Manfredo Velásquez, Mrs. Emma Guzmán Urbina, of the highest pension recognized by Honduran law;

  (ii) Payment to the children of Manfredo Velásquez, Héctor Ricardo, Nadia Waleska, and Herling Lizzett Velásquez Guzmán, of a pension or subsidy until they complete their university education; and

  (iii) Title to an adequate house, equivalent to the house of a middle class professional family.

  (b) Payment to the wife and children of Manfredo Velásquez of a cash amount corresponding to the resultant damages, loss of earnings, and emotional harm suffered by the family of Manfredo Velásquez, to be determined by the Illustrious Court based upon the expert opinion offered by the victim's family.

26.   Reparation of harm brought about by the violation of an international obligation consists of full restitution (*restitutio in integrum*), which includes the restoration of the prior situation, the reparation of the consequences of the violation, and indemnification for patrimonial and non-patrimonial damages, including emotional harm.

28.   Indemnification for human rights violations is supported by international instruments of a universal and regional character. The Human Rights Committee, created by the International Covenant on Civil and Political Rights of the United Nations, has repeatedly called for, based on the Optional Protocol, indemnification for the violation of human rights recognized in the Covenant (see, for example, communications 4/1977, 6/1977, 11/1977, 132/1982, 138/1983, 147/1983, 161/1983, 188/1984, 194/1985, etc. Reports of the Human Rights Committee, United Nations). The European Court of Human Rights has reached the same conclusion based upon Article 50 of the Convention for the Protection of Human Rights and Fundamental Freedoms.

46.   The Court notes that the disappearance of Manfredo Velásquez cannot be considered an accidental death for the purposes of compensation, given that it is the result of serious acts imputable to Honduras. The amount of compensation cannot, therefore, be based upon guidelines such as life insurance, but must be

calculated as a loss of earnings based upon the income the victim would have received up to the time of his possible natural death. In that sense, one can take as a point of departure the salary that, according to the certification of the Honduran Vice-Minister of Planning on October 19, 1988, Manfredo Velásquez was receiving at the time of his disappearance (1,030 lempiras per month) and calculate the amount he would have received at the time of his obligatory retirement at the age of sixty, as provided by Article 69 of the Law of the National Institute of Social Security for Teachers and which the Government itself considers the most favorable. At retirement, he would have been entitled to a pension until his death.

47.   However, the calculation of the loss of earnings must consider two distinct situations. When the beneficiary of the indemnity is a victim who is totally and permanently disabled, the compensation should include all he failed to receive, together with appropriate adjustments based upon his probable life expectancy. In that circumstance, the only income for the victim is what he would have received, but will not receive, as earnings.

48.   If the beneficiaries of the compensation are the family members, the situation is different. In principle, the family members have an actual or future possibility of working or receiving income on their own. The children, who should be guaranteed the possibility of an education that might extend to the age of twenty-five, could, for example, begin to work at that time. It is not correct, then, in these cases, to adhere to rigid criteria, more appropriate to the situation described in the above paragraph, but rather to arrive at a prudent estimate of the damages, given the circumstances of each case.

49.   Based upon a prudent estimate of the possible income of the victim for the rest of his probable life and on the fact that, in this case, the compensation is for the exclusive benefit of the family of Manfredo Velásquez identified at trial, the Court sets the loss of earnings in the amount of five hundred thousand lempiras to be paid to the wife and to the children of Manfredo Velásquez

---

Aloeboetoe et al. v. Suriname
10-Sep-1993
Series C No. 15—*Reparations and Costs*

39.   In view of the fact that more detailed information was required in order to be able to fix the amount of the compensation and costs, the President, after consulting with the Permanent Commission, on September 24, 1992, decided

to have the Court avail itself of the services of Mr. Christopher Healy and Ms. Merina Eduards as experts. By order of March 16, 1993, the Court decided to *"at the appropriate time make available to the parties the information supplied by the experts in this case."* The Court also requested clarifications and additional information of the parties.

50.   It has already been stated that insofar as the right to life is concerned, it is impossible to reinstate the enjoyment of that right to the victims. In such cases, reparation must take other, alternative forms, such as pecuniary compensation. This compensation refers primarily to actual damages suffered. According to arbitral case law, it is a general principle of law that such damages comprise both indirect damages and loss of earnings.

88.   In order to arrive at the amount of reparations for actual damages to be received by the victims' successors, the method employed was to relate it to the income that the victims would have earned throughout their working life had they not been killed. To that end, the Court decided to make inquiries in order to estimate the income that the victims would have earned during the month of June 1993, based on the economic activities pursued by each of them. That particular month was selected because it was then that a free exchange market was established in Suriname. In determining the amount of reparations, this made it possible to avoid the distortions produced by a system of fixed rates of exchange in the face of the inflationary process affecting the country's economy. That situation was in fact undermining confidence in long-term projections. In addition, the data provided by the Commission on the victims' income were not sufficiently documented; it was therefore impossible to use them as the basis for calculation without an *in situ* verification.

89.   The Court calculated the annual income of each victim in Surinamese Florins and then converted it into dollars at the rate of exchange in effect on the free market.

The annual figure was used to determine the wages that would have accrued during the period from 1988 to 1993, including both of those years. Interest was added as compensation to the sum obtained for each victim, in keeping with the rates in effect on the international market. The resulting amount was increased by the current net value of the expected income during the rest of the working life of each of the victims. In the case of Mikuwendje Aloeboetoe, an adolescent, it was assumed that he would begin to earn a living at the age of 18 and would receive an income similar to that of those listed as construction workers.

El Amparo v. Venezuela
14-Sep-1996
Series C No. 28—*Reparations and Costs*

2.   In its petition the Commission asserted that Venezuela had violated the following articles of the American Convention: 2 (Domestic Legal Effects), 4 (Right to Life), 5 (Right to Humane Treatment), 8(1) (Right to a Fair Trial), 24 (Right to Equal Protection), 25 (Right to Judicial Protection), and 1(1) (Obligation to Respect Rights), with the deaths of José R. Araujo, Luis A. Berrío, Moisés A. Blanco, Julio P. Ceballos, Antonio Eregua, Rafael M. Moreno, José Indalecio Guerrero, Arín O. Maldonado, Justo Mercado, Pedro Mosquera, José Puerta, Marino Torrealba, José Torrealba, and Marino Rivas, which occurred at the "La Colorada" Canal, Páez District in the State of Apure, Venezuela.

It also claimed in the petition that Articles 5, 8(1), 24, and 25 of the Convention had been violated to the detriment of Wolmer Gregorio Pinilla and José Augusto Arias, sole survivors of the aforementioned events.

3.   It further contended that the instant case referred to events that began on October 29, 1988. On that day sixteen fishermen from the village of "El Amparo", Venezuela, were on their way to the "La Colorada" canal along the Arauca river in Apure State on a "fishing trip." At approximately 11:20 a.m., when some of the fishermen were leaving the boat, members of the military and the police of the "José Antonio Páez Specific Command" (CEJAP) opened fire on them, killing fourteen of the sixteen fishermen.

Reparations and Costs

12.   In order to take an informed decision on the amount of the indemnities in a manner in keeping with the necessary technical considerations, the Court decided to avail itself of the professional services of an actuarial expert. To that end, *Licenciado* Eduardo Zumbado J., a consultant actuary in San José, Costa Rica, was engaged. The Secretariat of the Court received his report on August 5 and 9, 1996. The actuary simply made the arithmetical calculations on the basis of the data contained in the parties' briefs and the evidence presented in the docket.

25.   On April 29, 1996, the President requested the Commission to clarify some data on the subject. This information was furnished by way of briefs submitted on May 13 and 29, 1996. Moreover, in the first of the briefs, the Commission also indicated that "a factual error had been made in calculating the victims' loss of earnings" and changed the requested amount to a figure ranging between US$67,000.00 and US$197,000.00 for each of the victims, and approximately

US$5,000.00 for each of the survivors. The Commission also stated that the basic rural wage for the month of October 1988 was "1,700 Bolívares, [and that] the exchange rate at that time was 37.14 Bs/US$."

26.   By communication of June 14, 1996, the Government presented its observations on the Commission's aforementioned briefs of May 13 and 29, and alleged that

> it was not a simple factual error, but a new calculation that exceeded by more than 1,000 percent the calculations presented at the relevant stage of the proceedings by the victims' attorneys themselves and supported by the Delegates of the Commission, [and that the Government had in good faith] accepted the amount formally requested for loss of earnings at the hearing held on last January 27. [Only months later], the calculations [were] being radically altered . . . and astronomical figures [were] now being proposed.

27.   The representatives of the victims and their next of kin subsequently provided this Court with information on the victims' age and life expectancy, and the rural basic wage. They also estimated each person's personal expenses at 20 percent of their total earnings.

28.   On the basis of the information received, and of the calculations made by the actuary designated *ad effectum*, the Court calculated that the indemnity to be granted to each of the victims or their next of kin depended on their age at the time of death and the years remaining before they would have reached the age at which normal life expectancy is estimated in Venezuela, or the time during which the two survivors remained unemployed. In its calculations, the Court used as the base salary an amount not less than the cost of the basic food basket, which is higher than the minimum rural wage at the time of the events. Once the calculation was made, 25 percent was deducted for personal expenses, as in other cases. To this amount was added the interest accruing from the date of the events up to the present.

Myrna Mack Chang v. Guatemala

25-Nov-2003

Series C No. 101—*Merits, Reparations, and Costs*

Reparations and Costs

126.   Pursuant to the Order of the President, Carmen de León-Escribano

Schlotter and Clara Arenas Bianchi submitted their statements in writing and Bernardo Morales Figueroa submitted his expert opinion in writing, all of them made before a notary public. The Court will now summarize the significant parts of said statements:

c. Written expert opinion of Bernardo Morales Figueroa, a mathematician

The lost earnings of Myrna Mack Chang add up to US$949,934.78. This result was obtained applying the customary method of establishing the present value of an accrued amount of capital, adding the factor of professional experience. If one applies the method used by the Inter-American Court to determine lost earnings, the result would be US$561,384.64, so there is a difference of US$388,050.14 with respect to the calculation in his expert opinion. This arises from the differences in the terminal year of life expectancy, from not using average values but rather present values, operating in constant terms and carrying forward the information with the consumer price indexes, adding the use of the factor of professional maturity.

248.   The representatives of the next of kin of the victim asked the Court to order the State to pay the "lost earnings" of the victim, for which they pointed out that:

(a) to estimate the lost earnings, the Court should take into account that when she was murdered, the victim was an outstanding professional and intellectual, both in her country and in international circles, for which reason she had many professional opportunities before her;

(b) to estimate the non-earned salary of Myrna Mack Chang, the Court can base its calculations on the average of what she earned at the time of the facts, what the director of AVANCSO earns today, and the salary earned by persons in Guatemala with similar academic credentials employed in the field of social science. In the course of over ten years, Myrna Mack Chang's salary would have increased due to length of service, rising cost of living, and inflation in Guatemala;

(c) to estimate lost earnings in this case, they requested that the Court accept the calculation made by the expert witness offered before the Court, which adds up to US$949,434.78 (nine hundred forty-nine thousand four hundred thirty-four United States dollars and seventy-eight cents). In a subsidiary manner, they requested that an appropriate calculation be made in accordance with the traditional standards of the inter-American system and the specific situation of Myrna Mack Chang, in which case the amount for this item adds up to US$561,384.64 (five hundred sixty-one thousand three hundred eighty-four United States dollars and sixty-four cents);

250.   The Court will now establish the material damage, which includes loss or reduction of the income of the victim and expenses incurred by the next of kin of the victim due to the facts,[4] for which it will determine a compensation that seeks to redress the patrimonial consequences of the violations found in the instant Judgment. For this, it will take into account the evidence gathered in this case, the case law of the Court itself, and the pleadings of the representatives of the next of kin of the victim, of the Commission, and of the State.

a) Lost earnings

251.   The Commission and the representatives of the next of kin of the victim requested compensation for the lost earnings of Myrna Mack Chang. Specifically, said representatives requested that the Court adopt as a basis the average of what the victim earned at the time of the facts, what the director of AVANCSO earns today, the salary earned by persons with similar academic credentials to those of the victim, the salary increase of the victim over time, the rising cost of living, inflation in Guatemala, and life expectancy, among others.

252.   With respect to the lost earnings of Myrna Mack Chang, the Court, in fairness, sets the amount at US$235,000.00 (two hundred thirty-five thousand United States dollars) for this item. Said amount must be given to the daughter of the victim, Lucrecia Hernández Mack.

Ivcher Bronstein v. Peru

6-Feb-2001

Series C No. 74—*Merits, Reparations, and Costs*

3.   According to the facts described by the Commission, the State arbitrarily deprived Mr. Ivcher Bronstein, a naturalized Peruvian citizen and majority shareholder, director, and president of Channel 2—Frecuencia Latina (hereinafter "Channel 2", "the Channel" or "Frecuencia Latina") of the Peruvian television network, of his nationality title in order to remove him from the editorial control of the said channel and restrict his freedom of expression, which he manifested by denouncing grave violations of human rights and acts of corruption.

4.   The Commission therefore requested the Court to call on Peru to restore and guarantee to Mr. Ivcher the enjoyment of all his rights and, in particular, that it should:

(a) Order that Mr. Ivcher Bronstein's Peruvian nationality title be reinstated and that the full and unconditional recognition of his Peruvian nationality be restored, with all attendant rights and prerogatives.

(b) Order that Mr. Ivcher Bronstein's enjoyment and exercise of his right to own shares in Compañía Latinoamericana de Radiodifusión S.A. be restored along with all his prerogatives as a shareholder in and administrator of that company.

(c) Order that Peru must guarantee Mr. Ivcher Bronstein's enjoyment and exercise [of] his right to freedom of expression and, in particular, that the acts of harassment and persecution against him, including the acts against his family and his company [should] cease.

(d) Order that the Peruvian State must adopt the necessary legislative and administrative measures to make full reparation and compensate Mr. Ivcher Bronstein for all the material and moral damages that the acts of its administrative and judicial organs have caused him.

181.   With regard to the violation of Article 21 of the Convention, the Court believes that the State should facilitate the conditions so that Mr. Ivcher Bronstein, whose Peruvian nationality has been restored, may take the necessary steps to recover the use and enjoyment of his rights as majority shareholder of Compañía Latinoamericana de Radiodifusión S.A., as he was until August 1, 1997, in the terms of domestic legislation. As for the recovery of dividends and other receipts that would have corresponded to Mr. Ivcher as majority shareholder and officer of the Company, domestic law should also apply. To that end, the respective petitions should be submitted to the competent national authorities.

182.   With regard to Article 13 of the Convention, the Court considers that the State should guarantee Mr. Ivcher the right to seek, investigate, and disseminate information and ideas through Peruvian television's Channel 2—Frecuencia Latina.

Miguel Castro Castro Prison v. Peru
25-Nov-2006
Series C No. 160—*Merits, Reparations, and Costs*

Reparations and Costs

423.   The pecuniary damage entails the loss or detriment to the income of the victims and, in this case, of their next of kin, and the expenses incurred as a consequence of the facts in the case *sub judice*. The Tribunal will set a compensatory amount in this sense for the violations declared in the present

Judgment,[219] [5] taking into account the State's partial acknowledgment of responsibility, the circumstances of the case, the evidence offered, the arguments presented by the parties, and the criteria established in the jurisprudence of the Tribunal itself.[220] [6]

Deceased Inmates

424.   The Court considers it appropriate to set, in equity, the amount of US$10,000.00 (ten thousand United States dollars) in favor of the 41 deceased inmates identified as compensation for pecuniary damages for the income they could have perceived for the work they could have carried out in the future. Said amounts must be distributed among their next of kin. The State must make said payments within an 18-month term as of the notification of the present Judgment.

Surviving inmates

425.   It has been proven that as a consequence of the facts of the present case there are victims that suffer from physical and psychological damages that in many cases imply a permanent reduction in their ability to work due to a complete permanent handicap. Therefore, the Court sets, in equity, the amount of US$25,000.00 (twenty-five thousand United States dollars, or its equivalent in Peruvian currency) in benefit of the victims that due to the facts of the present case resulted in a complete and permanent handicap that made it impossible to work and the amount of US$10,000.00 (ten thousand United States dollars, or its equivalent in Peruvian currency) for those that resulted in a partial permanent handicap that affects their ability to work. Since the Tribunal does not have sufficient evidence to determine the individual handicap of each of the surviving victims, said determination must be made by the domestic bodies specialized in deciding on handicaps upon request of the interested parties, who must present their request within an 8-month term, as of the notification of the present Judgment. The State must make said payments within an 18-month period as of the notification of the present Judgment.

426.   The discrepancies regarding the determination indicated in the previous paragraph must be solved within the domestic realm following the corresponding national proceedings before the competent authorities, among them the domestic courts. The previous is without detriment to this Tribunal's competence to supervise compliance with the Judgment.

Ticona Estrada et al. v. Bolivia

27-Nov-2008

Series C No. 191—*Merits, Reparations, and Costs*

Reparations and costs

112.   The Commission requested the Court to equitably determine the amount of compensation for consequential damages and "loss of income" of Renato Ticona and his relatives. Moreover, the representative requested the Court to consider the following information when determining the loss of income of Renato Ticona during his remaining and probable life expectancy:

(a) *Renato Ticona as a music teacher.*[98][7] The income he would have received from July 1980 to December 1982 amounts to US$2,004.75 (two thousand four United States dollars and seventy-five cents),[99][8] and considering the fact that there is no supporting documentation on the salary that Renato Ticona received, the representative requested the Court to equitably determine a sum; and

(b) *Renato Ticona as future agricultural engineer* Mr. Ticona Estrada would have started working as an agricultural engineer in the year 1983 at the age of 28 years old and, in accordance with the life-expectancy of 64 years, would have worked until the year 2019, that is, 36 more years. The probable income, based on a monthly average of US$1,027.00 (one thousand twenty-seven United States dollars), that Renato Ticona would have received as agricultural engineer amounts to US$360,477.00 (three hundred sixty thousand four hundred seventy-seven United States dollars).[100][9]

113.   Furthermore, the State did not agree with the amount requested as reparation by the representative. It requested the Court to calculate the probable loss of income of Renato Ticona, bearing in mind the salary he received as a music teacher, based on the salary of Bs. 550.00 (five hundred fifty Bolivian pesos) for thirty-eight and a half years of work and the corresponding deduction of 25% as personal expenses, and not the probable and uncertain exercise of the profession of agricultural engineer. The State expressed that, maybe, if the Court decides to consider the compensation of an agricultural engineer, the calculation should be made since the year 1985, when he would start receiving the salary of a professional.[101][10] In this sense, it requested the Court to apply the same parameter used in the case of *Trujillo Oroza*, that is, to calculate the reparations of Renato Ticona as probable agricultural engineer in the amount of US$488.00 (four hundred and eighty-eight United States dollars), which corresponds to 50% of the salary proposed by the representatives less 25% of the total for personal expenses.

114.   This Court finds that the award for lost income includes income that the

victim would have received during his or her remaining life expectancy. That amount, therefore, is considered the property of the deceased victim, which shall be delivered to his or her next of kin.[102 11]

115.   As has been proven in this Judgment, Renato Ticona was a victim of forced disappearance, and therefore he had suffered damages inherent to such practice. As has been certified by the parties, Renato Ticona was 25 years old and eight months at the moment of his disappearance and he worked as a music teacher at the school "Mariano Baptista," he was also attending the seventh semester of a career of agricultural engineering and, as demonstrated by the several testimonies, was the economic support of his family, composed of his parents, two brothers, and one sister. In this sense, Renato Ticona suffered pecuniary damages consisting of the loss of income.

116.   This Tribunal observes that Renato Ticona was, at the moment of the events, attending the seventh semester, out of ten, of the course of study of agricultural engineering, therefore, there were only three more semesters left to conclude the university studies. Based on the foregoing, this Tribunal considers that such circumstance allows establishing, with sufficient certainty, the activity or profession that Renato Ticona would do in the future and, therefore, establishes the income corresponding to such profession. Based on the foregoing, the Court sets the amount of US$170,000.00 (one hundred seventy thousand United States dollars), on equitable grounds, as it has established in other cases.[103 12]   In order to do so, the Court has considered his job as a teacher as from the year 1980, his possible role as agricultural engineer as from the year 1985[104 13] until the year 2019, his age, and his life expectancy.[105 14]

Torres Millacura v. Argentina

26-Aug-2011

Series C No 229—*Merits, Reparations, and Costs*

2.   The application is related to the alleged "arbitrary detention, torture, and enforced disappearance of Iván Eladio Torres [Millacura], which took place starting on October 3, 2003, in the City of Comodoro Rivadavia, Province of Chubut, and the subsequent lack of due diligence in the investigation of the facts, as well as the denial of justice to the detriment of the victim's family members."

3.   The Commission requested that the Court rule that the State of Argentina is responsible for violations of Articles 3 (Right to Recognition of Juridical Personality), 4 (Right to Life), 5 (Right to Humane Treatment [Personal Integrity]), 7 (Right to Personal Liberty), 8 (Right to a Fair Trial [Judicial

Guarantees]), and 25 (Right to Judicial Protection) of the American Convention on Human Rights (hereinafter "convention" or "American Convention"), all with regard to Article 1(1) of the American Convention (Obligation to Respect Rights), as well as the noncompliance of the obligations established in Articles I and IX of the Inter-American Convention on Forced Disappearance of Persons (hereinafter "Convention on Forced Disappearance), and Articles 1, 6, and 8 of the Inter-American Convention to Prevent and Punish Torture (hereinafter "Convention Against Torture"), all to the detriment of Iván Eladio Torres. Likewise, the Commission requested that the Court declare a violation of Articles 5 (Right to Humane Treatment [Personal Integrity]), 8 (Right to a Fair Trial [Judicial Guarantees]), and 25 (Right to Judicial Protection) of the American Convention, with regard to Article 1(1) of the Convention (Obligation to Respect Rights), to the detriment of the family members of Iván Eladio Torres. In addition, the Commission alleged that the State failed to comply with its obligation to adapt domestic law to the Convention according to Article 2 of the Convention, with regard to Articles 3, 4, 5, 7, 8(1), 25, and 1(1) thereof. Finally, it requested the payment of certain reparations, as well as the payment of costs and expenses for the case's domestic and international litigation.

D.1   Pecuniary damages.

180.   This Tribunal has developed the concept of pecuniary damages in its jurisprudence and has established that they assume "the loss of or detriment to the victim's income, the expenses incurred as a result of the facts, and the monetary consequences that have a causal nexus with the facts of the case under review."[176][15]

D.1.1 Arguments of the parties.

181.   The Commission asked the Court to order the State "to grant full reparations to the family members of Iván Eladio Torres Millacura, including ... pecuniary damages.»

182.   The representatives asked the Court to order the State to pay, to the benefit of Iván Eladio Torres Millacura, the amount of US $695,000.00 (six hundred ninety-five thousand United States dollars) for pecuniary damages, as well as an additional monthly sum starting October 2010 of US $8,225.00 (eight thousand two hundred twenty-five United States dollars) "plus support and contributions for health insurance and Social Security from October 2003" until he appears.[177][16] Likewise, for pecuniary damages, they requested US $506,970.00 (five hundred six thousand nine hundred seventy United States dollars) plus US $5,955.00 (five thousand nine hundred fifty-five United States dollars) monthly, starting October 30, 2010, until Iván Eladio Torres Millacura appears, in favor of

María Leontina Millacura Llaipén, Fabiola Valeria Torres, and Marcos Alejandro Torres Millacura.[178][17]

183.   For its part, the State asserted that the representatives "have not used any of the rational, prudent, or measured parameters available to them for calculating a legally viable and morally just compensatory claim according to applicable domestic and international standards" on the issue of reparations. In addition, the State holds that the representatives "did not include any valid evidence to even minimally justify the source [or] the amounts of the requested pecuniary reparations." Consequently, the State asked the Court to reject the claims of the representatives and "in keeping with the circumstances of the case, establish the reparations due to the family members of Iván Eladio Torres Millacura based on the principle of equity and in keeping with applicable international standards on the subject."

D.1.2.   Considerations of the Court.

D.1.2.1. Iván Eladio Torres Millacura

184.   The Court notes that as can be deduced from the case file, particularly the testimony given by Mrs. Leontina Millacura Llaipén and Mr. Marcos Alejandro Torres Millacura, at the time of his disappearance, Mr. Torres Millacura was unemployed. Nevertheless, it can also be deduced from that testimony that Mr. Torres Millacura often did different construction work.[179][18] The representatives did not submit pleadings or evidence allowing the Court to verify Mr. Torres Millacura's income for the different activities that he carried out. Consequently, the Court rules to establish, in equity, the amount of US$40,000.00 (forty thousand United States dollars) or its equivalent in Argentine currency. This amount must be paid by the deadline that the Court establishes for doing so.

Gutiérrez and Family v. Argentina

25-Nov-2013

Series C No 229—*Merits, Reparations, and Costs*

1..   On August 19, 2011, under the provisions of Articles 51 and 61 of the American Convention, the Inter-American Commission on Human Rights (hereinafter "the Inter-American Commission" or "the Commission") submitted to the jurisdiction of the Court the case of *Jorge Omar Gutiérrez and family v. the Argentine Republic* (hereinafter "the State" or "Argentina"). According to the Commission, the case concerns "the murder, on August 29, 1994, of Assistant Commissioner Gutiérrez who was investigating a case of corruption, subsequently known as [the] 'case of the parallel customs house ...,' in which important businessmen and high-ranking government officials were involved." An investigation had been opened in the ordinary criminal jurisdiction into the events on which that case was based, in which presumably "there were fundamental irregularities." However, "[e]ven though the investigation was fraught with irregularities and concealment measures, and despite the creation of a special committee by the Chamber of Deputies [of the National Congress], the State failed to adopt the necessary measures to clarify the facts and the corresponding responsibilities." Thus, "17 years after the execution of Assistant Commissioner Jorge Omar Gutiérrez, there is still no certainty about the circumstances of his death, and no one has been sanctioned for the incident." Lastly, the Commission affirmed that the human rights violations committed against Jorge Omar Gutiérrez and his family persisted as a result of the alleged absence of an effective investigation by the judicial authorities "into the participation of State agents in the murder of Mr. Gutiérrez."

VIII-3. Right to Personal Integrity of the Victims Next of Kin

D. Compensation

D.1. Pecuniary damage

D.1.2. Loss of earnings

177.   The representatives indicated that Jorge Omar Gutiérrez was 41 years of age when he was murdered and that, according to statistical data for 1999 of the National Census and Statistics Institute (INDEC), average life expectancy in Argentina for men was 68.53 years; they therefore calculated that Jorge Omar Gutiérrez would have lived a further 27.53 years, and received 330.36 more in salary. However, the representatives indicated that the calculation should take into account not only the 931.00 Argentine pesos a month that he received in 1994, but this amount should be updated, taking into account his commitment and the quality of his work, so that it could be expected that, during his career, he would be promoted to at least the rank of Commissioner General, with a current monthly salary of 23,923.59 Argentine pesos. According to the representatives, 25% should be deducted from the estimated amount of the income as the sum that the victim would have used for his personal expenses. Finally, the representatives asked the Court to establish, in equity, the rate that should be used to calculate interest, which should include interest calculated from the date of the incident until the date the payment is made. The Commission did not refer to this matter.

178.   The State considered "unfounded the said expectation to assimilate the career in the police force of [Jorge Omar] Gutiérrez to a purported 'successful career' culminating in the achievement of one of the highest ranks and,

consequently, the highest income on the current pay scale." In addition, it asked that the "the items that the Court will consider be defined using strict criteria of equity," taking into account that both the widow and the children of Jorge Omar Gutiérrez "have received and continue to receive the corresponding pension from the social security institute, which has been taking the place of the income with which [Mr.] Gutiérrez covered the his family's living costs and, therefore, an essential part of what is sought to be understood by loss of earnings."

179.   The Court notes that the representatives forwarded a voucher for the salary of Jorge Omar Gutiérrez as Assistant Commissioner, [277][19][20] as well as tables of the National Census and Statistics Institute on life expectancy at birth by sex and by jurisdiction in Argentina for the years 1990/1992 and 2000/2001[278][20] For its part, the State indicated that both the widow and the children of Jorge Omar Gutiérrez have received and continue to receive the pension that corresponded to him from the social security institute, without providing any evidence in this regard. The representatives did not disprove this allegation by the State; however, this Court has verified that the Directorate General of Judicial Affairs of the Police of the province of Buenos Aires decided to declare "the death of Assistant Commissioner Jorge Omar Gutiérrez attributable to service [and] to notify the heirs [...] of the compensation provided," [278][20] and to provide certified copies to the "Retirement and Pension Fund," for the pertinent effects. Therefore, the Court will not order a compensatory amount for the next of kin of Jorge Omar Gutiérrez for the said loss of earnings as of his execution.

The Landaeta Mejías Brothers et al. v. Venezuela

27-Aug-2014

Series C No. 281—*Preliminary Objections, Merits, Reparations and Costs*

1.   On July 10, 2012, the Inter-American Commission on Human Rights (hereinafter "the Inter-American Commission" or "the Commission") submitted to the jurisdiction of the Inter-American Court of Human Rights the case of the *Landaeta Mejías Brothers et al. v. the Bolivarian Republic of Venezuela* (hereinafter "the State" or "Venezuela"). According to the Commission, the case concerns the alleged extrajudicial execution of the brothers Igmar Alexander Landaeta Mejías (hereinafter "Igmar Landaeta") and Eduardo José Landaeta Mejías (hereinafter "Eduardo Landaeta"), 18 and 17 years of age respectively, by officials of the Public Order and Security Corps of the state of Aragua, Venezuela (hereinafter "CSOP"). In this regard, the Commission indicated

that "following threats and harassment against him, Igmar Alexander Landaeta Mejías was extrajudicially executed on November 17, 1996, while six weeks later – on December 30, 1996 – his brother, the minor Eduardo José Landaeta Mejías was unlawfully and arbitrarily deprived of liberty and, the following day, during a supposed transfer, he was extrajudicially executed. These facts took place in the context of extrajudicial executions in Venezuela, especially in the state of Aragua. The death of the two brothers remains unpunished. In the case of Igmar Alexander Landaeta Mejías, the criminal proceedings against the authorities culminated in a dismissal, while in the case of Eduardo José Landaeta Mejías, the criminal proceedings are still underway 16 years after his death."

VIII. Reparations Application of Article 63(1) of the American Convention)

D. Compensation

> *D.1 Pecuniary damage*
>
> D.1.2 Consequential damage

321.   The representatives indicated that the death of the Landaeta Mejías brothers entailed unexpected expenses, all of which were covered by the family. Since the family does not have vouchers for these expenses, the representatives asked the Court to establish, in equity, the sum of US$500 (five hundred United States dollars) for funeral expenses. The representatives also indicated that the psychological problems of Maria Magdalena Mejías and Victoria Landaeta caused the family to incur different expenses to obtain medical care and medicines, because they had to visit a psychologist. Since they do not have documentation regarding these expenses, the representatives asked the Court to establish, in equity, the sum of US$500 (five hundred United States dollars). They also indicated that this treatment will be required in future, and therefore asked to Court to order the payment of compensation, in equity, of US$2,000 (two thousand United States dollars).

322.   Regarding the funeral expenses incurred by the Landaeta Mejías family, the Court notes that no vouchers were provided; nevertheless, the Court presumes, as it has in previous cases,[411] that the family incurred different expenses owing to the death of the Landaeta Mejías brothers. Bearing in mind that the State was found responsible for violations of the obligation to respect and to ensure the right to life (supra para. 147 and 204), the Court decides that the State must pay a proportionate sum of US$500 (five hundred United States dollars), as compensation for funeral expenses to Ignacio Landaeta Muñoz and María Magdalena Mejías Camero.

323.   Regarding the presumed health care expenses incurred, the Court has no evidence that would substantiate the disbursements alleged by the representatives.[412] In addition, the Court finds that future medical care is included in the measure of rehabilitation indicated above (*supra* para. 303). Consequently, it is not necessary to establish the compensation requested for health care expenses.

Expelled Dominicans and Haitians v. Dominican Republic
28-Aug-2014
Series C No 282— *Preliminary Objections, Merits, Reparations and Costs*

1.   On July 12, 2012, in accordance with Articles 51 and 61 of the Convention, the Inter-American Commission on Human Rights (hereinafter "the Inter-American Commission" or "the Commission") submitted to the Court case 12,271 against the State of the Dominican Republic (hereinafter "the State" or "the Dominican Republic"). According to the Commission, the case relates to the "arbitrary detention and summary expulsion from the territory of the Dominican Republic" of the presumed victims who are Haitians and Dominicans of Haitian descent, including children (infra para. 3.c.i), without following the expulsion procedure set out in domestic law. In addition, the Commission considered "that a series of obstacles prevented Haitian immigrants from registering their children born in Dominican territory," and persons of Haitian descent born in the Dominican Republic from obtaining Dominican nationality.

2.   According to the Commission the case "occurred in a tense climate of mass collective expulsions of individuals that involved Dominicans and aliens alike, both documented and undocumented, who had established permanent residence in the Dominican Republic, where they had close family and work-related ties." In addition, among other considerations, the Commission referred to:

(a)   "impediments to granting nationality to persons born in Dominican territory, despite the fact that the State follows the principle of ius soli";

(b)   that "the State failed to submit information demonstrating that the repatriation procedure in effect at the time of these events had been applied to the [presumed] victims," and

(c)   that the presumed victims "were not provided with legal assistance, and did not have the opportunity to appeal the deportation decision; furthermore, there was no order from a competent, independent, and impartial authority ruling on their deportation." In addition, "the State did not indicate a specific remedy the [presumed] victims could have accessed to protect their rights." Also, according to the Commission, "during their arbitrary detention and expulsion, [they] did not have the opportunity to present their documentation and, in those cases where it was presented, it was destroyed by the Dominican officials," which meant that the presumed victims "were deprived of the ability to demonstrate their physical existence and juridical personality." In addition, "during their detention, the [presumed] victims did not receive water, food, or medical assistance, and their expulsion led to the uprooting and breakdown of family structures and affected the normal development of familial relations, even for new members of the family."

C. 1. Pecuniary damage

479.   The Court has developed the concept of pecuniary damage in its case law and has established that it supposes "the loss of, or detriment to, the income of the victims, the expenses incurred because of the facts, and the consequences of a pecuniary nature that have a causal nexus with the facts of the case."[498 20]

480.   The information provided reveals that, owing to the detention and expulsion, the Medina family lost a horse valued at RD$3,400 Dominican pesos, a mule valued at RD$2,800 Dominican pesos, four cows valued at RD$5,000 Dominican pesos each, 43 hens valued at RD$200 Dominican pesos each, their house in Oviedo, which was worth approximately RD$50,000 Dominican pesos, and two beds, one table, four chairs, valued at RD$10,500 Dominican pesos. The Fils-Aimé family lost two beds, eight chairs, clothing, 19 pigs, one donkey, one goat, several hens, 36 turkeys valued at RD$500 Dominican pesos each, and a lot where Jeanty Fils-Aimé planted corn, pigeon peas and yam, all with an approximate value of RD$50,000 Dominican pesos. The Jean Mesidor family lost two beds, one table, four chairs, a refrigerator, a stove, a gas tank, fans, a television, a radio, clothing, and sheets for six people, and Victor Jean was unable to collect RD$1,000 Dominican pesos. Bersson Gelin lost approximately RD$3,000 Dominican pesos that were stolen from him during the expulsion, and, owing to the detention and expulsion, he was unable to collect three months of wages that his employer owed him, amounting to RD$42,000 Dominican pesos. Regarding the supposed disbursements made by the Medina family for the medical treatment of the child Awilda Ferreras Medina, the evidence provided to the Court does not reveal a causal nexus between the problems suffered by the child and the violations declared in this Judgment.

481.   In this regard, the Court considers, based on the facts, that the victims were summarily expelled by the State without being able to take their belongings with

them or to collect them or to dispose of them. Consequently, it can be presumed that they suffered financial losses on being expelled and, owing to the factual situation, it is evidently impossible for them to have probative elements to prove this. Taking into account that the Medina, Fils-Aimé and Jean Mesidor families, and Bersson Gelin were expelled when the Court had temporal competence, the Court establishes, in equity, the sum of US$8,000.00 (eight thousand United States dollars) for each family for pecuniary damage. The amount corresponding to each family must be delivered, respectively, to Willian Medina Ferreras, Janise Midi, Bersson Gelin, and Victor Jean. With regard to the request relating to the transport and accommodation expenses for the journeys made by Antonio Sensión and Rafaelito Pérez Charles, the Court rejects them, because it has not been proved that these expenses are connected to the violations declared to their detriment.

482.   Furthermore, with regard to the alleged loss of earnings of Antonio Sensión, Bersson Gelin, Rafaelito Pérez Charles, Jeanty Fils-Aimé, Willian Medina Ferreras and Victor Jean on losing their jobs and their means of subsistence, although the representatives referred to the different activities they carried out, they failed to submit any evidence relating to the income that the victims received, or to possible future income, or information relating to their wages. Consequently, the Court does not have sufficient elements to make this determination and therefore rejects this request.

Rodríguez Vera et al. ("the Disappeared from the Palace of Justice") v. Colombia

14-Nov-2014

Series C No 229—*Merits, Reparations, and Costs*

1.   On February 9, 2012, in accordance with Articles 51 and 61 of the American Convention and Article 35 of the Court's Rules of Procedure, the Inter-American Commission on Human Rights (hereinafter "the Inter-American Commission" or "the Commission") submitted the case entitled *Carlos Augusto Rodríguez Vera et al. (Palace of Justice) v. the Republic of Colombia* (hereinafter "the State" or "Colombia") to the jurisdiction of the Inter-American Court. According to the Commission the facts of this case occurred in the context of the events known as the taking and retaking of the Palace of Justice in Bogota, which took place on November 6 and 7, 1985. In particular, the case relates to the presumed forced disappearance of Carlos Augusto Rodríguez Vera, Cristina del Pilar Guarín Cortés, David Suspes Celis, Bernardo Beltrán Hernández, Héctor

Jaime Beltrán Fuentes, Gloria Stella Lizarazo, Luz Mary Portela León, Norma Constanza Esguerra Forero, Lucy Amparo Oviedo Bonilla, Gloria Anzola de Lanao, Ana Rosa Castiblanco Torres and Irma Franco Pineda during the operation to retake the building. The case also relates to the presumed disappearance and subsequent execution of Justice Carlos Horacio Urán Rojas, as well as to the presumed detention and torture of Yolanda Santodomingo Albericci, Eduardo Matson Ospino, Orlando Quijano and José Vicente Rubiano Galvis, and to the alleged failure of the courts to clarify all these events and to punish all those responsible.

XIV.   Reparations (Application of Article 63(1) of the American Convention)

E. Compensation

E.4) Considerations of the Court

E.4.1) Pecuniary damage

593.   This Court recognizes and assesses positively the efforts made by Colombia in relation to its obligation to make reparation in this case. The Court recalls that, if domestic mechanisms exist to determine forms of reparation, these procedures and results must be taken into account (*supra* para. 548). Thus, this Court finds it necessary to analyze whether the contentious-administrative courts ruled on the full scope of the State responsibility included in this case, [893][21] and also to determine whether the compensation awarded meets the criteria of being objective, reasonable and effective to make adequate reparation for the violations of the rights recognized in the Convention that have been declared by this Court. [894][22]

594.   In this regard, the Court notes that there are some differences of opinion in relation to the compensation awarded at the domestic level and the compensation that this Court usually awards in cases such as this one. The Colombian contentious-administrative jurisdiction does not grant compensation to persons who are disappeared or deceased, and compensation for "loss of earnings" is only awarded if the family members who depended on the disappeared or deceased victim apply for it. [895][23] Under this criterion, compensation was not awarded for the loss of earnings of the disappeared victim to any of the next of kin of Cristina del Pilar Guarín Cortés, Bernardo Beltrán Hernández, Irma Franco Pineda and Luz Mary Portela León. [896][24] Also, in the case of Irma Franco Pineda, the Council of State indicated that it was not in order to grant compensation for loss of earnings to her family members because "the loss of earnings or assistance resulting from unlawful activities such as those to which the person disappeared was dedicated does not constitute a source of compensation." [897][25]

595.   The Court emphasizes that the award of compensation for pecuniary damage in the contentious-administrative jurisdiction was made based on criteria that, although distinct, are objective and reasonable, so that the Court finds that, in keeping with the principle of complementarity on which the inter-American jurisdiction is based, [898 26] it is not in order for the Court to order additional compensation for pecuniary damage in the cases in which this compensation has already been awarded by the contentious-administrative jurisdiction. [899 27]

---

2. *Lucrum Cessans* For Children

"Street Children" (Villagrán-Morales et al.) v. Guatemala
19-Nov-1999
Series C No. 63—*Merits*

2.   When presenting the case to the Court, the Commission invoked Articles 50 and 51 of the American Convention on Human Rights (hereinafter "the Convention" or "the American Convention") and Articles 32 et seq. of the Rules of Procedure. The Commission referred this case for the Court to determine whether Guatemala had violated the following Articles of the Convention: 1 (Obligation to Respect Rights), 4 (Right to Life), 5 (Right to Humane Treatment), 7 (Right to Personal Liberty), 8 (Right to a Fair Trial), and 25 (Right to Judicial Protection). According to the application, these violations were the result of

the abduction, torture and murder of Henry Giovanni Contreras, Federico Clemente Figueroa Túnchez, Julio Roberto Caal Sandoval, and Jovito Josué Juárez Cifuentes; the murder of Anstraum [Aman] Villagrán Morales; and the failure of State mechanisms to deal appropriately with the said violations and provide the victim's families with access to justice.

3.   As two of the victims, Julio Roberto Caal Sandoval and Jovito Josué Juárez Cifuentes, were minors when they were abducted, tortured, and murdered and Anstraum Aman Villagrán Morales was a minor when he was killed, the Commission alleged that Guatemala had violated Article 19 (Rights of the Child) of the American Convention. The Commission requested the Court to order the State to take the necessary steps to conduct a prompt, impartial, and effective investigation into the facts "so that [the individual responsibilities for the alleged violations may be] recorded in an officially authorized report" and "those responsible may be punished appropriately." It also requested the Court

to order the State "to vindicate the names of the victims and make fair payment to the persons affected by the violations of the aforementioned rights" and to pay costs to the victims and their representatives. In its application, the Commission also cited the violation of Articles 1, 6, and 8 of the Inter-American Convention to Prevent and Punish Torture (hereinafter "Convention against Torture").

26-May-2001
Series C No. 77—*Reparations and Costs*

74.   The Commission argued:
(a) that, with regard to loss of earnings, in this case it had been proved that the victims provided emotional, affective, and financial support to their next of kin and that the fact that they were street children does not preclude the obligation to provide compensation for loss of earnings. It added that this concept cannot be eliminated because the victims did not work all the time. It also indicated that, when calculating the loss of earnings, and in order to estimate the loss of earnings corresponding to the requirements and circumstances of this case, the following factors should be taken into consideration: life expectancy,[69][28] the age of the victims, wages that would not be received based on the minimum wage for non-agricultural activities,[70][29] interest on past losses,[71][30] and discount to the current value[72][31]; and
(b) that it supported the requests submitted by the petitioners with regard to the damage suffered by the next of kin of Henry Giovanni Contreras, Julio Roberto Caal Sandoval, and Anstraun Aman Villagrán Morales as a result of the search for the victims, medical expenses, funeral services, and expenses related to the legal proceedings. With regard to the next of kin of Federico Clemente Figueroa Túnchez and Jovito Josué Juárez Cifuentes, it requested the Court to determine the compensation for such losses fairly, taking into account the circumstances of the case and all available information.

78.   Bearing in mind the information received during this proceeding, the facts that are considered proved, and its consistent jurisprudence, the Court finds that compensation for pecuniary damage in this case should include the items indicated in this section.

79.   With regard to loss of earnings, the representatives of the victims' next of kin and the Commission agree that, in order to make its calculation, the Court should take into account the minimum wage for non-agricultural activities

in Guatemala. The State, on the other hand, is opposed to using this basis and argues that the victims did not hold permanent, continuous employment. As it has on other occasions,[78][32] this Court considers that, in view of the lack of precise information on the victims, it should use the minimum wage for non-agricultural activities in Guatemala as a basis.

81.   The Court observes that the minimum wage for non-agricultural activities was Q348.00 (three hundred forty-eight quetzales) at the date of the death of the victims in this case, which, at the June 1990 exchange rate, is equal to US$80.93 (eighty United States dollars and ninety-three cents) as the monthly wage that would correspond to each of them. The calculation of the earnings that they will no longer receive will be made on the basis of 12 wages a year plus the corresponding annual bonuses under Guatemalan legislation. This will yield the earnings that each victim could presumably have enjoyed during his probable life—the period between his age at the time of the events and the end of his life expectancy in 1990, the year of the facts.[79][33] Twenty-five percent must be subtracted from this amount for personal expenses. The remaining amount must be adjusted to its current value at the date of the judgment.[80][34]

Bulacio vs. Argentina
18-Sep-2003
Series C No. 100—*Merits, Reparations, and Costs*
   a) Lost earnings

84.   The representatives of the victim and the Inter-American Commission requested compensation for Walter David Bulacio's lost earnings, based on the monthly salary that he received as a caddie at the golf course. This Court deems that it has been proven that youth Bulacio received a monthly income of $400 (four hundred pesos), equivalent to US$400.00 (four hundred United States dollars); however, it deems that given the nature of the activity he did not receive a complementary salary as his income came from tips given by the clients. The Court also deems that it is reasonable to assume that youth Bulacio would not have carried out this activity for the rest of his life, but there is no certain fact that makes it possible to ascertain the activity or profession that he would have exercised in the future, that is, that there are insufficient grounds to establish the loss of a definite chance, which "must be estimated on the basis of certain damage with sufficient grounds to establish the probable realization of said damage."[56]
[35] Due to the above, the Court decides to set, in fairness, US$100,000.00 (one

hundred thousand United States dollars) as compensation for Walter David Bulacio's lost earnings.

Juvenile Reeducation Institute vs. Paraguay
2-Sep-2004
Series C No. 112—*Preliminary Objections, Merits, Reparations, and Costs*

Reparations and Costs
284.   In the case of compensation for pecuniary damages, the Commission observed that:

   (a) absent proof to the contrary, the State has already covered the *damnum emergens,* as it paid various funeral expenses in the case of deceased victims; it also paid the medical expenses of the children injured in the fires; and

   (b) in order to determine the *lucrum cessans* in a just and equitable manner, the Court must consider the wages that the victims ceased to receive as a consequence of the State's violation of their right to life, their ages at the time of their deaths, the number of years before they would have reached the average life expectancy in Paraguay, and the minimum wage currently being paid. The Commission considered that upon their release, the deceased inmates would have joined the work force; inasmuch as at the time of their deaths the inmates were not working, the Commission reasoned that the Court should fix a sum in equity to determine the compensation owed to each deceased inmate, taking each victim's particular circumstances into account. Finally, the Commission was of the view that some monetary amount should be set to compensate for post-fire consequences sustained by the children injured in those fires, such as permanent injuries that will have an impact on future job performance.

287.   Based on the information received during the course of this proceeding, the facts proven, the violations established, and its *jurisprudence constante,* the Court finds that the compensation for pecuniary damages in the instant case should include the following:

   a) Lucrum cessans
288.   In the case of the income that deceased inmates Elvio Epifanio Acosta Ocampos, Marco Antonio Jiménez, Diego Walter Valdez, Sergio Daniel Vega

Figueredo, Sergio David Poletti Domínguez, Mario de Pilar Álvarez Pérez, Juan Alcides Román Barrios, Antonio Damián Escobar Morinigo, Carlos Raúl de la Cruz, Benito Augusto Adorno, Richard Daniel Martínez, and Héctor Ramón Vázquez ceased to receive, the Court considers that no definite fact has been established that would enable the Court to determine what activity or trade those inmates would have eventually practiced. This category of damages must be calculated on the basis of a definite injury that is sufficiently substantiated to find that the injury likely occurred.[206][36] Given the circumstances of the instant case, the evidence is not sufficient to prove the income lost. The Court will, therefore, grant an award in equity that uses the minimum wage in Paraguay to calculate the lost income.

289.   Given the considerations set out in the preceding paragraph and taking into account, *inter alia,* the circumstances of the specific case,[207][37] life expectance in Paraguay, and the legal minimum salary in Paraguay,[208][38] the Court grants in equity the sum of US$40,000.00 (forty thousand United States dollars) or its equivalent in the national currency of the State, to each of the deceased victims. Those amounts shall go to the next of kin of the twelve deceased inmates.

290.   As for the *lucrum cessans* of the injured former inmates,[209][39] all of whom were juveniles, this Court considers that it is possible to infer that the injuries these victims sustained meant, at the least, temporary work disability. But no evidence has been provided that would enable the Court to determine what trade or vocation these children might have practiced had they not been injured. In the absence of any other proof that the parties might have furnished, the Court will compute the injured inmates' lost income on the basis of the percentage of the body over which burns were sustained, as it regards this as the most objective criterion possible. It therefore grants in equity compensation for lost income in the following amounts: US$15,000 (fifteen thousand United States dollars) to those injured victims who sustained injuries on 20% or more of their bodies; US$13,000.00 (thirteen thousand United States dollars) for those who sustained burns over 10% but less than 20% of their bodies; US$11,000.00 (eleven thousand United States dollars) for who sustained injuries over 5% but less than 10% of their bodies, and US$9,000.00 (nine thousand United States dollars) to those who sustained injuries over less than 5% of their body.

292. As this Court does not have figures for 19 of the injured former inmates,[210][40] it will assume that they sustained burns over less than 5% of their body and award them the corresponding sum.

ANALYSIS AND QUESTIONS RAISED BY THE COURT'S JURISPRUDENCE

Compensation for lost earnings is a concept common to most of the world's legal systems, including the legal systems of the Americas. Pecuniary damages, and specifically *lucrum cessans* (loss of earnings), is generally the first category of reparations addressed by the Inter-American Court of Human Rights in cases involving human rights violations.

Lost earnings are amongst the most quantifiable damages, yet as evident from the above case excerpts, the Court must consider various objective factors to calculate appropriate compensation. Such factors include the victim's income prior to the violation; their profession, trade, or prospective occupation; their age and life expectancy; the victim's temporary or permanent disability, or death (in other words, the victim's ability to earn income after the violation); and the State's minimum wage or basic food basket (i.e., the cost of a nutritious diet). The Court has included all forms of income, including dividends, tips, and pensions, to compensate for loss of earnings. Additionally, when relevant, the Court has factored inflation, interest, and cost of living adjustments into its calculations.

In cases where the victim's income or occupation was unknown, or the victim was unemployed, the Court has utilized the State's minimum wage or basic food basket to determine *lucrum cessans* compensation and protect the integrity of reparations for the victim's next of kin.

The Court has also affirmed that children must be compensated for their lost earnings, regardless of whether the earnings were regular and regardless of the children's status in society (e.g., "street children" must be compensated for their lost earnings).

- Are there additional factors that the Court should consider in determining lost earnings, especially for children and younger adults whose occupations and incomes would likely change over time? Is it appropriate to assume that "street children" would have remained impoverished throughout their lifetimes?
- In certain cases, despite objective proof of lost earnings (for instance in *Myrna Mack Chang*), the Court has awarded compensation "in equity." Are such decisions possibly a result of conflicting expert testimony and other evidence, or might the Court be considering other factors?
- How should the Court determine lost earnings for a victim whose income or occupation was unknown? Is there an alternative to the minimum wage or basic food basket?

- Should the Court require expert calculations for lost earnings?
- In some cases, the Court has ordered that certain determinations be made by domestic tribunals (e.g., determinations of the specific handicaps suffered by each of the surviving victims in *Miguel Castro Castro Prison*), while in other cases it has relied upon expert testimony and other evidence presented for its consideration. What may account for these differences in whether the Court makes its own factual determinations or refers certain decisions to domestic tribunals?

B. OTHER DIRECT AND CONSEQUENTIAL DAMAGES (*DANNUM EMERGENS*)

Velásquez Rodríguez v. Honduras
21-Jul-1989
Series C No. 4—*Merits*

41. In this regard, the attorneys ask for compensation for patrimonial damages within the concept of damages and include . . . the expenses of the family related to the investigation of the whereabouts of Manfredo Velásquez.
42. The Court cannot grant that request in the present case. Though it is theoretically correct that those expenses come within the definition of damages, they cannot be awarded in the instant case because they were not pleaded or proven opportunely. No estimate or proof of expenses related to the investigation of the whereabouts of the victim was submitted during the trial. Likewise, with regard to litigation expenses in bringing the matter before the Court, the judgment on the merits already denied an award of costs because there was no pleading to support the request.

Aloeboetoe et al. v. Suriname
10-Sep-1993
Series C No. 15—*Reparations and Costs*

79. The Court considers it appropriate for the next of kin of the victims to be reimbursed for expenses incurred in obtaining information about them after they were killed and in searching for their bodies and taking up matters with the Surinamese authorities. In the specific case of victims Daison and Deede-Manoe

Aloeboetoe, the Commission claims equal sums to cover expenses relating to each of them. These victims were brothers. It would seem reasonable to conclude, therefore, that the next of kin took the same steps for both at one and the same time and incurred in a single outlay. The Court consequently finds it appropriate to approve a single reimbursement for the two victims.

In its brief, the Commission indicates that in all cases the expenditures were made by the mother of each victim. For lack of proof to the contrary, the reimbursement shall be paid to these persons.

80.   The Commission's brief states that the victims were stripped of some of their assets and belongings at the time of their detention. However, it does not present a claim in this regard and the Court will therefore refrain from analyzing this issue.

Bulacio vs. Argentina

18-Sep-2003

Series C No. 100—*Merits, Reparations, and Costs*

100.   Despite the fact that compensation for future medical expenses was not included in the requests made by the Inter-American Commission and the representatives, the Court finds that compensation for non-pecuniary damage should also include, based on information received, case law,[67 41] and the proven facts, an amount of money for future medical expenses of the next of kin of the victim: Lorena Beatriz Bulacio, Graciela Rosa Scavone, and María Ramona Armas de Bulacio as there is sufficient evidence to demonstrate that the suffering of the latter originated both in what happened to Walter David Bulacio and in the subsequent pattern of impunity. The Court deems it appropriate to set as compensation for said component, in fairness, the amount of US$10,000.00 (ten thousand United States dollars) to be distributed in equal parts among Lorena Beatriz Bulacio, Graciela Rosa Scavone, and María Ramona Armas de Bulacio.

Myrna Mack Chang v. Guatemala

25-Nov-2003

Series C No. 101—*Merits, Reparations, and Costs*

b) Consequential damages

253.   Taking into account the claims of the parties, the body of evidence,

the proven facts in the instant case, and its own case law, the Court finds that compensation for material damage in the instant case must also include the following:

(a) with respect to Helen Mack Chang, sister of the victim, it has been proven that, as a consequence of the extra-legal death of her sister, she undertook the task of searching for justice for over thirteen years through her active participation in the criminal proceedings to investigate the facts and to identify and punish all those responsible. Helen Mack Chang gave up her work as a consequence of the facts discussed in the instant case, established the Myrna Mack Foundation, and has spent much of her time struggling against impunity. The Court deems that Helen Mack Chang stopped receiving her customary income as a consequence of the facts, and, bearing in mind the specific circumstances of the *sub judice* case, in fairness, it sets the amount of compensation at US$25,000.00 (twenty-five thousand United States dollars);

(b) as regards the father and the daughter of the victim, it has been proven that due to the extra-legal death of Myrna Mack Chang and of the consequences stemming from this fact, they suffered various physical and psychological illnesses, for which they had to receive medical treatment. Therefore, the Court deems it pertinent to set US$3,000.00 (three thousand United States dollars) as compensation for medical expenses incurred by Yam Mack Choy and US$3,000.00 (three thousand United States dollars) for Lucrecia Hernández Mack, for this same item. Since Yam Mack Choy passed away on April 24, 1999, compensation in his favor must be paid in full to Zoila Chang Lau.

Juvenile Reeducation Institute v. Paraguay
2-Sep-2004
Series C No. 112—*Preliminary Objections, Merits, Reparations, and Costs*

b) Damnum emergens

293.   The Commission reported that the State had covered the *damnum emergens*, and the representatives did not provide evidence to support their counterclaim. The foregoing notwithstanding, the body of evidence in the present case contains various statements[211][42] demonstrating that the State did not in fact cover all the medical expenses of Francisco Ramón Adorno, or all the medical and funeral expenses of Sergio David Poletti Domínguez and Mario del Pilar Álvarez

Pérez. The State covered only a portion of those expenses. As no specific evidence was offered concerning the supposed expenses, this Court deems it appropriate to grant in equity the sum of US$1,000.00 (one thousand United States dollars) to the next of kin of each of the above-named former inmates.

Chaparro Álvarez and Lapo Íñiguez v. Ecuador
21-Nov-2007
Series C No. 170—*Preliminary Objections, Merits, Reparations, and Costs*

a) Pecuniary damage arising from the seizure and deposit of property

228.   The Court has established in this judgment that Mr. Chaparro's shares in the Plumavit factory had a financial value that formed part of his patrimony. This financial value was directly related to the value of the company itself. The State's actions, namely the unsatisfactory administration of the property, the delay in the return of the factory, the return of property in a deteriorated condition, and the misplacement of certain property, entailed an impediment to the use and enjoyment of those shares because the value of the company decreased considerably, and this had an impact on Mr. Chaparro's patrimony.

229.   Based on the above, the Court finds that the State must compensate Mr. Chaparro for the financial losses that the depreciation in the value of the company caused him.

230.   However, the only evidence presented on this aspect is the expert appraisal of Yasmín Kuri González. Regarding this appraisal, the representatives made general references without defining the amount they are requesting as compensation for this concept and without developing a logical reasoning that would allow the Court to assess the damage effectively caused. Indeed, the representatives submitted this evidence, but did not develop a line of reasoning about the expert appraisal that would allow this Court to understand it and assess it with the rest of the body of evidence using sound criticism. The Court finds that this reasoning was required in the instant case in order to clarify on what basis the Court could consider this expert's opinions to be valid. This is particularly necessary with regard to expert appraisals based on technical expertise outside that of the Court.

231.   What the Court can observe from the expert appraisal in question is that the expert made a calculation of the "operating flows" from 1997 to 2006, and the result was more than five million United States dollars.[157][43] No explanation has

been presented to the Court of why the calculations had to be up until 2006. As established previously, the factory was returned in 2002. Furthermore, during the public hearing held in this case, Mr. Chaparro stated that he sold the factory,[158][44] but he did not specify the exact date of the sale or the price obtained, and how much was remitted to him. Furthermore, when submitting the helpful evidence requested by the President, the representatives advised that the factory still exists and that Mr. Chaparro is the owner of almost all the shares; in other words, the factory has not been sold.[159][45] Lastly, the percentage of the company's losses that could be attributed to Mr. Chaparro, in relation to the number of shares he possessed at the time of his arrest, has not been explained.

232.   Based on the above, and given the complexity of determining the commercial value of a company, which could include, *inter alia*, its capital, the financial situation, the capital investments, property and securities, assets and liabilities, operating flows, market potential and other matters, the Court considers that an arbitration tribunal should determine the percentage of loss that Mr. Chaparro suffered as a result of the State's seizure and deposit of the Plumavit factory. Despite the foregoing, the Court takes into account that the said factory had been in operation for several years and that, at the time of the facts, had received some loans to improve its productivity; consequently, the Court establishes, based on the equity principle, the amount of US$150,000.00 (one hundred fifty thousand United States dollars) as value of this loss. If the amount decided during the arbitration procedure is greater than the amount ordered by the Court in this judgment, the State may deduct from the victim the amount established by this Court, based on the equity principle. If the amount decided in the arbitration procedure is less, the victim shall keep the US$150,000.00 (one hundred fifty thousand United States dollars) established in this judgment. The amount established by the Court shall be delivered to Mr. Chaparro within one year at the latest of notification of this judgment.

233.   The arbitration procedure indicated in the preceding paragraph must be of an independent nature, be carried out in the city in which Mr. Chaparro resides, and be pursuant to the applicable domestic laws concerning arbitration, provided that it does not contradict the decisions in this judgment. The procedure must commence within six months of notification of this judgment. The arbitration tribunal shall be composed of three arbitrators. The State and Mr. Chaparro shall each select an arbitrator. The third arbitrator shall be selected by mutual agreement between the State and Mr. Chaparro. If, within two months of notification of this judgment, the parties have not reached an agreement, the third arbitrator shall be selected by mutual agreement by the arbitrator selected by the State and the

one selected by Mr. Chaparro. If the two arbitrators do not reach an agreement within the following two months, the State and Mr. Chaparro's representatives must present this Court with a slate of no less than two and no more than three candidates. The Court will decide the third arbitrator from among the candidates proposed by the parties. The amount decided by the arbitration tribunal must be delivered to Mr. Chaparro within one year of notification of its decision, at the latest.

234.   With regard to Mr. Lapo, the only possession that was seized from him was his vehicle, which has not yet been returned. According to the expert appraisal made by Kuri González, the value of the vehicle was calculated "based on the valuation of the Guayas Transit Commission at US$1,150.09 [(one thousand one hundred fifty United States dollars and nine cents)]."[160 46] The State has not contested this conclusion and the Court finds it reasonable. Therefore, it decides that the State must deliver the amount of US$1,150.09 (one thousand one hundred and fifty United States dollars and nine cents) to Mr. Lapo, as compensation for the loss of his vehicle. This amount must be delivered within one year of notification of this judgment.

Salvador Chiriboga *v.* Ecuador
6-May-2008
Series C No. 179—*Preliminary Objection and Merits*

2.   In accordance with the facts invoked by the Inter-American Commission, between December 1974 and September 1977, Salvador Chiriboga siblings inherited from their father, Guillermo Salvador Tobar, a property of 60 hectares, designated under number 108 of lot "Batán de Merizalde". On May 13, 1991 the then Municipal Council of Quito (hereinafter, the "Municipal Council" or the "Council"), nowadays called Council of the Metropolitan District of Quito, declared the property of Salvador Chiriboga siblings to be of public utility in order to expropriate and take immediate possession of the property belonging to Salvador Chiriboga siblings. As a consequence of said municipal decision, Salvador Chiriboga siblings have filed several lawsuits and remedies with State's authorities in order to resolve the declaration of public utility, as well as to claim for a just compensation according to the terms of the Ecuadorian legislation and the American Convention.

5.   With regard to the expropriation proceedings, the Commission argued that 15 years have passed since the Municipal Council declared the property to

be of public use and that the possession of the property in order to expropriate it occurred on July 10, 1997, without a court order determining the final value of the property and ordering the payment of a compensation. The Commission further alleged that during that period of time, the Municipality has been in possession of the property. As a consequence, Salvador Chiriboga siblings have been barred from exercising their property rights, especially the right to use and enjoy the property they are entitled to as rightful owners. Furthermore, the Commission pointed out that according to the American Convention and the domestic legislation, the Court's order establishing the effective condemnation must be issued within a short period of time.

7.   Finally, the Commission requested the Court to declare that the State is responsible for the violation of the rights enshrined in Articles 8 (Right to a Fair Trial), 21 (Right to Private Property) and 25 (Right to Judicial Protection) of the American Convention, in relation to Articles 1(1) (Obligation to Respect Rights) and 2 (Domestic Legal Effects) therein, to the detriment of Maria Salvador Chiriboga. Furthermore, it requested the Court to order the State to adopt certain measures for reparations, as well as the payment of costs and expenses.

10.   On May 17, 2007, the State[1647] submitted a brief containing a preliminary objection, the answer to the complaint and observations to the brief of requests and arguments (hereinafter, the "answer to the complaint"). The State alleged that it did not violate Article 21 (Right to Property) of the Convention and that the deprivation of the property belonging to Salvador Chiriboga siblings was conducted "[...] in accordance with the American Convention, it was compatible to the right to property because it was based on reasons of public utility and social interest and was subjected to the payment of a fair compensation". In relation to the alleged violation of Article 8 (Right to a Fair Trial) of the Convention, to the detriment of Salvador Chiriboga siblings, the State indicated that the alleged victim initiated several proceedings, both before constitutional as well as administrative courts "[...] which have been decided by resolutions taking into account the factual, legal and consequential elements, [... and that] in the condemnation proceeding initiated by the Municipality of Quito, it is clearly the desire of the alleged victim's representatives to delay the trial". In relation to Article 25 (Right to Judicial Protection) of the Convention, the State argued that it has never hindered the access to the legal resources available at the domestic administrative courts in order to challenge, on countless occasions, the administrative orders that turned out to be prejudicial to the interests of Salvador Chiriboga siblings.

11.   With regard to the possible reparations, the State pointed out that it will only accept to pay "[…] a compensation […] fixed within the framework of the domestic or Inter-American proceedings and based on an impartial assessment, according to the real value of the property, regardless of the current increase in value, if it adjust to the reality of the country, and the annual municipal budget and above all, under the terms of [...] of the Court [...]". Lastly, it challenged the sums of money requested by the representatives as compensation, costs and expenses. In said brief, the State also raised a preliminary objection based on non-exhaustion of domestic remedies.

135.   Therefore:

THE COURT,

DECLARES:

Six votes against two, that:

2. The State violated the right to property in relation to Article 21(2) of the American Convention on Human Rights, in relation to the rights to judicial guarantees and protection enshrined in Articles 8(1) and 25(1) of the American Convention, all of that in relation to Article 1(1) therein, to the detriment of María Salvador Chiriboga [. . .]. Judge Quiroga Medina and Judge *ad hoc* Rodríguez Pinzón partially disagree with regard to the violation of Article 25(1) of the American Convention on Human Rights.

AND DECIDES:

Unanimously that:

4. The determination of the amount and payment of the just compensation for the expropriation of the legally protected interests, as well as any other measure intended to repair the violations declared in this Judgment, be made by common consent between the State and the representatives, within the term of six months as from notice of this Judgment [. . .].

Unanimously that:

5. The Court reserves the authority to verify whether such agreement is made in accordance with the American Convention on Human Rights and proceed accordingly. In case no agreement is reached, the Court shall determine the corresponding reparations and the costs and expenses, continuing with the corresponding procedure [. . .]. Judge Quiroga Medina and Judge *ad hoc* Rodríguez Pinzón advised the Court of their Partially Dissenting Opinions and Judge Ventura Robles advised the Court of his Concurring Opinion, which accompany this Judgment.

03-Mar.-11

Series C, No. 222

Reparations and Costs

C) Compensation

1. Pecuniary damage

86.   The Court has developed the standard of pecuniary damage and the situations in which it must be compensated. [137][48] However, in the present case the Tribunal will not analyze the pecuniary damage from the traditional perspective of consequential damages or loss of income, but derived from the non-compliance with the payment of a just compensation, which has resulted in an infringement of the victim's material condition and has led to the State's international responsibility.

87.   The representatives requested that as reparation "for the appropriation of the property [...] belonging [to María Salvador Chiriboga] the State be ordered to pay the interest accrued during the time in which it has not paid the just compensation." Based on the aforementioned, in its brief on reparations, the representatives demanded the payment of an annual compound interest computed as of the declaration of public interest dated May 13, 1991. Thus, they indicated that the State owed, up to May 13, 2009, the total amount of US$56,730,723.69 (fifty six million seven hundred and thirty thousand seven hundred and twenty three United States dollars and sixty nine cents) for that purpose. They added that if payment of the just compensation is made after that date, an estimate of the interest must be calculated under the same formula until payment is actually made, and that the interest rate will be the Libor rate in force in the month of May of each year.

88.   Later, in the public hearing the representatives stated that there were several agreements between them and the State, one of these being that an amount should be set in regard to interest, but that there was still a discrepancy regarding the interest rate and the date as of which it should be computed. They requested that the Court establish said standards. In this sense, they reiterated to the Tribunal that "it should define a formula for compound interests as has been done by several arbitration courts in matters of investments." [138][49] They added that "this is the same principle that should be applied, since even though the matter in dispute is not directly about investments, we cannot deny that it refers to an identical right, namely the right to property."

89.   On its part, at the public hearing the State expressed that on July 16, 1996, the Municipality of the Metropolitan District of Quito filed the complaint

before the "Court of Justice"[139][50] in order to obtain the occupation order, and that the Ecuadorian legislation states in these cases, that in order to be able to occupy the property, the just price must be recorded. According to the State, in this case, along with the filing of the complaint for expropriation it recorded the amount of the just price in the Municipality's opinion at that time at 225,990,625.00 Sucres.[140][51] This means that the Municipality has never failed to comply with its obligations, and that regarding the representatives' current expectation to receive interest, the legal actions set out by the Municipality are not being recognized, and they are trying to collect payment of an interest charge that does not correspond. Payment of interest is an additional payment, which results from not honoring an obligation. In this sense, the State provided evidence on the record that indicated and expressed that it has never wanted to diminish the agreement reached with the opposing party regarding the payment of interest, and it stated its willingness to respect it.

90.   Without detriment to the aforementioned, the State mentioned that any estimate of the interest made by the Court should be made as of the year 1997, between the 6th and 10th days of July 1997. Said date was determined by the Court in the Judgment on the Merits as the one on which the Municipality of Quito occupied the property, and not as of May 13, 1991, date of the declaration of public interest, as was requested by the representatives. Additionally, it reiterated that "acknowledging the differential initial amount sought by the victim is alien to the standard of justice."

91.   From that indicated by the representatives and the State at the public hearing, the Court observes that they agree that this Tribunal determine an interest as a consequence of the lack of payment of a just compensation for the expropriated property.[141][52] Therefore, the Tribunal will establish if the determination of the interest proceeds or not, and if it does, it will define the type of interest and the date as of which it shall be calculated.

92.   The Judgment on the Merits established that the subjective recourses or those of full jurisdiction filed by the Salvador Chiriboga brothers and the expropriation claim filed by the State were not resolved within a reasonable time period nor were they effective and that the expropriation proceedings had been arbitrary.[142][53] Additionally, the Court already ruled in said Judgment that the State has not paid the just compensation; thus it is not correct to reopen the discussion on this matter at this stage.

93.   The Court reiterates that, up to this date, the expropriation proceedings are still in process before the domestic jurisdiction, more than twelve years after they were started, and the payment of the just compensation is still pending,

despite the fact that María Salvador Chiriboga has lost possession of her property. In this sense the European Court of Human Rights has stated that the measures employed in combination with the excessive duration of the judicial action places the petitioners in a long situation of uncertainty, which worsens the damaging effects of these measures, which they have had to carry, a special burden that breaks the just balance between the demands of the public interest and the protection of the right to have property respected, [143][54] and in cases such as the present, the European Court has ordered the payment of interest calculated on the basis of a lawful rate. [144][55]

94. This Court observes that other international courts have determined, in cases of expropriation, the payment of simple[145][56] or compound[146][57] interest to repair the damage caused. For example the European Court, in matters of expropriation, has decided upon a simple interest, [147][58] while the arbitration courts in investment matters, from a commercial point of view, acknowledge that the granting of a compound interest[148][59] is justified under certain circumstances, in order to compensate in a comprehensive manner the losses suffered and grant additional protection to foreign investors within a global context.

95.　　　Additionally, the Court observes that the Organic Law of the Municipal Regimen in force, approved on December 5, 2005, in its Article 244[149][60] states that in cases of expropriation, besides the price determined either conventionally or judicially, the owner will be paid an additional five per cent as the affectation price.

96. On the other hand, it is also important to mention that the Ecuadorian Civil Code in force, approved on July 12, 2005 in Articles 1573 and 1575,[150][61] establishes rules on the compensation for damages due to default and, if the obligation consists in paying an amount of money, it provides guidelines for the charging of interest. The aforementioned indicates that, according to Ecuador's domestic legislation, it is possible to determine interest based on the non-compliance of obligations.

97.　　　In the present case, the State should have, as stated in Article 21 of the Convention, paid the just compensation, and it should have done so promptly, as indicated in the Judgment on the Merits. However, this did not happen, and it resulted in the violation of Articles 21(2), 8(1), and 25(1) of the Convention. It is the State's duty to respect and guarantee the protection of the right to private property, which in the case *sub judice* has been examined by the Court from the perspective of a human right, in light of the object and purpose of the American Convention, and not in consideration of commercial or investment interests which are characteristic of courts of another nature.

98.   The representatives argued the Libor rate for the estimation of the interest and the State did not specifically object to the use of this rate as a reference. In seeking to satisfy the purpose of complying with a just compensation and the payment of the corresponding interest, it is necessary to determine the latter, in order to avoid having to submit determination to another domestic process that would delay payment. Given the aforementioned and since there is no controversy between the parties in the application of said rate, as well as because of the fact that it is considered reasonable for the specific case, this Court considers it appropriate to apply to the present case the Libor rate for the estimation of the respective interests. Additionally, this Tribunal determines that a compound interest is inapplicable, due to the nature of the present case.

99.   As a consequence, the Court establishes that the interest that must be covered due to the lack of a timely payment by the State must be estimated based on a simple interest rate, applying the Libor rate as a reference and on the amount of the just compensation set by this Tribunal [. . .].

100.   Now, in what refers to the date as of which the interest should be computed, the representatives and the State disagree in this matter (*supra* paras. 87 and 90). In this regard, this Tribunal observes that in the present case, even though the declaration of public interest is dated May 13, 1991, the dispossession of said property did not occur until the year 1997. Likewise, the Court established in its Judgment on Merits that the occupation of Mrs. Salvador Chiriboga's property by the Municipality of Quito occurred between the 7th and 10th days of July 1997.[151 62] Since it was as of that date that the victim actually lost the right to enjoy possession of the property, this Tribunal considers it adequate to establish that the estimate of the corresponding interest must be done as of July 7, 1997.[152 63]

101.   This Court concludes that the State must pay the victim the simple interest accrued according to the Libor rate on the amount of the just compensation as of July 1997 until February 2011, which amount ascends to US$ 9,435,757.80 (nine million, four hundred and thirty-five hundred thousand, seven hundred and fifty-seven United States dollars and eighty cents).

ANALYSIS AND QUESTIONS RAISED BY THE COURT'S JURISPRUDENCE

The Inter-American Court of Human Rights has awarded compensation for a broad range of direct and consequential damages resulting from violations of the Convention. Over time, the Court's requirements have evolved for requesting compensation for *dannum emergens* and providing proof of such damages. In *Velásquez Rodríguez*, the Court decided that the damages were not pleaded or proven in time for the Court's consideration and thus, denied the request. However, in subsequent cases, the Court found that certain damages were self-evident and awarded compensation without requiring further proof (e.g., future medical expenses in *Bulacio*). Similarly, in certain cases, the Court awarded *dannum emergens* compensation in equity (as in *Juvenile Reeducation Institute*).

- Do *dannum emergens* include all monetary damages (aside from loss of earnings) resulting from the violation? How closely related must the damages be to the violation to be considered *dannum emergens*?

- Which types of *dannum emergens* should be considered self-evident, and which should require specific proof as to damage and amount? What types of *dannum emergens* should be valued by expert witnesses?

- Who, aside from the victim of the violation, should be able to seek and receive compensation for *dannum emergens*?

- The Court has awarded compensation in equity in some cases where an exact amount was not proffered in evidence (e.g., *Juvenile Reeducation Institute*) or could not otherwise be specifically determined (e.g., *Chaparro* Álvarez *and Lapo* Íñiguez). What other factors should the Court consider to potentially order compensation in equity and on what bases should the compensation amount be determined?

C.   LIFE PLAN ("PROYECTO DE VIDA")

Loayza Tamayo v. Peru
27-Nov-1998
Series C No. 42—*Reparations and Costs*

144.   The victim petitioned the Court for a ruling on the compensation, which might be due to her in the form of damage to her "life plan" and enumerated a number of factors that, in her judgment, should be taken into account to establish the scope of this ahead of damages and measure its consequences.

145.   The State alleged that the request for compensation for damages to a life plan was inadmissible and noted that compensation of that nature was implicit in the other categories for which damages were sought, such as the "indirect or consequential damages" and "lost earnings." It pointed out that the victim had already been re-instated as a history and geography teacher at the Rímac National

Women's High School and that she was free to apply to have her place in the law school saved; it maintained that reinstatement at the San Martín de Porres Private University was a decision that only the organs of that institution could make. The State further argued that both the victim and the Commission had attributed the alleged damages caused to Ms. Loayza-Tamayo to her detention. Its contention was, however, that the State could not be held liable for those damages inasmuch as the authorities that intervened in the case in question did so in the legitimate exercise of their authority under the laws in force at that time.

146.   The State's argument that the authorities acted in the legitimate exercise of their authority is inadmissible. The Court itself has established that the acts of which Ms. Loayza-Tamayo was victim were violations of provisions of the American Convention.

147.   The head of damages to a victim's "life plan" has been examined both in recent doctrine and case law. This notion is different from the notions of special damages and loss of earnings. It is definitely not the same as the immediate and direct harm to a victim's assets, as in the case of "indirect or consequential damages." The concept of lost earnings refers solely to the loss of future economic earnings that can be quantified by certain measurable and objective indicators. The so-called "life plan," deals with the full self-actualization of the person concerned and takes account of her calling in life, her particular circumstances, her potentialities, and her ambitions, thus permitting her to set for herself, in a reasonable manner, specific goals, and to attain those goals.

148.   The concept of a "life plan" is akin to the concept of personal fulfillment, which in turn is based on the options that an individual may have for leading his life and achieving the goal that he sets for himself. Strictly speaking, those options are the manifestation and guarantee of freedom. An individual can hardly be described as truly free if he does not have options to pursue in life and to carry that life to its natural conclusion. Those options, in themselves, have an important existential value. Hence, their elimination or curtailment objectively abridges freedom and constitutes the loss of a valuable asset, a loss that this Court cannot disregard.

149.   In the case under study, while the outcome was neither certain nor inevitable, it was a plausible situation—not merely possible—within the likelihood given the subject's natural and foreseeable development, a development that was disrupted and upset by events that violated her human rights. Those events radically alter the course in which her life was on, introduce new and hostile circumstances, and upset the kinds of plans and projects that a person makes

based on the everyday circumstances in which one's life unfolds and on one's own aptitudes to carry out those plans with a likelihood of success.

150.   It is reasonable to maintain, therefore, that acts that violate rights seriously obstruct and impair the accomplishment of an anticipated and expected result and thereby substantially alter the individual's development. In other words, the damage to the "life plan," understood as an expectation that is both reasonable and attainable in practice, implies the loss or severe diminution, in a manner that is irreparable or reparable only with great difficulty, of a person's prospects for self-development. Thus, a person's life is altered by factors that, although extraneous to him, are unfairly and arbitrarily thrust upon him in violation of laws in effect and in a breach of the trust that the person had in government organs duty-bound to protect him and to provide him with the security needed to exercise his rights and to satisfy his legitimate interests.

151.   For all these reasons, the claim seeking reparation, to the extent possible and by appropriate means, for the loss of options that the wrongful acts caused to the victim is entirely admissible. The reparation is thus closer to what it should be in order to satisfy the exigencies of justice: complete redress of the wrongful injury. In other words, it more closely approximates the ideal of *restitutio in integrum*.

152.   It is obvious that the violations committed against the victim in the instant Case prevented her from achieving her goals for personal and professional growth, goals that would have been feasible under normal circumstances. Those violations caused irreparable damage to her life, forcing her to interrupt her studies and to take up life in a foreign country far from the context in which her life had been evolving, in a state of solitude, poverty, and severe physical and psychological distress. Obviously this combination of circumstances, directly attributable to the violations that this Court examined, has seriously and probably irreparably altered the life of Ms. Loayza-Tamayo and has prevented her from achieving the personal, family, and professional goals that she had reasonably set for herself.

153.   The Court recognizes the existence of grave damage to the "life plan" of Ms. María Elena Loayza-Tamayo caused by violations of her human rights. Nevertheless, neither case law nor doctrine has evolved to the point where acknowledgment of damage to a life plan can be translated into economic terms. Hence, the Court is refraining from quantifying it. It notes, however, that the victim's recourse to international tribunals and issuance of the corresponding judgment constitute some measure of satisfaction for damages of these kinds.

154.   The condemnation represented by the material and moral damages ordered on other points of this Judgment should be some compensation for the victim for the suffering these violations have caused her; still, it would be difficult to restore or offer back to her the options for personal fulfillment of which she has been unjustly deprived.

Cantoral Benavides v. Peru
18-Aug-2000
Series C No. 69 – *Merits*

1.   The Inter-American Commission on Human Rights (hereinafter "the Commission" or "the Inter-American Commission"), in filing the application, invoked Articles 50 and 51 of the American Convention on Human Rights (hereinafter "the American Convention" or "the Convention") and Article 26 et seq. of the Rules of Procedure then in force[1 64] In filing said application, the Commission asked the Court to decide whether the State of Peru (hereinafter "the State" or "Peru") had violated the following Articles of the Convention: 1(1) (Obligation to Respect Rights); 2 (Domestic Legal Effects); 7(1) to 7(6) (Right to Personal Liberty); 5 (Right to Humane Treatment); 8(1), 8(2), 8(2)d), 8(2)f), 8.2.g), 8(3) and 8(4) (Right to a Fair Trial); and 25 (Right to Judicial Protection) and Articles 2 and 8 of the Inter-American Convention to Prevent and Punish Torture (hereinafter "Inter-American Convention Against Torture"). According to the application, these violations were suffered by Mr. Luis Alberto Cantoral-Benavides due to the unlawful deprivation of his liberty following his arbitrary detention and incarceration; cruel, inhuman, and degrading treatment; violation of the judicial guarantees; and double jeopardy based on the same facts. In its final written brief, the Commission added the alleged violation of Articles 8(2)(c), 8(5), and 9 of the American Convention, and 6 of the Inter-American Convention Against Torture.

3-Dec-2001
Series C No. 88 – *Reparations and Costs*

58.   The victim's representatives have made reference to various forms of non-pecuniary damages: the physical and mental suffering endured by the victim, the destruction of his life plan, the disintegration of the family, and the pain and suffering that the victim's mother and brothers endured.

60. It is obvious to the Court that the facts of this case dramatically altered the course that Luis Alberto Cantoral Benavides' life would otherwise have taken. The pain and suffering that those events inflicted upon him prevented the victim from fulfilling his vocation, aspirations, and potential, particularly with regard to his preparation for his chosen career and his work as a professional. All this was highly detrimental to his "life project."[47][65]

80.   The best way to restore Luis Alberto Cantoral Benavides' life plan is for the State to provide him with a fellowship for advanced or university studies to cover the costs of a degree preparing him for the profession of his choosing, and his living expenses for the duration of those studies, at a learning institution of recognized academic excellence, which the victim and the State select by mutual agreement.

Gutiérrez Soler v. Colombia
12-Sep-2005
Series C No. 132—*Merits, Reparations, and Costs*

2.   The Commission filed the application for the Court to determine whether the State had violated the rights in Articles 5(1), 5(2), and 5(4) (Right to Humane Treatment); 7(1), 7(2), 7(3), 7(4), 7(5), and 7(6) (Right to Personal Liberty); 8(1), 8(2)(d), 8(2)(e), 8(2)(g), and 8(3) (Right to a Fair Trial); and 25 (Right to Judicial Protection) of the Convention, in relation to the obligation set forth in Article 1(1) (Obligation to Respect Rights) of said treaty, to the detriment of Wilson Gutiérrez-Soler. In the application, the Commission pointed out that "the [alleged] deprivation of personal liberty and inhumane treatment of Wilson Gutiérrez-Soler was perpetrated by a State agent and a private individual (a former State agent himself) who[,] with the sufferance of government officers[,] used the means available to the Public Force to arrest the [alleged] victim and to try and exact from him a confession, using torture, for the alleged commission of a crime—in relation to which the domestic courts eventually found him innocent." With respect to local action, Mr. Gutiérrez-Soler "[allegedly] exhausted all domestic legal remedies in his pursuit of justice and relief"; his complaints were dismissed. In this respect, the Commission stated that "[t]he [alleged] impunity of those responsible and the lack of reparation ten years after the facts have not only destroyed Gutiérrez-Soler's life project and that of his family, but have also adversely impacted their safety and, in some cases, forced them into exile."

87.   The Commission argued that "the lack of redress and the fact that the

perpetrators are still unpunished destroyed Mr. Wilson Gutiérrez-Soler's life project." On the other hand, the representatives asserted that the events in the instant case changed his life "radically," rupturing "his personality and" causing the severance of "his family ties."

88.   The Court considers that the violations of Mr. Wilson Gutiérrez-Soler's rights prevented him from achieving his personal and vocational development expectations, which under normal circumstances would have been feasible. Furthermore, they caused irreparable damage to his life, forcing him to sever family ties and go abroad, in solitude, in financial distress, and physically and emotionally broken down. In Mr. Gutiérrez-Soler's own words, the consequences of torture and of the subsequent events were serious, to wit:

> my life was done with —and not just mine—my son's and my wife's as well . . .My family was lost, we lost the ties between parents and children . . . . Not only was I stripped of my self-worth, but of my family and my parents too.

Likewise, it is proven that the specific sort of torture the victim underwent not only left him physical scars, but has also permanently lowered his self-esteem and his ability to have and enjoy intimate relations of affection.

89.   Considering all of the foregoing, the Court finds that damage to Mr. Wilson Gutiérrez-Soler's "life project" has occurred as a result of the violation of his human rights. However, as in other cases,[37][66] the Court decides not to compensate for said damage financially, since the Judgment awarding damages herein contributes to compensate Mr. Wilson Gutiérrez-Soler for pecuniary and non-pecuniary damages. The complex and all-encompassing nature of damage to the "life project" calls for action securing satisfaction and guarantees of non-repetition that go beyond the financial sphere.[38][67] Notwithstanding the above, the Court considers that no form of redress could return Mr. Wilson Gutiérrez-Soler the personal fulfillment options of which he was unfairly deprived or provide him with fresh options.

ANALYSIS AND QUESTIONS RAISED BY THE COURT'S JURISPRUDENCE

The Inter-American Court of Human Rights has recognized and affirmed the concept of life plan ("proyecto de vida") in numerous cases. However, for the purposes of damages and compensation, this concept has not been fully distinguished from the categories encompassed by pecuniary and non-pecuniary damages. In fact, some scholars assert that damages to a victim's life plan are subsumed within pecuniary and non-pecuniary damages.

- In *Loayza Tamayo*, the Court defined damage to a victim's life plan as loss of their prospects for self-development, or a resulting inability to achieve personal fulfillment or self-actualization. In *Cantoral Benavides*, the Court determined that the specific harm suffered could be remedied by the provision of an academic fellowship to support the victim's self-development. In contrast, in *Gutiérrez Soler*, the Court declared that no measures of redress could restore the victim's life plan. Are the distinctions between these cases solely the result of the specific circumstances of each case?
- Would a more specific definition of life plan result in compensatory damages? How foreseeable should life plan damages be? Would this additional category of compensatory damages be beneficial?
- What specific distinctions might be drawn between *lucrum cessans* (loss of earnings) and *dannum emergens* (other direct and consequential damages) and the concept of life plan ("proyecto de vida")?
- Do all violations of human rights and freedoms result in damage to a victim's prospects for self-development, personal fulfillment, or self-actualization (i.e., to a victim's life plan)? Are all violations equally damaging to a victim's life plan?

IV.   NON-PECUNIARY DAMAGES

The Inter-American Court of Human Rights orders non-pecuniary, or moral, damages for emotional harm and pain and suffering resulting from the violation of a right or freedom protected by the Inter-American Convention on Human Rights. Again since its first decision ordering compensatory damages, in *Velásquez Rodríguez v. Honduras*, the Court has considered and ordered non-pecuniary damages, when appropriate, as fair compensation to remedy human rights violations. While non-pecuniary damages frequently are as evident as pecuniary damages, pain and suffering can be difficult to assess monetarily. As with all forms of reparations ordered, the Court considers the specific circumstances of each case to make its determinations regarding non-pecuniary damages. The following case excerpts demonstrate the Court's reasoning and the factors it has considered in arriving at its decisions regarding non-pecuniary damage.

Velásquez Rodríguez v. Honduras
21-Jul-1989
Series C No. 7 —*Reparations and Costs*

50.   The Court must now consider the question of the indemnification of the moral damages which are primarily the result of the psychological impact suffered by the family of Manfredo Velásquez because of the violation of the rights and freedoms guaranteed by the American Convention, especially by the dramatic characteristics of the involuntary disappearance of persons.

51.   The moral damages are demonstrated by expert documentary evidence and the testimony of Dr. Federico Allodi, psychiatrist and Professor of Psychology at the University of Toronto, Canada. According to his testimony, the above doctor examined the wife of Manfredo Velásquez, Mrs. Emma Guzmán Urbina de Velásquez, and his children, Héctor Ricardo, Herling Lizzett, and Nadia Waleska Velásquez. According to those examinations, they had symptoms of fright, anguish, depression, and withdrawal, all because of the disappearance of the head of the family. The Government could not disprove the existence of psychological problems that affect the family of the victim. The Court finds that the disappearance of Manfredo Velásquez produced harmful psychological impacts among his immediate family, which should be indemnified as moral damages.

52.   The Court believes the Government should pay compensation for moral damages in the amount of two hundred fifty thousand lempiras, to be paid to the wife and children of Manfredo Velásquez.

Aloeboetoe et al. v. Suriname
10-Sep-1993
Series C No. 15—*Reparations and Costs*

51.   In the instant case, the victims who died at Tjongalangapassi suffered moral damages when they were abused by an armed band that deprived them of their liberty and later killed them. The beatings received, the pain of knowing they were condemned to die for no reason whatsoever, and the torture of having to dig their own graves are all part of the moral damages suffered by the victims. In addition, the person who did not die outright had to bear the pain of his wounds being infested by maggots and of seeing the bodies of his companions being devoured by vultures.

52.   In the Court's opinion, it is clear that the victims suffered moral damages, for it is characteristic of human nature that anybody subjected to the aggression and abuse described above will experience moral suffering. The Court considers that no evidence is required to arrive at this conclusion; the acknowledgement of responsibility by Suriname suffices.

91.   As regards the reparations for moral damages, the Court believes that, bearing in mind the economic and social position of the beneficiaries, such reparations should take the form of a lump sum payment in the same amount for all the victims, with the exception of Richenel Voola, who was assigned reparation that exceeded that of the others by one third. As has already been stated, Richenel Voola was subjected to greater suffering as a result of his agony. There is nothing to indicate that there were any differences in the injuries and ill-treatment suffered by the other victims.

92.   For lack of other data and because it considers it fair, the Court has accepted the total amount claimed by the Commission for moral damages.

The amounts in Sf [Suriname florins] that the Commission claims for each victim have been adjusted by a coefficient representing the fluctuation of domestic prices in Suriname over the period in question. The value in florins was converted into dollars at the free market rate of exchange and then increased to include compensatory interest, calculated at the rate in effect on the international market. The total amount was then distributed among the victims as stipulated in the previous paragraph.

96.   The compensation fixed for the victims' heirs includes an amount that will enable the minor children to continue their education until they reach a certain age. Nevertheless, these goals will not be met merely by granting compensatory damages; it is also essential that the children be offered a school where they can receive adequate education and basic medical attention. At the present time, this is not available in several of the Saramaka villages.

Most of the children of the victims live in Gujaba, where the school and the medical dispensary have both been shut down. The Court believes that, as part of the compensation due, Suriname is under the obligation to reopen the school at Gujaba and staff it with teaching and administrative personnel to enable it to function on a permanent basis as of 1994. In addition, the necessary steps shall be taken for the medical dispensary already in place there to be made operational and reopen that same year.

El Amparo v. Venezuela
14-Sep-1996
Series C No. 28—*Reparations and Costs*

33.   The Court observes that while the Commission did rely for its calculation of moral damages on the Court's opinions in the *Velásquez Rodríguez* and *Godínez Cruz* cases in the judgments of July 21, 1989, it is also a fact that different awards were made in the judgment on reparations in the *Aloeboetoe et al.* case (US$29,070.00 for each of six families and US$38,155.00 for the seventh, in addition to other obligations to be discharged by the State).

34. The Court is of the opinion that, while case law may establish precedents, it cannot be invoked as a criterion to be universally applied; instead, each case needs to be examined individually. It should also be noted that in the present case, as in that of *Aloeboetoe et al.*, and unlike the *Velásquez Rodríguez* and *Godínez Cruz* cases, the State has acknowledged the facts and accepted responsibility.

35.   This having been said, there are numerous cases in which other international tribunals have decided that a condemnatory judgment per se constitutes adequate reparation for moral damages, as amply demonstrated by the case law of, among others, the European Court of Human Rights [citations omitted] However, it is the view of this Court that while a condemnatory judgment may in itself constitute a form of reparation and moral satisfaction, whether or not there has been recognition on the part of the State, it would not suffice in the instant case, given the extreme gravity of the violation of the right to life and of the moral suffering inflicted on the victims and their next of kin, who should be compensated on an equitable basis.

36.   As this Court has held in the past,

> [i]t is clear that the victims suffered moral damages, for it is characteristic of human nature that anybody subjected to the aggression and abuse described above will experience moral suffering. The Court considers that no evidence is required to arrive at this conclusion. (*Aloeboetoe et al. Case, Reparations*, para. 52).

37.   In the light of the above, the Court, taking all the special circumstances of the case into account, concludes that it is fair to award an indemnity of US$20,000.00 to each of the families of the deceased and to each of the survivors.

"Street Children" (Villagrán-Morales et al.) v. Guatemala
26-May-2001
Series C No. 77—*Reparations and Costs*

89.   The victims' next of kin and the Commission have referred to various types of non-pecuniary damage: the physical and mental suffering experienced by the direct victims and their families; the loss of life, considering life to be a value in itself, or an autonomous value; the destruction of the life plan of the youths who were assassinated and that of their next of kin; and the damage suffered by three of the direct victims, owing to their status as minors, by having been deprived of the special measures of protection that the State should have provided to them.

90.   Taking into consideration the different aspects of the above-mentioned damage that has been submitted as evidence by the victims' representatives and the Commission, insofar as they are pertinent and respond to the particularities of each individual case, the Court, in fairness, establishes the value of the compensation for non-pecuniary damage that must be made to each of the direct victims and their immediate next of kin, as indicated in the table that appears below (*infra* para. 93). The Court explains that, when making this calculation for non-pecuniary damage, it has also borne in mind the overall adverse conditions of abandonment endured by the five street children, who were in a high-risk situation and without any protection as regards their future.[83][68]

91.   In order to establish the compensation for non-pecuniary damage, the Court also considered:

   (a) with regard to Henry Giovanni Contreras, Julio Roberto Caal Sandoval, Federico Clemente Figueroa Túnchez, and Jovito Josué Juárez Cifuentes, that they were forcibly retained in secret, isolated from the external world, and subjected to extremely violent treatment, including severe abuse and physical and psychological torture before being assassinated;[84][69] and

   (b) with regard to Anstraum Aman Villagrán Morales, Julio Roberto Caal Sandoval, and Jovito Josué Suárez Cifuentes, that they were minors and, consequently, they were particularly vulnerable and should have been the object of special protection by the State.[85][70]

93. In accordance with the foregoing, the Court establishes the following amounts as compensation for the non-pecuniary damage suffered by the five youths who are the subject of this case, their mothers and grandmother, and their siblings who are listed in this table:

Reparation for non-pecuniary damage	
Direct victims	**Amount**
Anstraun Aman Villagrán Morales	US$ 23,000.00
Henry Giovanni Contreras	US$ 27,000.00
Julio Roberto Caal Sandoval	US$ 30,000.00
Federico Clemente Figueroa Túnchez	US$ 27,000.00
Jovito Josué Juárez Cifuentes	US$ 30,000.00
Mothers and grandmother	
Matilde Reyna Morales García	US$ 26,000.00
Ana María Contreras	US$ 26,000.00
Rosa Carlota Sandoval	US$ 26,000.00
Margarita Urbina	US$ 26,000.00
Marta Isabel Túnchez Palencia	US$ 26,000.00
Noemí Cifuentes	US$ 26,000.00
Siblings	
Reyna Dalila Villagrán Morales Lorena	US$ 3,000.00
Dianeth Villagrán Morales	US$ 3,000.00
Gerardo Adoriman Villagrán Morales	US$ 3,000.00
Mónica Renata Agreda Contreras Shirley	US$ 3,000.00
Marlen Agreda Contreras Osman Ravid	US$ 3,000.00
Agreda Contreras Guadalupe Concepción	US$ 3,000.00
Figueroa Túnchez	US$ 3,000.00
Zorayda Izabel Figueroa Túnchez	US$ 3,000.00

Juvenile Reeducation Institute v. Paraguay

2-Sep-2004

Series C No. 112—*Preliminary Objections, Merits, Reparations, and Costs*

301.   The inmates at the center endured inhuman detention conditions, which included, *inter alia,* overpopulation, violence, crowding, poor diet, lack of proper medical attention, and torture. They were confined in filthy cells, with few sanitary facilities and had little opportunity to engage in recreational activities. It was against this backdrop of inhuman detention conditions at the center that nine inmates[215][71] died and 42[216][72] were injured as a result of fires; another child[217][73] died from a bullet wound. Subsequently, two children[218][74] who had been transferred from the center to the Emboscada adult penitentiary died from wounds inflicted by a sharp instrument.

302.   This Court considers that their suffering is all the worse when one considers that the vast majority of the victims were children, and the State had special obligations regarding them, over and above those it has regarding adults.[219][75]

303.   Taking into account the various facets of the damages claimed by the Commission and the State and applying the foregoing inferences, the Court sets, in equity, the value of the compensation for non-pecuniary damages . . . based on the following parameters:

(a) in arriving at a figure for the compensation owed to the deceased inmates for the non-pecuniary damages they suffered,[220][76] the Court has considered that these victims suffered inhuman prison conditions; most of these victims were children who died violent deaths while in the custody of the State. The conditions at the center caused the children fear, anguish, desperation, and a sense of powerlessness as the situation in which they found themselves was unremitting, and in all likelihood they had no hope that their lot would change in the near term. This Court has also weighed the particularly traumatic circumstances of their deaths and the fact that the majority of the deceased did not die immediately, but instead were racked with terrible pain. In the case of the injured inmates as well,[221][77] the Court has considered the inhuman prison conditions of their internment, the severity of the injuries they sustained as a result of the fires, and that, with the major injuries they sustained, their lives were in many respects unalterably changed from the normal life they might otherwise have lived; and

(b) in determining the compensation owed to the identified next of kin of the deceased and injured inmates, whom this Court has declared to be victims, this Court must take account of the suffering that they have endured as a direct consequence of the inmates' injuries and/or deaths. These next of kin have experienced profound suffering and pain, detrimental to their mental and moral integrity. Moreover, the events that they had to endure caused them great pain and a sense of powerlessness, insecurity, grief, and frustration, which has profoundly altered their circumstances and their family and social relations, representing a serious blow to their lifestyle.

304.   For non-pecuniary damages sustained by the nine inmates who died in or as a result of the first fire, this Court awards compensation, in equity, in the amount of US$65,000.00 (sixty-five thousand United States dollars); in the cases of Benito Augusto Adorno, Héctor Ramón Vázquez, and Richard Daniel Martínez, whose deaths were not attributable to the fires, the Court orders compensation for non-material damages in the amount of US$50,000.00 (fifty thousand United States dollars).

305.   One of the criteria the Court used to compute the compensation owed to the injured former inmates was the percentage of the body that sustained burns. For these victims, the Court is awarding non-pecuniary damages, in equity, in the following amounts: US$50,000.00 (fifty thousand United States dollars) to those who sustained burns over 30% or more of their body; US$45,000.00 (forty-five thousand United States dollars) to those who sustained burns over an area ranging from 20% but less than 30%; US$40,000.00 (forty thousand United States dollars) to those who sustained burns over an area ranging from 10% but less than 20% of their body; US$30,000.00 (thirty thousand United States dollars) to those who sustained burns over an area ranging from 5% but less than 10% of their body, and US$22,000.00 to those whose burns cover less than 5% of their body. In the case of some children, the Court has already ascertained what percentage of their body sustained burns. The records appear in the body of evidence in the present case.

306.   With no information on 19 injured former inmates,[222][78] this Court assumes that they sustained burns over less than 5% of their body and assigns them the corresponding amount.

307.   As for the identified next of kin of the deceased inmates, this Court considers US$25,000.00 (twenty-five thousand United States dollars) for each parent to be an appropriate sum as compensation in equity for non-pecuniary damages. In the case of the identified next of kin of the inmates injured in or as a result of the fires, this Court considers the sum of US$15,000.00 (fifteen thousand United States dollars) to be an appropriate sum as compensation in equity for non-pecuniary damages.

Pueblo Bello Massacre *v.* Colombia
31-Jan-2006
Series C No. 140—*Merits, Reparations and Costs*

Findings of the Court

254.   Non-pecuniary damage can include the suffering and hardship caused to the direct victims and their next of kin, the harm of objects of value that are very significant to the individual, and also changes, of a non-pecuniary nature, in the living conditions of the victims. Since it is not possible to allocate a precise monetary equivalent for non-pecuniary damage, it can only be compensated in two ways in order to provide comprehensive reparation to the victims. First, by the payment of a sum of money that the Court decides by the reasonable exercise of judicial discretion and based on the principle of equity, or by means of compensation such as granting or providing specific goods or services. And, second, by acts or projects with public recognition or repercussion, such as broadcasting a message that officially condemns the human rights violations in question and makes a commitment to efforts designed to ensure it does not happen again. [257][79] Such acts have the effect of acknowledging the dignity of the victims and consoling their next of kin.

255.   As the Court has indicated in other cases, [258][80] the non-pecuniary damage inflicted on the victims is evident, because it is inherent in human nature that all those subjected to brutal acts in the context of this case experienced intense suffering, anguish, terror and insecurity, so that this damage does not have to be proved.

256.   As has been established, before being disappeared and deprived of life, the 43 persons were deprived of liberty and subjected to inhumane treatment (*supra* para. 95(33)). The next of kin of the persons disappeared and deprived of life have suffered harm as a result of their disappearance or death, owing to the lack of support from the State authorities in an effective search for the disappeared and the fear to begin or continue their own search for their family members. Since most of the victims are disappeared, their immediate family have not been able to honor their loved ones appropriately. The absence of a complete and effective investigation into the facts and the partial impunity constitute an additional source of suffering and anguish for the next of kin. All the foregoing, in addition to affecting their mental integrity, has had an impact on their social and labor relations, altered the dynamics of their families and, in some cases, jeopardized the life and physical integrity of some of the family members (*supra* para. 95(161)).

257.   With regard to the next of kin of the persons disappeared and deprived of life, the Court reiterates that the suffering caused to a victim "extends to the closest members of the family, particularly those who were in close affective contact with the victim." [259][81] In addition, the Court has presumed that the suffering or death of a person causes their children, spouse or companion, mother, father and siblings a non-pecuniary damage that need not be proved. [260][82]

258.   International case law has established repeatedly that the judgment constitutes *per se* a form of reparation. However, owing to the gravity of the facts in the instant case and the situation of partial impunity, the intensity of the suffering caused to the victims, the alterations in their living conditions, and the other consequences of a non-pecuniary nature, the Court considers it necessary to order the payment of compensation for non-pecuniary damage, based on the principle of equity, [261][83] which must be awarded as stipulated in paragraphs 236, 237 and 240 of this judgment, and in accordance with the following parameters:

(a) For each of the 37 victims disappeared and the six deprived of life, the Court established the amount of US$30,000.00 (thirty thousand United States dollars);

(b) At the time of their disappearance, three of the victims were minors: Manuel de Jesús Montes Martínez, José Encarnación Barrera Orozco and Miguel Antonio Pérez Ramos. Consequently, it can be presumed that the suffering caused by the facts of the case assumed particularly intense characteristics in their regard. Therefore, the damage referred to in the preceding paragraph must be compensated, based on equity, in each case, with the amount of US$5,000.00 (five thousand United States dollars), which will increase the amount indicated above;

(c) For the immediate next of kin of the victims, the Court considers that the corresponding damage must be compensated by payment in their favor of the amounts indicated below:

(i) US$10,000.00 (ten thousand United States dollars) in the case of the mother, father, wife or permanent companion and each child of the 37 victims disappeared;

(ii) US$8,000.00 (eight thousand United States dollars) in the case of the mother, father, wife or permanent companion and each child of the six victims deprived of life;

(iii) US$500.00 (five hundred United States dollars) in the case of each sibling of the disappeared and deprived of life, and

(iv) These amounts will be increased by the payment of US$2,000.00 (two thousand United States dollars) to Macrina

> Onelia Martínez Paternina, mother of Manuel de Jesús Montes Martínez, Dora Isabel Tuberquia Petro, companion of Genor José Arrieta Lora, Gloria de Jesús Petro Pérez, companion of Luis Miguel Salgado Berrío, and Dormelina Barba Monterrosa, companion of Andrés Manuel Perosa Jiménez, who were pregnant when the men disappeared.

259.   Based on the above, the amounts to be paid as compensation for the non-pecuniary damage caused by the violations declared in this case, in favor of the persons disappeared or deprived of life and of their next of kin, are indicated in Appendix II of this judgment.

Miguel Castro Castro Prison v. Peru

25-Nov-2006

Series C No. 160—*Merits, Reparations, and Costs*

432.   Taking into account the different violations declared by the Tribunal in the present Judgment, the Court sets, in equity, the compensations for non-pecuniary damage taking into consideration:

(a) that regarding the deceased inmates, the non-pecuniary damages suffered due to the manner in which they died within the context of the violent events of "Operative Transfer 1," which implied the illegitimate use of force, an attack of great magnitude employing weapons normally used at war, and the lack of a timely medical attention;

(b) that the deceased victim Julia Marlene Olivos Peña was tortured;

(c) that regarding the surviving inmates, the non-pecuniary damages suffered due to the violations to the right to a humane treatment within the context of the violent events of "Operative Transfer 1," which implied the illegitimate use of force, an attack of great magnitude employing weapons normally used at war, the lack of a timely medical attention to those injured, the treatments received after May 9, 1992, and during their transfers to other criminal centers and to hospitals, the treatments received in the health centers where they were transferred during the attack and once it had concluded, and the general detention conditions to which they were submitted after "Operative Transfer 1";

(d) that the Court determined that the totality of the aggressive acts and the conditions in which the State deliberately placed all inmates (those who died and those who survived) for the duration of the attack caused in them a serious psychological and emotional suffering and constituted a psychological torture for all of them;

(e) that the Court determined that the totality of the detention conditions and the treatment to which the inmates were submitted in the criminal centers to which they were transferred or relocated after the so-called "Operative Transfer 1," constituted physical and psychological torture inflicted on all of them;

(f) that the female inmates Eva Sofia Challco, Sabina Quispe Rojas, and Vicenta Genua López, at the time of the events, were 7, 8, and 5 months pregnant and that the State left the basic prenatal health needs of the first two unattended, as well as the pre- and postnatal health needs of Mrs. Quispe;

(g) that one female inmate was submitted to an alleged finger vaginal "examination", which constituted sexual rape;

(h) that six female inmates were forced to remain naked at the hospital, while watched over by armed men, which constituted sexual violence;

(i) that the next of kin of the deceased inmates were the victims of violations to Articles 8(1) and 25 of the Convention, in relation to Article 1(1) of said treaty, in connection to Articles 7(b) of the Inter-American Convention to Prevent, Punish, and Eradicate Violence Against Women and 1, 6, and 8 of the Inter-American Convention to Prevent and Punish Torture;

(j) that the Court declared that the right to humane treatment of the next of kin of the inmates stated in paragraphs 336, 337, 340, and 341 was breached due to the treatment suffered at the hands of the state agents while they were outside the criminal center between May 6 and 9, 1992, after that date when they went looking for their next of kin in hospitals and morgues, and due to the strict solitary confinement and visiting restrictions applied by the State on the inmates after the attack on the criminal center. Likewise, when declaring said breach, the Tribunal considered that said solitary confinement caused a special infringement on the inmates' children under the age of 18 during said confinement;

(k) that the remains of Mr. Francisco Aguilar Vega have not been handed over to his next of kin; and

(i) other factors that determine the seriousness of the facts indicated by the Court in Chapter IX on "the State's International Responsibility within the context of the present case."

433. Pursuant to the aforementioned, the Court sets, in equity, the following compensations for non-pecuniary damages:

(a) for each of the 41 deceased victims identified, the Court sets, in equity, the amount of US$50,000.00 (fifty thousand United States dollars or its equivalent in Peruvian currency). The State must make these payments within an 18-month period, as of the notification of the present Judgment

(b) for the next of kin of the 41 deceased victims identified, the Court considers that the corresponding damages must be compensated through the payment of the amounts stated below:

  (i) US $10,000.00 (ten thousand United States dollars or its equivalent in Peruvian currency) in the case of the father, mother, spouse, or permanent partner and of each son or daughter of the victims. In the case of these next of kin of the victim Mario Francisco Aguilar Vega, the Court sets the compensation at US$15,000.00 (fifteen thousand United States dollars or its equivalent in Peruvian currency);

  (ii) US$1,000.00 (one thousand United States dollars or its equivalent in Peruvian currency) in the case of each brother or sister of the victims. In the case of these next of kin of the victim Mario Francisco Aguilar Vega the Court sets the compensation at US$1,200.00 (one thousand two hundred United States dollars or its equivalent in Peruvian currency);

(c) regarding the surviving victims:

  (i) for each of the victims with injuries of physical or mental illnesses that imply a complete permanent handicap to work, the amount of US$20,000.00 (twenty thousand United States dollars or its equivalent in Peruvian currency);

  (ii) for each of the victims with injuries of physical or mental illnesses that imply a permanent partial handicap to work, the amount of US$12,000.00 (twelve thousand United States dollars or its equivalent in Peruvian currency);

  (iii) for each of the victims with permanent consequences due to injuries suffered that did not result in a complete or partial handicap, the amount of US$8,000.00 (eight thousand United States dollars or its equivalent in Peruvian currency);

  (iv) for each of the other surviving victims not included in any of the previously mentioned categories, the amount of US$4,000.00 (four thousand United States dollars or its equivalent in Peruvian currency);

(v) since the Tribunal does not have sufficient evidence to individually determine in which of the previous categories each of the surviving victims must be included, said determination must be made by the domestic bodies specialized in the classification of injuries and handicaps upon request of the interested parties, who must present their request within an 8-month term as of the notification of the present Judgment. Each of the victims may only be included in one of the four previous categories, which should be the one that represents the highest amount of compensation. The discrepancies regarding said determination must be solved within the domestic realm, following the corresponding national proceedings before the competent authorities, among them the domestic courts. The previous is without detriment to this Tribunal's competence to supervise compliance of the Judgment. The State must make said payments within an 18-month period as of the notification of the present Judgment;

(viii) the Court sets an additional compensation in favor of the victims Eva Challco, Sabina Quispe Rojas, and Vicenta Genua López at US $5,000.00 (five thousand United States dollars or its equivalent in Peruvian currency). The State must make said payments within an 18-month period as of the notification of the present Judgment;

(ix) the Court sets an additional compensation in favor of the victim of sexual rape, whose name is included in Appendix 2 of victims of this Judgment, which for these effects is considered part of the same, at US $30,000.00 (thirty thousand United States dollars or its equivalent in Peruvian currency). The State must make said payments within an 18-month period as of the notification of the present Judgment;

(x) the Court sets an additional compensation in favor of the six victims of sexual violence at US$10,000.00 (ten thousand United States dollars or its equivalent in Peruvian currency). The names of these victims are found in Appendix 2 of victims of this Judgment, which for these effects is considered part of the same. The State must make said payments within an 18-month period as of the notification of the present Judgment;

Saramaka People v. Suriname

28-Nov-2007

Series C No. 172—*Preliminary Objections, Merits, Reparations, and Costs*

A.1) The members of the Saramaka people as a distinct social, cultural and economic group with a special relationship with its ancestral territory

82.   Their culture is also similar to that of tribal peoples insofar as the members of the Saramaka people maintain a strong spiritual relationship with the ancestral territory[66][84] they have traditionally used and occupied. Land is more than merely a source of subsistence for them; it is also a necessary source for the continuation of the life and cultural identity of the Saramaka people.[67][85] The lands and resources of the Saramaka people are part of their social, ancestral, and spiritual essence. In this territory, the Saramaka people hunt, fish, and farm, and they gather water, plants for medicinal purposes, oils, minerals, and wood.[68][86] Their sacred sites are scattered throughout the territory, while at the same time the territory itself has a sacred value to them.[69][87] In particular, the identity of the members of the Saramaka people with the land is inextricably linked to their historical fight for freedom from slavery, called the sacred "first time."[70][88] During the public hearing in this case, Head Captain Wazen Eduards described their special relationship with the land as follows:

> The forest is like our market place; it is where we get our medicines, our medicinal plants. It is where we hunt to have meat to eat. The forest is truly our entire life. When our ancestors fled into the forest they did not carry anything with them. They learned how to live, what plants to eat, how to deal with subsistence needs once they got to the forest. It is our whole life.[71][89]

83.   Furthermore, their economy can also be characterized as tribal. According to the expert testimony of Dr. Richard Price, for example, "the very great bulk of food that Saramaka eat comes from . . . farms [and] gardens" traditionally cultivated by Saramaka women.[72][90] The men, according to Dr. Price, fish and "hunt wild pig, deer, tapir, all sorts of monkeys, different kinds of birds, everything that Saramakas eat."[73][91] Furthermore, the women gather various fruits, plants and minerals, which they use in a variety of ways, including making baskets, cooking oil, and roofs for their dwellings.[74][92]

84.   Thus, in accordance with all of the above, the Court considers that the members of the Saramaka people make up a tribal community whose social,

cultural, and economic characteristics are different from other sections of the national community, particularly because of their special relationship with their ancestral territories and because they regulate themselves, at least partially, by their own norms, customs, and/or traditions. Accordingly, the Court will now address whether and to what extent the members of the tribal peoples require special measures that guarantee the full exercise of their rights.

199.   According to the evidence submitted before the Tribunal, a considerable quantity of valuable timber was extracted from Saramaka territory without any consultation or compensation. Additionally, the evidence shows that the logging concessions awarded by the State caused significant property damage to the territory traditionally occupied and used by the Saramakas. For these reasons, and based on equitable grounds, the Court considers that the members of the Saramaka people must be compensated for the material damage directly caused by these activities in the amount of US$75,000.00 (seventy-five thousand United States dollars). This amount shall be added to the development fund.

200.   In the previous chapter the Court described the environmental damage and destruction of lands and resources traditionally used by the Saramaka people, as well as the impact it had on their property, not just as it pertains to its subsistence resources, but also with regards to the spiritual connection the Saramaka people have with their territory. Furthermore, there is evidence that demonstrates the suffering and distress that the members of the Saramaka people have endured as a result of the long and ongoing struggle for the legal recognition of their right to the territory they have traditionally used and occupied for centuries, as well as their frustration with a domestic legal system that does not protect them against violations of said right, all of which constitutes a denigration of their basic cultural and spiritual values. The Court considers that the immaterial damage caused to the Saramaka people by these alterations to the very fabric of their society entitles them to a just compensation.

201.   For these reasons, and on equitable grounds, the Court hereby orders the State to allocate US$600,000.00 (six hundred thousand United States dollars) for a community development fund created and established for the benefit of the members of the Saramaka people in their traditional territory. Such fund will serve to finance educational, housing, agricultural, and health projects, as well as provide electricity and drinking water, if necessary, for the benefit of the Saramaka people. The State must allocate said amount for this development fund in accordance with paragraph 208 of the present Judgment.

Xákmok Kásek Indigenous Community v. Paraguay
24-Aug-2010
Series C No. 214—*Merits, Reparations, and Costs*

2.   The application relates to the State's alleged international responsibility for the alleged failure to ensure the right of the Xákmok Kásek Indigenous Community (hereinafter "the Xákmok Kásek Indigenous Community," "the Xákmok Kásek Community," "the Indigenous Community," or "the Community") and its members' (hereinafter "the members of the Community") to their ancestral property, because the actions concerning the territorial claims of the Community were being processed since 1990 "and had not yet been decided satisfactorily." According to the Commission, "[t]his has meant that, not only has it been impossible for the Community to access the property and take possession of their territory, but also, owing to the characteristics of the Community, that it has been kept in a vulnerable situation with regard to food, medicine, and sanitation that continuously threatens the Community's integrity and the survival of its members."

3.   The Commission asked the Court to declare the State responsible for the violation of the rights established in Articles 3 (Right to Juridical Personality), 4 (Right to Life), 8(1) (Right to Judicial Guarantees), 19 (Rights of the Child), 21 (Right to Property), and 25 (Right to Judicial Protection) of the Convention, in relation to the obligations established in Articles 1(1) (Obligation to Respect Rights) and 2 (Domestic Legal Effects) of the Convention. The Commission asked the Court to order the State to adopt specific measures of reparation. The State and the representatives of the alleged victims were notified of the application on August 17, 2009.

65.   According to the evidence provided, the Xákmok Kásek Community is composed of 66 families with a total of 268 individuals;[93] [58] it was created from members of the Sanapaná villages who traditionally inhabited and roamed the area subsequently occupied by the Salazar Ranch, and members of the Enxet village located there who gave their name, which means "many little parrots,"[94] [59] to the Community, as well as by the Dermott family, of Enxet descent, who arrived in the area in 1947.[95] [60]

66.   When the indigenous people from different villages gathered near the core of the Salazar Ranch, which was close to the place called Xákmok Kásek, they gradually began to intermingle. Between 1953[96] [61] and March 2008, the Community's main settlement was in the core of the Salazar Ranch, at Km. 340

of the Trans-Chaco Highway, in the Pozo Colorado district, President Hayes department, in the western region of the Chaco.[97] [62]

67.   On December 28, 1990,[98] [63] the Community's leaders filed an administrative action before the Rural Welfare Institute (IBR) (currently Land and Rural Development Institute (INDERT), hereinafter "IBR" or "INDERT"), in order to recover their traditional lands under the provisions of Law No. 904/81 the "Indigenous Communities Statute."[99] [64]

68.   The Community is claiming an area of 10,700 hectares, which forms part of its traditional territory, located within the Salazar Ranch, on the outskirts of an area known as Retiro Primero or Mompey Sensap in the language of the Community.[100] [65] Although it forms part of the Community's ancestral territory, the Community's main settlement until early 2008 (*supra* para. 66) was not part of the area of 10,700 hectares claimed.

69.   When the claim was filed, the land in question formed part of a farm owned by Eaton y Cía. S.A.[101] [66] Towards the end of 2002, part of the territory claimed (3,293 hectares) was acquired by the Chortitzer Komitee Mennonite Cooperative.[102] [67] Consequently, the land claimed by the Community is currently the property of Eaton y Cía. S.A. and the Chortitzer Komitee Mennonite Cooperative.[103] [68]

70.   Following the failure of the administrative action, the leaders of the Community went directly to the Congress of the Republic on June 23, 1999, to request the expropriation of the lands claimed.[104] [69]

71.   In view of this request, the owner of the property presented a report to Congress stating that it was not necessary to expropriate the lands claimed, because "the heart of the ranch [was] established on that part of the land, [and that] land was available adjoining the area claimed."[105] [70]

72.   On November 16, 2000, the Paraguayan Senate rejected the bill to expropriate the land claimed by the Community.[106] [71]

73. According to the INDI President, society in general "opposes ceding to the claims of the indigenous peoples in this way," and "historically, the national Congress has opposed expropriations."[107] [72]

74.   The life of the members of the Community within the Salazar Ranch was conditioned by restrictions on the use of the land because the lands they occupied were privately owned. In particular, the members of the Community were prohibited from growing crops or possessing livestock.[108] [73] However, although they were settled on a small portion of their traditional territory, they roamed their lands[109] [74] and carried out certain activities such as hunting, even though this was difficult.[110] [75] Furthermore, many members of the Community worked on the Salazar Ranch.[111] [76]

75.   However, according to the testimony given before this Court, in recent years the members of the Community faced even more restrictions to their way of life and their mobility within the Salazar Ranch. Several deponents related that hunting had been prohibited completely;[112] [77] the landowner had hired private security guards to control their entrances, exits and movements,[113] [78] and they were unable to practice activities such as fishing and gathering food.[114] [79]

76.   In view of these difficulties, on April 16, 2005, the leaders of the Nepoxen, Saria, Tajamar Kabayu and Kenaten Communities, all of Angaité origin (hereinafter "the Angaité communities") agreed to cede 1,500 hectares to the members of the Xákmok Kásek Community.[115] [80] The INDI had restored 15,113 hectares to those communities in 1997.[116] [81] In September 2005, the Community leaders asked the INDI to grant title to this portion of land to the Community.[117] [82] Subsequently, when accepting the title for this portion of land, the members of the Community "reaffirmed [their] determination to continue the struggle to reclaim [their] remaining territory; that is, a total of 10,700 hectares."[118] [83]

77.   On February 25, 2008, due to the increase in difficulties on the Salazar Ranch, the members of the Community moved and settled on the 1,500 hectares ceded by the Angaité communities. This new settlement was called "25 de Febrero,"[119] [84] and is outside the lands claimed.[120] [85]

78.   To date, title to the "25 de Febrero" lands, where they are currently settled, has not been granted to the Xákmok Kásek Community.

79.   Upon moving from their old settlement, some members of the Community separated from it and moved to other communities.[121] [86]

6.2.   Non-pecuniary damage

321.   When establishing the non-pecuniary damage, the Court will assess the special meaning that land has for indigenous peoples in general and for the Xákmok Kásek Community in particular. This means that any denial of the enjoyment or exercise of property rights harms values that are very significant to the members of those peoples, who run the risk of losing or suffering irreparable harm to their life and identity and to the cultural heritage to be passed on to future generations.

322.   The Court also takes into consideration that the State committed itself "[to] the integral development of this Community by the design and execution of projects for the collective use of the property awarded, with either national or international funding."

323.   Based on the above and as it has in previous cases,[314] [122] the Court

considers it appropriate to order, in equity, that the State create a community development fund as compensation for the non-pecuniary damage that the members of the Community have suffered. . . . The State must allocate the sum of US$700,000.00 (seven hundred thousand United States dollars) to this fund, which must be used to implement educational, housing, nutritional, and health projects, as well as to provide drinking water and to build sanitation infrastructure, for the benefit of the members of the Community. These projects must be decided by an implementation committee, described below, and must be completed within two years of the delivery of the lands to the members of the Community.

324.   The committee mentioned in the preceding paragraph will be responsible for determining how the development fund is implemented and must be established within six months of the delivery of the lands to the members of the Community, with three members: a representative of the indigenous Community, a representative of the State, and a third member appointed by mutual agreement between the victims and the State. If the State and the representatives fail to reach agreement regarding the members of the implementation committee within the said time frame, the Court will decide.

325.   Moreover, in light of the conclusions reached in the chapter of this judgment on Article 4(1) of the Convention, the Court considers it appropriate, in accordance with the equity principle, and based on a prudent assessment of the non-pecuniary damage, that the State pay the sum of US$260,000.00 (two hundred and sixty thousand United States dollars) to the leaders of the Xákmok Kásek Community. This compensation for non-pecuniary damage for the members of the Community who died must be made available to the said leaders of the Community within one year of notification of this judgment, so that, in accordance with their customs and traditions, they may distribute the amount that corresponds to each family member of those who died or invest the money as the Community sees fit, in keeping with its own decision-making procedures.

Salvador Chiriboga v. Ecuador
03-Mar-2011
Series C No. 222—*Reparations and Costs*

2.   Non-pecuniary damage

105.   The Court has developed in its jurisprudence the standard of non-pecuniary damage and has established that it includes "both the suffering and grief caused to the direct victim and her next of kin, the damage to values very

important to the people, as well as the alterations, of a non-pecuniary nature, in the living conditions of the victim or their family.[153][123]

106.   The representatives expressed that in the present case the victim "has experienced a lot of concern [...] since she found herself in a situation of complete insecurity for several five-year periods with regard to the fate of her assets (and that of her family), due to the lack of resolution of the different judicial proceedings regarding her property." They requested the amount of US$25,000.00 (twenty-five thousand United States dollars) for the standard of non-pecuniary damages, as well as to repair the violation to the rights acknowledged in Articles 8(1) and 25 of the Convention.

107.   On its part, the State expressed that "it is aware that a violation to fundamental rights entails a moral damage; however, not all violations result in the same grave effects." The State considers that, even though human rights are interdependent and hierarchically of an equal value and importance, it cannot be considered that a violation as grave as an extrajudicial execution or torture deserves a monetary reparation of equal value for the standard of non-pecuniary damage as a violation to private property and due process, as this would delegitimize international justice and would seriously damage the credibility of the Inter-American system."

108.   The Commission considered that the non-pecuniary damage is evident, since the victim has been appealing to the State for more than "sixteen" years without obtaining a final resolution until now.

109.   The Court observes that Mrs. Salvador Chiriboga stated at the public hearing that the facts of the case have had a very strong impact on her, which has affected her health. [154][124] Likewise, Susana Salvador Chiriboga, in her statement rendered before a public notary, stated that "[her] mother has preferred to continue with the claims, despite her health, so that justice can be served." [155][125] On her part, the witness Guadalupe Jessica Salvador Chiriboga emphasized the fact that her mother has had to overcome heavy emotional pressure, which has affected her health. [156][126]

110.   Regarding the aforementioned, the State indicated that Mrs. Guadalupe Jessica Salvador Chiriboga "mentioned emotional aspects that deserve respect, but that are not relevant for the effects of this case, and the same thing has occurred with the other family members that have offered their statements as if it were a family of limited resources and whose health has deteriorated as a consequence of the municipal action, which is very far from the truth."

111.   The Court reintroduces that stated in the Judgment on the Merits, [157][127]

in the sense that Mrs. Salvador Chiriboga is in a state of juridical uncertainty as a result of the delay in the proceedings, since she has not been able to effectively exercise her right to property, since it has been occupied by the Municipality of Quito for more than a decade, without a decision being reached regarding who is the rightful owner of the property. A denial of justice has occurred since a final judgment determining the amount of the just compensation for the property has not been reached, which has resulted in an ineffective and arbitrary expropriation proceeding. Said situation persists today and has caused a disproportionate burden to the detriment of the victim and to the detriment of the just balance. [158][128]

112.   This Tribunal's jurisprudence has repeatedly stated that a judgment constitutes *per se* a form of reparation. [159][129]   However, in consideration of that stated, the circumstances of the case *sub judice,* and of the violation declared in the Judgment on the Merits of Articles 21(2), 8(1), and 25(1) of the Convention to the detriment of the victim, this Court considers it appropriate to determine the payment of a compensation, in equity, [160][130] in the amount of US$10,000.00 (ten thousand United States dollars) in favor of Mrs. María Salvador Chiriboga for the standard of non-pecuniary damages.

113. The State must make the payment of the compensation for the standard of non-pecuniary damages directly to the beneficiary within a one-year term computed as of the notification of the present Judgment.

Río Negro Massacres v. Guatemala
4-Sept-2012
Series C No. 250—*Preliminary objection, merits, reparations and costs*

I.   Introduction of the Case and Purpose of the Dispute

1.   On November 30, 2010, in keeping with the provisions of Articles 51 and 61 of the American Convention and Article 35 of the Court's Rules of Procedure, the Inter-American Commission on Human Rights (hereinafter "the Inter-American Commission" or "the Commission") submitted to the jurisdiction of the Court the case of the Río Negro Massacres with regard to the Republic of Guatemala (hereinafter "the State" or "Guatemala"). This case originated in the petition lodged by the *Asociación para el Desarrollo Integral de las Víctimas de la Violencia en las Verapaces* (hereinafter "ADIVIMA") on July 19, 2005. The Inter-American Commission approved Admissibility Report No. 13/08 on March 5, 2008, and, under Article 50 of the Convention, issued Merits Report No. 86/10

on July 14, 2010, with a series of recommendations to the State.[2][131] The Merits Report was notified to Guatemala on July 30, 2010, and the State was granted two months to report on compliance with the recommendations. On October 4, 2010, the State requested a one-month extension to submit information on compliance with the recommendations made by the Commission. This extension was granted on October 30, 2010, and the Commission ordered the State to submit information by November 20, 2010, at the latest. However, the State did not submit the necessary information and, consequently, the Commission submitted the case to the Court "owing to the State's failure to comply with the recommendations and the resulting need to obtain justice in the case." The Commission appointed Commissioner Dinah Shelton and the then Executive Secretary, Santiago A. Canton, as delegates, and Deputy Executive Secretary Elizabeth Abi-Mershed, and Karla I. Quintana Osuna and Isabel Madariaga Cuneo, lawyers of the Executive Secretariat, as legal advisors.

2.   According to the Inter-American Commission, this case deals with "the destruction of the Mayan community of Río Negro by means of a series of massacres perpetrated by the Guatemalan Army and members of the Civil Self-defense Patrols in 1980 and 1982; the persecution and elimination of its members and the subsequent violations directed against the survivors, including the failure to investigate the said events. In particular, the Commission submits this case due to the denial of justice ever since the acts were perpetrated, and the consequent impunity that persists to this day." In addition, the Commission indicated that "the facts reported to the Court include, among others, those relating to the forced disappearances, forced displacement, and violations of the personal integrity of the next of kin and survivors, the destruction of the community's social fabric, the failure to identify the persons executed and disappeared [...], the consequent failure to bury them in keeping with Mayan traditions, the impossibility of the survivors returning to their lands, the lack of protection for children, accusations of being 'guerrillas, the social base of the guerrillas, internal enemies and subversives,' discrimination, as well as the [alleged] failure to conduct an impartial and effective investigation into the multiple violations that occurred during and after the massacres." The Commission also alleged that the facts of this case "[...] fit within a more general context of massacres in Guatemala that were planned by State agents as part of a 'scorched earth' policy aimed by the Guatemalan State against the Mayan people, who were characterized as the 'internal enemy,' in a context of discrimination and racism [...]."

3.   Based on the above, the Inter-American Commission asked the Court to

declare the international responsibility of the State of Guatemala for the alleged violation of the rights recognized in the following articles of the American Convention: 3 (Right to Juridical Personality), 4 (Right to Life), 5 (Right to Humane Treatment), 6 (Freedom from Slavery), 7 (Right to Personal Liberty), 8 (Right to a Fair Trial), 11 (Right to Privacy), 12 (Freedom of Conscience and Religion), 16 (Freedom of Association), 17 (Rights of the Family), 19 (Rights of the Child), 21 (Right to Property), 22 (Freedom of Movement and Residence), 24 (Right to Equal Protection) and 25 (Right to Judicial Protection), in relation to the general obligation to respect and ensure human rights established in Article 1(1) of this instrument, to the detriment of the members of the Río Negro community. In addition, it asked the Court to declare that the State had failed to comply with the obligations established in Articles I of the Convention on Forced Disappearance of Persons (hereinafter "Convention on Forced Disappearance"); 1, 6 and 8 of the Inter-American Convention to Prevent and Punish Torture (hereinafter "Convention against Torture"), and 7(b) of the Inter-American Convention on the Prevention, Punishment, and Eradication of Violence against Women "Convention of Belem do Pará." In addition, the Inter-American Commission asked the Court to order the State to provide specific measures of reparation.

XIV. Reparations

D. Compensations for pecuniary and non-pecuniary damage

D.1. Compensation granted under the National Reparations Program

297.   The State asked that some of the victims who had been provided with reparation under the National Reparations Program be considered "duly compensated." The State also indicated its willingness to "provide financial redress" to the victims of this case who had not been compensated previously. During the public hearing the State reiterated its willingness to provide reparation to the victims who had not been compensated; however, it indicated that it would do so "includ[ing them] under the reparations items of the National Reparations Program."

298.   The Commission asked the Court to order the State to "[m]ake adequate reparation for the human rights violations declared in the [merits] report both in the form of pecuniary and non-pecuniary damage, including just compensation." In addition, it appreciated the measures taken by the State to implement the National Reparations Program (*supra* para. 300), under which compensation had been granted to some of the victims in the instant case. However, according to the Commission, "this program does not guarantee that [... the victims of human rights violations] will receive reparation in a manner consistent with inter-American

standards." Thus, it requested that, "once the receipt of certain compensatory amounts by some of the victims [under the PNR] has been proved, [the Court] take them into account when ordering compensation so that they can be subtracted from the final amount ordered [...] for the victims who are in the same situation."

299.   Regarding the list forwarded by the State of 102 persons or family units to whom reparations have presumably been awarded already under the PNR (*infra* para. 300), the representatives indicated that: (a) some of the individuals mentioned are not victims of the Río Negro massacres and were not individualized as presumed victims in this case; (b) others are victims and have already received a certain amount as compensation, and (c) others are victims but have not received any compensation as yet. The representatives also indicated that the National Reparations Program only awards reparations to some categories of victims; for example, it does not offer reparations to victims of violations of the rights to judicial protection and guarantees; and the program stipulates "that the maximum amount granted to each family unit will be of Q44,000.00, irrespective of the number of victims in the family, and this amount must therefore be divided among the different beneficiaries [...]." They also stated that reparations "of an individual and financial nature" could not be considered "integral" reparation.

300.   The Court observes, first, that the State has expressed its willingness to provide financial reparations to the victims of this case in keeping with the reparation items of the National Reparations Program. In addition, the State had forwarded with its answering brief a list of 102 people or family units who have apparently received financial reparations under the PNR and a copy of the pertinent administrative case files. For their part, the representatives recognized that some of the individuals on this list are victims in the instant case and have already received compensation under the said program.

301. In this regard, the Court recalls that under Article 63(1) of the American Convention, it must ensure that the consequences of the human rights violations declared in this Judgment are repaired, and must order the payment of just compensation to the injured party, in accordance with international standards and its consistent case law on this matter.

302.   The Court observes that the said National Reparations Program establishes:

> A maximum amount of financial reparation of forty-four thousand quetzales in cases in which the family unit has more than one fatal victim of extrajudicial execution, forced disappearance, or death during a massacre; this amount shall also be granted to the survivors of torture

or rape when, in addition to themselves, there are also another or other fatal victims in the same family unit.[365] [132]

303.   The foregoing reveals that the differences between the parties stem from the standards or criteria used by the National Reparations Program to calculate or allocate the compensatory amounts to the victims. The Court takes note that the State has a program of reparations under which it has already proceeded to compensate some of the victims of the massacres in this case.

304.   Based on the provisions of Article 63(1) of the American Convention, the Court will now order the measures required to repair the pecuniary and non-pecuniary damage arising from the violations declared in the preceding chapters. Nevertheless, the amounts that have already been awarded to the victims in this case at the domestic level under the PNR must be recognized as part of the reparation due to them and subtracted from the amounts established by the Court in this Judgment for compensation (*infra* para. 309). At the stage of monitoring compliance, the State must provide proof of the effective delivery of the amounts ordered under the said program.

Santo Domingo Massacre v. Colombia
30-Nov-2012
Series C No. 259— *Preliminary Objections, Merits and Reparations*

VIII. Reparations
   D. Compensation
   D.2 Considerations of the Court
334.   In this case, the Court notes that the next of kin of those who died in Santo Domingo received reparation under the Colombian contentious administrative proceeding (*supra* paras. 124 and *ff.*). Thus, 107 relatives of 16 of the 17 presumed victims who were killed[462] [133] have received compensation under the contentious administrative jurisdiction.[463] [134] These next of kin obtained reparation after signing a conciliation agreement with the Ministry of Defense that was endorsed by the Council of State. [464] [135] In addition, it appears that 5 family members have not received compensation under the contentious administrative jurisdiction for the death of their next of kin, even though they have exhausted this remedy. [465] [136]

335.   As regards those who were injured by the bombardment, 11 of these 27 victims received compensation under the Colombian contentious administrative jurisdiction. Some of them also received compensation as next of kin of those who died. [466] [137] In addition, two of the injured victims were not compensated,

even though they had recourse to the contentious administrative jurisdiction. [467] [138] There is no evidence whether the remaining 14 injured victims had recourse to this jurisdiction. [468] [139] Regarding the next of kin of the injured victims, with the exception of six family members of Amalio Neite González, [469] [140] none of them received compensation under the contentious administrative jurisdiction.

336.   Taking into account that the contentious courts have established reparations in this case based on what the victims claimed and even conciliated, and in keeping with the principle of complementarity, the Court finds that it is not appropriate to order additional monetary reparations, for either pecuniary or non-pecuniary damage in favor of the next of kin of the victims who died, or of those injured during the events, who have already received reparation under the domestic system of justice.

337.   Nevertheless, the Court must determine the situation of the injured victims (*supra* para. 335), as well as of five family members of two deceased victims, [470] [141] and the next of kin of the injured victims, who did not have recourse to the domestic contentious-administrative jurisdiction. In this regard, the Court finds that the State must grant and execute, within one year and using a prompt domestic mechanism, the pertinent compensation and indemnities for pecuniary and non-pecuniary damage, if appropriate, which must be established based on the objective, reasonable and effective criteria of the Colombian contentious-administrative jurisdiction. The next of kin of victims who consider that they are beneficiaries of the provisions of this paragraph should approach the corresponding State authorities within three months at the latest of notification of this Judgment.

338.   The preceding decision (*supra* para. 337) does not affect the next of kin of victims who were not petitioners, who have not been represented in the proceedings before the Commission and the Court, and who have not been included as victims or injured parties in this Judgment, insofar as it does not preclude any actions that they might file at the domestic level.

Rivera v. Peru

26- Nov-2013

Series C No. 274—*Preliminary Objections, Merits, Reparations and Costs*

I. Introduction of the Case and Purpose of the Dispute

1.   On June 10, 2012, the Inter-American Commission on Human Rights (hereinafter "the Inter-American Commission" or "the Commission") submitted to the jurisdiction of the Court (hereinafter "submission brief") the case of

Jeremías Osorio Rivera and others v. the Republic of Peru (hereinafter "the State" or "Peru"), indicating that:

(a) Jeremías Osorio Rivera had been detained by a Peruvian Army patrol in the province of Cajatambo, department of Lima, on April 28, 1991, and subsequently forcibly disappeared in a context of armed conflict, in which enforced disappearance had allegedly been used systematically by members of the State's armed forces; (b) Jeremías Osorio Rivera had been subject to alleged acts of torture during his transfer by members of the Cajatambo Counter-subversive Base on April 30, 1991;

(c) the soldiers had not provided information on his whereabouts and, subsequently, disseminated false information on this, and

(d) to date, "more than 20 years after the [presumed] victim's enforced disappearance, and with the entire truth about the events still not known, the domestic criminal proceedings ha[d] not provided an effective remedy to determine the fate of the [presumed] victim, or to ensure the rights of access to justice and to the truth through the investigation and eventual punishment of those responsible."

286.   International case law has established repeatedly that the judgment may constitute *per se* a form of reparation.[400][142] Nevertheless, in its case law, the Court has developed the concept of non-pecuniary damage and has established that this "may include the suffering and afflictions caused to the direct victim and his next of kin, the impairment of values that are of great significance to the individual, and also the changes of a non-pecuniary nature in the living conditions of the victim or his family."[401][143]

287.   Bearing in mind the circumstances of this case, the violations committed, the different degrees of suffering caused and experienced, the time that has elapsed, the denial of justice, and also the changes in the living conditions of some family members, the proven violations of the personal integrity of the victim's family, and the other consequences of a non-pecuniary nature they suffered, the Court will now establish, in equity, the compensation for non-pecuniary damage in favor of the victims.

288.   First, the Court considers that the circumstances that surrounded the detention and subsequent disappearance of Jeremías Osorio Rivera were such that they caused profound fear and suffering. In previous cases,[402][144] the Inter-American Court has found that similar circumstances had caused the victim serious non-pecuniary harm that had to be assessed in its full dimension when establishing compensation for this concept. In light of these criteria, the Court considers that Jeremías Osorio Rivera should be compensated for non-pecuniary damage and

orders, in equity, the payment of US$80,000.00 (eighty thousand United States dollars). Half this amount must be delivered to Santa Fe Gaitán Calderón, and the other half must be shared equally among the children of Jeremías Osorio Rivera, namely: Edith Laritza Osorio Gaytán, Neida Rocío Osorio Gaitán, Vannesa Judith Osorio Gaitán and Jersy Jeremías Osorio Gaitán.

289.   Second, the Court finds that Santa Fe Gaitán Calderón, Edith Laritza Osorio Gaytán, Neida Rocío Osorio Gaitán, Vannesa Judith Osorio Gaitán and Jersy Jeremías Osorio Gaitán have experienced great suffering or their life projects were affected as a result of the enforced disappearance of Jeremías Osorio Rivera. Consequently, the Court establishes, in equity, the sum of US$45,000.00 (forty-five thousand United States dollars), for non-pecuniary damage, in favor of Santa Fe Gaitán Calderón, and of each child of Jeremías Osorio Rivera, namely: Edith Laritza Osorio Gaytán, Neida Rocío Osorio Gaitán, Vannesa Judith Osorio Gaitán and Jersy Jeremías Osorio Gaitán.

290.   Lastly, considering the effects on their personal integrity suffered to different degrees as a result of the facts of this case, the Court establishes, in equity, the sum of US$20,000.00 (twenty thousand United States dollars) for Juana Rivera Lozano, and US$10,000.00 (ten thousand United States dollars) for each of the following siblings of Jeremías Osorio Rivera: Epifanía Alejandrina, Elena Máxima, Adelaida, Silvia, Mario and Efraín, all with the surnames Osorio Rivera. In addition, the Court establishes, in equity, the sum of US$45,000.00 (forty-five thousand United States dollars) for Porfirio Osorio Rivera, who has been the main promoter of the search for justice for the disappearance of his brother, Jeremías Osorio Rivera.

Rodríguez Vera et al. ("the Disappeared from the Palace of Justice") v. Colombia
14-Nov-2014
Series C No. 287—*Preliminary Objections, Merits, Reparations and Costs*

I. Introduction of the Case and Purpose of the Dispute

1.   On February 9, 2012, in accordance with Articles 51 and 61 of the American Convention and Article 35 of the Court's Rules of Procedure, the Inter-American Commission on Human Rights (hereinafter "the Inter-American Commission" or "the Commission") submitted the case entitled *Carlos Augusto Rodríguez Vera et al. (Palace of Justice) v. the Republic of Colombia* (hereinafter "the State" or "Colombia") to the jurisdiction of the Inter-American Court.

According to the Commission the facts of this case occurred in the context of the events known as the taking and retaking of the Palace of Justice in Bogota, which took place on November 6 and 7, 1985. In particular, the case relates to the presumed forced disappearance of Carlos Augusto Rodríguez Vera, Cristina del Pilar Guarín Cortés, David Suspes Celis, Bernardo Beltrán Hernández, Héctor Jaime Beltrán Fuentes, Gloria Stella Lizarazo, Luz Mary Portela León, Norma Constanza Esguerra Forero, Lucy Amparo Oviedo Bonilla, Gloria Anzola de Lanao, Ana Rosa Castiblanco Torres and Irma Franco Pineda during the operation to retake the building. The case also relates to the presumed disappearance and subsequent execution of Justice Carlos Horacio Urán Rojas, as well as to the presumed detention and torture of Yolanda Santodomingo Albericci, Eduardo Matson Ospino, Orlando Quijano and José Vicente Rubiano Galvis, and to the alleged failure of the courts to clarify all these events and to punish all those responsible.

XIV. Reparations

E. Compensation

E.4) Considerations of the Court

E.4.1) Pecuniary damage

593.   This Court recognizes and assesses positively the efforts made by Colombia in relation to its obligation to make reparation in this case. The Court recalls that, if domestic mechanisms exist to determine forms of reparation, these procedures and results must be taken into account (*supra* para. 548). Thus, this Court finds it necessary to analyze whether the contentious-administrative courts ruled on the full scope of the State responsibility included in this case,[893][145] and also to determine whether the compensation awarded meets the criteria of being objective, reasonable and effective to make adequate reparation for the violations of the rights recognized in the Convention that have been declared by this Court.[894][146]

594.   In this regard, the Court notes that there are some differences of opinion in relation to the compensation awarded at the domestic level and the compensation that this Court usually awards in cases such as this one. The Colombian contentious-administrative jurisdiction does not grant compensation to persons who are disappeared or deceased, and compensation for "loss of earnings" is only awarded if the family members who depended on the disappeared or deceased victim apply for it.[895][147] Under this criterion, compensation was not awarded for the loss of earnings of the disappeared victim to any of the next of kin of Cristina del Pilar Guarín Cortés, Bernardo Beltrán Hernández, Irma Franco Pineda and Luz Mary Portela León.[896][148] Also, in the case of Irma Franco Pineda, the Council of State indicated that it was not in order to grant compensation for

loss of earnings to her family members because "the loss of earnings or assistance resulting from unlawful activities such as those to which the person disappeared was dedicated does not constitute a source of compensation." [897] [149]

595. The Court emphasizes that the award of compensation for pecuniary damage in the contentious-administrative jurisdiction was made based on criteria that, although distinct, are objective and reasonable, so that the Court finds that, in keeping with the principle of complementarity on which the inter-American jurisdiction is based, [898] [150] it is not in order for the Court to order additional compensation for pecuniary damage in the cases in which this compensation has already been awarded by the contentious-administrative jurisdiction. [899] [151]

ANALYSIS AND QUESTIONS RAISED BY THE COURT'S JURISPRUDENCE

In determining non-pecuniary damages, the Inter-American Court of Human Rights has stated the difficulty in placing a precise monetary value on loss of life, violations of integrity, and the unalterable changes that occur to victims when their rights are violated. Nevertheless, as the Court affirms throughout its jurisprudence, psychological harm and suffering, the impact of a disappearance or killing upon next of kin, and the pain of torture, sexual violence and other extreme violence is evident and need not be proven. As demonstrated in the above case excerpts, the Court considers the circumstances of each case individually; and although the Court's case law provides precedent, there is no universal application of precedent to determine appropriate non-pecuniary compensation. In some cases the Court has attempted to distinguish certain objective factors in making its determinations regarding non-pecuniary compensation. These factors have included relative levels of suffering between victims in the same case (as in *Aloeboetoe et al.*), percentages of burns sustained over the victims' bodies (as in *Juvenile Reeducation Institute*), and partial or complete disabilities (as in *Miguel Castro Castro Prison*). The Court has also taken into consideration the vulnerability of particular victims or groups of victims, and the special obligations that States owe to children.

- Non-pecuniary damages are, by their nature, difficult to quantify and assess monetarily. Are there certain objective factors that the Court could consider?
- Should non-pecuniary compensation depend upon the type and egregiousness of the violation, or the impact upon the victim or their next of kin, or upon other factors?

- What types of vulnerabilities should the Court factor into its determinations of non-pecuniary compensation?
- What distinctions, if any, should the Court make in awarding non-pecuniary compensation to individual victims in contrast to groups of victims?
- In its judgments, the Court has affirmed that moral damages are evident and need not be proven. Are there moral damages that would need to be proven (e.g., pain and suffering experienced by someone not generally considered next of kin)? What expertise might be required to prove such moral damages?
- Are there human rights violations that do not lead to moral damages?

V.   PUNITIVE DAMAGES

In several cases, the Inter-American Court of Human Rights has considered the question of ordering punitive damages. Despite some debate reflected in concurring opinions, to date the Court majority has held that the term "fair compensation" as used in Article 63 of the American Convention on Human Rights does not contemplate punitive damages. In several opinions, the Court has stressed that it does not serve a penal function; rather that its competence is to provide reparations to address damages resulting from violations of rights and freedoms protected by the American Convention. Nevertheless, some scholars have asserted that the question of punitive damages may arise again as law and justice mechanisms continue to evolve. The following case excerpts demonstrate the Court's reasoning in not ordering punitive damages.

Velásquez Rodríguez v. Honduras
21-Jul-1989
Series C No. 7—*Reparations and Costs*

37.   The attorneys also request the payment by the Government of punitive damages as part of the indemnity, because this case involved extremely serious violations of human rights.

38.   The expression "fair compensation," used in Article 63(1) of the Convention to refer to a part of the reparation and to the "injured party," is compensatory and not punitive. Although some domestic courts, particularly the

Anglo-American, award damages in amounts meant to deter or to serve as an example, this principle is not applicable in international law at this time.

39.   Because of the foregoing, the Court believes, then, that the fair compensation, described as "compensatory" in the judgment on the merits of July 29, 1988, includes reparation to the family of the victim of the material and moral damages they suffered because of the involuntary disappearance of Manfredo Velásquez.

Garrido and Baigorria v. Argentina
27-Aug-1998
Series C No. 39—*Reparations and Costs*

43.   In certain passages of the submissions filed by the victims' families, they seek indemnification that would go beyond the realm of compensation for damages caused, and into the punitive realm. At the January 20, 1998 hearing, for example, the representative of the victims' relatives demanded "exemplary damages." Such functions are not in the nature of this Court and are not within its power. The Inter-American Court is not a penal court and, in this particular matter, its competence is to determine the reparations that States that have violated the Convention must make. As the word suggests, reparation is achieved through measures that serve to 'repair' the effects of the violation committed. Their quality and their amount depend on the damage done both at the material and at the moral levels. Reparations are not meant to enrich or impoverish the victim or his heirs (*Cf. del Ferrocarril de la Bahía de Delagoa* Case, La Fontaine, Pasicrisie Internationale, Berne, 1902, p. 406).

44.   In the cases against Honduras (*Velásquez Rodríguez* Case, Compensatory Damages, supra 40, para. 38, and *Godínez Cruz* Case, Compensatory Damages, *supra* 40, para. 36), the Court held that the expression "fair compensation" used in Article 63(1) of the Convention is "compensatory and not punitive" and that international law does not, at this time, use the principle of compensation "to deter or to serve as an example." Also, in the *Fairén Garbi and Solís Corrales* Case, this Court found that "the objective of international human rights law is not to punish those individuals who are guilty of violations, but rather to protect the victims and to provide for the reparation of damages" (*Fairén Garbi and Solís Corrales* Case, Judgment of March 15, 1989. Series C No. 6, para 136). The Court finds no reason to deviate from these precedents in the instant case.

ANALYSIS AND QUESTIONS RAISED BY THE COURT'S JURISPRUDENCE

To date, the Inter-American Court of Human Rights has determined that its judgments properly include compensation for damages, but not punitive damages, because international human rights law includes the reparation of damages suffered by victims, but not the punishment of perpetrators of the violations.

- In *Velásquez Rodríguez*, the Inter-American Court of Human Rights declared that "[a]lthough some domestic courts, particularly the Anglo-American, award damages in amounts meant to deter or to serve as an example, *this principle is not applicable in international law at this time*."[152] Does this statement reflect the Court's understanding of the evolving nature of international law and the possibility of future decisions that award punitive damages?
- Should punitive damages be awarded in cases involving human rights violations? If so, what criteria should be utilized to determine whether the case warrants punitive damages?
- Is the role of the Court simply to rule on cases involving alleged violations of human rights and freedoms, or is it also to prevent and deter future violations? Are judgments finding human rights violations and awarding compensatory damages sufficient to deter future violations?
- Do non-pecuniary, or moral, damages serve any purpose similar to punitive damages?

VI. CONDITIONS FOR PAYMENTS

Frequently, the Inter-American Court of Human Rights orders that payment of damages be made within a certain reasonable time period and it has developed procedural mechanisms to monitor compliance with its orders. Additionally, in certain cases, the Court has determined that damages must be paid to victims according to particular conditions. As demonstrated by the following case excerpts, these conditions are specific to the circumstances of each case.

Aloeboetoe et al. v. Suriname
10-Sep-1993
Series C No. 15—*Reparations and Costs*

99.   In order to comply with the monetary compensation fixed by this judgment, the Government shall deposit the sum of US$453,102.00 (four hundred fifty-three thousand one hundred two dollars) before April 1, 1994, in the *Surinaamse Trustmaatschappij N.V.* (Suritrust), Gravenstraat 32, in the city of Paramaribo.

The Government may also fulfill this obligation by depositing the equivalent amount in Dutch Florins. The rate of exchange used to determine the equivalent value shall be the selling rate for the United States dollar and the Dutch Florin quoted on the New York market on the day before the date of payment.

100.   With the funds received, Suritrust shall set up trust funds in dollars for the beneficiaries listed, under the most favorable conditions consistent with banking practice. Any deceased beneficiaries shall be replaced by their heirs.

Two trust funds shall be established, one on behalf of the minor children and the other on behalf of the adult beneficiaries.

A Foundation (hereinafter "the Foundation") . . . shall serve as trustee.

101.   The trust fund for the minor children shall be set up with the compensation payable to all those unmarried beneficiaries who have still not reached the age of 21.

This trust fund shall continue to operate until such time as the last of the beneficiaries comes of age or marries. As each of the minor beneficiaries meets those conditions, their contributions shall become subject to the provisions governing the trust fund for the adult beneficiaries.

102.   The adult beneficiaries may withdraw up to 25% (twenty-five percent) of the sum due to them at the time that the Government of Suriname makes the deposit. The trust fund for the adults shall be set up with the remaining funds. The duration of the trust fund shall be a minimum of three and a maximum of 17 years; semi-annual withdrawals shall be permitted. The Foundation may set up a different system in special circumstances.

103.   The Court hereby orders the creation of a Foundation, with a view to providing the beneficiaries with the opportunity of obtaining the best returns for the sums received in reparation. The Foundation, a non-profit organization, shall be established in the city of Paramaribo, the capital of Suriname, and shall be composed of the following persons, who have already accepted their appointments and shall carry out their functions *ad honorem*:

Albert Jozef Brahim
Ilse Labadie
John C. de Miranda
Antonius H. te Dorsthorst
John Kent
Rodney R. Vrede
Armand Ronald Tjong A Hung.

104. The Court expresses its appreciation to the persons who have agreed to participate in the Foundation, as a means of contributing to a true and effective protection of human rights in the Americas.

105. At a plenary meeting, the members of the Foundation shall, with the collaboration of the Executive Secretariat of the Court, define their organization, statutes, and by-laws, as well as the operational structure of the trust funds. The Foundation shall transmit these documents to the Court after final approval.

The role of the Foundation shall be to act as trustee of the funds deposited in Suritrust and to advise the beneficiaries as to the allocation of the reparations received or of the income they obtain from the trust funds.

106. The Foundation shall provide advice to the beneficiaries. Although the children of the victims are among the principal beneficiaries, this fact does not release their mothers, or their guardians in whose charge they may be, from the obligation of providing them with assistance, food, clothing, and education free of charge. The Foundation shall try to ensure that the compensation received by the minor children of the victims be used to cover subsequent study expenses, or else to create a small capital when they begin to work or get married, and that it only be used for ordinary expenses when grave problems of health or family finances require it.

107. For the operating expenses of the Foundation, the Government of Suriname shall, within 30 days of its establishment, make a one-time contribution in the amount of US$4,000 (four thousand dollars) or its equivalent in local currency at the selling rate of exchange in force on the free market at the time of such payment.

108. Suriname shall not be permitted to restrict or tax the activities of the Foundation or the operation of the trust funds beyond current levels, nor shall it modify any conditions currently in force nor interfere in the Foundation's decisions, except in ways that would be favorable to it.

Bulacio vs. Argentina

18-Sep-2003

Series C No. 100—*Merits, Reparations, and Costs*

157.   To comply with the instant Judgment, the State must pay the compensations and reimbursement of legal costs and expenses within six months from the date it receives notice of the instant Judgment.

158.   Pursuant to its case law,[109][153] the State can fulfill its pecuniary obligations by payment in United States dollars or an equivalent amount in Argentinean currency, using for this calculation the exchange rate between both currencies in the New York Exchange, in the United States of America, the day before the payment.

159.   Payment of the amount for pecuniary and non-pecuniary damages, as well as legal costs and expenses set forth in the instant Judgment, cannot be subject to currently existing taxes or levies or to any decreed in the future. In addition, if the State were to be in arrears, it must pay interest on the amount owed, according to the interest rate for arrearages in the Argentinean banking system. Finally, if for any reason it was not possible for the beneficiaries to collect the respective payments within twelve months, the State must deposit the respective amounts in the name of said beneficiaries in an account or certificate of deposit, at a solid financial institution, in United States dollars or their equivalent in Argentinean currency, and under the most favorable conditions allowed by banking laws and practices. If after ten years the payment has not been claimed, the amount will return to the State together with the interest accrued.

160.   With respect to the compensation ordered in favor of the children Tamara Florencia and Matías Emanuel Bulacio, the State must deposit the amounts in their name in an investment in a solid Argentinean banking institution, in United States dollars or their equivalent in Argentinean currency, within six months time, and under the most favorable financial conditions allowed by banking laws and practices while they are minors. If after five years from when said persons attain majority the compensation has not been claimed, the capital and interest earned will be distributed proportionally among the other beneficiaries of the reparations.

ANALYSIS AND QUESTIONS RAISED BY THE COURT'S JURISPRUDENCE

Following the well-established principle that reparations must address the specific circumstances of each case, the Inter-American Court of Human Rights has declared that, in some cases, compensation must be made under certain conditions.

- Are conditions on payment of compensation reflective of certain types of violations, or the vulnerability of victims, or other considerations?
- Should the Court always place conditions on payment of compensation, or only in particular cases?

VII. COSTS & EXPENSES

Because the costs and expenses victims incur to bring their case before the Inter-American human rights system are a direct consequence of the violation itself, the Inter-American Court of Human Rights typically orders States to reimburse victims for those costs and expenses as part of the reparations order. Such orders are common to civil code legal systems, and are also often ordered in common law systems. The following case excerpts demonstrate the Court's reasoning and considerations for such orders.

El Amparo v. Venezuela
14-Sep-1996
Series C No. 28—*Reparations and Costs*

21.   Although no proof of the expenses incurred has been presented, the Court considers it fair to grant an indemnity of US$2,000.00 to each of the families of the deceased victims and to each of the survivors, as compensation for the expenses they incurred in their various representations to the national authorities.
63.   With reference to the Commission's request to be awarded costs, the Court has stated on previous occasions that the Commission cannot demand that expenses incurred as a result of its own internal work structure be reimbursed through the assessment of costs.

Ivcher Bronstein v. Peru

06-Feb-2001

Series C No. 74—*Merits, Reparations, and Costs*

172.   On January 8, 2001, at the request of the Court, the Commission submitted arguments concerning the expenses and costs of this case and attached the evidentiary documents that it considered justified those expenses. These arguments are summarized below:

   (a) the expenses incurred in litigating this case at the national and international level were assumed by Mr. Ivcher from his personal accounts, and by his company, Productos Paraíso del Perú. These expenses include professional fees, office maintenance, payment of telephone services and communications, and medical attention for Rosario Lam;

   (b) *Productos Paraíso del Perú* incurred expenses of US$3,142,346.00 (three million one hundred and forty-two thousand three hundred and forty-six United States dollars) and 9,687,498.00 (nine million six hundred and eighty-seven thousand four hundred and ninety-eight) Peruvian soles, which is equal to US$3,104,967.00 (three million one hundred four thousand nine hundred sixty-seven United States dollars). Mr. Ivcher incurred expenses of US$1,557,513.00 (one million five hundred fifty-seven thousand five hundred thirteen United States dollars). This gives a total amount disbursed by Mr. Ivcher's company and from his personal accounts of US$7,804,826.00 (seven million eight hundred four thousand eight hundred twenty-six United States dollars); and

   (c) the amounts mentioned do not include the "remaining expenses" that Mr. Ivcher has had to incur, or the fees corresponding to this case and the actions filed in Lima, which amount to US$1,000,000.00 (one million United States dollars), or the fees corresponding to the reparations stage before the Inter-American Court.

188.   With regard to the expenses and costs in this case, the Court considers that it is appropriate to recall, as has been stated on other occasions,[115][154] that it must evaluate prudently the specific scope of the costs, taking into account not only their justification and the circumstances of the concrete case, but also the nature of the international jurisdiction for the protection of human rights and the characteristics of the respective proceeding, which has its own distinctive character that differs from that of other proceedings of a national or international nature, and observing the standards established by this Court in the resolution of other cases.

189.   To this effect, the Court considers that it is fair to grant the victim the amount of US$50,000.00 (fifty thousand United States dollars) in reimbursement of the costs and expenses incurred in the domestic and the international jurisdictions.

Cesti Hurtado v. Peru
29-Sep-1999
Series C No. 56 – *Merits*

2.   The Commission declared that the purpose of the application is that the Court should decide whether, in the case of Gustavo Adolfo Cesti Hurtado, the State violated Articles 5(1), (2), and (3) (Right to Humane Treatment); 7(1), (2), (3), and (6) (Right to Personal Liberty); 8(1) and 8(2) (Right to a Fair Trial); 11 (Right to Privacy); 21 (Right to Property); 25(1) and 25(2)(a) and 25(2)(c) (Right to Judicial Protection); and 51(2), all the foregoing in relation to Article 1 (Obligation to Respect Rights) and Article 2 (Domestic Legal Effects) of the Convention. Although the Court had been requested to pronounce judgment on a possible violation by the State of Article 17 (Rights of the Family), the Commission did not refer to this point again, nor did it provide any arguments, consequently the Court did not pronounce judgment in this respect.

3.   According to the Commission's submission, as a result of the violation of the rights indicated, Gustavo Cesti Hurtado was included in an action under the military justice system, in the course of which he was arrested, deprived of his liberty, and sentenced, despite the existence of a final decision in a habeas corpus action ordering that the alleged victim should be separated from the proceedings under the military justice system and that his freedom should be respected.

31-May-01
Series C No. 78—*Reparations and Costs*

68.   In his brief on reparations, the victim requested the Inter-American Court to approve the following amounts for reimbursement of costs and expenses:

(a)   US$34,939.00 (thirty-four thousand nine hundred thirty-nine United States dollars) for the fees of Javier Valle Riestra at the start of the proceeding under the military justice system;

(b)   US$94,892.24 (ninety-four thousand eight hundred ninety-two United

States dollars and twenty-four cents) and US$10,202.60 (ten thousand two hundred two United States dollars and sixty cents) for fees that have already been paid to Alberto Borea Odría and Miguel Borea Odría, respectively, for assuming his defense in the trial under the military justice system in Peru and for the application before the Inter-American Commission and the Inter-American Court;

(c) US$210,000.00 (two hundred ten thousand United States dollars) for pending fees for Alberto Borea Odría, for the proceedings at the merits and reparation stages before the Inter-American Court;

(d) US$45,000.00 (forty-five thousand United States dollars) for retaining a lawyer's office in the United States to provide legal advice;

(e) US$46,512.18 (forty-six thousand five hundred twelve United States dollars and eighteen cents) for air travel, owing to 12 journeys to the seat of the Court in San José, Costa Rica, and the seat of the Commission in Washington, D.C., by his lawyers and family, and also travel by other lawyers to different places to further his case; and

(f) US$55,836.56 (fifty-five thousand eight hundred thirty-six United States dollars and fifty-six cents) for expenses arising from these journeys, such as airport taxes, taxis, hotels, food, telephone calls, faxes, and translators.

Mr. Cesti stated that, although the Commission was formally responsible for submitting the case to the Court, the advice of the victim's lawyer was fundamental in order to process the case appropriately. Moreover, he requested the Court to determine Mr. Borea's fees for the reparation stage, since the latter had agreed that his fees would depend on the respective results and suggested that this amount should be no less than 15% of the amount that the Court ordered Peru to pay as reparation. Lastly, he observed that the disbursements he would have to make for the presence of his lawyer and the parties in San José, Costa Rica, were still pending.

69.   In its brief on reparations, the Commission requested the Court to order the State to pay Mr. Cesti the expenses that he had incurred at both the domestic level and before the inter-American system; to this end, it referred to the justification and the estimate of expenses that the victim had submitted in the instant case.

70.   In this respect, the State indicated that:

(a) the Commission represented Mr. Cesti's interests before the Inter-American Court, and its involvement was compensated by the contributions of the countries that form part of the Convention, which included Peru, and that the other expenses incurred in the said proceeding should be paid for by the interested parties;

(b) the amounts proposed by the victim, including those that he was attempting to collect for his defense before the military justice system, "[did] not harmonize with the table of fees established in [Peru]" and that it did not consider it viable for a *supra*national instance to establish the costs of an internal judicial proceeding; and

(c) the expenses for travel and per diems include travel to countries that have no relation to the proceeding in the instant case.

71.   It should be understood that costs and expenses are included in the concept of reparation established in Article 63(1) of the American Convention, because the measures taken by the victim or victims, their successors or their representatives to have access to international justice imply financial disbursements and commitments that should be compensated when a guilty verdict is delivered. Therefore, this Court considers that the costs referred to in Article 55(1) of the Rules of Procedure also include the various necessary and reasonable expenses that the victims make in order to have access to the inter-American system for the protection of human rights, and the fees of those who provide legal assistance are included among the expenses. Evidently, this only refers to the necessary and reasonable expenses, according to the particularities of the case, which are effectively incurred or defrayed by the victim or his representatives.[29][155] Owing to the foregoing, the Court must prudently assess the scope of the costs and expenses, bearing in mind the circumstances of the specific case, the nature of the international jurisdiction for the protection of human rights, and the characteristics of the respective proceeding, which are unique and differ from those of other proceedings of a national or international nature.[30][156]

72.   The disbursements that are strictly necessary to attend to the matters before the jurisdictional organs at the national and international level are included in the concept of expenses and costs.[31][157] With regard to professional fees, it is necessary to bear in mind the characteristics inherent in the international human rights proceeding, in which decisions are adopted on the violations of such rights, without examining all the extremes of the implications of these violations, which could involve questions of earnings related to the said fees, which are legitimate in themselves, but unrelated to the specific issue of the protection of human rights. Therefore, the Court must decide these claims with restraint. If the Court proceeded otherwise, international human rights litigation would be denatured. Consequently, the Court must apply criteria of equity in these cases.

73. To that end, the Court considers that it is fair to grant the victim the sum

of US$20,000.00 (twenty thousand United States dollars), in reimbursement of the expenses and costs generated in the domestic jurisdiction and in the inter-American jurisdiction; this amount includes professional fees.[32][158]

Juan Humberto Sánchez v. Honduras
7–Jun-2003
Series C No. 99—*Preliminary Objections, Merits, Reparations, and Costs*

1.   The Commission argued in its application that Juan Humberto Sánchez, the alleged victim, had twice been detained by the Honduran armed forces "for his alleged ties with the *Frente Farabundo Martí para la Liberación Nacional* (FMLN) of El Salvador."

The first capture allegedly took place on July 10, 1992, and was carried out by members of the Tenth Infantry Battalion of Marcala, La Paz, under the command of second lieutenant Ángel Belisario Hernández González, and [Mr. Sánchez] was released on July 11, 1992 for lack of evidence on the charges for which he was detained.

The second capture was allegedly carried out by members of the First Battalion of Territorial Forces at his home during the night of that same day, July 11. On July 22, 1992 the next of kin of the alleged victim heard that the body of Juan Humberto Sánchez had been found "in a deep pool of the 'Río Negro,' stuck between the stones and in a state of decay [,] . . . with a rope around the neck that crossed his chest and tied his hands toward the back, and there were signs of torture."

On the other hand, the Commission argued that on July 20, 1992, before the body of the alleged victim was found, a habeas corpus remedy had been filed before the Appellate Court of Comayagua for the "kidnapping and detention" of Juan Humberto Sánchez. This habeas corpus remedy was rejected on August 14, 1992.

Furthermore, the Commission pointed out that to date no person has been tried or punished for the "kidnapping, torture, and execution" of Juan Humberto Sánchez, for which reason there continues to be a situation of impunity with respect to the case. In this regard, the Commission also stated that the criminal proceeding followed there has been marked by a "lack of seriousness and effectiveness," that it has been insufficient and that from the start it has faced numerous obstacles, including intimidation and threats against witnesses and relatives of the alleged victim.

2.   In view of the above, the Commission asked the Court to find that the following rights were breached to the detriment of Juan Humberto Sánchez: Articles 4 (Right to Life), 5 (Right to Humane Treatment), 7 (Right to Personal Liberty), 8 (Right to Fair Trial), and 25 (Judicial Protection), in combination with the obligation set forth in Article 1(1) (Obligation to Respect and Ensure Rights) of the American Convention. The Commission also requested that the Court order the State to adopt a series of pecuniary and non-pecuniary measures of reparation.

190.   The representatives of the victim requested reimbursement of legal costs and expenses amounting to US$28,190.58 (twenty-eight thousand one hundred ninety United States dollars and fifty-eight cents) for expenses incurred in their search for justice in the instant case, both domestically and internationally. They specifically requested the following amounts: US$19,597.72 (nineteen thousand five hundred ninety-seven United States dollars and seventy-two cents) for legal costs and expenses incurred by COFADEH; US$8,592.86 (eight thousand five hundred ninety-two United States dollars and eighty-six cents) as reimbursement for expenses incurred by CEJIL; and to set an amount in fairness for CODEHUCA.

191.   The Commission argued that the Court must recognize reasonable costs incurred by the legal representatives in the domestic ambit and before the bodies of the inter-American system for the protection of human rights, and the Commission stated that it "endorse[d] the claims made by the representatives of [the next of kin of the victim regarding reparations]."

192.   The State pointed out that payment of "compensations" to the attorneys who intervened is not in order, such as those of the Inter-American Commission or those of the Center for Justice and International Law, CEJIL, since they "perform a function for a remuneration set for them by the [body] to which they belong."

193.   As this Court has pointed out before,[185 159] legal costs and expenses are included under the concept of reparations embodied in Article 63(1) of the American Convention because the activities carried out by the next of kin of the victim to establish his whereabouts and, subsequently, to attain justice both at the domestic and the international levels entail expenses which must be compensated for when the State is found to be internationally responsible by means of a condemnatory judgment. With respect to their reimbursement, the Court must judiciously assess their scope, which encompasses the expenses incurred before the authorities of the domestic jurisdiction as well as those incurred in the proceedings before the inter-American system, bearing in mind the circumstances of the specific case and the nature of international jurisdiction for protection of human rights.[186 160] This assessment must be based on the principle of fairness and take into account the expenses stated by the parties insofar as their quantum is reasonable.[187 161]

194. To this end, the Court deems it equitable to order payment of a total sum of US$16,000.00 (sixteen thousand United States dollars) for legal costs and expenses incurred by the representatives of the victim in the domestic proceedings and in the international proceedings before the inter-American system for protection of human rights. The respective payment must be distributed as follows: a) US$14,000.00 (fourteen thousand United States dollars) to COFADEH; and b) US$2,000.00 (two thousand United States dollars) to CEJIL.

195. As a consequence of the existing impunity in the instant case and of the reparation ordered by this Court to further the judicial investigations to establish the truth regarding what happened to Juan Humberto Sánchez and to punish those responsible, it will be necessary for the next of kin of the victim to incur expenses in the domestic system, for which reason the Court, in fairness, grants the sum of US$3,000.00 (three thousand United States dollars) to be distributed in equal parts between María Dominga Sánchez and Juan José Vijil Hernández.

Bulacio vs. Argentina
18-Sep-2003
Series C No. 100—*Merits, Reparations, and Costs*

Legal Costs and Expenses
Arguments of the representatives of the next of kin of the victim
146. The representatives asked the Court to order the State to pay legal expenses and costs, including those for two attorneys representing them in the domestic legal proceedings. This adds up to US$50,000.00 (fifty thousand United States dollars) each. With respect to the bodies intervening in the international proceedings, both before the Inter-American Commission and before the Court, they requested the following amounts: for CELS, US$15,000.00 (fifteen thousand United States dollars); for CEJIL, US$10,000.00 (ten thousand United States dollars); and for CORREPI, US$15,000.00 (fifteen thousand United States dollars).

Arguments of the Commission
147. The Commission asked the Court to order the State to pay the expenses and costs generated by processing of the case, both domestically and before the inter-American system, based on the following criteria:
   (a) the fees of attorneys María del Carmen Verdú and Daniel A. Stragá for their actions before the Argentinean and international courts during a ten-year period, as well as expenses for phone calls, photocopies, mail

services, travel to Washington, D.C., and Costa Rica, are estimated at US$50,000.00 (fifty thousand United States dollars) for each attorney, adding up to US$100,000.00 (one hundred thousand United States dollars); and

(b) the fees for the attorneys of CELS, CEJIL, and CORREPI for their participation in the case once it began under international jurisdiction, are as follows: for the attorneys of CORREPI, US$ 11,000.00 (eleven thousand United States dollars); for the attorneys of CELS, US$11.100.00 (eleven thousand one hundred United States dollars) and for the attorneys of CEJIL, US$4.050.00 (four thousand and fifty United States dollars).

Arguments of the State

148.   The State asked the Court to take into account the decision in the [*Aloeboetoe*] *et al.* Case, in that, considering that the State had explicitly acknowledged its international responsibility and had not obstructed the procedure to set reparations, the Commission's request to order the State to pay the costs was dismissed.

149.   Alternatively, the State requested that to establish costs and expenses it take into account the decision in the *Castillo Páez* Case regarding judicious assessment of the specific scope of the legal costs, considering to this end their timely verification.

Considerations of the Court

150.   As the Court has already stated several times before,[106 162] legal costs and expenses are included under the concept of reparation set forth in Article 63(1) of the American Convention, in view of the fact that the actions carried out by the next of kin of the victim to establish his whereabouts and, subsequently, to obtain justice both under domestic and international jurisdiction, involve expenses that must be compensated when the State is found to be internationally responsible in a judgment against it. With respect to the reimbursement, it is for the Court to judiciously assess the amount, which includes expenses incurred before the authorities under domestic jurisdiction and those incurred in the proceedings before the inter-American system, taking into account the certification of expenses made, the circumstances of the specific case, and the nature of international jurisdiction for protection of human rights.[107 163] This assessment can be based on the principle of equity and assessing the expenses stated by the parties, insofar as their quantum is reasonable.[108 164]

151.   In the instant case, the Court notes that there is a discrepancy between the Inter-American Commission and the representatives of the next of kin of the victim regarding legal costs and expenses. On the one hand, the Commission requested

payment of certain amounts in its January 4, 2002 brief on reparations. In it, the Commission pointed out that "continuation of the processing of the case before the . . . Court will require new legal costs and expenses in the near future [that] should also receive . . . compensation," but in the brief with its final arguments, on July 4, 2003, it ratified the amounts requested on January 4, 2002. In their July 4, 2003 brief with their final arguments, the representatives, in turn, demanded substantially higher amounts than those requested by the Commission with regard to legal costs and expenses, pointing out that "continuation of the processing of the case before the . . . Court has required new legal costs and expenses." Finally, the Court notes that neither the Commission nor the representatives supplied receipts or vouchers to substantiate their claims regarding this aspect of the compensation.

152.   The Court deems it equitable to order payment of US$40,000.00 (forty thousand United States dollars) for legal costs and expenses in the domestic proceedings and in the international human rights proceedings. Payment must be distributed as follows: a) US$12,000.00 (twelve thousand United States dollars) to María del Carmen Verdú; b) US$12,000.00 (twelve thousand United States dollars) to Daniel A. Stragá; c) US$7,000.00 (seven thousand United States dollars) to CORREPI; d) US$7,000.00 (seven thousand United States dollars) to CELS; and e) US$2,000.00 (two thousand United States dollars) to CEJIL.

153.   This Court deems that to further the proceedings regarding investigation of the facts, the next of kin of the victim will need to incur expenses under domestic jurisdiction, and for this it grants in equity US$5,000.00 (five thousand United States dollars) to Graciela Rosa Scavone.

---

19 Merchants v. Colombia
5-Jul-2004
Series C No. 109—*Merits, Reparations and Costs*

Costs and Expenses
283.   As the Court as indicated on previous occasions,[237][165] costs and expenses are included in the concept of reparation embodied in Article 63(1) of the American Convention, because the measures taken by the next of kin of the victims in order to obtain justice, at the domestic and the international level, imply expenditure that must be compensated when the State's international responsibility has been declared by means of a conviction. Regarding reimbursement, the Court must prudently assess their scope, which includes the expenses incurred before the authorities of the domestic jurisdiction, and also those incurred during

the proceedings before the Inter-American System, taking into account the circumstances of the specific case and the nature of the international jurisdiction for the protection of human rights. [238][166] This assessment may be based on the principle of fairness and by evaluating the expenses indicated by the Inter-American Commission, provided that the amount is reasonable. [239][167]

284.   With regard to recognition of costs and expenses, legal assistance to the victim does not begin merely at the reparations stage, but starts before the domestic judicial bodies and continues in the successive instances of the Inter-American System for the protection of human rights; namely, in the proceedings before the Commission and before the Court. Consequently, in the concept of costs, for these purposes, both those that correspond to the stage of access to justice at the national level, as those that refer to justice at the international level before the two instances, the Commission and the Court, are included. [240][168]

285.   To this end, the Court considers that, in fairness, the following amounts may be ordered for costs and expenses: the sum of US$10,000.00 (ten thousand United States dollars) or the equivalent in Colombian currency, to be delivered to the Colombian Jurists Commission, and the sum of US$3,000.00 (three thousand United States dollars) or the equivalent in Colombian currency, to be delivered to the Center for Justice and International Law (CEJIL).

Chaparro Álvarez y Lapo Íñiguez. v. Ecuador

21-Nov-2007

Series C No. 170—*Preliminary Objections, Merits, Reparations, and Costs*

278.   The representatives requested reimbursement of the sum of US$235,813.21 (two hundred thirty-five thousand eight hundred thirteen United States dollars and twenty-one cents) to Mr. Chaparro and US$9,941.55 (nine thousand nine hundred forty-one United States dollars and fifty-five cents) to Mr. Lapo for legal advice and representation and the procedural costs they incurred during the proceedings in the domestic sphere and in these international proceedings. In turn, Mr. Lapo provided a statement of expenses that exceeds the amount requested by the representatives and indicated that he had not kept some of the receipts for those expenses. The State requested the Court to "abide by its case law on costs and expenses and establish reasonable amounts based on the equity principle."

279.   From the documentation provided, it can be seen that the victims agreed with their representatives that they would pay the latter the sum of US$150,000.00 (one hundred fifty thousand United States dollars) for professional fees, "when the Ecuadorean State pays the pecuniary reparations that the Inter-American Court

orders in favor of Messrs. Chaparro Álvarez and Lapo Íñiguez in its judgment."[181]
[169] In this regard, the State declared that "the amount . . . 'agreed' for the payment
of professional fees cannot be recognized by the Inter-American Court in the
case of an eventual judgment against the State and, instead, the amount should
be established, based on the equity principle, without taking into account the
arrangements and conditions under which the lawyers have assumed the legal
representation of the alleged victims."

280.　　The Court has indicated previously that it does not have competence to
rule on the agreements that victims reach with their representatives concerning
professional fees.[182][170] However, if, as in the instant case, it is requested that this
agreement between the victims and their representatives be assumed by the State,
the Court must examine whether the agreed amount is reasonable. In this regard,
in *Cantoral Benavides v. Peru*, the Court stated that the costs "include the various
necessary and reasonable expenses that the victim or victims incurred in order to
have access to the Inter-American system for the protection of human rights, and
these expenses include the fees of those who provide legal assistance."[183][171]

281.　　Bearing in mind the foregoing considerations, the evidence provided,
the State's observations on this evidence, and the equity principle, the Court
determines that the State shall deliver the sum of US$30,000.00 (thirty thousand
United States dollars) to Mr. Chaparro and the sum of US$5,000.00 (five thousand
United States dollars) to Mr. Lapo for costs and expenses. These amounts shall
be delivered to the victims within one year of notification of this judgment, and
they shall deliver the amount they consider appropriate to their representatives, in
keeping with the assistance provided by the latter.

282.　　Furthermore, the representatives requested reimbursement of
approximately $5,000.00 (five thousand United States dollars) to Mr. Lapo and
US$3,500.00 (three thousand five hundred United States dollars) to Mr. Chaparro
for supposed food and maintenance expenses while they were deprived of their
liberty and for paying for "security to other inmates." In this regard, the Court
observes, first, that these allegations were presented together with the helpful
evidence, in other words, when the appropriate procedural opportunity had
expired. According to the Court's case law, the request for helpful evidence does
not grant a fresh opportunity for expanding or completing arguments.[184][172] Second,
the said concepts do not conform to what the Court understands by costs and
expenses, which are: "the disbursements that are strictly necessary to attend the
matters before the jurisdictional organs at the national and international level."[185]
[173] Consequently, it decides not to grant reimbursement for these concepts.

Artavia Murillo et. al ("In Vitro Fertilization") v. Costa Rica
28-Nov-2012
Series C No. 257— *Merits, Reparations and Costs*

1.   On July 29, 2011, the Inter-American Commission on Human Rights (hereinafter the "Inter-American Commission" or "the Commission") submitted a brief to the jurisdiction of the Inter-American Court (hereinafter "brief submitting the case"), under the provisions of Articles 51 and 61 of the Convention, against the State of Costa Rica (hereinafter "the State" or "Costa Rica") in relation to case 12,361. The initial petition was submitted to the Commission on January 19, 2001, by Gerardo Trejos Salas. On March 11, 2004, the Inter- American Commission approved Admissibility Report No 25/04. [3][174] On July 14, 2010, the Commission approved Report on Merits No. 85/10, [4][175] under the terms of Article 50 of the American Convention (hereinafter also "the Merits Report" or "Report No. 85/10"), in which it made a number of recommendations to the State. Having granted the State three extensions to allow it to comply with the said recommendations, the Commission decided to submit the case to the Court. The Commission designated Rodrigo Escobar Gil, Commissioner, and Santiago A. Canton, then Executive Secretary, as delegates and appointed Elizabeth Abi-Mershed, Deputy Executive Secretary, and the lawyers Silvia Serrano Guzmán, Isabel Madariaga, Fiorella Melzi and Rosa Velorio as legal advisers.

2.   The Commission indicated that this case concerned alleged human rights violations resulting from the presumed general prohibition of the practice of *in vitro* fertilization (hereinafter "IVF"), which had been in effect in Costa Rica since 2000, following a ruling of the Constitutional Chamber of the Costa Rican Supreme Court of Justice (hereinafter "Constitutional Chamber"). Among other aspects, the Commission alleged that this absolute prohibition constituted arbitrary interference in the right to private life and the right to found a family. It further alleged that the prohibition violated the right to equality of the victims, inasmuch as the State had denied them access to a treatment that would have enabled them to overcome their disadvantage with regard to the possibility of having biological children. It also argued that this ban had a disproportionate impact on women.

3.   The Commission asked the Court to declare the international responsibility of the Costa Rican State for the violation of Articles 11(2), 17(2) and 24 of the American Convention, in relation to Articles 1(1) and 2 of this instrument, to the detriment of Gretel Artavia Murillo, Miguel Mejías Carballo, Andrea Bianchi Bruno, German Alberto Moreno Valencia, Ana Cristina Castillo

León, Enrique Acuña Cartín, Ileana Henchoz Bolaños, Miguel Antonio Yamuni Zeledón, Claudia María Carro Maklouf, Víctor Hugo Sanabria León, Karen Espinoza Vindas, Héctor Jiménez Acuña, Maria del Socorro Calderón P., Joaquina Arroyo Fonseca, Geovanni Antonio Vega, Carlos E. Vargas Solórzano, Julieta González Ledezma and Oriester Rojas Carranza.

VIII. Reparations

D) Costs and expenses

369. Regarding the reimbursement of costs and expenses, it corresponds to the Court to evaluate their scope prudently; they include the expenses generated before the authorities of the domestic jurisdiction, as well as those arising during the proceedings before the inter-American system, taking into account the circumstances of the specific case and the nature of the international jurisdiction for the protection of human rights. This assessment may be made based on the equity principle and taking into account the expenses indicated by the parties, provided that the *quantum* is reasonable. [517][176] Moreover, the Court reiterates that it is not enough to submit evidentiary documents, but rather the parties must also provide arguments relating the evidence to the fact it is considered to represent and, since this relates to alleged financial disbursements, the items and their justification must be established clearly. [518][177]

370. In the instant case, the Court observes that representative Trejos, who represented the victims during the proceedings before the Commission (*supra* paras. 1 and 8), died before these contentious proceedings were completed. Nevertheless, in his pleadings and motions brief, he was able to describe his claims for costs and expenses.

371. Furthermore, the Court observes that representative Trejos presented expense vouchers for US$1,376.96. [519][178] With his final arguments, representative May provided invoices corresponding to five affidavits for a total of US$2,500.00 dollars, without indicating why the cost of each notarial service had been calculated at US$500.00. In addition, in his final arguments, representative May requested the same amount that representative Trejos had asked for in his pleadings and motions brief, without clarifying whether these were two autonomous requests, or else, which part of the latter request corresponded to fees for Mr. Trejos and which part to fees for Mr. May. For his part, representative Molina provided expense vouchers for the sum of US$9,243.00, which corresponds mostly to the partial calculation of some professional services. [520][179]

372. The Court observes that the case file does not contain any supporting evidence to justify the sums that the representatives are requesting for professional fees and services. Indeed, the amounts requested for fees were not accompanied by specific proof of their reasonableness and scope. [521][180]

373.   Therefore, the Court establishes, in equity, the sum of US$10,000.00 (ten thousand United States dollars) for costs and expenses in favor of representative Gerardo Trejos, which must be paid directly to his heirs, in keeping with the applicable domestic law. Furthermore, the Court establishes, in equity, the sum of US$2,000.00 (two thousand United States dollars) for costs and expenses in favor of representative May, and the sum of US$3,000 (three thousand United States dollars) for costs and expenses in favor of representative Molina.

Mendoza v. Argentina
14-May-2013
Series C No. 260—*Merits, Reparations and Costs*

1.   On June 17, 2011, pursuant to the provisions of Articles 51 and 61 of the American Convention, the Inter-American Commission on Human Rights (hereinafter "the Inter-American Commission" or "the Commission") submitted to the Court's jurisdiction the case of *César Alberto Mendoza et al. v. the Argentine Republic* (hereinafter "the State" or "Argentina"). The case of *Mendoza et al. v. Argentina* refers to the supposed imposing of life sentences ("life imprisonment" [privación perpetua de la libertad] on César Alberto Mendoza, Lucas Matías Mendoza, Ricardo David Videla Fernández and Saúl Cristian Roldán Cajal, and "reclusion for life" [reclusión perpetua] on Claudio David Núñez), "for facts that occurred when they were children [...] in application of a juvenile justice system that allowed them to be treated as adult offenders." The case also refers to supposed "restrictions in the scope of the review by means of the remedies of cassation filed by the [presumed] victims" and to "a series of [presumed] violations that occurred while they were serving their sentences in the custody of the State." Thus, the Commission argued that Saúl Cristian Roldán Cajal and Ricardo David Videla were subjected to detention conditions that were "incompatible with their human dignity," which led to the latter's death and which has not been investigated effectively; that Claudio David Núñez and Lucas Matías Mendoza were victims of "acts of torture," and that the latter lost his sight "without the State providing [adequate] medical care."

XIII. Reparations

E) Costs and expenses

E.1. Pleadings of the representative

356.   The representative requested the reimbursement of 39,429 Argentine pesos corresponding to the disbursements she had incurred during the international

litigation, and that had not been covered by the Victims' Legal Assistance Fund. This amount corresponds to 2,500 Argentine pesos for "[o]ffice expenses"; 10,551 Argentine pesos for travel and per diems for meetings with the victims in the provinces of La Pampa and Mendoza during the preparation of the expert opinions, and 26,378 Argentine pesos for the expenses incurred by officials from the national Ombudsman's Office during the visit to Costa Rica for the public hearing held in this case.

357. The Commission did not submit any observations in this regard. The State indicated that it was "surprised [that the representative had] request[ed] reimbursement of costs and expenses], because [the amounts claimed] c[ame] from the budget of the Argentine State."

E.2. Considerations of the Court

358. As the Court has indicated, costs and expenses are part of the concept of reparation, because the victims' activities to obtain justice at both the national and the international level involve disbursements that must be compensated when the international responsibility of the State is declared in a judgment.

359. However, in this case, the Court observes that the representative of the victims is the head of the Argentine national Office of the Ombudsman, which is an organ of the State. The representative did not justify how, despite this circumstance, it would be appropriate to reimburse the amounts requested. Therefore, the Court will not order the reimbursement of the expenses claimed.

ANALYSIS AND QUESTIONS RAISED BY THE COURT'S JURISPRUDENCE

In numerous decisions, the Inter-American Court of Human Rights has declared that victims must be compensated for legal costs and expenses, a necessary component of litigation, when States are found to be responsible for violations of their rights and freedoms. In other words, the Court has stated that legal costs and expenses are included in the concept of reparations as set forth in Article 63(1) of the American Convention because victims incur these costs and expenses in seeking justice. The Court has further stated that the term costs as referred to by Article 55(1) of the Rules of Procedure includes the legal costs and expenses which make it possible for victims to access the Inter-American human rights system and to secure legal assistance.

As with the determination of non-pecuniary damages, the Court applies the principle of equity to its determinations of what constitutes necessary and reasonable, and therefore compensable, legal costs and expenses. And, as with all reparations judgments, the Court considers the specific circumstances of each case to make its decisions regarding compensable legal costs and expenses.

- What distinctions can be drawn between *dannum emergens* (direct and consequential damages resulting from human rights violations) and legal costs and expenses incurred in seeking justice for such violations?

- What types of legal costs and expenses should be compensable? Should all incurred legal costs and expenses be compensated? When the Court awards partial compensation for legal costs and expenses, should it specify which costs and expenses are to be compensated, or should victims decide how to utilize the partial reimbursement?

- Could the Court set specific monetary limits (e.g., limits on compensable legal fees) and predetermined categories of compensable legal costs and expenses? Would such limits discourage potentially high legal fees, for instance, or would such predeterminations potentially limit legal assistance in complex and extended legal proceedings?

- Are the Court's considerations of equity, prudence, and the specific circumstances of each case sufficiently clear? Should the Court's considerations include the economic situation of the State, the financial situation of the victim, or the financial situation of the victim's legal representatives, or would such considerations undermine the upholding of human rights law?

- Do partial awards of legal costs and expenses discourage individual or private attorneys from representing clients before the Court? Would full awards of costs and expenses impact State participation in the Inter-American human rights system? Are non-government organizations best able to absorb the potential costs and expenses of litigation and therefore the best option for legal representation? Do such monetary considerations potentially impact the legal representation a victim or group of victims may be able to secure?

- What are the other possible consequences when the Court does not award all legal costs and expenses? Do such decisions potentially impact who pursues justice through the Inter-American human rights system? Does the Court's establishment of the Victims' Legal Assistance Fund[181] address some of these accessibility concerns?

Endnotes

1 *Bámaca-Velásquez v. Guatemala*, Reparations and Costs, February 22, 2002 Judgment, C Series No. 91, para. 41.

2 9 I.L.M. 673 (1970) (signed Nov. 22, 1969; entry into force June 1, 1978)

3 United Nations General Assembly, A/RES/60/147 Adopted at the 64th plenary meeting, 16th December 2005.

4 *Cf.* Juan Humberto Sánchez Case, *supra* note 9[Judgment of June 7, 2003. Series C No. 99], para. 162; Trujillo Oroza Case. Reparations, *supra* note 277[(Art. 63(1) American Convention on Human Rights). Judgment of February 27, 2002. Series C No. 92], para. 65; and Bámaca Velásquez Case. Reparations, [(Art. 63(1) American Convention on Human Rights). Judgment of February 22,, 2002. Series C No. 91] *supra* note 277, para. 43.

5 219 *Cfr.* case of Vargas Areco, [Judgment of September 26, 2006. Series C No. 155] *supra*, para. 146; case of Almonacid Arellano et al, [Judgment of September 26, 2006. Series C No. 154] *supra*, para. 158; and case of Goiburú et al., [Judgment of September 22, 2006. Series C No. 153] *supra*, para. 150.

6 220 *Cfr.* case of Vargas Areco, *supra* note [219], para. 146; case of Goiburú et al., *supra* note [219], para. 150; and case of Montero Aranguren et al. (Detention Center of Catia), [Judgment of July 5, 2006. Series C No. 150] para. 126.

7 98 In accordance with the information provided by the relatives, Renato Ticona would have stopped working as a music teacher once he would have obtained his professional degree. The foregoing means that he would have continued working as a music teacher for two and a half years more, until December 1982.

8 99 The representative stated that the salary of Renato Ticona as music teacher in the years 1977 and 1978 amounted to Bs. 866.71 (eight hundred sixty-six Bolivian pesos and seventy-one cents). Nevertheless, it was impossible to determine the salary he received between 1979 and June 1980 and the salary he would have received from July 1980 to December 1982. As a consequence, in order to estimate the salary of a music teacher, it was considered the minimum salary in force on September 19, 2008, which amounted to Bs. 575.00 (five hundred seventy-five Bolivian pesos), which is equal to US$81.00 (eighty-one United States dollars).

9 100 According to the representative, in order to do the corresponding estimation, it requested information to the Society of Engineers of Bolivia ("SIB") and the Professional Association of Agricultural Engineers of Bolivia—District of La Paz ("CIAB-LP"). The SIB pointed out that the average salary, per month, would be US$950.00 (nine hundred fifty United States dollars) and the CIAB-LP pointed out that said salary would amount to 7.830.00 Bs. (seven thousand eight hundred thirty Bolivian pesos) which, according to the exchange rate as of September 17, 2008, equals US$1,104.00 (one thousand one hundred four United States dollars). The representative, based on the foregoing, made a new estimation of the salary of an agricultural engineer, with more than 20 years of experience, that would amount to US$1,027.00 (one thousand twenty-seven United States dollars), which was used as the basis for the estimation.

10 101 According to the State, the Technical University of Oruro was closed due to the coup d'etat carried out by General Luis García Meza from July 17, 1980 to May 21, 1982. As a consequence, Renato Ticona could have continued studying as from the middle of 1982, and he would have obtained his degree in the year 1984; therefore, any calculation as an alleged agricultural engineer should be considered as from the year 1985. The State objected to the estimation made by the representative since it cannot consider the 20 years of seniority of Renato Ticona for the professional income of all his professional life. It was a lineal calculation of the income received. The State forwarded to the Court a report from the School of Agricultural and Livestock Sciences of August 18, 2008, which evidences that those students, who entered to the university on the second semester of 1974, obtained

their degree between 1985 and 1995.

11 102   *Cf.* case of *Velásquez Rodríguez V. Honduras. supra* [Reparations and Costs. Judgment of July 21, 1989. Series C N°. 7], para. 49; and *case of Cantoral Huamani and García Santa Cruz*, Preliminary Objection, Merits, reparations, and costs. Judgment of July 10, 2007. Series C, N° 41, para. 166; and *case of Escué Zapata v. Colombia, supra* [Merits, reparations, and costs. Judgment of July 4, 2007. Series C N°. 165], para. 141.

12 103   *Cf.* case of Trujillo Oroza v. Bolivia, *supra* [Reparations and Costs. Judgment of February 27, 2002. Series C N° 92], para. 73, case of *Ituango Massacres* [*v. Colombia*. Preliminary Objection, Merits, Reparations, and Costs. Judgment of July 1, 2006. Series C N° 148] *supra*, para. 373; case of *La Rochela Massacre v. Colombia*. Merits, reparations, and costs. Judgment of May 11, 2007. Series C N°. 163, para. 248.

13 104   The Court took into account the information provided by the State and the representative regarding the graduation date of Renato Ticona, since the University Ticona Estrada was studying at, remained closed during some time. As a consequence, the Tribunal considers pertinent to establish the year 1985 as the year from which the victim initiated his profession as agricultural engineer.

14 105   *Cf.* case of the "White Van" (*Paniagua Morales et al.*) *v. Guatemala, supra* [Reparations and Costs. Judgment of May 25, 2001. Series C N° 76], para. 94; case of *Molina Theissen v. Guatemala.* Reparations and Costs. Judgment of July 3, 2004. Series C N°. 108, para. 57, and case of *La Rochela Massacre v. Colombia*, [Merits, reparations, and costs. Judgment of May 11, 2007. Series C N°. 163] *supra*, para. 248.

15 176   *Cf.* case of *Bámaca Velásquez v. Guatemala. Reparations and Costs.* Judgment of February 22, 2002. Series C No. 91, para. 43; case of *Chocrón Chocrón v. Venezuela,* [Preliminary Objection, Merits, Reparations and Costs. Judgment of July 1, 2011. Series C No. 227], and *case of Mejía Idrovo v. Ecuador,* [Preliminary Objections, Merits, Reparations and Costs. Judgment of July 5, 2011 Series C No. 228], para. 129.

16 177   They argued that "[g]iven the deprivation of [Mr. Torres Millacura's] right to work and to plan his future, [...] the Collective Work Agreement N° 605/10, should be used as [reference], approved on September 10, 2010, in the [highest] branch of production," in order to calculate the amount corresponding to this.

17 178   In this regard, they held that Mr. Torres Millacura "was the breadwinner," and that Mrs. Millacura Llaipén now "[d]edicates her life to the search for her son." According to the representatives, Mrs. Millacura Llaipén has suffered much harm to her health "since [...] the moment of the enforced disappearance" of her son; Fabiola Valeria Torres "[l]ives marked by [...] the desperation of finding Iván [Eladio...]", and neither her nor Marcos Alejandro Torres Millacura find work given that they are his siblings.

18 179   *Cf.* Testimony of María Leontina Millacura Llaipén rendered at the public hearing before this Court; Testimony rendered before notary public by Marcos Alejandro Torres Millacura on May 9, 2011 (case file on the merits, tome II, folio 1173). See also, the testimony rendered before notary public by Fabiola Valeria Torres on May 12, 2011 (case file on the merits, tome II, folio 1110).

19   The voucher is for a net sum of 931.76 Argentine pesos and for a paid sum of 899.46 Argentine pesos. Cf. Voucher for the salary of Jorge Omar Gutiérrez (file of annexes to the pleadings and motions brief, folio 2030).\
† Cf. INDEC tables on life expectancy at birth, by sex and by jurisdiction, in Argentina, 1990/92 and 2000/2001 (file of annexes to the pleadings and motions brief, folio 2032).
‡ Cf. Decision No. 104097 (file of annexes before the Commission, folio 101).

20 498   case of *Bámaca Velásquez v. Guatemala. Reparations and costs.* Judgment of February 22, 2002. Series C No. 91, para. 43, and *case of Norín Catrimán et al. (Leaders, members and activist of the Mapuche Indigenous People) v. Chile*, para. 441.

21 893   *Cf.* case of *Cepeda Vargas v. Colombia. Preliminary objections, merits, reparations and costs.* Judgment of May 26, 2010, Para. 246, *and case of the Santo Domingo Massacre*

v. Colombia. Preliminary objections, merits and reparations. Judgment of November 30, 2012. Series C No. 259, para. 37.

22 894   Cf. case of Cepeda Vargas v. Colombia. Preliminary objections, merits, reparations and costs. Judgment of May 26, 2010, paras. 139 and 140, and case of the Santo Domingo Massacre v. Colombia. Preliminary objections, merits and reparations. Judgment of November 30, 2012. Series C No. 259, para. 37.

23 895   The Court also observes that, when determining the pecuniary compensation at the domestic level, the calculation of the compensation corresponding to the children was made based on the time that had elapsed between their age at the time of the events and the time until they achieved their majority.

24 896   See, with regard to: (1) Cristina del Pilar Guarín Cortés, the judgment of the Council of State of October 13, 1994 (evidence file, folios 3190 to 3245); (2) Bernardo Beltrán Hernández, the judgment of the Council of State of October 13, 1994 (evidence file, folios 2906 to 2952); (3) Irma Franco Pineda, the judgment of the Council of State of September 11, 1997 (evidence file, folios 3247 to 3262), and (4) Luz Mary Portela León, the judgment of the Council of State of September 6, 1995 (evidence file, folios 3049 to 3094).

25 897   Judgment of the Council of State of September 11, 1997, in the proceedings instituted by the next of kin of Irma Franco Pineda (evidence file, folio 3260).

26 898   Cf. case of Manuel Cepeda Vargas v. Colombia. Preliminary objections, merits, reparations and costs. Judgment of May 26, 2010. Series C No. 213, para. 246, and case of Tarazona Arrieta et al. v. Peru. Preliminary objection, merits, reparations and costs. Judgment of October 15, 2014. Series C No. 286, para. 137.

27 899   This refers to the cases of: (1) Gloria Stella Lizarazo Figueroa, (2) Carlos Augusto Rodríguez Vera, (3) David Suspes Celis, (4) Héctor Jaime Beltrán Fuentes, (5) Norma Constanza Esguerra, (6) Ana Rosa Castiblanco Torres and (7) Carlos Horacio Urán Rojas.

28 69   According to the Commission, indicators produced by the National Institute of Statistics for 1990-1995, indicate that "the average remaining life expectancy for men from 15 to 19 years of age would have been 50.04 years". In view of the similarities in ages (which ranged from 15 to 20 years) and circumstances of the victims, "the Commission has made a single calculation and considers that it should be applied to each of them."

29 70   According to the Commission, reference to the minimum legal wage for workers in the nonagricultural sector is an appropriate minimum limit for calculations in this case, in accordance with the provisions of Article 103 of the Labor Code, with the legal bonuses (Q0.30 per hour) and the periodic modifications to the minimum wages in force. The Commission traced the increase in the minimum wages from the time of the events up until 1999 and established that the average annual increase for that period had been 6.9%; it then applied this increase to the projection for non-perceived future wages.

30 71   The Commission has applied the rate of passive compound interest in force for each year, published by the Banco de Guatemala.

31 72   The Commission used a discount rate of 3% for calculating the current value of the loss of earnings.

32 78   Cf. Neira Alegría et al. case. Reparations, [(Article 63(1) American Convention on Human Rights). Judgment of September 19, 1996. Series C No. 29], para. 49; El Amparo case. Reparations, [(Article 63(1) American Convention on Human Rights). Judgment of September 14, 1996. Series C No. 28], para. 28; and Aloeboetoe et al. case. Reparations, [(Article 63(1) American Convention on Human Rights). Judgment of September 10, 1993. Series C. No 15], paras. 88 and 89.

33 79   To calculate life expectancy, the Court took into account the document entitled "Guatemala: Tablas Abreviadas de Mortalidad (Período 1990–1995)"; it also considered data such as age, sex and geographical zone of residence.[80] To this end, the Court used a 6% annual rate of interest.

34 80   To this end, the Court used a 6% annual rate of interest.

35 5   *Cf. Castillo Páez Case, Reparations,* [(Art. 63(1) American Convention on Human Rights). Judgment of November 27, 1998, Series C No. 43], para. 74.

36 206   *Cf.* case of *Molina Theissen,* [Reparations (Art. 63(1) American Convention on Human Rights). Judgment of July 3, 2004. Series C No. 108], para. 57; *case of Bulacio,* [Judgment of September 18, 2003. Series C No. 100], para. 84; and case of *Castillo Páez, Reparations* (Art. 63(1) American Convention on Human Rights). Judgment of November 27, 1998. Series C No. 43, para. 74.

37 207   *Cf.* case of the 19 Tradesmen, *supra* note 2[0]6, para. 240; case of Juan Humberto Sánchez. Interpretation of the Judgment on Preliminary Objections, Merits and Reparations. (Art. 67 American Convention on Human Rights). Judgment of November 26, 2003. Series C No. 102, para. 56; and case of Bulacio, *supra* note [20]6, para. 150.

38 208   *Cf.* case of the 19 Tradesmen, [Judgment of July 5, 2004. Series C No. 109], para. 240; case of the Caracazo, [*Reparations* (Art. 63(1) American Convention on Human Rights). Judgment of August 29, 2002. Series C No. 95], para. 88; and case of the "Street Children" (Villagrán Morales et al.). Reparations (Art. 63(1) American Convention on Human Rights). Judgment of May 26, 2001. Series C No. 77, para. 79.

39 209   [The Court lists the names of the deceased inmates.]

40 210   [The Court lists the names of the injured inmates.]

41 67   *Cf. Cantoral Benavides Case, Reparations,* [(Art. 63(1) American Convention on Human Rights). December 3, 2001 Judgment. Series C No. 88], para. 51; *Blake Case, Reparations.* [(Art. 63(1) American Convention on Human Rights). January 22, 1999 Judgment. Series C No. 48], para. 50; and *Loayza Tamayo Case, Reparations,* [(Art. 63.1 American Convention on Human Rights), November 27, 1998 Judgment. Series C No. 42], para. 129(d).

42 211   *Cf.* Statements made in the presence of a person authorized by law to authenticate documents and statements (affidavits) by Francisco Ramón Adorno and María Teresa de Jesús Pérez and the testimony given by Ms. Teofista Domínguez Riveros before this Court on May 3, 2004.

43 157   *Cf.* statement made before notary public (affidavit) by Yazmín Kuri González on April 16, 2007 (file on merits, Volume I, folio 374).

44 158   *Cf.* testimony of [Juan Carlos] Chaparro [Álvarez] at the public hearing [held before the Inter-American Court on May 17, 2007].

45 159   *Cf.* brief submitted by the representatives on October 3, 2007, as helpful evidence requested by the President of the Court (file on merits, volume III, folio 1096).

46 160   *Cf.* [statement made before notary public (affidavit) by] Yazmín Kuri González [on April 16, 2007 (file on merits, Volume I,] folio 374).

47 16   The State appointed Erick Roberts, Deputy Director on Human Rights' matters for the Attorney General's Office, Principal Agent and Salim Zaidán, Office of the Deputy Director on Human Rights' matters of the Attorney General's Office, Deputy Agent.

48 137   *Cf.* case of *Bámaca Velásquez V. Guatemala. Reparations and Costs.* Judgment of February 22, 2002. Series C No. 91, para. 43; *case of Gomes Lund et al. ("Guerrilha do Araguaia") V. Brazil, supra* note 8, para. 298, and *case of Cabrera García and Montiel Flores V. México, supra* note 8, para. 248.

49 138   In this regard, they cited the example of the Judgment rendered by the Centre for Settlement of Investment Disputes (ICSID) in the *Compañía del Desarrollo Santa Elena S.A. V. Costa Rica, supra* note 92.

50 139   It is worth mention that in the Judgment of Merits it was established that the expropriation filed by the Metropolitan Municipality of Quito against María and Julio Guillermo Salvador Chiriboga was presented on July 16, 1996. The expropriation trial was listed under No. 1300-96, which was initiated that same day before the Ninth Court. *Cf.* case of *Salvador Chiriboga V. Ecuador, supra* note 24, paras. 4 and 103.

51 140   In the main documents, the representatives as well as the State, made statements regard-

ing the amount of the payment consigned with the lawsuit of expropriation in the process No. 1300-96. The representatives indicated that the amount of Sucres assigned with the writ of the lawsuit of expropriation corresponded to the date of the presentation of that writ, and the amount of $9.032.00 (nine thousand and thirty two dollars of the United States of America) (written brief containing pleadings, motions, and evidence, file on preliminary objections and merits, Volume II, pp. 145) On the other hand, the State indicated that the value of the amount consigned at the moment of payment, when the lawsuit of expropriation was presented, represented almost US$ 300.000,00 (three hundred thousand dollars of the United States of American) (the States plea, file on preliminary objections and merits, Volume II, page 219).

52 141   It is important to note that the State in its note of January 13, 2009, stated yet again that there is no liquidation obligation nor is there a default by the Municipality, to which the payment of interest does not follow. It recalled that stated in the hearing on the appropriation of an amount since the declaration of public interest (case file of Reparations and Costs, tome V, folio 1069). Both the Commission and the representatives noted that the State could not change its opinion, given that it had acknowledged in the public hearing the payment of interests. In this regard, the Commission requested *estoppel* be applied (case file of Reparations and Costs, tome VI, folios 1242 and 1248).

53 142   *Cf.* case of *Salvador Chiriboga V. Ecuador, supra* note 24, para. 113.

54 143   *Cf.* Eur. Court H.R., *Tsirikakis v. Greece.* Judgment of January 17, 2002, para. 60 and 61.

55 144   *Cf.* Eur. Court H.R., *Tsirikakis v. Greece.* Judgment of January 23, 2003, para. 11.

56 145   The following is meant by simple interest: in any period, interest rate multiplied by the invariable amount of the principal.

57 146   The following is meant by compound interest: in any period, the interest rate is multiplied by a varying amount of the principal. Unpaid interest is added to principal outstanding and converted to principal in the new period.

58 147   *Cf.* Eur. Court H.R., case of *Stran Greek Refineries and Stratis Andreadis v. Greece.* Judgment of December 9, 1994, para. 83; Eur. Court H.R., *Case Guiso-Gallisay v. Italy, supra* note 82, para. 105, and Eur. Court H.R., *Case Schembri and others s v. Malta, supra* note 83, para. 18.

59 148   At the International Centre for Settlement of Investment Disputes (ICSID) cases are filed that have a distinct legal relevance, where the matters involve commercial motives and investment. *Cf.* ICSID, *Compañía del Desarrollo Santa Elena S.A. V. Costa Rica, supra* note 92, paras. 96 -107; *Metalclad Corporation V. México.* Judgment of August 30, 2000, ARB (AF)/97/1, para. 128, and *Middle East Cement Shipping and Handling Co. S.A. V. República Árabe de Egipto.* Judgment of April 12, 2002. ARB/99/6, paras. 173-175.

60 149   It corresponds to Article 256 of the prior Organic Law of the Municipal Regimen, approved on October 15,1971, which states "in all cases of expropriation the owner shall be paid, in addition to the conventional or judicially established price, five percent as for the price of the damage. The ultimate value shall be delivered to the owner in cash in the amounts and within the time limits set by the municipality, in agreement with the expropriated, and such intervals shall not exceed five years. The fees payable in installments compound legal interest. The price paid will be exempt from all duties, taxes or other tax levies, municipal or any other."

61 150   Corresponds to Articles 1600 and 1602 of the prior Civil Code, which was codified on November 20, 1970. Article 1600 literally notes that "damages should be compensated since the debtor defaulted, or, if the obligation is to not, from the time of the contravention." Article 1602 states that "if the obligation is to pay an amount of money, the compensation for damages for default is subject to the following norms: 1) the conventional interests are still owed, if an interest superior to the legal interest is operational, or the legal interests are owed, in the contrary; keeping, nevertheless, in force the special provisions that authorize the cost of current interests, in some cases; 2.) The creditor does not need to justify when

only interests are collected. In such cases, the delay suffices, 3.) the interest in arrears do not generate interests, and 4.) This rule applies to all kinds of rents, royalties, and periodic pensions."

[62 151] *Cf.* case of *Salvador Chiriboga v. Ecuador, supra* note 24, para. 72.

[63 152] *Cf.* Eur. Court H.R., *Case Guiso-Gallisay v. Italya, supra* note 82, para. 105, and Eur. Court H.R., *Case Schembri and others v. Malta, supra* note 83, para. 18.

[64 1] Rules of Procedure approved by the Court at its Twenty-third Regular Session, held January 9 – 18, 1991; amended on January 25, 1993; July 16, 1993; and December 2, 1995.

[65 47] Loayza Tamayo Case. Reparations (Art. 63(1) American Convention on Human Rights). Judgment of November 27, 1998. Series C No. 42, paragraph 147.

[66 37] *Cf.* case of Cantoral Benavides. Reparations (Article 63(1) American Convention on Human Rights). Judgment of 3 December 2001. Series C No. 88, para. 80; and case of Loayza Tamayo. Reparations (Article 63(1) American Convention on Human Rights). Judgment of 27 November 1998. Series C No. 42, para. 153.

[67 38] *Cf.* case of Cantoral Benavides, *supra* note 37, paras. 63 and 80.

[68 83] *Cf. Villagrán Morales et al. case (The "Street Children" case).* Judgment of November 19, 1999. Series C No. 63, paras. 188 to 191.

[69 84] *Cf. Villagrán Morales et al. case (The "Street Children" case), supra* note 8[3], paras. 157 to 163.

[70 85] *Cf. Villagrán Morales et al. case (The "Street Children" case), supra* note 8[3], paras. 195 to 197.

[71 215] [The Court names the victims.]

[72 216] [The Court names the victims.]

[73 217] [The Court names the victims.]

[74 218] [The Court names the victims.]

[75 219] *Cf.* case of the "Street Children" (Villagrán Morales et al.), [*Reparations* (Art. 63(1) American Convention on Human Rights). Judgment of May 26, 2001. Series C No. 77] *supra,* para. 91.b); and Juridical Condition and Human Rights of the Child, [Advisory Opinion OC-17/02 of August 28, 2002. Series A No. 17] *supra,* paragraphs 54, 60, and 93.

[76 220] [The Court names the victims.]

[77 221] [The Court names the victims.]

[78 222] [The Court names the victims.]

[79 257] *Cf.* case of *Blanco Romero et al., supra* note 10, para. 86; case of *García Asto and RamírezRojas, supra* note 10, para. 267, and case of *Gómez Palomino, supra* note 10, para. 130.

[80 258] *Cf.* case of the *"Mapiripán Massacre", supra* note 7, para. 283; case of *Tibi, supra* note 192, para. 244, and case of the *"Juvenile Reeducation Institute", supra* note 17, para. 300.

[81 259] *Cf.* case of the *Serrano Cruz Sisters, supra* note 214, para. 159; case of *the Gómez Paquiyauri Brothers, supra* note 188, para. 218, and case of *19 Merchants, supra* note 192, para. 249.

[82 260] *Cf.* case of the *19 Merchants, supra note* 192, para. 229; case of *Maritza Urrutia, supra note* 190, para. 169; case of *Myrna Mack Chang, supra note* 197, paras. 245 and 264, *and* case of *Bulacio, supra* note 192, para. 98.

[83 261] *Cf.* case of *Blanco Romero et al., supra* note 10, para. 87; case of *García Asto and Ramírez Rojas, supra* note 10, para. 268, and case of *Gómez Palomino, supra* note 10, para. 131.

[84 66] By using the term "territory" the Court is referring to the sum of traditionally used lands and resources. In this sense, the Saramaka territory belongs collectively to the members of the Saramaka people, whereas the lands within that territory are divided among and vested in the twelve Saramaka clans * * *.

85 67 *Cf.* Professor Richard Price, "Report in support of Provisional Measures", *supra* note 6[6], (folios 17-18).

86 68 *Cf.* Testimony of Captain Cesar Adjako during the public hearing at the Court held on May 9 and 10, 2007 (transcription of public hearing, p. 15); Expert opinion of Professor Richard Price, *supra* note 6[6] (transcription of public hearing, p. 55); Report of Professor Richard Price, September 30, 2000 (case file of appendices to the application and Appendix 1, appendix 1, folio 4), and Professor Richard Price, "Report in support of Provisional Measures", *supra* note 6[7], (folio 16).

87 69 *Cf.* Professor Richard Price, "Report in support of Provisional Measures", *supra* note 6[7], (folio 14), and Affidavit of Dr. Peter Poole of April 30, 2007 (case file of affidavits and observations, appendix 8, folio 1961).

88 70 *Cf.* Professor Richard Price, "Report in support of Provisional Measures", *supra* note 6[7].

89 71 Testimony of Head Captain and Fiscali Wazen Eduards, [during the public hearing at the Court held on May 9 and 10, 2007] (transcription of public hearing, p.5).

90 72 *Cf.* Expert opinion of Professor Richard Price, *supra* note 6[6] (transcription of public hearing, p. 55); Report of Professor Richard Price, *supra* note 68, and Professor Richard Price, "Report in support of Provisional Measures", *supra* note 6[7], (folio 16).

91 73 *Cf.* Expert opinion of Professor Richard Price, *supra* note 6[6] (transcription of public hearing, p. 55); Report of Professor Richard Price, *supra* note 68, and Professor Richard Price, "Report in support of Provisional Measures", *supra* note 6[7], (folio 16).

92 74 *Cf.* Expert opinion of Professor Richard Price, *supra* note 6[6] (transcription of public hearing, p. 55); Report of Professor Richard Price, *supra* note 68, and Professor Richard Price, "Report in support of Provisional Measures", *supra* note 6[7], (folio 16).

93 58 *Cf.* Census of the Community updated to October 16, 2009, (file of attachments to the pleadings and motions brief, tome VI, attachment 10, folios 2762 to 2783); Census of the Xákmok Kásek Community, settled on 1,500 hectares, undated (file of attachments to the answer, attachment 6(2), tome VIII, folios 3618 to 3626); Census of the Indigenous Community prepared by the representatives, updated to August 30, 2008 (file of appendices to the application, appendix 3, tome I, folios 320 to 336), and Salazar Indigenous Peoples Census, February 2008 (file of attachments to the answer, attachment 6(2), tome VIII, folios 3221 to 3617).

94 59 On some occasions, it was translated as "little parrots' nest" (application brief, merits file, folio 23); on other occasions "little birds' nest" (testimony of Maximiliano Ruíz, [provided during the public hearing on April 14, 2010, during the forty-first special session held in Lima, Peru]). Also, the private landowners explained that the Salazar Ranch has been known by different names, including, "Estancia Laguna Koncit," which appears to mean "place of many parrots" in Enlhet. *Cf.* "Una breve reseña histórica de los Kent, Mobsbye, Eaton en el Chaco." Fortin Juan de Salazar and Espinoza (file of attachments provided by the State at the public hearing, attachment X, tome IX, folio 3836).

95 [60] *Cf.* Testimony of Tomás Dermott [before notary public (merits file, tome II] folios 594 to 596). The State indicated that the Xákmok Kásek Community was relatively new and had separated from a pre-existing community "whose original place of residence was constituted by an area known as Misión Inglesa and 'El Estribo.'" However, it did not provide evidence to support this argument (answer to the application, merits file, tome 1, folios 370 and 371).

96 61 *Cf.* Socio-Anthropological Report on the Xakmok Kasek Community [by the INDI Legal Department (file of appendices to the application, appendix 3, tome II], folio 841), and testimony of Tomás Dermott, *supra* note [60], folio 597.

97 62 *Cf.*[Anthropological Report of the Center for Anthropological Studies of the Universidad Católica Nuestra Señora de la Asunción, signed by Miguel Chase Sardi, dated December

21, 1995 (file of appendices to the application, appendix 3, tome II], folios 735); Socio-Anthropological Report on the Xákmok Kásek Community, *supra* note [61], folios 838 to 853; Report of site visit carried out by Pastor Cabanellas (engineer) on May 17, 1991 (file of appendices to the application, appendix 3, tome II, folios 791 to 793), and report of the expanded site visit on September 22, 1992 (file of appendices to the application, appendix 3, tome III, folio 883).

98 63 According to the representatives, in 1986, Ramón Oviedo, leader of the indigenous community, asked the INDI for 200 hectares, part of its ancestral lands; however, the INDI did not process this request. This affirmation was not denied or contested by the State (merits file, folio 231). Moreover, according to Community leaders Marcelino López and Clemente Dermott, deponents before this Court, the case file corresponding to this initial request was mislaid and a new request was therefore filed in 1990. *Cf.* Testimony of Marcelino López before to notary public (pleadings and motions brief, merits file, tome II, folios 231 and 582, and testimony of Clemente Dermott before a notary public on March 25, 2010 (merits file, tome II, folio 645).

99 64 *Cf.* Law 904/81 Indigenous Communities Statute of December 18, 1981 (file of appendices to the application, appendix 7, folios 2399 to 2425).

100 65 The Community originally requested 6,900 hectares, then increased its request to 20,000 hectares, and ultimately reduced its request to 10,700 hectares, "because it seemed that if we reduced it, the State would be persuaded to return the land to us and also because some members of the Community, who could not hold out any longer left." Testimony of Marcelino López, *supra* note 63, folio 582. Similarly, communication of the leaders of the Community addressed to the President of the IBR on November 11, 1993 (file of appendices to the application, appendix 3, tome III, folio 898), and request of the Community to the IBR on September 28, 1990 (file of appendices to the application, appendix 3, tome II, folio 780).

101 66 *Cf.* Report on the site visit carried out by Pastor Cabanellas (engineer), *supra* note 62, folios 791 to 795.

102 67 *Cf.* Testimony of Roberto Carlos Eaton Kent before notary public (merits file, tome II], folio 662); testimony of Clemente Dermott, *supra* note 63, folio 647; press release of April 3, 2003, entitled, "*Sawatzky dice que desconocia reclamo de Enxet*" [Sawatzky says he was not aware of Enxet claim] (file of appendices to the application, appendix 3, tome IV, folio 1584); press release of April 1, 2003, entitled "*Menonitas ofrecen al INDI tierra reclamada por nativos*" [Mennonites offer the INDI land being claimed by indigenous peoples] (file of appendices to the application, appendix 3 tome IV, folio 1583); press release of January 7, 2003, entitled "*Eaton & Cía. vendió tierra reclamada por indígenas*" [Eaton & Co. sold land claimed by the indigenous peoples] (file of appendices to the application, appendix 3, tome IV, folio 1576), and press release of February 7, 2003, entitled "*Nativos insisten en recuperar tierras vendidas a menonitas*" [Indigenous peoples insist in recovering land sold to Mennonites] (file of appendices to the application, appendix 3, tome IV, folio 1575).

103 68 *Cf.* Testimony of Roberto Carlos Eaton Kent, *supra* note [67], folio 662; testimony of Marcelino López, *supra* note 63, folio 581; expert testimony of Sergio Iván Braticevic [by affidavit (file of attachments to the State's final arguments, tome X], folios 948 and 949), and expert testimony of Antonio Spiridinoff before notary public (merits file, tome II, folio 614).

104 69 *Cf.* Expropriation request made by the Community on June 23, 1999, addressed to the Senate of the Congress of the Republic (file of appendices to the application, appendix 3, tome IV, folios 1837 to 1846).

105 70 *Cf.* Report entitled "*Salazar Ranch frente a un pedido de expropiación*" [file of attachments provided by the State at the public hearing, tome IX, attachment X, 3785 to

3811, and testimony of Roberto Carlos Eaton Kent before notary public (merits file, tome II], folio 3792).

106 71   *Cf.* Resolution No. 693 of the Senate of the national Congress (file of appendices to the application, attachment 5, folio 2384). On September 23, 2000, the Senate's Agrarian Reform and Rural Welfare Committee recommended the approval of the expropriation in favor of the Community; however, on November 9, 2000, it retracted this opinion (*Cf.* Opinion No. 11-2000/2001 of November 9, 2000, of the Agrarian Reform and Rural Welfare Committee, file of appendices to the application, attachment 5, folio 2382); bill presented to the Senate on June 25, 1999 (file of appendices to the application, attachment 5, folio 2381), and Opinion No. 18-2000-2001 of the Agrarian Reform and Rural Welfare Committee (file of appendices to the application, attachment 5, folio 2383).

107 72   *Cf.* Testimony of Lida Acuña [provided during the public hearing on April 14, 2010, during the forty-first special session held in Lima, Peru] and testimony of Rodrigo Villagra Carron [provided during the public hearing on April 14, 2010, during the forty-first special session held in Lima, Peru].

108 73   *Cf.* CEADUC Anthropological Report, *supra* note [62], folios 741 and 743, and testimony of Tomás Dermott, *supra* note [60], folio 598.

109 74   *Cf.* Testimony of Marcelino López, *supra* note 63, folio 580.

110 75   *Cf.* Testimony of Gerardo Larrosa before notary public on March 25, 2010 (merits file, tome II, folios 604 to 609), and Testimony of Tomás Dermott, *supra* note [60], folio 595.

111 76   *Cf.* Testimony of Maximiliano Ruíz, *supra* note [59]; testimony of Marcelino López, *supra* note [63], folio 586, and CEADUC Report, *supra* note [62], folio 712 and 713.

112 77   *Cf.* Testimony of Marcelino López, *supra* note 63, folio 580; testimony of Gerardo Larrosa, *supra* note 75, folio 605; testimony of Lida Beatriz Acuña, *supra* note [72]; testimony of Maximiliano Ruíz, *supra* note [63], and testimony of Antonia Ramírez, *supra* note 28 folio 1151.

113 78   *Cf.* Testimony of Gerardo Larrosa, *supra* note 75, folio 505; testimony of Marcelino López, *supra* note 63, folio 580; testimony of Antonia Ramírez [provided during the public hearing on April 14, 2010, during the forty-first special session held in Lima, Peru], folios 1151, 1152 and 1156, and testimony of Clemente Dermott, *supra* note 63, folio 650.

114 79   *Cf.* Testimony of Gerardo Larrosa, *supra* note 75, folio 605, and testimony of Rodrigo Villagra Carron, *supra* note [72].

115 80   *Cf.* Agreement signed by the leaders of the communities of Nepoxen, Saria, Tajamar Kabayu, Kenaten, and Xákmok Kásek on April 16, 2005 (case file of documents provided by the State at the public hearing, tome IX, attachment VI, folios 3731 and 3732); testimony of Maximiliano Ruíz, *supra* note [59]. The said communities were also known as the Cora-í (*Cf.* Testimony of Rodrigo Villagra Carron, *supra* note [72]).

116 81   *Cf.* Testimony of Roberto Carlos Eaton Kent, *supra* note [67], folio 659, and testimony of Rodrigo Villagra Carron, *supra* note [72].

117 82   *Cf.* Letter from the Community of September 9, 2005, addressed to the INDI (case file of documents provided by the State at the public hearing, tome IX, attachment VI, folio 3730).

118 83   *Cf.* Minutes of the meeting of the Community of May 2, 2009 (file of attachments to the pleadings and motions brief, attachment 7, tome VI, folio 2736).

119 84   *Cf.* Testimony of Marcelino López, *supra* note 63, folio 580; testimony of Gerardo Larrosa *supra* note 75, folio 605; testimony of Maximiliano Ruíz, *supra* note [59]; testimony of Clemente Dermott, *supra* note 63, and testimony of Antonia Ramírez, *supra* note [7]8.

120 85   Rodrigo Villagra Carron indicated that the "25 de Febrero" settlement was 35 Km from the Salazar Ranch; while Clemente Dermott indicated that it was 35 Km from the Trans-Chaco Highway. *Cf.* Testimony of Rodrigo Villagra Carron, *supra* note [72], and

testimony of Clemente Dermott, *supra* note 63, folio 645.

121 86 *Cf.* Testimony of Marcelino López, *supra* note 63, folios 586 and 587.

122 314 case of *the Yakye Axa Indigenous Community v. Paraguay*, [Merits, reparations and costs, Judgment of June 17, 2005, Series C No. 125], para. 234; case of *Escué Zapata v. Colombia. Merits, reparations and costs.* Judgment of July 4, 2007. Series C No. 164, para. 16, and case of *the Saramaka People v. Suriname*, [Preliminary objections, merits, reparations and costs. Judgment of November 28, 2007. Series C No. 172], paras. 201 and 202.

123 153 *Cf.* case of *the "Street Children" (Villagrán Morales et al.) V. Guatemala. Reparations and Costs.* Judgment of May 26, 2001. Series C No. 77, para. 84; case of *Gomes Lund et al. ("Guerrilha do Araguaia") V. Brazil*, *supra* note 8,para. 305, and case of *Cabrera García and Montiel Flores V. México*, *supra* note 8, para. 255.

124 154 *Cf.* Statement of María Salvador Chiriboga rendered in the public hearing held on October 19, 2007 in the city of Bogota, Colombia.

125 155 *Cf.* Statement of Susana Salvador Chiriboga rendered before a public notary on October 1, 2007 (case file of Preliminary Objection and Merits, tome IV, f. 494).

126 156 *Cf.* Statement of Guadalupe Jessica Salvador Chiriboga rendered before a public notary on October 1, 2007 (case file of Merits, tome IV, folio 479).

127 157 *Cf.* case of *Salvador Chiriboga V. Ecuador*, *supra* note 24, paras. 111 to 113.

128 158 As was indicated in paragraph 76 of the present Judgment, by limiting the right to private property, the State shall fulfill with the objective of achieving a just equilibrium in between the public interest and the owners interest, so that in the present case the State should have used the least burdensome means to reduce the detriment of the right to private property of the victim.

129 159 *Cf.* case of *Suárez Rosero V. Ecuador. Reparations and Costs.* Judgment of January 20, 1999. Series C No. 44, para. 72; case of *Gomes Lund et al. ("Guerrilha do Araguaia") V. Brazil*, *supra* note 8, para. 310, and case of *Cabrera García and Montiel Flores V. México*, *supra* note 8, para. 260.

130 160 *Cf.* case of *Neira Alegría et al. V. Perú. Reparations and Costs.* Judgment of September 19, 1996. Series C No. 29, para. 56; case of *Gomes Lund et al. ("Guerrilha do Araguaia") V. Brazil*, *supra* note 8, para. 310, and case of *Cabrera García and Montiel Flores V. México*, *supra* note 8, para. 260.

131 2 In Admissibility Report No. 86/10, the Commission concluded that the State was responsible for the violation of Articles 3, 4, 5, 6, 7, 8, 11, 12, 16, 17, 19, 21, 22, 24 and 25 of the American Convention on Human Rights; as well as for failure to comply with the obligations established in Articles 1, 6 and 8 of the Inter-American Convention to Prevent and Punish Torture, Article 7(b) of the Convention of Belém do Pará, and Article I of the Inter-American Convention on Forced Disappearance of Persons, to the detriment of the presumed victims indicated in the said Report.

132 365 Opinion-PNR-BVRB-03-2011 of April 27, 2011, of the PNR, in relation to the file corresponding to Celestina Osorio Ixpata and María Osorio Chen (file of annexes to the submission of the case, tome XXXVI, folio 24596).

133 462 In the case of victim 17, according to the representatives, the young man Luis Enrique Parada Ropero was raised from an early age by Myriam Soreira Tulibila Macualo (merits file, tome 1, folio 240). However, she has received reparation for the death of her son, Oscar Esneider Vanegas Tulibila, and not for the death of Luis Enrique Parada Ropero. This means that she did not have recourse to the contentious-administrative jurisdiction in relation to the death of the youth Parada. In addition, according to the representatives, some members of the family of Luis Enrique Parada live in the state of Barinas in the Bolivarian Republic of Venezuela, and they listed the names of uncles (brothers of his father); Isidro, Andres and Isaías Paradas, however, they do not appear as victims (merits file, tome 1, folio 240).

134 463   *Cf.* Judgment of the Contentious Administrative Court of Arauca, Mario Galvis Gelvez *et al.*, case file No. 81-001- 23-2000-348, May 20, 2004 (evidence file, tome 20, folio 10180 to 10274), the Conciliation Agreement, Third Section, Council of State, Mario Galvis Gelves *et al.*, proceedings No. 28259, November 8, 2007 (evidence file, tome 3, folios 1044 and 1045), and the approval of the Conciliation Agreement, Judgment of the Third Section, Council of State, Mario Galvis Gelves *et al.*, case file No. 07001-23-31-000-2000-0348-01, December 13, 2007(evidence file, tome 2, folios 751-806). In this judgment, the conciliation was approved between the Nation and 19 of the 23 joint litigators, it was declared that the proceedings were terminated with regard to them, and the agreement was not approved with regard to the remaining four, ordering that the proceedings should continue in their regard. Subsequently, in a judgment of November 19, 2008, the Nation-Ministry of Defense was declared materially responsible for the damage caused to the four remaining co-litigants. See Third Section, Council of State, Mario Galvis Gelves *et al.*, case file No. 07001-23-31-000-2000-0348-01, November 19, 2008 (evidence file, tome 3, folios 1047-1127).

135 464   By Decision 979 of the Ministry of National Defense of March 18, 2009, the conciliation agreement approved on December 13, 2007, was complied with (evidence file, tome 2, folios 1129 to 1146), and by Decision 1560 of the Ministry of National Defense of April 27, 2009, the Judgment of November 19, 2008, was complied with (evidence file, tome 3, folios 1148-1155), so that the Nation-Ministry of Defense paid the representative of the presumed victims a total of five thousand seven hundred and fifty-eight million seven hundred and fifty-nine thousand and nineteen pesos and twenty cents (5,758,759,019.20 pesos). Decision 979 provided compensation to 79 family members and Decision 1560 provided compensation to 30 family members. Two family members of a deceased victim (Carmen Edilia González Ravelo, wife of Salomón Neite; and Marcos Neite González, son of Salomón Neite) were compensated in both decisions.

136 465   Nerys Duarte Cárdenas, Andersson Díaz Duarte and Davinson Duarte Cárdenas had recourse to the contentious administrative jurisdiction, but did not receive reparation because they had not proved the family relationship. In addition, Lucero Talero Sánchez, companion of Levis Orlando Martínez, did not receive compensation either, because she had not proved that she lived with the victim; however, her children did receive reparation as his children. In the case of María Elena Carreño, she did not prove that she was the sister of the deceased victim Levis Orlando Martínez (evidence file, tome 2, folios 782 and 783).

137 466   Namely: Edwin Fernando Vanegas Tulibila (brother of Oscar Esneider Vanegas Tulibila), Milciades Bonilla Ostos (permanent companion of Nancy Ávila Abaunza), Mario Galvis Gelves (husband of Teresa Mojica Hernández), Mónica Bello Tilano (mother of Egna Margarita Bello Tilano and sister of Katherine Cárdenas Tilano), Amalio Neite González (son of Salomón Neite), Marcos Aurelio Neite Méndez (brother of Luis Carlos Neite Méndez), Erinson Olimpo Cárdenas Tilano (brother of Katherine Cárdenas Tilano) and Neftalí Neite González (son of Salomón Neite).

138 467   They are María Cenobia Panqueva and Neftalí Neite González. In the case of the former, the loss of employment capacity was not determined, and in that of the latter, no medical record was provided so that it was not possible to determine the loss of employment capacity. See Judgment of the Contentious Administrative Court of Arauca, Mario Galvis Gelvez et al., case file No. 81-001-23-2000-348, May 20, 2004 (evidence file, tome 20, folio 10253); Judgment of the Third Section, Council of State, Mario Galvis Gelves et al., case file No. 07001-23-31-000-2000-0348-01, December 13, 2007 (evidence file, tome 2, folio 783), and Judgment of the Third Section, Council of State, Mario Galvis Gelves et al., case file No. 07001-23-31-000-2000-0348-01, November 19, 2008 (evidence file, tome 3, folio 1081-1082).

139 468   The State only referred to the sisters Maribel Daza Rojas and Rusmira Daza Rojas, as

injured victims who had not had recourse to the contentious administrative jurisdiction.

140 469 They are Carmen Edilia González Ravelo, who received compensation for the injuries to her son Amalio Neite González, as well as her siblings Neftalí, Neila, Salomón, Elizabeth and Marcos Neite González.

141 470 Nerys Duarte Cárdenas (permanent companion of Carmen Antonio Díaz), Andersson Duarte Cárdenas (son of Carmen Antonio Díaz), Davinson Duarte Cárdenas (son of Carmen Antonio Díaz), Lucero Talero Sánchez (permanent companion of Levis Orlando Martínez Carreña) and María Elena Carreño (sister of Levis Orlando Martínez Carreña).

142 400 *Cf.* case of *Suárez Rosero v. Ecuador. Reparations and costs*. Judgment of January 20, 1999. Series C No. 44, para. 72, and case of *the Constitutional Tribunal (Camba Campos et al.) v. Ecuador*, supra, para. 250.

143 401 case of the Street Children (Villagrán Morales et al.) v. Guatemala. Reparations and costs. Judgment of May 26, 2001. Series C No. 77, para. 84, and case of Luna López v. Honduras, supra, para. 251.

144 402 *Cf.* case of *Aloeboetoe et al. v. Suriname. Reparations and costs*. Judgment of September 10, 1993. Series C No. 15, para. 51, and case of *Gómez Palomino v. Peru. Merits, reparations and costs*, supra, para. 132.

145 893 *Cf.* case of *Cepeda Vargas v. Colombia. Preliminary objections, merits, reparations and costs*. Judgment of May 26, 2010, Para. 246, and case of *the Santo Domingo Massacre v. Colombia. Preliminary objections, merits and reparations*. Judgment of November 30, 2012. Series C No. 259, para. 37.

146 894 *Cf.* case of *Cepeda Vargas v. Colombia. Preliminary objections, merits, reparations and costs*. Judgment of May 26, 2010, paras. 139 and 140, and case of *the Santo Domingo Massacre v. Colombia*. Preliminary objections, merits and reparations. Judgment of November 30, 2012. Series C No. 259, para. 37.

147 895 The Court also observes that, when determining the pecuniary compensation at the domestic level, the calculation of the compensation corresponding to the children was made based on the time that had elapsed between their age at the time of the events and the time until they achieved their majority.

148 896 See, with regard to: (1) Cristina del Pilar Guarín Cortés, the judgment of the Council of State of October 13, 1994 (evidence file, folios 3190 to 3245); (2) Bernardo Beltrán Hernández, the judgment of the Council of State of October 13, 1994 (evidence file, folios 2906 to 2952); (3) Irma Franco Pineda, the judgment of the Council of State of September 11, 1997 (evidence file, folios 3247 to 3262), and (4) Luz Mary Portela León, the judgment of the Council of State of September 6, 1995 (evidence file, folios 3049 to 3094).

149 897 Judgment of the Council of State of September 11, 1997, in the proceedings instituted by the next of kin of Irma Franco Pineda (evidence file, folio 3260).

150 898 *Cf.* case of *Manuel Cepeda Vargas v. Colombia. Preliminary objections, merits, reparations and costs*. Judgment of May 26, 2010. Series C No. 213, para. 246, and case of *Tarazona Arrieta et al. v. Peru. Preliminary objection, merits, reparations and costs*. Judgment of October 15, 2014. Series C No. 286, para. 137.

151 899 This refers to the cases of: (1) Gloria Stella Lizarazo Figueroa, (2) Carlos Augusto Rodríguez Vera, (3) David Suspes Celis, (4) Héctor Jaime Beltrán Fuentes, (5) Norma Constanza Esguerra, (6) Ana Rosa Castiblanco Torres and (7) Carlos Horacio Urán Rojas.

152 *Velásquez Rodríguez v. Honduras, Reparations and Costs*, Judgment of July 21, 1989, Series C No. 7, para. 38 (emphasis added).

153 109 *Cf. Juan Humberto Sánchez Case, supra* note 4, para. 197; *"Five Pensioners" Case*, [June 7, 2003 Judgment. Series C No. 99], para. 183; *Las Palmeras Case, Reparations*, [(Art. 63(1) American Convention on Human Rights). November 26, 2002 Judgment. Series C No. 96], para. 92; *El Caracazo Case, Reparations*, [(Art. 63(1) American Convention on Human Rights). August 29, 2002 Judgment. Series C No. 95], para. 139;

Trujillo Oroza Case, Reparations, [(Art. 63(1) American Convention on Human Rights). February 27, 2002 Judgment. Series C No. 92], para. 137; *Bámaca Velásquez Case, Reparations,* [(Art. 63(1) American Convention on Human Rights). February 22, 2002 Judgment. Series C No. 91], para. 100; *Durand and Ugarte Case, Reparations,* [(Art. 63(1) American Convention on Human Rights). December 3, 2001 Judgment. Series C No. 89], para. 28; *Cantoral Benavides Case, Reparations,* [(Art. 63(1) American Convention on Human Rights). December 3, 2001 Judgment. Series C No. 88], para. 95; *Barrios Altos Case. Reparations* (Art. 63(1) American Convention on Human Rights). November 30, 2001 Judgment. Series C No. 87, para. 40; *Mayagna (Sumo) Awas Tingni Community Case,* [August 31, 2001 Judgment. Series C No. 79], para. 170; *Cesti Hurtado Case, Reparations,* [*Reparations* (Art. 63(1) American Convention on Human Rights). May 31, 2001 Judgment. Series C No. 78], para. 76; *"Street Children" Case (Villagrán Morales at al.), Reparations,* [(Art. 63(1) American Convention on Human Rights). May 26, 2001 Judgment. Series C No. 77], para. 119; *"White Van" Case (Paniagua Morales et al.). Reparations,* [(Art. 63(1) American Convention on Human Rights). May 25, 2001 Judgment. Series C No. 76], para. 225; *Blake Case, Reparations,* [(Art. 63(1) American Convention on Human Rights). January 22, 1999 Judgment. Series C No. 48], para. 71; *Suárez Rosero Case, Reparations,* [(Art. 63(1) American Convention on Human Rights). January 20, 1999 Judgment. Series C No. 44], para. 109; *Castillo Páez Case, Reparations,* [(Art. 63(1) American Convention on Human Rights). November 27, 1998 Judgment. Series C No. 43], para. 114; *Loayza Tamayo Case, Reparations,* [(Art. 63.1 American Convention on Human Rights), November 27, 1998 Judgment. Series C No. 42], para. 188; *Garrido and Baigorria Case, Reparations,* [(Art. 63(1) American Convention on Human Rights). August 27, 1998 Judgment. Series C No. 39], para. 39; *Caballero Delgado and Santana Case, Reparations,* [(Art. 63(1) American Convention on Human Rights). January 29, 1997 Judgment. Series C No. 31], para. 31; *Neira Alegría et al. Case, Reparations,* [(Art. 63(1) American Convention on Human Rights). September 19, 1996 Judgment. Series C No. 29], para. 64; and *El Amparo Case, Reparations,* [(Art. 63(1) American Convention on Human Rights). September 14, 1996 Judgment. Series C No. 28], para. 45.

154 115 *Cf. Constitutional Court case,* [Judgment of January 31, 2001. Series C No. 71], para. 125; and *Suárez Rosero* Case, *Reparations,* [(Article 63(1) American Convention on Human Rights). Judgment of January 20, 1999. Series C No. 44], paras. 92 and 97.

155 29 *Cf. Loayza Tamayo case. Reparations,* [(Article 63(1) of the American Convention on Human Rights). Judgment of November 27, 1998. Series C No. 42], para. 177; and *Garrido and Baigorria case. Reparations,* [(Article 63(1) of the American Convention on Human Rights). Judgment of August 27, 1998. Series C No. 39], para. 80.

156 30 *Cf. Villagrán Morales et al.* Case. *Reparations,* [(Article 63(1) of the American Convention on Human Rights). Judgment of May 26, 2001. Series C No. 77], para. 107; *Paniagua Morales et al. case. Reparations* (Article 63(1) of the American Convention on Human Rights). Series C No. 76, para. 212; *and Garrido and Baigorria case. Reparations, supra* note [29], para. 82.

157 31 Also, *Cf. Loayza Tamayo case. Reparations, supra* note [29], para. 178; and *Garrido and Baigorria case. Reparations, supra* note [29], para. 81.

158 32 Also *Cf. Ivcher Bronstein case,* [Judgment of February 6, 2001. Series C No. 74], para. 189; *Baena Ricardo et al. case,* [Judgment of February 2, 2001, Series C No. 72], para. 209 and *The Constitutional Court case,* [Judgment of January 31, 2001. Series C No. 71], para. 126.

159 185 *Las Palmeras Case, Reparations,* [(Art. 63(1) American Convention on Human Rights). Judgment of November 26, 2002. Series C No. 96], para. 82; *El Caracazo Case, Reparations,* [(Art. 63(1) American Convention on Human Rights). Judgment of August 29, 2002. Series C No. 95], para. 130; and *Trujillo Oroza* Case, *Reparations,* [(Art. 63(1)

American Convention on Human Rights). Judgment of February 27, 2002. Series C No. 92], para. 126.

160 186   *"Five Pensioners" Case*, [Judgment of February 28, 2003. Series C No. 98], para. 181, *Cantos* Case, [Judgment of November 28, 2002. Series C No. 97], para. 72; and *Las Palmeras* Case, *Reparations, supra* note [185], para. 83.

161 187   *"Five Pensioners" Case, supra* note [186], para. 181, *Cantos* Case, *supra* note [186], para. 72; and *El Caracazo* Case, *Reparations, supra* note [185], para. 131.

162 106   *Cf., Juan Humberto Sánchez* Case, [June 7, 2003 Judgment. Series C No. 99], para. 193; *Las Palmeras Case, Reparations,* [(Art. 63(1) American Convention on Human Rights). November 26, 2002 Judgment. Series C No. 96], para. 82; and *El Caracazo Case, Reparations,* [(Art. 63(1) American Convention on Human Rights). August 29, 2002 Judgment. Series C No. 95], para. 130.

163 107   *Cf., Juan Humberto Sánchez* Case, *supra* note [106], para. 193; *"Five Pensioners" Case*, [February 28, 2003 Judgment. Series C No. 98], para. 181; and *Cantos* Case, [November 28, 2002 Judgment. Series C No. 97], para. 72.

164 108   *Cf., Juan Humberto Sánchez* Case, *supra* note [106], para. 193; *"Five Pensioners" Case*, *supra* note [107], para. 181; and *Cantos Case, supra* note [107], para. 72.

165 237   *Cf.* case of Maritza Urrutia, supra note 3, para. 182; case of Myrna Mack Chang, supra note 3, para. 290; and case of Bulacio, supra note 3, para. 150.

166 238   *Cf.* case of Maritza Urrutia, supra note 3, para. 182; case of Myrna Mack Chang, supra note 3, para. 290; and case of Bulacio, supra note 3, para. 150.

167 239   *Cf.* case of Maritza Urrutia, supra note 3, para. 182; case of Myrna Mack Chang, supra note 3, para. 290; and case of Bulacio, supra note 3, para. 150.

168 240   *Cf.* case of Maritza Urrutia, supra note 3, para. 183; case of Loayza Tamayo. Reparations (Art. 63(1) American Convention on Human Rights). Judgment of November 27, 1998. Series C No. 42, para. 178; and Garrido and Baigorria case. Reparations (Art. 63(1) American Convention on Human Rights). Judgment of August 27, 1998. Series C No. 39, para. 81.

169 181   Certification issued by the lawyers Xavier A. Flores Aguirre and Pablo J. Cevallos Palomeque on September 20, 2007 (file on merits, volume III, folio 944).

170 182   *Cf.* case of *de the Gómez Paquiyauri Brothers. Monitoring compliance with judgment.* Order of the Inter-American Court of Human Rights of September 22, 2006, sixteenth considering paragraph.

171 183   *Cf.* case of *Cantoral Benavides,* [*v. Peru. Reparations and Costs.* Judgment of December 3, 2001. Series C No. 88], para. 85. Also, in case of *Cesti Hurtado v. Peru*, the Court stated that "[w]ith regard to professional fees, it is necessary to bear in mind the characteristics inherent in international human rights proceedings, in which decisions are adopted on the violations of such rights, without examining all the extremes of the implications of these violations, which could involve questions of profit related to the said fees, which are legitimate in themselves, but unrelated to the specific issue of the protection of human rights. Therefore, the Court must decide these claims with restraint. If the Court proceeded otherwise, international human rights litigation would be denatured. Consequently, the Court must apply criteria of equity in these cases."

172 184   *Cf.* case of *Molina Theissen,* [*v. Guatemala. Reparations and costs.* Judgment of July 3, 2004. Series C No. 108], para. 22; case of *Acosta Calderón,* [*v. Ecuador. Merits, reparations, and costs.* Judgment of June 24, 2005. Series C No. 129], para. 41.[185] *Cf.* case of *Cesti Hurtado, supra* note 183, para. 72.

173 185   *Cf.* case of *Cesti Hurtado, supra* note 183, para. 72.

174 3   In this Report the Inter-American Commission declared admissible the petition regarding the alleged violation of Articles 11, 17 and 24 of the American Convention, in relation to Articles 1(1) and 2 thereof. Cf. Admissibility Report No. 25/04, Case 12,361, Ana Victoria Sánchez Villalobos et al., Costa Rica, March 11, 2004 (file of attachments to

the pleadings and motions brief of the representative Gerardo Trejos, tome I, annex 2, folios 3900 to 3914). In this report, the Commission declared that the "complaint was inadmissible with regard to the firms *"Costa Rica Ultrasonografía S.A. and the Instituto Costarricense de Fertilidad."*

175 4   Merits Report No. 85/10, Case No. 12,361, Gretel Artavia Murillo et al. v. Costa Rica, July 14, 2010 (merits file, folios 7 to 37).

176 517   *Cf.* case of *Garrido and Baigorria v. Argentina. Reparations and costs.* Judgment of August 27, 1998. Series C No. 39, para. 82; case of *the Río Negro Massacres v. Guatemala. Preliminary objection, merits, reparations and costs.* Judgment of September 4, 2012 Series C No. 250, para. 314.

177 518   *Cf.* case of *Chaparro Álvarez and Lapo Íñiguez. v. Ecuador. Preliminary objections, merits, reparations and costs.* Judgment of November 21, 2007. Series C No. 170, para. 277, and case of *Vélez Restrepo and family v. Colombia,* para. 307.

178 519   In his pleadings and motions brief, representative Trejos presented as expenses during the proceedings: (i) the invoice for the purchase of a plane ticket in the name of Andrea Bianchi (US$439.72); (ii) the invoice for the purchase of a plane ticket in the name of Gerardo Trejos Salas (US$468.62), and (iii) the invoice for the purchase of a plane ticket in the name of Gloria Mazariegos (US$468.62),totaling US$1,376.96 (file of annexes to the pleadings and motions brief, volume I, folios 4071 and 4072).

179 520   In his pleadings and motions brief, representative Boris Molina Acevedo presented as expenses during the proceedings: (i) invoice for professional services issued to María Lorna Ballestero Muñóz por US$6,000.00; (ii) receipt of payment for professional services to Gabriela Darsié and Enrique Madrigal for US$1,375, (iii) receipt for payment of professional services for advice and assistance provided by William Vega for US$1,600, and (iv) and for photocopies and administrative expenses 131,850 colones (file of annexes to the pleadings and motions brief, volume VI, folios 6537 a 6364).

180 521   *Cf.* case of *Chitay Nech et al. v. Guatemala. Preliminary objections, merits, reparations and costs.* Judgment of May 25, 2010. Series C No. 212, para. 287.

181   *See generally,* Section VII "The Victims' Legal Assistance Fund" in Chapter One "Defining Victim, Beneficiary, and the Right of Action."

Chapter Three

BEYOND COMPENSATION: *RESTITUTIO IN INTEGRUM*

I. INTRODUCTION

"*Restitutio in integrum*" literally means restoration to a whole or uninjured condition (i.e., restoration to the *status quo ante*). The principle of *restitutio in integrum* requires the full restoration of the victim to the situation that existed prior to violation of his or her human rights and freedoms, and full reparation of the consequences of the violation. Although monetary compensation can address and alleviate some of the financially quantifiable consequences of violations, full restoration of a victim's rights and freedoms most often requires holistic and comprehensive measures that provide redress and seek to remedy the violation. These forms of reparation involve restitution, rehabilitation, satisfaction, and guarantees of non-repetition.

Reparations orders address the specific circumstances of each case, and consequently each case may involve different measures of reparations. Restitution seeks to restore the victim to the situation that would have existed had the violation of their rights and freedoms not occurred. Restitution may involve *inter alia* restoration of a victim's liberty and enjoyment of his or her human rights, or the return of his or her employment status or property. However, restitution cannot be made fully, or sometimes even partially, in certain cases. Rehabilitation may be required, as another measure of reparation, to remedy the physical, mental and other consequences of the violation.

Throughout its jurisprudence, the Inter-American Court of Human Rights has affirmed that the Court's decision may constitute *per se* a form of reparation. This declaration recognizes the importance of satisfaction as a measure of reparation and the value of truth in remedying violations. Satisfaction also may take the form of, *inter alia,* investigation, public disclosure, acknowledgment and acceptance of responsibility by the perpetrators, commemoration of the victims, and other effective measures directed at the cessation of continuing violations. Guarantees of non-repetition are explicitly directed at ensuring that future violations do not occur. Such measures frequently address the underlying causes of violations and circumstances that permit or encourage violations of human rights and freedoms to occur.

Under Article 63(1) of the American Convention on Human Rights, "[i] f the Court finds that there has been a violation of a right or freedom protected by this Convention, the Court shall rule that the injured party be ensured the enjoyment of his right or freedom that was violated [and] if appropriate, that the consequences of the measure or situation that constituted the breach of such right or freedom be remedied." As the Court has noted throughout its jurisprudence, "this provision reflects a customary norm that constitutes one of the fundamental principles of contemporary International Law on State responsibility."[1]

The Basic Principles and Guidelines on the Right to a Remedy and Reparation for Victims of Gross Violations of International Human Rights Law and Serious Violations of International Humanitarian Law, as adopted in 2005 by the United Nations General Assembly, codified the customary international norm that violations of rights require remedy and reparation, and that reparation measures include restitution, rehabilitation, satisfaction and guarantees of non-repetition. The following case excerpts demonstrate the Court's analysis and decisions regarding the provision of full and effective reparations to address specific human rights violations in the forms of restitution, rehabilitation, satisfaction and guarantees of non-repetition.

II. NORMATIVE FRAMEWORK

A. Basic Principles and Guidelines on the Right to a Remedy and Reparation for Victims of Gross Violations of International Human Rights Law and Serious Violations of International Humanitarian Law[2]

18.   In accordance with domestic law and international law, and taking account of individual circumstances, victims of gross violations of international human rights law and serious violations of international humanitarian law should, as appropriate and proportional to the gravity of the violation and the circumstances of each case, be provided with full and effective reparation, as

laid out in principles 19 to 23, which include the following forms: restitution, compensation, rehabilitation, satisfaction and guarantees of non-repetition.

19.   *Restitution* should, whenever possible, restore the victim to the original situation before the gross violations of international human rights law or serious violations of international humanitarian law occurred. Restitution includes, as appropriate: restoration of liberty, enjoyment of human rights, identity, family life and citizenship, return to one's place of residence, restoration of employment and return of property.

20.   *Compensation* should be provided for any economically assessable damage, as appropriate and proportional to the gravity of the violation and the circumstances of each case, resulting from gross violations of international human rights law and serious violations of international humanitarian law, such as:

    (a) Physical or mental harm;

    (b) Lost opportunities, including employment, education and social benefits;

    (c) Material damages and loss of earnings, including loss of earning potential; Moral damage;

    (d) Costs required for legal or expert assistance, medicine and medical services, and psychological and social services.

21.   *Rehabilitation* should include medical and psychological care as well as legal and social services.

22.   *Satisfaction* should include, where applicable, any or all of the following:international human rights law and international humanitarian law training and in educational material at all levels.

23.   *Guarantees of non-repetition* should include, where applicable, any or all of the following measures, which will also contribute to prevention:

    (a) Ensuring effective civilian control of military and security forces;

    (b) Ensuring that all civilian and military proceedings abide by international standards of due process, fairness and impartiality;

    (c) Strengthening the independence of the judiciary;

    (d) Protecting persons in the legal, medical and health-care professions, the media and other related professions, and human rights defenders;

    (e) Providing, on a priority and continued basis, human rights and international humanitarian law education to all sectors of society and training for law enforcement officials as well as military and security forces;

    (d) Promoting the observance of codes of conduct and ethical norms, in particular international standards, by public servants, including law enforcement, correctional, media, medical, psychological, social service and military personnel, as well as by economic enterprises;

    (e) Promoting mechanisms for preventing and monitoring social conflicts and their resolution;

    (f) Reviewing and reforming laws contributing to or allowing gross violations of international human rights law and serious violations of international humanitarian law.

B. Draft Articles on State Responsibility for Internationally Wrongful Acts with Commentaries[3]

ARTICLE 30. CESSATION AND NON-REPETITION

The State responsible for the internationally wrongful act is under an obligation: to cease that act, if it is continuing; to offer appropriate assurances and guarantees non-repetition, if circumstances so require.

Commentary

(1) Article 30 deals with two separate but linked issues raised by the breach of an international obligation: the cessation of the wrongful conduct and the offer of assurances and guarantees of non-repetition by the responsible State if circumstances so require. Both are aspects of the restoration and repair of the legal relationship affected by the breach. Cessation is, as it were, the negative aspect of future performance, concerned with securing an end to continuing wrongful conduct, whereas assurances and guarantees serve a preventive function and may be described as a positive reinforcement of future performance.

(7) The question of cessation often arises in close connection with that of reparation, and particularly restitution. The result of cessation may be indistinguishable from restitution . . . . Nonetheless, the two must be distinguished. Unlike restitution, cessation is not subject to limitations relating to proportionality. It may give rise to a continuing obligation, even when literal return to the *status quo ante* is excluded or can only be achieved in an approximate way.

(11) Assurances of guarantees of non-repetition may be sought by way of satisfaction (e.g. the repeal of the legislation which allowed the breach to occur) and there is thus some overlap between the two in practice.

(12) Assurances are normally given verbally, while guarantees of non-repetition involve something more—for example, preventive measures to be taken by the responsible State designed to avoid repetition of the breach.

ARTICLE 31. REPARATION

1. The responsible State is under an obligation to make full reparation for the injury caused by the internationally wrongful act.

2. Injury includes any damage, whether material or moral, caused by the internationally wrongful act of a State.

Commentary

(3) The obligation placed on the responsible State by Article 31 is to make "full reparation" . . . . In other words, the responsible States must endeavor to "wipe out all the consequences of the illegal act and reestablish the situation which would, in all probability, have existed if that act had not been committed"[4] though the provision of one or more of the forms of reparation . . . .[5]

ARTICLE 34. FORMS OF REPARATION

Full reparation for the injury caused by the internationally wrongful act shall take the form of restitution, compensation and satisfaction, either singly or in combination . . . .

ARTICLE 35. RESTITUTION

A State responsible for an internationally wrongful act is under an obligation to make restitution, that is, to re-establish the situation which existed before the wrongful act was committed, provided and to the extent that restitution:

(a) is not materially impossible;

(b)   does not involve a burden out of all proportion to the benefit deriving from restitution instead of compensation.

Commentary

(1) Restitution involves the re-establishment as far as possible of the situation which existed prior to the commission of the internationally wrongful act, to the extent that any changes that have occurred in that situation may be traced to that act.

(2) The concept of restitution is not uniformly defined. According to one definition, restitution consists in re-establishing the *status quo ante*, i.e. the situation that existed prior to the occurrence of the wrongful act. Under another definition, restitution is the establishment or re-establishment of the situation that would have existed if the wrongful act had not been committed. The former definition is the narrower one; it does not extend to the compensation which may be due to the injured party for loss suffered . . . . The latter definition absorbs into the concept of restitution other elements of full reparation and tends to conflate restitution as a form of reparation and the underlying obligation of reparation itself.

(3) [B]ecause restitution most closely conforms to the general principle that the responsible State is bound to wipe out the legal and material consequences of its wrongful act by re-establishing the situation that would exist if that act had not been committed, it comes first among the forms of reparation.

(6) What may be required in terms of restitution will often depend on the content of the primary obligation which has been breached. Restitution, as the first of the forms of reparation, is of particular importance where the obligation breached is of a continuing character, and even more so where it arises under a peremptory norm of general international law.

(7) The obligation to make restitution is not unlimited. In particular, under Article 35, restitution is required "provided and to the extent that" it is neither materially impossible nor wholly disproportionate.

(8) ... On the other hand, restitution is not impossible merely on grounds of legal or practical difficulties, even though the responsible State may have to make special efforts to overcome these.

ARTICLE 36. COMPENSATION

1. The State responsible for an internationally wrongful act is under an obligation to compensate for the damage caused thereby, insofar as such damage is not made good by restitution.

2. The compensation shall cover any financially assessable damage including loss of profits insofar as it is established.

Commentary

(3) Restitution, despite its primacy as a matter of legal principle, is frequently unavailable or inadequate . . . . Even where restitution is made, it may be insufficient to ensure full reparation. The role of compensation is to fill in any gaps so as to ensure full reparation for damage suffered.

(4) As compared with satisfaction, the function of compensation is to address the actual losses incurred as a result of the internationally wrongful act. Compensation corresponds to the financially assessable damage suffered . . . . It is not concerned to punish the responsible State, nor does compensation have an expressive or exemplary character. Thus, compensation generally consists of a monetary payment, though it may sometimes take the form, as agreed, of other forms of value. Monetary compensation is intended to offset, as far as may be, the damage suffered . . . as a result of the breach. Satisfaction is concerned with non-material injury . . . on which a monetary value can be put only in a highly approximate and notional way.

ARTICLE 37. SATISFACTION

1. The State responsible for an internationally wrongful act is under an obligation to give satisfaction for the injury caused by that act insofar as

it cannot be made good by restitution or compensation.

2. Satisfaction may consist in an acknowledgment of the breach, an expression of regret, a formal apology or another appropriate modality.

3. Satisfaction shall not be out of proportion to the injury and may not take a form humiliating to the responsible State.

Commentary

(1) Satisfaction . . . is not a standard form of reparation, in the sense that in many cases the injury caused by an internationally wrongful act of a State may be fully repaired by restitution and/or compensation.

(3) In accordance with paragraph 2 of Article 31, the injury for which a responsible State is obliged to make full reparation embraces "any damage, whether material or moral . . ." Material and moral damage resulting from an internationally wrongful act will normally be financially assessable and hence covered by the remedy of compensation. Satisfaction, on the other hand, is the remedy for those injuries, not financially assessable, which amount to an affront . . . . These injuries are frequently of a symbolic character, arising from the very fact of the breach of the obligation, irrespective of its material consequences.

(5) [S]atisfaction may consist in an acknowledgment of the breach, an expression of regret, a formal apology or another appropriate modality. * * * The appropriate form of satisfaction will depend on the circumstances and cannot be prescribed in advance. Many possibilities exist . . . . Assurances or guarantees of non-repetition, which are dealt with in the articles in the context of cessation, may also amount to a form of satisfaction.

(6) One of the most common modalities of satisfaction provided in the case of moral or non-material injury . . . is a declaration of the wrongfulness of the act by a competent court or tribunal.

III. RESTITUTION

As the term implies, "restitution" seeks to restore the victim of the human rights violation to the situation that would have existed had the violation not occurred. As demonstrated in the following case excerpts, the Inter-American Court of Human Rights has ordered restitution to restore the rights of individual and groups of victims to employment and various related benefits, as well as to restore the rights of entire communities to their homes and livelihoods, as in the below cases involving restoration of ancestral lands to indigenous communities.

All forms of reparation are fundamentally directed at remedying the harm suffered by the victim as a result of the violation of their human rights. Restitution, as a form of reparation, is directed at restoring the specific rights and freedoms that were violated and restoring the victim[s] insofar as possible to their situation prior to violation of their rights.

Aloeboetoe et al. v. Suriname
10-Sep-1993
Series C No. 15—*Reparations and Costs*

96.   The compensation fixed for the victims' heirs includes an amount that will enable the minor children to continue their education until they reach a certain age. Nevertheless, these goals will not be met merely by granting compensatory damages; it is also essential that the children be offered a school where they can receive adequate education and basic medical attention. At the present time, this is not available in several of the Saramaka villages.

Most of the children of the victims live in Gujaba, where the school and the medical dispensary have both been shut down. The Court believes that, as part of the compensation due, Suriname is under the obligation to reopen the school at Gujaba and staff it with teaching and administrative personnel to enable it to function on a permanent basis as of 1994. In addition, the necessary steps shall be taken for the medical dispensary already in place there to be made operational and reopen that same year.

Loayza Tamayo v. Peru
27-Nov-1998
Series C No. 42—*Reparations and Costs*

113.   It is the view of this Court that the State does have an obligation to make every effort within its power to have the victim reinstated in the teaching positions she held in public institutions at the time of her detention. Her salaries and other benefits should be equal to the full amount she was receiving for teaching in the public and private sectors at the time of her detention, adjusted to its value as of the date of this Judgment. The Court has had before it a resolution ordering the victim's reinstatement in the teaching service, so that Peru has already partially complied with this obligation.

114.   The Court further considers that the State is under the obligation to re-enter the victim's name on the proper retirement records, retroactive to the date

on which she was removed from those records, and to ensure that she enjoys the same retirement rights to which she was entitled prior to her detention.

115.   However, judging from the evidence, particularly the medical reports on the victim's health and the victim's own statement, circumstances are such that, for the present, it would be difficult for her to fully re-immerse herself in her former jobs.

116.   The State, therefore, has an obligation to do everything necessary to ensure that the victim receives her salaries, social security, and employment benefits as of the date of issuance of this Judgment and until such time as she is able to effectively re-join the teaching service. The Court believes the prudent course of action would be to use the domestic mechanisms that apply in cases of employment disability or any other suitable means that will ensure that this obligation is honored.

117.   The Court believes that, strictly speaking, the victim's claims regarding her career prospects and promotion would not be measures of restitution; it will, therefore, examine them when it evaluates the damages the victim is claiming to her "life plan" (*proyecto de vida*).

Apitz Barbera et al. v. Venezuela
5-Aug-2008
Series C No. 182—*Preliminary Objections, Merits, Reparations, and Costs*

2.   The application is related to the removal from office of former judges of the *Corte Primera de lo Contenciso Administrativo* (First Court of Administrative Disputes) (hereinafter "the First Court") Ana María Ruggeri Cova, Perkins Rocha Contreras, and Juan Carlos Apitz Barbera on October 30, 2003, on the grounds that they had committed an inexcusable judicial error when they granted an *amparo* (protection of constitutional guarantees and rights) against an administrative act that had denied a request for protocolization of a land sale. The Commission asserted that the removal based on this error "is contrary to the principle of judicial independence and undermines the right of judges to decide freely in accordance with the law" and that they were removed "on the grounds that they had committed an [alleged] inexcusable judicial error when what existed was a reasonable and reasoned difference of possible legal interpretations concerning a particular procedural feature. This was a serious violation of their right to due process because of the lack of justification of the decision to remove them and their lack of access to any simple, swift, and effective recourse for obtaining a determination on the disciplinary measure to which they had been subjected." Moreover, the Commission stated that the First Court had adopted decisions "that had generated adverse reactions among senior officials of the executive branch"

and that "the indicia as a whole" supported the inference that the body that ordered the removal was not independent and impartial and that such removal resulted from a "misuse of power" originating in the "cause-and-effect relationship between the statements of the President of the Republic and senior government officials concerning the decisions that went against government interests and the disciplinary investigation that was initiated and that culminated in the victims' removal."

3.   In its application, the Commission requested the Court to declare the State responsible for the violation of the rights enshrined in Article 8 (Right to a Fair Trial) and Article 25 (Right to Judicial Protection) of the American Convention in conjunction with the duties established in Article 1(1) (Obligation to Respect Rights) and Article 2 (Obligation to Adjust Domestic Legislation to Human Rights Standards) thereof, to the detriment of the victims. Furthermore, it requested the Court to order certain measures of reparation.

244.   The Commission requested that "the victims be reinstated in their position as judges of the First Court. . . or a position of similar hierarchy if it were not possible to reinstate them in the court where they sat." It added that "should they be reinstated in a temporary position, the pertinent public competitive selection processes should be conducted as soon as possible through an adequate and effective procedure." In turn, the representative requested that "in order to secure the independence of the Judiciary, . . . the victims' removal from office be set aside and reinstatement in their positions be effected."

245.   The State [alleged] that setting aside removal from office and reinstating the judges in their position "is no reparation" since if "the State's responsibility were determined, the prior situation of the judges would be restored, and taking the facts regarding the appointment defects as proven" this, "far from being reparative, is clearly 'condemnatory.'"

246.   The Court has determined that the removal of the victims from their position was the result of a process that was in violation of judicial guarantees and judicial protection. Consequently, taking into consideration that the irremovability of judges, whether they be temporary or permanent, must ensure that those who were arbitrarily removed from their position as judges be reinstated therein, the Court deems that as a reparation measure the State must reinstate the victims, if they so desire, in a position in the Judiciary in which they have the same rank, salary, and related social benefits as they had prior to their removal. If, due to legitimate reasons that are beyond the will of the victims, the State could not reinstate them in the Judiciary within the term of six months as from notice of this Judgment, it shall pay each of the victims the amount set in equity of US$100,000.00 (one hundred thousand United States dollars), or its equivalent amount in national currency, within eighteen months as from notice of this Judgment.

González et al. ("Cotton Field") v. Mexico
16-Nov-2009
Series C No. 205—*Preliminary Objections, Merits, Reparations, and Costs*

2.   [The Inter-American Commission presented the Court an application alleging Mexico's] international responsibility for "the disappearance and subsequent death" of Mss. Claudia Ivette González, Esmeralda Herrera Monreal, and Laura Berenice Ramos Monárrez (hereinafter "Mss. González, Herrera, and Ramos"), whose bodies were found in a cotton field in Ciudad Juárez on November 6, 2001. The State is considered responsible for "the lack of measures for the protection of the victims, two of whom were minor children, the lack of prevention of these crimes, in spite of full awareness of the existence of a pattern of gender-related violence that had resulted in hundreds of women and girls murdered, the lack of response of the authorities to the disappearance . . .; the lack of due diligence in the investigation of the homicides . . ., as well as the denial of justice and the lack of an adequate reparation."

3.   The Commission asked that the Court declare the State responsible for the violation of the rights embodied in Articles 4 (Right to Life), 5 (Right to Humane Treatment), 8 (Right to a Fair Trial), 19 (Rights of the Child), and 25 (Right to Judicial Protection) of the Convention, in relation to the obligations established in Articles 1(1) (Obligation to Respect Rights) and 2 (Domestic Legal Effects) thereof, together with failure to comply with the obligations arising from Article 7 of the Convention on the Prevention, Punishment, and Eradication of Violence against Women (hereinafter "the Convention of Belém do Pará"). The application was notified to the State on December 21, 2007, and to the representatives on January 2, 2008.

228.   In the instant case, the Court takes note, firstly, of the State's acknowledgement of the situation of violence against women in Ciudad Juárez and also its statement that the murders of women in Ciudad Juárez "are influenced by a culture of discrimination against women."

229.   Secondly, the Court notes that it has established . . . that the reports of the IACHR Rapporteur, CEDAW, and Amnesty International, among others, indicate that many of the killings of women in Ciudad Juárez are manifestations of gender-based violence.

230.   Thirdly, the three victims in this case were young, underprivileged women, workers or students, as were many of the victims of the murders in Ciudad Juárez. They were abducted and their bodies appeared in a cotton field. It has been accepted as proved that they suffered physical ill-treatment and very probably sexual abuse of some type before they died.

231.   All of this leads the Court to conclude that Mss. González, Ramos, and

Herrera, were victims of violence against women according to the American Convention and the Convention of Belém do Pará. On the same basis, the Court considers that the murders of the victims were gender-based and were perpetrated in an acknowledged context of violence against women in Ciudad Juárez.

450.   The Court recalls that the concept of "integral reparation" (*restitutio in integrum*) entails the re-establishment of the previous situation and the elimination of the effects produced by the violation, as well as the payment of compensation for the damage caused. However, bearing in mind the context of structural discrimination in which the facts of this case occurred, which was acknowledged by the State, the reparations must be designed to change this situation, so that their effect is not only of restitution, but also of rectification. In this regard, re-establishment of the same structural context of violence and discrimination is not acceptable.

Yakye Axa Indigenous Community v. Paraguay
17-Jun-2005
Series C No. 125—*Merits, Reparations, and Costs*

1.   On March 17, 2003 the Inter-American Commission on Human Rights (hereinafter "the Commission" or "the Inter-American Commission") filed before the Inter-American Court an application against the State of Paraguay (hereinafter "the State" or "Paraguay"), originating in complaint No. 12.313, received at the Secretariat of the Commission on January 10, 2000.

2.   The Commission filed the application, based on Articles 51 and 61 of the American Convention, for the Court to decide whether Paraguay breached Articles 4 (Right to Life), 8 (Right to Fair Trial), 21 (Right to Property), and 25 (Judicial Protection) of the American Convention, in combination with the obligations set forth in Articles 1(1) (Obligation to Respect Rights) and 2 (Domestic Legal Effects) of that same Convention, to the detriment of the Yakye Axa Indigenous Community of the Enxet-Lengua People (hereinafter the "Yakye Axa Indigenous Community," the "Yakye Axa Community," the "Indigenous Community," or the "Community") and its members. The Commission [alleged] that the State has not ensured the ancestral property rights of the Yakye Axa Indigenous Community and its members because, while said Community's land claim has been processed since 1993, no satisfactory solution has been attained. According to the Commission in its application, this has made it impossible for the Community and its members to own and possess their territory and has kept it in a vulnerable situation in terms of food, medical, and public health care, constantly threatening the survival of the members of the Community and of the [Community] as such.

D) OTHER FORMS OF REPARATION (MEASURES OF SATISFACTION AND GUARANTEES OF NON-RECIDIVISM

210.   In this section, the Court will now establish measures of satisfaction to redress non-pecuniary damage and will also order measures that are public in their scope or repercussions. Said measures are especially relevant in the instant case due to the collective nature of the damage caused.[219 6]

a)   Handing over of traditional territory to the Yakye Axa Indigenous Community

211.   The common basis of the human rights violations against the members of the Yakye Axa Community found in the instant Judgment is primarily the lack of materialization of the ancestral territorial rights of the members of the Community, whose existence has not been challenged by the State. Furthermore, the State has expressed throughout this proceeding before the Court its willingness to grant lands to the members of the Community. Thus, in the brief with its reply to the application, it stated that

> [b]earing in mind the general interest sought by the substantive matter, even though the State of Paraguay does not agree with the grounds for the application, it acquiesces to the request for reparations and, therefore, through the appropriate authorities, it will order the granting of lands to the applicant [C]ommunity, within the [C]ommunity's traditional territory, with the area authorized by the legislation in force, that is, 100 hectares per family, for which purpose it will allocate financial resources that it has already requested from the Legislative . . . .

> The property that will be granted to the [C]ommunity will be purchased by the State in the manner and under the conditions authorized by the legislation in force, without affecting the rights of third parties who are likewise protected by that legislation and the American Convention, for which reason it undertakes no commitment to conduct an unlawful expropriation or confiscation . . . .

212.   The State added that

> it ratifies its willingness to grant a title deed, free of cost, to the Yakye Axa Community, in accordance with the Constitution and the legislation in force, to 7,901 hectares in favor of said [C]ommunity, within the delimited territory in the Paraguayan Chaco, subject to what national legislation allows and without affecting the rights of third parties who justify property rights and rational use, whether by means of a negotiated purchase from the owners of said lands or by expropriation in accordance with domestic legislation . . . .

213.   In its oral pleadings at the public hearing of the instant case, the State pointed out that

> what the State . . . plans to give the members of this [C] ommunity is not just any land. It is the land they decide at the appropriate time within their ancestral territory and within what this Chanawatsan community has stated is part of their territory, which . . .is much broader than the eighteen thousand hectares that they claim today as irreplaceable territory . . . .

214.   In its final written pleadings the State reiterate[d] its sustained willingness to reach a definitive solution to this case by means of direct negotiations with the Community . . . to grant the Yakye Axa Community an area of land in accordance with its communal needs, pursuant to the Constitution, to ILO Agreement [No.] 169, and to the respective special legislation, within the CHANAWATSAN territory.

215.   It is not for the Court to define the traditional territory of the Yakye Axa Indigenous Community, but rather to establish whether the State has respected and guaranteed its members' right to communal property, and it has done so in the instant Judgment. Therefore, the State must delimit, demarcate, grant title deed, and transfer the land, pursuant to paragraphs 137 to 154 of the instant Judgment.

216.   For this, it is necessary to consider that the victims of the instant case have to date an awareness of an exclusive common history; they are the sedentary expression of one of the bands of the Chanawatsan indigenous peoples, of the Lengua-Maskoy linguistic family, whose traditional form of occupation was as hunter-gatherers. Possession of their traditional territory is indelibly recorded in their historical memory, and their relationship with the land is such that severing that tie entails the certain risk of an irreparable ethnic and cultural loss, with the ensuing loss of diversity. In the process of sedentarization, the Yakye Axa Community took on an identity of its own that is connected to a physically and culturally determined geographic space, which is a specific part of what was the vast Chanawatsan territory.

217.   For the aforementioned reasons, the State must identify said traditional territory and give it to the Yakye Axa Community free of cost, within a maximum period of three years from the date of notification of the instant Judgment. If the traditional territory is in private hands, the State must assess the legality, necessity, and proportionality of expropriation or non-expropriation of said lands to attain a legitimate objective in a democratic society, as set forth in paragraphs 144 to 154 of this Judgment. For this, it must take into account the specificities of the Yakye Axa Indigenous Community, as well as its values, practices, customs, and customary law. If for objective and well-founded reasons the claim to ancestral territory of the members of the Yakye Axa Community is not possible, the State must grant them alternative land, chosen by means of a consensus with

the community, in accordance with its own manner of consultation and decision-making, practices, and customs. In either case, the area of land must be sufficient to ensure preservation and development of the Community's own manner of life.
218.   To comply with the requirement set forth in the previous paragraph, the State, if necessary, will establish a fund exclusively for the purchase of the land to be granted to the Yakye Axa Community, within a maximum period of one year from the date of notification of the instant Judgment, and that fund will be used either to purchase the land from private owners or to pay fair compensation to them in case of expropriation, as appropriate.

b)   Providing basic services and goods

219.   The Commission and the representatives, in their main briefs, expressed the need to provide basic services to the members of the Yakye Axa Indigenous Community, including drinking water and sanitary infrastructure, a public health center, and a school. They also mentioned the need for medical and educational services to be provided permanently to the members of the Community in a culturally pertinent manner, taking into account its customs and traditions. The State, in turn, pointed out that

> it also acquiesces to the request to establish a health post, a school, drinking water supply, and sanitary infrastructure for the Community at the place where the State is able to establish said services and as close as possible to a provisional settlement.

220.   The State added that

> insofar as possible it acquiesces [to the request to provide] medical care and education to the members of the Community, in accordance with existing educational and healthcare plans of the State.

221.   In view of the above, the Court orders that, as long as the Community remains landless, given its special state of vulnerability and the impossibility of resorting to its traditional subsistence mechanisms, the State must supply, immediately and on a regular basis, sufficient drinking water for the consumption and personal hygiene of the members of the Community; it must provide regular medical care and appropriate medicine to protect the health of all persons, especially children, the elderly, and pregnant women, including medicine and adequate treatment for worming of all members of the Community; it must supply food in quantities, variety, and quality that are sufficient for the members of the Community to have the minimum conditions for a decent life; it must provide latrines or any other type of appropriate toilets for effective and healthy management of the biological waste of the Community; and it must supply sufficient bilingual material for appropriate education of the students at the school in the current settlement of the Community.

c)   Adapting domestic legislation to the American Convention

225.   The Court deems it necessary for the State to guarantee effective exercise of the rights set forth in its Constitution and in its legislation, pursuant to the American Convention. Therefore, the State, within a reasonable term, must adopt in its domestic legislation, pursuant to the provisions of Article 2 of the American Convention, such legislative, administrative, and any other measures as may be necessary to create an effective mechanism for indigenous peoples' claims to ancestral lands such that it makes their right to property effective, taking into account their customary law, values, practices, and customs.

Sawhoyamaxa Indigenous Community v. Paraguay
29-Mar-2006
Series C No. 146—*Merits, Reparations, and Costs*

2.   The Commission filed the application pursuant to Article 61 of the American Convention, in order that the Court should decide whether Paraguay had violated Articles 4 (Right to Life), 5 (Right to Humane Treatment), 8 (Right to a Fair Trial), 21 (Right to Property), and 25 (Right to Judicial Protection) of the American Convention, with relation to the obligations set forth in Articles 1(1) (Obligation to Respect Rights) and 2 (Obligation to Adopt Domestic Law Measures) thereof, to the detriment of the Sawhoyamaxa Indigenous Community of the Enxet-Lengua people (hereinafter, the "Sawhoyamaxa Indigenous Community," the "Sawhoyamaxa Community," the "Indigenous Community," or the "Community," irrespectively) and its members (hereinafter, "the members of the Community"). The Community [alleged] that the State has not ensured the ancestral property right of the Sawhoyamaxa Community and its members, inasmuch as their claim for territorial rights is pending since 1991 and it has not been satisfactorily resolved to date. As stated in the Commission's application, this has barred the Community and its members from title to and possession of their lands and has implied keeping it in a state of nutritional, medical, and health vulnerability, which constantly threatens their survival and integrity.

B)   RESTITUTION OF TRADITIONAL LANDS TO THE MEMBERS OF THE SAWHOYAMAXA COMMUNITY

210.   In view of its conclusions contained in the chapter related to Article 21 of the American Convention, the Court considers that the restitution of traditional lands to the members of the Sawhoyamaxa Community is the reparation measure that best complies with the *restitutio in integrum* principle; therefore, the Court orders that the State shall adopt all legislative, administrative, or other types of measures necessary to guarantee the members of the Community ownership

rights over their traditional lands and, consequently, the right to use and enjoy those lands.

211.   As it has been proven, the lands claimed before the domestic jurisdiction by the members of the Community are part of their traditional habitat and are suitable for their ultimate settlement. However, restitution of such lands to the Community is barred, since these lands are currently privately owned.

212.   On that matter, pursuant to the Courts precedent,[234][7] the State must consider the possibility of purchasing these lands or the lawfulness, need, and proportionality of condemning these lands in order to achieve a lawful purpose in a democratic society, as reaffirmed in paragraphs 135 to 141 of the instant Judgment and paragraphs 143 to 151 of the judgment entered by the Court in the case of the Indigenous Community *Yakye Axa*. If restitution of ancestral lands to the members of the Sawhoyamaxa Community is not possible on objective and sufficient grounds, the State shall make over alternative lands, selected upon agreement with the aforementioned Indigenous Community and in accordance with the community's own decision-making and consultation procedures, values, practices, and customs. In either case, the extension and quality of the lands must be sufficient to guarantee the preservation and development of the Community's own way of life.

213.   In the instant case, the Court notes that the State has expressed that it "intends to make over, for no consideration to the Sawhoyamaxa Community, as provided in the Constitution and in the statutes in force, an extension of land consistent with the number of stable and permanent members of the Community, in favor of such Community, within their lands delimited in the Paraguayan Chaco, where the Enxet-Lengua people has traditionally been settled, always to the extent permitted by domestic legislation and without affecting any third party who accredits to hold ownership title and a rational exploitation, either by acquisition, upon agreement with the owners of those lands, or by condemnation pursuant to the laws of the Republic."

214.   In this regard, it must be taken into account that, pursuant to paragraphs 135 to 141 of the instant Judgment, the fact that the Community's traditional lands are currently privately held or reasonably exploited, is not in itself an "objective and sufficient ground" barring restitution thereof.

215.   The State shall, within three years as from notice of the instant Judgment, formally and physically grant tenure the lands to the victims, irrespective of whether they be acquired by purchase or by condemnation or whether alternative lands are selected. The State shall guarantee all the necessary funds for the purpose.

D) NON-PECUNIARY DAMAGE

221.   This Court finds that the non-enforcement of the right to hold title to the communal property of the members of the Sawhoyamaxa Community and the

detrimental living conditions imposed upon them as a consequence of the State's delay in enforcing their rights over the lands must be taken into account when assessing the value of the non-pecuniary damage sustained.

222.   Similarly, the Court finds that the special meaning that these lands have for indigenous peoples, in general, and for the members of the Sawhoyamaxa Community, in particular, implies that the denial of those rights over land involves a detriment to values that are highly significant to the members of those communities, who are at risk of losing or suffering irreparable damage to their lives and identities, and to the cultural heritage of future generations.

223.   In the instant case, the State recognized "the need of the members of the Community to generate a productive yield out of the lands to be made over to them in order to cater for the needs of the Community and to allow the adequate development of such lands. To such effect, the State will implement a project for the adequate development of such lands immediately after consultations with and acceptance by the Community."

224.   Based on the above the Court considers meet, on equitable grounds, to order the State to establish a community development fund in the lands to be made over to the members of the Community, as set forth in paragraph 207 of the instant Judgment. The State shall allocate the amount of US$1,000,000.00 (one million United States Dollars) to such fund, which will be used to implement educational, housing, agricultural, and health projects, as well as to provide drinking water and to build sanitation infrastructure, for the benefit of the members of the Community. These projects must be established by an implementation committee, as described below, and must be completed within two years as from delivery of the lands to the members of the Indigenous Community.

225.   The abovementioned committee will be in charge of defining the ways in which the development fund is to be implemented and will be made up of three members: a representative appointed by the victims, a representative appointed by the State, and another representative jointly appointed by the victims and the State. Should the State and the representatives fail to reach an agreement as to the members of the implementation committee within six months after notice of the instant Judgment, the Court will convene a meeting to discuss the matter.

E)   OTHER FORMS OF REPARATION (MEASURES OF SATISFACTION AND NON-REPETITION GUARANTEES)

228.   In this subparagraph, the Court will determine those measures of satisfaction aimed at redressing non-pecuniary damage as well as other measures with a public scope or impact.[238 8] These measures are especially relevant in the instant case, given the collective nature of the damage caused.

a)   Delivery of property and basic services

229.   In the instant case, Paraguay stated its intention to satisfy the request of the Commission and the representatives regarding the establishment of a health

care center and a school, as well as the provision of drinking water, sanitation facilities, medical care, and educational services, in favor of the members of the Community.

230.   With the foregoing in mind and in view of the conclusions contained in the chapter related to Article 4 of the American Convention, the Court orders that, while the members of the Community remain landless, the State shall immediately, regularly, and permanently adopt measures to: a) supply sufficient drinking water for consumption and personal hygiene to the members of the Community; b) provide medical check-ups, tests, and care to all members of the Community, especially children, elder people, and women, together with periodic parasite removal and vaccination campaigns, respecting their practices and customs; c) deliver sufficient quantity and quality of food; d) set up latrines or other type of sanitation facilities in the settlements of the Community, and e) provide the school of the "Santa Elisa" settlement with all necessary material and human resources and establish a temporary school with all necessary material and human resources for the children of the "Kilómetro 16" settlement. The education provided must, inasmuch as possible, respect the cultural values of the Community and of Paraguay and is to be bilingual: in the [Enxet] language and, at the discretion of the members of the Community, either in Spanish or in Guarani.

231.   Likewise, in view of the conclusions contained in the chapter related to Article 3 of the Convention, the Court orders the State to implement, within one year as from the date notice of the instant Judgment be served, a registration and documentation program aimed at offering the members of the Community the possibility to register and to obtain their identification documents.

232.   Lastly, given the difficulties encountered by the members of the Community to access health care centers, the State shall set up in the Santa Elisa and Kilómetro 16 settlements of the Sawhoyamaxa Community a communication system to allow victims to contact health authorities competent to address emergency cases. If necessary, the State shall provide transportation. The State shall establish such communication system within six months as from the date notice of the instant Judgment is served.

233.   To comply with the provisions of the preceding paragraphs, the State shall secure participation and informed consent by the victims, which must be expressed by their representatives and leaders.

Saramaka People v. Suriname
28-Nov-2007
Series C No. 172—*Preliminary Objections, Merits, Reparations, and Costs*

C)   Measures of Redress

C.1)   Measures of Satisfaction and Guarantees of Non-Repetition

194.   In order to guarantee the non-repetition of the violation of the rights of the members of the Saramaka people to the recognition of their juridical personality, property, and judicial protection, the State must carry out the following measures:

(a) delimit, demarcate, and grant collective title over the territory of the members of the Saramaka people in accordance with their customary laws and through previous, effective, and fully informed consultations with the Saramaka people, without prejudice to other tribal and indigenous communities. Until said delimitation, demarcation, and titling of the Saramaka territory has been carried out, Suriname must abstain from acts which might lead the agents of the State itself, or third parties acting with its acquiescence or its tolerance, to affect the existence, value, use, or enjoyment of the territory to which the members of the Saramaka people are entitled, unless the State obtains the free, informed, and prior consent of the Saramaka people. With regards to the concessions already granted within traditional Saramaka territory, the State must review them, in light of the present Judgment and the Court's jurisprudence, in order to evaluate whether a modification of the rights of the concessionaires is necessary in order to preserve the survival of the Saramaka people. The State must begin the process of delimitation, demarcation, and titling of traditional Saramaka territory within three months from the notification of the present Judgment and must complete this process within three years from such date;

(b) grant the members of the Saramaka people legal recognition of their collective juridical capacity, pertaining to the community to which they belong, with the purpose of ensuring the full exercise and enjoyment of their right to communal property, as well as collective access to justice, in accordance with their communal system, customary laws, and traditions. The State must comply with this reparation measure within a reasonable time;

(c) remove or amend the legal provisions that impede protection of the right to property of the members of the Saramaka people and adopt, in its domestic legislation and through prior, effective, and fully informed consultations with the Saramaka people, legislative, administrative, and other measures as may be required to recognize, protect, guarantee, and give legal effect to the right of the members of the Saramaka people to hold collective title of the territory they have traditionally used and occupied, which includes the lands and natural resources necessary for their social, cultural, and economic survival, as well as manage, distribute, and effectively control such territory in accordance with their customary laws and traditional collective land tenure system and without prejudice to other tribal and indigenous communities. The State must comply with this reparation measure within a reasonable time;

(d) adopt legislative, administrative, and other measures necessary to recognize and ensure the right of the Saramaka people to be effectively consulted, in accordance with their traditions and customs, or when necessary, the right to give or withhold their free, informed, and prior consent, with regards to development or investment projects that may affect their territory, and to reasonably share the benefits of such projects with the members of the Saramaka people, should these be ultimately carried out. The Saramaka people must be consulted during the process established to comply with this form of reparation. The State must comply with this reparation measure within a reasonable time;

(e) ensure that environmental and social impact assessments are conducted by independent and technically competent entities prior to awarding a concession for any development or investment project within traditional Saramaka territory, and [the State must] implement adequate safeguards and mechanisms in order to minimize the damaging effects such projects may have upon the social, economic, and cultural survival of the Saramaka people, and

(f) adopt legislative, administrative, and other measures necessary to provide the members of the Saramaka people with adequate and effective recourses against acts that violate their right to the use and enjoyment of property in accordance with their communal land tenure system. The State must comply with this reparation measure within a reasonable time.

12-Aug-2008
Series C No. 185—*Interpretation of the Judgment on Preliminary Objections, Merits, Reparations, and Costs*

10.   The Court observes that some of the State's requests lack precision as to which issues require the Court's interpretation relating to the meaning or scope of the judgment. Nonetheless, the Court considers that the issues raised indicate that the State requires further guidance in order to fully comply with the Court's orders. Thus, to provide a comprehensive response to the State's concerns, and in light of the interrelatedness of some of the issues raised by the State, the Court declares the request admissible as a whole and will proceed to analyze those issues in the following order:

(a) questions regarding
    (i) the establishment of a mechanism for the "effective participation" of the Saramaka people, and

(ii) the determination of the beneficiaries of a "just compensation";

(b) questions regarding the circumstances in which the State may not execute a proposed developmental and investment plan in Saramaka territory, particularly regarding prior environmental and social impact assessments; (3) questions regarding concessions the State may grant in Saramaka territory, and (4) whether the Court took into consideration the State's arguments related to the violation of Article 3 of the Convention.

IV. The Requirements of "Effective Participation" and "Benefit Sharing"

14. The issues raised by the State refer to

(a) the establishment of a consultation mechanism with the Saramaka people, and

(b) the determination of the beneficiaries of a "just compensation" in relation to development and investment projects in Saramaka territory.

The Court considers that both concerns are addressed in the Judgment, particularly, but not exclusively, in paragraphs 81, 100, 101, 129-140, 147, 155, 164, 170, 171, 174, and 194 and in Operative Paragraphs 5 through 9. Nevertheless, the Court deems that a reiteration of how the Judgment addresses these issues is pertinent.

a) Regarding the establishment of a consultation mechanism with the Saramaka people

15. Regarding the first issue, the Court reiterates that the State has a duty to consult with the Saramaka people in order to comply with several of the Court's orders and that the Saramaka must determine, in accordance with their customs and traditions, which tribal members are to be involved in such consultations.

16. In this regard, the Judgment orders the State to consult with the Saramaka people regarding at least the following six issues:

(a) the process of delimiting, demarcating, and granting collective title over the territory of the Saramaka people;[6][9]

(b) the process of granting the members of the Saramaka people legal recognition of their collective juridical capacity, pertaining to the community to which they belong;[7][10]

(c) the process of adopting legislative, administrative, and other measures as may be required to recognize, protect, guarantee, and give legal effect to the right of the members of the Saramaka people to the territory they have traditionally used and occupied;[8][11]

(d) the process of adopting legislative, administrative, and other measures necessary to recognize and ensure the right of the Saramaka people to be effectively consulted, in accordance with their traditions and customs;[9][12]

(e) ... the results of prior environmental and social impact assessments,[10][13] and

(f) ... any proposed restrictions of the Saramaka people's property rights, particularly regarding proposed development or investment plans in or affecting Saramaka territory.[11][14]

17.   In paragraph 133 of the Judgment, the Court further clarified this last issue, stating that "in ensuring the effective participation of members of the Saramaka people in development or investment plans within their territory, the State has a duty to actively consult with said community according to their customs and traditions." In paragraphs 133 through 137 the Court gave specific guidelines as to what issues must be the subject of consultation, when the consultation must take place, why the Saramaka people must be consulted, and how the consultation must be carried out. Accordingly, the State has a duty, from the onset of the proposed activity, to actively consult with the Saramaka people in good faith and with the objective of reaching an agreement, which in turn requires the State to both accept and disseminate information in an understandable and publicly accessible format. Furthermore, depending upon the level of impact of the proposed activity, the State may additionally be required to obtain consent from the Saramaka people. The Tribunal has emphasized that when large-scale development or investment projects could affect the integrity of the Saramaka people's lands and natural resources, the State has a duty not only to consult with the Saramakas, but also to obtain their free, prior, and informed consent in accordance with their customs and traditions.[12 15]

18.   The Court deliberately omitted from the Judgment any specific consideration as to who must be consulted. By declaring that the consultation must take place "in conformity with their customs and tradition," the Court recognized that it is the Saramaka people, not the State, who must decide which person or group of persons will represent the Saramaka people in each consultation process ordered by the Tribunal.[13 16]

19.   Accordingly, the Saramaka people must inform the State which person or group of persons will represent them in each of the aforementioned consultation processes. The State must then consult with those Saramaka representatives to comply with the Court's orders.[14 17] Once such consultation has taken place, the Saramaka people will inform the State of the decisions taken, as well as their basis.

20.   In a related issue, the Tribunal observes that the State seems to misunderstand the difference between the State's obligation to consult with the Saramaka people, pursuant to their customs and traditions, and the content and purpose of the petitioning system described in Article 44[15 18] of the Convention.

21.   In paragraphs 22 through 24 of the Judgment, the Court addressed whether, in light of Article 44 of the Convention, the original petitioners had standing to file a petition before the Commission. The Court declared that any person or group of persons other than the [alleged] victims may file a petition before the Commission without first obtaining authorization from the *Gaa'man*, or, for example, from each member of the community. That analysis of the petitioning system under the American Convention bears no relation to the State's

obligation under the Judgment to consult with the Saramaka in accordance with their customs and traditions.

22.	Thus, the decision as to whom should be consulted regarding each of the various issues mentioned above (*supra* para. 16) must be made by the Saramaka people, pursuant to their customs and traditions. The Saramaka people will then communicate to the State who must be consulted, depending on the issue that requires consultation.

b) Regarding the determination of beneficiaries of a "just compensation" in relation to development and investment projects in Saramaka territory

23.	The second issue addressed by the State, pertaining to the determination of the beneficiaries of a "just compensation"[19] for development and investment projects in Saramaka territory, is closely related to the previous issue and is also addressed in the Judgment.

24.	In Operative Paragraph 8 of the Judgment, read in conjunction with paragraph 194(d), the Court ordered the State to

> adopt legislative, administrative, and other measures necessary to recognize and ensure the right of the Saramaka people to . . . reasonably share the benefits of [development and investment] projects with the members of the Saramaka people, should these be ultimately carried out. The Saramaka people must be consulted during the process established to comply with this form of reparation.

25.	Thus, the determination of those beneficiaries must be made in consultation with the Saramaka people, and not unilaterally by the State. In any case, as the representatives mentioned in their written submissions, "these matters can be discussed and addressed during the consultations and process of reaching agreement on the legislative and administrative measures required to give effect to, *inter alia*, the benefit sharing requirement."

26.	Furthermore, regarding the State's concern that there may be internal divisions among the Saramaka as to who can benefit from development projects, the Court observes that, pursuant to paragraph 164 of the Judgment, in the event that any internal conflict arises between members of the Saramaka community regarding this issue, it "must be resolved by the Saramaka people in accordance with their own traditional customs and norms, not by the State or this Court in this particular case."

27.	Consequently, the Tribunal reiterates that all issues related to the consultation process with the Saramaka people, as well as those concerning the beneficiaries of the "just compensation" that must be shared, must be determined and resolved by the Saramaka people in accordance with their traditional customs and norms and as ordered by the Court in its Judgment.

V. Prior Environmental and Social Impact Assessments
a)   General requirements and safeguards

31.   The Court deems that the issues raised indicate that the State may require further guidance in order to appropriately implement the Judgment. To ensure clarity on both the meaning and scope of the Judgment, and to ensure its appropriate application, the Court will address the State's concerns related to the issue of the environmental and social impact assessments.

32.   As the Court indicated in the Judgment, pursuant to Article 21 of the Convention, the State must respect the special relationship that members of the Saramaka people have with their territory in a way that guarantees their social, cultural, and economic survival.[17 20] The Court stated in paragraph 121 of its Judgment:

> the aim and purpose of the special measures required on behalf of the members of indigenous and tribal communities is to guarantee that they may continue living their traditional way of life, and their distinct cultural identity, social structure, economic system, customs, beliefs, and traditions are respected, guaranteed, and protected by the states.

33.   Such protection of property under Article 21 of the Convention, read in conjunction with Articles 1(1) and 2 of said instrument, poses a positive obligation on the State to adopt special measures that guarantee the members of the Saramaka people the full and equal exercise of their right to the territories they have traditionally used and occupied.

34.   Any attempt to restrict the property rights of the members of the Saramaka people must adhere to the strict requirements established by the Court in the Judgment and the Tribunal's jurisprudence. In the context of restrictions of property rights in general, the Court has previously held that,

> in accordance with Article 21 of the Convention, a State may restrict the use and enjoyment of the right to property where the restrictions are: a) previously established by law; b) necessary; c) proportional, and d) with the aim of achieving a legitimate objective in a democratic society.[18 21]

35.   In paragraph 128 of the Judgment, the Court stated that

> in analyzing whether restrictions on the property right of members of indigenous and tribal peoples are permissible, especially regarding the use and enjoyment of their traditionally owned lands and natural resources, another crucial factor to be considered is whether the restriction amounts to a denial of their traditions and customs in a way that endangers the very survival of the group and of its members. That is, under Article 21 of the

> Convention, the State may restrict the Saramakas' right to use and enjoy their traditionally owned lands and natural resources only when such restriction complies with the aforementioned requirements and, additionally, when it does not deny their survival as a tribal people . . . .[19][22]

36.   These safeguards are intended to preserve, protect, and guarantee the special relationship that the members of the Saramaka community have with their territory, which in turn ensures their survival as a tribal people. Thus, the State must satisfy each of the requirements mentioned above.

37.   The Court emphasized in the Judgment that the phrase "survival as a tribal people" must be understood as the ability of the Saramaka to "preserve, protect, and guarantee the special relationship that [they] have with their territory,"[20][23] so that "they may continue living their traditional way of life, and that their distinct cultural identity, social structure, economic system, customs, beliefs, and traditions are respected, guaranteed and protected . . . ."[21][24] That is, the term "survival" in this context signifies much more than physical survival.

38.   In order to guarantee their survival as a tribal people, the Court established a series of complementary requirements applicable to the Saramaka in particular, and indigenous and tribal peoples in general. To this end, the Court stated in paragraph 129 that

> in accordance with Article 1(1) of the Convention, in order to guarantee that restrictions to the property rights of the members of the Saramaka people by the issuance of concessions within their territory does not amount to a denial of their survival as a tribal people, the State must abide by the following three safeguards: First, the State must ensure the effective participation of the members of the Saramaka people, in conformity with their customs and traditions, regarding any development, investment, exploration, or extraction plan . . . within Saramaka territory. Second, the State must guarantee that the Saramaka will receive a reasonable benefit from any such plan within their territory. Thirdly, the State must ensure that no concession will be issued within Saramaka territory unless and until independent and technically capable entities, with the State's supervision, perform a prior environmental and social impact assessment. These safeguards are intended to preserve, protect, and guarantee the special relationship that the members of the Saramaka community have with their territory, which in turn ensures their survival as a tribal people.

39.   Additionally, in Operative Paragraph 9 of the Judgment, the Court

ordered the State to "implement adequate safeguards and mechanisms in order to minimize the damaging effects such projects may have upon the social, economic, and cultural survival of the Saramaka people."

b)   Prior environmental and social impact assessments (ESIAs)

40.   To respond with greater precision to the State's concerns related to the prior environmental and social impact assessments ordered in the Judgment, the Court will further elaborate upon this safeguard.[22][25] ESIAs serve to assess the possible damage or impact a proposed development or investment project may have on the property in question and on the community. The purpose of ESIAs is not only to have some objective measure of such possible impact on the land and the people, but also, as stated in paragraph 133 of the Judgment, to "ensure that members of the Saramaka people are aware of possible risks, including environmental and health risks, in order that the proposed development or investment plan is accepted knowingly and voluntarily."

41.   In order to comply with the Court's orders, the ESIAs must conform to the relevant international standards and best practices,[23][26] and must respect the Saramaka people's traditions and culture. In conjunction with said standards and best practices, the Judgment established that the ESIAs must be completed prior to the granting of the concession, as one of the objectives for requiring such studies is to guarantee the Saramaka's right to be informed about all the proposed projects in their territory. Hence, the State's obligation to supervise the ESIAs coincides with its duty to guarantee the effective participation of the Saramaka people in the process of granting concessions. Furthermore, the ESIAs must be undertaken by independent and technically capable entities, with the State's supervision. Finally, one of the factors the environmental and social impact assessment should address is the cumulative impact of existing and proposed projects. This allows for a more accurate assessment on whether the individual and cumulative effects of existing and future activities could jeopardize the survival of the indigenous or tribal people.

c)   Acceptable level of impact

42.   In response to the State's question as to what is an acceptable level of impact, as demonstrated through ESIAs, that would permit the State to grant a concession, the Court observes that what constitutes an acceptable level of impact may differ in each case. Nonetheless, the guiding principle with which to analyze the results of ESIAs should be that the level of impact does not deny the ability of the members of the Saramaka people to survive as a tribal people (*supra* para. 37).

43.   The Court also highlights that, in addition to the ESIAs, the State must comply with the other requirements stated in the Judgment when evaluating whether it should grant concessions for development and investment activities within or that affect the Saramaka territory.

VI. Concessions in the Territory of the Saramaka People

47.　　The Court observes that some of the issues raised by the State fall outside the factual scope of the Judgment, and therefore of this interpretation, particularly in relation to [alleged] tourism activities within Saramaka territory. Nonetheless, in order to avoid potential misinterpretations of the Judgment, the Court will address the issues raised by the State, insofar as they pertain to the Operative Paragraphs or the considerations that support the Court's orders.

48.　　In paragraph 194(c) and Operative Paragraph 7 of the Judgment, the Court observed that the members of the Saramaka people have the "right to manage, distribute, and effectively control such territories, in accordance with their customary laws and traditional collective land tenure system."[24][27] To that end, the Court ordered the State, *inter alia*, to delimit, demarcate, and give collective title over the territory of the Saramaka people and to adopt legislative, administrative, and other measures as may be required to recognize, protect, guarantee, and give legal effect to the right of the members of the Saramaka people to the territory they have traditionally used and occupied.[25][28] The process of adopting such measures, as well as the content of said legislative and administrative measures, must be determined by the State and the Saramaka people jointly in accordance with the Court's Judgment (*supra* para. 16).

49.　　The Judgment also stated that the right to property is not absolute and, thus, may be restricted by the State under very specific, exceptional circumstances, particularly when indigenous or tribal land rights are involved.[26][29] In this sense, the Judgment states in paragraph 127 that in "accordance with [Article 21 of the Convention] and the Court's jurisprudence, the State will be able to restrict, under certain circumstances, the Saramakas' property rights, including their rights to natural resources found on and within the territory," by granting concessions for development or investment projects within or that affect Saramaka territory. The Court discussed in the previous chapter those specific and exceptional circumstances in which the State may restrict the rights to property of the members of the Saramaka people (*supra* paras. 34 and 38).

50.　　In accordance with the aforementioned, the grant of concessions for development or investment projects within or that affect Saramaka territory constitutes a type of restriction on the use and enjoyment of such property. To the extent that this property corresponds to the members of the Saramaka people, they have the "right to manage, distribute, and effectively control such territories, in accordance with their customary laws and traditional collective land tenure system,"[27][30] as well as in conformity with domestic legislation, insofar as it is compatible with the American Convention and the jurisprudence of this Tribunal.

51.　　The Judgment addressed the issue of concessions in the context of proposed development, investment, exploration, or extraction plans within

Saramaka territory. In the footnote accompanying the three safeguards stated in paragraph 129 of the Judgment, the Tribunal specified that by

"development or investment plan" the Court means any proposed activity that may affect the integrity of the lands and natural resources within the territory of the Saramaka people, particularly any proposal to grant logging or mining concessions.

52.   The Court specifically addressed in the Judgment two types of concessions, that is, those involving logging or mining. As to these types of concessions, the Court held that the timber and gold mining concessions previously granted by the State generated a violation of the right to property of the members of the Saramaka people. Regarding timber, the Court explicitly stated in paragraph 146 of its Judgment:

> in accordance with the above analysis regarding the extraction of natural resources that are necessary for the survival of the Saramaka people[28 31] and consequently, its members, the State should not have granted logging concessions within Saramaka territory unless and until the three safeguards of effective participation, benefit-sharing, and prior environmental and social impact assessments were complied with.

53.   Regarding gold mining, the Court stated in paragraph 156 that:

the State failed to comply with the three safeguards when it issued small-scale gold-mining concessions within traditional Saramaka territory. That is, such concessions were issued without performing prior environmental and social impact assessments and without consulting the Saramaka people in accordance with their traditions or guaranteeing their members a reasonable share in the benefits of the project. As such, the State violated the members of the Saramaka people's right to property under Article 21 of the Convention, in conjunction with Article 1(1) of that judgment.

54.   The Tribunal did not specifically address other types of development or investment activities within or that affect Saramaka territory. Nonetheless, the Tribunal reiterates that, in the process of issuing concessions within or that affect Saramaka territory, or any other indigenous or tribal territory, the State has a duty to comply with its obligations under the American Convention as interpreted by the Court in its jurisprudence, particularly in light of the case of the *Saramaka People* and other cases involving indigenous and tribal peoples' land rights.

55.   In this sense, the Court observes that in Operative Paragraph 5 of the Judgment, in which the Tribunal ordered the State to delimit, demarcate, and grant collective title over the territory of the members of the Saramaka people, the Court further stated that

> [u]ntil said delimitation, demarcation, and titling of the Saramaka territory has been carried out, Suriname must abstain

from acts which might lead the agents of the State itself, or third parties acting with its acquiescence or its tolerance, to affect the existence, value, use or enjoyment of the territory to which the members of the Saramaka people are entitled, unless the State obtains the free, informed and prior consent of the Saramaka people. With regards to the concessions already granted within traditional Saramaka territory, the State must review them, in light of the present Judgment and the Court's jurisprudence, in order to evaluate whether a modification of the rights of the concessionaires is necessary in order to preserve the survival of the Saramaka people.

56.   Furthermore, the Tribunal hereby reiterates the text of paragraph 213, which states that

[in] accordance with its constant practice, the Court retains its authority, inherent to its attributions and derived from the provisions of Article 65 of the American Convention, to monitor full execution of this Judgment. The instant case shall be closed once the State has fully complied with the provisions ordered herein.

57.   Hence, considering that some of the issues raised by the State pertain to matters that are better suited to be treated by the Tribunal under its authority to monitor the full execution of the Judgment, the Court considers it sufficient, for purposes of the present request for interpretation, to reiterate the aforementioned content of the Judgment, and will supervise the implementation of the Court's orders pursuant to the relevant monitoring procedure.

VII. VIOLATION OF ARTICLE 3 OF THE CONVENTION

62.   The right of the members of the Saramaka people to the recognition of their juridical personality was addressed in the Judgment in paragraphs 159 through 175, and again in paragraphs 176 through 185 with regards to their right to judicial protection. In essence, the Court observed in paragraph 164 that "the Saramaka people can be defined as a distinct tribal group . . . whose members enjoy and exercise certain rights, such as the right to property, in a distinctly collective manner . . . ."

63.   Furthermore, in paragraph 174, the Court declared that

the members of the Saramaka people form a distinct tribal community in a situation of vulnerability, both as regards the State as well as private third parties, insofar as they lack the juridical capacity to collectively enjoy the right to property and to challenge before domestic courts [alleged] violations of such right. The Court considers that the State must recognize the juridical capacity of the members of the Saramaka people to fully exercise these rights in a collective manner. This may be achieved by implementing legislative or other measures that recognize and take into account the particular way in which the Saramaka people view themselves as a collectivity capable of exercising and enjoying the right to property. Thus, the State must establish, in consultation with the Saramaka people and fully respecting their traditions and customs, the judicial and administrative conditions necessary to ensure the recognition of their juridical personality, with the aim of guaranteeing them the use and enjoyment of their territory in accordance with their communal property system, as well as the rights to access to justice and equality before the law.[29][32]

64.   Likewise, the Court observed in paragraphs 171 and 172, that [t]he recognition of their juridical personality is a way, albeit not the only one, to ensure that the community, as a whole, will be able to fully enjoy and exercise their right to property, in accordance with their communal property system, and the right to equal access to judicial protection against violations of such right.

The Court considers that the right to have their juridical personality recognized by the State is one of the special measures owed to indigenous and tribal groups in order to ensure that they are able to use and enjoy their territory in accordance with their own traditions. This is a natural consequence of the recognition of the right of members of indigenous and tribal groups to enjoy certain rights in a communal manner.

65.   Thus, to fulfill its obligation under Operative Paragraph 6 of the Judgment, the Tribunal declared in paragraph 168 that the State must "take into account the manner in which members of indigenous and tribal peoples in general, and the Saramaka in particular, enjoy and exercise . . . the right to use and enjoy property collectively in accordance with their ancestral traditions." The same considerations must be taken into account to guarantee their right to equal access to judicial protection against violations of their right to property.

Xákmok Kásek Indigenous Community v. Paraguay
24-Aug-2010
Series C No. 214—*Merits, Reparations, and Costs*

2.   Measures of restitution

2.1.   Return of the traditional territory claimed

281.   In light of the conclusions in Chapter VI concerning Articles 8(1), 21(1) and 25(1) of the Convention, the Court considers that the return to the members of the Xákmok Kásek Community of their traditional land is the measure of reparation that comes closest to *restitutio in integrum*, and therefore it decides that the State must take all the necessary legislative, administrative, and any other measures to ensure the Community members' right to ownership of their traditional lands and, consequently, to the use and enjoyment of those lands.

282.   The Community's connection to those lands is indissoluble and fundamental for its cultural subsistence and its food supply, which is why its return is so important. Contrary to what the State has indicated, the land to be returned to the members of the Community is not just any piece of property "within the historical territory of the Enxet Lengua people," but rather the territory that, in this case, the members of the Community have proved is their specific traditional territory and the most suitable for the indigenous settlement.

283.   Consequently, the State must return to the members of the Community the 10,700 hectares claimed by them and identified as *Mopey Sensap* (today *Retiro Primero*) and *Makha Mompena* (today *Retiro Kuñataí*). The specific identification of this territory and its borders must be made by the State within one year of notification of this judgment, using the appropriate technical mechanisms for this purpose, and with the participation of the leaders of the Community and their freely chosen representatives.

284.   Once the traditional territory of the members of the Community is fully identified in the manner and within the time frame indicated in the preceding paragraph, if it is owned by private entities, whether natural or legal persons, the State, through its competent authorities, must decide whether it is possible to expropriate the land for the indigenous peoples. To decide this question, the State authorities must follow the criteria established in this judgment, taking very much into account the special relationship that the indigenous peoples have with their lands for the preservation of their culture and their survival. At no time should the decision of the domestic authorities be based exclusively on the fact that the land is owned privately or that it is being rationally exploited, based on the considerations presented in paragraph 149 of this judgment. To do this would be to ignore this ruling and constitute a violation of the commitments assumed by Paraguay of its own free will.

285.   The State has three years from notification of this judgment to return the traditional lands to the members of the Community. To this end, it must take a decision on the possibility of expropriation and, if appropriate, implement this. The State must carry out the necessary measures to achieve this objective within the said time frame. Moreover, within this time frame, the State can, if necessary, expedite the negotiations to purchase the corresponding lands.

286.   If, for objective and well-founded reasons—which, the Court reiterates, cannot be, exclusively, the fact that the land is in private hands or being rationally exploited—the Paraguayan authorities decide to give priority to the right to property of the private entities rather than to the right to property of the members of the Community, it must provide the latter with alternate land within the traditional territory of their ancestors. The selection of this land must be made with the consensus of the members of the Community, in keeping with their own ways of making decisions. The Court reiterates that the offer of alternate lands will only be admissible when it has been adequately assessed, as indicated in this judgment, that the expropriation is not appropriate and that the negotiations to purchase the land have failed.

287.   Following a well-founded request from the State, the Court may grant it an extension of one year to continue the respective domestic procedures commenced for the return of the traditional land. The request for an extension must be presented to the Court at least three months before the expiry of the three-year time limit established in paragraph 285 of this judgment. If the State does not present its request for an extension as indicated above, the Court will understand that it has waived its possibility of requesting it. The Court will reject any request that is time-barred. If the request for an extension is presented opportunely, the Court will forward it to the Commission and the representatives of the victims so that they can submit any observations they deem pertinent. The Court will decide whether or not to grant the extension, taking into account the reasons put forward by the State in its request, the observations of the Commission and the representatives, and the measures already taken by the State to comply with its obligation to deliver the land to the members of the Community. The Court will not grant the extension if, in its opinion, the State has not taken sufficient steps to comply with this measure of reparation. Lastly, the State must report in a precise and detailed manner every six months on the measures taken to return the traditional territory to the victims.

288.   Based on the above, the Court orders that, if the three-year time frame established in this judgment expires, or if the extension granted in keeping with paragraph 287 expires or is denied by the Court, without the State having delivered the traditional lands or, if applicable, the alternate lands, in keeping with the provisions of paragraphs 283 to 286, it must pay the leaders of the Community, on behalf of its members, the sum of US$10,000.00 (ten thousand United States dollars) for each month of delay. The Court understands this reparation as compensation to the victims for the State's failure to comply with the time limits established in this judgment and the resulting pecuniary and non-pecuniary damage, so that it does not constitute compensation that replaces the return of the traditional or alternate lands to the members of the Community.

289.   The calculation of the months for which the State must compensate the Community for its delay in complying with this judgment will cease when the traditional land, or if applicable, the alternate land, is finally awarded to them.

290.   During the procedure of monitoring compliance with this judgment, the Court will establish the dates on which the State must make the respective payments to the leaders of the Community for the delay in complying with this measure of reparation. These payments must be made in keeping with the guidelines stipulated in the section on "method of payment" of this judgment. If the State fails to comply with the dates established by the Court for making these payments, it must pay interest on arrears, in keeping with the provisions of paragraph 336 *infra*. The corresponding amounts shall be delivered to the duly recognized leaders of the Community, who will distribute the money as the Community decides based on its own decision-making methods.

2.2.   Protection of the territory claimed

291.   The State must not carry out any action that further obstructs the effects of this judgment. In this regard, until the traditional territory has been awarded to the Community, the State must ensure that the territory is not harmed by the actions of the State itself or of private third parties. Thus, the State shall ensure that the area is not deforested, that the sites that are of cultural importance to the Community are not destroyed, that the land is not transferred, and that it is not exploited in such a way as to cause irreparable harm to the area or to its natural resources.

2.3.   Granting title to the "25 de Febrero" lands

292.   The State indicated that it was processing the granting of title to the 1,500 hectares of the place known as "25 de Febrero," where the Community is currently located. However, it underlined certain obstacles to the granting of title and registration of the land owing to formal problems concerning the representation and registration of community leaders.

293.   In this regard, the Court considers that the State itself must resolve all these formal obstacles to the granting of title to this land, in keeping with the provisions of paragraphs 48 and 49. Specifically, through the competent authorities, the State must guarantee the rectification of the discrepancies regarding the registration of the leaders of the Community for the necessary legal effects. The State must do this within six months of notification of this judgment.

294.   Furthermore, this Court orders the State, within one year of notification of this judgment, to grant title to the 1,500 hectares ceded to the members of the Xákmok Kásek Community by the Angaité communities (*supra* paras. 76 to 78). This will allow the members of the Community to have a territory and ensure their survival provisionally, while its traditional land is demarcated and title is granted. The Court considers it relevant to stress the solidarity and unity of the Angaité communities with the Xákmok Kásek Community.

295.   The Court emphasizes that the granting of title to the said 1,500 hectares does not affect or influence the return of the traditional territory to which the members of the Xákmok Kásek Community have a right, in accordance with paragraphs 281 to 290 of this judgment.

4.   Rehabilitation measures: Provision of goods and basic services

301.   Based on the conclusions presented in Chapter VII with regard to Article 4 of the American Convention, the Court orders that, until the traditional territory or, if applicable, alternate land is delivered to the members of the Community, the State must take the following measures immediately, periodically, or permanently: (a) provision of sufficient potable water for the consumption and personal hygiene of the members of the Community; (b) medical and psycho-social attention to all the members of the Community, especially the children and the elderly, together with periodic vaccination and deparasitization campaigns that respect their ways and customs; (c) specialized medical care for pregnant women, both pre- and post-natal and during the first months of the baby's life; (d) delivery of food of sufficient quality and quantity to ensure an adequate diet; (e) installation of latrines or any other adequate type of sanitation system in the Community's settlement, and (f) provision of the necessary materials and human resources for the school to guarantee the Community's children access to basic education, paying special attention to ensuring that the education provided respects their cultural traditions and guarantees the protection of their own language. To this end, the State must consult the Community as necessary.

302.   The obligations indicated in the preceding paragraph must be complied with immediately.

303.   Notwithstanding the foregoing, to ensure that the provision of basic supplies and services is adequate and regular, the State must prepare a study within six months of notification of this judgment that establishes the following:

(a) Regarding the provision of potable water:

(i) the frequency of the deliveries;

(ii) the method to be used to deliver the water and ensure its purity, and

(iii) the amount of water to be delivered per person and/or per family;

(b) Regarding the medical and psycho-social care, and the delivery of medicines:

(i) the frequency required for the medical personnel to visit the Community;

(ii) the main illnesses and diseases suffered by the members of the Community;

(iii) the medicines and treatment required for those illnesses;

(iv) the required pre- and post-natal care, and

(v) the manner and frequency with which the vaccination and deparasitization should be carried out;

    (c) Regarding the supply of food:

        (i) the type of food to be supplie[d] to the members of the Community to guarantee a nutritious diet;

        (ii) the frequency with which the deliveries should be made;

        (iii) the amount of food to be supplied per person and/or family.

    (d) Regarding the effective and hygienic management of biological waste: the type and number of latrines to be provided, and

    (e) Regarding the supply of materials and human resources to the Community's school:

        (i) the physical and human resources that the school needs to guarantee an adequate bilingual education;

        (ii) the materials that each student needs for an adequate education, and

        (iii) the inputs that the school's teachers require in order to give their classes.

304.   To prepare the study mentioned in the preceding paragraph, the experts in charge of it must have the specific technical knowledge required for each task. In addition, the experts must always include the point of view of the members of the Community, expressed in keeping with their decision-making practices. This study could be prepared by the Inter-institutional Commission (CICSI).[308] [33]

305.   When the State forwards the report to the Court, it will be forwarded to the Commission and the representatives so that they can submit any observations they deem pertinent. Taking the opinions of the parties into account, the Court may order the State to require its experts to complete or expand the study. From then on, the State must adapt the delivery of basic supplies and services to the members of the Community, ordered in paragraph 301, to the conclusions reached by the experts in their report.

306.   Lastly, given the difficulties that the members of the Community have to access health clinics, the State must establish, in the place where the Community is temporarily located, namely, "25 de Febrero," a permanent health clinic with the necessary medicines and supplies to provide adequate health care. To do this, the State has six months as of notification of this judgment. In addition, it must establish immediately a system of communication in the said settlement that allows the victims to contact the competent health-care authorities for attention to emergency cases. If necessary, the State must provide transportation for the individuals who require this. Subsequently, the State must ensure that the health clinic and the communication system are moved to the place where the Community settles permanently.

5.   Guarantees of non-repetition

5.1.   *Implementation of registration and documentation programs*

308.   Based on the conclusions established in Chapter IX concerning Article

3 of the Convention, the Court orders the State to implement, within one year of notification of this judgment at the most, a registration and documentation program, so that the members of the Community can register and to obtain their identity documents.

5.2. *Adapting domestic law to the Convention*

309.   Based on the Court's conclusions in Chapter VI of this judgment, the Court finds it necessary that the State ensure the effective enjoyment of the rights recognized by the American Convention, by its Constitution and by its laws. The Court considers that the State's international responsibility in this case has resulted from the fact that it had failed to adapt its laws in order to guarantee the indigenous communities' right to ownership of their traditional territory, and also that institutional practices limit or fail to guarantee fully the effective application of the laws that have been established formally to guarantee the rights of the members of the indigenous communities. In the Court's opinion, the social interest of property for the indigenous communities should signify that the circumstance that it is indigenous ancestral land should be taken into account, and should be reflected at both the substantive and the procedural levels.

310.   Consequently, in accordance with Article 2 of the American Convention, within two years, the State must adopt in its domestic law the necessary legislative, administrative, and any other measures to establish an effective system for indigenous peoples to claim their ancestral or traditional lands, which makes it possible to implement their right to property. This system must establish substantive norms that guarantee: (a) that the importance to the indigenous peoples of their traditional lands is taken into account, and (b) that it is not enough that the land claimed is owned privately and is being exploited rationally to reject any land claim. Furthermore, this system must establish that a judicial authority has the competence to decide the disputes that arise between the right to property of private entities and that of the indigenous peoples.

5.3. *Regarding the decree declaring part of the land claimed by the members of the Community a protected wooded area*

311.   With regard to judicial practice, this Court has established that it is aware that domestic judges and tribunals are subject to the rule of law and, therefore, they are obliged to apply the legal provisions in force.[309][34] However, when a State has ratified an international treaty such as the American Convention, its judges, as part of the State apparatus, are also subject to it, which obliges them to ensure that the effects of the provisions of the Convention are not weakened by the application of laws contrary to its object and purpose. In other words, the Judiciary must *ex officio* exercise "control that domestic laws are in accordance with the American Convention, evidently, within the framework of its respective competences and the corresponding procedural regulations. In this task, the Judiciary must take

into account not only the treaty, but also the interpretation given to it by Inter-American Court, ultimate interpreter of the American Convention.[310][35]

312.   In this case, Decree No. 11,804 issued on January 31, 2008, declaring part of the land claimed by the Community a protected wooded area under private ownership, disregarded the indigenous peoples' claim to the land filed with the INDI and, according to the State's own specialized domestic agencies, it should be considered null.

313.   Consequently, the State must take the measures necessary to ensure that Decree No. 11,804 is not an obstacle to returning the traditional land to the members of the Community.

The Kichwa Indigenous People of Sarayaku v. Ecuador
27-Jun-2012
Series C No. 245—*Merits and reparations*

2. According to the Commission, this case concerns, among other matters, the granting by the State of a permit to a private oil company to carry out oil exploration and exploitation activities in the territory of the Kichwa Indigenous People of Sarayaku (hereinafter "the Sarayaku People" or "the People" or "Sarayaku") in the 1990s, without previously consulting them and without obtaining their consent. Thus, the company began the exploration phase, and even introduced high-powered explosives in several places on indigenous territory, thereby creating an [alleged] situation of risk for the population because, for a time, this prevented them from seeking means of subsistence and limited their rights to freedom of movement and to cultural expression. In addition, this case relates to the [alleged] lack of judicial protection and the failure to observe judicial guarantees.

3. Based on the foregoing, the Commission asked the Court to declare the international responsibility of the State for the violation of:

(a) The right to private property, recognized in Article 21, in relation to Articles 13, 23, and 1(1) of the American Convention, to the detriment of the Kichwa People of Sarayaku and its members;

(b) The right to life, judicial guarantees and judicial protection, established in Articles 4, 8, and 25, in relation to Article 1(1) of the American Convention, to the detriment of the People and its members;

(c) The right to freedom of movement and residence recognized in Article 22, in relation to Article 1(1) of the American Convention, to the detriment of the members of the People;

(d) The right to personal integrity recognized in Article 5 of the American Convention, in relation to Article 1(1) thereof, to the detriment of 20 members of the Kichwa People of Sarayaku;4 and

(e) The obligation to adopt domestic legal measures established in Article 2 of the American Convention, and

Lastly, the Commission asked the Court to order the State to adopt specific measures of reparation.

REPARATIONS
(Application of Article 63(1) of the American Convention) [335] [36]
B.1 Restitution
Removal of explosives and reforestation of the affected areas

289. With regard to the explosives buried in the territory of the Sarayaku People, the Court appreciates that, since 2009, the State has taken several steps to deactivate or remove the explosives, at times in consultation with the Sarayaku People. In addition, the State has proposed several options to neutralize the explosives buried in the territory.

290. In particular, the State provided a certificate of approval by the Sub-Secretary for Environmental Quality of a "Comprehensive Environmental Assessment" of Block 23, indicating that the CGC representative should, *inter alia*, "[s]ubmit a schedule with specific deadlines for executing the activities contemplated in the Plan of Action, including those related to the information process on the way in which the pentolite was dealt with [...], the current situation of this explosive; environmental impacts of the attempts to find and evaluate the buried material." [347] [37] Also, in the terms of the contract termination agreement, in clause 8.4, the parties (Petroecuador and CGC) "accept and ratify that there is no environmental liability in the [concession] area that can be attributed to the contractor" (*supra* para. 123).

291. In relation to the removal of the pentolite from the territory of the Sarayaku People, the Court observes that, according to the parties, two different situations exist: first, the pentolite near the surface (approximately 150 kilograms) is buried at a depth of up to five meters and it would be possible to remove it completely. Second, the pentolite buried at a greater depth – at about 15 to 20 meters – would be difficult to remove without causing significant environmental damage or even potential safety risks for those removing it.

292. Regarding the pentolite located near the surface, the State indicated that its removal by physical means posed serious safety risks for the people responsible for carrying out the operation. In addition, it would entail damage to the integrity of the territory, because it would have to be carried out with heavy machinery. For their part, representatives and the Commission requested the removal of all surface explosives, which would entail a search of at least 500 meters on each side of the E16 seismic line running through the Sarayaku territory.

293. The Court stipulates that the State must neutralize, deactivate and, as

appropriate, completely remove the surface pentolite, searching at least 500 meters on each side of the E16 seismic line running through the Sarayaku territory, as proposed by the representatives. The ways and means used for this purpose must be chosen after a process of prior, free and informed consultation with the People so that it may authorize the entry and presence on its territory of the equipment and people required in this regard. Lastly, since the State has argued that a risk exists to the physical integrity of the people responsible for removing the explosives, it is for the State, in consultation with the People, to select the methods for removing the explosives that pose the least possible risk to the ecosystems in the area, consistent with the Sarayaku worldview and the safety of the team performing the operation.

294. As for the pentolite buried at a greater depth, the Court notes that, based on the technical appraisals that have been conducted, the representatives themselves have proposed a solution to neutralize its danger. [348 38] The State did not present any observations in this regard. The case file contains no specific arguments, or technical appraisals or evidence of a different nature, which would indicate that the Sarayaku Peoples' proposal is not an appropriate and safe option in keeping with their worldview for neutralizing the buried explosives. Therefore, the Court decides that, in accordance with the technical appraisals presented in these proceedings, and unless a better solution is agreed upon by the parties at the domestic level, the State must: (i) determine the number of points where the pentolite is buried; (ii) bury the detonator cables so that they are inaccessible and the explosive can degrade naturally, and (iii) mark the burial locations appropriately, even planting local tree species that do not grow roots deep enough to cause an accidental explosion of the pentolite. In addition, the State must adopt the necessary measures to remove any machinery, structures and non-biodegradable waste that have remained as a result of the oil company's activities, and reforest the areas that may still be affected by the opening up of trails and campsites for the seismic survey. These tasks must be carried out following a process of prior, free and informed consultation with the Sarayaku People, who must authorize the entry and presence on its territory of the material and persons required to this end.

295. Compliance with this measure of reparation is an obligation of the State, and it must complete it within no more than three years. For the purposes of compliance, the Court decides that, within six months, the State and the Sarayaku People must establish by mutual agreement a schedule and a work plan that includes, among other aspects, the determination of the location of the superficial pentolite and of the material buried at a greater depth, as well as the specific and effective steps to deactivate, neutralize and, as appropriate, remove the pentolite. Within the same period, the parties must provide the Court with information in

this regard. Once this information has been submitted, the State and the Sarayaku People must report on the measures taken to comply with the work plan every six months.

The Massacres of El Mozote and Nearby Places v. El Salvador
25-Oct-2012
Series C No. 252—*Merits, reparations and costs*

2. The case relates to the [alleged] successive massacres committed between December 11 and 13, 1981, in the context of a military operation by the Atlacatl Battalion, together with other military units, in seven places in the northern part of the department of Morazán, Republic of El Salvador, during which approximately 1,000 people were killed, "including an alarming number of children," as well as to the [alleged] investigation that was opened into these events and the "decision of September 27, 1993, to halt it based on the Law of General Amnesty for the Consolidation of Peace, which is still in force in El Salvador" and, finally, to the [alleged] exhumations performed over the following years, without leading to the reactivation of the investigations, "despite reiterated requests to the corresponding authorities."

3. According to the Commission, the [alleged] massacres of the instant case occurred during the ruthless period of the so-called "counterinsurgency" operations, deployed against civilians on a massive scale by the Salvadoran army during the armed conflict. It was the systematic and generalized nature of this type of action, designed to terrorize the population, which allows it to be concluded that the [alleged] massacres of the instant case constituted "one of the most heinous manifestations of the crimes against humanity committed at the time by the Salvadoran military." However, owing to the [alleged] validity of the Law of General Amnesty for the Consolidation of Peace, as well as reiterated omissions by the State, these grave events remain unpunished.

4. In its merits report, the Commission reached the conclusion that the State of El Salvador was internationally responsible for violating:

(a) The rights to life, to personal integrity and to personal liberty established in Articles 4, 5, and 7 of the American Convention in relation to Article 1(1) thereof, to the detriment of the victims who were extrajudicially executed;

(b) The special obligations with regard to children, established in Article 19 of the American Convention, in relation to Article 1(1) of this instrument, to the to the detriment of the children who were extrajudicially executed;

(c) The rights to personal integrity and to privacy established in Articles

5 and 11 of the American Convention, to the detriment of the women who were raped in the village of El Mozote;

(d) The right to property established in Article 21 of the American Convention in relation to Article 1(1) of this instrument, to the detriment of the executed victims who were stripped of their possessions, as well as of the survivors whose homes were destroyed or whose means of subsistence were seized or eliminated;

(e) The right to personal integrity set forth in Article 5 of the American Convention in relation to Article 1(1) thereof, to the detriment of the survivors and next of kin of the executed victims;

(f) The right to freedom of movement and residence set forth in Article 22 of the American Convention, in relation to Article 1(1) of this instrument, to the detriment of those who were forcibly displaced, and

(g) The rights to judicial guarantees and judicial protection established in Articles 8 and 25 of the American Convention, in relation to the obligations established in Articles 1(1) and 2 of this instrument; Articles 1, 6, and 8 of the Inter-American Convention to Prevent and Punish Torture; and Article 7 of the Inter-American Convention for the Prevention, Punishment, and Eradication of Violence against Women or "Convention of Belém do Pará," to the detriment of the survivors and next of kin of the executed victims.

5. The Commission submitted to the Inter-American Court the State's acts and omissions that occurred after June 6, 1995, the date on which El Salvador accepted the compulsory jurisdiction of the Court. These include: the application of the Law of General Amnesty for the Consolidation of Peace; the failure to reopen the investigations; the absence of continued and sustained efforts to exhume as many mortal remains as possible; the lack of judicial follow-up on the exhumations performed and on the information obtained from them; the lack of response to the requests to re-open the investigations; the effects of the massacres and their impunity on the surviving next of kin; the failure to make reparation to them, and the situation of displacement of some presumed victims. The foregoing, without prejudice to the State of El Salvador accepting the Court's competence to hear this case in full, under the provisions of Article 62(2) of the American Convention. Consequently, the Commission asked that the State be ordered to adopt certain measures of reparation.

REPARATIONS (Application of Article 63(1) of the American Convention)

303. Taking into consideration the violations of the American Convention, the Inter-American Convention to Prevent and Punish Torture, and the Inter-American Convention for the Prevention, Punishment and Eradication of Violence against Women "Convention of Belém do Pará" declared in this Judgment, the Court will

proceed to analyze the claims presented by the Commission and the representatives, as well as the arguments of the State, in light of the criteria established in the Court's case law regarding the nature and scope of the obligation to repair, [489 39] in order to establish measures designed to repair the damage caused to the victims.

305. Before this, the Court finds it pertinent to reiterate that the denial of justice to the detriment of the victims of grave human rights violations, such as a massacre, results in a variety of impacts in both the individual and the collective spheres. [491 40] Thus, it is evident that the victims of prolonged impunity suffer different adverse effects owing to the search for justice, not only of a pecuniary nature, but also sufferings and damage of a psychological and physical nature, and to their life project, as well as other possible alterations in their social relationships and their families and community dynamics. [492 41] This Court has indicated that this damage is increased by the absence of support from the State authorities in the effective search for and identification of the remains, and the impossibility of honoring their loved ones appropriately. [493 42] Accordingly, the Court has considered the need to grant different measures of reparation, in order to redress the damage fully; thus, in addition to pecuniary compensation, measures of satisfaction, restitution and rehabilitation, and guarantees of non-repetition have special relevance owing to the severity of the effects and the collective nature of the damage suffered. [494 43]

C. Measures of restitution, rehabilitation and satisfaction, and guarantees of non-repetition

335. International case law and, in particular, that of the Court, has established repeatedly that the judgment may constitute *per se* a form of reparation. [509 44] However, based on the circumstances of the case and the adverse effects on the victims as a result of the violations of the American Convention declared to their detriment, the Court considers it pertinent to determine the following measures of reparation.

1) Measures of restitution

a) Development program for the village of El Mozote and nearby places

339. The Court assesses positively the State's willingness to institute a social development program in favor of the victims in this case. In view of the harm caused by the facts of this case to the members of the communities belonging to the village of El Mozote, the canton of La Joya, the villages of Ranchería, Los Toriles, and Jocote Amarillo, and the canton of Cerro Pando, this Court establishes, as it has in other cases, [510 45] that, in these communities and irrespective of the public works included in the national budget destined to that region or municipality, the State must implement in these communities in full coordination with the victims and their representatives, a development program that includes the following:

(a) improvements to the public road system;
(b) access to public services of water and electricity;

(c) establishment of a health care center in a place accessible for most of the villages, with adequate personnel and conditions, that can provide medical, psychological or psychiatric care to the people who have been affected and who require this type of treatment in keeping with paragraphs 350 to 353 of the Judgment;

(d) construction of a school in a place accessible for most of the villages, and

(e) construction of a center for the elderly.

340. The State must implement the development program within five years of notification of this Judgment.

b) Provide adequate conditions for the victims who are still displaced to return to their place of origin

344. The evidence presented in this case reveals that most of the victims who survived the massacres displaced from their places of origin to other municipalities and even outside El Salvador, losing their homes and, in some cases, their crops, possessions, farm animals and livestock during the massacres and the displacement (*supra* paras. 175 and 183). As determined, some of the displaced victims have returned to their place of origin, while others have not yet returned and, in some cases, there is no information on their current location (*supra* paras. 189 and 190).

345. In order to contribute to the reparation of the victims who were forcibly displaced from their communities of origin; namely, the village of El Mozote, the canton of La Joya, the villages of Ranchería, Los Toriles, and Jocote Amarillo, and the canton of Cerro Pando, the Court orders that the State must guarantee adequate conditions so that the displaced victims can return to their communities of origin permanently, if they so wish. If these conditions do not exist, the State must provide the necessary and sufficient resources to enable the victims of enforced displacement to resettle in similar conditions to those they had before the events, in the place that they freely and willingly indicate within the department of Morazán, in El Salvador. The Court recognizes that the State's compliance with this measure of reparation entails, in part, that the beneficiaries indicate their intention of returning to their places of origin in El Salvador. Therefore, the Court establishes that, within two years of notification of this Judgment, the State and the beneficiaries should reach the pertinent agreement in order to comply with what the Court has ordered if the forcibly displaced victims identified in Annex "D" of this Judgment wish to return to their communities of origin.

346. In addition, given that the inhabitants of the said communities lost their homes as a result of the facts of this case (*supra* paras. 175 to 178), this Court orders the State to implement a housing program in the areas affected by the massacres of this case, under which adequate housing is provided to the displaced victims who require this. [511] [46] The forcibly displaced victims identified in Annex "D" of this Judgment who request this measure of reparation, or their legal

representatives, have one year from notification of this Judgment to inform the State of their intention to be part of the housing program.

Wong Ho Wing v. Peru
30-June-2015
Series C No. 297—*Preliminary Objection, Merits, Reparations and Costs*

1.. On October 30, 2013, in accordance with the provisions of Articles 51 and 61 of the American Convention and Article 35 of the Court's Rules of Procedure, the Inter-American Commission on Human Rights (hereinafter "the Inter-American Commission" or "the Commission") submitted the case of *Wong Ho Wing v.t the Republic of Peru* (hereinafter "the State" or "Peru") to the jurisdiction of the Inter-American Court. According to the Commission, the facts of this case related to a series of presumed violations of the rights of Wong Ho Wing, a national of the People's Republic of China, from the time of his detention on October 27, 2008, and throughout the extradition process that continues to date. According to the Commission, Wong Ho Wing has been and continues to be subjected to an [alleged] arbitrary and excessive deprivation of liberty that is not justified by procedural requirements. The Commission also concluded that, at different stages of the extradition proceedings, the domestic authorities had presumably been responsible for a series of omissions and irregularities in the processing of the case, which constituted, in addition to presumed violations of several aspects of due process, [alleged] non-compliance with the obligation to ensure the right to life and to humane treatment of Wong Ho Wing. In addition, it concluded that, since May 24, 2011, the date on which the Peruvian Constitutional Court ordered the Executive Branch to refrain from extraditing Wong Ho Wing, the State authorities had [alleged]ly failed to comply with a court ruling, which was incompatible with the right to judicial protection.

B. Measures of integral reparation: restitution and satisfaction
B.1) Restitution
a) Extradition process
301. The Commission asked the Court to order the State "[t]o establish the measures necessary to ensure that the extradition process is brought to a conclusion as soon as possible, in accordance with the procedures set forth in the Peruvian Code of Criminal Procedure, denying the extradition request in strict compliance with the judgment of the Constitutional Court of May 24, 2011." In addition, it asked that in compliance with this measure, the State ensure that none of its authorities implement mechanisms that would obstruct or delay execution of that judgment. The representative asked the Court to order the State to take a decision in the extradition

process as soon as possible, "denying the extradition request." He also asked that, in no circumstance, should Wong Ho Wing be extradited to the People's Republic of China where his life and personal integrity were at risk and, as a result, the total disintegration of his immediate family." The State advised that the extradition process was at the final stage, so that the Commission's request would "be assessed by the corresponding entities, in accordance with the laws of Peru in force and the regular domestic procedures, based on the Court's decision" in this case.

302. The Court recalls that it has concluded that the State has not acted with the necessary due diligence in the extradition process, which has resulted in the excessive duration of the extradition proceedings and of the deprivation of Wong Ho Wing's liberty. This constitutes a violation of the guarantee of a reasonable time in the processing of the extradition proceedings and of his detention in violation of Articles 7(1), 7(5) and 8(1) of the Convention, in relation to Article 1(1) of this instrument, as decided in Chapters X and XI of this Judgment. Consequently, the Court finds that the State should take the final decision in the extradition process as soon as possible, taking into account paragraphs 193 to 223 of this Judgment.

303. In addition, bearing in mind the nature of the provisional measures ordered in this case, the Court considers that the State's obligations under these measures is replaced by the measures ordered in this Judgment as of the date of its notification.

b) Review of the provisional arrest

304. The Commission asked that the Court order the State to review *ex officio* the provisional detention of Wong Ho Wing, taking into consideration his legal situation following the conclusion of the extradition proceedings. In particular, it asked that any judicial decision on the personal liberty of Wong Ho Wing should be made "in strict compliance with the principles of exceptionality, necessity and proportionality." The representative requested the immediate release of Wong Ho Wing. The State asserted that, on March 10, 2014, the Seventh Criminal Court of El Callao had revoked the provisional arrest warrant and issued the measure of an order to appear in court periodically: house arrest, establishing a financial surety and the prohibition to leave the country. It argued that the court had taken into consideration the time Wong Ho Wing had spent in the Sarita Colonia Prison, and considered it appropriate to modify the measures; hence, the State considered that it had complied with the Commission's request.

305. The Court recalls that Wong Ho Wing has been deprived of liberty since October 2008. Even though he has been kept under house arrest since March 2014, the Court reiterates its findings in this Judgment as regards the arbitrary nature of the detention, the excessive time taken to process the extradition proceedings, and the duration of the provisional arrest. The Court recalls that the purpose of the actual deprivation of liberty of Wong Ho Wing is his extradition. Therefore, taking into account the measure of reparation according to which the State must take a final decision in the extradition proceedings (*supra* para. 302), the Court orders

the State to review, immediately, the deprivation of liberty of Wong Ho Wing, taking into account the standards established in Chapter XI of this Judgment. In addition, the State should take into consideration the time that he has remained deprived of his liberty to date and his actual situation and health care needs.

ANALYSIS AND QUESTIONS RAISED BY THE COURT'S JURISPRUDENCE

Restitution is the primary form of reparation because, when possible, it holds the greatest possibility of reestablishing the *status quo ante* or restoring the victim to the situation that existed prior to the violation of their rights and freedoms, which is the aim of all reparations. As demonstrated by the above case excerpts, orders of restitution may be relatively simple, as in *Apitz Barbera*, which involved reinstatement of the victims to their positions of employment as a remedy for wrongful and arbitrary removal. In other cases, reinstitution may involve more complex and multiple steps, as in the cases involving the restoration of land and territory to indigenous communities. In such cases, restitution may require the support of other measures of reparation, such as guarantees of non-repetition ordering legal reforms to uphold land rights.

For instance, a number of the Court's decisions have involved the restitution of ancestral lands to indigenous communities. *Kichwa Indigenous People of Sarayaku* involved the literal restoration of the People's land through the removal of explosives used for oil exploration and exploitation, as well as the restoration of the People's control over the territory. As also detailed in the Court's decisions in *Sawhoyamaxa Indigenous Community*, *Saramaka People*, and *Xákmok Kásek Indigenous Community*, restitution of these communities' ancestral lands also required legal reforms to ensure the protection of the communities' rights to property and to ensure effective consultation by the State with the respective community, as well as free prior informed consent by the community for any decisions that would impact their lands and their use of their lands. Such decisions demonstrate the interconnected nature of reparations where, for example, restitution measures require guarantees of non-repetition.

- In *Aloeboetoe*, the Inter-American Court of Human Rights stated that compensation was not sufficient to repair the violation and that the establishment of a school and medical dispensary were necessary. In *Loayza Tamayo*, the Court determined that the victim would not be able to fully return to her previous employment, and that monetary benefits were necessary. Then, in *Apitz Barbera*, the Court ordered that the victims be reinstated in their former judicial positions, but allowed the possibility that if it were not legitimately possible to return the victims to their positions, that they be monetarily compensated. In what other circumstances may restitution require supplementary compensation? Under what circumstances may compensation substitute for restitution?

- In *Apitz Barbera*, restitution involved the return of victims to their former judicial positions. The Court's restitution order also served to uphold judicial independence. What other circumstances involving restitution may repair the violations a victim has suffered while also upholding broader principles of law and justice?

- In *"Cotton Field,"* the Court stated that "bearing in mind the context of structural discrimination in which the facts of this case occurred . . . reparations must be designed to change this situation, so that their effect is not only of restitution, but also of rectification. In this regard, re-establishment of the same structural context of violence and discrimination is not acceptable." Here, the Court emphasized that *restitutio in integrum* "entails the re-establishment of the previous situation and the *elimination of the effects produced by the violation.*"[47] Thus, the Court stresses here that restitution, then, is not simply a return to the prior state, particularly in circumstances where the prior state itself involved human rights violations; rather, restitution requires remediation of the violations that the victim suffered. What does this understanding of restitution imply for cases that involve ongoing or long-standing violations of human rights? What is the meaning of restitution if the victim's prior state involved violations of their rights?

- In *Yakye Axa Indigenous Community*, as in several other cases involving the restitution of ancestral lands to an indigenous community, the Court ordered the restoration of the community's lands and required the State to ensure that the lands be protected from harm by the State itself or by private third parties. The Court further ordered that until the lands were restored to the community, that the State ensure the provision of water, food, sanitation systems, health care and treatment, and educational materials in the community's own language. In what other circumstances might restitution involve multiple steps or take long periods of time? Should the State be responsible for these provisions in all cases where victims are deprived of their means of subsistence?

- Also in *Yakye Axa Indigenous Community*, while the Court ordered the restoration of the community's land to them, it suggested that "[i]f for objective and well-founded reasons the claim to ancestral territory of the members of the Yakye Axa Community is not possible, the State must grant them alternative land, chosen by means of a consensus with the community, in accordance with its own manner of consultation and decision-making, practices, and customs. In either case, the area of land must be sufficient to ensure preservation and development of the Community's own manner of life." What would constitute "objective and well-founded reasons"?

- In *Massacres of El Mozote*, the Court ordered the State to institute a social development program, along with housing, to include roads improvement, access to public services of water and electricity, a health center, a geographically accessible school, and a center for elderly community members. This order was designed to provide adequate conditions to support the return of community members in the aftermath of successive massacres and forced displacement. What other circumstances might necessitate a social development program as restitution?

IV. REHABILITATION

Rehabilitation is a fundamental form of reparation awarded when victims require medical and psychological treatment and care as a result of the violations they suffered. The Inter-American Court of Human Rights has also awarded other types of rehabilitation, such as vocational and educational training that would assist victims to reintegrate into their community and society following the violation and when violations have damaged the victim's life project. The following case excerpts demonstrate the range of the Court's rehabilitation orders.

Plan de Sanchez Massacre v. Guatemala
19-Nov-2004
Series C No. 116—*Reparations and Costs*

1.   On July 31, 2002, the Inter-American Commission on Human Rights (hereinafter "the Commission" or "the Inter-American Commission") filed an application against the State of Guatemala (hereinafter "the State" or "Guatemala") before the Inter-American Court, originating from petition No. 11,763 and received by the Secretariat of the Commission on October 25, 1996.

2.   The Commission submitted the application, based on Article 61 of the American Convention, for the Court to "declare that the State was internationally responsible . . . for violations to the rights to humane treatment, judicial protection,

a fair trial, . . . equal protection, freedom of conscience and religion, and . . . property, in relation to the obligation to respect rights, which are embodied in Articles 5, 8, 25, 24, 12, 21, and 1[(1)] of the American Convention." In the application, the Commission [alleged] "denial of justice and other acts of intimidation and discrimination affecting the rights to humane treatment, freedom of conscience and religion, and property of the survivors and the next of kin of the victims of the massacre of 268 individuals . . . mostly members of the Maya indigenous people of the village of Plan de Sánchez, Municipality of Rabinal, Department of Baja Verapaz, perpetrated by members of the Guatemalan Army and civilian collaborators, under the guidance of the Army, on Sunday, July 18, 1982.

g)   *Housing program*

105.   Since the inhabitants of Plan de Sánchez lost their homes as a result of the facts of this case, the Court considers that the State must implement a housing program to provide adequate housing[272 48] to the surviving victims who live in that village and who require it. The State must implement this program within five years of notification of this judgment.

f)   *Medical and psychological treatment*

106.   The victims who have given testimony before the Court or by affidavit have stated that they suffer from physical and psychological problems as a result of the facts of this case. Also, the expert witness, Nieves Gómez Dupuis, stated during the public hearing that the surviving victims of the massacre have mental health problems and psychosomatic ailments. The Court notes that it should order a measure designed to reduce the physical and mental sufferings of the victims in this case, resulting from the violations, if they so wish.[273 49]

107.   To help repair this damage, the Court decides that the State shall provide, free of charge, through its specialized health institutions, the medical treatment that the victims require, including, inter alia, any necessary medication. The State shall also create a specialized program of psychological and psychiatric treatment, which should also be provided free of charge. When providing the psychological and psychiatric treatment, the special circumstances and needs of each person must be taken into account, in order to provide collective, family, and individual treatment. This treatment should be implemented following an assessment of each individual and as agreed with each of them.

108.   To this end, the State must set up a committee to evaluate the physical and mental condition of the victims, and also the treatment that each one requires. The non-governmental organization, Community Studies and Psychosocial Action Team, must play an active part in this committee and, should this organization not agree or be unable to assume the task, the State must identify another non-governmental organization, with experience in treating victims, to replace it.

Guatemala must inform the Court about the constitution of this committee within six month. With regard to the medical and psychological treatment, this should be started immediately after the constitution of the committee for a period of five years.

h)   Development program (health, education, production and infrastructure)

109.   In their arguments, the Commission and the representatives noted the need to develop programs on health, education, production, and infrastructure that would benefit the members of the communities affected by the facts of this case. The State also indicated that the measures of reparation could comprise the obligation of the State to provide social services, in accordance with international standards. Also, the witnesses, Juan Manuel Jerónimo and Buenaventura Manuel Jerónimo, in particular, mentioned that educational and infrastructure programs (for example, highways, paved roads, potable water) should be implemented as a measure of reparation.

110.   Given the harm caused to the members of the Plan de Sánchez community and to the members of the communities of Chipuerta, Joya de Ramos, Raxjut, Volcanillo, Coxojabaj, Las Tunas, Las Minas, Las Ventanas, Ixchel, Chiac, Concul, and Chichupac, owing to the facts of this case, the Court decides that the State shall implement the following programs in these communities (in addition to the public works financed by the national budget allocated to that region or municipality): a) study and dissemination of the Maya-Achí culture in the affected communities through the Guatemalan Academy of Mayan Languages or a similar organization; b) maintenance and improvement of the road systems between the said communities and the municipal capital of Rabinal; c) sewage system and potable water supply; d) supply of teaching personnel trained in intercultural and bilingual teaching for primary, secondary and comprehensive schooling in these communities, and e) the establishment of a health center in the village of Plan de Sánchez with adequate personnel and conditions, as well as training for the personnel of the Rabinal Municipal Health Center so that they can provide medical and psychological care to those who have been affected and who require this kind of treatment.

111.   The State must implement these programs within five years of notification of this judgment and present the Court with a detailed implementation report every year.

Radilla-Pacheco v. Mexico
23-Nov-2009
Series C No. 209—*Preliminary Objections, Merits, Reparations, and Costs*

C7. Psychological attention

358. This Tribunal, having verified the damages suffered by the victims in the present case, which were established in Chapter VIII of the present Judgment, considers it convenient to order that the State offer free psychological and/ or psychiatric attention immediately, adequately, and effectively, through its specialized public health institutions, to the victims that so request it. For this, it shall take into consideration the special sufferings of the beneficiaries through the prior realization of a physical and psychological assessment. Likewise, the corresponding treatments shall be offered for as long as considered necessary and it shall include the free supply of the medications that could eventually be required.

Rosendo Cantú et al. v. Mexico
31-Aug-2010
Series C No. 216—*Preliminary Objections, Merits, Reparations, and Costs*

2. According to the Inter-American Commission, the application refers to the [alleged] international responsibility of the State for the "rape and torture" of Mrs. Rosendo Cantu that took place on February 16, 2002; the "lack of due diligence in the investigation and punishment of the perpetrators" of these facts; "the consequence caused by the facts in the case to the daughter of the [[alleged]] victim"; "the failure to make adequate reparation to the [[alleged]] victim and her next of kin"; the "use of the military justice system to investigate and prosecute human rights violations," and "the difficulties encountered by indigenous people, particularly indigenous women, to obtain access to justice and health care."
3. Based on the above, the Inter-American Commission asked the Court to declare the State responsible for the violation of Articles 5 (Right to Personal Integrity), 8 (Right to a Fair Trial), 25 (Right to Judicial Protection), 11 (Right to Privacy [Honor and Dignity]), and 19 (Rights of the Child) of the American Convention, in relation to the general obligation to respect and ensure human rights established in Article 1(1) thereof, to the detriment of Mrs. Rosendo Cantu. In addition, it indicated that Mexico is responsible for the violation of Article 5 (Right to Personal Integrity) of the Convention to the detriment of Yenys Bernardino Rosendo, daughter of Mrs. Rosendo Cantu. In addition, it noted that Mexico is responsible for the violation of Article 7 of the Inter-American Convention on the Prevention, Punishment, and Eradication of Violence against Women (hereinafter also "the Convention of Belém do Pará") and Articles 1, 6, and 8 of the Inter-American Convention to Prevent and Punish Torture (hereinafter "the Convention against Torture"), all to the detriment of Mrs. Rosendo Cantu. Based on the

abovementioned, the Inter-American Commission asked the Court to order the State to make certain reparations.

ARTICLES 5 (RIGHT TO HUMANE TREATMENT) [49][50] **AND 11 (RIGHT TO PRIVACY)** [50][51]**, IN RELATION TO ARTICLE 1(1) (OBLIGATION TO RESPECT RIGHTS),** [51][52] **OF THE AMERICAN CONVENTION AND 1, 2, AND 6 OF THE INTERAMERICAN CONVENTION TO PREVENT AND PUNISH TORTURE,** [52][53] **AND 7 OF THE CONVENTION OF BELEM DO PARA.** [53][54]

A. Facts relating to the [alleged] rape of Mrs. Rosendo Cantú

70. The facts of the present case occurred in the context of a significant military presence in the state of Guerrero, [54][55] aimed at repressing unlawful activities such as organized crime. It has been reported that fundamental rights were violated during the repression of such activities. [55][56] In the state of Guerrero, most of the population belongs to indigenous communities, who conserve their traditions and cultural identity and reside in the poorest and most marginalized municipalities. [56][57] In general, the indigenous population is in a situation of vulnerability, and this is reflected in various forums, such as in the administration of justice and health care services. Especially, the members of this population are defenseless because they do not speak Spanish and do not have interpreters, because of the absence of financial resources to hire a lawyer, to travel to health care centers or to the organs of justice, and also because they are often victims of abusive practices or practices that violate due process. [57][58] Owing to this situation, members of the indigenous communities do not use the organs of justice or the public agencies engaged in the protection of human rights, because they distrust them or because they fear reprisals, [58][59] and in the case of indigenous women, the situation is even worse, because filing complaints concerning certain acts has become a challenge that requires them to overcome many obstacles, such as rejection from their community and other "harmful traditional practices." [59][60]

71. Among the forms of violence that affect women in the state of Guerrero, there exists "institutional violence by the Military." [60][61] The presence of the Army performing police work in the state of Guerrero has been a polemic issue because it conflicts with individual and communitarian rights and freedoms, and has placed the population, particularly the women, in a situation of extreme vulnerability. [61][62] According to the Secretariat for Women's Affairs in the state of Guerrero in this setting, "[i]ndigenous women continue to suffer the consequences of a patriarchal structure that is blind to gender equity, particularly within institutions such as the Armed Forces or police, whose members are trained to defend the nation, and to combat or attack criminals, but who are not sensitized to the human rights of the community and of women." [62][63] In this context, between 1997 and 2004, complaints were filed in six cases of the rape of indigenous women attributed

to members of the Army in the state of Guerrero, which were all heard in the military justice system, [63] [64] and there is no evidence that those responsible have been punished in any of these cases.

72. Mrs. Rosendo Cantú is an indigenous woman and a member of the Me´phaa indigenous community, [64] [65] originally from the Caxitepec community, state of Guerrero. [65] [66] At the time of the facts, she was 17 years of age, [66] [67] and she was married to Mr. Fidel Bernardino Sierra[67] [68] with whom she lived with, approximately one-hour walking distance from Barranca Bejuco, [68] [69] with their daughter, Yenys Bernardino Rosendo, born November 23, 2001. [69] [70] The community of Barranca Bejuco is located in an isolated mountainous area, and consequently, access is difficult. [70] [71]

73. Mrs. Rosendo Cantú stated that on February 16, 2002, at around three in the afternoon, she was at a stream near her home where she had gone to wash clothes. When she went to bathe, eight soldiers, accompanied by a civilian they had detained, approached her and surrounded her. Two of them questioned her about "the hooded men" ["los encapuchados"] and they showed her a picture of a person and a list of names of other people while one of them threatened her with a weapon. She indicated that "because of the fear that they do something to her" she responded that she did not know of the people they questioned her about. The soldier, who aimed at her, hit her in the stomach with the weapon, making her fall to the ground and lose consciousness for a moment. She narrated that when she regained consciousness, she sat up and one of the soldiers grabbed her by the hair and insisted about the required information, telling her that if she did not answer they would kill her along with all of the people in Barranca Bejuco. She stated that, afterwards, "using [...] violence they scratched her face," they took off her skirt and her underwear, and they knocked her to the floor, and one of them sexually penetrated her, and once he was done, the other soldier who had questioned her proceeded to sexually penetrate her. [71] [72]

74. Upon arriving at her home, Mrs. Rosendo Cantú told what had happened to her sister-in-law, Mrs. Estela Sierra Morales, and to her husband, Mr. Fidel Bernardino Sierra, when he arrived home after work. [72] [73] He then went to Barranca Bejuco to file a complaint with the authorities of the community. [73] [74]

75. On February 18, 2002, Mrs. Rosendo Cantú, accompanied by her husband, went to a health care clinic in the community of Caxitepec to be seen for the blows she had received, and no evidence exists that she indicated having been raped. [74] [75] The doctor gave her some painkillers and anti-inflammatory pills for the pain. [75] [76] On February 26, 2002, they went to Ayutla de los Libres to be attended at the Hospital, to which they had to walk for eight hours. [76] [77] There, she was attended by the "general consultation service, with the record of trauma to her abdomen," where it was stated that "10 days prior, a trunk of wood had fallen [there], causing

the pain," without stating she had been raped. In said consultation, "lab studies" were requested, [77][78] which consisted of a general urine exam. [78][79]

REPARATIONS
(Application of Article 63(1) of the American Convention[267][80])

205. The Court will proceed to examine the claims submitted by the Commission and the representatives, as well as the State's arguments, so as to order measures designed to repair the damage caused to the victims. Regarding the State's arguments, the Court observes that it presented specific arguments with regard to only some of the requested measures of reparation. Notwithstanding, Mexico requested in a general manner that the Court reject "any claim for reparation presented by the [Commission] or the petitioners." In addition, it requested that the measures ordered "should be designed to repair the violation [...] committed and not to make the victims more rich, [...] nor to provide a double reparation." Lastly, it requested that the Court consider the measures of public policy implemented by the State as guarantees of non-repetition.

206. The Court does not lose sight that Mrs. Rosendo Cantú is an indigenous woman, a girl child at the time the violations occurred, and whose situation of particular vulnerability will be taken into account in the reparations awarded in this Judgment. Furthermore, the Court finds that the obligation to repair in a case that involves victims belonging to an indigenous community may call for measures that encompass the entire community[271][81] (*infra* para. 226).

B. Measures of satisfaction, rehabilitation, and guarantees of non-repetition
vi) Multidisciplinary health services for women victims of sexual abuse

233. The Commission requested that the Court order the State to design and implement multidisciplinary health services for women victims of rape, which encompass the specific necessities of indigenous women for their recuperation, rehabilitation, and reinsertion into the community.

234. The State presented information during the public hearing and in its final written arguments regarding the public policy, programs, norms, and actions that it has implemented at a federal and local level in order to "reduce the prevalence and severity of the harm caused by violence against women, with a particular emphasis on those women in situations of major risk and vulnerability." Among other aspects, it presented information regarding Mexican Norm-046-SSA2-2005, "Domestic and sexual violence against women. The criteria for prevention and attention," which strives to establish the criteria for detention, prevention, medical care, and the orientation for the service users of the general health care services, and particularly, those involved in circumstances of domestic or sexual violence. In this manner, it strives to provide medical care to the victim of violence that involves the promotion, protection, and restoration—to the highest

degree possible—of physical and mental health via treatment, rehabilitation, or referrals to specialized places. Likewise, it reported on the creation in the state of Guerrero of institutions that intervene in cases of sexual violence against women such as the Investigation of Sexual Offenses and Domestic Violence, the municipal offices specialized in assistance and prevention of violence against women, made up of lawyers, social workers, doctors, and psychologists, and the State System to Prevent, Attend, Punish, and Eradicate Violence against Women" as well as the creation, at a federal level of: i) four Integral Attention Centers for victims of gender-based violence, "with the hopes of expanding the number [...] to all the federal entities," and ii) a national network of refuge for women victims of violence, where they offer "specialized and interdisciplinary protection and attention to women and children in conditions of domestic, sexual violence or trade."

235. In this regard, the Court notes that the State gave specific information regarding the institutions, norms, programs, and actions developed in this sphere, whose existence or validity was not questioned by the Commission, and to which the Commission also did not present information regarding possible deficiencies or problems. As such, the Court states that the duty to provide motive and establish the claims for reparations and costs is not satisfied with generic requests where there is no attached evidence or supporting argumentation (*supra* para. 232). The abovementioned prevents the Court from addressing the requested measures.

vii) Participatory programs to contribute to the reinsertion in the community of indigenous women victims of rape

236. The Commission requested the Court to order the State to design participatory programs to contribute to the reinsertion of indigenous women victims of rape into the community.

237. The State presented information regarding some public policies initiated at a federal level as well as within the state of Guerrero regarding the participation of indigenous women in the diagnosis of the situation of violence against women and the "socialization of the legal instruments that recognize said women's' rights." In particular, the State reported on training workshops for indigenous women, indigenous authorities, indigenous organizations and those who offer services regarding violence, municipal authorities, and government employees of the judicial branch so as to, *inter alia,* "sensitize [them] in regard to the attention of women and their development in conditions that promote equal protection and freedom from violence."

238. In this regard, the State provided definite information regarding programs and actions developed on this subject, and the existence and validity were not objected to by the Commission, and to which the Commission also did not raise information regarding their possible problems. As such, the Court states

that the duty to provide motive and establish the claims for reparations and costs is not satisfied with generic requests where there is no attached evidence or argumentation (*supra* paras. 232 and 238). The abovementioned prevents the Court from addressing the requested measures.

xi) Medical and psychological care

250. The Commission asked the Court to order the State to adopt measures of medical and psychological rehabilitation for the victim and her next of kin, which should include the design and implementation of a mental health care plan, in consensus with mental health professionals and women victims of rape, for the recuperation, rehabilitation, and full reinsertion back into their communities.

251. The representatives asked the Court to order the State to guarantee to Mrs. Rosendo Cantú and her daughter, medical and psychological care provided by competent and trustworthy professionals for both of them, that take into consideration their status as an indigenous woman victim of violence, her culture, and her address. Moreover, they requested that the State incur all expenses related to treatment, including transportation or other necessities.

252. The Court finds, as it has in other cases, [288] [82] that a measure of reparation must be ordered that provides appropriate care for the physical and psychological effects suffered by the victims, which attend to their gender and ethnicity. Consequently, having verified the violations and the harm suffered by the victims in the present case, the Court decides that the State is obliged to provide them, free of charge and immediately, with the medical and psychological care they require. Prior, clear, and sufficient information should be offered to the victims so as to obtain their consent. The treatments should be provided for the time that is necessary, and should include the provision of medication, and where applicable, transportation, interpreters, and other costs that are directly related and strictly necessary.

253. In particular, the psychological or psychiatric treatment must be provided by State personnel and institutions specialized in attending to victims of acts of violence such as those that occurred in this case. If the State does not have this type of service available, it must have recourse to specialized private or civil society institutions. When providing this treatment, the specific circumstances and needs of each victim must be considered, so that they are offered individual and family treatment, as agreed upon by each of them, and following an individual evaluation. [289] [83] Lastly, this treatment must be provided, insofar as possible, in the institutions nearest to their place of residence. The victims that request this measure of reparation, or their legal representatives, have six months as of the notification of this Judgment to inform the State of their specific requests for psychological or psychiatric treatment. The Court highlights the need for the State and the representatives to offer their best collaborative efforts and to provide

the victims with all the information necessary for said victims to receive the psychological treatment in order to advance the implementation of this measure in an agreed upon manner.

xiii) Award of scholarships

256. The representatives asked the Court to order the State to award scholarships to Mrs. Rosendo Cantú and her daughter, given that they considered that "the only way they can improve their lives is to continue with their studies."

257. The Court has established in this Judgment that the facts of the case harmed Mrs. Rosendo Cantú and her daughter and this harm continues and has resulted in significant alterations to their lives and also to their domestic relations and their relations with the community, which have affected their personal development (*supra* paras. 130, 131, 138, and 139). Based on the foregoing, and bearing in mind the representatives' request, the Court finds it appropriate to order as a measure of satisfaction in this case, as it has in other cases, [290][84] that the State awards scholarships in Mexican public establishments to Mrs. Rosendo Cantú and her daughter, Yenys Bernardino Rosendo, that cover all the costs of their education until the completion of their higher education, whether of technical or university studies. The State's compliance with the obligation implies that the beneficiaries must take certain measures to exercise their right to this measure of reparation. [291][85] Consequently, those who requested this measure of reparation, or their legal representatives, have six months from notification of this Judgment, to advise the State of their request of scholarships.

xiv) Health care center for the victim's community

258. The representatives requested the Court to order the State, in the framework of a policy of access to health care for women in indigenous communities in Mexico, to give Mrs. Rosendo Cantu's indigenous community a comprehensive health care center, with specialized personnel in the treatment of women victims of violence, that provides translators and the necessary resources and medication, so as to guarantee increased access to said services for women in the community to actively participate, promoting human rights of women victims of violence, if the victim wishes so.

259. The Court notes that the State reported on various public policies aimed at attending to women victims of sexual violence, that have been implemented by means of a National Program of Prevention and Attention to Domestic and Sexual Violence, which has been implemented in 32 federal states and which establishes as its objective an organized social response to the needs of women victims of violence regarding medical and psychological care. It also reported that the state of Guerrero has carried out multiple actions to attend to women in Guerrero, through various agencies, including the Secretariat of Women and the Secretariat of Indigenous Affairs, and the provision of services such as mobile units traveling

to attend to the problems of women in the community. It also reported that in indigenous areas, policies and programs have been designed and implemented to expand coverage of health services. The State also indicated that health personnel "constantly receives training on human rights [...] to ensure adequate provision of health services to people," and made reference to works that have been carried out to improve health care infrastructure in the state of Guerrero and special services for women victims of sexual violence. On the other hand, of the evidence presented in the current case, it is evident that the nearest health care center to the Barranca Bejuco community is found in the community of Caxitepec.

260. In the present case, the Court notes that the rape of Mrs. Rosendo Cantú has demonstrated the need to strengthen attention and the health care centers that treat women who have suffered violence. Notwithstanding the aforementioned, the Court notes that there is a health care center in Caxitepec, and the representatives have not provided the Court with sufficient information for it to consider the need of ordering to create a new health care center. The services for treating women victims of sexual violence can be guaranteed within the current center, which should be fortified by way of the provision of material resources and staffing, including the provision of a translator who speaks Me'paa, as well as the use of an appropriate protocol, to take the appropriate actions; all this in the context of the implementation of programs regarding care for victims of violence and investment efforts in improving the services that the State indicated that it has been carrying out.

Atala Riffo and Daughters v. Chile
24-Feb-2012
Series C No. 239—*Merits, Reparations and Costs*

3. According to the Commission, the present case concerns the [alleged] international responsibility of the State for discriminatory treatment and arbitrary interference in the private and family life suffered by Ms. Atala due to her sexual orientation, in the legal process that resulted in the loss of care and custody of her daughters M., V and R. The case also concerns the [alleged] failure to take into account the best interests of the girls, whose custody and care were determined without having regard to their rights, and on the basis of [alleged] discriminatory prejudices. The Commission requested the Court to declare the violation of Articles 11 (Right to Privacy), 17.1 and 17.4 (Rights of the Family), 19 (Rights of the Child), 24 (Right to Equal Protection) and 25 (Right to Judicial Protection) of the Convention, in relation to Article 1.1 thereof. Likewise, the Commission requested the Court to order the State to adopt reparation measures.

REPARATIONS
(APPLICATION OF ARTICLE 63.1 OF THE AMERICAN CONVENTION)

239. Based on the provisions of Article 63.1 of the American Convention,[263] [86] the Court has indicated that any violation of an international obligation that has caused damage entails the duty to provide adequate reparation,[264] [87] and that this provision reflects a customary norm that constitutes one of the fundamental principles of contemporary International Law on State responsibility. [265] [88]

240. The State argued that this case "has not entailed a violation of the human rights of Ms. Karen Atala's or those of her three daughters." However, taking into account the violations of the American Convention declared in the preceding chapters, the Court will now consider the requests for reparations made by the Commission and the representatives, as well as the State's observations thereof, in light of the criteria embodied in the Court's case law regarding the nature and scope of the obligation to make reparations, in order to adopt the measures [ ] required to redress the damage to the victims.

241. The reparation of damage caused by a breach of an international obligation requires, wherever possible, full restitution (*restitutio in integrum*), which consists of reinstating the situation prior to the violation. Where this is not feasible, as happens in the majority of cases involving human rights violations, the Court shall decide measures to guarantee the infringed rights, repair the damage caused by the violations and establish an amount in compensation to make good on the damage caused.[266] [89] Therefore, the Court has considered the need to order several measures of reparation in order to fully redress the damage caused, and therefore, in addition to pecuniary compensation, the measures of restitution, satisfaction and guarantees of non-repetition are especially relevant.[267] [90]

242. This Court has held that reparations must have a causal nexus with the facts of the case, the violations declared, the damages verified and the measures requested to repair the consequences of those damages. Therefore, based on the considerations of the merits and the violations of the Convention declared in the preceding chapters, the Court must adhere to this concurrence in order to rule properly and according to law.[268] [91]

A. Injured Party

246. International jurisprudence, and in particular the case law of the Inter-American Court, has repeatedly held that a judgment *per se* constitutes a form of reparation. [272] [92] Nonetheless, considering the circumstances of the case under examination and the burdens placed upon the victims due to the violations of Articles 8(1), 11(2), 17(1), 17(4), 19, and 24 of the American Convention committed against Ms. Atala and the girls M., V. and R., the Court deems it appropriate to order certain measures of reparation, as explained in the following paragraphs.

C. Other measures of full redress: satisfaction and guarantees of non-repetition

1. Rehabilitation: Medical and psychological treatment for the victims

253. The Court notes that the evidence offered by the psychiatrists shows several indications that Ms. Atala and her daughters suffer as a consequence of the human rights´ violations that occurred in this case.

254. As in other cases[274][93] the Court deems it necessary to order a measure of reparation that provides adequate care for the physical and mental ailments suffered by the victims, addressing their specific needs. Therefore, having confirmed the violations and damages suffered by the victims in the present case, the Court orders the State to provide them, freely and immediately, with appropriate and effective medical and psychological care for up to four years. In particular, the psychological treatment must be provided by State institutions and personnel specialized in treating victims of acts such as those that occurred in the instant case. When providing said treatment, the specific circumstances and needs of each victim must be take into account, so that they are offered family and individual treatment, as agreed upon with each one, after an individual evaluation[275][94]. The treatments must include the provision of medicines and, where appropriate, transportation or other expenses that are directly related and are strictly necessary.

255. In particular, and where possible, the treatment must be provided at the health centers nearest to the victims' places of residence. The victims who request this measure of reparation have a period of six months from notification of this Judgment to advise the State, either in person or through their legal representatives, of their wish to receive medical or psychological care.

Furlan and Family v. Argentina

31-Aug-2012

Series C No. 246—*Preliminary Objections, Merits, Reparations and Costs*

3. According to the Commission, this application is related to the State's [alleged] international responsibility for the "lack of timely response by the Argentinean judicial authorities, who incurred in an excessive delay in the resolution of a civil action against the State, whose response depended on the medical treatment of the [[alleged]] victim, as a child with disabilities." The Commission requested that the Court declare the violation of Articles 8(1) (Right to a Fair Trial) and 25(1) (Right to Judicial Protection) in relation to Article 1(1) (Obligation to Respect Rights) of the American Convention to the detriment of Sebastián Furlan and Danilo Furlan. In addition, it requested that the Court declare the violation of Article 25(2.c) (Judicial Protection) in relation to Article 1(1) (Obligation to Respect Rights) of the Convention, to the detriment of Sebastián Furlan. Furthermore, it [alleged]

the violation of Articles 5(1) (Right to Personal Integrity) and 19 (Rights of the Child) in relation to Article 1(1) (Obligation to Respect Rights) of the Convention to the detriment of Sebastián Furlan. Also, it requested that the Court declare the violation of Article 5(1) (Right to Personal Integrity), in relation to Article 1(1) (Obligation to Respect Rights) of the Convention to the detriment of Danilo Furlan, Susana Fernández, Claudio Erwin Furlan and Sabina Eva Furlan. Finally, pursuant to Article 35(1.g) of the Rules of Procedure, in its brief submitting the case, the Commission requested that the Court order the State to implement reparation measures.

RIGHT TO A FAIR TRIAL, RIGHT TO JUDICIAL PROTECTION AND RIGHT TO PROPERTY IN RELATION TO THE RIGHTS OF THE CHILD, RIGHTS OF PERSONS WITH DISABILITIES AND THE RIGHT TO EQUALITY

2. Preliminary considerations on the rights of children and of persons with disabilities

124. First, the Court notes that in the instant case, the [alleged] violations of the rights enshrined in the American Convention are in relation to the fact that Sebastián Furlan was a child at the time of the accident and that, consequently, this accident resulted in his becoming an adult with disabilities. Taking these two facts into account, the Court considers that the [alleged] violations must be analyzed in light of: i) the international body of law on the protection of children, and ii) the international standards on the protection and guarantee of the rights of persons with disabilities. These two legal frameworks should be considered as cross-references in the analysis of the instant case.

B.2. Children and persons with disabilities

128. Since the creation of the Inter-American System, in the American Declaration on the Rights and Duties of Man, adopted in 1948, the rights of persons with disabilities have been protected. [259][95]

129. In subsequent decades, the Additional Protocol to the American Convention on Economic, Social and Cultural Rights ("Protocol of San Salvador") [260][96] stated that "everyone affected by a diminution of his physical or mental capacities is entitled to receive special attention designed to help him achieve the greatest possible development of his personality."

130. Later, in 1999, the Inter-American Convention on the Elimination of All Forms of Discrimination against Persons with Disabilities[261][97] (hereinafter "CIADDIS") was adopted, which stated in its Preamble that States Parties reaffirm "that persons with disabilities have the same human rights and fundamental freedoms as other persons; and that these rights, which include freedom from discrimination based on disability, flow from the inherent dignity and equality of each person." In addition, this Convention established a list of obligations that States must comply with in order to achieve "the prevention and elimination of

all forms of discrimination against persons with disabilities and to promote their full integration into society." [262 98] This Convention was ratified by Argentina on January 10, 2001.[263 99] Recently, the OAS General Assembly approved the "Declaration on the Decade of the Americas for the Rights and Dignity of Persons with Disabilities (2006-2016)." [264 100]

131. Moreover, in the universal system the Convention on the Rights of Persons with Disabilities (hereinafter "CRPD") entered into effect on May 3, 2008, establishing the following guiding principles on this matter: [265 101] i) respect for inherent dignity, individual autonomy including the freedom to make one's own choices, and independence of persons; ii) non-discrimination; iii) full and effective participation and inclusion in society; iv) respect for difference and acceptance of persons with disabilities as part of human diversity and humanity; v) equality of opportunity; vi) accessibility; vii) equality between men and women; and viii) respect for the evolving capacities of children with disabilities and the right of children with disabilities to preserve their identity. Argentina ratified this Convention on September 2, 2008. [266 102]

132. CIADDIS defines the term "disability" as "physical, mental, or sensory impairment, whether permanent or temporary, that limits the capacity to perform one or more essential activities of daily life, and which can be caused or aggravated by the economic and social environment," [267 103] whilst the CRPD established that persons with disabilities "include those who have long-term physical, mental, intellectual or sensory impairments which in interaction with various barriers may hinder their full and effective participation in society on an equal basis with others." [268 104]

133. In this regard, the Court notes that in the aforementioned Conventions the social model for disability is taken into account, which implies that disability is not only defined by the presence of a physical, mental, intellectual or sensory impairment, but is interrelated with the barriers or limitations that exist socially for persons to exercise their rights effectively. The types of limitations or barriers commonly encountered by people with functional diversity in society are, among others, [269 105] physical or architectural[270 106] types of barriers, communication, [271 107] attitudinal, [272 108] or socioeconomic[273 109] barriers.

134. In this regard, the Inter-American Court reiterates that any person who is in a vulnerable situation is entitled to special protection, based on the special duties that the State must comply with to satisfy the general obligation to respect and ensure human rights. The Court calls to mind that it is not sufficient for States to refrain from violating rights, and that it is imperative to adopt affirmative measures to be determined according to the particular protection needs of the subject of rights, whether on account of his personal situation or his specific circumstances, [274 110] such as disability. [275 111] Moreover, States have the obligation to promote the inclusion of persons with disabilities through equality of conditions, opportunities

and participation in all spheres of society[276][112] to ensure that the limitations described above are removed. Consequently, it is necessary for States to promote social inclusion practices and adopt affirmative measures to remove such barriers. [277][113]

135. The Court also considers that people with disabilities are often subject to discrimination because of their condition; therefore, States must adopt the appropriate legislative, social, [278][114] educational, [279][115] employment[280][116] or other measures necessary to prevent all discrimination associated with mental disabilities, and to promote the full integration of such persons into society. [281][117] Appropriate access to justice plays a fundamental role to address these types of discrimination. [282][118]

136. Regarding the strengthened obligations of States in relation to children with disabilities, the CRPD established that: [283][119] i) "States Parties shall take all necessary measures to ensure the full enjoyment by children with disabilities of all human rights and fundamental freedoms on an equal basis with other children"; ii) "in all actions concerning children with disabilities, the best interests of the child shall be a primary consideration"; and iii) "that children with disabilities h[ave] the right to express their views freely on all matters affecting them, their views being given due weight in accordance with their age and maturity, on an equal basis with other children, and to be provided with disability and age-appropriate assistance to realize that right." Meanwhile, General Comment No. 9 states that "the leading principle for the implementation of the Convention with respect to children with disabilities [is] the enjoyment of a full and decent life in conditions that ensure dignity, promote self-reliance and facilitate active participation in the community." [284][120]

137. Likewise, the CRPD contains a specific article on the scope of the right to access to justice and the obligations that States must assume regarding people with disabilities. In particular, it establishes that:[285][121] i) States Parties shall ensure effective access to justice for persons with disabilities on an equal basis with others, including through the provision of procedural and age-appropriate accommodations, in order to facilitate their effective role as direct and indirect participants, including as witnesses, in all legal proceedings, including at investigative and other preliminary stages, and ii) States Parties shall promote appropriate training for those working in the field of administration of justice, including police and prison staff.

138. Likewise, the Convention on the Rights of the Child requires States to adopt special measures of protection with regard to health[286][122] and social security,[287][123] which should be even greater for children with disabilities. [288][124] Regarding children with disabilities, the Committee for the Rights of the Child has stated that:

Attainment of the highest possible standard of health as well as access and affordability of quality healthcare is an inherent right for all children. Children with disabilities are often left out because of several challenges, including discrimination, inaccessibility due to the lack of information and/or financial resources, transportation, geographic distribution and physical access to health care facilities. [289] [125]

139. Having established these general standards, the Court considers that since Sebastián was a child and is currently an adult with disabilities, it is necessary to analyze the dispute between the parties based on an interpretation of the rights of the American Convention and their related obligations, in light of the special protection measures stemming from those standards. This framework provides mechanisms to guarantee and adequately protect the rights of persons with disabilities, in conditions of equality, taking into account their specific needs.

B) Comprehensive measures of reparation: rehabilitation, satisfaction and guarantee of non-repetition

278. The Court stresses that the violations declared in the preceding chapters were committed to the detriment of a child and, subsequently, an adult with a disability, which means that the reparations awarded in the instant case must be in keeping with the social model relating to disability established in the international treaties on this matter (*supra* para. 133 to 135). This means that the measures of reparation do not focus exclusively on rehabilitation measures of a medical nature, but include measures that help persons with a disability overcome the obstacles or limitations imposed so that they can "achieve and maintain the maximum independence, physical, mental, social and vocational capacity, and full inclusion and participation in all aspects of life." [439] [126]

B.1) Measures of rehabilitationConsiderations of the Court

B.1.1. Physical and mental rehabilitation

282. The Court emphasizes that health care must be available to everyone who needs it. All treatment for people with disabilities should be in the best interest of the patient, should aim to preserve their dignity and independence, reduce the impact of the disease, and improve their quality of life. [440] [127] As to the scope of the right to rehabilitation under international law, Article 25 of the CRPD establishes the right to enjoy the highest attainable standard of health without discrimination on the basis of disability and the obligation by States to take all appropriate measures to ensure access for persons with disabilities to health services, including health-related rehabilitation. [441] [128] Likewise, Article 23 of the Convention on the Rights of the Child refers to the measures that States should adopt regarding children with disabilities. [442] [129]

283. This Court has confirmed the harm caused to Sebastián Furlan by the delay

in the proceedings that prevented him from obtaining access to medical and psychological treatment that could have had a positive impact on his life (*supra* paras. 197 to 203), as demonstrated by the expert medical opinions presented during the proceedings (*supra* paras. 197 to 203). The effects on Sebastián Furlan's household have also been demonstrated (*supra* paras. 252 to 265) and are supported by the socio-economic studies and the relevant expert opinions submitted in this case (*supra* paras. 252 to 265). In this regard, the Court stresses that the expert opinion provided in the instant case emphasizes that highlights in such cases, rehabilitation must be provided in an early and timely manner to achieve ideal results, [443][130] that it must be continuous and must go beyond the initial stage of greater complexity. Rehabilitation must take into account the type of disability that the person has and be coordinated by a multidisciplinary team that addresses all the aspects of a person as whole. [444][131]

284. Consequently, the Court finds, as it has in other cases [445][132] that it is appropriate to order a measure of reparation that provides adequate treatment for the psychological and physical problems suffered by the victims as a result of the violations declared in this judgment. Therefore, the Court considers it necessary to order the State to provide, free of charge and immediately, through its specialized health care services, adequate and effective medical, psychological and psychiatric treatment to the victims, with their prior informed consent, including the provision of any medicines they may eventually require, also free of charge, taking into consideration the health problems of each one. Furthermore, the respective treatments must be provided, to the extent possible, at the facilities nearest to their places of residence and for as long as necessary. [446][133] In addition, when providing the psychological or psychiatric treatment, the specific circumstances and needs of each victim must be considered, so that they are provided with family and individual treatments, as agreed with each one, following an individual assessment. [447][134] The victims who require this measure of reparation, or their legal representatives, have six months as of notification of this Judgment to advise the State of their intention to receive medical, psychological or psychiatric treatment. [448][135]

B.1.2) Rehabilitation in relation to the life project

285. Regarding the presumed "damage to personal relationships" [alleged] by the representatives in the case of Sebastián Furlan, the Court, taking into account the reasoning underlying this argument, interprets this expression as an allusion to the so-called damage to the "life project", which relates to the full self-realization of the person affected, taking into account his vocation, aptitudes, circumstances, potential and aspirations, which allow him to reasonably establish certain expectations for himself and achieve them. [449][136] The life project is expressed in expectations for personal, professional and family development that are possible

under normal conditions. [450] [137] This Court has indicated that "damage to the life project" entails the loss or very serious impairment of personal development opportunities that are irreparable or very difficult to repair. [451] [138] It arises from the limitations suffered by a person in relating to and enjoying his personal, family or social environment owing to serious problems of a physical, mental, psychological or emotional nature. Comprehensive reparation of damage to the "life project" generally calls for reparation measures that go beyond mere monetary compensation, and involve measures of rehabilitation, satisfaction and non-repetition. [452] [139] In some recent cases, the Court has assessed this type of damage and has repaired it. [453] [140] Likewise, the Court notes that some of the higher domestic courts recognize relatively similar damages associated with "life relationships" or other analogous or complementary concepts. [454] [141]

286. In this respect, Mr. Danilo Furlan described the abrupt change in Sebastián Furlan's life as follows:

[t]he changes in Sebastian's life due to the lack of timely and comprehensive rehabilitation assistance were dramatic and total. He went from being a good student to being the last in the class, where he was allowed to sit in as a listener out of pity. He went from being a basketball player in the youth team of Club Ciudadela Norte to being barely able to walk. He went from talking fast to barely mumbling. For those who did not know him, the first impression was that he was drunk, therefore he couldn't even answer the phone. He went from having friends and classmates to being sidelined, discriminated against and absolutely alone without any social relationships. He went from having extraordinary agility in karate, basketball, swimming and other sports to being barely a shadow of his former self. He went from being invited to all the birthdays of neighbors and friends to being excluded and only attending a birthday when it was his or his brother's. He went from being free and independent to being limited, controlled, medicated and dependent. He went from having a tremendous will to live to trying to kill himself twice. He went from having a large family to nobody caring about him because he was not 'socially reliable.'" [455] [142]

287. In short, Sebastian Furlan's life project was severely affected. Considering the difficulties that a child with a disability must face as regards their own limitations and possible integration difficulties, particularly in the social sphere and in school, the expert opinion emphasized that Sebastian Furlan should have received specialized care. In fact, expert witness Rodriguez indicated that:

A psychologist should have intervened to supervise learning and social aspects with his peers at school. There are no school reports, nor do we know if there was a school department to intervene. The school team and the health team should have worked together, considering that this is a child who finished a school year healthy and began the next year in a situation of Disability. [456][143]

288. Also, bearing in mind that the lack of appropriate rehabilitation has had a negative impact on Sebastián Furlan in the different social, work and educational spheres (*supra* paras. 197 to 203), the Court finds that he must be offered access to rehabilitation and training services and programs based on a multidisciplinary assessment of his needs and capabilities. [457][144] This should take into consideration the social model to address disability (*supra* paras. 133 to 135), since this provides a broader approach to the rehabilitation measures for persons with disabilities. Therefore, the Court orders the Argentine State to create a multidisciplinary team which, taking into account the opinion of Sebastián Furlan, will determine the most appropriate measures of protection and assistance for his social, educational, vocational and labor insertion. Also, in determining these measures, the assistance required to facilitate their implementation must be taken into account, so that, by mutual consent, treatment can be provided at home or in locations near his place of residence. The State shall submit annual reports on the implementation of this measure for a period of three years, once implementation of said mechanism begins.

The Massacres of El Mozote and Nearby Places v. El Salvador
25-Oct-2012
Series C No. 252—*Merits, reparations and costs*

2) Measures of rehabilitation
a) Medical, psychological or psychiatric care for the victims
350. First, the Court appreciates the general initiatives taken by the State regarding the public health care systems. Despite this, it considers it pertinent to indicate that the social services that the State provides to individuals should not be confused with the reparations to which the victims of human rights violations are entitled, based on the specific damage caused by the violation. [512][145]
351. Regarding the psychosocial impact and emotional consequences suffered by the victims, expert witness Yáñez de La Cruz explained that "the massacre [...] dissolved the social networks in which the life project of both the individual and the community was inserted [...]. There was a loss of the collective subject that identifies an individual with the community, and there was a significant impact on the collective dignity." [513][146] In this regard, she pointed out that the violence took place in the village squares and churches and, just as it destroyed the land and the animals, it also destroyed "the core of the collective way of life," "the identity and

symbols of the peasant universe." [514][147] Thus, when the victims hear the massacre discussed or see something that reminds them, "98% of them describe feeling ill, dizzy, chest pains and generally depressed." [515][148] In addition, many have been diagnosed with illnesses such as cancer, multiple sclerosis and other terminal diseases. [516][149] For their part, the individuals and families who were displaced from their place of origin "lost their community and affective ties to their identifying roots, in addition to their property," as well as "what had been, until then, the life project of each of them." [517][150] Therefore, they feel "anger, sadness, fear, nostalgia, helplessness, shame, abandonment, and loss of their place in the universe, all of which may result in the appearance of psychological symptoms." [518][151] The expert witness noted that, in general, the victims "have not been able to process their sorrow owing to lack of mechanisms for the social validation of their pain, as a result of the lack of institutional and collective support. It is a very deep and private sorrow, which paralyzes many healthy aspects, such as giving or receiving affection, and having a plan for the future." [519][152] All of this must be repaired at both the individual and the collective levels. [520][153]

352. Having verified the violations and the harm suffered by the victims, as it has in other cases, [521][154] the Court considers it necessary to order measures of rehabilitation in this case. In this regard, it finds that comprehensive attention to the physical, mental and psychosocial problems suffered by the victims in this case is the appropriate reparation. Indeed, given the characteristics of this case, the Court finds that psychosocial treatment is an essential component of reparation, because it has been verified that the harm suffered by the victims refers not only to parts of their individual identity, but also to the loss of their community roots and ties. Consequently, the Court finds it necessary to establish the obligation of the State to implement, within one year, a permanent program of comprehensive care and attention to their physical, mental and psychosocial health. This program must have a multidisciplinary approach and be headed by experts in this area, who have been sensitized and trained in attention to victims of human rights violations, and also a collective approach.

353. Thus, under the said program ordered for the comprehensive care and attention to health, the State must provide, free of charge, through its specialized health care institutions in El Salvador, adequately and effectively, medical, psychological or psychiatric, and psychosocial treatment to the surviving victims of the massacres and the next of kin of the victims who were executed, who request this, following their informed consent, including the supply, free of charge, of the medicines and tests they may eventually require, taking into consideration the ailments of each of them. If the State is unable to provide this treatment, it must have recourse to specialized private or civil society institutions. Furthermore, the respective treatments must be provided, to the extent possible, in the centers nearest to their

places of residence[522] [155]in El Salvador for as long as necessary. When providing the psychological or psychiatric treatment, the specific circumstances and needs of each victim must also be taken into consideration, so that they may be provided with collective, family or individual treatments, as agreed with each of them and after individual evaluation. [523] [156] This medical, psychological or psychiatric, and psychosocial treatment must include simple and differentiated registration and updating procedures by the corresponding health care system, and the State officials responsible for providing it must know that they are designed to provide reparation. The surviving victims and the next of kin of the executed victims identified in Annexes "B" and "C" of this Judgment who request this measure of reparation, or their legal representatives, have one year from notification of this Judgment to inform the State of their intention of receiving medical, psychological or psychiatric, and psychosocial treatment.

Artavia Murillo et al. ("In Vitro Fertilization") v. Costa Rica
28-Nov-2012
Series C No. 257—*Preliminary objections, merits, reparations and costs*

2. The Commission indicated that this case concerned [alleged] human rights violations resulting from the presumed general prohibition of the practice of *in vitro* fertilization (hereinafter "IVF"), which had been in effect in Costa Rica since 2000, following a ruling of the Constitutional Chamber of the Costa Rican Supreme Court of Justice (hereinafter "Constitutional Chamber"). Among other aspects, the Commission [alleged] that this absolute prohibition constituted arbitrary interference in the right to private life and the right to found a family. It further [alleged] that the prohibition violated the right to equality of the victims, inasmuch as the State had denied them access to a treatment that would have enabled them to overcome their disadvantage with regard to the possibility of having biological children. It also argued that this ban had a disproportionate impact on women.

3. The Commission asked the Court to declare the international responsibility of the Costa Rican State for the violation of Articles 11(2), 17(2) and 24 of the American Convention, in relation to Articles 1(1) and 2 of this instrument, to the detriment of Gretel Artavia Murillo, Miguel Mejías Carballo, Andrea Bianchi Bruno, German Alberto Moreno Valencia, Ana Cristina Castillo León, Enrique Acuña Cartín, Ileana Henchoz Bolaños, Miguel Antonio Yamuni Zeledón, Claudia María Carro Maklouf, Víctor Hugo Sanabria León, Karen Espinoza Vindas, Héctor Jiménez Acuña, Maria del Socorro Calderón P., Joaquina Arroyo

Fonseca, Geovanni Antonio Vega, Carlos E. Vargas Solórzano, Julieta González Ledezma and Oriester Rojas Carranza.

318. Based on the provisions of Article 63(1) of the American Convention, [486 157] the Court has indicated that every violation of an international obligation which causes damage entails the obligation to provide adequate reparation[487 158] and that this provision reflects a customary law that is one of the fundamental principles of contemporary international law on State responsibility. [488 159]

319. The reparation of the damage caused by the violation of an international obligation requires, whenever possible, full restitution (*restitutio in integrum*), which consists of the re-establishment of the previous situation. If this is not feasible, as in most cases of human rights violations, the Court will determine measures to guarantee the rights infringed and to repair the consequences of the violations. [489 160] Consequently, the Court has considered the need to award different measures of reparation in order to redress the damage comprehensively, so that, in addition to pecuniary compensation, measures of restitution and satisfaction and guarantees of non-repetition have special relevance for the damage caused. [490 161]

320. The Court has established that reparations must have a causal nexus to the facts of the case, the violations declared, the damage proved, and the measures requested to repair the respective damage. Therefore, the Court must observe that these requirements have been met in order to rule appropriately and in keeping with the law. [491 162]

B) Measures of rehabilitation and satisfaction and guarantees of non-repetition

B.1) Measures of psychological rehabilitation

Considerations of the Court

326. The Court has indicated that this case is not related to a presumed right to have children or a right to have access to IVF. To the contrary, the case has focused on the impact of a disproportionate interference in decisions regarding private and family life, and the other rights involved, and the impact that this interference had on mental integrity. Consequently, the Court finds, as it has in other cases, [495 163] that it is necessary to establish a measure of reparation that provides adequate attention to the psychological problems suffered by the victims, addressing their specific needs, provided they have requested this. The Court observes different problems suffered by the victims owing to the arbitrary interference in access to an assisted reproduction technique. Therefore, having verified the violations and the damage suffered by the victims in this case, the Court establishes the State's obligation to provide them with the psychological treatment they require, free of charge and immediately, for up to four years. In particular, the psychological treatment must be provided by State institutions and personnel specialized in attending victims of events such as those that occurred in

this case. When providing this treatment, the specific circumstances and needs of each victim should also be considered, so that they are provided with family and individual treatment, as agreed with each of them, after an individual assessment. [496] [164] The treatments must include the provision of medicines and, if appropriate, transportation and other expenses that are directly related and strictly necessary.

Mendoza et al. v. Argentina
14-May-2013
Series C No. 260—*Preliminary objections, merits and reparations*

1. On June 17, 2011, pursuant to the provisions of Articles 51 and 61 of the American Convention, the Inter-American Commission on Human Rights (hereinafter "the Inter-American Commission" or "the Commission") submitted to the Court's jurisdiction the case of *César Alberto Mendoza et al. v. the Argentine Republic* (hereinafter "the State" or "Argentina"). The case of *Mendoza et al. v. Argentina* refers to the supposed imposing of life sentences ("life imprisonment" [*privación perpetua de la libertad*] on César Alberto Mendoza, Lucas Matías Mendoza, Ricardo David Videla Fernández and Saúl Cristian Roldán Cajal, and "reclusion for life" [*reclusión perpetua*] on Claudio David Núñez), "for facts that occurred when they were children [...] in application of a juvenile justice system that allowed them to be treated as adult offenders." The case also refers to supposed "restrictions in the scope of the review by means of the remedies of cassation filed by the [presumed] victims" and to "a series of [presumed] violations that occurred while they were serving their sentences in the custody of the State." Thus, the Commission argued that Saúl Cristian Roldán Cajal and Ricardo David Videla were subjected to detention conditions that were "incompatible with their human dignity," which led to the latter's death and which has not been investigated effectively; that Claudio David Núñez and Lucas Matías Mendoza were victims of "acts of torture," and that the latter lost his sight "without the State providing [adequate] medical care."

2. The proceedings before the Commission were as follows:

c. *Merits report.* Under the terms of Article 50 of the Convention, on November 2, 2010, the Commission issued Report on merits No. 172/10 (hereinafter "the Merits Report" or "Report No. 172/10"), in which it reached a series of conclusions and made several recommendations to the State:

(i) *Conclusions.* The Commission concluded that the State was responsible for the violation of the rights recognized in the following Articles of the American Convention:

(a) to the detriment of César Alberto Mendoza, Claudio David Núñez, Lucas Matías Mendoza, Saúl Cristian Roldán Cajal and Ricardo David Videla Fernández, Articles 5(1), 5(2), 5(6), 7(3) and 19, as well as Article 8(2)(h)) of the Convention, all in relation to Articles 1(1) and 2 thereof;

(b) to the detriment of César Alberto Mendoza and Saúl Cristian Roldán Cajal, Article 8(2)(d) and (e) of the Convention, in relation to Article 1(1) thereof;

(c) to the detriment of Saúl Cristian Roldán Cajal and Ricardo David Videla Fernández, Article 5(1) and 5(2) of the Convention, in relation to Article 1(1) thereof;

(d) to the detriment of Ricardo David Videla Fernández, Articles 4(1) and 5(1) of the Convention, and to the detriment of their next of kin, Articles 8(1) and 25(1) thereof, all in relation to Article 1(1) of this instrument;

(e) to the detriment of Lucas Matías Mendoza, Articles 5(1), 5(2) and 19 of the Convention, in relation to Article 1(1) thereof;

(f) to the detriment of Lucas Matías Mendoza and Claudio David Núñez, Articles 5(1), 5(2), 8(1) and 25(1) of the Convention, in relation to Article 1(1) thereof, as well as non-compliance with the obligations established in Articles 1, 6 and 8 of the Inter-American Convention to Prevent and Punish Torture, and

(g) to the detriment of the next of kin of the presumed victims, Article 5(1) of the Convention.

ii. *Recommendations.* Consequently, the Commission recommended that the State:

(a) "Take the necessary measures so that César Alberto Mendoza, Claudio David Nuñez, Lucas Matías Mendoza and Saúl Cristián Roldán Cajal are able to file an appeal to obtain a broad review of the sentences convicting them in compliance with Article 8(2)(h) of the American Convention [… during which] the international standards for juvenile criminal justice are applied as described in the [… Merits R]eport and that the victims' legal situation is established observing those standards";

(b) "Ensure that, while they are deprived of liberty, they have the medical attention they require;

(c) "Prescribe the legislative and other measures to ensure that the criminal justice system applicable to adolescents, for crimes committed while under 18 years of age, is compatible with the international obligations concerning the special protection for children and the purpose of the punishment, in keeping with the parameters set out in the [… Merits R]eport";

(d) "Prescribe the legislative and other measures to ensure effective

compliance with the right recognized in Article 8(2)(h) of the Convention
[...] in keeping with the standards described in the [... Merits R]eport";

(e) "Conduct a complete, impartial and effective investigation, within a
reasonable time, to clarify the death of Ricardo Videla Fernández and, as
appropriate, impose the corresponding punishments. This investigation
must include the possible responsibility for omissions or failures to
comply with the obligation of prevention of the officials who were in
charge of the custody of the [presumed] victim";

(f) "Conduct a complete, impartial, and effective investigation, within a
reasonable time, to clarify the acts of torture suffered by Lucas Matías
Mendoza and Claudio David Nuñez and, as appropriate, impose the
corresponding punishments";

(g) "Organize measures of non-repetition that include training programs for
prison personnel on international human rights standards, in particular on
the right of persons deprived of liberty to be treated with dignity, as well
as on the prohibition of torture and other cruel, inhuman or degrading
treatment";

(h) "Take the necessary measures to ensure that the detention conditions
in the Mendoza Provincial Prison meet the relevant inter-American
standards, and";

(i) "Provide adequate compensation for the human rights violations declared
in the [... Merits R]eport" for both the pecuniary and the non-pecuniary
aspects. [4 165]

d. *Notification to the State.*
The Merits Report was notified to the Argentine State on November 19,
2010, and the State was granted two months to report on compliance with the
recommendations. In response to Argentina's requests and its express waiver
of the possibility of filing preliminary objects with regard to the time frame
established in Article 5(1) of the American Convention, the Commission granted
three extensions so that the State could adopt the corresponding measures.

e. *Submission to the Court.*
Once the above-mentioned time frame and the extensions had expired, the
Commission submitted the instant case to the Inter-American Court "in order to
obtain justice for the victims owing to the Argentine State's failure to make any
substantial progress in complying with the recommendations." The Commission
appointed Commissioner Luz Patricia Mejía and then Executive Secretary,
Santiago A. Canton, as delegates, and Deputy Executive Secretary Elizabeth Abi-
Mershed, and María Claudia Pulido, Silvia Serrano Guzmán and Andrés Pizarro,
Executive Secretariat lawyers, as legal advisors.

3. Based on the foregoing, the Inter-American Commission asked the Court to
declare the international responsibility of the Argentine State for the violation of:

(a) "The rights recognized in Articles 5(1), 5(2), 5(6), 7(3) and 19 of the American Convention in relation to the obligations established in Articles 1(1) and 2 of the Convention, to the detriment of César Alberto Mendoza, Claudio David Nuñez, Lucas Matías Mendoza, Saúl Cristian Roldán Cajal and Ricardo David Videla Fernández";

(b) "The right recognized in Article 8(2)(h) of the American Convention in relation to the obligations established in Articles 1(1) and 2 of the Convention, to the detriment of César Alberto Mendoza, Claudio David Nuñez, Lucas Matías Mendoza, Saúl Cristian Roldán Cajal and Ricardo David Videla Fernández";

(c) "The rights recognized in Article 8(2)(d) and (e) of the American Convention in relation to the obligations established in Articles 1(1) of the Convention, to the detriment of César Alberto Mendoza and Saúl Cristian Roldán Cajal";

(d) "[...the] rights recognized in Articles 5(1) and 5(2) of the American Convention in relation to the obligations established in Article 1(1), to the detriment of Saúl Cristian Roldán Cajal and Ricardo David Videla Fernández;"

(e) "[... the] rights recognized in Articles 4(1) and 5(1) of the American Convention to the detriment of Ricardo David Videla Fernández, and 8(1) and 25(1) of the American Convention to the detriment of his next of kin, all in relation to the obligations established in Article 1(1) of this instrument";

(f) "[... the] rights recognized in Articles 5(1), 5(2) and 19 of the American Convention in relation to the obligations established in Article 1(1), to the detriment of Lucas Matías Mendoza;"

(g) "[... the] rights recognized in Articles 5(1), 5(2), 8(1) and 25(1) of the American Convention in relation to the obligations established in Article 1(1) [of this instrument], to the detriment of Lucas Matías Mendoza and Claudio David Nuñez." Also, the obligations contained in Articles 1, 6 and 8 of the Inter-American Convention to Prevent and Punish Torture," and

(h) "The right recognized in Article 5(1) [of the American Convention] to the detriment of the next of kin of the victims."

PROVEN FACTS

F.1. Situation of violence in the Mendoza provincial prisons

103. In the context of the request for provisional measures filed by the Inter-American Commission on October 14, 2004, in favor of those detained in the Mendoza Provincial Prison, among other matters, the Argentine State acknowledged that the situation inside the prison, which included a high rate of violent deaths, was "critical," and provided information on the measures it

was implementing to safeguard the life and integrity of the inmates, such as regular inspections in order to find objects that could be used as weapons. [128] [166] The Inter-American Court ordered the adoption of provisional measures in the Order of November 22, 2004, and this decision was reiterated by the Court in its Orders of June 18, 2005, March 30, 2006, and November 27, 2007, because it considered that the situation of extreme gravity and urgency subsisted within this prison. It should be noted that, in an official document signed by the State, the Inter-American Commission, and the representatives of the beneficiaries of the provisional measures on the occasion of the public hearing held in Asuncion, Paraguay, on May 11, 2005, Argentina undertook, *inter alia,* to create an *ad hoc* Investigation Committee "in order to investigate the acts of violence and deaths that had occurred in the prisons of the province of Mendoza between January 2004 [...] and [that] date," and "to take measures in order to seize weapons of any type that might be found in the establishments, [... and] to prevent the clandestine entry of weapons [...]."[129] [167]The provisional measures remained in force until November 26, 2010, when they were lifted following "the adoption of several decisions at the domestic level that ha[d] ordered the rectification of the situation in the Mendoza Prisons." [130] [168]

B. Measures of integral reparation: rehabilitation, satisfaction, and guarantees of non-repetition

B.1. Rehabilitation

B.1.1. Physical and psychological

B.1.1.2. Considerations of the Court

310. In this judgment the Court has established the psychological impact of the life sentences imposed on César Alberto Mendoza, Claudio David Núñez, Lucas Matías Mendoza and Saúl Cristian Roldán Cajal, based on which the Court considered them cruel and inhuman treatment (*supra* para. 183). Expert witness Laura Sobredo concluded that "all those experiences [suffered by the youths] should be considered traumatic [... and] indelible events." The Court also noted that, owing to the inadequate medical attention to his visual problems, Lucas Matías suffered permanent damage while in State custody (*supra* paras. 187 to 195). In addition, the Court established that Claudio David Núñez and Lucas Matías Mendoza had been victims of torture in the Federal Prison Complex (*supra* para. 211).

311. Therefore, the Court finds, as it has in other cases, [381] [169] that the State must provide, immediately and free of charge, through its specialized health care institutions and personnel, the necessary, adequate and effective medical, and psychological or psychiatric care to Lucas Matías Mendoza and Claudio David Núñez, and the necessary psychological or psychiatric care to César Alberto Mendoza and Saúl Cristian Roldán Cajal, if they all request this, including

the free provision of any medication they may eventually require, taking into consideration the ailments of each one related to this case. In particular, in the case of Lucas Matías Mendoza, the Court orders that the State provide immediately the ophthalmological, surgical and/or specialized therapeutic treatment that may alleviate or improve his visual problems.

312. If the State lacks adequate health care institutions or personnel, it must have recourse to specialized private institutions or institutions of civil society. Also, in the case of the victims who have been released, the respective treatments must be provided, to the extent possible, in the centers closest to their place of residence in Argentina for as long as necessary. [382][170] When providing the treatment, the specific circumstances and needs of each victim must also be considered, as agreed with each of them and following an individual assessment. The victims who request this measure of reparation, or their legal representatives, have six months from notification of this Judgment, to advise the State of their intention to receive the medical and psychological or psychiatric care ordered. [383][171]

B.1.2. Education and/or training
B.1.2.2. Considerations of the Court

314. The Court finds, as it has in other cases, that the life project relates to the integral self-realization of the person concerned, taking into consideration their vocation, skills, circumstances, potential and aspirations that allow them to establish certain reasonable expectations and to achieve them. [384][172] It is also expressed in the expectations for personal, professional and family development that are possible under normal conditions. [385][173] The Court has indicated that "harm to the life project" involves the loss or severe impairment of opportunities for personal development, in a way that is irreparable or very difficult to repair. [386][174] This harm is derived from the constraints suffered by a person to relate to and to enjoy their personal, family or social environment due to serious injuries caused to them of a physical, mental, psychological or emotional nature. The integral reparation of the damage to the "life project" generally calls for measures of reparation that go beyond mere pecuniary compensation, consisting of measures of rehabilitation, satisfaction and a guarantee of non-repetition. [387][175] In some recent cases, the Court has assessed this type of damage and provided reparation for it. [388][176] Furthermore, the Court observes that some domestic high courts recognize relatively similar damage associated with "relationships" or other similar or complementary concepts. [389][177]

315. In this case, César Alberto Mendoza, Claudio David Núñez, Lucas Matías Mendoza and Saúl Cristian Roldán Cajal were sentenced to life imprisonment for crimes committed while under 18 years of age. During the public hearing, expert witness Sofía Tiscornia mentioned that this sentence imposed on them "a life project, but for a life that implies the end, the closure, of all autonomy and

decent social existence." She also indicated that "all of them have described how the imposing of the life sentence closed off any future perspectives," because "the number of years of imprisonment imposed was more than any adolescent has lived." The expert witness also indicated that the State "is responsible for restoring human dignity to [the victims]." Life imprisonment means the end of the road of life when it has barely begun. [390] [178] According to expert witness Tiscornia, when adolescents realize the magnitude of their punishment, "the effect is devastating; they feel that life is over and, in many cases, they think that the only thing that can happen with their life, is to end it" (*supra* para. 180).

316. In this Judgment, it has been established that the life sentences imposed on the victims did not meet the standards of the rights of the child as regards criminal justice, and had harmful effects that ended their future expectations of life (*supra* paras. 177 and 183). Unlike an adult, a minor has not had the complete opportunity to plan his work or studies in order to address the challenges posed by today's societies. [391] [179] However, the Court finds it evident that imposing life sentences on these minors, and the absence of any real possibility of achieving social rehabilitation, annulled their possibility of forming a life project at a crucial stage of their education and their personal development. Also, since the victims were sentenced to imprisonment for crimes committed as children, the State had the obligation to provide them with the possibility of schooling or vocational training, so that they could undergo social rehabilitation and develop a life project. Thus, the Court considers that the most appropriate way to ensure a decent life project for César Alberto Mendoza, Claudio David Núñez, Lucas Matías Mendoza and Saúl Cristian Roldán Cajal is through training that enables them to develop appropriate skills and abilities for their autonomy, insertion in the workforce, and social integration.

317. Therefore, the Court decides that, as soon as possible, the State should provide the said victims with the educational or formal training options they request, including university education, through the prison system or, if they are released, through its public institutions. Regarding the latter, the State must also provide them with a comprehensive scholarship while they are studying, which should include travel expenses and suitable educational materials for their studies until these are completed, to enable them to meet the requirements of an adequate education. The State must implement this measure of reparation within one year of notification of this Judgment.

318. Since, according to the information provided by the parties, Saúl Cristian Roldán Cajal and Lucas Matías Mendoza are deprived of their liberty for the supposed perpetration of other offenses (*supra* paras. 92, 96 and 97), the State must ensure that they receive the educational training ordered in the preceding paragraph in the places where they are detained. In the case of Lucas Matías

Mendoza, the State must consider his special needs due to his loss of vision and ensure that his place of detention has suitable facilities for him to carry out his studies, if he so wishes. Furthermore, the Court considers that the educational grant described in the preceding paragraph must also be provided to Saúl Cristian Roldán Cajal and to Lucas Matías Mendoza in the event that they are released and continue their studies outside the prison.

F.2 *Other measures of reparation requested*

360. The representative asked the Court to order the State to release the victims by commuting the sentences, and to eliminate their names from the criminal records; to grant them housing and facilities for work and study; to prepare and implement educational, training and employment programs during the prison and post-prison stages; to prepare and implement plans that encourage the strengthening of the ties between individuals deprived of liberty and their next of kin and the community, and to organize awareness-raising campaigns and protocols for the actions of journalists. The representative and the Commission also requested the improvement of detention conditions in the Mendoza Prisons.

361. The Court finds that the measures of reparation ordered in this Judgment are sufficient as regards the facts and the human rights violations established, among other factors, because César Alberto Mendoza and Claudio David Núñez have been released, and Saúl Cristian Roldán Cajal and Lucas Matías Mendoza are detained for the supposed perpetration of other offenses.

García Lucero et al. v. Chile
28-Aug-2013
Series C No. 297—*Preliminary Objection, Merits and Reparations*

1. On September 20, 2011, the Inter-American Commission on Human Rights (hereinafter "the Inter-American Commission" or "the Commission"), under the provisions of Articles 51 and 61 of the American Convention and Article 35 of the Court's Rules of Procedure, submitted to the jurisdiction of the Court Case No. 12,519 relating to García Lucero *et al.* against the Republic of Chile (hereinafter "the State" or "Chile").

2. According to the Commission, this case concerns the State's [alleged] international responsibility for the failure to investigate and to make integral reparation for the various acts of torture suffered by Leopoldo Guillermo García Lucero (hereinafter also "Leopoldo García Lucero," "Leopoldo García," "Mr. García Lucero" or "the presumed victim" [1 180]) from the time of his arrest on September 16, 1973, until June 12, 1975, the date on which he left Chilean territory

by a decision of the Ministry of the Interior. Since 1975, Mr. García Lucero has been living in the United Kingdom. According to the Commission, Chile "has failed to provide integral reparation for Mr. García Lucero, from an individualized perspective and taking into account that he lives in exile, as well as the permanent disability he suffers as a result of the torture he endured." In addition, it indicated that the State had failed to comply with its obligation to investigate the said torture, *ex officio*, and had kept Decree-Law No. 2,191, which was incompatible with the American Convention, in force. The Commission added that, while the facts of the case related to the failure to investigate and make reparation for the acts of torture began before Chile had accepted the contentious jurisdiction of the Court on August 21, 1990, these omissions had continued after that acceptance, and continued to this day.

3. The Commission asked the Court to declare the violation of the rights to judicial guarantees and protection and to humane treatment, in relation to the general obligation to guarantee human rights, as well as the obligation to adapt its domestic legislation (Articles 1(1), 2, 5(1), 8(1) and 25(1) of the American Convention) and the obligation to investigate established in Article 8 of the Inter-American Convention to Prevent and Punish Torture (hereinafter also "the Inter-American Convention against Torture"), to the detriment of Leopoldo García Lucero and his family; also, the violation of the right to integral, adequate and effective reparation under the general obligation to ensure rights in keeping with Article 5(1) of the American Convention, in conjunction with Article 1(1) of this treaty, to the detriment of Mr. García Lucero. In addition, it asked that the Court declare the violation of the right to humane treatment established in Article 5(1) of the Convention, in relation to the general obligation to ensure human rights established in Article 1(1) of this instrument, to the detriment of Elena Otilia García (hereinafter also "Elena García"), wife of Mr. García Lucero, of her daughters, María Elena Klug and Gloria Klug, and of Francisca Rocío García Illanes. [2][181] Furthermore, the Commission asked the Court to order the State to adopt specific measures of reparation.

IX. REPARATIONS
C. Measures of satisfaction and rehabilitation
C.2) Rehabilitation

227. The Commission asked the Court to order the State to "[f]ully and adequately compensate Leopoldo García Lucero and his next of kin [...], in a manner that takes into account his specific condition, as he is in exile and permanently disabled." It asked that the Court ensure that "Leopoldo García Lucero and his next of kin have access to the medical and psychiatric/psychological treatment needed to assist in their physical and mental recovery at a specialized facility of his choosing, or the means to secure this recovery."

228. The representatives asked that Mr. García Lucero and his wife be provided with "the purchase of health insurance that covers pre-existing [conditions] [...] and that is recognized in the United Kingdom." They also stipulated that "if there is no insurance that covers pre- existing conditions, the [...] Court should order the State of Chile to pay the costs of those treatments that are not covered by health insurance." The representatives asserted that this was the most viable way of providing Mr. García Lucero with a measure of rehabilitation owing to the failure to redress the acts of torture in a way that was prompt, effective and of good quality, bearing in mind his vulnerable situation. In conclusion, the representatives also asked that the State grant a housing allowance as a measure of rehabilitation.

229. Regarding the measures of rehabilitation, the State contested the request for medical treatment submitted by the Commission and by the representatives. It indicated that the representatives had based their request, "mainly, on the effects of the acts of torture, rather than on the presumed failure of the State to comply with the obligation to investigate and to provide reparation to the victims." In addition, as already indicated (*supra* para. 73), it argued that it would be impossible to implement the PRAIS Program outside Chile.

C.2.2) Considerations of the Court

230. The Court notes that the representatives and the Commission, in their requests for measures to provide medical and psychological treatment for the victim, argue harm that could be related to facts that fall outside the temporal competence of the Court and, therefore, regarding which the Court has not ruled.

231. Despite this, the Court notes that Mr. García Lucero is in a particularly vulnerable situation. [226] [182] In this regard, the Court observes that it has been proved that Mr. García Lucero is 79 years old and suffers from a permanent disability. Also, it has not been contested that Mr. García Lucero was a victim of torture and "political imprisonment," as recognized by the Valech Commission, with both physical and psychological repercussions. Indeed, the Court takes note that, in 2004, the State acknowledged that Mr. García Lucero was a victim of torture and has indicated that it is not the State's intention to "avoid its obligation to repair the harm caused to don Leopoldo's physical and mental health." In addition, the State has implemented public reparation policies for victims of torture and "political imprisonment" that include measures of rehabilitation. However, Mr. García Lucero resides in the United Kingdom and, consequently, currently has no access to these programs.

232. Nevertheless, the Court appreciates that the State has provided Mr. García Lucero with '*Multistim Sensor*' "medical equipment" to treat his condition.

233. Based on the preceding considerations and the particularities of this case, the Court assesses positively the State's initiative to take measures to improve Mr. García Lucero's well-being and urges the State to provide a discretionary

sum of money in pounds sterling that is reasonably adequate to cover the costs of his medical and psychological treatments in his current place of residence in the United Kingdom.

J. v. Peru
27-Nov-2013
Series C No. 275—*Preliminary Objection, Merits, Reparations and Costs*

1. On January 4, 2012, under Articles 51 and 61 of the American Convention and Article 35 of the Court's Rules of Procedure, the Inter-American Commission on Human Rights (hereinafter "the Inter-American Commission" or "the Commission") submitted the case of *J. v. the Republic of Peru* (hereinafter "the State" or "Peru") to the jurisdiction of the Inter-American Court. The case concerns the [alleged] "illegal and arbitrary detention of J. and the searches of her home on April 13, 1992, by State agents, who [presumably] committed acts of torture and cruel, inhuman and degrading treatment, including the [[alleged]] rape of the [presumed] victim." According to the Commission, "[t]hese acts were followed by the transfer of Ms. J. to the National Counter-terrorism Directorate (DINCOTE) and her [[alleged]] deprivation of liberty there for 17 days, without judicial oversight and in inhuman detention conditions," as well as "by a series of [[alleged]] violations of due process and the principle of legality and non-retroactivity during the criminal proceedings against the [presumed] victim for supposed acts of terrorism while Decree-Law 25,475 was in force. Ms. J. was exonerated in June 1993, following which she left Peru." According to the Commission, "[o]n December 27, 1993, the 'faceless' Supreme Court of Justice annulled the acquittal without explaining its reasons and ordered a new trial. At the present time, proceedings against Ms. J. remain pending in Peru, and an international warrant has been issued for her arrest."

X. REPARATIONS

C) Other measures of integral reparation: rehabilitation, satisfaction and guarantees of non-repetition

C.1) Rehabilitation

395. The Court notes that, when she arrived in the United Kingdom, Ms. J. had tuberculosis, which she probably contracted while she was in prison (*supra* para. 114). In addition, she was unable to endure being in small spaces and frequently cried when confronted with memories of her past experiences. [556][183] According to a psychological report prepared by the Traumatic Stress Clinic, Ms. J. suffers from complex chronic post-traumatic stress (*supra* para. 114). The report indicated that, as described by Ms. J., she relives the events through images, nightmares and flashbacks. This may be caused by internal or external stimuli that represent

an aspect of her traumatic experience. These circumstances are accompanied by intense psychological stress with tachycardia, sweating, dizziness, nausea and, sometimes, vomiting. In addition, Ms. J. states that she avoids certain thoughts, feelings or situations related to the events; for example, she avoids people from her country and speaking her own language. Ms. J. also suffers from moderate to severe depression and severe anxiety. [557] [184] This diagnosis was corroborated by Thomas Wenzel, Chair of the World Psychiatric Association, Section on "Psychological Consequences of Torture and Persecution." [558] [185]

396. Notwithstanding the foregoing, the Court notes that, based on the information provided, it is not possible to determine precisely whether the psychological and psychiatric effects described are a consequence of the facts of this case or of the case of the *Miguel Castro Castro Prison v. Peru,* in which Ms. J. was also declared a victim of the violation of her personal integrity, in particular of torture and other forms of cruel, inhuman and degrading treatment. [559] [186] The Court recalls that, in the case of the *Miguel Castro Castro Prison v. Peru,* the Court ordered:

> With regard to the victims who substantiate that they are domiciled abroad and prove before the competent domestic organs, in the manner and within the time frames established in paragraph 433.c.v) and vii) of [that] judgment, that as a result of the facts of [that] case they need to receive appropriate medical or psychological treatment, the State must deposit in a bank account indicated by each victim the sum of US$5,000 (five thousand United States dollars), so that this sum can contribute to the said treatment. [560] [187]

397. The Court has not received any information that the State has complied with this measure of reparation. In the instant case, the Court has established that Ms. J. was a victim of a violation of Article 5(2) of the Convention at the time of her initial arrest (*supra* paras. 313 to 368). The Court considers that, owing to the severity of the said facts, it is possible that they resulted in medical consequences that must be remedied, without prejudice to the reparation established in the case of the Miguel Castro Castro Prison. Consequently, as it has in other case, [561] [188] the Court finds it necessary to establish a measure of reparation that provides appropriate treatment for the psychiatric or psychological problems caused to the victim. The Court observes that Ms. J. does not live in Peru, so that, if she requests psychological or psychiatric treatment, the State must award her, once, the sum of US$7,000.00 (seven thousand United States dollars) for the expenses of psychological or psychiatric treatment, as well as for medicines and other related expenses, so that she may receive this treatment in the places where she resides. [562] [189] Ms. J. must advise whether she wishes to receive psychological or psychiatric treatment within six months of notification of this Judgment.

Espinoza Gonzáles v. Peru
20-Nov-2014
Series C No. 289—*Preliminary Objections, Merits, Reparations and Costs*

1. On December 8, 2011, the Inter-American Commission on Human Rights (hereinafter "the Inter-American Commission" or "the Commission") presented a brief (hereinafter "submission brief") in which it submitted the case of Gladys Carol Espinoza Gonzáles against the Republic of Peru (hereinafter "the State" or "Peru") to the jurisdiction of the Inter-American Court. According to the Commission, this case relates to the supposed unlawful and arbitrary arrest of Gladys Carol Espinoza Gonzáles on April 17, 1993, as well as to the [alleged] rape and other acts constituting torture that she endured while in the custody of agents of the former Abduction Investigation Division (DIVISE) and of the National Counter-terrorism Directorate (DINCOTE), both attached to the Peruvian National Police. The Commission affirmed that, in addition to the [alleged] acts of torture that took place at the beginning of 1993, Gladys Espinoza had been subjected to inhuman detention conditions during her incarceration in the Yanamayo Prison from January 1996 to April 2001, presumably without access to adequate medical care and food, and denied the possibility of receiving visits from members of her family. It also indicated that, in August 1999, agents of the National Special Operations Directorate of the Peruvian National Police (DINOES) had beaten her on sensitive parts of her body, without the presumed victim having access to prompt medical care. Lastly, it stated that the facts of the case had not been investigated and punished by the competent judicial authorities, and remained in impunity.

IX. REPARATIONS (Application of Article 63(1) of the American Convention)

C) Measures of rehabilitation and satisfaction, and guarantees of non-repetition
  C.3.4. Rehabilitation of women victims of sexual violence during the Peruvian conflict

331. In this case, the Court has established that the generalized practice of rape and other forms of sexual violence was used as a war strategy and particularly affected women in the context of the Peruvian conflict from 1980 to 2000 (*supra* paras. 67, 228 and 229). Consequently, the Court considers that, if it does not already have one, the State must implement a mechanism that allows all women victims of such violations who request this to have access free of charge, through the State's public institutions, to specialized medical, psychological and/or psychiatric rehabilitation to redress this type of violation.

Gonzalez Lluy et al. v. Ecuador
1-Sept-2015
Series C No. 298—*Preliminary Objections, Merits and Reparations*

1. On March 18, 2014, in accordance with Articles 51 and 61 of the American Convention and Article 35 of the Court's Rules of Procedure, the Inter-American Commission on Human Rights (hereinafter "the Inter-American Commission" or "the Commission") submitted to the Court the case of *TGGL and family v. Ecuador* (hereinafter "the State" or "Ecuador"). The case relates to the presumed international responsibility of the State for the adverse effects on a decent life and the personal integrity of Talía Gabriela Gonzales Lluy (hereinafter "Talía"), "as a result of infection with HIV following a blood transfusion performed on her [...] when she was three years of age." According to the Commission, the State had not complied adequately with its obligation to ensure rights, specifically, it had failed to perform "its role of supervision and control over private entities that provide health care services." The Commission also concluded that the State's failure to respond adequately, mainly by failing to provide specialized medical care, has continued to affect the exercise of the rights of the presumed victim, and it considered that the domestic investigation and criminal proceedings did not meet the basic standards of due diligence to provide an effective remedy for the presumed victim and her family, Teresa and Iván Lluy, and also failed to comply with the duty to provide special protection to Talía Gonzales Lluy owing to her status as a minor.

XII. REPARATIONS

C. Measures of restitution, rehabilitation and satisfaction, and guarantees of non- repetition

> *C.2) Measures of rehabilitation*

358. The Court underlines that, in this Judgment, it has been declared that Talía acquired the HIV virus as a direct result of acts and omissions of the State in the context of inspection, supervision and control of the provision of health services by the State. Consequently, although the Court considers it a positive element, and appreciates the institutional effort that has been made to provide quality medical care through the public sector, the Court finds it pertinent that, for the health care to fulfill a reparatory function in this specific case, the State must provide the level of prevention, treatment, care and support that Talía's health care requires.

359. Therefore, the Court finds, as it has in other cases, [377] that it is necessary to establish a measure that provides adequate treatment for the physical and psychological problems suffered by Talía as a result of the violations established in this Judgment. Thus, the Court establishes the State's obligation to provide immediately and free of charge, through specialized public health institutions or specialized health care personnel, prompt, adequate and effective medical and

psychological or psychiatric treatment to Talía Gonzales Lluy, including the provision, also free of charge, of the medicines that she may require, taking into consideration her ailments. If the State lacks such resources, it must have recourse to private or specialized civil society institutions. In addition, the respective treatment must be provided, insofar as possible, in the center nearest to her place of residence in Ecuador for as long as necessary. The victim or her legal representatives have six months from notification of this Judgment to advise the State of her intention to receive psychological and/or psychiatric treatment.

360. Furthermore, in emergency situations, the Court establishes that the State must adopt the recommendations of the doctor indicated by Talía. Also, if that doctor determines that there is a well-founded reason for Talía to receive treatment under the private health care system, the State must cover the required expenses to restore her health. It will be for the State to prove before the Court that this measure remains in place and, every three months, it must present a report on the measure.

ANALYSIS AND QUESTIONS RAISED BY THE COURT'S JURISPRUDENCE

As demonstrated in the above case excerpts, the Inter-American Court of Human Rights awards rehabilitation as reparation when victims have suffered physically, mentally or emotionally as a result of the violation. These orders require the State to provide adequate and effective rehabilitative treatment and care that is free of charge, as close as possible to the victim's residence, and available for varying or indefinite time periods depending on the case circumstances. Where relevant, the Court also orders that such rehabilitation be offered with informed consent, in the victim's language or via interpretation, and that it be otherwise culturally competent and sufficiently specialized to meet the victim's needs, as in *Mendoza et al.* In certain cases, the Court has also ordered rehabilitative social services and rehabilitative training to support the victim's educational and vocational reintegration.

- The Court has recognized the need for rehabilitative treatment and care for victims, as well as for their next of kin, as in *Rosendo Cantú et al*, where the Court recognized the medical and psychological harm done to the victim, as well as her next of kin. In *Plan de Sanchez Massacre* and *The Massacres of El Mozote and Nearby Places*, the Court also recognized the harm done to the victims' next of kin. What are the relevant criteria when the Court decides to award rehabilitative treatment and care for victims' next of kin?

- Also in *Plan de Sanchez Massacre* and *The Massacres of El Mozote and Nearby Places*, the Court recognized the need to provide individual, family and collective rehabilitation. What circumstances might lead the Court to articulate the need for collective rehabilitation in future cases?

- In *Rosendo Cantú et al*, the Court ordered medical and psychological treatment and care (with interpretation and cultural competent services) for the victim and her next of kin. However, the Court declined to order the State to create multidisciplinary health services for women victims of sexual assault, participatory programs to contribute to the reinsertion in the community of indigenous women victims of rape, or the creation of a health care center for the victim's community, citing the State's current programs and policies addressing these concerns. Nevertheless, the Court recognized the necessity of such programs and services and highlighted the importance of increasing resources and improving the services that the State was already providing, especially in light of the rape of Mrs. Rosendo Cantú. Was the Court's decision solely based on the State's current provision of services and programs? Was there a sufficient causal nexus to allow the Court to order additional services and programs?

- In *Rosendo Cantú et al*, the Court also recognized that the victim and her daughter were suffering continuing harm and that the violation that damaged the victim's relationship to her community. As a rehabilitation measure, the Court ordered educational scholarships for both the victim and her daughter to address the impact of the violation on their personal development. In *Furlan and Family* and *Mendoza et al.*, the Court also ordered educational and vocational training as rehabilitative measures to address the impairment of the victim's life project as a result of the violation. What criteria does the Court use to determine whether the victim's life project is altered as a result of the violation? How do such rehabilitation orders differ from compensatory damage orders in addressing the impact on a victim's life project?

- In deciding *Furlan and Family*, the Court cited several international human rights conventions and treaty bodies, including the Convention on the Rights of Persons with Disabilities, the Convention on the Rights of the Child, and the Convention on Economic, Social and Cultural Rights, as well as regional human rights instruments, namely the Additional Protocol to the American Convention on

Economic, Social and Cultural Rights ("Protocol of San Salvador") and the Inter-American Convention on the Elimination of All Forms of Discrimination against Persons with Disabilities. Did the Court cite the international conventions to bolster its analysis, to demonstrate the normative nature of its decision or for another reason? In what cases might the Court want to cite to international as well as regional instruments?

V. SATISFACTION

Satisfaction is a form of reparation aimed at remedying moral, or non-material, harm caused by violations of human rights. As demonstrated in the following case excerpts, the Inter-American Court of Human Rights orders satisfaction measures in cases where other forms of reparation may not be able to fully repair the harm caused.

Amongst the most common measures of satisfaction ordered are official acknowledgment of the facts and acceptance of responsibility, public apology for the violations, and commemorations to the victims. Thus, in cases where the Court has determined that violations have occurred, it often states that its "judgment constitutes *per se* a form of reparation."[190] Because full disclosure of the truth is central to the purpose of satisfaction, and to the full reparation and restoration of the rights of victims, the Court also may order investigation, prosecution and, where applicable, punishment. Satisfaction may also include measures designed to cease ongoing violations and consequently may involve guarantees of non-repetition.

A. OBLIGATION TO INVESTIGATE, PROSECUTE AND PUNISH

Velásquez Rodríguez v. Honduras
29-Jul-1988
Series C No. 4—*Merits*

174.   The State has a legal duty to take reasonable steps to prevent human rights violations and to use the means at its disposal to carry out a serious investigation of violations committed within its jurisdiction, to identify those

responsible, to impose the appropriate punishment, and to ensure the victim adequate compensation.

175.   This duty to prevent includes all those means of a legal, political, administrative, and cultural nature that promote the protection of human rights and ensure that any violations are considered and treated as illegal acts, which, as such, may lead to the punishment of those responsible and the obligation to indemnify the victims for damages. It is not possible to make a detailed list of all such measures, since they vary with the law and the conditions of each State Party. Of course, while the State is obligated to prevent human rights abuses, the existence of a particular violation does not, in itself, prove the failure to take preventive measures. On the other hand, subjecting a person to official, repressive bodies that practice torture and assassination with impunity is itself a breach of the duty to prevent violations of the rights to life and physical integrity of the person, even if that particular person is not tortured or assassinated, or if those facts cannot be proven in a concrete case.

176.   The State is obligated to investigate every situation involving a violation of the rights protected by the Convention. If the State apparatus acts in such a way that the violation goes unpunished and the victim's full enjoyment of such rights is not restored as soon as possible, the State has failed to comply with its duty to ensure the free and full exercise of those rights to the persons within its jurisdiction. The same is true when the State allows private persons or groups to act freely and with impunity to the detriment of the rights recognized by the Convention.

177.   In certain circumstances, it may be difficult to investigate acts that violate an individual's rights. The duty to investigate, like the duty to prevent, is not breached merely because the investigation does not produce a satisfactory result. Nevertheless, it must be undertaken in a serious manner and not as a mere formality preordained to be ineffective. An investigation must have an objective and be assumed by the State as its own legal duty, not as a step taken by private interests that depends upon the initiative of the victim or his family or upon their offer of proof, without an effective search for the truth by the government. This is true regardless of what agent is eventually found responsible for the violation. Where the acts of private parties that violate the Convention are not seriously investigated, those parties are aided in a sense by the government, thereby making the State responsible on the international plane.

178.   In the instant case, the evidence shows a complete inability of the procedures of the State of Honduras, which were theoretically adequate, to carry out an investigation into the disappearance of Manfredo Velásquez, and its failure to fulfill its duties to pay compensation and punish those responsible, as set out in Article 1 (1) of the Convention.

180.   Nor did the organs of the Executive Branch carry out a serious investigation to establish the fate of Manfredo Velásquez. There was no investigation of public allegations of a practice of disappearances nor a determination of whether Manfredo Velásquez had been a victim of that practice. The Commission's requests for information were ignored to the point that the Commission had to presume, under Article 42 of its Regulations, that the allegations were true. The offer of an investigation in accord with Resolution 30/83 of the Commission resulted in an investigation by the Armed Forces, the same body accused of direct responsibility for the disappearances. This raises grave questions regarding the seriousness of the investigation. The Government often resorted to asking relatives of the victims to present conclusive proof of their allegations even though those allegations, because they involved crimes against the person, should have been investigated on the Government's own initiative in fulfillment of the State's duty to ensure public order. This is especially true when the allegations refer to a practice carried out within the Armed Forces, which, because of its nature, is not subject to private investigations. No proceeding was initiated to establish responsibility for the disappearance of Manfredo Velásquez and apply punishment under internal law. All of the above leads to the conclusion that the Honduran authorities did not take effective action to ensure respect for human rights within the jurisdiction of that State as required by Article 1(1) of the Convention.

181.   The duty to investigate facts of this type continues as long as there is uncertainty about the fate of the person who has disappeared. Even in the hypothetical case that those individually responsible for crimes of this type cannot be legally punished under certain circumstances, the State is obligated to use the means at its disposal to inform the relatives of the fate of the victims and, if they have been killed, the location of their remains.

21-Jul-89

Series C No. 7—Reparations and Costs

7.   Citing paragraph 2 of the Resolution of January 20, 1989, Mrs. Emma Guzmán de Velásquez, the wife of Angel Manfredo Velásquez Rodríguez (also known as Manfredo Velásquez), submitted a pleading dated February 26, 1989, in which she asked the Court to order the Government to comply with the following points:

(2)   An investigation of each of the 150 cases.

(3)   A complete and truthful public report on what happened to the disappeared persons.

(4)   The trial and punishment of those responsible for this practice.

8.   As required by the Resolution of January 20, 1989, the Commission submitted its opinion on March 1, 1989. It asserted that the just compensation to be paid by Honduras to the family of Manfredo Velásquez should include the following:

(1)   The adoption of measures by the State of Honduras that express its emphatic condemnation of the facts that gave rise to the Court's judgment. In particular, it should be established that the Government has an obligation to carry out an exhaustive investigation of the circumstances of the disappearance of Manfredo Velásquez and bring charges against anyone responsible for the disappearance.

9.   On March 10, 1989, the attorneys submitted a pleading in which they assert that, in conformity with Article 63 of the Convention, reparation should be moral as well as monetary. The measures they request as moral reparation are the following:

- An exhaustive investigation of the phenomenon of involuntary disappearances in Honduras, with special attention to the fate of each of the disappeared. The resulting information should be made known to the family and the public;
- Prosecution and appropriate punishment of those responsible for inciting, planning, implementing, or covering up disappearances, in accord with the laws and procedures of Honduras.

34.   However, in its judgment on the merits, the Court has already pointed out the Government's continuing duty to investigate so long as the fate of a disappeared person is unknown. The duty to investigate is in addition to the duties to prevent involuntary disappearances and to punish those directly responsible

35.   Although these obligations were not expressly incorporated into the resolutory part of the judgment on the merits, it is a principle of procedural law that the bases of a judicial decision are a part of the same. Consequently, the Court declares that those obligations on the part of Honduras continue until they are fully carried out.

36.   Otherwise, the Court understands that the judgment on the merits of July 29, 1988, is in itself a type of reparation and moral satisfaction of significance and importance for the families of the victims.

El Ámparo v. Venezuela
14-Sep-1996
Series C No. 28—*Reparations and Costs*

53.   In the same brief the Commission called for an investigation and "effective punishment of the physical and intellectual authors, of the accomplices, and of those who sought to cover up the events that gave rise to the instant case."
55.   With regard to the investigation and effective punishment of the perpetrators of the acts, the State argued that

it is clear that the Judgment of the Inter-American Court can do more than order the appropriate indemnities without infringing the rights of those [alleged]ly implicated. Compensation of the victims and their next of kin, recognition of the international responsibility of the Venezuelan state, and the condemnatory judgment of the Inter-American Court of Human Rights are the ideal means of making reparation—as far as possible—for the damages caused to the victims and their next of kin.

61. Continuation of the process for investigating the acts and punishing those responsible is an obligation incumbent upon the State whenever there has been a violation of human rights, an obligation that must be discharged seriously and not as a mere formality.

62. As far as the other non-pecuniary reparations requested by the Commission are concerned, the Court considers that Venezuela's recognition of its responsibility, the January 18, 1995 judgment on the merits of this case and the present judgment rendered by this Court constitute adequate reparation in themselves.

Bulacio v. Argentina
18-Sep-2003
Series C No. 100—*Merits, Reparations, and Costs*

110. This Court has stated several times that:
> [t]he State party to the American Convention has the duty to investigate human rights violations and to punish those responsible and the accessories after the fact. And all persons who consider themselves to be victims of said violations, as well as their next of kin, have the right to resort to justice to ensure that this duty of the State is fulfilled, for their benefit and that of society as a whole.[68][191]

111. Active protection of the right to life and of the other rights enshrined in the American Convention is set within the framework of the duty of the State to ensure free and full exercise of the rights of all persons under the jurisdiction of a State, and it requires that the latter take such steps as may be necessary to punish deprivation of the right to life and other human rights violations, as well as to prevent abridgment of any of these rights by its own security forces or by third parties acting with its acquiescence.[69][192]

112. This Court has repeatedly stated that the obligation to investigate must be carried out "in all seriousness and not as a mere formality destined beforehand to be fruitless."[70][193] The investigation conducted by the State to comply with this obligation "[m]ust have a purpose and be undertaken by [it] as a juridical

obligation of its own and not as a mere processing of private interests, subject to procedural initiative of the victim or his or her next of kin or to evidence privately supplied, without the public authorities effectively seeking the truth."[71][194]

113.   The Court notes that since May 23, 1996, the date on which the defense counsel was notified of the request by the public prosecutor of a 15-year prison sentence against Police Captain Espósito, for the reiterated crime of aggravated illegal imprisonment, the defense counsel for the accused filed a large number of diverse legal questions and remedies (requests for postponement, challenges, incidental pleas, objections, motions on lack of jurisdiction, requests for annulment, among others) that have not allowed the proceedings to progress toward their natural culmination, which has given rise to a plea for extinguishment of the criminal action.

114.   This manner of exercising the means that the law makes available to the defense counsel has been tolerated and allowed by the intervening judiciary bodies, forgetting that their function is not exhausted by enabling due process that guarantees defense at a trial, but that they must also ensure, within a reasonable time,[72][195] the right of the victim or his or her next of kin to learn the truth about what happened and for those responsible to be punished.

115.   The right to effective judicial protection therefore requires that the judges direct the process in such a way that undue delays and hindrances do not lead to impunity, thus frustrating adequate and due protection of human rights.

116.   With respect to the extinguishment invoked with respect to an ongoing case under domestic law this Court has stated that extinguishment provisions or any other domestic legal obstacle that attempts to impede the investigation and punishment of those responsible for human rights violations are inadmissible.[73][196] The Court deems that the general obligations enshrined in Articles 1(1) and 2 of the American Convention require that the States Party adopt timely provisions of all types for no one to be denied the right to judicial protection,[74][197] enshrined in Article 25 of the American Convention.

117.   In accordance with the obligations undertaken by the States pursuant to the Convention, no domestic legal provision or institution, including extinguishment, can oppose compliance with the judgments of the Court regarding investigation and punishment of those responsible for human rights violations. If that were not the case, the rights enshrined in the American Convention would be devoid of effective protection. This understanding of the Court is in accordance with the language and the spirit of the Convention, as well as the general principles of law; one of these principles is that of *pacta sunt servanda*, which requires ensuring *effective application* of the provisions of a treaty in the domestic legal system of the States Party.[75][198]

118.   Pursuant to the general principles of law and as follows from Article 27 of the 1969 Vienna Convention on the Law of Treaties, domestic legal rules

or institutions can in no way hinder full application of decisions by international bodies for protection of human rights.

119.   It is also appropriate to emphasize that the State has acknowledged its international responsibility in the instant case for violation of Articles 8 and 25 of the American Convention, which protect the rights to fair trial and to judicial protection, respectively, to the detriment of Walter David Bulacio and his next of kin. Furthermore, this Court has deemed it proven that despite commencement of several judicial proceedings, to date—over twelve years after the facts—no one has been punished for his responsibility in them. Therefore, there exists a situation of grave impunity.

120.   The Court deems that impunity is:

> the overall lack of investigation, pursuit, capture, trial and conviction of those responsible for violations of rights protected under the American Convention, as the State has the obligation to combat said situation by all legal means within its power, as impunity fosters chronic recidivism of human rights violations and total defenselessness of the victims and of their next of kin.[76][199]

121.   In light of the above, it is necessary for the State to continue and conclude the investigation of the facts and to punish those responsible for them. The next of kin of the victim must have full access and the capacity to act at all stages and levels of said investigations, pursuant to domestic legislation and the provisions of the American Convention. The results of the aforementioned investigations must be made known publicly, for Argentinean society to know the truth about the facts.

Almonacid-Arellano et al. v. Chile

26-Sep-2006

Series C No. 154—*Preliminary Objections, Merits, Reparations, and Costs*

2.   The Commission filed the application in the instant case before the Court so that it can decide whether the State has violated the rights enshrined in Articles 8 (Judicial Guarantees) and 25 (Judicial Protection) of the American Convention, in relation to Article 1(1) (Obligation to Respect Rights) thereof, to the prejudice of Luis Alfredo Almonacid-Arellano's next of kin. Furthermore, the Commission requested the Court to declare that the State has violated the obligation arising from Article 2 (Obligation to Adopt Domestic Legal Remedies) of the Convention.

3.   The facts set forth in the application filed by the Commission are related to the [alleged] failure to investigate and punish all those persons responsible for

the extra-legal execution of Mr. Almonacid-Arellano, based on the Amnesty Law enacted in Chile by Decree Law No. 2.191 of 1978, as well as to the [alleged] lack of reparation in favor of his next of kin.

4.   Furthermore, the Commission requested the Inter-American Court to order the State, under Article 63(1) of the Convention, to take the measures of reparation detailed in the application. Lastly, the Commission requested the Court to order the State to pay the costs and expenses arising from the domestic legal proceedings and from the proceedings before the Inter-American System of Human Rights.

146.   The Court has found that the State has violated the rights established in Articles 8 and 25 of the American Convention in relation to Article 1(1) thereof, to the detriment of Elvira del Rosario Gómez-Olivares and Alfredo, Alexis, and José Luis Almonacid-Gómez. This violation occurred for two reasons: i) the granting of jurisdiction to the military courts to hear the case of Mr. Almonacid-Arellano's death, and ii) the application of Decree Law No. 2.191. The first violation resulted from Order of the Supreme Court of December 5, 1996, whilst the second one was a consequence of the judgments of January 28, 1997 of the Second Military Court of Santiago and of March 25, 1998 of the Court-Martial.

147.   In view of the foregoing, the Court hereby orders that the State set aside the above-mentioned domestic decisions and judgments, and refer the case file to a regular court, so that, by way of criminal proceedings, all those responsible for Mr. Almonacid-Arellano's death are identified and punished.

148.   The Court has previously ruled that the right to know the truth is included in the right of victims or their next of kin to have the harmful acts and the corresponding responsibilities elucidated by competent State bodies through the investigation and prosecution provided for in Articles 8 and 25 of the Convention.[159][200]

149.   Once more, the Court wishes to highlight the important role played by the different Chilean Commissions in trying to collectively build the truth of the events that occurred between 1973 and 1990. Likewise, the Court appreciates that the Report of the *Comisión Nacional de Verdad y Reconciliación* (National Truth and Reconciliation Commission) includes Mr. Almonacid-Arellano's name and a brief summary of the circumstances of his execution.

150.   Notwithstanding the foregoing, the Court considers it relevant to remark that the "historical truth" included in the reports of the above-mentioned Commissions is no substitute for the duty of the State to reach the truth through judicial proceedings. In this sense, Articles 1(1), 8, and 25 of the Convention protect truth as a whole, and hence, the Chilean State must carry out a judicial investigation of the facts related to Mr. Almonacid-Arellano's death, attribute responsibilities, and punish all those who turn out to be participants. Indeed, the

Report of the *Comisión Nacional de Verdad y Reconciliación* (National Truth and Reconciliation Commission) concludes that:

> From the standpoint of prevention alone, this Commission believes that for the sake of achieving national reconciliation and preventing the recurrence of such events it is absolutely necessary that the government fully exercise its power to mete out punishment. Full protection of human rights is conceivable only within a state that is truly subject to the rule of law. The rule of law means that all citizens are subject to the law and to the courts, and hence that the sanctions contemplated in criminal law, which should be applied to all alike, should thereby be applied to those who infringe the laws [that] safeguard human rights.[160][201]

151. The State may not invoke any domestic law or provision to exonerate itself from the Court's order to have a criminal court investigate and punish those responsible for Mr. Almonacid-Arellano's death. The Chilean State may not apply Decree Law No. 2.191 again, on account of all the considerations presented in this Judgment, . . . Additionally, the State may not invoke the statute of limitations, the non-retroactivity of criminal law or the *ne bis in idem* principle to decline its duty to investigate and punish those responsible.

152. Indeed, as a crime against humanity, the offense committed against Mr. Almonacid-Arellano is neither susceptible of amnesty nor extinguishable. As explained in paragraphs 105 and 106 of this Judgment, crimes against humanity are intolerable in the eyes of the international community and offend humanity as a whole. The damage caused by these crimes still prevails in the national society and the international community, both of which demand that those responsible be investigated and punished. In this sense, the Convention on the Non-Applicability of Statutory Limitations to War Crimes and Crimes Against Humanity[161][202] clearly states that "no statutory limitation shall apply to [said internationally wrongful acts], irrespective of the date of their commission."

153. Even though the Chilean State has not ratified said Convention, the Court believes that the non-applicability of statutes of limitations to crimes against humanity is a norm of general international law (*ius cogens*), which is not created by said Convention, but it is acknowledged by it. Hence, the Chilean State must comply with this imperative rule.

154. With regard to the *ne bis in idem* principle, although it is acknowledged as a human right in Article 8(4) of the American Convention, it is not an absolute right and, therefore, is not applicable where: i) the intervention of the court that heard the case and decided either to dismiss it or to acquit a person responsible for violating human rights or international law, was intended to

shield the accused party from criminal responsibility, ii) the proceedings were not conducted independently or impartially in accordance with due procedural guarantees, or iii) there was no real intent to bring those responsible to justice.[162] [203] A judgment rendered in the foregoing circumstances produces an "apparent" or "fraudulent" *res judicata* case.[163] [204] On the other hand, the Court believes that if there appear new facts or evidence that make it possible to ascertain the identity of those responsible for human rights violations or for crimes against humanity, investigations can be reopened, even if the case ended in an acquittal with the authority of a final judgment, since the dictates of justice, the rights of the victims, and the spirit and the wording of the American Convention supersede the protection of the *ne bis in idem* principle.

155. In the instant case, two of the foregoing conditions are met. Firstly, the case was heard by courts that did not uphold the guarantees of jurisdiction, independence, and impartiality. Secondly, the application of Decree Law No. 2.191 did actually prevent those [alleged]ly responsible from being brought before the courts and favored impunity for the crime committed against Mr. Almonacid-Arellano. The State cannot, therefore, rely on the *ne bis in idem* principle to avoid complying with the order of the Court (*supra* para. 147).

156. On the other hand, the State, in order to fulfill its duty to investigate, must guarantee that the necessary facilities shall be provided by all public institutions to the regular court trying Mr. Almonacid-Arellano's case (*supra* para. 147). Hence, the former shall forward to said court any information or documents it may request, bring before it the persons it may subpoena, and perform the actions it may order.

157. Finally, the State must guarantee that Elvira del Rosario Gómez-Olivares and Alfredo, Alexis, and José Luis Almonacid-Gómez have full access to and capacity to act at all stages and instances of said investigation, pursuant to the domestic law and the provisions of the American Convention.[164] [205] The results of the investigation shall be publicly disclosed by the State, so that the Chilean society may know the truth about the events of the instant case.[165] [206]

Saramaka People v. Suriname

28-Nov-2007

Series C No. 172—*Preliminary Objections, Merits, Reparations, and Costs*

196. Furthermore, as a measure of satisfaction, the State must do the following:
   (a) translate into Dutch and publish chapter VII of the present Judgment, without the corresponding footnotes, as well as operative paragraphs one through fifteen, in the State's Official Gazette and in another national daily newspaper, and

(b) finance two radio broadcasts, in the Saramaka language, of the content of paragraphs 2, 4, 5, 17, 77, 80-86, 88, 90, 91, 115, 116, 121, 122, 127-129, 146, 150, 154, 156, 172, and 178 of the present Judgment, without the corresponding footnotes, as well as Operative Paragraphs 1 through 15 hereof, in a radio station accessible to the Saramaka people. The time and date of said broadcasts must be informed to the victims or their representatives with sufficient advance notice.

197.   The State must publish the relevant parts of the Judgment, in accordance with paragraph 196(a) of the present Judgment, at least once in each publication within a year of notification of the present Judgment. The State must also broadcast the relevant parts of the Judgment, in accordance with paragraph 196(b), within a year of notification of the present Judgment.

Valle Jaramillo et al. v. Colombia
27-Nov-2008
Series C No. 192—*Merits, Reparations, and Costs*

232.   The Court recalls that, in compliance with its obligation to investigate and, if applicable, to punish those responsible for the facts *sub judice*, the State must remove all the obstacles, *de facto* and *de jure*, that prevent adequate investigation into the facts and use all available means to expedite that investigation and the respective proceedings in order to avoid a recurrence of facts as grave as those of this case.

233.   At the same time, taking into account the Court's case law,[165 207] the State must ensure that the next of kin of the victims have full access and capacity to act at all stages and in all instances of these investigations and proceedings so that they may submit pleas and motions, receive information, offer evidence, formulate arguments, and, in brief, assert their interests. Domestic law must organize the respective proceedings in accordance with the American Convention and this judgment. The purpose of this participation must be access to justice, knowledge of the truth about what happened, and fair reparation. In addition, the result of the proceedings must be publicized so that Colombian society is informed of the judicial determination of the facts and of those responsible in the instant case.[166 208]

González et al. ("Cotton Field") v. Mexico
16-Nov-2009
Series C No. 205—*Preliminary Objections, Merits, Reparations, and Costs*

146.   According to the Commission and the representatives, another factor that characterizes these murders of women is the failure to clarify them and the irregularities in the respective investigations that, they consider, have given rise to a climate of impunity. In this regard, the Tribunal takes note of the State's acknowledgement of "the commission of several irregularities in the investigation and processing of the murders of women perpetrated between 1993 and 2004 in Ciudad Juárez." The State also regretted "the mistakes committed up until 2004 by public servants who took part in some of these investigations."

150.   According to the evidence provided, the irregularities in the investigations and the proceedings included delays in starting investigations; slowness of the investigations or absence of activity in the case files; negligence and irregularities in gathering evidence and conducting examinations, and in the identification of victims; loss of information; misplacement of body parts in the custody of the Public Prosecutor's Office; and failure to consider the attacks on women as part of a global phenomenon of gender-based violence. According to the U.N. Rapporteur on Judicial Independence, following a visit to Ciudad Juárez in 2001, he "was amazed to learn of the total inefficiency, incompetency, indifference, insensitivity, and negligence of the police who investigated these cases earlier." For its part, the Special Prosecutor's Office indicated in its 2006 report that, in 85% of 139 earlier investigations analyzed, it had detected responsibilities that could be attributed to public servants, serious deficiencies, and omissions that "prevent resolving the respective murders, causing impunity."

154.   Evidence provided to the Court indicates, *inter alia*, that officials of the State of Chihuahua and the municipality of Juárez made light of the problem and even blamed the victims for their fate based on the way they dressed, the place they worked, their behavior, the fact that they were out alone, or a lack of parental care.[152 209] In this regard, it is worth noting the assertion by the CNDH in its Recommendation 44/1998 that it had documented statements by officials and authorities of the State Attorney's Office that revealed an "absence of interest or willingness to pay attention to and remedy a serious social problem, as well as a form of discrimination" that constituted a "form of sexist denigration."[153 210]

164. Based on the foregoing, the Court concludes that, since 1993, there has been an increase in the murders of women, with at least 264 victims up until 2001 and 379 up to 2005. However, besides these figures, which the Tribunal notes are unreliable, it is a matter of concern that some of these crimes appear to have involved extreme levels of violence, including sexual violence, and that, in general, they have been influenced, as the State has accepted, by a culture of gender-based discrimination, which, according to various probative sources, has had an impact on both the motives and the method of the crimes, as well as on the response of the authorities. In this regard, the ineffective responses and the

indifferent attitudes that have been documented in relation to the investigation of these crimes should be noted, since they appear to have permitted the perpetuation of the violence against women in Ciudad Juárez. The Court finds that, up until 2005, most of the crimes had not been resolved, and murders with characteristics of sexual violence present higher levels of impunity.

3.   ***Obligation to investigate the facts and identify, prosecute and, if appropriate, punish those responsible for the violations***

3.1.   Identification, prosecution and punishment of those responsible for the gender-based disappearance, ill-treatment, and murder of Mss. González, Ramos and Herrera

455.   Therefore, the Tribunal orders that the State must conduct effectively the criminal proceedings that are underway and, if applicable, those that may be opened in the future, to identify, prosecute, and punish the perpetrators and masterminds of the disappearance, ill-treatments, and deprivation of life of Ms. González, Ms. Herrera, and Ms. Ramos, in keeping with the following directives:

(a) All factual or juridical obstacles to the due investigation of the facts and conduct of the respective judicial proceedings shall be removed and all available means used to ensure that the investigations and judicial proceedings are conducted promptly in order to avoid a repetition of the same or similar acts as those in the instant case;

(b) The investigation shall include a gender perspective; undertake specific lines of inquiry concerning sexual assault, which must involve lines of inquiry into the corresponding patterns in the area; be conducted in accordance with protocols and manuals that comply with the directives set out in this judgment; provide the victims' next of kin with information on progress in the investigation regularly and give them full access to the case files; and. . . be carried out by officials who are highly trained in similar cases and in dealing with victims of discrimination and gender-based violence;

(c) The different entities that take part in the investigation procedures and in the judicial proceedings shall have the necessary human and material resources to perform their tasks adequately, independently, and impartially, and those who take part in the investigations shall be given due guarantees for their safety; and

(d) The results of the proceedings shall be published so that Mexican society is aware of the facts that are the purpose of the instant case.

3.2.   Identification, prosecution and, if applicable, sanction of the officials who committed irregularities

459.   In the instant case, the Court finds that none of the officials who committed serious irregularities during the first stage of the investigations have been sanctioned

460.   The Tribunal finds that, as a means of combating impunity, the State shall, within a reasonable time, investigate the officials accused of irregularities through the competent public institutions and, following a due procedure, apply the corresponding administrative, disciplinary, or criminal sanctions to those found responsible.

3.3.   Investigation of the complaints filed by the victims' next of kin who have been harassed and persecuted

462.   Since the Court found that, in the instant case, Mrs. Monárrez suffered various acts of harassment from the time her daughter disappeared until she abandoned her country to go into exile abroad, a situation also suffered by her other three children and grandchildren, and that Adrián Herrera Monreal suffered various acts of harassment, the Court orders that the State shall, within a reasonable time, conduct the corresponding investigations and, if applicable, punish those responsible.

463.   The three gender-based murders in this case took place in a context of discrimination and violence against women. It does not correspond to the Tribunal to attribute responsibility to the State merely for the context; however, it cannot refrain from noting the extreme importance that the rectification of this situation signifies for the general measures of prevention that the State must adopt so that women and girls in Mexico can enjoy their human rights, and it invites the State to consider this.

4.2. Guarantees of non-repetition

4.2.1. Regarding the request for a comprehensive, coordinated and long-term policy to ensure that cases of violence against women are prevented and investigated, those responsible prosecuted and punished, and reparation made to the victims

477.   The Tribunal observes that the State listed all the institutions, actions, and legal measures undertaken from 2001 to date, at both the federal and local level to prevent and investigate the murder of women in Ciudad Juárez, as well as the support granted to the victims by the government.

493.   The Tribunal observes that, in their briefs, neither the Commission nor the representatives challenged the existence or the validity of the above organizations and programs mentioned by the State, or the State's evaluation of each one. Moreover, neither the Commission nor the representatives provided sufficient arguments on practical problems encountered with the actions implemented by the State to date, or clarified why the series of measures adopted by the State cannot be considered an "integral, coordinated policy." In this regard, the Court recalls that, under Article 34(1) of the Rules of Procedure, the Commission must indicate its claims for reparations and costs in the application, together with the justification and the pertinent conclusions. This obligation to provide the rationale

and the justification is not fulfilled by general requests with no factual or legal arguments or evidence that would allow the Tribunal to examine their purpose, reasonableness and scope. The same applies to the representatives.

494.   The Court appreciates the efforts made by the Mexican State to formally adapt its legislation and other legal actions and institutions and to implement different actions designed to combat gender-based violence, both in the State of Chihuahua and at the federal level, as well as its efforts to adapt its criminal justice system at the local and federal levels. These advances are structural indicators of the adoption of norms that, in principle, are aimed at tackling the violence and discrimination against women in a context such as the one that has been proved in the instant case.

495.   Nevertheless, the Tribunal does not have sufficient, recent information to be able to assess whether these laws, institutions, and actions have: (i) resulted in the effective prevention and investigation of cases of violence against women and gender-based murder; (ii) ensured that those responsible have been prosecuted and sanctioned, and (iii) ensured that reparation has been made to the victims; all this bearing in mind the context established in the instant case. Thus, for example, none of the parties offered precise information on the occurrence of similar crimes to those of this case from 2006 to 2009.[478][211] In particular, the Court is unable to rule on the existence of an integral policy to overcome the situation of violence against women, discrimination, and impunity without information on any structural defects that crosscut these policies, any problems in their implementation, and their impact on the effective enjoyment of their rights by the victims of this violence. In addition, the Tribunal does not have result indicators in relation to how the policies implemented by the State could constitute reparations with a gender perspective to the extent that they: (i) question and, by means of special measures, are able to modify, the status quo that causes and maintains violence against women and gender-based murders; (ii) have clearly led to progress in overcoming the unjustified legal, political, social, formal, and factual inequalities that cause, promote, or reproduce the factors of gender-based discrimination, and (iii) raise the awareness of public officials and society on the impact of the issue of discrimination against women in the public and private spheres.

496.   The fact that the Commission, the representatives, and the State have not provided sufficient arguments prevents the Court from ruling on whether the public policies currently being implemented really represent a guarantee of non-repetition of what happened in this case.

> 4.2.2. Standardization of protocols, federal investigation criteria, expert services and provision of justice to combat the disappearances and murders of women and the different types of violence against women

502.   In other cases, the Court has ordered that the parameters for

investigations, forensic analyses, and prosecution should be harmonized with international standards.[482][212] The Tribunal considers that, in this case, the State must, within a reasonable time, continue harmonizing all its protocols, manuals, judicial investigation criteria, expert services[,] and delivery of justice used to investigate all crimes concerning the disappearance, sexual abuse, and murder of women with the Istanbul Protocol, the United Nations Manual on the Effective Prevention and Investigation of Extralegal, Arbitrary, and Summary Executions, and the international standards for searching for disappeared people, based on a gender perspective. In this regard, it must provide an annual report for three years.

4.2.3. Implementation of a program to look for and find disappeared women in the State of Chihuahua

504. The Court observes that, on July 22, 2003, the State implemented Operation Alba "to establish special surveillance, in addition to the surveillance that already existed, in areas of high risk for women and where murder victims had been found." Subsequently, on May 23, 2005, the Protocol for Reception, Reaction, and Coordination between municipal, state and federal authorities in cases of missing women and girls in the Municipality of Juárez, or the "Alba Protocol," was implemented. Based on agreement and consensus among the participating institutions, the protocol established a mechanism for reception, reaction, and coordination among authorities of the three spheres of government when women or girls went missing in Ciudad Juárez. In October 2006, the protocol had been "activated 8 times [since its creation], and had led to the discovery of 7 women and 2 children who had gone missing or disappeared."[483][213]

505. The Tribunal assesses positively the creation of Operation Alba and the Alba Protocol as a way of paying increased attention to the disappearance of women in Ciudad Juárez. Nevertheless, it observes that these search programs are only put in practice when a "high-risk" disappearance occurs, a criterion that, according to information from several sources, is only met in the case of reports with "specific characteristics";[484][214] namely, that "it is certain that [the women] had no reason to abandon their home," a young girl disappeared,[485][215] "the young woman [had] a stable routine,"[486][216] and that the report had "characteristics associated with the 'serial' killings."[487][217]

506. The Court considers that the Alba Protocol, or any analogous mechanism in Chihuahua, should include the following parameters: (i) implement searches *ex officio* and without any delay in cases of disappearance as a measure to protect the life, personal liberty, and personal integrity of the disappeared person; (ii) coordinate the efforts of the different security agencies to find the person; (iii) eliminate any factual or legal obstacle that reduces the effectiveness of the search or that prevents it from starting, such as requiring preliminary inquiries or

procedures; (iv) allocate the human, financial, logistic, scientific, or any other type of resource required for the search to be successful; (v) crosscheck the missing person report with the database of missing persons mentioned in section 4.2.4 and (vi) give priority to searching areas where reason dictates that it is most probable to find the disappeared person, without arbitrarily disregarding other possibilities or areas. All of the above must be even more urgent and rigorous when a girl has disappeared. In this regard, an annual report must be presented for three years.

507.   The Ciudad Juárez Commission advised that, in March 2005, it set up the web page: www.mujeresdesaparecidascdjuarez.gob.mx with information on some of the young women and girls who had disappeared in Ciudad Juárez.[488 218] The Court notes that the page has not been updated since December 2006.

508.   In this regard, and bearing in mind that an electronic network where anyone can provide information on a disappeared woman or girl child could be useful to trace that individual, the Tribunal orders, as it has on other occasions,[489] [219] the creation of a web page with the necessary personal information on all the women and girls who have disappeared in Chihuahua since 1993 and who are still missing. This web page must allow anyone to communicate with the authorities by any means, including anonymously, in order to provide relevant information on the whereabouts of the disappeared women or girls or, if applicable, of their remains. The information on the web page must be updated constantly.

> 4.2.4 Comparison of genetic information from the bodies of unidentified women or girls deprived of life in Chihuahua with missing persons on a national level

511.   Although the Court observes that the State created a register with data on women who are missing in the Municipality of Juárez and a forensic DNA databank,[490 220] the Tribunal has no probative elements to allow it to conclude that the State created a national database of disappeared persons. Furthermore, even though the Court observes that there is a forensic DNA database with genetic information on some of the next of kin of victims of gender-based murder and of some bodies that were found,[491 221] it has no evidence that the State has compared the information on disappeared women at the national level, or the genetic information of the next of kin of those disappeared women, with the genetic information extracted from the bodies of any women or girl deprived of life and unidentified in Chihuahua. Moreover, there is no information in the case file to allow the Tribunal to determine whether the information contained in said databases is sufficient, or their level of effectiveness and results in relation to the investigations of the disappearances and murders of women in Ciudad Juárez.

512.   The Court finds that the rationale for creating a database of disappeared women and girls at the national level, and updating and comparing the genetic information from the relatives of missing persons with that of unidentified bodies, is the possibility that the bodies of some of the women or girls found in Chihuahua

belong to individuals who disappeared in other states of the Federation, and even in other countries. Consequently, as it has in other cases,[492 222] the Court orders: (i) the creation or updating of a database with the personal information available on disappeared women and girls at the national level; (ii) the creation or updating of a database with the necessary personal information, principally DNA and tissue samples, of the next of kin of the disappeared who consent to this—or that is ordered by a judge—so that the State can store this personal information with the sole purpose of locating a disappeared person, and (iii) the creation or updating of a database with the genetic information and tissue samples from the body of any unidentified woman or girl deprived of life in the State of Chihuahua. The State must protect the personal information in these databases at all times.

4.2.5.　Creation of a legal mechanism for transferring cases from the civil courts to the federal jurisdiction when impunity exists or when serious irregularities are proven in the preliminary investigations

519.　The Court observes that the activity of the Special Prosecutor's Office was limited to systematizing the information on the murders of women in Ciudad Juárez and investigating only those crimes that fell within the federal jurisdiction.[501 223] In this regard also, the Tribunal does not have recent information on the functioning and effectiveness of the modified FEIHM.

520.　The representatives did not support their request for redress with clear, pertinent and sufficient arguments concerning the problems of access to justice that could have arisen from domestic law applicable to the mechanism of transfer to the federal jurisdiction. In addition, they did not provide arguments on the specific evidence about the policies designed by the State to resolve the problem in recent years. The foregoing prevents the Court from ruling on this request for reparation.

4.2.6.　Prohibition for any official to discriminate based on gender

525.　The representatives did not submit arguments about the possible lacunae and deficiencies in this type of laws, programs, and actions; consequently, the Tribunal does possess any elements on which it can rule with regard to this request.

4.2.7. Law regulating support for victims of gender-based murders

528.　The Court observes that the Head of the Ciudad Juárez Commission recognized that, in 2005, when establishing the Financial Support Fund for the Families of Victims of Murders of Women, it was not considered a means of redressing the damage. The assistance was offered based on the criminal acts of the murderer and not on the State's responsibilities, and the support was conditioned to the filing of civil or family lawsuits.[508 224]

529.　The Tribunal considers that the social services that the State provides to individuals cannot be confused with the reparations to which the victims of human rights violations have a right based on the specific damage arising from the violation. Hence, the Court will not consider any government support that was not specifically addressed at repairing the lack of prevention, impunity and discrimination that can be attributed to the State in the instant case as part of the reparation that the State alleges to have made.

530.   In addition, the Court finds that it cannot tell the State how it should regulate the support it offers to the individual as part of a social assistance program; accordingly, it abstains from ruling on this request by the representatives.

Radilla-Pacheco v. Mexico
23-Nov-2009
Series C No. 209—*Preliminary Objections, Merits, Reparations, and Costs*

2. The facts of the present case refer to the [alleged] forced disappearance of Mr. Rosendo Radilla-Pacheco, which supposedly occurred since August 25, 1974, in the hands of members of the Army in the State of Guerrero, Mexico. According to the Inter-American Commission, the [alleged] violations derived from this fact "continue to exist up to this date, since the State of Mexico has not established the whereabouts of the [[alleged]] victim, nor have his remains been found." According to that argued by the Commission, "more than 33 years after the occurrence of the facts, there is complete impunity since the State has not criminally punished those responsible, nor has it guaranteed the next of kin an adequate reparation."

A. Background: Facts regarding the arrest and subsequent disappearance of Mr. Radilla-Pacheco

A1. The [alleged] victim, Rosendo Radilla-Pacheco

120. Mr. Rosendo Radilla-Pacheco was born on March 20, 1914 at Las Clavellinas, State of Guerrero, Mexico.[2585] On September 13, 1941 he married Victoria Martínez Neri,[2686] with whom he had twelve children, namely: Romana, Andrea, Evelina, Rosa, Tita, Ana María, Agustina,

María del Carmen, María del Pilar, Judith, Rosendo, and Victoria, all of surnames Radilla Martínez.[87 227]

121. Rosendo Radilla-Pacheco was involved in different activities of the political life and in social works in Atoyac de Álvarez, Guerrero, specifically in the organization of coffee growers and farmers of the area. [88 2287] Thus, Mr. Rosendo Radilla-Pacheco was part of the Agricultural Unit of the Coffee Sierra of Atoyac de Álvarez. Between June 1, 1955 and August 31, 1956, he was president of the Municipal Council of Atoyac de Álvarez. In September 1956, he carried out actions as Municipal President. From 1956 to 1960 he was the general secretary

of the Regional Farmers' Committee. In 1961, he was president of the parent association of the Board in Favor of the Federal School Modesto Alarcón. In 1965, he participated in the foundation of the Agricultural League of the South Emiliano Zapata. [89][228] Among his different occupations, we can also mention the growing of coffee and coconut, as well as the purchase and sale of cattle. [90][229]

122. Mr. Rosendo Radilla-Pacheco composed "corridos", a popular musical Mexican expression that recounts epic verses accompanied by a guitar. The corridos composed by Mr. Rosendo Radilla-Pacheco talk about different facts that occurred in Atoyac de Álvarez, and the peasants' social battles of the time.[230][91]

123. According to that stated by the representatives, there are reports from the "Federal Security Office", included in preliminary inquiry SIEDF/CGI/453/07, that detail the activities carried out by Mr. Radilla-Pacheco. The Court verified that in a document dated September 26, 1965 of the Federal Security Office, reference is made to Mr. Rosendo Radilla-Pacheco's participation in presiding over the "inaugural act of the Extraordinary Peasant Congress of the Revolutionary League of the South 'Emiliano Zapata' and of the C.C.I."[92][231] Likewise, the representatives stated that in a document dated "21 VI 82", whose heading states "Background of Rosendo Radilla-Pacheco", it is established that: On February 17, 1962, he attended the signing of the Summons of the Civic War Committee of which he is a member and in which the people in general were invited to a rally that would be held in Boca de Arroyo, municipality of Atoyac de Álvarez, Guerrero[.]Later, on June 23rd of the same year, he signed a manifesto of the Civic War Association, of which he was also a member. In said document he tried to influence public opinion, so it would not choose bad leaders, evoking the times of General Raúl Caballero Aburto and he invited to the mentioned Association's State Convention to be held in Acapulco, Guerrero. From 13.45 to 17.10 hours of September 26, 1965, Radilla-Pacheco presided over the inaugural act of the Peasant Congress of the Revolutionary Agricultural League of the South "Emiliano Zapata" and of the CCI holding the meeting at the former Bullring of Iguala, Guerrero [...].[93][232]

A2. Arrest and subsequent disappearance of Mr. Rosendo Radilla-Pacheco

124. On August 25, 1974 Rosendo Radilla-Pacheco, 60 years old, and his son Rosendo Radilla Martínez, 11 years old, were traveling on a bus from Atoyac de Álvarez to Chilpancingo, Guerrero. The bus was stopped at a military checkpoint where soldiers made all the passengers get out to inspect them and their belongings. Later, all the passengers got on the bus again and continued their journey. [94][233]

125. The bus was stopped at a second military checkpoint located "at the entrance of the Cuauhtémoc Colony [between] Cacalutla and Alcholoa." The soldiers asked the passengers to get off the bus so they could check it inside. After the review, the soldiers informed the passengers they could get on the bus again, except for Mr. Rosendo Radilla-Pacheco, who was arrested because "he composed corridos"

(*supra* para. 122). Mr. Radilla-Pacheco stated that was not a crime, however, a soldier responded: *"in the meantime you're screwed."* [95] [234]

126. Mr. Rosendo Radilla-Pacheco asked the soldiers to let his son, Rosendo Radilla Martínez, go since he was a minor, which the soldiers accepted. At the same time, he asked his son to inform his family that the Mexican Army had arrested him. [96] [235] Mr. Radilla-Pacheco "[w]as put in the custody of the Military Zone of [Guerrero]." [97] [236]

127. In this sense, both the National Commission and the Special Prosecutors' Office considered the case of Mr. Rosendo Radilla-Pacheco as a fully proven forced disappearance. Specifically, the Report made by the Special Prosecutors' Office refers to Mr. Rosendo Radilla-Pacheco's arrest at the "[c]heckpoint of the Col. Cuauhtémoc (Chilpancingo), [...] on August 25, 1974. The reason argued was because he composed corridos. He continues to be missing." [98] [237] On its part, the National Commission stated that "[m]embers of the Mexican army, attached to the State of Guerrero, illegally exercised their functions on September 28, 1974 [*sic*] in the illegal exercise of their position, upon arbitrarily arresting Mr. Rosendo Radilla-Pacheco, who far from being put at the disposal of the immediate authority [...] was check[ed] into military installations, being this the last time news was recorded on his whereabouts, reason for which besides the illegal detention, the mentioned military members are considered responsible for [his] disappearance [...]." [99] [238]

128. After his arrest, Mr. Radilla-Pacheco was seen at the Military Barracks of Atoyac de Álvarez with signs of physical abuse. Mr. Maximiliano Nava Martínez testified that:

"Four days after his arrival [at the military barracks of Atoyac de Álvarez], Mr. Rosendo Radilla-Pacheco was taken away [...] one of the detainees said: 'that man composed a corrido on the massacre of May 18th', which caught their attention and they separated him from the rest of the group. [...]" "They separated him once again from the group and when they brought him back he had his hands tied and his eyes were covered with his handkerchief, a red paliacate. [T]hey tried to put cotton that had been wet with an unknown substance in his eyes, under the bandage; he was telling them not to put anything in his eyes; that his crime did not call for that, reason for which he resisted. For the time being they resisted. When they took someone out they told us that the heavy players were going to enjoy a banquet." "Two days later they took him away [...], in a red pick-up truck [*sic*], saying that in a little while they would come back for those of us left there, once 'they were finished with these bodies'. From that point on [he] did not see [him] again." [100] [239]

129. In that same sense, in a statement offered before the Special Prosecutors' Office, Mr. Nava Martínez indicated that:

"[…] on August 25, 1974, he heard a male singing a corrido, he was singing loudly with a guitar [...], it was the first time he had heard the corrido he was singing [...] singing [at the military barracks of Atoyac de Álvarez] against the government[;] the person was at a distance of about ten meters [...] he remembers him and saw him because they would act as if they got tired and they would put their hands on the blindfolds and however they could they would remove the blindfolds from their eyes and he could observe it was a male, with a mustache who was singing and was not wearing the blindfold on his eyes and who was singing and playing the guitar […] once outside the barracks [… some people] came to comment on who the person who had been singing the corrido was, saying among them that it was Mr. Rosendo Radilla-Pacheco, who lived in San Vicente de Benítez with his wife[,] but he never saw him again […]."[101 240]

130. Likewise, the case file includes the statement of Mr. Enrique Hernández Girón, who expressed he was detained on August 25, 1974 along with Mr. Radilla-Pacheco at the Barracks of Atoyac de Álvarez, Guerrero. Specifically, he stated that "[h]e was put in a long room in which […] he could see […] there were more people […] of the male sex […], but they were all blindfolded[,] there were so many they did not fit inside [… there], through the blindfold he was able to see [that] Mr. Rosendo Radilla-Pacheco, who he had met a long time ago since he was from [Atoyac,] was next to [him], that he even talked to [him …], that he was also blindfolded, […] that after talking on that first night they took him outside and beat him, and that they took all of them outside in that same way to beat them at night, [Mr. Hernández Girón] was there for approximately one month and five days[,] but that when he left [Rosendo Radilla-Pacheco] remain[ed] there[,] he saw him all those days in the inside of the room […] and that up to this date he is still missing […]."[102 241]

131. Upon knowing of his arrest, the next of kin of Mr. Rosendo Radilla-Pacheco took a series of steps in order to determine his whereabouts, especially through contact with relatives or friends that worked for the State. However, the next of kin have adduced that, due to the conditions of repression that existed at that time, acknowledged by the State, they refrained from filing formal accusations regarding the facts (*infra* paras. 194 and 196). In this regard, Mrs. Tita Radilla, upon filing a complaint on May 14, 1999 (*infra* para. 183), indicated that "[t]he person who came forward to demand news regarding any relative at that time was detained, we had to disappear from the region in order to avoid being arrested." [103 242]

B. *The context in which the facts of the present case occurred*

132. It has been documented that at the time at which Mr. Rosendo Radilla-Pacheco was detained and disappeared numerous forced disappearances of persons occurred throughout the Mexican territory. [104 243] Thus, it can be concluded from the body of evidence that the National Human Rights Commission of Mexico, [105 244] within the framework of the Special Program for [alleged] Disappeared Persons, [106 245] examined 532 case files of complaints regarding the forced disappearance of persons perpetrated during the "[p]henomena classified as the 'Dirty war of the seventies'." [107 246] Based on that investigation, the National Commission issued Recommendation 026/2001, [108 247] in which it indicated that it had sufficient elements to conclude that in at least 275 cases of those examined that several of the rights of those people reported as disappeared were violated. [109 248]

133. The forced disappearances examined occurred in specific political, social, and economic circumstances. [110 249] In this regard, the National Commission established that [...] in the scenario of the presidential succession of 1970, while a political-electoral battle was being developed in plain sight without surprises, scores of activists were found in secrecy, dedicated full-time to their own tasks, as a prior and necessary step for the subsequent development of the actions. [...] Between 1973 and 1974 the guerrilla actions and the counter insurgence were exacerbated. The Communist League 23 de Septiembre went on to occupy the top position in the confrontation with the federal government as of the failed kidnapping and subsequent murder of the businessman from Nuevo Leon, Eugenio Garza Sada, in September 1973. This event is followed by a time marked by drastic measures against the guerrilla: the illegal arrest, torture, and forced disappearance and, even, probable extralegal executions of militants and leaders. [...][...] Other important groups of the Mexican guerilla were the "Agricultural Brigade for Executions of the Party of the Poor", led by Professor Lucio Cabañas, whose presence was basically in the State of Guerrero. [...] Its main actions were, besides ambushes of the Army and the security forces, the kidnapping in 1974 of the governor elect of Guerrero, Rubén Figueroa.

The group commanded by Professor Genaro Vázquez Rojas, the "National Civic Revolutionary Association" (ACNR) also had impact on public opinion, with its main presence also in Guerrero; it was an organization that did not survive, as part of the guerrilla, the death of its leader in February 1972. Its most well-known action was the kidnapping of Jaime Castrejón Díez, at that time rector of the Universidad Autónoma de Guerrero, who was exchanged for a dozen inmates of the armed movement, who were sent to Cuba by the Mexican government.[...]

Against these groups, the anti-subversive policy was characterized, at least until 1981, as having practically unlimited powers. Its operation was the responsibility of groups specially formed by some corporations for the [S]tate's safety (White

Brigade or Special Brigade) led by the Federal Security Office [...] [...] the violence continued until the beginning of the eighties and it was translated into armed actions, confrontations, with the continuance of the excessive behavior of anti-subversive organizations and the subsequent forced disappearances that increased the occurrence of illegal facts [...].[111][250]

134. From the investigations carried out, the National Commission observed that in those times "[t]he government instances that constitutionally had the task of seeking justice and protecting the rights of citizens, showed their incapacity and failure to prevent, investigate, and punish the facts, as well as offer the necessary help to the people interested in investigating the whereabouts of the victims of arbitrary arrests and forced disappearances."[112][251]

135. The Court observes that the National Human Rights Commission has not been the only body of the State dedicated to the documentation and investigation of this type of facts. The National Commission recommended to the Executive, *inter alia,* "[t]hat it issue instructions to the Attorney General of the Republic to appoint a special prosecutor, so it c[ould] take charge of the investigation and prosecution, in its case, of the crimes that [could] result from the facts to which Recommendation [026/2001] [made] refer[ence]."[113][252] The Federal Executive adopted the recommendation and once this Special Prosecutors' Office was created in the year 2002, it examined the 532 case files processed by the National Commission, and received different complaints throughout 2002 and up to 2006.[114][253]

136. In the year 2006, the Special Prosecutors' Office presented a "Historic Report to the Mexican Society" (*supra* paras. 73 through 75), in which it made reference to the existence, at the time at which Rosendo Radilla-Pacheco was arrested, of a pattern of arrests, torture, and forced disappearances of militant members of the guerrilla or people identified as its supporters. In the same, it indicated that:

> In a one-year term – from November 22, 1973 through November 19, 1974- we found in the reports of the National Defense Secretary, the recording of 207 detainees by the Army reported as 'packages'. All these arrests were illegal. The detainees were interrogated, tortured, and many of them were forced to be informants. They were not put at the orders of a competent authority. They were kept in military prisons and clandestine detention centers for very long periods of time and many of them are missing.[115][254]
>
> [...] The explicit objective of torturing detainees was to obtain information. The methods were not important. Since the inmate was never handed over to the competent authority, he could be submitted to all types of torture, including, damage to their faces, third-degree burns, making them drink gasoline,

breaking the bones of the body, cutting or slicing of the bottom of their feet, giving them electrical shocks on different parts of their bodies, tying them from their testicles and hanging them, introducing glass bottles in women's vaginas and submitting them to humiliation, introducing hoses in their anus in order to fill them with water and then beat them. [116][255]

137. The Report of the Special Prosecutors' Office documented military actions deployed in the State of Guerrero that reveal what could have been the background for the arrest of Mr. Radilla-Pacheco. That report indicated that "[i]t was estimated that for 1971 the Army had 24,000 soldiers, a third part of all its members, concentrated in Guerrero" and that, during that time, the Peasant Brigade for Executions of the Communist Party of the Poor, led by Lucio Cabañas "was who had control of an ample area" of the sierra, which was the reason for which "[t]he army harass[ed] the communities [and] arrest[ed] the inhabitants accusing them of supplying Lucio." [117][256] In this regard, it points out that after the kidnapping of the then governor elect of the State of Guerrero, Rubén Figueroa, by the Peasant Brigade, which occurred on June 6, 1974, weeks before the arrest of Mr. Rosendo Radilla-Pacheco (*supra* paras. 124 through 126), "[t]he Army's response was brutal against the peasant communities, which it considered the bases of the guerrilla movement." [118][257] According to the report, the Army sought "[t]he annihilation of any traces of the guerrilla, throwing blood and fire to anyone who was a member or suspicious of being a supporter of the guerrilla, either within the Party of the Poor or the left wing […]."[119][258]

REPARATIONS (*Application of Article 63(1) of the Convention*) [312][259]

B. Obligation to investigate the facts and identify, prosecute, and, in its case, punish the responsible parties

331. In the present case the Court established that the investigation regarding the arrest and subsequent forced disappearance of Mr. Rosendo Radilla-Pacheco has not been carried out with due diligence. Likewise, the Tribunal considers that upon expanding the competence of the military jurisdiction to acts that constitute a forced disappearance of persons, the State has violated the right of the next of kin of Mr. Rosendo Radilla-Pacheco to a competent tribunal. All this in detriment to the right to know the truth regarding those facts (*supra* paras. 166 and 313). Therefore, as it has done on other occasions,[315][260] the Court rules that the State shall effectively and with the proper due diligence carry out the investigation and, if it were the case, the criminal proceedings that are in process with regard to the facts of the present case, in order to determine the corresponding criminal responsibilities and effectively apply the punishments and consequences established by law. This obligation shall be complied with within a reasonable period of time, following the criteria established regarding investigations in this type of cases (*supra* paras. 142 through 145).

332. Similarly, the State shall guarantee, through its competent institutions, that the ongoing preliminary inquiry on the facts that constitute the forced disappearance of Mr. Rosendo Radilla is kept before the ordinary jurisdiction. Whenever new criminal cases are opened against [alleged] responsible parties who are or have been military officers, the authorities in charge shall guarantee that they will be brought before the common or ordinary jurisdiction and, under no circumstance, in the military or war courts. Additionally, in order to comply with that ordered, the State shall guarantee that the future references made to the facts of this case will be in reference to the crime of forced disappearance. In this sense, it is important to reiterate that since it is a crime of a permanent execution, that is, whose consummation is prolonged in time, when it comes into force in the domestic criminal law, if the criminal behavior continues, the new law is applicable (*supra* para. 239).

333. The Court considered as established that the forced disappearance of Mr. Radilla-Pacheco occurred within a context of forced disappearances of persons (*supra* para. 132 through 137). In this sense, as it has done in other cases, it determined that the authorities in charge of the investigations have the duty to guarantee that in the course of the same the systematic patterns that allowed the commission of grave violations of human rights in the present case and the context in which they occurred will be assessed taking into account the complexity of this type of facts and of the structure in which the people probably involved in the same are located, thus avoiding omission in the gathering of the evidence and in the following of logical lines of investigation. [316][261] (*supra* paras. 221 through 222)

334. Finally, the Court reiterates that during the investigation and the prosecution, the State shall guarantee the victims full access and the capacity to act during all the stages (*supra* para. 247). Additionally, the results of the proceedings shall be made public with the objective of informing the Mexican society of the truth of the facts. [317][262]

C. Measures of satisfaction and guarantees of non-repetition

C1. Determination of the whereabouts of Rosendo Radilla-Pacheco

335. The Commission requested that the Court order the State to locate the whereabouts of Mr. Radilla-Pacheco, or, in its defect, hand over his remains to his next of kin. The representatives requested to the Court that the State comply with the aforementioned, through the corresponding exhumations in presence of his next of kin, their experts, and legal representatives. The State, on its part, informed that it has performed certain diligences to determine the whereabouts of the victim or his remains (*supra* paras. 207 through 208).

336. In the present case it has been established that Mr. Rosendo Radilla-Pacheco continues to be missing (*supra* para. 158). Therefore, the State shall, as a means of reparation of the victims' right to the truth, [318][263] continue with an effective search

and immediate location of him, or that of his remains, either through a criminal investigation or through another adequate and effective procedure. The diligences performed by the State in order to determine the whereabouts of Mr. Radilla-Pacheco or, if it were the case, the exhumations in order to locate his remains shall be carried out in agreement and the presence of the next of kin of Mr. Rosendo Radilla, as well as the experts, and legal representatives. Additionally, in the event that the remains of Mr. Radilla-Pacheco are located, they shall be delivered to his next of kin prior to genetic proof of the relationship, as soon as possible and without any cost whatsoever. The State shall cover the funeral costs, according to the beliefs of the Radilla Martínez family and in common agreement with them.

Rosendo Cantú et al. v. Mexico
31-Aug-2010
Series C No. 216—*Preliminary Objections, Merits, Reparations, and Costs*

76. On February 27, 2002, Mrs. Rosendo Cantú and Mr. Bernardino Sierra filed a complaint "against members of the Mexican Army [...] for violating human rights" before the National Human Rights Commission[79][264] (hereinafter "the National Commission" or "NHRC"). On March 7th of the same year, the Director General of the National Commission informed the [alleged] victim of the admission of the complaint, and consequently, the initiation of the Preliminary Investigations and corresponding proceedings. [80][265] On March 11, 2002, Mrs. Rosendo Cantu and her husband requested the intervention of the Constitutional Governor of Guerrero, wherein aside from requesting justice be served, they asked that disciplinary actions be made to the health care services "which they had a right to in the Caxitepec clinic." [81][266]
77. On March 7, 2002, the Mexican League for the Defense of Human Rights [*Liga Mexicana por la Defensa de los Derechos Humanos*] filed a claim before the Commission for the Defense of Human Rights for the state of Guerrero (hereinafter also, "Human Rights Commission of Guerrero" or "CODDEHUM"), in regard to the case of Mrs. Rosendo Cantú, for "[alleged] violations [...], which consist of torture, wounds, and rape by members of the army." [82][267] That same day, the Secretary of National Defense issued a press release stating that "members of the Mexican Army and Armed Forces, engaged in a permanent campaign against drug trafficking in the state of Guerrero, did not at said time or location, carry out an operation in the area of the Barranca [...] Bejuco community." [83][268] On March 8, 2002, the Inspector General of the Human Rights Commission of Guerrero, took the statement of Mrs. Rosendo Cantú and her husband, and in addition, found out that in the records of the Public Prosecutor's Agency in

Allende there was no criminal complaint for the rape of Mrs. Rosendo Cantú. [84]
[269] That same day the agent of the Public Prosecutor's Office of Allende received the communication dated March 7, 2002 of the Inspector General to start the preliminary investigation, in which he stated "that [Mrs.] Rosendo Cantú [...] was the victim of acts of torture and rape on [...] February 16 of the year in course, in accordance with the complaint presented before the National Human Rights Commission." [85][270]

78. On March 8, 2002, Mrs. Rosendo Cantú, accompanied by Mr. Lugo Cortés and others, turned to the Allende Public Prosecutor's Office to file a complaint for the crime of rape. [86][271] That same day the Public Prosecutor initiated Preliminary Investigation ALLE/SC/02/62/2002 "for the crime of [...] rape." [87][272] Initially, "they did not want to receive the complaint [...] stating that the attorney in charge of said complaints related to sexual violence, [...] was out business hours [...] and that she had been instructed by her superior to not take in the complaint." Given the abovementioned, the Inspector General of the CODDEHUM "had to insist that [...] it was necessary to take in the complaint," a procedure which was finally taken on by "an agent of the Public Prosecutor's Office outside of Me'paa, [that] did not speak their language [without the assistance of an] expert translator," [88][273] whom Mrs. Rosendo Cantu's husband had to assist with the translation of what she could not communicate in Spanish. [89][274] The Inspector General, moreover, requested that "she would undergo a medical gynecological exam by a female doctor," as it was the wish of the victim. [90][275] The agent of the Public Prosecutor, only counting on a male forensic expert, who was located outside of the district, requested that the Director of Expert Services of Chilpancingo Guerrero " [an] expert in gynecological matters be designated, preferably female, as requested by the victim, so as to carry out the physical examination and issue the corresponding report." [91][276]

79. On March 12, 2002, Mrs. Rosendo Cantú went to the Ayutla Hospital accompanied by an agent of the Human Rights Commission of Guerrero for a medical gynecological examination. The [female] doctor requested several laboratory tests. [92][277] On March 15, 2002, the General Office for Expert Services reported to the agent of the Public Prosecutor's Office, as a response to the request made on March 12, 2002, that they did not have personnel specialized in gynecology, rather that they only had "medical experts in legal medicine (general medicine)." [93][278] On March 19, 2002, Mrs. Rosendo Cantú was administered a gynecological evaluation at the installations of the Public Prosecutor in Tlapa of Comonfort, by a medical examiner connected with said common public prosecutor's agency. [94][279]

i) Obligation to investigate the facts and to identify, prosecute, and eventually punish those responsible

208. The Commission and the representatives substantially coincided in what regards the obligation to investigate the facts, and where applicable, to punish those responsible. In sum, they requested the Court to order the State to carry out an investigation with due diligence, on the facts of the present case, so as to ascertain the historical truth of what occurred, identify those responsible, and apply the appropriate punishment. Moreover, they noted that the victim and her next of kin should have full access and means to act in all the stages of the investigation according to domestic law and the American Convention. In addition, they requested that security be guaranteed to the victim, her next of kin, and the representatives in relation to the threats and persecution experienced as a consequence of the search for justice.

209. The Commission added that the State must adopt all the legal and administrative measures necessary in order to complete the investigation in the ordinary forum, forwarding to it all of the prior antecedents of the military investigation. Furthermore, it indicated that the State must investigate and punish all those responsible for the obstruction of justice, cover-up, and impunity that have prevailed in relation to this case.

210. The representatives added that the State must adopt affirmative measures that guarantee access to justice of Mrs. Rosendo Cantú, taking into account the cultural, social, economic, and other obstacles faced and offer the means to overcome them. Finally, they also requested administrative sanction of the public agents responsible for the irregularities verified in the investigation.

211. The Court has established in the present Judgment, bearing in mind the State's partial acknowledgement of responsibility, that the investigation of the rape of Mrs. Rosendo Cantú was not conducted, to date, with due diligence or under the appropriate jurisdiction, and consequently, that Mexico has violated the rights to judicial guarantees and to judicial protection established in Articles 8 and 25 of the American Convention (*supra* para. 162). Consequently, as it has done on other occasions,[272 280] the Court finds that the State must efficiently conduct the criminal investigation into the facts of this case, in order to determine the corresponding criminal responsibilities and apply the punishments and consequences established by law. This obligation must be complied with within a reasonable time, respecting the criteria mentioned above concerning investigations in this type of case.[273 281]

212. In particular, the State must guarantee, through its competent institutions, that the preliminary investigation that is being conducted into the facts that constituted the rape of Mrs. Rosendo Cantú remain within the ordinary [non-military] jurisdiction. Furthermore, if new criminal actions based on the facts of this case are filed against [alleged] perpetrators, who are or have been members of the military, the authorities in charge of the case must ensure that they are conducted under the ordinary jurisdiction and, in no circumstances, under the military forum.[274 282]

213. The Court reiterates that during the investigation and prosecution, the State must ensure the victim full access and capacity to act at all stages. In a case such as this in which the victim, a woman and indigenous person, has had to face various obstacles in order to access justice, the State has the obligation to continue to offer the means by which the victim may fully access and participate in all the proceedings of the case and, to this end, it must ensure that an interpreter is provided and that she counts on assistance with a gender-based perspective; all the foregoing is based on her circumstance of special vulnerability. Lastly, if Mrs. Rosendo Cantú offers her consent, the results of the proceedings must be publicized, so that Mexican society learns the truth about the incident.

214. In addition, on other occasions, [275][283] the Court has ordered the State to initiate disciplinary, administrative, or criminal actions under its domestic law with regard to those responsible for the different procedural and investigative irregularities in a case. In the present case, taking into account that in this case agents at the Ayutla Public Prosecutor's Office complicated matters when receiving the complaint filed by Mrs. Rosendo Cantú (*supra* para. 179) and that it does not appear that one of the doctors had given the corresponding authorities the legal warning, (*supra* para. 192) the Court orders the State to examine this fact, and where applicable, the conduct of the respective government employees, in keeping with the appropriate disciplinary norms.

215. Finally, in regard to the request to guarantee the security of the victims, the next of kin, and the representatives, the Court recalls that the provisional measures ordered opportunely by this Court remain in force (*supra* para. 15).

viii) Protocol for the diligent investigation of acts of violence

239. The Commission requested the Court to order the State to design protocols to facilitate and promote the effective, standardized, and transparent investigation of acts of physical, sexual, and psychological violence, which should include a description of the complex nature of the evidence, and details of the minimum evidence that must be collected in order to provide adequate probative grounds, according to the provisions of the Istanbul Protocol.

240. The State reported on the adoption of distinct protocols related to the investigation of the violence against women in the state of Guerrero, such as the protocols of care to women in situations of violence and of the investigation of crimes of homicide with a focus on feminicides. Moreover, it reported on the publication of two manuals entitled, "Detection Networks, Support and Reference of Cases of Violence Against Indigenous Women of Guerrero," and "Reference Models of Cases of Gender Violence for the state of Guerrero," as well as other instruments related to the investigation and attention to violence against women, among others, the "Integrated Model for the Prevention and Attention of Family and Sexual Violence," model used by health units, and the Program of "Medical

Attention to Raped Persons." Likewise, the State provided information on the process of fitting the Istanbul Protocol to the national context through elaboration and application of the Special Medical/Psychological Report for Cases of Possible Torture and/or Mistreatment, issued by the Office of the Attorney General of the Republic, as well as by publication of institutional guidelines for the application of this Report to be followed by the agents of the Office of the Public Prosecutor of the Federation, and the forensic experts and/or criminal pathologists of the Office of the Attorney General of the Republic. Furthermore, it advised that 29 federative entities had received training on this report and three federative entities were in the process of training the attorney general's offices on the implementation of the Istanbul Protocol. Lastly, the State provided information on the elaboration of Mexican Official Norm NOM-046-SSA2-2005 on domestic and sexual violence and violence against women, which contains criteria to prevent and deal with this. This norm establishes various obligations for personal health, among others, to inform the Public Prosecutor's Office to carry out the corresponding investigations, and it was created pursuant to a friendly settlement with the Inter-American Commission.

241. The Court takes note of the information provided by the State concerning the existence of the mentioned instruments, and the training activities that the federative entities have been holding. However, the State did not attach the document on the "national contextualization" of the Istanbul Protocol or on its application in the state of Guerrero. Furthermore, the Court positively notes the existence of Mexican Official Norm NOM-046-SSA2-2005, which contains criteria for preventing and dealing with sexual abuse and violence against women, as well as detection and investigation standards for health personnel. Nevertheless, the Court notes that despite that in its introduction it states that "with the [elaboration] of this Mexican Official Norm [the State] complies with the commitments acquired in the international forum," and despite that the Norm is the result of an agreement with the Inter-American Commission, Article 8 of the Norm demonstrates that it "does not meet Mexican and international guidelines or recommendations," namely, that it does not conform to international standards. The Inter-American Commission and the representatives did not address any of the instruments indicated by the State.

242. The Court has ordered in other cases that the parameters for investigations and for performing forensic analyses be harmonized with international standards. [285] [284] In the present case, the Court finds it necessary that the State continue with a standardized action protocol for the investigation of sexual abuse, for the federal forum and the state of Guerrero, based on the parameters established in the Istanbul Protocol and the World Health Organization's guidelines mentioned above.

xv) Office for women victims of violence of the Public Prosecutor's Office

261. The representatives asked the Court to order the Mexican State to create a Special Office of the Public Prosecutor to provide attention to women victims of violence in the state of Guerrero, of easy access, which should have appropriate technical and financial resources and personnel trained to handle cases such as this one who are conversant with the international standards for treating women victims of violence and torture.

262. Mexico reported that in the state of Guerrero there exists, among others, a Special Prosecutor's Office for the Investigation of Crimes of Sexual and Domestic Violence, of which seven agencies specialized in attention to sexual violence depend, and which are strategically located in the territory of the state, one in the Mountain Region, all of which are staffed by female personnel, trained on matters of gender and violence, and the Special Prosecutor for Crimes of Violence Against Women and Human Trafficking, adjoined to the Attorney General of Justice of the Republic. Moreover, Mexico reported that the state of Guerrero has carried out multiple actions to take care of indigenous women of Guerrero, noting the work of various agencies, among others, the Secretariat for Women and the Secretariat of Legal Matters in the state of Guerrero, the creation of 36 municipal [councils] for assistance and prevention of the same specialization located in the Mountain area. In addition, it reported that in order to provide psychological and legal attention and social work-oriented attention for women in the Mountain and Costa Chica region, in municipalities and localities of greater marginalization that have higher numbers of indigenous population, it counts on two mobile units. Similarly, it reported on a program of consultancy, orientation in gender violence and legal representation in family matters, whose actions are aimed at providing, among other services, free legal representation and assistance to women, and it also reported on the program of defense and legal aid of the attorney general of defense of the rights of women, which, among other matters, offers economic aid to women to cover costs in jurisdictional proceedings and provides representation and legal aid in the criminal procedures in which they may be involved. Lastly, it reported on the actions taken in regard to the dissemination of women's rights information, among which it noted the distribution of leaflets to raise awareness of the functions, services, and location of the municipal units specialized in the care for women victims of violence.

263. The Court values the information presented by the State and notes that the representatives have not given their observations on the diverse actions, mobile units, or institutions referred to by Mexico, nor have they provided information noting the possible failures with these organizations. Based on the aforementioned, the Court does not have specific and sufficient information to assess the situation and order the creation of the requested office by the representatives. Nevertheless,

the services for women victims of sexual violence must be offered by the institutions noted by the State, among others, the Public Prosecutor's Office of Ayutla de los Libres, by way of the provision of material resources and personnel, whose activities should be strengthened through trainings ordered in the present Judgment.

264. Lastly, the Court observes that the diagnostic report carried out by the Secretariat for Women of the state of Guerrero identifies, among other barriers that complicate attention to the violence in indigenous and rural zones, the fact that said services are centered in cities, and the difficulties regarding access and moving of the location of the services. [292][285] Said diagnostic report recommends, among other measures to decentralize the services and to promote roaming services of sensitization, detection, and attention to violence and to improve access to telephone services for the indigenous communities of Guerrero, so as to allow better attention to women victims of violence. The Court understands that the first of these measures shall be attended to by the informed mobile units. Notwithstanding the foregoing, the Court appreciates the document and considers it useful to indicate the State willingness to discuss the need for progress in implementing these two recommendations in the area where the events of this case occurred.

Torres Millacura v. Argentina
26-Aug-2011
Series C No. 229—*Merits, Reparations, and Costs*

B. Obligation to investigate the facts and determine the whereabouts of Iván Eladio Torres Millacura.

B.1.   Arguments of the parties.

161.   The Commission asked the Court to order the State to "carry out a full, impartial, effective, and prompt investigation of the facts, with the purpose of identifying all the masterminds and perpetrators who participated in the facts related to the arbitrary detention, torture, and enforced disappearance of Iván Eladio Torres Millacura, establishing their responsibility, and punishing them." Likewise, it requested that the Court order the State "to fully, impartially, and effectively investigate the fate or whereabouts of Iván Eladio Torres Millacura," and that, "in the event it is established that the victim is no longer alive . . . to take the necessary measures to turn over his remains to [his] family members."

162.   The representatives agreed with the Commission. Moreover, they held that "not a single person in Argentina has been accused of the crime of forcibly disappearing Iván Eladio Torres Millacura[, and that] the State remains inactive[,]

guaranteeing impunity in this case." In this way, they requested that the Court order the State to "denounce the facts of this case . . . before the International Criminal Court . . . for investigation." Also, the representatives stated that "the expectations [of the relatives of Iván Eladio Torres Millacura] do not lie in the Court ordering the State to 'look for Iván,' but rather that the Court order . . . the State to return him alive, exactly how they took him [sic]."

163.   The State rejected the representatives' claims "as they do not meet international standards on reparations." In addition, it stated that "the facts of this case are being investigated currently by domestic judicial authorities." Likewise, the State expressed the view that "parallel to the judicial action toward establishing the facts [and] identifying and punishing those responsible, a 'Search Dossier' is being processed in which several investigative measures have been taken."

B.2.   Considerations of the Court.

164.   Taking this into account, the Court orders the State to remove allobstacles, de facto and de jure, that keep this case in impunity[169 286] and orders that all those investigations that may be necessary be launched in order to identify and, where appropriate, punish those responsible for the facts that took place with regard to Mr. Torres Millacura. The State shall direct and complete the pertinent investigations and proceedings within a reasonable period of time in order to establish the truth of the facts. In particular, the State shall:

(a) start and/or conclude the pertinent investigations with regard to the facts to which Mr. Iván Eladio Torres Millacura was a victim, taking into account the systematic pattern of police abuse that exists in the Province of Chubut, with the goal that the proceeding and the pertinent investigations be conducted in consideration of these facts, avoiding omissions in the collection of evidence and the pursuit of logical lines of investigation. Those investigations must be directed toward determining the masterminds and perpetrators behind the facts of this case, and

(b) ensure that the competent authorities carry out the corresponding investigations *ex officio*; that for doing so, they have and use all the logistical and scientific resources necessary to collect and process evidence and, in particular, that they have the means to access documentation and information that is pertinent to the investigation of the facts denounced and to promptly carrying out the actions and inquiries that are essential for bringing what happened to Iván Eladio Torres Millacura to light; and that the individuals who participate in the investigation—among them, the family members of the victims and witnesses—have all due guarantees for their security.

165.   The Court finds that, based on its jurisprudence,[170 287] the State must ensure both full access for family members of victims and their capacity to

take action at all stages of the investigation and trial of those responsible, in accordance with domestic law and the provisions of the American Convention. In addition, the results of the corresponding proceedings must be made public so that Argentine society can learn about the facts that are the subject of this case, as well as who is responsible for them.[171 288]

166.   In addition, the Court notes that the State has launched actions toward establishing the whereabouts of Mr. Iván Eladio Torres Millacura. Thus, taking into account the jurisprudence of this Court,[172 289] the Tribunal orders the State to continue with this search, and in doing so to make all efforts possible as quickly as possible. The Tribunal highlights that Mr. Torres Millacura disappeared almost eight years ago, and thus it is a fair expectation of his family members that the State take all effective actions to determine his whereabouts, and to adopt the measures necessary.

167.   In addition, the Court notes that in the application's list of petitions, the Commission asked the Court to order the State to carry out an investigation "with regard to the individuals who are part of the various State bodies that have been involved in the investigations and proceedings carried out with regard to the facts of this case," in order to determine responsibility for deficiencies "that have resulted in impunity." However, in the considerations of fact and law in the application, the Commission did not make any arguments on this point. For this reason, the Court will not rule on this request.

168.   Finally, with regard to the representatives' request that the Court order the State to denounce the facts of this case before the International Criminal Court, this Tribunal does not have jurisdiction to order a State to bring a complaint against itself before any Tribunal or Court, whether national or international. Therefore, the representatives' request is clearly inadmissible.

The Massacres of El Mozote and Nearby Places v. El Salvador
25-Oct-2012
Series C No. 252—*Merits, reparations and costs*

B. Obligation to investigate the facts that gave rise to the violations and to identify, prosecute and punish, as appropriate, those responsible, and also to locate, identify and, return to their next of kin the remains of the victims of the massacres
1) Complete investigation, determination, prosecution and eventual punishment of all the masterminds and perpetrators of the massacres
315. In Chapter VIII of this Judgment, the Court declared the violation of the

rights to judicial guarantees and to judicial protection, as well as the failure to comply with Articles 1, 6 and 8 of the Inter-American Convention to Prevent and Punish Torture and 7(b) of the Convention of Belém do Pará, because it had not opened an investigation *ex officio*, because of the lack of diligence in the criminal investigation conducted by the Second First Instance Court of San Francisco Gotera, and because of decision to dismiss the proceedings in application of the Law of General Amnesty for the Consolidation of the Peace, as well as because of the violation of the guarantee of a reasonable term. Thus, the said investigation has not constituted an effective remedy to ensure the rights of access to justice and to know the truth by the investigation, prosecution and eventual punishment of those responsible for the massacres, in a way that examines, completely and exhaustively, the numerous adverse effects caused to the victims in this case, or to ensure the full reparation of the consequences of the violations. Accordingly, 32 years after the events, and 19 years after the decision was issued to dismiss the only proceedings that had been opened for the facts of this case, without any of those responsible having been identified or indicted during the investigation, total impunity prevails.

316. The Court assesses positively the work of the Truth Commission for El Salvador and the publication of its report, as an effort that has contributed to the search for and determination of the truth of a historic period in El Salvador. In addition, the Truth Commission underlined the importance of holding judicial proceedings to prosecute and punish those responsible, so the Court considers it pertinent to reiterate that the "historic truth" contained in the said report neither completes nor substitutes for the State's obligation to establish the truth and to ensure the judicial determination of individual or State responsibilities also by judicial proceedings. [496] [290]

317. The Court reiterates that investigation is a peremptory obligation of the State, and also the importance that such actions be conducted in conformity with international standards. Therefore, the Court considers that the State must adopt clear and specific strategies to overcome impunity in the prosecution of the masterminds and perpetrators of the massacres of El Mozote and nearby places committed during the Salvadoran armed conflict.

318. First, since the Law of General Amnesty for the Consolidation of Peace lacks effectiveness according to the considerations made in paragraphs 283 to 296, the State must ensure that this law never again represents an obstacle to the investigation of the events that are the subject of this case or to the identification, prosecution and eventual punishment of those responsible for these events and other similar grave human rights violations that occurred during the armed conflict in El Salvador. This obligation is binding on all the State's powers and organs as a whole, which are obliged to exercise *ex officio* the control of conformity

between the domestic norms and the American Convention; evidently, within the framework of their respective competences and the corresponding procedural regulations. [497][291]

319. Based on the foregoing and also on its case law, [498][292] this Court establishes that the State must, within a reasonable time, initiate, promote, re-open, direct, continue and conclude, as appropriate, with the greatest diligence, the pertinent investigations and proceedings in order to establish the truth of the events and to determine the criminal responsibilities that may exist, and remove all the obstacles *de facto* and *de jure* that maintain total impunity in this case, taking into account that around 31 years have passed since the said massacres took place. In this regard, the State must investigate effectively all the facts of the massacres including, in addition to the extrajudicial executions, other possible serious violations of personal integrity and, in particular, the acts of torture, and the rape of the women, as well as the enforced displacements. To this end, the State must:

(a) Abstain from resorting to mechanisms such as amnesty in favor of the perpetrators, as well as any other similar provision, prescription, non-retroactivity of the criminal law, *res judicata*, *ne bis in idem,* or any other mechanism that exempts responsibility, to waive this obligation;

(b) Take into account the systematic pattern of human rights violations in the context of the Salvadoran armed conflict, as well as the large-scale military operations within which the events of this case took place, so that the pertinent investigations and proceedings are conducted bearing in mind the complexity of these events and the context in which they occurred, avoiding omission in the collection of evidence in following logical lines of investigation based on a correct assessment of the systematic patterns that gave rise to the events investigated;

(c) Identify and individualize all the masterminds and perpetrators of the massacres in this case. Due diligence in the investigation signifies that all the State authorities are obliged to collaborate in the collection of evidence; therefore they must provide the judge, prosecutor or other judicial authority with all the information required and abstain from actions that entail an obstruction to the progress of the investigation;

(d) Ensure that the competent authorities conduct the corresponding investigations *ex officio* and, to that end, that they have available and use all the necessary logistic and scientific resources to obtain and process the evidence and, in particular, that they have the authority to access the pertinent documentation and information to investigate the events denounced and to carry out the essential actions and inquiries to clarify what happened in this case;

(e) Guarantee that the investigations into the events that constitute the massacres in this case remain, at all times, in the ordinary jurisdiction;

(f) Ensure that the different organs of the justice system involved in the case have the necessary human, financial, logistic, scientific or any other type of resources necessary to perform their tasks adequately, independently and impartially, and take the necessary measures to ensure that judicial officials, prosecutors, investigators and other agents of justice have an adequate safety and protection system, taking into account the circumstances of the cases under their responsibility and the place where they are working, that will allow them to perform their functions with due diligence, and also to ensure the protection of witnesses, victims and next of kin, and

(g) Ensure full access and legal standing at all the stages of the investigation and prosecution of those responsible to the victims or their next of kin.

320. In addition, the results of the corresponding proceedings must be published so that Salvadoran society knows the facts that are the purpose of this case, and also those responsible.

321. As decided in the case of *Contreras et al v. El Salvador*, [499] [293] the State must adopt pertinent and adequate measures to guarantee to agents of justice, and also to Salvadoran society, public, technical and systematized access to the archives that contain relevant and useful information for the ongoing investigations in the cases concerning human rights violations during the armed conflict; measures that it must support with the appropriate budgetary allocations.

2) Administrative, disciplinary or criminal measures for the State officials responsible for obstructing the investigations

325. In previous cases, [500] [294] when dealing with certain violations, the Court has established that the State must file disciplinary, administrative or criminal actions, as appropriate, according to its domestic laws, against those responsible for the different procedural and investigative irregularities. In the instant case, it has been proved that various State authorities obstructed the progress of the investigations and delayed the judicial inspections and exhumations, and this culminated with the application of the Law of General Amnesty for the Consolidation of Peace, thus perpetuating the impunity in this case (*supra* para. 299). Also, despite requests to re-open the proceedings made by the representatives, the investigation remains closed and archived (*supra* para. 300).

326. Consequently, this Court considers that, as a way of combating impunity, the State must, within a reasonable time, investigate, through its competent public institutions, the conduct of the officials who obstructed the investigation and permitted the facts to remain unpunished since they occurred and then, following an appropriate proceeding, apply the corresponding administrative, disciplinary or criminal punishments, as appropriate, to those found responsible.

3) Discovery, identification and return to their next of kin of the remains of the persons executed in the massacres of El Mozote and nearby places

330. The Court appreciates the work performed by the Argentine Forensic Anthropology Team to recover the remains of those who had been executed, as well as the return of remains that was carried out by the judicial authorities as a result of this work (*supra* paras. 230 to 241). Nevertheless, the Court observes that the Second First Instance Court of San Francisco Gotera decided to terminate the exhumation procedures once the Law of General Amnesty for the Consolidation of Peace had been enacted and applied to this case (*supra* paras. 229 and 276). The subsequent exhumations were only performed on the initiative of *Tutela Legal del Arzobispado (supra* para. 234). Moreover, no other measures have been taken since 2004 to seek and locate other individuals who died in the massacres.

331. This Court has established that the right of the victims' next of kin to know the whereabouts of the remains of their loved ones constitutes, in addition to a requirement of the right to know the truth, a measure of reparation and, therefore, gives rise to a correlated obligation of the State to meet this fair expectation. In addition, for the next of kin, it is very important to receive the bodies of those who died in the massacre, because it allows them to bury them in accordance with their beliefs, as well as to close the process of mourning that they have endured all these years.[295][501] In the words of expert witness Yáñez de la Cruz, "certain cultural and social rituals contribute to the mourning process through practices such as the wake, the burial, consolation, all the actions that confirm that the loved ones will not return"; and these rituals could not be performed with regard to the massacres of El Mozote and nearby places.[502][296] It is also worth underlining that the remains can provide useful information to clarify the facts, because they provide details of the treatment that the victims received, the way in which they were executed, and the *modus operandi*. Similarly, the place where the remains are found may provide valuable information on the perpetrators or the institution to which they belonged.[503][297]

332. The Court considers that, within six months of notification of this Judgment, the State must collect the available information on possible interment or burial sites, which must be protected in order to preserve them so that, following up on the work already undertaken by the Argentine Forensic Anthropology Team, any other action that is necessary in order to exhume and identify other individuals who were executed is initiated systematically and rigorously, with adequate human and financial resources.[504][298] To this end, the State must use all necessary technical and scientific means, taking into account the pertinent national and international standards[505][299] and must endeavor to complete all the exhumations within two years of notification of this Judgment. In this regard, the Court considers that the informed consent of the victims' families and coordination with them through

their representatives is a fundamental element of this process. [506] [300]

333. If the remains are identified, they must be delivered to the next of kin, after a genetic corroboration of relationship or testing using adequate and suitable methods, as appropriate, as soon as possible and at no cost to the next of kin. The State must also cover the expenses for transportation and burial in accordance with the beliefs of their family. [507] [301] Should the remains not be identified or claimed by any next of kin, the State must bury them individually in an acceptable cemetery or place that is known to the communities that were victims of the massacres. A specific identifiable area in this place shall be reserved for their burial with the indication that these are individuals who have not been identified or claimed who died in the massacres of El Mozote and nearby places, with information on the place where the remains were found.

334. To ensure that the individualization of those exhumed is effective and viable, this Court establishes, as it has in other cases, [508] [302] that the State must provide written information to the victims' representatives on the process of identification and return of the remains of those who died in the massacres and, as appropriate, request their collaboration for the pertinent purposes. Copies of these communications must be presented to the Court to be considered during the monitoring of compliance with this Judgment.

Mendoza et al. v. Argentina
14-May-2013
Series C No. 260—*Preliminary objections, merits and reparations*

C. Obligation to investigate the facts and to identify, prosecute and, as appropriate, punish those responsible
C.1. Investigation into the death of Ricardo David Videla Fernández
C.1.2. Considerations of the Court

340. According to the considerations on the merits set out in Chapter X of this Judgment, the Argentine State has the obligation to investigate with due diligence, the possible responsibilities of the personnel of the Mendoza Prison for the presumed failure to comply with their duty to prevent violations of the right to life of Ricardo David Videla (*supra* paras. 216 to 229). Therefore, the State must comply with the said obligation to investigate and, as appropriate, sanction, by means of the pertinent judicial, disciplinary or administrative mechanisms, the acts that could have contributed to the death of Ricardo David Videla in that prison. [403] [303]

341. Furthermore, the victim's next of kin or their representatives must have

full access and legal standing at all stages and levels of the domestic criminal proceedings held in this case, in accordance with domestic legislation and the American Convention. The results of these proceedings must be published by the State, so that the Argentine society can know the truth regarding the facts of this case. [404 304]

C.2. Investigation into the acts of torture suffered by Lucas Matías Mendoza and Claudio David Núñez

C.2.2. Considerations of the Court

343. In this Judgment, the Court has determined that the State violated, to the detriment of Claudio David Núñez and Lucas Matías Mendoza, Articles 5(1), 5(2), 8 and 25 of the American Convention, in relation to Article 1(1) of this treaty, as well Articles 1, 6 and 8 of the Inter-American Convention to Prevent and Punish Torture, because the State closed the investigations opened into the torture committed against them, without Argentina having provided a satisfactory and convincing explanation of what happened (*supra* paras. 232 to 236).

344. Accordingly, as the Court has decided on other occasions, [405 305] these facts must be investigated effectively by means of proceedings held against those presumably responsible for the attacks on personal integrity that occurred. Consequently, the Court decides that the State must conduct a criminal investigation into the acts of torture committed against Claudio David Núñez and Lucas Matías Mendoza in order to determine the eventual criminal responsibilities and, as appropriate, apply the punishments and consequences established by law. This obligation must be complied with within a reasonable time and taking into consideration the criteria established concerning investigations in this type of case. [406 306] Also, if the investigation into the said acts reveals procedural and investigative irregularities related to them, the pertinent disciplinary, administrative or criminal action must be undertaken. [407 307]

B. PUBLIC APOLOGY, ACKNOWLEDGMENT OF RESPONSIBILITY AND COMMEMORATION OF THE VICTIM

The Mayagna (Sumo) Awas Tingni Community v. Nicaragua
31-Aug-2001
Series C No. 79—*Merits, Reparations, and Costs*

2.   The Commission presented this case for the Court to decide whether the State violated Articles 1 (Obligation to Respect Rights), 2 (Domestic Legal

Effects), 21 (Right to Property), and 25 (Right to Judicial Protection) of the Convention in view of the fact that Nicaragua has not demarcated the communal lands of the Awas Tingni Community, nor has the State adopted effective measures to ensure the property rights of the Community to its ancestral lands and natural resources, and also because it granted a concession on community lands without the assent of the Community, and the State did not ensure an effective remedy in response to the Community's protests regarding its property rights.

[*Reparations and Costs*]

163.　In the instant case the Court established that Nicaragua breached Articles 25 and 21 of the Convention in relation to articles 1(1) and 2 of the Convention. In this regard, the Court has reiterated in its constant jurisprudence that it is a principle of international law that any violation of an international obligation that has caused damage carries with it the obligation to provide adequate reparation for it.[163 308]

164.　For the aforementioned reason, pursuant to Article 2 of the American Convention on Human Rights, this Court considers that the State must adopt the legislative, administrative, and any other measures required to create an effective mechanism for delimitation, demarcation, and titling of the property of indigenous communities, in accordance with their customary law, values, customs, and mores. Furthermore, as a consequence of the aforementioned violations of rights protected by the Convention in the instant case, the Court rules that the State must carry out the delimitation, demarcation, and titling of the corresponding lands of the members of the Awas Tingni Community, within a maximum term of 15 months, with full participation by the Community, and taking into account its customary law, values, customs, and mores. Until the delimitation, demarcation, and titling of the lands of the members of the Community have been carried out, Nicaragua must abstain from acts that might lead the agents of the State itself, or third parties acting with its acquiescence or its tolerance, to affect the existence, value, use, or enjoyment of the property located in the geographic area where the members of the Awas Tingni Community live and carry out their activities.

Plan de Sanchez Massacre v. Guatemala
19-Nov-2004
Series C No. 116—*Reparations and Costs*

b) Public act acknowledging international responsibility to make reparation to the victims and to commemorate those executed in the massacre

100.　In its judgment on merits of April 29, 2004, the Court stated that the

State's acknowledgment of responsibility made a positive contribution to the evolution of this proceeding and to the application of the principles that inspire the American Convention. The Court also recognizes that, during the public hearing held on April 24, 2004, the State manifested "its profound regret for the events endured and suffered by the Plan de Sánchez community on July 18, 1982, [and] apologize[d] to the victims, the survivors, and the next of kin as an initial sign of respect, reparation, and guarantee of non-repetition." However, for this declaration to be fully effective as reparation to the victims and serve as a guarantee of non-repetition, the Court considers that the State must organize a public act acknowledging its responsibility for the events that occurred in this case to make reparation to the victims. The act should be carried out in the village of Plan de Sánchez, where the massacre occurred, in the presence of high-ranking State authorities and, in particular, in the presence of the members of the Plan de Sánchez community and the other victims in this case, inhabitants of the villages of Chipuerta, Joya de Ramos, Raxjut, Volcanillo, Coxojabaj, Las Tunas, Las Minas, Las Ventanas, Ixchel, Chiac, Concul, and Chichupac; the leaders of these affected communities must also take part in the act. The State must provide the means to facilitate the presence of these persons in the said act. Also, Guatemala must conduct this act in both Spanish and in Maya-Achí and publicize it in the media. The State shall carry out this activity within one year of notification of this judgment.

101.   Bearing in mind the characteristics of the case as regards those who were executed in the Plan de Sánchez massacre, carried out by State agents on July 18, 1982, the Court considers that, during this act, the State must honor publicly the memory of those executed, most of them members of the Mayan indigenous people belonging to the Achí linguistic community, who were the inhabitants of the village of Plan de Sánchez and also the villages of Chipuerta, Joya de Ramos, Raxjut, Volcanillo, Coxojabaj, Las Tunas, Las Minas, Las Ventanas, Ixchel, Chiac, Concul and Chichupac. The State must take into account the traditions and customs of the members of the affected communities in this act.

c) Translation of the judgments of the Court into the Maya-Achí language

102.   The Court considers that the State must translate the American Convention on Human Rights into the Maya-Achí language, if this has not been done already, as well as the judgment on merits delivered by the Court on April 29, 2004, and this judgment. Guatemala must also provide the necessary resources to publicize these texts in the municipality of Rabinal and deliver them to the victims of the instant case. To this end, the State has one year from notification of this judgment.

d) Publication of the pertinent parts of the judgments of the Court

103.   Furthermore, and as it has ordered on other occasions,[270][309] the Court considers that, as a measure of satisfaction, the State must publish, at least once,

in the official gazette and in another daily newspaper with national circulation, in Spanish and in Maya-Achí, the section entitled Proven Facts in Chapter V, . . . the first to fourth operative paragraph of the judgment on merits delivered by the Court on April 29, 2004, . . . Chapter VII entitled Proven Facts (without the footnotes), and the first to ninth operative paragraph of this judgment, within one year of notification of this judgment.

e) Guarantee of non-repetition by providing resources for the collective memory

104.   With regard to the guarantees of non-repetition of the facts of this case, the Court establishes, in fairness, the sum of US $25,000.00 (twenty-five thousand United States dollars) or its equivalent in national currency, for maintenance and improvements to the infrastructure of the chapel in which the victims pay homage to those who were executed in the Plan de Sánchez massacre. Within one year of notification of this judgment, this sum must be delivered to the members of the Plan de Sánchez community or their chosen representatives, who will be responsible for administering it. This will help raise public awareness to avoid repetition of events such as those that occurred in this case and keep alive the memory of those who died.[271][310]

Yakye Axa Indigenous Community v. Paraguay
17-Jun-2005
Series C No. 125—*Merits, Reparations, and Costs*

d)   Public act of acknowledgment of international responsibility

226.   As the Court has ordered in other cases,[220][311] the Court deems it necessary, with the aim of redressing the damage caused to the victims, for the State to conduct a public act of acknowledgment of its responsibility, one that is previously agreed upon with the victims and their representatives and is in connection with the violations found in this Judgment. This act must be conducted at the current seat of the Yakye Axa Community, at a public ceremony attended by high State authorities and the members of the Community living in other areas, and with participation by the leaders of the Community.[221][312] The State must provide the means for said persons to attend the aforementioned act.[222][313] The State must conduct said act both in the Enxet language and in Spanish or Guaraní and make it known to the public by means of the media.[223][314] At this act, the State must take into account the traditions and customs of the members of the Community. To do this, the State has one year's time from the date of notification of the instant Judgment.

e)   Publication and dissemination of the pertinent parts of the Judgment of the Court

227.   As it has ordered in previous cases,[224][315] the Court deems that, as a measure of satisfaction, the State must publish, within one year of the date of notification of the instant Judgment, at least once, in the Official Gazette and in another nationally distributed daily, both the section on Proven Facts and operative paragraphs One to Fourteen of this Judgment. The State must also cover the cost of radio broadcasting the content of paragraphs 50(12) to 50(16), 50(18), 50(22), 50(24), 50(58), 50(59), and 50(92) to 50(100) of chapter VI on Proven Facts; of paragraphs 135, 154, 155, 161, 162, 169, 172, and 175 of chapters IX and X; and of operative paragraphs One to Fourteen of the instant Judgment, in Enxet language and in Guaraní or Spanish, on a radio station to which the members of the Yakye Axa Community have access. The radio broadcast must be made at least four times, with two weeks time between each broadcast.

YATAMA v. Nicaragua
23-Jun-2005
Series C No. 127 — *Preliminary Objections, Merits, Reparations and Costs*

2.   The Commission presented the application for the Court to decide whether the State had violated Articles 8 (Right to a Fair Trial), 23 (Right to Participate in Government), and 25 (Judicial Protection) of the American Convention, all of them in relation to Articles 1(1) (Obligation to Respect Rights) and 2 (Domestic Legal Effects) thereof, to the detriment of the candidates for mayors, deputy mayors, and councilors presented by the indigenous regional political party, Yapti Tasba Masraka Nanih Asla Takanka (hereinafter "YATAMA"). The Commission [alleged] that these candidates were excluded from participating in the municipal elections held on November 5, 2000, in the North Atlantic and the South Atlantic Autonomous Regions (hereinafter "RAAN" and "RAAS") as a result of a decision issued on August 15, 2000, by the Supreme Electoral Council. The application stated that the [alleged] victims filed several recourses against this decision and, finally, on October 25, 2000, the Supreme Court of Justice of Nicaragua declared that the application for *amparo* that they had filed was inadmissible. The Commission indicated that the State had not provided a recourse that would have protected the right of these candidates to participate and to be elected in the municipal elections of November 5, 2000, and it had not adopted the legislative or other measures necessary to make these rights effective; above all, it had not provided for "norms in the electoral law that would facilitate the political participation of the indigenous organizations in the electoral

processes of the Atlantic Coast Autonomous Region of Nicaragua, in accordance with the customary law, values, practices and customs of the indigenous people who reside there."

C) Other Forms of Reparation (Measures of Satisfaction and Guarantees of Non-Repetition)

a)   Publication of the judgment

253.   The Court takes into account that "the communities use community radio as a means of information"; it therefore considers it necessary for the State to publicize, on a radio station with broad coverage on the Atlantic Coast, paragraphs 124(11), 124(20), 124(28), 124(31), 124(32), 124(39), 124(40), 124(46), 124(51), 124(62), 124(68), 124(70), and 124(71) of Chapter VII (Proven Facts); paragraphs 153, 154, 157 to 160, 162, 164, 173, 175, 176, 212, 218, 219, 221, 223, 224, 226, and 227, which correspond to Chapters IX and X on the violations declared by the Court; and the operative paragraphs of this judgment. This should be done in Spanish, Miskito, Sumo, Rama and English. The radio broadcast should be made on at least four occasions with an interval of two weeks between each broadcast. To this end, the State has one year from notification of this judgment.

González et al. ("Cotton Field") v. Mexico
16-Nov-2009
Series C No. 205—*Preliminary Objections, Merits, Reparations, and Costs*

4.1.3.   Commemoration of the victims of gender-based murder

471.   The Tribunal considers that, in the instant case, it is pertinent for the State to erect a monument to commemorate the women victims of gender-based murder in Ciudad Juárez, who include the victims in this case, as a way of dignifying them and as a reminder of the context of violence they experienced, which the State undertakes to prevent in the future. The monument shall be unveiled at the ceremony during which the State publicly acknowledges its international responsibility and shall be built in the cotton field in which the victims of this case were found.

472.   Since the monument relates to more individuals than those considered victims in this case, the decision on the type of monument shall correspond to the public authorities, who must consult the opinion of civil society organizations by means of an open, public procedure in which the organizations that represented the victims in this case shall be included.

Radilla-Pacheco v. Mexico

23-Nov-2009

Series C No. 209—*Preliminary Objections, Merits, Reparations, and Costs*

C4. Publication of the relevant parts of the present Judgment

350. As stated by this Tribunal in other cases, [323] [316] the State shall publish in the Official Gazette of the Federation and in another newspaper of ample national circulation, for a single time, paragraphs 1 through 7, 52 through 66, 114 through 358 of the present Judgment, without the footnotes, and its operative paragraphs. Additionally, as has been ordered by the Tribunal on previous occasions, [324] [317] the present Judgment shall be published in its totality on the official website of the Attorney General of the Republic and be available for a one-year period. For the publications in the newspapers and on the Internet the terms of six and two months, respectively, computed as of the notification of the present Judgment, are set.

C5. Public act of acknowledgment of international responsibility

352. The Court values positively the offering made by the State regarding this form of reparation, given the importance and positive effects this modality of reparations has for the victims of violations of human rights. On previous occasions, the Court has valued favorably those acts that seek to recover the memory of the victims, the acknowledgment of their dignity, and the consolation of their relatives. [325] [318]

353. Taking into account the aforementioned, this Tribunal considers it necessary that the State hold a public act of acknowledgment of responsibility with regard to the facts of the present case and in satisfaction of the memory of Rosendo Radilla-Pacheco. Reference shall be made, in that act, to the violations of human rights declared in the present Judgment. Likewise, it shall be carried out through a public ceremony in the presence of high national authorities and the next of kin of Mr. Radilla-Pacheco. The State and the next of kin of Mr. Radilla-Pacheco and/ or their representatives, shall agree on the modality of compliance with the public act of acknowledgment, as well as the specific aspects required, such as the place and date on which it will be held.

354. Additionally, with the objective of preserving the memory of Mr. Rosendo Radilla-Pacheco within the community to which he belonged, in the same act of acknowledgment of responsibility, if possible, or after it, the State shall, in coordination with the victims, place a commemorative plaque of the facts of his forced disappearance in some part of the city of Atoyac de Álvarez.

C6. Reestablishment of the memory: bibliographic sketch of the life of Mr. Rosendo Radilla-Pacheco.

356. The Court considers that the historical vindication and the dignity of Mr. Rosendo Radilla-Pacheco is of utmost importance, and the reason for which

it values and accepts the proposal made by the State in the present case, as a guarantee of non-repetition, since these initiatives are important both for the preservation of the memory and satisfaction of the victims, and the recovery and reestablishment of the historical memory within a democratic society. Based on the aforementioned, the Court considers that the State shall execute the proposal to prepare a bibliographical sketch of the life of Mr. Radilla-Pacheco, in the terms proposed in the previous paragraph, through a publication, as of the investigation *in situ* and of the reproduction of the corresponding official sources. Said publication shall be made within a one-year term. Additionally, this measure shall be fulfilled with the participation of the victims.

Xákmok Kásek Indigenous Community v. Paraguay
24-Aug-2010
Series C No. 214—*Merits, Reparations, and Costs*

3.   Measures of Satisfaction

3.1   Public act of acknowledgement of international responsibility

297.   As it has ordered in other cases,[304][319] in order to repair the damage caused to the victims, the Court finds it necessary that the State carry out a public act to acknowledge its international responsibility for the violations declared in this judgment. This act must be agreed upon previously with the Community. Furthermore, the act must take place at the current site of the Community, during a public ceremony attended by senior State authorities and the members of the Community, including those who live in other areas; to this end, the State must provide the necessary means to facilitate transportation. The leaders of the Community must be permitted to participate in the said act. Moreover, the State must conduct this act in the Community's languages, and in Spanish and Guaraní, and must broadcast it on a radio station with wide coverage in the Chaco. The State must organize this act within one year of notification of this judgment.

3.2   Publication and broadcast of the judgment

299   Moreover, as it has previously,[307][320] the Court finds it appropriate that the State publicize the official summary of the judgment delivered by the Court on a radio station with wide coverage in the Chaco. To this end, the State must have the official summary of the judgment translated into the Sanapaná, Enxet, and Guaraní languages. The radio broadcasts must be made on the first Sunday of the month at least four times and a recording of the broadcasts must be forwarded to the Court when they have been made. The State has six months to complete this, as of notification of this judgment.

Rosendo Cantú et al. v. Mexico
31-Aug-2010
Series C No. 216—*Preliminary Objections, Merits, Reparations, and Costs*

iii) Public act of acknowledgement of responsibility

224. The Commission asked the Court to order the State to publicly acknowledge its State responsibility for the harm caused.

225. The representatives also asked that an act should be held during which the State would publicly acknowledge its responsibility, in the Spanish and Me'paa languages, with the participation of high-ranking officials, and where the President of Mexico would offer an apology for the violations committed. Said act must be "covered by the princip[al] media that reach the national and community sector," and be held according to the victim's wishes and that she should indicate the place where the act should be held, as well as other aspects related to the content and conditions in which the act will be carried out. Lastly, they requested that, in the act, the reality of marginalization, exclusion, and discrimination of indigenous peoples be acknowledged, with particular emphasis made on the situation of indigenous women, as well the important work of human rights organizations.

226. The Court recalls that the State made a partial acknowledgement of its international responsibility at the public hearing held in this case (*supra* para. 16). The Court has determined that the State's acknowledgement of responsibility makes a positive contribution to the development of this [procedure] and to validity of the principles that inspire the American Convention (*supra* para. 25). However, as in other cases, [279] [321] for this acknowledgement to achieve its full effect, the Court considers that the State must organize a public act of acknowledgement of international responsibility in relation to the facts of the present case. During this act, reference should be made to the human rights violations declared in this Judgment. The act should be carried out in a public ceremony, held in the Spanish and Me'paa languages, in the presence of high-ranking national authorities and of the state of Guerrero, the victims in this case, and authorities and members of the victims' community. The State, together with Mrs. Rosendo Cantú, and/or her representatives, must agree on how the public act of acknowledgement is to be organized, as well as other details, such as the place and date. If Mrs. Rosendo Cantú agrees, this act should be broadcast by a radio station of the state of Guerrero. The State has one year from the notification of this Judgment to carry out said act.

iv) Publication of the Judgment

227. The Commission requested the Court to order the State to publish the Judgment in a national means of circulation.

228. The representatives asked the Court to order the publication of the pertinent

parts of the Judgment, in the Spanish and the Me'paa languages, "in both radio broadcast with statewide coverage as well as coverage in the community, on four occasions [...], and in a newspaper of national circulation and another in statewide circulation, in the Official Gazette of the Federation and on the webpage of the National Secretary of Defense."

229. As it has ordered on other occasions, [280] [322] the Court considers that, as a measure of satisfaction, the State must publish once, in Spanish, in the Official Gazette, paragraphs 1 to 5, 11, 13, 16 to 18, 24, 25, 70 to 79, 107 to 121, 127 to 131, 137 to 139, 159 to 167, 174 to 182, 184, 185, 200 to 202, 206 and 207 of this Judgment, including the titles of each chapter and of the respective section— without the corresponding footnotes—and including the operative paragraphs hereto. Moreover, if Mrs. Rosendo Cantú authorizes it, the State must: i) publish the official summary issued by the Court in a newspaper with widespread national circulation, in Spanish, and in a newspaper with widespread circulation in the state of Guerrero, in Spanish and Me'paa; [281] [323] ii) publish this Judgment in its entirety, [282] [324] together with the translation into Me'paa of the official summary, which should be made on an appropriate web site of the federal State and of the state of Guerrero, taking into account the characteristics of the publication ordered to be carried out, and this must remain available for at least one year, and iii) broadcast the official summary once, in both languages, on a radio station [283] [325] with coverage in Barranca Bejuco. The State has six months from the notification of this Judgment to make the publications and broadcasts indicated above.

Atala Riffo and Daughters v. Chile
24-Feb-2012
Series C No. 239—*Merits, Reparations and Costs*

2. Satisfaction

a) Publication of the Judgment

259. In this regard, the Court considers that, as it has ordered in other cases,[276] the State shall publish the following, within six months from the notification of this Judgment:

    i.   the official summary of the Judgment written by the Court, once only, in the Official Gazette;

    ii.   the official summary of the Judgment written by the Court, once only, in a newspaper of broad national circulation, and

    iii.   the present Judgment in its entirety, to be posted on a government website for a period of one year.

b) Public act acknowledging international liability

263. The Court has determined that in certain cases it is justified that the States acknowledge their responsibility through a public act, in order to achieve its full effect. [277][326] In this particular case, it is appropriate to adopt a measure of that nature and the State shall make reference to the human rights violations described in this Judgment. The State shall ensure the participation of those victims who wish to be present, and shall invite the organizations that represented the victims in national and international proceedings. The conduct and other details of the public ceremony shall be duly discussed in advance with the victims' representatives. The State is granted a period of one year from the notification of this Judgment to comply with this obligation.

264. Regarding the State authorities who should be present or participate in this act, the Court, as it has done in other cases, states that these authorities must be of high rank. It will be up to the State to decide to whom this task should be entrusted. However, the Judicial Branch must be represented at the ceremony.

The Kichwa Indigenous People of Sarayaku v. Ecuador
27-Jun-2012
Series C No. 245—*Merits and reparations*

B.3 Measures of satisfaction

a) Public act of acknowledgment of international responsibility

305. Although, in this case, the State has already acknowledged its responsibility on Sarayaku territory, as it has in other cases [350][327] and in order to repair the damage caused to the Sarayaku People by the violation of their rights, the Court finds that the State must organize a public act to acknowledge its international responsibility for the violations declared in this Judgment. The determination of the place and method of carrying out this act must be previously consulted and agreed with the People. The act must take place in a public ceremony, in the presence of senior State officials and the members of the People, in the Kichwa and Spanish languages, and must be widely publicized in the media. The State has one year from notification of the Judgment to comply with this measure.

b) Publication and broadcasting of the judgment

306. The representatives asked that "the relevant parts of the judgment be published at least once in the Official Gazette and in another national newspaper, in both Spanish and Kichwa." The Commission and the State did not refer to this aspect.

307. In this regard, the Court finds, as it has in other cases, [351][328] that the State must publish, within six months of notification of this Judgment:

    i.   the official summary of this Judgment prepared by the Court, once, in the Official Gazette;

ii.   the official summary of this Judgment prepared by the Court, once, in a newspaper with wide national circulation; and

iii.   this Judgment, in its entirety, on an official website, available for one year.

308. Furthermore, the Court considers it appropriate that the State publicize, through a radio station with widespread coverage in the southeastern Amazonian region, the official summary of the Judgment, in Spanish, Kichwa and other indigenous languages of this sub-region, with the relevant translation. The radio broadcast must be made on the first Sunday of the month, on at least four occasions. The State has one year from notification of this Judgment to comply with this measure.

The Massacres of El Mozote and Nearby Places v. El Salvador
25-Oct-2012
Series C No. 252—*Merits, reparations and costs*

3) Measures of Satisfaction
a) Public acknowledgment of responsibility
357. In the instant case, the Court notes that the act of acknowledgment of responsibility held at the domestic level and before the delivery of this Judgment was agreed with the victims or their representatives and was executed as follows: (a) publicly; (b) at the place where the events occurred; (c) responsibility for the extrajudicial execution of the victims was acknowledged as well as for the other violations committed in this case; (d) it was held in the presence, and with the participation, of a considerable number of survivors and next of kin; (e) it was headed by the highest State authority – namely, the President of the Republic – and senior State officials took part in it, and (f) it was broadcast and disseminated fully throughout the country. In this regard, the Inter-American Court considers that the ceremony conducted by El Salvador is appropriate and proportionate to the severity of the violations whose reparation is sought and that the declarations of the President of the Republic were designed to recover the memory of the victims, recognize their dignity, and console their relatives. [525] [329] Therefore, the Court considers that it is not necessary to order another public act of acknowledgment of international responsibility in relation to the facts of this case and, in addition, it assesses positively the State's initiative to hold talks with the victims on the other measures of reparation to be implemented. Lastly, the Court urges the State to continue making the necessary arrangements to comply with the measures announced in the said speech.
b) Publication of the Judgment

361. Based on the nature and scale of the violations declared, the Court finds it appropriate to establish, as it has in other cases, [526][330] that the State must publish, within six months of notification of this Judgment:

    i.   The official summary of this Judgment prepared by the Court, once, in the Official Gazette;

    ii.   The official summary of this Judgment prepared by the Court, once, in a national newspaper with extensive circulation, and

    iii.   This Judgment in its entirety, available for one year, on an official website.

c) Production and diffusion of audiovisual material

362. In general terms, the Commission asked the Court to order the State to establish and disseminate the historical truth of the facts and to recover the memory of the deceased victims.

363. The representatives considered that it was essential that the State produce a video in which it informed society of the grave acts committed during the massacres of El Mozote and nearby places, which must also refer to the "scorched earth" policy, "in the context of which the events of the massacre occurred, and include information regarding the failure to investigate these grave events, [and also] an undertaking by the State that such events will not happen again." In this regard, they asked that all expenses for the production of the video be assumed by the State and that its content be approved by the victims and their representatives, before its transmission. They also asked that this video be broadcast in the audiovisual media with greatest national coverage, on at least three occasions separated by a month, at prime time, and that it be uploaded to the web page of the Salvadoran Armed Forces.

364. The State expressed its willingness to agree to, and to produce and disseminate an audiovisual presentation, within the reasonable time required by its nature.

365. The Court assesses positively the State's willingness to comply with the measure of reparation requested by the representatives in this aspect of the Judgment. In view of the circumstances of this case, the Court requires the preparation of an audiovisual documentary on the grave acts committed during the massacres of El Mozote and nearby places, which must also refer to the "scorched earth" policy in the context of the armed conflict in El Salvador, with specific mention of this case; its content must be agreed previously with the victims and their representatives. The State must assume all the expenses arising from the production and distribution of this video. The Court considers that the video must be distributed as extensively as possible among the victims, their representatives, and the country's schools and universities for its subsequent promotion and impact with the ultimate objective of informing Salvadoran society of these facts. The said video must be transmitted, at least once, on a national channel and during prime time, and

it must be uploaded to the web page of the Armed Forces of El Salvador. The State has two years from notification of this Judgment to comply with this measure.

___

Mendoza et al. v. Argentina
14-May-2013
Series C No. 260—*Preliminary objections, merits and reparations*

B.2. Satisfaction
B.2.1. Publication and dissemination of the pertinent parts of the judgment
   B.2.1.2. Considerations of the Court
320. The Court decides, as it has ordered in other cases, [392 331] that the State must publish once, within six months of notification of this Judgment, the official summary of the Judgment prepared by the Court in the official gazette and in a national newspaper with widespread circulation. The State must ensure that this newspaper also circulates widely in the province of Mendoza. In addition, Argentina must publish the complete judgment on an official website of the Judiciary of the Autonomous City of Buenos Aires and of the province of Mendoza, and of the prisons and juvenile institutions in both locations.

___

Gonzalez Lluy et al. v. Ecuador
1-Sept-2015
Series C No. 298—*Preliminary Objections, Merits and Reparations*

XII. REPARATIONS
C. Measures of restitution, rehabilitation and satisfaction, and guarantees of non-repetition
   C.3) Measures of satisfaction
      C.3.3) Scholarship
372. This Court notes that, in 2013, Talía entered the Universidad Estatal de Cuenca to study graphic design, but had to withdraw owing to health problems resulting from activities inherent in this field of study. Consequently, starting in 2015, Talía began to study social psychology at this university. Taking this into consideration, the Court appreciates the State's observation during the public hearing regarding the possibility of Talía being awarded a scholarship based on academic excellence. However, the Court observes that the scholarship that the State referred to corresponds to a general offer that the State makes to all Ecuadorian students who perform well academically; thus, it does not respond specifically to an acknowledgement of Talía's situation as a victim. Therefore, the

Court establishes that the State must grant Talía Gonzales Lluy a scholarship to continue her university studies that is not conditional on obtaining the marks that would earn her a scholarship based on academic excellence. The said scholarship must cover all the expenses until she concludes her studies, for both academic materials and living costs if necessary. The victim or her legal representatives have six months from notification of this Judgment to inform the State of her intention to receive this scholarship.

373. In addition, the State must award Talía a scholarship to undertake postgraduate studies "in any university in the world in which she is accepted." This scholarship must be awarded regardless of Talía's academic performance during her undergraduate studies, and must be awarded based on her condition of victim of the violations declared in this Judgment. To this end, once she graduates, Talía must inform the State and this Court within 24 months of the postgraduate studies she has decided to pursue, and that she has been accepted. The State must cover academic and living costs in advance, in keeping with the cost of living in the country in which Talía will pursue her studies,[380][332] so that the victim does not have to disburse the amounts corresponding to these items and then be reimbursed.

ANALYSIS AND QUESTIONS RAISED BY THE COURT'S JURISPRUDENCE

As demonstrated by the above case excerpts, the Inter-American Court of Human Rights frequently orders investigation as a measure of satisfaction in cases where the circumstances surrounding violations remain unknown or have been purposely obfuscated, as in many cases involving disappearances and killings, and including cases where families and communities seek the recovery of victims and the bodies of victims. Where impunity prevails and may have compounded the harm of human rights violations, the Court may order prosecution and, where applicable, punishment of those responsible for the violations. Such measures serve generally to uphold the rule of law and justice and specifically to help rectify the harm caused by the violations.

Central to the goal of satisfaction, as evidenced by the Court's jurisprudence, is the full disclosure of the facts surrounding violations (insofar as such disclosures do not cause further harm to victims, their next of kin, and witnesses and advocates). Satisfaction measures such as public apology, official acknowledgments of responsibility and tributes to victims are designed to rectify the moral harm caused by the violations and to restore the dignity, reputation and rights of the victims. The Court's consistent practice of including detailed factual accounts in its judgments and its frequent declaration that its "judgment constitutes *per se* a form of reparation" affirm the importance of the facts for victims whose rights have been violated. The discovery and disclosure of facts surrounding violations are equally important to the cessation of ongoing violations and are a fundamental basis for another form of reparation, that of guarantees of non-repetition. As with all forms of reparation, satisfaction measures are tailored to remedy the specific violations in each case and vary accordingly.

- Numerous cases before the Court have involved disappearances and killings, including *Velásquez Rodríguez*, *El Ámparo*, *Bulacio*, *Almonacid-Arellano et al.* and, more recently, *Radilla-Pacheco*, *Torres Millacura* and *Mendoza et al.* In each of these cases, the Court has ordered measures of satisfaction, specifically regarding the duty to conduct full, impartial and effective investigations into the facts of the disappearance or killing, and that such investigations may not be "mere formalit[ies] destined beforehand to be fruitless."[333] The Court has ordered effective punishment of the perpetrators, as in *El Ámparo*, and has emphasized that impunity is unacceptable. Similarly, in *Bulacio*, the Court also ordered effective judicial protection, such that human rights were protected and that impunity did not prevail. In *Almonacid-Arellano*, the Court emphasized these points further in stating that "the State may not invoke the statute of limitations, the non-retroactivity of criminal law or the *ne bis in idem* principle to decline its duty to investigate and punish those responsible," and that crimes against humanity are "neither susceptible of amnesty nor extinguishable."[334] Effective, impartial and full investigations, effective judicial protections, and sanctions against those responsible for violations are essential measures of satisfaction in cases where the facts and circumstances surrounding the violations remain unknown or have been obscured. Are there circumstances in which a full, impartial and effective investigation legitimately may not result in a full revelation of the facts surrounding the violations, or in the identification, prosecution and punishment of all of the perpetrators of a violation?
- A central concern of satisfaction is the revelation of truth, including the facts and circumstances surrounding the violations of human rights, and the full and public disclosure of the truth in each case. In *Saramaka People*, *Valle Jaramillo*, and the *"Cotton Field"* case, the Court ordered that the facts and circumstances of the violation be made public so that society was informed. Such judgments emphasize the importance of the truth not only to the victims and their families, but also to society at large. The Court has also stated

that the disclosure of the truth is necessary to prevent repetitions of such violations. What commonalities do these cases share? Based on these commonalities, in what other circumstances may the Court determine that society must be informed regarding the facts of a case?

- In each case in which the Court has ordered publication of a public apology or official acknowledgement of responsibility, or the creation of a memorial or tribute to the victims, the Court has deemed that such measures of satisfaction are necessary to restore the dignity of the victims, to serve as symbolic reparation to the victims, their families and their communities, and to provide victims, as well as society, with the truth and a greater awareness regarding the violations of human rights. Are such measures appropriate in all cases involving human rights violations? What commonalities exist amongst the cases in which the Court has ordered such measures? In what cases may such measures be unnecessary or inappropriate? In what circumstances may partial or full disclosures of the truth potentially cause further harm to victims, their families, or their communities? Should the Court determine whether partial or full disclosures of the truth are appropriate, or should victims and their advocates make such determinations?

VI. GUARANTEES OF NON-REPETITION

Guarantees of non-repetition are aimed at ensuring that further violations do not occur. As demonstrated by the following case excerpts, the measures ordered by the Inter-American Court of Human Rights as guarantees of non-repetition address the underlying causes of human rights violations and the circumstances that allow or encourage violations to occur. As measures of reparation, guarantees of non-repetition serve to prevent future violations, to cease ongoing violations, and to assure victims of past violations of recognition of the harm they have suffered and of action to prevent its repetition.

A. ORDERING LEGAL REFORM

El Ámparo v. Venezuela
14-Sep-1996
Series C No. 28—*Reparations and Costs*

52.   In the aforementioned brief of November 3, 1995, the Commission requested the reform of the Military Code of Justice, specifically Article 54(2) and (3), and of any military regulations and instructions that are incompatible with the Convention. That article states in its operative part that:

> [t]he President of the Republic, as a functionary of military justice, is empowered . . . 2) To order that a military trial not be held in certain cases, when he deems it in the national interest.
> 3) To order the discontinuance of military trials, when he deems it advisable, in any circumstances.

54.   In its aforementioned brief of January 3, 1996, the State claimed that the Commission's request bore no relation to the events and to the State's responsibility, inasmuch as redress necessitates restoring the situation that existed prior to the events that gave rise to its responsibility. It maintained that "*[n]othing that the Commission seeks in this regard can represent this type of restoration. The Code of Military Justice is not, per se, incompatible with the American Convention on Human Rights.*"

56.   In short, the Commission defines the non-pecuniary reparations as: reform of the Code of Military Justice and those military regulations and instructions that are incompatible with the Convention . . ..

57.   The State, for its part, contends that the impugned articles of the Code of Military Justice were not enforced in the instant case and merely constitute a prerogative of the President of the Republic, that the victims have received satisfaction through Venezuela's acceptance of responsibility, and that the non-pecuniary reparations are inconsistent with international jurisprudence in general and with that of this Court in particular.

58.   In connection with the foregoing, the Court considers that, in effect, Article 54 of the aforementioned Code, which grants the President of the Republic the power to order that a military trial not be held in specific cases when he deems it in the national interest and to order the discontinuance of military trials at any stage, has not been enforced in the instant case. The military authorities charged and prosecuted those responsible for the El Amparo case, and the President of the Republic never ordered the cessation, or any discontinuance, of the trial.

59.   In Advisory Opinion OC-14/94, this Court stipulated:

> The contentious jurisdiction of the Court is intended to protect the rights and freedoms of specific individuals, not to resolve abstract questions. There is no provision in the Convention authorizing the Court, under its contentious jurisdiction, to determine whether a law that has not yet affected the guaranteed rights and freedoms of specific individuals is in violation of the Convention. As has already been noted, the Commission has

that power and, in exercising it, would fulfill its main function of promoting respect for and defense of human rights. The Court also could do so in the exercise of its advisory jurisdiction, pursuant to Article 64(2) [of the Convention]. [International Responsibility for the Promulgation and Enforcement of Laws in Violation of the Convention (Arts. 1 and 2, American Convention on Human Rights) Advisory Opinion OC-14/94 of December 9, 1994. Series A No. 14, para. 49.]

60.   The Court, pursuant to the above Advisory Opinion, abstains from making a pronouncement in the abstract on the compatibility of Venezuela's Code of Military Justice, and its regulations and instructions, with the American Convention, and therefore does not deem it appropriate to order the Venezuelan State to undertake the reforms sought by the Commission.

CONCURRING OPINION OF JUDGE A. A. CANÇADO TRINDADE

I concur with the decision of the Court. I understand that at this stage an express clarification should have been added to the effect that the faculty reserved by the Court, in item 4 of the judgment, also extends to examining and deciding upon the request made by the Inter-American Commission on Human Rights (point 5) as to the incompatibility or otherwise of sections 2 and 3 of Article 54 of the Code of Military Justice of Venezuela with the object and purpose of the American Convention on Human Rights.

"The Last Temptation of Christ" (Olmedo Bustos et al.) v. Chile
5-Feb-2001
Series C No. 73—*Merits, Reparations, and Costs*

1.   . . . The Commission filed this case for the Court to decide whether Chile had violated Articles 13 (Freedom of Thought and Expression) and 12 (Freedom of Conscience and Religion) of the Convention. The Commission also requested the Court to declare that, as a result of the [alleged] violations of the said articles, Chile had failed to fulfill Articles 1(1) (Obligation to Respect Rights) and 2 (Domestic Legal Effects) of the Convention.

2.   According to the petition, the said violations were committed to the detriment of Chilean society and, in particular, Juan Pablo Olmedo Bustos, Ciro Colombara López, Claudio Márquez Vidal, Alex Muñoz Wilson, Matías Insunza Tagle, and Hernán Aguirre Fuentes, as a result of the "judicial censorship of the cinematographic exhibition of the film "The Last Temptation of Christ", confirmed by the Supreme Court of Chile . . . on June 17, 1997."

[Reparations and Costs]

84.   While Article 2 of the Convention establishes that:

Where the exercise of any of the rights or freedoms referred to in Article 1 is not already ensured by legislative or other provisions, the States Parties undertake to adopt, in accordance with their constitutional processes and the provisions of this Convention, such legislative or other measures as may be necessary to give effect to those rights or freedoms.

85.   The Court has indicated that the general obligations of the State, established in Article 2 of the Convention, include the adoption of measures to suppress laws and practices of any kind that imply a violation of the guarantees established in the Convention, and also the adoption of laws and the implementation of practices leading to the effective observance of the said guarantees.[20][335]   [See *Castillo Petruzzi et al. v. Peru*, Series C No. 52]

86.   The Court observes that, in accordance with the findings of this judgment, the State violated Article 13 of the American Convention to the detriment of Juan Pablo Olmedo Bustos, Ciro Colombara López, Claudio Márquez Vidal, Alex Muñoz Wilson, Matías Insunza Tagle, and Hernán Aguirre Fuentes because it has failed to comply with the general obligation to respect the rights and freedoms recognized in the Convention and to guarantee their free and full exercise, as established in its Article 1(1).

87.   In international law, customary law establishes that a State that has ratified a human rights treaty must introduce the necessary modifications to its domestic law to ensure the proper compliance with the obligations it has assumed. This law is universally accepted and is supported by jurisprudence.[21][336]   The American Convention establishes the general obligation of each State Party to adapt its domestic law to the provisions of this Convention, in order to guarantee the rights that it embodies. This general obligation of the State Party implies that the measures of domestic law must be effective (the principle of *effet utile*). This means that the State must adopt all measures so that the provisions of the Convention are effectively fulfilled in its domestic legal system, as Article 2 of the Convention requires. Such measures are only effective when the State adjusts its actions to the Convention's rules on protection.

88.   In this case, by maintaining cinematographic censorship in the Chilean legal system (Article 19(12) of the Constitution and Decree Law 679), the State is failing to comply with the obligation to adapt its domestic law to the Convention in order to make effective the rights embodied in it, as established in Articles 2 and 1(1) of the Convention.

97.   With regard to Article 13 of the Convention, the Court considers that the State must modify its legal system in order to eliminate prior censorship and allow

the cinematographic exhibition and publicity of the film "The Last Temptation of Christ" because it is obliged to respect the right to freedom of expression and to guarantee its free and full exercise to all persons subject to its jurisdiction.

98.	With regard to Articles 1(1) and 2 of the Convention, the norms of Chilean domestic legislation that govern the exhibition and publicity of cinematographic production have still not been adapted to the provision of the American Convention that prior censorship is prohibited. Therefore, the State continues to fail to comply with the general obligations referred to in those provisions of the Convention. Consequently, Chile must adopt the appropriate measures to reform its domestic laws, as set out in the previous paragraph, in order to ensure the respect and enjoyment of the right to freedom of thought and expression embodied in the Convention.

Herrera-Ulloa v. Costa Rica
2-Jul-2004
Series C No. 107—*Preliminary Objections, Merits, Reparations and Costs*

1. On January 28, 2003, the Inter-American Commission on Human Rights (hereinafter "the Commission" or "the Inter-American Commission") filed an application with the Court against the State of Costa Rica (hereinafter "the State" or "Costa Rica") based on petition No. 12,367, received at the Commission's Secretariat on March 1, 2001.

2. The Commission filed the application pursuant to Article 51 of the American Convention, for the Court to decide whether the State had violated Article 13 (Freedom of Thought and Expression), in combination with the obligations set forth in articles 1(1) (Obligation to Respect Rights) and 2 (Domestic Legal Effects) of the Convention, to the detriment of Mauricio Herrera Ulloa and Fernán Vargas Rohrmoser by its criminal conviction of Mr. Herrera Ulloa on four counts of publishing insults constituting defamation of a public official. His conviction carried with it all the attendant consequences under Costa Rican law, including civil liabilities.

3. The facts submitted by the Commission concern violations [alleged] to have been committed by the State by virtue of the November 12, 1999 conviction. That conviction was a consequence of the fact that on May 19, 20 and 21, and December 13, 1995, the newspaper *"La Nación"* had carried a number of articles by journalist Mauricio Herrera Ulloa that partially reproduced several articles from the Belgian press. The Belgian press reports had attributed certain illegal acts to Félix Przedborski, Costa Rica's honorary representative to the International Atomic Energy Agency in Austria. The November 12, 1999 judgment, delivered by the Criminal Court of the First Judicial Circuit of San José, found Mr.

Mauricio Herrera Ulloa guilty on four counts of publishing insults constituting defamation and ordered him to pay a fine; *La Nación* was ordered to publish the "Now Therefore" portion of the court's judgment. The court also upheld the claim for civil damages. It found Mr. Mauricio Herrera Ulloa and *La Nación* jointly and severally liable and ordered them to pay a compensation for the moral damage caused by the articles carried in *La Nación,* and to pay court costs and personal damages as well. The judgment also ordered *La Nación* to remove the link at the *"La Nación Digital"* website between the surname Przedborski and the impugned articles, and to create a link between those articles and the operative part of the court's judgment. Finally, the Commission pointed out that under Costa Rican law, Mr. Herrera Ulloa's conviction meant that his name was entered into the Judiciary's Record of Convicted Felons. In addition to the foregoing, the Commission reported that on April 3, 2001, the Criminal Court of the First Judicial Circuit of San José issued an order demanding that Mr. Fernán Vargas Rohrmoser, legal representative of the *"La Nación"* newspaper, pay the penalty the court imposed on that newspaper in the November 12, 1999 judgment, warning that failure to do so might constitute the crime of contempt of authority.

4. The Commission also asked the Court to order the State to award compensation for the damages caused to the [alleged] victims; to nullify and eliminate all the consequences that followed from Mr. Mauricio Herrera Ulloa's conviction, and the effects the Costa Rican domestic court's judgment had *vis-à-vis* Mr. Fernán Vargas Rohrmoser: to vacate the order to remove the link at the *"La Nación" Digital* website between the surname Przedborski and the impugned articles; to eliminate the link between those articles and the operative part of the court's decision to convict; to remove Mr. Herrera Ulloa's name from the Judiciary's Record of Convicted Felons; and to vacate the order to establish a link at the *"La Nación" Digital* website between the articles and the operative part of the judgment. The Commission also asked the Court to order the State to amend its criminal laws to comport with the provisions of the American Convention. Finally the Commission asked the Court to order the State to pay the legal costs and expenses incurred by the [alleged] victims.

XIII
REPARATIONS (Application of Article 63(1) of the Convention)
Considerations of the Court

191. As recounted in the preceding chapters, the Court has found that by the events in this case, the State violated articles 13 and 8(1) of the American Convention, in relation to articles 1(1) and 2 thereof, to the detriment of Mr. Mauricio Herrera Ulloa. In its case law, this Court has established that it is a principle of international law that any violation of an international obligation that has caused damage creates a new obligation, which is to adequately redress the wrong done.

[124][337] Here, the Court stands on Article 63(1) of the American Convention, which holds that [i]f the Court finds that there has been a violation of a right or freedom protected by this Convention, the Court shall rule that the injured party be ensured the enjoyment of his right or freedom that was violated. It shall also rule, if appropriate, that the consequences of the measure or situation that constituted the breach of such right or freedom be remedied and that fair compensation be paid to the injured party.

192. Reparation of the wrong caused by the violation of an international obligation requires, whenever possible, full restitution (*restitutio in integrum*), which is to restore the situation as it was prior to the violation.

193. The obligation to repair, which is regulated in all its aspects (scope, nature, modes and establishment of beneficiaries) by international law, cannot be modified by the State nor can the latter avoid complying with it by invoking provisions of its domestic law. [125][338]

194. As the term implies, reparations are measures intended to erase the effects of the violations committed. In this respect, the reparations established should be in relation to the violations that have previously been declared.

195. The Court has determined that the November 12, 1999 judgment delivered by the Criminal Court of the First Judicial Circuit of San José that convicted Mr. Mauricio Herrera Ulloa of a crime, had the effect of violating his right to freedom of thought and expression (*supra* paragraphs 130, 131, 132, 133 and 135). For that reason, the State must nullify that judgment and all the measures it ordered, including any involving third parties. The effects of the Criminal Court of the First Judicial Circuit of San Jose judgment re as follows: 1) Mr. Mauricio Herrera Ulloa was declared guilty on four counts of the crime of publishing offenses constituting defamation; 2) the penalty imposed on Mr. Herrera Ulloa consisted of 40 days' fine per count, at ¢2,500.00 (two thousand five hundred colones) a day, for a total of 160 days' fine. In application of the rule of *concurso material* (where a number of related crimes are combined to reduce the penalty that would have been required had each separate crime carried its own weight), "the fine [wa]s reduced to be three times the maximum imposed"; in other words, the fine was reduced from 160 to 120 days, for a total of ¢300,000.00 (three hundred thousand colones); 3) in the civil award, Mr. Mauricio Herrera Ulloa and the newspaper "*La Nación,*" represented by Mr. Fernán Vargas Rohrmoser, were held jointly and severally liable and ordered to pay ¢60,000,000.00 (sixty million colones) for the moral damages caused by the articles carried in "*La Nación*" on March 19, 20, and 21, 1995, and then again on December 13, 1995; 4) Mr. Mauricio Herrera Ulloa was ordered to publish the "Now, Therefore" portion of the judgment in the newspaper "*La Nación*", in the section called "El País," in the same print face used for the articles about which the criminal complaint was filed; 5) "*La*

Nación" was ordered to take down the link at the *La Nación Digital* website on the internet, between the surname Przedborski and the articles about which the criminal complaint was filed; 6) *"La Nación"* was ordered to create a link at the *La Nación Digital* website on the internet between the articles about which the complaint was filed and the operative part of the judgment; 7) Mr. Herrera Ulloa and the newspaper *"La Nación,"* represented by Mr. Fernán Vargas Rohrmoser, were ordered to pay court costs in the amount of ¢1,000.00 (one thousand colones) and personal damages totaling ¢3,810,000.00 (three million eight hundred ten thousand colones); and 8) Mr. Mauricio Herrera Ulloa's name was entered into the Judiciary's Record of Convicted Felons. The Court finds that the State must take all necessary judicial, administrative and any other measures to nullify and abolish any and all effects of the November 12, 1999 judgment.

196. By an order dated September 7, 2001, the Court ordered the State to adopt provisional measures on behalf of Mr. Mauricio Herrera Ulloa (*supra para.* 17), as follows: "a) to adopt forthwith those measures necessary to suspend the entry of Mauricio Herrera Ulloa's name in the Judiciary's Record of Convicted Felons; b) to suspend the order for *"La Nación"* to publish the "Now Therefore" portion of the conviction handed down by the San José First Circuit Criminal Trial Court on November 12, 1999; c) to suspend the order to create a "link" at the *La Nación Digital* website between the disputed articles and the operative part of that court judgment. In other words, the Court had ordered a stay of some of the effects of the November 12, 1999 ruling, and had further ordered that it should remain in place "until such time as the bodies of the inter-American system for the protection of human rights ha[d] arrived at a final decision on the case." Given what the Court set out in the preceding paragraph, it considers that the State's obligations vis-à-vis the ordered provisional measures are now replaced by the obligations ordered in the present judgment, effective as of the date of its notification.

197. The Court further considers that the State must respect and ensure the right to freedom of thought and expression, in the terms of Article 13 of the American Convention and the present judgment.

198. The Court also considers that within a reasonable period of time, the State must adapt its domestic legal system to conform to the provisions of Article 8(2) (h) of the Convention, in relation to Article 2 thereof.

199. With regard to the claim seeking reimbursement of the payment that would be made if the civil damages, court costs and personal damages ordered in the November 12, 1999 court judgment are enforced, the Court understands that this claim has been settled by the Court's decision regarding nullification of the effects of that judgment (*supra para.* 195).

Moiwana Community v. Suriname
15-Jun-2005
Series C No. 124—*Preliminary Objections, Merits, Reparations, and Costs*

D) Other Forms of Reparation (Satisfaction measures and non-repetition guarantees)

201. In this chapter, the Court will determine the measures of satisfaction to repair non-pecuniary damages; such measures seek to impact the public sphere.[108] [339] These measures have special significance in the instant case, given the extreme gravity of the facts and the collective nature of the damages suffered.

b) Collective title to traditional territories

209. In light of its conclusions in the chapter concerning Article 21 of the American Convention, the Court holds that the State shall adopt such legislative, administrative, and other measures as are necessary to ensure the property rights of the members of the Moiwana community in relation to the traditional territories from which they were expelled, and provide for their use and enjoyment of those territories. These measures shall include the creation of an effective mechanism for the delimitation, demarcation, and titling of said traditional territories.

210. The State shall take these measures with the participation and informed consent of the victims as expressed through their representatives, the members of the other Cottica N'djuka villages and the neighboring indigenous communities, including the community of Alfonsdorp.

211. Until the Moiwana community members' right to property with respect to their traditional territories is secured, Suriname shall refrain from actions—either of State agents or third parties acting with State acquiescence or tolerance—that would affect the existence, value, use, or enjoyment of the property located in the geographical area where the Moiwana community members traditionally lived until the events of November 29, 1986.

c) State guarantees of safety for those community members who decide to return to Moiwana Village

212. The Court is aware that the Moiwana community members do not wish to return to their traditional lands until: 1) the territory is purified according to cultural rituals, and 2) they no longer fear that further hostilities will be directed toward their community. Neither of these elements is possible without an effective investigation and judicial process, leading to the clarification of the facts and punishment of the responsible parties. As these processes are carried out and led to conclusion, only the community members themselves can decide when exactly it would be appropriate to return to Moiwana Village. When community members eventually are satisfied that the necessary conditions have been reached so as to permit their return, the State shall guarantee their safety. To that effect,

upon the community members' return to Moiwana Village, the State shall send representatives every month to Moiwana Village during the first year, in order to consult with the Moiwana residents. If the community members express concern regarding their safety during those monthly meetings, the State must take appropriate measures to guarantee their security, which shall be designed in strict consultation with said community members.

d) Developmental fund

213.   As the 1986 military operation destroyed Moiwana Village property and forced survivors to flee, both the representatives and the Commission have emphasized the necessity of implementing a developmental program that would provide basic social services to the community members upon their return. The State, for its part, has shown willingness "to pay for the reasonable costs of survivors and family members to commence cultural activities,. . . with regard to the occurrences (of November 29, 1986)."

214.   In that regard, this Court rules that Suriname shall establish a developmental fund to consist of US$1,200,000 (one million, two hundred thousand United States dollars), which will be directed to health, housing, and educational programs for the Moiwana community members. The specific aspects of said programs shall be determined by an implementation committee, which is described in the following paragraph, and shall be completed within a period of five years from the date of notification of the present judgment.

215.   The above-mentioned committee will be in charge of determining how the developmental fund is implemented and will be comprised of three members. The committee shall have a representative designated by the victims and another shall be chosen by the State; the third member shall be selected through an agreement between the representatives of the victims and the State. If the State and the representatives of the victims have not arrived at an agreement regarding the composition of the implementation committee within six months from the date of notification of the present judgment, the Court will convene them to a meeting in order to decide upon the matter.

8-Feb-2006

Series C No. 145—*Interpretation of the June 15, 2005 Judgment on the Preliminary Objections*

19.   . . . The Court deems it pertinent to point out that, by recognizing the right of the Moiwana community members to the use and enjoyment of their traditional lands, the Court has not made any determination as to the appropriate boundaries of the territory in question. Rather, in order to render effective "the property rights of the members of the Moiwana community in relation to the traditional territories from which they were expelled," and having acknowledged the lack of "formal legal title," the Court has directed the State, as a measure of reparation,

to "adopt such legislative, administrative, and other measures as are necessary to ensure" those rights, after due consultation with the neighboring communities. If said rights are to be properly ensured, the measures to be taken must naturally include "the delimitation, demarcation, and titling of said traditional territories" with the participation and informed consent of the victims as expressed through their representatives, the members of the other Cottica N'djuka villages, and the neighboring indigenous communities. In this case, the Court has simply left the designation of the territorial boundaries in question to "an effective mechanism" of the State's design.

YATAMA v. Nicaragua
23-Jun-2005
Series C No. 127—*Preliminary Objections, Merits, Reparations and Costs*

c)   **Reforms to Electoral Act No. 331 of 2000 and other measures**
259.   The State must reform the regulation of the requirements established in Electoral Act No. 331 of 2000 that, it has been declared, violate the Convention and adopt, within a reasonable time, the necessary measures to ensure that the members of the indigenous and ethnic communities may participate in the electoral processes effectively, . . . taking into account their traditions, practices, and customs, within the framework of a democratic society. The requirements established should permit and encourage the members of these communities to have adequate representation that allows them to intervene in decision-making processes on national issues that concern society as a whole and on specific matters that pertain to these communities; therefore, these requirements should not constitute barriers for such political participation.

Girls Yean and Bosico v. Dominican Republic
8-Sep-2005
Series C No. 130—*Preliminary Objections, Merits, Reparations, and Costs*

2.   The Commission submitted the application based on Article 61 of the American Convention, for the Court to declare the international responsibility of the Dominican Republic for the [alleged] violation of Articles 3 (Right to Juridical Personality), 8 (Right to a Fair Trial), 19 (Rights of the Child), 20 (Right to Nationality), 24 (Right to Equal Protection) and 25 (Right to Judicial Protection) of the American Convention, in relation to Articles 1(1) (Obligation to Respect Rights) and 2 (Domestic Legal Effects) thereof, to the detriment of the children Dilcia Oliven Yean and Violeta Bosico Cofi[1] (hereinafter "the children Dilcia

Yean and Violeta Bosico", "the Yean and Bosico children," "the children Dilcia and Violeta," "the children" or "the [alleged] victims"), with regard to the facts that have occurred and the rights that have been violated since March 25, 1999, the date on which the Dominican Republic accepted the contentious jurisdiction of the Court.

3.   In its application, the Commission [alleged] that the State, through its Registry Office authorities, had refused to issue birth certificates for the Yean and Bosico children, even though they were born within the State's territory and that the Constitution of the Dominican Republic (hereinafter "the Constitution") establishes the principle of *ius soli* to determine those who have a right to Dominican citizenship. The Commission indicated that the State obliged the [alleged] victims to endure a situation of continued illegality and social vulnerability, violations that are even more serious in the case of children, since the Dominican Republic denied the Yean and Bosico children their right to Dominican nationality and let them remain stateless persons until September 25, 2001. According to the Commission, the child Violeta Bosico was unable to attend school for one year owing to the lack of an identity document. The Commission also alleges that the absence of a mechanism or procedure for an individual to appeal a decision of the Registry Office before a judge of first instance, and also the discriminatory acts of the Registry Office officials, who did not allow the [alleged] victims to obtain their birth certificate, violate specific rights embodied in the Convention. The Commission requested the Court to order the State to grant reparations that make full amends for the [alleged] violations of the children's rights. It also requested that the State adopt the legislative and other measures necessary to ensure respect for the rights embodied in the Convention and establish guidelines that contain reasonable requirements for the late registration of births and do not impose excessive or discriminatory obligations, so as to facilitate the registration of Dominican-Haitian children. Lastly, the Commission requested the Court to order the State to pay the reasonable costs and expenses arising from processing the case in the domestic jurisdiction and before the organs of the Inter-American System.

c)   **Regarding the norms on late birth registration in the civil status registry**

236.   The State should adopt "the legislative or other measure necessary to make effective" the rights established in the American Convention. This is an obligation the State should fulfill because it has ratified this legal instrument.[120][340]

237.   Given the characteristics of this case, the Court finds it necessary to refer to the context of late registration of birth in the Dominican Republic. In this regard, the United Nations Committee on the Rights of the Child has recommended that the Dominican Republic:

strengthen and increase its measures to ensure the immediate registration of the birth of all children. Special emphasis should be placed on the registration of children belonging to the most vulnerable groups, including children of Haitian origin or belonging to Haitian migrant families.[121 341]

238.   The Court has noted that the Dominican Republic modified its legislation and, in particular, the norms applicable to late registration of birth, while this case was being heard by the organs of the Inter-American system for the protection of human rights.

239.   The Court finds that, pursuant to Article 2 of the American Convention and within a reasonable time, the Dominican Republic should adopt within its domestic laws, the legislative, administrative and any other measures needed to regulate the procedure and requirements for acquiring Dominican nationality by late declaration of birth. This procedure must be simple, accessible, and reasonable, because, to the contrary, applicants could remain stateless. Furthermore, there must be an effective recourse for cases in which the request is refused.

240.   The Court finds that, when establishing the requirements for late registration of birth, the State should take into consideration the particularly vulnerable situation of Dominican children of Haitian origin. The requirements should not constitute an obstacle for obtaining Dominican nationality and should be only those essential for establishing that the birth occurred in the Dominican Republic. In this regard, the identification of the father or the mother of the child cannot be restricted to the presentation of the identity card; rather, for this purpose, the State should accept another appropriate public document, since the said identity card is only held by Dominican citizens. Moreover, the requirements should be specified clearly and be standardized, and their application should not be left to the discretion of State officials, in order to guarantee the legal certainty of those who use this procedure and to ensure an effective guarantee of the rights embodied in the American Convention, pursuant to Article 1(1) of the Convention.

241.   The State should also take the permanent measures necessary to facilitate the early and opportune registration of children, irrespective of their parentage or origin, so as to reduce the number of individuals who resort to the procedure of late registration of birth.

Sawhoyamaxa Indigenous Community v. Paraguay
29-Mar-2006
Series C No. 146—*Merits, Reparations, and Costs*

c)   Adapting domestic legislation to the American Convention
234.   In the answer to the application, the State "acquiesced" to the request made

by the Inter-American Commission and the representatives "for the enactment and enforcement of legislation contemplating an effective and expedient remedy to solve conflicts of rights as those at issue in the instant case."

235.   Based on the above and in view of the conclusions reached by the Court in the chapters relating to Articles 8, 21, 25, and 2 of the American Convention, the Court finds that the State shall guarantee the effective exercise of the rights contemplated in its Political Constitution and domestic legislation, pursuant to the American Convention. Consequently, the State shall, within a reasonable time, enact into its domestic legislation, as per Article 2 of the American Convention, the legislative, administrative, and other measures necessary to provide an efficient mechanism to claim the ancestral lands of indigenous peoples, enforcing their property rights and taking into consideration their customary law, values, practices, and customs.

Yvon Neptune v. Haití
6-Jul-2008
Series C No. 180—*Merits, Reparations, and Costs*

2.   The Commission considered that "a Court judgment in this case [the first contentious case filed before the Court against Haiti,] would not only seek to redress the violations against Mr. Neptune, . . . but also has the potential to improve the situation of all detainees in Haiti suffering from similar circumstances of arbitrary arrest, prolonged pretrial detention, due process irregularities, and poor prison conditions, through the implementation of the necessary and appropriate reforms to the Haitian judicial system." The Commission requested the Court to declare the State responsible for the violation of Articles 5(1), 5(2), and 5(4) (Right to Humane Treatment), 7(4), 7(5)[,] and 7(6) (Right to Personal Liberty), 8(1), 8(2)(b), and 8(2)(c) (Right to a Fair Trial), 9 (Freedom from Ex Post Facto Laws) and 25(1) (Right to Judicial Protection) of the American Convention, all "in conjunction with" Article 1(1) (Obligation to Respect Rights) thereof, to the detriment of Mr. Yvon Neptune, [alleged] victim in this case. As a result of the above, the Commission requested the Court to order the State to adopt certain measures of reparation.

10.   With specific reference to Mr. Neptune, his mandate ended on March 12, 2004.[18 342] In this regard, the Commission indicated in its application that "the petitioners also claimed . . . that, shortly thereafter, threats made against Mr. Neptune's life forced him into hiding."[19 343] In March 2004, an investigating magistrate of the Court of First Instance of St. Marc issued an arrest warrant

against Mr. Neptune, "accused of having ordered and participated in the massacre of the population of La Scierie (Saint-Marc) and in the arson of several houses in February 2004."[20 344] Two days later, the Government of Haiti issued an order banning Mr. Neptune from leaving the country. Mr. Neptune was detained on June 27, 2004, when he turned himself into the police.[21 345] According to the Commission, at the time of his arrest, he was not informed of the reasons for his detention, nor was he informed of his rights.[22 346] The application also refers, inter alia, to the fact that the State did not bring Mr. Neptune promptly before a judge or other judicial official authorized by law to exercise judicial power; he was not granted recourse to a competent court to decide on the lawfulness of his arrest; his physical, mental and moral integrity was not guaranteed, nor his right to be separated from convicted criminals, given the conditions of his detention and the treatment he received. Mr. Neptune remained detained until July 27, 2006, first in the National Penitentiary of Port-au-Prince and later in the Annex to the National Penitentiary, from which he was released on humanitarian grounds.[23 347] The criminal proceedings against him remained open.

[*Reparations and Costs*]

181.   The appalling conditions of Haitian prisons and detention centers have been brought to light in this case. It is pertinent to recall that international human rights treaties, particularly the American Convention, oblige States to provide decent living conditions for persons deprived of liberty.

182.   Regarding the lack of security in the National Penitentiary, the Court has recognized that the State's international obligation to ensure to all persons the full exercise of their human rights includes the obligation "to design and apply a penitentiary policy that prevents critical situations" that endanger the fundamental rights of the prisoners in their custody.[227 348]

Radilla-Pacheco v. Mexico

23-Nov-2009

Series C No. 209—*Preliminary Objections, Merits, Reparations, and Costs*

C2. Reforms to legal stipulations

    i)   *Constitutional and legislative reforms in matters of military jurisdiction*

338. For this Tribunal, not only the suppression or issuing of the regulations within the domestic legislation guarantee the rights enshrined in the American Convention, pursuant with the obligation included in Article 2 of that instrument. The development of State practices leading to the effective observance of the

rights and liberties enshrined in the same is also required. Therefore, the existence of a regulation does not guarantee in itself that its application will be adequate. It is necessary that the application of the regulations or their interpretation, as jurisdictional practices and a manifestation of the state's public order, be adjusted to the same purpose sought by Article 2 of the Convention. [319] [349] In practical terms, the interpretation of Article 13 of the Political Constitution of Mexico shall be coherent with the conventional and constitutional principles of the due process of law and the right to a fair trial, included in Article 8(1) of the American Convention and the relevant regulations of the Mexican Constitution.

339. With regard to judicial practices, this Tribunal has established, in its jurisprudence, that it is aware that the domestic judges and tribunals are subject to the rule of law and that, therefore, they are compelled to apply the regulations in force within the legal system. [320] [350] But once a State has ratified an international treaty such as the American Convention, its judges, as part of the State's apparatus, are also submitted to it, which compels them to make sure that the provisions of the Convention are not affected by the application of laws contrary to its object and purpose, and that they do not lack legal effects from their creation. In other words, the Judiciary shall exercise a "control of conventionality" *ex officio* between domestic regulations and the American Convention, evidently within the framework of its respective competences and the corresponding procedural regulations. Within this task, the Judiciary shall take into consideration not only the treaty but also the interpretation the Inter-American Court, final interpreter of the American Convention, has made of it. [321] [351]

340. Therefore, it is necessary that the constitutional and legislative interpretations regarding the material and personal competence criteria of military jurisdiction in Mexico be adjusted to the principles established in the jurisprudence of this Tribunal, which have been reiterated in the present case (*supra* paras. 272 through 277).

341. As per this understanding, this Tribunal considers that it is not necessary to order the modification of the regulatory content included in Article 13 of the Political Constitution of the United Mexican States.

342. Despite the aforementioned, the Court stated in Chapter IX of the present Judgment that Article 57 of the Military Criminal Code is incompatible with the American Convention (*supra* paras. 287 and 289). Therefore, the State shall adopt, within a reasonable period of time, the appropriate legislative reforms in order to make the mentioned provision compatible with the international standards of the field and of the Convention, pursuant with paragraphs 272 through 277 of this Judgment.*ii) Adequate definition of the crime of forced disappearance of persons: reforms to Article*

215-A of the Federal Criminal Code pursuant with international instruments

344. In the present Judgment the Court established Article 215 A of the Federal

Criminal Code, which punishes the crime of forced disappearance of persons, does [not] fully and effectively adjust to international regulations in force in this subject (*supra* para. 324). Therefore, the State shall adopt all the measures necessary to make that legal classification compatible with the international standards, paying special attention to that stated in Article II of the CIDFP, pursuant with the criteria previously established in paragraphs 320 through 324 of the present judgment. This obligation is binding for [all] the state's powers and bodies as a whole. In that sense, the State shall not limit its actions to "promoting" the corresponding bill, but it shall guarantee its prompt sanction and entry into force, pursuant with the procedures established in its domestic legal system in that sense.

Fernandez Ortega et al. v. Mexico
30-Aug-2010
Series C No. 215—*Preliminary Objections, Merits, Reparations, and Costs*

ii) Adaptation of domestic law to the international standards of justice
233.   The Commission asked the Court to order Mexico to limit and restrict the scope of the military jurisdiction, excluding it from hearing cases in which human rights violations have been committed and, particularly, cases of sexual abuse.
234.   On its behalf, the representatives asked the Court to order the State to reform Article 13 of the Political Constitution and Article 57 of the Code of Military Justice in order to establish clearly and without any ambiguity that the military system of justice must abstain, whatsoever the circumstances, from hearing cases of human rights violations attributed to members of the Mexican armed forces, whether or not they are on active service. Furthermore, they asked the Court to order the Mexican State to carry out legislative reforms in order to provide the victims of an offense or the aggrieved parties with access to an effective remedy for the protection of their rights and, specifically, to contest the submission of their case to the military jurisdiction.
235.   In the Court's opinion, it is not only the enactment or the suppression of domestic legal provisions that guarantee the rights contained in the American Convention. Pursuant to the obligation established in its Article 2 of said instrument, the State must also develop practices leading to the effective observance of the rights and freedoms embodied in the Convention. The existence of a norm does not, in and of itself, guarantee that its application will be adequate. The application of the norms or their interpretation, as jurisdictional practices and expressions of the State's public order, must be adapted to the objective sought by Article 2 of the Convention. In practical terms, as the Court has already established, the

interpretation of Article 13 of the Mexican Constitution must be coherent with the constitutional and the treaty-based principles of due process and access to justice contained in Article 8(1) of the American Convention and the pertinent provisions of the Mexican Constitution.[245][352]

236.   In its jurisprudence, the Court has established its awareness that domestic authorities are subject to the rule of law and, consequently, that they are obliged to apply the provisions of the laws that are in force in the legal code.[246] [353] Nevertheless, when a State is a party to an international treaty such as the American Convention, its judges, as part of the State apparatus, are also subject to such a treaty, and this obliges them to ensure that the effects of the provisions of the Convention are not diminished by the application of norms contrary to its object and purpose. The Judicial branch must exercise control *ex officio* of the harmonization of the domestic norms with the American Convention, evidently within the framework of their respective competences and the corresponding procedural rules. In this task, the judicial branch should bear in mind not only the treaty, but also the interpretation of it made by the Inter-American Court, definitive interpreter of the American Convention.[247][354]

237.   Hence, the constitutional and legislative interpretations concerning the criteria for the personal and subject matter jurisdiction of the military jurisdiction in Mexico needs to be adapted to the principles established in the Court's jurisprudence, which have been reiterated in the present case. This implies that, irrespective of the reforms to the law that the State may adopt (*infra* paras. 239 and 240), in this case, it is incumbent on the judicial authorities, based on the "control of the harmonization of domestic law with the Convention," to order immediately and *ex officio* that the facts be heard by the ordinary criminal justice system.

238.   On the other hand, the Court recalls that it has already found, in the case of *Radilla Pacheco*, that it is not necessary to order the amendment of the normative content that regulates Article 13 of the Political Constitution of the United Mexican States.

239.   Furthermore, in Chapter IX of this Judgment, the Court has declared that Article 57.II.a of the Code of Military Justice is incompatible with the American Convention. Consequently, the Court reiterates to the State its obligation to harmonize, within a reasonable time, said provision with the international standards in this regard and with the Convention, in conformity with what is established in this Judgment.

240.   Finally, pursuant to that established in Chapter IX of this Judgment, Mrs. Fernández Ortega did not have an appropriate and effective remedy to contest the intervention of the military justice system. As a consequence, Mexico must adopt, also within a reasonable time, the relevant legislative reforms to allow those

affected by the intervention of the military forum to have available an effective remedy to contest its jurisdiction.

Rosendo Cantú et al. v. Mexico
31-Aug-2010
Series C No. 216—*Preliminary Objections, Merits, Reparations, and Costs*

ii) Adaptation of domestic law to the international standards of justice
216. The Commission requested the Court to order Mexico to limit and restrict the scope of the military jurisdiction, excluding it from hearing cases in which human rights violations have been committed and, particularly, in cases of sexual abuse.
217. The representatives asked the Court to order the State to reform Article 13 of the Constitution and Article 57 of the Code of Military Justice in order to establish clearly and without any ambiguity that the military system of justice must abstain, whatsoever the circumstances, from hearing cases of human rights violations attributed to members of the Mexican Armed Forces, whether or not they are on active duty, being that it considered the State has not fulfilled this obligation.
218. In the Court's opinion, it is not only the suppression or expedition of domestic legal provisions that guarantee the rights contained in the American Convention. Pursuant to the obligation established in its Article 2 thereof, the State must also develop practices leading to the effective observance of the rights and freedoms embodied in the Convention. The existence of a norm does not, in and of itself, guarantee that its application will be adequate. It is necessary that the application of the norms or their interpretation, as jurisdictional practices and expressions of the State's public order, must be adapted to the objective sought by Article 2 of the Convention. In practical terms, as the Court has already established, the interpretation of Article 13 of the Mexican Constitution must be coherent with the constitutional and the treaty-based principles of due process and access to justice contained in Article 8(1) of the American Convention and the pertinent provisions of the Mexican Constitution. [276][355]
219. In its jurisprudence, the Court has established its awareness that domestic authorities are subject to the rule of law, and consequently, that they are obliged to apply the provisions of the laws that are in force in the legal code. [277][356] Nevertheless, when a State has ratified an international treaty such as the American Convention, all of its organs, including its judges, as part of the State apparatus, are also subject to such a treaty, and this obligates them to ensure that the effects of the provisions of the Convention are not diminished by the application of norms contrary to its object and purpose. The Judicial Branch must exercise control *ex officio* of the harmonization of the domestic norms with the American

Convention, evidently within the framework of their respective jurisdictions and the corresponding procedural rules. In this task, the Judicial Branch should bear in mind not only the treaty, but also the corresponding interpretation made by the Inter-American Court, the definitive interpreter of the American Convention. [278][357]

220. Hence, the constitutional and legislative interpretations concerning the criteria for the personal and subject matter jurisdiction of the military jurisdiction in Mexico need to be adapted to the principles established in the Court's jurisprudence, which have been reiterated in the present case. This implies that, irrespective of the reforms to the law that the State may adopt (*infra* para. 222), in this case, it is incumbent on the judicial authorities, based on the control of the harmonization of domestic law with the Convention, to order immediately and *ex officio* that the facts be heard by the ordinary criminal justice system.

221. Moreover, the Court recalls that it has already found, in the case of *Radilla Pacheco*, that it is not necessary to order the amendment of the normative content that regulates Article 13 of the Political Constitution of the United Mexican States.

222. Furthermore, in Chapter IX of this Judgment, the Court has declared that Article 57 of the Code of Military Justice is incompatible with the American Convention (*supra* paras. 162 and 163). Consequently, the Court reiterates to the State its obligation to adopt, within a reasonable time, the legislative reforms applicable in order to harmonize the mentioned provision with the international standards in this regard and with the Convention, in keeping with that established in this Judgment.

223. Finally, pursuant to that established in Chapter IX of this Judgment, Mrs. Rosendo Cantú did not have an appropriate and effective remedy to contest the intervention of the military justice system (*supra* paras. 164 to 167). As a consequence, Mexico must adopt, also within a reasonable time, the relevant legislative reforms to allow those affected by the intervention of the military forum to have available an effective remedy to contest its jurisdiction.

v) Policy that guarantees access to justice of indigenous women and that respects their cultural identity

230. The Commission asked the Court to order the State to guarantee access to justice to indigenous women by way of the design of a policy that respects their cultural identity.

231. The State presented a large amount of information on the various actions and measures it has adopted to eradicate discriminatory practices, particularly against women and indigenous persons. The State made reference to, among other programs, the Intercultural Model for the Development of the Indigenous Peoples, facilitated by the Secretariat of Indigenous Affairs of the state of Guerrero. This program includes as one of its central points the legal reform and indigenous recognition, and its services are aimed at reviewing and systematizing laws to

formulate a reform proposal and bill on rights and culture in the state of Guerrero. Moreover, the Intercultural Model includes a Defense and Legal Aid Program for Indigenous Peoples, whose actions are aimed at offering defense services, legal aid, and administrative procedures in favor of the indigenous population. Likewise, Mexico also reported on the Program for the promotion of collaboration on justice in which projects have been carried out with civil organizations and the United Nations Fund for Women in order to promote the leadership of indigenous women in public matters. Lastly, during the public hearing, the State presented documentation relating to actions and programs in the area of gender and of indigenous peoples, including the Institutional and Social Enhancement Program for the Exercise of the Human Rights of Indigenous Women, prepared by the Government of the state of Guerrero, which proposes an "Intercultural and gender equity model for the exercise of the human rights of indigenous women."

232. The Court notes that the State provided certain information on programs and actions implemented in this sphere, whose existence or validity was not contested by the Commission, and to which the Commission did not provide any information indicating possible shortcomings. In this respect, the Court has already established that the obligation to motivate and establish a foundation for the Commission's claims for reparations and costs is not fulfilled by general requests without any legal or factual argumentation or evidence that would allow the Court to analyze their purpose, reasonableness, and scope. [284][358] This prevents the Court from ruling on the measure requested.

xii) Codification of the crime of torture in the Criminal Code of the state of Guerrero

254. The representatives requested the Court to order the State to appropriately codify the crime of torture in the criminal legislation of the state of Guerrero so that those involved in judicial operations of said state can effectively investigate and punish those responsible for the conducts that fall into said penal codification. In their final written arguments, the representatives requested that the Court order the State to "reform the norms in which the crime of torture in Guerrero is legislated," which "do not satisfy the minimum conventional standards, and which have been included in a normative body different from the state Criminal Code."

255. The Court determined in this case that the investigation for the crime of rape is not incompatible with the obligations of the Inter-American Convention to Prevent and Punish Torture (*supra* para. 186). For this reason, the Court considers that it is not necessary to address this requested measure of reparation.

xvii) Other measures requested

268. In its final written arguments, the Commission requested that Court to order the following additional measures of reparations from the State: i) to adopt, as a

priority, a comprehensive and coordinated policy, backed-up with the appropriate resources, to guarantee that cases of violence against women are properly prevented, investigated, punished, and that the victims receive reparations, and ii) to implement public policies and institutional programs designed to quash stereotypes regarding the role of women in society and to promote the eradication of socio-cultural discrimination patterns that prevent full access to justice for women, including training programs for government employees in all branches of the administration of justice, the police, and the comprehensive prevention policies. Furthermore, the representatives, also in their final written arguments, asked the Court to order the State of Mexico: i) to establish adequate and effective mechanisms for prior, free, and informed consent of the indigenous peoples or communities of Guerrero whenever legislative or administrative measures are adopted that would result in the presence of security forces, including soldiers, on their territory, or on the territory in which these communities reside, and ii) to establish adequate conditions for the victims to return to their native community, to which they request, *inter alia,* the restitution of their cultural heritage, the eradication of the risk and threat factors, the design of preventive and not culturally deterrent measures, and the provision of psycho emotional accompaniment that the victim so requires.

269. The Court observes that the Commission and the representatives did not submit these requests at the appropriate procedural opportunity, namely, in the brief containing the application and written brief of pleadings and motions. Consequently, the requests for these measures of reparation are time-barred and the Court will not consider them.

Atala Riffo and Daughters v. Chile
24-Feb-2012
Series C No. 239—*Merits, Reparations and Costs*

b. Adoption of domestic measures, reforms, and adaptation of laws against discrimination
Considerations of the Court
279. The Court recalls that Article 2 of the Convention requires States Parties to adopt, in accordance with their constitutional processes and the provisions of the Convention, the legislative or other measures necessary to render effective the rights and freedoms protected by the Convention. [281][359] In other words, the States not only have the positive obligation to adopt the legislative measures necessary to guarantee the exercise of the rights enshrined therein, but they must also avoid promulgating laws that may impede the free exercise of these rights, as well as prevent the amendment or suppression of any laws which protect those rights. [282][360]

280. In the case at hand, the Court limited itself to examining the relationship between the legal application of certain laws with possible discriminatory practices. The Court did not analyze the compatibility of a particular law with the American Convention, nor was this matter pertinent to the case. Also, the representatives did not provide sufficient facts that would suggest that the violations resulted from a problem with the laws *per se*. Therefore, the Court considers that it is not appropriate, in the circumstances of the present case, to order the adoption, modification or adjustment of specific domestic laws.

281. Furthermore, as previously established in its case law, this Court recalls that it is cognizant that the State authorities are subject to the rule of law and, therefore, are required to apply the provisions in force in their legal system. [283][361] But when a State is Party to an international agreement such as the American Convention, all its organs, including its judges and all other entities linked to the administration of justice, are also subject to it. This obliges them to remain vigilant and to ensure that the effects of the Convention's provisions are not impaired by the application of other laws contrary to its purpose and aim.

282. The judges and entities engaged in the administration of justice at all levels are required to undertake "Convention control" *ex officio* between domestic law and the American Convention in the context of their respective competencies and the corresponding procedural regulations. In this task, the judges and other organs of the justice system must take into account not only the Convention, but also the interpretation thereof by the Inter-American Court, in its role as the final authority on the interpretation of the American Convention.[284][362]

283. Thus, for example, the region's highest Courts, such as the Constitutional Chamber of the Supreme Court of Costa Rica,[285][363] the Constitutional Court of Bolivia,[286][364] the Supreme Court of Justice of the Dominican Republic,[287][365] the Constitutional Court of Peru,[288][366] the Supreme Court of Justice of Argentina,[289][367] the Constitutional Court of Colombia,[290][368] the Supreme Court of Mexico,[291][369] and the Supreme Court of Panama[292][370] have cited and applied such a control, taking into account the interpretations offered by the Inter-American Court.

284. In conclusion, based on the treaty control mechanism, legal and administrative interpretations and proper judicial guarantees should be applied in accordance with the principles established in the jurisprudence of this Court in the present case. [293][371] This is of particular importance in relation to sexual orientation as one of the prohibited categories of discrimination pursuant to Article 1.1 of the American Convention (*supra* paragraph C.2).

The Kichwa Indigenous People of Sarayaku v. Ecuador
27-Jun-2012
Series C No. 245—*Merits and reparations*

B.2 Guarantees of non-repetition
a) Due prior consultation

296. The Court has been informed by the State and the representatives that, in November 2010, PETROECUADOR and the CGC signed an Act of Termination by Mutual Agreement of the partnership contract for the exploration of hydrocarbons and exploitation of crude oil in Block 23 (*supra* para. 123). In addition, the representatives referred to several announcements by authorities of the State's hydrocarbons sector regarding a call for new bids for oil exploration in the south-central Amazonian region of Ecuador, in the provinces of Pastaza and Morona Santiago. In particular, it was [alleged] that at least eight blocks were to be exploited in the southeastern part of Amazonia, which includes the province of Pastaza, and that the new bidding round would include the Sarayaku territory.

297. Furthermore, it was reported that, in November 2010, the State had signed a "Contract modifying the contract for provision of services for the exploration and exploitation of hydrocarbons (crude oil) in Block 10" of the Ecuadorian Amazonian region [349] [372] with a company holding the concession for this new "Block 10," the redefined area of which would include a portion of around 80,000 hectares of Block 23. This would affect the territory of Kichwa communities in the upper watershed of the Bobonaza River and the Achuar Association of Shaime, as well as a portion of the Sarayaku territory.

298. In this regard, it should be recalled that, when acknowledging the State's responsibility in this case, the Secretary for Legal Affairs of the Presidency of the Republic of Ecuador stated that:

> [...] There will be no oil exploitation here without prior consultation. [...] No new round will begin without informed consultation. [...] We will not do any oil exploitation behind the back of the communities, but rather through the dialogue that will take place at some point, if we decide to begin oil exploitation [...] here. There will be no oil development without an open and frank dialogue; not a dialogue undertaken by the oil company, as has always been denounced. We have changed the law so that the dialogue is initiated by the Government and not by the extractive sector [...].

299. While it is not incumbent on the Court to rule on new oil bidding rounds that the State may have initiated, in the present case, the Court has determined that the State is responsible for the violation of the right to communal property of the Sarayaku People, because it failed to guarantee their right to consultation adequately. Consequently, as a guarantee of non-repetition, the Court stipulates that, in the event that the State should seek to carry out activities or projects for the exploration or extraction of natural resources, or any type of investment or

development plans that could eventually have an impact on the Sarayaku territory or affect essential aspects of their worldview or their life and cultural identity, the Sarayaku People shall be previously, adequately and effectively consulted, in full compliance with the relevant international standards.

300. In this regard, the Court recalls that the processes of participation and prior consultation must be conducted in good faith at all the preparation and planning stages of any project of this nature. Moreover, in keeping with the international standards applicable in such cases, the State must truly ensure that any plan or project that involves, or could potentially affect the ancestral territory, includes prior comprehensive studies on the environmental or social impact, prepared by independent, technically qualified entities, with the active participation of the indigenous communities concerned.

b) Regulation of prior consultation in domestic law

301. Regarding domestic laws that recognize the right to prior, free and informed consultation, the Court has already observed that, in the evolution of the international *corpus juris*, the 2008 Ecuadorian Constitution is one of the most advanced in the world in this area. However, the Court has also noted that the right to prior consultation has not been sufficiently and adequately regulated through appropriate norms for its practical implementation. Thus, under Article 2 of the American Convention, the State must adopt, within a reasonable time, any legislative, administrative or other type of measures that may be necessary to implement effectively the right to prior consultation of the indigenous and tribal peoples and communities, and amend those measures that prevent its full and free exercise and, to this end, the State must ensure the participation of the communities themselves.

Furlan and Family v. Argentina

31-Aug-2012

Series C No. 246—*Preliminary Objections, Merits, Reparations and Costs*

B.3) Guarantees of non-repetition

 B.3.1) Access to information on health and social security

Considerations of the Court

294. The Court has already confirmed the impact produced on the right to personal integrity of Sebastián Furlan due to lack of access to timely rehabilitation which would have provided him with better opportunities in life (*supra* paras. 197 to 203). Bearing in mind that the State has a legal framework that could prevent situations such as this from being repeated, the Court considers it important to enforce the obligation of active transparency in relation to the health and social security benefits to which people with disabilities are entitled in Argentina. This

imposes on the State the obligation to provide the public with the maximum amount of information, in a proactive manner, regarding the information needed to obtain said benefits. This information should be comprehensive, easily understood, available in simple language and up to date. Also, given that large segments of the population do not yet have access to new technologies, and yet many of these rights may depend on their obtaining information on how to exercise them, in these circumstances the State must find efficient ways to fulfill its obligation of active transparency. [459 373]

295. Consequently, the Court considers that within the framework of the implementation of Argentine laws that regulate access to health and social security benefits, the State must adopt the necessary measures to ensure that as soon as a person is diagnosed with serious problems or aftereffects related to disability, that person or his family is provided with a charter of rights that summarizes, in a concise, clear and accessible manner, the benefits contemplated in the aforementioned rules, the standards for the protection of persons with mental disabilities established in this Judgment and other related public policies, as well as the institutions that can provide assistance in demanding the fulfillment of their rights. The State shall report annually on the implementation of this measure for a period of three years, once implementation of said mechanism begins.

> *B.3.2) Legal reforms to civil proceedings and the execution of judgments in cases involving minors and persons with disabilities*

Considerations of the Court

300. The Court recalls that Article 2 of the Convention requires States Parties to adopt, based on their constitutional processes and the provisions of the Convention, such legislative or other measures as may be necessary to give effect to the rights or freedoms protected by the Convention. [460 374] In other words, States not only have the positive obligation to adopt the necessary legislative measures to guarantee the exercise of the rights embodied in the Convention, but they must also avoid promulgating laws that prevent the free exercise of those rights, and eliminate or amend laws that protect them. [461 375] Therefore, the Court recalls that, in the context of the obligations stemming from Articles 1(1) and 2 of the Convention, and according to the standards described in this Judgment (*supra* paras. 125 to 139), the States must take steps to reduce structural barriers or limitations and to give the appropriate preferential treatment to persons with disabilities, in order to achieve the objective of their full participation and equality within society.

301. In this case, the Court merely examined the duration of the judicial proceedings and the obstacles to access to health care, rehabilitation and social security services. The Court did not analyze the compatibility of a specific provision with the American Convention, which was not an element of this case. Moreover, the representatives did not provide sufficient evidence to allow the Court to infer that the violations declared in this case stem from a problem in the laws themselves.

Other proposed reforms relate to fundamental matters that are intrinsic to the regulation of the Argentine civil procedure. The representatives did not provide further information that would allow the Court to conclude that the regulation of the Argentine civil procedure, as established by the law, contains normative flaws in relation to the disputes examined in this case. Therefore, the Court abstains from ordering the legislative reforms requested by the representatives in respect of the amendment of the National Code of Civil and Commercial Procedure.

302. Furthermore, as established in its case law, the Court recalls that it is aware that the domestic authorities are subject to the rule of law and, thus, are obliged to apply the legislative provisions in force. [462 376] However, when a State is a party to an international treaty such as the American Convention, all its organs, including the judges and other bodies involved in the administration of justice, are also subject to it, which obliges them to ensure that the effects of the Convention's provisions are not lessened by the application of norms that are contrary to its object and purpose.

303. The judges and organs responsible for the administration of justice at all levels are obliged to exercise *ex officio* control to ensure that domestic norms are in line with the American Convention, within their respective spheres of competence and the corresponding procedural regulations. In this task, the judges and organs for the administration of justice must take into account not only the treaty, but also its interpretation by the Inter-American Court, as the final interpreter of the American Convention. [463 377]

304. Thus, for example, the highest courts of the region, such as the Constitutional Chamber of the Supreme Court of Justice of Costa Rica, [464 378] the Constitutional Court of Bolivia, [465 379] the Supreme Court of Justice of the Dominican Republic, [466 380] the Constitutional Court of Peru, [467 381] the Supreme Court of Justice of the Nation of Argentina, [468 382] the Constitutional Court of Colombia, [469 383] the Supreme Court of the Nation of Mexico, [470 384] and the Supreme Court of Panama[471 385] have all referred to and applied this control of compatibility with the Convention, taking into account interpretations made by the Inter-American Court.

305. In conclusion, based on the control of compatibility with the convention, and judicial and administrative interpretations, judicial guarantees must be applied in this case in accordance with the principles established in this Court's jurisprudence. [472 386] This is of particular relevance in light of the Court's observations concerning the need to take into account any situation of vulnerability facing a person, especially in the case of minors or persons with disabilities, in order to guarantee them a differentiated treatment with regard to the duration of judicial proceedings and also in the context of the proceedings in which the payment of court-ordered compensation is established (*supra* para. 204, 217 and 222).

Artavia Murillo et al. ("In Vitro Fertilization") v. Costa Rica
28-Nov-2012
Series C No. 257—*Preliminary objections, merits, reparations and costs*

B.3) Guarantees of non-repetition
    B.3.1) State measures that do not prevent the practice of IVF
Considerations of the Court
334. The Court recalls that the State must prevent the recurrence of human rights violations such as those that have occurred and, therefore, adopt all necessary legal, administrative and other measures to prevent similar events from occurring in the future, in compliance with its obligation of prevention and to guarantee the fundamental rights recognized by the American Convention. [497][387]
335. In particular, and in accordance with Article 2 of the Convention, the State has the obligation to adopt the necessary measures to ensure the enjoyment of the rights and freedoms recognized in the Convention. [498][388] In other words, States have not only the positive obligation to adopt the necessary legislative measures to ensure the enjoyment of the rights established in the Convention, but must also avoid enacting those laws that prevent the free exercise of these rights, and avoid the elimination or amendment of laws that protect them. [499][389]
336. First, and taking into account the considerations in this Judgment, the pertinent State authorities must take the appropriate measures to ensure that the prohibition of the practice of IVF is annulled as rapidly as possible so that those who wish to use this assisted reproduction technique may do so without encountering any impediments to the exercise of the rights that this Judgment has found to have been violated (*supra* para. 317). The State must provide information on the measures taken in this regard within six months.
337. Second, the State must, as soon as possible, regulate those aspects it considers necessary for the implementation of IVF, taking into account the principles established in this Judgment. In addition, the State must establish systems for the inspection and quality control of the qualified professionals and institutions that perform this type of assisted reproduction technique. The State must provide information every year on the gradual implementation of these systems.
338. Third, in the context of the considerations made in this Judgment (*supra* paras. 285 to 303), the Costa Rica Social Security Institute must make IVF available within its health care infertility treatments and programs, in accordance with the obligation to respect and guarantee the principle of non-discrimination. The State must provide information every six months on the measures adopted in order to make these services available gradually to those who require them and on the plans that it draws up to this end.

Mendoza et al. v. Argentina
14-May-2013
Series C No. 260—*Preliminary objections, merits and reparations*

B.3. Guarantees of non-repetition
B.3.1. Juvenile Criminal Regime
B.3.1.2. Considerations of the Court

323. The Court recalls that Article 2 of the Convention obliges the States Parties to adopt, in accordance with their constitutional processes and the provisions of the Convention, such legislative or other measures as may be necessary to give effect to those rights and freedoms protected by the Convention. [393][390] In other words, the States not only have the positive obligation to adopt the necessary legislative measures to guarantee the exercise of the rights established in the Convention, but must also avoid enacting laws that preclude the free exercise of those rights, and prevent the annulment or amendment of laws that protect them. [394][391] Nevertheless, in its case law, the Court has established that it is aware that domestic authorities are subject to the rule of law. [395][392] However, as indicated in this Judgment (*supra* para. 218), when a State is a party to an in international treaty, such as the American Convention, all its organs, including its judges, are also bound by that treaty; accordingly, they must exercise, *ex officio,* "control of the conformity" of domestic norms with the American Convention. [396][393]

324. The Court assesses positively the issue of the Maldonado judgment by the State, which establishes important criteria concerning the incompatibility of life imprisonment with the rights of the child. [397][394] In addition, the Court appreciates that, in the instant case, the decisions handed down on the applications for review that ultimately annulled the life sentences imposed on Saúl Cristian Roldán Cajal, César Alberto Mendoza, Lucas Matías Mendoza and Claudio David Núñez applied this judgment, among other elements (*supra* paras. 92 and 94).

325. Also, the Court observes that Law 26,061, on the comprehensive protection of children and adolescents, establishes that application of the Convention on the Rights of the Child is mandatory in every administrative, judicial or any other type of act, decision or measure adopted in their regard. [398][395] Nevertheless, in this Judgment, it was determined that Law 22,278, which currently regulates the juvenile criminal regime in Argentina and which was applied in this case, contains provisions contrary to the American Convention and to the international standards applicable to juvenile criminal justice (*supra* paras. 157 and 298). The Court has also established that, under Articles 19, 17, 1(1) and 2 of the Convention, the State is obliged to guarantee, by the adoption of the necessary legislative or other measures, the protection of the child by the family, society and the State. In this way, the Court considers that, in order to comply with these obligations,

Argentina must adapt its legal framework to the international standards indicated previously concerning juvenile criminal justice (*supra* paras. 139 to 167) and design and implement public policies with clear goals and timetables, as well as with the allocation of sufficient budgetary resources for the prevention of juvenile delinquency by means of effective programs and services that encourage the integral development of children and adolescents. Thus, Argentina must, among other matters, disseminate information on the international standards concerning the rights of the child, and provide support to the most vulnerable children and adolescents, and also their families. [399][396]

B.3.2. Ensure that life imprisonment and reclusion for life are never again imposed

326. In this Judgment, it has been mentioned that on September 4, 2012, the Prosecutor General of the Nation filed a special appeal against the decision of the Federal Criminal Cassation Chamber of August 21, 2012 (*supra* para. 95), in favor of César Alberto Mendoza, Claudio David Núñez and Lucas Matías Mendoza, arguing, basically, that the principle of *res judicata* had been violated and that the declaration of the unconstitutionality of paragraph 7 of article 80 of the Criminal Code was "arbitrary." [400][397] On September 27, 2012, the Second Chamber of the Federal Criminal Cassation Chamber declared that the special remedy filed by the Prosecutor General of the Nation was inadmissible. Therefore, on October 5, 2012, the Prosecutor General filed a remedy of complaint before the Supreme Court of Justice of the Nation. [401][398] It has also been indicated that, at the date of this Judgment, the said remedy had not yet been resolved; thus, the decision of the Second Chamber of the Federal Criminal Cassation Chamber of August 21, 2012, is still not final.

327. Based on the human rights violations declared in this case, particularly those related to the imposing of life sentences on César Alberto Mendoza, Claudio David Núñez and Lucas Matías Mendoza and the denial of the appeal in cassation after their conviction (*supra* para. 256), the Court decided that the State must ensure that the sentences of life imprisonment and reclusion for life are never again imposed on César Alberto Mendoza, Claudio David Núñez and Lucas Matías Mendoza, or on any other person for crimes committed while minors. Likewise, Argentina must guarantee that anyone currently serving such sentences for crimes committed while they were minors may obtain a review of the sentence adapted to the standards described in this Judgment (*supra* paras. 240 to 261). The foregoing is in order to avoid the need for cases such as this one being lodged before the organs of the inter-American system for the protection of human rights and, instead, that they can be decided by the corresponding State organs.

B.3.3. Right to appeal the judgment

B.3.3.2. Considerations of the Court

330. In this Judgment, the Court has already established that the State did not guarantee Saúl Cristian Roldán Cajal, César Alberto Mendoza, Claudio David Núñez, Lucas Matías Mendoza and Ricardo David Videla Fernández the right to appeal the judgment by filing the appeals in cassation regulated by Article 474 of the Code of Criminal Procedure of the province of Mendoza and Article 456 of the national Code of Criminal Procedure, respectively (*supra* paras. 240 and 261). The Court emphasizes that these facts occurred before the delivery of the Casal judgment (*supra* paras. 252 to 261).

331. The Court assesses positively the Casal judgment mentioned by the State with regard to the criteria it reveals on the scope of the review comprised by the appeal in cassation, in accordance with the standards derived from Article 8(2)(h) of the American Convention. The Court also underscores that the said judgment was cited by the courts when deciding the appeals for review filed by Saúl Cristian Roldán Cajal, César Alberto Mendoza, Claudio David Núñez and Lucas Matías Mendoza, and that control of compliance with the Convention was performed with regard to the scope of the right to appeal the judgment before a higher judge or court. Regarding the Casal judgment, the State explained how the system of constitutional control functions, based on which the criteria established in the said ruling regarding the right to appeal a judgment must be applied by Argentine judges at all levels.

332. The Court considers that judges in Argentina must continue exercising control of conformity with the Convention in order to ensure the right to appeal a judgment pursuant to Article 8(2)(h) of the American Convention and this Court's case law. Nonetheless, the Court refers to its considerations on the obligations derived from Articles 2 and 8(2)(h) of the American Convention (*supra* paras. 293 to 298 and 301 to 303), and considers that within a reasonable time, the State must adapt its domestic laws to the parameters set forth in this Judgment.

Human Rights Defender *et al.* v. Guatemala
28-Aug-2014
Series C No. 283—*Preliminary Objections, Merits and Reparations*

1. On July 17, 2012, pursuant to the provisions of Articles 51 and 61 of the American Convention and Article 35 of the Court's Rules of Procedure, the Inter-American Commission on Human Rights (hereinafter "the Inter- American Commission" or "the Commission") submitted a brief to the jurisdiction of the Inter-American Court (hereinafter "submission brief") in the case of *Human Rights Defender et al. v. Guatemala* (hereinafter the "State" or "Guatemala"). According to the Commission, this case concerns the State's [alleged] "failure

to prevent the murder of the human rights defender [A.A.], on December 20, 2004, [which] remains in impunity as a result of the irregularities committed at the beginning of the investigation and the lack of diligence in investigating hypotheses related to the motive for the killing. Furthermore, it [alleged] that the investigation did not take place within a reasonable time and was compromised by the lack of protection afforded to the persons who were actively involved in the process." The Commission held that the State's failure to provide protection for the victims' family members led to their displacement, in violation of the right to freedom of movement and residence. It also [alleged] that Guatemala failed in its duty to guarantee political rights, in view of the public position held by Mr. A.A., and the fact that it became impossible for his daughter, B.A., to continue to exercise those rights.

IX. REPARATIONS

C) Comprehensive measures of reparation: restitution, rehabilitation, satisfaction and guarantees of non-repetition

C.4. Guarantees of non-repetition

C.4.1. Public policy for the protection of human rights defenders

262. The **Commission** and the **representatives** asked the Court to order the State to adopt measures of a legislative, institutional, judicial or, in the case of the representatives, administrative nature, aimed at reducing the risks faced by human rights defenders. The **State** reiterated that it was not proven that Mr. A.A. was a human rights defender or that his death was "related to his supposed role as a defender [...]." It also held that it "has already adopted the measures required in this regard by the Commission [...]".

263. In relation to the adoption of measures to reduce the risks faced by human rights defenders, this Court has established that the State has planned and/or implemented various measures aimed at addressing those risks (*supra* note 74). However, Guatemala did not provide the Court with information about their effectiveness. Consequently, the State must implement, within a reasonable time, a public policy for the protection of human rights defenders, taking into account, at least, the following requirements: [372] [399]

(a) the participation of human rights defenders, civil society organizations and experts in the formulation of standards for the regulation of a program for the protection of the group in question;

(b) the protection program should adopt a comprehensive and inter-institutional approach to this problem, based on the risk posed by each situation and adopt immediate measures to address complaints by defenders;

(c) the creation of a risk analysis model to adequately determine the risk and the protection needs of each defender or group;

(d) the creation of an information management system on the status of the prevention and protection of human rights defenders;

(e) the design of protection plans in response to specific risks faced by each defender and to the nature of his/her work;

(f) the promotion of a culture of legitimization and protection of the work of human rights defenders, and

(g) the provision of sufficient human and financial resources to respond to the real needs for protection of human rights defenders.

264. Similarly, the State must present annual reports within a period of one year on the actions taken to implement said policy.

B. INCOMPATABILITY OF AMNESTY LAWS WITH HUMAN RIGHTS

Barrios Altos v. Peru
14-Mar-2001
Series C No. 75—*Merits*

41.   This Court considers that all amnesty provisions, provisions on prescription, and the establishment of measures designed to eliminate responsibility are inadmissible because they are intended to prevent the investigation and punishment of those responsible for serious human rights violations such as torture; extrajudicial, summary, or arbitrary execution; and forced disappearance, all of them prohibited because they violate non-derogable rights recognized by international human rights law.

42.   The Court, in accordance with the arguments put forward by the Commission and not contested by the State, considers that the amnesty laws adopted by Peru prevented the victims' next of kin and the surviving victims in this case from being heard by a judge, as established in Article 8(1) of the Convention; they violated the right to judicial protection embodied in Article 25 of the Convention; they prevented the investigation, capture, prosecution and conviction of those responsible for the events that occurred in Barrios Altos, thus failing to comply with Article 1(1) of the Convention; and they obstructed clarification of the facts of this case. Finally, the adoption of self-amnesty laws that are incompatible with the Convention meant that Peru failed to comply with the obligation to adapt internal legislation that is embodied in Article 2 of the Convention.

43.   The Court considers that it should be emphasized that, in the light of the general obligations established in Articles 1(1) and 2 of the American Convention, the States Parties are obliged to take all measures to ensure that no one is deprived of judicial protection and the exercise of the right to a simple and effective

recourse, in the terms of Articles 8 and 25 of the Convention. Consequently, States Parties to the Convention that adopt laws that have the opposite effect, such as self-amnesty laws, violate Articles 8 and 25, in relation to Articles 1(1) and 2 of the Convention. Self-amnesty laws lead to the defenselessness of victims and perpetuate impunity; therefore, they are manifestly incompatible with the aims and spirit of the Convention. This type of law precludes the identification of the individuals who are responsible for human rights violations because it obstructs the investigation and access to justice and prevents the victims and their next of kin from knowing the truth and receiving the corresponding reparation.

44.   Owing to the manifest incompatibility of self-amnesty laws and the American Convention on Human Rights, the said laws lack legal effect and may not continue to obstruct the investigation of the grounds on which this case is based or the identification and punishment of those responsible, nor can they have the same or a similar impact with regard to other cases that have occurred in Peru, where the rights established in the American Convention have been violated.

THE COURT,

DECIDES:

unanimously,

3.   To find, in accordance with the terms of the State's recognition of international responsibility, that the State failed to comply with Articles 1(1) and 2 of the American Convention on Human Rights as a result of the promulgation and application of Amnesty Laws No. 26479 and No. 26492 and the violation of the articles of the Convention mentioned in operative paragraph 2 of this judgment.

4.   To find that Amnesty Laws No. 26479 and No. 26492 are incompatible with the American Convention on Human Rights and, consequently, lack legal effect.

Almonacid-Arellano et al. v. Chile
26-Sep-2006
Series C No. 154—*Preliminary Objections, Merits, Reparations, and Costs*

b)   Impossibility to grant an amnesty for crimes against humanity

105.   According to the International Law *corpus iuris,* a crime against humanity is in itself a serious violation of human rights and affects mankind as a whole. In the case of *Prosecutor v. Erdemovic,* the International Tribunal for the Former Yugoslavia stated that:

> Crimes against humanity are serious acts of violence that harm human beings by striking what is most essential to them: their life, liberty, physical welfare, health, and or dignity. They are inhumane acts that by their extent and gravity go beyond

the limits tolerable to the international community, which must perforce demand their punishment. But crimes against humanity also transcend the individual because when the individual is assaulted, humanity comes under attack and is negated. It is therefore the concept of humanity as victim that essentially characterizes crimes against humanity.[127 400]

106.   Since the individual and the whole mankind are the victims of all crimes against humanity, the General Assembly of the United Nations has held since 1946 [128 401] that those responsible for the commission of such crimes must be punished. In that respect, they point out Resolutions 2583 (XXIV) of 1969 and 3074 (XXVIII) of 1973. In the former, the General Assembly held that the "thorough investigation" of war crimes and crimes against humanity, as well as the punishment of those responsible for them "constitute an important element in the prevention of such crimes, the protection of human rights and fundamental freedoms, the encouragement of confidence, the furtherance of cooperation among peoples, and the promotion of international peace and security." [129 402] In the latter, the General Assembly stated the following:

War crimes and crimes against humanity, wherever they are committed, shall be subject to investigation and the persons against whom there is evidence that they have committed such crimes shall be subject to tracing, arrest, trial, and, if found guilty, to punishment.

. . . .

States shall not take any legislative or other measures that may be prejudicial to the international obligations they have assumed in regard to the detection, arrest, extradition, and punishment of persons guilty of war crimes and crimes against humanity.[130 403]

107.   Likewise, Resolutions 827 and 955 of the Security Council of the United Nations,[131 404] together with the Charters of the Tribunals for the Former Yugoslavia (Article 29) and Rwanda (Article 28), impose on all Member States of the United Nations the obligation to fully cooperate with the Tribunals for the investigation and punishment of those persons accused of having committed serious international law violations, including crimes against humanity. Likewise, the Secretary General of the United Nations has pointed out that in view of the rules and principles of the United Nations, all peace agreements approved by the United Nations can never promise amnesty for crimes against humanity.[132 405]

108.   The adoption and enforcement of laws that grant amnesty for crimes against humanity prevents the compliance of the obligations stated above. The Secretary General of the United Nations, in his report about the establishment of the Special Tribunal for Sierra Leona stated the following:

> While recognizing that amnesty is an accepted legal concept
> and a gesture of peace and reconciliation at the end of a civil
> war or an internal armed conflict, the UN has consistently
> maintained the position that amnesty cannot be granted in
> respect of international crimes such as genocide, crimes against
> humanity, or violations of international humanitarian law.[133 406]

109.   The Secretary General also informed that the legal effects of the amnesty granted in Sierra Leone had not been taken into account "given their illegality pursuant to international law."[134 407]   Indeed, the Charter for the Special Tribunal for Sierra Leone stated that the amnesty granted to persons accused of crimes against humanity, which are violations of Article 3 of the Geneva Conventions and Additional Protocol II,[135 408] as well as of other serious violations of international humanitarian law, "shall not be an impediment to subject [them] to trial."

110.   The obligation that arises pursuant to international law to try, and, if found guilty, to punish the perpetrators of certain international crimes, among which are crimes against humanity, is derived from the duty of protection embodied in Article 1(1) of the American Convention. This obligation implies the duty of the States Parties to organize the entire government system, and in general, all agencies through which the public power is exercised, in such manner as to legally protect the free and full exercise of human rights. As a consequence of this obligation, the States must prevent, investigate, and punish all violations of the rights recognized by the Convention and, at the same time, guarantee the reinstatement, if possible, of the violated rights, and as the case may be, the reparation of the damage caused due to the violation of human rights. If the State agencies act in a manner that such violation goes unpunished and it prevents the reinstatement, as soon as possible, of such rights to the victim of such violation, it can be concluded that such State has not complied with its duty to guarantee the free and full exercise of those rights to the individuals who are subject to its jurisdiction. [136 409]

111.   Crimes against humanity give rise to the violation of a series of undeniable rights that are recognized by the American Convention, which violation cannot remain unpunished. The Court has stated on several occasions that the State has the duty to prevent and combat impunity, which the Court has defined as "the lack of investigation, prosecution, arrest, trial, and conviction of those responsible for the violation of the rights protected by the American Convention." [137 410]   Likewise, the Court has determined that the investigation must be conducted resorting to all legal means available and must be focused on the determination of the truth and the investigation, prosecution, arrest, trial, and conviction of those persons that are responsible for the facts, both as perpetrators and instigators, especially when State agents are or may be involved in such events. [138 411]   In that respect, the Court has pointed out that those resources that, in view of the general conditions of the

country or due to the circumstances of the case, turn to be deceptive, cannot be taken into account. [139 412]

112.   In the case of *Barrios Altos* the Court has already stated that:
all amnesty provisions, provisions on prescription, and the establishment of measures designed to eliminate responsibility are inadmissible; because they are intended to prevent the investigation and punishment of those responsible for serious human rights violations such as torture; extra-legal, summary, or arbitrary execution; and forced disappearance, all of them prohibited because they violate non-derogable rights recognized by international human rights law.[140 413]

113.   It is worth mentioning that the State itself recognized in the instant case that "amnesty or self-amnesty laws are, in principle, contrary to the rules of international human rights law."[141 414]

114.   In view of the above considerations, the Court determines that the States cannot neglect their duty to investigate, identify, and punish those persons responsible for crimes against humanity by enforcing amnesty laws or any other similar domestic provisions. Consequently, crimes against humanity are crimes that cannot be susceptible of amnesty.

The Court Rules,

Unanimously, that:

5.   The State must ensure that Decree Law No. 2.191 does not continue to hinder further investigation into the extra-legal execution of Mr. Almonacid-Arellano as well as the identification and, if applicable, punishment of those responsible, as set forth in paragraphs 145 to 157 herein.

6.   The State must ensure that Decree Law No. 2.191 does not continue to hinder the investigation, prosecution, and, if applicable, punishment of those responsible for similar violations in Chile, in accordance with paragraph 145 herein.

Gomes Lund et al. (Guerrilha do Araguaia) v. Brazil
24-Nov-2010
Series C No. 219—*Preliminary Objections, Merits, Reparations, and Costs*

1.   On March 26, 2009, in accordance with the provisions of Articles 51 and 61 of the American Convention, the Inter-American Commission on Human Rights (hereinafter, "the Inter-American Commission" or "the Commission") submitted an application against the Federal Republic of Brazil (hereinafter, "the State," "Brazil," or "the Union") to the Court, which originated from the petition

presented on August 7, 1995 by the Center for Justice and International Law (CEJIL), Human Rights Watch/Americas, in the name of disappeared persons in the context of the *Guerrilha do Araguaia* (hereinafter, also "the Guerrilla") and their next of kin.[2][415] On March 6, 2001, the Commission issued Admissibility Report No. 33/01[3][416] and, on October 31, 2008, approved the Report on the Merits No. 91/08, pursuant to Article 50 of the Convention, in which it made a series of recommendations for the State.[4][417] This report was notified to Brazil on November 21, 2008, and the State was granted a period of two months to provide information on any actions taken to implement the recommendations of the Commission. Despite the two extensions afforded to the State, the period of time for it to present information regarding compliance with the recommendations elapsed without there having been "satisfactory implementation of [them]." As such, the Commission decided to submit the case to the Court, considering that it represented "an important opportunity for the Court to consolidate the Inter-American jurisprudence on amnesty laws in relation to enforced disappearances and extrajudicial executions and on the State's consequential obligation to provide society with the truth and to investigate, prosecute, and punish serious human rights violations." Likewise, the Commission emphasized the historical value of the case and the possibility that the Court could affirm the non-compatibility of not only the amnesty laws, but also of the laws on confidentiality of documents with the American Convention. The Commission designated as delegates Mr. Felipe González, Commissioner, and Santiago A. Canton, Executive Secretary, and as legal advisors the Deputy Executive Secretary, Mrs. Elizabeth Abi-Mershed, and the lawyers, Lilly Ching Soto and Mario López Garelli, Executive Secretariat specialists.

2.   According to the Commission, the application refers to the [alleged] "responsibility [of the State] for the arbitrary detention, torture, and enforced disappearance of 70 persons, members of the Communist Party of Brazil . . . and peasants of the region . . . as a result of the operations of the Brazilian Army between 1972 and 1975, whose purpose it was to eradicate the *Guerrilha do Araguaia*, in the context of the military dictatorship in Brazil (1964–1985)." Moreover, the Commission submitted the case to the Court because, "under Law No. 6.683/79 . . ., the State did not carry out a criminal investigation so as to prosecute and punish the persons responsible for the enforced disappearance of 70 victims and the extrajudicial execution of Maria Lúcia Petit da Silva . . . because the judicial remedies of a civil nature aimed at obtaining information regarding the facts have not been effective in guaranteeing that the next of kin of the disappeared and executed persons have access to information on the *Guerrilha do Araguaia*; because the legislative and administrative measures adopted by the State have unduly restricted the next of kin's right to access information; and because the disappearance of the victims,

the execution of Maria Lúcia Petit da Silva, the impunity of those responsible, and the lack of access to justice, the truth, and information, have negatively affected the personal integrity of the next of kin of the disappeared and executed person." The Commission requested the Court to declare that the State is responsible for the violation of the rights established in Articles 3 (Right to Juridical Personality), 4 (Right to Life), 5 (Right to Humane Treatment (personal integrity)), 7 (Right to Personal Liberty), 8 (Right to a Fair Trial (judicial guarantees)), 13 (Freedom of Thought and Expression), and 25 (Right to Judicial Protection) of the American Convention on Human Rights (hereinafter, "the American Convention" or "the Convention"), in relation with the obligations enshrined in Articles 1(1) (obligation to respect rights) and 2 (domestic legal effects) of the same. The Commission requested that the Court order the State to adopt specific measures of reparation.

3.   On July 18, 2009, the *Grupo Tortura Nunca Más de Rio de Janeiro* (Group on Torture Never Again of Rio de Janeiro), the *Comisión de Familiares de Muertos y Desaparecidos Políticos del Instituto de Estudios de la Violencia del Estado* [Commission of the Next of Kin of Politically Deceased and Disappeared Persons of the Institute of Studies on State Violence], and the Center for Justice and International Law (hereinafter, "the representatives") presented their brief of pleadings, motions, and evidence (hereinafter, "brief of pleadings and motions"), pursuant to Article 24 of the Court Rules of Procedure. In said brief, the representatives requested that the Court declare "[i]n relation to the enforced disappearance of the [[alleged]] victims . . . and the total impunity regarding the facts," the international responsibility of the State of Brazil for the violation of Articles 3, 4, 5, 7, 8, and 25 of the Convention, all in relation to Article[s] 1(1) and 2 of the same instrument, as well as Articles 1, 2, 6, and 8 of the Inter-American Convention to Prevent and Punish Torture (hereinafter, also "Inter-American Convention against Torture"]; of Articles 8 and 25, in relation to Articles 1(1) and 2 of the American Convention and Articles 1, 6, and 8 of the Inter-American Convention against Torture for the failure to investigate and lack of due diligence in the domestic proceedings; of Articles 1(1), 2, 13, 8, and 25 of the Convention for the undue restrictions on the right to access information; of Articles 1(1), 8, 13, and 25 of the Convention for the violation of the right to the truth, and Article 5 of the Convention for the violation of the personal integrity of the next of kin of the [[alleged]] disappeared victims. As a consequence, they requested the Court to order various measures of reparation. The next of kin of forty-eight [alleged] victims, through power of attorney granted on various dates, assigned the abovementioned organizations as their legal representatives, those of which are represented, in turn, by Mrs. Cecília Maria Bouças Coimbra, Elizabeth Silveira e Silva, and Victória Lavinia Grabois Olimpio (*Grupo Tortura Nunca Más* (Group Torture Never Again)); Criméia Alice Schmidt de Almeida (Commission of the

Next of Kin of the Politically Deceased and Disappeared Persons of the Institute of Studies on State Violence); Viviana Krsticevic, Beatriz Affonso, Helena Rocha, and Mr. Michael Camilleri (CEJIL).

4.   On October 31, 2009, the State presented a brief wherein it filed three preliminary objections, responded to the application, and made observations to the brief of pleadings and motions (hereinafter "response to the application"). The State requested the Court to consider the preliminary objections founded, and as a consequence, to: a) recognize the lack of jurisdiction *ratione temporis* to examine the [alleged] violations which occurred prior to Brazil's recognition of the contentious jurisdiction of the Court; b) declare it lacks jurisdiction because of the failure to exhaust domestic remedies, and c) immediately archive the present case given that the representatives do not have a legal interest in the proceedings. Alternatively, in regard to the merits, Brazil requested the Court to recognize "all the measures taken in the domestic forum" and "to declare as inadmissible the requests of the [Commission and representatives] given that within the country a solution is unfolding, compatible with its peculiarities, for the definitive consolidation of national reconciliation." The State assigned Mr. Hildebrando Tadeu Nascimento Valadares as Agent and Mrs. Márcia Maria Adorno Calvalcanti Ramos, Camila Serrano Giunchetti, Cristina Timponi Cambiaghi, and Bartira Meira Ramos Nagado and Mr. Sérgio Ramos de Matos Brito and Mr. Bruno Correia Cardoso, as Deputy Agents.

B. Obligations to investigate the facts, prosecute, and where necessary, punish those responsible and determine the whereabouts of the victims

  1. Obligation to investigate the facts, prosecute, and where necessary, punish those responsible

253.   The Commission requested that the Court order the State to carry out, by means of the civil (ordinary) law jurisdiction, a comprehensive, effective, and impartial legal investigation of the enforced disappearances of the present case and of the execution of Mrs. Petit da Silva, in accordance with legal due process, in order to identify the intellectual and physical perpetrators of said violations and to criminally punish them. To this end, the State must take into account that said crimes are not bound by a statute of limitations and not subject to amnesties. As such, Brazil must adopt all the necessary measures to assure that the Amnesty Law and the secrecy laws do not continue to represent an obstacle for the criminal prosecution of gross violations of human rights. In addition, it requested the publication of said investigation in order for Brazilian society to be aware of what occurred during this period of its history.

254.   The representatives requested the Court to order Brazil to investigate the facts, as well as to prosecute and punish all those responsible in a reasonable period of time, and to order the State not to use provisions of its domestic law, such as the

statute of limitations, *res judicata*, non-retroactivity of criminal law, and *ne bis in idem*, or any other exceptions to responsibility, to be exempt from its obligation. The State must remove all the de facto and de jure obstacles that maintain the impunity of the facts, such as those related to the Amnesty Law. In addition, they requested that the Court order the State to: a) judge all the proceedings in relation to gross violations of human rights in the ordinary justice system; b) allow all the next of kin of the victims full access and legitimacy to act in all the procedural stages of the case, pursuant to domestic laws and to the American Convention, and c) publicly and widely disclose the results of the investigations for the knowledge of Brazilian society.

255.   The State did not specifically address the investigation of the facts and only noted that the analysis of the Amnesty Law cannot be separated from the moment in which it was enacted nor from the foundations from which it is established. On the other hand, it recalled that the decision of the Federal Supreme Court in the Non-compliance Action of the Fundamental Principle 153 considered the Amnesty Law to be entirely legitimate in light of the new constitutional legal system.

256.   In Chapter VIII of the present Judgment, the Court established the violation of the right to judicial guarantees and due judicial protection for the failure to investigate, prosecute, and eventually punish those responsible for the facts of the present case. Taking into account the foregoing, as well as its jurisprudence, this Court orders that the State must effectively conduct a criminal investigation of the facts of the present case in order to ascertain them, determine the corresponding criminal responsibility, and to effectively apply the punishment and consequences provided by law.[372 418] This obligation must be satisfied in a reasonable period of time, considering the criteria on investigations indicated in cases of this type,[373 419] *inter alia*:

(a) to initiate the corresponding investigations in relation to the facts of the present case, taking into account the systematic violations of human rights that existed in said period, in order to allow for the proceeding and appropriate investigations to be carried out in consideration of the complexity of these facts and the context in which they occurred, thereby avoiding omissions in the gathering of evidence and in the logical lines of investigation;

(b) to determine the physical and intellectual perpetrators of the enforced disappearances of the victims and of the extrajudicial execution. Furthermore, as this deals with gross violations of human rights, and taking into account the nature of the facts and the continued or permanent nature of enforced disappearances, the State many not apply the Amnesty Law to the benefit of the perpetrators, as well as other analogous provisions; the statute of limitations; non-retroactivity of the criminal law; *res judicata*; *ne bis in idem*; or any other similar exception that excuses responsibility of this obligation, in the terms of paragraphs 171 to 179 of this Judgment, and

(c) to ensure that: (i) the competent authorities carry out the corresponding investigations *ex officio*, and that in this manner they have at their disposition and use all the logistical and scientific resources that may be necessary to collect and process the evidence, and in particular, that they have the means to access the relevant documentation and information in order to investigate the allegations and promptly carry out the essential actions and investigations to ascertain what happenedto the deceased person and to the disappeared person of the present case; (ii) those who participate in the investigations, among them, the next of kin of the victims, witnesses, and operators of justice, have at their disposition the due guarantees for security, and (iii) the authorities abstain from carrying out acts that imply an obstruction to the development of the investigative process.

257.   In particular, the State must guarantee that the criminal cases initiated due to the facts of the present case against the [alleged] perpetrators who were or are military officials be carried out within the ordinary jurisdiction and not within the military jurisdiction.[374][420] Finally, the Court considers that, based on its jurisprudence, the State must ensure the next of kin of the victims full access and the capacity to take part in all the stages of the investigation and trial of those responsible, pursuant to domestic law and to the American Convention. In addition, the results of the corresponding procedures should be publicly disclosed thereby permitting Brazilian society to know the facts of the present case, as well as those responsible.

Gelman v. Uruguay
24-Feb-2011
Series C No. 221—*Merits and Reparations*

1.   On January 21, 2010, the Inter-American Commission on Human Rights (hereinafter "the Commission" or "the Inter-American Commission") presented, pursuant to Articles 51 and 61 of the Convention, an application against the Eastern Republic of Uruguay in relation to the case of Juan Gelman, María Claudia García de Gelman, and María Macarena Gelman García[2][421] (hereinafter "the case of *Gelman v. Uruguay*").[3][422] On March 9, 2007, the Commission adopted Admissibility Report No. 30/07, wherein it declared the admissibility of the case and on July 18, 2008, approved, under the terms of Article 50 of the Convention, the Report on the Merits No. 32/08.[4][423]

2.   The facts [alleged] by the Commission relate to the enforced disappearance of María Claudia García Iruretagoyena de Gelman since late 1976, subsequent to her detention in Buenos Aires, Argentina, during the advanced stages of her pregnancy, to which it is presumed that she was then transported to Uruguay where she gave birth to her daughter, who was then given to an Uruguayan family—actions which the Commission notes were committed by Uruguayan and Argentine State agents in the context of "Operation Cóndor," and, to date, the whereabouts of María Claudia García as well as the circumstances in which the disappearance took place remain unknown. Furthermore, the Commission [alleged] the suppression of identity and nationality of María Macarena Gelman García Iruretagoyena, daughter of María Claudia García de Gelman and Marcelo Gelman and the denial of justice, impunity, and in general, the suffering caused to Juan Gelman, his family, María Macarena Gelman, and the next of kin of María Claudia García, as a consequence of the failure to investigate the facts, prosecute, and punish those responsible under Law No. 15.848 or the Expiry Law (hereinafter "the Expiry Law"), promulgated in 1986 by the democratic government of Uruguay.

3.   The Commission requested that the Court, as a consequence, conclude and declare that the State is responsible for the violation of:

(a) The right to a fair trial and judicial protection recognized in Articles 8(1) and 25 in relation to Articles 1(1) and 2 of the American Convention on Human Rights, and in relation to Articles I(b), III, IV, and V of the Inter-American Convention on Forced Disappearance of Persons, as well as Articles 1, 6, 8, and 11 of the Inter-American Convention to Prevent and Punish Torture, to the detriment of Juan Gelman, María Claudia García de Gelman, María Macarena Gelman, and their next of kin;

(b) the right to juridical personality, life, personal liberty, humane treatment, and the obligation to punish these violations in a serious and effective manner, recognized in Articles 3, 4, 5, 7, and 1(1) of the American Convention in relation to Articles 1(b), III, IV, and V of the Inter-American Convention on Forced Disappearance of Persons and Articles 6 and 8 of the Inter-American Convention to Prevent and Punish Torture, to the detriment of María Claudia García;

(c) the right to personal integrity, recognized in Article 5(1), in relation to Article 1(1) of the American Convention, regarding Juan Gelman, María Macarena Gelman, and their next of kin;

(d) the right to the recognition of juridical personality, the protection of honor and dignity, the right to a name, special measures of protection for the child, and the right to nationality, recognized in Articles 3, 11, 18, 19, and 20, respectively, in relation to Article 1(1) of the American

Convention, regarding María Macarena Gelman; and,

(e) the right of protection of the family, recognized in Article 17 of the American Convention and Article XII of the Inter-American Convention on Forced Disappearance of Persons, in relation to Article 1(1) of the American Convention, regarding Juan Gelman, María Macarena Gelman, and their next of kin.

F. Amnesty laws and the Jurisprudence of this Court.

225.   This Court has established that "amnesty provisions, the statute of limitation provisions, and the establishment of exclusions of responsibility that are intended to prevent the investigation and punish those responsible for serious violations to human rights such as torture; summary, extrajudicial, or arbitrary executions; and enforced disappearance are not admissible, all of which are prohibited for contravening irrevocable rights recognized by international human rights law."[288 424]

226.   In this sense, amnesty laws are, in cases of serious violations of human rights, expressly incompatible with the letter and spirit of the Pact of San José, given that they violate the provisions of Articles 1(1) and 2, that is, in that they impede the investigation and punishment of those responsible for serious human rights violations and, consequently, impede access to victims and their families to the truth of what happened and to the corresponding reparation, thereby hindering the full, timely, and effective rule of justice in the relevant cases. This, in turn, favors impunity and arbitrariness and also seriously affects the rule of law; therefore, in light of international law, they have been declared to have no legal effect.

227.   In particular, amnesty laws affect the international obligation of the State in regard to the investigation and punishment of serious human rights violations because they prevent the next of kin from being heard before a judge, pursuant to that indicated in Article 8(1) of the American Convention, thereby violating the right to judicial protection enshrined in Article 25 of the Convention precisely for the failure to investigate, . . . capture, prosecute, and punish those responsible for the facts, thereby failing to comply with Article 1(1) of the Convention.

228.   Under the general obligations enshrined in Articles 1(1) and 2 of the American Convention, the States Parties have the obligation to take measures of all kinds to assure that no one is taken from judicial protection and the exercise of their right to a simple and effective remedy, in the terms of Articles 8 and 25 of the Convention, and once the American Convention has been ratified, it corresponds to the State to adopt all the measures to revoke the legal provisions that may contradict said treaty as established in Article 2 thereof, such as those that prevent the investigation of serious human rights violations given that it leads to the defenselessness of victims and the perpetuation of impunity and prevents the next of kin from knowing the truth regarding the facts.

229.   The incompatibility with the Convention includes amnesties of serious human rights violations and is not limited to those that are denominated, "self-amnesties," and the Court, more than the adoption process and the authority which issued the Amnesty Law, refers to its *ratio legis*: to leave unpunished serious violations committed in international law.[289][425] The incompatibility of the amnesty laws with the American Convention in cases of serious violations of human rights does not stem from a formal question, such as its origin, but rather from the material aspect as regards the rights enshrined in Articles 8 and 25, in relation to Articles 1(1) and 2 of the Convention.

G. The investigation of the facts and the Uruguayan Expiry Law.

230.   The way in which, at least for a period of time, the Expiry Law adopted in Uruguay has been interpreted and applied, on the one hand, has affected the State's international obligation to investigate and punish human rights violations relating to the enforced disappearance of María Claudia García Iruretagoyena and of María Macarena Gelman García, as well as the situation regarding the latter in relation to her abduction and the concealment of her identity, due to the prevention of the victim's next of kin from being heard by a judge, pursuant to that right stated in Article 8(1) of the American Convention and has, on the other hand, violated the right to judicial protection enshrined in Article 25 of that instrument because of the failure to investigate, . . . capture, prosecute, and punish those responsible for the facts, thereby also failing to comply with Articles 1(1) and 2 of the Convention, referring to the adaption of domestic law to the Convention.[290][426]

231.   The failure to investigate the serious human rights violations committed in the present case, which occurred in the context of systematic patterns, evinces the noncompliance with international obligations of the State, established by non-extendible norms.[291][427]

232.   Given its express incompatibility with the American Convention, the provisions of the Expiry Law that impede the investigation and punishment of serious violations of human rights have no legal effect and, therefore, cannot continue to obstruct the investigation of the facts of this case and the identification and punishment of those responsible, nor can they have the same or similar impact on other cases of serious violations of human rights enshrined in the American Convention that may have occurred in Uruguay.[292][428]

233.   The obligation to investigate the facts in the case of enforced disappearance is specified in the provisions of Articles III, IV, V, and XII of the Inter-American Convention on Forced Disappearance of Persons, in regard to the investigation of enforced disappearance as a continuing offense, the establishment of jurisdiction to investigate said crime, the cooperation between States for the criminal prosecution and possible extradition of the [alleged] perpetrators, and access to information regarding the places of detention.

234.   Similarly, given the involvement, not only of a systematic pattern in which multiple authorities may have been involved, but also of a cross-border/interstate operation, the State should have used and applied the appropriate legal instruments for the analysis of the case, the criminal codifications that are in-line with the facts, and the design of an appropriate investigation able to collect and systematize the vast and diverse information that has been reserved or made not easily accessible and includes the necessary inter-state cooperation.

235.   In the same sense, the procedures initiated by Juan Gelman and the one opened in 2008 through the efforts of Maria Macarena Gelman, were brought under the crime of homicide, thereby excluding other crimes such as torture, enforced disappearance, and theft of identity, which allows the claim to be declared, by the domestic tribunal, as prescribed by law.

236.   It is necessary to reiterate that this is a case of serious violations of human rights, particularly enforced disappearance, and therefore it is this codification that should have priority in the investigations that appropriately should be opened at the domestic level. As established by this Court, given the involvement of a crime of a permanent nature, namely, a crime that is prolonged in time, when the codification of enforced disappearance enters into force, the new law applies, without this implying a retroactive application.[293 429]   In this sense, tribunals of the highest levels of the States of the American continent have rendered rulings and applied criminal norms in cases concerning acts that began to toll before the respective criminal codification entered into force.[294 430]

237.   In order for, in the present case, the investigation to be effective, the State should have and must apply an appropriate regulatory framework to develop it, which implies the regulation and application in domestic law of enforced disappearance of persons, given that criminal prosecution is an appropriate instrument to prevent future human rights violations of this nature,[295 431] and furthermore, the State must ensure that no normative or any other obstacles prevent the investigation of such acts and, where appropriate, the sanction of those responsible.[296 432]

238.   The fact that the Expiry Law of the State has been approved in a democratic regime and further ratified or supported by the public, on two occasions, namely, through the exercise of direct democracy, does not automatically or by itself grant legitimacy under international law. The participation of the public was in relation to the law, using methods of direct exercise of democracy—referendum (paragraph 2 of Article 79 of the Constitution of Uruguay) in 1989 and "plebiscite" (letter A of Article 331 of the Constitution of Uruguay) regarding a referendum that declared as null Articles 1 and 4 of the Law—therefore, October 25, 2009, should be considered as an act attributable to the State that gave rise to its international responsibility.

239.   The bare existence of a democratic regime does not guarantee, per se, the permanent respect of international law, including the international law of human rights, and which has also been considered by the Inter-American Democratic Charter.[297][433] The democratic legitimacy of specific facts in a society is limited by the norms of protection of human rights recognized in international treaties, such as the American Convention, in such a form that the existence of one true democratic regime is determined by both its formal and substantial characteristics, and therefore, particularly in cases of serious violations of nonrevocable norms of international law, the protection of human rights constitutes an impassable limit to the rule of the majority, that is, to the forum of the "possible to be decided" by the majorities in the democratic instance, those who should also prioritize "control of conformity with the Convention," which is a function and task of any public authority and not only the judicial branch.   In this sense, the Supreme Court of Justice has exercised an appropriate control of conformity with the Convention in respect to the Expiry Law, by establishing, *inter alia*, that "the limits of the sovereignty of the majority lies, essentially, in two aspects: the guardianship of the fundamental rights (first, amongst all, the right to life and personal liberty, and there is no will of the majority, nor the general interest, nor the common good wherein these can be sacrificed) and the subjection of the public authorities to the law."[298][434]   Other domestic courts have also referred to the limits of democracy in relation to the protection of fundamental rights.[299][435]

240.   In addition, in applying the provisions of the Expiry Law (which, for all [intents and] purposes constitutes an amnesty law) and thereby impeding the investigation of the facts and the identification, prosecution, and possible punishment of the possible perpetrators of continued and permanent injuries such as those caused by enforced disappearance, the State fails to comply with its obligation to adapt its domestic law as enshrined in Article 2 of the Convention.

H. Conclusion

241.   The interpretation of the executive branch of the State, dated June 23, 2005, that the case subject to this proceeding be expressly excluded from the application of the Expiry Law, means that, regarding the specific case of María Claudia García de Gelman, the law is no longer to be an obstacle that prevents the investigation and punishment of those responsible.   Nonetheless, the main obstacle for the investigations in this case has been the validity and application of the Expiry Law, which, as stated by various domestic authorities, the State does not contest the necessity to revoke, although, however, it does not do so.

242.   It is evident that the investigations in the State related to this case have exceeded any standard of reasonableness regarding the length of the proceedings, to which, notwithstanding that this entails a case of serious violations of human rights, it has not given priority to the principle of effectiveness in the investigation

of the facts, the determination and, where applicable, the necessary punishment for those responsible. [300 436]

243.   All persons, including the next of kin of the victims of gross human rights violations, have, pursuant to Articles 1(1), 8(1), and 25, as well as in certain circumstances Article 13 of the Convention,[301 437] the right to know the truth. As a consequence, the next of kin of the victims and society must be informed of all that occurred in regard to said violations. [302 438] This right has also been recognized in various instruments of the United Nations and by the General Assembly of the Organization of American States,[303 439] and whose content, in particular cases of enforced disappearance, is part of the "right of the next of kin to know the fate of the victims, and where possible, the location of their remains," [304 440] encompassed in the right to access to justice and the obligation to investigate — forms of reparation to know the truth in the specific case. [305 441]

244.   The Inter-American Court concludes that the State violated the Rights to Fair Trial (judicial guarantees) and Judicial Protection provided for in Articles 8(1) and 25(1) of the American Convention, in relation to Articles 1(1) and 2 thereof, and of the mentioned norms of the Inter-American Convention on Forced Disappearance of Persons, for failing to effectively investigate the disappearance of María Claudia García Iruretagoyena, and the abduction, suppression of identity, and delivery of María Macarena Gelman to a third party, to the detriment of Juan and Maria Macarena Gelman.

246.   Due to the interpretation and application that has been given to the Expiry Law, which lacks legal effect in regard to human rights violations in the terms indicated above (*supra* para. 232), the State has not fulfilled its obligation to adapt its domestic legislation to the Convention, contained in Article 2 thereof, in relation to Articles 8(1), 25, and 1(1) thereof and Articles I(b), III, IV, and V of the Inter-American Convention on Forced Disappearance of Persons.

VII. REPARATIONS

B.   *Obligation to investigate the facts and to identify, prosecute and, where appropriate, punish those responsible and adopt all the necessary domestic legislative measures*

> *B.1   Investigation, prosecution and, where appropriate, punishment of those responsible*

253.   . . . Given that the Expiry Law lacks the effects because of its incompatibility with the American Convention and the Inter-American Convention on Forced Disappearance of Persons, in as much as it can impede the investigation and possible sanction of those responsible for serious human rights violations,

the State must guarantee that this never again becomes an impediment for the investigation of the facts at hand and of the identification, and, if applicable, punishment of those responsible for the facts and similar serious violations of human rights that took place in Uruguay.

254.   Consequently, the State should ensure that no other analogous norm, such as a statute of limitations, non-retroactivity of the criminal law, *res judicata*, *ne bis in idem*, or any other similar law exonerating responsibility, be applied and that the authorities refrain from carrying out acts that would implicate the obstruction of the investigative process.

255.   The State must conduct the investigation in an effective manner so that it is done in a reasonable amount of time, be it by ordering either the necessary speed to the existing open claim or by ordering a new one, depending on what is most beneficial to the investigation, and furthermore, ensuring that the competent authorities conduct the corresponding *ex officio* investigations, having at their disposal the necessary authorization and remedies, allowing those who are part of the investigation, among them the victim's relatives, witnesses, and administrators of justice, to be assured the due guarantees of security.[309][442]

256.   Particularly, the Court considers that, with basis in its jurisprudence, [310][443] the State must ensure the full access and capacity to act of the next of kin of the victims in every stage of the investigation and prosecution of those responsible. Additionally, the result of the corresponding proceedings should be disseminated publicly in order for Uruguayan society to know of the facts of the present case, as well as to know those responsible for them. [311][444]

Espinoza Gonzáles v. Peru
20-Nov-2014
Series C No. 289—*Preliminary Objections, Merits, Reparations and Costs*

IX. REPARATIONS

B) Obligation to investigate the facts that gave rise to the violations and to identify, prosecute and punish, as appropriate, those responsible

309. As it has established on other occasions relating to this type of case,[483][445] both the respective investigation and the criminal proceedings should include a gender perspective, undertake specific lines of investigation with regard to the sexual violence in order to avoid omissions in the collection of evidence, and provide the victim with information on any progress in the investigation and criminal proceedings pursuant to domestic law and, as appropriate, adequate participation at all stages of the investigation and trial. In addition, the investigation must be conducted by officials with experience in similar cases and in attention to victims

of gender-based discrimination and violence. Furthermore, it must be ensured that those in charge of the investigation and the criminal proceedings, as well as, when appropriate, other persons involved such as witnesses, experts, or members of the victim's family, have due guarantees for their safety. Likewise, since a gross violation of human rights is involved, because torture was a generalized practice in the context of the conflict in Peru, the State must abstain from using mechanisms such as amnesty to benefit the perpetrators, or any other similar provision, such as prescription, non-retroactivity of the criminal law, *res judicata, ne bis in idem* or any other similar extenuating circumstance in order to evade this obligation. [483] [446]

C. HUMAN RIGHTS EDUCATION AND TRAINING

Myrna Mack Chang v. Guatemala
25-Nov-2003
Series C No. 101—*Merits, Reparations, and Costs*

281.   The characteristics of the facts in this case reveal that the armed forces, the police corps, and the security and intelligence agencies of the State acted exceeding their authority by applying means and methods that were not respectful of human rights. It is imperative to avoid recidivism of the circumstances and facts described with respect to this same Judgment.

282.   The State must adopt the necessary provisions for this and, specifically, those tending to educate and train all members of its armed forces, the police, and its security agencies regarding the principles and rules for protection of human rights, even under a state of emergency. The State must specifically include education on human rights and on International Humanitarian Law in its training programs for the members of the armed forces, of the police, and of its security agencies.

Girls Yean and Bosico v. Dominican Republic
8-Sep-2005
Series C No. 130—*Preliminary Objections, Merits, Reparations, and Costs*

242.   The Court also finds that the State should implement, within a reasonable time, a program to provide training on human rights, with special emphasis on the right to equal protection and non-discrimination, to the State officials responsible for registering births, during which they should receive guidance on the special situation of children so that a culture of tolerance and non-discrimination is fostered.

d)   *Regarding education*

244.   The State should comply with its obligation to guarantee access to free primary education for all children, irrespective of their origin or parentage, which arises from the special protection that must be provided to children.

"Mapiripán Massacre" v. Colombia
15-Sep-2005
Series C No. 134—*Merits, Reparations, and Costs*

2. The Commission filed the application in this case for the Court to decide whether the State breached Articles 4 (Right to Life), 5 (Right to Humane Treatment) and 7 (Right to Personal Liberty) of the American Convention, to the detriment of the [[alleged]] victims of the [alleged] massacre carried out in Mapiripán, stated in the application. The Commission also asked the Court to decide whether the State breached Articles 8.1 (Right to Fair Trial) and 25 (Right to Judicial Protection) of the Convention, in combination with Article 1(1) (Obligation to Respect Rights) of said treaty, to the detriment of the [alleged]victims of the [alleged]massacre and their next of kin. When it filed the application, the Commission pointed out that "between July 15 and 20, 1997 [...] approximately one hundred members of the Autodefensas Unidas de Colombia [, ...] with the collaboration and acquiescence of agents of the [...] State, deprived of their liberty, tortured, and murdered at least 49 civilians, after which they destroyed their bodies and threw their remains into the Guaviare River, in the Municipality of Mapiripán, Department of Meta". The Commission also pointed out that the [alleged]victims were "approximately 49 individuals", of whom it identified ten individuals and some of their next of kin.

B) OTHER FORMS OF REPARATION
(Measures of satisfaction and guarantees of non-recidivism)
h) Human rights education
316. Bearing in mind that the Mapiripán Massacre was committed by paramilitary who acted with the collaboration, tolerance and acquiescence of State agents, breaching the imperative provisions of International Law, the State must take steps to train the members of its armed forces and of its security agencies regarding the principles and provisions for protection of human rights and of international humanitarian law and on the limits to which it must be subject. Therefore, the State must implement, within a reasonable time, permanent education programs on human rights and international humanitarian law within the Colombian Armed Forces, at all hierarchical levels.
317. Said programs must specifically refer to the instant Judgment, to international human rights instruments and to international humanitarian law. In this regard, the

Constitutional Court of Colombia has pointed out, with regard to the obligations derived from Protocol II to disseminate international humanitarian law, that knowledge of said law "is an essential requirement for it to be respected by the parties that oppose each other. Therefore [...] all humanitarian law agreements attach a special importance to the task of disseminating humanitarian rules, not only among the opposing parties but also among the civilian population, for the latter to be aware of its rights in the context of the armed conflict. Furthermore, [...] the State must disseminate them [and] and they must be studied in educational institutions [...] Specifically, [it is] indispensable for the members of the security forces to be familiar with humanitarian rules, not only because they are natural addressees of said regulations but also because the Constitution itself states that they must receive human rights education [...]."[294][447]

Ximenes-Lopes v. Brazil
4-Jul-2006
Series C No 149—*Merits, Reparations, and Costs*

2.   The Commission filed the application for the Court to determine whether the State had violated the rights embodied in Articles 4 (Right to Life), 5 (Right to Humane Treatment), 8 (Right to a Fair Trial), and 25 (Right to Judicial Protection) of the American Convention in relation to the obligation set forth in Article 1(1) (Obligation to Respect Rights) of said treaty, to the detriment of Damião Ximenes-Lopes (hereinafter "Damião Ximenes-Lopes," "Ximenes-Lopes," or "the [alleged]victim"), for the [alleged] inhuman and degrading hospitalization conditions of Damião Ximenes-Lopes, a person with mental illness; the [alleged] beating and attack against the personal integrity of the [alleged] victim as a result of the action of the Officers of *Casa de Reposo Guararapes* (Guararapes Rest Home) (hereinafter "*Casa de Reposo Guararapes*" or "the hospital"); his death while held under psychiatric treatment; and the [alleged] lack of investigation and respect for the right to a fair trial that derived from the impunity surrounding such case. The [alleged] victim was hospitalized on October 1, 1999, as part of a psychiatric treatment in *Casa de Reposo Guararapes*, which is a private psychiatric clinic that operated in the public health system of Brazil, called the Uniform Health System (hereinafter "the Uniform Health System" or "the SUS"), in the Municipality of Sobral, state of Ceará. Ximenes-Lopes died on October 4, 1999, in *Casa de Reposo Guararapes* after three days of hospitalization.

3.   The Commission further stated that the events in the instant case are particularly relevant given the situation of vulnerability of persons with mental illness and the special obligation of the State to provide protection to individuals held in health centers operating within the State Uniform Health System.

[Reparations and Costs]

250.   It has been proved in the instant case that at the time of the events there was no adequate service for treating and hospitalizing persons with mental disabilities, such as in the *Casa de Reposo Guararapes* (Guararapes Rest Home), an institution that provided such service under the Single Health System. Although the fact that the State has adopted several measures to improve the service is worthy of note, this Court considers that the State must continue developing a training and education program for physicians, psychiatrists, psychologists, nurses, auxiliary nurses, and all other persons working in Mental Health Care institutions, particularly on the principles that must govern the treatment to be afforded to persons who suffer from a mental disability, pursuant to the international guidelines governing the subject and those set forth in this Judgment

---

Miguel Castro-Castro Prison v. Peru
25-Nov-2006
Series C No. 160—*Merits, Reparations, and Costs*

451.   The violations attributable to the State in the present case were perpetrated by police and army personnel, as well as special security forces, in violation of imperative norms of international law. Likewise, the Court has indicated [230][448] that in order to adequately guarantee the right to life and integrity, the members of the security forces must receive adequate training.

452.   Therefore, the State must design and implement, within a reasonable period of time, human rights education programs, addressed to agents of the Peruvian police force, on the international standards applicable to matters regarding treatment of inmates in situations of altercations of public order in penitentiary centers.

González et al. ("Cotton Field") v. Mexico
16-Nov-2009
Series C No. 205—*Preliminary Objections, Merits, Reparations, and Costs*

4.2.8.   Training with a gender perspective for public officials and the general public of the state of Chihuahua

531.   The Commission asked that the Court order the State to organize training programs for public officials in all branches of the administration of justice and the police, as well as comprehensive prevention policies. Furthermore, it asked that the Tribunal order the implementation of public policies and institutional

programs to overcome existing stereotypes of the role of women among the society of Ciudad Juárez and to promote the elimination of discriminatory socio-cultural patterns that prevent women from obtaining full access to justice.

532.   The representatives recognized that, although the State has made significant efforts with regard to training public officials, especially those whose work has a direct impact on the cases of disappearances and murders of women, these efforts have not been entirely satisfactory because they did not include a cross-cutting gender perspective and did not incorporate a gender perspective in every activity implemented by the State's authorities. They added that, although they had received training, the officials who appeared at the hearing "do not understand the implications of the Conventions. . . as regards the rights" of the victims.

533.   The State indicated that "it is aware that some of the irregularities committed at the onset of the investigations into the murders of Claudia Ivette González, Esmeralda Herrera Monreal, and Laura Berenice Ramos Monárrez were due to the lack of training of the public officials involved." However, the State [alleged] that, starting in October 2004, the Office of the Attorney General for the state of Chihuahua, in coordination with local institutions and universities, had designed a specialized training program on investigation techniques and procedures, and the professionalization of expert services, in which it invested more than 14 million pesos. No proof of the investment of this capital sum has been provided to the Court. The program includes "master's programs with the collaboration of Spanish universities and the National Human Rights Commission." [509][449] In 2005, more than 122 training programs were provided through the Center for Criminal and Forensic Studies, representing an investment of more than 12 million pesos. [510][450] The Tribunal observes that this investment has not been authenticated.

534.   On the issue of training, since 2006, the Organic Law of the Judiciary of the state of Chihuahua has accorded special importance to training officials of the Chihuahua state Judiciary in human rights and gender equality. [511][451]

535.   The State affirmed that it has provided training with a gender perspective for public officials of the states of the Mexican Republic, including the state of Chihuahua, through training courses for multipliers under the Gender Equity Subprogram. [512][452] It also mentioned that it had offered training to federal public officials under the awareness-raising program with a gender perspective offered by INMUJERES, as well as to public officials from the Federal Government's Public Security Secretariat under the Gender Equity Subprogram. Furthermore, it indicated that, in 2003 and 2004, it had trained personnel of the Public Security Secretariat in basic and specialized topics relating to human rights and public security. The State did not provide evidence of which public officials had been trained.

536.   The State indicated that, under strategy 5.4 ("to combat gender-based violence and to sanction it more severely") of the 2007-2012 National Development Plan, the Federal Government would implement programs of "awareness-raising and training for the police, doctors, public prosecutors, and judges, and for all those responsible for protecting and providing services to women who suffer any type of violence."[513 453]

537.   The State also referred to the following training provided in 2007: an "International Diploma on Gender and the Criminal System," attended by 41 public officials; [514 454] a "Diploma on Domestic Violence and Human Rights," for 69 members of the state Attorney General's Office; [515 455] the course "Advanced Specialization in the Basics and Principles of Procedural Law and Gender"; [516 456] and the course "Domestic Violence: a Problem for Everyone," for personnel of the Alternative Justice Center, the Rapid Response Unit, and the Specialized Unit for Crimes against Liberty, Sexual Safety, and the Family. [517 457] For 2008, the State referred to the course on "Forensic Reports in cases of Gender-Based Violence," which was offered to psychologists of the "Directorate to Provide Services to Victims." [518 458] In addition, the "Licentiate in the Provision of Justice" is offered in the state of Chihuahua, and the curriculum includes a course on "Gender Perspective." [519 459]

538.   The Court observes that witness Castro Romero testified that the diploma course on "Gender and Human Rights" was offered by the network of public institutions that provide services to women in abusive situations from October 14 to November 26, 2005. She also referred to the seminar on "International Human Rights Law: Litigation strategies" with the participation of around "60 people, including the Deputy State Attorney-General for the Northern Region and personnel of FEVIM (Office of the Special Prosecutor for Crimes related to Acts of Violence against Women)." [520 460]

539.   In addition, witness Caballero Rodríguez, an official of the Public Prosecutor's Office in charge of the investigations in this case, stated that he had received training on the American Convention and the Belem do Pará Convention, among other topics. [521 461]

540.   The Tribunal appreciates all the training programs with a gender perspective that the State has offered to public officials since 2004, as well as the possible investment of significant resources in this effort. However, since training is an ongoing activity, it must be maintained for a considerable period of time in order to achieve its objectives. [522 462] In addition the Court indicates that training with a gender perspective involves not only learning about laws and regulations, but also developing the capacity to recognize the discrimination that women suffer in their daily life. In particular, the training should enable all officials to recognize the effect on women of stereotyped ideas and opinions in relation to the meaning and scope of human rights.

541.   Consequently, notwithstanding the existence of programs and training sessions for public officials responsible for providing justice in Ciudad Juárez, as well as courses on human rights and gender, the Court orders the State to continue implementing permanent education and training programs and courses in: (i) human rights and gender; (ii) a gender perspective for due diligence in conducting preliminary investigations and judicial proceedings in relation to the discrimination, abuse, and murder of women based on their gender, and (iii) elimination of stereotypes of women's role in society.

542.   The programs and courses will be addressed to the police, prosecutors, judges, military officials, public servants responsible for providing services and legal assistance to victims of crime, and any local or federal public officials who participate directly or indirectly in prevention, investigation, prosecution, punishment, and reparation.   These permanent programs must make special mention of this Judgment and of the international human rights instruments, specifically those concerning gender-based violence, such as the Convention of Belém do Pará and CEDAW, taking into account how certain norms or practices of domestic law, either intentionally or by their results, have discriminatory effects on the daily life of women.   The programs must also include studies on the Istanbul Protocol and the United Nations Manual on the Effective Prevention and Investigation of Extralegal, Arbitrary, and Summary Executions.   The State must provide an annual report on the implementation of the courses and training sessions for three years.

543.   In addition, taking into account the situation of discrimination against women acknowledged by the State, the State must offer a program of education for the general public of the State of Chihuahua in order to overcome this situation. To this end, the State must submit an annual report indicating the activities it has implemented in this regard for three years.

Radilla-Pacheco v. Mexico
23-Nov-2009
Series C No. 209—*Preliminary Objections, Merits, Reparations, and Costs*

C3. Training legal agents and education in human rights
345. The representatives requested that this Tribunal order that the State train "[a]ll public officials who in the normal development of their tasks are in contact with the next of kin of victims of forced disappearance [...] so they know how to deal with the considerations necessary [...]" with those people.
346. Given the specific circumstances of the present case, this Tribunal considers it important to strengthen the institutional capacities of the State of Mexico, through

the training of public officials, in order to avoid facts as those analyzed in the present case from happening again. With regard to the training in matters of the protection of human rights, the Court, in it[s] jurisprudence, has considered that this is one form of offering public officials new knowledge, of developing their capacities, allowing their specialization in certain innovative areas, preparing them to fill different positions and adapting their abilities in order to offer a better performance in the tasks assigned. [463] [322]

347. Similarly, this Tribunal has reiterated that the State's obligation to adequately investigate and punish, in its case, those responsible, shall be diligently complied with in order to avoid impunity and the repetition of this type of facts. Therefore, the Court orders that, without detriment to the training programs for public officials in matters of human rights that already exist in Mexico, the State shall implement, within a reasonable period of time and with the corresponding budgetary stipulation:

(a) Programs or permanent courses regarding the analysis of the jurisprudence of the Inter-American Human Rights Protection System in reference to the limits of military criminal jurisdiction, as well as the rights to judicial guarantees and judicial protection, as a way of preventing that cases of violations of human rights be investigated and prosecuted by that jurisdiction. Those programs will be addressed to the members of all the Military's Forces, including agents of the Public Prosecutors' Office and judges, as well as the agents of the public prosecutors' office of the Attorney General of the Republic and judges of the Judiciary of the Federation, and

(b) A training program on the due investigation and prosecution of facts that constitute the forced disappearance of persons, addressed to agents of the Public Prosecutors' office of the Attorney General of the Republic and judges of the Judiciary of the Federation, who have jurisdiction in the investigation and prosecution of facts such as the ones that occurred in the present case, in order to provide those officials with the legal, technical, and scientific elements necessary to comprehensively evaluate the phenomenon of forced disappearance. Specifically, in this type of cases the authorities in charge of the investigation shall be trained in the use of circumstantial evidence, indicia, and presumptions, the assessment of the systematic patterns that may lead to the facts under investigation and the location of persons who have suffered a forced disappearance. (*supra* para. 206 and 222).

348. Within the aforementioned programs, special reference shall be made to the present Judgment and to the human rights international instruments to which Mexico is a Party.

Rosendo Cantú et al. v. Mexico
31-Aug-2010
Series C No. 216—*Preliminary Objections, Merits, Reparations, and Costs*

ix) Training programs for officials

243. The Commission asked that the Court order the State to develop training programs for government employees in accordance with the Istanbul Protocol, to provide said officials with the necessary scientific and technical elements to evaluate possible situations of torture or cruel, inhuman, or degrading treatment.

244. The State presented information and documentary evidence about the implementation of training programs and courses, as well as operating manuals for officials of the public administration, the judiciary branch, and health sector employees. Among other initiatives, Mexico reported that in 2009, a procedure of institutional and social fortification for attention to violence against indigenous women was developed, training government employees of the state of Guerrero in human rights, gender equity, and interculturality. Moreover, the Attorney General of Justice of the state of Guerrero provides training courses in human rights, with the goal of raising awareness amongst the employees on the importance of prevention of sexual assaults, highlighting seminars on criminal investigations of sexual violence, forensic medicine, and attention to victims of sexual violence. In addition, during the 2008-2009 period, the General Secretariat of the Government of Guerrero, carried out two training workshops called "Networks of development of detention, support, and reference of gender-based violence cases in indigenous areas of Guerrero" directed, among others, at indigenous authorities and care providers to the violence. Ten workshops on professionalism of public employees of the judiciary branch of the state of Guerrero were carried out. Finally, Mexico also made reference to other training initiatives of general reach, including the training of translators in the agencies of the Public Prosecutor's Office in indigenous communities.

245. The Court assesses positively the existence of training programs and courses developed by the State. In this regard, it considers that they should include the provisions of the Istanbul Protocol and the guidelines of the World Health Organization, and should pay special attention to the response to [alleged] victims of rape, particularly when they belong to vulnerable groups, such as indigenous women and children.

246. As it has done previously, [286] [464] the Court orders the State to continue implementing permanent training programs and courses on the diligent investigation of cases of the sexual abuse of women that include a gender and ethnicity perspective. These courses must be offered to officials at the federal level and in the state of Guerrero, particularly to officials within the Public Prosecutor's Office, the judicial branch, the police, and health sector personnel

with competence in this type of case who, owing to their functions, constitute the first line of response to women victims of violence.

x) Permanent educational programs on human rights within the Armed Forces

247. The Commission asked that the Court order the State to implement permanent educational programs on human rights within the Mexican Armed Forces, for all ranks, which should include special mention of international human rights instruments, specifically those related to the protection of women's rights, *inter alia*, their right to live without violence, and to non-discrimination.

248. The State presented information on the human rights training programs and international humanitarian law programs implemented by the Mexican Secretariat of National Defense. Likewise, it indicated the creation of the General Office of Human Rights of said Secretariat, responsible for promoting a culture of human rights within the Armed Forces and to follow the complaints and recommendations that the National Human Rights Commission puts forward for the probable violations of human rights imputed to military personnel. Regarding a gender-based perspective, it manifested that said Secretariat is currently developing a Training and Sensitization Program for Gender-Based Perspectives.

249. The Court assesses the information offered by the State regarding the training programs. This Court considers it important to develop the State's institutional capacities by training members of the Armed Forces on the principles and norms for the protection of human rights and on the limits to which they should be subject,[287][465] in order to avoid a repetition of acts such as those that occurred in the present case. To this end, the State must implement, within a reasonable period of time, a permanent program or course of obligatory human rights training, that includes, among other topics, the limits in the interaction between military personnel and the civilian population, gender, and indigenous rights, for members of the Armed Forces in all hierarchical ranks.

xvi) Campaign for the awareness and sensitization of the prohibition and effects of violence and discrimination against the indigenous woman

265. The representatives requested the Court to order the State of Mexico to carry out a campaign for the awareness and sensitization of the prohibition and effects of violence and discrimination against indigenous women in all aspects of their lives, which should be directed at the population in general, and particularly at the education and public health facilities in the state of Guerrero, such as federal, state, municipal and communitarian employees.

266. In this regard, the State presented evidence of campaigns regarding the prohibition and effects of violence and discrimination against women in all aspects of their lives. In particular, it reported on two programs of dissemination, through several media outlets, addressed to population, public officers and social actors that attend to victims of gender related violence and human trafficking. The State also reported on campaigns, implemented by the National Women's Institute

and the National Commission for the Development of Indigenous Peoples, on the prevention—in print and electronic media—to promote nonviolence as the right of women in indigenous areas, which include radio programs covering topics such as gender violence, sexual harassment, domestic violence, and sexual rights, among others. Finally, the State noted that the said Department of Indigenous Affairs of the state of Guerrero has promoted radio broadcasting in indigenous radios, of the rights enshrined in Law 533 of Access of Women to a Life Free From Violence in four indigenous languages that exist throughout the state of Guerrero.

267. The Court does not have information on behalf of the representatives that indicates the deficiencies in this campaign. As such, the Court does not find that it is necessary to carry out a new awareness and sensitization campaign of the population in general regarding the prohibition and effects of violence and discrimination against indigenous women in all aspects of their lives, rather that the measure should be guaranteed by means of the continuation of the already established campaign. Regarding the government employees, the Court considers that the publication of the present Judgment and the reparations ordered in sections *ix)* and *x)* of this chapter are sufficient and adequate, and as such, the Court will not declare additional measures regarding the present request for reparation.

Atala Riffo and Daughters v. Chile
24-Feb-2012
Series C No. 239—*Merits, Reparations and Costs*

3. Guarantees of non-repetition
267. The Court emphasizes that some discriminatory acts analyzed in the previous chapters relate to the perpetuation of stereotypes that are associated with the structural and historical discrimination suffered by sexual minorities (*supra* para. 92), particularly in matters concerning access to justice and the application of domestic law. Therefore, some reparations must have a transformative purpose, in order to produce both a restorative and corrective effect [279] [466] and promote structural changes, dismantling certain stereotypes and practices that perpetuate discrimination against LGBT groups. It is on this basis that the Court will analyze the requests of the Commission and the representatives.

a. Training for public officials
271. The Court takes note of the advances made by the State in its training programs and activities directed at public officials. Notwithstanding this progress, the Court orders the State to continue implementing continuous educational programs and training courses in: i) human rights, sexual orientation, and non-discrimination; ii) protection of the rights of LGBTI community; and iii) discrimination, overcoming

gender stereotypes of LGBTI persons and homophobia. The courses must be directed at public officials at the regional and national levels, and particularly at judicial officials of all areas and levels of the judicial branch.

272. In these programs and training courses, special mention must be made of both the present Judgment and the various precedents of the *corpus iuris* of human rights related to the prohibition of discrimination based on sexual orientation and the obligation of all authorities and officials to guarantee that all persons, without discrimination based on sexual orientation, may enjoy each and every one of the rights established in the Convention. To this end, special attention should be paid to norms or practices in domestic law which, either intentionally or because of their results, may have discriminatory effects on the exercise of rights by persons belonging to sexual minorities.

The Kichwa Indigenous People of Sarayaku v. Ecuador
27-Jun-2012
Series C No. 245—*Merits and reparations*

c) Training of State officials on the rights of indigenous peoples
302. In this case, the Court has determined that the violations of the rights to prior consultation and cultural identity of the Sarayaku People resulted from the acts and omissions of different officials and institutions that failed to guarantee those rights. The State must implement, within a reasonable time and with the corresponding budgetary allocation, mandatory programs or courses that include modules on the domestic and international standards concerning the human rights of indigenous peoples and communities, for military, police and judicial officials, as well as others whose functions involve relations with indigenous peoples, as part of the general and continuing training of officials in the respective institutions, at all hierarchical levels.

Furlan and Family v. Argentina
31-Aug-2012
Series C No. 246—*Preliminary Objections, Merits, Reparations and Costs*

B.3.3) Training for public officials and cooperation between State institutions
Considerations of the Court
308. The Court takes cognizance of the actions carried out by the State with regard to training for officials, information campaigns and inter-institutional cooperation to strengthen services for persons with disabilities. Nevertheless, bearing in mind the violations that have been declared to the detriment of a person

with disabilities in relation to the duration of judicial proceedings (*supra* para. 204) and the execution of the judgment (*supra* para. 219), the Court considers it necessary that the State continue to provide training courses to officials of the Executive and the Judiciary and public information campaigns on the protection of the rights of persons with disabilities. [473 467] The training programs should reflect the principles of full participation and equality, [474 468] and be conducted in consultation with organizations for persons with disabilities. [475 469] In addition, the Court considers that the State should continue to strengthen cooperation between State institutions and non-governmental organizations in order to improve the care provided to persons with disabilities and their families. To this end, it should ensure that the organizations of persons with disabilities can play a significant role so as to guarantee that their concerns are duly taken into account and processed appropriately. [476 470]

The Massacres of El Mozote and Nearby Places v. El Salvador
25-Oct-2012
Series C No. 252—*Merits, reparations and costs*

4) *Guarantees of non-repetition*
a) Training for the Armed Forces of the Republic of El Salvador
368. In the instant case, the State has acknowledged and the Court has determined that, during the military operation in which the Atlacatl BIRI was the main participant, with the support of other military units, including the Salvadoran Air Force, successive massacres were perpetrated at seven places in the north of the department of Morazán (*supra* paras. 17, 19 and 151). In this regard, the Court considers it pertinent to recall that it is crucial that human rights education programs are implemented effectively within the security forces and have an impact in order to create guarantees of non-repetition of events such as those of the instant case. Such programs must be reflected in results of action and prevention that demonstrate their effectiveness, regardless of the fact that they must be evaluated by suitable indicators. [527 471]
369. Consequently, this Court considers it important to strengthen the State's institutional capacities by training the members of the Armed Forces of the Republic of El Salvador on the principles and norms of protection of human rights and on the constraints to which they must be subject. Therefore, the State must implement, within one year of notification of this Judgment and with the respective budgetary provision, a permanent and compulsory program or course on human rights, including a children- and gender-based perspective, for all ranks of the Armed Forces of the Republic of El Salvador. This Judgment and the

case law of the Inter-American Court on grave human rights violations must be included in the training.

Artavia Murillo et al. ("In Vitro Fertilization") v. Costa Rica
28-Nov-2012
Series C No. 257—*Preliminary objections, merits, reparations and costs*

B.3.2) Campaign on the rights of persons with reproductive disabilities
Considerations of the Court
341. The Court observes that the State did not specify the existing mechanisms to raise awareness on reproductive health. [500][472] Therefore, it orders the State to implement permanent education and training programs and courses on human rights, reproductive rights and non-discrimination for judicial employees in all areas and at all echelons of the Judiciary. [501][473] These programs and training courses should make special mention of this Judgment and the different precedents in the *corpus iuris* of human rights relating to reproductive rights and the principle of non-discrimination.

Mendoza et al. v. Argentina
14-May-2013
Series C No. 260—*Preliminary objections, merits and reparations*

B.3.4. Training for State authorities
B.3.4.2. Considerations of the Court

336. The Court assesses positively the progress made by the State to apply a mechanism to prevent torture and urges the State to expedite the implementation of specific and effective measures in this regard. However, the State did not explain whether this mechanism is also applicable in detention centers and prisons.
337. Thus, in order to guarantee the non-repetition of the human rights violations declared in this case, the Court finds it important to strengthen the institutional capacities of federal prison personnel and prison personnel of the province of Mendoza, as well as of the judges with competence for offenses committed by juveniles, by providing them with training on the principles and norms of the protection of human rights and the rights of the child, including those relating to humane treatment and torture. To this end, the State must implement, within a reasonable time, if they do not exist at present, obligatory programs or courses

on the above-mentioned points as part of the general and ongoing education of the said State officials. These programs or courses must include references to this Judgment, to the Inter-American Court's case law on personal integrity, torture, and the rights of the child, as well as the international human rights obligations derived from the treaties to which Argentina is a Party. [402][474]

ANALYSIS AND QUESTIONS RAISED BY THE COURT'S JURISPRUDENCE

As demonstrated by the above case excerpts, the Inter-American Court of Human Rights orders a range of measures designed to guarantee the non-repetition of human rights violations. Such measures frequently involve legal reforms, ranging from ensuring civilian control over military and security forces, judicial independence, and the protection of potential victims, advocates and other human rights defenders, to the observance of international standards of due process, fairness and impartiality in civilian and military proceedings, as well as the observance of ethical norms and codes of conduct by public servants and officials in all sectors of society. A significant category of legal reform is the review of laws which directly or indirectly permit gross violations of human rights law, and particularly amnesty laws which the Court has judged repeatedly to be incompatible with the upholding of human rights.

Another fundamental measure ordered by the Court to guarantee non-repetition of violations is human rights education and training for all sectors of society, and particularly law enforcement, military and security forces. Such education and training measures, as with other measures designed to guarantee non-repetition seek to address and remedy widespread, systematic or gross violations of human rights and recognize that individual violations may be part of a pattern or practice of violations. And, while the core of guarantees of non-repetition is to prevent future violations, such guarantees necessarily relate to the cessation of ongoing violations and the official acknowledgement of past violations, thus offering a form of reparation for victims who have suffered the harm of violations of their human rights.

- Throughout its jurisprudence, the Court has addressed legal reforms necessary to bring domestic law into accord with the American Convention on Human Rights and other applicable international norms, as in *"The Last Temptation of Christ," Radilla-Pacheco, Fernandez Ortega, Rosendo Cantú, Atala Riffo and Daughters,* and *Mendoza et al.* In *El Amparo*, it affirmed that international standards must be applied in both civilian and military settings. And in several cases, including *Furlan and Family* and *Artavia*

Murillo et al., the Court has emphasized that States not only have the positive obligation to adopt the necessary legislative measures to guarantee the exercise of the rights embodied in the Convention, but they must also avoid promulgating laws that prevent, restrict, or eliminate, the free exercise of those rights.[475] In some cases, the legal reform ordered by the Court addresses the violation of the victim's rights very specifically, as in the removal of Herrera-Ulloa's name from the registry of convicted felons. In other cases, the Court has addressed collective rights, such as in *Moiwana Community* and *Sawhoyamaxa Indigenous Community* where collective title and right to property was at issue, in *Yatama* where access and participation in the electoral process was at issue, and in *Kichwa Indigenous People of Sarayaku* where the Court ordered that prior consultation be regulated within domestic law. In numerous cases, the Court has addressed the violations in the instant case and simultaneously shed light upon larger societal issues, such as in *Girls Yean and Bosico* in which the Court ordered the facilitation of birth registrations for Dominican children of Haitian origin, and in *Yvon Neptune* in which the Court addressed the conditions within Haitian prisons and detention centers. Even specific legal reforms directed at addressing the violations suffered by one victim, as in *Herrera-Ulloa*, set a legal precedent and may thus impact larger numbers of victims. Is legal reform always necessary to address violations suffered by large numbers of victims or communities, or are there circumstances in which the Court could order measures to address large-scale harm without legal reforms?

- In each of the above case excerpts involving amnesty laws, the Court has declared that such amnesties are incompatible with the observance of human rights. These cases involved disappearances, extrajudicial executions and other killings, and crimes against humanity. Are there any other types of violations that could be subject to amnesty laws?

- The Court frequently orders human rights education and training to raise awareness and knowledge amongst relevant officials and agencies and to counter the underlying causes of various human rights violations. In numerous cases, the education and training ordered is to address a range of human rights issues, as in the training of security forces (as addressed in *Myrna Mack Chang*, *"Mapiripán Massacre"*, and *El Mozote*). The Court has also addressed specific education and training issues in many of its cases, such as equal protection and non-discrimination (*Girls Yean and Bosico*), mental health (*Ximenes-Lopes*), the humane treatment of inmates (*Miguel Castro-Castro*), violence against women (*"Cotton Field"*), disappearances (*Radilla-Pacheco*), sexual assault (*Rosendo Cantú*), LGBT rights (*Atala* Riffo), indigenous peoples' rights (*Kichwa Indigenous People of Sarayaku*), disability issues (*Furlan and Family*), reproductive rights (*Artavia Murillo*), and torture and the rights of the child (*Mendoza et al.*). In several cases, the Court has addressed pervasive and systematic discrimination and violence against women and has ordered that education and trainings involve a "gender perspective" and serve to raise awareness regarding such issues within society (*"Cotton Field"*), particularly amongst service providers such as doctors and law enforcement officials, including prosecutors, police and judges. In some cases, the Court has explicitly noted the necessity for permanent education programs and ongoing trainings (as in *Rosendo Cantú* and *Mendoza et al.*), as well as awareness-raising and sensitization campaigns. In what circumstances is it more effective to order human rights education and training for a specific sector of society, and when is it more effective to order such education and training for an entire community or society? Is ongoing human rights education and training always appropriate? And does the Court have a mandate or right to promote cultural change?

- The Court has also declared that "some reparations must have a transformative purpose, in order to produce both a restorative and corrective effect and promote structural changes, dismantling certain stereotypes and practices that perpetuate discrimination."[476] Is this type of transformation the purpose of all human rights education and training measures, as well as guarantees of non-repetition in general? Are there any types of guarantees of non-repetition that do not need to serve a transformative purpose?

Endnotes

1   *See Atala Riffo and Daughters v. Chile*, Merits, Reparations and Costs, Judgment of February 24, 2012, Series C, No. 239, para. 239.

2   United Nations General Assembly, A/RES/60/147, adopted at the 64th plenary meeting on 16 December 2005.

3   Adopted by the International Law Commission (ILC) at its fifty-third session, 2001.

4   *Factory at Chorzów, Merits, Judgment No. 13, 1928, P.C.I.J., Series A, No. 17*, p.47.

5   *See* Draft Articles on State Responsibility for Internationally Wrongful Acts with Commentaries, *Art. 34-37.*

6 219 See *Case of Caesar,* [Judgment of March 11, 2005. Series C No. 123], para. 129; *Case of Huilca Tecse,* [Judgment of March 3, 2005. Series C No. 121], para. 102, and *Case of the*

7 234   *Serrano Cruz Sisters*, [Judgment of March 1, 2005. Series C No. 120], para. 165. *Cf. Case of Indigenous Community Yakye Axa*. Interpretation of the Judgment on the Merits, Reparations, and Costs (art. 67(1) American Convention on Human Rights). Judgment of February 6, 2006. Series C No. 142, para. 26, and *Case of Indigenous Community Yakye Axa*, [Judgment of June 17, 2005. Series C No. 125], para. 144 to 154 and 217.

8 238   *Cf. Case of the Pueblo Bello Massacre*, [Judgment of January 31, 2006. Series C No. 140], para. 264, *Case of Blanco-Romero et al.* Judgment of November 28, 2005. Series C[,] No. 138, para. 93; and Case of *Gómez Palomino [v. Perú*. Judgment of November 22, 2005, Series C No. 136], para. 136.

9 6   In Operative Paragraph 5 of the Judgment, read in conjunction with paragraph 194(a), the Court ordered the State to "delimit, demarcate, and grant collective title over the territory of the members of the Saramaka people, in accordance with their customary laws and through previous, effective, and fully informed consultations with the Saramaka people, without prejudice to other tribal and indigenous communities." *Cf. Case of the Saramaka People v. Suriname. Preliminary Objections, Merits, Reparations, and Costs.* Judgment of November 28, 2007. Series C No. 172], para. 194(a).

10 7   In Operative Paragraph 6 of the Judgment, read in conjunction with paragraph 174, the Court ordered the State to "establish, in consultation with the Saramaka people and fully respecting their traditions and customs, the judicial and administrative conditions necessary to ensure the recognition of their juridical personality[] with the aim of guaranteeing them the use and enjoyment of their territory in accordance with their communal property system, as well as the rights to access to justice and equality before the law." *Cf. Case of the Saramaka People, supra* note [6], para. 174.

11 8   In Operative Paragraph 7 of the Judgment, read in conjunction with paragraph 194(c), the Court ordered the State to "remove or amend the legal provisions that impede protection of the right to property of the members of the Saramaka people and adopt, in its domestic legislation, and through prior, effective[,] and fully informed consultations with the Saramaka people, legislative, administrative, and other measures as may be required to recognize, protect, guarantee[,] and give legal effect to the right of the members of the Saramaka people to hold collective title of the territory they have traditionally used and occupied." *Cf. Case of the Saramaka People, supra* note [6], para. 194(c).

12 9   In Operative Paragraph 8 of the Judgment, read in conjunction with paragraph 194(d), the Court ordered the State to "adopt legislative, administrative[,] and other measures necessary to recognize and ensure the right of the Saramaka people to be effectively consulted, in accordance with their traditions and customs, or when necessary, the right to give or withhold their free, informed[,] and prior consent[] with regards to development or investment projects that may affect their territory[] and to reasonably share the benefits of such projects with the members of the Saramaka people, should these be ultimately carried out. The Saramaka people must be consulted during the process established to comply with this form of reparation." *Cf. Case of the Saramaka People, supra* note [6], para. 194(d).

13 10   In Operative Paragraph 9 of the Judgment, read in conjunction with paragraph 133, the Court ordered the State to "ensure that members of the Saramaka people are aware of possible risks, including environmental and health risks, in order that the proposed development or investment plan is accepted knowingly and voluntarily." *Cf. Case of the Saramaka People, supra* note [6], para. 133.

14 11   In paragraph 129 of the Judgment, the Court declared that "in accordance with Article 1(1) of the Convention, in order to guarantee that restrictions to the property rights of the members of the Saramaka people by the issuance of concessions within their territory does not amount to a denial of their survival as a tribal people, the State must . . . ensure the[ir] effective participation . . ., in conformity with their customs and traditions . . . ." *Case of the Saramaka People, supra* note 1, para. 129.

15 12   *Cf. Case of the Saramaka People, supra* note [6], paras. 133 through 137.

16 13   *Cf. Case of the Saramaka People, supra* note [6], para. 133.

17 14   The Court declared in paragraph 137 that, "in addition to the consultation that is always required when planning development or investment projects within traditional Saramaka territory, the safeguard of effective participation that is necessary when dealing with major development or investment plans that may have a profound impact on the property rights of the members of the Saramaka people to a large part of their territory must be understood to additionally require the free, prior, and informed consent of the Saramakas, in accordance with their traditions and customs." *Case of the Saramaka People, supra* note [6], para. 137.

18 15   Article 44 of the Convention provides that "any person or group of persons, or any nongovernmental entity legally recognized in one or more member states of the Organization, may lodge petitions with the Commission containing denunciations or complaints of violation of this Convention by a State Party."

19   In paragraph 138 of the Judgment the Court declared that the "concept of benefit-sharing, which can be found in various international instruments regarding indigenous and tribal peoples' rights,[...] can be said to be inherent to the right of compensation recognized under Article 21(2) of the Convention . . . .." *Case of the Saramaka People, supra* note 1, para. 138.

20 17   *Cf. Case of the Saramaka People, supra* note [6], Operative Paragraphs 5, 7, and 9, and paras. 81, 86, 90, 91, 103, 120-123, 126-129, 139-141, 146, 148, 155, 157, 158, 194(a), 194(c), and 194(e).

21 18   *Cf. Case of the Saramaka People, supra* note [6], paras. 127 and 137; *Case of the Yakye Axa Indigenous Community v. Paraguay. Merits, Reparations and Costs.* Judgment of June 17, 2005. Series C No. 125, paras. 144-145 citing (*mutatis mutandi*) *Case of Ricardo Canese v. Paraguay. Merits, Reparations and Costs.* Judgment of August 31, 2004. Series C No. 111, para. 96; *Case of Herrera Ulloa v. Costa Rica. Preliminary Objections, Merits, Reparations and Costs.* Judgment of July 2, 2004. Series C No. 107, para. 127, and *Case of Ivcher Bronstein v. Peru. Merits, Reparations and Costs.* Judgment of February 6, 2001. Series C No. 74. para. 155.

22 19   *Cf. Case of the Saramaka People, supra* note [6], para. 128; and *mutatis mutandis*, UNHRC, *Länsman et al. v. Finland (Fifty-second session, 1994)*, Communication No. 511/1992, U.N. Doc. CCPR/C/52/D/511/1994, November 8, 1994, para. 9.4 (allowing States to pursue development activities that limit the rights of a minority culture as long as the activity does not fully extinguish the indigenous people's way of life).

23 20   *Case of the Saramaka People, supra* note [6], paras. 91 and 129.

24 21   *Case of the Saramaka People, supra* note [6], para. 121.

25 22   The ninth Operative Paragraph of the Judgment indicates that the State shall "ensure that environmental and social impact assessments are conducted by independent and technically competent entities prior to awarding a concession for any development or investment project within traditional Saramaka territory, and [it shall] implement adequate safeguards and mechanisms in order to minimize the damaging effects such projects may have upon the social, economic and cultural survival of the Saramaka people, in the terms of paragraphs 129, 133, 143, 146, 148, 155, 158, and 194(e) of [the] Judgment." *Case of the Saramaka People, supra* note 6, Operative Paragraph 9.

26 23   One of the most comprehensive and used standards for ESIAs in the context of indigenous and tribal peoples is known as the *Akwé:Kon Guidelines for the Conduct of Cultural, Environmental and Social Impact Assessments Regarding Developments Proposed to Take Place on, or which are Likely to Impact on, Sacred Sites and on Lands and Waters Traditionally Occupied or Used by Indigenous and Local Communities*, which can be found at www.cbd.int/doc/publications/akwe-brochure-pdf.

27 24   The Court has also previously held that "traditional possession of their lands by indigenous people has equivalent effects to those of a state-granted full property title." *Cf. Case of the Sawhoyamaxa Indigenous Community v. Paraguay. Merits, Reparations and Costs.* Judg-

ment of March 29, 2006. Series C No. 146, para. 128.

28 25   *Cf. Case of the Saramaka People, supra* note [6], Operative Paragraphs 5 and 7.

29 26   *Cf. Case of the Saramaka People, supra* note [6], paras. 127 and 129 of the Judgment.

30 27   *Case of the Saramaka People, supra* note [6], para. 194(c).

31 28   In paragraph 122 of the Judgment, the Court stated that "the natural resources found on and within indigenous and tribal people's territories that are protected under Article 21 are those natural resources traditionally used and necessary for the very survival, development, and continuation of such people's way of life." *Case of the Saramaka People, supra* note 6, para. 122. [29] *Cf. Case of the Sawhoyamaxa Indigenous Community [v. Paraguay. Merits, Reparations and Costs.* Judgment of March 29, 2006. Series C No. 146], para. 189.

32 29   *Cf. Case of the Sawhoyamaxa Indigenous Community [v. Paraguay. Merits, Reparations and Costs.* Judgment of March 29, 2006. Series C No. 146], para. 189.

33 308   *Cf.* Decree No. 1,595 of February 26, 2009, "creating and appointing the members of the Inter-institutional Commission responsible for implementing the necessary measures to Comply with the International Judgments (CICSI) delivered by the Inter-American Court of Human Rights and the recommendations issued by the Inter-American Commission on Human Rights" (attachments to the answer to the application, attachment 5(5), tome VIII, folios 3591 to 3595).

34 309   *Cf. Case of Almonacid-Arellano et al. v. Chile,* [Preliminary objections, merits, reparations and costs. Judgment of September 26, 2006. Series C No. 154], para. 124; *Case of La Cantuta v. Peru. Merits, reparations and costs.* Judgment of November 29, 2006. Series C No. 162, para. 173, and *Case of Radilla Pacheco v. Mexico,* [Preliminary objections, merits, reparations and costs. Judgment of November 23, 2009. Series C No. 209], para. 339.

35 310   *Cf. Case of Almonacid-Arellano et al. v. Chile, supra* note 3[0]9, para. 124; *Case of La Cantuta v. Peru, supra* note 30[9], para. 173, and *Case of Radilla Pacheco v. Mexico, supra* [309], para. 339.

36 335   Article 63(1) of the American Convention states: "If the Court finds that there has been a violation of a right or freedom protected by this Convention, the Court shall rule that the injured party be ensured the enjoyment of his right or freedom that was violated. It shall also rule, if appropriate, that the consequences of the measure or situation that constituted the breach of such right or freedom be remedied and that fair compensation be paid to the injured party."

37 347   Evidence file, tome 17, folio 9595.

38 348   The representatives asked the Court to require the State "to remove all the explosives on the surface of the territory […], as the Sarayaku requested during the proceeding on provisional measures." To this end, "the State must search at least 500 meters on both sides of the E16 seismic line which passes through Sarayaku territory." In addition, they asked the Court to "order the Ecuadorian State to deal with the pentolite underground in accordance with the plan proposed by Professor Kanth, which is based on determining the number of points where the pentolite is buried, burying the detonator cables, marking the points where these are buried, and declaring the area as a recovery zone." Lastly, they indicated that "the process described must be executed by the State as soon as possible," and that "[e]very phase of this management plan must be submitted for consultation and agreed with the Kichwa People of Sarayaku, who should continue receiving external advice on the process."

39 489   *Cf. Case of Velásquez Rodríguez v. Honduras. Reparations and costs,* paras. 25 to 27, and *Case of Vélez Restrepo and family members v. Colombia,* para. 257.

40 491   *Cf. Case of the Las Dos Erres Massacre v. Guatemala,* para. 226.

41 492   *Cf. Case of the Las Dos Erres Massacre v. Guatemala,* para. 226.

42 493   *Cf. Case of the Las Dos Erres Massacre v. Guatemala,* para. 226.

43 494   *Cf. Case of the Las Dos Erres Massacre v. Guatemala,* para. 226.

44 509   *Cf. Case of El Amparo v. Venezuela. Reparations and costs.* Judgment of September 14,

45 510 1996. Series C No. 28, para. 35, and *Case of Furlan and family v. Argentina*, para. 319.
Cf. Case of Masacre Plan de Sánchez v. Guatemala. Reparations and costs. Judgment of November 19, 2004. Series C No. 116, para. 105, and *Case of the Río Negro Massacres v. Guatemala*, para. 284.

46 511 *Cf. Case of Masacre Plan de Sánchez v. Guatemala. Reparations and costs*, para. 105, and *Case of the Ituango Massacres v. Colombia*, para. 407.

47 *See González et al. ("Cotton Field") v. Mexico*, Preliminary Objections, Merits, Reparations, and Costs, Nov. 16, 2009, Series C No. 205, para. 450 (emphasis added).

48 272 *Cf.* Application of the International Covenant on Economic, Social and Cultural Rights, General Comment 4, The right to adequate housing (paragraph 1 of Article 11 of the Covenant) (Sixth session, 1991), U.N. Doc. E/1991/23.

49 273 *Cf. Case of the "Juvenile Reeducation Institute"*, *supra* note [270], para. 318; *Case of the Gómez Paquiyauri Brothers, supra* note 2[7]1, para. 207, and *Case of the 19 Tradesmen*, *supra* note 2[71], para. 277.

50 49 Article 5 of the American Convention establishes, in what is pertinent, that: 1. Every person has the right to have his physical, mental, and moral integrity respected. 2. No one shall be subjected to torture or to cruel, inhuman, or degrading punishment or treatment. All persons deprived of their liberty shall be treated with respect for the inherent dignity of the human person.

51 50 Article 11 of the Convention establishes, *inter alia,* that: 1. Everyone has the right to have his honor respected and his dignity recognized.
2. No one may be the object of arbitrary or abusive interference with his private life, his family, his home, or his correspondence, or of unlawful attacks on his honor or reputation.

52 51 Article 1(1) establishes that: "[t]he States Parties to this Convention undertake to respect the rights and freedoms recognized herein and to ensure to all persons subject to their jurisdiction the free and full exercise of those rights and freedoms, without any discrimination for reasons of race, color, sex, language, religion, political or other opinion, national or social origin, economic status, birth, or any other social condition."

53 52 The Inter-American Convention to Prevent and Punish Torture establishes, *inter alia*, that: Article 1 The State Parties undertake to prevent and punish torture in accordance with the terms of this Convention. Article 2 For the purposes of this Convention, torture shall be understood to be any act intentionally performed whereby physical or mental pain or suffering is inflicted on a person for purposes of criminal investigation, as a means of intimidation, as personal punishment, as a preventive measure, as a penalty, or for any other purpose. Torture shall also be understood to be the use of methods upon a person intended to obliterate the personality of the victim or to diminish his physical or mental capacities, even if they do not cause physical pain or mental anguish. Article 6. In accordance with the terms of Article 1, the States Parties shall take effective measures to prevent and punish torture within their jurisdiction.
The States Parties shall ensure that all acts of torture and attempts to commit torture are offenses under their criminal law and shall make such acts punishable by severe penalties that take into account their serious nature.

54 53 Article 7(a) and (b) of the Convention of Belém do Pará, establishes, in what is pertinent, that: The States Parties condemn all forms of violence against women and agree to pursue, by all appropriate means and without delay, policies to prevent, punish and eradicate such violence and undertake to: a. refrain from engaging in any act or practice of violence against women and to ensure that their authorities, officials, personnel, agents, and institutions act in conformity with this obligation[, and] b. apply due diligence to prevent, investigate and impose penalties for violence against women[.]

55 54 *Cf. Report 2003*, United Nations Office of the High Commissioner for Human Rights in Mexico, *supra* note 34, folio 293); *Report regarding violence against women in the Municipalities of the Mountain region of Guerrero* [Diagnóstico sobre violencia contra las mu-

jeres en los Municipios de la región de la Montaña de Guerrero], Secretariat for Women's Affairs in the state of Guerrero and others (file of annexes presented by the State during the public hearing, tome VI, annex 13, folio 19709), and sworn statement made before a public notary by the expert witness Stavenhagen on March 29, 2010, (case file on the merits, tome II, folio 1178), and press release No. 026 issued by the Secretariat of National Defense on March 7, 2002 (case file of annexes to the answer to the application, tome I, folio 7617).

56 55 *Cf. Report 2003,* United Nations Office of the High Commissioner for Human Rights in Mexico, *supra* note 34, folio 293; *Report,* Secretariat for Women's Affairs of the state of Guerrero and others, *supra* note 54, folios 19716 and 19717; *Always close, always far: The Armed Forces in Mexico* [Siempre cerca, siempre lejos: Las fuerzas armadas en México], Global Exchange, CIEPAC and CENCOS, *supra* note 34, folios 5033, 5034, and 5036 to 5039, and sworn statement made before a public notary by expert witness Rodolfo Stavenhagen, *supra* note 54, folio 1178.

57 56 *Cf. Model of Reference of Cases of Gender Violence for the state of Guerrero* [Modelo de Referencia de Casos de Violencia de Género para el Estado de Guerrero], Secretariat of Women's Affairs for the state of Guerrero, December 2008 (file of annexes presented by the State at the public hearing, tome V, annex 8, folios 19249 and 19250); *Report,* Secretariat for Women's Affairs of the state of Guerrero and others, *supra* note 54, folio 19696; and sworn statement made before a public notary by expert witness Rodolfo Stavenhagen, *supra* note 54, folio 1178.

58 57 *Cf. Reference Model 2008.* Secretariat of the Women's Affairs by the state of Guerrero, *supra* note 56, folio 19249, and *Development of Networks for the detection, support, and reference of cases of violence against indigenous women of Guerrero* [Desarrollo de Redes de detección, apoyo y referencia de casos de violencia contra las mujeres indígenas de Guerrero], Secretariat for Women's Affairs of the state of Guerrero and National Network of Shelters, December 2008 (file of annexes submitted by the State at the public hearing, tome V, annex 7, folios 19081 to 19090).

59 58 *Cf. Report 2003,* United Nations Office of the High Commissioner for Human Rights in Mexico, *supra* note 34, folios 293 and 294; sworn statement of expert Rodolfo Stavenhagen rendered before a public notary, *supra* note 54, folio 1179, and sworn statement of expert Bonfil Sanchez rendered before a public notary, *supra* note 54, folios 1413 and 1416.

60 59 *Cf. Network Development 2008,* Secretariat for Women's Affairs of the state of Guerrero and National Network of Shelters, *supra* note 57, folio 19087, and sworn statement rendered by expert witness Rodolfo Stavenhagen before a public notary, *supra* note 54, folio 1179 to 1181.

61 60 *Cf. Report,* Secretariat for Women's Affairs of the state of Guerrero and others, *supra* 54, folio 19715, and *Report 2003,* United Nations Office of the High Commissioner in Mexico, *supra* note 34, folio 293.

62 61 *Cf. Report,* Secretariat for Women's Affairs of the state of Guerrero and others, *supra* note 54, folio 19716.

63 62 *Network Development 2008,* Secretariat for Women's Affairs of the state of Guerrero and National Network of Shelters, *supra* note 57, folio 19086.

64 63 *Cf. Report,* Secretariat for Women's Affairs of the state of Guerrero and others, México, *supra* note 54, folios 19716 and 19717, and sworn statement rendered before a public notary by expert witness Stavenhagen, *supra* note 54, folio 1180.

65 64 *Cf.* Sworn statement rendered by Mrs. Rosendo Cantú in the public hearing on May 27, 2010; brief of complaint filed by Mrs. Rosendo Cantú and Mr. Bernardino Sierra before the National Human Rights Commission (NHRC) on February 27, 2002 (case file of annexes to the answer to the application, tome I, annex 1, folio 7556).

66 65 *Cf.* Complaint filed by Mrs. Rosendo Cantú before the Public Prosecutor of the Common Jurisdiction of the Judicial District of Allende, Ayutla de los Libres, Guerrero, on March 8, 2002 (case file of annexes to the application, tome V, annex 1, folios 9262 and 9268

to 9270), and birth certificate of Mrs. Rosendo Cantú (case file of annexes to the brief of motions and pleadings, tome I, annex 23, folio 5469).

67 66   *Cf.* Birth certificate of Mrs. Rosendo Cantú, *supra* note 65, folio 5469.

68 67   *Cf.* Marriage Certificate of Mr. Bernardino Sierra and Mrs. Rosendo Cantú of July 31, 2001 (case file of annexes to the brief of pleadings and motions, tome II, annex 27, folio 5501). In 2005, Mr. Bernardino Sierra abandoned his family and moved to another city. *Cf.* Statement by Mrs. Correa González rendered before a public notary on May 6, 2010 (case file on the merits, tome III, folio 1148), and statement of Mrs. Alejandra Gonzalez Marin rendered before a public notary on October 22, 2009 (case file of annexes to the brief of pleadings and motions, tome I, annex 26, folios 5481 and 5482).

69 68   *Cf.* Complaint filed by Mrs. Rosendo Cantú before the Public Prosecutor of the Common Jurisdiction, *supra* note 65, folio 9268.

70 69   *Cf.* Birth Certificate of Yenys Bernardino Rosendo (case file of annexes to brief of motions and pleadings, tome II, annex 27, folio 5469).

71 70   *Cf.* Written final arguments of the State (case file on the merits, tome IV, folio 2004).

72 71   *Cf.* Brief of complaint filed by Mrs. Rosendo Cantú and Mr. Bernardino Sierra before the NHRC, *supra* note 64, folios 7556 to 7561; communication of Mrs. Rosendo Cantú and Mr. Bernardino Sierra addressed to the Constitutional Governor of Guerrero on March 11, 2002 (case file of annexes to the application, tome I, annex 6, folios 343 to 345); statement by Mrs. Rosendo Cantú before the Military Public Prosecutors of the 35th Military Zone, on March 6, 2002 (case file of annexes to the answer to the application, tome II, annex 1, folios 7824 to 7829), complaint filed by Mrs. Rosendo Cantú before the Public Prosecutor of the Common Jurisdiction, *supra* note 65, folios 9268 and 9269, and statement of Mrs. Rosendo Cantú before the Inspector General of the CODDEHUM on March 8, 2002 (case file of annexes to the answer to the application, tome I, folios 7588 and 7589).

73 72   *Cf.* Statement of Mr. Bernardino Sierra before the Public Prosecutor of the Common Jurisdiction Specialized in Sexual Offenses and Domestic Violence, on April 22, 2002 (case file of annexes to the application, tome I, annex 10, folio 357bis); statement of Mrs. Fidel Bernardino Sierra rendered before the Chief Agent of the Office of the Public Prosecutor of the Common Jurisdiction of Morelos Judiciary District, Specialized in Sexual Offenses and Domestic Violence, on May 9, 2002 (case file of annexes to the brief of pleadings and motions, tome II, annex 56, folio 5739).

74 73   At this time, he spoke of what happened to Mr. Encarnación Sierra Morales, and subsequently, both went to the Municipal Delegate of the Barranca Bejuco community, Mr. Ezequiel Sierra Morales, to tell him what had [occurred] and to proceed with a complaint. Mr. Ezequiel Sierra Morales summoned the indigenous community of Barranca Bejuco to tell them about what had [occurred]. Mr. Bernardino Sierra stated: "we found the delegate in his home [and] I told him about what had [occurred] to my wife […] to which the delegate showed concern and we went to the delegation together with Encarnación Morales Sierra, and the delegate began to speak […] so that the people of the village would come together […] people were at the delegation at that time, and […] and he [reported] what had [occurred] to my wife," statement of Mr. Bernardino Sierra before the Public Prosecutor of the Common Jurisdiction, *supra* note 72, folio 5739.

75 74   *Cf.* Clinical history of the family Bernardino Rosendo, II notes of the evolution of Mrs. Rosendo Cantú on [February] 18, 2002 (case file of annexes to the answer to the application, tome, folio 7756).

76 75   *Cf.* Clinical history of the family Bernardino Rosendo, *supra* note 74, folio 7756; Mrs. Rosendo Cantú noted in her communication addressed to the Constitutional Governor of Guerrero that "[her] husband explained to the doctor that the soldiers had hit her and requested assistance," communication addressed to the Constitutional Governor, *supra* note 71, folio 345.

77 76   *Cf.* Communication addressed to the Constitutional Governor of the state of Guerrero,

supra note 71, folio 343 to 345, and sworn statement of Mrs. Rosendo Cantú in the public hearing, *supra* note 64.

78 77   *Cf.* Medical note provided by physician of the General Hospital of Ayutla on February 26, 2002, (case file of annexes to the answer to the application, tome I, appendix 1, folio 7624); Evidence provided by a social worker of the General Hospital of Ayutla on February 27, 2002, (case file of annexes to the answer to the application, tome I, appendix 1, folio 7625); note of the Director of the General Hospital of Ayutla, submitted to the Inspector General of the CODDEHUM on March 12, 2002, (case file of annexes to the answer to the application, tome I, appendix 1, folio 7623); sworn statement of the doctor of the area of general medicine, who attended to Mrs. [Rosendo] Cantú on February 26, 2002 at the General Hospital of Ayutla, rendered on March 7, 2002 before the Military Public Prosecutor's Office adjoined to the 35th Military zone (case file of annexes to the brief of pleadings and motions, tome II, annex 42, folio 5692).

79 78   *Cf.* Results of the general urine exam provided by the laboratory of clinical analysis of the General Hospital of Ayutla on February 27, 2002 (case file of annexes to the answer to the application, tome I, appendix 1, folio 7626).

80 267   Article 63(1) of the American Convention establishes that: "If the Court finds that there has been a violation of a right or freedom protected by [the] Convention, the Court shall rule that the injured party be ensured the enjoyment of his right or freedom that was violated. It shall also rule, if appropriate, that the consequences of the measure or situation that constituted the breach of such right or freedom be remedied and that fair compensation be paid to the injured party."

81 271   *Cf. Aloeboetoe et al. v. Suriname.* Reparations and costs. Judgment of September 10, 1993. Series C. No. 15, paras. 96 and 97; *Case of the Plan of Sánchez Massacre v. Guatemala. Reparations and Costs.* Judgment of November 19, 2004. Series C No. 116, para. 86, and *Case of the Moiwana Community v. Suriname. Preliminary Objections, Merits, Reparations, and Costs.* Judgment of June 15, 2005. Series C No. 124, para. 194.

82 288   288 *Cf. Case of Barrios Altos, supra* note 277, para. 45; *Case Chitay Nech et al., supra* note 25, para. 255, and *Case of Manuel Cepeda Vargas, supra* note 25, para. 235.

83 289   289 *Cf. 19 Tradesmen v. Colombia.* Merits, Reparations, and Costs. Judgment of July 5, 2004. Series C No. 109, para. 278; *Case of Chitay Nech et al., supra* note 25, para. 256, and *Case of Manuel Cepeda Vargas, supra* note 25, para. 235.

84 290   *Cf. Case of the Gómez Paquiyauri Brothers v. Perú. Merits, Reparations, and Costs.* Judgment of July 8, 2004. Series C No. 110, para. 237; *Case of Cantoral Huamaní and García Santa Cruz v. Perú. Preliminary Objections, Merits, Reparations, and Costs.* Judgment of July 10, 2007. Series C No. 167, para. 194, and *Case of Valle Jaramillo et al., supra* note 234, paras. 227 subsection (f) and 231.

85 291   *Cf. Case of Escué Zapata v. Colombia. Interpretation of the Judgment of Merits, Reparations, and Costs.* Judgment of May 5, 2008 Series C No. 178, paras. 27 and 28; *Case of Valle Jaramillo et al., supra* note 234, para. 229, and *Case of Valle Jaramillo et al. v. Colombia. Interpretation of the Judgment of Merits, Reparations, and Costs.* Judgment of July 7, 2009 Series C No. 201, [para]. 38.

86 263   Article 63 provides: 1. If the Court finds that there has been a violation of a right or freedom protected by this Convention, the Court shall rule that the injured party be ensured the enjoyment of his right or freedom that was violated. It shall also rule, if appropriate, that the consequences of the measure or situation that constituted the breach of such right or freedom be remedied and that fair compensation be paid to the injured party.

87 264   264 *Cf. Case of Velásquez Rodríguez v. Honduras. Reparations and Costs.* Judgment of July 21, 1989. Series C No. 7, para. 25; *Case of Fontevecchia and D`Amico, supra* note 28, para. 97.

88 265   *Cf. Case of Castillo Páez v. Peru. Reparations and Costs.* Judgment of November 27, 1998. Series C No. 43, para. 50 and *Case of Fontevecchia and D`Amico, supra* note 28,

para. 97.

89 266 *Cf. Case of Velásquez Rodríguez v. Honduras. supra* [note 264], para. 26 and *Case of Fontevecchia and D'Amico, supra* note 28, para. 98.

90 267 *Cf. Case of the Mapiripán Massacre supra* note 93, para. 294 and *Case of Barbani Duarte et al., supra* note 91, para. 2.

91 268 *Cf. Case of Baldeón García v. Peru. Merits, Reparations, and Costs.* Judgment of April 6, 2006. Series C No. 183 and *Case of Fontevecchia and D'Amico, supra* note 28, para. 101.

92 272 *Cf. Case of Neira Alegría et al. v. Peru. Reparations and Costs.* Judgment of September 19, 1996. Series C No. 29, para. 56 and *Case of Fontevecchia and D'Amico, supra* note 28, para. 102.

93 274 *Cf.* Case *Barrios Altos v. Peru. Reparaciones and Costs.* Judgment of November 30, 2001. Series C No. 87, paras. 42 and 45 and *Case of Barrios Family, supra* note 31, para. 329.

94 275 *Cf.* Case *19 Comerciantes V. Colombia.* Merits, Reparations and Costs. Judgment of July 5, 2004. Series C No. 109, para. 278 and *Case of Barrios Family, supra* note 31, para. 329.

95 259 259 Article XVI of the American Declaration on the Rights and Duties of Man states: Every person has the right to social security which will protect him from the consequences of unemployment, old age and any disabilities arising from causes beyond his control that make it physically or mentally impossible for him to earn a living.

96 260 Article 18 (Protection of the Handicapped) of the Additional Protocol to the American Convention on Human Rights in the Area of Economic, Social and Cultural Rights, "Protocol of San Salvador" establishes: Everyone affected by a diminution of his physical or mental capacities is entitled to receive special attention designed to help him achieve the greatest possible development of his personality. The States Parties agree to adopt such measures as may be necessary for this purpose and, especially, to: a. Undertake programs specifically aimed at providing the handicapped with the resources and environment needed for attaining this goal, including work programs consistent with their possibilities and freely accepted by them or their legal representatives, as the case may be; b. Provide special training to the families of the handicapped in order to help them solve the problems of coexistence and convert them into active agents in the physical, mental and emotional development of the latter; c. Include the consideration of solutions to specific requirements arising from needs of this group as a priority component of their urban development plans; d. Encourage the establishment of social groups in which the handicapped can be helped to enjoy a fuller life.

97 261 Inter-American Convention for the Elimination of All Forms of Discrimination Against Persons with Disabilities, AG/RES. 1608 (XXIX-O/99).

98 262 Article 2 of the Convention on the Elimination of All Forms of Discrimination Against Persons with Disabilities.

99 263 Information available on the Web site of the Department of International Law of the Organization of American States at the following link: http://www.oas.org/juridico/spanish/firmas/a-65.html, consulted for the last time on August 31, 2012. See also, Merits file, volume II, page 225.

100 264 AG/DEC. 50 (XXXVI-O/06) Adopted at the fourth plenary session held on June 6, 2006. This resolution was adopted under the motto: "Equality, Dignity, and Participation," in order to achieve the recognition and full exercise of the rights and dignity of persons with disabilities and their right to participate fully in economic, social, cultural and political life and in the development of their societies, without discrimination and on an equal basis with others."

101 265 Article 3 of the Convention on the Rights of Persons with Disabilities

102 266 Information available on the United Nations web site at the link: http://treaties.un.org/Pages/ViewDetails.aspx?src=TREATY&mtdsg_no=IV-15&chapter=4&lang=en, last consulted on August 31, 2012. This Convention was approved through Law 26.378, which was ratified on May 21, 2008 and promulgated in June 6, 2008 (file of appendices to brief of pleadings and motions volume VII, page 3233).

103 267   Article I of Inter-American Convention for the Elimination of All Forms of Discrimination Against Persons with Disabilities.

104 268   Article I of the CPDP

105   [269] *Cf.* Committee on the Rights of the Child, General Comment No. 9, The rights of children with disabilities, CRC/C/GC/9, 27 of February 27, 2007, para. 5 ("The Committee emphasizes that the barrier is not the disability itself but rather a combination of social, cultural, attitudinal and physical obstacles which children with disabilities encounter in their daily lives.").

106 270   General Comment No. 9, para. 39. "The physical inaccessibility of public transportation and other facilities, including governmental buildings, shopping areas, recreational facilities among others, is a major factor in the marginalization and exclusion of children with disabilities and markedly compromises their access to services, including health and education."

107 271   General Comment No. 9, para. 37 "Access to information and means of communication, including information and communication technologies and systems, enables children with disabilities to live independently and participate fully in all aspects of life."

108 272   UN General Assembly, Standard Rules on the Equalization of Opportunities for Persons with Disabilities, 0A/RES/48/96, March 4, 1994, 85th plenary meeting, para. 3. "In the disability field, however, there are also many specific circumstances that have influenced the living conditions of persons with disabilities. Ignorance, neglect, superstition and fear are social factors that throughout the history of disability have isolated persons with disabilities and delayed their development."

109 273   *Cf. Case of Ximenes Lopes v. Brazil. Merits, Reparations and Costs.* Judgment of July 4, 2006. Series C No. 149, para. 104. *Cf.* also Article III.2 of the Inter-American Convention on the Elimination of all Forms of Discrimination against Persons with Disabilities, and Committee on Economic, Social and Cultural Rights, General Comment No. 5, "Persons with Disabilities." U.N. Doc. E/C.12/1994/13 (1994), September 12, 1994, para. 9.

110 274   *Cf. Case of the "Massacre of Mapiripán" v. Colombia. Merits, Reparations and Costs.* Judgment of September 15, 2005. Series C No. 134, paras. 111 and 113, and *Case of the Kichwa Indigenous People of Sarayaku v. Ecuador. Merits and Reparations.* Judgment of June 27, 2012. Series C No. 245, para. 244.

111 275   *Cf. Case of Ximenes López v. Brazil*, para. 103.

112 276   *Cf.* UN General Assembly Standard Rules on the Equalization of Opportunities for Persons with Disabilities

113 277   Committee on Economic Social and Cultural Rights, General Comment No. 5, para. 13.

114 278   By way of an example, it emphasizes that "under the general principles of international human rights law," persons with disabilities have the right "to marry and have their own family. These rights are frequently ignored or denied, especially in the case of persons with mental disabilities." Committee on Economic Social and Cultural Rights, General Comment No. 5, "Persons with Disabilities." United Nations, Document E/1995/22 (1994), para. 30. Similarly, Rule 9(2) of the Standard Rules on the Equalization of Opportunities for Persons with Disabilities establishes that: "persons with disabilities must not be denied the opportunity to experience their sexuality, have sexual relationships and experience parenthood. Taking into account that persons with disabilities may experience difficulties in getting married and setting up a family, States should encourage the availability of appropriate counseling."

115 279   In this regard, it is worth noting that "children with disabilities have the same right to education as all other children and shall enjoy this right without discrimination on the basis of equal opportunity, as stipulated in the Convention." Furthermore, "inclusive education should be the goal of educating children with disabilities. The manner and form of inclusion must be dictated by the individual educational needs of the child, since the education of some children with disabilities requires a kind of support which may not be

readily available in the regular school system." General Comment No. 9, paras. 62 and 66. Also, "the principle of equal primary, secondary and tertiary educational opportunities for children, youth and adults with disabilities [imply that they must take place] in integrated settings." Art. 6, the Standard Rules on Equalization of Opportunities.

116 280   In this regard, "the integration of persons with disabilities into the regular labour market should be actively supported by States." Committee on Economic Social and Cultural Rights, General Comment No. 5, "Persons with Disabilities." United Nations, Document E/1995/22 (1994), para. 20. Similarly, "in both rural and urban areas they must have equal opportunities for productive and gainful employment in the labour market." General Assembly of the UN, Standard Rules on the Equalization of Opportunities for Persons with Disabilities, 0A/RES/48/96, March 4, 1994, Forty-eighth session, Rule 7. See also: ILO Convention No. 159 (1983) on Vocational Rehabilitation and Employment (Disabled Persons), Recommendation No. 99 (1955) concerning the vocational rehabilitation of disabled persons, and Recommendation No. 168 (1983) on employment of disabled persons.

117 281   *Cf. Caso Ximenes Lópes Vs. Brazil*, para. 105. See also Article I.2.of the American Convention on the Elimination of All Forms of Discrimination against Persons with Disabilities, which states: The term "discrimination against persons with disabilities" means any distinction, exclusion, or restriction based on a disability, record of disability, condition resulting from a previous disability, or perception of disability, whether present or past, which has the effect or objective of impairing or nullifying the recognition, enjoyment, or exercise by a person with a disability of his or her human rights and fundamental freedoms." Similarly, Article 2(1) of the Convention on the Rights of the Child states: States Parties shall respect and ensure the rights set forth in the present Convention to each child within their jurisdiction without discrimination of any kind, irrespective of the child's or his or her parent's or legal guardian's [...] disability, [...] or any other status.

118 282   Article 13 of the Convention on the Rights of Persons with Disabilities specifies various points regarding access to justice for persons with disabilities.

119 283   Article 7 of the Convention on the Rights of Persons with Disabilities.

120 284   Committee on the Rights of the Child, General Comment No. 9, para. 11.

121 285   *Cf. Article* 13 of the CRPD.

122 286   *Cf. Article* 24 Convention on the Rights of the Child.

123 287   *Cf. Article* 26 Convention on the Rights of the Child.

124 288   *Cf. Article* 23 Convention on the Rights of the Child.

125 289   Committee on the Rights of the Child, General Comment No. 9, para. 51.

126 439   Article 26 of the CRDP.

127 440   *Cf. Case of Ximenes Lopes Vs. Brasil. Merits, Reparations and Costs.* Judgment of July 4, 2006. Series C No. 149, para. 109. See also: World Health Organization. Department of Mental Health and Substance Abuse. Ten Basic Principles of the Mental Health Care Law (1996), principles 2, 4 and 5. The CESCR has stated that the "right to physical and mental health also implies the right to have access to, and to benefit from, those medical and social services - including orthopedic devices - which enable persons with disabilities to become independent, prevent further disabilities and support their social integration. Similarly, such persons should be provided with rehabilitation services which would enable them "to reach and sustain their optimum level of independence and functioning." All such services should be provided in such a way that the persons concerned are able to maintain full respect for their rights and dignity." Committee on Economic, Social and Cultural Rights, General Comment No. 5, "Persons with Disabilities." United Nations Document E/1995/22 (1994), para. 34.

128 441   Similarly, Article 25 of the CRPD establishes, *inter alia*, that States must: i) Provide persons with disabilities with the same range, quality and standard of free or affordable health care and programmes as provided to other persons, including in the area of sexual and reproductive health and population-based public health programs; ii) Provide those

health services needed by persons with disabilities specifically because of their disabilities, including early identification and intervention as appropriate, and services designed to minimize and prevent further disabilities, including among children and older persons; iii) Provide these health services as close as possible to people's own communities, including in rural areas; and iv) Require health professionals to provide care of the same quality to persons with disabilities as to others, including on the basis of free and informed consent by, *inter alia,* raising awareness of the human rights, dignity, autonomy and needs of persons with disabilities through training and the promulgation of ethical standards for public and private health care. With regard to the rehabilitation of persons with disabilities, the Principles for the Protection of Persons with Mental Illness and the Improvement of Mental Health Care define mental health care as the analysis and diagnosis of a person's mental condition, and the treatment, care and rehabilitation provided for a mental illness or suspected mental illness; the treatment and care of every patient shall be based on an individually prescribed plan, discussed with the patient, reviewed periodically revised as necessary and provided by qualified professional staff (Principle 9) and the consequences of refusing or stopping treatment must be explained to the patient (Principle 11). Adopted by the United Nations General Assembly. Resolution 46/119 of December 17, 1991.

129 442   Article 23 establishes that: "[…] 2. States Parties recognize the right of a mentally or physically disabled child to receive special care and shall ensure the extension, subject to available resources, to the eligible child and to those responsible for his or her care, of assistance for which application is made and which is appropriate to the child's conditions and to the circumstances of the parents or others caring for the child. 3. Recognizing the special needs of a disabled child, assistance extended in accordance with paragraph 2 of this article shall be provided free of charge, whenever possible, taking into account the financial resources of the parents or others caring for the child, and shall be designed to ensure that the disabled child has access to and receives education, training, health care services, rehabilitation services, preparation for employment and recreational opportunities in a manner conducive to the child's achieving the fullest possible social integration and individual development, including his or her cultural and spiritual development."

130 443   In this regard, the expert witness Estela Rodríguez stated that: "[the] sooner the rehabilitation is started, the better the results will be because it prevents the brain from perpetuating the malfunction (it always does) during the recovery process." Affidavit rendered by medical expert Estela del Carmen Rodríguez of February 10, 2012 (Merits file, volume II, page 753).

131 444   *Cf.* Statement by expert witness Laura Beatriz Subies at the public hearing in this case.

132 445   *Cf. Case of Cantoral Benavides v. Peru. Reparations and Costs.* Judgment of December 3, 2001. Series C No. 88. para. 57, *and Case of González Medina v. Dominican Republic,* para. 293.

133 446   *Cf. Case of the Dos Erres Massacre v. Guatemala. Preliminary Objection, Merits, Reparations and Costs.* Judgment of November 24, 2009. Series C No. 211. para. 270, and *Case of González Medina v. Dominican Republic,* para. 293.

134 447   *Cf. Case of the 19 Tradesmen v. Colombia. Preliminary Objection.* Judgment of June 12, 2002. Series C No. 93, para. 278, and *Case of González Medina v. Dominican Republic,* para. 293.

135 448   *Cf. Case of Fernández Ortega et al. v. Mexico,* para. 252, and *Case of González Medina v. Dominican Republic,* para.293.

136 449   *Cf. Case of Loayza Tamayo v. Peru. Reparations and Costs.* Judgment of November 27, 1998. Series C No. 42, para. 147.

137 450   *Cf. Case of Tibi v. Ecuador. Preliminary Objections, Merits, Reparations and Costs.* Judgment of September 7, 2004. Series C No. 114, para. 245.

138 451   *Cf. Case of Loayza Tamayo v. Peru. Reparations and Costs,* para. 150.

139 452   *Cf. Case of Cantoral Benavides v. Peru. Reparations and Costs.* Judgment of December 3, 2001. Series C No. 88, para. 80, and *Case of Valle Jaramillo et al. v. Colombia.* paras. 227,

231.

^{140 453} *Cf. Case of the Dos Erres Massacre v. Guatemala. Preliminary Objection, Merits, Reparations and Costs.* Judgment of November 24, 2009. Series C No. 211, para. 284 and 293, and *Case of Mejía Idrovo v. Ecuador*, para. 134.

^{141 454} *Cf.* Council of State of Colombia: Administrative Law Chamber, Third Section, Judgment of July 19, 2000, Case file 11,842, and Administrative Law Chamber, Third Section, Judgment of September 14, 2011, Case file 38,222. Also, see: Judgments of the Supreme Court of Justice of Colombia, Civil Court of Appeals, Judgment of May 13, 2008 and Criminal Cassation Chamber, Judgment of August 25, 2010.

^{142 455} Affidavit of Danilo Furlan (Merits file, volume II, folios 692 and 693). For her part, the witness Violeta Jano also expressed her views on this point: "Sebastian's life was never the same. As he could not walk or speak properly, he could no longer play sports or anything. He also lost all his friends because it was difficult to be with Sebastián. He did inappropriate things and was constantly in danger." Affidavit of Violeta Jano (Merits file, volume II, page 738).

^{143 456} Affidavit of Doctor Estela del Carmen Rodríguez of February 10, 2012 (Merits file, volume II, page 760). In this regard, the expert Alejandro Morlacchetti said "... that the State's obligations with respect to persons with disabilities is to provide, facilitate and enable educational centers where that person, according to their degree of disability, is integrated to the school system [...] so he is as close as possible and as little as possible excluded of the existing educational system." Statement by expert Alejandro Morlacchetti at the public hearing.

^{144 457} Article 26 of the Convention on the Rights of Persons with Disabilities

^{145 512} *Cf. Case of González et al. ("Cotton Field") v. Mexico*, para. 529.

^{146 513} Expert opinion provided by María Sol Yáñez De La Cruz before the Inter-American Court during the public hearing held on April 23, 2012.

^{147 514} Expert opinion provided by María Sol Yáñez De La Cruz before the Inter-American Court during the public hearing held on April 23, 2012.

^{148 515} Expert opinion on psychosocial impacts and recommendations for reparations in the case of "The Massacres of El Mozote and nearby places" provided by María Sol Yáñez De La Cruz, undated (evidence file, tome XVIII, annex 2 to the final written arguments of the representatives, folio 10548).

^{149 516} *Cf.* Expert opinion provided by María Sol Yáñez De La Cruz before the Inter-American Court during the public hearing held on April 23, 2012.

^{150 517} Expert opinion on psychosocial impacts and recommendations for reparations in the case of "The Massacres of El Mozote and nearby places" provided by María Sol Yáñez De La Cruz, undated (evidence file, tome XVIII, annex 2 to the final written arguments of the representatives, folios 10549 to 10550).

^{151 518} Expert opinion on psychosocial impacts and recommendations for reparations in the case of "The Massacres of El Mozote and nearby places" provided by María Sol Yáñez De La Cruz, undated (evidence file, tome XVIII, annex 2 to the final written arguments of the representatives, folios 10548 to 10550).

^{152 519} Expert opinion on psychosocial impacts and recommendations for reparations in the case of "The Massacres of El Mozote and nearby places" provided by María Sol Yáñez De La Cruz, undated (evidence file, tome XVIII, annex 2 to the final written arguments of the representatives, folio 10548).

^{153 520} *Cf.* Expert opinion on psychosocial impacts and recommendations for reparations in the case of "The Massacres of El Mozote and nearby places" provided by María Sol Yáñez De La Cruz, undated (evidence file, tome XVIII, annex 2 to the final written arguments of the representatives, folio 10550).

^{154 521} *Cf. Case of Cantoral Benavides v. Peru. Reparations and costs.* Judgment of December 3, 2001. Series C No. 88, para. 51(e), and *Case of the Río Negro Massacres v. Guatemala,*

para. 287.

[155 522]   *Cf. Case of the Las Dos Erres Massacre v. Guatemala,* para. 270, and *Case of Uzcátegui et al. v. Venezuela. Merits and reparations.* Judgment of September 3, 2012. Series C No. 249, para. 253(d).

[156 523]   *Cf. Case of the Las Dos Erres Massacre v. Guatemala,* para. 270, and *Case of Uzcátegui et al. v. Venezuela,* para. 253(b).

[157 486]   Article 63(1) of the American Convention establishes that "[i]f the Court finds that there has been a violation of a right or freedom protected by this Convention, the Court shall rule that the injured party be ensured the enjoyment of his right or freedom that was violated. It shall also rule, if appropriate, that the consequences of the measure or situation that constituted the breach of such right or freedom be remedied and that fair compensation be paid to the injured party."

[158 487]   *Cf. Case of Velásquez Rodríguez v. Honduras. Reparations and costs.* Judgment of July 21, 1989. Series C No. 7, para. 25, and *Case of Nadege Dorzema et al. v. Dominican Republic,* para. 238.

[159 488]   *Cf. Case of Velásquez Rodríguez v. Honduras. Reparations and costs,* para. 25, and *Case of Nadege Dorzema et al. v. Dominican Republic,* para. 238.

[160 489]   *Cf. Case of Velásquez Rodríguez v. Honduras. Reparations and costs,* para. 25, and *Case of the Río Negro Massacres v. Guatemala. Preliminary objection, merits, reparations and costs.* Judgment of September 4, 2012 Series C No. 250, para. 245.

[161 490]   *Cf. Case of Velásquez Rodríguez v. Honduras. Reparations and costs,* para. 25, and *Case of the Río Negro Massacres v. Guatemala,* para. 248.

[162 491]   *Cf. Case of Ticona Estrada v. Bolivia. Merits, reparations and costs.* Judgment of November 27, 2008. Series C No. 191, para. 110, and *Case of the Massacres of El Mozote and nearby places v. El Salvador.* Merits, reparations and costs. Judgment of October 25, 2012 Series C No. 252.493 *Cf. Case of the "Street Children" (Villagrán Morales et al.) v. Guatemala. Reparations and costs.* Judgment of May 26, 2001. Series C No. 77, para. 84, and *Case of Vélez Restrepo and family v. Colombia,* para. 259.

[163 495]   *Cf. Case of Barrios Altos v. Peru. Reparations and costs.* Judgment of November 30, 2001. Series C No. 87, para. 42 and 45 and *Case of the Río Negro Massacres v. Guatemala,* para. 287.

[164 496]   *Cf. Case of the 19 Tradesmen v. Colombia.* Merits, reparations and costs. Judgment of July 5, 2004. Series C No. 109, para. 278, and *Case of the Barrios Family v. Venezuela. Merits, reparations and costs.* Judgment of November 24, 2011. Series C No. 237, para. 329.

[165 4]   *Cf.* Merits Report No. 172/10 of November 2, 2010 (merits file, tome I, folios 83 and 84).

[166 128]   *Cf. Matter of the Mendoza Prisons.* Provisional measures with regard to Argentina. Decision of the Inter-American Court of Human Rights of November 22, 2004, twelfth having seen paragraph and ninth considering paragraph.

[167 129]   *Cf. Matter of the Mendoza Prisons.* Provisional measures with regard to Argentina. Order of the Inter-American Court of Human Rights of March 30, 2006, fourth and fifth having seen paragraphs.

[168 130]   *Cf. Matter of the Mendoza Prisons.* Provisional measures with regard to Argentina. Order of the Inter-American Court of Human Rights of November 26, 2010, forty-fourth considering paragraph.

[169 381]   *Cf. Case of Barrios Altos v. Peru. Reparations and costs.* Judgment of November 30, 2001. Series C No. 87, paras. 42 and 45, and *Case of Artavia Murillo et al. (In vitro fertilization) v. Costa Rica,* para. 326.

[170 382]   *Cf. Case of the Las Dos Erres Massacre v. Guatemala. Preliminary objection, merits, reparations and costs.* Judgment of November 24, 2009. Series C No. 211, para. 270, and *Case of the Massacre of Santo Domingo v. Colombia,* para. 309.

[171 383]   *Cf. Case of the 19 Tradesmen v. Colombia. Merits, reparations and costs.* Judgment of July 5, 2004. Series C No. 109, para. 278, and *Case of the Massacre of Santo Domingo v. Colombia,* para. 309.

172 384   *Cf. Case of Loayza Tamayo v. Peru. Reparations and costs.* Judgment of November 27, 1998. Series C No. 42, para. 147, and *Case of Furlan and family members v. Argentina,* para. 285.

173 385   *Cf. Case of Loayza Tamayo v. Peru. Reparations and costs,* para. 148, and *Case of Furlan and family members v. Argentina,* para. 285.

174 386   *Cf. Case of Loayza Tamayo v. Peru. Reparations and costs,* para. 150, and *Case of Furlan and family members v. Argentina,* para. 285.

175 387   *Cf. Case of Cantoral Benavides v. Peru. Reparations and costs,* para. 80, and *Case of Furlan and family members v. Argentina,* para. 285.

176 388   *Cf. Case of the Las Dos Erres Massacre v. Guatemala,* paras. 284 and 293, and *Case of Furlan and family members v. Argentina,* paras. 285 and 286.

177 389   *Cf.* Council of State of Colombia: Contentious Administrative Chamber, Third Section, Judgment of July 19, 2000, Case file No. 11,842, and Contentious Administrative Chamber, Third Section, Judgment of September 14, 2011, Case file 38,222. See, also: Judgments of the Supreme Court of Justice of Colombia, Civil Cassation Chamber, Judgment No. 1100131030061997-09327-01 of May 13, 2008, and Criminal Cassation Chamber, Judgment No. 33833 of August 25, 2010.

178 390   *Cf. Amicus curiae* submitted by the *Asociación Pro Derechos Civiles* (merits file, tome III, folio 1943).

179 391   *Cf. Amicus curiae* submitted by the *Asociación Pro Derechos Civiles* (merits file, tome III, folio 1943).

180 1   According to Article 2(25) of the Court's Rules of Procedure, the expression "alleged victim" refers to the person whose rights under the Convention or another treaty of the inter-American system have allegedly been violated." In this case, although the State acknowledged that Mr. García Lucero was a victim of torture, for the purpose of examining this case, the Court will understand that he is a presumed victim of the alleged violations indicated by the Commission and the representatives owing to the State's violation of certain articles of the American Convention and the Inter-American Convention to Prevent and Punish Torture

181 2   See *infra* para. 61 of this Judgment with regard to María Elena and Gloria Klug, and to Francisca Rocío García Illanes.

182 226   Regarding the characterization of Mr. García Lucero as a vulnerable person, it should be indicated that Articles 17 and 18 of the Protocol to the American Convention on Human Rights in the Area of Economic, Social and Cultural Rights, "Protocol of San Salvador," indicate the pertinence of the "protection" of the "elderly" and the "handicapped." Also, on December 16, 1991, the General Assembly of the United Nations adopted the "United Nations Principles for Older Persons" (Resolution 46/91).

183 556   *Cf.* Letter from Dr. Gill Hinshelwood dated October 26, 1994 (file of annexes to the Merits Report, annex 9, folio 93).

184 557   *Cf.* Report of the Traumatic Stress Clinic dated November 28, 1996 (file of annexes to the Merits Report, annex 7, folios 81 a 89).

185 558   *Cf.* Medical report of Dr. Thomas Wenzel dated March 10, 2008 (file of annexes to the motions and arguments brief, annex 60, folio 3192).

186 559   *Cf. Case of the Miguel Castro Castro Prison v. Peru. Merits, reparations and costs, supra,* para. 293, 300, 333.

187 560   *Case of the Miguel Castro Castro Prison v. Peru. Merits, reparations and costs, supra,* para. 450.

188 561   *Cf. Case of Barrios Altos v. Peru. Reparations and costs.* Judgment of November 30, 2001. Series C No. 87, paras. 42 and 45, and *Case of Mendoza et al. v. Argentina, supra,* para. 311.

189 562   *Cf. Case of the Las Dos Erres Massacre v. Guatemala. Preliminary objection, merits, reparations and costs.* Judgment of November 24, 2009. Series C No. 211, para. 270, and *Case of Gudiel Álvarez et al. ("Diario Militar") v. Guatemala, supra,* para. 340.

190   *See, e.g., González et al. ("Cotton Field") v. Mexico*, Preliminary Objections, Merits, Reparations, and Costs, Nov. 16, 2009, Series C No. 205, p. 147, para. 11.

191 68   *Cf., Juan Humberto Sánchez Case,* [June 7, 2003 Judgment. Series C No. 99] 4, para. 184; *El Caracazo Case, Reparations,* [(Art. 63(1) American Convention on Human Rights). August 29, 2002 Judgment. Series C No. 95], para. 115; *Las Palmeras Case, Reparations,* [(Art. 63(1) American Convention on Human Rights). November 26, 2002 Judgment. Series C No. 96], para. 66; *Trujillo Oroza Case, Reparations,* [(Art. 63(1) American Convention on Human Rights). February 27, 2002 Judgment. Series C No. 92], para. 99; *Bámaca Velásquez Case, Reparations,* [(Art. 63(1) American Convention on Human Rights). February 22, 2002 Judgment. Series C No. 91], paras. 76 and 77; and *Cantoral Benavides Case, Reparations,* [(Art. 63(1) American Convention on Human Rights). December 3, 2001 Judgment. Series C No. 88], paras. 69 and 70.

192   *Cf., Juan Humberto Sánchez Case, supra* note [68], para. 110; *Bámaca Velásquez Case, supra* note [68], para. 172; and *"Street Children" Case (Villagrán Morales at al.).* November 19, 1999 Judgment. Series C No. 63, paras. 144-145. Likewise, General Comment No. 6 (Sixteenth session, 1982), para. 3, supra note 123; María Fanny Suárez de Guerrero v. Colombia. Brief No. R.11/45 (February 5, 1979), U.N. Doc. Supp. No. 40 (A/37/40) in 137 (1982), page 137.

193 70   *Cf., Juan Humberto Sánchez Case, supra* note [68], para. 144; *Bámaca Velásquez Case, supra* note [68], para. 212; and *"Street Children" Case (Villagrán Morales at al.), supra* note 69, para. 226.

194 71   *Cf., Juan Humberto Sánchez Case, supra* note [68], para. 144; *Bámaca Velásquez Case, supra* note [68], para. 212; and *"Street Children" Case (Villagrán Morales at al.), supra* note 69, para. 226.

195 72   *Cf., Hilaire, Constantine and Benjamin et al. Case,* [June 21, 2002 Judgment. Series C No. 94], paras. 142 to 144; *Suárez Rosero Case.* November 12, 1997 Judgment. Series C No. 35, paras. 71 and 72; and *Genie Lacayo Case.* January 29, 1997 Judgment. Series C No. 30, para. 77.

196 73   *Cf., Trujillo Oroza Case, Reparations, supra* note [68], para. 106; *Barrios Altos Case,* [March 14, 2001 Judgment. Series C No. 75], para. 41; and *Barrios Altos Case. Interpretation of the Judgment on the Merits.* (Art. 67 American Convention on Human Rights). September 3, 2001 Judgment. Series C No. 83, para. 15

197 74   *Cf., Barrios Altos Case, supra* note [7]3, para. 43.

198 75   *Cf., "Five Pensioners" Case,* [February 28, 2003 Judgment. Series C No. 98], para. 164; *Hilaire, Constantine and Benjamin et al. Case, supra* note [72], para. 112; and *Trujillo Oroza Case, Reparations, supra* note [68], para. 96.

199 76   *Cf., Juan Humberto Sánchez Case, supra* note [68], paras. 143 and 185; *Las Palmeras Case, Reparations, supra* note [68], para. 53.a); and *El Caracazo Case, Reparations, supra* note [68], paras. 116 and 117.

200 159   *Cf. Case of Barrios Altos,* [Judgment of March 14, 2001. Series C No. 75], para. 48. *Case of Bámaca-Vélasquez.* Judgment of November 25, 2000. Series C No. 70, para. 201.

201 160   *Cf.* Report of the *Comisión Nacional de Verdad y Reconciliación* (National Truth and Reconciliation Commission) (record of appendixes to the final written arguments of the State, Appendix 2, p. 2520).

202 161   Adopted by the General Assembly of the United Nations through Resolution 2391 (XXIII) of November 26, 1968, entered into force on November 11, 1970.

203 162   *Cf.* UN, Rome Statute of the International Criminal Court, adopted by the United Nations Diplomatic Conference of Plenipotentiaries on the Establishment of an International Criminal Court, UN Doc. A/CONF.183/9, July 17, 1998, Art. 20; Statute of the International Criminal Tribunal for the former Yugoslavia, S/Res/827, 1993, Art. 10, and Statute of the International Criminal Tribunal for Rwanda, S/Res/955, November 8, 1994, Art. 9.

204 163   *Cf. Case of Carpio-Nicolle et al.* Judgment of November 22, 2004. Series C No. 117, para.

131.

205 164   *Cf. Case of Montero-Aranguren et al.,* [Judgment of July 5, 2006. Series C No. 150], para.
139; *Case of Baldeón-García,* [Judgment of April 6, 2006. Series C No. 147], para. 199;
and *Case of Blanco-Romero et al.* Judgment of November 28, 2005. Series C No. 138,
para. 97.

206 165   *Cf. Case of Montero-Aranguren et al., supra* note 1[64], para. 139; *Case of Baldeón-
García, supra* note 1[64], para. 199; and *Case of the Pueblo Bello Massacre,* [Judgment of
January 31, 2006. Series C No. 140], para. 267.

207 165   *Cf. El Caracazo v. Venezuela. Reparations and costs.* Judgment of August 29, 2002. Series
C No. 95, para. 118; *Case of Bayarri v. Argentina,* [*Preliminary objection, merits, repara-
tions and costs. Judgment of October 30 2008.* Series C No. 187], para. 176, and *Case of
Heliodoro Portugal, supra* note 13, para. 247.

208 166   *Cf. Las Palmeras v. Colombia. Reparations and costs.* Judgment of November 26, 2002.
Series C No. 96, para. 67; *Case of Heliodoro Portugal* [*v. Panama. Preliminary objections,
merits, reparations and costs.* Judgment of August 12, 2008. Series C No. 186], para. 247,
and *Case of Cantoral Huamaní and García Santa Cruz* [*v. Peru. Preliminary objection,
merits, reparations and costs.* Judgment of July 10, 2007. Series C No. 167], para. 191.

209 152   Cf. IACHR, The Situation of the Rights of Women in Ciudad Juárez, [Mexico: The Right
to be Free from Violence and Discrimination, OEA/Ser.L/V//II.117, Doc. 44, March 7,
2003 (case file of attachments to the application, volume VII, attachment 1,] folio 1765;
[United Nations, Report on Mexico produced by the Committee on the Elimination of
Discrimination against Women under Article 8 of the Optional Protocol of the Convention,
and reply from the Government of Mexico, CEDAW/C/2005/OP.8/MEXICO, 27 January
2005 (case file of attachments to the application, volume VII, attachment 3b],folio 2052;
CNDH, Recomendación 44/1998, [issued on May 15, 1998 (case file of attachments to the
application, volume VII, attachment 4, folios 2113 to 2164)] folio 2139, and testimony of
expert witness Mónárrez Fragoso, *supra* note 101, folios 3938 and 3940.

210 153   CNDH, Recomendación 44/1998, *supra* note 72, folio 2155.

211 478   In their final written arguments of June 2009, the representatives indicated that "from 2008
to date, 24 girls and women of Ciudad Juárez have disappeared; there is no information
on their whereabouts and the authorities have not taken sufficiently exhaustive and conscientious measures to find them," according to "an estimated figure based on official information recorded" by the NGO, *Nuestras Hijas de Regreso a Casa A.C.* However, no
specific information was provided to the Court on what this official information was, or the
methodology used to obtain this figure. Moreover, no relevant documentary evidence was
attached.

212 482   *Cf. Case of Gutiérrez Soler v. Colombia. Merits, Reparations and Costs.* Judgment of September 12, 2005. Series C No. 132, paras. 109 and 110.

213 483   *Cf. Comisión para Prevenir y Erradicar la Violencia contra las Mujeres en Ciudad Juárez*
[Commission for the Prevention and Erradication of Violence Against Women in Ciudad
Juarez], *Tercer informe de gestión* [Third Annual Report], [May 2005-September 2006],
folio 9054.

214 484   *Cf.* Office of the Attorney General for the state of Chihuahua, official letter addressed to the
Director of Human Rights of the Ministry of Foreign Affairs, February 17, 2003 (case file
of attachments to the answer to the application, volume XLII, attachment 75, folio 15381).

215 485   *Cf.* [United Nations, Report on Mexico produced by the Committee on the Elimination of
Discrimination against Women under Article 8 of the Optional Protocol of the Convention,
and reply from the Government of Mexico, CEDAW/C/2005/OP.8/MEXICO, 27 January
2005 (case file of attachments to the application, volume VII, attachment 3b,] folio 1929[)]

216 486   Cf. [CNDH, Informe Especial de la Comisión Nacional de los Derechos Humanos sobre
los Casos deHomicidios y Desapariciones de Mujeres en el Municipio de Juárez, Chihuahua, 2003 [Special Report of theNational Human Rights Commission on the Cases of

Homicides and Disappearances of Women in the Municipalityof Juarez, Chihuahua, 2003] (case file of attachments to the application, volume VII, attachment5,] folio 2174[)],and Amnesty International, [Mexico: Intolerable killings: 10 years of Abductions and Murders or Women in CiudadJuárez and Chihuahua, AMR 41/027/2003 (case file of attachments to the application, volume VII, attachment 6,]folio 2274[)].

217 487   *Cf.* IACHR, *The Situation of the Rights of Women in Ciudad Juárez* [*Mexico: The Right to be Free from Violence and Discrimination*, OEA/Ser.L/V//II.117, Doc. 44, March 7, 2003 (case file of attachments to the application, volume VII, attachment 1], folio 1746[)].

218 488   *Cf. Comisión para Prevenir y Erradicar la Violencia contra las Mujeres en Ciudad Juárez, Tercer informe de gestión, supra* note [487], folio 9200.

219 489   *Cf. Case of the Serrano Cruz Sisters v. El Salvador.* [*Merits, Reparations and Costs*. Judgment of March 1, 2005. Series C No. 120] para. 190.

220 490   *Cf.* Office of the Special Prosecutor for the Investigation of Crimes related to the Murders of Women in Ciudad Juárez, [Chihuahua, Informe Final, issued in January 2006 (case file of attachments to the answer to the application, volume XL, attachment 59], folios 14582 and 14587 to 14594[)].

221 491   *Cf.* Office of the Special Prosecutor for the Investigation of Crimes related to the Murders of Women in Ciudad Juárez, *Informe Final, supra* note [490] folios 14582 and 14587 to 14594.

222 492   *Cf. Case of Molina Theissen v. Guatemala. Reparations and Costs.* Judgment of July 3, 2004. Series C No. 108, para. 91; *Case of the Serrano Cruz Sisters v. El Salvador, supra* note 4[89] para. 193, and *Case of Servellón García et al. v. Honduras*, [*Merits, Reparations and Costs*. Judgment of September 21, 2006. Series C No. 152], para. 203.

223 501   *Cf.* Office of the Special Prosecutor for the Investigation of Crimes related to the Murders of Women in Ciudad Juárez, *Informe Final, supra* note [490], folios 14532, 14538, 14539 and 14544.

224 508   *Cf. Comisión para Prevenir y Erradicar la Violencia contra las Mujeres en Ciudad Juárez, Tercer informe de gestión*, note [487], folio 9185.

225 85   *Cf.* Copy of the baptism certificate of Mr. Rosendo Radilla-Pacheco, issued by the Parrish of Santa María de la Asunción de Atoyac de Álvarez, Guerrero, on September 5, 2007 (dossier of appendixes to the application, appendix 5, folio 911).

226 86   *Cf.* Copy of the marriage certificate issued by the Parrish of Santa María de la Asunción de Atoyac de Álvarez, Guerrero, undated (dossier of appendixes to the application, appendix 6, folio 913).

227 87   *Cf.* copy of each of their voter's cards (dossier of appendixes to the application, appendix 7, folios 915 through 926, and dossier of merits, volume I, appendix 7, folio 265).

228 89   *Cf.* Radilla Martínez, Andrea. *Voces Acalladas (Vidas Truncadas)*, 2nd ed., Mexico, Editorial Program Nueva Visión 2007-Secretariat of Women of Guerrero-Universidad Autónoma de Guerrero-UAFyL, 2008 (dossier of appendixes to the application, appendix 8, folios 946, 952, 955, 956, and 965; dossier of appendixes to the brief of pleadings and motions, appendix B(12), pages 41, 53, 58, 61, and 79).

229 90   *Cf.* Statement offered by Andrea Radilla Martínez before notary public (affidavit) on June 10, 2009 (dossier of merits, volume IV, folio 1156); statement offered by Mrs. Ana María Radilla Martínez before notary public (affidavit) on June 10, 2009 (dossier of merits, volume IV, folio 1164); statement offered by Mr. Rosendo Radilla Martínez during the public hearing held before the Inter-American Court on July 7, 2009, and statement offered by Mrs. Tita Radilla Martínez during the public hearing held before the Inter-American Court on July 7, 2009.

230 91   *Cf.* Compact disc that includes "corridos" of Mr. Rosendo Radilla-Pacheco (dossier of appendixes to the application, appendix 9; dossier of appendixes to the brief of pleadings and motions, appendix B(11)) and Radilla

Martínez, Andrea. *Voces Acalladas (Vidas Truncadas)*, 2nd ed., Mexico, Editorial Program Nueva Visión 2007- Secretariat of Women of Guerrero-Universidad Autónoma de Guerrero-UAFyL, 2008 (dossier of appendixes to the application, appendix 8, folios 958 through 962; dossier of appendixes to the brief of pleadings and motions, appendix B(12), pages 65 through 72).

231 92   *Cf.* Record of the receipt of the document and authenticity of documents. A.P. PGR/FE-MOSPP/033/2002 (dossier of appendixes to the brief of pleadings and motions, appendix D(13), folios 1870 through 1872), and document identified as "D.F.S.-26-IX-65. State of Guerrero", signed by Fernando Gutiérrez Barrios, Federal Security Director, included in Preliminary Inquiry PGR/FEMOSPP/033/2002 (dossier of appendixes to the brief of pleadings and motions, appendix D(13), folios 1873 through 1874).

232 93   The State did not object the existence of this document, proven only based on the dossier of preliminary inquiry SIEDF/CGI/454/2007, copy of which it did not forward to the Tribunal (*supra* para. 92).

233 94   *Cf.* Statement offered by Mr. Rosendo Radilla Martínez during the public hearing held before the Inter-American Court on July 7, 2009; statement offered on July 31, 2003 by Mr. Rosendo Radilla Martínez before the Special Prosecutors' Office for Social and Public Movements of the Past, in Preliminary Inquiry PGR/FEMOSPP/051/2002 (dossier of appendixes to the brief of pleadings and motions, appendix D(19), folio 1898), and Case File CNDH/PDS/95/GRO/S00228.000, Case of Mr. Radilla-Pacheco Rosendo, Civic War Association and Revolutionary League of the South "Emiliano Zapata", Special Report on the Complaints in Matters of Forced Disappearances Occurred in the Decade of the 70s and Beginning of the 80s (dossier of appendixes to the application, appendix 2, folios 868 through 869, and dossier of appendixes to the brief of pleadings and motions, appendix C, folios 1681 through 1682).

234 95   *Cf.* Statement offered by Mr. Rosendo Radilla Martínez during the public hearing held before the Inter-American Court on July 7, 2009; statement offered on July 31, 2003 by Mr. Rosendo Radilla Martínez before the Special Prosecutors' Office for Social and Public Movements of the Past, in Preliminary Inquiry PGR/FEMOSPP/051/2002 (dossier of appendixes to the brief of pleadings and motions, appendix D(19), folio 1899), and Case File CNDH/PDS/95/GRO/S00228.000, Case of Mr. Radilla-Pacheco Rosendo, Civic War Association and Revolutionary League of the South "Emiliano Zapata", Special Report on the Complaints in Matters of Forced Disappearances Occurred in the Decade of the 70s and Beginning of the 80s (dossier of appendixes to the application, appendix 2, folios 868 through 869, and dossier of appendixes to the brief of pleadings and motions, appendix C, folios 1681 through 1682).

235 96   *Cf.* Statement offered by Mr. Rosendo Radilla Martínez during the public hearing held before the Inter-American Court on July 7, 2009 and statement offered on July 31, 2003 by Mr. Rosendo Radilla Martínez before the Special Prosecutors' Office for Social and Public Movements of the Past, in Preliminary Inquiry PGR/FEMOSPP/051/2002 (dossier of appendixes to the brief of pleadings and motions, appendix D(19), folio 1899).

236 97   *Cf.* Record of the receipt of the document and authenticity of documents. A.P. PGR/FE-MOSPP/033/2002 (dossier of appendixes to the brief of pleadings and motions, appendix D(14), folios 1875 through 1877), and document of the Secretariat of the Interior identified as "D.F.S.-8-VIII-75", included in Preliminary Inquiry PGR/FEMOSPP/033/2002 (dossier of appendixes to the brief of pleadings and motions, appendix D(14), folios 1881).

237 98   *Cf.* [Historical] Report for the Mexican Society, Special Prosecutors' Office for Social and Political Movements of the Past, Attorney General of the Republic, 2006 (dossier of appendixes to the application, appendix 4, page 640).

238 99   *Cf.* File CNDH/PDS/95/GRO/S00228.000, Case of Mr. Radilla-Pacheco Rosendo, Civic War Association and Revolutionary League of the South "Emiliano Zapata", Special Report on Complaints in Matters of Forced Disappearances Occurred in the Decade of the 70s

and Beginning of the 80s (dossier of appendixes to the application, appendix 2, folio 869 and dossier of appendixes to the brief of pleadings and motions, appendix C, folio1682).

239 100   *Cf.* Hand-written statement signed by Maximiliano Nava Martínez on September 30, 1982 (dossier of appendixes to the brief of pleadings and motions, appendix D(22), folios 1914 and 1915).

240 101   *Cf.* Statement of Mr. Maximiliano Nava Martínez offered before the Special Prosecutors' Office on September 26, 2003 (dossier of appendixes to the brief of pleadings and motions, appendix D(25), folios 1925 and 1926).

241 102   *Cf.* Statement of Mr. Enrique Hernández Girón offered before the Special Prosecutors' Office on December10, 2003 (dossier of appendixes to the brief of pleadings and motions, appendix D(29), folios 1947 through 1948).

242 103   *Cf.* Complaint filed before the Agent of the Public Prosecutors' Office of the Common Jurisdiction of the city of Atoyac de Álvarez, Guerrero, on May 14, 1999 (dossier of appendixes to the brief of pleadings and motions, appendix D(20), folios 1906 through 1907).

243 104   *Cf.* Recommendation 026/2001 of the National Human Rights Commission (dossier of appendixes to the application, appendix 3, folio 871; dossier of appendixes to the respondent's plea, appendix V(2), page 1) and Historical Report for the Mexican Society, Special Prosecutors' Office for Social and Political Movements of the Past. Attorney General of the Republic, 2006 (dossier of appendixes to the application, appendix 4, pages 503 through 530).

244 105   On June 6, 1990 the National Human Rights Commission was created through a presidential decree as a decentralized body of the Secretariat of the Interior (dossier on merits, volume III, appendix V(1), folios 845 and 846). Subsequently, through a reform to Article 102, section B, of the Political Constitution of the United Mexican States, published in the Official Gazette of the Federation on September 13, 1999, said body was granted constitutional status (dossier of appendixes to the respondent's plea, appendix V(4), pages 1 and 2).

245 106   The Constituent Council of the National Human Rights Commission agreed the "[c]reation of a program addressed to the search of missing persons," after which on September 18, 1990 the Special Program for the Alleged Disappeared Persons was created. *Cf.* Recommendation 026/2001 of the National Human Rights Commission (dossier of appendixes to the respondent's plea, appendix V(2), page 1).

246 107   To these effects, said National Commission carried out field investigations and had direct contact with the next of kin of the disappeared, gathered documents in the General Archive of the Nation, the National Library and Newspaper Library, the Library of the Attorney General of the Republic, the Mexico Library, and the Archives of the Center of National Research and Security Center, requested information from the Attorney General of the Republic on aggrieved parties and the complaints filed, it analyzed case files and carried out visual inspections at different governmental instances, among others. *Cf.* Recommendation 026/2001 of the National Human Rights Commission (dossier of appendixes to the application, appendix 3, folios 871, 872, and 889, and dossier of appendixes to the respondent's plea, appendix V(2), pages 1, 2, 17, and 18). The Report of the Special Prosecutors' Office states that the period called "dirty war" is named this way in direct reference to the way in which the counterinsurgence actions were carried out to contain armed groups considered violators of the law. *Cf.* Historical Report for the Mexican Society, Special Prosecutors' Office for Social and Political Movements of the Past. Attorney General of the Republic, 2006 (dossier of appendixes to the application, appendix 4, page 279).

247 108   The recommendation was issued based on that stated in Articles 102, section B, of the Political Constitution of the United Mexican States; 1, 3, 6, fractions I, II, III; 15, fraction VII; 24, fraction IV, 44, 46, and 51 of the Law of the National Human Rights Commission. *Cf.* Recommendation 026/2001 of the National Human Rights Commission (dossier of appendixes to the application, appendix 3, folio 873, and dossier of appendixes to the respondent's plea, appendix V(2), page 3).

248 109   *Cf.* Recommendation 026/2001 of the National Human Rights Commission (dossier of appendixes to the application, appendix 3, folio 872; dossier of appendixes to the respondent's plea, appendix V(2), page 2).

249 110   In that sense, the Commission indicated that it does not seek to "[p]resent a specific story or chronicle regarding the events occurred in [that] period, instead[,] it ma[de] reference to the context in which the disappearances object of the investigation of [the] National Commission occurred and[,] due to the diversity of the sources consulted, [the] statements could lack precision, which [did] not imply any judgment of value on behalf of [the] Commission regarding the groups referr[ed] to therein." Recommendation 026/2001 of the National Human Rights Commission (dossier of appendixes to the application, appendix 3, folio 877 and dossier of appendixes to the respondent's plea, appendix V(2), pages 6 and 7).

250 111   *Cf.* Recommendation 026/2001 of the National Human Rights Commission (dossier of appendixes to the application, appendix 3, folios 879 through 881, and dossier of appendixes to the respondent's plea, appendix V(2), pages 8 through 10).

251 112   *Cf.* Recommendation 026/2001 of the National Human Rights Commission (dossier of appendixes to the application, appendix 3, folio 891 and dossier of appendixes to the respondent's plea, appendix V(2), pages 19).

252 113   *Cf.* Recommendation 026/2001 of the National Human Rights Commission (dossier of appendixes to the application, appendix 3, folio 909 and dossier of appendixes to the respondent's plea, appendix V(2), page 36).

253 114   *Cf.* Statement offered by Attorney Martha Patricia Valadez Sanabria before notary public (affidavit) on June 18, 2009 (dossier on merits, volume IV, folio 1423), and Evaluation Report on the Follow-up of Recommendation 26/2001, National Human Rights Commission, of August 25, 2009 (dossier on merits, volume IX, folio 3014). In the respondent's plea, the State mentioned that "[t]he Special Prosecutors' Office [...] started working in 2002 with the initial receipt of the 532 case file gathered by the [National Commission] and, later, with the different complaints they received during 2002 and up to 2006, year in which through an agreement of the Attorney General of the Republic [...]" the Special Prosecutors' Office was closed and the investigations were transferred to the General Investigation Coordination (dossier on merits, volume II, folio 659).

254 115   *Cf.* Historical Report to the Mexican Society, Special Prosecutors' Office for Social and Political Movements of the past. Attorney General of the Republic, 2006 (dossier of appendixes to the application, appendix 4, page 606).

255 116   *Cf.* Historical Report to the Mexican Society, Special Prosecutors' Office for Social and Political Movements of the past. Attorney General of the Republic, 2006 (dossier of appendixes to the application, appendix 4, page 612).

256 117   *Cf.* Historical Report to the Mexican Society, Special Prosecutors' Office for Social and Political Movements of the past. Attorney General of the Republic, 2006 (dossier of appendixes to the application, appendix 4, page 333 and 342).

257 118   *Cf.* Historical Report to the Mexican Society, Special Prosecutors' Office for Social and Political Movements of the past. Attorney General of the Republic, 2006 (dossier of appendixes to the application, appendix 4, page 367).

258 119   *Cf.* Historical Report to the Mexican Society, Special Prosecutors' Office for Social and Political Movements of the past. Attorney General of the Republic, 2006 (dossier of appendixes to the application, appendix 4, page 368).

259 312   Article 63(1) of the Convention states that: If the Court finds that there has been a violation of a right or freedom protected by this Convention, the Court shall rule that the injured party be ensured the enjoyment of his right or freedom that was violated. It shall also rule, if appropriate, that the consequences of the measure or situation that constituted the breach of such right or freedom be remedied and that fair compensation be paid to the injured party.

260 315   *Cf. Velásquez Rodríguez, supra* note 24, para. 174; *Case of Kawas Fernández v. Honduras, supra* note 40, para. 191, and *Case of Garibaldi v. Brazil, supra* note 32, para. 169.

261 316   *Cf. Case of the Massacre of la Rochela v. Colombia, supra* note 83, para. 157.

262 317   *Cf. Case of the Carcazo v. Venezuela. Reparations and Costs.* Judgment of August 29, 2002. Series C No. 95, para. 118; *Case of Kawas Fernández v. Honduras, supra* note 40, para. 194, and *Case of Anzualdo Castro v. Peru, supra* note 44, para. 183.

263 318   *Cf. Case of the Caracazo v. Venezuela. Reparations and Costs, supra* note 317, para. 122; *Case of Ticona Estrada v. Bolivia, supra* note 23, para. 84, and *Case of Anzualdo Castro v. Peru, supra* note 44, para. 185.

264 79   *Cf.* Brief of complaint filed by Mrs. Rosendo Cantú and Mr. Bernardino Sierra before the NHRC, *supra* note 64, folios 7556 to 7561.

265 80   *Cf.* Communication of acceptance issued by the Director General of the National Human Rights Commission on March 7, 2002 (case file of annexes to the answer to the application, tome I, annex 1, folio 7581).

266 81   *Cf.* Communication addressed to the Constitutional Governor of Guerrero, *supra* note 71, folio 345.

267 82   *Cf.* Act of receipt of complaint by President of the Mexican League for the Defense of Human Rights of March 7, 2002 (case file of annexes to the answer to the application, tome I, annex 1, folio 7583).

268 83   *Cf.* Press Release No. 026 issued by the Secretariat of National Defense, *supra* note 54.

269 84   *Cf.* Procedures carried out by the Inspector General of CODDEHUM on March 8, 2002 (case file of annexes to the application, tome I, annex 1, folios 7587 to 7591).

270 85   *Cf.* Order No. 722/2002 issued by the CODDEHUM on March 7, 2002, received by the Clerk of the Public Prosecutor of the Common Jurisdiction on March 8, 2002 (case file of annexes to the answer to the [application], tome I, annex 1, folio 5767).

271 86   *Cf.* Complaint filed by Mrs. Rosendo Cantú before the Public Prosecutor of the Common [Jurisdiction], *supra* note 65, folio 9262.

272 87   *Cf.* Complaint filed by Mrs. Rosendo Cantú before the Public Prosecutor of the Common [Jurisdiction], *supra* note 65, folio 9262, and information card issued by the Public Prosecutor of the Judicial District of Allende, addressed to the President of the CODDEHUM on March 11, 2002, (case file of annexes to the answer to the application, tome 1, annex 1, folio 7658).

273 88   Sworn statement rendered by Mr. Lugo Cortés during the public hearing on May 27, 2010.

274 89   Sworn statement rendered by Mr. Lugo Cortés during the public hearing, *supra* note 88.

275 90   *Cf.* Certificate of procedures issued by the CODDEHUM on March 8, 2002 (case file of annexes to the answer to the application, tome I, annex 1, folios 7604 and 7607), and sworn statement rendered by Mr. Lugo Cortés during the public hearing, *supra* note 88.

276 91   Order No. 235 issued by the Public Prosecutor of the Common Jurisdiction, addressed to the Director of Investigation Services of Chilpancingo on March 8, 2002 (case file of annexes to the brief of pleadings and motions, tome I, folio 5069); complaint filed by Mrs. Rosendo Cantú before the Public Prosecutor of the Common Jurisdiction, *supra* note 65, folios 9262 and 9271, and certificate of procedures issued by the CODDEHUM, *supra* note 90, folio 7607.

277 92   *Cf.* Medical note of March 12, 2002, sent by a female doctor of the Emergency Services of the General Hospital of Ayutla (case file of annexes to the brief of pleadings and motions, tome I, annex 3, folio 5118). The doctor requested the following laboratory tests: "EGO," pregnancy test, HIV test and cultures of cervical secretion. Nevertheless, there is only proof of the urine studies, "VDRL," and a pregnancy test.

278 93   *Cf.* Order No. PGJE/DGSP/ND/XXVIII-2/207/2002 issued by the General Office of Investigatory Services on March 15, 2002 (case file of annexes to the application, tome I, annex 7, folio 348).

279 94   *Cf.* Order No. 130/2002 issued by medical examiner assigned to the Judicial District of Morelos on 19 March 2002 (case file of annexes to the answer to the [application], tome V, annex 1, folio 9297).

280 272   272 *Cf. Velásquez Rodríguez, supra* note 33, para. 174; *Case of Chitay Nech et al., supra*

note 25, para. 235, and *Case of Manuel Cepeda Vargas, supra* note 25, para. 216.

281 273   273 *Cf. Case of Radilla Pacheco, supra* note 36, para. 331. See *Case of the Dos ErresMassacre, supra* note 27, para. 233; *Case of Chitay Nech et al., supra* note 25, para. 235, and *Case of Manuel Cepeda Vargas, supra* note 25, para. 216.

282 274   274 *Cf. Case of Radilla Pacheco, supra* note 36, para. 332.

283 275   *Cf. Case of the Dos Erres Massacre, supra* note 27, para. 233, subsection d.

284 285   *Cf. Case of González et al. ("Cotton Field"), supra* note 21, para. 502

285 292   *Cf. Network Development 2008*, Secretariat for Women and National Network of Shelters, *supra* note 57, folio 19159.

286 169   Cf. Case of Myrna Mack Chang v. Guatemala. Merits, Reparations and Costs. Judgment of November 25, 2003. Series C No. 101, para. 277; Case of Manuel Cepeda Vargas v. Colombia. Preliminary Objections, Merits, Reparations and Costs. Judgment of May 26, 2010. Series C No. 213, para. 216, and Case of Ibsen Cárdenas and Ibsen Peña v. Bolivia, [Merits, Reparations and Costs. Judgment of September 1, 2010. Series C No. 217], para. 273.

287 170   Cf. Case of the Caracazo v. Venezuela. Reparations and Costs. Judgment of August 29, 2002. Series C No. 95, para. 118; Case of Gomes Lund et al. (Guerrilha do Araguaia) v. Brazil, [Preliminary Objections, Merits, Reparations and Costs. Judgment of November 24, 2010. Series C No. 219], para. 257, and Case of Gelman v. Uruguay, [Merits and Reparations. Judgment of February 24, 2011. Series C No. 221], para. 256.

288 171   Cf. Case of the Caracazo v. Venezuela. Reparations and Costs, supra note 170, para. 118; Case of Gomes Lund et al. (Guerrilha do Araguaia) v. Brazil, supra note [1]70, para. 257, and Case of Gelman v. Uruguay, supra note [170], para. 256.

289 172   Cf. Case of Velásquez Rodríguez v. Honduras. Merits, [Judgment of July 29, 1988. Series C No. 4], para. 181; Case of Gomes Lund et al. (Guerrilha do Araguaia) v. Brazil, supra note [1]70, para. 262, and Case of Gelman v. Uruguay, supra note [170], para. 259.

290 496   *Cf. Case of Almonacid Arellano et al. v. Chile,* para. 150, and *Case of the Río Negro Massacres v. Guatemala,* para. 259.

291 497   *Cf. Case of Almonacid Arellano et al. v. Chile,* para. 124, and *Case of Cabrera García and Montiel Flores v. Mexico. Preliminary objection, merits, reparations and costs.* Judgment of November 26, 2010. Series C No. 220, para. 225.

292 498   *Cf. Case of Velásquez Rodríguez v. Honduras. Merits,* para. 174, and *Case of the Río Negro Massacres v. Guatemala,* para. 257.

293 499   *Cf. Case of Contreras et al. v. El Salvador,* para. 212.

294 500   *Cf. Case of the Las Dos Erres Massacre v. Guatemala,* para. 233(d), and *Case of the Río Negro Massacres v. Guatemala,* para. 257(d).

295 501   *Cf. Case of the Las Dos Erres Massacre v. Guatemala,* para. 245.

296 502   *Cf.* Expert opinion on psychosocial impacts and recommendations for reparations in the case of "The Massacres of El Mozote and nearby places" provided by María Sol Yáñez De La Cruz, undated (evidence file, tome XVIII, annex 2 to the final written arguments of the representatives, folio 10550).

297 503   *Cf. Case of the Las Dos Erres Massacre v. Guatemala,* para. 245.

298 504   *Cf.* Joint expert opinion provided by affidavit by Luis Fondebrider, Mercedes C. Doretti and Silvana Turner on April 18, 2012 (evidence file, tome XVII, affidavits, folios 10313 and 10322).

299 505   Such as those established in the United Nations Manual on the Effective Prevention and Investigation of Extra-Legal, Arbitrary and Summary Executions.

300 506   *Cf.* Joint expert opinion provided by affidavit by Luis Fondebrider, Mercedes C. Doretti and Silvana Turner on April 18, 2012 (evidence file, tome XVII, affidavits, folio 10318), and Expert opinion on psychosocial impacts and recommendations for reparations in the case of "The Massacres of El Mozote and nearby places" provided by María Sol Yáñez De La Cruz, undated (evidence file, tome XVIII, annex 2 to the final written arguments of the representatives, folio 10559).

301 507   *Cf. Case of the Las Dos Erres Massacre v. Guatemala,* para. 248.

302 508   *Cf. Case of the Las Dos Erres Massacre v. Guatemala,* para. 249.

303 403   *Cf. Case of the Las Dos Erres Massacre v. Guatemala,* para. 233, and *Case of Fornerón and daughter v. Argentina. Merits, reparations and costs.* Judgment of April 27, 2012. Series C No.242, para. 172.

304 404   *Cf. Case of El Caracazo v. Venezuela. Reparations and costs.* Judgment of August 29, 2002. Series C No. 95, para. 118, and *Case of García and family members v. Guatemala. Merits, reparations and costs.* Judgment of November 29, 2012. Series C. No. 258, para. 197.

305 405   *Cf. Case of Velásquez Rodríguez v. Honduras. Merits,* para. 174, and *Case of Cabrera García and Montiel Flores v. Mexico,* para. 215.

306 406   *Cf. Case of Radilla Pacheco v. Mexico. Preliminary objections, merits, reparations and costs.* Judgment of November 23, 2009. Series C No. 209, para. 331, and *Case of Cabrera García and Montiel Flores v. Mexico,* para. 215.

307 407   *Case of Cabrera García and Montiel Flores v. Mexico,* para. 215.

308 163   *Cfr. Cesti Hurtado case. Reparations, [(art. 63.1 American Convention on Human Rights.* Judgment of May 31, 2001. C Series No. 78], para. 32; *"Street Children" case (Villagrán Morales et al. vs. Guatemala). Reparations,* [(art. 63.1 American Convention on Human Rights). Judgment of May 26, 2001. C Series No. 77], para. 59; *"White van" case (Paniagua Morales et al. vs. Guatemala). Reparations, [(art. 63.1 American Convention on Human Rights).* Judgment of May 25, 2001. C Series No. 76], para. 75; *Ivcher Bronstein case,* [Judgment of February 6, 2001. C Series No. 74], para.177; *Baena Ricardo et al. case* [Judgment of February 2, 2001. C Series No. 72], para.201; *Case of the Constitutional Court,* [Decision of January 31, 2001. C Series No. 71], para.118; *Suárez Rosero case. Reparations* (art. 63.1 American Convention on Human Rights). Judgment of January 20 1999. C Series No. 44, para.40; *Loayza Tamayo Case. Reparations* (Art. 63.1 American Convention on Human Rights), Judgment of November 27, 1998. C Series No. 42, para.84; *Caballero Delgado and Santana case. Reparations* (art. 63.1 American Convention on Human Rights). Judgment of January 29, 1997. C Series No. 31, para.15; *Neira Alegría et al. case. Reparations* (art. 63.1 American Convention on Human Rights). Judgment of September 19, 1996. C Series No. 29, para.36; *El Amparo case. Reparations* (art. 63.1 American Convention on Human Rights). Judgment of September 14, 1996. C Series No. 28, para.14; and *Aloeboetoe et al. case. Reparations* (art. 63.1 American Convention on Human Rights). Judgment of September 10, 1993. C Series No. 15, para.43. In this same direction, *cfr.,* Reparation for Injuries Suffered in the Service of the United Nations, Advisory Opinion, I.C.J. Reports 1949, p. 184; *Factory at Chorzów, Merits,* Judgment No. 13, 1928, P.C.I.J., Series A, No. 17, p. 29; and *Factory at Chorzów, Jurisdiction,* Judgment No. 8, 1927, P.C.I.J., Series A, No. 9, p. 21.

309 270   *Cf. Case of Tibi,* [Judgment of September 7, 2004. Series C No. 114], para. 260; *Case of the "Juvenile Reeducation Institute,"* [Judgment of September 2, 2004. Series C No. 112], para. 315, and *Case of Ricardo Canese.* [Judgment of August 31, 2004. Series C No. 111], para. 209.

310 271   *Cf. Case of the Gómez Paquiyauri Brothers* [*Merits, reparations and costs,* Judgment of July 8, 2004. Series C No. 110], para. 236; *Case of the 19 Tradesmen,* [Judgment of July 5, 2004. Series C No. 109], para.273, and *Case of Molina Theissen. Reparations,* [(Art. 63(1) American Convention on Human Rights). Judgment of July 3, 2004. Series C No. 108], para. 88.

311 220   See *Case of Huilca Tecse* [Judgment of March 3, 2005. Series C No. 121], para. 111; *Case of the Serrano Cruz Sisters, supra* note 2[19], para. 194, and *Case of Carpio Nicolle et al.,* [Judgment of November 22, 2004. Series C. No. 117], para. 136.

312 221   See *Case of the Plan de Sánchez Massacre. Reparations,* [(Art. 63(1) American Convention on Human Rights). Judgment of November 19, 2004. Series C No. 116], para. 100.

313 222   See *Case of the Serrano Cruz Sisters, supra* note 2, [19] para. 194, and *Case of the Plan de Sánchez Massacre. Reparations, supra* note [221], para. 100.

314 223   See *Case of the Serrano Cruz Sisters, supra* note 2[19], para. 194; *Case of the Plan de Sánchez Massacre. Reparations, supra* note [221], para. 100, and Case of Myrna Mack Chang, [Judgment of November 25, 2003. Series C No. 101], para. 278.

315 224   See *Case of Huilca Tecse, supra* note 2[20], para. 96; *Case of the Serrano Cruz Sisters, supra* note 2[19], para. 194, and *Case of Lori Berenson Mejía,* [Judgment of November 25, 2004. Series C No. 119], para. 240.

316 323   *Cf. Case of Barrios Altos v. Peru. Reparations and Costs.* Judgment of November 30, 2001. Series C No. 87, Operative Paragraph 5(d); *Case of Escher et al., supra* note 64, para. 239, and *Case of Garibaldi v. Brazil, supra* note 32, para. 157.

317 324   *Cf. Case of the Serrano Cruz Sisters v. El Salvador, supra* note 82, para. 195; *Case of Escher et al. v. Brazil, supra* note 64, para. 239, and *Case of Garibaldi v. Brazil, supra* note 32, para. 157.

318 325   *Cf. Case of the Pueblo Bello Massacre v. Colombia, supra* note 133, para. 254; *Case of Ximenes Lopes v.Brazil, supra* note 319, para. 227, and *Case of the Miguel Castro Castro Prison v. Peru, supra* note 51, para. 430.

319 304   *Cf. Case of Huilca Tecse v. Peru. Merits, reparations and costs.* Judgment of March 3, 2005. Series C No. 121, para. 111; *Case of the "Dos Erres" Massacre v. Guatemala,* [Preliminary objection, merits, reparations and costs. Judgment of November 24, 2009. Series C No. 211], para. 261, *and Case of Manuel Cepeda Vargas v. Colombia,* [Preliminary objections, merits and reparations. Judgment of May 26, 2010. Series C No. 213], para. 222.

320 307   *Cf. Case of Yatama v. Nicaragua,* [Preliminary objections, merits, reparations and costs. Judgment of June 23, 2005. Series C No. 127], para. 253; *Case of Tiu Tojín v. Guatemala,* [Merits, reparations and costs. Judgment of November 26, 2008. Series C No. 190], para. 108, and *Case of Chitay Nech et al. v. Guatemala,* [Preliminary objections, merits, reparations, and costs. Judgment of May 25, 2010. Series C No. 212], para. 245.

321 279   *Cf. Case of Kawas Fernández v. Honduras, supra* note 117, para. 202; *Case of Anzualdo Castro, v. Perú. Preliminary Objections, Merits, Reparations, and Costs.* Judgment of September 22, 2009. Series C No. 202, para. 200, and *Case of González et al. ("Cotton Fields"), supra* note 21, para. 469.

322 280   *Cf. Barrios Altos v. Peru.* Reparations and Costs. Judgment of November 30, 2001. Series C No. 87, Operative paragraph 5(d); *Case of Chitay Nech et al. v. Guatemala. supra* note 25, para. 244, and *Case of Manuel Cepeda Vargas, supra* note 21, para. 220.

323 281   *Cf. Case of Chitay Nech et al., supra* note 25, para. 244 and 245.

324 282   *Cf. Serrano Cruz Sisters v. El Salvador. Merits, Reparations, and Costs.* Judgment of March 1, 2005. Series C No. 120, para. 195; *Case of Chitay Nech et al., supra* note 25, para. 244, and *Case of Manuel Cepeda Vargas, supra* note 25, para. 220.

325 283   *Cf. Yakye Axa Indigenous Community supra* note 254, para. 227; *Case of Tiu Tojín, supra* note 254, para. 108, and *Case of Chitay Nech et al., supra* note 25, para. 245.

326 277   *Cf. Case of Cantoral Benavides v. Peru. Reparations, and Costs.* Judgment *of December* 3, 2001. Series C No. 88, para. 81 and *Case of the Massacre of Pueblo Bello v. Colombia. Merits, Reparations and Costs.* Judgment of January 31, 2006. Series C No. 140, para. 254.

327 350   *Cf. Case of Cantoral Benavides v. Peru. Reparations and costs.* Judgment of December 3, 2001. Series C No. 88, para. 81, and *Case of Atala Riffo and daughters,* para. 263. See also *Case of the Moiwana Community, Preliminary objections, merits, reparations and costs,* paras. 216 and 217 and *Case of the Xákmok Kásek Indigenous People v. Paraguay,* para. 297.

328 351   *Cf. Case of Cantoral Benavides v. Peru. Reparations and costs,* para. 79, and *Case of Forneron and daughter v. Argentina,* para. 183.

329 525   *Cf. Case of Trujillo Oroza v. Bolivia. Reparations and costs.* Judgment of February 27, 2002. Series C No. 92, para. 77, and *Case of Gelman v. Uruguay,* para. 265.

330 526   *Cf. Case of Cantoral Benavides v. Peru. Reparations and costs,* para. 79, and *Case of Fur-*

lan and family v. Argentina, para. 290.

331 392   *Cf. Case of the Massacre of Santo Domingo v. Colombia,* para. 303, and *Case of Cantoral Benavides v. Peru. Preliminary objections.* Judgment of September 3, 1998. Series C No. 40, para. 79.

332 380   To this end, the State could take as a basis the estimates used by the university in which Talís would undertake her postgraduate studies to determine the amount of the scholarships it awards to students for their living costs.

333   *See, e.g., Bulacio v. Argentina,* Merits, Reparations, and Costs, Sept. 18, 2003, Series C No. 100, para. 112.

334   *See Almonacid-Arellano et al. v. Chile,* Preliminary Objections, Merits, Reparations, and Costs, Sept. 26, 2006, Series C No. 154, paras. 151-52.

335 20   *Cf. Durand and Ugarte case,* Judgment of August 16, 2000, Inter-Am. Ct. H.R. (ser. C) No. 68, para. 137.

336 21   *Cf. "principe allant de soi"* ["principle taken for granted"]; *Echange des populations grecques et turques [Exchange of Greek and Turkish Populations],* advisory opinion 1925, C.P.J.I., series B, no. 10, p. 20; and *Durand and Ugarte case, supra* note 20, para. 136.

337 124   *Cf. Case of Maritza Urrutia, supra* note 7, para. 141; *Case of Myrna Mack-Chang, supra* note 7, para. 234; and *Case of Bulacio, supra* note 7, para. 70.

338 125   *Cf. Case of Maritza Urrutia, supra* note 7, para. 143; *Case of Myrna Mack-Chang, supra* note 7, para. 236; and *Case of Bulacio, supra* note 7, para. 72.

339 108   *Cf. Case of the Serrano-Cruz Sisters.* [Judgment of March 1st, 2005. Series C No. 120], para. 165; *Case of Plan de Sánchez Massacre. Reparations,* [(Art. 63.1 American Convention on Human Rights). Judgment of November 19, 2004. Series C No. 116], para. 93; and *Case of De la Cruz-Flores.* [Judgment of November 18, 2004. Series C No. 115], para. 164.

340 120   *Cf. Case of Yatama, supra* note 13, para. 254; *Case of Fermín Ramírez, supra* note 13, para. 130(d), and *Case of Yakye Axa Indigenous Community, supra* note 16, para. 225.

341 121   *Cf.* United Nations, Committee on the Rights of the Child, Examination of the Reports presented by the States Parties under Article 44 of the Convention. Concluding Observations of the Committee on the Rights of the Child. The Dominican Republic. UN Doc. CRC/C/15/Add.150, of 21 February 2001, para. 27.

342 18   *Cf.* Statement made before notary public (affidavit) by Yvon Neptune [on September 20, 2007], para. 1 ([evidence file, Volume III,] folio 405).

343 19   *Cf.* Application submitted by the Commission, [December 14, 2006], para. 29 (merits file, volume I, folio 108).

344 20   *Cf.* Arrest warrant issued by the investigating magistrate of the Court of First Instance of St. Marc on March 25, 2004 (evidence file, Volume II, folio 254).

345 21   *Cf.* Application submitted by the Commission, *supra* note [19], para. 30 (folio 108) and statement made before notary public (affidavit) by Yvon Neptune, *supra* note [18], para. 30 (folio 456).

346 22   *Cf.* Application submitted by the Commission, *supra* note [19], para. 87 (folio 123), and final written arguments presented by the Commission, October 2, 2007, para. 36 (merits file, volume II, folio 307).

347 23   *Cf.* Application submitted by the Commission, *supra* note [18], paras. 31, 42, 48 and 49 (folios 109, 111 and 112).

348 227   The "Juvenile Reeducation Institute" v. Paraguay, *supra* note 137, para. 178. See also Matter of the Urso Branco Prison. Provisional measures with regard to Brazil. Order of the Inter-American Court of Human Rights of April 22, 2004, eleventh considering paragraph. Likewise, the European Court has established that Article 3 of the European Convention establishes the State's obligation to adopt preventively concrete measures to protect the physical integrity and health of those deprived of liberty. Cf. Eur. Court H.R., *Pantea v. Romania,* judgement of 3 June 2003, Reports of Judgments and Decisions 2003-VI (extracts), para. 190.

349 319   *Cf. Case of Castillo Petruzzi et al. v. Peru, supra* note 54, para. 207; *Case of Ximenes Lopes v. Brazil. Merits, Reparations, and Costs.* Judgment of July 4, 2006. Series C No. 149, para. 83, and *Case of Almonacid Arellano et al. v. Chile, supra* note 19, para. 118.

350 320   *Cf. Case of Almonacid Arellano et al. v. Chile, supra* note 19, para. 124, and *Case of La Cantuta v. Peru, supra* note 51, para. 173.

351 321   *Cf. Case of Almonacid Arellano et al. v. Chile, supra* note 19, para. 124; *Case of La Cantuta v. Peru, supra* note 51, para. 173, and *Case of Boyce et al. v. Barbados. Preliminary Objection, Merits, Reparations, and Costs.* Judgment of November 20, 2007. Series C No. 169, para. 78. The Tribunal observes that the conventionality control has already been exercised in the domestic judicial realm in Mexico. *Cf.* Direct Administrative Appeal of Relief 1060/2008, First Collegiate Court in Administrative and Labor Matters of the Eleventh Circuit, judgment of July 2, 2009. That decision established that: "the local courts of the State of Mexico shall not limit themselves to the mere application of local laws but they are also compelled to apply the Constitution, international treaties or conventions, and the jurisprudence issued by the Inter-American Court of Human Rights, among other bodies, which forces them to exercise a control of conventionality among domestic regulations and supranational ones, as was considered by the First Chamber of the Supreme Court of Justice of the Nation […]."

352 245   *Cf. Case of Radilla Pacheco* [v. Mexico. Preliminary Objections, Merits, Reparations, and Costs. Judgment of November 23, 2009. Series C No. 209], para. 338.

353 246   *Cf. Case of Almonacid-Arellano et al. v. Chile. Preliminary Objections, Merits, Reparations, and Costs.* Judgment of September 26, 2006. Series C No. 154, para. 124; *Case of La Cantuta v. Perú. Merits, Reparations, and Costs.* Judgment of November 29, 2006. Series C No. 162, para. 173, and *Case of Radilla Pacheco, supra* note [245], para. 339.

354 247   *Cf. Case of Almonacid-Arellano, supra* note 246, para. 124; *Case of Boyce et al. v. Barbados. Preliminary Objections, Merits, Reparations, and Costs.* Judgment of November 20, 2007, Series C No. 169, para. 78, and *Case of Radilla Pacheco, supra* note [245], para. 339.

355 276   *Cf. Case of Radilla Pacheco, supra* note 36, para. 338.

356 277   *Cf. Case of Almonacid Arellano et al. v. Chile. Preliminary Objections, Merits, Reparations, and Costs.* Judgment of September 26, 2006. Series C No. 154, para. 124; *Case of La Cantúta v. Perú. Merits, Reparations, and Costs.* Judgment of November 29, 2006. Series C No. 162, para. 173, and *Case of Radilla Pacheco, supra* note 36, para. 339.

357 278   *Cf. Case of Almonacid Arellano, supra* note 282, para. 124; *Case of Boyce et al. v. Barbados. Preliminary Objections, Merits, Reparations, and Costs.* Judgment of November 20, 2007, Series C No. 169, para. 78, and *Case of Radilla Pacheco, supra* note 36, para. 339.

358 284   *Cf. Case of González et al. ("Cotton Field"), supra* note 21, para. 493.

359 281   *Cf. Case Gangaram Panday v. Suriname. Preliminary Objections.* Judgment of December 4, 1991. Series C No. 12, para. 50 and *Case Chocrón Chocrón, supra* note 26, para. 1

360 282   *Cf. Case Gangaram Panday, supra note* 281, para. 50 and *Case Chocrón Chocrón, supra* note 26, para. 1

361 283   *Cf. Case of Almonacid Arellano et al. v. Chile. Preliminary Objections, Merits, Reparations, and Costs.* Judgment of September 26, 2006. Series C No. 154, para. 124 and *Case of Fontevecchia and D'Amico, supra* note 28, para. 93

362 284   *Cf. Case Almonacid Arellano et al., supra* note [283], para. 124 and *Case Fontevecchia and D'Amico, supra* note 28, para. 93.

363 285   *Cf.* Judgment of May 9, 1995 issued by the Constitutional Chamber of the Supreme Court of Costa Rica. Held unconstitutional. Vote 2313-95 (File 0421-S-90), considering clause VII.

364 286   *Cf.* Judgment issued on May 10, 2010 by the Constitutional Court of Bolivia (File No. 2006-13381-27- RAC), para. III.3 on "The Inter-American System of Human Rights. Basis and effects of the Judgments issued by the Inter-American Court of Human Rights."

365 287   *Cf.* Order No. 1920-2003 issued on November 13, 2003 by the Supreme Court of the Do-

minican Republic.

366 288   Judgment issued on July 21, 2006 by the Constitutional Court of Peru (File No. 2730-2006-PA/TC), consideration 12 and judgment 00007-2007-PI/TC issued on June 19, 2007 by the plenary of the Constitutional Court of Peru (Callao College of Lawyers, Congress of the Republic), consideration 26.

367 289   *Cf.* Judgment issued on December 23, 2004 by the Supreme Court of Argentina (File No. 224. XXXIX), "Espósito, Miguel Angel s/ Incidental Proceeding of Limitation on the Criminal Action commenced by the Defense," considering clause 6 and Judgment of the Inter-American Court of Human Rights of the Supreme Court of Argentina, Mazzeo, July Lilo, et al., cassation recourse and unconstitutionality. M. 2333. XLII. Et al. of July 13, 2007, para. 20.

368 290   *Cf.* Judgment C-010/00 issued on March 19, 2000 by the Constitutional Court of Colombia, para. 6.

369 291   *Cf.* Plenary of the Supreme Court of Justice of Mexico, Record 912/2010, Decision of July 14 2011.

370 292   *Cf.* Supreme Court of Justice of Panama, Decision No. 240 of May 12, 2010 in compliance with the Judgment of the Inter-American Court of Human Rights, of January 27, 2009, in the case of Santander Tristan Donoso v. Panama.

371 293   *Cf. Case López Mendoza v. Venezuela. Merits Reparations and Costs.* Judgment of September 1, 2011. Series C No. 233, para. 228.

372 349   Final Negotiation Report. "Contract for the provision of services for the exploration and exploitation of crude oil in Block 10. AGIP ECUADOR OIL B.V, of November 21, 2010 (evidence file, tome 18, folios 9711 and 9736).

373 459   *Mutatis mutandi, Case of Claude Reyes et al. v. Chile. Merits, Reparations and Costs.* Judgment of September 19, 2006. Series C No. 151, para. 79. Also, the extent of this obligation is specified in the resolution of the Inter-American Juridical Committee on the "Principles on the Right of Access to Information," which establishes that "Public bodies should disseminate information about their functions and activities —including [...] their policies, opportunities for consultation, activities which affect members of the public, their budget, and subsidies, benefits and contracts— on a routine and proactive basis, even in the absence of a specific request, and ensure that the information is accessible and understandable." Inter-American Juridical Committee, "Principles on the right of access to information", 73° Regular Session, August 7, 2008, OAS/Ser. Q CJI/RES.147 (LXXIII-O/08), operative paragraph 4.

374 460   *Cf. Case of Gangaram Panday v. Suriname. Preliminary Objections.* Judgment of December 4, 1991. Series C No. 12, para. 50 and *Case of the Kichwa Indigenous People of Sarayaku v. Ecuador,* para. 221.

375 461   *Cf. Case of Gangaram Panday. Preliminary Objections,* para. 50 and *Case of the Kichwa Indigenous People of Sarayaku v. Ecuador,* para. 221.

376 462   *Cf. Case of Almonacid Arellano et al. v. Chile. Preliminary Objections, Merits, Reparations and Costs.* Judgment of September 26, 2006. Series C No. 154, para. 124 and *Case of Atala Riffo and Daughters v. Chile. Merits, Reparations and Costs.* Judgment of February 24, 2012. Serie[s] C No. 239, para. 281.

377 463   *Cf. Case of Almonacid Arellano et al.,* para. 124 and *Case of Atala Riffo and Daughters v. Chile,* para. 282.

378 464   *Cf.* Judgment of May 9, 1995 delivered by the Constitutional Chamber of the Supreme Court of Justice of Costa Rica. Action of unconstitutionality. Opinion 2313-95 (File 0421-S-90), considering paragraph VII.

379 465   *Cf.* Judgment of May 10, 2010, delivered by the Constitutional Court of Bolivia (Case file No. 2006-13381-27 RAC), section III.3. on "the Inter-American Human Rights System. Grounds for and effects of the judgments delivered by the Inter-American Court of Human Rights."

380 466   *Cf.* Decision No. 1920-2003 issued by the Supreme Court of Justice of the Dominican Republic on November 13, 2003.

381 467   *Cf.* Judgment delivered by the Constitutional Court of Peru on July 21, 2006, (Case file No. 2730-2006-PA/TC), reasoning #12 and judgment 00007-2007-PI/TC issued on June 19, 2007 by the Constitutional Court of Peru in Plenary (Lawyers' Professional Association of El Callao v. Congress of the Republic), reasoning #26.

382 468   *Cf.* Judgment issued on December 23, 2004, by the Supreme Court of Justice of the Argentine Nation (Case file 224. XXXIX), "Espósito, Miguel Angel re/incidental plea of prescription of the criminal action filed by his defense counsel," considering paragraph 6 and Judgment of the Supreme Court of Justice of the Argentine Nation, Mazzeo, Julio Lilo et al., appeal for annulment and unconstitutionality. M. 2333. XLII. and others of July 13, 2007, para. 20.

383 469   *Cf.* Judgment C-010/00 delivered by the Constitutional Court of Colombia on January 19, 2000, para. 6.

384 470   *Cf.* Plenary of the Supreme Court of Justice of Mexico, Case file "Miscellaneous" 912/2010, ruling of July 14, 2011.

385 471   *Cf.* Supreme Court of Justice of Panama, Decision No. 240 of May 12, 2010, ordering compliance with the judgment of January 27, 2009, of the Inter-American Court of Human Rights in the case of Santander Tristan Donoso *v.* Panama.

386 472   *Cf. Case of López Mendoza v. Venezuela. Merits, Reparations and Costs.* Judgment of September 1, 2011. Series C No. 233, para. 228 and *Case of Atala Riffo and Daughters v. Chile*, para. 284.

387 497   *Cf. Case of Velásquez Rodríguez. Merits,* para. 166, and *Case of the Kichwa Indigenous People of Sarayaku v. Ecuador,* para. 221.

388 498   *Cf. Case of Gangaram Panday v. Suriname. Preliminary objections.* Judgment of December 4, 1991. Series C No. 12, para. 50, and *Case of Furlan and family v. Argentina,* para. 300.

389 499   *Cf. Case of Gangaram Panday v. Suriname. Preliminary objections,* para. 50, and *Case of Furlan and family v. Argentina,* para. 300.

390 393   *Cf. Case of Garrido and Baigorria v. Argentina. Reparations and costs.* Judgment of August 27, 1998. Series C No. 39, para. 68, and *Case of the Massacre of Santo Domingo v. Colombia,* para. 245.

391 394   *Cf. Case of Castillo Petruzzi et al. v. Peru,* para. 207, and *Case of Furlan and family members v. Argentina,* para. 300.

392 395   *Cf. Case of Almonacid Arellano et al. v. Chile. Preliminary objections, merits, reparations and costs.* Judgment of September 26, 2006. Series C No. 154, para. 124, *and Case of Atala Riffo and daughters v. Chile. Merits, reparations and costs.* Judgment of the February 24, 2012. Series C No. 239, para. 281.

393 396   *Cf. Case of Almonacid Arellano et al. v. Chile,* para. 124, and *Case of Gudiel Álvarez et al. ("Diario Militar") v. Guatemala,* para. 330.

394 397   The pertinent parts of this judgment indicate that: "absolute punishments, such as life imprisonments, are characterized, precisely, because they do not admit aggravating or attenuating circumstances of any nature. This means that the legislator declares, *de iure,* that any answer to the charges is irrelevant [...]. However, in the case of acts committed by juveniles, the situation is different, because, if the court decides to apply a punishment, it must still decide whether it is applicable to reduce the punishment for that for an attempted offense. Consequently, it is no longer sufficient to merely indicate the legal definition of the conduct in order to decide the applicable punishment. [...] Furthermore, in the case of juveniles, the specific emotional situation when committing the act, his or her real possibilities of controlling the course of events, or even, the possibility of having acted impulsively or at the urging of companions, or any other element that could affect guilt, acquires a different significance that must be examined when determining the punishment. [...] Law 22,278 contains an element that does not appear in the Criminal Code: the authority

and obligation of the judge to ponder the "need for punishment.' […T]he reasons why the legislator granted the judge such broad powers when handing down a sentence to an individual who committed an offense when he or she was under 18 years of age is related to the mandate to ensure that these punishments, above all, seek social reinsertion or, in the words of the Convention on the Rights of the Child, 'the desirability of promoting the child's reintegration and the child's assuming a constructive role in society" (art. 40(1)). […] The constitutional mandate ordering that punishments consisting of deprivation of liberty shall have as an essential aim the reform and social rehabilitation of the prisoners (art. 5(6), American Convention) and that the essential aim of the treatment of prisoners shall be their reformation and social rehabilitation (art. 10(3) ICCVP) requires that the sentencing judge should not disregard the possible effects of the punishment from the point of view of special prevention. This mandate, in the case of juveniles, is much more constructive and translates into the obligation to provide grounds for the need for the deprivation of liberty imposed from the standpoint of the possibilities of resocialization, which supposes the need to weigh carefully in this consideration of need the potential adverse effects of imprisonment." *Cf.* Supreme Court of Justice of the Nation. Maldonado, Daniel Enrique *et al.*, case No.1174, judgment of December 7, 2005 (file of annexes to the submission of the case, tome VIII, folio 4333).

395 398 "Article 2. Mandatory Application. The Convention on the Rights of the Child is of mandatory application in the conditions under which it is in force, in every administrative, judicial or any other type of action, decision or measure adopted concerning persons under eighteen years of age. Children and adolescents have the right to be heard and responded to in whatever form they express themselves, in all spheres." *Cf.* Law 26,061 (merits file, tome IV, folio 2458).

396 399 *Cf.* United Nations, Committee on the Rights of the Child, General Comment No. 10, Children's rights in juvenile justice, 25 April 2007, CRC/C/GC/10, para. 18.

397 400 *Cf.* Special federal appeal submitted by the Prosecutor General of the Nation on September 4, 2012, against the decision of the Federal Criminal Cassation Chamber of August 21, 2012 (file of annexes to the representative's final written arguments, folios 8365 and 8374).

398 401 *Cf.* Remedy of complaint filed by the Prosecutor General of the Nation before the Supreme Court of Justice of the Nation on October 5, 2012 (merits file, tome III, folio 2354).

399 372 *Cf. Case of Luna López v. Honduras, supra*, para. 243.

400 127 *Cf.* International Criminal Tribunal for the Former Yugoslavia, *Prosecutor v. Erdemovic*, Case No. IT-96-22-T, Sentencing Judgment, November 29, 1996, at para. 28. * * *

401 128 *Cf.* UN, Extradition and punishment of war criminals, adopted by the General Assembly of the United Nations in Resolution 3 (I) of February 13, 1946; Confirmation of the Principles of International Law recognized by the Charter of the Nuremberg Tribunal, adopted by the General Assembly of the United Nations in Resolution 95 (I) of December 11, 1946; Extradition of war criminals and traitors, adopted by the General Assembly of the United Nations in Resolution 170 (II) of October 31, 1947; Question of the punishment of war criminals and of persons who have committed crimes against humanity, adopted by the General Assembly of the United Nations in Resolution 2338 (XXII) of December 18, 1967; Convention on the Non-Applicability of Statutory Limitations to War Crimes and Crimes against Humanity, adopted by the General Assembly of the United Nations in Resolution 2391 (XXIII) of November 25, 1968; Question of the punishment of war criminals and of persons who have committed crimes against humanity adopted by the General Assembly of the United Nations in Resolution 2712 (XXV) of December 14, 1970; Question of the punishment of war criminals and of persons who have committed crimes against humanity adopted by the General Assembly of the United Nations in Resolution 2840 (XXVI) of December 18, 1971, and Crime Prevention and Control, adopted by the General Assembly of the United Nations in Resolution 3021 (XXVII) of December 18, 1972.

402 129 *Cf.* UN, Question of the punishment of war criminals and of persons who have committed

crimes against humanity, adopted by the General Assembly of the United Nations in Resolution 2583 (XXIV) of December 15, 1969.

403 130   *Cf.* UN, Principles of International Cooperation in the Detection, Arrest, Extradition and Punishment of Persons Guilty of War Crimes and Crimes against Humanity, adopted by the General Assembly of the United Nations in Resolution 3074 (XXVIII) December 3, 1973.

404 131   *Cf.* UN Resolution of the Security Council S/RES/827 for the establishment of the International Criminal Tribunal for the Former Yugoslavia of March 25, 1993; and Resolution of the Security Council S/RES/955 for the establishment of an International Criminal Case for Rwanda of November 8, 1994.

405 132   *Cf.* UN Report of the Secretary General S/2004/616 on the Rule of Law and Transitional Justice in conflict and post-conflict societies of August 3, 2004, para. 10.

406 133   *Cf.* UN Report of the Secretary General S/2000/915 on the establishment of a Tribunal for Sierra Leona, of October 4, 2000, para. 22.

407 134   *Cf.* UN Report of the Secretary General S/2000/915 on the establishment of a Tribunal for Sierra Leona, of October 4, 2000, para. 24.

408 135   *Cf.* UN Additional Protocol to the Geneva Conventions of August 12, 1949 regarding the protection of victims of non-international armed conflicts (Protocol II).

409 136   *Cf. Case of Velásquez Rodríguez.* Judgment of July 29, 1988. Series C No. 4, para. 166, and *Case of Godínez-Cruz.* Judgment of January 20, 1989. Series C No. 5, para. 175.

410 137   *Cf. Case of the Ituango Massacres,* [Judgment of July 1, 2006. Series C No. 148], para. 299; *Case of the "Mapiripán Massacre,"* Judgment of September 15, 2005. Series C No. 134, para. 237; *Case of the Moiwana Community,* Judgment of September 15, 2005. Series C No. 134, para. 203.

411 138   *Cf. Case of Ximenes-Lopes,* [Judgment of July 4, 2006. Series C No. 149], para. 148; *Case of Baldeón-García,* [Judgment of April 6, 2006. Series C No. 147], para. 94; and *Case of the Pueblo Bello Massacre,* Judgment of January 31, 2006. Series C No. 140, para. 143.

412 139   *Cf. Case of Baldeón-García, supra* note 1[38], para. 144; *Case of the 19 Merchants,* Judgment of July 5, 2004. Series C No. 109, para. 192; and *Case of Baena Ricardo et al. Jurisdiction.* Judgment of November 28, 2003. Series C No. 104, para. 77.

413 140   *Cf. Case of Barrios Altos.* Judgment of March 14, 2001. Series C No. 75, para. 41.

414 141   *Cf.* Final written arguments of the State (record on the Merits of the Case, Volume III, folio 723.)

415 2   Subsequently, the Next of Kin of the Politically Deceased and Disappeared Persons of the Institute of Studies on State Violence, Angela Harkavy, and the *Grupo Tortura Nunca Más de Río de Janeiro* [Group Torture Never Again from Rio de Janeiro], joined as petitioners.

416 3   In the Admissibility Report No. 33/01[,] the Commission declared admissible the case No. 11.552 in regard to the alleged violation of Articles 4, 8, 12, 13, and 25, in accordance with 1(1), all of the American Convention, as well as Articles I, XXV, and XXVI on the American Declaration on the Rights and Duties of Man (hereinafter, "American Declaration"), (case file of annexes to the petition, appendix 3, tome III, folio 2322).

417 4   In the Report on the Merits No. 91/08[,] the Commission concluded that the State was responsible for the violations of the human rights established in Articles I, XXV, and XXVI of the American Declaration and 4, 5, and 7 in relation with Article 1(1) of the American Convention, to the detriment of the disappeared victims; in Articles XVII of the American Declaration, and 3 in relation with Article 1(1) of the American Convention, to the detriment of the disappeared persons; in Articles I of the American Declaration and 5 of the American Convention, in connection with Article 1(1) to the detriment of the next of kin of the disappeared persons; in Article 13 of the American Convention, in relation with Article 2 of the same, to the detriment of the next of kin of the disappeared; in Articles XVIII of the American Declaration, and 8(1) and 25 of the American Convention in relation with Articles 1(1) and 2 of the same, to the detriment of the disappeared persons and their next of kin of the disappeared persons in virtue of the application of the amnesty law to the dis-

appeared persons; [and in] Articles XVIII of the American Declaration and 8(1) and 25 of the American Convention, in relation with Article 1(1) of the same, to the detriment of the disappeared persons and their next of kin, in virtue of the ineffectiveness of the non-criminal judicial actions filed in the framework of the present case (case file of annexes to the petition, appendix 3, tome VII, folio 3655).

418 372   *Cf. Velásquez Rodríguez. Merits,* [Judgment of July 29, 1988. Series C No. 4], para. 174; *Case of Rosendo Cantú et al. [v. México. Preliminary Objection, Merits, Reparations and Costs.* Judgment of August 31, 2010. Series C No. 216], para. 211, and *Case of Ibsen Cárdenas and Ibsen Peña [v. Bolivia. Merits, Reparations, and Costs.* Judgment of September 1, 2010 Series C No. 217], para. 237.

419 373   *Cf. Case of the Dos Erres Massacre [v. Guatemala. Preliminary Objection, Merits, Reparations and Costs.* Judgment of November 24, 2009. Series C No. 211], para. 233; *Case of Manuel Cepeda Vargas [v. Colombia. Preliminary Objections, Merits, Reparations, and Costs.* Judgment May 26, 2010. Series C No. 213], para. 216 and *Case of Ibsen Cárdenas and Ibsen Peña, supra* note [372] para. 237.

420 374   Pursuant to its jurisprudence, the Inter-American Court refers to the ordinary or common jurisdiction as being the criminal and non-military jurisdiction. *Cf. Case of Radilla Pacheco [v. México. Preliminary Objections, Merits, Reparations, and Costs.* Judgment of November 23, 2009. Series C No. 209], para. 332; *Case of Fernández Ortega et al. [v. México. Preliminary Objection, Merits, Reparations, and Costs.* Judgment of [August] 30[,] 2010. Series C No. 215], para. 229, and *Case of Rosendo Cantú et al., supra* note [372], para. 212.

421 2   Also mentioned as María Macarena Tauriño Vivian, due to the facts of the case.

422 3   The Commission appointed as delegate[e]s Ms. Luz Patricia Mejía, Commissioner, and Mr. Santiago A. Canton, Executive Secretary[,] and as legal advisors Ms. Elizabeth Abi-Mershed, Deputy Executive Secretary, Christina Cerna[,] and Lilly Ching, attorneys of the Executive Secretary.

423 4   In this report, the Commission concluded that the State is responsible for the violation of Articles 3, 4, 5, and 7, in relation to Article 1(1) of the American Convention, with Articles I.b, III, IV, and V of the Inter-American Convention on the Forced Disappearance of Persons and with Articles 6 and 8 of the Inter-American Convention to Prevent and Punish Torture and Articles I, XVIII[,] and XXVI of the American Declaration on the Rights and Duties of Man, to the detriment of María Claudia García; of Articles 1(1), 2, 8(1) and 25 of the American Convention, Articles I.b, III, IV, and V of the Inter-American Convention on Forced Disappearance of Persons and Articles 1, 6, 8, and 11 of the Inter-American Convention to Prevent and Punish Torture, to the detriment of the next of kin of María Claudia García; Articles 5(1) and 1(1) of the Convention to the detriment of Juan Gelman, his family and María Macarena Gelman; Articles 3, 11, 17, 18, 19, 20, and 1(1) of the American Convention, Article XII of the Inter-American Convention on Forced Disappearance of Persons and Articles VI, VII, and XVII of the American Declaration on the Rights and Duties of Man, to the detriment of Juan Gelman and his family and of María Macarena Gelman. In this report, the Commission made the following recommendations to the State: a) carry out a complete and impartial investigation in order to identify and punish those responsible for the human rights violations in the case; b) adopt the legislative or any measures necessary to revoke Law 15.848 or the Expiry Law of the State; c) create a domestic mechanism, with binding legal powers and authority over all the State bodies to supervise these recommendations; and d) order full reparation for the next of kin that includes compensation and symbolic acts that guarantee the non-repetition of the acts committed.

424 288   *Cf. Case of Barrios Altos v. Perú. Merits.* Judgment of March 14, 2001. Series C No. 75, para. 41; *Case of The Dos Erres Massacre [v. Guatemala. Preliminary Objection, Merits, Reparations and Costs.* Judgment of November 24, 2009. Series C No. 211], para. 129, and *Case of Gomes Lund et al. (Guerrilha do Araguaia) [v. Brazil. Preliminary Objections,*

Merits, Reparations and Costs. Judgment of November 24, 2010. Series C No. 219], para. 171.

425 289   *Cf. Case of Almonacid-Arellano et al. v. Chile. Preliminary Objections, Merits, Reparations and Costs.* Judgment of September 26, 2006. Series C No. 154, para. 120, and *Case of Gomes Lund et al. (Guerrilha do Araguaia), supra* note [288], para. 175.

426 290   *Cf. Case of Gomes Lund et al. (Guerrilha do Araguaia), supra* note [288], para. 175.

427 291   *Cf. Case of Goiburú et al.,* [v. *Paraguay. Merits, Reparations and Costs.* Judgment of September 22, 2006. Series C No. 153], paras. 93 and 128; *Case of Ibsen Cárdenas and Ibsen Peña,* [v. *Bolivia. Merits, Reparations and Costs.* Judgment of September 1, 2010 Series C No. 217], para. 61 and 197, and *Case of Gomes Lund et al. (Guerrilha do Araguaia), supra* note [288], para. 137.

428 292   *Cf. Case of Barrios Altos. Merits, supra* note 288, para. 44; *Case of La Cantuta v. Perú. Merits, Reparations and Costs.* Judgment of November 29, 2006. Series C No. 162, para. 175, and *Case of Gomes Lund et al. (Guerrilha do Araguaia), supra* note [288], para. 174.

429 293   *Cf. Case of Tiu Tojín,* [v. *Guatemala. Merits, Reparations and Costs.* Judgment of November 26, 2008. Series C No. 190], para. 44, para. 87; *Case of Ibsen Cárdenas and Ibsen Peña, supra* note [291], para. 201, and *Case of Gomes Lund et al. (Guerrilha do Araguaia), supra* note [288], para. 179.

430 294   *Cf.* Supreme Court of Justice of Peru, Judgment of March 18, 2006, Exp: 111-04, D.D Cayo Rivera Schreiber; Constitutional Tribunal of Peru, Judgment of March 18, 2004, Case file No. 2488-2002-HC/TC, para. 26 and Judgment of December 9, 2004, Case file No. 2798-04-HC/TC, para. 22; Supreme Court of Justice of México, Thesis: P./J. 49/2004, Federal Judicial Weekly and its Gazette, Novena Época, Plenum,Constitutional Chamber of the Supreme Tribunal of Justice of the Bolivarian Republic of Venezuela, Judgement of August 10, 2007,and Constitutional Court of Colombia, Judgment C-580/02 of July 31, 2002.

431 295   *Cf. Case of Goiburú et al., supra* note 2[91], para. 92; *Case of Ibsen Cárdenas and Ibsen Peña, supra* note [291], para. 66, and *Case of Gomes Lund et al. (Guerrilha do Araguaia), supra* note [288], para. 109.

432 296   *Cf. Case of Gomes Lund et al. (Guerrilha do Araguaia), supra* note 16, para. 109. In this regard, see the Statement of the Acting Minister of Foreign Affairs of Uruguay before the Parliamentary Commission, regarding the Gelman Case, which indicated "there is a worrisome point that must be considered: the legal investigations open in the year 2008 are still in the pre-summarial stage, without any formal accusations against any of the alleged perpetrators," that "this procedural situation of the claim exposes her to risk of being affected by a possible new application of the Expiry Law," that "if the investigations close without the presentation of an accusation, it could be that a new attempt to reopen by the family members would allow for a new request for an opinion by the executive power in the terms established by Article 3 of the Expiry Law, and because it involved an act by the Government, it is possible that it would change its position as it did before in these same actions considering, for example, that the case may be deemed protected by the Expiry Law," "that is, that in the actual state of the claim, the possibility exists that the report by the executive branch be reversed, declaring that this claim is not protected by the law. In this way, a new request by the families could be protected by the law and could finish this process without an accusation."

433 297   *Cf.* General Assembly of the OAS, Resolution AG/RES. 1 (XXVIII-E/01) of September 11, 2001.

434 298   Supreme Court of Justice del Uruguay, *Case of Nibia Sabalsagaray Curutchet,* [Judgment No. 365, of October 19, 2009]: The ratification that took place in the referendum appeal brought against the Law in 1989 does not project any significant consequence in relation to the constitutional analysis to be performed . . . .Moreover, the direct exercise of popular sovereignty by way of a derogatory referendum derogatory of the laws sanctioned by the

Legislature only have the aforementioned possible range, but the rejection of the waiver by the public does not extend its effectiveness to the point of providing coverage to a rule of constitutional law flawed "*ab origine*" for violating rules or principles laid down or approved by the Charter. As Luigi Ferrajoli says, constitutional rules that establish principles and fundamental rights guarantee the material dimensions of the "substantial democracy," which refers to that which can not be decided or is to be decided by the majority, linking the legislation, under penalty of invalidity, with the enforcement of fundamental rights and other axiological principles established by it . . . . The author characterizes as the metajuridical fallacy the confusion between the paradigm of the rule of law and a political democracy, in which a rule is legitimate only if it is desired by the majority."

Because domestic tribunals have ruled, based on international obligations, with respect to the threshold value of, be it, the legislative branch or the mechanisms of direct democracy, as in the cases of a). The Constitutional Chamber of the Supreme Court of Costa Rica, on August 9, 2010, stated that it was not constitutionally valid to subject to popular vote (referendum) a bill that would allow for civil unions between persons of the same sex that was pending before the Legislative Assembly, because such a means could not be used to decide issues of human rights guaranteed in international treaties. In this regard, the Constitutional Court noted, "The human rights enshrined in the instruments of public international law — declarations and conventions on the matter—are a substantial bulwark of the freedom configuration of the legislature, both ordinary and eminently popular through the referendum. . . . The reforming or constituent power-derived—in regard to the constituting power — is limited by the essence of human and fundamental rights, so that, by way of partial amendment of the constitution, can not reduce or curtail the essence of those . . . . It is necessary to add that the rights of the minorities, because of their undeniable nature, are an eminently technical legal issue that must be held by the ordinary legislative majorities and not prone to denial "Constitutional Chamber of the Supreme Court of Costa Rica, Judgment No 2010013313 on August 10, 2010, Case File 10-008331-0007-CO, Considering clause VI. b). The Constitutional Court of stated that a democratic process requires certain rules that limit the power of the majority expressed in the polls to protect the minority: "the old identification of the people with the majority expressed in the polls is not enough to attribute a democratic nature to a regime that, in actuality, is also based in the respect of the minority. . . . The institutionalization of the people prevents sovereignty that lies within from functioning as a pretext for the exercise of its power unknown to any legal limit and detached from any form of control. The democratic process, if genuine and truly so, requires the establishment and maintenance of rules that channel the manifestations of popular will and prevent a majority from speaking on behalf of the people to the exclusion of some. . . ." Constitutional Court of Colombia, Judgment C-141 of 2010 of February 26, 2010, M.P. Humberto Antonio Sierra Porto, where it decides on the constitutionality of Law 1354 of 2009, of the summons to a constitutional referendum. c) The Federal Constitution of the Swiss Confederation in Article139.3 states that "when a popular initiative does not respect the principle of unity of form, the unit of matter, or the mandatory provisions of international law, the Federal Assembly will declare it totally or partially void." The Swiss Federal Council, in a report by March 5, 2010 on the relationship between international law and domestic law, ruled on the norms it considered as imperative to international law. In that regard, it noted that these standards are: rules prohibiting the use of force between states, the prohibitions on torture, genocide, and slavery, as well as the core of international humanitarian law (prohibition of attacks on physical integrity, hostage taking, attacks on the dignity of persons and carrying out of executions without trial by a regularly constituted court) and the intangibles of the guarantees of the European Convention of Human Rights. http://www.eda.admin.ch/etc/medialib/downloads/edazen/topics/intla/cintla.Par.0052.File.tmp/ La%20relation%20entre%20droi %20international%20et%20droit%20interne.pdf, last accessed on February 23, 2011(translation of the Secretariat of the Court). d) The jurisprudence of various courts of the United States, for example in the case Perry v. Schwarzenegger, in which it states that the referendum on same-sex couples was unconstitutional because it prevented the State of California from meeting its obligation not to discriminate against people who wanted to marry in accordance with Amendment 14 of the Constitution. In this way, the Supreme Court declared "the fundamental rights cannot be put to a vote; they do not depend on the outcome of elections." *Perry v. Schwarzenegger* (Challenge to Proposition 8) 10-16696, Court of Appeals for the Ninth Circuit, United States. In the Case of *Romer v. Evans*, the Supreme Court overturned the initiative that would have prevented the legislature from adopting a standard that would protect gays and lesbians from anti-discrimination. *Romer, Governor of Colorado, et al. v. Evans et al. (94-1039), 517 U.S. 620 (1996).* United States Supreme Court. Finally, in the Case of West Virginia State Board of Education v Barnette, the United States Supreme Court ruled that the right to freedom of expression protected the students from the rule that required them to salute the flag of the United States and of the oath of allegiance to it. In that vein, the Court held that the essential purpose of the Bill of Rights was to withdraw certain subjects from the vicissitudes of political controversy, placing them beyond the reach of majorities and officials, and conferring the status of legal principles to be applied by the courts. The right of individuals to life, liberty and property, freedom of expression, freedom of press, freedom of worship and assembly, and other fundamental rights may not be voted on, do not depend on election results." *West Virginia State Board of Education v Barnette*, 319 U.S. 624, (1943), 319 U.S. 624, June 14, 1943, Supreme Court of the United States. e) The Constitutional Court of South Africa refused a referendum on capital punishment, considering that a majority can not decide on the rights of the minority, which in this case are those marginalized by society were identified by the Court, as people who could be subject to the corporal punishment: "In the same sense, the issue of constitutionality of the death penalty can not be put to a referendum, where the opinion of the majority would prevail over the wishes of any minority. The main reason for establishing the new legal order, and to vest the judicial power to review all legislation in the courts, is to protect the rights of minorities among other people who are not in a position to adequately protect their rights through the democratic process. Those entitled to claim this protection include the socially excluded and marginalized people in our society. Only if there is a will to protect those who are worse off and the weakest among us, then we can be sure that our rights will be protected. *Constitutional Court of South Africa, State v. Tand M Makwanyane Mchunu,* Case No. CC/3/94, June 6, 1995, para. 88. f) The Constitutional Court of Slovenia, in the Case of the so-called "Erased" (people who do not have a legal immigration status), decided that it is not possible to hold a referendum on the rights of an established minority; the Court struck down a referendum that sought to revoke the legal residency status of a minority. In this regard, the court noted: "the principles of a State governed by the principle of legality, the right to equality before the law, the right to personal dignity and security, the right to seek redress for violations of human rights, and the authority of the Constitutional Court, should be prioritized over the right to make decisions in a referendum." Judgement of the Constitutional Court of Slovenia June 10, 2010, U-II-1/10. *Referendum on the confirmation of the Act on Amendments and Modifications of the Act on the Regulation of the Status of Citizens of Other Successor States to the Former SFRY in the Republic of Slovenia,* para. 10.

436 300   *Cf. Case of the Pueblo Bello Massacre, [v. Colombia. Merits, Reparations and Costs.* Judgment of January 31, 2006. Series C No. 140], para. 171; *Case of the Mapiripan Massacre, [v. Colombia. Merits, Reparations and Costs.* Judgment of September 15, 2005. Series C No. 134], para. 214; and *Case of La Cantuta, [v. Perú. Merits, Reparations and Costs.* Judgment of November 29, 2006. Series C No. 162], para. 149. See, also, *mutatis mutandi, Case of Ibsen Cárdenas and Ibsen Peña, supra* note [291], para. 166.

437 301   Recently, in the Case of Gomes Lund et al., the Court noted that under the facts involved,

the right to know the truth was related to an action brought by relatives to access certain information, related to access to justice and the right to seek and receive information as enshrined in Article 13 of the Convention; therefore it was analyzed under this norm.

438 302   *Cf.* Case of *Myrna Mack Chang* [*v. Guatemala. Merits, Reparations and Costs.* Judgment of November 25, 2003. Series C No. 101], para. 274; *Case of Carpio Nicolle et al. v. Guatemala. Merits, Reparations and Costs.* Judgment of November 22, 2004. Series C No. 117, para. 128, and *Case of Gomes Lund et al. (Guerrilha do Araguaia), supra* note [288], para. 200.

439 303   *Cf. inter alia,* Report of the Office of the High Commissioner of the United Nations for Human Rights. *Study on the Right to the Truth,* U.N. Doc. E/CN.4/2006/91 of January 9, 2006; General Assembly of the OAS, Resolutions: AG/RES. 2175 (XXXVI-O/06) of June 6, 2006, AG/RES. 2267 (XXXVII-O/07) of June 5, 2007; AG/RES. 2406 (XXXVIII-O/08) of June 3, 2008; AG/RES. 2509 (XXXIX-O/09) of June 4, 2009, and AG/RES. 2595 (XL-O/10) of July 12, 2010, and Report of Diane Orentlicher, Independent expert responsible for updating the set of principles to combat impunity (E/CN.4/2005/102) of February 18, 2005. In the same sense, the former Human Rights Commission of the United Nations, in the Set of Principles for the Protection and Promotion of Human Rights Through Action to Combat Impunity of 2005, established, *inter alia,* that: (i) "Every people has the inalienable right to know the truth about past events concerning the perpetration of heinous crimes and about the circumstances and reasons that led, through massive or systematic violations, to the perpetration of those crimes, *(principle 2); (ii)* A people's knowledge of the history of its oppression is part of its heritage and, as such, must be ensured by appropriate measures in fulfillment of the State's duty to preserve archives and other evidence concerning violations of human rights and humanitarian law and to facilitate knowledge of those violations. Such measures shall be aimed at preserving the collective memory from extinction and, in particular, at guarding against the development of revisionist and negationist arguments, (principle 3); (iii) Irrespective of any legal proceedings, victims and their families have the imprescriptible right to know the truth about the circumstances in which violations took place and, in the event of death or disappearance, the victims' fate, (principle 4), and (iv) States must take appropriate action, including measures necessary to ensure the independent and effective operation of the judiciary, to give effect to the right to know. Appropriate measures to ensure this right may include non-judicial processes that complement the role of the judiciary. Regardless of whether a State establishes such a body, it must ensure the preservation of, and access to, archives concerning violations of human rights and humanitarian law. *Cf.* the Set of Principles for the protection and promotion of human rights through action to combat impunity (E/CN.4/2005/102/Add.1) of February 8, 2005.

440 304   *Case of Velásquez Rodríguez. Merits,* [*v. Honduras. Merits.* Judgment of July 29, 1988. Series C No. 4], para. 181; *Case of Anzualdo Castro,* [*v. Perú. Preliminary Objection, Merits, Reparations and Costs.* Judgment of September 22, 2009. Series C No. 202], para. 118, and *Case of Gomes Lund et al. (Guerrilha do Araguaia), supra* note [288], para. 201.

441 305   *Cf. Case of Velásquez Rodríguez. Merits, supra* note [304], para. 181; *Case of Anzualdo Castro, supra* note [304], para. 118, and *Case of Gomes Lund et al. (Guerrilha do Araguaia), supra* note [288], para. 201.

442 309   *Cf. Velásquez Rodríguez. Merits, supra* note [304], para. 174; *Case of Rosendo Cantú et al.,* [*v. México. Preliminary Objection, Merits, Reparations and Costs.* Judgment of August 31, 2010 Series C No. 216], para. 211; *Case of Ibsen Cárdenas and Ibsen Peña, supra* note [291], para. 237-c, and *Case of Gomes Lund et al. (Guerrilha do Araguaia), supra* note [288], para. 256-c.

443 310   *Cf. Case of del Caracazo v. Venezuela. Reparations and Costs.* Judgment of August 29, 2002. Series C No. 95, para. 118; *Case of Ibsen Cárdenas and Ibsen Peña, supra* note [291], para. 238, and *Case of Gomes Lund et al. (Guerrilha do Araguaia), supra* note

[288], para. 257.

444 311   *Cf. Case of del Caracazo. Reparations and Costs*, supra note 310, para. 118; *Case of Manuel Cepeda Vargas*, [*v. Colombia. Preliminary Objections, Merits and Reparations.* Judgment of May 26, 2010. Series C No. 213], para. 217, and *Case of Ibsen Cárdenas and Ibsen Peña*, supra note [291], para. 238.

445 483   *Cf. Case of González et al. ("Cotton Field") v. Mexico*, supra, para. 455, and *Case of Veliz Franco et al. v. Guatemala*, supra, para. 251.

446 484   *Cf. Case of Barrios Altos v. Peru. Merits.* Judgment of March 14, 2001. Series C No. 75, para. 41, and *Case of Osorio Rivera and family members v. Peru*, supra, para. 244.

447 294   See judgment C-225/95 of May 18, 1995, issued by the Constitutional Court.

448 230   *Cfr. Case of Montero Aranguren et al. (Detention Center of Catia).* [Judgment of July 5, 2006. Series C No. 150], para. 147.

449 509   The State attached various contracts signed from 2005 to 2008 with national and international institutions, such as the UNAM[;] the Instituto de Mediación de Mexico, S.C.[;] the Universidad Autónoma de Chihuahua[;] the Universidad Autónoma de Ciudad Juárez[;] the Universidad de Barcelona[;] the Universidad de Gerona[;] the IMCAA, S.A. de C.V.[;] and the Latin American Forum for Urban Security and Democracy, A.C., in collaboration with local institutions such as the Office of the Attorney General for the state of Chihuahua and the State Human Rights Commission, as well as federal institutions, such as the National Human Rights Commission (case file of attachments to the final written arguments of the State, volume L, folios 17565 17833).

450 510   The State exhibited a list of courses offered over the period of 2005 to 2009[] with the name of each course, the place and date it was held, and the names of those who were trained (*Cf.* Office of the Attorney General for the state of Chihuahua, Center for Criminal and Forensic Studies, [Courses taught during] 2005-2009, case file of attachments to the final written arguments of the State, volume XLIX, folios 17537 to 17564).

451 511   *Cf.* Articles 135 and 145-k of the Organic Law of the Judiciary of the state of Chihuahua [published in the Official Gazette on August 9, 2006 (case file of attachments to the answer to the application, volume XXXIX, attachment 54], folios 14220 and 14226[)].

452 512   The Court observes that the case file contains a supporting document for a national training course for multipliers, under the Subprogram on Equity and Application of the Gender Equity Manual; on "Prevention of Domestic Violence," for authorities of the state of Chihuahua Public Security Secretariat, and on "Women's Human Rights and Self-esteem," "Masculinity and Self-esteem," and "Domestic Violence and Assertiveness," or Chihuahua public officials (*Cf.* Progress and results of actions within the framework of "PROEQUIDAD", organized by the National Women's Institute, Directorate General of Evaluation and Statistics, Evaluation Directorate, from January to December 2005, case file of attachments to the answer to the application, volume XLI, attachment 6, folios 15014 to 15016).

453 513   *Cf.* 2007-2012 National Development Plan, strategy 5.4 [of focal point 1, and objective 16 of focal point 3 (case file of attachments to the answer to the application, volume XLII, attachment 84], folio 15495 to 15792[)].

454 514   *Cf.* agreement signed by the Executive Secretary General of the Latin American Forum for Urban Security and Democracy and the Office of the Attorney General for the state of Chihuahua on May 15, 2007 (case file of attachments to the final written arguments of the State, volume L, folios 17675 to 17688).

455 515   *Cf.* cooperation agreement for the diploma course "Domestic violence and human rights" signed by the Office of the Attorney General for the state of Chihuahua and the Universidad Nacional Autónoma de Mexico on April 9, 2007 (case file of attachments to the final written arguments of the State, volume L, folio 17689) and report on institutional policies implemented to prevent, investigate, sanction and eliminate violence against women issued by the Office of the Attorney General for the state of Chihuahua (case file of attachments to the answer to the application, volume XL, attachments 60, folio 14960).

456 516   *Cf.* contract for providing services signed by the Office of the Attorney General of the state of Chihuahua and the Mexican Institute of Applied Sciences and Arts (INMCAA S.A. de C.V.) on February 1, 2007 (case file of attachments to the final written arguments of the State, volume L, folio 17696).

457 517   The State attached a list from the Center for Criminal and Forensic Studies with the courses offered from 2005 to 2009. It states that a 12-hour course entitled "Domestic violence: a problem for everyone," was offered to 26 people from June 26 to 28, 2007 (case file of attachments to the final written arguments of the State, volume XLIX, folio 17551).

458 518   On the list of courses held from 2005 to 2009, the State indicated that, in October 2008, the Chihuahua Women's Institute offered the course "Forensic reports in cases of gender-based violence" to 8 psychologists from the state Attorney General's Office who treat victims (Cf. Office of the Attorney General for the state of Chihuahua, Center for Criminal and Forensic Studies, supra note 510, folio 17563).

459 519   The State attached a list of the training offered in 2005, which refers to a "Licentiate in the provision of justice" involving 549 people (case file of attachments to the final written arguments of the State, volume XLIX, folio 17535).

460 520   Cf. statement made before notary public by witness Castro Romero on April 27, 2009, attachment 1 (merits case file, volume VIII, folios 2927 and 2928).

461 521   *Cf.* [T]estimony of witness Caballero Rodríguez [at the public hearing held on April 28, 2009].

462 522   *Cf. Case of Escher et al. v. Brazil.* [*Preliminary Objections, Merits, Reparations and Costs.* Judgment of July 6, 2009. Series C No. 199], para. 251.

463 322   *Cf. Case of Claude Reyes et al. v. Chile. Monitoring of Compliance with Judgment.* Order of the Inter-American Court of Human Rights of November 24, 2008, Considering clause number nineteen, and Case of *Escher et al. v. Brazil, supra* note 64, para. 251.

464 286   *Cf. Case of González et al. ("Cotton Field"), supra* note 21, para. 541.

465 287   *Cf. Case of the Rochela Massacre, supra* note 219, para. 303.

466 279   *Cf. Case González et al. ("Cotton Field "), supra* note [127], para. 450.

467 473   This aspect is also related to the provisions of Article 13 of the United Nations Convention on the Rights of Persons with Disabilities, which establishes, in relation to access to justice, that States Parties shall promote appropriate training for those working in the field of administration of justice, including police and prison staff.

468 474   *Cf.* Article 19(2) of the Standard Rules for the Equalization of Opportunities for Persons with Disabilities, resolution approved by the United Nations General Assembly, Forty-Eighth Period of Sessions, March 4, 1994, A/RES/48/96.

469 475   *Cf.* Article 19(3) of the Standard Rules for the Equalization of Opportunities for Persons with Disabilities, resolution approved by the United Nations General Assembly, Forty-Eighth Period of Sessions, March 4, 1994, A/RES/48/96.

470 476   *Cf.* Article 18 of the Standard Rules for the Equalization of Opportunities for Persons with Disabilities, resolution approved by the United Nations General Assembly, Forty-Eighth Period of Sessions, March 4, 1994, A/RES/48/96.

471 527   *Cf. Case of Goiburú et al. v. Paraguay. Monitoring compliance with judgment.* Order of the Inter-American Court of Human Rights of November 19, 2009, forty-ninth considering paragraph, and *Case of the Las Dos Erres Massacre v. Guatemala,* para. 252.

472 500   The State merely mentioned the existence of a "Workshop on monitoring the MDG in Latin America" (merits report, volume III, folio 1253).

473 501   Similarly *Cf. Case of Atala Riffo and daughters v. Chile,* para. 271.

474 402   *Cf. Case of El Caracazo v. Venezuela. Reparations and costs.* Judgment of August 29, 2002. Series C No. 95, para. 127, and *Case of the Massacres of El Mozote and nearby places v. El Salvador. Merits, reparations and costs.* Judgment of October 25, 2012. Series C No.252, para. 369.

475   *See, e.g., Furlan and Family v. Argentina,* Preliminary Objections, Merits, Reparations and

Costs, Aug. 31, 2012, Series C No. 246, para. 300.

476   *See, e.g., Atala Riffo and Daughters*, Merits, Reparations and Costs, Feb. 24, 2012, Series C No. 239, para. 267.

Chapter Four

ENSURING EFFECTIVENESS: ORDERING PROVISIONAL MEASURES AND MONITORING COMPLIANCE

I. INTRODUCTION

The Inter-American Court of Human Rights utilizes two types of mechanisms to ensure the effectiveness of the Court's work: orders of provisional measures and the monitoring of compliance with judgments on the merits of contentious cases decided by the Court. Orders of provisional measures are utilized by the Court when necessary to ensure that various parties to contentious cases, including alleged victims, witnesses, advocates and others, are protected from irreparable harm. The Court also routinely monitors compliance with its judgments in contentious cases. Both provisional measures and monitoring compliance are essential to ensuring the effectiveness of the Court's work and, by extension, upholding the human rights principles that are at the foundation of the American Convention on Human Rights. The Convention, as well as the Rules of Procedure of the Inter-American Court of Human Rights, articulate the Court's competence and the legal bases for orders of provisional measures and the monitoring of compliance with its judgments.

II. NORMATIVE FRAMEWORK

A. RULES OF PROCEDURE OF THE INTER-AMERICAN COURT OF HUMAN RIGHTS[1]

ARTICLE 26. PROVISIONAL MEASURES

1. At any stage of the proceedings involving cases of extreme gravity and urgency, and when necessary to avoid irreparable damage to persons, the Court may, at the request of a party or on its own motion, order such provisional measures as it deems pertinent, pursuant to Article 63(2) of the Convention.

2. With respect to matters not yet submitted to it, the Court may act at the request of the Commission.

3. In contentious cases already submitted to the Court, the victims or alleged victims or their duly accredited representatives, may present a request for provisional measures in relation to the cases directly to the Court.

4. The request may be made to the President, to any judge of the Court, or to the Secretariat, by any means of communication. In every case, the recipient of the request shall immediately bring it to the President's attention.

5. The Court, or if the Court is not sitting, the President, when he considers it is possible and essential, may require the State, the Commission, or the representatives of the beneficiaries to provide information on a request for provisional measures before deciding on the measure requested.[92]

6. If the Court is not sitting, the President, in consultation with the Permanent Commission and, if possible, with the other judges, shall call upon the government concerned to adopt such urgent measures as may be necessary to ensure the effectiveness of any provisional measures that may be ordered by the Court at its next session.

7. The monitoring of urgent or provisional measures ordered shall be carried out by means of the submission of State's reports and the filing of the corresponding observations to those reports by the representatives of the beneficiaries.[103] The Inter-American Commission on Human Rights shall present observations to the State's reports and to the observations of the beneficiaries of the measures or their representatives.

8. When it considers it pertinent, the Court shall require from other sources of information, any relevant data on the matter that allows the assessment of the gravity and urgency of the situation and the effectiveness of the measures. To that end, it may require expert reports and any other report it considers appropriate.[114]

9. The Court, or its President if the Court is not sitting, may convene the parties to a public or private[125] hearing on provisional measures.

10. In its Annual Report to the General Assembly, the Court shall include a statement concerning the provisional measures ordered during the period covered by the report. If those measures have not been duly implemented, the Court shall make such recommendations as it deems appropriate.

ARTICLE 54. PROTECTION OF ALLEGED VICTIMS, WITNESSES, AND EXPERT WITNESSES

States may not institute proceedings against alleged victims, witnesses, or expert witnesses, nor exert pressure on them or on their families on account of declarations or opinions they have delivered before the Court.

ARTICLE 63. PROCEDURE FOR MONITORING COMPLIANCE WITH THE JUDGMENTS AND OTHER DECISIONS OF THE COURT[356]

1. The procedure for monitoring compliance with the judgments and other decisions of the Court shall be carried out by means of the submission of reports by the State and observations to those reports by the victims or their legal representatives. The Commission shall present observations to the State's reports and to the observations of the victims or their representatives.

2. The Court may require from other sources of information relevant data regarding the case in order to evaluate compliance therewith. To that end, the Tribunal shall also require expert declarations or reports it considers appropriate.

3. When it deems appropriate, the Tribunal may convene the parties to a hearing in order to monitor compliance with its decisions.

4. Once the Tribunal has obtained all the relevant information, it shall determine the state of compliance with its decisions and issue the pertinent orders.

B. AMERICAN CONVENTION ON HUMAN RIGHTS [7]
ARTICLE 63

1. If the Court finds that there has been a violation of a right or freedom protected by this Convention, the Court shall rule that the injured party be ensured the enjoyment of his right or freedom that was violated. It shall also rule, if appropriate, that the consequences of the measure or situation that constituted the breach of such right or freedom be remedied and that fair compensation be paid to the injured party.

2. In cases of extreme gravity and urgency, and when necessary to avoid irreparable damage to persons, the Court shall adopt such provisional

measures as it deems pertinent in matters it has under consideration. With respect to a case not yet submitted to the Court, it may act at the request of the Commission.

ARTICLE 65

To each regular session of the General Assembly of the Organization of American States shall submit, for the Assembly's consideration, a report on its work during the previous year. It shall specify, in particular, the cases in which a state has not complied with its judgments, making any pertinent recommendations.

ARTICLE 68

1. The States Parties to the Convention undertake to comply with the judgment of the Court in any case to which they are parties.

2. That part of a judgment that stipulates compensatory damages may be executed in the country concerned in accordance with domestic procedure governing the execution of judgments against the state.

III. PROVISIONAL MEASURES

At any stage in proceedings before the Inter-American Court of Human Rights, including *prior* to the Court's consideration of preliminary objections and *after* the Court's judgment on the merits of a given case, the Court may consider and order provisional measures to protect alleged victims, potential witnesses, legal advocates and others related to the case from irreparable harm, as well as to put the State and alleged perpetrators on notice that they will be held responsible for any harm visited upon those whom the provisional measures are ordered to protect. Such measures serve to protect individual victims and to uphold the effectiveness of the Inter-American human rights system by acting to prevent and minimize further harm and allowing the Court and parties involved in litigation to effectively focus their attention on the human rights violations already at issue in the case. The below-excerpted orders from the Inter-American Court of Human Rights and the President of the Court illustrate the various procedural avenues through which requests for provisional measures are made to the Court, and whom the measures are ordered to protect, as well as the range of substantive issues on which the Court bases its decisions to order provisional measures.

Provisional Measures regarding Peru in the Matter of the Constitutional Court

7-Apr-2000

Order of the President of the Inter-American Court of Human Rights

HAVING SEEN:

1.   The communication of April 3, 2000, and its annexes, in which Delia Revoredo Marsano de Mur (hereinafter "Mrs. Revoredo") submitted to the Inter-American Court of Human Rights (hereinafter "the Court" or "the Inter-American Court") a request for provisional measures for her husband, Jaime Mur Campoverde, and herself, in connection with the Constitutional Tribunal case before the Court against Peru (hereinafter "Peru" or "the State"), pursuant to Article 63.2 of the American Convention on Human Rights (hereinafter "the Convention" or "the American Convention") and Article 25 of the Rules of Procedure of the Court hereinafter "the Rules of Procedure"). In this communication, Mrs. Revoredo requests the Court:

    (a) That while the proceeding on the restitution of the Magistrates of the Constitutional Tribunal is being heard, the Peruvian State shall abstain from harassing [her] directly or harassing [her] husband, by exercising control over the manipulation of judges and tribunals.

    (b) That, specifically, the judicial proceedings filed against [her] before the Fifteenth Court specializing in the crimes included in Administrative Resolution No. 744-CME-PJ - File. No. 1607-2000, for the alleged crimes of misappropriation, fraud and crime against the authority to attest documents, shall be suspended until the action for restitution to [her] function of Constitutional Magistrate shall have been decided.

    (c) That the spouses Delia Revoredo de Mur and Jaime Mur Campoverde shall be guaranteed their right to the judicial protection of their proprietary interests, allowing their company Corporación de Productos Alimenticios Nacionales PYC S.A. the legal recourse of contesting in court an adverse decision of an arbitrator.

2.   Mrs. Revoredo based her request for provisional measures on the following considerations:

    (a) That during the proceeding in which she participated as a member of the Constitutional Tribunal of her country, where the action on the unconstitutionality of a law "interpreting" the Constitution of the State, which allowed the actual President of Peru to be a candidate to a third consecutive presidential mandate, was examined, three of the seven magistrates present, who maintained the unconstitutionality of this "interpretative law", were dismissed and suffered "all kinds of pressure: offers, threats, harassment".

    (b) That, as far as she is concerned, she may not be tried or condemned, due to her constitutional immunity; therefore, the attacks were focused on her husband, and a proceeding that had been filed for the alleged contraband of a vehicle was reopened. During this period, she and her husband suffered attacks on their property and their telephones were intercepted, while there was also interference in her husband's business activities.

(c) That, following her dismissal as a magistrate of the Constitutional Tribunal, she was appointed Dean of the Lima Lawyers Professional Association and President of the Board of Deans of the Peruvian Lawyers Professional Associations and instructed by civil society entities to lodge a complaint with the Inter-American Commission on Human Rights due to the interference of the Executive in the constitutional functions of other State organs. In consequence, she was informed that her husband was going to be condemned "and that he would be arrested", so they went into exile.

(d) That, following declarations of the President of Peru in which he referred negatively to the good reputation of Mr. and Mrs. Mur, they decided to give up exile and return to Peru.

(e) That, due to a recent public declaration, which she signed together with various other Peruvians in order to create a Front for the Defense of Democracy, the following events have occurred: the criminal action aimed at impeding her from leaving the country was reactivated, she has been requested to pay a pledge of 20,000 soles and the public registries have been requested to supply a list of her property so that it may be embargoed; one of her husband's companies lost a case and both the case and subsequent appeals for review that were presented were processed irregularly in order to prejudice them.

(f) That all the previous acts against her have a twofold objective: on the one hand, to take away her freedom and her property, and on the other, to impede her reincorporation into the Constitutional Tribunal, due to legal impediment.

(g) That the Government, through the judges or prosecutors, uses family or company problems to impose arbitrary judicial penalties that jeopardize the honour and freedom of the persons involved.

CONSIDERING:

1.   That Peru has been a State Party to the American Convention since July 28, 1978, and that it accepted the jurisdiction of the Court on January 21, 1981.

2.   That Article 63.2 of the American Convention provides that, in cases of "extreme gravity and urgency and when necessary to avoid irreparable damage to persons", the Court may take the provisional measures that it deems pertinent, in matters it has under consideration.

3.   That, in the words of Article 25.1 and 25.4 of the Rules of Procedures of the Court,

> [a]t any stage of the proceedings involving cases of extreme gravity and urgency, and when necessary to avoid irreparable damage to persons, the Court may, at the request of a party or on its own motion, order such provisional measures as it deems pertinent, pursuant to Article 63.2 of the Convention.
> [...]
> [i]f the Court is not sitting, the President, in consultation with the PermanentCommission and, if possible, with the other judges, shall call upon the Government concerned to adopt such urgent measures as may be necessary to ensure the effectiveness of any provisional measures subsequently ordered by the Court at its next session.

4.   That, from these provisions, it is evident that the Court, or, when appropriate, its President, may act *ex officio* in cases of extreme gravity and urgency to avoid irreparable damage to persons. The Court has already done so previously (Order of January 15, 1988, Provisional Measures in the *Velásquez Rodríguez, Fairén Garbi and Solís Corrales,* and *Godínez Cruz cases*, fourth and fifth preambular paragraphs). As the Court is not sitting, the President is authorized to adopt urgent measures *ex officio* in such cases of extreme gravity and urgency to avoid irreparable damages to persons.

5.   That Article 1.1 of the Convention establishes the obligation of States Parties to respect the rights and freedoms recognized therein and to ensure their free and full exercise to all persons subject to their jurisdiction.

6.   That the Court is authorized to adopt provisional measures in cases of extreme gravity and urgency to avoid irreparable damage to persons (Article 63.2 of the Convention). In this case, in relation to the request contained in the section "Having Seen", 1.a (*supra*), this implies safeguarding the personal integrity of Mrs. Revoredo.

7.   That the information submitted in this case reveals a *prima facie* threat to the integrity of Mrs. Revoredo. The standard of *prima facie* appreciation of a case and the application of assumptions in view of the needs of protection have led this Court to order provisional measures on various occasions (*cf. inter alia*, Order of the Inter-American Court of Human Rights of November 17, 1999, Provisional Measures in the *Digna Ochoa y Plácido et al case*, fifth preambular paragraph; Order of the Inter-American Court of Human Rights of June 3, 1999, Provisional Measures in the *Cesti Hurtado case*, fourth preambular paragraph; Order of the Inter-American Court of Human Rights of May 27, 1999, Provisional Measures in the *James et al case*, eighth preambular paragraph; Order of the Inter-American

Court of Human Rights of June 19, 1998, Provisional Measures in the *Clemente Teherán et al case*, fifth preambular paragraph; Order of the President of the Inter-American Court of Human Rights of July 22, 1997, Provisional Measures in the *Alvarez et al case*, fifth preambular paragraph; Order of the President of the Inter-American Court of Human Rights of August 16, 1995, Provisional Measures in the *Blake case*, fourth preambular paragraph; Order of the President of the Inter-American Court of Human Rights of July 26, 1995, Provisional Measures in the *Carpio Nicolle case*, fourth preambular paragraph; Order of the President of the Inter-American Court of Human Rights of June 4, 1995, Provisional Measures in the *Carpio Nicolle case*, fifth preambular paragraph; Order of the Inter-American Court of Human Rights of December 7, 1994, Provisional Measures in the *Caballero Delgado and Santana case*, third preambular paragraph; and Order of the Inter-American Court of Human Rights of June 22, 1994, Provisional Measures in the *Colotenango case*, fifth preambular paragraph).

8.   That, in its jurisprudence, this Court has protected witnesses who have made statements before it by adopting provisional measures *(cf. inter alia*, Order of the Inter-American Court of Human Rights of January 15, 1988, Provisional Measures in the *Velásquez Rodríguez, Fairén Garbi and Solís Corrales,* and *Godínez Cruz cases*; Order of the Inter-American Court of Human Rights of December 7, 1994, Provisional Measures in the *Caballero Delgado and Santana case*; Orders of the Inter-American Court of Human Rights of September 22, 1995, and April 18, 1997, Provisional Measures in the *Blake case*; Order of the President of the Inter-American Court of Human Rights of June 30, 1998, and Order of the Inter-American Court of Human Rights of August 29, 1998, both as to the Provisional Measures in the *Bámaca Velásquez case*); with all the more reason is the adoption of provisional measures justified when it is a petitioner in a contentious case pending before the Court who claims that she fears for her personal integrity.

9.   That, on this point, as this Court has already stated, "it is the responsibility of the State to adopt security measures to protect all those who are subject to its jurisdiction; this obligation is even more evident as regards those who are involved in proceedings before the supervisory organs of the American Convention" (*cf.* Order of the Inter-American Court of Human Rights of November 17, 1999, Provisional Measures in the *Digna Ochoa y Plácido et al case*, seventh preambular paragraph).

10.   That the purpose of provisional measures, under the national legal systems (domestic procedural law) in general, is to preserve the rights of the contending parties, ensuring that the future judgement on merits is not prejudiced by their actions *pendente lite.*

11.   That, under the International Law of Human Rights, the purpose

of provisional measures goes further, as, besides their essentially preventive character, they effectively protect fundamental rights, inasmuch as they seek to avoid irreparable damage to persons.

12.   That (further requests) refer to legal proceedings that are not directly linked to the facts of the *Constitutional Tribunal case* under consideration by this Court and, if these facts were to be submitted to the Court, it would not be in order for it to take a decision with regard to ordering provisional measures, since this would imply prejudging the merits. In view of its specific object and legal nature, the granting of provisional measures may under no circumstances prejudge the merits of a case.

13.   That, in accordance with Article 25.4 of the Rules of Procedure, the President of the Court is only authorized to order such urgent measures as may be necessary to ensure the effectiveness of any provisional measures subsequently ordered by the Court at its next period of sessions (*cf. inter alia,* Order of the President of the Inter-American Court of Human Rights of February 10, 1998, in the *Paniagua Morales et al* and *Vásquez et al cases*; and Order of the President of the Inter-American Court of Human Rights of July 29, 1997, Provisional Measures in the *Cesti Hurtado case*).

THEREFORE:

THE PRESIDENT OF THE INTER-AMERICAN COURT OF HUMAN RIGHTS

Based on Article 63.2 of the American Convention on Human Rights and on the use of the attributes conferred on him by Article 25.4 of the Rules of Procedure, after having consulted all the Judges of the Court,

DECIDES:

1.   To call upon the State to adopt immediately all necessary measures to ensure effectively the physical, psychological and moral integrity of Delia Revoredo Marsano de Mur, petitioner in the *Constitutional Tribunal* case under consideration by the Court, in order that any provisional measures that the Inter-American Court of Human Rights may decide to order shall have the pertinent effects.

2.   To call upon the State and the Inter-American Commission on Human Rights to provide detailed information on the situation of Delia Revoredo Marsano de Mur, at the latest by April 25, 2000, so that the Inter-American Court of Human Rights may take a decision in this respect in due course.

3.   To call upon the State to present to the Court a report on the measures taken pursuant to resolutory point 1 of the present Order, at the latest by April 25, 2000, so that it may inform the members of the Court during the next period of sessions, and to continue providing information on these once every six weeks.

4.   To call upon the Inter-American Commission on Human Rights to

present its observations on the reports summited by the State, within thirty days of having been notified that these have been received.

14-Aug-2000
Order of the Inter-American Court of Human Rights
Provisional Measures Requested by the Inter-American Commission on Human Rights

CONSIDERING:

5.   That the Order of the President of April 7, 2000, was adopted according to law and is consistent with the merits of the facts and circumstances that justified the adoption of urgent measures, and that this Court ratifies it in every respect.

6.   That the Commission has asked this Court to maintain the provisional measures in the instant case, because "the extreme gravity and urgency of the situation have become evident in the account of the facts."

7.   That the request for provisional measures is related to the case of the *Constitutional Court*, currently under consideration before the Court.

8.   That the Court considers that the State had the obligation, in conformity with the Order of the President, of April 7, 2000, to order the adoption of whatever measures were necessary to "ensure effectively the physical, psychological and moral integrity of Delia Revoredo-Marsano-de-Mur, petitioner in the *Constitutional Court Case* under consideration by the Court."

9.   That the Court has established that "it is the responsibility of the State to adopt security measures to protect all those who are subject to its jurisdiction; this obligation is even more evident as regards those who are involved in proceedings before the supervisory organs of the American Convention."[1][8]

10.   That this Court has drawn the attention of some States to the omissions incurred with respect to their obligation to take steps relative to the provisional measures ordered by the Tribunal.[2][9]

11.   That, to date, the State has failed to submit the urgent report requested by the Order of the President of April 7, 2000, both on the measures adopted to ensure effectively the physical, psychological and moral integrity of Delia Revoredo-Marsano-de-Mur, and on her situation.

12.   That the event of default by the State is particularly serious given the legal nature of the provisional measures, which are intended to prevent irreparable damage to persons in a situation of extreme gravity and urgency.

13.   That, as pointed out by this Court, "the States Parties to the Convention must guarantee compliance with its provisions and its effects *(effet utile)* within their own domestic laws.[3][10]

14.   That the provision established in Article 63(2) of the Convention makes it

mandatory for the State to adopt the provisional measures ordered by this Tribunal, since there stands "a basic principle of the law of international state responsibility, supported by international jurisprudence, according to which States must fulfil their conventional international obligations in good faith (*pacta sunt servanda*)."[4][11]

15.   That, in like manner, the State has the obligation to investigate the facts that have given rise to this request for provisional measures, in order to identify those responsible and impose upon them the pertinent punishment.

NOW, THEREFORE,

THE INTER-AMERICAN COURT OF HUMAN RIGHTS,

In exercise of the powers conferred upon it by Article 63(2) of the American Convention on Human Rights, and Article 25 of its Rules of Procedure,

DECIDES:

1.   To ratify the Order of the President of the Inter-American Court of Human Rights of April 7, 2000, in all of its aspects and, therefore, to request that the State adopt the necessary measures to protect the physical, psychological and moral integrity of Ms. Delia Revoredo-Marsano-de-Mur, in order to prevent her from suffering irreparable damage.

2.   To request that the State and the Inter-American Commission on Human Rights provide detailed information no later than September 14, 2000, on the situation of Ms. Delia Revoredo-Marsano-de-Mur and, as regards the State, that it also provide information on the measures adopted for her protection, as it should have done on April 25, 2000, in conformity with the Order of the President of the Inter-American Court of Human Rights of April 7, 2000.

3.   To request that the State investigate the facts that gave rise to the adoption of the current provisional measures, and that it punish the persons responsible.

4.   To request that, as of the date of notification of this Order, the State submit reports on the provisional measures adopted in the instant case every two months.

5.   To request that the Inter-American Commission on Human Rights submit to the Inter-American Court of Human Rights its observations on said reports by the State, within six weeks of receiving them.

31-Jan-2001

Merits, Reparations and Costs

THE COURT, unanimously,

1.   finds that the State violated the right to a fair trial embodied in Article 8 of the American Convention on Human Rights, with regard to Manuel Aguirre Roca, Guillermo Rey Terry and Delia Revoredo Marsano.

2.   finds that the State violated the right to judicial protection embodied in Article 25 of the American Convention on Human Rights, with regard to Manuel Aguirre Roca, Guillermo Rey Terry and Delia Revoredo Marsano.

3.   finds that the State failed to comply with the general obligation of Article 1(1) of the American Convention on Human Rights, with regard to the violation of the substantive rights indicated in the previous operative paragraphs of this judgment.

4.   decides that the State must order an investigation to determine the persons responsible for the human rights violations referred to in this judgment and also publish the results of this investigation and punish those responsible.

5.   decides that the State must pay the amounts corresponding to the arrears of salary and other benefits that, by law, correspond to Manuel Aguirre Roca, Guillermo Rey Terry and Delia Revoredo Marsano, in the terms of paragraphs 121 and 128 of this judgment.

6.   decides that, in fairness, the State must reimburse the victims in the instant case, for costs and expenses, in the way and under the terms set out in paragraphs 126 and 128 of this judgment, the following amounts: Manuel Aguirre Roca, US$25,000.00 (twenty-five thousand United States dollars) or the equivalent in Peruvian money when the payment is made; Guillermo Rey Terry, US$25,000.00 (twenty-five thousand United States dollars) or the equivalent in Peruvian money when the payment is made; and Delia Revoredo Marsano, US$35,000.00 (thirty-five thousand United States dollars) or the equivalent in Peruvian money when the payment is made.

7.   decides that it will monitor that this judgment is complied with and only then will it close the case.

14-Mar-2001
Order of the Inter-American Court of Human Rights
Provisional Measures Requested by the Inter-American Commission on Human Rights

HAVING SEEN:
4.   The judgment in this case delivered by the Court on January 31, 2001.

5.   The communication of the Inter-American Commission on Human Rights (hereinafter "the Commission") of February 2, 2001, in which it stated that "although [...] there has been a political change in the country, the precautionary measures corresponding to the legal proceedings filed against Dr. Delia Revoredo de Mur, have still not been executed and, for this reason, it is important that these measures should continue to be maintained".

6.   The State's communication of February 27, 2001 indicated that it had executed the necessary actions to comply with the judgment of January 31, 2001, and with the provisional measures adopted by the Court on August 14, 2000. It also stated that it had take[n] steps to eliminate the political manipulation of the Judiciary and this had created "favorable conditions for deciding the cases

that are being processed" before the said organ. Furthermore, it stated that on November 17, 2000, the Congress of Peru had reinstated Manuel Aguirre Roca, Guillermo Rey Terry and Delia Revoredo Marsano in their functions as justices of the Constitutional Court and on February 26, 2001, a meeting had been held with the latter in order to coordinate compliance with the judgment on merits. In view of the foregoing, and considering that the presumption of extreme gravity and urgency no longer exists, it concluded that "there is currently no threat against the safety of Mrs. Revoredo" and requested that the provisional measures should be suspended in the instant case.

2.   That Article 63.2 of the American Convention provides that, in cases of "extreme gravity and urgency, and when necessary to avoid irreparable damage to persons", the Court may adopt such provisional measures as it deems pertinent in matters it has under consideration.

3.   That provisional measures have an exceptional nature and are therefore ordered having regard to the needs for protection and, once ordered, they must be maintained while the basic requirements mentioned in the previous considering paragraph exist.

4.   That the changes that have occurred in Peru and the developments in the Constitutional Court case, in particular, Mrs. Revoredo's reinstatement as a Constitutional Court justice, lead this Court to conclude that the circumstances of "extreme gravity and urgency" and the probability of irreparable damage required by Article 63.2 of the Convention do not exist and, therefore, the reasons that caused this Court to order provisional measures in the instant case have terminated. The declarations of the Inter-American Commission . . . that legal proceedings are still pending do not bear any relation to the purpose of the provisional measures adopted by the Court on August 14, 2000, in its first operative paragraph; moreover, they do not constitute circumstances of extreme gravity and urgency that would warrant maintaining the actual provisional measures.

THEREFORE:

THE INTER-AMERICAN COURT OF HUMAN RIGHTS

in exercise of the powers conferred upon it by Article 63.2 of the American Convention on Human Rights and Article 25 of its Rules of Procedure,

DECIDES:

1.   To lift the provisional measures ordered by the Inter-American Court of Human Rights in its order of August 14, 2000, in favor of Delia Revoredo Marsano.

2.   To communicate this order to the State of Peru and to the Inter-American Commission on Human Rights.

3. To close the file.

Provisional Measures regarding Costa Rica in the Matter of La Nación Newspaper
6-Apr-2001
Order of the President of the Inter-American Court of Human Rights
Request for Provisional Measures by the Inter-American Commission on Human Rights

HAVING SEEN:

The communication of the Inter-American Commission on Human Rights (hereinafter "the Commission" or "the Inter-American Commission") of March 28, 2001, in which it filed a request for provisional measures in favor of Mauricio Herrera Ulloa and Fernán Vargas Rohrmoser, respectively, journalist and legal representative of the Costa Rican newspaper, *La Nación*, "for [the Court to call on] the Republic of Costa Rica to protect the freedom of expression" of the said persons.

CONSIDERING:

4.   That, on examining the Commission's communication of March 28, 2001 (*supra* having seen 1), the President considers that the request includes elements that appear to be related to the merits of the case and deems it necessary to request additional information from the Inter-American Commission and the State of Costa Rica (hereinafter "the State" or "Costa Rica"). Accordingly, both parties should submit information to the Court in writing on the following aspects: a) the urgency of the situation; b) the gravity of the situation; c) the probability of irreparable damage to the alleged victims, and d) the implications that a decision by the Court on the adoption of the provisional measures requested by the Commission could have when deciding the merits of the case.

5.   That, as a result of the elements indicated in considering paragraph 4, the President deems that it is necessary to hear the arguments of the State and the Commission on this matter at a public audience.

6.   That, in view of the foregoing, it is also necessary, as an urgent measure, to request the State to abstain from executing any action that would alter the *status quo* of the matter until this public audience has been held and the Court is able to deliberate and decide on the admissibility of the provisional measures requested by the Commission.

THEREFORE:

THE PRESIDENT OF THE INTER-AMERICAN COURT OF HUMAN RIGHTS,

DECIDES:

1. To grant the Inter-American Commission on Human Rights and the State of Costa Rica until May 12, 2001, to submit the information referred to in considering paragraph 4 of this order.

2.   To convene the Inter-American Commission on Human Rights and the State of Costa Rica to a public hearing to be held at the seat of the Inter-American Court of Human Rights on May 22, 2001, at 10 a.m., so that the Court may hear their points of view on the facts and circumstances that motivated the request for provisional measures.

3.   To request the State, as an urgent measure, to abstain from executing any action that would alter the *status quo* of the matter until this public hearing has been held and the Court is able to deliberate and decide on the admissibility of the provisional measures requested by the Commission.

21-May-2001
Order of the President of the Inter-American Court of Human Rights
Request for Provisional Measures by the Inter-American Commission on Human Rights

HAVING SEEN:
3.   The communication of the Commission of May 9, 2001, in which it proposed that Mauricio Herrera Ulloa should appear as a witness in the hearing convened for May 22, 2001.

4.   The communication of the State of Costa Rica (hereinafter "the State" or "Costa Rica") of May 15, 2001, in which it indicated that "it [did] not object to [the] request" of the Commission mentioned in the previous paragraph, "in the understanding that the said hearing would not address the merits of the matter that was under consideration by" the Inter-American Commission.

CONSIDERING:
3.   That, according to the statements of the State and the Commission, Mr. Herrera Ulloa is one of the alleged victims in the case; the Court therefore agrees that he may testify as a witness, in the understanding that this testimony must be limited to the subject of the hearing convened by the President (*supra* having seen 2).

4.   That the fact that a person has a direct interest in the result of a case or may have taken part in the proceeding before the Commission is not *per se* a factor that prevents him from making a statement before the Court, which, in its practice, has even admitted the testimony of the victim and his next of kin *(ICourtHR, Loayza Tamayo case. Judgment of September 17, 1997. Series C No. 33; ICourtHR, Castillo Páez case. Judgment of November 3, 1997. Series C No. 34; ICourtHR, Suárez Rosero case. Judgment of November 12, 1997. Series C No. 35; ICourtHR, Blake case. Judgment of January 24, 1998. Series C No. 36; ICourtHR, Paniagua Morales et al. case. Judgment of March 8, 1998. Series C No. 37; ICourtHR, Villagrán Morales et al. case. Judgment of November 19, 1999. Series C No. 63)* [112].

THEREFORE:
THE INTER-AMERICAN COURT OF HUMAN RIGHTS,
DECIDES:
1.   To summon Mauricio Herrera Ulloa to appear before the Inter-American Court of Human Rights to give testimony at 10.00 a.m. on May 22, 2001.
2.   That the testimony must be limited exclusively to what has been indicated in the fourth considering paragraph of the order of the President of the Court of April 6, 2001; that is, to the gravity and urgency of the situation and the probability of irreparable damage that could be caused to the witness.

23-May-2001
Order of the President of the Inter-American Court of Human Rights
Request for Provisional Measures by the Inter-American Commission on Human Rights

HAVING SEEN:
1.   The communication of the Inter-American Commission on Human Rights (hereinafter "the Commission" or "the Inter-American Commission") of March 28, 2001, in which it submitted a request for provisional measures in favor of Mauricio Herrera Ulloa and Fernán Vargas Rohrmoser, respectively journalist and legal representative of the Costa Rican newspaper, *La Nación*, "for [the Court to request] the Republic of Costa Rica to protect the freedom of expression" of the said persons. The grounds for the Commission's request were that:
   (a) the journalist, Mauricio Herrera Ulloa, had been criminally convicted of four offenses in the sphere of libel, owing to articles published in the newspaper, *La Nación*, which reproduced what had been published in the European press concerning a "controversial" Costa Rican public official accredited by the Costa Rican foreign service to the International Atomic Energy Agency (IAEA) in Vienna;
   (b) the judgment of the Criminal Trial Court of the First Judicial Circuit of San José ordered: 40 days of fines at two thousand five hundred colones a day for each of the four offenses, for a total of one hundred and sixty days of fines and, in application of the rules for this type of proceeding, the penalty was reduced to three times the highest fine imposed, that is to one hundred and twenty days of fines, which would amount to three hundred thousand colones; the civil action for compensatory damages was declared admissible and Mauricio Herrera Ulloa and *Periódico La Nación, S.A.,* represented by Fernán Vargas Rohrmoser, as the persons jointly liable, were condemned to pay sixty million colones for the non-pecuniary damage caused by the publications in the newspaper, *La Nación*, on May 19, 20 and 21 and December 13, 1995; publication

of the operative paragraphs of the judgment in the same section of the newspaper, *La Nación*, that is, "*El País*", and with the same typeface as the articles that were the subject of the dispute, under the responsibility of Mauricio Herrera Ulloa, as the person responsible for the unlawful acts that were committed; that *La Nación S.A.* withdraw the link that existed between the last name Przedborski and the disputed articles in *La Nación Digital* on Internet, and that it establish a link between those articles and the operative paragraphs of the judgment. Furthermore, the judgment condemned the defendants to pay one thousand colones towards the procedural costs and the sum of three million eight hundred and ten thousand colones for personal costs;

(c) the Third Chamber of the Supreme Court of Justice admitted the appeal for annulment filed against the judgment of the Criminal Trial Court of the First Judicial Circuit of San José, but rejected this appeal and, in a judgment of January 24, 2001, confirmed the decision that had been appealed;

(d) the execution of the criminal judgment convicting the victims was ordered in a "comminatory, non-postponable[,] executable" manner and "forthwith" by the Criminal Trial Court of the First Judicial Circuit of San José, to be executed within three days of notification, which took place on February 27, 2001;

(e) in response to a petition received on March 1, 2001, the Commission adopted the following precautionary measures: that the State of Costa Rica (hereinafter "the State" or "Costa Rica") suspend the execution of the guilty verdict until the Commission had examined the case and adopted a final decision on the merits of the matter, o[r] until the State had adopted the necessary measures to annul the judgment voluntarily; that the State abstain from taking any measure addressed at including the journalist, Mauricio Herrera Ulloa, in the Judicial Record of Offenders of Costa Rica, and that it abstain from executing any other act or action that would affect the right to freedom of expression of the journalist, Mauricio Herrera Ulloa, and the newspaper, *La Nación*;

(f) in a decision of March 20, 2001, a remedy filed in order to enforce compliance with the precautionary measures of the Commission was declared inadmissible;

(g) the situation of the journalist, Mauricio Herrera Ulloa, and of Fernán Vargas Rohrmoser, legal representative of *La Nación*, has deteriorated since the precautionary measures were ordered and is currently "precarious and of imminent risk"; and that the statements of the different judges who are intervening in the case, disregarding the precautionary measures, lead to the conclusion that the judgment may be executed in any moment and that any decision of the Commission, or eventually of the Inter-American Court of Human Rights (hereinafter "the Court" or "the Inter-American Court") will be ineffective since "grave, irreparable damage to freedom of expression" will have been perpetrated; in other words, it will not produce any "useful effect"; and

(h) that the damage to freedom of expression is clear and imminent, not only with regard to the individual freedom of Herrera Ulloa and Vargas Rohrmoser, but to that of the entire Costa Rican society.

(i) consequently, the Commission requested the Court to adopt forthwith the following provisional measures:

(i) that Costa Rica suspend the execution of the condemnatory judgment delivered by the Criminal Trial Court of the First Judicial Circuit of San José on November 12, 1999, until the Commission has examined the case and, in accordance with Article 50 of the American Convention on Human Rights (hereinafter "the Convention" or "the American Convention"), has adopted a final decision on the merits of the matter or, should the case be referred to the Court, the latter has delivered the corresponding judgment;

ii) that Costa Rica abstain from executing any action addressed at including the journalist, Mauricio Herrera Ulloa, in the Judicial Register of Offenders of Costa Rica, and

(iii) that Costa Rica abstain from executing any act or action that would affect the right to freedom of expression of the journalist, Mauricio Herrera Ulloa, and the newspaper, *La Nación.*

2.   The order that the President of the Court (hereinafter "the President") delivered on April 6, 2001, in consultation with the judges of the Court, in which he decided:

1. To grant the Inter-American Commission on Human Rights and the State of Costa Rica until May 12, 2001, to submit the information referred to in considering paragraph 4 of this order.

2. To summon the Inter-American Commission on Human Rights and the State of Costa Rica to a public hearing to be held at the seat of the Inter-American Court of Human Rights on May 22, 2001, at 10 a.m., so that the Court may hear their points of view on the facts and circumstances that motivated the request for provisional measures.

3. To request the State, as an urgent measure, to abstain from executing any action that would alter the *status quo* of the matter until this public hearing has been held and the Court is able to deliberate and decide on the admissibility of the provisional measures requested by the Commission.

3.   The Commission's communication of May 10, 2001, submitted in response to the decisions in the order of the President (*supra* having seen 2.1). In brief, the Commission indicated in this communication:

(a) that, essentially, the Convention establishes a system for the protection of human rights and not a system to compensate the violation of such rights, which would operate as a result of violation of the Convention;

(b) that the principal objective of the protective measures adopted by the Commission and the Court is to avoid a violation being committed or, if applicable, continuing to be committed, until the mechanisms of the inter-American system of human rights have finished processing the case.

(c) that the urgency of the provisional measures is self-explanatory, because there is a criminal judgment, an "Order of Execution and Injunction", an order of the Inter-American Commission adopting precautionary measures, two domestic judicial decisions that disregard the precautionary measures ordered by the Commission and reiterate the court order for the immediate execution of the judgment, a decision of the tribunal that heard the case "warning" the alleged victims that "they could become guilty of the offense of disobedience to authority (*Disobediencia a la autoridad*)", there is an order of the President of April 6, 2001, adopting urgent measures, and a decision of the Trial Court of the First Judicial Circuit of San José, the tribunal that heard the case, delivered a few days later, on April 24, 2001, establishing the following in its operative section:

> [i]n compliance with the order issued by [the President of] the Inter-American Court of Human Rights[,] concerning the application of provisional precautionary measures of an urgent nature[,] the suspension of the execution of the judgment and the respective decisions that depend on it are ordered.

An imminent threat looms over the alleged victims that a judgment will be executed peremptorily that, *prima facie*, appears to have aspects that are incompatible with Article 13 of the Convention. The only factor that protects the alleged victims from the violation of their human rights being consummated and preserves them from the "threats" of the Costa Rican court is the order for urgent measures issued by the President;

(d) that the gravity and the irreparability of the situation refer to individual rights recognized in the Convention that the States Parties have assumed an obligation to respect and guarantee. A serious threat to their right to express themselves freely hangs over the alleged victims, should judgment No. 1320-99 be executed. The explanatory statement of the draft Law for the Protection of the Freedom of the Press, which the President of the Republic of Costa Rica proposed to the Legislative Assembly on November 30, 1998, states that "[i]t has been maintained ... that the press is obliged to confirm the veracity of all the news that it obtains from its sources, which is evidently impossible, unless it applies a real self-censorship that would impair the freedom to disseminate information." If the suspension of the execution of judgment is lifted, freedom of expression and democratic values will be harmed by the necessary delay in processing the case (*periculum in mora*). There is a reasonable possibility of a risk that the rights alleged by the petitioners will be violated (*fumus boni iuris*) if the judgment is executed, so that the requirement of extreme gravity is met by the threat to the freedom of expression of the alleged victims;

(e) that if the judgment is executed, it would cause irreparable damage, effects that could never be eliminated retroactively. The execution of judgment would entail the registration of Mauricio Herrera Ulloa in the "Judicial Register of Offenders", which would cause him an irreparable harm. The reparation, if appropriate, would not serve for the *restitutio in integrum* of the harm that could be caused to the alleged victims. Suspension of the execution of judgment until the case has been processed before the inter-American system also promotes the State's interests, because if it is established that the petitioners were right and that the criminal sentence violates the Convention, the result would be that the payments resulting from the proceeding on compensation that the journalist, Herrera Ulloa, and *La Nación* must pay to Mr. Przedborski, according to the judgment, would imply that the State and not Mr. Przedborski would be obliged to compensate those who had paid the compensation to the complainant. Although this is not entirely irreparable for the alleged victims, it could entail an unnecessary prolongation of the harmful situation. Moreover, the State would suffer irreparable harm by reimbursing an amount that had been collected by the complainant, over whom the Court lacks jurisdiction; and

(f) that, with regard to the implications that a decision by the Court on the adoption of provisional measures could have for deciding the merits of the case, the urgent or provisional measures are not an advance notice of the opinion on the merits of the case, but rather a summary pronouncement, based on incomplete knowledge. The suspension of the execution of judgment is required in order to conserve the possibilities of success of the friendly settlement procedure before the Commission; it will also be useful to avoid irreparable damage to the alleged victims and to the State itself, if the organs of the system conclude that the judgment of the domestic courts violated the Convention. Even if the organs of the system conclude that the Convention was not violated, nothing would stand in the way of the subsequent execution of the said judgment, nor would anyone have been caused an irreparable damage. If the Court does not adopt the measures, the judgment is executed and the decision on merits concludes that the said judgment violates the Convention, there will have been an unjustified violation of the human rights of the alleged victims, because a compensatory indemnification would not provide them with the *restitutio in integrum* of the damages that had been caused.

4.   The State's communication of May 16, 2001, submitted in response to the decisions in the order of the President (*supra* having seen 2.1), which indicate:

(a) that the purpose of the Commission's request is to suspend the effects of a judgment delivered by an independent Judiciary with absolute respect for the norms of due process and for the individual and collective rights and freedoms guaranteed by the Constitution and the human rights conventions;

(b) that, should the Court order provisional measures, this could prejudge the merits of the matter inasmuch as it is assumed, a priori, that the Court has competence to hear it. The Court could be advancing too far in a proceeding that is only just beginning, and would be indicating that this case has merits to be heard by it;

(c) that, if the provisional measures are accepted, this could legitimate the use of an extraordinary remedy to annul the execution of a judgment in which neither the life nor the physical integrity of a person is at stake;

(d) with regard to the extreme gravity, that almost all the Court's provisional measures have been ordered in order to protect the life or the physical integrity of a person. In the instant case, the sanctions imposed by the Costa Rican criminal court are pecuniary penalties and not burdens that those affected are unable to assume. The registration of Mauricio Herrera Ulloa in the Judicial Registry of Offenders could evidently entail certain limitations or difficulties, but *per se* does not prevent him from exercising his profession or carrying on his life in society. The fact of being ordered to publish the operative part of the judgment and to link it to the disputed texts does not appear to entail a situation of any gravity or impose a considerable financial burden, but rather it is part of an exercise that could be deemed normal in the context of the same right to information alleged by the Commission in its communication requesting provisional measures. The order to suppress the link in *La Nación Digital* between the disputed articles and the last name, Przedborski, does not entail a situation of extreme gravity for the company, *La Nación S.A.*, but its suspension could affect Mr. Przedborski's name;

(e) with regard to the extreme urgency, the urgency of the required measure is the result of the nature of the situation that motivates it. The Court must evaluate whether there is a situation of urgency where the right to life or to physical integrity is being threatened or violated, which are the grounds that the Court has previously considered in order to call for provisional measures; and

(f) as for irreparable damage to persons, the possibility of an irreparable damage that could be caused to the alleged victims is not evident. If the Inter-American Court eventually decides that the judgment of the Costa Rican criminal court violated human rights protect by the Convention, Article 63 of this instrument authorizes the Court to order that the consequences of the situation that constituted the violation of those rights be repaired and fair compensation paid to the injured party.

5.   The following persons appeared at the public hearing on this request that was held at the Inter-American Court on May 22, 2001:

For Costa Rica:

     Farid Beirute, Prosecutor General

     José Enrique Castro, from the Office of the Prosecutor General

     Arnoldo Brenes, from the Ministry of Foreign Affairs and Worship

     Carmen Claramunt, from the Ministry of Foreign Affairs and Worship

For the Inter-American Commission on Human Rights:

     Pedro Nikken, delegate

     Carlos Ayala Corao, delegate

     Ariel Dulitzky, Principal Specialist of the Secretariat of the Commission

     Debora Benchoam, lawyer of the Secretariat of the Commission

     Fernando Guier, assistant

Witness proposed by the Inter-American Commission:

     Mauricio Herrera Ulloa

6.   The statements made by Costa Rica in the said public hearing, reiterating the arguments set out in its communication of May 16, 2001 (*supra* having seen 4), and declaring its willingness to comply with whatever the Court decides concerning the request for provisional measures under consideration by the Court.

7.   The statements of the delegates of the Inter-American Commission, who indicated that they appeared at the hearing as representatives of the victims, in accordance with the pertinent provisions of the new Rules of Procedure of the Commission, which entered into force on May 1, 2001, and repeated the contents of the Commission's communication of May 10, 2001 (*supra* having seen 3).

8.   The testimony of Mauricio Herrera Ulloa, who stated that the registration

of his name in the Judicial Registry of Offenders of Costa Rica would affect his future exercise of his profession and, in his opinion, also prejudice all his colleagues in the performance of their professional duties, since they would exercise self-censorship for fear of being accused before the courts of justice. [113]

CONSIDERING:

1.   That Costa Rica has been a State Party to the American Convention since April 8, 1970, and recognized the obligatory jurisdiction of the Court on July 2, 1980.

2.   That Article 63.2 of the Convention establishes that:

> In cases of extreme gravity and urgency, and when necessary to avoid irreparable damage to persons, the Court shall adopt such provisional measures that it deems pertinent in the matters it has under consideration. With respect to a case not yet submitted to the Court, it may act at the request of the Commission.

3.   That on this issue, Article 25.1 of the Rules of Procedure of the Court establishes that:

> At any stage of the proceedings involving cases of extreme gravity and urgency, and when necessary to avoid irreparable damage to persons, the Court may, at the request of a party or on its own motion, order such provisional measures as it deems pertinent, pursuant to Article 63.2 of the Convention.

4.   That, under international human rights law, provisional measures are, essentially, not only precautionary in character, in the sense that they preserve a juridical relationship, but also protective, since they protect human rights. Provided that the basic requirements of extreme gravity and urgency and the prevention of irreparable damage to persons are met, provisional measures become a true jurisdictional guarantee of a preventive nature.

5.   That, as a result of the public hearing (*supra* having seen 5), it is necessary to obtain further information regarding the irreparability of the damage that Mauricio Herrera Ulloa might suffer if his name is included in the Judicial Register of Offenders of Costa Rica.

6.   That, to this end, the State should submit a report indicating the possibilities contained in the domestic legislation of Costa Rica to avoid or repair, if applicable, the damage referred to, through the powers granted to any of the State's organs.

7.   That, in view of the foregoing, the Court deems that, as a provisional measure, it should maintain the decisions of the President in his order of April 6, 2001 (*supra* having seen 2), which the Court ratifies in its entirety.

8.   That, consequently, the State of Costa Rica must abstain from executing any action that would alter the *status quo* in the case *sub judice* until it submits

the report referred to in the sixth considering paragraph of this order, by August 16, 2001, at the latest, and this can be considered by the Court in its next regular session to be held from August 27 to September 8, 2001.

THEREFORE:

THE INTER-AMERICAN COURT OF HUMAN RIGHTS,

DECIDES:

1.   To grant the State of Costa Rica until August 16, 2001, to submit the report referred to in the sixth and eighth considering paragraphs of this order.

2.   To ratify the order of the President of the Inter-American Court of Human Rights of April 6, 2001, and, consequently, to call on the State of Costa Rica to abstain from executing any action that would alter the *status quo* of the matter until it has submitted the requested report and the Court can deliberate and decide on this during its next regular session.

7-Sep-2001

Order of the President of the Inter-American Court of Human Rights

Request for Provisional Measures by the Inter-American Commission on Human Rights

HAVING SEEN:

1.   The brief that the Inter-American Commission on Human Rights (hereinafter "the Commission" or "the Inter-American Commission") filed on March 28, 2001, wherein it submitted a request seeking provisional measures on behalf of Mauricio Herrera Ulloa, attorney, and Fernán Vargas Rohrmoser, journalist with the Costa Rican newspaper *La Nación*. Specifically, the Commission was petitioning the Court to call upon the State of Costa Rica (hereinafter "the State" or "Costa Rica") to:

    (a) suspend execution of the November 12, 1999 conviction handed down by the San José First Circuit Criminal Trial Court until such time as the Commission has examined the case and, pursuant to Article 50 of the American Convention on Human Rights (hereinafter "the Convention" or "the American Convention"), has arrived at a final decision on the merits of the case or, should the Court admit the case, until such time as it has delivered its judgment on the matter;

    (b) refrain for taking any action designed to enter the name of journalist Mauricio Herrera Ulloa in the Costa Rican Judiciary's Record of Convicted Felons, and

    (c) refrain from taking any measure or action that might infringe the right to freedom of expression that journalist Mauricio Herrera Ulloa and the newspaper *La Nación* enjoy;

The Commission based its request on the following:

(a) journalist Mauricio Herrera Ulloa was convicted on four counts of varying degrees of libel because of articles he published in the newspaper *La Nación* that quoted reports carried in a European newspaper about a "controversial" Costa Rican Foreign Service official accredited to the International Atomic Energy Organization, headquartered in Vienna; and

(b) the judgment of the San José First Circuit Criminal Trial Court was: to order a forty-day fine on each of the four counts, at a rate of two thousand five hundred colones per day, for a total fine of 160 days which, when the rule for appearance in court was applied, was reduced to three times the greatest fine, in other words, a fine of 120 days for a total of three hundred thousand colones; to find for the plaintiff in the civil damages suit, ordering Mauricio Herrera Ulloa and the newspaper *La Nación, S.A.*, represented by Fernán Vargas Rohrmoser, as jointly and severally liable, to pay moral damages of sixty million colones as compensatory damages for the stories reported in *La Nación* on May 19, 20 and 21 and December 13, 1995; to order that the court's ruling be published in the newspaper *La Nación*, in the same section where the articles were printed—the section titled *"El País"*—using the same size and typeface used in the articles against which the suit was brought, all at the expense of Mauricio Herrera Ulloa as the author of the crimes committed; to order *La Nación S.A.* to break the existing link that exists online at *La Nación Digital* between the surname Przedborski and the articles that prompted the complaint, and that a link be established connecting those articles to the operative part of the judgment. The court also ordered the civil defendants to pay court costs of one thousand colones, and the sum of three million eight hundred ten thousand colones in personal expenses;

2.   The Order that the President of the Court (hereinafter "the President") delivered on April 6, 2001, after conferring with all other judges on the Court, to the following effect:

1. To grant the Inter-American Commission on Human Rights and the State of Costa Rica until May 12, 2001, to submit the information referred to in considering paragraph 4 of this order.

2. To convene the Inter-American Commission on Human Rights and the State of Costa Rica to a public hearing to be held at the seat of the Inter-American Court of Human Rights on May 22, 2001, at 10:00 a.m., so that the Court may hear their points of view on the facts and circumstances that motivated the request for provisional measures.

3. To request the State, as an urgent measure, to abstain from

executing any action that would alter the *statu[s] quo* of the matter until this public hearing has been held and the Court is able to deliberate and decide on the admissibility of the provisional measures requested by the Commission;

3.   The submission of Mr. Féliz Przedborski Chawa, dated April 23, 2001, wherein he asks the Court to "hear [his] attorneys," Francisco Castillo González and Gonzalo Facio Segrega, at the public hearing to be held in San José;

4.   The May 21, 2001 note from the Secretariat of the Court (hereinafter "the Secretariat), sent on instructions from the Inter-American Court of Human Rights, wherein it informed Mr. Féliz Przedborski Chawa that no provision in "the American Convention on Human Rights, the Court's Statutes or its Rules of Procedure allows third parties interested in a matter that the Court has under consideration to intervene in the matter" and that "since those conditions are not met, the Court decide[d] that it cannot accede to your request";

5.   The Commission's submission of May 10, 2001, presented in response to the President's Order (*supra,* paragraph 2.1 under *Having Seen:*);

6.   The State's May 16, 2001 submission, presented in response to the President's Order (*supra,* paragraph 2.1 under *Having Seen:*);

7.   The public hearing on the present request, held at the Inter-American Court on May 22, 2001

8.   The statements made by Costa Rica and by the Inter-American Commission at that public hearing, and the testimony given by Mauricio Herrera Ulloa;

9.   The May 23, 2001 Order of the Court, wherein it resolved:

1. To grant the State of Costa Rica until August 16, 2001, to submit the report referred to in the sixth and eighth considering paragraphs of this order.

2. To ratify the order of the President of the Inter-American Court of Human Rights of April 6, 2001, and, consequently, to call on the State of Costa Rica to abstain from executing any action that would alter the *status quo* of the matter until it has submitted the requested report and the Court can deliberate and decide on this during its next regular session;

10.   The State's August 16, 2001 report on the nature and ramifications of the Judiciary's Record of Convicted Felons;

11.   The Commission's August 24, 2001 observations on the State's August 16, 2001 brief;

12.   The Secretariat's August 28, 2001 note whereby, following instructions from the Court *en banc*[,] it informed the parties that:

[[h]aving studied and considered [the] certifications [from the Judiciary Criminal

Records Office—one supplied by the State, the other by the Commission], the Court note[d] that the two certifications differ[ed] as to their content. It therefore request[ed] the State to clarify whether Mr. Mauricio Herrera Ulloa is or is not listed in the Judiciary's Record of Convicted Felons. If so, the Court request[ed] that the State indicate the date on which his name was entered into that record and the implications and effects of being so listed. It also asked the State to indicate when the notation was entered ordering "suspension of execution of the judgment and orders," "pursuant to the Order of the Inter.-American Court."

Costa Rica was given until September 1, 2001, to submit that information, but with no extensions, in order that the Court might deliberate and reach a decision on the matter at its LII regular session;

13.   The Commission's August 29, 2001 brief wherein it requested a copy of any brief the State might file in response to the Secretariat's note of August 28, 2001, "with the understanding that [...] it reserves its right to make the observations it deems pertinent within the 24-hour period following actual receipt of that transmission";

14.   The State's August 31, 2001 filing, wherein it presented the report requested by the Secretariat on August 28, 2001 (*supra,* paragraph 12 under *Having Seen:*) and which stated that:

[b]y an unfortunate internal administrative error made when preparing [the certification requested by Mr. Mauricio Herrera Ulloa for employment purposes], the notation states that there are no entries in [that gentleman's] name; the correct certification is the one issued by the Office of the Attorney General of the Nation.

... no measure has been taken here that could be prejudicial to either MAURICIO

HERRERA ULLOA or to the Office of the Attorney General, as [...] this was an internal administrative error uncommon for this office.

... MAURICIO HERRERA ULLOA's conviction by the San José First Circuit Criminal Trial Court was duly entered into the record on March 1, 2001, and the notation ordering that execution of the judgment and orders be suspended pursuant to the Order of the Inter-American Court, was entered on April 26, 2001.

15.   The Secretariat's August 31, 2001 note where, in accordance with the

Court's instructions, it gave the Commission until September 1, 2001 to present its observations on the State's August 31, 2001 report.

16.   The Commission's brief of September 1, 2001, wherein it presented its observations on the State's August 31, 2001 brief. In summation, it stated that:

(a)   that contradiction by the State itself points up the insecurity and lack of legal certainty that Mauricio Herrera Ulloa is experiencing, which is justification for the provisional measures the Commission seeks; and

(b)   for Costa Rica even to suggest that this Court settle the matter of an egregious contradiction between two finalized State documents on the strength of its argument that one of the two was supposedly not "valid" because of an internal administrative error committed by no less than the highest authority within the Judiciary Criminal Records Office, is itself an infringement of Mauricio Herrera Ulloa's right of self defense and to due process of law, upheld in the American Convention, and

CONSIDERING:

5.   That in requesting provisional measures to protect the freedom of expression of "journalist Mauricio Herrera Ulloa and the newspaper *La Nación*", represented by Fernán Vargas Rohrmoser, the Commission is seeking three things:

(a)   that execution of the judgment of conviction delivered by the San José First Circuit Criminal Trial Court on November 12, 1999, be suspended;

(b)   that Mauricio Herrera Ulloa's name not be listed in the Judiciary's Record of Convicted Felons, and c) that the State refrain from taking any measure that would be prejudicial to the right to freedom of expression that Mauricio Herrera Ulloa and the newspaper *La Nación* enjoy.

6.   That freedom of expression, recognized in Article 13 of the Convention, is a cornerstone upon which the very existence of a democratic society rests. It is indispensable for the formation of public opinion. It is also a *condition sine qua non* for the development of political parties, trade unions, scientific and cultural societies and, in general, those who wish to influence the public. It represents, in short, the means that enable the community, when exercising its options, to be sufficiently informed. Consequently, it can be said that a society that is not well informed is not a society that is truly free.[114]

7.   That an order must be given to suspend *La Nación's* publication of the operative paragraphs of the judgment of conviction that the San José First Circuit Criminal Trial Court delivered on November 12, 1999 and its creation of a "link" at the *La Nación Digital* website between the contested newspaper articles and the operative paragraphs of that judgment, since such a publication and such a link would cause irreparable harm to Mauricio Herrera Ulloa. No irreparable harm would be done, however, if the other operative paragraphs of that judgment were enforced. Execution of those paragraphs should be suspended until the case is

finally settled by the organs of the inter-American system for the protection of human rights;

8.   That the Court will not rule on the matter of the removal of the link at *La Nación Digital* that connects the surname Przedborski to the contested articles—delinkage ordered in the judgment of the San José First Circuit Criminal Trial Court on November 12, 1999—since the question of delinkage goes to the merits of the petition now before the Inter-American Commission, and is not material to provisional measures;

9.   That the entry of Herrera Ulloa's name in the Judiciary's Record of Convicted Felons, created by Law No. 6723 of March 10, 1982, warrants special attention. The Court observes that it is the State's claim, one not refuted by the Commission, that the name in question was entered into the record on March 1, 2001, which was prior to the date on which the request seeking provisional measures was filed with this Court. This information was supplied to the Court after the public hearing was held;

10.   That the profession that journalists practice is the mass media business. The practice of professional journalism is indistinguishable from the exercise of freedom of expression. In fact, the two are inextricably intertwined, for the professional journalist is not, nor can he be, anything but someone who has decided to exercise freedom of expression in a continuous, regular and paid manner;[215] and

11.   That entering his name in the Judiciary's Record of Convicted Felons causes irreparable damage to the journalist Herrera Ulloa, since it is prejudicial to his practice of his journalistic profession and poses an imminent threat of irreparable damage to his to reputation. The fact that this matter involves a journalist— someone practicing a profession where credibility is essential to performance—ischarged with a crime related to the practice of his profession, persuades the Court that his name should not be entered into any such record until such time as the bodies of the inter-American system for the protection of human rights have decided the case, so as to avoid doing damages that are irreparable in nature, as opposed to other damages that are essentially monetary in nature.

NOW, THEREFORE,
THE INTER-AMERICAN COURT OF HUMAN RIGHTS
RESOLVES:

1.   To call upon the State of Costa Rica to adopt forthwith those measures necessary to suspend the entry of Mauricio Herrera Ulloa's name in the Judiciary's Record of Convicted Felons until such time as the bodies of the inter-American system for the protection of human rights have arrived at a final decision on his case.

2.   To call upon the State of Costa Rica to suspend the order for *La Nación*

to publish the "Now Therefore" portion of the conviction handed down by the San José First Circuit Criminal Trial Court on November 12, 1999, and to suspend the order to create a "link" at the *La Nación Digital* website between the disputed articles and the operative part of that court ruling.

3.   To call upon the State of Costa Rica to inform the Inter-American Court of Human Rights, within 30 days of notification of this Order, of the measures it has taken pursuant to the order, and to call upon the Inter-American Commission on Human Rights to submit its observations on that report within 30 days of receiving it.

6-Dec-2001
Order of the President of the Inter-American Court of Human Rights
Provisional Measures in the Matter of the Republic of Costa Rica

HAVING SEEN:
16.   The State's brief of October 5, 2001, in which it advised that "it had ordered that execution of the judgment delivered against Mauricio Herrera Ulloa should remain suspended until the Inter-American Court of Human Rights [had] made the corresponding final decision." Costa Rica also indicated that the registration in the Judicial Record of Offenders had been suspended.

17.   The Commission's brief of November 8, 2001, in which it stated that "it [had] no objections to make to the information provided by the State" and that "it [would] remain attentive to the evolution of the situation in order to inform the Court of any change that might arise."

18.   The Commission's brief of November 30, 2001, in which it indicated that "in flagrant disregard of the provisional measures decided by [the] Court, in a certification dated November 29, 2001, the original of which is attached, it was once again certified, also by the official, Hernán Esquivel Salas, and in the same words as those that preceded the provisional measures decided unanimously" by the Court, that the following entry appears against Mauricio Herrera Ulloa: "the Criminal Court of the First Judicial Circuit, November 12, 1999, sentenced him to one hundred and twenty days of fines for the offense(s) of publication of offenses in the form of libel...."

19.   The Secretariat's note of December 3, 2001, in which, on the instructions of the Court, it granted the State until December 5, 2001, to present its observations on the Commission's brief of November 30, 2001.

20.   The State's brief of December 4, 2001, in which it advised that "[o]wing to an erroneous interpretation [...] there has been some confusion when certifying the criminal record of Mauricio Herrera Ulloa." It added that "the Judicial Files and Records Department has already taken the necessary measures to terminate

once and for all the uncertainty surrounding the situation of Mr. Herrera Ulloa and ensure [...] that, as of this date, such a situation with regard to the certifications issued will never, in any circumstances, be repeated."

CONSIDERING:

5.   That the Court, in the order of September 7, 2001 (*supra* Having Seen 15), called on the State to adopt the necessary measures to annul the registration of Mauricio Herrera Ulloa in the Judicial Record of Offenders until the case had been decided finally by the supervisory organs of the American Convention.

6.   That, owing to existing circumstances, this Court deems it is necessary to clarify that it adopted provisional measures and ordered the State to annul the registration of Mr. Herrera Ulloa in the Judicial Record of Offenders, so that the entry concerning the judgment delivered by the Criminal Trial Court against the above-mentioned journalist would be eliminated from this Record—until the case had been finally decided by the organs of the inter-American human rights system. Consequently, when a certification of the criminal record of Mauricio Herrera Ulloa is requested, it should not contain any entry relating to the facts and acts that gave rise to these provisional measures.

7.   That the brief presented by the State on December 4, 2001 (*supra* Having Seen 20) indicates that the necessary measures to comply with the decisions of this Court have now been adopted and, consequently, the registration of Mauricio Herrera Ulloa in the Judicial Record of Offenders has been annulled.

THEREFORE:

THE INTER-AMERICAN COURT OF HUMAN RIGHTS
DECIDES:

1.   To take note of the information contained in the State of Costa Rica's note of December 4, 2001.

2.   To call on the State of Costa Rica to continue to apply the provisional measures ordered by the Inter-American Court of Human Rights in the order of September 7, 2001, and, in particular, to maintain the annulment of the registration of Mauricio Herrera Ulloa in the Judicial Record of Offenders.

26-Aug-2002
Order of the President of the Inter-American Court of Human Rights
Provisional Measures Regarding the Republic of Costa Rica

HAVING SEEN:

1.   The facts stated in the "Having seen" paragraphs of the December 6, 2001 Order of the Inter-American Court of Human Rights (hereinafter "the Court" or "the Inter-American Court").

2.   The September 7, 2001 Order of the Court, in which it decided:

1. To order the State of Costa Rica to adopt forthwith those measures necessary to suspend the entry of Mauricio Herrera Ulloa's name in the Judiciary's Record of Convicted Felons until such time as the bodies of the inter-American system for the protection of human rights have arrived at a final decision on his case.

2. To order the State of Costa Rica to suspend the order for *La Nación* to publish the "Therefore" portion of the conviction handed down by the San José First Circuit Criminal Trial Court on November 12, 1999, and to suspend the order to create a "link" at the *La Nación Digital* website between the disputed articles and the operative part of that court ruling.

3. To order the State of Costa Rica to inform the Inter-American Court of Human

Rights, within 30 days of notification of this Order, of the measures it has taken pursuant to the order, and to call upon the Inter-American Commission on Human Rights to submit its observations on that report within 30 days of receiving it.

3.   The brief filed on July 30, 2002, in which the Ministry of Foreign Affairs of the State of Costa Rica (hereinafter "the State" or "Costa Rica") forwarded the rogatory letter issued on June 27, 2002 by the Examining Justice of the Criminal Court of the First Judicial Circuit of San José. According to the letter rogatory, on June 17, 2002 the Trial Court of the First Judicial Circuit of San José ordered that the Inter-American Court be consulted about "whether the Provisional Measures adopted then in the case of the daily '*La Nación*' refer [to] the whole judgment, both criminal and civil, or whether they refer only to the criminal judgment."

CONSIDERING:

5.   Due to the existing doubts and circumstances, the Court deems it necessary to specify the provisional measures ordered by the Court.

6.   In its brief requesting provisional measures, the Inter-American Commission on Human Rights (hereinafter "the Commission" or "the Inter-American Commission") requested that the Court order the State to stay execution of the November 12, 1999 conviction decided by the Criminal Trial Court of the First Circuit in San José, Costa Rica, until the Commission has reached a final decision on the merits of this matter or until the Inter-American Court has rendered judgment.

7.   The November 12, 1999 judgment of the Criminal Trial Court of the First Circuit in San José decided:

(a)   to convict the accused on four counts of libel;

(b)   to order a forty-day fine on each of the four counts, to be paid by Mauricio Herrera Ulloa, at a rate of ¢2,500.00 (two thousand five hundred colones) per day, for a total fine of 160 days which, when the rule for appearance in court was applied, was "reduced to three times the greatest fine," in other words, a fine of 120 days for a total of ¢300,000.00 (three hundred thousand colones);

(c) to find for the plaintiff in the civil damages suit, ordering Mauricio Herrera Ulloa and the newspaper *La Nación,* as jointly and severally liable, to pay moral damages of ¢60,000,000.00 (sixty million colones) as compensatory damages for the stories reported in *La Nación* on March 19, 20 and 21 and December 13, 1995;

(d) to order Mauricio Herrera to publish the "Therefore" section of the court's ruling in the newspaper *La Nación,* in the section titled "*El País*", using the same size and typeface used in the articles against which the suit was brought;

(e) to order *La Nación* to break the existing online link at *La Nación Digital* between the surname Przedborski and the articles that prompted the complaint;

(f) to order *La Nación* to establish a link in *La Nación Digital* between the articles that prompted the complaint and the operative part of the judgment; and

(g) to order Mauricio Herrera and the daily *La Nación* to pay court costs of ¢1,000.00 (one thousand colones) and ¢3,810,000.00 (three million eight hundred ten thousand colones) in personal expenses.

8.   In its September 7, 2001 Order, the Court ordered only the following three provisional measures:

(a) to order the State of Costa Rica to adopt forthwith those measures necessary to suspend the entry of Mauricio Herrera Ulloa's name in the Judiciary's Record of Convicted Felons until such time as the bodies of the inter-American system for the protection of human rights have arrived at a final decision on his case;

(b) to order the State of Costa Rica to suspend the order for *La Nación* to publish the "Therefore" portion of the conviction handed down by the San José First Circuit Criminal Trial Court on November 12, 1999; and

(c) to order the State of Costa Rica to suspend the order to create a "link" at the *La Nación Digital* website between the disputed articles and the operative part of that court ruling.

9.   In view of the query by the State, and as part of the required follow-up on measures ordered by the Court, it is appropriate to specify that the measures set forth by the latter in its September 7, 2001 Order refer only to three of the points ordered by the Criminal Trial Court of the First Circuit in San José, specifically the following:

to point (a), with the aim of annulling the entry of Mauricio Herrera Ulloa's name in the Judicial Record of Convicted Felons until a final decision has been reached on the case by the bodies of the inter-American human rights system;

to point (d), with the aim of suspending the order to publish in the daily *La Nación* the "Therefore" section of the conviction decided by the Criminal Trial Court of the First Circuit in San José on November 12, 1999; and

to point (f), to suspend the order to establish a "link", in *La Nación Digital*, between the Articles referred to in this action and the operative paragraphs of the aforementioned judgment.

The measures ordered by the Court seek to obtain the effects stated above, independently of the civil, criminal, or other projections of points 1), 4), and 6) of the aforementioned judgment by the Criminal Trial Court of the First Circuit of San José.

THEREFORE:
THE INTER-AMERICAN COURT OF HUMAN RIGHTS
DECIDES:

1.   To stipulate that the provisional measures ordered refer specifically to:

   (a) taking, without delay, whatever steps are required to annul the entry of Mauricio Herrera Ulloa's name in the Judiciary's Record of Convicted Felons until a final decision is reached on this case by the bodies of the inter-American human rights system;

   (b) suspending the order to publish in the daily *La Nación* the "Now Therefore" section of the conviction decided by the Criminal Trial Court of the First Circuit of San José on November 12, 1999; and

   (c) suspending the order to establish a "link", in *La Nación Digital*, between the articles referred to in the action and the operative paragraphs of that judgment.

2.   To stipulate that the aforementioned provisional measures were decreed to attain the effects stated in the ninth Whereas of that Order, independently of the civil, criminal, or other projections of points 1), 4), and 6) of the aforementioned judgment by the Criminal Trial Court of the First Circuit in San José.

3.   To order the State of Costa Rica, within one month of notification of the instant resolution, to report to the Inter-American Court of Human Rights on compliance with the provisional measures, and likewise for the Inter-American Commission on Human Rights to submit its observations on that report within 30 days of the date they are received.

Provisional Measures regarding Ecuador in the Matter of Pueblo Indígena Sarayaku
6-Jul-2004
Order of the Inter-American Court of Human Rights
Provisional Measures regarding Ecuador

HAVING SEEN:

1.   The June 15, 2004 brief of the Inter-American Commission on Human Rights (hereinafter "the Commission" or "the "the Inter-American Commission"") where, pursuant to Article 63(2) of the American Convention on Human Rights (hereinafter "the Convention" or "the American Convention") and Article 25 of the Rules of Procedure of the Inter-American Court of Human Rights (hereinafter "the Court" or "the Inter-American Court"), it submitted to the Court a request seeking the adoption of provisional measures on behalf of the members of the Kichwa indigenous community of Sarayaku (hereinafter "the community" or "the indigenous people") and its defenders, with respect to the Republic of Ecuador (hereinafter "the State" or "Ecuador"), to protect their lives, integrity of person, freedom of movement and the special relationship they have to their ancestral land, in connection with a petition that the *Asociación del Pueblo Kichwa de Sarayaku*, the Center for Justice and International Law and the Center for Economic and Social Rights (hereinafter "the petitioners") filed with the Inter-American Commission.

2.   The Commission based its request on the following allegations of facts:

   (a) In 1992, Ecuador legally recognized the Sarayaku community's ancestral territory by granting it the title to that territory. On July 26, 1996 the State concluded a participation contract with the Argentine business, *Compañía General de Combustible* (hereinafter the "CGC") granting a concession for oil exploration and drilling over an area of 200,000 hectares, called Block 23, in the province of Pastaza, Ecuador. Some 65% of this block is within the ancestral territory of the Kichwa indigenous community of Sarayaku. The contract was allegedly signed without consulting the Sarayaku people and without having obtained their informed consent.

   (b) According to the information supplied by the petitioners, between 1996 and 2002, the CGC made several attempts to negotiate to enter Sarayaku territory and, using questionable means, tried to exact from the indigenous people their consent for the oil drilling.

   (c) Despite a court order in which the Pastaza Civil Law Judge of First Instance ordered precautionary measures for the Kichwa people of Sarayaku, and an order from the Ombudsman's Office protecting that community's rights, CGC employees and agents of the State have taken measures detrimental to that people's interests.

(d) On January 13, 2003, villagers from Jatún Molino, which neighbors Sarayaku territory, were shot at from the bank of the Bobonaza River as they were traveling in canoes. As trees were cut down, the river, which is the Sarayaku people's principal communication route, was eventually blocked, making it difficult for the Sarayaku to get from one place to another.

(e) On January 25, 2003, within the perimeter of Sarayaku territory, members of the Ecuadorian Army and CGC security personnel detained indigenous leaders Elvis Fernando Gualinga, Marcelo Gualinga, Reinaldo Gualinga and Fabián Grefa, after which they allegedly tortured them. It is alleged that the indigenous leaders' hands and feet were tied with rope and their eyes blindfolded. They were thrown on the ground and forced to remain in that position for an hour. Fabián Grefa was forced to kneel alongside a rifle, whereupon they took photographs of him, apparently with the idea of accusing him of illegal possession of weapons. Later, Army agents put the four indigenous leaders aboard a CGC helicopter, flew them to a CGC base and handed them over to CGC security personnel, who also tortured the indigenous leaders. The four were then taken to Police facilities until the Sarayaku leaders managed to negotiate their release.

(f) On January 26, 2003, members of Ecuador's armed forces, wielding firearms, allegedly attacked the Peace and Life Camp at Tiutihualli, which is within Sarayaku territory. They are also alleged to have attacked the Peace and Life Camp at Panduro. Approximately 60 indigenous people from the community were there at the time, among them women, children and elderly people who kept watch so that the CGC workers would not enter their territory. When this happened, the Sarayaku scattered into the rainforest, where they stayed for a week, too afraid to return, and living off of what they could gather from the rainforest. In that period, some members of the community were reportedly abducted by CGC personnel and reappeared in March 2003.

(g) On January 29, 2003, Marisela Yuri Gualinga-Santi and Tatiana Gualinga-Dacha, both 12 years of age, were stopped by an Ecuadorian Army patrol, along with workers from the CGC. They were questioned about why they were there and threatened by the CGC workers. The petitioners alleged that before the two girls were released, they were sexually molested.

(h) On May 5, 2003, the Commission asked Ecuador to adopt precautionary measures on behalf of the Kichwa indigenous community of Sarayaku. It also requested that Ecuador adopt all measures it deemed pertinent to protect the life and physical, mental and moral integrity of the members of the indigenous community of Sarayaku, especially Franco Viteri, José Gualinga, Francisco Santi, Cristina Gualinga, Reinaldo Alejandro Gualinga and the two girls whom Army personnel or civilians having no ties to the community might threaten or intimidate; investigate the events that occurred on January 26, 2003, at the Sarayaku Community's Peace and Life Camp at Tiutilhualli and the aftermath of those events; prosecute and punish those responsible; take the necessary measures to protect the special bond between the Sarayaku Community and its territory; and, in consultation with the community and its representatives vis-à-vis the inter-American system for the protection of human rights, agree upon precautionary measures.

(i) When it requested the precautionary measures on May 5, 2003, the Commission gave the State a 15-day period in which to report on the measures adopted. On June 17, 2003, Ecuador reported that it had sent a number of communications to the appropriate authorities with instructions to comply with the precautionary measures, and that the armed forces were investigating the events that occurred on January 26, 2003.

(j) On July 18, 2003, the petitioners reported that the State was not complying with the precautionary measures; the memorandums sent to various authorities were all that had been done. They also reported that no one had contacted the leaders of the community to determine what type of protection the persons named in the order for precautionary measures would receive. In that same submission, the petitioners also stated that navigation on the Bobonaza River had been stopped, which meant that the Sarayaku people were unable to get to their own territory or to have contact with other villages.

(k) On August 5, 2003, the State sent the Commission a copy of a memorandum signed by the Deputy Secretary of Defense, in which he reported that as the oil exploration and drilling work was getting underway in the zone, the Sarayaku people had threatened neighboring communities and that Amazonas' IV Command had allegedly launched a security operation to prevent "criminal activity" on the part of the indigenous peoples. The memorandum reported that on January 25, 2003, a patrol doing reconnaissance in the area "was taken by surprise by a band of 30 armed indigenous people." The military personnel were stripped of their weapons. The note added the following: "the complaint that they [the petitioners] have filed with the Inter-American Commission on Human Rights is not true; these things, like the military attack on the 'TIUTIHUALLI PEACE AND LIFE CAMP', which never happened, are "the *comuneros'* exaggerations".

(l) On September 27, 2003, the State submitted information on implementation of the measures and attached a memorandum from the Attorney General which read as follows:

> [t]he report prepared by the police reveals that arrest warrants had been issued for certain members of the Sarayaku Community because of complaints filed by the CGC Oil Company alleging acts of vandalism committed by the *comuneros.* The Ecuadorian State, through the Office of the Attorney General, has had to do a thorough investigation of the information received—information the petitioners did not report so that the protection afforded by the Inter-American Commission would not become a vehicle that the above-named persons could use [...] to circumvent their appearance in domestic courts to answer the charges filed.

With its letter, the State enclosed a plan of operations for protection of the members of the Sarayaku community; however, that report did not indicate whether the security measures had actually been implemented.

(m) On October 16, 2003, during its 118th regular session, the Commission held a hearing to discuss issues related to the precautionary measures. At that hearing, the petitioners alleged that the State was not in full compliance with the precautionary measures; they stated further that rather than protect the Sarayaku community, the actions undertaken by the State had been prejudicial to it. They added that Ecuador had never contacted the Community's representatives to agree on the implementation of those measures, as the Commission had requested. At that hearing, the State contended that the increased military presence in the area in question had to do with the border situation with Colombia, and not with the Sarayaku community.

(n) On December 5, 2003, the petitioners informed the Commission that on December 4, 2003, approximately 120 people from the Sarayaku communit—women and children included—who were traveling along the Bobonaza River en route to the city of Puyo to participate in a march protesting the government's oil policy, were attacked and assaulted by workers from the CGC. The indigenous people were hit with sticks, stones and machetes and their belongings were hacked to pieces. Many of the inhabitants of Sarayaku sustained very serious injuries; the assailants abducted four others, one of whom was a boy, and released them the following day.

(ii) On December 17, 2003, the Commission extended the precautionary measures for another six months. It also gave the State 15 days in which to report to the Commission on the precautionary measures adopted. Ecuador requested an extension, but when the new deadline expired, it had still not provided the requested information.

(o) On April 8, 2004, the petitioners supplied the Commission with information on the failure to implement the precautionary measures and asked it to request the Inter-American Court to adopt provisional measures. In that request, the petitioners reported that on March 31, 2004, a military command allegedly launched a surprise incursion into the community's territory. That very same day, the Chief of the Joint Command of the Ecuadorian Armed Forces, General Octavio Romero, had flown aboard an Army helicopter into the populated center of Sarayaku, accompanied by two military police and ten Army officers, all heavily armed. The purpose of the General's visit was allegedly to tell the authorities of the Sarayaku community that if the community adopted a more extreme position and refused to allow the oil company to enter, "decisions will be made in Quito and the territory will be militarized".

(p) In that same communication of April 8, 2004, the petitioners reported on nine attacks against the lives and physical person of members of the indigenous community and its defenders.

- On February 1, 2004, unknown persons attempted to assassinate Leonidas Iza, President of the Confederation of Indigenous Nationalities of Ecuador (CONAIE) and his family; the attempt left one of his children gravely wounded. These events prompted the Commission to grant precautionary measures on February 26, 2004. Leonidas Iza has consistently expressed CONAIE's opposition to the militarization of the Sarayaku indigenous territory.

- On March 1, 2004, as he was getting off public transportation in Quito, Marlon Santi, President of the Sarayaku, was attacked and physically assaulted as his assailants punched and kicked him. Mr. Santi was about to travel to Washington, D.C., to a working meeting convened by the Commission. His assailants called him an Indian and made specific references to Sarayaku, the oil business and the country's development, and warned him to abandon his opposition to the oil exploration and drilling. After hitting him, they threw him on the ground and opened his bag, stealing his passport and other identification papers.

- Some days after Marlon Santi was physically assaulted, police searched the Sarayaku offices in Puyo. The search was done "by order of the Ministry of Defense." The police questioned everyone there, but no record of the interrogation was prepared.

- On April 6, 2004, the Pachamama Foundation and the Amazanga Institute received a telephone call warning them of a bomb in their facilities. These organizations have consistently supported the Sarayaku community.

- With regard to the obligation to investigate the attacks upon the Sarayaku people, the petitioners reported that the January 26, 2003 attack, the violence committed against villagers on December 4 and 5, 2003, and the other acts of violence and intimidation reported have not been investigated by any State authority;

(q) On April 28, 2004, the petititioners reported that on April 23, 2004, José Serrano Salgado, attorney and legal representative of the Sarayaku people, was attacked and physically assaulted by three armed and hooded men, while he was on his way to a meeting with the Sarayaku leaders in Puyo. Holding a pistol to his head, his assailants threatened him and warned him to abandon his work on behalf of the Sarayaku indigenous people.

(r) On April 30, 2004, the Commission forwarded to the State the additional information that the petitioners had supplied, with the request that the precautionary measures be extended to include the Sarayaku people's attorney, Mr. José Serrano-Delgado.

(s) On May 28, 2004, the State reported on the implementation of measures of protection in the case of the persons specifically named in the May 5, 2003 request for precautionary measures: Messrs. Franco Viteri, José Gualinga, Elvis Fernando Gualinga-Malavar, Fabian Grefa and Marcelo Gualinga. The State indicated that the Pastaza police had interviewed leaders of the indigenous people to coordinate those measures. The only statement Ecuador made regarding the request that the necessary measures be taken to ensure the life and physical, mental and moral integrity of all members of the indigenous people was that the topography of the territory "makes it difficult to fully comply with the precautionary measures; compounding the difficulty is the fact that there is no police station for the police assigned to provide the needed protection and security." The State explained further that "all the complaints that representatives of the CGC oil company filed against members of the Community have been investigated," adding that "the Second Criminal Law Judge of Pastaza dismissed, once and for all, criminal case No. 52-2003 against the Sarayaku leaders".

(t) On June 9, 2004, the petitioners stated that it was untrue that the State was taking steps to comply with the precautionary measures requested by the Commission; they went on to say that quite the contrary, "the measures taken were for the purpose of keeping the Sarayaku leaders' activities under surveillance, intimidating them, and continuing the pressure on the Community to allow the oil people into their territory." The petitioners added that the State has not taken any steps to protect the lives and personal safety of the members and leaders of the Sarayaku community and their attorneys.

(u) The explosives being detonated have destroyed forests, water sources, caves, underground rivers and sacred sites, and have driven animals away. The explosives planted in the traditional hunting areas have thus made it more difficult for the indigenous people to find food, thereby affecting their ability to secure the means to ensure the members' subsistence and altering their life cycle. All this has been detrimental to the Sarayaku indigenous people's right to use and enjoy their ancestral territory.

3.   The Commission's observations to the effect that when taken together, the facts alleged constitute a situation of extreme gravity and urgency that could result in irreparable harm to the members of the Kichwa indigenous community of Sarayaku and its defenders, which justifies the Court's ordering of provisional measures under Article 63(2) of the Convention. The Commission stated further that Ecuador had not complied with the precautionary measures that the Commission had ordered in this case.

In light of the foregoing, the Commission requested that the Court call upon Ecuador to:

[...] adopt without delay whatever measures are needed to:

1. [p]rotect the life and the integrity of the person of the members of the indigenous community of Sarayaku and their defenders[;]

2. [r]efrain from unlawfully restricting the right to freedom of movement of the members of the Sarayaku indigenous people[;]

3. [i]nvestigate the assaults committed on members of the Sarayaku Indigenous People[; and]

4. [p]rotect the special relationship that the Kichwa community of Sarayaku have with their ancestral territory; in particular, protect the use and enjoyment of their collective title to the property and its natural resources and take the measures necessary to avoid immediate and irreparable damage resulting from the activities of third parties who enter the Sarayaku people's territory or who exploit the existing natural resources within that territory, until such time as the

organs of the inter-American system for the protection of human rights have adopted a final decision on the matter.

Further, these measures are to be planned by mutual agreement between the State and the representatives of the Kichwa indigenous people of Sarayaku and, given the very grave and delicate situation, implemented immediately.

4. The June 28, 2004 note from the Secretariat of the Court where, on instructions from the full Court, it requested that the State submit to the Court, by July 1, 2004 at the latest, its comments on the Commission's request for provisional measures and any information it might it have on the situation of "extreme gravity and urgency" and the possibility that "irreparable harm" might be done to the members of the Sarayaku indigenous people and their defenders.

5. The July 2, 2004 communication where the State requested a 15-day extension to file its comments on the Commission's request seeking provisional measures.

6. The July 5, 2004 note from the Secretariat where, following instructions from the full Court, it informed the State that the extension had not been authorized "as this was a request seeking provisional measures, in which a situation of 'extreme gravity and urgency' is alleged, as is the possibility that 'irreparable harm' might be caused to the members of the Sarayaku indigenous people and their defenders."

CONSIDERING THAT:

1. The State ratified the American Convention on December 28, 1977 and, pursuant to Article 62 thereof, recognized the Court's binding jurisdiction on July 24, 1984.

2. Article 63(2) of the American Convention provides that "[i]n cases of extreme gravity and urgency, and when necessary to avoid irreparable damage to persons, the Court shall adopt such provisional measures as it deems pertinent in matters it has under consideration. With respect to a case not yet submitted to the Court, it may act at the request of the Commission."

3. Article 25(1) of the Court's Rules of Procedure provides that "[a]t any stage of the proceedings involving cases of extreme gravity and urgency, and when necessary to avoid irreparable damage to persons, the Court may, at the request of a party or on its own motion, order such provisional measures as it deems pertinent, pursuant to Article 63(2) of the Convention."

4. Article 1(1) of the Convention establishes the duty of States parties to respect the rights and freedoms recognized therein and to ensure their free and full exercise to all persons subject to their jurisdiction.

5.   The purpose of provisional measures in domestic legal systems (domestic procedural law) in general, is to preserve the rights of the parties to a dispute, thereby ensuring that execution of the judgment on the merits is not obstructed or otherwise prejudiced by their actions *pendente lite*.

6.   Under the International Law of Human Rights, urgent and provisional measures serve a further purpose, which is to protect fundamental human rights, thereby avoiding irreparable harm to persons.

7.   The information presented by the Commission in this case reveals *prima facie*, a threat to the life and integrity of the persons of the members of the Kichwa indigenous community of Sarayaku and its defenders. On a number of occasions, when protective measures were called for, this Court has ordered provisional measures based on the standard of *prima facie* assessment of a case and on the basis of presumptive evidence. [116]

8.   The Inter-American Commission has adopted precautionary measures that have not produced the needed effects; to the contrary, recent events indicate that the members of the Sarayaku Kichwa indigenous community and their defenders are in grave peril.

9.   Heretofore, the Court has ordered protection of a group of people not previously named, but who are identifiable and whose identity can be determined, and who are in grave peril by virtue of the fact that they belong to a given community. [217] In the instant case, as the Commission has indicated, the Kichwa indigenous community of Sarayaku, composed of approximately 1200 persons, is an organized community located in a specific geographic area comprising the villages of Shiguacoca, Chontayaku, Sarayakillo, Cali Cali, Teresa Mama, Llanchama and Sarayaku Centro, in the province of Pastaza. Its members are identifiable and can be named. Furthermore, as they are all members of that community, they are exposed to the same threat of aggression against the integrity of their person and lives. This Court therefore deems that provisional measures must be ordered to protect all members of the Kichwa indigenous community of Sarayaku.

10.   To effectively ensure the rights recognized in the American Convention, the State Party has an obligation, *erga omnes*, to protect all persons subject to its jurisdiction. As this Court has previously held, this general obligation applies not only with respect to the power of the State but also with respect to actions by third parties, including groups of armed irregulars of any kind. [318] The Court observes that given the characteristics of the instant case, provisional measures are needed to protect all members of the Kichwa indigenous community of Sarayaku, in accordance with the provisions of the American Convention.

11.   In this regard, the Court has held that:

[t]he right to life is a fundamental human right, and the

> exercise of this right is essential for the exercise of all other human rights. If it is not respected, all rights lack meaning. Owing to the fundamental nature of the right to life, restrictive approaches to it are inadmissible. In essence, the fundamental right to life includes not only the right of every human being not to be deprived of his life arbitrarily, but also the right that he will not be prevented from having access to the conditions that guarantee a dignified existence. States have the obligation to guarantee the creation of the conditions required in order that violations of this basic right do not occur and, in particular, the duty to prevent its agents from violating it. [4][19]

12.   The case to which the Commission's request refers is not now pending with the Court for a decision on the merits; therefore, adoption of provisional measures does not imply a decision on the merits of the dispute between the petitioners and the State. [5][20] In adopting provisional measures, the Court is merely guaranteeing that it is able to faithfully discharge its mandate under the Convention for cases of extreme gravity and urgency that require measures of protection to avoid irreparable harm to persons.

13.   As of the date of issuance of the present Order, July 6, 2004, the State has still not submitted its comments in response to the Secretariat's note of June 28, 2004 (*supra* '*Having Seen*' 4, 5 and 6).

NOW, THEREFORE,

THE INTER-AMERICAN COURT OF HUMAN RIGHTS,

in exercise of its authorities under Article 63(2) of the American Convention on Human Rights and Article 25 of the Court's Rules of Procedure,

DECIDES:

1.   To call upon the State to adopt, forthwith, the measures necessary to protect the life and integrity of person of the members of the Kichwa indigenous community of Sarayaku and of those who represent and defend them in proceedings ordered before the authorities.

2.   To call upon the State to guarantee the right to freedom of movement of the members of the Kichwa community of Sarayaku.

3.   To call upon the State to investigate the facts that necessitated the adoption of these provisional measures so as to identify those responsible and impose the appropriate punishments.

4.   To call upon the State to allow the beneficiaries of these measures to participate in their planning and implementation and, in general, to keep them informed of the progress made with execution of the measures ordered by the Inter-American Court of Human Rights.

5.   To call upon the State to report to the Inter-American Court of Human

Rights, within the ten-day period following notification of the present Order, on the provisional measures it has adopted in compliance therewith.

6.   To call upon the Inter-American Commission on Human Rights to forward this Order to the beneficiaries of these measures and to inform them that they may submit their comments within the five-day period following notification of the State's report.

7.   To call upon the Inter-American Commission on Human Rights to submit its comments within the seven-day period following notification of the State's report.

8.   To call upon the State, subsequent to its first communication (*supra* operative paragraph 5), to continue reporting to the Inter-American Court of Human Rights every two months on the provisional measures adopted, and to call upon the representatives of the beneficiaries of these measures to submit their observations on the State's reports within one month of receiving them; to also call upon the Inter-American Commission on Human Rights to submit its observations on the State's reports within six weeks of receiving them.

4-Feb-2010
Order of the Inter-American Court of Human Rights
Provisional Measures Regarding the Republic of Ecuador
Matter of the Kichwa Indigenous People of Sarayaku

HAVING SEEN:

1.   The Order issued by the Inter-American Court of Human Rights (hereinafter, the "Inter-American Court", the "Court" or the "Tribunal") of July 6, 2004, by which it was decided, *inter alia* "[t]o call upon the State to adopt [...] the measures necessary to protect the life and integrity of person of the members of the Kichwa indigenous community of Sarayaku and of those who represent and defend them [...]," "[t]o call upon the State to guarantee the right to freedom of movement of the members of the Kichwa community of Sarayaku," to call upon the State to investigate the facts that necessitated the adoption of these provisional measures so as to identify those responsible and impose the appropriate punishments," "to call upon the State to allow the beneficiaries of these measures to participate in their planning and implementation and, in general, to keep them informed of the progress made with execution of the measures ordered by the [...] Court [...]."

2.   The Order of the then President of the Court of March 18, 2005, by which it was decided to convene the Commission, the representatives and the State to a public hearing, which was held in Asunción, Paraguay, at the seat of the Supreme Court of Justice of that country, on May 11, 2005.

3.   The Order issued by the Tribunal on June 17, 2005, by which it was decided to repeat to the State to maintain the measures adopted, in the terms of the Order of July 6, 2004, (*supra* Having Seen clause 1) and to adopt, forthwith, the measures necessary:

  (a) To comply strictly and immediately with the measures ordered by the Inter-American Court to protect effectively the lives, personal integrity and freedom of movement of all the members of the Sarayaku Indigenous People;

  (b) To enable the members of the Sarayaku Indigenous People to carry out their activities and make use of the natural resources that exist in the territory where they are settled; specifically, the State must adopt those measures tending to avoid immediate and irreparable damage to their lives and personal integrities as a result of third parties' activities who live near the community or who exploit the natural resources within the community. In particular, the State must remove the explosive material placed in the territory where the Sarayaku Indigenous People is settled, if this has not already been done;

  (c) To ensure the protection and safety of the beneficiaries of these measures, without any type of coercion or threat;

  (d) To ensure the freedom of movement of the members of the Sarayaku Indigenous People, especially down the Borbonaza River;

  (e) To maintain the airstrip located on the land where the Sarayaku Indigenous People is settled to ensure that this means of transport is not suspended;

  (f) To investigate the facts that gave rise to the adoption and maintenance of these provisional measures, and the threats and acts of intimidation against some of the members of the Sarayaku Indigenous People, especially Marlon Santi, in order to identify those responsible and impose the corresponding sanctions, in keeping with the parameters established in the American Convention;

  (g) To continue allowing the beneficiaries of the provisional measures or their representatives to take part in planning and implementing these measures, so as to identify those that are most appropriate for the protection and safety of the members of the Sarayaku Indigenous People and, in general, to keep them informed about progress in the adoption of the measures ordered by the Inter-American Court; and

(h) To inform the neighboring indigenous communities about the meaning and scope of the provisional measures for both the State and third parties, in order to promote a climate of peaceful coexistence.

4.   The different reports presented by the State between June 2005 and October 2009, as well as the different observations submitted by the representatives and the Inter-American Commission in that regard.

5.   The Order of the Presidency of the Court issued on December 18, 2009, by which the Inter-American Commission, the State and the representatives were convened to a public hearing, in order to obtain information on the implementation of said provisional measures.

6.   The arguments put forward by the parties at the public hearing on the implementation of these provisional measures, held on February 3, 2010, at the seat of the Tribunal.

CONSIDERING THAT:

1.   Ecuador has been a State Party to the American Convention on Human Rights (hereinafter, the "American Convention" or the "Convention") since December 28, 1977, and that it accepted the binding jurisdiction of the Court on July 24, 1984.

2.   According to Article 63(2) of the Convention, three conditions must be met in order for the Court to be able to order provisional measures, namely: i) "extreme gravity;" ii) "urgency" and iii) when necessary to avoid "irreparable damage to people." These three conditions must coexist and must be present in every situation where the intervention of the Tribunal is required . . . and, by the same token the conditions must persist in order for the Court to maintain the protection so ordered.

3.   In the scope of provisional measures, the Court must only consider those arguments strictly and directly related to said conditions. Therefore, in order to decide whether it keeps the provisional measures in force, the Tribunal must analyze if the situation of extreme gravity and urgency which led to their adoption still persists, or whether new equally serious and urgent circumstances deserve their maintenance. . . . All other issues may be brought to the Court's attention solely through the procedure for contentious cases.

4.   The case that gave rise to these provisional measures has not been brought to the Court's attention as to the merits; instead, the measures have been ordered in the context of a case that is being processed, at the merits stage, before the Inter-American Commission. Therefore, the maintenance of the provisional measures does not imply an eventual decision on the merits of the existing controversy between the petitioners and the State. By keeping the provisional measures in force, the Court is merely ensuring that it can exercise its mandate pursuant to the Convention.

5.   In relation to the measures to effectively protect and void irreparable damage to the life, physical integrity and security of the members of the Sarayaku People, in order to form to carry out their activities and make use of the existing natural resources, in the recent public hearing, the State informed that, by the end of August 2009, it was delivered to the people, who the Community itself identified as the most vulnerable people, some cards and prior to this event, the State provided training to the beneficiaries and the personnel of the Police Headquarters of Pastaza, in charge of providing protection, on how to use such cards. The State clarified that if the community identifies other vulnerable people, the State shall immediately deliver a card to them. Moreover, the State sustained that it provides protection 24 hours per day at the offices of the Sarayaku community as well as at the community tourism agency located in Puyo. Likewise, it alleged that it is conducting a police operation with permanent patrols in other areas, including the inland port of Latasas. As to the right to freedom of circulation down the Borbonaza River and the maintenance of the airstrip located in the territory of the Sarayaku Indigenous People, the State informed that it is taking steps for the implementation of a permanent police post in the inland port of Latasas and that it has made progress to determine the necessary maintenance measures of the airstrip.

6.   Moreover, the representatives pointed out that even though those cards were delivered, the cards "only identify their bearers as beneficiaries of the protective measures but do not guarantee *per se* their security." In this respect, the Commission alleged that "the State does not inform on the protection provided to all the members" of the community. In relation to the police post in the inland port of Latasas, the representatives sustained that such post has not been implemented and that the security is not provided on a permanent basis. Furthermore, the airstrip has been improved and maintained by the members of the community themselves. The Commission agreed with what was expressed regarding this last aspect.

7.   As to the obligation to remove the explosive material placed in the territory where the Sarayaku community is settled, it is necessary to recall that since January 9, 2001, by means of resolution of the Board of Directors of "Petroecuador", the agreement entered into with CGC Petroleum Company has been suspended, due to *force majeure*; therefore, the company is not carrying out any activity. Then, on May 8, 2009, the Ministry of Mines and Petroleum issued a resolution by which CGC Petroleum Company was informed that the *force majeure* was lifted and that it had to immediately resume the prospecting and exploitation operations and activities. In that respect, the representatives indicated that this resolution was issued without holding any previous consultation with the Sarayaku People and that it could have serious implications for the security

and integrity of the beneficiaries. In response to the above mentioned, the State indicated that, in August 2009, the Board of Directors of "Petroecuador" decided to cancel the suspension of the activities in blocks 23 and 24 and ordered to immediately resume the activities stipulated in the contracts for the prospecting and exploitation of the hydrocarbons of said blocks. However, the State informed that it had entered into negotiations with CGC to consider such contracts terminated and that, in the course of said negotiations, it is not contemplated the commencement of the operations of the company. The representatives expressed that said resolution had affected the trust earned. The Commission indicated that the scope of such negotiation is not clear.

8.   Specifically, the State informed that the removal of the pentolite is conducted in two phases: the first one regarding the material found in the surface, a phase already completed, and the second one, regarding the material found under the surface of the earth. As to the first phase, the State had previously informed that, in December 2007, an Inter-institutional Cooperation Agreement was entered into between the Ministry of Mines and Petroleum and the Sarayaku People, which was terminated in April 2008 with approximately 40% of those preliminary works. To complete the rest of the preliminary works, a second agreement was entered into between Sarayaku and the Ministry in April 2008. In October and December 2009, a new cooperation agreement was signed. In the first phase, the State informed that the removal of the explosives from the surface was completed in three sub-phases—visual search by the explosive technicians of the Intervention and Rescue Group (GIR) of the National Police of Ecuador, search with technological equipments and search with the help of explosive detection dogs. Hence, in July 2009, the GIR personnel entered the territory of the Sarayaku People and proceeded to conduct a visual search and manual removal of 14 kilograms of pentolite, explosive material that was burn[ed] and detonated in a controlled manner on August 24, 2009, at the Provincial Police Headquarters of Pastaza, in the presence of a representative of the Government Attorney's Office of Pastaza, leaders of the Sarayaku people, representatives of the Ministry of Justice and Human Rights and press media. The State further alleged that the search for explosives was conducted in an area demarcated according to the information provided by the community. The second phase, that is, the removal of the material from the subsurface, is still incomplete due to disagreements with the members of the community regarding the method to be used, but the State sustained that such material placed in the subsurface does not represent a danger for the community, given the depth in which the explosives are buried. Finally, the State indicated that it does not have specific information regarding the amount of explosive buried in the territory in question, given that there is only one report of the CGC company which would account for the explosives admitted at a military

base used as operations center, but that there is no information on the entry of said explosives in the territory.

9.   The representatives expressed that the removal of the pentolite is urgent and that it must be conducted as soon as possible, given that the territory, in which the Sarayaku Indigenous People is settled, constitutes a legacy of their survival and existence. To this end, the representatives alleged that the removal activities that ended up in the destruction of barely 14 kilograms of explosive, out of the 1400 kilograms there would be buried in there, had negative consequences for the community insofar as such destruction had serious environmental and, as a result, cultural impacts which seem out-of-proportion in relation to the amount of explosives the State would have removed so far. In this respect, they presented an evaluation of the socio-cultural impact of the removal of explosives from the surface. Therefore, they expressed their concern about the impact that the completion of the next phases may have. They maintain that it is the technical responsibility of the State to determine the areas where the explosives were placed and that it is necessary to hold consultations with other experts in order to identify the manner to proceed with the removal of the explosives that is less intrusive and more respectful to the environment and the worldview of the Sarayaku People. Furthermore, they expressed that it falls upon the State to determine the location of the explosives, given that the inspection of the land and the determination of the level of danger of the explosives was completed five years ago and yet the State indicates it has uncertain information.

10.   Prior to the hearing, the Commission had valued, on different occasions, the efforts made by the State and the representatives to remove the explosive material placed in the Sarayaku territory, but it expressed its concern about the declaration of the gradual progress considering that this should have been done as soon as practicable, given that the explosives represent a potential danger and a very important environmental liability which hinder the access to an vast area of the territory and entail a permanent risk to the life and integrity of the members of Sarayaku. At the hearing, in response to the doubts expressed by the State regarding the existence and quantity of explosive in the area, the Commission made reference to a document of the National Direction of Environmental Protection [Dirección Nacional de Protección Ambiental], furnished within the framework of the processing of the merits of the case before it, by which it was informed that explosive charges were distributed in Block 23.

11.   As to the obligation to investigate into the facts that gave rise to the adoption of these provisional measures, the State advised that it requested the members of the community to present a report regarding the complaints they filed for a follow-up and, if applicable, to launch the investigations. Furthermore, the State maintained that there are only two complaints before the Government

Attorney's Office of Pastaza and that said complaints are filed given that it was impossible to identify the accused people. However, the State argued that it seeks to declare the non-applicability of statutory limitation to the crimes of torture, mistreatment and assault, according to the terms of the Constitution of Ecuador, in order to conduct the investigations that correspond in coordination with the Ombudsman. In that respect, the representatives indicated that the progress is nonexistent and the Commission emphasized that the State had expressed the fact that "it has no updated information and does not know all the investigations that needed to be launched," but that the State has, in effect, the information related to this measure.

12.	Moreover, the Court notes that no acts of violence had been recently reported against the members of the Sarayaku Indigenous People, or acts that hindered the access to the Borbonaza River. Furthermore, it valued the distribution of beneficiaries' cards to certain members of the Community, as well as the disposition shown by the State in order to work together with the beneficiaries in the planning and implementation of the provisional measures adopted and to be adopted. However, it is relevant to require the State to present specific information on the real benefits that those cards provide to the members of the Community; the materialization of the surveillance posts; the security of the access roads to the community; the current situation of the alleged inter-community conflicts in the area and the feasibility of implementing other types of protection.

13.	In addition, the Tribunal values that the state authorities and the representatives of the Sarayaku People had entered into agreements for the removal of the explosive material and that the State has completed the first phase of removal of explosives that were over the surface of the territory, of which the Sarayaku community was informed and coordinated efforts were made to that end. However, even though the State has given explanations about the delay in the adoption of this procedure, it does not clearly justify why the implementation of said procedure began more than four years after the Tribunal expressly ordered it (*supra* Having Seen clause 3). Under the particular circumstances in which these provisional measures were ordered, the protection of the right to life and human treatment of the members of the Sarayaku Indigenous Community required and requires the guarantee that the explosives will be removed from the territory where the community is settled, given that this situation has hindered their freedom of circulation and the use of the natural resources existing in the area. In these circumstances, it is clear that the main concern, at this moment, is focused on the current and potential risk that the existence of high explosives buried in their territory implies for the Sarayaku community. On the one hand, the State has expressed its disposition to continue with the next phase of removal of explosive material buried in the territory, for which it pointed out two alternative procedures, namely, the controlled denotation of the pentolite or its "precipitation".

On the other hand, the representatives expressed the need to look for technical alternatives, referring to the need to seek the advice of other experts and, if the indigenous community does not have means for that, they trusted that the State will support their search. That is to say, it is clear there is no agreement between the State and the beneficiaries as to the adequate technical procedures to do it, particularly because of the possible environmental, social and cultural impact that the methods suggested so far could represent for the Sarayaku community.

14.   The Court emphasizes the spirit of coordination and agreement shown at the hearing by the State and the representatives, to determine whether there is a technical solution different to the ones mentioned. The Tribunal highlights the need and importance of finding ways to communicate in order to determine the procedure to remove the explosives that best suits the security needs in technical and personal terms, on the part of the authorities in charge and, at the same time, in cultural terms acceptable to the worldview of the Sarayaku community. Therefore, it is appropriate to maintain the order for the State to adopt the provisional measures necessary to protect the life, physical integrity and personal security of the members of the Kichwa People of Sarayaku. To this end, it is relevant to require the State to define, in particular, the technical procedures, the specific program and schedule to effectively remove all the explosive material buried in the territory, by mutual agreement with the Sarayaku community, and to continue submitting updated and specific information on the existing or future plans related to the prospecting and exploitation of oil in Blocks 23 and 24, as well as on the possibility the CGC company has to resume the operations, and the amount and precise location of the explosives existing in the area where the Sarayaku community is settled.

15.   The Tribunal values the effectiveness of the hearing held to learn about the current status of implementation of these provisional measures.

THEREFORE:

THE INTER-AMERICAN COURT OF HUMAN RIGHTS,

by virtue of the authority granted by Article 63(2) of the American Convention on Human Rights, and in accordance with Articles 24(2) and 25 of the Court's Statutes and Articles 15(2), 27 and 31(2) of the Court's Rules of Procedure of the Court,

DECIDES:

1.   To ratify the provisional measures ordered in its Order of June 17, 2005, particularly as to the obligation for the State to adopt the provisional measures to protect the life, physical integrity and personal security of the members of the Kichwa People of Sarayaku and, therefore, to require the State to adopt the appropriate measures to promptly and effectively remove the explosive material buried in the territory where said community is settled.

2.   To repeat the urgent need for the State to establish a clear and permanent system so that the Kichwa People of Sarayaku may participate in the planning, implementation and evaluation of said provisional measures.

3.   To require the State to inform Inter-American Court, no later than May 1, 2010, on the provisional measures it has adopted in compliance with this Order and to continue informing this Court, every two months, on the measures adopted to that end. In its report, the State shall present updated information on the compliance with what was ordered and, in particular, on the technical procedures, the specific program and schedule to effectively remove all the explosive material buried in the territory where the Sarayaku community is settled, as well as information on existing or future plans related to the prospecting and exploitation of oil in Blocks 23 and 24, in the terms of Considering clauses twelve to fourteen.

4.   To call upon the representatives of the beneficiaries of these provisional measures and the Inter-American Commission on Human Rights to submit their observations to the State reports within a term of four and six weeks, respectively, as of receipt of said reports.

5.   To require the Secretariat of the Court to notify the State, the Inter-American Commission and the representatives of the beneficiaries of these measures of this Order.

Provisional Measures regarding Argentina in the Matter of Mendoza Prisons
30-Mar-2006
Order of the Inter-American Court of Human Rights
Provisional Measures in the Matter of Mendoza Prisons

HAVING SEEN:

1.   The submission dated October 14, 2004, and its Appendixes, whereby the Inter-American Commission on Human Rights (hereinafter "the Inter-American Commission" or "the Commission") filed with the Inter-American Court of Human Rights (hereinafter "the Court", "the Inter-American Court," or "the Tribunal") a petition for provisional measures, pursuant to the provisions of Article 63(2) of the American Convention on Human Rights (hereinafter "the Convention" or "the Inter-American Convention"), Article 25 of the Court's Rules of Procedure (hereinafter "the Rules of Procedure") and Article 74 of the Commission's Rules of Procedure, seeking *inter alia* that the Argentine Government (hereinafter, the "State" or "Argentina") protect the life and personal integrity of "the persons held in custody in the Mendoza Provincial Prison, those in custody in the Gustavo André Unit, located at *Lavalle*, and all persons hereinafter imprisoned in such units, and the employees and officials rendering services on the said premises."

2.   The letter of the President of the Inter-American Court of Human Rights

(hereinafter "the President") dated November 5, 2004, whereby the President acknowledged the position taken by the State of Argentina (hereinafter "the State" or "Argentina") concerning the petition for provisional measures as well as other several measures that had been implemented in connection with the facts under review and as a response to the precautionary measures requested by the Inter-American Commission. In turn, the President was concerned to notice that over a period of seven months a number of untried prisoners and inmates as well as several penitentiary guards had been injured or killed in the Mendoza Provincial Prison and in the Gustavo André penitentiary unit, located at *Lavalle*. Particularly, the President considered it a serious matter that after the submission of the petition for provisional measures and during the effectiveness of the precautionary measures requested by the Commission, one person was killed and another was injured as they were held in custody in the Mendoza Provincial Prison. In this regard, the President advised he was convinced that the State would abide by the precautionary measures requested by the Commission pending the Court's decision on the petition for provisional measures, which the President decided to submit to the consideration of the full Court. Finally, the President urged that the State take all necessary steps to protect the life and personal integrity of the persons in favor of whom the provisional measures were requested.

3.   The Order of the Inter-American Court of Human Rights (hereinafter, the "Court" or "the Inter-American Court") of November 22, 2004, wherein the Court resolved:

> 1. to request that the State immediately adopt all necessary measures to protect the life and personal integrity of all detainees and inmates of the Mendoza Provincial Prison and of the Gustavo André Unit, located at *Lavalle*, as well as all other persons found within the premises.
>
> 2. to request that, as a protective measure adequate to the present situation, the State investigate the facts that gave rise to the adoption of these provisional measures in order to identify the persons to be held liable for said events and punish them accordingly.
>
> [...]

4.   The Order of the President of the Court of March 18, 2005, whereby the President resolved to summon the Inter-American Commission, the representatives of the beneficiaries of the provisional measures and the State, to a public hearing to be held in Asunción, Paraguay, at the seat of the Supreme Court of Justice of such country, as from May 11, 2005, so that the Court would hear the arguments on the facts and circumstances relating to the implementation of said measures.

5.   The public hearing on the provisional measures held in Asunción,

Paraguay, at the seat of the Supreme Court of Justice of said country, on May 11, 2005.

6.   The record signed by the representatives of the Inter-American Commission on Human Rights (hereinafter "the Commission" or "the Inter-American Commission), the representatives of the beneficiaries of the provisional measures (hereinafter "the representatives") and the State, submitted on May 11, 2005, to the Court during said public hearing, in which they expressed their agreement on keeping the provisional measures in full force, and further agreed to "remit to the consideration of the [...] Inter-American Court [...] the following set of measures so that the Court could evaluate the possibility of specifying the content of the Order dated November 22, 2004, with a view to safeguarding the life and physical integrity of the beneficiaries to said order:"

1. Measures regarding the penitentiary staff:

a. In the short-term, to increase the number of penitentiary staff to safeguard the security of the institutions;

b. To introduce changes in the surveillance pattern in a manner such that it assures adequate control and the actual presence of personnel in the cellblocks;

c. In the mid-term, to carry out a purge of the penitentiary corps in order to assure adequate service provision;

d. As a permanent measure, to assure the recruitment and continuous training of penitentiary staff; and

e. to request that the authorities of the General Security Council of the Province report the outcome of investigations on the individuals directly responsible for the dead and injured in the Mendoza Prison and the Gustavo André Unit during 2004/2005, and to describe the status of administrative proceedings in course.

2. Separation of prisoners by categories:

a. In the short-term, to adopt necessary measures to segregate untried prisoners from convicted prisoners, and juvenile adults from adults; and

b. As a progressive measure, to develop a classification mechanism taking into consideration at least the criteria established in Article 8 of the UN Standard
Minimum Rules for the Treatment of Prisoners.

3. Measures to avoid the entrance of weapons into the institutions:

To take actions to sequestrate weapons of all kinds that could be found within the institutions, and to set up adequate surveillance—with the involvement and under the control of the judiciary—in order to guarantee the legality of said measures. Furthermore, to adopt necessary measures to bar the clandestine entrance of weapons, including surveillance over the spaces designed for the use by penitentiary agents.

4. Disciplinary Actions:

a. In the short-term, adoption of all measures necessary to notify —as soon as practicable— the defense of any person subjected to administrative investigations for the imposition of sanctions so that said person's right to defense is safeguarded; and

b. In the mid-term, adoption of legislative or any other type of measures needed to set up a disciplinary action scheme in keeping with the terms of the American Convention on Human Rights and other applicable international instruments on human rights.

5. Increasing Improvement on Detention Conditions:

a. A survey on the individuals held in custody under the Province penitentiary system, which shall be conducted by the Ministry of Justice and Security of Mendoza; access to showers and sanitary units in working condition; weekly provision of hygiene gear; guaranteed access to sufficient drinking water; adoption of necessary measures so that all areas of the institution are well-lit; barring of prolonged cell confinement, repression of groups of hooded individuals and restriction of visitation; barring of access of personnel with dogs to cellblocks and to areas for the use by visitors;

b. In the mid-term, expansion of the registry of prisoners, in accordance with the guidelines of the Inter-American Court of Human Rights in the case of *Bulacio*, paragraph 132;

c. A bimonthly report on the outcome of the survey on prisoners' health conditions identifying the clinical charts prepared, treatment prescribed and ensuring that medicine and food are provided as prescribed;

d. In the mid-term, psychological, psychiatric, dental and ophthalmologic assistance will be provided;

e. Prisoners' equitable access to work, recreational, formal and non-formal educational programs will be guaranteed, and other programs related to reinstatement will be created;

f. Actions to diminish overcrowding by means of reducing the number of persons held in custody under pretrial detention (in accordance with the criteria established in a recent decision of the Supreme Court of Justice on prisons in Buenos Aires); this will call for mechanisms other than pretrial detention such as programs for provisional release on parole; and

g. Concerning overcrowding, full compliance with sentencing guidelines for progressive computation must be guaranteed.

6. Involvement of the Judicial System

a. Full compliance with the terms of duration of judicial proceedings, in accordance with the standards laid out in the Pact of San Jose, Costa Rica, and in the Mendoza Code of Criminal Procedure;

b. Investigations on the incidents of violence that took place in the Mendoza Prison and Gustavo André penitentiary unit; and

c. Full compliance with the obligation on the part of Judges, Prosecutors and Official Defense Attorneys to visit—on a periodic basis—prisons with untried or convicted prisoners the responsibility for whom rests with the judiciary body under the charge of said officials.

7. Creation of an *Ad Hoc* Investigation Committee:

a. The Committee shall be in charge of investigating the incidents of violence and death that took place in the prisons located in the Province of Mendoza from January 2004 to date;

b. The Committee shall be created as a special, independent and impartial unit; it shall carry on activities within the framework of principles of efficient prevention and investigation of extralegal, arbitrary or summary executions, as per recommendations stated in resolution 1989/65 of United Nations Economic and Social Council, dated May 24, 1989; and

c. The Committee shall be composed of members appointed by the national government and the provincial government pursuant to the foregoing guidelines.

8. Reinforcement of the Follow-up Committee:

The number of members of the follow-up committee created in November 2004, composed of the national government, the government of Mendoza, Senator Marita Perceval, the Supreme Court of Justice in and for the Province and the petitioners, shall be increased in order to broaden the committee's operating horizons, assessing the possibility to appoint to the committee the National Ministry of the Interior, the Cabinet Chief Office and the Secretariat of Justice reporting to the National Ministry of Justice and Human Rights.

9. Assistance and Cooperation:

The National Government undertakes to provide the Province of Mendoza with assistance and resources needed to implement the measures established in this document.

6.   Order of the Court of June 18, 2005, wherein the Court resolved:

1. to request once again that the State keep in full force and effect the provisional measures adopted by virtue of the Order of the Inter-American Court of Human Rights dated November 22, 2004, and that the State order forthwith those measures needed to efficiently protect the life and integrity of all persons held in custody in the Mendoza Provincial Prison and the Gustavo André Unit, located in *Lavalle*, as well as all other persons found within the premises. Among the measures to be adopted by the State are the ones described in the agreement signed by the Inter-American Commission, the representatives of the beneficiaries of the measures and the State [(*supra* Having Seen Clause No. 5)].

2. To request that the State continue informing the Inter-American Court of Human Rights —every two month next following its latest report—on the actions taken in compliance with all issues ordered by the Inter-American Court, and request the representatives of the beneficiaries of the provisional measures ordered and the Inter-American Commission on Human Rights to submit their comments to said State's reports within a term of four weeks and six weeks, respectively, next following receipt of the referenced State's reports.

7.   The submission dated June 21, 2005, wherein the representatives filed a document entitled "report on the visit of June 13, 2005, to the Mendoza Prison and request for a visit of the Inter-American Commission to said penitentiary."

8.   The submission dated June 22, 2005, in which the representatives reported the alleged death of the inmate Ricardo David Videla.

9.   The note of June 23, 2005, whereby the Secretariat requested that the State and the Commission present relevant comments to the submission made on June 22, 2005 (*supra* Having Seen Clause No. 8).

10.   The submissions made on June 22 and 23, 2005, wherein the representatives filed three news articles in connection with the alleged suicide of Ricardo David Videla-Fernandez, a young man who allegedly died on June 21, 2005, as well as another document whereby "the young man's defense attorney reported this incident [to the Inter-American Court]."

11.   The submission of June 23, 2005, in which the State reported the

"unfortunate death of inmate Ricardo Videla-Fernandez [who had allegedly] committed suicide while confined in his cell."

12.   The submission of June 28, 2005, wherein Argentina filed a copy of the "report of the Follow-up Commission on the conditions of the Mendoza Provincial Prison," in which *inter alia* Argentina reported that no cellblock lack proper lighting devises; that some inmates reported that prolonged confinement is still being used; that there are no juvenile adults living together with adult prisoners; that the main issues affecting education are lack of space and lack of resources; and that access of prisoners to workshops is limited. Furthermore "the Follow-up Commission prepared a bill modifying the Mendoza Code of Criminal Procedure providing for a second instance in matters of execution before the Court of Appeals for cases where the decisions passed by the jail oversight judge bring about a substantive alteration of the sentence imposed."

13.   The submission of July 1, 2005, wherein the representatives filed a "criminal report [allegedly] presented by the petitioners to the Director of Prisons in Mendoza, Sergio Miranda, so that officials would investigate the [alleged] crimes of torture, harsh treatment, unlawful harassment or coercion, breach of duties inherent in public officials, disobedience [and] abuse of authority."

14.   The submission of July 4, 2005, wherein the representatives produced a news article stating that "the prisoners [allegedly held in custody in the maximum security units] were sewing up their mouths because they had been confined in individual cells for 23 hours."

15.   The submission of July 5, 2005, whereby the representatives requested that the present case "be treated in the next following term of Court […], as the national and provincial authorities showed great commitment to the issue but in fact the Asunción Agreement and the Order of the Inter-American Court of June 18, 2005, were not being complied with. Furthermore, the alleged suicide of Videla-Fernández—the young man sentenced to life imprisonment—in cellblock 11 of the local penitentiary, after 22-hour confinement periods, makes this an issue worth being tried before the Inter-American Court [as the petition regarding Mr. Videla-Fernández] is pending before the Inter-American Commission."

16.   The submission of July 15, 2005, wherein the representatives remitted the order passed on July 14, 2005, by the Jail Oversight Judge in and for the Province of Mendoza resolving to compel the Executive of the Province of Mendoza to take actions so that the Complex *Boulonge Sur Mer*, *inter alia*, will offer minimum hygiene conditions, provide prisoners with mattresses and adequate and necessary bedding, extend prisoners' recreational time schedules, provide water to cell-blocks, repair electric installations, refurnish gas connections, repair existing sanitary installations and build new ones as necessary, and refurbish existing facilities and create new lodging sectors.

17.   The submission of July 18, 2005, wherein the Inter-American Commission filed its observations to the third and fourth State's report, claiming *inter alia* that although it valued the State's willingness to comply with mid-term and long-term measures, the Commission was worried about the current status of compliance with said measures as there had been no concrete changes, and prison overcrowding, absence of segregation of untried prisoners from convicted prisoners, lack of adequate control and security as well as of basic services of hygiene and health care, were still an issue. Furthermore, the Commission remitted order of July 14, 2005, passed by the Jail Oversight Judge in and for the Province of Mendoza (*supra*, Having Seen Clause No. 16).

18.   The submission of July 28, 2005, wherein the representatives forwarded information about alleged actions of "repression carried out [by the State] during the last riot".

19.   The submission of August 5, 2005, wherein the representatives presented its "comments on the observations made by the Inter-American Commission on Human Rights on July 18, 2005" (*supra* Having Seen Clause No. 17). In this regard, the Secretariat understood that said submission corresponded with the representative's observation to the fourth State's report.

20.   The submission of August 8, 2005, whereby the State requested an extension for an additional ten days for the State to submit its fifth State's report, which was granted.

21.   The submission of August 12, 2005, wherein the Inter-American Commission "express[ed] its profound concern ... for the status of implementation of provisional measures ... and commitments undertaken by the State at the public hearing held in Asunción, Paraguay, on May 11, 2005, as well as for a series of recent incidents uncovering security pitfalls in both correctional institutions ...." In this regard, the Commission made particular reference to two riots and to the alleged "deployment of forces in order to quell these riots."

22.   The submission of August 15, 2005, whereby the representatives reported on "... a new questionable death of an inmate at the Mendoza Prison ...who had allegedly been electrocuted as he was handling a clandestine connection".

23.   The submission of August 26, 2005, wherein Argentina presented its fifth State's report describing *inter alia* the measures adopted in order to protect the penitentiary personnel; the procedures to compile a complete registry of inmate data; to segregate prison populations; to sequester weapons; to notify defense attorneys of any sanction imposed on inmates; to make surveys on prison crowding conditions; to improve sanitary, lighting, and the general condition of the correctional institutions. Furthermore, the State claimed that it "is strongly committed to complying with the provisional measures in full." On September 23, 2005, Argentina submitted the original report along with its exhibits.

24.   The submission of August 29, 2005, wherein the representatives filed its observations to the third and fourth State's reports pointing out—among other things—the existence of impunity, overcrowding, uncleanliness, cohabitation of untried prisoners and convicted prisoners, poor conditions of cleanliness and labor security, unsafeness and repression. This creates a "tense environment exclusively created from the [alleged] inoperativeness of provincial authorities working without a Plan of Penitentiary Policy that should —in order of priority— be based on international commitments."

25.   The submission of September 21, 2005, wherein the representatives remitted a "note drafted by the UNC on [the alleged repression and abuses committed] in the Mendoza Prison."

26.   The submission of October 20, 2005, whereby the Inter-American Commission filed its observations to the fifth State's report point out—among other things—its concern for the status of compliance with the provisional measures ordered, as their implementation "has been deficient". Therefore, compliance with the order of the Court calls for "an immediate improvement on safety conditions."

27.   The submission of November 3, 2005, wherein Argentina requested an extension for an additional 30-day period within which to submit its sixth report.

28.   The note of November 7, 2005, wherein the Secretariat informed the State that the request for extension of terms had been disallowed owing to the fact that the term for submission of the State's report had expired on October 26, 2005. Consequently, the Secretariat requested that the State send its report as soon as practicable.

29.   The submission of November 23, 2005, wherein the representatives requested that a memorandum by Amnesty International addressed to the Governor of the Province of Mendoza, lodged on the website of said organization, be added to the file. Furthermore, they reported that Mr. Alfredo Ramón-Guevara had died, and therefore he was no longer a representative of the beneficiaries.

30.   The submission of December 5, 2005, wherein the representatives reported on the alleged offences to their law firm.

31.   The submission of December 6, 2005, wherein the representatives reported that a week before, "Sebastian Pablo Matías Esquivel had been injured by stabbing [...] and that inmate Antonio Gil Caballero [had died]."

32.   The note of December 9, 2005, wherein the Secretariat, following the instructions of the President, requested that Argentina report not later than December 19, 2005, on the alleged incidents described in the submissions made by the representatives on December 6, 2005 (*supra* Having Seen Clause No. 31).

33.   The submission of December 12, 2005, wherein the representatives filed information "[on the judicial proceedings instituted against on the penitentiary

guards of the penal farm Gustavo André in connection with the death of five inmates in 2004.]" Furthermore, they reported that "inmate [...] Ángel Bernardo Flores suffered minor injuries in the said Mendoza Prison."

34. The submission of December 16, 2005, wherein the Inter-American Commission made reference to the implementation of provisional measures and to the State's failure to submit its sixth report, which Argentina should have submitted on October 26, 2005 (*supra* Having Seen Clause No. 28).

35. The submission of December 16, 2005, whereby the representatives reported on the alleged intimidation and threats sustained by Pablo Salinas, one of the representatives.

36. The note of December 19, 2005, wherein the Secretariat, following instructions of its President, requested that Argentina comment—in its next report—on the information filed by the representatives on December 12, 2005 (*supra* Having Seen Clause No. 33).

37. The submission of December 19, 2005, in which Argentina made reference to the information submitted by the representatives that "Sebastian Pablo Matías Esquivel was injured by stabbing [...] and that inmate Antonio Gil Caballero [had died]," as requested from the Government by way of Secretariat's note of December 9, 2005 (*supra* Having Seen Clause No. 32). In this regard, Argentina claimed that the death of inmate Antonio Gil-Caballero was due to "natural causes" and that there were no evidences whatsoever of the injuries reported in connection with inmate Sebastián Pablo Matías-Esquivel.

38. The submission of December 19, 2005, wherein the representatives filed a document concerning a decision of Amnesty International in connection with the alleged threats reported by the representatives, particularly in connection with Mr. Pablo Salinas.

39. The note of December 20, 2005, wherein the Secretariat requested once again the submission of the sixth State's report, as it had not been filed by its due date. Consequently, following instructions of the President of the Court, Argentina was requested to enlarge on the implementation of provisional measures, as well as on the presumed intimidation suffered by Mr. Pablo Salinas, in the report Argentina had to submit on December 26, 2005. Furthermore, the Inter-American Commission was requested to include comments on said information among its observations to the sixth State's report.

40. The Secretariat's note of January 9, 2006, requesting the State to submit its sixth and seventh reports, as the terms had expired on October 26, 2005, and December 26, 2005, respectively, and these reports had not been received. Furthermore, as part of those reports, the State was required to include comments as requested by way of Secretariat's note of December 20, 2005 (*supra* Having Seen Clause No. 39).

41.   The submission of January 11, 2006, whereby the State filed its sixth and seventh State's reports, describing inter alia the state of investigations, the condition of the criminal juvenile adult population, as well as the actions taken in order to set off the quantity imbalance between inmates and penitentiary staff members, and to train penitentiary personnel. Furthermore, the State stated once again its willingness to comply with the provisional measures ordered. Moreover, the State made reference to the information requested by way of Secretariat's note of December 20, 2005, on the presumed intimidations sustained by Mr. Pablo Salinas, one of the representatives of the beneficiaries. In this regard, the State claimed that it had "requested from competent authorities ... all the information ... concerning such incidents, as well as ... information on the measures actually taken to both safeguard the safety and physical integrity of [Mr.] Salinas, and ... to investigate the said reported threats." On January 20, 2006, the State submitted the original report along with its exhibits.

42.   The submission of January 24, 2006, wherein the Inter-American Commission stated that "owing to the importance of the Exhibit [that was missing in the State's report] for a correct assessment of the progress on the implementation process of [said] provisional measures, the Commission understands that the term within which the Commission must file its observations shall commence on the date said exhibit is forwarded." On January 25, 2006, following the instructions of its President, the Secretariat informed the representative and the Commission of a 10-day extension next following the date of expiration of the original terms of four and six weeks, respectively, for them to file their observations to said State reports.

43.   The submission of February 1, 2006, wherein the State reported the death of inmate Federico Alberto Minatti. On the same day, the representatives reported said death and submitted information about the implementation of provisional measures.

44.   The submission of February 1, 2006, wherein the State reported "the incidents of violence that had taken place at Units No. 4 on [...] December 12, 2005," in respect of which the State informed of the measures and actions taken by the Penitentiary Board. Furthermore, the State referred to "the situation associated with the threats sustained by Pablo Salinas, María Angélica Escayola and Alfredo Guevara," in respect of which the State claimed that "both [Mr.] Pablo Salinas and his colleagues have been awarded adequate protection by the authorities and immediate and useful actions were taken so as to identify the aggressors."

45.   The Order of the Court of February 7, 2006, summoning the Inter-American Commission, the representatives of the beneficiaries of the provisional measures and the State to a public hearing to be held in the city of Brasilia, Brazil, at the seat of the Superior Tribunal of Justice of said country, on March 30, 2006,

so that the Court could hear their arguments on the facts and circumstances relating to the implementation of said measures.

46.   The submissions of February 14 and 16, 2006, wherein the representatives filed information about inmate Ricardo Vilca, who "was found [severely] injured within the same cellblock where a few days before [inmate Federico Alberto] Minatti had been found dead."

47.   The submission of February 21, 2006, wherein the State requested an extension of time for the submission of its eighth State's report. The extension due date was set for March 17, 2006.

48.   The submissions of February 27, 2006, in which the representatives filed a "copy of the [alleged] *habeas corpus* filed owing to the incidents that had taken place in the cellblock for juvenile adults" of the *De Boulonge Sur Mer* Correctional Institution, as well as copy of the "Order [passed by the jail oversight judge] in the proceedings identified with No. 8732 – Habeas Corpus – Cellblock No.2, Mendoza Provincial Prison."

49.   The submission of March 6, 2006, wherein the Inter-American Commission submitted its observations to the sixth and seventh State's reports.

50.   The public hearing on provisional measures held on the date hereof in Brasilia, Brazil, at the seat of the Superior Tribunal of Justice of that country, with the presence of:

from the Inter-American Commission:

> Florentín Meléndez, Commissioner;
> Santiago Canton, Secretary;
> Víctor H. Madrigal-Borloz, Advisor;
> Elizabeth Abi-Mershed, Advisor;
> Juan Pablo Albán, Advisor, and
> Manuela Cuvi, Advisor;

of the representatives:

> Carlos Eduardo Varela Álvarez, y
> Pablo Gabriel Salinas;

from the State:

> Jorge Nelson Cardozo, advisor to the Cabinet of Foreign Office;
> Alejandro Acosta, Deputy Secretary of Justice of the Province of Mendoza;
> Alberto Javier Salgado, from the Human Rights Division of the Foreign Office;
> Andrea Gualde, from the Ministry of Justice;
> Ciro Annichiaricco, from the Ministry of Justice, and
> Pilar Mayoral, from the Ministry of Justice.

51.   The arguments presented by the Commission at the referenced public meeting. Among other issues, the Commission stated as follows:

(a) The Commission stated once again its concern for the exposure of persons within prisons to a position of risk of extremely gravity and urgent nature threatening their lives and personal integrity. The position of risk has not changed substantially, and violence is still in place as it may be evidenced—among other instances—by injured prisoners, questionable deaths, riots, hanger strikes, fights, escapes and sequestration of weapons;

(b) Some progress has been made in the implementation of provisional measures, such as the appointment of new penitentiary agents, the creation of a new jail oversight criminal court and the office for the defense of inmates' human rights. Furthermore, the Commission values both the projection of measures in the long term on the part of the State and the political willingness of the national government and of the provincial government, and the talks between the parties. However, progress has been inadequate and misdirected as concrete substantive measures have not been implemented in order to overcome the crisis;

(c) Security controls are deficient and management of prisons is erratic in the hands of the custody bodies as the incidents that have taken place inside the cellblocks have passed unnoticed to the authorities. Furthermore, the use of force to quell riots has been excessive;

(d) Judicial authorities have allowed two petitions for habeas corpus presented by the representatives and several inmates and their families, in connection with prolonged periods of confinement and sanitary and health care issues;

(e) The severity of the situation has been acknowledged by the highest Argentine authorities;

(f) It is necessary to take measures as part of an integral reform, such as more skilled personnel, proper cellblock lighting, actions against overcrowding, segregation of convicted prisoners from untried detainees, sanitary measures for the provision of proper toilets and drinking water for the use by the inmates, and barring of entrance of weapons to the facility;

(g) Overcrowding is not fought against only by building new cellblocks but also by providing for measures as an alternative to pretrial detention;

(h) The agreed-upon short-term commitments as per the record signed in Asunción have not been met. In this regard:

    (i) the Commission acknowledges the recruitment of new penitentiary agents, but the profile and training status of said new employees are unknown;

    (ii) Investigations are not carried out effectively or impartially, and the system does not provide for legal, criminal penalties, it only provides for disciplinary actions. Furthermore, the legislative and governmental provincial authorities have taken a fairly passive stance when compared to judicial authorities' involvement;

(iii) Follow-up Commission entrusted with provisional measures is inactive;

(iv) In spite of the fact that the Commission acknowledges that the number of deaths has decreased, the severe risk of violent death has not been eradicated;

(i) The Commission requests that the Court make use of all its conventional power to enforce the provisional measures, and force the State's both national and provincial governments to assume their responsibility,

(j) This case is not about determining who should be held internationally responsible when dealing with a federal State, as this issue has already been dealt with in the Convention and previous court decisions;

(k) It is necessary to implement a political compliance strategy considering:

(i) the effective implementation of provisional measures in the provincial scenario;

(ii) federal government's assumption of direct responsibility as part of the process;

(iii) the existence of effective and transparent coordination of process of compliance between the federal government and the provincial government;

(iv) a call for consultations among the political sectors of the Province of Mendoza that do not acknowledge the provisional measures or the need for said measures or transparency, in order to have them involved in the process of implementation and compliance; and

(v) involvement of other governmental agencies in addition to the Foreign Office and the Government of the Province of Mendoza, who may provide technical advi[c]e, resources, and concrete short-term solutions to overcome the current scenario of violence.

(l) There is a need for a concrete State commitment to immediate action the results of which could be verified in the short term, and for the Court to be informed, in within a month, by way of the State's ninth report, of the implementation of the commitments undertaken as per the Record of Asunción, including:

(i) Change in security patterns so that guards will make rounds on a regular basis in the facilities and not outside.

(ii) Immediate reactivation of the Ad Hoc Investigation Commission and the Follow-up Commission; and

(iii) Barring of prolonged periods of confinement, completion of lighting works in all cells and a reactivation meeting as soon as practicable.

52. The arguments posed by the representatives at such public hearing, in agreement with the ones presented by the Commission, including further:

(a) Their dissent with the Commission concerning the alleged political willingness on the part of the federal government and the provincial government, and the alleged improvement on the conditions prevailing in the prisons involved in this case. Although the representatives were aware of the personal efforts of many governmental agents, the actions taken do not suffice to argue that provisional measures have been complied with.

(b) Discontinuance of the work of the Follow-up Commission or the Ad Hoc Commission entrusted with investigating the deaths occurred, which favors impunity;

(c) Uncertainty about the conditions under which the office of the defense of the rights of inmates works;

(d) The federal judicial authorities are responsible for lodging over 60% of untried prisoners in the penitentiaries located in Mendoza, while the provincial judicial authorities are responsible for lodging 45% of said inmates;

(e) In spite of the fact that judicial authorities have allowed several submissions for habeas corpus, prolonged periods of confinement and torture are still used inside the cellblocks;

(f) Regarding education and resocialization, only four young prisoners take lessons in a small classroom. Furthermore, when they turn 21 years old, they are relocated with the other adult prisoners, and the authorities no longer provide them with education;

(g) Penitentiary guards are under pressure to work without rest;

(h) In spite of the precautionary and provisional measures, and a recent decision of the Argentine Supreme Court, the rate of persons detained in the Province of Mendoza has increased, while penitentiary conditions and facilities are still the same;

(i) The S[t]ate must prepare a plan to comply with the commitments undertaken in Paraguay, providing for a budget and readily access to information, means of control of compliance with provisional measures, as well as the involvement of the highest national and provincial authorities; and

(j) A request to the Court seeking that provisional measures are detailed and kept in force.

53. The arguments presented by the State in connection with the public hearing, including *inter alia*:

(a) The need to take into account the social context calling for a hand of iron on inmates, as well as more severe penalties and fewer possibilities to apply for releases;

(b) As a special measure, state agents have met with the investigation judge to "convince him of the measure that should be taken" in order to grant beneficiaries to inmates, as well as with federal and provincial authorities. However, progress in this area at the judicial level is slow;

(c) An assessment of the persons who are in the condition to obtain provisional release from prison by way of the benefit of discharge;

(d) At present, there are no inmates subjected to prolonged periods of confinement;

(e) Regarding the Follow-up Commission, it is difficult for the members who compose it to meet owing to the distances between Buenos Aires and the Province of Mendoza;

(f) The national government has not provided an answer to the provincial government in connection with the issues affecting the penitentiaries located in said province;

(g) Out of the inmates imprisoned in the penitentiaries located in Mendoza, 300 places are used by the federal government, and the Province provides the necessary funding for those places;

(h) The judiciary of the Province of Mendoza keeps 44% of its prisoners in custody far beyond the due date set for trials, without any prospects for trial commencement;

(i) The Federal Government is willing to work together with the parties, the Inter-American Court and the province of Mendoza so as to try and find a solution to the problem affecting the case and Argentina;

(j) Although it admits that the issue of overcrowding is severe, the State makes a point of the fact that there has been an improvement on this issue;

(k) Argentina has prepared a declaration concerning the prisoners held in custody, which is "ready" to be presented before the General Assembly of the OAS, and has ratified the Optional Protocol to the UN Convention against Torture;

(l) In the case pending before the Commission, an amicable solution was proposed in that the State creates a trust fund destined to the implementation of the provisional measures relating to the penitentiaries located in Mendoza and administered by the Follow-up Commission; and

(m) The State shares some of the proposals made by the Inter-American Commission such as the barring of prolonged periods of confinement and the reactivation of the Follow-up Commission, and welcomes new proposals for their consideration. Furthermore, the State made it clear that it is not avoiding responsibility for the present case.

CONSIDERING:

1.   That Argentina has been a State Party to the American Convention from September 5, 1984, and that pursuant to Article 62 of said Convention, Argentina has accepted the contentious jurisdiction of the Court upon ratifying said instrument;

2.   That Article 63(2) of the American Convention sets forth that "[I]n cases of extreme gravity and urgency, and when necessary to avoid irreparable damage to persons, the Court shall adopt such provisional measures as it deems pertinent in matters it has under consideration. With respect to a case not yet submitted to the Court, it may act at the request of the Commission."

3.   That, in the terms of Article 25 of the Court's Rules of Procedure,

> [...]
>
> 2. With respect to matters not yet submitted to it, the Court may act at the request of the Commission.
>
> 6. The beneficiaries of provisional measures or urgent measures ordered by the President may address their comments on the report made by the State directly to the Court. The Inter-American Commission of Human Rights shall present observations to the State's report and to the observations of the beneficiaries or their representatives.
>
> [...]

4.   That International Law on Human Rights considers that provisional measures are not only of a precautionary nature in that they preserve a juridical situation, but fundamentally of a shielding nature as they protect human rights. As long as the basic requirements of extreme gravity and urgency and the necessity to avoid irreparable damage to persons are met, provisional measures become a true jurisdictional guarantee of a preventive nature.

5.   That the merits of the case in connection with which these provisional measures were granted are not being tried before this Court, and that the adoption of provisional measures do not amount to passing judgment on the merits of the dispute between the petitioners and the State. [1 21] That in adopting provisional measures, the Court is only fulfilling its mandate in conformity with the terms of the Convention, in cases of extreme gravity and urgency calling for protective measures in order to avoid irreparable damage to persons.

6.   That Article 1(1) of the Convention provides for the State Parties' general obligation to respect the rights and freedoms contained therein, and to ensure to all persons subject to their jurisdiction the free and full exercise of those

rights and freedoms. In furtherance of this obligation, any State Party has the *erga omnes* obligation of protecting all the persons subject to their jurisdiction. This Court has held that said general obligation is imposed in connection not only with the power of the State, but also with the acts and conduct of private third parties. [222]

7.   That this Court has held that every State has a special role as guarantor in respect of the persons held in custody in penitentiary institutions or detention units, as penitentiary authorities exert control over these persons. [323] Furthermore, "[o]ne of the obligations that a State must unavoidably assume in its role as guarantor—in order to protect and guarantee the right to life and personal integrity of the inmates—is to [provide] them with minimum conditions compatible with their dignity while they remain in said detention units." [424]

8.   That, during the effective term of these provisional measures—according to the information submitted by the Commission, the representatives and the State—the inmates of the Mendoza Provincial Prison and those in custody in the André Gustavo Unit, located in Lavalle, as well as the person found within these facilities, are still exposed to a situation that puts—or has directly put—their life and personal integrity at stake. Particularly, from the information forwarded by the parties, it can be concluded that—in spite of the good faith and the endeavors taken by State authorities throughout 2005 and up to date—serious acts of violence have taken place, and four persons have died in the former penitentiary center under circumstances not yet fully clear; there were two riots in which the force used to subdue them has been excessive and in which a number of inmates have been injured and/or received different harsh treatments; and that generally, the state of overcrowding and the deterioration levels inside such centers have not undergone any change at all. As emphasized by the Commission, the risk of violent death has not been eradicated; investigations made have not yielded any actual outcome; and deficient conditions of security and internal control are still the same, including lack of segregation of inmates and detainees by categories, and that entry and possession of weapons inside the penitentiary centers is still an issue. These incidents are still happening at present in spite of the effective term of the provisional measures previously ordered by the Court, despite the fact that they have been addressed expressly at the public hearing held on the date hereof in Brasilia (*supra*, Having Seen Clause No. 50), and although some of them had been noticed by the Jail Oversight Court in determining a number of petitions for *habeas corpus*.

9.   That the Court has already established that the international responsibility of the States within the framework of the American Convention arises from the commission of violations to general *erga omnes* obligations to respect and caused to be respected and guarantee rules of protections and ensure the efficacy of the

rights contemplated therein in all circumstances and in respect of any person, pursuant to Articles 1(1) and (2) of said treaty.[525] These general obligations create special duties that may be determined in accordance with the particular needs of protection of any law-abiding subject, whether due to their personal capabilities or to the specific situation they are in. In fact, Article 1(1) of the Convention imposes on every State Party fundamental rights of respect and guarantee of rights, in a manner such that any detriment to human rights acknowledged by the Convention that may be attributed, as per the rules of International Law, to the actions or act of omissions of governmental authorities, amounts to an act attributable to any such State and therefore the State's international responsibility is compromised pursuant to the terms of the Convention itself and the general provisions of International Law.[626]

10.   That the provision established in Article 63(2) of the Convention makes it compulsory for any State to adopt the provisional measures that may be ordered by this Court, insofar as the States must meet their conventional obligations in good faith in accordance with the basic law principle of international responsibility of the States, which is supported by international case law *(pacta sunt servanda)*. Any breach to the order of enforcement of provisional measures passed by the Court in proceedings before the Commission and the Court may trigger international responsibility of the States.[727]

11.   That this Court is aware of the fact that the correction of and solution to the situation affecting the Mendoza Prisons is a process with short-, mid-, and long-term goals; that this takes a set of actions on the part of federal and provincial authorities, with administrative, judicial or even legislative powers, to cure the conditions of defective confinement and detention. However, given the order of this Court to adopt provisional measures, the subject-matter of which is the protection of life and integrity of the persons held in custody in said penitentiary units and of those found within such facilities, the State cannot assert defenses based on the State's domestic law to avoid taking firm, concrete, and effective action in compliance with the measures ordered so that no further deaths occur. Nor can the State rely on the defense of lack of coordination between federal and provincial authorities in order to prevent the deaths and acts of violence that have taken place during the effective term of these provisional measures. Regardless of the unitary or federal structure of government of any State Party to the Convention, in the international jurisdiction scenario it is the State as such that is to be held accountable to the oversight bodies created in said treaty and it is the only State that is obliged to adopt such measures. Failure of the State to adopt said provisional measures triggers such State's international responsibility.

12.   That under the circumstances of this case, the measures adopted by the State must include those directly designed to protect the right to life and

integrity of the beneficiaries, considering the relationship both among them and with penitentiary and governmental authorities. Particularly, and in light of the allegations made by the parties at the public hearing held on the date hereof in Brasilia (*supra* Having Seen Clause No. 50), it is essential for the State to adopt— in an immediate and inexcusable fashion— effective and necessary measures to actually eradicate the risk of violent death and serious assaults to personal integrity, especially in connection with the deficient conditions of security and internal control affecting confinement centers. The measures to implement, notwithstanding the adoption of others referred to elsewhere herein (*supra* Having Seen Clause No. 5) and others that may be deemed pertinent, are described below:

- An increase in the number of penitentiary personnel in order to guarantee security in the institutions;
- Elimination of weapons within the facilities;
- Changes in surveillance pattern in such a manner that they ensure adequate control and actual presence of penitentiary personnel inside the facilities;
- Those actions identified as measures of immediate implementation for the "progressive improvement in detention conditions" (*supra* Having Seen Clause No. 5); and
- Immediate reactivation of the so-called "follow-up commission" (*supra* Having Seen Clauses No. 5 and 12).

13.   That, to these effects, the Court deems it of paramount importance that the measures are implemented in effective and transparent joint efforts of provincial and federal authorities, with the involvement of bodies with the capability of providing the technical criteria to determine the immediate measures designed to overcome the situation that has been the basis for the petition of said provisional measures.

14.   That the duty to report to the Court on the implementation of measures is twofold in that compliance with said duty requires the formal submission of a document within the term set as well as the specific, true, current and detailed material reference to the issues that fall within the scope of said obligation.[28] Any breach to this State's duty is particularly serious because of the juridical nature of these measures.[29] Even though the State has submitted—when and as required— most of its reports, it is necessary that the State keep on reporting to the Court specifically and concretely on the results obtained from the implementation of the measures. It is paramount that the priority measures referred to in Considering Clause No. 12 get reflected in the State's reports describing the means, actions and goals set by the State in agreement with the specific needs of protection of the beneficiaries thereof, in such a manner that they give real sense and provide a continuum in those reports. In this sense, the role of the Inter-American Commission is particularly important so as to adequately and effectively follow up the implementation of the measures so ordered.

15.   That, based on the foregoing, it is relevant to keep the provisional measures in force, by virtue of which the State has the obligation to protect the life and integrity of all the persons held in custody in the Mendoza Provincial Prison and those in the Gustavo André Unit, located in Lavalle, as well as any person found within said facilities, especially by means of the measures described both in the previous and in this present Order, among others (*supra* Having Seen Clauses No. 3 and 6). In this regard, the Court highlights the fact that at the hearing held on the date hereof in Brasilia (*supra* Having Seen Clause No. 50) the representatives, the Commission and the State agreed on the fact that the conditions of the referenced confinement centers have not undergone tangible improvement and on the need to keep said measures in full force and effect.

THEREFORE:

THE INTER-AMERICAN COURT OF HUMAN RIGHTS,

by virtue of the authority granted by Article 63(2) of the American Convention on Human Rights and Article 25 and 29 of its Rules of Procedure,

DECIDES:

1.   To order the State to adopt—in an immediate and inexcusable manner— the effective and necessary provisional measures to efficiently protect the life and integrity of all the persons held in custody in the Mendoza Provincial Prison and those in the Gustavo André Unit of Lavalle, as well as every person found within those facilities, especially to eradicate the risk of violent death and the deficient conditions of security and internal control in confinement centers, pursuant to the provisions set out in Considering Clauses 11 and 12 of this Order.

2.   To order the State to implement the provisional measures ordered in effective and transparent coordination with federal and provincial authorities, pursuant to the provisions of Considering Clauses No. 11 and 13 of this Order, in order to ensure the effectiveness of such measures.

3.   To order the State to report to the Inter-American Court every two months next following its latest report concretely and specifically on the actions taken in compliance with the orders of this Court. Especially, it is essential that the adoption of the priority measures described in this Order get reflected in reports containing concrete results in terms of the specific needs of protection for the beneficiaries of such measures, pursuant to the provisions set out in Considering Clause No. 14 of this Order. In this regard, the oversight role of the Inter-American Commission is radical for an adequate and effective follow-up on the implementation of the measures so ordered.

4.   To order the representatives of the beneficiaries and the Inter-American Commission to submit their observations to the State's reports within a term of four and six weeks, respectively, next following receipt of the referenced State's reports.

5.   To notify this Order to the Inter-American Commission, the representatives and the State.

22-Aug-2007
Order of the President of the Inter-American Court of Human Rights
Request for the Broadening of Provisional Measures in the Matter of the Mendoza Prisons

CONSIDERING:

6.   That on March 24, 2007, the representatives filed before the Court—pursuant to Article 63(2) of the Convention and Article 25 of the Rules of Procedure—a "request to broaden" the provisional measures granted, so as to extend the same to those persons who have been deprived of their liberty at the *Complejo Penitenciario III (Almafuerte)* (III Penitentiary Complex [Almafuerte]) located at Cacheuta, "taking into account that the persons that are deprived of their liberty at the Mendoza Penitentiary are being referred to this new detention center" (*supra* Having Seen clause 8.) The representatives expressed, *inter alia*, that in Sectors I and II the inmates are subject to 21-hour confinement in individual cellblocks. As regards health conditions, several inmates reported the lack of medical treatment and also requests for medical assistance that have not been addressed. There is almost no communication with the penitentiary agents, and such officers refuse to refer requests for hearings and *habeas corpus* petitions. There are several inmates fasting to protest because they denounce that they cannot communicate with their families. They are not allowed to have radios, watches or television sets. Searches are carried out by "stripping visitors and inmates and they include rectal tact," as a condition to let the visitor in (*supra* Having Seen Clauses N° 8, 9 and 11.) Furthermore, they sent a copy of a "corrective writ of *habeas corpus*" filed with regard to the inmate Carlos Molina-Ponce, who might be incarcerated in the *Complejo Penitenciario III (Almafuerte)* (III Penitentiary Complex [Almafuerte]) "since his detention, conditions have seriously worsened and they requested such conditions to be ceased." According to the statements made in such writ of *habeas corpus* filed "[Molina-Ponce] is subject to extended confinement periods, and sanctions or punishments are applied to him without serving notice to his defense attorney; he has to endure inhuman cruel and degrading treatment, he is not assisted with any labor therapy and needs urgent psychological treatment. He does not have any access to a free communication with the outside world and the authorities."

7.   That in the objections to such petition to broaden the provisional measures, the State pointed out that "the said petition was filed by the representatives of the petitioners and not by the Commission", and it further pointed out that it considered that "any request to broaden the scope of the provisional measures, for facts other than those occurring in the penitentiaries stated in the Order of November 22, 2004, should be filed by the Commission" (*supra* Having Seen Clause N° 14.)

8.   That the Inter-American Commission considered that, "in view of the information sent by the representatives of the beneficiaries; and considering the court order issued by the Criminal Sentence Execution Judge of the Province of Mendoza regarding the writ of *habeas corpus* filed with respect to the inmate Carlos Molina-Ponce, wherein certain facts affecting the personal integrity of the inmates at the "Almafuerte" penitentiary are proved; and further taking into account the information published by the newspapers in Mendoza, regarding the invasive physical searches which are conducted on the inmates referred to the "Almafuerte" penitentiary in a so-called "rubber room" within the penitentiary center, there exists a serious risk of causing irreparable damage to the personal integrity; and therefore, the request for provisional measures is found to be appropriate." The Commission requested that the measures to be ordered include: "the protection to the right to life and humane treatment of the inmates incarcerated in the "Almafuerte" penitentiary; to protect inmates against cruel, inhuman and degrading treatment such as, *inter alia*, extended confinement periods and mistreatment; to suspend invasive physical searches on inmates and persons visiting the penitentiary; to investigate the facts (*supra* Having Seen Clause N° 13.) The President shall proceed to determine if the material facts concur in order to direct the broadening of the said provisional measures.

9.   That in the objections to the request to broaden the provisional measures, the State reported, *inter alia*, that back then, in the *Complejo Penitenciario III (Almafuerte)* (III Penitentiary Complex [Almafuerte]) only Module V was in use, such unit was designed with a maximum security level, and at that time there were 42 inmates, all of them convicted, 17 of whom were recidivists, all of them of Argentine nationality and of age, and each lodged in an individual cell. The State further reported that the construction of the Complex had not finished yet and that it was contemplated to operate at full capacity by July, 2007; that it would have five modules, one maximum security and four medium security modules respectively, totaling 938 lodging places; the State further pointed out that recreational activities were carried on in three wings of the operating module and also that inmates had one hour of recreational activities in the indoors yard of the penitentiary; and further stated that a system of rules for the registration of persons and property was being drafted to be approved and applied to the whole penitentiary system. Meanwhile, the Complex Director issued Memorandum 001/07 on March, 26, 2007, to fix standards to be applied to the registration of visitors. Among such standards, it was stated that "staff making the searches shall be of the same gender as the visitor. If the visitor does not consent to the search, the visitor shall be allowed to contact the inmate through a phone cabin. It is strictly forbidden to apply degrading treatment and to carry on rectal or vaginal tact; [...] and as regards inmates, [... it is forbidden] to conduct searches by rectal tact,

this shall only be allowed in extreme circumstances and shall be completed by medical staff;" pursuant to Memorandum 003/07, any petitions made by inmates, whether orally or in writing, must be received by security personnel, and must be delivered to the Penitentiary Director by the Module Chief Officer. All inmates confined therein have been interviewed by the Director [or] by Officers, and there are 6 medical doctors on duty 24 hours a day, psychological and dental assistance is also provided. As regards the request to broaden the provisional measures, the State further declared that the inmates confined at the Almafuerte Complex are duly classified (only convicts are confined therein), no events have occurred that may allow to believe that the physical integrity of the inmates is endangered, since they are properly watched over and medical checks are conducted. There is no overcrowding, no lack of hygiene, or improper feeding. The request of the petitioners is based on the writ of *habeas corpus* upheld by the Criminal Sentence Execution Judge, and the State has complied with all the measures ordered by the said judge. Therefore, there are no reasons that may justify the international jurisdiction, and thus, the intervention of the Court. Due to the aforesaid, the State considered that all the information available is not enough to conclude that there exists a situation of extreme seriousness and urgency and that irreparable harm can be caused, so as to justify a possible broadening of the provisional measures so as to extend their effects to all those inmates confined in the *Complejo Penitenciario III (Almafuerte)* (III Penitentiary Complex [Almafuerte])

10.   That the request to broaden the provisional measures was brought before the Court during its previous Extraordinary Session, as well as the observations and notes directed to the Presidents of both the Court and the Commission in May 2007, by means of which the State invited "the President [of the Commission...] to pay a personal visit [to the *Complejo Penitenciario III (Almafuerte)* (III Penitentiary Complex [Almafuerte]]." At that time, the Court considered it proper that, before making any decision regarding the request to broaden the provisional measures, the Inter-American Convention informed its decision as to the invitation extended by the State, as well as its current opinion on the need to broaden the provisional measures at issue (*supra* Having Seen Clause No. 19). The Commission replied, after the last Regular Session of the Court, that "...should it gather the necessary resources it would prepare a visit for the end of the year..." (*supra* Having Seen Clauses No. 20 and 24).

11.   That the representatives filed an *habeas corpus* remedy at domestic level based on the same grounds alleged for requesting the broadening of these measures (*supra* Having Seen Clauses No. 8 and 9 and Considering Clause No. 6). A provincial court of criminal enforcement accepted the *habeas corpus* remedy filed through a decision dated March 23, 2007, in which "apart from Medina Ponce, other 40 inmates institutionalized therein are also benefited after having been interviewed, after having requested reports and after having paid a

visit to the Detention Center." As informed by the representatives, in the above mentioned Judgment, *inter alia*, it was decided,

> TO SUMMON the Director of the *Complejo Penitenciario III (Almafuerte)* (III Penitentiary Complex [Almafuerte]) in Cacheuta, in order that he immediately starts the negotiations, gives orders and/or executes the necessary proceedings so that any cruel, inhuman and degrading treatment to which the inmates confined in SECTORS 1 and 2 of the said Complex are subjected to comes to an end [...; to] ensure their right to petition, thus instrumenting a fast and effective channel to forward the different writs and/or mail directed—without previous censorship—to the judicial and/or administrative authorities [...;] so that he effects the proceedings necessary to provide and/or allow the access of radio and/or television sets to grant the right to information that the inmates have [...;] so that within [five days] he effects all the negotiations necessary to provide any means of telephone communication to the inmates confined in Complex III in order to guarantee their right to communication [...] TO RECOMMEND the Director of the *Complejo Penitenciario III (Almafuerte)* (III Penitentiary Complex [Almafuerte]) in Cacheuta to reorganize the activities of the inmates confined in SECTORS 1 and 2 of that Complex so that they are allowed to have more breaks and consequently reduce the number of hours they remain confined, provided the Institution security so allows.

12.   That as informed by the State, after this decision of the Criminal Enforcement Court, the Director of the III Penitentiary Complex issued several memos ordering a series of measures and guidelines aimed to correct the situations of fact which gave rise to the request for broadening the provisionary measures (*supra* Considering Clause No. 9).

13.   That before the request to broaden the provisional measures ordered by this Court, according to information added to the case file, the domestic courts—including the Argentinean Supreme Court— passed several judgments regarding the facts that originated them and which order the protection of the people deprived of liberty in the Province of Mendoza in general. This Presidency considers the attention of the domestic courts to the above described situation to be of utmost importance and in that sense and it enhances the following decisions:

(a) In a judgment of February 13, 2007, the National Supreme Court considered, *inter alia*, that "[...] as custodian of the constitutional safeguards and due to the lack of results regarding the order issued by the Inter-American Court of Human Rights, it sees itself in the inevitable obligation to order the National State to adopt the measures to put an end to the situation of the penitentiary facilities of the Province of Mendoza within twenty days, and to take the measures that shall be stated in the operative part of this judgment [...]" and it decided:

> "I.- To order the National State to adopt the necessary measures to put an end to the situation of the penitentiary facilities of the Province of Mendoza within twenty days; II.- To order the Supreme Court of Mendoza as well as the courts of all instances of that province, in their respective jurisdictions and by decision of this Supreme Court—considering the urgency of the case—to cause any eventual aggravation of a detention situation which may imply cruel, inhuman or degrading treatment or any other kind of treatment susceptible of entailing the international liability of Federal State, to come to an end; III.- To order that every twenty days the National Executive Power informs the Court on the measures it adopts to improve the situation of the detainees. Serve notice upon [...] the National Executive Power (Ministry of Justice and Human Rights); and the governor of the Province of Mendoza [...]"

(b) In a Decision of February 14, 2007, the Supreme Court of Mendoza ruled:

> 1. To serve notice and inform on the content of the decision [of the National Supreme Court of February 13, 2007], to all the Courts of the Province of Mendoza for its fulfillment and to cause any eventual aggravation of the detention conditions which may imply a violation of Article 18 of the National Constitution to come to an end; 2. To order an extraordinary visit to female penitentiaries *Boulogne Sur Mer* and *Gustavo André*, which shall be conducted by the Justices of this Court to all the penitentiary facilities of the Province; 3. To order the immediate verification of the conditions in the penitentiary institutions through Criminal Enforcement Judges; 4. To set [a] hearing for February 19 [2007] so that the Governor of the Province of Mendoza appears before this Court to inform on the degree of fulfillment of the provisional measures [sic] set by the Inter-American Court of Human Rights; and to request the National Supreme Court to subpoena the

National Executive Power so that it immediately proceeds to relocate the federal inmates institutionalized in the Provincial Penitentiary.

(c) In an administrative order issued on March 1, 2007, the Supreme Court of Mendoza, "[a]nalyzing the content of the judgment passed by the National Supreme Court in the case of 'Lavado Diego et al vs. the Province of Mendoza', [...] as it is the duty of this Court to cause any situation implying any cruel, degrading treatment to come to an end, or the end of any other treatment contrary to the National Constitution", *inter alia*, considered

"That from the visit paid on February 10 of this year it was possible to verify the state of precariousness and lack of hygiene of the facilities of "Bulogne Sur Mer" Penitentiary institution, " [...]

The deplorable state of the restrooms and the spots aimed for personal hygiene purposes has also been verified, as well as that they are completely insufficient in number for their physiological needs, without any respect whatsoever for the basic right to privacy as they have no doors; in fact, bags and plastic bottles are actually used for that matter.

That the minimum dignity conditions suppose, at least, the existence of a bed to rest and a proper place for hygiene purposes, conditions absolutely nonexistent within Bulogne Sur Mer facility, and impossible to correct with the necessary urgency they require.-

Notwithstanding that, and considering the above mentioned peremptoriness, it is not impossible to mitigate the extremely serious situation by means of some urgent and immediate measures, while expecting the activation of penitentiary institution "Almafuerte".

[AND] DECID[ed]:

A. To communicate the Provincial Executive Power that with the highest possible degree of urgency it shall;

(1) Proceed to disinfect Bulogne Sur Mer penitentiary in order to eradicate insects (cockroaches) taking the proper measures for the permanent cleansing of the cellblocks.

(2) Provide chemical toilets, substitute or other type of toilets in a sufficient number in the different cellblocks which allow the privacy and dignity for the physiological needs of the inmates.

(3) Cause the situation of excessive overcrowding to cease, relocating the inmates in dignified conditions.

(4) Adopt the measures to efficiently guarantee the inmates physical integrity so as to avoid situations which may risk their life.

(5) Provide permanent control, care and medical assistance for the inmates, especially those of cellblock No. 15.

[...]

(d) In a decision of March 20, 2007, the National Supreme Court ruled on the merits of the lawsuit filed (*supra* Considering Clause No. 13(a)). Although it decided that the case "is not of the original jurisdiction of this National Supreme Court" and it ordered "to forward the case file to the *Cámara Nacional de Apelaciones en lo Contencioso Administrativo Federal* (National Appellate Court on Federal Administrative Matters) for the pertinent purposes [... and] certified copies of the case file to the Supreme Court of Mendoza", it considered, *inter alia*:

(13) That, in effect, it is convenient to remember that the National Executive Power has the power to represent the State in the context of matters which may involve the responsibility of the country within the international scope, as that branch has been constitutionally granted the exercise of the foreign affairs of the Nation.

(14) That among those hypotheses we find this case, where the National Executive Power –as custodian of the interests of the National State- shall act for an interest of its own regarding the consequences that the fulfillment or the non-fulfillment of the recommendations and decisions adopted by the Commission and the Inter-American Court of Human Rights with respect to the facts denounced may entail. It is the National Executive Power which has passive legal standing in the claim, and not the Province of Mendoza. The matter has exceeded the domestic scope of the State, and that prevents the above mentioned provincial State from being one of the bearers of the legal relationship on which the above mentioned claims are based, regardless of their fundament [...] The provincial State can not be granted the capacity to contradict the specific matter the proceeding shall be about [...]

(15) That even the tenor of the decisions and communications of the international bodies which take part in the claims that give rise to this proceedings—attached hereto—reveal

that the legal relationship invoked, and on which basis it is sought to enforce the fulfillment of the recommendations and decisions adopted by the Commission and by the Inter-American Court of Human Rights, directly links the claimants to the National State and not to the Province of Mendoza.

(16) That for that matter it is proper to emphasize that the Inter-American Court of Human Rights itself stated—when analyzing the admissibility of the provisional measures requested, the purpose of which is to alter the denounced situation of fact— that "...it is aware that the relief and the improvement of the situation of the penitentiaries of Mendoza constitutes a short, medium and long-term process, which requires a set of actions of administrative, judicial and eventually legislative nature by the federal and provincial authorities so as to correct the imprisonment and detention conditions. However, before this Court's order to adopt provisional measures, the purpose of which is the protection of the life and the integrity of the inmates detained in those penitentiaries and of the people within the facilities, the State can not allege domestic law grounds to refrain from taking firm, concrete and effective courses of action so as to fulfill the ordered measures to prevent any additional deaths. Neither can the State allege the lack of coordination between the federal and the provincial authorities to avoid the deaths and acts of violence which have continued to exist during their enforcement. Regardless of the unitary of federal structure of a State Party to the Convention, before the international jurisdiction it is the State as such which appears before the bodies which supervise that treaty, and the State is the only one obliged to adopt the measures. The lack of adoption of the provisional measures on the part of the State compromises its international liability" (judgment of March 30, 2006, Considering Clause No. 11, page 98). It is not pointless to state that in that same sense was the judgment of the Inter-American Court in the case of "Garrido and Baigorria vs. Argentina", judgment of August 27, 1998; and in Advisory Opinion Number 16 of October 1, 1999, on "the Right to Information on Consular Assistance in the Context of the Guarantees of Due Process of Law."

(17) That in that way, a decision contrary to the one sought, and as a consequence of which it would be possible to pursue the enforcement of the provisional measures adopted by the Inter-American Court—by means of the alleged accumulation—both against the National State and the Province of Mendoza, would imply as much as emptying the content of Article 99, subparagraph 1, of the National Constitution, and the international commitments undertaken by the Argentine Nation. [...]

(20) That regardless of all the above, it is important to enhance that, as a consequence of the decision of this Court of February 13, 2007, the Supreme Court of Mendoza issued decision No. 20,037, dated February 14, 2007, by means of which—among other provisions—it requested this Court to "subpoena the National Executive Power so that it proceeds to the immediate and urgent relocation of the federal inmates incarcerated in the Provincial Penitentiary"; and this Court must adjudge on the matter as the request is directed to it.

(21) That the request must not be received through the alleged way. According to the provisions stated in law 24,660, regarding the points of interest herein, the State and the provinces may enter into agreements aimed to receive or transfer convicts from their respective jurisdictions, and the said transfer shall be charged to the petitioning State (Articles 212 and subsequent of the above mentioned law). The Province of Mendoza adhered to that provision by passing law 6,513. Consequently, the National Executive Power could barely be summoned to perform the above mentioned "immediate and urgent relocation" by request of just one of the powers of the local State when these institutionalizations exist on the basis of agreements entered into by the States, which legitimate representatives understood that the application of the system was convenient to guarantee a better individualization of the penalty and an effective integration of the Republic's penitentiary system (Article 212 quoted above).

14.   That in view of the principle of subsidiarity informed by the Inter-American System of human rights, an order for the adoption (or the broadening) of provisional measures under Article 63(2) of the American Convention is justified

in situations of extreme seriousness and urgency and before the possibility of irreparable damage to the people respect to whom the ordinary guarantees existing in the State where they are requested turn out to be insufficient or not effective, or where the domestic authorities can not or do not want to make them prevail.

15.   That regarding the people deprived of liberty in the Provincial Penitentiary of Mendoza who were then transferred to the *Complejo Penitenciario III (Almafuerte)* (III Penitentiary Complex [Almafuerte]) in Cacheuta, a provincial Criminal Enforcement Judge ordered the adoption of measures and the Director of the Penitentiary Complex issued several provisions on the matter (*supra* Having Seen Clauses No. 8, 9, 12, 17 and 18 and Considering Clauses No. 6, 8, 9, 11 and 12). According to what has been informed, the construction of this Complex and the transfer of people thereto are solutions to which the State has turned to deal with the overcrowding problem in other penitentiaries, which is precisely one of the situations of fact which gave rise to the provisional measures at issue. In its last report, the State pointed out that at present there are 131 people deprived of liberty in the *Complejo Penitenciario III (Almafuerte)* (III Penitentiary Complex [Almafuerte]), who were transferred from the Provincial Penitentiary; the assisting professional staff that works there amounts to 23 people and the security guards would total 108 officers (*supra* Having Seen Clause No. 22). The representatives informed that a person who was confined in Almafuerte might have died on July 17, 2007 in a hospital, "after being assisted due to a diagnosis of pneumonitis" (*supra* Having Seen Clause No. 23). Thus, the Court has not been informed on facts which reveal or imply a situation of extreme seriousness and urgency for the life and the integrity of the people deprived of liberty within that Penitentiary Complex.

16.   That although it is not admissible to broaden the provisional measures herein referred to, it is convenient to remember that Article 1(1) of the Convention sets forth the general obligations that the States Party have to respect the rights and liberties consecrated therein, and to guarantee their free and total exercise to any person subjected to their jurisdiction, which are imposed not only with respect to the power of the State, but also with respect to the actions of third parties. This Court has considered that the State is in a special position of guarantor of the people deprived of their liberty in penitentiaries or detention centers, due to the fact that penitentiary authorities exercise total control over them. [130] Furthermore, "[o]ne of the obligations that the State must inevitably assume in its position as guarantor, and in order to protect and guarantee the right to life and physical integrity of those deprived of liberty, is that of [seeking] them the minimum conditions compatible with their dignity as they remain in detention centers". [231] Thus, regardless of the existence of specific provisional measures, the State is especially obliged to guarantee the rights of the people in circumstances of deprivation of liberty.

NOW THEREFORE:

THE PRESIDENT OF THE INTER-AMERICAN COURT OF HUMAN RIGHTS,

Exercising the authority conferred upon him by Article 63(2) of the American Convention on Human Rights and Articles 25 and 29 of its Rules of Procedure, and in consultation with the other Magistrates of the Court,

DECIDES:

1.   To overrule the request for broadening the provisional measures ordered in the case of the Penitentiaries of Mendoza filed by the beneficiaries' representatives and backed-up by the Inter-American Commission on Human Rights, in the terms of operative paragraphs 10 to 16 herein.

2.   To request the State to maintain the provisional measures ordered by the Inter-American Court of Human Rights in its Orders of November 22, 2004, of June 18, 2005 and of March 30, 2006.

3.   To serve notice of this Order to the Inter-American Commission, the representatives and the State.

27-Nov-2007

Order of the Inter-American Court of Human Rights

Provisional Measures Regarding Argentina

Matter of Mendoza Prisons

THEREFORE:

THE INTER-AMERICAN COURT OF HUMAN RIGHTS,

by virtue of the authority granted by Article 63(2) of the American Convention on Human Rights and Article 25 and 29 of its Rules of Procedure,

DECIDES:

1.   To fully ratify the Order of the President of the Court of August 22, 2007.

2.   To order the State to continue adopting the effective and necessary provisional measures to efficiently protect the life and integrity of all the persons held in custody in the Mendoza Provincial Prison and those in the Gustavo André Unit of Lavalle, as well as every person found within those facilities, especially to eradicate the risk of violent death and the deficient conditions of security and internal control in confinement centers, pursuant to the provisions set out in the Order of the Court of March 30, 2006.

3.   To order the State to report to the Inter-American Court every two months next following its latest report, specifically on the actions taken in compliance with the orders of this Court. In particular, it is paramount that the adoption of the priority measures established in [. . .] this Order gets reflected in the State's reports describing the specific results obtained in agreement with the specific needs of protection of the beneficiaries thereof. In this sense, the role of the Inter-American

Commission is particularly important so as to adequately and effectively follow up the implementation of the measures so ordered.

4.   To request the representatives of the beneficiaries and the Inter-American Commission to submit their observations to the State's reports within a term of four and six weeks, respectively, next following receipt of the referred State's reports.

5.   No notify this Order to the Inter-American Commission, the representatives and the State.

26-Nov-2010
Order of the Inter-American Court of Human Rights
Provisional Measures Regarding the Republic of Argentina
Matter of Mendoza Penitentiaries

CONSIDERING THAT:

3.   These provisional measures were initially ordered through an Order dated November 22, 2004, in which the Court found that "from the background presented by the Commission on this matter, as well as from the State's statements, it can be deduced *prima facie* that […] a situation of extreme gravity and urgency prevail[ed] in [the Mendoza provincial penitentiary and Gustavo André Unit in Lavalle] such that the lives and integrity of the individuals deprived of liberty in [those facilities] and of the individuals found within them were at grave risk and vulnerable." Later, that judgment was reiterated by the Court in rulings dated June 18, 2005, March 30, 2006, and November 27, 2007, which maintain the order for provisional measures upon considering that the situation of extreme gravity and urgency persisted. In addition, a request by the representatives for the provisional measures to be broadened to the benefit of individuals imprisoned in another penitentiary (Penitentiary Complex III "Almafuerte" in Cacheuta) was dismissed (*supra* Having Seen 7). Also, case No. 12.532, "Inmates of the Mendoza Penitentiary," is being processed in the merits stage before the Inter-American Commission. In the context of that case, the petitioners and the State have reached a friendly settlement agreement that is pending approval of the corresponding proceeding on the part of the Commission (*infra* Considering 10). In its latest reports submitted during the year 2010, the State has asked that the provisional measures be lifted.

4.   Given the period during which these provisional measures are in force, the results of the *in situ* visit to the penitentiaries carried out by a delegation of the Commission in April of 2009 and its corresponding report (*supra* Having Seen 13), and the aforementioned request for the measures to be lifted, it is necessary to carry out an examination of the progress made in the implementation of the provisional measures before weighing the need to maintain them, as follows: i)

information beyond the purpose of the provisional measures; ii) analysis on the implementation of the provisional measures; and iii) the request that the measures be lifted.

(i) Information submitted that is beyond the purpose of the provisional measures

5.   The Tribunal has already established on prior occasions that in the context of provisional measures, it does not fall to the Court to consider the merits of any argument that is not strictly related to extreme gravity, urgency and the need to avoid irreparable damages to the beneficiaries. Any other matter can be brought before the Court in an adversarial case or in requests for advisory opinions. [11][32]

6.   The representatives have submitted a variety of information on the legislative measures adopted with regard generally to individuals deprived of liberty in the Province of Mendoza. Regarding this, they expressed their concern over legislation that they consider to be "repressive or in violation of human rights," indicating that Law No. 7.929 on prisoner releases restricts the right to freedom during criminal proceeding, which according to them brings with it a "considerable increase in the prison population." They also indicated that the program of the Ministry of the Government for the chemical castration of sex offenders established both medical and therapeutic treatment through Decree No. 308 of March 3, 2010, a decree intended to prevent parliamentary debate on it. Also, even when the Tribunal decided not to broaden the provisional measures to cover Penitentiary Complex III "Almafuerte" in Cacheuta (*supra* Having Seen 7), the representatives continued to submit information on it.

7.   For its part, the State made detailed reference to the manner in which the legal defense of the inmates was carried out in administrative disciplinary proceedings in the penitentiaries via a team of public defenders staffed by officials operatively and functionally answering to the Human Rights Directorate, under the Subsecretariat of Justice and Human Rights[.] Those defenders took charge of reporting to the Human Rights Directorate of the Province on any problems taking place in any penitentiary unit, along with attending to the complaints brought by the inmates before that directorate via petitions prepared in writing or through their relatives. It also indicated that recently, an Office of the Attorney General Law was passed providing for the creation of ombudsman's offices for sentence execution. Regarding this, the Commission held, *inter alia*, that "justice is being neglected" as the judicial administrative penitentiary sentence execution proceedings are slow; it indicated that there are only two sentence execution judges and that the slowness of the proceedings prevent the application of the differentiated regimen while the inmates of the Gustavo André prison facility, in Lavalle, did not receive prompt attention to their requests for temporary leave and other benefits.

8.   Elsewhere, the State indicated that in the San Felipe prison, 325 inmates are "being educated" and 350 work; and in the Boulogne Sur Mer prison, 325 inmates are studying and 351 participate in labor activities. In the André complex, in Lavalle, they have satellite classrooms with 75 lecture hours to implement various courses. Although the representatives did not make specific reference to this point, the Commission indicated that "one of the frequent causes of violence among the prisoners continues to be the lack of activities to occupy them during recreational hours." The Commission also observed during its *in loco* visit carried out in 2009 that there is "a high percentage of inmates who do not have access to any kind of labor, educational, or recreational activity, nor access to telephones to communicate with the outside world" and, with regard to the inmates in the Prison Farm, observed "with satisfaction that all of them benefit from technical training programs in agricultural work, programs that are run by professionals."

9.   With regard to sanitary and health conditions, the State indicated that it had taken several measures to improve the situation of those deprived of liberty in the penitentiaries. [12][33] The representatives observed that "it is true that a health program has been implemented that has improved coverage with regard to the physical health of the inmates. However, the greater concern is the mental health of the penitentiary population" due to the high number of suicides. For its part, although the Commission viewed positively information provided by the State, it highlighted that suicides continue to take place and observed that the State failed to present "precise information with regard to the conditions of the sanitary facilities, access to portable water, and hygiene measures."

10.   These provisional measures arose out of the situation of extreme urgency and gravity characterized by intra-prison violence that put the lives and integrity of the inmates in grave risk due to the grave overcrowding situation, security and guard deficiencies, and the existence of weapons held by the inmates, among other factors. Specifically, in its order handed down on March 30, 2006, the Court found that the goal of these measures is focused on effectively protecting the life and integrity of all the persons held in custody in the Mendoza Provincial Prison and those in the Gustavo André Unit of Lavalle, as well as every person found within those facilities, especially to "eradicate the risk of violent death and the deficient conditions of security and internal control in confinement centers." [13][34] At that time it was found that, among other measures necessary to overcome that situation, the State must prioritize the following: An increase in the number of penitentiary personnel intended to guarantee security in the facilities; the elimination of weapons within the facility; a change in guard patterns in such a way as to ensure adequate oversight, and the effective presence of penitentiary personnel in the blocks; and to apply these measures immediately in order to "progressively improve the conditions of detention." Subsequent to that Order,

the Court has viewed positively the agreements reached between the State, the Commission, and the representatives, expressed in the so-called "Asunción Accords," establishing a series of measures to be applied immediately, along with other measures to be applied more gradually and progressively, without this implying that the Court must supervise those agreements given the purpose of the measures and the fact that an open petition exists before the Inter-American System.[14 35]

11.   Taking this into account, the Court views positively the information submitted by the State on the different measures taken to improve detention conditions through programs to educate individuals deprived of liberty in the penitentiaries,[15 36] along with the efforts to improve the educational and recreational activities, as well as measures related to sanitary and health conditions and other additional measures to improve the security situation inside the prisons (*supra* Considering 8 and 9). However, a significant part of the information presented by the representatives, the Commission, and the State is outside the purpose of these provisional measures, such as the information referencing aspects of due process in administrative proceedings launched in connection with incidents taking place inside the penitentiaries; incidents allegedly having taken place in a different penitentiary named Almafuerte; the issuing of rules authorizing methods of chemical castration for individuals convicted of sex crimes; and a law that allegedly restricts personal liberty during criminal proceedings, among others. Therefore, the Court will not rule on this and will hereinafter rule only on aspects pertaining to the central protective purpose of these measures (*supra* Considering 10).

(ii) Analysis of the implementation of the provisional measures

1. Measures to correct overcrowding

12.   The State reported that in order to confront the situation of overcrowding through the restructuring of the penitentiary system, the Province of Mendoza built a totally new prison facility called the Almafuerte complex with holding capacity for 940 inmates; it inaugurated the Borbollón prison unit intended exclusively for the imprisonment of women; and it built the San Felipe II prison complex, which currently has capacity for 960 inmates and as of the issuing of this order contained 551 inmates. Likewise, the State reported that it inaugurated two new modules in the Gustavo André prison complex in Lavelle where "inmates are housed who have reached the final stage in the progressive imprisonment regimen." That prison has the capacity to hold 130 inmates. In addition, Blocks 4 and 12 of the Boulogne Sur Mer complex were demolished in order to be reconstructed. This complex is part of the Mendoza Provincial Penitentiary. Regarding this penitentiary, the State reported that the inmate population of the Boulogne Sur Mer complex has

been reduced from 1650 inmates in 2004, when the measures were ordered, to 872 inmates, with its holding capacity at 890 slots. This capacity will be increased to 960 slots when the "locative arrangements" reach their conclusion.

13.   The State indicated that it continues to implement short, medium, and long term measures toward achieving the total restructuring of its penitentiary system. In this way, it indicated that, in order to improve the overcrowding situation, the Province of Mendoza and the Nation of Argentina have agreed on the construction of a federal prison with a capacity to receive 520 federal inmates, thus lessening the crowding in the provincial prisons. The Province of Mendoza has already ceded land that will be used for this facility and a public tender is being opened. The project is expected to begin in March of 2011. Likewise, building renovations are pending in order to totally restructure the Boulogne Sur Mer complex over a period of three years. The State also reported that it completed the construction of the kitchen, bakery, and occupational therapy and maintenance workshops in the San Felipe complex. In addition, it has built a new micro hospital within the San Felipe complex. This will allow for full first aid care and postsurgical internment for all the inmates of units one and two of Boulogne Sur Mer and San Felipe.

14.   With regard to that issue, the representatives of the beneficiaries indicated that the capacity of the penitentiary facilities of Mendoza "is being exceeded [...] by a total of 615 inmates," with a constant increase in the capacity deficit in the majority of the penitentiary units between 2008 at 2009. The representatives argued that it is crucial for the Mendoza government to effectively carry out the total reconstruction of the Boulogne Sur Mer facilities, as any kind of partial renovations do nothing but prolong the agony of that building. They say that it should be totally demolished, as ordered by the Supreme Court of Mendoza toward the end of 2009.

15.   The Commission viewed positively the fact that block seven of the provincial beneficiary was demolished, as this had been the most problematic in terms of violence, and that block four is partially demolished. It noted that block two has been shut down, that currently its future functions are being weighed, and that a block for homosexual inmates has been set up and is in excellent condition. The Commission indicated that at the time of its *in loco* visit, the population of the Provincial Penitentiary equaled more than 1500 inmates, 883 of them being held in the "interior" area, and the remaining in the "San Felipe complex," known previously as the "exterior area." The Commission expressed its concern over what the representative had expressed with regard to the overpopulation of the Boulogne Sur Mer Penitentiary by more than 200%. In contrast, it stated that the situation had been overcome in the Gustavo André facility, in Lavalle, following the remodeling of the block affected by the fire in May of 2004.

16.   The Court notes that the State has reported on several structural modifications to the facilities of the provincial penitentiaries and that the Supreme

Court of Justice of Mendoza had ordered the remodeling of the Boulogne Sur Mer complex (*supra* Considering 14). The Tribunal highlights that the State has provided information on measures adopted to remedy the overcrowding in the penitentiaries that have been the object of the provisional measures ordered by the Tribunal. Consequently, although the overcrowding situation has not been completely remedied, as problems remain in various areas of the penitentiary complexes, the situation has substantially improved and is different from the prevailing situation when the measures were ordered in the year 2004[.] This allows the Tribunal to consider that one of the purposes of the provisional measures has been complied with, although the elimination of all overcrowding in the penitentiaries has not taken place. This is of course necessary but it exceeds the central protective purpose of the measures.

2. Separation of individuals deprived of liberty

17.   The State reported that in order to comply with international standards, it has separated the inmates according to categories as follows:

- Complex number one, Boulogne Sur Mer, is reserved only for inmates who are on trial, with specific exceptions in cases in which the life or integrity of an individual faces risk in facilities for inmates who have been sentenced.
- Complexes numbers two and three, San Felipe and Almafuerte, are reserved for inmates whose final sentences have been issued and are at the disposal of the Sentence Execution judges of the Province or the Federal courts.
- Unit number three, El Borbollón, is reserved exclusively for women. For their part, young adults between the ages of 18 and 21 are held in the San Felipe complex in an area totally separated from the rest of the prison population. In the same way, the inmates undergoing a test period for execution of sentences of deprivation of liberty under the regimen provided for in Law No. 24.660 are housed in the San Felipe complex.
- Finally, the ones serving the final stages of their sentences are housed in unit number four, Gustavo André. Likewise, the State reported that the Gustavo André unit, in Lavalle, is housing 54 convicted inmates who enjoy "test period privileges" where they do occupational therapy tasks —principally of a rural kind: farm work and maintenance.

18.   Regarding this, both the representatives and the Commission recognized the progress with regard to the separation of the inmates into categories. However, the Commission highlighted that completion of this task is still pending, considering that as of the end of 2009 more than 80 individuals on trial were

still located in the internal section and the inmates who had been convicted did not receive differentiated treatment according to their ages, status of completion of the sentence, or the nature of the crime for which they were convicted. It also highlighted that a small percentage of the detainees in that penitentiary system are elderly individuals who could benefit from measures that are alternatives to deprivation of liberty and commented that a small percentage of the penitentiary population of a homosexual orientation is being housed in a special block with detention conditions that are "very different" from the others.

19.   The Court highlights the progress made by the State with regard to separating the inmates into different categories, noting that this progress has had positive effects with regard to the security situation of the inmates and denotes the State's willingness to comply with international standards on the treatment of individuals deprived of liberty.

3. Internment measures with security and guard personnel

20.   The State expressed that in order to achieve the peaceful coexistence of the inmates, it has distributed the penitentiary population among different blocks that themselves have several levels of security. In the Boulogne Sur Mer complex there are 471 security personnel officers and 196 individuals assigned to the administrative personal. Likewise, the complex has 287 inmates who are isolated because of problems with communal living, of which 192 have done so voluntarily and 95 under court order. In this context, the prison facility has 14 blocks, the majority of which allow free movement from 0700 hrs. to 1900 hrs. and three of which have night lockdown. Only two blocks allow free movement 24 hours, one reserved for inmates without behavioral problems and the other for those "with a different sexual condition." Likewise, the State indicated that it has set up a unit there with capacity to hold 60 convicted inmates facing exceptional circumstances. The rest of the blocks are intended to hold isolated inmates for reasons of security and based on the nature of the crime committed. For its part, the San Felipe Penitentiary Complex II has eight modules, each module with capacity for 60 inmates divided into two floors, each one with 40 cells. Both cells have a common patio that is partially open featuring natural and artificial light. As regarding young adults, in order to facilitate communal living, a maximum of 30 inmates is permitted per unit. The hours of free movement and lockdown within the complex varies between 0700 hrs. and 2200 hrs., taking into account "that [L]aw [No.] 24.660 requires that inmates in the advanced stage of the progressive sentence regimen have access to open detention spaces to educate the inmates on self-discipline, for which reason the San Felipe complex is intended specifically for that purpose. This means that the adults housed in that unit have flexible rules and few hours of cell lockdown."

21.   Additionally, the State indicated that in order to improve the security situation in the penitentiary complexes, currently a total of 2,020 individuals are guarding them as penitentiary personnel, compared to 2,719 inmates currently. In this process, the State expressed that in 2008 a total of 338 penitentiary personnel were hired. Of them, 260 hold positions of security personnel and carry out guard duties. The remaining 78 agents work as administrative and professional personnel. In 2009, a total of 318 penitentiary personnel were hired. Of them, 271 hold positions of security personnel and carry out guard duties. The remaining 47 agents work as administrative and professional personnel. In 2010, the State has hired 70 members of the administrative personnel, and in the [. . .] month of December 2010, 220 agents were hired as security personnel, representing a total of approximately 200 hirings in the year 2010. In particular, the State reported that the Boulogne Sur Mer complex has 667 officers, of which 471 correspond to the security corps and 196 to the administrative corps. Likewise, that includes 96 individuals providing in-wall guard services divided into three companies with rotating shifts of 24 hours of work and 48 hours of rest. Additionally, in the San Felipe II penitentiary complex, 282 personnel currently provide services, of which 221 work in the security corps. The internal security division includes 120 guards distributed in 32 officials per guard shift, working 24 hours on and 48 hours off.

22.   Likewise, the State indicated that it has created a specific department for training penitentiary personnel where the different courses that have been provided in human rights, narco criminality, crisis management, criminal intelligence, transportation of inmates, guarding of high-risk inmates, and inspection training have been planned and coordinated. The State also expressed that it has trained the penitentiary security officers on specific methods of treatment and respect of human rights and that a budget for the penitentiary school has been established within the action plan budget, a school that currently does not exist in the Province.

23.   In addition, in order to prevent the presence of weapons in the facilities, the State indicated that it has set up inspection divisions, implementing them in the places where the inmates are housed. The Boulogne Sur Mer Penitentiary has a division composed of 52 officers, while the San Felipe facility has an inspection division with nine officers who carry out inspections. The inspections are carried out on a daily basis and follow a protocol with a "detailed methodological, juridical, and technical process intended to preserve respect for the inmates and prevent any kind of excesses." In addition, the inspections and Boulogne Sur Mer are recorded on video and remain at the disposal of the authorities for a period of three months. The entrance of visitors is also regulated by personnel trained to do so. The State indicated that "inspections are carried out on a daily basis and general inspections are carried out occasionally," all with the presence of General Security Inspection authorities "in order to provide all guarantees, both for the prison population and

for the penitentiary personnel." Likewise, it indicated that in advisory support of the Province, the federal penitentiary system has outlined a work methodology with the purpose of improving security patterns through greater presence in the cellblocks and increased patrols. Also, the State indicated specifically that the Boulogne Sur Mer complex has an inspection section made up of an official and 52 officers, allowing the inspections to be carried out on a daily basis. Likewise, the San Felipe II Penitentiary Complex has an inspection division made up of eight officers. They inspect the cells one at a time without using any violent methods.

24.   The representatives of the beneficiaries indicated regarding this that the State has carried out "a clear policy of increasing the number of penitentiary personnel in order to be able to provide services in the various facilities," thus allowing for an increase in the number of inmates transferred from the Boulogne Sur Mer penitentiary to the Almafuerte facility." Nevertheless, they specified that the penitentiary personnel are still not adequately trained and therefore not suitable, in addition to being subjected to exhausting work hours, and therefore the inspections they carry out are inadequate. Likewise, they reiterated that overcrowding still exists in some blocks and that penitentiary policies do not attend to the individuals in isolation. Finally, with regard to the young adults, they highlighted that the daily lockdown is more than 18 to 20 hours, as this population is the one with the most problems with violence, and violent incidents persist. According to the representatives and in accordance with the information provided by the sentence execution judge to the Mendoza Supreme Court, as regards the Gustavo André prison in Lavalle, it still does not meet security standards on its emergency sprinkler system for fires and it lacks communication equipment like telephones.

25.   Also, with regard to separation according to block, the representatives hold that information provided by the State "contradicts reality," as it cannot state that the situation has improved "in such a short time" after the Commission's visit, especially when intra-prison violence continues to be reported.

26.   In its report dated November 16, 2009, after its *in situ* visit, the Commission indicated that conditions in the Mendoza Provincial Penitentiary were deficient in terms of security and fostered violence among the inmates. This was recognized by the prison guards themselves; they confirmed that the penitentiary personnel was insufficient and that due to fear, the guards did not regularly visit the blocks, for which reason they cannot monitor what happens in places away from the yard. Also, it confirmed that the work shifts were excessive, and the guard personnel expressed that the greater need at the moment, in terms of security, was for an increase in the number of personnel. In the same way, it reported that the training provided was not sufficient and indicated that said training should "include preparation for responding to emergency situations and

for the treatment of the penitentiary population in accordance with international standards." In the same way, and although it viewed positively the increase in the number of penitentiary personnel reported by the State, the Commission requested that the State be required to provide "the details of the number of guard officials specifically assigned to the departments at issue in these provisional measures."

27.   The Court observes that while these measures have been in effect, there has been a steady increase in the number of security personnel designated for guarding inmates deprived of liberty in the penitentiaries, although it could very well be insufficient. Additionally, certain mechanisms have been implemented to improve the security conditions inside the jails, including an increase in the frequency of the inspections of the detained individuals. In turn, the concern over the correct and regular carrying out of inspections and their effectiveness in the prevention of violence and adequate and effective control of the interior of the blocks on the part of the penitentiary guards is manifest, in addition to the lack of information on the results of these inspections.

4. Incidents of prison violence and suicide

28.   In response to the suicides that have taken place in the prisons, the State indicated that it has increased care and assistance for the inmates in all the penitentiary complexes in the areas of psychological and social services, providing intensive care for the inmates at risk of committing suicide. Likewise, in the San Felipe complex it has created the Psychosocial Division, a treatment program that has made progress in the communal living of inmates, preventing disciplinary problems inside the complex. The State added that incidents of violence that put at risk the life or physical integrity of the inmates housed in the penitentiaries— like the ones that took place near the middle of 2004—have not been repeated; and that in 2010 no deaths due to fights or violent incidents have taken place, while with regard to suicides, there were two cases that took place in the months of March and May of 2010, respectively. The State also reported that the deaths and suicides that took place in previous years were attended to immediately by personnel of the general security inspectorate and by officials with the public prosecutor's offices in charge of the judicial investigations, with all cases being investigated. The State also reported that in 2009, there were four violent deaths in the Boulogne Sur Mer and San Felipe prisons, as well as four incidents of suicide.

29.   For their part, the representatives submitted specific information on grave incidents in Mendoza prisons and observed that according to news items from the year 2009, at least 15 inmates died violently in different detention places in the province, of which nine were reported as suicides and six as homicides, adding to those the six suicides and five homicides that took place during the year 2008. This brings the total to 26 deaths in the penitentiary complexes (15 suicide 11

homicides) during those years. They also made reference to two alleged suicides reported during the first months of 2010, attributing them to "the terrible and deplorable conditions of detention of individuals deprived of liberty" where poor guard and detention conditions persist. The representatives also indicated that, in accordance with indications from the place's chaplain, "it is alarming that an inmate spends 20 out of 24 hours of the day locked up and alone in a cell, without any activity to do," which "tempts them to suicide, undoubtedly." Likewise, the representatives reported on the recent incidents of violence in 2010 between the months of August and November, when at least 11 inmates were injured due to fights with knives and at least one was injured with a firearm by penitentiary guard officials during an inspection. The representatives highlighted that in addition, in accordance with the Center for the Study of Crime Policies and Human Rights in Buenos Aires, the province of Mendoza is in second place according to the metric of "number of deaths per location" in penitentiary centers in Argentina, with 15.

30.   In this sense, the Commission indicated that the urgency and gravity of the provisional measures persist, as the urgency is demonstrated "in kind by the continuation of the situation of violence and insecurity that has been partially but not completely overcome." In addition, it indicated that there has been an increase in the number of cases of homicides and suicides since 2008, many of which have not been solved. Following its visit, the Commission concluded that the nonexistence of a contingency plan for violent or unforeseen situations, the lack of control of the entry and possession of knives, the insufficient and poorly trained penitentiary personnel, the failure to separate prisoners by categories, and the deficient sanitary and physical conditions, are, among other things, factors that increase the risk for individuals imprisoned or working in the detention centers.

31.   The Court observes that, according to the information provided, two kinds of factual situations can be distinguished in which the lives or integrity of the inmates have been at risk or have been affected, namely, and according to seriousness: on one hand, incidents of violence, and on the other, suicides. It should be recalled that since 2005 and through the present day, serious incidents of violence have taken place and numerous individuals have died in the provincial penitentiary under circumstances that are not fully clear; that several inmates have been wounded and/or have suffered various kinds of humiliations in situations of violence that could have been prevented; that deficient detention conditions are still in place; that the investigations carried out have not produced solid results and that deficiencies in the security conditions and internal controls persist, including with regard to the entry and possession of weapons in the penitentiary facilities. During 2010, incidents of suicide and other incidents of violence have taken place in which several individuals have been injured due to fights with knives. It is reprehensible that while these provisional measures have been in

effect, incidents have taken place in which the lives and integrity of individuals deprived of liberty have been irreparably affected. That is to say, it should be clarified that despite the fact that the efforts of several State authorities to improve the situation have had positive results, the provisional measures have not been completely effective. Although the incidents that supposedly took place in the Almafuerte penitentiary—highlighted by the representatives—are not the subject of these measures (*supra* Considering 6), the Court observes that violent deaths have taken place in that facility even though it was built by the State precisely in order to alleviate the situation of overcrowding in the other penitentiaries. This could reveal a situation in which the violence is being transferred and the situation in question is not being truly addressed. However, the Tribunal notes that currently, a significant reduction has taken place in the incidents of violent deaths in comparison with previous years. In sum, the Court notes that although incidents of violence continue to take place, the situation of prison violence has generally improved, as it has notably diminished in the last year.

iii) On the request to lift the measures submitted by the State

32.   The State has requested on several occasions since December of 2008 (*supra* Having Seen 11) that these provisional measures be lifted on considering that the situation originating the measures has disappeared. The State indicated that "the specific actions taken by the Provincial State toward addressing the overcrowding, the separation of inmates into categories, and the training and noteworthy increase in the number of penitentiary personnel and education, among other things, [have] been demonstrated. [These elements] have tended to diminish intra-prison violence and ensure the physical integrity of inmates, preventing incidents of violence thereby also protecting the physical integrity of penitentiary personnel." It highlighted that since the six deaths that took place during the fire in 2004 in the Gustavo André Prison Colony, incidents of violence have not been repeated in that facility, and a sprinkler system has been installed there as well. The State also highlighted the increase in the number of penitentiary officers since 2004 to 2020 officers as of November 2010, of which 1411 are guards, for a total population of 2719 individuals deprived of liberty. The State indicated that "it has adopted and continues to implement short-, medium-, and long-term measures to deal with the structural problems and in order to improve and correct the situation of the Mendoza penitentiaries in the understanding that the duty to adopt those measures derives from its general obligations to respect and guarantee rights, acquired by Argentina upon ratification of the American Convention." Also, the State indicated that these provisional measures "run the risk of becoming permanent."

33.   The State also highlighted that the Supreme Court of Justice of the

Province is monitoring the prison situation. It specified that "the Constitution of the province of Mendoza specifically establishes [that] the Supreme Court of Justice of Mendoza has the obligation to supervise the conditions faced by individuals deprived of liberty, both those on trial and those convicted." In this way, "in compliance with this function and through the intermediary of its office on prison matters, which is under the Administrative Chamber of the [Supreme Court of Justice], permanent monitoring is carried out on the progress of the refurbishing and improvements [to the buildings] and sanitary [improvements] of the blocks via periodic visits to the prison and the submission of reports that the administrative authority [...] brings before the [Supreme Court of Justice]."

34. The representatives indicated that "the lifting of the measures would be legitimate only as long as the situation of violence and insecurity that [led] to their adoption has been remedied." However, they noted that "during the time the measures have been in force, the deaths of various inmates have taken place and many others have been seriously injured," for which reason they alleged that "the situation of risk to life and physical integrity of the inmates continues to exist." The representatives "recognize that certain progress has been made on the situations of violence and lack of security that originated the adoption of the provisional measures, to the point that the number of violent deaths seen during 2004 has been reduced." However, they indicated that "the conditions for those deaths to occur, whether homicide or suicide, continue to be in place" and that "it is therefore necessary to maintain the protective measures." They also indicated that "despite viewing positively the progress made in implementing specific actions with regard to the inmates in the Gustavo André prison farm in Lavalle toward improving the general conditions of the penitentiary population in the province, such as the construction of new facilities, [they highlight] that the situation of risk has not been overcome."

35. Likewise, the representatives indicated that the internment conditions seen at the time of the Inter-American Commission's *in loco* visit in 2009 are the same. However, they recognize that due to the provisional measures ordered by the Court, the situation of individuals deprived of liberty has improved. Finally, they asked the Court to maintain the provisional measures "for a time longer" and that they be lifted only when the State has complied with certain requirements— such as, for example, compliance with the "Asuncion Accords"—and indicated that the best result of the measures has been the strengthening of democratic institutions, a project contained in the friendly settlement in order to resolve the situation domestically (*supra* Having Seen 3).

36. For its part, the Commission considered that "the risk faced by the beneficiaries remains" and that the "measures taken by the State have not been sufficient to eradicate the risk faced by the beneficiaries." It added that it has been

demonstrated that "the continuation of the situation of insecurity and the deficient health, physical, and sanitary conditions, while they have improved, have not done so sufficiently to eradicate the risk." The Commission also indicated following its visit in April 2009 that "although progress has been made, the alleged lack of security and violence that led to the request for provisional measures persist[ed]." The Commission indicated that "with regard to the Lavalle farm prison, [...] [there was] a radical change in the situation of the beneficiaries held [there], for which reason [...] it recognize[d] the significant efforts of the State [...] to adequately implement the provisional measures." However, it indicated that the State has not fully implemented the measures ordered by the Tribunal and that it did not have "sufficient evidence—for example the implementation of the orders of the national and provincial Supreme Courts—to reach the conclusion that the State has taken sufficient measures."

37.   The Commission viewed positively the increase in security personnel, the separation of inmates, the improvements to the facilities, the progress in medical care, and the resocialization programs, and the continuation of the short-, medium-, and long-term measures taken are a sign of the State's willingness to comply with provisional measures. However, it specified that the request to lift the measures should evaluate the direct relationship between the measures and improvements made in the elimination of the situation of risk that led to the adoption of the measures. It specified that it is crucial for the evaluation to focus on the risk factors that introduced the violent incidents and the loss of human lives. The Commission emphasized that among the risk factors to be highlighted are the penitentiary security and guard conditions—particularly the lack of effective control in the blocks—in the Gustavo André prison in Lavalle; the risk factors related to the lack of security and emergency situations; the presence of weapons in the provincial penitentiary; and overcrowding. It observes that there is not a close relationship between the measures taken and the elimination of the risk factors indicated. Therefore, the Commission highlighted that despite the increase in the number of penitentiary personnel, it cannot be established whether this has resulted in an improvement in the security situation inside the prison and that there is not detailed information on new guard patterns. With regard to the presence of weapons in the prison, the Commission indicated that it does not have specific information on the results of the inspections implemented nor on the more general measures that have been adopted to diagnose and eliminate the causes leading to the rearming of the penitentiary population. It also observed that the State has not submitted information on the complaints of mistreatment during inspections. With regard to the overcrowding, the Commission indicated that the State must make reference to what the representatives have reported as far as the high level of overcrowding in some of the blocks. Likewise, the Commission

indicated that with regard to the incidents of suicide that have taken place in the prison, they "have taken place in a context of violence in which the inmates have a limited opportunity to avoid the violence to which they see themselves exposed, for which reason they decided to isolate themselves," with the State failing to provide detailed information on the measures taken to prevent or avoid those incidents.

38.   Based on this, the Commission noted that there is no information allowing for a reasonable degree of certainty on the elimination of risk; it recognized that there has been a reduction in the incidents of violence, however acts of violence and fights among the inmates still take place, causing an increase in the number of inmates in isolation. It therefore indicated that the nonexistence of violent incidents is not the only factor that should govern the lifting of the measures and underscored that the situation of improvements in the conditions is due precisely to the measures adopted. It thus highlighted that another criteria for lifting measures is the existence of internal oversight measures on the situation inside the penitentiary. The Commission found that the conditions for lifting the measures are still not right and asked that the measures be maintained "for a reasonable period" until the Court has better informational elements toward lifting them.

39.   The Court recalls that when handing down protective measures, the standard of the Tribunal or its head for evaluating these requirements is *prima facie*, as on occasion the application of assumptions is necessary given the need for protection. [16][37] Without prejudice to this, maintaining protective measures requires the Court to perform a more rigorous evaluation of the persistence of the situation that led to the measures. [17][38] Should the State request the lifting or modification of the provisional measures ordered, it must present sufficient evidence and argumentation allowing for the Tribunal to see that the risk or the threat no longer meets the standards of extreme gravity and urgency of avoiding irreparable damage. At the same time, the burden of the beneficiaries and the Commission to present evidence and pleadings increases with the passage of time and the lack of new threats. Certainly the fact that new threats do not arise can be due precisely to the effectiveness of the protection provided or the deterrence of the threats with the Tribunal's order. Nevertheless, the Tribunal has considered that the passage of a reasonable period of time without threats or intimidation, added to a lack of risk, can lead to the lifting of the provisional measures. [18][39]

40.   At the same time, the Court must take into account that, in keeping with the preamble of the American Convention, international protection under the Convention "reinforc[es] or complement[s] the protection provided by the domestic law of the American States." Thus, on confirming that the State in question has established effective protective mechanisms or taken effective protective actions for the beneficiaries of the provisional measures, the Tribunal can decide to lift the provisional measures and place the obligation to protect on

the party principally responsible, that being the State.[19][40] Upon the Court lifting the provisional measures for this reason, it is up to the State, in keeping with its duty to guarantee human rights, to maintain the protective measures that it has adopted and that the Tribunal found effective during a period of time warranted by the circumstances.

41.   In this matter, the Tribunal highlights that almost six years have passed since the provisional measures have been adopted. These measures have undoubtedly had a positive effect toward overcoming the grave situation that has principally characterized the Mendoza Provincial Penitentiary since the year 2004, taken into account the grave incidents of violence inside the prisons and the loss of control and security by the authorities in charge of guarding the inmates at certain times or periods. These effects have been recognized by both the Commission and the representatives. The progress on issues of security and detention conditions has already been indicated, as have the improvements in the infrastructure of the complexes and the construction of another maximum-security penitentiary (Almafuerte in Cacheuta) to allow for greater control the overcrowding situation, in addition to other projects that are in progress. Although the violent deaths continued during the years 2008 and 2009 (*supra* Considering 29), the rate of violent incidents has steadily and significantly decreased, although it has also been confirmed that suicides continue to take place in the penitentiary. Actions have been taken to prevent overcrowding, such as the one tending toward the separation of inmates in the various complexes according to category; the number of penitentiary personnel have been increased; and the inspection system has been implemented for controlling weapons and other objects prohibited within the prison.

42.   The Court highlights the different commitments and agreements reached between the State and the representatives of the beneficiaries, such as the document signed on May 11, 2005, in Asuncion,[20][41] (*supra* Having Seen 3), as well as the recognition by the representatives and the Commission of the actions carried out by the State (*supra* Considering 18, 24, and 26).

43.   It is important to note that the State has complied with its duty to report to the Tribunal periodically on the steps taken to implement these measures.

44.   Additionally, it is particularly relevant in this matter to highlight the impact that the measures ordered have had on the actions of domestic legal authorities such as the Supreme Court of Justice of the Nation and the Supreme Court of Justice of Mendoza, as well as the attention of international oversight mechanisms like the United Nations Committee against Torture and the United Nations Working Group on Arbitrary Detention. Thus, for example, the Court recalls the adoption of several rulings on the domestic level ordering the correction of the situation in the Mendoza Penitentiaries:

(a) through writs of *habeas corpus*, the first one granted on March 23, 2007[21][42] and the other granted on June 18, 2008, by the Second Oversight Court of the Judicial Branch of Mendoza, ordering to immediately provide all "corrective measures to safeguard at all times the physical and psychic integrity of the inmates housed in Block 3 of the Provincial Penitentiary of the Province of Mendoza."[22][43] It also ordered "to attend immediately to the needs of the inmates and resolve the conditions of overcrowding and treatment, education, work, and psychiatric, medical, social and spiritual care." The first of these rulings established, *inter alia*,

> TO CALL UPON the director of Penitentiary Complex No. III (Almafuerte) in Cacheuta to immediately take the steps, issue the orders, and/or execute the proceedings necessary for the cruel, inhuman, and degrading treatment suffered by the inmates housed in SECTORS 1 and 2 of the Complex to cease [...; to] ensure the inmates their right to petition, having the duty to establish an effective and rapid means of attending to the different briefs and/or correspondence sent, without prior restraint, to judicial and/or administrative authorities [...;] to take the steps toward providing and/or allowing the entry of radio and/or television devices that ensure the right to information enjoyed by the inmates [...;] within the period of [5 days], to take steps toward providing some means of telephonic communication to the inmates housed in Complex III in order to ensure the inmates their right to communicate [...] TO RECOMMEND that the director of Penitentiary Complex No. III (Almafuerte) of Cacheuta reorganize the activities of the inmates housed in SECTORS I and II of the complex in such a way as to permit them to enjoy more recreation and thereby decrease the number of hours under lockdown to the extent permitted by the safety conditions of the facility.

(b) In a ruling dated February 13, 2007, the Supreme Court of Justice of the Nation found, *inter alia*, that "[...] as custodian of constitutional guarantees and attending to the lack of results obtained by the order issued by the Inter-American Court of Human Rights, it finds itself with the unavoidable obligation to call upon the National State to, within 20 days, take those measures necessary to put an end to the situation being faced in the prison units of the province of Mendoza and to take the measures hereinafter indicated in the operative part of this judgment [...]" and ruled:

II. To instruct the Supreme Court of Justice of the Province of Mendoza and provincial tribunals of all levels, within their corresponding jurisdictions and by order of the Supreme Court and considering the urgency of the case, to put an end to all eventual situations of aggravation of detention that amount to cruel, inhuman, or degrading treatment or any other situation possibly leading to international responsibility of the Federal State; III. To order the National Executive Branch to report to the Tribunal every 20 days on the measures adopted to improve the situation of those detained. Notify [...] the National Executive Branch— the Ministry of Justice and Human Rights—; and the Governor of the Province of Mendoza of this order [...]

(c) In an Order dated February 14, 2007, the Supreme Court of Mendoza ruled:

1. To notify and report on the contents of the resolution [of the CSJN dated February 13, 2007], to all the Tribunals of the Province of Mendoza for their compliance and in order to cease any eventual situation of aggravation of detention that would violate Article 18 of the National Constitution; 2. To order an extraordinary visit to the women's prison facilities, Boulogne Sur Mer, and Gustavo André to be led by the magistrates of this Tribunal to all the penitentiary units in the Province; 3. To order the immediate confirmation of the conditions of the prison facilities via the Sentence Execution Judges; 4. To call [a] hearing for February 19, [2007,] in order to call the governor of the province of Mendoza before this Tribunal to report on the degree of compliance with the precautionary measures [sic] ordered by the Inter-American Court of Human Rights; and 5. To ask the Supreme Court of Justice of the Nation to call on the National Executive Branch to immediately and urgently relocate the federal inmates housed in the Provincial Penitentiary.

(d) In an administrative order issued on March 1, 2007, the Supreme Court of Justice of the Province of Mendoza, "examining the contents of the ruling handed down by the Supreme Court of Justice of the Nation in the orders entitled *Lavado Diego et al. v. the Province of Mendoza*[...] instructing this Tribunal to make cease all situations implying cruel, degrading, or other treatment capable of violating the national Constitution," *inter alia*, ruled

A. To inform the executive branch of the province that it must, with all possible urgency;

(1) Move to disinfect the Boulogne Sur Mer penitentiary facility to eradicate the insects (cockroaches), taking measures leading to the permanent cleanliness of the blocks;

(2) Provide chemical, substitute, or other bathrooms in sufficient quantities in the different blocks to allow for the inmates' privacy and dignity while attending to their physiological needs;

(3) Eliminate the situation of excessive overcrowding, relocating the inmates in dignified conditions;

(4) Adopt measures to effectively guarantee the physical integrity of the inmates, tending to prevent situations that put their lives at risk;

5. Provide permanent medical control, care, and assistance for the inmates, especially in block 15.-

[...]

(e) An order of the Supreme Court of Justice of the Nation dated March 20, 2007, ruled on the merits of the action brought (*supra* Considering 41(a)). Although it ruled that the case does not fall under its "native jurisdiction" and ordered "to move the proceedings to the National Appeals Chamber in the Adversarial Administrative Federal Court for all pertinent purposes [... and] to the Supreme Court of the Province of Mendoza," it found, *inter alia*, the following:

(14) That this situation is among those possible, and that given it, the National Executive Branch, in supervision of the interests of the National State, shall act in its own interest with regard to the consequences entailed in the compliance or noncompliance with the recommendations and rulings made by the Commission and the Inter-American Court of Human Rights on the facts denounced. That it is the legitimate bearer of the obligation related with the claim and not the Province of Mendoza. The issue has left the domestic scope of the Republic of Argentina, meaning that the aforementioned provincial state is one of the bearers of the juridical relationship on which the above-referenced claims are based, disregarding its grounds [...] The provincial state cannot be recognized as suitable for

contesting the specific subject this proceeding is dealing with [...]

(15) That the tone itself of the orders and communication of the international bodies intervening in the complaints leading to this proceeding—attached to this ruling—reveal that the juridical relationship invoked based on which it is sought to order compliance with recommendations and rulings made by the Commission and the Inter-American Court of Human Rights links the actors directly with the National State and not the Province of Mendoza.

(17) That in this way, a ruling contrary to the one brought about and as a consequence of which the execution of the provisional measures adopted by the Inter-American Court could be pursued—via the sought-after joinder—both against the National State and against the Province of Mendoza would mean emptying Art. 99, subparagraph 1st of the National Constitution as well as the international commitments assumed by the Nation of Argentina of their content. [...]

(20) That without prejudice to all this, it should be highlighted that as a consequence of the ruling of this Court dated February 13, 2007, the Supreme Court of Justice of the Province of Mendoza has handed down order 20.037, of February 14, 2007, through which—among the other provisions with which it concerns itself—it has requested that this Tribunal "call upon the National Executive Branch to move immediately and urgently to relocate the federal inmates housed in the Provincial Penitentiary;" and this Court must rule on this given that it was presented with the request.

(21) That the request shall not b[e] received via the intended route. Pursuant to the provisions contained in Law 24.660 applicable herein, the Nation and the provinces shall reach agreements on the receipt or transfer of convicts from their corresponding jurisdictions, and the transfer in question must paid for by the State requesting it (arts. 212 and following, cited law). The Province of Mendoza joined that provision through the passage of law 6513. In this way, the National Executive Branch cannot be called upon to carry out the aforementioned "immediate and urgent relocation"—at the request of only one of the branches

of authority of the local state—when the housing of the inmates takes place based on agreements signed by the States, with the legitimate representatives of that system of application understanding it to be advisable in order to ensure better individualization of sentences and the effective integration of the Republic's penitentiary system (art. 212 cited).

(f) On October 21, 2009, the Supreme Court of Justice of Mendoza issued a ruling ordering the provincial government to prepare an annual and comprehensive working plan in no more than 60 days that would include the renovation or replacement of all the Boulogne Sur Mer prison facilities.

45.   Attending to the principle of complementary and subsidiary nature that guides the Inter-American Human Rights System, an order to adopt or maintain original measures is justified in situations contemplated under Article 63(2) of the American Convention, with regard to which the ordinary guarantees existing in the State are insufficient or ineffective when the domestic authorities cannot or do not wish to make them prevail. [23][44] Although there is no information on the record indicating the way in which the rulings of the domestic judicial authorities have been complied with or implemented, the truth is that the domestic authorities have been attentive to the situation of the Mendoza Penitentiaries since the Tribunal ordered the provisional measures. This allows for the reasonable assumption that they will continue adequately exercising all due Convention related oversight, [24][45] likewise with regard to the protective measures to be required going forward.

46.   For all these reasons, the Court views positively the efforts made by the State and the active participation of the representatives of the beneficiaries and finds that the factual situation that led to the adoption and maintenance of these measures to the benefit of individuals deprived of liberty in the Mendoza Provincial Penitentiary and the Gustavo André unit, in Lavalle, does not persist. The situation of risk facing these individuals has evidently not been eliminated, but the situation of vulnerability faced by individuals deprived of liberty is a characteristic of any detention center. The information presented by the State, the Commission, and the representatives does not allow for the conclusion that the situation currently facing the inmates in the Mendoza Provincial Penitentiaries or the specific factors of risk that they could be facing meet the standard of gravity verified previously. In any case, the urgency and imminence of the situation no longer coincide.

47.   This Tribunal is aware that the alleviation and correction of the situation present in the Mendoza penitentiaries is a short, medium, and long term process requiring a collection of actions directed toward rectifying prison and detention

conditions on the part of federal and provincial authorities in the administrative, judicial, and legislative areas. Many of these issues do not fall under the supervision of the implementation of provisional measures. Because of this and for the aforementioned reasons, the Court finds it appropriate to lift the provisional measures.

48.   Finally, the Court has been informed that in the petition submitted to the Inter-American Commission known as "case of the Inmates of the Mendoza Penitentiary," the State and the representatives reached a friendly settlement agreement on August 28, 2007. [25][46] According to information provided by the State, that agreement was approved domestically through "Decree No. 2740 ratified through [L]aw [No.] 7.930 of September 16, 2008." The State reported on the measures taken toward complying with that agreement, in particular measures of pecuniary and legal reparations and measures of satisfaction; [26][47] it expressed that the Commission has not issued the corresponding report under Article 49 of the Convention. According to the Commission, the petitioners recently requested "that the agreement not be approved." Regarding this, the State highlighted that it has been requesting approval of the agreement for two years and has gotten no response.

49.   Representatives indicated that, in their judgment, the "Friendly Settlement Agreement on the issue of the Mendoza Penitentiary does not cover the Provisional Measures, and the petitioners will not block their removal if the Nation and the Province fully comply with the agreement." They indicated that "in this case, the petitioners and the State want the [Commission] to evaluate and supervise the agreement, not put an end to the matter with its signature," for which reason "if the National State has sent its request for [the application of Article] 49 of the Convention, it does so within the framework of the commitments made," but they indicated that "it is the [Commission] that must decide if the agreement meets inter-American standards and if it has been complied with." During the public hearing in November of 2010, they indicated that although the friendly settlement does not form part of the provisional measures, Law No. 17.930 establishing compliance with it came out of these provisional measures, for which reason it is closely linked, and the measures on which they have reached an agreement would help to improve democratic institutions in order to rectify the situation of individuals deprived of liberty.

50.   For its part, the Commission highlighted that the provisional measures were requested independently and "apart from the existence of the case," with their purpose being to protect rights rather than to prevent the result of the petitions brought before the Commission. It indicated that it is true that there is a friendly settlement agreement presented by "one of the petitioning groups" and the Commission "is evaluating it in order to issue a report pursuant to Article

49 of the Convention." In particular, it found that the State request for the Court to rule on the urgency of the approval of the friendly settlement agreement is inadmissible given that the preceding is independent of the provisional measures and it falls solely and exclusively to the Commission under its independence and autonomy to rule on cases being processed before it.

51.   The Court views positively the conciliatory attitude of the petitioners and the State, manifested in this matter through the agreements reached in the so-called "Asuncion Accords," (*supra* Having Seen 3) as it reflects a commitment to comply with obligations under the Convention. The Court observes that the Commission indicated that it has not yet approved the agreement but that it is studying the possibility of doing so pursuant to Article 49 of the Convention. It is possible for some of the measures agreed upon between the State and the petitioners in the "friendly settlement" intended to remedy situations apparently not compatible with the American Convention taking place in the Mendoza penitentiaries to include elements also pertaining to the purpose of these provisional measures. Although the provisional measures proceeding should not imply a forum for debate on questions of the merits that could imply a pre-judgment in a case, it is clear that the jurisdiction to weigh and supervise that friendly settlement agreement falls exclusively to the Inter-American Commission. Consequently, upon lifting these provisional measures, the Tribunal limits itself to ruling on whether the situation of risk that led to this proceeding persists in the terms indicated (Considering 39), for which reason it does not fall to the Tribunal to rule on what the State has indicated as far as the need to approve the aforementioned agreement. It is enough to find that the Inter-American Human Rights System remains attentive to the situation of the Mendoza Penitentiaries through the action of one of its bodies, to which corresponds the duty to determine the future course of the proceeding.

52.   Without prejudice to what this Tribunal rules, it should be reiterated that Article 1(1) of the American Convention sets forth the general obligations of States Parties to respect the rights and liberties enshrined in the Convention and to guarantee the free and full exercise of these rights for all individuals subject to their jurisdiction. The Court especially highlights the State's position to guarantee with regard to individuals deprived of liberty, [27][48] by virtue of which penitentiary authorities exercise total control over them, making the general obligations take on a particular shade of meaning that obliges the State to provide inmates with the minimum conditions compatible with their dignity during the time they remain in the detention centers, with the purpose of protecting and guaranteeing their rights to life and personal integrity. [28][49] Because of this, and independent of the existence of specific provisional measures, [29][50] the State is especially obligated to guarantee the rights of individuals under circumstances of deprivation of liberty. [30][51] Likewise, in this particular matter, the Court recalls that in keeping with

international law, the State must ensure that the security measures taken in prison facilities include adequate training of the penitentiary personnel who provide security in the prison and the effectiveness of those mechanisms for preventing prison violence, such as the ability to react to incidents of violence or emergencies inside the blocks. The State must ensure that the inspections are done properly and carried out periodically, intended to prevent violence and eliminate risk through adequate and effective control of the interior of the blocks on the part of the penitentiary guards, and that the results of these inspections be duly and quickly communicated to the competent authorities.

53.   As far as the minimum conditions of detention, it is important to recall that the State must in principle maintain adequate installations, the separation of inmates into categories, and access to adequate health, hygiene, and education services, as well as offer measures for recreation and mental and physical health to the individuals deprived of liberty. [31] [52] Likewise, the State must ensure that the personnel in charge of security have the training and tools necessary to do their jobs with respect for the rights of those detained, in particular that they use force in an exceptional, planned, and limited manner in order to prevent prison violence. For this reason, the measures to be taken by the State must prioritize a system of preventive action—intended *inter alia* to prevent arms trafficking and an increase in violence—over a system of repressive action. [32] [53]

THEREFORE:

THE INTER-AMERICAN COURT OF HUMAN RIGHTS,

by way of the authority conferred by Article 63(2) of the American Convention on Human Rights and Article 27 of the Rules of Procedure,

DECIDES:

1.   To lift the provisional measures ordered by the Inter-American Court of Human Rights on November 22, 2004, and later ratified, to protect the life and integrity of all the persons held in custody in the Mendoza Provincial Prison and those in the Gustavo André Unit, in Lavalle, as well as every person found within those facilities.

2.   To clarify that under the terms of Article 1(1) of the American Convention, the lifting of provisional measures does not imply that the State is relieved of its obligations under the Convention to protect.

3. To request that the Secretariat of the Court notify the State, the Inter-American Commission on Human Rights, the representatives of the beneficiaries, and the State of Argentina of this Order.

4. To close the case file on this matter.

1-Jul-2011

Order of the Inter-American Court of Human Rights

Provisional Measures with Regard to the Republic of Argentina
Matter of the Mendoza Prisons

CONSIDERING THAT:

4.   The Commission requested the "re-opening" of the provisional measures that the Court had ordered in the matter of the Mendoza Prisons as of November 22, 2004, which were in force until December 15, 2010, the date of notification of the order of November 26, 2010. In order to determine the admissibility of this request, the Court will examine the information and justification presented by the Commission, together with its observations and those of the State in this regard.

A.   Information presented by the Commission and the State

(a) Regarding the alleged acts of torture or violence

5.   The Commission has presented information to the Court regarding alleged acts that could be classified as torture against inmates of the San Felipe Unit, which is part of the Mendoza prison system. It indicated that, during the first half of January 2011, a mobile telephone owned by a prison official was found outside the Boulogne Sur Mer Prison Unit, [6] [54] with several videos and photographs that show acts of torture inflicted on inmates of the San Felipe Prison Unit by members of the prison staff, as well as other "violent and irresponsible [types of conduct] among the members of the prison staff and 5 towards those deprived of liberty for whom they are responsible." The Commission's request was accompanied by audiovisual material, which it described as follows:

(i)   The first video "appeared to have been made on September 4, 2010, and in [...] it can be seen at least five prison officials in the San Felipe complex wearing boxing gloves and practicing fighting, during evening hours";

(ii)   The second video was apparently made on "December 3, 2010, and in [...] it can be seen that [two] prison officials are punching and kicking an inmate, possibly a young adult–in other words, older than 18 and less than 21 years of age–in a room next to the San Felipe Unit that accommodates this prison population, with the connivance of the individual filming the incident; and, when an attempt is made to hide the beating by closing the door, the latter indicates his disappointment at being unable to continue filming. The moans emitted by the defenseless inmate in response to the beating he is receiving on his abdomen and legs can be heard in the audio";

(iii) The third video is composed of two files of June 6, 2010, "where it is possible to observe at least [five] prison officials who are forcing an as yet unknown inmate to kneel on the floor, handcuffed and tied to a window of the pavilion, with his arms stretched up contrary to their natural flexion. In this macabre scenario, the prison officials punch and kick the inmate, especially on the ribs, which, according to the inmate's protests, appear to have been broken. Moreover, the officials ask him where it hurts and then punish him there";

(iv) The video "*light for a fag end*" [...] records how, following an inmate's request for a light for his cigarette, prison staff use a flame-throwing device against the that cell's peephole. The prison officials film this situation, joking and boasting about their actions";

(v) The last video "films the actions of the prison staff locking the cells of the pavilion." The video appears to show that the staff "take advantage [that] the inmates [...] are bathing and [it can also be seen that] they push them violently into the cells using anti-regulatory means such as wooden and iron batons. Furthermore, the prison officials boast jokingly about what they are doing in front of the device used to make the video."

6.   According to the Commission, the representatives of the petitioners indicated that the inmates who appear in the videos being subjected to the alleged acts of torture are Walter Fabián Correa and William Vargas García, and the inmates who contacted the representatives are Andrés Yacante and Matías Marcelo Tello Sánchez. According to the information provided by the Commission, during a visit to the San Felipe Unit on February 6, 2011, by the lawyer, Carlos Varela, the inmates Andrés Yacante and Matías Tello had stated that "[a] young man named Emanuel had been placed in cell 12, apparently accused of rape, and this person [...] was constantly [and severely] tortured with blows to the head; they say that, once, they heard [him] shouting that they had dislocated his shoulder and thrown pepper gas in his face."

(b) *Regarding the alleged systemic or general nature of the reported acts of torture*

7.   The Inter-American Commission indicated that the acts of torture and ill-treatment recorded in the videos that came to light were not isolated events, but reveal a systematic practice by the agents of the Mendoza Prison Service. In relation to the briefs of the petitioners' representatives of February 2, 6 and 10, 2011, the Commission provided the following elements:

(i)   Statement made by William Vargas to *Diario UNO* on February 10, 2011;

(ii) Statements made by Walter Fabián Correa during a visit to the San Felipe Unit by the legal advisers of the Assistant Secretariat of Justice and Human Rights and of the Human Rights Directorate on February 8, 2011, in which Carlos Varela also participated;

(iii) Accounts given by the inmates, Andrés Yacante and Matías Marcel Tello Sánchez, during a visit to the San Felipe Unit by the lawyer Carlos Varela on February 6, 2011;

(iv) Audiovisual information;

(v) Letter from the President of the Human Rights and Guarantees Commission of the Chamber of Deputies of the province of Mendoza addressed to the Executive Secretary of the Inter-American Commission dated February 14, 2011, stating that he had received complaints of mistreatment and appalling detention conditions from next of kin of inmates, before the videos came to light, and that it had been "possible to verify that this was not an isolated event because the videos that were found reveal that the inmates are mistreated in different places and also the incidents happened during different periods of time";

(vi) Statements made to the press in Mendoza by the Prison Attorney, Francisco Mugnolo, on February 10, 2011, in which he asserted "that episodes of torture such as those recorded are common in Argentine prisons, and that one of the reasons why this happens is the deficient training of prison agents." In other declarations, the Attorney stated that "the violation of the human rights of detainees is a daily practice," and

(vii) Other complaints concerning similar acts filed by inmates after the alleged acts of torture committed against William Vargas and Walter F. Correa had become public.

8.   In addition, the Commission indicated that there is a culture of violence, irresponsibility and indiscipline among the members of the Provincial Penitentiary Service. They presented the following elements in support of this affirmation:

(i) "A video recorded on September 5, 2010, that shows the prison staff of the San Felipe Unit fighting with gloves at night, in the absence of any sporting or training context. This is happening while they smoke and drink *mate*. In the background can be heard the voice of the person filming who repeats phrases such as: "the first man who fails to get up loses";

(ii) "Another two videos in which prison staff, in an undisciplined and irresponsible manner, annoy each other and end up hitting and kicking each other 'fraternally' but visibly arousing their tempers";

(iii) Three groups of photographs in which the prison staff can be observed in various obscene situations or justifying violence during the exercise of their functions;

(iv) Newspaper articles according to which, in November 2009, a candidate for the Mendoza Prison Service reported that one of the instructors submitted his students to physical abuse. The "existence of this complaint was confirmed by the Director of the Prison

Service and the instructor has been removed from his post while an investigation is undertaken."

9.   Regarding the foregoing, the State argued that "[t]he specific acts of violence that came to light in February 2011, and regarding which the Commission bases its request to re-open provisional measures, do not constitute a systematic pattern of torture and cruel, inhuman or degrading treatment of the inmates by prison staff. These are isolated acts of violence, whose common denominator is the identity of the authors who have been deprived of their liberty and charged with the offenses committed."

10.   With regard to the elements provided by the Commission, and in relation to the petitioners' allegations of a possible systematic practice of torture based on a letter from a deputy reproduced by the Commission, the State acknowledged that the alleged acts took place in different parts of the establishment, but indicated that the same prison staff intervened in each of the alleged acts. Consequently, the fact that the acts occurred in different places within the establishment could not prove that a general pattern exists, but merely that they were acts of "a specific and identified group of prison guards who are being investigated by the provincial system of justice." It indicated that these individuals are being processed under the most severe administrative charges possible and are no longer able to affect the rights of the inmates.

11.   With regard to the declarations of the Prison Attorney, the State indicated that his powers relate to federal rather than provincial inmates; that the last time the Prison Attorney visited the Mendoza prisons was in 2007, and that he had not visited any of the prisons of the province of Mendoza since then. Regarding the complaints mentioned by the President of the Human Rights and Guarantees Commission of the Chamber of Deputies of the province of Mendoza, the State affirmed that it was unaware of these complaints and that, although it had requested them, it had not yet received a response to the said request; hence, the "provincial Executive Branch is unaware of the content of the said complaints received from the [said] Deputy or of how they have been dealt with."

12.   Lastly, in its observations on the State's brief, the Commission added, with regard to the evidence of a systematic practice that, in the context of the provisional measures, it was "sufficient that there is *prima facie* evidence of the extreme gravity, urgency and irreparability of the damage." Furthermore, it mentioned that the State had merely established that "only seven guards were responsible for torturing the inmates, and that they were being prosecuted, without offering any other information on the measures taken in response to the affirmations at the domestic level that what happened was part of a systematic practice." In addition, even though the Commission did not indicate the specific information to which it was referring, it alleged that, in the context of the provisional measures,

"information [existed] concerning the actions of the prison guards against the inmates," to which should be added "the information reported to the Court in March 2011 concerning torture committed by prison guards—not only as regards seven of them—as well as concerning the numerous statements by inmates, their next of kin, and public officials indicating that what was recorded on video was not a[n] isolated event but is a constant within the prisons and that the inmates do not report it for fear of reprisals." Finally, it alleged that the "information on the culture of violence, irresponsibility and indiscipline of the prison guards, as well as the deficient training of prison staff" should be added to the case file.

(c) *Regarding the alleged actual detention conditions in the Mendoza Prisons*

13.   The Commission advised that problems still exist arising from the actual detention conditions of the inmates of the San Felipe and Boulogne Sur Mer Units, such as the failure to provide cleaning materials and adequate food, together with the absence of activities for the prisoners, except for a two-hour visit once a week.

14.   The Commission also indicated that, added to the alleged acts of torture and the evidence of a systematic pattern of violence by state agents, "the most recent information regarding fights and mistreatment reveals that violence continues among the inmates—the central issue of the provisional measures while they were in force—and this means that the threats to life and integrity persist." In particular, the Commission, based on the reports of the petitioners, advised of confrontations among inmates in the San Felipe and Boulogne Sur Mer Units.

15.   Regarding the detention conditions, the State referred to several projects that are being implemented in the province of Mendoza that relate to the prison situation. In particular, it mentioned: (i) the "Mendoza Penitentiary School" project to provide prison personnel with permanent education and training on the relevant international human rights standards, and (ii) implementation of health care programs for the inmates.

16.   With regard to the fights and acts of violence, the State declared that: (i) they constitute "conflicts within the prisons, which do not involve the responsibility of prison staff"; (ii) effective measures had been taken to ensure the integrity of the inmates affected by acts of violence, and (iii) the inmates had been attended by health professionals, both at the time of the events and also in the following days to monitor the evolution of the injuries suffered.

17.   In its latest report, the State referred to diverse construction and repair work in several pavilions of the Boulogne Sur Mer Unit and the San Felipe Unit that would result in improved conditions and increased capacity. In addition, it provided figures on the numbers of inmates who were working or receiving job training and indicated that, by monitoring their health and introducing preventive health care, it had been possible to make considerable improvements in the quality of life of the inmates, their next of kin, and the prison staff.

(d) Regarding the alleged measures adopted by the State in relation to the reported facts

18.   The State alleged that it had taken a series of measures to put an end to the acts that had occurred and been reported by the Inter-American Commission. It submitted a report by the province of Mendoza in which, it alleged, the individualized acts of torture and mistreatment against inmates of the Mendoza prisons were not tolerated or justified in any way. The State indicated that, owing to the actions taken, the safety, life and integrity of the inmates "are ensured as evaluated in November 2010."

19.   With regard to William Vargas García, Walter Fabián Correa, Andrés Yacante and Matías Marcelo Tello Sanchez, the State alleged that it had adopted the following measures:

(i)   The Treatment Department of the San Felipe Prison Complex had conducted an "exhaustive physical, mental and legal review" of them. They had undergone an "individual psychological interview to verify their situation as regards their transit through the progressive punishment regime, their actual mental conditions, and the possibility of and/or need for temporary relocation." The provincial report indicated that, owing to the time that has elapsed and despite the notoriety of the facts, no visible aftereffects had been identified.

(ii)   Regarding the legal situation, the judicial files and records of each inmate were reviewed.

(iii)   In relation to the above, on February 9, 2011, William Vargas García was released on parole.

(iv)   The other three accused, who are being prosecuted for different offenses, are awaiting their respective oral trial. As a safeguard measure, and in order to ensure a "comprehensive containment scheme," they were incorporated into a module without inmates and with a special guard composed of guards from other units. Subsequently, and at the request of their next of kin and the representative, they were transferred to Unit VII of Tunuyán (the Transit Prison), to await the conclusion of the preliminary administrative proceedings of all those eventually found responsible for the facts. In this unit, they receive a weekly medical inspection. In its latest report, the State indicated that, on April 28, 2011, Walter Fabián Correa, Andres Yacante and Matías Marcelo Tello Sánchez had been transferred to Almafuerte Prison Complex III. They are in a module for inmates who are "Young Adults – on trial" and have access to food, central heating, a public telephone, different types of recreational activities, and a once-weekly seven-hour visiting regime. This module has internal and external exercise yards, individual cells and appropriate conditions. The "Social Action Division" has provided them with specialized professional attention. On May 27, 2011, Walter Fabián Correa was transferred back the San Felipe Unit, at his mother's express request, and

(v) According to a medical evaluation in May 2011, Andrés Yacante and Marcelo Tello Sánchez are in good health. And Walter Fabián Correa, who has repeatedly tried to commit suicide, has been provided with permanent psychological monitoring and assistance; on 11 occasions, he has received attention in the Medical Assistance Division and, although he was treated in the El Sauce Hospital for a fresh suicide attempt on May 19 and 20, four days later he was re-evaluated by the psychiatric services and it was determined that he had been "compensated, and was no longer considering suicide." The State also presented conclusions of reports on these three individuals prepared by the Psychological Treatment Division.

20.   In its latest brief (*supra* twenty-first Having Seen paragraph), the Commission stated that William Vargas García was allegedly continuing to receive threats, even though he had been accepted into the witness protection program when he was released on parole and the State has not given him any protection. In addition, although the provincial government had apparently obtained a house for him, he does not live in it "because there is no furniture." Furthermore, one of his former cellmates had also been a victim of torture that had been reported, and he does not have protection either. Regarding Walter Fabián Correa, "who reported harassment and being beaten in Almafuerte, he asked to be released, but his request was refused," and the authorities have taken no action in relation to his suicide attempts. Regarding Andrés Yacante and Marcelo Tello Sánchez, the application for habeas corpus filed in their favor owing to the alleged beating received in the Almafuerte Unit, and orders had been issued to transfer them to the San Felipe Unit. The Commission reiterated that they are in a situation of aggravated risk, not necessarily owing to the fact that they remain detained in the place where the reported facts occurred, but rather owing to the complaint itself, which revealed what happens in the said prison units. Lastly, the Commission stated that, during the investigation into the acts of torture, it was reported that an inmate had been forced to sign a statement affirming that it was he who had obtained the mobile telephone with the films.

21.   The State indicated that it had taken several measures with regard to those who had been identified as "allegedly responsible for the acts of torture and ill-treatment against the inmates of the San Felipe Prison Complex"; in particular:

(i)   Administrative proceedings by the General Security Inspectorate, a decentralized body responsible for investigating and initiating pre-trial proceedings for administrative errors, with the consequent determination of responsibility of the members of the provincial security forces. Ten preliminary administrative procedures have been conducted, in which the opening of preliminary administrative proceedings and the application of preventive suspension or removal has been ordered for seven of the agents involved;

(ii) Those exercising supervisory tasks were charged and removed from their functions based on failure to comply with their control obligations;

(iii) Administrative case files have been opened owing to complaints received by telephone from next of kin of inmates based on newspaper articles, and owing to complaints forwarded by the Human Rights Directorate of the Ministry of Governance;

(iv) The Provincial Deputy Secretariat of Human Rights took statements from inmates of the pavilion where the acts allegedly occurred, and these were incorporated into the administrative and judicial investigations;

(v)   Following the filing of the complaints by the Human Rights Directorate of the Ministry of Governance of the province of Mendoza, the office of the Prosecutor for Complex Crimes of the province of Mendoza initiated the corresponding investigations. Currently, there are: (i) three individuals accused of the crime of torture; (ii) one individual charged with the offense of harsh and humiliating treatment; (iii) one individual charged with the crime of torture compounded by the offense of harsh and humiliating treatment, and (iv) two individuals charged with the offense of omissions in the performance of their functions, which allowed the torture to occur. These seven individuals are currently detained, based on the justified fear that, owing to their condition of prison agents, they could obstruct the investigation."

(vi) In its last report, the State specified that the agent accused of the offense of harsh and humiliating treatment had been released and that the other six agents were located in Prison Unit No. 6 of the Boulogne Sur Mer Complex. In addition, the Prosecutor had requested pre-trial detention for these six agents who had been charged, but no decision had been taken in this regard. Even though the case has not been brought to trial, "the probative aspect is quite complex" and there has been "permanent procedural activity by the defense counsel of each of the accused," and (vii)The province of Mendoza–represented by the Minister of Governance, Justice and Human Rights, the Deputy Secretary for Human Rights, the Director of Human Rights and the Director General of the Prison Service, together with the Argentine State, through the national Human Rights Secretariat, are the complainants in the case.

22.   The State has referred to other measures undertaken based on the facts reported by the Commission and the representatives of the beneficiaries of the measures that were lifted. In particular, it mentioned the following:

(i)   In order to increase its presence in the prisons, to inspect the cells without prior notice, and to guarantee the right of the inmates to report this type of ill-treatment, the Provincial Human Rights Directorate has created delegations in each of the prisons with the daily presence of lawyers attached to the Directorate to tour the facilities, and to receive statements and complaints of different types, and

(ii) In order to identify whether there have been other acts of a similar nature that have not been reported, as well as to advance the investigation of the facts denounced, the individualization of those responsible, and the application of the corresponding legal sanction, the Deputy Secretariat of Justice and Human Rights has instructed its advisors to receive testimony from the inmates lodged in the pavilion where the incidents allegedly occurred. These recorded statements are useful for advancing the administrative investigations and were also provided to the legal proceedings.

B. Regarding the request to "re-open" the provisional measures.

(a) Regarding the "re-opening" of the provisional measures and other procedural aspects

23.   The State questioned the concept of "re-opening" provisional measures, arguing that it was not supported by any procedural norm in force. It added that the provisional measures ordered by the Court in 2004, "concluded automatically with the decision to lift them adopted in November 2011, so that any ruling on the matter would require a new and detailed examination of the situation reported and, eventually, the issue of a new order that would assess whether a situation of extreme gravity and urgency existed that could justify the issue of an exceptional measure such as the one proposed by the Commission."

24.   The State underscored that the request did not denounce any new act, but "attempts to justify the order of a new provisional measure based on events that had already taken place, precisely while the order of November 22, 2004,

was in force." The report of the province of Mendoza indicates that the State was unaware of these events until February 2, 2011, when the videos were publicized by the media and, although the videos were made before the request to lift the measures, the expert assessment had not been made to determine the date on which the files were created. Moreover, the State mentioned that it should be stressed that "the general situation in the establishments covered by the measures was widely discussed during the public hearing [...] which resulted in the decision duly made to lift the provisional measures" and that, all things considered, "the events [in question] had occurred in 2010, were reported in 2011 and, in addition, the local authorities had not been unresponsive to them; to the contrary, the facts had resulted in the detention and prosecution of those allegedly responsible."

25.   Thirdly, the State observed that the Commission had submitted the request for measures to the Court "*inaudita parte*," without requesting any information from the Argentine State, based merely on the information provided by the petitioners and on newspaper articles, and without previously invoking the powers granted to it by Article 25 of its Rules of Procedure, which allows it to request the State to adopt precautionary measures in serious and urgent situations. The State argued that, anyway, it was unable to present its observations on the information provided by the petitioners.

26.   Lastly, the State argued that, based on the petitioners' complaint, the province of Mendoza had coordinated a series of measures that demonstrate that the State was determined to find a solution to the events that took place in the prison prior to the request, so that, in observance of the principle of the subordination of the inter-American system, the request to re-open the measures was inadmissible.

27.   The Commission indicated in this respect that its request to re-open the measures was based "on the nature of the facts reported to the Court in March 2011, on events that occurred during the second half of 2010 in the context of the serious situation that was reported to the Inter-American Court throughout the six years that the measure were in force." It added that it was particularly relevant that the events occurred while the provisional measures ordered by the Court were in force and that those events were not known when the Court ordered the lifting of the provisional measures on November 26, 2010, but were provided as supervening evidence and would clearly have had an impact on the assessment made by the Court. In this regard, "the fact that the Court and the Commission were unaware of these events is precisely because the State was not exercising the necessary supervision or implementing the measures to protect the beneficiaries of the provisional measures in force at the time. Consequently, the Commission considered that it was unnecessary to make a new, separate analysis of the matter, as the State claimed, because the events occurred while the provisional measures were in force, without the State providing the appropriate protection." Lastly, the

Commission stated that, irrespective of the name given to the concept of "re-opening," the situation that occurred reveals the concurrence of the elements of extreme gravity and urgency, and the need to avoid irreparable harm to persons.

28.   With regard to the State's observations concerning whether the Commission should have issued precautionary measures before submitting the request that is being decided, this Court recognizes that, in several matters, when ordering provisional measures, the Court has found it relevant that, previously, the Commission had ordered the State to adopt precautionary measures and that these had not produced the required protection or the State had not adopted them.[557] Moreover, the Court has recognized the importance of the precautionary measures ordered by the Commission as an instrument of prevention and protection and, in numerous cases, the Commission's practice has been to order them before submitting a request for provisional measures to the Court. Despite this, Article 63(2) of the Convention does not require as a prerequisite for the Court to order provisional measures that the Commission should have previously ordered precautionary measures or any other requisites that could delay or prevent their issue, thus increasing the risk to the human rights that should be protected. Consequently, the observations of the State in this regard are without merit.

29.   The Court also observes that, as the State has noted, the concept of "re-opening" provisional measures is not established in the Court's Rules of Procedure. Nevertheless, this does not prevent the Court from examining the Commission's arguments in view of the alleged needs for protection of persons by provisional measures, in the terms of Article 63(2) of the Convention. Regardless of the name used by the Commission to submit its request, the request is founded on the alleged existence of acts that took place while the provisional measures recently lifted in the matter of the Mendoza Prisons were in force, and the beneficiaries of those measures were the same individuals whose protection is now requested. Therefore, the Court can consider the Commission's request as a simple request for provisional measures, just as it has in previous matters where the Court has ordered such measures even when they had already been lifted.[8 56] In this situation, even if the Commission did not hear the State before submitting this request, it would be consistent with its own understanding of the procedure to be followed in the situation described and, in any case, the State has had many opportunities to manifest its position and arguments when the Court forwarded it the Commission's request. Consequently, the Court must examine whether the specific requirements for ordering provisional measures concur.

(b) Regarding the need to order provisional measures

30.   Article 63(2) of the Convention requires that three conditions must be met for the Court to be able to order provisional measures: (i) "extreme gravity"; (ii) "urgency," and (iii) that the purpose is to "avoid irreparable damage." Likewise,

these three conditions must persist for the Court to maintain the protection ordered. If one of them is no longer valid, the Court must assess the pertinence of continuing the protection ordered, without prejudice to ordering the measures again if, in the future, the three conditions are again met. In addition, although, when ordering the measures of protection, the standard of assessment of these requirements by the Court or its President is *prima facie*, [9][57] the maintenance of the measures of protection requires a more rigorous evaluation by the Court of the persistence of the situation that gave rise to them. [10][58]

31.   The Court has established on previous occasions that, under provisional measures, it is not appropriate to consider the merits of any argument other than those strictly related to the extreme gravity, urgency and need to avoid irreparable harm to the beneficiaries. Any other matter can only be submitted to the consideration of the Court in a contentious case or in a request for an advisory opinion. [11][59] Furthermore, the Court has recognized that provisional measures are of a protective rather than a merely precautionary nature. [12][60] Consequently, the Court will not refer to the observations of the State on the execution of a friendly settlement agreement that has apparently been reached in the proceedings on the petition before the Commission.

32.   In relation to the requirement of "gravity" for the adoption of provisional measures, the Convention calls for this to be "extreme"; in other words, that it is to its most intense and severe degree. [13][61] As for the requirement concerning the "urgency" of the situation that is the subject of the request for provisional measures, this implies that the danger or threat involved is imminent, which requires that the response to remedy them be immediate. When analyzing this aspect, the opportuneness and the duration of the requested precautionary or protective measures must be assessed. [14][62]

33.   In this matter, in addition to requesting protection for four individuals, the Inter-American Commission asked the Court to order the protection of those deprived of liberty in the San Felipe and Boulogne Sur Mer Units (*supra* seventh Having Seen paragraph); thus the potential beneficiaries are identifiable, because they are individuals imprisoned in the said detention centers, or who may enter them in the future as inmates, or who enter them, regularly or eventually, either as officials or as visitors. [15][63]

34.   In this matter, the gravity arises from the documentary and audiovisual elements provided, which consist of videos and photographs from a mobile telephone allegedly owned by a prison agent, as well as from the testimony of those deprived of liberty and of public officials (*supra* fifth considering paragraph), which reveal *prima facie* the existence of violent acts perpetrated against inmates of the San Felipe Prison Unit by members of the prison staff, which could even be classified as acts of torture. In addition, further elements may reveal other types

of undue and violent conduct among members of the prison staff and towards those deprived of liberty for whom they are responsible. These acts allegedly took place while the provisional measures were in force, although the Commission and the Court were not advised of them, because the alleged acts had not yet been revealed, which is, in turn, evidence of a lack of internal monitoring by the State of the actions of the prison staff, actions that should be monitored by the State in its capacity as guarantor in prisons and detention centers.

35.   According to the arguments and information provided by the Commission and the representatives, while the provisional measures in this matter were in force numerous tense and violent situations arose in the relations between inmates and prison staff. [16][64] In particular, information was provided on reports of inhuman and degrading treatment inflicted on inmates in the provincial prisons, the investigation of which suffered long delays and gave rise to fears that it was neither independent nor exhaustive. [17][65] The representatives argued that, even though the judicial authorities had declared several applications for habeas corpus admissible, prolonged detention and acts of torture within the pavilions continued. [18][66] The report of the visit made to the prisons by the Inter-American Commission's Rapporteur for the Rights of Persons Deprived of Liberty at the end of April 2009, stated that prison staff inspection teams comprised only a few officials, so that, given their numerical disadvantage, they used very violent procedures to carry out the inspections. [19][67]

36.   Although the facts alleged on this occasion refer to acts committed by several prison agents against two inmates of the San Felipe Unit, the reported situation of acts that could be classified as inhuman or degrading treatment, and even forms of torture, could indicate the possible existence within the prisons of certain practices incompatible with the State's obligations under the Convention. In any case, this should be an obvious line of investigation into the facts by the domestic authorities during the administrative and criminal proceedings. Although the State may be adopting measures to investigate and prosecute the alleged perpetrators of the acts, in both the administrative and the criminal jurisdictions, together with measures to prevent similar acts (*supra* twenty-second considering paragraph), it did not report whether all its investigative mechanisms were trying to determine specifically whether similar practices or acts exist within the prisons, because it alleged that such practices do not exist.

37.   With regard to the individual or specific protection requested by the Commission, according to the information provided by the Commission and by the State, the latter appears to have adopted a series of measures in order to protect the life and physical integrity of William Vargas García, Walter Fabián Correa, Andrés Yacante and Matías Marcelo Tello Sanchez (*supra* nineteenth considering paragraph). Nevertheless, the Commission has advised that these individuals have

been attacked in the places of detention to which they were transferred and that the witnesses of the acts are not receiving adequate protection, and the State has not provided any response to this.

38.   In relation to the measures adopted with regard to the "alleged perpetrators of the acts of torture and ill-treatment against the inmates of the San Felipe Prison Complex," together with other measures, the State underscored:

(i)   The opening of 10 administrative procedures (investigation and pre-trial proceedings for possible administrative offenses) by the General Security Inspectorate, during which it was decided to open a summary administrative proceeding and apply preventive suspension or removal in the case of seven prison agents who were involved; as well as charges against and the dismissal of those exercising supervisory tasks based on failure to comply with their control obligations;

(ii) The opening of administrative case files based on complaints made by the next of kin of inmates, newspaper articles, and complaints forwarded by the Human Rights Directorate of the Ministry of Governance;

(iii) The opening of a criminal investigation by the office of the Prosecutor for Complex Crimes of the province of Mendoza, whose current status is: (a) three individuals charged with the crime of torture; (ii) one person charged with the offense of harsh and humiliating treatment; (iii) one person charged with the crimes of torture in conjunction with the offense of harsh and humiliating treatment, and (iv) two individuals charged with the offense of omission in performance of functions which permitted torture. The six accused are currently detained in the Boulogne Sur Mer Complex (the agent accused of the offense of harsh and humiliating treatment has been released). The Minister of Governance, Justice and Human Rights, the Deputy Secretary for Human Rights, the Director of Human Rights and the Director General of the Prison Service, all of the province of Mendoza, and also the federal State–through the national Human Rights Secretariat–are the complainants in the case;

(iv) The creation of delegations of the Provincial Human Rights Directorate in each prison to receive statements and complaints of different kinds.

39.   The irreparable nature of possible harm to the rights of those deprived of liberty is evident if pertinent measures of prevention and protection are not adopted at the domestic level. In view of the special severity of the situation denounced, the obligation to ensure the protection of those directly involved in

the facts must be stressed, as well as of other inmates who could be victims or witnesses should similar acts occur, and also not to thwart their due investigation owing to the presence of other prison staff and the possible obstacles this could represent, including to prevent threats, intimidation or reprisals.

40.   Irrespective of whether the requirements concur to order the protection of those deprived of liberty in these prisons, the Court has reiterated that, based on the principle of complementarity and subordination that governs the inter-American human rights system, an order to adopt or maintain provisional measures is only justified in situations established in Article 63(2) of the American Convention, in which the ordinary guarantees that exist in the State regarding which they are requested are insufficient or ineffective, or the domestic authorities cannot or do not want to ensure their effectiveness. [20][68] The State has provided information on numerous, significant measures that its administrative and judicial authorities are adopting as a result of the reported facts (*supra* twenty-first and twenty-second considering paragraphs), which would indicate the willingness of the authorities to set in motion specific mechanisms of prevention and investigation at the domestic level. In other words, the domestic authorities have responded to the situation in the Mendoza Prisons since the Court ordered the provisional measures, and have reacted to the facts that caused the Commission to request the re-opening of the provisional measures. This leads to the reasonable assumption that they will continue exercising due control of respect for the provisions of the Convention, [21][69] and also as regards the measures of protection that may be required in future. Consequently, the Court finds that, at this time, it is not appropriate to order provisional measures of protection.

41.   Nevertheless, it is worth underlining what this Court indicated in its last order of November 26, 2010, when requiring the lifting of the measures decided in the matter of the Mendoza Prisons:

> 52. Notwithstanding the Court's decision, it must be reiterated that Article 1(1) of the Convention establishes the general obligations of the States Parties to respect the rights and freedoms recognized therein and to ensure to all persons subject to their jurisdiction the free and full exercise of those rights and freedoms in all circumstances. In particular, the Court emphasizes the State's position as guarantor with regard to those deprived of liberty, [...] because the prison authorities exercise total control over them, and consequently those general obligations acquire a special nuance that obliges the State to provide the interns with the minimum conditions compatible with their dignity while they remain in a detention center, in order to protect and guarantee their rights to life and personal

integrity.[...] Consequently, irrespective of the existence of specific provisional measures,[...] the State is specifically obliged to guarantee the rights of those deprived of liberty. [...] Moreover, in this particular matter, the Court recalls that in conformity with international norms, the State must ensure that the measures of security adopted in the prison centers include the appropriate training of the penitentiary personnel who provide the security in the prison and the effectiveness of the said mechanisms for the prevention of intra-prison violence, such as the possibility of their having to react to acts of violence or emergencies within the pavilions. The State must ensure that searches and carried out periodically and appropriately, in order to prevent violence and eliminate danger, in function of an adequate and effective control within the pavilions by the penitentiary guards, and that the results of these searches are duly and opportunely communicated to the competent authorities.

53. Regarding minimum detention conditions, it is important to recall the principle that the State must provide adequate facilities, separate interns by categories, provide access to satisfactory health, hygiene and education services, and offer activities for recreation and the mental and physical health of persons deprived of liberty.[...] Furthermore, the State must ensure that the personnel responsible for the custody of interns have the necessary capabilities and tools to perform their work respecting the rights of the detainees, especially that they only use planned and limited force exceptionally, in order to avoid violence within the prison. To this end, the measures that the State must adopt should give priority to a system of preventive measures, addressed, *inter alia*, at avoiding arms smuggling and an increase in violence, rather than a system of repressive measures.[...]

42.   In addition, it should be emphasized that, when lifting these provisional measures, the Court merely determines whether the situation of risk that gave rise to the proceeding subsists, in the terms indicated (*supra* thirtieth considering paragraph), and that the inter-American human rights system will continue to address the situation of the Mendoza Prisons through the actions of one of its organs [the Inter-American Commission], which must determine the next step in the proceedings, either within the framework of the petition pending definition, or by means of other mechanisms, such as the Inter-American Commission's Rapporteur for the Rights of Persons Deprived of Liberty.

THEREFORE:
THE INTER-AMERICAN COURT OF HUMAN RIGHTS,
in exercise of the authority conferred by Article 63(2) of the American Convention on Human Rights and Article 27 of its Rules of Procedure,
DECIDES:
1.   To reject the request to re-open the provisional measures ordered by the Inter-American Court on November 22, 2004, subsequently ratified, and lifted on December 15, 2010, to protect the life and integrity of all those deprived of liberty in the Mendoza Provincial Prison and in the Gustavo André Unit, of Lavalle, as well as all those who are within these prisons.
2.   In keeping with the principle of complementarity and subordination that regulates the inter-American human rights system, not to order the State on this occasion to adopt provisional measures to protect the life and personal integrity of the persons deprived of liberty in the San Felipe and Boulogne Sur Mer Units of the Mendoza Provincial Prison, despite the information included in the forty-first and forty-second considering paragraphs.
3.   To require the Secretariat of the Court to notify this order to the Inter-American Commission on Human Rights and to the Republic of Argentina.
4.   To close the case file of this matter.

Provisional Measures regarding Colombia in the Matter of La Rochela Massacre
19-Nov-2009
Order of the Inter-American Court of Human Rights
Provisional Measures regarding Colombia Case of the Rochela Massacre

CONSIDERING:
1.   That Colombia has been a State Party to the American Convention since July 31, 1973, and according to its Article 62, it has accepted the adjucatory jurisdiction of the Court on June 21, 1985.
2.   That Article 63(2) of the Convention establishes that in "cases of extreme gravity and urgency, and when necessary to avoid irreparable damage to persons," the Court may, with regard to a it is hearing, order such provisional measures as it deems pertinent".
3.   That, in this regard, Article 26 of the Rules of Procedure establishes that:
        1. During any stage of the procedure, as long as regarding cases of extreme gravity, urgency, and when necessary to avoid irreparable damage to persons, the Court, by its own initiative or at the request of a party, may order provisional measures that it considers pertinent, in the terms of Article 63(2) of the

Convention.

[...]

3. In contentious cases already submitted to the Court, the victims or alleged victims, their next of kin, or their duly accredited representatives may present a request for provisional measures directly to the Court.

4.　　That Article 1(1) of the Convention establishes the obligation of the State Parties to respect the rights and freedoms recognized therein and to ensure to all persons subject to their jurisdiction the free and full exercise of those rights and freedoms, which are imposed not only in relation to the power of the State but also in relation with actions of third parties. [170]

5.　　That on October 3, 4, and 6, 2009, Paola Martínez Ortiz, Luz Nely Carvajal Londoño and Esperanza Uribe Mantilla, respectively, received at their homes a pamphlet entitled with the acronym "A.U.C." and signed by the "Agilas (sic) Negras Bloque Capital" group, that signaled that "the past must be left behind" and that they must "think more in those which are and not in those that left." [271] Also, in these pamphlets were the words "MILITARY OBJECTIVE" (capital letters within the text). In the pamphlet received by Ms. Martinez, it said: "do whatever is possible to enjoy your future grandchild."

6.　　That the representatives alleged, without presenting any specific proof in this respect, the following harassments and threats related to Ms. Luz Nelly Carvajal:

　　(a) On September 29 and October 3, 2009, she had received "intimidating calls, as well as threats by telephone," where the "speaker did not talk or hung up in the moment she answered." Also, they alleged that in said opportunities she could have identified the numbers sent, but "when investigating into the calls, [they had appeared] as deactivated or permanently busy," and

　　(b) On October 10, 2009, she received a call on her cell phone in which a voice called her by her name and said "stop bothering."

7.　　That the representatives alleged, without presenting any specific proof in this respect, the following harassments and threats related to Ms. Esperanza Uribe Mantilla:

　　(a) On October 10, 2009, she received a call on her cell phone, in which a "masculine voice" said "Esperanza Uribe Mantilla, this call is with the purpose that you stay quiet, don't talk anymore, if you love your sons, be quiet." An hour later, there was another call with a different voice that said, "Esperanza Uribe Mantilla, I hope that you have clear what I just informed you, if you love your sons, be quiet and don't bother anymore," and

　　(b) In "the past weeks" Ms. Uribe "has been realizing that the trash from her house has been picked through."

8.   That the representatives alleged, without presenting any specific proof in this respect, that on October 10, 2009, Ms. Paola Martinez Ortiz also received a call "approximately at the same time" as Ms. Carvajal and Ms. Uribe, in which a masculine voice said "Didn't you understand the message, old SoB stop bothering."

9.   That the representatives considered that these threats "have placed the victims and their next of kin in a state of permanent terror and anxiety." According to them, even though the State has developed some actions, "it has not provided permanent, structural, and efficient measures that allow a response to the situation of threat." It has resulted that the "threats, harassments, and following warnings are registered in the context of advances in judicial processes [of investigation of the massacre] that have been produced this year," as well as in the "visibility that the next of kin of the victims have acquired" due to "the television programs on which they have participated recently that emphasize the connection to the criminal process of the ex-employees of the State, among those generals of the National Army, who are presumably involved in the planning, development, and execution of the massacre." In the same way, they reiterated that "there exists a risk that similar acts continue to happen and is also extended to other next of kin." They added that the threats received came from self-designated "Aguilas Negras" (Black Eagles) groups, which are "structures that correspond to the actual phase of rearmament and configuration of the paramilitary groups."

10.   That the representatives informed that previously they had presented acts of harassment against Ms. Martinez, Carvajal and Uribe. In this respect, they indicated, without providing proof in this respect, that:

(a) on September 28, 2005, before the public act of recognition of partial State responsibility for the acts of the *Massacre of La Rochela*, some men that were unidentified were asking for Ms. Martinez and Carvajal;

(b) on February 2, 2006 Ms. Uribe, Carvajal and Martínez had been "harassed" by a person that was taking [their] pictures and two youngsters that walked around them and looked at them insistently. Afterwards, a man had looked at them defiantly, and after that he met a person that looked very like the one that had taken [their] pictures;

(c) on February 27, 2006, when Ms. Uribe arrived at her apartment, she perceived "a red-wine colored vehicle that appeared to be watching her." Weeks later, at her place of work, she received a call in which a masculine voice said that they "were to cut the little chain;"

(d) on December 1, 2007, a daughter of Ms. Carvajal had been attacked in the street by a man that sprayed her face with pepper gas, which led to her being incapacitated for several days, and

(e) on December 31, 2007, Ms. Carvajal had received a call to her cellular number, in which a "choked" masculine voice had said: "we are going to kill you." As a consequence of these acts, Ms. Carvajal was forced to change residence along with her family.

11.   That the representatives indicated that the respective criminal reports have been presented before the Attorney General of the Nation, but there have still been no news of the assignment of a prosecutor. They added that they had organized meetings with the Board of Human Rights of the National Police, of the Presidential Program of Human Rights of the Vice-Presidency of the Republic, and with the Ministry of Foreign Relations. They signaled as well that "no measures of adequate protection had been adopted in the understanding that, in accordance with the state authorities, the families of the victims of the Massacre of La Rochela cannot be the object of the Program for Protection of the Ministry of the Interior, nor of the Program of Protection to victims of the public prosecutor's office, because they were not part of a criminal process, nor of the measures in favor of the operators of justice, unless the three victims were workers of the Attorney General of the Nation."

12.   That the State did not present specific proof of any kind. Nevertheless, the State informed regarding the criminal investigation that had been initiated by the Attorney General of the Nation in relation with the threats mentioned. The State specified that the investigation had been assigned to diverse units of the Prosecutor (units 330, 209, 32 and 125). Also, the State maintained that the public prosecutor's office made a "re-evaluation of threat and risk" regarding Ms. Martinez, Carvajal and Uribe, and the results were presented "in the following days" and regarding which the Office of Protection and Assistance of the Attorney General adopted "the decision that it was pertinent." Also, the Board of Protection and Special Services of the National Police had been in charge of executing "technical studies on the level of risk and threat" to the women mentioned. Likewise, Colombia informed that the Metropolitan Police of Bogota had made police rounds for a period of one month at the place of residence of the women.

13.   That the State informed that it made available a "direct [l]ink with the National Police" with the goal that the victims "could contact them in case of an emergency through their cellular phones." Also, they had facilitated contact numbers of the person in charge of the Police Station in the respective zone and the telephone numbers of the Coordinator of the Group of Human Rights of the National Police. Finally, the State "reject[ed] all the acts of intimidation" that occurred.

14.   That Article 63(2) of the Convention demands that for the Court to grant provisional measures, three conditions must concur: i) "extreme gravity," ii) "urgency," and iii) when necessary to "avoid irreparable damage to persons." These three conditions are co-existing and must be present in each situation in which the intervention of the Tribunal is sought. In the same way, the three

conditions described must persist for the Court to maintain the protection ordered. If one of them is no longer in effect, the Tribunal will again evaluate the pertinence of continuing with the protection ordered.

15.   That the standard of interpretation of a *prima facie* case and the application of presumptions before the necessities of protection have led this Court to order measures in distinct occasions.[372] Nevertheless, with the goal of maintaining the measures, it is necessary that the situation of extreme gravity, urgency, and the need to avoid irreparable damage subsists,[373] for which, before the requirements of the Court to evaluate the maintenance of the same, said information must be duly accredited and founded.

16.   That the pamphlets received by Ms. Martinez, Carvajal and Uribe in October of 2009, in which a military objective by an illegal armed group is declared, constitute a situation that generates extreme gravity and urgency of risk for the life and personal integrity of said persons, for which it is pertinent to order measures of protection in their favor.

17.   That the information regarding the risk of the next of kin of the women mentioned is still insufficient and only counted with the general mention of the attack suffered by the daughter of Ms. Carvajal and the mention of the grandson of Ms. Martinez in the pamphlet that threatened death on October 3, 2009. Therefore, the Tribunal will [e]valuate its pertinence after learning of the risk studies that currently are being carried out by the state institutions.

18.   That the State must carry out the pertinent steps so that the provisional measures ordained in the present Order are planned and applied with the participation of the beneficiaries of the same or their representatives, in such a way that the measures referred to are offered in a diligent and effective manner.

NOW THEREFORE:

THE INTER-AMERICAN COURT OF HUMAN RIGHTS,

pursuant to the authority conferred by Article 63(2) of the American Convention on Human Rights and Article 26 and 30 of its Rules of Procedure,[574]

DECIDES:

1.   To require the State to adopt immediately the measures necessary to protect the life and personal integrity of Ms. Paola Martínez Ortiz, Luz Nelly Carvajal Londoño, and Esperanza Uribe Mantilla.

2.   To require the State to carry out all the pertinent steps for the ordained measures of protection in the present Order to be planned and implemented with the participation of the beneficiaries of the same or their representatives, in such a way that the measures referred to are offered in a diligent and effective manner and that, in general, to keep the Court informed about the advancement of their execution.

3.   To require the State to inform the Court, no later than January 20, 2010, about the steps that it has taken to implement the provisional measures that this

Order has ordained and to continue informing the Court with respect to the measures each two months.

4.   To request the representatives of the beneficiaries of the present measures and the Inter-American Commission on Human Rights to present their observations to the State's reports referred to the previous resolution point, in a time period of four and six weeks, respectively, beginning from the notification of the same.

5.   To require the Secretary of the Court to notify this Order to the Inter-American Commission on Human Rights, the representatives of the beneficiaries of these measures, and to the Republic of Colombia.

Provisional Measures regarding Mexico in the Matter of Rosendo Cantú et al.

2-Feb-2010
Order of the President of the Inter-American Court of Human Rights
Provisional Measures regarding Mexico

HAVING SEEN:
1.   The Order issued by the then-President (hereinafter "the President") of the Inter-American Court of Human Rights (hereinafter "the Inter-American Court," "the Court" or "the Tribunal") on April 9, 2009, by which it required the United Mexican States (hereinafter "Mexico" or "the State") to immediately adopt the measures that were necessary to protect the life and personal integrity of Obtilia Eugenio Manuel and certain next of kin; of Inés Fernández Ortega and certain next of kin, of 41 members of the Tlapaneco Indigenous People Organization and of 29 members of the Montaña Tlachinollan Organization, and the next of kin of Raúl Lucas Castro and Manuel Ponce Rosas, in the case of Fernandez Ortega *et al.*

2.   The Order issued by the Tribunal on April 30, 2009, by which it ratified the Order of the President of the Inter-American Court of April 9, 2009.

3.   The brief of December 18, 2009, and its appendixes, by which the Tlapaneco Indigenous People Organization A. C. (OPIT), the Center for Human Rights of the Montaña Tlachinollan, A. C. (Tlachinollan) and the Center for Justice and International Law (CEJIL) (all together hereinafter "the representatives"), submitted to the Inter-American Court a request for the extension of the provisional measures in the procedure related with the Inés Fernández Ortega *et al.* case, in conformity with Article 63 of the American Convention on Human Rights (hereinafter "the American Convention" or "the Convention") and Article 26 of the Rules of the Court then in force, with the purpose of Mexico protecting the life and personal integrity of Valentina Rosendo Cantú and her daughter Yenis Bernardino Rosendo.

4.   The alleged facts upon which the request for provisional measures was based presented by the representatives, namely:

(a) Valentina Rosendo Cantú (hereinafter also "Ms. Rosendo") and her daughter, Yenis Bernardino Rosendo, live alone in the city of Chilpancingo (the capital of the state of Guerrero) far from their community, "as a consequence of the [alleged] sexual violation suffered by [the first] at the hands of the military;"

(b) On October 12, 2009, when Ms. Rosendo left her work, she noticed a man in the sidewalk in front observing the house from which she had left and he followed her. When she stopped in a store, such person continued watching her, so she chose to return to the house where she worked. Four hours later, when she again left for her home, Ms. Rosendo noticed the presence of the same person that had been watching her. Due to "[t]hese facts, caused her a grave fear," she returned to her work-place. She communicated with a next of kin for him to accompany her, and as she left her work-place, she noticed that "the man was still outside" and he photographed her with a cell phone. The following morning, when Ms. Rosendo left her other job, "the person that had been watching her" the day before was outside the house. Consequently, on November 17, 2009, Ms. Rosendo brought a complain[t] for the offense of threats, for which the prior investigation GRO/SC/125/2009 was begun;

(c) On December 11, 2009, at approximately 6:20 pm, Ms. Rosendo went to pick up her daughter Yenis Bernardino from the school where she studied and a few meters before arriving, her daughter "left running with her backpack on her back, crying and very upset," because two men that had tried to take her away, had stolen her cell phone. For this, the aforementioned inquiry incorporated the new criminal facts against Ms. Rosendo and her daughter for the offense of threats, robbery, minors or disabled persons abduction, and child abduction.

(d) On February 13, 2009, "in the framework of the disappearance of Raúl Lucas Lucía and Manuel Ponce Flores, as well as of the aggressions committed against Obtilia Eugenio, Ms. Rosendo informed her representatives "that she identified two persons that were watching her and following her from her house to her work." She added that Ms. Rosendo "could recognize that one of the persons watching her [had] been identifie[d] as an assistant of the Army." The next of kin of Ms. Rosendo, who are in another community, had manifested her that they fear for her life, because in such place "information exists that members of the Army, which are connected with other members of the community, are in Chilpancingo with the objective of following her."

5.   The arguments of the representatives to support their request for measures of protection, among which they provided that:

(a) "the facts are grave attempts against life, security, and tranquility of Valentina [Rosendo Cantu] and her daughter" and occurred in a context of the re-activation of the case of Ms. Rosendo before the Tribunal, "for which a well-founded fear exists that reprisals may be taken against her or against her family,"

(b) Ms. Rosendo and her daughter do not have on a security measure that allows them to be protected. As a result of the sexual violation and the work that she initiated to denounce it on an internal and international level, Ms. Rosendo "was obligated to radically change her life and to reside in the city of Chilpancingo, where she does not have social networks of support." Initially, they estimated that the change of city was a measure to give her protection, nevertheless "[the] response and [the] measures of protection towards her were slower" when provided by the representatives, since Tlachinollan is located 4 and a half hours of distance by vehicle from Chilpancingo;

(c) The facts suffered by Ms. Rosendo and her daughter are similar to those that were denounced by the beneficiaries of the related provisional measures in the case of Fernández Ortega *et al.*, namely "following and the taking of photos by persons with similar profiles and complexion; incidents of robbery to close next of kin [and] threats," and

(d) The situation of extreme gravity and urgency is manifested in that since 2002, the year in which the facts occurred, to the present date, the investigations had not advanced. They affirmed that "[t]he impunity for the authors of these acts leads to repetition and worsening of the acts against the beneficiaries." Additionally, said situation "is directly linked with the work of denounce that [Ms. Rosendo] has made in relation to her case, whose pattern and context have much in common with the case of Inés Fernández [Ortega]."

6.   The Order of the President of the Tribunal of December 23, 2009, through which it resolved, *inter alia*:

> 1. To dismiss the request for extension of the provisional measures, according to that indicated in the eighth Considering paragraph of the [...] Order.
>
> 2. To require the State to inform the Inter-American Court of Human Rights, no later than January 8, 2010, about the situation of extreme gravity and urgency of Ms. Valentina Rosendo Cantú and her daughter Yenis Bernardino Rosendo, within the case of Rosendo Cantú v. México.

7.   The brief of January 5, 2010, through which the State requested "an extension of 15 days to complete the report regarding the situation" of Valentina Rosendo Cantú and Yenis Bernardino Rosendo requested by the President.

8.   The communications of January 7 and 21, 2010, through which the Secretary of the Inter-American Court (hereinafter "the Secretary"), following the instructions of the President of the Tribunal, respectively: a) granted an extension to the State until January 15, 2010, to present said report, and b) reminded the State that, at the expiration of the extension granted, the mentioned report had not been received, for which the Secretary requested its submission as soon as possible.

9.   The brief of January 26, 2010, through which the State presented information about the alleged situation of extreme gravity and urgency of Valentina Rosendo Cantú and Yenis Bernardino Rosendo.

CONSIDERING:

1.   That Mexico is a State Party to the American Convention since March 24, 1981, and, according to Article 62 of the Convention, recognized the adjudicatory jurisdiction of the Court on December 16, 1998.

2.   That Article 63(2) of the American Convention provides that, "[i]n cases of extreme gravity and urgency, and when necessary to avoid irreparable damage to persons, the Court shall adopt such provisional measures as it deems pertinent in matters it has under consideration. With respect to a case not yet submitted to the Court, it may act at the request of the Commission."

3.   That Article 27 of the Rules of the Court[175] provides:

> 1. At any stage of the proceedings involving cases of extreme gravity and urgency, and when necessary to avoid irreparable damage to persons, the Court may, at the request of a party or on its own motion, order such provisional measures as it deems pertinent, pursuant to Article 63(2) of the Convention.
>
> [...]
>
> 3. In contentious cases already submitted to the Court, the victims or alleged victims or their duly accredited representatives, may present directly to the Court a request for provisional measures in relation to [. . .] the object of the case.
>
> [...]

4.   That Article 1(1) of the Convention establishes the general obligations of the State Parties to respect the rights and liberties protected in it and to guarantee their free and full exercise to each person that is subject to its jurisdiction, which are imposed not only in relation to the power of the State but also in relation with the actions of third persons.[276]

5.   That under International Human Rights law, provisional measures are not only precautionary, in the sense of preserving a juridical situation; they are also safeguards inasmuch as they protect human rights. When the requisite basic conditions of extreme gravity and urgency are present and when necessary to prevent irreparable harm to persons, provisional measures become a true jurisdictional guarantee that is preventive in nature.[377]

6.   That the regulation established in Article 63(2) of the Convention confers an obligatory character to the adoption, on the part of the State, of the provisional measures that this Tribunal orders, so that according to the basic principle of the law of international responsibility of the State, supported by international jurisprudence, the States must comply with their convention obligations in good faith (*pacta sunt servanda*).[478]

7.   That the request for amplification of provisional measures in favor of Ms. Rosendo and her daughter was denied in the framework of the case of Fernández Ortega *et al.* Nevertheless, the Court observes that, just as signaled by the President in the Order of December 23, 2009,[579] that the beneficiaries of the provisional measures correspond to the presumed victims of the case of Rosendo Cantú *et al.*, for which the facts and arguments shown by the representatives in their brief, as well as the information presented by the State, will be analyzed in the present case.

8.   That of the information supplied by the representatives, it follows that Ms. Rosendo and her daughter, due to the sexual violation that Ms. Rosendo suffered, have moved from the city and are living far from their family. In such location, Ms. Rosendo has been the object of followings from her two places of work and photographed on one of these occasions by one same person of "military appearance;" previously, two unknown persons had tried to deprive the child of Ms. Rosendo of her liberty and had robbed her cell phone. These facts have been put into the knowledge of the Public Ministry and a prior inquiry has been begun (*supra* Having Seen 4).

9.   That the State transmitted to this Tribunal "the information obtained by the Secretary of the Interior, the institution responsible for implementing and monitoring the provisional [...] measures." Of the information submitted, it follows that:

   (a) for the General Director of International Cooperation of the Attorney General of the Republic, "the requirements of gravity and urgency are not fulfilled, elements which are necessary for the implementation of provisional measures," given that "there is no background of these facts regarding whether they have been denounced before the Agent of the Public Ministry of the Federation, given that [...] the facts referred to were made to the knowledge of the Agent of the Public Ministry of the Common Jurisdiction in the state of Guerrero;"

   (b) the Special Prosecutor for the Protection of Human Rights of the

Attorney General of Justice of the State of Guerrero indicated that on November 17, 2009, it began the prior inquiry GRO/SC/125/2009 for the offense of threats against Ms. Rosendo Cantu, "in which the Ministry attest[ed] to the accuracy of the initiative and the brief of the accusation, the ratification of the brief of the claim by [the offended party] and the declaration of [a] witness." Also, on December 15, 2009, Ms. Rosendo Cantu extended the claim "for new criminal facts against her minor daughter [...] which took place on December 11, 2009, but to this date, the brief has not been ratified by the offended party," and

(c) the person in charge of the Police Station of Sector 41-XII Chilapancingo of the State of Guerrero manifested that "no request for help [...] nor any incident by the part of [Ms. Rosendo and her daughter] has been received or registered."

10.   That Article 63(2) of the Convention demands that for the Court to provide provisional measures, three conditions must coincide: i) "extreme gravity," ii) "urgency," and iii) and to "avoid irreparable damage to persons." These three conditions are coexistent and must be present in every situation in which the intervention of the Tribunal is requested. [6 80]

11.   That when issuing measures of protection, the Tribunal or whoever is presiding is not required, in principle, to find evidence of the facts that *prima facie* appear to fulfill the requirements of Article 63 of the Convention. On the contrary, the maintenance of the measures of protection demand an evaluation by the Court regarding the persistence of the situation of extreme gravity and urgency to avoid irreparable damage that gave origin to the measures, [7 81] on the basis of the evidentiary information. [8 82]

12.   That the information presented by the representatives and the State (*supra* Considering 8 and 9) demonstrate, *prima facie*, that Ms. Rosendo and her daughter, who are the presumed victims in a case before the Court regarding, *inter alia*, the alleged sexual violation against Ms. Rosendo, supposedly committed by military personnel, and with the lack of an investigation of such facts, are found in a situation of extreme gravity and urgency, so that their lives and personal integrity shall be threatened and in grave risk. This results from the alleged followings carried out, the photographs taken, and the attempt to deprive the liberty of the girl. Consequently, the Tribunal finds necessary the protection of said persons through provisional measures, in light of that provided in the Convention.

13.   That without prejudice to the aforementioned and in consideration of that put forth, the Court deems appropriate to order: a) that the State present a report that identifies and establishes the risk of threat for the beneficiaries of the present provisional measures, and timely defines the measures and means of specific, adequate, and sufficient protection to avoid that the risk materializes, and b) that the representatives

present information that permits the Tribunal to evaluate the persistence of the situation of extreme gravity and urgency and of the need to avoid irreparable damage to the beneficiaries. Also, the Court finds it necessary that the representatives clarify their account of the facts. In this sense, the Court warns that, on one hand, it declares that in October of 2009, on two opportunities, Ms. Rosendo was followed by the same person (*supra* [Having Seen] 4.b), while, on the other hand, they indicate that in February 2009, Ms. Rosendo had identified "the two persons that were watching and following her from her house to her job," (*supra* [Having Seen] 4.d).

14.   That the State must carry out the pertinent steps so that the provisional measures ordered in the present Order are planned and applied with the participation of their beneficiaries, or their representatives, in such a manner that the measures are offered in a diligent and effective manner. The Court emphasizes that it is essential the positive participation of the State, and particularly of the representatives, with the goal of coordinating the implementation of the provisional measures in the present case.

15.   That the Tribunal finds it timely to remember that when dealing with provisional measures, it corresponds to the Court to consider only and strictly those arguments that relate directly with extreme gravity, urgency, and the need to avoid irreparable damage to persons. Any other fact or argument can only be analyzed and resolved during the consideration of the merits of a contentious case. [9][83]

16.   The adoption of provisional measures does not imply an eventual decision regarding the merits of the existing controversy between the beneficiaries and the State, [10][84] nor prejudges the State's responsibility for the facts denounced. When adopting provisional measures, the Tribunal is only exercising its mandate according to the Convention, in cases of extreme gravity and urgency that require measures of protection in order to avoid irreparable damage to persons. [11][85]

THEREFORE:

THE INTER-AMERICAN COURT OF HUMAN RIGHTS,

In use of the powers conferred upon it in Article 63(2) of the American Convention on Human Rights and Article 27 of the Rules of the Tribunal,

DECIDES:

1.   To require the State to adopt, immediately, the measures necessary to protect the life and personal integrity of Valentina Rosendo Cantú and Yenis Bernardino Rosendo, taking into consideration the situation and the particular circumstances of this case.

2.   To require the State to submit to the Inter-American Court the report indicated in the Considering thirteenth of the present Order, as well as information regarding the implementation of the measures no later than March 22, 2010. Also, the State must submit a bi-monthly report about the implementation and effects of the present measures, a time period that must begin on the aforementioned date.

3.   To request the representatives of the beneficiaries and the Inter-American Commission on Human Rights to present their observations in a time period of two and four weeks, respectively, from the notification of the reports of the State that are indicated in the second operative paragraph. Also, the representatives must respond to the request for clarification indicated in the Considering thirteenth of the present Order.

4.   To request the Secretary to notify the present Order to the State, the Inter-American Commission on Human Rights and the representatives of the beneficiaries.

1-Jul-2011
Order of the Inter-American Court of Human Rights
Provisional Measures regarding the United Mexican States
case of *Rosendo Cantú et al.*

(a) Assessment of the risk

5.   The State reported that on March 8, 2010, a meeting was held between the representatives of the beneficiaries and the authorities involved in the present case, in which Mexico accepted the offer made by the representatives to have the risk assessment carried out by Peace Brigades International of Mexico (hereinafter "Peace Brigades") or by the United Nation's Office of the High Commissioner of Human Rights in Mexico (hereinafter "Office in Mexico of the High Commissioner). It reported that Peace Brigades expressed that it would be able to carry out risk assessment to the beneficiaries, and that the Office of the High Commissioner in Mexico noted that "it would follow the process of the presentation of the study of the analysis of the risk." It affirmed that the document drafted by Peace Brigades "is accepted by the State as the appropriate mechanism to comply with the [operative] paragraph of the Order of February 2, 2010."

(b) Measures of protection in favor of the beneficiaries

15.   The State reported that "[on] March 8, 2010 [...] it presented the representative[s] with three sets of NEXTEL radio phones[,] requested [by the beneficiaries]." It added that on May 5, 2010, the representatives required the State to install a satellite telephone at the home of the family members of the beneficiaries. In this regard, it noted that, although the family members of Mrs. Rosendo Cantú are not beneficiaries of the present provisional measures, the State "in good faith [...] is carrying out the necessary administrative procedures to implement the requested measure." It stated that on August 31, 2010, it signed a contract with a telephone company for its services, despite there having been some administrative difficulties with the company." Given the foregoing, "a [...] new contract was requested," where the possibility existed "of acquiring other sets that could better satisfy the requirements [...] of the provisional measures." It

subsequently reported that new steps have been taken in this regard and noted that "once there is a result, it will inform the Court on the matter."

16.   Regarding the other measures of protection, it indicated that on July 15, 2010, it presented the representatives with a "preliminary work plan," wherein it included the proposals of the State regarding the implementation of the recommendations issued by Peace Brigades in its risk assessment of May 21, 2010. On September 13, 2010, it presented the representatives with a work plan for the comprehensive implementation of measures, so that the representatives could submit their comments in order to begin the implementation. On March 23, 2011, it reported that, once the observations of the representatives were received, Mexico began taking the pertinent steps, in such a way that:

(a) on February 8, 2011, the beneficiaries were provided with specific security equipment for their home;

(b) the representatives are in contact with a public employee of the Unit for the Promotion and Defense of Human Rights, who—at any time—responds to situations related to the security of the beneficiaries and implements specific actions of to coordinate with agencies to attend to the complaints;

(c) a "guarantee letter" was provided to the beneficiaries, signed by the head of the Unit for the Promotion and Defense of Human Rights, which establishes the special situation of protection of the beneficiaries, and which allows for an immediate response of any security body if they encounter risk;

(d) a "guarantee letter" was provided to the beneficiaries, signed by the head of the Unit for the Promotion and Defense of Human Rights, addressed to the authorities at a federal, state, and municipal level, with a message of support recognizing the responsibility of the State to protect the integrity of Mrs. Rosendo Cantú, and

(e) together with the Ministry of Federal Public Security, efforts were made to provide the beneficiaries with a "Workshop on Stalking Detection and Response Actions to any harassment" and a "Course on Self Defense," in the terms requested by the representatives, without receiving a response from the mentioned agency. In regard to the measures pending implementation, "it considers that due to the change in circumstances both regarding the initiation of efforts by State authorities of Guerrero as well as the initiation of the execution of the [J]udgement [...], it is necessary to establish, in consensus with the beneficiaries, a new path for the care of the provisional measures, to which [...] it will summon [...] a work meeting [with the representatives]." In regard to the measures that have not yet been agreed upon by the representatives, it expressed "its commitment and willingness to continue with the pertinent negotiations and to promptly reach an agreement regarding the handling of the matter."

17.   The representatives noted that the State, upon taking on the recommendations proposed by Peace Brigades in its report, this would "allow for [...] the creation of a comprehensive security plan that in a preventive manner mitigates the gravity and urgency of the risk and creates the conditions necessary to avoid, as little as possible, incidents associated with the security of the beneficiaries and their family." They indicated that "the proposals of the State do not address the pressing needs facing the beneficiaries, according to the assessment prepared by Peace Brigades." To that extent, the creation of security conditions continued to fall on the beneficiaries and their representatives. They indicated that the state "has failed to report [...] that the implementation of those measures not covered by its proposal remains pending [, as well as] the appropriateness of those, which being covered, do not meet the specifications and the purpose of the evaluation of risk undertaken." They confirmed that "in terms of the security infrastructure for the home of the beneficiaries [...] the State presented [specific] equipment [...] on February 8, 2011." They added that several of the measures proposed by the State have not been accepted, without there being a counteroffer by the State representatives to date.

18.   Likewise, they confirmed that the State gave the requested cellular phones on March 8, 2009, one of which was stolen from the sister of Mrs. Rosendo Cantú, to which they requested "that the stolen radio phone be returned and the necessary change of number be done for the two phones that continue to work, in order to ensure the security of the beneficiaries." They indicated that the State had not complied with the request to install a satellite telephone in the home of the family members of the beneficiary and that "for her, the isolation of her father and mother in her native community, increases the risk and founded fear. [One] of the satellite telephones would allow Mrs. Rosendo Cantú to monitor the situation regarding the security of her parents and family." They specified that "her family, [although they are not beneficiaries of the present measures,] have suffered threats and intimidations, which are intended to impact the search for justice that [Mrs.] Rosendo Cantu has lived for a duration of [...] eight years. They noted that the conduct of the State in regard to the installation of the satellite telephone demonstrates reluctance to comply with this measure.

19.   They concluded that the actions that to date the State has carried out "are administrative actions that consist of the submission of two official letters, and [...] it has provided specific infrastructure, which is only part of that requested. [Nevertheless,] it has not implemented actions that remove the administrative or financial obstacles that would allow for prompt specific actions or to pay for the expenses to guarantee the security of the beneficiaries. Based on the foregoing,

they anticipate a summons by the State for a follow-up meeting, recalling that the last meeting was carried out in July 2010."

20.   The Commission expressed "the need for the State to adopt the necessary measures to protect the life and integrity of the beneficiaries as promptly as possible and the importance of the participation of representatives in the design of its implementation." It added that "the design of the sufficient and appropriate provisional measures for [her] protection [...]should not be subject to obtaining resources from the Mexican State, and [should be implemented] as soon as possible." It valued the implementation of agreements between the parties and that the State "is responding to the requests of [the representatives]," waiting "for the limitations posed to be overcome" regarding those measures for which no agreements have been reached. It concluded that the "proceed[u]res carried out by the [State] can be of use, but do not constitute the most substantive or specific measures required for the effective protection of the beneficiaries."

21.   In regard to the measures of protection adopted to date, first, the Court values that State provided equipment for the protection of the beneficiaries at their home, as well as the provision of three phones requested for use by the beneficiaries and the sister of Mrs. Rosendo Cantú, and its willingness to replace the stolen phone. Nevertheless, the Court does not have sufficient information on the progress made regarding the delivery of the stolen phone and the change of number requested by the representatives, to which it asks the State to submit up to date information on this point.

22.   As for the satellite phone to be installed in the home of the parents of Mrs. Rosendo Cantú, the Court appreciates the willingness of the State to provide this measure in order for the beneficiary to monitor the situation of her family in the community where they reside, as requested by the representatives, notwithstanding that it notes that the family members of Mrs. Rosendo Cantú are not beneficiaries of the provisional measures, to which the Court is not able to analyze the measure (*supra* Considering clause 12).

23.   For the measures of protection related to the proposal made by Peace Brigades in its report, the Court will refer, first, to those which have already been implemented by agreement between the parties, second, to those where there has been an agreement by the parties but have not yet been implemented, third, to the measures where there is no agreement between the parties, and finally, to the specific measures that, although requested, are not related to the provisional measures.

24.   On the first point, the Court notes that the representatives and the State have come to an agreement and have implemented the following measures of protection, in addition to the those regarding the delivery of the radio equipment and the protection of the home: a) delivery of security infrastructure for the home

of the beneficiaries (*supra* Considering clause 21); b) the provision of the contact information of a public employee to the beneficiaries of the Unit for the Promotion and Defense of Human Rights of the Ministry of the Interior; c) delivery of a "guarantee letter" to the beneficiaries, signed by the head of the Unit for the Promotion and Defense of Human Rights, which establishes the special situation of protection of the beneficiaries, and which allows for an immediate response of any security body if they encounter risk; d) delivery of a "guarantee letter," signed by the head of the Unit for the Promotion and Defense of Human Rights, addressed to the authorities at a federal, state, and municipal level, with a message of support recognizing the responsibility of the State to protect the integrity of the beneficiaries, and e) efforts to assure the participation of the beneficiary in a "Workshop on Stalking Detection and Response Actions to any harassment" and a "Course on Self Defense." The Court appreciates the steps taken by Mexico to reach a compromise with the representatives that has allowed for the implementation of these measures and requests that the State submit an update on the progress of the measure referred to in paragraph e) of this paragraph.

25.   Second, the Court notes from that reported by the parties that there are certain measures of protection where there is no apparent controversy between the parties, but the State has not reported on implementation of these measures. In this regard, the Court notes that the representatives do not specify all of the measures, but rather they indicate "among them, for example, [...] the support of the Ministry of Education for the security of Yenis Bernardino at the school, and the establishment of bi-monthly meetings to assess compliance with the provisional measures." Consequently, the Court asked the representatives to specify the specific measures proposed by the State that have been accepted without question by the beneficiaries, and also requires the State to submit specific information on this point.

26.   As regards the other measures of protection on which the parties have not reached an agreement, the Court recalls that in its previous Order it determined that the State should take the steps necessary to ensure that the provisional measures are planned and implemented with the participation of the beneficiaries or their representatives, so that the measures are provided for in a diligent and effective manner. The Court emphasized that the positive involvement of the State and particularly of the representatives is essential to coordinate the implementation of provisional measures in this case. Consequently, the Court considers it necessary that the process for determining these protective measures continue to be performed in joint form, constructively and promptly, and with the constant communication and agreement between the parties. In this regard, the Court notes that the parties agree on the need to hold meetings in order to specify the pertinent actions to continue to implement appropriate security measures, given

the current circumstances, and therefore calls on the State and representatives to come together to promptly carry out the relevant meetings, with the participation of all authorities and agencies involved, and to submit to the Court an updated reported on the progress that results therein.

27.   Lastly, the Court considers that specific measures of protection have been proposed that are not directly related to the adoption of urgent and effective provisional measures that guarantee the protection of the integrity or life of the beneficiaries, but rather that involve measures related to the general situation suffered by Mrs. Rosendo Cantu and her daughter, as a consequence of the facts related to the contentious case and that, in large part, concern the measures of reparation ordered in the Judgment; or, where applicable, involve measures in favor of third parties that are not beneficiaries of these provisional measures. For this reason, the Court will not rule on the following measures of protection:

(a) the provision of a computer and highspeed internet connection for the home of the beneficiaries and computer and internet use training;

(b) delivery of a photographic camera;

(c) facilitate the registration of the daughter in a study center for her to continue her school year, cover expenses related to her education, and fund a babysitter or a trustworthy person to care for the child when Mrs. Rosendo Cantú is not around;

(d) permanent lighting system on the outside of Mrs. Rosendo Cantú's parents home, and a monitoring system camera and security plates in the her sister's home,

(e) cover of the costs of psychological care until the beneficiary no longer wants such services;

(f) coverage of expenses related to professional training that will enable her to have stable employment while she manages the situation of exile she is in;

(g) coverage of the beneficiaries travel expenses for trips made to visit their relatives and members of their organization, and

(h) accountability of the military operations in the Mountains of Costa Chica de Guerrero.

(c) Investigation of the facts that led to the provisional measures

28.   In regard to the investigation of the threats and harassment experienced by the beneficiaries, the State noted that in the framework of the preliminary investigation GRO/SC/125/2009, a site-visit was carried out at the place where the events occurred that was turned over to the Ministerial Police of the State for the investigation of what occurred, nevertheless, "[i]n order to continue with the investigations], it is necessary that the injured parties [...] ratify and expand their statements," not appearing when summoned. In response to the representatives,

Mexico noted that it is not its intention to apply, to her detriment, any measures, enshrined in domestic legislation, to pressure her to appear; on the contrary, "it is willing to offer the necessary legal guarantees to adapt the proceedings to any special needs" and preserve her security when she decides to go before the authorities. Notwithstanding the foregoing, it reiterated that as this regards crimes challenged on a complaint, the participation of the victims is essential to continue with the integration of the investigations. Subsequently, it reported that the Attorney General of Guerrero "stated that the all steps to continue the preliminary investigation have been exhausted [...] without the appearance of the beneficiaries, to which it reiterates its willingness that the ministerial authorities be moved to where the [beneficiaries] are to seek the expansion of their statements." Consequently, Mexico "will await, within the limits permitted by law, the necessary time for the [beneficiaries] to provide the information they already have about the events that gave rise to the provisional measures." Finally, it required the psychologist who has carried out the psychological studies on Mrs. Rosendo Cantu to go before the Attorney General of the Republic to ratify her expert report made, in order for "the corresponding legal effects to follow-suit." Regarding the investigation of events surrounding the rape of Mrs. Rosendo Cantú, the State indicated that it is the subject of the Judgment delivered by the Court in this case, and therefore "it will be processed as part of the monitoring of compliance of [it]." 29. The representatives reported that the identification of those responsible cannot depend solely on a sketch or of the direct recognition of the victim, but rather that the investigation can move forward based on the extensive investigations carried out by the ministerial police. Nevertheless, "the State has not shown that it has developed a line of investigation to establish the truth of what happened. By contrast, it only lists two procedures taken and seems to depend on the progress of the investigation only on the initiative of the victim." They indicated that the beneficiary is in a situation of PTSD and the psychologist that is treating her recommends "that she avoid revictimizing events or meetings, [including] to appear before authorities in the procurement and administration of justice." That is why, even though Mrs. Rosendo Cantu is "entirely willing to appear before the authorities and to help clarify the facts," such appearance should "not to be required" if her security and psycho-emotional integrity do not allow for it. They noted that "the Mexican constitutional framework establishes that the security and support of the victims is a right, and as such possible coercive measures that can be applied to the detriment of the [beneficiary] are incomprehensible." Subsequently, they reported that "the work of accompaniment carried out for [Mrs. Rosendo Cantú] have confirmed that both beneficiaries do not have any information to contribute to the investigation. Therefore, it is unnecessary that they go before the prosecuting authority." On the other hand, they stated that "the forwarding of the investigation to the civil justice system regarding the rape by members of the Army against [Mrs.] Rosendo Cantú is essential to add to her security."

30.   The Commission noted that there is not enough information regarding the possible link between the case of Mrs. Rosendo Cantu before the Court, the threats against her that led to the provisional measures, and the case before the Court of Mrs. Fernández Ortega, and the threats that she and her defenders suffer, without sufficient information regarding "whether the investigations of the preliminary investigation are linked with the investigation into the facts of the case or regarding possible lines of investigation." It also emphasized the importance of investigating the threats made in a comprehensive manner, considering that "the implementation of [the] measures of protection, together with the investigation to determine the source of the risk in which the beneficiaries are in, and the effective punishment, are crucial factors to prevent the occurrence of more irreparable harm." It stressed that "the impunity in which the case remains [regarding the rape of Mr. Rosendo Cantu], including the failure to forward the case to the ordinary jurisdiction, is one of the elements that has not allowed for substantial progress regarding the elimination of risk factors for the beneficiaries [...] through the administration of justice." It affirmed that "it is not clear from the information provided by the State whether it is necessary that the beneficiaries have to go to ratify the expert report of the psychologist or whether it is enough that said professional ratifies it."

31.   The Court first notes that the representatives and the Commission refer in this aspect both to the investigation of the events that led to the adoption of provisional measures, as well as to the investigation of the facts related to the case on the merits resolved by the Court through the Judgment on preliminary objections, merits, reparations and costs, issued on August 31, 2010 in the *case of Rosendo Cantú et al.* In this regard, and notwithstanding any relationship that might exist between the two procedures, the analysis of the effectiveness of the investigation carried out domestically on the facts related to this Judgment, as well as the intervention of the ordinary criminal courts, should be done under the monitoring of compliance with the Judgment.

32.   In relation to the obligation to investigate the facts in the complaint that resulted in the present measures, the Court recalls that Article 1(1) of the American Convention establishes that the State has the general obligation to respect the rights and liberties recognized therein and to guarantee their free and full exercise to each person subject to its jurisdiction. As a consequence, independent of the existence of specific provisional measures, the State is especially obligated to guarantee the rights of the persons in situations of risk and must promote the necessary investigations in order to clarify the facts, and where necessary, punish those responsible.[11][86] Nevertheless, this Court has noted that the analysis of the effectiveness of investigations and proceedings

concerning the facts that motivate the provisional measures should be done in the examination of the merits of the case.[12 87]

33.　　The Court notes that in this case, the State, although it has only reported on some procedures taken in connection with the investigation of the allegations, confirmed that it is willing to provide the legal guarantees necessary to adapt the procedure to the special needs of the beneficiaries in order for them to appear before a court to continue with the respective proceeding (*supra* Considering clause 28).

Moreover, the representatives initially demonstrated the "broad willingness of [Mrs. Rosendo Cantú] to appear before the authorities to contribute to the clarification of the facts." In this manner, the Court considers it convenient for the parties to agree on appropriate mechanisms for a possible statement of the beneficiaries that does not imply any damage to the emotional or psychological state, which could involve the taking of a statement by female personnel of the public prosecutor's office, in a trustworthy environment for the beneficiaries, in a tranquil environment and with psychological assistance by the professionals that usually accompany her.

THEREFORE:
THE INTER-AMERICAN COURT OF HUMAN RIGHTS,
In use of the powers conferred upon it in Article 63(2) of the American Convention on Human Rights and Article 27 of the Rules of the Tribunal,
DECIDES:
1.　　To require the State to continue adopting the measures that may be necessary to protect the life and personal integrity of Valentina Rosendo Cantú and Yenis Bernardino Rosendo, taking into account the situation and specific circumstances of the case.
2.　　To require the State to continue reporting to the Inter-American Court of Human Rights, every two months, as of legal notice of this Order, on the provisional measures adopted in conformity with this decision.
3.　　To request the representatives of the beneficiaries and the Inter-American Commission on Human Rights to present their observations in a period of two and four weeks, respectively, as of legal notice of the reports of the State noted in operative paragraph 2. Moreover, the representatives should respond to the request for information noted in Considering clause 25 of this Order.
4.　　To request the Secretariat to provide legal notice of the present Order to the United Mexican States, the Inter-American Commission on Human Rights, and the representatives of the beneficiaries. Judge Vio Grossi presented his Dissenting Vote before the Court, and Judges García-Sayán, Franco, Ventura Robles, Macaulay and Abreu Blondet presented their Concurring Opinion, which accompany this Order.

23-June-2015
Order of the Inter-American Court of Human Rights
Provisional Measures regarding the United Mexican States

THE INTER-AMERICAN COURT OF HUMAN RIGHTS,
DECIDES:
By five votes to one:
1.   To maintain the provisional measures ordered in favor of Valentina Rosendo Cantú and of Yenis Bernardino Rosendo for an additional period of time that expires on the 23 of December of 2015, and thus asks the State to continue adopting the necessary measures to protect their life and personal integrity, taking into consideration the particular situation and circumstances in this case.
2.   To reiterate that the State take all necessary steps so that the measures ordered in this Resolution are planned and implemented with the participation of the beneficiaries or their representatives and that, in general, the State inform them before the execution of the measures.

23-Feb-2016
Order of the Inter-American Court of Human Rights
Provisional Measures regarding the United Mexican States

THE INTER-AMERICAN COURT OF HUMAN RIGHTS, pursuant to its attributions conferred by Article 63.2 of the American Convention on Human Rights and Articles 27 and 31 of the Court's Rules of Procedure
DECIDES:
1.   To lift and conclude these provisional measures ordered by the Court in its February 2, 2010 Resolution with regards to Valentina Rosendo Cantú and Yenis Bernardino Rosendo.
2.   As indicated in the terms of article 1.1 of the American Convention, the cancellation of provisional measures does not imply that the State is relieved of its conventional obligations to protect, in conformity with Considering 26 of this present Resolution.
3.   To ask the Secretary of the court to notify the State of Mexico, the Inter-American Commission on Human Rights, and the representatives of the beneficiaries of this Resolution.
4.   To close the file on this matter.

Provisional Measures regarding Paraguay in the Matter of L.M.
1-July-2011
Order of the Inter-American Court of Human Rights
Provisional Measures regarding Paraguay

HAVING SEEN:

1.   The brief of the Inter-American Commission on Human Rights (hereinafter "the Inter-American Commission" or "the Commission") of May 23, 2011 and its attachments, whereby it submitted to the Inter-American Court of Human Rights (hereinafter "the Court" or "the Inter-American Court") a request for provisional measures in accordance with Articles 63(2) of the American Convention on Human Rights (hereinafter "the American Convention" or "the Convention") and 27 of the Court's Rules of Procedure (hereinafter "the Rules of Procedure"), for the Court to require the Republic of Paraguay (hereinafter "Paraguay" or "the State") to "expedite the domestic proceedings and the decisions concerning the best interest of the child L.M. – one and a half years old - including, as soon as possible, the decisions concerning contact with his biological family."

2.   The background information submitted by the Commission related to the request for provisional measures, namely:

(a) The child L.M. was born on August 2, 2009, in Asunción, Paraguay. According to the petitioners, L.M. is the son of L.S. (26 years) and V.H.R. (22 years), who were in a relationship for about one year and decided to separate in April 2009 when L.S. was unaware of her pregnancy. Due to family circumstances, L.S. hid her pregnancy from her family and from the father of the child. According to the information provided, L.S. left the hospital two days after her son was born and, owing to her vulnerable emotional state, she handed L.M. over at the door of the San Bautista Church in Asunción;

(b) After learning what had occurred from a couple who took L.M. in, on August 5, 2009, the Public Prosecutor's Office opened a case called "Newborn Male [...] without Measures of Protection and Support" before the Judge of First Instance for Children and Adolescents (hereinafter "the First Instance Judge"). The judge ordered a search for the next of kin of L.M. and, on August 10, 2009, granted provisional custody of the child to the B.I. family. The B.I. family was appointed the "foster family," "as an essentially precautionary measure" until his legal situation was defined, and after the Adoption Center had proposed the family owing to its previous experience in this role;

(c) On September 17, 2009, the married couple composed of E.A.P. (who is a judge of the Republic among other activities) and O.O.Z - who were taking steps to adopt a child – asked for provisional custody of L.M.

(d) On November 10, 2009, after a "social and environmental study" of the O-A family had been conducted, a judicial ruling was issued revoking the provisional custody exercised by the B.I. family, and granting custody to the O-A family. The same ruling ordered that L.M. be registered in the Registry Office;

(e) On November 12, 2009, the same day that the child was given to the O-A family, the Adoption Center attached to the Children and Adolescents Secretariat reported that it had found the child's biological parents, and indicated, *inter alia,* the following: [...] understanding that the child has not yet been transferred, that the biological parents have been found, and that the possibility of reinsertion exists, we believe that, at this time, it would not be appropriate to transfer the child from a foster family to a family that intends to adopt;

(f) On November 16, 2009, L.S. and V.H.R. registered L.M. as their son in the Civil Registry Directorate General;

(g) On November 18, 2009, V.H.R. appeared before the court, presented the registration he had filed, and expressed his intention of assuming responsibility for L.M., explaining that he had been unaware of the situation and requesting that the child to be handed over to him. Specifically, he asked that the provisional custody granted to the O-A family be revoked;

(h) On November 19, 2009, in a petition filed by the couple O-A, a proceeding for forfeit of parental authority (*patria potestad*) was initiated against L.S. Regarding this proceeding, the State indicated that "all of the files from the Children and Adolescents Jurisdiction were sent to the Second Criminal Court for Adolescents, because this was the appropriate body, since all the other Children and Adolescents Courts had disqualified themselves;

(i) On November 20 and 25, 2009, the Technical Team for Maintenance of Family Relationships of the Children and Adolescents Secretariat's Adoption Center, and the *"Corazones por la Infancia"* Foundation, respectively, issued reports in which they indicated the pertinence of reinserting L.M. into his biological family;

(j) In view of the request by V.H.R. to revoke the provisional custody, on December 14, 2009, a hearing was held before the Third First Instance Judge for Children and Adolescents, during which V.H.R. and L.S. ratified before this judicial authority their request to assume responsibility for the child. In this procedure, the First Instance Judge ordered the intervention of the Judiciary's Office for Maintenance of Relationships and for "social and environmental studies" to be conducted;

(k) After the hearing, L.S. asked the First Instance Judge to order the necessary measures to allow her to visit her son during the end-of-year festivities. She also stated expressly that she would not give her consent to an adoption and, as a precautionary measure, requested that L.M. be prohibited from leaving the country;

(l) On February 19, 2010, based on the petition filed by the O-A couple, proceedings to challenge paternity were initiated against V.H.R. After several judges had disqualified themselves, the file was forwarded to the Adolescents Criminal Court on August 31, 2010;

(m) On July 2, 2010, the First Instance Judge issued a ruling in first instance revoking the custody granted to the O-A couple, and ordering the restitution of the child L.M. to V.H.R., with temporary monitoring by a social worker. In addition, a contact and visits regime was established for the child with his mother and his extended maternal family;

(n) As the State reported to the Commission, criminal proceedings were opened for abandonment and others offenses against V.H.R. and L.S., and are being processed by the Sixth Criminal Guarantee Court. Although the date when the proceedings were initiated was not mentioned, the investigation began by a court order of July 7, 2010;

(o) On August 18, 2010, the Children and Adolescents Court of Appeal annulled the July 2, 2010, decision of the First Instance Judge. In this decision the Court of Appeal indicated that there were a number of proceedings that, in its opinion, should be conducted simultaneously, because their effects were interrelated. In addition, it mentioned that the court hearing the case could establish an interim measure regarding contact with the biological family. In the words of the Court of Appeal: Given that the guardians have filed an action for forfeit of parental authority against [L.S.], and to challenge the paternity of V.H.R. [...] and the parents have been charged in criminal proceedings for the offenses of abandonment and violation of educational or civic obligations, [...] we cannot predict what the criminal court will decide; however, it cannot be ignored that the criminal charges, the forfeit of parental authority, and the challenge to paternity in this jurisdiction are interconnected owing to their effects and, consequently, the judgment appealed conflicts with the appropriate procedures in the three lawsuits, whose results cannot be known until there are judicial decisions accepting or rejecting the actions and, naturally, that these are final. [...] The court that follows in the order of rotation is empowered to establish, according to the circumstances, some type of interim contact while the actions are being processed;

(p) On September 16, 2010, the file was sent again to the Second Court whose regular judge had been disqualified from the case. On September 20, 2010, the file was pending transfer to the Adolescents Criminal Court, which at the time of the presentation of the Commission's request was "on a leave due to travel";

(q) On October 8, 2010, L.S. asked the First Adolescents Criminal Court to establish contact between L.M. and his parents and maternal grandparents; to require the guardians to provide information on the child's condition, and that the measures ordered previously of the psychological, social and environmental studies of the biological parents be conducted, to give continuity to the process of maintaining the relationship. V.H.R. made a similar request on the same date;

(r) On October 19, 2010, the Adolescents Criminal Court rejected these requests, and ordered that the social worker be present in the home of the O-A family to monitor the custody granted. The Commission indicated that, as of January 2011, this measure had not been executed;

(s) The decision of October 19, 2010, was appealed by L.S., and is currently pending a ruling;

(t) On November 5, 2010, L.M.'s parents filed requests for a contact regime with the child before the Children and Adolescents Court, regarding which disqualifications and recusals also occurred. The results of these actions was not provided, and

(u) The maternal grandparents of L.M. filed a request for custody of the child and requested a provisional contact regime. The results of this action were not provided;

(v) On March 21, 2011, the National Children and Adolescents Secretariat's Adoption Center submitted the report on the psychosocial and legal aspect of maintaining the relationship within the framework of the main custody proceeding; based on this, it indicated that "it would be desirable that the Court:

    (i) Revoke the provisional custody of the child [L.M.] granted to O.Z. and E.A.P.

    (ii) Order the reinsertion of the child [L.M.] with his maternal grandparents, [A.S.] and [T.M. de S], or with the biological father [V.H.R.], or the biological mother L.S, who are able to assume responsibility for raising and caring for the child, mainly because the current family group encourages mutual help and shared responsibilities."

3.   The processing of the request for precautionary measures and the petition before the Inter-American Commission:

(a) On June 17, 2010, the *Coordinadora por los Derechos de la Infancia y la Adolescencia* [Coordinator of the Rights of Children and Adolescents] (hereinafter "CDIA") and the Center for Justice and International Law (hereinafter "CEJIL") filed a request for precautionary measures before the Commission. Petition 1474/10 was opened;

(b) On July 26, 2010, the Commission asked the State to submit information on the following aspects within 10 days:

   (i) Whether the biological parents have access to the child while the judicial proceedings take place. If not, the State should provide the reasons;

   (ii) Based on the best interests of the child and the alleged effects that this situation could have on the relationship of the proposed beneficiary and his parents, indicate the duration of the proceedings to decide on the custody of the child, and whether there is any expedite procedure under Paraguayan law so that his situation can be decided as soon as possible; and

   (iii) Any information that the State deems pertinent with regards to the situation described by the petitioner;

(c) On August 23, 2010, the State submitted its response confirming the essential elements of the proceedings indicated by the petitioners, and adding the following information on the points raised by the Commission:

   (i) At the date of presentation of the report, "the Court of the original proceedings ha[d] not ordered the precautionary measure of a provisional contact regime while the trial was being held," and the file remained at the Children and Adolescents Appeals Chamber, based on the judgment of first instance.

   (ii) The judge of the original proceedings disqualified herself from the case in question, "forwarding it to the next corresponding judge, who also disqualified himself, and so on, until it reached the Second Children and Adolescents Court";

   (iii) Regarding the procedural time frames, the State's response indicates that "all the procedural norms governing the children and adolescents jurisdiction establish a summary procedure, under which the court of first instance has only six days to issue a decision. In addition, the courts of appeal have 10 days from the start of the appeal proceedings to deliver a ruling";

(d) On November 10, 2010, the Commission decided to grant precautionary measures, after analyzing the situation and "in view of a lack of progress in the proceedings and the irreparable effects that these delays could cause and were causing, to the detriment of L.M." In its communication, the Commission indicated that: Based on the principle of the best interests of the child, it is appropriate to grant precautionary measures in the terms of Article 25(1) of [the Commission's] Rules of Procedure so as to ensure that the time factor does not become a determining element for the domestic courts, to the detriment to the rights of the child, L.M. Consequently it asks the Government to: 1. Take the necessary measures to ensure that the proceedings concerning the custody and care of the child L.M. are decided within three months, and 2. To report on the steps taken to comply with this precautionary measure.

(e) On December 29, 2010, in response to the request for precautionary measures, the State confirmed the existence of the different domestic proceedings relating to this matter, and the fact that none had achieved a final ruling on the situation and custody of L.M., or on his contact with his biological nuclear or extended family. In addition, it indicated that "since December this year (referring to 2010), most of the case files, with the exception of the criminal case file, are at the same court due to the joinder of actions and to assist the judge in examining them." In addition, "all the parties have taken advantage of the rights granted them by law, and have requested the judicial authorities to make different rulings, which has resulted in disqualifications, recusals, appeals, discontinuation of appeals, all of which are being decided at the request of the parties in the different proceedings," and that "these are following their normal procedural course";

(f) On February 22, 2011, the representatives of the possible beneficiary submitted additional information indicating that, in the last three months, the main custody file has been paralyzed because, owing to the recusals and disqualifications, it had not been possible to assemble three judges who accepted competence to decide the appeal filed against the judgment of October 19, 2010. In addition, they indicated that the contact proceedings initiated in November 2010 remained without a decision and that, in these proceedings, six judges from the children's and adolescents' jurisdiction had disqualified themselves, which had resulted in a delay "of around 40 days to begin processing the cases." They added that, in the proceedings to challenge the paternity of V.H.R., a DNA test had not been carried out, even though the latter had asked that it be conducted as soon as possible in order to end this litigation;

(g) On March 26, 2011, a working meeting was held at the seat of the Commission, attended by the petitioners and representatives of the proposed beneficiary, the State of Paraguay, and L.S., biological mother of L.M. At this meeting, the petitioners reiterated that the precautionary measures ordered by the Commission had not been complied with, and underscored the absence of progress in the domestic proceedings. The State indicated that there had been delays in the judicial proceedings because the parties – petitioners and guardians – had taken advantage of the procedural guarantees provided by domestic law and, also, a series of children's judges had disqualified themselves "for reasons attributed to each of the parties."

4. The Commission's arguments to support its request for provisional measures, including the following:

(a) From a preliminary assessment of the proceedings, there are, *prima facie*, a series of elements that, taken together, constitute a situation of extreme gravity that, to date, has been causing irreparable damages to the child L.M., namely:

(i) One year and nine months have elapsed since the main proceeding for the custody of L.M. began, and to date no first instance decision has been taken regarding his situation. This proceeding has been almost paralyzed since October 2010, when an appeal was filed against the decision of October 19, 2010;

(ii) The stalling of the proceeding has resulted, among other factors, from the impossibility of establishing an appeals court to decide the appeal, due to the judges disqualifying themselves;

(iii) The legal time limits within which the State indicated these cases must be resolved expired a long time ago;

(iv) There are other related proceedings in which the judges have also disqualified themselves, and other incidents that have prevented a final ruling;

(v) the State has not adopted any measure to expedite the proceedings, and has not complied with the Commission's precautionary measures;

(b) In the said exceptional circumstances, in which the domestic authorities must take decisions on these aspects, the principle of special protection measures for children is closely related to the timeliness of the respective decisions. This exceptional diligence is due to the fact that the passage of time inevitably becomes a defining element for emotional ties that are difficult to undo without harming the child;

(c) On several opportunities there have been unjustified delays in the proceedings and throughout the proceedings a number of the judicial authorities from the children and adolescents' jurisdiction have disqualified themselves;

(d) Despite the precautionary measures ordered by the Commission, which included a specific time frame to conclude the proceedings, the State has failed to adopt measures aimed at expediting the domestic proceedings;

(e) The situation of delay and absence of decisions in the domestic proceedings entails a risk that is not only imminent but is also materializing, without any likelihood that the situation will change unless the mechanism of provisional measures is activated; and

(f) The special celerity of the proceedings, their swift resolution, and the urgent decision concerning contact with the biological family, in addition to being requirements under the Convention, analysis of which corresponds to the merits of the matter, become the means for the urgent protection and safeguard of L.M.'s rights, and the way to ensure that the measures of comprehensive restitution eventually recommended by the Commission or ordered by the Court can be truly effective.

5.   The Secretariat's note of May 25, 2011, in which, based on Article 27(5) of the Rules of Procedure and on the instructions of the Court in plenary, the State was asked to submit, by June 6, 2011 at the latest, any observations it deemed pertinent, as well as any other relevant information and documentation. In this communication the State was asked to keep the identity of the child L.M. confidential.

6.   The brief of June 9, 2011, in which the State responded to the request for observations (*supra* having seen paragraph 5) and indicated the following:

(a) The parties' right to file petitions before the authorities had been respected, and "it had acted with due diligence in all the proceedings, complying with the provisions of the Constitution and international treaties";

(b) The measures taken by the domestic authorities should be taken into account, as they reveal the State's interest and willingness to guarantee the comprehensive protection of the child L.M. The State, through its courts, has adopted all existing legal measures to resolve the disputes surrounding the child, respecting constitutional guarantees and due process;

(c) The seven proceedings concerning the child L.M. that are currently active must be studied and analyzed thoroughly, "because there are various differences of opinion that, if taken lightly, could cause significant harm to the child." The State referred specifically to the criminal proceeding opened for the offense of abandonment against L.S., "birth mother of the child L.M.," the investigative phase of which had concluded and the accusation against her had been filed by the Public Prosecutor's Office, with a request to hear the case in public oral proceedings. The preliminary hearing was set for June 7, 2011. It also mentioned the case challenging paternity, which was at the stage of receiving evidence;

(d) To ensure that "situations such as that of the child L.M. do not occur again," on May 23, 2011, the National Children and Adolescents Secretariat (SNNA) submitted a request for examination of a bill to amend Articles 7, 18 and 21 of Law 1136/97, Adoption Law.

7.　　The Secretariat's note of June 13, 2011, in which, on the instructions of the President, the Inter-American Commission was granted until June 16, 2011, to submit any observations it deemed pertinent.

8.　　The brief of June 16, 2011, in which the Commission submitted its observations on the State's report and argued that "it was abstract"; that it did not change in any way the grounds for the Commission's request for provisional measures but rather, to the contrary, it reflected the lack of celerity in the proceedings. In addition, the Commission argued that the report revealed that the State continued to give normal treatment to this matter, which "is characterized by the fact that the urgency does not derive from a threat of harm, whose appearance can be anticipated in the future, but from harm that is already being caused and the prospects of repairing it are inversely proportional to the passage of time."

9.　　The brief of June 23, 2011, in which the Commission "expanded the [preceding] observations." It indicated that "the main custody case remains paralyzed owing to the impossibility of establishing a court of appeal," and this "extends to the three cases on contact filed by different members of L.M.'s biological family, as well as the case on forfeit of parental authority, because decisions on an appeal are pending in all the cases." The Commission stated that this situation "reveals *prima facie* the inability of the institutions to provide a prompt response to disputes that, owing to the nature of the interests at stake and the grave damage that could be caused to the beneficiary, warrant exceptional diligence." In addition, it reported that, of the three DNA tests, it had only been possible to perform one, because the O-A family had not come forward with the child L.M. for the second test that had been ordered, and had appealed the decision ordering that the DNA tests be conducted by two specialized laboratories.

CONSIDERING THAT:

1.　　Paraguay has been a State Party to the American Convention since August 24, 1989, and pursuant to Article 62 of the Convention, accepted the compulsory jurisdiction of the Court on March 11, 1993.

2.　　Article 63(2) of the American Convention establishes that "[i]n cases of extreme gravity and urgency, and when necessary to avoid irreparable damage to persons, the Court shall adopt such provisional measures as it deems pertinent in matters it has under consideration. With respect to a case not yet submitted to the Court, it may act at the request of the Commission."

3.　　According to Article 27 of the Court's Rules of Procedure:

(a) At any stage of proceedings involving cases of extreme gravity and urgency, and when necessary to avoid irreparable damage to persons, the Court may, on its own motion, order such provisional measures as it deems appropriate, pursuant to Article 63(2) of the Convention.

(b) With respect to matters not yet submitted to it, the Court may act at the request of the Commission. [...]

(c) The Court, or if the Court is not sitting, the Presidency, upon considering that it is possible and necessary, may require the State, the Commission, or the representatives of the beneficiaries to provide information on a request for provisional measures before deciding on the measure requested.

(d) If the Court is not sitting, the Presidency, in consultation with the Permanent Commission and, if possible, with the other Judges, shall call upon the State concerned to adopt such urgent measures as may be necessary to ensure the effectiveness of any provisional measures that may be ordered by the Court during its next period of sessions.

4.   This request for provisional measures does not arise from a case before the Court, but rather the measures have been requested within the framework of petition 1474/10 being processed by the Inter-American Commission since September 1, 2010, which is currently at the admissibility stage.

5.   The Court has established that under international human rights law, provisional measures are not only preventive, in the sense that they preserve a juridical situation, but rather they are fundamentally protective, because they protect human rights insofar as they seek to avoid irreparable damage to persons. The preventive nature of provisional measures relates to the context of international litigations. In this regard, the object and purpose of these measures is to preserve the rights potentially at risk until the dispute is settled, and to guarantee the integrity and effectiveness of the decision on merits, so as to prevent the violation of the rights in litigation, a situation which could make the final decision ineffective or impair its practical effects. Thus, provisional measures allow the State concerned to comply with the final decision and, if appropriate, to make the reparation ordered. As regards the protective nature, the Court has indicated that, provided that the basic requirements are met, provisional measures become a real jurisdictional guarantee of a preventive nature, because they protect human rights insofar as they seek to prevent irreparable damage to persons.

6.   The three conditions that Article 63(2) of the Convention requires for the Court to be able to grant provisional measures must be present in any situation in which they are requested. Based on its competence, in the context of provisional measures the Court may only consider those arguments directly related to the extreme gravity, urgency, and need to prevent irreparable damage to persons. Any other fact or argument may only be examined and decided during consideration of the merits of a contentious case.

7.   Regarding the requirement of "gravity," for purposes of the adoption

of provisional measures, the Convention requires it to be "extreme"; in other words, at its highest or most intense level. The "urgent" nature implies that the risk or threat involved must be imminent, which also supposes that the response to remedy it must be immediate. Finally, with regard to the damage, there must be reasonable probability that it will be caused, and it must not involve legal rights or property that can be repaired.

8.   The Court observes that, from the information provided by the Commission and not opposed by the State with regard to the facts and background of this matter (*supra* having seen paragraph 2), it can be inferred that:

(a) The O-A family has currently and since November 10, 2009, provisional custody of the child L.M., aged one year and ten months, under a ruling by the Third Children and Adolescents Court of First Instance;

(b) The preceding decision was adopted within the main proceeding concerning the custody of L.M., initiated on August 5, 2009 (almost since the child's birth). All those involved are participating in this proceeding. According to information provided by the State to the Commission, all the procedural norms that govern the children and adolescents jurisdiction establish summary proceedings, so that the first instance court has merely six days to deliver a ruling, and the courts of appeal have only 10 days in which to rule. This case is paralyzed owing to the current apparent impossibility of establishing an appeals court.

(c) On November 16, 2009, L.S. and V.H.R., apparently the biological mother and father, registered L.M. as their son with the Civil Registration Directorate General;

(d) In November 2009 and February 2010, respectively, the O-A family filed two petitions against L.S. and V.H.R., namely: for forfeit of parental authority against the former and to challenge the paternity of the latter. In the second proceeding, the court ordered three DNA tests to confirm the biological relationship; only one of these had been performed (the results of which were not advised), because the O-A family has not come forward with the child for the second test and has filed an appeal against the decision expanding the evidence.

(e) Since July 2010, a criminal proceeding has apparently been underway for "abandonment and other" offenses against V.H.R. and L.S., in which charges have been filed as well as a request to hear the case in a public oral proceeding.

(f) In November 2010, members of the child's biological and "extended" family, in other words his father, mother and maternal grandparents, filed petitions requesting custody of the child, and a "provisional contact regime" with him, in three judicial proceedings, which have not been decided;

(g) Seven domestic judicial proceedings are underway in relation to the matter of the child L.M., and no final decision has been reached in any of them. In several of these proceedings there have been a number of disqualifications and recusals of the judges from the children and adolescents jurisdiction, whose turn it was to hear the case, and this has caused major delays.

9.   The Court observes that the child L.M. is in the provisional custody of a family that, when custody was granted, was taking steps to adopt a child. Thus, since the birth of the child L.M.—who is almost two years old—he has been separated from his biological family, without, currently, having any type of contact with the alleged family members; in other words, in the terms used in the request for provisional measures, with his biological "nuclear" and "extended" family. This is occurring because no final judgment has been handed down in the said proceedings and owing to the alleged lack of response by the domestic courts to the specific requests for custody and for a "contact regime" that would allow the child and his family of origin to maintain a relationship through a visiting regime.

10.   Regarding this failure to "decide the proceedings," the State indicated that this was not due "to the indifference of the domestic courts, but rather to compliance with the current laws, which are in keeping with the international treaties signed by the Republic of Paraguay." Although it is not incumbent on the Court, within the framework of a request for provisional measures, to assess the compatibility of the laws of Paraguay with the Convention or other treaties, it is relevant that the State submitted as an attachment to its observations a bill to amend several articles of the Adoption Law as an "example of steps taken by the State to prevent the repetition of situations such as that of the child L.M."

11.   Thus, the explanatory statement for the bill presented by the State indicates that the current Adoption Law "gives rise to a situation that enables the custody of children not yet declared available for adoption to be granted to families with clear intentions to adopt, omitting the technical procedures relating to the maintenance of the ties between the child and his or her biological family, without having exhausted the mechanisms for maintaining the biological ties and, in most cases, giving priority to using adoption as a first measure rather than as an exceptional measure." In this regard, the text adds that "the possibility granted by the Law [...] to families awarded custody to be able to adopt children after custody has been in effect for two years, tacitly gave rise to the appearance of a mechanism known as pre-adoption custody [which is] incompatible with the comprehensive protection doctrine, because it does not respect the child's right and best interest to live with his or her family of origin as a first measure, in which the child and its family receive sufficient support to strengthen and maintain the original ties." The

text continues, by indicating that, "[c]ompletely to the contrary, the concept of pre-adoption custody is used in a discretionary manner as an abbreviated method to obtain and legitimize irregular situations very closely related to the sale and trafficking of boys, girls, and adolescents; this is clearly revealed by the statistics of the Adoption Center, which show that, in 2010, 82% of the adoption judgments were granted based on pre-adoption custody." The explanatory statement concludes by indicating that, in view of the description of the background facts relating to the jurisdictional and administrative procedures that establish the mechanism of pre-adoption custody, in clear violation of the best interest of the child, the comprehensive protection doctrine, and the specific functions of the Adoption Center, the jurisdictional legal framework must be amended."

12.   In the instant matter, as the Commission has indicated, "the main point of the request is that no decision has been reached in any of the cases regarding the custody and care of L.M., and no decision has been reached regarding the biological relationship with his nuclear and/or extended family." In other words, "his custody and care situation remains unresolved, while the requests that seek to establish contacts with his biological family remain undecided." Consequently, the Commission argues that this "series of elements constitutes a situation of extreme gravity that may affect, irreparably, the proposed beneficiary's rights to identity, mental integrity, and to a family" and, consequently, requests the State to "expedite the domestic proceedings and decisions regarding L.M.'s best interest, including, as soon as possible, the required decisions on his contact with his biological family."

13.   The Court does not have to rule on whether the different proceedings in the domestic sphere are being processed in keeping with the American Convention, or in accordance with the special obligations of protection for children and adolescents. If appropriate, these aspects could be debated in the context of the petition filed before the Inter-American Commission. In this matter, the Court is only called on to determine whether the proposed beneficiary is in a situation of extreme gravity and urgency that responds to the need to prevent irreparable damage. The request presented in favor of L.M. intends to protect his rights to mental integrity, identity, and a family.

14.   Regarding the right to protection of the child's family, recognized in Article 17 of the American Convention, the Court has underscored that this means that the State is obliged not only to establish and directly execute measures for the protection of children, in accordance with Article 19 of the Convention, but also to encourage, in the broadest possible way, the development and strength of the family unit. Consequently, the separation of children from their family may constitute, in certain circumstances, a violation of the said right to protection of the family, as even the legal separation of a child from his or her biological

family is only applicable when duly justified in the best interest of the child, and is exceptional and, insofar as possible, temporary. In addition, given that during early childhood children exercise their rights through their next of kin, and that the family plays an essential role in their development, the separation of a minor from his biological parents may affect his right to personal integrity, contained in Article 5(1) of the Convention, insofar as it may jeopardize his or her development.

15.   In relation to the right to identity, the Court has indicated, quoting the Inter-American Juridical Committee, that "it is a fundamental right" that "can be conceptualized, in general, as the series of attributes and characteristics that allow the individualization of a person in society and, in this regard, it comprises several other rights included in the Convention, according to the subject of rights in question and the circumstances of the case." Thus, with regard to boys, girls, and adolescents, based on the provisions of Article 8 of the Convention on the Rights of the Child, the right to identity comprises, among other matters, the right to family relationships.

16.   Due precisely due to the foregoing, and in view of the importance of the interests at stake, the right to physical integrity, the right to identity, and the right to the protection of the family, the administrative and judicial proceedings relating to the protection of the human rights of the child, particularly those judicial proceedings concerning the adoption, guardianship and custody of boys and girls in early childhood, must be handled by the authorities with exceptional diligence and celerity. The foregoing reveals a need to defend and to protect the best interest of the child, as well as to guarantee the rights that are potentially at risk until the dispute on merits has been resolved, and to ensure the practical effects of the decision eventually adopted.

17.   As indicated, the child L.M. is currently almost 2 years old, and the proceedings concerning his guardianship, custody, parental authority, paternity, and family contact, are still being processed. The State attributes this length of time to the due observance by the domestic courts of domestic law and, indeed, when annulling the decision of the first instance judge that had ordered the restitution of the child to his biological father, the Children and Adolescents Court of Appeal found that a series of proceedings existed that needed to be conducted simultaneously, since their effects were interrelated (*supra* having seen paragraph 2(o)). It is worth noting that, also and notwithstanding the decision, the Court of Appeal itself indicated that the court appointed to hear the case could establish an interim measure of contact with the biological family. In addition, the domestic courts have received several technical reports, mainly from the Adoption Center of the Children and Adolescents Secretariat of the Ministry of Justice, recommending that the child L.M. not be separated from his family of origin.

18.   Based on the above, the mere passage of time may be a factor that favors the creation of ties with the foster family, which, in an eventual decision regarding the rights of the child, may become the main grounds for not changing the child's actual situation, principally because the risk of seriously affecting the child's emotional and psychological balance increases. In other words, the passage of time would inevitably constitute a defining element of ties of affection that would be hard to revert without causing damage to the child. This situation entails a risk that is not only imminent but may already be occurring. Consequently, greater delays in the proceedings, irrespective of any decision on the determination of his rights, may determine the irreversible or irreparable nature of the actual situation, and render invalid and detrimental to the interests of the child L.M. any decision to the contrary.

19.   Therefore, although it is not applicable to order, as the Commission has requested, the acceleration of the domestic proceedings, since the analysis of the rapidity and effectiveness of the proceedings concerning the facts that give rise to the request for provisional measures corresponds to the examination of the merits of the case, the Court observes that the delay or lack of response may imply an irreparable damage to the rights to psychological integrity, identity, and protection of the family of the child L.M.. Therefore, while the judicial proceedings to define his legal situation are resolved, the Court deems it pertinent to order, as a provisional measure to prevent the child's rights being affected, that the State take the necessary, adequate, and effective measures to allow him to maintain contact with his family of origin, with the support of appropriate professional personnel to monitor the child's emotional condition. In this regard, this Court recalls that the Court of Appeal itself established that an interim measure could be established for contact with the biological family, without this entailing anticipating a decision in relation to the proceedings underway concerning the child L.M.; in other words, without broaching the merits of those proceedings.

20.   In addition, the State must take the pertinent measures to ensure that the provisional measures required in this order are planned and implemented with the participation of the beneficiary's representatives, the respective members of his biological family, and when appropriate, of the family with custody, so that the said measures are adopted diligently and effectively.

21.   Consequently, noting that the Inter-American Commission received the request for precautionary measures on June 17, 2010, and that petition 1474/10, received on September 1, 2010, is at the admissibility stage, the Court considers that the Inter-American Commission should decide on the petition as promptly as possible, based on the urgency alleged in the request for provisional measures.

22.   The adoption of urgent or provisional measures does not imply a decision on the merits of the case if it were to be considered by the Court, nor does it prejudge the State's responsibility for the reported facts.

THEREFORE:
THE INTER-AMERICAN COURT OF HUMAN RIGHTS,
in exercise of the authority granted by Article 63(2) of the American Convention and 27 of its Rules of Procedure,
DECIDES:
1.   To require the State of Paraguay to adopt forthwith the measures necessary, adequate, and effective to protect the rights to personal integrity, identity, and protection of the family of the child L.M., allowing him to be in contact with his family of origin, with the support of appropriate professional personnel to monitor the child's emotional condition, as established in considering paragraphs 16 and 18 to 20 of this order.
2.   To require the State to report to the Inter-American Court, by August 20, 2011, at the latest, on the provisions of the first operative paragraph of this Order.
3.   To require the representatives of the beneficiary and the Inter-American Commission to submit to the Inter-American Court, within two and four weeks, respectively, any observations they deem pertinent on the report mentioned in the second operative paragraph of this order.
4.   To require the State, also, to report to the Inter-American Court every two months as of August 20, 2011, on the provisional measures adopted in accordance with this decision.
5.   To request the representatives of the beneficiary and the Inter-American Commission to submit their observations within four and six weeks, respectively, of notification of the reports of the State indicated in the fourth operative paragraph.
6.   To require the Secretariat to notify this order to the State and the Inter-American Commission and, through the latter, to the representatives of the beneficiary.

23-Jan-2012
Order of the President of the Inter-American Court of Human Rights
Provisional Measures regarding Paraguay

CONSIDERING THAT:
5.   In relation to the situation of the child L.M., the State and the representatives reported the following:
  (a) On August 2, 2011, the Supreme Court of Justice of Paraguay issued a resolution addressed to the Ombudsman for Children and Adolescents, wherein it ordered that all the necessary measures be implemented in order that the provisional measure of the Inter-American Court be satisfied;
  (b) On August 23, 2011, the Ombudsman for Children and Adolescents requested that the Courts of First Instance for Children and Adolescents

implement the provisional measures ordered by the Inter-American Court of Human Rights and confirmed by the Supreme Court;

(c) On that same date, the judge of the court of first instance in charge of the processing of matter, summoned the parents, maternal grandparents, and the guardians of child L.M. to a hearing for August 31, in order for them to appear and be heard. A psychologist and social worker were also summoned, both of the judiciary;

(d) On that same day, the attorney for couple O-A challenged the presiding judge, filed an action for annulment of the actions, and requested the suspension of the set hearing;

(e) On August 31, 2011, all those summoned appeared in court, except the couple O-A, guardians of child L.M. The hearing was held, and at the end of the hearing, immediate compliance was ordered with the operative provisions ordered by the Inter-American Court in its Order of July 1, 2011, as well as establishment of a temporary visitation schedule with the extended family (maternal grandparents) as of September 6, 2011;

(f) On September 5, 2011, couple O-A once again filed an action for annulment and an appeal against the decision of August 31, considering that the "procedural actions subject to appeal are null as they were declared in violation of the rules of due process" and in contravention with the legal provisions that require the mandatory and ineludible presence of the representatives of the child in proceedings of this nature;

(g) On September 6, 2011, the day the first encounter should have taken place among the maternal grandparents and child L.M., the guardians did not appear in the place established for the reunion, to which the visitation ordered in the judicial ruling of August 31;

(h) On September 27, 2011, the first meeting between child L.M. and his grandparents took place, in the presence of a forensic psychologist and a social worker, in compliance with that established in the resolution of September 31, 2011.

(i) Since then, other visits have taken place between the child and his maternal grandparents and requests to expand the visitation schedule to other members of the biological family of the child have been rejected.

6. The representatives noted that the encounter constitutes "a first step in the implementation of the provisional measures" but that it "is not in any respects effective compliance," in that the measure involves an "isolated encounter between the boy and his maternal grandparents," and that this has not "yet been [...] regulated [...]." They added that "it is important to highlight that the provisional measure has not yet been met, since the schedule has not been made effective between child L.M. and his [biological] parents." With regard to the

judicial resolution of August 31, 2011, they considered that "the measure ordered by the judge has led to weekly encounters between child L.M. and his maternal grandparents, without mention of the possibility of expanding the visits to the parents, which thereby does not satisfy compliance with the provisional measure." Moreover, the representatives considered that, in general terms, there has not been effective compliance with that ordered by the Court and they have requested the Court to summon the parties to a hearing.

7.   The President values the measures to implement the measures ordered in favor of child L.M. carried out by the domestic authorities, but also notes that the information that the State has provided is incomplete.

8.   Moreover, the President states that encounters have taken place between child L.M. and his maternal grandparents as of September 27, 2011. While the State has expressed that it is complying with the provisional measure ordered, the Commission and the representatives have expressed that child L.M. has not yet had contact with his biological parents, and there is no clarity with respect to the modality of the measures regarding visitation.

9.   It is important to recall what the Court stated in the mentioned order, that "in view of the importance of the interests at stake, the right to physical integrity, the right to identity, and the right to the protection of the family, the administrative and judicial proceedings relating to the protection of the human rights of the child, particularly those judicial proceedings concerning the adoption, guardianship and custody of boys and girls in early childhood, must be handled by the authorities with exceptional diligence and celerity."

10.   The President deems it necessary for the Court to receive, in a private hearing, up- to-date information from the State, the Inter-American Commission, and the representatives, on the status and prospects of the implementation of the provisional measures ordered in the Order of the Court of July 1, 2011.

THEREFORE:

THE PRESIDENT OF THE INTER-AMERICAN COURT OF HUMAN RIGHTS,

in exercise of the authority granted by Article 63(2) of the American Convention on Human Rights, and Articles 4, 15(1), 27(2), 27(9), and 31(2) of the Rules of Procedure of the Court,

DECIDES:

1.   To summon to the Inter-American Court of Human Rights the representatives of the beneficiaries of these provisional measures and the State of Paraguay to a private hearing that will be held at the seat of the Inter-American Court on February 20, 2012, as of 3:00 p.m until 5:00 p.m., in order for the Court to receive information and observations on the implementation of the provisional measures, pursuant to the considering paragraphs 7 to 10 of this Order.

2.　　　To request the Secretariat of the Court to provide legal notice of this Order to the Inter-American Commission, the representatives of the beneficiaries of the provisional measures, and the State.

27-Apr-2012
Order of the Inter-American Court of Human Rights
Provisional Measures regarding Paraguay

CONSIDERING THAT:
5.　　　In relation to the situation of the child LM, the State and the representatives have essentially reported the following:

(a) On August 2, 2011 the Supreme Court of Justice of Paraguay issued a decision addressed to the "Defensoría de la Niñez y la Adolescencia" (Ombudsman's Office for Children and Adolescents) in which it ordered the implementation of all means necessary to comply with the provisional measure of the Inter-American Court;

(b) On August 23, 2011 the Ombudsman's Office for Children and Adolescents requested that the Court of First Instance for Children and Adolescents implement the provisional measure ordered by the Inter-American Court and confirmed by the Supreme Court;

(c) On that same date the judge of first instance in charge of the proceedings summoned the parents, the grandparents and the family with custody of LM to a hearing on August 31. On this occasion a psychologist and a social worker of the judicial branch were also summoned;

(d) That same day the attorney of the O-A couple objected to the acting judge, filed a motion for the annulment of the proceedings and requested that the hearing be suspended;

(e) On August 31, 2011 all the summoned parties appeared before the Court, except for the O-A couple, with custody of the child. The hearing took place and the judge ordered immediate compliance with the operative paragraphs established by the Inter-American Court in the Order of July 1, 2011, and called for provisional visiting arrangements to be made with the extended family (maternal grandparents) as of September 6, 2011;

(f) On September 5, 2011 the O-A couple filed another motion of annulment and appealed against the ruling of August 31, considering that "the procedural acts performed are invalid since they were in violation of the rules of due process" and contravene the legal provisions that stipulate the mandatory and unavoidable presence of children's representatives in proceedings of this nature;

(g) On September 6, 2011, the date on which the first meeting between the maternal grandparents and the child LM was to be held, the custodial family did not arrive at the indicated place, and therefore the contact arrangement ordered in the judicial decision of August 31 did not take place;

(h) On September 20, 2011 the Court of Appeal for Children and Adolescents rejected the appeal for annulment filed by the custodial family and confirmed the order of August 31, 2011 in full, providing no further information on the grounds of the decision;

(i) On September 27, 2011 the first meeting took place between the child LM and the maternal grandparents, in the presence of a forensic psychologist and a social worker, in compliance with the order of September 31, 2011;

(j) On November 7, 2011 the Ombudsman's Office for Children and Adolescents filed a brief before the Judge of first instance requesting that the measure be extended to the biological parents;

(k) On November 8, 2011 the Judge confirmed the court's decision of August 31 (to not extend the contacts), providing no information on the grounds for the decision;

(l) On November 14, 2011 the Ombudsman filed a motion for reconsideration of the previous decision, which was "ambiguously resolved without interaction between the child and his parents," according to the representatives.

(m) On February 20 the O-A couple communicated to the Court for Children and Adolescents that they had relinquished their role as the custodial family of the child. In a hearing on this matter, which took place on the same day that this Court held the hearing (*supra* Having Seen 6), the maternal grandparents indicated that they would accept custody of the child LM, and

(n) On February 24 the court issued an order revoking the custody of the child held by the O-A couple and granted custody to the maternal grandparents.

6. During the private hearing held in the instant matter, the State reported on the contact arrangements made between the child LM and his biological family, which it considered should be implemented in a gradual manner, starting with the child's maternal grandparents in order to prevent any harm to the child, and claimed that it had complied with the provisional measures. Subsequently, the State presented the order issued by the Court of Children and Adolescents of February 24, 2012 which revoked the custody of the child LM awarded to the O-A couple and granted said custody to the maternal grandparents, and established the method and conditions for the handover of the child. Consequently, the State requested that the Court lift the provisional measures.

7.   The representatives, while acknowledging that a rapprochement had taken place between the child LM and his biological family, claimed that the contact arrangements ordered had not been implemented gradually, but rather minimally, given that the arrangements only applied to meetings with the maternal grandparents, at a shopping center, and that since the first meeting they had only spent a total of 20 hours with the child. The representatives pointed out that the Ombudsman for Children and Adolescents had requested, on several occasions, that the contact arrangements be extended to include the parents of the child, something that was rejected by the Court for Children and Adolescents, which interpreted that the interaction with the "biological family" as indicated in the Order of the Inter-American Court of July 1, 2011 did not include the parents. With regard to the comments made by the State during the hearing, the representatives stated that no final decision had yet been made and that the contact arrangements had not changed, neither in fact nor in law. Therefore, they requested that the provisional measures be continued. However, in March 2012 they confirmed that the child LM was living with his maternal grandparents and had daily contact with his mother and father, for which reason they requested the lifting of the provisional measures. Notwithstanding the foregoing, the representatives noted that the maternal grandparents did not have formal documents certifying that they are the child's guardians and that "the State ha[d] not provided the support of specialized personnel to monitor the child LM's process of interaction with and incorporation into his biological family."

8.   The Inter-American Commission pointed out that there was no court ruling revoking of the custody of the child from the O-A couple and, although it viewed the gradual rapprochement between the child and his family in a favorable light, it considered that the process had not been carried out appropriately. During the hearing it stated that it felt it necessary for the Court to continue monitoring the child's relationship with his biological family until a final court ruling is issued. However, in its last brief it "deemed admissible the lifting of the provisional measures under the terms requested by both parties."

9.   The Court notes that since the provisional measures have been in force, the State has provided incomplete information regarding their implementation and without the required frequency. As to the facts, the first meeting of the child and his maternal grandparents took place on September 27, 2011, almost three months after the provisional measures were ordered. Subsequently, there was no contact between the child LM and his biological parents given that the domestic courts did not order it, in spite of repeated requests by the Office of the Ombudsman for Children, a body appointed by the Supreme Court to implement the measures. On the day of the hearing convened by the President of the Court (*supra* Having Seen 6) the State reported that the O-A couple had communicated to the domestic

courts their decision to relinquish custody of the child, and that during a court hearing held on that same day the maternal grandparents had agreed to accept custody. Indeed, on February 24, 2012 the aforementioned court issued a ruling in this regard, and therefore, since the maternal grandparents of the child were appointed as guardians, the child LM currently maintains a relationship with the extended family and also with his biological parents given that his mother lives in the same house as the grandparents.

10.   The purpose of these provisional measures has been the need for the State to adopt the measures necessary, adequate and effective to protect the rights to humane treatment, identity and protection of the family of the child LM, allowing him to interact with his family of origin while the judicial proceedings to define his legal status were being resolved. The Court notes that there was a lack of clear information regarding the manner and circumstances in which the child's transition from the custodial family to the family of origin was carried out, which occurred in an immediate and not a gradual manner. Nor was the Court provided with information indicating that this rapprochement was carried out with the support of appropriate professional personnel to monitor the child's emotional situation. Nevertheless, the fact is that the circumstances that gave rise to the adoption of these provisional measures no longer exist, and that the State, the representatives and the Commission agree that the lifting of the measures is appropriate. Accordingly, the Court deems it admissible to lift the provisional measures, on the understanding that the parties agree to this and without any detriment to the proceedings in the case admitted for consideration by the Inter-American Commission. The Court points out that, under the terms of Article 1.1 of the American Convention, the lifting of provisional measures does not mean that the State is exonerated from its conventional obligations to afford protection to the child LM.

THEREFORE:

THE INTER-AMERICAN COURT OF HUMAN RIGHTS,

In the exercise of the authority granted by Article 63(2) of the American Convention on Human Rights and Articles 27 and 31 of its Rules of Procedure,

DECIDES:

1.   To lift the provisional measures ordered by the Inter-American Court on July 1, 2011 in favor of the child LM.

2.   To require the Secretariat of the Inter-American Court to notify the State of Paraguay, the Inter-American Commission on Human Rights and the representatives of the beneficiary of this Order.

3.   To close the file on this matter.

ANALYSIS AND QUESTIONS RAISED BY THE COURT'S JURISPRUDENCE

As the above excerpts demonstrate, the Inter-American Court of Human Rights considers and orders provisional measures in circumstances ranging from requests made by victims and representatives in contentious cases before the Court, as well as from requests referred to the Court by the Inter-American Commission on Human Rights, and in circumstances ranging from threats to life and personal integrity, to threats to freedom of expression. Regardless of the types of threats involved and how the request for provisional measures is made to the Court, the three-fold criteria of irreparable harm, extreme gravity and urgency remains the same. The Court maintains (and, when necessary, adjusts) the orders for provisional measures whenever these criteria are met, and lifts the orders of provisional measures when the circumstances which led to the order are no longer present. The ordering and lifting of provisional measures is a determination that the Court makes independently of its consideration and judgment on the merits of the case. In other words, if the three-fold criteria of irreparable harm, extreme gravity and urgency are not present, the Court will not order (or will lift prior orders of) provisional measures, even if the facts of the case indicate other violations of human rights and the American Convention on Human Rights.

As the Court emphasizes in its orders of provisional measures, these orders are based on and limited to the facts relevant to determining the potential for irreparable harm and circumstances of extreme gravity and urgency; its decisions to order provisional measures are not preemptive decisions on the merits and are independent from its consideration and judgments on the merits of the contentious cases before it. For example, in the Court President's order of provisional measures regarding Peru in the matter of the Constitutional Court, the Court explicitly stated that the information submitted to it in *Constitutional Court v. Peru* presented a *prima facie* threat warranting provisional measures and stated, equally clearly, that an order of provisional measures in no way prejudged the merits of the case.

The Court also emphasizes that while the primary purpose of provisional measures is to prevent irreparable harm to persons, these measures also serve to protect fundamental human rights. For instance, the Court summarized the Commission's communication to the Court in its request for provisional measures regarding Costa Rica in the matter of La Nación Newspaper (Order of the President of the Inter-American Court of Human Rights, 23 May 2001) by stating:

  (a) that, essentially, the Convention establishes a system for the protection of human rights and not a system to compensate the violation of such rights, which would operate as a result of violation of the Convention;

  (b) that the principal objective of the protective measures adopted by the Commission and the Court is to avoid a violation being committed or, if applicable, continuing to be committed, until the mechanisms of the inter-American system of human rights have finished processing the case.

Consequently, orders of provisional measures function in two ways to ensure the effectiveness of the Court's work: (1) broadly, by upholding fundamental human rights as stipulated in the American Convention on Human Rights, and (2) specifically, by preventing violations of the human rights of those associated with the given case and thereby allowing the case to proceed.

In its orders of provisional measures, the Court emphasizes that the State is responsible for protecting parties and witnesses involved in proceedings before the supervisory organs of the American Convention on Human Rights (i.e., the Inter-American Commission on Human Rights and the Inter-American Court of Human Rights). The Court importantly emphasizes, as in its order of provisional measures regarding Ecuador in the matter of Pueblo Indígena Sarayaku, that the State is equally responsible for the actions of third parties.

- Each order of provisional measures is reflective of the given circumstances and the Court routinely orders the State to report back to the Court within a specific time frame on the steps it has undertaken to ensure the safety of those the measures are ordered to protect. In some orders, the Court charged the State to take "all necessary measures" and in some orders, the Court ordered specific measures that the State must undertake to comply with the provisional measures. Based on the above excerpts, under what circumstances does the Court order specific measures and under what circumstances does the Court order the State to take "all necessary measures"?

- Compare the factual circumstances initially presented in the matter of the Constitutional Court and in the matter of Mendoza Prisons with those initially presented in the matter of La Nación Newspaper. What distinctions led the Court to determine that there was a *prima facie* threat in the former two matters, but that there was a need for more information and a hearing in the latter matter?

- Compare the Court's orders of provisional measures and necessary reporting by the State and by the representatives in its order of provisional measures regarding Colombia in the matter of La Rochela Massacre and in its order of provisional measures regarding Mexico in the matter of Rosendo Cantú et al. In the matter of La Rochela Massacre, the Court noted that representatives and the State each made allegations "without proof." The Court then ordered the State to take "all necessary" and "all pertinent steps" though it previously allowed that the risk assessment to be conducted by State institutions rather than requiring a public hearing or further reports to be submitted to the Court for its own deliberation. Might the Court's decision have been based on its confidence in the impartiality of the State's institutions and history of human rights observance or compliance with the Court's orders, or might there be other reasons for the Court's decision? By contrast, in the matter of Rosendo Cantú, the Court ordered further reports from the State and the representatives for its consideration, while it also ordered the State to take all necessary measures. Under what circumstances would it be reasonable for the Court to order certain factual determinations to be made by the State, or by representatives, or both, rather than by the Court itself?

- Under what circumstances may provisional measures be necessary in addition to the Court's judgment in a contentious case (i.e., under what circumstances may the merits decision not remedy "cases of extreme gravity and urgency and . . . avoid irreparable damage")?
- Consider the factual circumstances presented in the matter of Pueblo Indígena Sarayaku, where the Court ordered provisional measures to protect the entire community (in contrast to certain named individuals as in other above excerpts), and the factual circumstances presented in the matter of Mendoza Prisons, where the Court ordered provisional measures to protect all inmates. In both orders, the Court referenced the States' *erga omnes* obligation to protect all persons subject to its jurisdiction. Did the Court emphasize this obligation because of the vulnerable status of indigenous peoples in the former matter and imprisoned individuals in the latter matter, or because of the involvement of private third party actors, or for other reasons? In what circumstances may it be particularly important for the Court to reference *erga omnes* obligations?

IV.   MONITORING COMPLIANCE

Although judgment on the merits is frequently the procedural culmination of a contentious case, it is also usually the beginning of the process of remedying human rights violations. Throughout its jurisprudence, the Court has become increasingly systematic in its monitoring of compliance with its final judgments. In addition to detailing specific reparations measures, whenever possible and relevant, the Court indicates timeframes for State compliance with each measure. This allows victims, States and the Court itself to readily monitor full or partial compliance with the judgment, and to pursue additional compliance measures if necessary. The Court, along with victims, advocates and legal scholars, has identified the monitoring of compliance as an essential component of reparations orders. While the Court has often stated that its decisions are *per se* a form of reparation, of course, the decision by itself also is insufficient. Thus, it is crucial to the effectiveness of reparations orders to monitor whether the Court's rulings have been implemented. The below excerpts illustrate the range of compliance issues that the Court addresses and monitors following its merits judgments.

Monitoring Compliance with Judgment in the Case of the Constitutional Court v. Peru
1-Jun-2001
Order of the Inter-American Court of Human Rights
The Castillo Páez, Loayza Tamayo, Castillo Petruzzi et al., Ivcher Bronstein and Constitutional Court Cases

HAVING SEEN:
1.   The decisions of the Inter-American Court of Human Rights (hereinafter "the Court" or "the Inter-American Court") in the judgment on reparations of November 27, 1998, in the *Castillo Páez case*.

2.   The decisions of the Court in the judgment on reparations of November 27, 1998, in the *Loayza Tamayo case*.

3.   The decisions of the Court in the judgment of May 30, 1999, in the *Castillo Petruzzi et al. case*.

4.   The note of July 16, 1999, received by the Secretariat of the Court on July 27, 1999, in which the General Secretariat of the Organization of American States (OAS) advised that, on July 9, 1999, the State of Peru (hereinafter "the State" or "Peru") had presented an instrument in which it communicated the "withdrawal" of its declaration consenting to the optional clause concerning recognition of the contentious jurisdiction of the Court. It also remitted a copy of the original of this instrument, dated July 8, 1999, in Lima. In this document, the Minister for Foreign Affairs of Peru indicated that the Congress of the Republic, in Legislative Resolution No. 27,152 of the same date, had adopted the "withdrawal", as follows:

> [...] that, pursuant to the American Convention on Human Rights, the Republic of Peru is withdrawing the declaration consenting to the optional clause concerning recognition of the contentious jurisdiction of the Inter-American Court of Human Rights, which the Government of Peru had made at one time.
> The withdrawal of the recognition of the contentious jurisdiction of the Inter-American Court shall take immediate effect and

shall apply to all cases in which Peru has not answered the application filed with the Court.

5.　　The judgments on competence delivered in the *Constitutional Court* and *Ivcher Bronstein cases* of September 24, 1999, in which the Inter-American Court decided unanimously:

   (a) To declare that:

      (i) the Inter-American Court of Human Rights is competent to take up [these cases];

      (ii) Peru's purported withdrawal of the declaration recognizing the contentious jurisdiction of the Inter-American Court of Human Rights is inadmissible.

   (b) To continue to examine and process [these cases].

      [...]

6.　　The orders on compliance with judgment of November 17, 1999, in which the Court decided that, "in accordance with the principle of *pacta sunt servanda,* and in conformity with the provisions of Article 68(1) of the American Convention on Human Rights, the State has a duty to comply promptly" with the judgments of November 27, 1998, in the *Loayza Tamayo case,* and of May 30, 1999, in the *Castillo Petruzzi et al. case* (*supra* Having seen 2 and 3).

7.　　Legislative Resolution No. 27,401 of January 18, 2001, by which the State derogated Legislative Resolution No. 27,152 and resolved to commission "the Executive to take all necessary measures to annul any possible results of the said Legislative Resolution, fully re-establishing the contentious jurisdiction of the Inter-American Court of Human Rights for the State of Peru".

8.　　The decisions of the Court in the judgment of January 31, 2001, in the *Constitutional Court case.*

9.　　The decisions of the Court in the judgment of February 6, 2001, in the *Ivcher Bronstein case.*

10.　　The note transmitted by the Minister for Foreign Affairs of Peru, Javier Pérez de Cuéllar, to the Secretary General of the Organization of American States, César Gaviria Trujillo, in which Peru declared that:

    the recognition of the contentious jurisdiction of the Court [...], made by Peru on October 20, 1980, is fully in force and the State of Peru is bound by all its legal effects; and it should be understood that this declaration has been in force without interruption since it was deposited with the General Secretariat of the Organization of American States (OAS), on January 21, 1981.

11.　　The notes dated February 1, 2001, which the Minister of Justice of Peru presented to the President of the Court during his visit to this Court on February 9, 2001. In these notes, the State indicated that it expressly recognized the responsibility that it had incurred by violating the rights of the justices of the Constitutional Court and of Baruch Ivcher Bronstein and provided information on the measures that the State was taking to re-establish the rights of the said persons.

12.   The communication of February 9, 2001, with which Peru forwarded Supreme Resolution No. 062-2001-RE, published in the official gazette *El Peruano* on February 8, 2001, in which it appointed agents for the State in the *Durand and Ugarte, Neira Alegría et al., Castillo Páez, Loayza Tamayo, Castillo Petruzzi et al., Cantoral Benavides, Barrios Altos, Cesti Hurtado, Constitutional Court* and *Ivcher Bronstein cases.*

13.   The State's briefs of March 30 and May 7, 2001, in the *Castillo Páez case,* February 16, and April 10 and 11, 2001, in the *Loayza Tamayo case,* April 18 and May 8 and 16, 2001, in the *Castillo Petruzzi et al. case,* April 18, 2001, in the *Ivcher Bronstein case* and April 18 and May 25, 2001, in the *Constitutional Court case,* informing the Court about progress in compliance with the judgment in each of these cases.

CONSIDERING:

1.   That Article 68(1) of the Convention establishes that "[t]he States Parties to the Convention undertake to comply with the judgment of the Court in any case to which they are parties".

2.   That this obligation corresponds to a basic principle of the law of State international responsibility, firmly supported by international jurisprudence, according to which States must comply with their obligations under international conventions in good faith (*pacta sunt servanda*)[288].

3.   That the measures adopted by the State of Peru (*supra* Having Seen 7, 10 and 11) imply compliance with the decisions of the Court in the judgments on competence of September 24, 1999, in the *Constitutional Court* and *Ivcher Bronstein cases.*

4.   That the information that this Court has received implies that progress has been made in compliance with the judgments in the *Castillo Páez, Loayza Tamayo, Castillo Petruzzi et al., Ivcher Bronstein* and *Constitutional Court cases.*

THEREFORE:

THE INTER-AMERICAN COURT OF HUMAN RIGHTS,

in accordance with Articles 67 and 68(1) of the American Convention on Human Rights, Article 25 of the Statute of the Inter-American Court of Human Rights and Article 29 of its Rules of Procedure,

DECIDES:

1.   To take note of the compliance by the State of Peru of the judgments on competence of September 24, 1999, in the *Constitutional Court* and *Ivcher Bronstein cases,* and of the progress made, up until the date that this order was

issued, in compliance with the judgments delivered by the Court in the *Castillo Páez, Loayza Tamayo, Castillo Petruzzi et al., Ivcher Bronstein* and *Constitutional Court cases.*

2.   To notify this order to the State of Peru, the Inter-American Commission on Human Rights and the victims or their representatives, as appropriate.

Monitoring Compliance with Judgment
17-Nov-2004
Order of the Inter-American Court of Human Rights

HAVING SEEN:

1.   The January 31, 2001 Judgment of the Inter-American Court of Human Rights (hereinafter "the Court" or "the Inter-American Court"), in which it:

   1.   f[ound] that the State violated the right to a fair trial embodied in Article 8 of the American Convention on Human Rights, with regard to Manuel Aguirre Roca, Guillermo Rey Terry and Delia Revoredo Marsano.

   2.   f[ound] that the State violated the right to judicial protection embodied in Article 25 of the American Convention on Human Rights, with regard to Manuel Aguirre Roca, Guillermo Rey Terry and Delia Revoredo Marsano.3. f[ound] that the State failed to comply with the general obligation of Article 1(1) of the American Convention on Human Rights, with regard to the violation of the substantive rights indicated in the previous operative paragraphs of th[e] judgment.

   4.   decide[d] that the State [should] order an investigation to determine the persons responsible for the human rights violations referred to in th[e] judgment and also publish the results of this investigation and punish those responsible.

   5.   decide[d] that the State [should] pay the amounts corresponding to the arrears of salary and other benefits that, by law, correspond to Manuel Aguirre Roca, Guillermo Rey Terry and Delia Revoredo Marsano [...].

   6.   decide[d] that, in fairness, the State [should] reimburse the victims in the instant case, for costs and expenses [...] the following amounts: Manuel Aguirre Roca, US$25,000.00 (twenty-five thousand United States dollars) or the equivalent in Peruvian money when the payment is made; Guillermo Rey Terry, US$25,000.00 (twenty-five thousand United States dollars) or the equivalent in Peruvian money when the

payment is made; and Delia Revoredo Marsano, US$35,000.00 (thirty-five thousand United States dollars) or the equivalent in Peruvian money when the payment is made.

7. decide[d] that it will monitor that th[e] judgment is complied with and only then w[ould] it close the case.

2.   The November 27, 2003 Order of the Court on compliance with the judgment in the instant case, in Whereas seven and eight of which it ordered:

7. [...] in supervising comprehensive compliance with the judgments on the merits and on reparations issued in the instant case, and after analyzing the information supplied by the State, by the victims, and by the Inter-American Commission, the Court [...] verif[ied] that the State ha[d] paid the compensations for legal costs and expenses of the victims before the Court, pursuant to operative paragraph six of the Judgment on reparations.

8. [...] after analyzing the information supplied by the State, by the victims and by the Inter-American Commission, the Court deem[ed] it indispensable for the State to report to the Court on the following with respect to compliance:

(f) the outcome of the investigation to identify and punish the persons responsible for the human rights violations committed against the victims in this case [...] *(Operative paragraph four of the November 27, 2003 Judgment);* and

(b) payment of the back pay and other benefits owed, according to domestic legislation, to Manuel Aguirre Roca, Guillermo Rey Terry and Delia Revoredo Marsano *(Operative paragraph five of the November 27, 2003 Judgment).*

In this regard, the Court decided:

6. To urge the State to take such measures as m[ight] be necessary to make those reparations ordered in the January 31, 2001 Judgment with which compliance [wa]s pending effective and to promptly comply with them, pursuant to Article 68(1) of the American Convention on Human Rights.

3.   The April 2, 2004 brief, in which the State asserted that a complaint regarding the facts of the instant case was transferred to the Prosecutor's Office Specializing in Unlawful Enrichment and Constitutional Complaints on September 4, 2002. On April 1, 2003, according to a March 29, 2003 order, said complaint was forwarded to the

Congress of the Republic, and it was subsequently transferred to the Presidency of Congress. On April 23, 2003 the Directorate ordered said complaint shelved, and up to the date when the brief by the State was drafted, there had been no report on what was agreed. However, the State expressed that it would ask Congress to reconsider said decision, given the judgment by the Court. The State also reported that it had requested—and would do so once again—that the necessary administrative steps be taken to effect "the payment ordered in the judgment of the Court" through the Special Fund for Management of Monies Unlawfully Obtained to the Detriment of the State, bearing in mind the provisions of Law No. 27,775, which regulates the procedure to implement judgments issued by international courts.

4.   The May 18, 2004 brief, in which Delia Revoredo Marsano de Mur reported that Guillermo Rey Terry, one of the victims in the instant case, died on May 2, 2004.

5.   The May 25, 2004 brief in which Manuel Aguirre Roca stated that there had been no progress in the investigation, identification, and punishment of those responsible for the violation of the human rights of the three justices. On the other hand, regarding payment of the back pay and other benefits due to them, Mr. Aguirre Roca explained that the amount of compensation set by the State was based on Law No. 27,775. However, he deemed that said law is not pertinent, as it did not exist when the Court issued the January 31, 2001 Judgment. Therefore, the intention to subject payment to said law is unacceptable, as it "eludes" payment of the interest that should be paid after the sixth month, since once that term expired, the State should have deposited the amount, guaranteeing payment of the interest. Therefore, he concluded that payment of the compensation cannot be subject to or conditioned by said Law; instead, payment should be made in accordance with the provision in force at the time said Judgment was issued.

6.   The June 14, 2004 brief, in which the Inter-American Commission on Human Rights (hereinafter "the Commission" or "the Inter-American Commission") pointed out that "since November 27, 2003 there ha[d] been no progress in compliance with the judgment in the [...] case."

7.   The August 17, 2004 brief, in which Herlinda Ibáñez reported that her husband, Manuel Aguirre Roca, one of the victims in the instant case, died on June 20, 2004.

WHEREAS:

1.   Oversight of compliance with its decisions is an authority inherent to the judicial functions of the Court.

2.   Peru has been a State Party to the American Convention (hereinafter "the American Convention" or "the Convention") since July 28, 1978, and it accepted the adjudicatory jurisdiction of the Court on January 21, 1981.

3.   Article 68(1) of the American Convention sets forth that "[t]he States Parties to the Convention undertake to comply with the judgment of the Court

in any case to which they are parties." For this, the States must ensure domestic implementation of the orders issued by the Court in its rulings. [189]

4.   In view of the final and unappealable nature of the judgments of the Court, pursuant to Article 67 of the American Convention, the State must fully and promptly comply with them.

5.   The obligation to comply with the orders issued by the Court in its rulings is in accordance with a basic principle of Law regarding the international responsibility of the State, backed by international jurisprudence, according to which the States must carry out their international treaty obligations in good faith *(pacta sunt servanda)* and, as this Court has stated and is set forth in Article 27 of the 1969 Vienna Convention on the Law of Treaties, they may not refuse to undertake the international responsibility already set forth by arguing domestic reasons. [290] The treaty obligations of the States Party are binding for all the branches and bodies of the State.

6.   The States Party to the Convention must ensure compliance with the treaty provisions and their effective application (*effet utile*) in their respective domestic legal systems. This principle applies not only to substantive provisions of the human rights treaties (that is, those containing provisions regarding the rights protected), but also with respect to the procedural provisions, such as those pertaining to compliance with the decisions of the Court. These obligations must be interpreted and applied in a manner that ensures that the right protected is truly practical and effective, taking into account the special nature of human rights treaties. [391]

7.   The States Party to the Convention that have accepted the adjudicatory jurisdiction of the Court have the duty to obey the obligations established by the Court. In this regard, Peru must take such steps as may be necessary to comply with the orders issued by the Court in the January 31, 2001 Judgment (*supra* Having Seen 1).

8.   In the process of overseeing comprehensive compliance with the January 31, 2001 Judgment, and after analyzing the documents supplied by the State, by the representatives of the victim and by the Commission in their briefs on compliance with reparations (*supra* Having Seen 3, 5 and 6), the Court notes that it does not have sufficient information on the following points currently pending compliance:

(f)   The current status of the investigations to identify and punish the persons responsible for the human rights violations committed against the victims in the case *(operative paragraph four of the January 31, 2001 Judgment);* and

(g)   Payment of the back pay and other benefits due, according to domestic legislation, to Manuel Aguirre Roca, Guillermo Rey Terry and Delia Revoredo Marsano (*operative paragraph five of the January 31, 2001 Judgment*).

9.   This Court has asserted that the State that is found responsible and is in arrears regarding payment of the compensation ordered by the Court must pay interest on the amount owed.[492] It is an obligation of the State found responsible to pay the compensation ordered by the Court within the term set for this purpose, and non-compliance with this obligation entails consequences for the State. When it pays after the deadline, the State incurs the obligation to pay interest on the amount owed, so as to maintain the value of the compensation and ensure that that said amounts retain their purchasing power. The Court has declared that the States have said obligation to pay interest even when the judgment in which the Court ordered the reparations did not explicitly state said obligation.[593]

6.   The Court will consider the general status of compliance with its January 31, 2001 Judgment, as well as with its November 27, 2003 Order and the instant Order, once it receives the respective information on the measures with respect to which compliance is pending.

NOW THEREFORE:

THE INTER-AMERICAN COURT OF HUMAN RIGHTS,

exercising its authority to oversee compliance with its decisions, pursuant to Articles 33, 62(1), 62(3), 65, 67 and 68(1) of the American Convention on Human Rights, 25(1) and 30 of its Statute, and 29(2) of its Rules of Procedure,

FINDS:

1.   That it will continue to oversee compliance with the points currently pending compliance in the instant case, namely:

   (f) investigation to identify and punish the persons responsible for the human rights violations committed against the victims in this case; and

   (g) payment of the back pay and other benefits due, according to domestic legislation, to Manuel Aguirre Roca, Guillermo Rey Terry and Delia Revoredo Marsano.

AND DECIDES:

1.   To order the State to take such measures as may be necessary to put into effect and promptly comply with those points currently pending compliance that were ordered by the Court in the January 31, 2001 Judgment, as well as the provisions of the November 27, 2003 Order and the instant Order, pursuant to the provisions of Article 68(1) of the American Convention on Human Rights.

2.   To order the State to fix and pay, in accordance with the domestic legislation most favorable to the victims and respecting due process guarantees, the interest due from the time it incurred in arrears regarding payment of the back pay and other benefits of Manuel Aguirre Roca, Guillermo Rey Terry and Delia Revoredo Marsano.

3.   To ask the State to submit a detailed report, no later than January 31, 2005, on the current status of investigations to identify and punish the persons

responsible for the human rights violations committed against the victims in this case—as well as regarding steps taken to pay the back pay, other benefits and interest due, according to domestic legislation, to Manuel Aguirre Roca, Guillermo Rey Terry and Delia Revoredo Marsano—as set forth in Whereas eight and nine of the instant Order.

4.   To ask the Inter-American Commission, as well as Delia Revoredo Marsano and the next of kin and/or representatives of the deceased victims, to submit their comments on the report by the State mentioned in the previous operative paragraph, within six and four weeks, respectively, of the date when they receive said report.

5.   To continue overseeing compliance with the January 31, 2001 Judgment.

6.   To notify the instant Order to the State, to the Inter-American Commission, and to Delia Revoredo Marsano and the next of kin and/or representatives of the deceased victims.

7-Feb-2006

Ruling of the Inter-American Court of Human Rights

Case of the Constitutional Court (Aguirre Roca, Rey Terry & Revoredo Marsano) v. Peru

WHEREAS:

1.   That the supervision of the compliance of its decisions is a power inherent to the jurisdictional functions of the Court.

2.   That Peru is a State Party in the American Convention on Human Rights (hereinafter "the American Convention" or "the Convention") since July 28, 1978 and it acknowledged the Court's competence on January 21, 1981.

3.   That Article 68(1) of the American Convention states that "[t]he States Parties to the Convention undertake to comply with the judgment of the Court in any case to which they are parties." For this the States must ensure the implementation at a domestic level of that ordered by the Tribunal in its decisions. [194]

4.   That in virtue of the definitive and unappealable nature of the judgments of the Court, pursuant to that established in Article 67 of the American Convention, these must be complied with in a prompt manner by the State in a comprehensive manner.

5.   That the obligation to comply with that stated in the decisions of the Court correspond to a basic principle of law on the State's international responsibility, backed up by the international jurisprudence, according to which the States must comply with their international conventional obligations with good faith *(pacta sunt servanda)* and, as has already been stated by this Court and in Article 27 of the Vienna Convention on the Law of the Treaties of 1969, they may not, due to reasons of domestic law, ignore the international responsibility already established. [295] The conventional obligations of the States Parties are binding for all the powers and bodies of the State.

6.   That the States Parties to the Convention must guarantee compliance of the conventional stipulations and their effects (*effet utile*) in the realm of their respective domestic law. This principle is applied not only in relation to the substantive norms of the human rights treaties (that is, those that include stipulations regarding the protected rights), but also in relation to procedural norms, such as those that refer to the compliance of the decisions of the Court. These obligations must be interpreted and applied in such a way that the protected guarantee is actually practical and efficient, having present the special nature of the human rights treaties.[3 96]

7.   That the States Parties to the Convention that have acknowledged the Court's obligatory jurisdiction have the duty to comply with the obligations established by the Tribunal. In this sense, Peru must adopt all the necessary measures in order to effectively comply with that ordered by the Court in its Judgment of January 31, 2001.

8.   That when supervising the comprehensive compliance of the Judgment on merits and reparations issued in the present case, and after analyzing the information provided by the State, the Commission, and by the victims or their next of kin, the Tribunal has verified that Peru made several payments in the concept of the arrears of salary and other benefits ordered in favor of the victims: as can be concluded from the briefs presented by Mrs. Delia Revoredo Marsano de Mur, Pilar Vega Alvear de Rey, and Herlinda Ibáñez viuda de Aguirre Roca on January 14, 2005, February 21, 2005, and March 11, 2005, respectively; the State made a partial payment of S/ 322,000.00 new soles, equal to US$ 100,000.00 (one hundred thousand dollars of the United States of America), in favor of these women, in the concept of compensation for the arrears of salary. Likewise, on January 12, 2006 the mentioned victim and the next of kin informed the Court that on December 28, 2005 the State made a payment in the amount of S/ 517,496.20 new soles, in favor of each of them, in the concept of said compensation. Mrs. Revoredo Marsano, Vega Alvear viuda de Rey, and Ibáñez viuda de Aguirre Roca stated that with this last payment, added to the aforementioned partial payment, the State had paid the totality of the compensation, which had been set at S/ 839,496.22 new soles in favor of each of the former senior judges, without taking into consideration the interests for delayed payments. Finally, through a brief received on January 26, 2006, Mrs. Delia Revoredo Marsano de Mur informed that in the month of January 2006 the State had paid her the amount of S/ 45,749.06 new soles, equal to US $13,455.76 [dollars of the United States of America] in the concept of interests

9.   That Mrs. Delia Revoredo Marsano de Mur, Pilar Vega Alvear viuda de Rey, and Herlinda Ibáñez viuda de Aguirre Roca have stated that, even though they did receive the compensatory payment, the amount of the interests for delayed payments has not yet been determined or paid since there is a disagreement with the State regarding the date as of which they should start to be computed.

Besides, Mrs. Delia Revoredo Marsano de Mur stated that the payment received on December 28, 2005, as well as the last payment received in the month of January 2006, was assigned to the payment of interests until their amount is determined, since Article 1257 of the Peruvian Civil Code grants the creditor the power to assign the partial payment to the interests due and then to the capital. In relation to the above, the victims also stated their disagreement with the State, in the sense that, according to the latter, the funds required to make the pending payments had to be provided by the Ministry of Economy, in application of law 27775 (Law that regulates the procedure for the execution of judgments issued by supranational courts), since they considered that those payments should come from the FEDADOI, where they have not been budgeted and they do not require the authorization of the Ministry of Economy and Finances for the corresponding "budgetary availability".

10.   That the State presented a request of opinion before the Court in order to determine the exact date as of which the interests for delayed payments should be computed. In this sense, the State mentioned that, according to the Peruvian Ministry of Justice, "the amount it must pay the former senior judges as compensation generates interests as of the date in which the amount of the compensation was determined," that is, as of the date on which the ruling of July 1, 2003 was issued by the 64° Court Specialized in Civil Matters of Lima, for which it proceeded to issue the check corresponding to the interests for delayed payments for the period from July 2, 2003 to December 15, 2005. On its part, the victims or their next of kin considered that the interests for delayed payments should be computed as of August 1, 2001, that is, six months after the expiration of the term given to comply with the payments set in the Judgment of January 31, 2001 issued in the present case. At the same time, the Inter-American Commission estimated that said interests should be computed as of the moment in which the six-month period after the Judgment was notified had expired.

11.   That in the last ruling of supervision of the Judgment issued in the present case, the Court mentioned, the same as in other cases,[497] that the State responsible that incurs delays regarding the payment of the compensations ordered by the Tribunal must pay interest over the amount due. It is an obligation of the State responsible to comply with payment of the compensations ordered by the Tribunal in its judgments within the time period established for it, and failure to comply with this obligation brings about consequences for the State. When payment is made after the period has expired, the consequent obligation arises for the state to pay interest over the amounts due, thus maintaining the value of the compensation and ensuring that said amounts maintain their purchasing power. The Court has declared that the States have the mentioned obligation to pay interest even when said obligation is not expressly established in the judgment in which the Tribunal ordered the reparations.[598]

12.   That according to the fifth operative paragraph of the Judgment of January 31, 2001, the State should pay the compensatory amounts corresponding to the arrears of salary and other compensations that, pursuant to their legislation, corresponded to the victims, which should be set following the corresponding domestic procedures, and payments should be made within a six-month period as of the date on which the Judgment was notified. According to the information provided by the parties, the Court observes that the State has made some payments, in a differed manner, in the concept of the compensations owed to the victims, that in their totality add up to . . . the whole amount determined through the domestic procedures mentioned.

13.   That even though the amounts of the compensations were set afterwards, it was the State's obligation to determine and pay the corresponding compensations within a 6-month term as of the notice of the Judgment, that is, prior to August 7, 2001. Therefore, the calculation of the interests for delayed payments must be computed as of the expiration of the term mentioned in order to comply with the Judgment, regardless of when the compensatory amounts were set. Likewise, as stated in the previous Ruling of supervision of compliance with judgment in this case . . . the State must determine and pay the interests generated during the time in which in incurred in delay regarding the payment of the arrears of salary and other benefits of Messrs. Manuel Aguirre Roca, Guillermo Rey Terry, and Delia Revoredo Marsano, pursuant to the most favorable domestic law applicable to the victims and observing the guarantees of the due process. The amount that the State already paid Mrs. Revoredo Marsano de Mur must be deducted from that determination.

14.   That in relation to the obligation to investigate and punish the people responsible for the violations of human rights committed in the present case, the victims, their next of kin, and the Commission consider that the State has not complied with the due investigation, since it has not proven effective progress in this sense. On its part, the State has mentioned that in April 2005 the Peruvian Ombudsman considered that it corresponded to the Congress of the Republic to decide the initiation of the political trial against certain public officials, in order to apply political sanctions for violations to the Constitution. To this effect, the State had requested information in this regard to the Congress' Council of Directors, without there being evidence of the results of that procedure. The Court considers that from the information provided no important progress can be concluded on the State's part in compliance of that obligation to investigate and punish those responsible, since it simply reiterates that stated in previous reports, reason for which the supervision regarding this point of the Judgment must be kept open.

15.   That the Court will once again supervise the general state of compliance of its Judgment of January 31, 2001, as well as of its Rulings of November 27,

2003 and November 17, 2004, and the present Ruling, once it has received the corresponding information on the matters where compliance is still pending.

THEREFORE:

THE INTER-AMERICAN COURT OF HUMAN RIGHTS,

in exercise of its powers of supervision of compliance with its decisions, pursuant to Articles 33, 62(1), 62(3), 65, 67, and 68(1) of the American Convention on Human Rights, 25(1) and 30 of the Statutes and 29(2) of its Rules of Procedures,

DECLARES:

1.   That the State has complied with the totality of payment of the compensations for the arrears of salary and other benefits that, pursuant to domestic legislation, correspond to Messrs. Manuel Aguirre Roca, Guillermo Rey Terry y Delia Revoredo Marsano de Mur (*fifth operative paragraph of the Judgment of January 31, 2001*).

2.   That it will maintain the procedure of supervision of compliance of the pending matters in the present case open, specifically:

(a) investigation to determine the people responsible for the violations of human rights against the victims of the case and their punishment (*fourth operative paragraph of the Judgment of January 31, 2001*), and

(b) the determination and payment, pursuant to the most favorable domestic legislation applicable to the victims and observing the guarantees of the due process, of the interests generated during the time in which it incurred in delay regarding the payment of the arrears of salary and other benefits of Messrs. Manuel Aguirre Roca, Guillermo Rey Terry, and Delia Revoredo Marsano (*fifth operative paragraph of the Judgment of January 31, 2001 and ruling of Compliance with Judgment of November 17, 2004*).

AND DECIDES:

1.   To urge the State to adopt all the measures necessary to give effect and prompt compliance to the matters pending of compliance that were ordered by the Tribunal in the Judgment of January 31, 2001, as well as that stated in the Rulings of November 27, 2003 and November 17, 2004 * * * and the Eighth to Fourteenth Whereas Clauses of the present Ruling, pursuant to that stipulated in Article 68(1) of the American Convention on Human Rights.

2.   To request the State to present, no later than May 26, 2006, a detailed report on the status of compliance of the pending matters mentioned.

3.   To ask the Inter-American Commission, as well as Mrs. Delia Revoredo Marsano and the next of kin and/ or representatives of the deceased victims, to present their observations to the State report mentioned in the previous operative paragraph within the term of six and four weeks, respectively, as of its receipt.

4.   To continue to supervise compliance with the Judgment of January 31, 2001.

5.   To notify the present Ruling to the State, the Inter-American Commission of Human Rights, as well as the victims and their next of kin or representatives.

5-Aug-2008
Order of the Inter-American Court of Human Rights
Case of the Constitutional Court (Aguirre Roca, Rey Ferry & Revoredo Marsano) v. Peru
Monitoring Compliance with Judgment

CONSIDERING:

5.   That those States Parties to the American Convention that have accepted the binding jurisdiction of the Court are under a duty to fulfill the obligations set by the Tribunal. This obligation includes the State's duty to report on the measures adopted to comply with such decisions of the Court. Timely fulfillment of the State's obligation to report to the Court on the exact manner in which it is complying with each of the aspects ordered by the latter is essential to evaluate the status of compliance in this case.[4 99] Furthermore, the General Assembly of the OAS repeated that, in order for the Court to fully meet its obligation to report to the General Assembly on compliance with its judgments, the States Parties need to provide, in timely fashion, the information requested by the Court.[5 100]

6.   That, the Secretary of the Court sent notes to the States on several occasions . . . , reminding it of the obligation to report on the measures adopted to comply with the Judgment.

7.   That, pursuant to section 67 of the American Convention, State parties must fully comply with the judgments entered by the Court in time fashion. Furthermore, section 68(1) of the American Convention stipulates that "[t]he States Parties to the Convention undertake to comply with the judgment of the Court in any case to which they are parties". The treaty obligations of States Parties are binding on all the States' powers and organs.[6 101]

8.   That, the Peruvian State has not reported on the compliance with the Judgment and, therefore, had failed to fulfill its conventional obligation.

9.   That, without the proper information submitted by the State, this Court cannot exercise its role to oversight compliance with the Judgments delivered by it. That, for the sake of safeguarding and guaranteeing the application of the measures of reparations so delivered, this Tribunal must be able to verify execution of the Judgment and count with information related thereto. As a consequence, the Court considers it is necessary that the State informs on the status of compliance with the determination and payment in full of the amounts corresponding to the interest accrued during the time the State incurred in arrears with respect to the payment of the back salaries and other benefits of Manuel Aguirre Roca, Guillermo Rey Terry and Delia Revoredo Marsano,

as has been established in the operative paragraph five of the Judgment. In relation to the other aspects of the Judgment so delivered, the Court reserves the possibility of duly assessing them in a possible public hearing to be convened to such end.

10.   That, when monitoring full compliance with the Judgment delivered in the instant case, the Court considers it is vital that the State submit information on the operative paragraphs pending compliance in accordance with the provisions of this Order

11.   That the Court will assess the general status of compliance with such Judgment, once it is provided with relevant information on the operative paragraphs related to the reparations of an economic nature that are still pending compliance.

THEREFORE:

THE INTER-AMERICAN COURT OF HUMAN RIGHTS,

by virtue of its authority to monitor compliance with its own decisions pursuant to Articles 33, 62(1), 62(3), 65, 67 and 68(1) of the American Convention on Human Rights, and Articles 25(1) and 30 of its Statute and 29(2) of its Rules of Procedure,

DECLARES:

1.   That, in accordance with the provisions of Considering Clauses No. 6 to 10 of this present Order, the State has not fulfilled the obligation of informing this Court on the measures adopted to comply with the terms set forth in the Judgment on the merits, reparations and costs, issued by the Tribunal on January 31, 2001.

2.   That it will maintain open the procedure to monitor compliance with those operative paragraphs pending compliance of the Judgment of January 31, 2001, reserving the possibility of convening a public hearing in due time in order to assess the compliance with such Judgment.

AND DECIDES:

1.   To call upon the State to adopt such measures as may be necessary to promptly and effectively comply with the pending operative paragraphs ordered by the Court in the Judgment on the merits, reparations and costs of the case at hand, pursuant to the terms of this Order and the provisions of Article 68(1) of the American Convention on Human Rights.

2.   To order the State to submit to the Inter-American Court of Human Rights, not later than September 26, 2008, a report describing all the measures adopted to comply with the decisions ordered by this Court.

3.   To require the Secretariat of the Court to notify this Order to the State, the Inter-American Commission on Human Rights and the representatives of the victims.

Monitoring Compliance with Judgment in the Case of Herrera Ulloa v. Costa Rica
22-Sep-2006
Order of the Inter-American Court of Human Rights

CONSIDERING:

8.   That, in monitoring comprehensive compliance with the Judgment on preliminary objections, merits, reparations and costs delivered in the instant case, and after having analyzed the information supplied by the State, the Inter-American Commission and the victim's representatives in their briefs on compliance with the judgment . . . , the Court has verified which aspects of such Judgment are still pending compliance and which ones have been partially complied with.

9.   That, in its Order of September 12, 2005 . . . the Court verified that Costa Rica has partially complied with its obligations to pay non-pecuniary damages and reimburse expenses, and that only payment of arrearage interest is still pending. Pursuant to the ninth operative paragraph of the Judgment of the Court, the State is required to pay arrearage interest accrued from February 6, 2005 to the date of actual payment. As per the information provided to the Court, payment of said interest is still pending. Through its Brief of January 30, 2006 . . . the State reported that, on October 20, 2005, it requested that the Minister of the Treasury "take all appropriate measures to secure effective payment of the amount due on account of arrearage interest," totaling ¢ 155,799.00 (one hundred and fifty-five thousand, seven hundred and ninety-nine colones), computed at an arrearage interest rate of 2% p.a. from February 6, 2005 to August 24, 2005. In its brief of February 28, 2006 . . . the representatives confirmed that the State has not yet made payment of such arrearage interest, further indicating that it intentionally failed to advise the victim of the amount of interest payable, merely informing that "the payment order was already [ready]." Consequently, it is necessary for the State to submit updated information on compliance with this obligation.

10.   That, as regards the State's obligation to nullify the judgment rendered on November 12, 1999, whereby Mauricio Herrera-Ulloa was criminally convicted, and all the measures it orders, in its Order of September 12, 2005 . . ., the Court requested the parties to submit information and observations in order to obtain clear information regarding which of the obligations defined in the domestic judgment and referred to in paragraph 195[4][102] of the Court's Judgment . . . had actually been nullified. The Court noted that the ruling of the Criminal Court of the First Judicial Circuit of San José of August 24, 2004 apparently nullifies the sections of the aforementioned domestic criminal judgment referred to in paragraphs 195(1), (2), (4), (5), (6) and (8) of the Court's Judgment.

11.   That, based on the information supplied by the parties . . ., Costa Rica

has complied with its obligation to nullify the measures ordered in the domestic judgment of November 12, 1999 and referred to in paragraph 195(1), (2), (4), (5), (6) and (8) of the Court's Judgment.

12.   That in its Judgment of July 2, 2004 . . ., the Court ruled that the State is to nullify the domestic criminal judgment delivered on November 12, 1999 "and all the measures it ordered, including any involving third parties."

13.   That, in paragraph 195 of the Judgment of July 2, 2004 . . ., the Court ruled that the State is to nullify, *inter alia*, the civil award of non-pecuniary damages jointly and severally payable by Mauricio Herrera-Ulloa and the *La Nación* newspaper, in the amount of ¢60,000,000.00 (sixty million colones) for the moral damages caused; and to nullify the award of court costs in the amount of ¢1,000.00 (one thousand colones) and personal damages in the amount of ¢3,810,000.00 (three million, eight hundred and ten thousand colones) against Mauricio Herrera-Ulloa and the *La Nación* newspaper.[5][103]

14.   That, based on the information provided to the Court, on June 25, 2004, the First Civil Large Claims Court of San José enforced the civil damages award and the award of court costs and personal damages under the domestic criminal judgment of November 12, 1999. Said civil court endorsed to Przedborski the certificate of deposit in the amount of ¢63,811,000.00 (sixty three million, eight hundred and eleven thousand colones) that *La Nación* had deposited in the context of the civil enforcement of said domestic judgment.

15.   That both the State . . . and the victim's representatives . . . have reported to the Court on the different writs and appeals and the proceeding instituted before the domestic courts in order to have such money reimbursed to La Nación S.A. As per the information submitted to the Court, La Nación S.A. has not yet been reimbursed for the ¢63,811,000.00 (sixty three million, eight hundred and eleven thousand colones) that it deposited with the First Civil Large Claims Court of San José in the context of the civil proceeding for the enforcement of the domestic judgment of November 12, 1999.

16.   That, given the difficulties that have hindered compliance with the obligation to nullify the civil damages award and the award of court costs and personal damages made in the domestic criminal judgment of September 12, 1999, the Court considers it worth noting that, in its Judgment . . ., it ruled that said domestic judgment is in conflict with the American Convention, thus finding that Costa Rica "must take all necessary judicial, administrative and any other measures" to nullify and abolish any and all effects of said domestic judgment. It should be noted that the States Parties' obligations under the Convention are binding on all branches of government and organs of the State. Therefore, given that a State court enforced two of the measures provided for in the aforementioned domestic judgment, it is the State's duty to adopt all measures required to comply

with the orders of this Court, which should be done on its own motion and in a period of six months as from the date of notice of the Judgment of the Court. Accordingly, it is necessary for the State to submit updated information on compliance with this specific obligation.

17.   That, as regards the obligation to adjust its domestic legal system to the provisions of Article 8(2)(h) of the American Convention, in relation to Article 2 thereof, within a reasonable period of time, the Court notes that, as far as the developments in connection with bill No. 15.856, for the enactment of the "Relaxation of Criminal Cassation Requirements Law" are concerned, on October 4, 2005 such bill was approved upon the favorable unanimous opinion of the Permanent Commission on Legal Affairs of the Legislative Assembly . . . Moreover, the Inter-American Commission stated that said bill "does, to a certain extent, relax [said remedy]" to bring it in line with Article 8(2)(h) of the American Convention, and that it is a part of a "process for compliance 'within a reasonable time period' that is to be monitored by the Court" . . . The victim's representatives' view is that the State has not complied with this obligation; they noted that the bill has not been voted on by the Legislative Assembly *en bloc*, and expressed their concern in connection with the provisions of the second temporary article of the bill . . ..

18.   That, in order to assess whether the adjustment of the domestic laws is taking place within a reasonable period of time, the Court has deemed it necessary for Costa Rica to provide updated information on any domestic measures adopted therefor, including developments in connection with the enactment of the bill into a law and the administrative and any other measures it may have adopted in that regard. On this subject, the Court considers it worth noting that about two years have elapsed since the State was notified of the Judgment, and pointing out that such adjustment to conform to the Convention is particularly important at the Costa Rican legal level.

19.   That the Court has verified Costa Rica's partial compliance with its obligation to nullify the judgment rendered on November 12, 1999 by the Criminal Court of the First Judicial Circuit of San José *(fourth operative paragraph of the Judgment of July 2, 2004)*. The State has complied with its obligation to nullify those effects of the domestic judgment of November 12, 1999 that were referred to in paragraph 195(1), (2), (4), (5), (6) and (8) of the Court's Judgment; this means that it has nullified the following effects: 1) Mauricio Herrera-Ulloa was declared guilty on four counts of the crime of publishing offenses constituting defamation; 2) the penalty imposed on Mauricio Herrera-Ulloa of 120 days' fine, for a total of ¢300,000.00 (three hundred thousand colones); 4) Mauricio Herrera-Ulloa was ordered to publish the "Now, Therefore" portion of the judgment in the newspaper *La Nación*, in the section called "El País," in the same print face used for the articles about which the criminal complaint was filed; 5) *La Nación* was ordered to take down the link at the *La Nación Digital* website on the Internet, between

the surname Przedborski and the articles about which the criminal complaint was filed; 6) *La Nación* was ordered to create a link at the *La Nación Digital* website on the Internet between the articles about which the complaint was filed and the operative part of the judgment; and 8) Mauricio Herrera-Ulloa's name was entered into the Judiciary's Record of Convicted Felons.

20.   That it is the Court's view that it is essential for the State to provide it with up-to-date information on the following aspects, compliance with which is still pending:

(a) nullify the November 12, 1999 judgment of the Criminal Court of the First Judicial Circuit of San José and all the measures it orders *(fourth operative paragraph of the Judgment of July 2, 2004).* The State has not complied with its obligation to nullify the points of the domestic judgment of November 12, 1999 referred to in paragraph 195(3) and (7) of the Court's Judgment, *i.e.* it has not nullified the following points: 3) in the civil award, Mauricio Herrera-Ulloa and newspaper "La Nación," represented by Fernán Vargas-Rohrmoser, were held jointly and severally liable and ordered to pay ¢60,000,000.00 (sixty million colones) for the moral damages caused by the articles carried in *La Nación* on March 19, 20 and 21, 1995 and then again on December 13, 1995; and 7) Mauricio Herrera-Ulloa and the newspaper "La Nación," represented by Fernán Vargas-Rohrmoser, were ordered to pay court costs in the amount of ¢1,000.00 (on thousand colones) and personal damages totaling ¢3,810,000.00 (three million eight hundred and ten thousand colones);

(b) within a reasonable period, adjust its domestic system to conform to the provisions of Article 8(2)(h) of the American Convention, in relation to Article 2 thereof *(fifth operative paragraph of the Judgment of July 2, 2004);* and

(c) pay interest accrued on the payment of the compensation for nonpecuniary damages and the reimbursement of expenses to Mauricio Herrera-Ulloa after expiration of the term prescribed in the Judgment *(sixth, seventh and ninth operative paragraphs of the Judgment of July 2, 2004).*

21.   That the Court will consider the general status of compliance with the Judgment on preliminary objections, merits and reparations of July 2, 2004 once it is provided with the relevant information on the pending reparations.

THEREFORE:

THE INTER-AMERICAN COURT OF HUMAN RIGHTS,

by virtue of its authority to monitor compliance with its own decisions pursuant to Articles 33, 62(1), 62(3), 65, 67 and 68(1) of the American Convention on Human Rights, and Articles 25(1) and 30 of its Statute and 29(2) of its Rules of Procedure,

DECLARES:

1.   That, in accordance with Considering clauses No. 11 and 19 of this Order, the State has partially complied with its obligation to nullify the Judgment issued by the Criminal Court of the First Judicial Circuit of San José on November 12, 1999 *(fourth operative paragraph of the Judgment of July 2, 2004)*.

2.   That it will keep open the proceeding for monitoring compliance with the points pending compliance in the instant case, namely:

   (a) to nullify the November 12, 1999 judgment of the Criminal Court of the First Judicial Circuit of San José and all the measures it orders *(fourth operative paragraph of the Judgment of July 2, 2004)*, pursuant to Considering clauses No. 11 to 16 and 20(a) of this Order;

   (b) to adjust its domestic legal system to the provisions of Article 8(2)(h) of the American Convention on Human Rights, in relation to Article 2 thereof *(fifth operative paragraph of the Judgment of July 2, 2004)*; and

   (c) to pay interest accrued on account of the payment of the compensation for non-pecuniary damages and reimbursement of expenses to Mauricio Herrera-Ulloa after expiration of the term prescribed in the Judgment *(sixth, seventh and ninth operative paragraphs of the Judgment of July 2, 2004)*.

AND DECIDES:

1.   To call upon the State to adopt such measures as may be necessary to promptly and effectively comply with the pending measures ordered by the Tribunal in the Judgment on preliminary objections, merits and reparations, pursuant to Article 68(1) of the American Convention on Human Rights.

2.   To request that, by January 19, 2007, the State submit to the Inter-American Court of Human Rights a report specifying such measures as may have been adopted to comply with the reparations ordered by this Court and which are still pending fulfillment, as established in Considering clauses No. 11 to 18 and 20 and the declarative paragraphs of this Order.

3.   To call upon the representatives of the victim and the Inter-American Commission on Human Rights to submit their observations to the State's report referred to in the preceding operative paragraph, within a period of four and six weeks, respectively, as from the date of receipt of the report.

4.   To continue monitoring those sections of the Judgment on preliminary objections, merits and reparations of July 2, 2004 that are still pending compliance.

5.   To request that the Secretariat of the Court notify this Order to the Inter-American Commission on Human Rights, the representatives of the victim and the State.

9-Jul-2009
Order of the Inter-American Court of Human Rights
Monitoring Compliance with Judgment

CONSIDERING:

7.   That the States Parties to the Convention who have acknowledged the Court's contentious jurisdiction have the duty to comply with the obligations imposed by the Court. Such obligations include the duty of the State to report to the Court on the measures adopted in compliance with the Court's rulings. The prompt observance of a State's obligation to inform the Court on the manner in which it is carrying out each of the instructions set out by the Court is essential to evaluate compliance with the Judgment as a whole.[6 104]

8.   That the Court finds the hearing held to monitor the issues pending compliance in this case very instrumental.

9.   That, with regard to the obligation to annul in whole the judgment issued on November 12, 1999 by the Criminal Court for the First Court Circuit of San José, in connection with the damages and court and other costs awarded against Mr. Mauricio Herrera-Ulloa and the La Nación newspaper, represented by Mr. Fernán Vargas Rohrmoser (*operative paragraph No. 4 of the Judgment*), the State informed that "failed action was taken before civil courts seeking the recovery of sixty-three million eight hundred and eleven thousand colones, plus interest as damages and court costs for La Nación S.A. corporation". Said corporation filed ordinary fiscal civil proceedings against the State before a Contentious-Administrative and Civil Fiscal Court.

10.   That, afterwards, Costa Rica informed that, through judgment No. 823-2007 of June 22, 2007, the Contentious-Administrative and Civil Fiscal Court had granted relief to La Nación S.A., compelling the State to reimburse "principal in the amount of sixty-three million eight hundred and eleven thousand colones, pursuant to the certificate of deposit [...], plus statutory interest and default interest owed"; furthermore, the State was compelled to "pay personal and court costs incurred in pursuing this action". Upon issuing such judgment, Costa Rica informed that, among other steps being taken, "funds [were] being applied into the 'compensation' item to provide for [...] the payment of the damages award against the State", which implied "taking unavoidable legal steps which require from two to three months to be effective, when the deposit into La Nación S.A.'s account will be made".

11.   That, finally, on January 29, 2009 the State reported that it had made two deposits into La Nación S.A.'s account for sixty-three million, eight hundred and eleven thousand colones (CRC 63,811,000.00) and sixty-seven million, seven hundred and fifty thousand, three hundred and sixty colones (CRC 67,750,360.00), as "the principal owed for the annulment of the aforementioned judgment and [the] amount [arising from] costs and statutory and default interest". The State attached copies of the certificates of the deposits made on September 19 and December 10, 2008.

12.   That the representatives pointed out that they had to file an action against the State in view of "the Ministry of Finance's refusal to comply with the judgment reimbursing the compensation award paid when required [...]. The Ministry alleged that such payment should be ordered by the Supreme Court of Justice *en banc*. The Supreme Court, for its part, failed to comply with the requirement and expressed its opinion that contentious administrative proceedings should be carried out previously, refusing to comply with the Inter-American Court's Judgment pursuant to the Convention and the Headquarters Agreement. Finally, the State as defendant in the aforementioned proceedings has not been particularly cooperative either, since, in light of its undeniable international obligations in this regard, in compliance with the Judgment it should have appeared at least upon commencement of the proceedings rather than confining itself to refrain from raising challenges. Had the State acted properly, the contentious-administrative proceedings would very likely have ended by now and the Judgment would have been enforced in whole".

13.   That the representatives added that the State "has failed to comply on its own with its duty to abide by a final international judgment almost five years old[, which] is even more inexplicable considering that section 27 of the Headquarters Agreement between [the State] and [the Court provides that] 'once the orders of the Court and its President have been notified to the appropriate administrative or judicial authorities of the Republic, they shall have the same binding force as the orders issued by Costa Rican courts'". The representatives stated that the action filed by La Nación S.A. against the State was encouraged by them "in an attempt to cure the State's contradictions and breaches of duties and to offer the State further opportunity to comply with international duties which it has failed to perform on its own". This made the State's breach of duties even worse, as "[the State] continues making excuses such as difficulties and defects in its domestic system for its delay in complying with a money judgment issued by a Costa Rican court along the same lines as [the Court's order of] July 2004".

14.   That, with regard to the amounts deposited in late 2008 (*supra* Considering clause No. 11), the representatives stated that "they do not cover the interest accrued between the date of the Costa Rican court's judgment and the payment date", which must be paid not only pursuant to the Costa Rican contentious-administrative court's judgment, but also pursuant to operative paragraph No. 9 of the Court's Judgment. Additionally, they stated that "the amounts deposited by the State are not enough to cover the costs incurred in claiming payment in the Costa Rican domestic courts", referring to the proceedings commenced in view of the State's failure to comply with its legal duty to pay on its own the amounts it was compelled to pay. The same domestic court order compelled the State to pay personal and court costs incurred in pursuing the domestic proceedings, which constitutes an "ancillary obligation inseparable from the Court's Judgment", as

such costs had to be incurred as a result of the State's failure to comply with the Judgment. The Judgment remains "pending compliance" and the "State still owes eleven million, two hundred and sixty-eight thousand, nine hundred and forty-one colones with forty cents (CRC 11,268,941.40), as unpaid interest accrued during eighteen months, calculated at the basic interest rate of the Central Bank of Costa Rica, which is currently 12%. The State also owes fees in the amount of six million nine hundred thousand colones (CRC 6,900,000.00), for collecting in court the sums ordered in the Judgment". The representatives submitted a pleading on February 5, 2009, in which they claimed for the aforesaid amounts before the Contentious-Administrative Civil Fiscal Court.

15.   That the Inter-American Commission "positively value[d] the payments made by Costa Rica to the La Nación newspaper". Notwithstanding the foregoing, the Commission considered it would be useful for the State "to make a statement on the representatives' allegations [...] of February 17, 2009 that the payments made fail to fully comply with their obligation", so that the Court may decide whether to consider such obligation fulfilled.

16.   That at the private hearing for monitoring compliance the State pointed out that "indeed, a claim is still pending for some amounts owed as interest and costs" and that "a court decision is expected ordering payment of such amounts; the amounts [...] do not represent principal or the initial amounts, but constitute ancillary sums deriving from such original amounts". The representatives agreed on the fact that the amounts owed are the result of "engaging in a contentious-administrative proceeding to enforce the Judgment, as such judgment was not spontaneously complied with [...], which gave rise to additional procedural complications and caused further costs which could have been avoided if the Judgment had been complied with simultaneously. For its part, the Commission referred to its written observations on the above-mentioned differences.

17.   That the Inter-American Court notices that in September and December 2008 the State deposited the amounts owed in connection with the principal amount owed as a result of the annulment of the aforementioned judgment and personal costs and current and default interest (*supra* Considering clause No. 11).

18.   That the Court notices the difficulties and delays in complying with this reparation measure. The deadline for complying with this obligation expired six months after the Judgment was notified, on February 6, 2005, while the State made the aforesaid deposits in September and December 2008 (*supra* Considering clause No. 11), that is, more than three years and seven months, and three years and ten months, respectively, after the expiry of the term. Additionally, the Court also notices that the State failed to comply on its own with this reparation measure, so the representatives had to file an action with the domestic courts. Costa Rica has paid the amount due as principal in connection with the civil

damages award; however, such civil proceeding gave rise to additional costs, expenses and interest, which had not been fully paid. The State pointed out that it is waiting for a domestic court decision ordering payment of such amounts. In view of the foregoing, the State in its next report must refer to the observations of the representatives and the Commission (*supra* Considering clauses No. 14 and 15) and furnish current information on the compliance with this item.

19.   That with regard to the obligation to adjust its domestic legal system within a reasonable term to conform to the provisions of Article 8(2)(h) of the American Convention in relation to Article 2 thereof (*operative paragraph No. 5 of the Judgment)*, the State informed that on April 28, 2006, the Legislative Assembly enacted Law No. 8503, called "Law Extending Criminal Review Proceedings" (hereinafter, also "Criminal Review Proceedings Law"), published on June 6, 2006 in the official gazette La Gaceta No. 108. The State attached a copy of such publication and, additionally, pointed out that:

(a) pursuant to the Judgment issued by the Inter-American Court, "both the Third Division of the Supreme Court of Justice and the Criminal Cassation Court adjusted their case law [...] with administrative and legal interpretation action, even before amending the Code of Criminal Procedure through the Criminal Review Proceedings Law". Among other "immediate measures", the rules governing admissibility of evidence were made more flexible and expanded, and factual evidence was admitted in criminal review proceedings;

(b) by enacting the Criminal Review Proceedings Law, "Costa Rica complied with the Inter-American Court's order in its judgment of July 2, 2004," since the law: "(a) Relaxes the formalities of the motion for review; both in terms of admissibility requirements and other formalities typical of review proceedings; (b) expressly provides for the possibility for alleging a violation of due process or of the right to defense, so full provision is made for the possibility of reviewing any kind of defects or violations to the rights of convicts; (c) provides an opportunity to receive factual evidence through the review proceedings, provided one of the causes for a review proceeding is present, including the rising of new facts or new evidence; (d) offers an opportunity to produce evidence that was not admitted at trial, because it was arbitrarily dismissed or rejected; even the Court or Division may *ex officio* order that evidence be produced when it deems it necessary, appropriate or instrumental to settle the case; (e) extensively provides for the analysis to be carried out on review, allowing the moving party to rely on the sound or video recording of the trial as grounds for its motion for review; (f) reduces the formalities of the review procedure; and (g) provides an opportunity to file a motion for appeal when the motion for review has been rejected based on the admissibility criteria in force before the law was enacted";

(c) as to the requirement that the review relief be accessible and simple, pursuant to section 447 of the Criminal Review Proceedings law the Court may reject a motion for review if it considers that the order being challenged may not be reviewed pursuant to review proceedings, that the motion for review has been filed after the term to do so or that the moving party has no right to move for review. In the event the motion is admissible, it shall proceed, and the Court shall issue a decision on the merits, even when it considers that there are defects in the way the motion has been framed. The Criminal Review Proceedings law, together with section 15 of the Code of Criminal Procedure, also amended by the aforementioned law, which provides for the possibility of curing formal defects, "significantly reduces the formalities involved in criminal review proceedings, so that a court hearing an appeal on the grounds of error must consider the motion, even if there are defects in the way the motion has been framed. Only where the defects are such that the Court cannot satisfy the motion, the moving party is given an opportunity to correct such defects at a hearing. Thus, even in such a case a court may not declare a motion for review inadmissible without giving the moving party an opportunity to cure any defects";

(d) as regards the requirement that the review proceedings allow for comprehensive review of the judgment, international law rules provide that "the right to review clearly does not necessarily mean that […] there must be a right to appeal in the narrow sense". Any conviction requires two operations: Firstly, the 'proven fact' must be determined (finding of facts); secondly—after the facts have been established—the facts must fit one or more legal rules (finding of law). Both operations can be strictly controlled through a motion for review of a criminal judgment pursuant to an error, the former by examining the causes of the facts and the latter by examining how the law was applied to the facts in the criminal judgment. The motion for review of a criminal judgment on the grounds of error "provides a measure of control over the factual findings by the higher court […]. The Costa Rican review system can normally provide ordinary and effective recourse that is accessible and comprehensive so as to allow a higher court to carry out a comprehensive examination of all the issues of fact and of law disputed and analyzed by a trial court, which does ensure a comprehensive examination of the challenged decision through which the higher court may reconsider a court decision that runs counter to the law". The American Convention does not guarantee "the right to two successive trials by two different courts so that the second trial preempts the first one, but rather is intended to guarantee control or review of the conviction entered in the single instance trial, so as to prevent an error from causing harm to the accused". The Convention is complied with by establishing a remedy against an allegedly erroneous conviction, regardless of its name (i.e., appeal or review) provided that such remedy makes it possible to determine: (a) whether the procedural rules set out for the benefit of the accused have been observed in determining the facts that the lower court deemed to be proven in its judgment, and (b) the law applied to the proven fact. A "repetition or extension of the trial to a second instance would not satisfy [the international obligation]; at any rate would unnecessarily protract the process, and would aggravate the accused's situation by putting him twice in jeopardy, which can bring about a vicious circle, because if the repetition (i.e., the second instance) results in a new conviction, the process—following this rationale—would need to be repeated and then trial would have to be carried out once again (i.e., a third instance) so as to comply with the instruments in question";

(e) the Law Extending Criminal Review Proceedings incorporated subsection (j) into section 369 of the Code of Criminal Procedure, which established a defect in the judgment justifying review by a higher court *"where the judgment has not been issued pursuant to a due process or with an opportunity for defense"*. The introduction of this provision "ratifies the wide variety of grounds for granting a motion for review of a criminal judgment in Costa Rica, including any violation of the right of due process or the right to defense, thus allowing for a comprehensive review of the judgment";

(f) the Law Extending Criminal Review introduced section 449 bis into the Code of Criminal Procedure. Contrary to the classical views of cassation, "review of criminal judgments [in Costa Rica] allows supervision of the facts and evidence". Particularly "in the case of requests for review based on a lack of justification and violation of the rules of sound judgment, the goal is to challenge the proven facts and argue aspects of the evidence received. Those actions allow for a wide variety of options for requesting review, which becomes evident upon the incorporation of section 499 bis to the Code of Criminal Procedure". Additionally, the Law Extending Criminal Review provides that "the higher court may even rely on audio and visual recordings in reviewing the challenged decision". Furthermore, as regards the possibility that the Higher Court receives new evidence or evidence rejected at trial, the newly incorporated section 449 bis of the Code of Criminal Procedure allows for evidence to be submitted. The State further pointed out that "[i]n addition to the general opportunity afforded the accused to offer evidence supporting his case, the accused may also offer such evidence if it is essential to the request for review, provided such evidence has been previously rejected; which, although expressly provided only with respect to the Attorney General, the complainant and the civil plaintiff, it must be interpreted so that the accused may do it too";

(g) additionally, pursuant to the terms of the Law Extending Criminal Review, a person who was convicted prior to the effective date of such law may challenge the conviction on the grounds of violation to the right of due process or the right to defense by filing a motion for review on the grounds of error, which covers a wide range of situations. A person who "has been convicted prior to the effective date of the Law Extending Criminal Review may file a motion for review to argue the issues of fact and of law which could not be argued upon review because of the rules governing the admissibility of the motion for review"; and

(h) the statistical data submitted by the State with regard to the review proceedings show "substantially low inadmissibility rates, [...] which reflects the broader criteria currently adopted and the total abandonment of the excessive attachment to formality which the Costa Rican courts themselves have set out to abolish". Additionally, the effectiveness of the supervision by criminal review courts "is reflected in the high rate of court orders granting" motions for review.

20.   The State concluded that "in Costa Rica the motion for criminal review has departed from what this method for challenging decisions has been in Europe and Latin-America" and that the reform has resulted in "a complete reduction in formalities, which guarantees the right to simple recourse to carry out a comprehensive review of the judgment convicting a defendant". The Costa Rican review proceedings "have ceased to be strictly a review proceeding to acquire a number of features of appellate proceedings".

21.   That the representatives "celebrate[d] the State's efforts to comply with this part of the Court's Decision by enacting the aforementioned legislation. A legislative reform process entails the complications inherent in a debate in a democratic society, so it is always comforting to know that such a process is entertained pursuant to the judgment of an international human rights court such as the Inter-American Court". Additionally, among other considerations, the representatives pointed out that:

(a) "the new criminal review law keeps the same instances which were disapproved by the Court in its Judgment, that is, first instance and review by a higher court. However, the second instance is intended to be less formal and restricted than the typical review proceedings, which distinguished them from an appeal to a higher court pursuant to Article 8(2)(h) of the Convention". Thus, the Law Extending Review Proceedings "relaxes the requirements for admission of a motion for review; vests the Review Court with powers to carry out a more comprehensive review of a lower court's decision; provides an opportunity, albeit limited, to offer and receive evidence upon review; and increases the number of members of the Criminal Review Court. Additionally, temporary provision I provides an opportunity for the review of previous cases in which a motion for review by a higher court on grounds of error has been rejected on the basis of the former legislation repealed by the statutory reform in question. Doubtless, these are positive aspects aimed at curing the insufficiency of the motion for review to satisfy the requirements of Article 8(2)(h) of the Convention";

(b) however, "it cannot be overlooked that the reform represents a sort of compromise between the system criticized in the Court's Judgment (i.e., one instance with review proceedings limited to classical review proceedings) and the clearer system consisting of two-instance proceedings for the full examination of the case plus one review instance. Such compromise [...] does not seem to make up for the inobservance of the Costa Rican criminal procedure system of the Convention [...]. Indeed, the aforementioned enactment does not suffice to comply with the Court's Judgment [...]. Not only does the newly enacted legislation maintain the same review structure, but also, owing to the very nature of the motion for review on the grounds of error, the system remains unchanged inasmuch as it provides for a review of the judgment rather than a full review of the case actually allowing for an assessment of all the aspects involved in a conviction, including issues of fact as well as issues of law. The defects in the Costa Rican review system pointed out by the Court [are] not cured simply by admitting all motions for review, but by providing for legal and procedural mechanisms allowing for a full review of the judgment being challenged";

(c) the "new law has not modified section 443 of the Code of Criminal Procedure, which sets out the grounds upon which a motion for review may be granted". Such provision should have been modified "to provide for wider possibilities of obtaining review from a cassation court, or its content [should have been] modified so that it ceases to entertain a formalistic interpretation of the motion for review". The same might be predicated of section 449 bis of the Law Extending Criminal Review; even though it true that such provision provides greater possibilities for offering evidence, "it provides that the Cassation Court must evaluate the manner in which the trial court judges assessed the evidence and justified their decision, which confirms the supervisory role of the higher court rather than vesting it with the power to carry out 'a full and comprehensive review of all the issues presented to the lower court' pursuant to the Judgment";

(d) given that such "limitations, paired with the circumstance that the legislative reform does not touch on the structure of criminal procedure, which continues to be confined to a first instance plus review by a higher court, [the representatives] conclude that hardly will the Law Extending Criminal Review make Costa Rican criminal procedure comply with the requirements set out in Article 8(2)(h) of the Convention pursuant to the terms of the Judgment". This abstract consideration, however, "could be corrected in practice if the newly enacted rules were applied broadly to satisfy the requirements of the international law on human rights. Otherwise, if a restrictive stance is adopted—as did happen in the past—the goal of adjusting procedural roles to the Convention would be thwarted. In such a case, the Convention would be violated again in future cases submitted to this Court". Therefore, "the determination [whether the State has complied with its obligation to adjust its domestic legal system to Article 8(2)(h) of the Convention] will be made by the domestic courts, interpreting the law in accordance with its purpose and intent and pursuant to the State's international obligations";

(e) with regard to temporary section II of the Law Extending Review Proceedings providing that the newly enacted law will become effective as soon as sufficient economic resources are secured to meet the new task imposed upon the Cassation Court, it is "inadmissible [...] to make the effective protection of an individual right (i.e., the right to due process under Article 8 of the Convention) conditional upon the existence or availability of material resources", inasmuch as "the protection of the rights enshrined in the Convention may not be subordinated to the availability of economic resources". As long as such protection continues to be conditioned upon material resources, "the State [shall] not have fully satisfied this item of the Judgment", and

(f) the statistical data provided by the State to show the behavior of the courts after the Law Extending Review Proceedings is "partial and limited" and provides no grounds to conclude that the Judgment is being complied with. Pursuant to the analysis of the annual reports of the Planning and Statistics Department of the Judiciary, changes have not been substantial in practice. Court statistics clearly point at confirming the perception that "not only legislative reform is insufficient, but also there have been no major changes in practice". The representatives further stated that the statistical analyses "must be supplemented with qualitative analysis, scrutinizing past judgments to check whether there was a effectively [...] a full and comprehensive review of the court rulings and whether the moving parties were allowed to submit new evidence".

22.   That, based on the foregoing, the representatives concluded that the Law Extending Review Proceedings "constitutes a measure intended to comply with the Judgment [...] but contains formal limitations that do not assure that the higher court [will] carry out a full or comprehensive analysis of all the issues presented to the lower court, so its effectiveness will depend on its future application; therefore, the law must still be supervised by the Court". Furthermore, the condition contained in temporary section II of the aforementioned law is incompatible with the duties imposed by Articles 1(1) and 8(2)(h) of the Convention; therefore, "such Law does not constitute *per se* compliance with the Judgment [...] and fails to comply operative paragraph No. 5 [thereof]".

23.   That the Inter-American Commission analyzed the Law Extending Review Proceedings and found that "it extends to a certain degree criminal review proceedings in order to adjust review proceedings to Article 8(2)(h) of the Convention by introducing three fundamental changes:

(a) the relaxation of formal requirements for granting a motion for review on the grounds of error;

(b) the granting of additional powers to the authorities who must rule upon the motion to review in whole the lower court's judgment; and

(c) the relaxation of formalities as to the admission of evidence. The Commission took notice of "these significant reforms propounded by the State [...]; at the same time, it f[ound] that their effectiveness and the corresponding compliance with the Court's order in its judgment of July 2, 2004 must be assessed based on the application of the new system to specific cases".

24.   That, with regard to the statistical data furnished by the State, the Inter-American Commission found that it has not been proved that the State's rules of procedure have been redesigned to provide citizens with further judicial safeguards. Finally, the Commission asked the Court to "declare that the State enacted legislation aimed at adjusting the Costa Rican legal system to the terms of Article "8(2)(h) of the Inter-American Convention in relation to Article 2 thereof, which still must be analyzed for effective application and compliance, so the monitoring proceedings must be kept open with regard to this item".

25.   That, in the private hearing for monitoring compliance, the State provided explanations and clarifications regarding the representatives' and the Inter-American Commission's observations regarding the changes introduced to

review proceedings under the Law Extending Review Proceedings. Furthermore, it made reference to the "[B]ill to *establish the motion for appeal, introduce other amendments to appellate proceedings and adopt new trial rules (Legislative File No.)* 17.143)". The State informed that "this proposed legislative reform propounded by the Third Division of the Supreme Court of Justice and approved in a preliminary report by the [Supreme] Court *en banc*, raises the need to conclude a lengthy process of partial reforms dating back to the 1980s and intended to bring Costa Rica's domestic legal system into compliance with the obligations imposed by the American Convention, particularly Article 8(2)(h) in relation with Article 2 thereof". The Commission pointed out that "the propounders of this proposal [are] convinced that it will settle a long-lasting controversy" and added that the reform is aimed at:

(a) designing "a single uniform appellate system in criminal courts";

(b) "[c]reating a motion for appeal to the existing cassation courts against criminal judgments";

(c) creating a motion "to be filed before a judgment becomes final", which would be given "the largest possible broadness, accessibility and flexibility, so as to settle any doubts and objections presented so far in the face of a motion for review which, even though it has evolved substantially, remains the subject of much controversy by foreign commentators";

(d) ruling out asymmetries and self-defeating outcomes emerging from this long process of reform, which has included temporary fixes resulting from the evolution and the efforts to adjust the domestic criminal legal system to the terms of the American Convention"; and

(e) "[e]stablishing a [m]otion for [r]eview designed in a more classical fashion, and providing guidance in conflicting issues".

26.   That in the hearing for monitoring compliance the representatives summarized their observations submitted in their briefs and pointed out that the Law Extending Review Proceedings represented an effort by the State "to comply in good faith with the Judgment, but [...] such effort has proven to be insufficient in practice, and to that end a bill has been introduced which is now under consideration by the Legislative Assembly, which, in the view of that legislative body, satisfies the requirements set out in the Judgment for review by a higher court pursuant to the Convention". Even though the representatives once again acknowledged the efforts, they requested the Court to declare that the State has failed to comply with this reparation measure pursuant to the Judgment.

27.   That in the hearing for monitoring compliance the Inter-American Commission celebrated and acknowledged the State's efforts, recalled the observations set out in its various briefs and pointed out that "[the] reforms should

be reflected in a more effective procedure" and that it expects a qualitative change. It stated that, before deeming this item in the Judgment complied with, "in view of the fact that a new bill has been introduced in the Legislative Assembly [...], it is necessary to [wait] for the outcome of that new process of reform first and then for more appropriate information on the effectiveness of the procedural law reform, not in numerical terms but in real terms".

28.   That the Inter-American Court positively values the passage of Law No. 8503 called the "Law Extending Criminal Review Proceedings" and the fact that such law was enacted one year and seven months after the Judgment was notified. Furthermore, the Court also values the fact that the Costa Rican Judiciary adopted "immediate measures", even before enacting the Law Extending Criminal Review Proceedings in order to bring judicial practice into conformity with the terms of the Judgment (*supra* Considering clause No. 19.i).

29.   That the Court observes that the representatives and the Inter-American Commission have positively valued the State's efforts associated with the reform introduced through the Law Extending Criminal Review Proceedings, even though they find such modifications inadequate in terms of deeming this reparation measure complied with. For its part, the Court appreciates the information furnished by the State that a legislative process is currently underway in connection with compliance with the Judgment, among other aspects. In view of the information provided by the parties, the Inter-American Court takes notice of the evolution of the compliance process and deems it convenient to defer its evaluation until the State furnishes current information on the progress and outcome thereof.

30.   That, with regard to the obligation to pay default interest incurred by virtue of paying Mr. Mauricio Herrera-Ulloa compensation for non-pecuniary damage and the reimbursing him for expenses after the expiration of the term set forth in the Judgment (*operative paragraphs No. 6, 7 and 9*), the State informed that, through tender No. 06T20 of May 24, 2006, it deposited one hundred and fifty-five thousand, seven hundred and ninety-nine colones (CRC 155,799.00) for Mr. Herrera-Ulloa as default interest. The State attached the documents evidencing the deposit.

31.   That the representatives ratified that the above-mentioned amount was indeed deposited in favor of the victim. However, they reported that Mr. Herrera-Ulloa stated that such amount failed to cover the entire default interested owed, surely owing to a time lapse between the time the payment order was issued and the time the funds were made available. In spite of this, Mr. Herrera-Ulloa considered that, even though there is a small balance of outstanding default interest and in spite of the delays, the State has evidenced a will to compensate him and has covered almost the entirety of the amounts owed on these grounds, so he is "willing to consider the Judgment to be complied with as to this aspect". Therefore, they

requested the Court to "declare that the State has complied with [this] obligation".

32.   That the Inter-American Commission took notice of the briefs of the State.

33.   That, in accordance with the parties' briefs and the victim's intention, the Court deems it appropriate to consider the State to have complied with the obligation to pay default interest owed to Mr. Herrera-Ulloa pursuant to operative paragraphs No. 6, 7 and 9 of the Judgment.

THEREFORE:

THE INTER-AMERICAN COURT OF HUMAN RIGHTS,

In exercise of its powers to supervise compliance with its decisions under Articles 33, 62(1), 62(3), 65, 67 and 68(1) of the American Convention on Human Rights, Articles 25(1) and 30 of the Statute and Article 30 and 63 of its Rules of Procedure,[7][105]

DECLARES,

1.   That, pursuant to Considering clause No. 33 hereof, the State has implemented the following reparation measure:

    (a) Payment of interest incurred as a result of having paid Mr. Mauricio Herrera-Ulloa compensation for non-pecuniary damage and reimbursed him for expenses incurred after expiry of the term set out in the Judgment (*operative paragraphs No. 6, 7 and 9 of the Judgment*).

2.   That, pursuant to Considering clauses No. 17, 18, 28 and 29 hereof, the Court shall keep open the compliance with judgment proceedings for the following items:

    (a) repealing the judgment issued on November 12, 1999 by the Criminal Court for the First Judicial Circuit of San José (*operative paragraph No. 4 of the Judgment*). The State has paid the principal associated with the damages award, though there is an outstanding balance of interest and costs as explained in Considering clause No. 18 hereof.

    (b) adjusting its domestic legal system to the terms of Article 8(2)(h) of the American Convention on Human Rights, in relation to Article 2 thereof (*operative paragraph No. 5 of the Judgment*).

3.   That it will continue to monitor compliance with the following items pending compliance in this case, to wit:

    (a) repealing in full the judgment issued on November 12, 1999 by the Criminal Court for the First Judicial Circuit of San José (*operative paragraph No. 4 of the Judgment*), with regard to the balance of interest and costs pursuant to Considering clause No. 18 hereof, and

    (b) adjusting its domestic legal system to the terms of Article 8(2)(h) of the American Convention on Human Rights, in relation to Article 2 thereof (*operative paragraph No. 5 of the Judgment*).

AND DECIDES:

1.   To require the State to adopt all such measures as are necessary to effectively and promptly comply with the pending operative paragraphs in the Judgment on the Merits, Reparations and Costs of July 2, 2004, pursuant to Article 68(1) of the American Convention on Human Rights.

2.   To require the State to submit to the Inter-American Court of Human Rights, no later than October 15, 2009, a report stating the measures adopted to comply with the reparation measures ordered by this Court which are pending compliance, pursuant to Considering clauses No. 18 and 29 and in declaratory paragraph No. 2 hereof.

3.   To require the Inter-American Court of Human Rights and the victim's representatives to submit such comments to the State's report mentioned in the above operative paragraph as they deem appropriate, within two and four weeks, respectively, from receipt of the State's report.

4.   To continue monitoring compliance with the operative paragraphs of the Judgment on the merits, reparations and costs of July 2, 2004, pending compliance.

5.   To request the Court's Secretariat to notify this Order to Costa Rica, the Inter-American Commission on Human Rights and the victims' representatives.

22-Nov-2010
Order of the Inter-American Court of Human Rights
Supervision of Compliance with Judgment

CONSIDERING:

. . .

3.   Article 68.1 of the American Convention stipulates that "[t]he State Parties to the Convention promise to comply with the decision of the Court in any case to which they are parties." Therefore, the States must ensure that decisions of the Tribunal are implemented domestically. [1 106]

4.   Given the judgments of the Court are final and definitive, in accordance with Article 67 of the American Convention, they shall be promptly and fully complied with by the State. [2 107]

5.   The duty to comply with that established in the decisions of the Tribunal corresponds to a basic principle of the law of international responsibility of the State, supported by international jurisprudence; according to which the States shall fulfill their international treaty obligations in good faith (*pacta sunt servanda*) and, as put forth by this Court and under Article 27 of the Vienna Convention on the Law of Treaties of 1969, they cannot, for internal reasons, stop assuming the international responsibility already established. [3 108] The treaty obligations of States Parties are binding on all State bodies and organs. [4 109]

6.   The State Parties to the Convention shall guarantee compliance with treaty dispositions and *effet utile* within their respective domestic law. This principle is applied, not only regarding substantive rules of human rights treaties (namely, the ones that contain dispositions regarding the protected rights), but also in relation to procedural norms, such as those concerning compliance with decisions of the Court. These obligations shall be interpreted and applied within their respective domestic law. This principle applies, not only to the substantive rules of human rights treaties (namely, those containing dispositions on protected rights), but also regarding procedural norms, such as those referring to compliance with the decisions of the Court. These obligations shall be interpreted and applied in such a manner that the protected guarantee is truly practical and effective, taking into account the special nature of human rights treaties[5][110].

(a) Obligation to nullify the judgment issued on November 12, 1999, by the Criminal Court of the First Circuit of San Jose

7.   Regarding the obligation to nullify, in every respect, the judgment issued on November 12, 1999, by the Criminal Tribunal of the First Judiciary Circuit of San Jose (fourth operative paragraph of the Judgment), the State reported the following: a) regarding the amount owed in interests, the Contentious Administrative and Civil Court of the Treasury Department approved, by means of a judgment on September 8, 2009, the payment of legal and moratorium interests to the amount of ¢8.447.457,44 colones, paid to *La Nación* on November 13, 2009, and b) regarding the amount owed in personal costs, the Contentious Administrative Tribunal, First Section of the Second Circuit of San Jose approved by means of a resolution on February 23, 2010, the amount of ¢422,372.87 colones, which "is available to [the company] by drawing from the expenses fund that the State sets aside for this purpose." Also, it manifested that it has requested the processing of the corresponding procedures so that said amount be deposited in the bank account of the company. For the aforementioned, the State considered that "it has fulfilled the obligations arising from the Judgment of July 2, 2004; therefore, it request[ed that] full compliance with this issue be declared."

8.   The representatives informed that "the State has paid in full the amounts that were owed as compensation [...] as well as all outstanding interests and [the] costs, in such a way that the issues concerning capital in the Judgment can be considered satisfied."

9.   The Inter-American Commission stated that, "from the available information, it can be gathered that the total fulfillment of payments for compensation, interests and costs are still outstanding."

10.   From the information provided by the parties, the Tribunal concludes that the State has complied with the obligation to nullify, in every respect, the judgment issued on November 12, 1999, by the Criminal Court of the First Circuit

of San Jose, pursuant to the fourth operative paragraph of the Judgment, having complied fully with the payment of interests and costs owed pursuant to the eighteenth paragraph of the Order of the Inter-American Court of July 9, 2009.

(b) Obligation to bring its domestic legal system into conformity with the provisions of Article 8(2)(h) of the American Convention

11.   Regarding the obligation to bring its domestic legal system into conformity with the provisions of Article 8(2)(h) of the American Convention, in conjunction with Article 2, within a reasonable time period (fifth operative paragraph of the Judgment), Costa Rica reported that on April 29, 2010, the Legislative Assembly approved Law No. 8.837, "Law for the Creation of Appeal Proceedings for Judgments, additional amendments to the system of appeals and implementation of new orality rules in criminal proceedings" (hereinafter also "Law No. 8.837"), whose text was published on June 9, 2010, in *La Gaceta*, the official newspaper for the State of Costa Rica. Also, it included a copy of the official publication of said law, which:

(a) made various amendments to the Code of Criminal Procedure, such as expanding the judgment appeals system by adding a criminal judgment appeals proceeding; reforming the review procedure; and, strengthening the principle of orality in criminal proceedings;

(b) created the judgment appeals recourse so that all judgments and dismissals issued in the trial phase are appealable.[6][111] The appeals recourse "would enable the complete examination of the judgment when the interested party disagrees with the facts established, the incorporation and evaluation of evidence, the legal foundation or the drawing up of the sentence. The High Court will pronounce the points that are explicitly questioned, as well as stating, even ex officio, the absolute defects and violations of due process found in the judgment."[7][112] Also, Law No. 8.837 provides for a reduced number of reasons for inadmissibility of judgment appeals recourses as well as stating that the procedure must be resolved even when defects exist in its drafting. If such defects were to completely impede that the claim be heard, the Tribunal of Appeal may act so that the party rectify them, pointing out the aspects that must be clarified and corrected.[8][113] Regarding evidence in the Tribunal of Appeal, it provides that, "[for] a full review of the trial or sentence issued by the trial court, through the judgment appeals recourse, the Tribunal, at the request of the party, will have the power to examine the record of evidence presented at the trial, as long as it is necessary, pertinent and useful for the goals of the appeal, the object of the case or for the verification of an offense. The same procedure would be applied with everything the accused says." Also, Law 8.837 states that regarding testimony evidence and expert witnesses that, exceptionally, it shall be given directly before the Tribunal of Appeal, as well as in circumstances under which certain evidence can be considered to be new. Additionally, it provides for the possibility for said Tribunal of Appeal to use the available documentation system, so as to more readily monitor what happened in the trial court.[9][114] The Tribunal of Appeal would determine the legality and grounds of the claims made during the appeal proceedings, so as to assess that the way the trail judges weighed the evidence and on what they based their decision.[10][115] Finally, it regulates everything related to the order of the Tribunal of Appeal and the retrial;[11][116] and,

(c) it modified the judicial review proceeding, which shall act against the judgment issued by the tribunals of appeal[12][117]: i) when the existence of contradictory orders issued by said tribunals are alleged, or by said tribunals and by the Court of Criminal Review,[13][118] or ii) when the judgment does not comply with or erroneously applies a substantive or procedural legal precept.[14][119]

12.   The representatives took positive note of the sanction made on April 29, 2010 by the Legislative Assembly of Costa Rica to the "Law for the Creation of Appeal Proceedings for Judgments, additional amendments to the provisions of appeals and implementation of new orality rules in criminal proceedings," which became the Law of the Republic No. 8.837 after its publication in the "La Gaceta", Costa Rica's Official State Newspaper, on June 9, 2010. Also, they stated that although "full compliance with this chapter of the Judgment will only be achieved when the new procedural system gains complete practical enforcement," it must, however, be assumed that the State will apply this system appropriately and in good faith. Also, they manifested that "with the introduction of the new procedural system, the State has complied formally with that set forth by the Judgment and that any divergence that may arise during the application of said system would relate to general compliance with duties that Costa Rica must undertake in accordance with the Convention, rather than the execution of the Judgment on the [present case]." Finally, the representatives stated that with "the complete and definitive execution of the Judgment, [...] Costa Rica honors once again its recognized commitment to the international protection of human rights."

13.   The Inter-American Commission "evaluat[ed] the progress stemming from the approval of the Law No. 8.837 and consider[ed] that it incorporates elements taken into account by the Court in its [J]udgment regarding the scope of Article 8(2)(h) [...] of the American Convention." Also, it observed that, in relation to this progress, it is necessary to assess its practical implementation, since the Commission "has a great number of petitions related to the issue set forth in the present operative paragraph of the [J]udgment."

14.　　The Tribunal positively values the various measures adopted by Costa Rica to comply with the Judgment of the present case, fundamentally, taking into account the high complexity of the material —the system of appeals for criminal matters— and the measures which are necessary to comply with this goal. Notwithstanding the difficulties, since the issuance of the Judgment, the State adopted various measures in order to advance toward full compliance with it provisions. Accordingly, the Inter-American Court viewed the approval of Law. No. 8.503 "Law of Opening of Criminal Cassation" (hereinafter "Law of Opening") positively and the fact that said law was approved one year and seven months after the notification of the Judgment. Also, the Tribunal valued that the Judicial Power adopted "immediate measures," even before the approval of the Inaugural Law, so as to bring judicial practice in to line with the provisions of the Judgment. [15] [120]

15.　　On this occasion, the Court also positively views the actions of the State that considered it necessary to strengthen the amendments implemented by the Inaugural Law, and, *motu propio,* initiated a new process of legal reform, which concluded with the approval of Law. No. 8.837. Through this law, in addition to maintaining the judicial review recourse, an appeals proceeding for criminal judgments is created which, *inter alia*: a) provides for the revision of a judgment before a superior tribunal; b) consists of a simple procedure, free of major formalities, that avoids any requirements or restrictions that infringe upon the essence of the right to appeal, and c) makes it possible to fully weigh up all the issues debated and analyzed by the trial court.

16.　　The Inter-American Court concludes that, by ensuring increased monitoring of judgments issued by a trial court in criminal law matters at the domestic level, Costa Rica has fully complied with operative paragraph five of the Judgment, and thus, concludes the present case. The future application of the appeal proceeding does not concern the supervision of compliance with the case of Herrera Ulloa.

THEREFORE:

THE INTER-AMERICAN COURT OF HUMAN RIGHTS,

in exercising its powers of supervision of compliance with its decisions, pursuant to Articles 67 and 68(1) of the American Convention on Human Rights, Article 30 of the Statute, and Article 31(1) of its Rules of Procedure,

DECLARES:

1.　　That in accordance with the provisions set in paragraphs 10, 14, 15, and 16 of the present Order, the State has fully complied with the operative paragraphs of the Judgment issued in the present case. These operative paragraphs stipulate that the State shall:

(a) nullify, in every respect, the November 12, 1999 judgment of the

Criminal Court of the First Judicial Circuit of San José, as provided for in paragraphs 195 and 204 of the Judgment *(operative paragraph four of the Judgment),* and

(b) bring its domestic legal system in to line with the provisions of Article 8(2)(h) of the American Convention on Human Rights, in conjunction with Article 2. *(operative paragraph five of the Judgment).*

2. That, consequently, the Republic of Costa Rica has fully complied with the Judgment issued on July 2, 2004, in the case of Herrera Ulloa, in accordance with that set forth in Article 68(1) of the American Convention on Human Rights, that obliges the State Parties to the American Convention to comply with the judgments issued by the Court.

AND RESOLVES:

1. To conclude the case of Herrera Ulloa, given that the Republic of Costa Rica has fully complied with the provisions of the Judgment issued by the Inter-American Court of Human Rights on July 2, 2004.

2. To close the present case.

3. To communicate this Order to the General Assembly of the Organization of American State during its next ordinary period of sessions through the 2010 Annual Report of the Inter-American Court of Human Rights.

4. To Secretariat of the Inter-American Court of Human Rights shall notify the Republic of Costa Rica, the Inter-American Commission on Human Rights, and the representatives of the victim of this present order.

Monitoring Compliance with Judgment in the Case of Almonacid-Arellano et. al v. Chile
26-Sep-2006
Preliminary Objections, Merits, Reparations and Costs

METHOD OF COMPLIANCE

165. In order to comply with this judgment, the State shall reimburse costs and expenses within a year from the date notice of the judgment is served upon it. Regarding the publication of this judgment . . ., the State shall comply with such measure within six months from the date notice of the judgment is served upon it. The remaining reparation measures ordered by the Court shall be complied with by the State within a reasonable time .

166. If the beneficiary of the reimbursement of costs and expenses were not able to receive the payment within the term specified above due to causes attributable thereto, the State shall deposit said amount into an account or certificate of deposit in favor of the beneficiary with a reputable Chilean financial institution, in United

States dollars, and under the most favorable financial terms permitted by law and banking practice. If after ten years compensation has not been claimed, these amounts shall be returned to the State together with accrued interest.

167   . The State may discharge its obligations by tendering United States dollars or an equivalent amount in Chilean currency, at the New York, USA, exchange rate as quoted on the day prior to the day payment is made.

168.   The amounts allocated in this Judgment as reimbursement of costs and expenses shall not be affected, reduced, or conditioned by current taxes or any taxes that may be levied in the future. Consequently, said amount shall be paid in full to the beneficiary in accordance with the provisions set forth in this judgment.

169.   Should the State fall into arrears with its payments, interest shall be paid on any amount due at the current bank default interest rate in Chile.

170.   In accordance with its constant practice, the Court retains the authority which derives from its jurisdiction and the provisions of Article 65 of the American Convention, to monitor full compliance with this judgment. The instant case shall be closed once the State has fully complied with the provisions herein set forth. Within one year from the date of notice of this judgment, the Chilean State shall submit to the Court a report on the measures adopted in compliance herewith.

XI. OPERATIVE PARAGRAPHS

171. Therefore,

THE COURT,

DECIDES:

Unanimously,

1.   To dismiss the preliminary objections raised by the State.

DECLARES:

Unanimously, that:

2.   The State did not comply with its obligations derived from Articles 1(1) and 2 of the American Convention on Human Rights and violated the rights enshrined in Articles 8(1) and 25 thereof, to the detriment of Elvira del Rosario Gómez-Olivares and Alfredo, Alexis, and José Luis Almonacid-Gómez * * *.

3.   Insofar as it was intended to grant amnesty to those responsible for crimes against humanity, Decree Law No. 2.191 is incompatible with the American Convention and, therefore, it has no legal effects.

4.   This judgment is, in and of itself, a form of reparation.

AND RULES:

Unanimously, that:

5.   The State must ensure that Decree Law No. 2.191 does not continue to hinder further investigation into the extra-legal execution of Mr. Almonacid-Arellano as well as the identification and, if applicable, punishment of those responsible . . .

6.   The State must ensure that Decree Law No. 2.191 does not continue to hinder the investigation, prosecution, and, if applicable, punishment of those responsible for similar violations in Chile . . .

7.   The State shall reimburse costs and expenses within one year from the date notice of this Judgment is served upon it . . .

8.   The State shall cause this Judgment to be published . . . within six months from the date notice of this judgment is served upon it.

9.   The State shall monitor full compliance with this Judgment and the instant case shall be closed once the State has fully complied with the provisions set forth herein. Within one year from the date of notice of this Judgment, the State shall submit to the Court a report on the measures adopted in compliance herewith.

18-Nov-2010
Order of the Inter-American Court of Human Rights
Monitoring Compliance with Judgment

HAVING SEEN:
1. The Judgment on preliminary objections, merits, reparations and costs (hereinafter "the Judgment") issued by the Inter-American Court of Human Rights (hereinafter "the Inter-American Court", "the Court" or "the Tribunal") on September 26, 2006, whereby, regarding reparations, it ruled the following:

> 5. The State must ensure that Decree Law 2.191 does not continue to hinder the continuation of investigations into the extrajudicial execution of Mr. Almonacid-Arellano and the identification and, where appropriate, the punishment of those responsible, as stated in paragraphs 145 to 157 of [the] Judgment.
>
> 6. The State must ensure that Decree Law 2.191 does not continue to hinder the investigation, prosecution and, if applicable, the punishment of those responsible for other similar violations in Chile, as stated in paragraphs 145 to 157 of [the] Judgment.
>
> 7. The State must reimburse the costs and expenses within one year following the notification [of the] Judgment, in accordance with paragraph 164 of [the] Judgment.
>
> 8. The State must execute the publications listed in paragraph 162 of the [...] Judgment, within six months following the notification thereof.

CONSIDERING:

I.   In relation to the obligation to investigate, identify, try and, where appropriate, punish those responsible for the extrajudicial execution of Mr. Almonacid-Arellano and the duty to ensure that Decree Law No. 2.191 does not continue to hinder the continuation of investigations (operative paragraph five and paragraphs 145 to 157 of the Judgment)

6.   The State provided information on actions that "have nullified resolutions and judgments that dismissed the cause through the enforcement [of] the Decree Law 2.191 (Amnesty DL)," the remanding of the case to the ordinary courts and the progress of the criminal proceedings. Chile reported that:

(a) In October 2007, it ordered the reopening of the judicial investigation into the death of Mr. Almonacid, and the Rancagua Appeals Court appointed a special visiting judge as the judge to hear the case on the murder of Mr. Almonacid. Subsequently, a peremptory challenge was lodged between said judge and the Second Military Court of Santiago. On December 3, 2008, the Supreme Court of Chile ruled that "regarding case No. 876-96 (40.184) of the First Criminal Court of Rancagua, on the homicide of Luis Almonacid-Arellano, a peremptory challenge [could] not be lodged with military justice "based on a report issued by the Prosecutor of the Supreme Court, whereby it stated that the ruling of the Inter-American Court "deemed it necessary to reopen proceedings before the ordinary judiciary and manifested the inapplicability of the amnesty for the accused." Therefore, consequently, the Supreme Court ruled that the case should be heard by the special visiting judge appointed by the Court of Appeals of Rancagua. On December 24, 2008, the judge issued a resolution in which he decided that, in compliance with the Judgment of the Inter-American Court, it [was] necessary "to pursue —in a civil court— the preliminary criminal investigation No. 40.184 of the First Criminal Court of Rancagua on the murder of Luis Almonacid-Arellano." The Home Under-Secretary and the Human Rights Program of the Ministry of the Interior "have participated in said criminal case," which "will make it possible to access the investigation and request measures that contribute to the clarification of the death of Mr. Almonacid-Arellano;"

(b) Through the Resolution of December 24, 2008, said Judge also ordered: the reopening of case No. 40.184 of the First Criminal Court of Rancagua to continue its processing; the nullification of the Resolution of the Second Military Court of Santiago of 28 January, 1997, that acquitted two suspects in the murder case of Mr. Almonacid-Arellano, and nullify the Resolution of March 25, 1998, which confirmed the acquittal; and, reestablish the indictment against one of them, who is the retired Major of the Carabineros, on suspicion of murder. As regards to the other accused party, a retired *Suboficial Mayor* [Chief Non Commissioned Officer] of the Carabineros, the State reported that he had died on June 21, 2005. In relation to the progress of criminal case No. 40.184, the State explained that: "this case had to be heard according to the rules that formerly governed criminal proceedings;" it is in the preliminary stage, which is secret; on July 6, 2009, it requested that the preliminary investigation be heard and it was waiting for the respective judicial resolution; and, in August 2010, it added that as a result of the inquiries carried out by the Examining Magistrate, it was possible to determine "the identity of the officer who drove the vehicle in which a badly wounded Mr. Almonacid was transported to the hospital in Rancagua," and the involvement of the defendant in the present case was established "through oral testimonies, confrontations, and his own confession, [which] is extremely relevant because [the defendant] has always denied any involvement with the death of Luis Almonacid"; and,

(c) Similarly, Chile sent a copy of the amendment bill for the Code of Military Justice, which "was submitted for consideration before the National Congress" on July 3, 2007. As indicated in the bill, one of the proposed amendments suggested that, as a rule of jurisdiction for military justice, said jurisdiction should be exercised "over military when ruling on cases pertaining to military jurisdiction" and that "the jurisdiction of military courts only be applied to military crimes against the sovereignty of the State and its domestic and foreign security, when such crimes are committed by soldiers," which would be subject to certain exceptions.

7.   The representatives did not make observations on any of the State reports, despite the various submission requests that were made, following the President of the Court's instructions, stating that such submissions be made as promptly as possible given the expiration of the submission deadlines . . ., and the only information submitted to the Court were copies of two decisions adopted domestically in relation to the investigation of the facts in this case,[5 121] without making any assessment about it.

8.   The Commission stated that it "positively value[d] the information provided by the State in relation to justice measures taken" but it noted that this information showed that, "the investigation is still in its early stages, only one person was accused [...], and no detailed information has been submitted about the investigative measures that had been exhausted to determine other possible perpetrators." It also positively valued proceedings carried out as part of the investigation initiated in civil courts and it believed the State should continue to report on progress in the investigation.

9.   When ordering the reparation measure concerning the obligation to investigate, the Court took into account that the violation of judicial guarantees and judicial protection in this case were based on two factors: i) the granting of jurisdiction to military courts, by means of a Supreme Court decision, to hear the case concerning the death of Mr. Almonacid-Arellano; and, ii) the enforcement of Decree Law No. 2.191 by which the military tribunals that ruled on the case granted themselves amnesty.[6][122] Consequently, in order to ensure that these violations are not repeated in this case, the Court ordered that the State, so as to fulfill its obligation to investigate the extrajudicial execution of Mr. Almonacid-Arellano and to identify and, where appropriate, punish those responsible, should: i) ensure that the Decree Law does not continue to hinder the investigation into what happened to Mr. Almonacid-Arellano, ii) nullify the decisions and judgments issued domestically that authorize jurisdiction to the military courts and allowed the investigation to be closed under the Decree Law; and, iii) refer the case to the courts, so that as part of criminal proceedings those responsible for the death of Mr. Almonacid-Arellano be identified and punished.[7][123]

10.   The Court also stated, *inter alia*, that the investigation should comply with the following: not enforce the Decree Law No. 2.191, not invoke prescription periods, non-retroactivity of criminal law, the principle of *ne bis in idem,* as well as not implementing any other measures to eliminate responsibility, or avoid the duty to investigate and punish those responsible;[8][124] ensure that all public institutions provide the necessary facilities to the ordinary court that hears the case of Mr. Almonacid-Arellano;[9][125] and ensure that Ms. Elvira del Rosario Gómez Olivares and Alfredo, Alexis and José Luis Almonacid Gómez have full access and ability to participate in all phases and stages of the investigations, in accordance with domestic law and the norms of the American Convention.[10][126]

11.   To assess the state of compliance with the obligation to investigate what happened to Mr. Almonacid-Arellano, the Court has referred to the information provided by Chile, which was not disputed by the representative or the Commission. However, the Court notes that, with the exception of two decisions taken in December 2008 in domestic criminal proceedings,[11][127] the Court does not have copies of the rulings and proceedings taken in connection with said investigation, both with respect to granting jurisdiction to ordinary courts and the execution of criminal proceedings pending before said jurisdiction, since the State has not provided copies of these actions and rulings. The Court also considers that the only occasion when the representative addressed the Tribunal in relation to monitoring compliance with the Judgment was to present a copy of the two judicial resolutions that relate specifically to the progress reported by the State (*supra* Considering Clause 7). The Court also notes that, regarding the rulings and proceedings carried out in the preliminary stage of the criminal proceedings

pending before the ordinary courts, the State explained that such a stage is secret and on July 6, 2009, it was ordered that the investigation be heard and it was awaiting the respective court resolution. Subsequently, in August 2010, it reported on some progress in the investigation (*supra* Considering Clause 6(b)).

12.   The Court notes that during the monitoring compliance with the Judgment stage it is essential that the State provide the Court information and complete documentation that makes it possible to verify compliance by the responsible State with the obligations ordered in the ruling. In order to fulfill the role of monitoring compliance with the reparation measures for the violations committed against the victims, and in view of the principle of adversary proceedings, in each case the Court will assess the need, suitability or appropriateness of upholding the confidentiality of information provided with regard to its use in the Order, but not regarding the Parties' access to it.[12][128]

13.   Firstly, regarding the duty to ensure that Decree Law No. 2.191 does not continue to hinder the investigation of the extrajudicial execution of Mr. Almonacid, the Court believes that from the information provided by the State it can be deduced that this duty has been guaranteed in this case to date through actions taken by judicial authorities who have not implemented said Decree, respecting the provisions of the Court to the effect that the Decree Law has no legal effect as it is incompatible with the American Convention. Because the criminal proceedings recently started the preliminary stage, it must be stressed that the State must take steps to continue to ensure this factor in all phases and stages of said proceedings, including the total and effective fulfillment of the obligation to investigate, prosecute and, where applicable, punish those responsible for the extrajudicial execution of Mr. Almonacid.

14.   Secondly, the Court acknowledges that Chile has fulfilled the duties to rescind the resolutions and judgments issued domestically which in turn gave jurisdiction to the military courts and led to the conclusion of the investigation pursuant to Decree Law No. 2.191 and that, consequently, allowed the case to be referred to ordinary courts in order to continue with the criminal investigation. In this regard, the Court values that in December 2008 the Chilean Supreme Court took the important decision to rule that in this case "it is not possible to lodge a peremptory challenge with a military court." As a result, the case was brought before the ordinary criminal courts. Furthermore, in that same month the special visiting judge, designated by the Rancagua Appeals Court to hear the investigation, issued a resolution ruling to "pursue —in a civil court— the criminal preliminary investigation of case No. 40.184 of the First Court of Rancagua into the murder of Luis Almonacid-Arellano." Furthermore, said Judge also ordered: the reopening of case No. 40.184 of the First Criminal Court of Rancagua to continue with its processing; the nullification of the Resolution of the Second Military Court of

Santiago of 28 January, 1997, that acquitted two suspects in the murder case of Mr. Almonacid-Arellano, and nullify the Resolution of March 25, 1998, which confirmed the acquittal; and, prosecute one of them, who is the retired Major of the Carabineros, on suspicion of murder. As reported by the State, the case is at the preliminary stage before the ordinary criminal courts and the Examining Magistrate has taken some steps to investigate the death of Mr. Almonacid, in particular to determine the corresponding liability, whereby it has been possible to prove the sole defendant's participation in the case concerning the execution of Mr. Almonacid (*supra* Considering Clause 6(b)). The State has not submitted information on what specific actions were taken as a result of said attestation. However, the Court believes the aforementioned domestic decisions comply with an important point of the obligation to investigate provided for in the Judgment.

15.   Similarly, regarding the obligation to ensure the investigation be executed in ordinary courts, the State sent a copy of the amendment bill for the Military Justice Code, which "was submitted for consideration before the National Congress" on July 3, 2007, and is yet to be approved. The Court values that the Executive Branch proposed this initiative and that it has been submitted to the Chilean Legislative Branch for its consideration, particularly due to the effects that an appropriate and complete legislative reform could have on the State's appropriate compliance with its general obligation to ensure the rights to judicial guarantees and judicial protection, and in particular the principle of natural law. However, bringing the Chilean legal system into conformity with international standards on military criminal jurisdiction and the creation of legal restrictions for jurisdiction of military courts in terms of subject matter and people is part of monitoring compliance with the ruling issued by this Court in the case of *Palamara Iribarne v. Chile*. [13] [129]

16.   The Court considers that the information provided by the State reflects Chile's principle of compliance with its international obligations to investigate and punish those responsible for the human rights violations identified in this case. Accordingly, the Court is waiting for complete and updated information on ongoing criminal proceedings covering: (i) information on compliance with the criteria established by the Court regarding the proper way to fully comply with the obligation to effectively investigate, including those highlighted in Considering Clause ten of this Order; and, (ii) information on measures or actions taken by the authorities, as a result of proving the participation of the only defendant in this case in the extrajudicial execution of Mr. Almonacid (*supra* Considering Clause 14).

> ## II.   *Regarding the obligation to ensure that Decree Law 2.191 does not continue to hinder the investigation, prosecution and, if applicable, the punishment of those responsible for other similar violations in Chile (operative paragraphs 145 of [the] Judgment)*

17.   The State indicated that it had studied "various ways" to comply with this aspect of the Judgment and that "it [had] deemed that the enactment of a bill to interpret Article 93 of the Penal Code to be the most viable option." Said article stipulates the grounds for the extinction of criminal liability. Furthermore, the State indicated that it had sought to "harmonize the non-enforcement of DL 2191, an Amnesty law, with the principles of *res judicata* and *ne bis in idem*, [and thus], in that sense, it [had] entered into a legal course of action." With respect to the first legislative amendment mentioned, Chile reported that in May 2008 "a bill intended to interpret Article 93 of the Penal Code [was] pending, with a view to preventing the enforcement of amnesty, pardon and prescription periods in cases on war crimes, genocide and crimes against humanity." According to the State, this bill "seeks to comply with the [J]udgment of [the] Court regarding the provision that Decree Law 2.191 must not hinder the investigation, prosecution and, where appropriate, punishment of those responsible for the human rights violations that occurred in Chile between 1973-1978." It added that the bill strives to enact an interpretive law to clarify the true meaning and scope of existing domestic laws relating to "the extinction of criminal liability in light of International Law on Human Rights." In its August 2010 report, it submitted a copy of that bill[14][130] and said it was in the second constitutional procedural stage in the Senate, where it had been submitted on May 6, 2009.[15][131] With respect to the second legislative procedure mentioned, the State also submitted a copy of its text, along with its August 2010 report, and indicated that it was a bill to "[m]odif[y] Article [657] of the Criminal Procedure Code, providing a new review channel for human rights violations."[16][132] It added that the bill was in the first stage of consideration and that it "mark[ed] the first report of the Lower House Committee on Human Rights, Nationality and Citizenship as a substage." The State also noted that both legislative procedures referred to the Judgment of the Court in this case.

18.   The representative of the victim and his family did not make observations on any of the State reports.

19.   In its observations, the Commission did not refer to the information provided by Chile regarding compliance with operative paragraph six of the Judgment.

20.   The Court notes that the State took a first step towards fulfilling its duty to ensure that the Decree Law does not continue to represent an obstacle to guaranteeing the right to judicial guarantees and judicial protection in Chile. The Court notes that the effective implementation of this reparation measure is an essential part of complying with the Judgment, as it aims to ensure that violations, such as those in the present case, do not recur by adopting domestic legal measures (legislative, administrative or otherwise) to correct the root causes of violations. While there may be different domestic law measures through which the State could ensure such an outcome, the Court notes that the State considers

the most appropriate way to do so is through a legislative amendment.

21.   Regarding the possibility of establishing specific grounds for filing a recourse to review in cases of serious human rights violations, the Court notes that, in such a case, a judicial review of these cases would be possible, so long as the review is not impeded by the enforcement of the principle of legality and retroactivity of criminal law.

22.   Because of the foregoing, the Court deems that Chile needs to explain how the two aforementioned legislative amendments would ensure that Decree Law No. 2.191 is not enforced by domestic bodies and authorities in the investigation and punishment of violations similar to those that took place in the this case. On the other hand, the Court notes that the State reported on the initiation of the processing of the bill to interpret the grounds for the exclusion of criminal responsibility in May 2008 (*supra* Considering Clause 17) and more than two years later, this bill is still pending before the Senate. Since this reparation measure should be fulfilled within a reasonable time, the Court urges the State to take any steps that may be necessary to promptly and effectively comply with this reparation measure. Accordingly, the Court believes that paragraph six of the Judgment is pending compliance and requests the State to continue to report in detail, timely and completely on the progress made with the processing of the bills and the measures taken, or those that will be taken, so that they be adopted, as well as the effectiveness of the aforementioned legislative amendments for the compliance with this reparation measure. Chile also must disclose whether it has adopted any administrative action or otherwise aimed at fulfilling the guarantee of non-repetition.

III. In relation to the obligation to reimburse the costs and expenses (operative paragraph seven and paragraph 164 of the Judgment)

23.   The State reported that on May 30, 2007 it paid the amount awarded by the Court as costs and expenses, depositing said amount "in the Savings Account of the State Bank, whose holder is Ms. Elvira del Rosario Gómez Olivares."

24.   The representative of the victim and his family did not make observations on any of the State reports.

25.   The Committee noted "with satisfaction the fulfillment of what was ordered by the Court in operative paragraph seven of the [J]udgment."

26.   The State reported that it had complied fully with this point in the report submitted on June 29, 2007, which was duly transmitted by the Court to the representative, who, despite repeated requests by the President of the Tribunal to submit observations on this report and other reports . . ., did not make any observations. Taking into account the observations of the Commission, as well as the fact that more than three years have passed since the State reported that it had reimbursed all costs and expenses, without the representative submitting any comments or objections thereto, the Court concludes that Chile has complied with

the provisions of operative paragraph seven of the Judgment within the one year timeframe set forth in the Judgment.

IV. In relation to the obligation to publish the Judgment in the Official Gazette and another newspaper that is widely circulated nationally (operative paragraph eight and paragraph 162 of the Judgment)

27.   In its first report, the State manifested that it made such publication "in the Official Gazette of Chile and in the *La Nación* newspaper on May 14 and 13, [2007] respectively," and provided copies of these publications.

28.   The representative of the victim and his family did not make observations on any of the State reports.

29.   The Committee noted "with satisfaction the fulfillment of what was ordered by the Court in operative paragraph eight of the [J]udgment."

30.   In its first report on June 5, 2007, the State reported that it had complied fully with this point. Said report was duly transmitted by the Court to the representative, who, despite repeated requests by the President of the Tribunal to submit observations on this report and other reports . . ., did not make any observations. Taking into account the proof of publication in the Official Gazette of Chile—and in a newspaper that is widely circulated nationally—provided by the State, the Commission's observations, as well as the fact that more than three years have passed since the State reported the execution of said publications without the representative making any comments or objections thereto, the Court concludes that Chile has complied with the provisions of operative paragraph eight of the Judgment.

V. In relation to the obligation to inform the Court of compliance with the Judgment

31.   To monitor the total compliance with the Judgment issued in this case, the Court has reviewed the information provided by the State in their reports and the Inter-American Commission in its observations on the reports. However, the Court notes that on September 23, 2009, following instructions of the President of the Court, the State was requested to submit a further report on compliance with the Judgment, which was not presented until August 23, 2010, almost a year after it was requested . . .

32.   The Court reminded that the obligation to respect the rulings of the Court includes the State's duty to inform the Court about the measures taken to comply with the Court's provisions in aforementioned Judgment. The obligation to inform the Court about compliance with the Judgment requires, for its effective implementation, the formal presentation of a document, within time limits, as well as specific, accurate, up-to-date and detailed reference material on the issues related to the obligation. [17 133] Timely fulfillment of the State's obligation to advise the Court how it is complying with each of the reparations it ordered is essential in order to assess the status of compliance with the Judgment. [18 134]

33.   The Court also highlights the particular importance of the observations of the Commission and the representatives of the victims in order to assess the implementation, by the State, of the measures to comply with the Judgment. [19] [135] Consequently, for proper and complete assessment of compliance with the Judgment it is essential that the representative present observations without any delay . . . —as seen in this proceeding—on the information provided by the State and requested by this Court regarding compliance with the reparations measures ordered.

THEREFORE:

THE INTER-AMERICAN COURT OF HUMAN RIGHTS,

in exercising its authority to monitor compliance with its decisions in accordance with Articles 33, 61(1), 62(3), 65, 67, and 68(1) of the American Convention on Human Rights, Article 25(1) and 30 of the Statue, and Article 31 and 69 of its Rules of Procedure,

DECLARES:

1.   The State has complied fully with the following points:

(a) To reimburse costs and expenses (*operative paragraph seven of the Judgment*); and,

(b) To publish the Judgment in the Official Gazette and another newspaper that is widely circulated nationally (*operative paragraph eight of the Judgment*).

2.   It shall keep the monitoring process open for the following outstanding points:

(a) To investigate, identify, try and, where appropriate, punish those responsible for the extrajudicial execution of Mr. Almonacid-Arellano and the duty to ensure that Decree Law No. 2.191 does not continue to hinder the continuation of investigations (*operative paragraph five and paragraphs 145 to 157 of the Judgment); and,*

(b) To ensure that Decree Law No. 2.191 does not continue to hinder the investigation, prosecution and, if applicable, the punishment of those responsible for other similar violations in Chile (*operative paragraphs six and paragraph 145 of [the] Judgment*)

Monitoring Compliance with Judgment in the Case of La Cantuta v. Peru
29-Nov-2006
Merits, Reparations and Costs

(F) METHOD OF COMPLIANCE

246.   In order to comply with the instant Judgment, the State must pay the compensations for pecuniary and non pecuniary damage, and reimburse costs and

expenses, within the term of one year following notice of this Judgment . . . With regard to the publication of the instant Judgment and the public acknowledgement of liability and apology . . ., the State has a six-month term, following notice of this Judgment, to comply with said obligations. As regards the adequate treatment of the disappeared victims' next of kin, the State must provide for the same from the date of notice of this Judgment and for the period of time deemed necessary . . .. Furthermore, Perú must take without delay the necessary actions to effectively conduct and complete, within a reasonable time, the ongoing investigations and the criminal proceedings pending in the domestic courts, and to carry out, as the case may be, the necessary investigations to determine the criminal liability of the perpetrators of the violations committed to the detriment of the victims . . .. The State must forthwith carry out the search and localization of the remains of the victims and, once located, the State must deliver them as soon as practicable to the next of kin and give them dignified burial . . . With regard to the education programs on human rights, the State must implement them within a reasonable time . . .

247.   The compensations established to the benefit of the relatives of the 10 executed or disappeared victims shall be delivered directly to each beneficiary. If a beneficiary dies before the date of payment, the compensation must be paid to the heirs according to applicable domestic laws. [188] [136]

248.   If the beneficiaries of compensations are not able to receive the payments within the specified term, due to causes attributable to them, the State shall deposit said amounts in an account to the beneficiary's name or draw a certificate of deposit from a reputable Peruvian financial institution, in United States dollars, under the most favorable financial terms the laws in force and customary banking practice allow. If after ten years compensations were still unclaimed, these amounts plus any accrued interest shall be returned to the State.

249.   Payment of the costs and expenses incurred by the representatives in said proceedings shall be made to Andrea Gisela Ortiz-Perea and Alejandrina Raida Cóndor-Saez, who will in turn make the pertinent payments . . .

250.   The State may discharge its pecuniary obligations by tendering United States dollars or an equivalent amount in the currency of Perú, at the New York, USA exchange rate between both currencies on the day prior to the day payment is made.

251.   The amounts allocated in this Judgment as compensations and reimbursement of costs and expenses, shall not be affected, reduced or conditioned by taxing conditions now existing or hereafter created. Therefore, beneficiaries shall therefore receive the total amount as per the provisions herein.

252.   Should the State fall into arrears with its payments, Peruvian banking default interest rates shall be paid on the amount owed.

253.   In accordance with its constant practice, the Court retains the authority

emanating from its jurisdiction and the provisions of Article 65 of the American Convention, to monitor full compliance with this judgment. The instant case shall be closed once the State implements in full the provisions herein. Perú shall, within a year, submit to the Court a report on the measures adopted in compliance with this Judgment.

20-Nov-2009
Order of the Inter-American Court of Human Rights
Monitoring Compliance with Judgment

HAVING SEEN:

1.   The judgment on the merits, reparations and costs rendered on November 29, 2006 (hereinafter, the "Judgment") by the Inter-American Court of Human Rights (hereinafter, the "Inter-American Court" or the "Court",) whereby the Court ordered the following, to wit:

> [...]9. The State must take without delay the necessary actions to effectively conduct and complete, within a reasonable time, the ongoing investigations and the criminal proceedings pending in the domestic courts, and to carry out, as the case may be, the necessary investigations to determine the criminal liability of the perpetrators of the violations committed to the detriment of Hugo Muñoz-Sánchez, Dora Oyague-Fierro, Marcelino Rosales Cárdenas, Bertila Lozano-Torres, Luis Enrique Ortiz-Perea, Armando Richard Amaro-Cóndor, Robert Edgar Teodoro-Espinoza, Heráclides Pablo-Meza, Juan Gabriel Mariños-Figueroa and Felipe Flores-Chipana, as set forth in paragraph 224 of the instant Judgment. The State must adopt all judicial and diplomatic measures to prosecute and, in turn, punish the perpetrators of the violations committed in the instant case and file any corresponding extradition request under applicable domestic and international rules, as set forth in paragraphs 224 to 228 of the instant Judgment.
>
> 10. The State must forthwith carry out the search and localization of the mortal remains of Hugo Muñoz-Sánchez, Dora Oyague-Fierro, Marcelino Rosales-Cárdenas, Armando Richard Amaro-Cóndor, Robert Edgar Teodoro-Espinoza, Heráclides Pablo-Meza, Juan Gabriel Mariños-Figueroa and Felipe Flores-Chipana and, once located, the State must deliver them as soon as practicable to the relatives and bear the burial costs, as set forth in paragraph 232 of the instant Judgment.

11. The State must publicly acknowledge its liability within a term of six months, as set forth in paragraph 235 of the instant Judgment.

12. The State must ensure that, within the term of one year, the 10 individuals declared executed or forcefully disappeared victims in the instant case shall be represented in the memorial named "*El Ojo que Llora*" (The Crying Eye) if they are not represented so far and provided their relatives so desire; in doing so, the State must coordinate the victims' relatives' efforts to place a sign with the name of each victim, in the manner that may best fit the characteristics of the memorial, as set forth in paragraph 236 of the instant Judgment.

13. The State must publish, within the term of six months, at least once in the Official Gazette and in another national daily newspaper, paragraphs 37 to 44 and 51 to 58 of the chapter related to the partial acknowledgement, the proven facts in the instant Judgment, without the corresponding footnotes, and paragraphs 81 to 98, 109 to 116, 122 to 129, 135 to 161 and 165 to 189, and the operative paragraphs thereof, as set forth in paragraph 237 of the instant Judgment.

14. The State must provide the relatives of Hugo Muñoz-Sánchez, Dora Oyague-Fierro, Marcelino Rosales-Cárdenas, Bertila Lozano-Torres, Luis Enrique Ortiz-Perea, Armando Richard Amaro-Cóndor, Robert Edgar Teodoro-Espinoza, Heráclides Pablo-Meza, Juan Gabriel Mariños-Figueroa and Felipe Flores-Chipana, at their discretion and for as long as necessary, free of charge and at national health-care facilities, with any necessary treatment which shall comprise provision of medicines, as set forth in paragraph 238 of the instant Judgment.

15. The State must implement, on a permanent basis and within a reasonable time, human rights-oriented programs for the members of intelligence services, the Armed Forces and the National Police, as well as for prosecutors and judges, as set forth in paragraphs 240 to 242 of the instant Judgment.

16. The State must pay Andrea Gisela Ortiz-Perea, Antonia Pérez-Velásquez, Alejandrina Raida Cóndor-Saez, Dina Flormelania Pablo-Mateo, Rosario Muñoz-Sánchez, Fedor Muñoz-Sánchez, Hilario Jaime Amaro-Ancco, Magna Rosa Perea de Ortiz, Víctor Andrés Ortiz-Torres, José Ariol Teodoro-León, Bertila Bravo-Trujillo and José Esteban Oyague-Velazco,

within the term of one year, the amounts set out in paragraphs 214 and 215 of the instant Judgment, as compensation for pecuniary damage, as set forth in paragraphs 246 to 248 and 250 to 252 thereof.

17. The State must pay Antonia Pérez-Velásquez, Margarita Liliana Muñoz-Pérez, Hugo Alcibíades Muñoz-Pérez, Mayte Yu yin Muñoz-Atanasio, Hugo Fedor Muñoz-Atanasio, Carol Muñoz-Atanasio, Zorka Muñoz-Rodríguez, Vladimir Ilich Muñoz-Sarria, Rosario Muñoz-Sánchez, Fedor Muñoz-Sánchez, José Esteban Oyague-Velazco, Pilar Sara Fierro-Huamán, Carmen Oyague-Velazco, Jaime Oyague-Velazco, Demesia Cárdenas-Gutiérrez, Augusto Lozano-Lozano, Juana Torres de Lozano, Víctor Andrés Ortiz-Torres, Magna Rosa Perea de Ortiz, Andrea Gisela Ortiz-Perea, Edith Luzmila Ortiz-Perea, Gaby Lorena Ortiz-Perea, Natalia Milagros Ortiz-Perea, Haydee Ortiz-Chunga, Alejandrina Raida Cóndor-Saez, Hilario Jaime Amaro-Ancco, María Amaro-Cóndor, Susana Amaro-Cóndor, Carlos Alberto Amaro-Cóndor, Carmen Rosa Amaro-Cóndor, Juan Luis Amaro-Cóndor, Martín Hilario Amaro-Cóndor, Francisco Manuel Amaro-Cóndor, José Ariol Teodoro-León, Edelmira Espinoza-Mory, Bertila Bravo-Trujillo, José Faustino Pablo-Mateo, Serafina Meza-Aranda, Dina Flormelania Pablo-Mateo, Isabel Figueroa-Aguilar, Román Mariños-Eusebio, Rosario Carpio-Cardoso-Figueroa, Viviana Mariños-Figueroa, Marcia Claudina Mariños-Figueroa, Margarita Mariños-Figueroa de Padilla, Carmen Chipana de Flores and Celso Flores-Quispe, within the term of one year, the amounts set out in paragraph 220 of the instant Judgment, as compensation for non pecuniary damage, as set forth in paragraphs 219, 246 to 248 and 250 to 252 thereof.

18. The State must pay, within the term of one year, the amounts set out in paragraph 245 of the instant Judgment, as reimbursement for costs and expenses, which shall be delivered to Andrea Gisela Ortiz-Perea and Alejandrina Raida Cóndor-Saez, as set forth in paragraphs 246 and 249 to 252 thereof.

19. The Court shall monitor full compliance with this Judgment and the instant case shall be closed once the State implements in full the provisions herein. Within one year of the date of notification of this judgment, the State shall furnish the Court with a report on the measures taken in compliance therewith, in

the terms of paragraph 253 of said judgment. Within one year from the notification of [the] Judgment, the State shall submit a report to the Court on the measures adopted in compliance therewith, as set forth in paragraph 253 [there]of.

Obligation to investigate the events, prosecute and, in turn, punish those responsible for the violations

7.   That, in relation to the duty to immediately adopt the measures necessary to effectively conduct and complete, within a reasonable time, the ongoing investigations and criminal proceedings in regular criminal courts, and to order, if applicable, the necessary investigations to determine the criminal liability of those responsible for the violations committed against the victims (*operative paragraph nine of the Judgment,*) the State informed that three separate criminal proceedings in relation to compliance with this operative paragraph were then pending: i) judicial proceedings N° 03-2003, in the First Special Criminal Division of the Lima Superior Court of Justice, against certain members of the Colina Group; ii) judicial proceedings N° 19-2001-AV, in the Special Criminal Division of the Supreme Court, against former president Alberto Fujimori, and iii) judicial proceedings N° 68-2007, in the Fifth Special Criminal Anticorruption Court, based on report N° 08-2004 against Vladimiro Montesinos-Torres, Nicolás de Bari Hermoza-Ríos, Luis Augusto Pérez-Documet and José Adolfo Velarde-Astete. In the course of the proceedings, the accusation was extended against eight additional defendants. In relation to these investigations, the State subsequently reported that: i) in judicial proceedings N° 03-2003, April 8, 2008, the former Chief of the National Intelligence Service Julio Rolando Salazar-Monroe was convicted to 35 years' imprisonment, and former members of the Colina Group Gabriel Orlando Vera-Navarrete, José Alarcón-Gonzáles and Fernando Lecca-Esquén were convicted to 15 years' imprisonment on the charges of aggravated murder and forced disappearance of persons; ii) in judicial proceedings N° 19-2001-AV, after the extradition granted on September 21, 2007 by the Supreme Court of Justice of Chile, on April 7, 2009, the former president of the Republic Alberto Fujimori-Fujimori was convicted to 25 years' imprisonment "as mediate perpetrator of the crime of murder with perfidy and treachery, as aggravating circumstances, against the victims [in the instant case,"] and iii) in judicial proceedings N° 68-2007, an order of detention and restricted appearance was issued against the reported individuals.

8.   That the representatives welcomed the advances made in furtherance of compliance with this operative paragraph. Accordingly, they highlighted three issues: i) that in judicial proceedings N° 03-2003 against former members of the Colina Group, on April 27, 209, the Second Criminal Division ruled on

the appeal for annulment affirming the acquittal of Aquilino Portella-Núñez and the conviction of Gabriel Orlando Vera-Navarrette, José Alarcón-Gonzáles and Fernando Lecca Esquén to 15 years' imprisonment, and affirming the conviction of Julio Rolando Salazar-Monroe, while reducing his sentence from 35 to 25 years' imprisonment; ii) that the Special Criminal Anticorruption Division decided on appeal to deliver copies of the case file to the Attorney General's Office to conduct an investigation of those responsible for crime concealment in relation to these proceedings; and iii) that, through "efficient collaboration agreements," former members of the Colina Group agreed to surrender information concerning the events under investigation. In relation to the delays in the investigation, they pointed out that: i) judicial proceedings N° 68-2007 against Vladimiro Montesinos were still pending resolution, and the case file was forwarded to the Third Special Criminal Anticorruption Division after expiration of the investigation deadline; ii) that the judgment delivered in judicial proceedings N° 19-2001-AV against Alberto Fujimori-Fujimori was appealed against for annulment; and iii) that the State should furnish information on the measures adopted to locate and arrest the fugitive defendants in proceedings N° 03-2003, on whom prosecution reserve was imposed. Furthermore, they stated that the First Criminal Special Division was conducting a criminal process, undisclosed by the State, against Alberto Pinto-Cárdenas and Wilmen Yarlequé-Ordinola, who were convicted on July 3, 2008 to 20 years' imprisonment for the events in the instant case. Upon filing of an appeal for annulment, the conviction and sentence imposed on Wilmen Yarlequé-Ordinola was affirmed, the conviction against Alberto Pinto-Cárdenas was declared null and void, and an order granting a new trial was entered. Therefore, they considered that monitoring compliance with this measure of reparation should remain open.

9.   That, concerning the measures adopted by the State, the Commission considered that important actions aiming to complete the investigation, prosecute and punish those responsible were taken, while it is awaiting information on the progress thereof.

10.   That the Court highly appreciates the efforts made in furtherance of the investigation of the events. Thus, the criminal liability of several individuals responsible for the violations committed in the instant case, including former high-rank State officers, has been declared, while some proceedings are still pending final resolution. For this reason, the Tribunal understands that even though the State has made great progress in the investigation of the complex structure of the individuals involved in the planning and execution of the grave human rights violations in the instant case, further investigation should be made. Consequently, in order to continue monitoring compliance with this paragraph, the Court requires the State to keep informing on the progress of the ongoing investigations and/or on any new investigative actions, as well as on the results of the "efficient

collaboration agreements," on the fugitive defendants, on the process reported by the representatives, and on the appeal for annulment filed in judicial proceedings N° 19-2001-AV.

Search for and identification of disappeared victims

11.   That in relation to the duty to forthwith search and identify the mortal remains of the victims and, in turn, deliver them as soon as practicable to their relatives and bear the burial costs (*operative paragraph ten of the Judgment,*) the State informed that on July 17, 2008, at the premises of the *Equipo Peruano de Antropolgía Forense* (Peruvian Anthropological Forensic Team), six funerary coffins were delivered to the victims' next of kin, through their representatives, who were also offered burial services consisting of two funeral hearses, a funeral chapel and transportation for funeral and burial services. The evidence furnished by the State shows that the expert witnesses "determined that the remains were incomplete and that they belonged to 8 adult individuals, there were two bone parts of two females, the remains of a third individual did not match the saliva samples taken from eight out of ten next of kin, for there was a likelihood that this bone part belonged to Felipe Flores-Chipana or Manuel [Marcelino Máximo] Rosales-Cárdenas. They ruled that the female pelvis and femur bone parts did not belong to Bertila Lozano, but to Dora Ayague, the only woman among the victims. Luis Ortiz-Perea and Bertila Lozano were positively identified."[4][137]

12.   That the representatives agreed with the information submitted by the State, but pointed out that by July 19, 2008, the date set by the victims' next of kin to inhume the victims' remains, the State had failed to make "the necessary arrangements with the authorities of the cemetery 'El Ángel' to cause the remains inhumation to be authorized and order the cleaning of the mausoleum of the victims" and that fortunately they could rely on the good will of the cemetery authorities as a last resort to proceed with the inhumation. They further pointed out that the mortal remains of the other four victims had not been located and identified and that the outcome of the examinations conducted to identify the remains exhumed in 1993 was not reported, so they considered that the State had not fully complied with this operative paragraph. In this sense, they suggested that the State should keep informing the Court "on the actions taken to fully comply with this measure of reparation."

13.   That the Commission welcomed the efforts made by the State, but regretted its lack of diligence in making the necessary arrangements for the burial of the victims' remains. Moreover, it restated to the Court that the State should be required to furnish information on the domestic coordinating measures and concrete actions taken to locate the victims' remains which are still missing.

14.   That the Court highly appreciates the actions taken by the State to search for

and locate the victims; in particular, it underlines the fact that the inhumation of six of them was possible. To this effect, the Court requests the State to specify the names of the victims whose remains have been inhumed, as well as those who are still to be located. Accordingly, it is imperative that the State continue with the actions aimed at locating the four missing victims, resorting to all available means to immediately resume the search for the victims and, in turn, the identification of their remains, applying an action plan and the adequate technology, for which it is essential that the State proceed to reinforce its search and identification capacity gathering the professional and technical resources that the case requires. For the reasons stated above, the Court finds that the State has partly complied with this obligation and urges the State to keep up search efforts according to the provisions set out in paragraph 232 of the Judgment.

Public act of acknowledgement of responsibility
15.   That, in relation to the duty to perform, within the term of six months, a public act of acknowledgment of responsibility (*operative paragraph eleven of the Judgment*,) the State informed that the act was performed on October 25, 2007, at the seat of the Ministry of Justice, with the presence of the victims' next of kin, their legal representatives from APRODEH, members of other non-governmental organizations of human rights, newspapers, the radio and the television, the Ministry of Justice and other State officers. The ceremony was broadcasted on television and radio, the press media and on-line sites of many communications media. The State informed that a representative of the victims joined up with the organizers and coordinated the event planning. For this reason, the State considers that it has fully complied with operative paragraph eleven of the Judgment.
16.   That the representatives chose to make "no comments" on this issue.
17.   That the Commission values "the significance and prominence of the ceremony performed by the State [...] in order to mitigate the damage and to recognize the hardship inflicted on the victims and their next of kin."
18.   That the Court praises the actions taken so far and the willingness to coordinate the planning of the event with the victims, as well as the enthusiastic participation of state authorities. Furthermore, the Tribunal desires to highlight the generous broadcasting that the act of acknowledgment enjoyed in many communications media, because it helps preserve the historic memory about human rights violations, while promoting a means to prevent these acts from happening again. In this sense, the Court highly welcomes the actions taken by the State and considers that it has fully complied with this operative paragraph.

Representation of the victims on "El Ojo que Llora" (The Crying Eye) memorial
19.   That in relation to the duty to ensure, within the term of one year, that

the victims in the instant case are represented in the memorial named "*El Ojo que Llora*" (The Crying Eye) if they are not represented so far and provided their relatives so desire (*operative paragraph twelve of the Judgment,*) the State informed that the names of ten victims were engraved on the monument on December 20, 2007 and that, therefore, it considers that it has complied with this operative paragraph.

20.   That the representatives chose to make no comments on this issue.

21.   That the Commission welcomed that all the difficulties surrounding compliance with this operative paragraph have been overcome.

22.   That the Court praises that the names of the victims have been engraved on the "*El Ojo que Llora*" (The Crying Eye) memorial within the term set out in the Judgment, this way complying with this operative paragraph.

Publication of the Judgment

23.   That in relation to the duty to publish certain sections of the Judgment in the Official Gazette and in another national daily newspaper (*operative paragraph thirteen of the Judgment,*) the State informed that the publication was made in the Official Gazette "El Peruano" on June 24, 2007 in the terms of Supreme Resolution No. 120-2007-JUS dated June 23, 2007, that also authorized the publication of the relevant parts of the Judgment in a national daily newspaper, while the financial resources for said publication are still to be awarded. Later, the State reported that "the authorities [...] are currently devoted to the necessary arrangements for the publication" which is still pending. For this reason, the State considered that it has partly complied with this operative paragraph.

24.   That the representatives pointed out that, even though the relevant parts of the Judgments were published in the Official Gazette, the publication was made beyond the deadline set out by the Court. They also concluded that the State had failed to fully comply with this operative paragraph because the publication in a national daily newspaper was still pending.

25.   That the Commission, in turn, noted that the restrictions mentioned by the State should not be an obstacle to comply with the decision of the Court. Thereupon, the Commission "hopes that the State will make the publication in the near future."

26.   That the Court observes that, according to the provisions of the Judgment, the State should make the corresponding publications within a six-month term. That the State, the Commission and the representatives reported that the publication in the Official Gazette was effectively made, and furnished evidence thereof. Nonetheless, the publication in a national daily newspaper is still pending. As more than two years have elapsed since expiration of the deadline set out in the Judgment for the publications, the Court urges the State to take the

necessary steps to finance the pending publication in order to fully comply with its obligation.

Adequate treatment to the victims' next of kin

27.   That, in relation to the duty to confer an adequate treatment to the victims' next of kin (*operative paragraph fourteen of the Judgment,*) the State informed that the Ministry of Health "completed" the membership proceedings to enlist all the relatives in the *Sistema Integral de Salud* (Health Care Global System) (hereinafter, the "SIS") and that this was informed to their legal representatives by Notices No. 2044 and 2042 – 2007/JUS/CNDH-SE of November 21, 2007; for this reason, the State requested that this measure as ordered by the Court be considered fully complied with. Later, the State informed that the SIS had joined forces with the representative of the victims to collect the updated addresses of the next of kin so that they might have access to the health system, renewing the "request of collaboration to the Ministry of Health concerning the registration of the beneficiaries in the *Sistema Integral de Salud* (Health Care Global System)."

28.   That the representatives noted that "even though all inter-institutional proceedings have been conducted to cause the next of kin to be enlisted in the SIS, the mere registration does not guarantee provision of an adequate treatment and supply of medicines." They also noted that, even though the Judgment was delivered more than two years ago, the next of kin were not registered in the health system. For those reasons, they requested the Court to require the State to comply forthwith with this obligation and to submit updated information, taking into account that compliance with this obligation should "be monitored on an ongoing basis" to secure fulfillment thereof.

29.   That the Commission considered that the information furnished by the State "fails to include specific data, which are deemed conclusive for compliance with the decision of the Tribunal with regard to this obligation, fulfillment of which is immediate and periodic," and in this respect it found it necessary that "significant action" should be taken to provide adequate and comprehensive health assistance to the victims' next of kin.

30.   That the Court praises the actions taken in furtherance of compliance with this measure; however, it pointed out that provision of an adequate treatment and supply of medicines for as long as it is necessary is an obligation of immediate and periodic fulfillment, which is not satisfied with the mere registration of the victims' next of kin in the *Sistema Integral de Salud* (Health Care Global System.) In this sense, the Tribunal urges the State to continue submitting information on the progress of the implementation and maintenance of this measure.

Implementation of human rights education programs

31.   That, in relation to the duty to implement, within a reasonable time, human

rights oriented programs for the members of intelligence services, the Armed Forces and the National Police, as well as for prosecutors and judges (*operative paragraph fifteen of the Judgment,*) the State provided information about the application of human rights programs in the training centers of the Armed forces and reported that, subsequently, it implemented the necessary changes to cause the *Centro de Derecho Internacional Humanitario* (International Humanitarian Law Center) of the Armed Forces, within the *Comando Conjunto de las Fuerzas Armadas* (Armed Forces Joint Staff,) to provide training in the field of human rights. The State affirmed that the Judiciary carried out academic activities aimed at disseminating human rights information and that the Judiciary Academy "organizes on an ongoing and permanent" basis seminars and distant learning courses in human rights in the administration of justice for judges, prosecutors and other judicial officers. Furthermore, it highlighted that the Academy decided to include the Judgment of the Court in the instant case as mandatory material in the courses, together with international human rights instruments. It further reported on the human rights courses of the professional development, training, specialization, and continuing education centers of the *Sistema Educativo Policial* (Police Educational System.) Therefore, the State considers that it has partly complied with this operative paragraph based on the progress mentioned above.

32.   That the representatives suggested that it was necessary to continue monitoring compliance with this operative paragraph on an ongoing basis. They considered that the reports submitted by the State showed that a series of human rights education activities were organized, but that this should not be considered *per se* "sufficient and efficient" in training members of the intelligence service, the Armed Forces and the National Police, as well as prosecutors and judges. Therefore, the representatives concluded that, despite the progress made in training police officers, it is necessary that the State provide more detailed and comprehensive information on the education of other public officers as ordered in the Judgment, and requested that "ongoing monitoring" be made of both the frequency of the courses and the syllabus and evaluation methods to assess their effectiveness and to fully comply with this operative paragraph.

33.   That the Commission greatly appreciated "the actions taken to implement human rights education programs," but noted that the information on said courses of study failed to detail their permanent nature, and suggested that the State should keep on implementing the necessary measures to fully comply with its obligation. Subsequently, the Commission expressed its concerns about the lack of updated information and reiterated that the information then furnished "was not sufficient to assess the syllabus, scope, maintenance and impact of the activities carried out by the State."

34.   That the Court reminds that human rights education in the organizations involved in national security, as well as in those associated with justice

administration, is vital to secure that acts similar to the events occurred in the instant case will not happen again. The Tribunal highly praises the information submitted and the progress referenced in relation to human rights training courses in justice administration departments, the Armed Forces and the National Police. In particular, the Court notes that the human rights courses have been designed to the members of police and military forces of different hierarchy, and that international human rights instruments have been included in the syllabus of those courses, as required. Moreover, the State has included as mandatory reference in the training of judges the Judgment delivered by the Court in this case and has forwarded it to the *Consejo Superior de Justicia Militar* (Military Justice Supreme Council.)

35.   That despite the foregoing, the Court observes that the State has failed to address all the aspects of operative paragraph fifteen of the Judgment, as required; in particular, it has failed to furnish information on the education imparted in state intelligence agencies. Furthermore, the reported information omits reference to how the Judgment issued in the instant case has been incorporated as mandatory material in the training courses offered in security forces institutions. Therefore, the Court considers that the State has partly complied with this obligation. The State is then required to submit updated and detailed information in relation to the aspects not covered by the reports, in particular, those aspects concerning the state intelligence agencies.

Payment of compensations and reimbursement of costs and expenses

36.   That in relation to the payment of damages and compensations ordered in favor of the victims and their next of kin, as well as the reimbursement of the costs and expenses to the representatives (*operative paragraphs sixteen, seventeen and eighteen of the Judgment,*) the State informed that the Ministry of Justice had conducted the necessary proceedings aimed at gathering the resources through the *Oficina General de Economía y Desarrollo* (Finance and Development General Office) (OGED,) the *Fondo de Administración del Dinero Ilícitamente Obtenido en Perjuicio del Estado* (Fund for the Administration of Money Obtained Illicitly to the Detriment of the State) (FEDADOI), and the Ministry of Economy and Finance, but that the necessary measures to allocate in the budget the money to pay compensations and reimburse costs and expenses had not been taken. Subsequently, it reported that it had authorized the transfer of US$90,000.00 to the Ministry of Justice to pay pending reparations as pecuniary damage in favor of Antonia Pérez-Velásquez, Andra Gisela Ortiz-Perea, Alejandrina Raida Cóndor-Sáez and Dina Flor Melania Pablo-Meza, which was effectively made on May 12, 2009.

37.   That the representatives confirmed that payment of US$90,000.00 as pecuniary damage in favor of some relatives was effectively made and verified payment

by minutes of delivery of May 12, 2009. Nonetheless, they observed that the State had failed to mention that the whole group of relatives had been paid the compensations for pecuniary damage and reimbursed the costs and expenses as ordered. Additionally, they pointed out that the judgment of April 8, 2008, rendered in judicial proceedings No. 03-2003 "directed that the convicted defendants should pay, jointly and severally with the State, as civil reparation, the compensations ordered by the Court;" therefore, the next of kin filed an appeal for annulment, which is up to date pending resolution, based on the rationale that, notwithstanding any individual criminal liability, the international liability rests solely with the State. For this reason, the representatives concluded that the State had failed to fully comply with this operative paragraph and required detailed information on the coordinating actions taken to fully comply with all the payment obligations as soon as practicable.

38.   That the Commission expressed concerns about the lack of effective action in relation to this obligation "after the deadline set by the Court has long expired." Therefore, it is still waiting that, as soon as possible, the proceedings "to allocate the necessary resources" are conducted and the information on the actions taken in furtherance of the compliance with these operative paragraphs of the Judgment is submitted.

39.   That this Court notes that after three years from the Judgment, only the payments as pecuniary damage have been made in favor of some victims, but no mention has been made as to the proceedings aimed at effecting payment of pecuniary damage in favor of the remaining victims, payment of non-pecuniary damage and reimbursement of costs and expenses. Furthermore, the Court reiterates that the State should honor the unfulfilled payment obligations, the resolution achieved in the domestic criminal proceedings notwithstanding. In the light of the foregoing, the Tribunal reminds the State of the importance of strictly complying with this operative paragraph and, to this effect, it urges the State to resort to all available resources to effectively pay the amounts as ordered in the Judgment, including payment of any accrued interest.

THEREFORE:

THE INTER-AMERICAN COURT OF HUMAN RIGHTS,

in exercise of its authority to monitor compliance with its decisions and in accordance with Articles 62(3), 67 and 68(1) of the American Convention on Human Rights, Article 25(2) of its Statute and Articles 30(2) and 63 of its Rules of Procedure,

DECLARES:

1.   That pursuant with that stated in Considering clauses No. 18 and 22 of this Order, the State has complied with the obligation to:

   (a) To organize, within six months, a public act acknowledging responsibility (*operative paragraph eleven* and paragraph 235 of the Judgment), *and*

(b) to ensure, within the term of one year, that the 10 persons declared as victims of execution or forced disappearance in the Judgment are represented in the memorial named "*El Ojo que Llora*" (The Crying Eye) if they are not represented so far and provided their relatives so desire (*operative paragraph twelve of the Judgment* and paragraph 236 of the Judgment.)

2. That the State has partly complied with the obligations to:

(a) to take without delay the necessary actions to effectively conduct and complete, within a reasonable time, the ongoing investigations and the criminal proceedings pending in the domestic courts, and to carry out, as the case may be, the necessary investigations to determine the criminal liability of the perpetrators of the violations committed to the detriment of the victims in the instant case (*operative paragraph nine* and paragraphs 224 to 228 of the Judgment;)

(b) to forthwith carry out the search for and localization of the mortal remains of Hugo Muñoz-Sánchez, Dora Oyague-Fierro, Marcelino Rosales-Cárdenas, Armando Richard Amaro-Cóndor, Robert Edgar Teodoro-Espinoza, Heráclides Pablo-Meza, Juan Gabriel Mariños-Figueroa and Felipe Flores-Chipana and, once located, to deliver them as soon as practicable to their relatives and to bear the burial costs, (*operative paragraph ten* and paragraph 232 of the Judgment;)

(c) to publish, within the term of six months, at least once in the Official Gazette and in another national daily newspaper, paragraphs 37 to 44 and 51 to 58 of the chapter related to the partial acknowledgement, the proven facts in the instant Judgment, without the corresponding footnotes, and paragraphs 81 to 98, 109 to 116, 122 to 129, 135 to 161 and 165 to 189, and the operative paragraphs thereof, (*operative paragraph thirteen* and paragraph 237 of the Judgment;)

(d) to implement, on a permanent basis and within a reasonable time, human rights-oriented programs for the members of intelligence services, the Armed Forces and the National Police, as well as for prosecutors and judges (*operative paragraph fifteen* and paragraphs 240 to 242 of the Judgment,) and

(e) to pay, within the term of one year, the amounts set out in paragraphs 214 and 215 of the [...] Judgment, as compensation for pecuniary damage (*operative paragraph sixteen* and paragraphs 246 to 248 and 250 to 252 of the Judgment.)

3. That it will keep open the monitoring compliance proceedings with regard to the paragraphs, which are pending compliance in the instant case, to wit:

(a) to take without delay the necessary actions to effectively conduct and complete, within a reasonable time, the ongoing investigations and the criminal proceedings pending in the domestic courts, and to carry out, as the case may be, the necessary investigations to determine the criminal liability of the perpetrators of the violations committed to the detriment of the victims in the instant case (*operative paragraph nine* and paragraphs 224 to 228 of the Judgment;)

(b) to forthwith carry out the search and localization of the mortal remains of Hugo Muñoz-Sánchez, Dora Oyague-Fierro, Marcelino Rosales-Cárdenas, Armando Richard Amaro-Cóndor, Robert Edgar Teodoro-Espinoza, Heráclides Pablo-Meza, Juan Gabriel Mariños-Figueroa and Felipe Flores-Chipana and, once located, to deliver them as soon as practicable to the relatives and to bear the burial costs, (*operative paragraph ten* and paragraph 232 of the Judgment;)

(c) to publish, within the term of six months, at least once in the Official Gazette and in another national daily newspaper, paragraphs 37 to 44 and 51 to 58 of the chapter related to the partial acknowledgement, the proven facts in the instant Judgment, without the corresponding footnotes, and paragraphs 81 to 98, 109 to 116, 122 to 129, 135 to 161 and 165 to 189, and the operative paragraphs thereof, (*operative paragraph thirteen* and paragraph 237 of the Judgment;)

(d) to provide all the victims' next of kin, at their discretion and for as long as necessary, free of charge and at national health-care facilities, with any necessary treatment which shall comprise provision of medicines (*operative paragraph fourteen* and paragraph 238 of the Judgment;)

(e) to implement, on a permanent basis and within a reasonable time, human rights-oriented programs for the members of intelligence services (*operative paragraph fifteen* and paragraphs 240 to 242 of the Judgment,) and

(f) to pay the amounts set as compensation for pecuniary damage, compensation for non-pecuniary damages, and costs and expenses (*operative paragraphs sixteen, seventeen and eighteen* and paragraphs 215, 219, 246 to 248 and 250 to 252 of the Judgment.)

AND DECIDES:

4.   To require that the State adopt all the measures necessary to fully and promptly comply with the matters pending compliance that were ordered by the Tribunal in the Judgment on merits, reparations, and costs of November 29, 2006, pursuant with the stipulations of Article 68(1) of the American Convention on Human Rights.

5.   To request that the State present to the Inter-American Court, no later than March 1st, 2010, a report indicating all the measures adopted to comply with

the reparations ordered by this Court that are pending compliance, pursuant to the provisions of Considering clauses No. 10, 14, 26, 30, 35 and 39, and declarative paragraphs 2 and 3 of this Order.

6.   To request that the representatives of the next of kin of the victims and the Commission present their observations to the State's report mentioned in the previous operative paragraph, within a four and six-week term, respectively, computed as of the receipt of that report.

7.   To continue monitoring the matters pending compliance of the Judgment on merits, reparations, and costs of November 29, 2006.

8.   To request that the Secretariat notify the present Order to the State, the Inter-American Commission, and the representatives of the victims and their next of kin.

Monitoring Compliance with Judgment in the Case of Kimel v. Argentina
18-May-2010
Order of the Inter-American Court of Human Rights

THE INTER-AMERICAN COURT OF HUMAN RIGHTS,
in exercise of its authority to monitor compliance with its decisions and in accordance with
Articles 33, 62(1), 62(3), 65, 67 and 68(1) of the American Convention on Human Rights, 25(1) and 30 of its Statute, and 31 and 69 of its Rules of Procedure,[9][138]
DECLARES THAT:
1.   In accordance with Considering Paragraphs 11, 19, 23 and 35 of the instant Order, the State has fully complied with the following obligations:

(a) to pay the amounts set in the Judgment as compensation for pecuniary and non-pecuniary damage, and reimbursement of legal costs and expenses (*sixth operative paragraph of the Judgment);*

(b) to remove immediately the name of Mr. Kimel off all public records wherein he has been entered as having a criminal record in relation to the present case (*eighth operative paragraph of the Judgment*);

(c) to carry out the publications indicated in paragraph 125 of the Judgment (*ninth operative paragraph of the Judgment*), and

(d) to bring its domestic legislation into conformity with the provisions of the Inter-American Convention on Human Rights, so that the lack of accuracy acknowledged by the State be amended, in order to comply with the requirements of legal certainty so that, consequently, they do not affect the exercise of the right to freedom of thought and expression (*eleventh operative paragraph*).

2.   The monitoring proceedings will remain open until full compliance with the measures pending, in accordance with Considering Paragraphs 15 and 29 of the instant Order, is achieved, namely to:

(a) set aside the criminal sentence imposed on Mr. Kimel and all the effects deriving therefrom *(seventh operative paragraph of the Judgment),* and

(b) hold a public act of acknowledgement of its responsibility *(tenth operative paragraph of the Judgment).*

15-Nov-2010
Order of the Inter-American Court of Human Rights
Monitoring Compliance with Judgment

I.   **Regarding the obligation to nullify the criminal sentence imposed on Mr. Kimel and all the effects thereof (operative paragraph seven of the Judgment).**

7.   The State reported that it had consulted different State entities about "the possibility that the State [would] promote the adoption of a ruling that [would] declare the illegality of the sentence imposed on Mr. Kimel." It indicated that the Supreme Court of Justice of the Nation had manifested that, "the aspects related to the operative paragraph in question '...must [be] processed in the respective judicial proceedings following our legal system's most suitable proceedings...'" In light of this recommendation, the Board of Legal Matters of the Ministry of Foreign Affairs issued a ruling on the legal viability of the State filing an application for review of the judgment imposed on Mr. Kimel, by which it explained that "it may file an application for review through the retrospective application of a criminal law more benign than that applied in the judgment." Also, in said ruling, the State manifested that "the persons able to [exercise said recourse would be:] 1) the convicted and/or his defense, if he were unable, his legal representatives, or, if he had died, his spouse, his ancestors, descendants or siblings[, and] 2) the Public Prosecutor." Following this ruling, on February 5, 2010, the administrative proceedings were sent to the Attorney General's Office of the Nation "for the purposes of considering the possibility that the Public Prosecutor's Office [would] present the corresponding application for review." On April 13, 2010, the Attorney General's Office indicated that "it deem[ed] that [said] petition [would] not be an issue that concerns [the] Attorney General given that slander is privately actionable [, and that a]ccording to [the] criminal system and criminal proceedings [ofArgentina], the Public Prosecutor's Office [would] not be procedurally competent for such crimes and therefore, [would] not have the power to file a[n] application for review for a condemnatory judgment." According to the Attorney General's Office, the following persons are qualified to file such an application for review, "the convicted, and if he had died, his spouse,

his ancestors, descendants or siblings." In virtue of the conclusions of these bodies, Argentina manifested that "the State lacks the procedural legitimacy to file an application for review in the present case." Nevertheless, the State manifested "its determination to send [...] an *amicus curiae* to the respective court in the eventuality that the petitioners decide to file the aforementioned application for review."

8.   The representatives manifested their concern for, and rejection of, "the stance adopted by certain Argentine state-run agencies that maintain that it is the victim himself—or, in this case, his next of kin—that must make new legal and procedural efforts so that the State can comply with this point of the [J]udgment of the Court." They consider that the State "has not made sufficient efforts to comply, in a comprehensive and holistic manner, with the [J]udgment." They consider that, in light of an international duty, "reasons related to the limitations of domestic law do not justify the non-compliance;" therefore, the different State agencies must adapt their practices so as to effectively comply with the measures set forth by the Inter-American Court, including encouraging any necessary legal amendments. They expressed their concern regarding the State's inability to nullify a civil or criminal sentence when ordered to do so by an international human rights body; however, they insist that this does not constitute an excuse to cease implementing the decisions. Accordingly, they referred to the jurisprudence of the Supreme Court of Justice of the Nation of Argentina, according to which "the lack of guarantees or mechanisms to uphold these rights must addressed by the Judicial Power that acts as the final guarantor of [such] rights." They stated that the solution proposed by the State "implies imposing on the victim, once again, the burden of ensuring compliance with a judgment, in their favor, after years of litigation before both national and international courts." Notwithstanding the prior considerations, they stated that in the coming days they would file the respective application for review, "so as to speed up full compliance with the [J]udgment." To this end, they expressed that "they [undertook] the [State's] commitment to either act as *amicus curiae* or interested third party in the case" after filing the application, and they would also inform the Court of the stance held by those judicial authorities that must take part in the case. They added that the State "[must], at least, bear the costs and expenses that this work entail[ed]," manifesting that they hoped the Court would set an amount "as it has been doing in recent judgments, making evidentiary standards flexible and executed [in] an fair manner."

8.   The Commission stated that "as a general rule, it is not acceptable that the State cites domestic legal obstacles as a reason to not comply with their international obligations," which include the orders issued by the Inter-American Court. Nevertheless, the Commission observed that given, *inter alia*,

the representatives stated that they would file an application for review and that the State manifested that it would support said filing as an *amicus curiae*, they were following the development of the proceeding and hoped that it would be processed promptly so that that the Tribunal could acknowledge compliance with all the reparation measures ordered in the present case. Also, the Commission considered that Argentina must pay the expenses incurred by the representatives throughout the judicial proceedings.

9.   The Court reminds that in paragraph 123 of the Judgment it ordered that the State must, within six months of its notification, "nullify [the condemnatory judgment imposed on Mr. Kimel that constituted a violation of his right to the freedom of expression], in every aspect, including the implications that it [would] have upon third parties, namely: 1) labeling Mr. Kimel as the author of slander; 2) imposing a one year suspended prison sentence, and 3) the order to pay $20,000 (twenty thousand Argentine pesos)."

11.   The Tribunal values the willingness shown by the representatives to file an application for review in order to advance towards compliance with the aforementioned reparation, given that the State would not do so on its own accord. Nevertheless, the Court deems it appropriate to remind that the duty established in operative paragraph seven of the Judgment is an obligation of the State, and it cannot ignore its pre-established international responsibility based on domestic order grounds. [3][139] Accordingly, the Tribunal notes that in other cases in which this Court also ordered, as a reparation measure, to nullify the criminal conviction imposed on a victim for slander, in violation of his rights, the State proceeded on its own accord to comply with the reparation ordered, but rather the intervention of the victim or his next of kin is also necessary. [4][140] Accordingly, the Court notes that the present obligation is not fulfilled by the mere intervention of the State as an *amicus curiae* in the appropriate proceedings, but it requires that the corresponding State authorities nullify the criminal sentence imposed against Mr. Kimel, as well as all the effects thereof, as set forth in the Judgment. Likewise, the Court reminds that the treaty obligations of the State Parties bind all the branches and bodies of the State, [5][141] including the bodies of the Judicial Branch. Consequently, although it positively values the collaboration offered by the representatives of the victim to comply with this duty, the Court reiterates that it is the State's, by means of the appropriate bodies, responsibility to adopt the necessary measures to fully comply with that set forth by the Court, even if there is a recourse that may be initiated by the victim or his next of kin, under domestic law. However, due to the willingness shown by the representatives regarding the filing of the aforementioned recourse so as to expedite compliance with the Judgment and the willingness of the State to send the aforementioned *amicus curiae*, the Tribunal continues to await information from the representatives and the State regarding the development and result of the aforementioned application for review, in the understanding that it is the

duty of the State to adopt the measures necessary to comply, through its own initiative[6] [142], with that set forth by this Court, complying within six months from the notification of the Judgment.

12.   Furthermore, the Tribunal takes note of the request of the representatives regarding the incidental expenses that could be incurred through the aforementioned application for review (*supra* Considering Clause 0). Accordingly, the Court considers that compliance with the reparation measures provided for in the Judgment shall not entail new expenditure for the victim and his next of kin, such as those entailed by filing a new judicial application and its processing.[7] [143] Therefore, the Tribunal requires the State, in its next report on Compliance with the Judgment, to refer specifically to this request of the representatives.

13.   By virtue of the foregoing considerations, the Court deems that the reparation ordered in operative paragraph seven of the Judgment is pending compliance, and requests the State to submit detailed and complete information regarding the measures and actions adopted for the effective and total compliance with this reparation measure.

II. Regarding the obligation to perform a public act of acknowledgement of responsibility (operative paragraph ten of the Judgment)

14.   The State reported that on July 5, 2010, it performed a public act of acknowledgement of responsibility, that took place in the offices of the Legal and Social Studies Center (hereinafter "CELS"), an organization that acts as the representative in this case, and it was led by the President of the Argentinean Nation. Likewise, it stated that the Minister of Foreign Affairs, International Trade and Worship; the Minister of Justice, Security, and Human Rights; the Secretary of Human Rights; and the President of CELS were also present. By virtue of the foregoing, it requested that the present operative paragraph is deemed to be complied with.

15.   The representatives agreed with the information submitted by the State and added that the mother and the daughter of Mr. Eduardo Kimel, and recognized journalists and representatives of the social organization, attended the aforementioned act. Likewise, they highlighted some of the most relevant parts of the speech made by the President of the Nation in this act. The representatives expressed their profound satisfaction with the attitude of the State by carrying out an act with the presence of the highest political authority of the country. Furthermore, they stated that the decision to perform the act at CELS was mutually agreed upon by the petitioners and high-ranking officials of the federal government, due to the resistance shown by members of the Church of San Patricio.

16.   The Commission observed that Argentina had fulfilled this reparation measure.

17.   The Court values highly the act performed on July 5, 2010, in the offices of CELS, in accordance with that provided for by the State as well as the representatives, and also takes note of the conformity expressed by the representatives with such act. Likewise, it observes with satisfaction that such act was presided over by the President of the Nation and that other high-ranking officials of the government were also present, as well as the next of kin of the victim, and that the planning of such act had the due participation, cooperation, and agreement of the latter (*supra* Considering Clause 15), pursuant to the Order of the Court of May 18, 2010.[8 144] Furthermore, the Tribunal deems that the words of the President, according to that established by the representatives, achieved the purpose of the State acknowledging responsibility for the Human Rights violations committed against Mr. Eduardo Kimel, and, therefore, they contribute to dignify the memory of the victim. Furthermore, the Court deems it important to highlight the widespread coverage that such act received, through several means of communication,[9 145] because this contributes to a greater preservation of the historical memory of the human rights violation carried out, promoting, at the same time, the non-repetition of facts such as those seen in the present case.[10 146] Based on the foregoing, the Tribunal deems that the State has fully complied with operative paragraph ten of the Judgment.

THEREFORE:

THE INTER-AMERICAN COURT OF HUMAN RIGHTS,

in exercising its power of monitoring compliance with its decisions, pursuant to Articles 33, 62(1), 62(3), 65, 67 and 68(1) of the American Convention on Human Rights, and Articles 25(1) and 30 of the Statute, and Articles 31 and 69 of its Rules of Procedure,[11 147]

DECLARES:

1.   That the State has fully complied with the obligation to perform a public act to acknowledge its responsibility *(operative paragraph ten of the Judgment),* according to that set forth in the Considering Clause 17 of the present Order.

2.   That it will keep the monitoring procedure open until compliance with the outstanding obligations in the present case, namely, nullifying the criminal sentence imposed on Mr. Kimel and all the effects thereof *(operative paragraph seven of the Judgment),* according to that set forth in paragraphs 11 and 13 of the present Order.

5-Feb-2013

Order of the Inter-American Court of Human Rights

Monitoring Compliance with Judgment

5.   According to the provisions of the Order of the Court of November 15, 2010 * * *, the only measure of reparation pending compliance by the State is the

one relating to annulling the criminal sentence imposed on Mr. Kimel and any ensuing consequences (seventh operative paragraph the Judgment). This Order placed on record that the State had expressed its willingness to comply with the measure of reparation and informed the Court that it had consulted different State bodies in order to find out the appropriate way to achieve this. According to the State, its domestic organs concluded that an appeal for review of the criminal sentence should be filed, but that the State lacked procedural standing to file the appeal; however, it indicated "its firm intention to submit [...] an *amicus curiae* to the corresponding court," "in the event that the petitioners decided to file this appeal for review."[6][148] In addition, in this Order, this Court took into account the intention expressed by the representatives to file the appeal for review in order to expedite compliance with the said reparation, but also recalled that the obligation established in the seventh operative paragraph of the Judgment was an obligation of the State, which may not, for domestic reasons, fail to assume the international responsibility that has been established.[7][149] In this regard, the Court indicated that it was awaiting information from the representatives and the State concerning the execution and results of the said appeal for review, and asked the latter to provide complete and detailed information "on the measures and actions taken to ensure total and effective compliance with the said measure of reparation."[8][150]

6.   The State provided a copy of the *amicus curiae* that the National Human Rights Secretariat had submitted to the National Criminal Cassation Chamber,[9][151] which heard the appeal for review filed by the representatives of Mr. Kimel's daughter. Subsequently, it presented a copy of the judgment deciding this appeal for review, which was delivered by the Third Chamber of the National Criminal Cassation Chamber on November 10, 2011, and asked the Court to "consider that the seventh operative paragraph of the Judgment had been complied with [...] and [... to] order the closure of the case because it [had been] complied with fully." Regarding the request of the representatives that the State assume the expenses and costs arising from the appeal for review they had filed, Argentina indicated that "it had no objections in this regard and [...] awaited the decision adopted by the Court [...]." When referring to the amount requested by the representatives for expenses arising from the processing of this appeal, Argentina asked the Court to "determine the [said expenses] based on equity and the criteria [...] set out [in its brief]." These criteria referred to the way in which the representatives calculated the costs and expenses, the laws regulating the way in which this calculation should have been made, the amount requested by the representatives during the processing of the case before the Court, and that the amount awarded by this Court in the Judgment for costs and expenses included "the *future* expenses that Mr. Kimel might incur at the domestic level or during monitoring compliance with [the] Judgment."

7.   The representatives affirmed that, "in view of the obstacles described by the Argentine State" to compliance with this pending obligation, "the conditions should have been established to make [the said] compliance possible, since a further appeal had to be filed." They provided a copy of the appeal for review filed on November 15, 2010, "against the judgment handed down in the case of 'Kimel, Eduardo Gabriel ref./libel'" before the National Criminal Cassation Chamber and, on June 3, 2011, before the Court, asked that Argentina pay the expenses and costs arising from this proceeding. After the State had indicated that it had no objections with regard to the representatives' request (*supra* considering paragraph 6), they asked the Court to "consider that the Argentine State had indicated its decision" and to "establish an amount" in equity. When the Third Chamber of the National Criminal Cassation Chamber had delivered judgment deciding the appeal for review, the representatives reiterated the said request to the Court and also expressed their "concern" because the Chamber had "refuted that the appeal for review was admissible based on the existence of the judgment of the [Inter-American] Court," and annulled the sentence convicting Mr. Kimel based on "a more favorable criminal law which determined that the conduct was not criminalized." Regarding the amount of the costs incurred by the representatives in processing the appeal for review (*supra* having seen paragraph 4), they mentioned that "the Chamber [...] did not [...] establish costs" and explained the reasons why, in their opinion, these amounted to US$4,000 (four thousand United States dollars). [10] [152]

8.   The Commission indicated that the State should "pay the expenses incurred by [the representatives] in the judicial processing of the appeal for review." It indicated that "the State failed to take measures *ex officio* to comply with this aspect of the Judgment and that the mechanism used to try and eliminate the effects of the conviction [placed] an unwarranted burden on the representatives." In addition, it took note of "the State's willingness to cover the costs incurred by the representatives as a result of processing the appeal for review before the National Criminal Cassation Chamber" (*supra* considering paragraph 4). After it had been informed of the said judgment handed down by the Third Chamber of the National Criminal Cassation Chamber deciding the appeal for review, the Commission indicated that all the measures of reparation ordered by the Court had been fulfilled and stated that, once the representatives had forwarded the information on the costs they incurred, the State should reimburse them.

9.   The Court recalls that, in its Judgment, it ordered the State to annul "every aspect" of the criminal judgment delivered against Mr. Kimel, [11] [153] "including its implications for third parties, namely: (1) the accusation of Mr. Kimel as the author of the offense of libel; (2) the imposition of a suspended sentence to one year's imprisonment, and (3) the sentencing to pay $20,000.00 (twenty thousand

Argentine pesos)," which had to be paid within six months of notification of that judgment.[12][154]

10.   The Court has verified that, because the State considered that domestic law prevented it from taking measures *ex officio* to annul the judgment convicting Mr. Kimel, the representatives had to file an appeal for review before the National Criminal Cassation Chamber on November 15, 2010. In this appeal, they argued as grounds for its admissibility both "the obligation of the Argentine State to comply with the judgment delivered by the Inter-American Court in this case" and also the "principle of the most favorable law" ("paragraph 5 of article 479 of the National Code of Criminal Procedure"), because "a subsequent law [had been enacted] that decriminalized the act based on which the guilty verdict was handed down." The Court notes that, when filing the said appeal, the representatives asked that "[the court] order that the name of Eduardo Gabriel Kimel be eliminated immediately from any public record in which he appears with a criminal record in relation to this case." On this point, the Court recalls that, in its Order of May 18, 2010 * * *, it declared that the State "had complied fully with the eighth operative paragraph of the Judgment"; in this regard, it took into account both the evidence provided and the fact that the representatives had confirmed that "Mr. Kimel's name had, indeed, been eliminated from the public records of individuals with criminal records."

11.   Furthermore, it has been proved that, on November 10, 2011, the Third Chamber of the National Criminal Cassation Chamber delivered judgment ruling on the said appeal for review. In this judgment, it decided:

> [...]

> (2) To annul the ruling [...] condemning [Mr.] Kimel to a suspended sentence of one year's imprisonment, with costs of both instances, considering him criminally responsible for the offense of libel [...] and, consequently, to acquit [Mr.] Kimel of the act attributed to him;

> (3) To annul the ruling condemning [Mr.] Kimel to pay the complainant, Guillermo Federico Rivarola, the sum of twenty thousand pesos ($20.000), as compensation to repair the non-pecuniary damage caused.

12.   Taking into account that the said judicial decision of November 10, 2011, decided to annul the judgment against Mr. Kimel, with regard to both the attribution of criminal responsibility and the payment of civil compensation for non-pecuniary damage, and also taking into consideration the observations of the parties and of the Commission, the Court finds that the State has complied with the measure of reparation established in the seventh operative paragraph of the Judgment.

13.   Nevertheless, the Court notes that, although this was an obligation that the State should have fulfilled, the latter did not comply *ex officio* with the measures

of reparation ordered in the seventh operative paragraph of the Judgment, but rather the representatives had to file an appeal for review at the domestic level in order to obtain the annulment of the criminal judgment against Mr. Kimel.

14.   Regarding the costs requested by the representatives because they had to file the said judicial remedy, the Court does not find it appropriate to establish an additional amount for this concept at the actual stage of monitoring compliance with judgment. The additional costs and expenses incurred by the representatives owing to the filing and processing of the said remedy can be claimed in the domestic sphere, in keeping with the pertinent national procedures under domestic law.

THEREFORE:

THE INTER-AMERICAN COURT OF HUMAN RIGHTS,

in exercise of its attributes for monitoring compliance with its decisions under Articles 33, 62(1), 62(3), 65, 67 and 68(1) of the American Convention on Human Rights, 24 and 30 of its Statute, and 31 and 69 of its Rules of Procedure,[13][155]

DECLARES THAT:

1.   The State has complied fully with the obligation to annul the criminal conviction imposed on Mr. Kimel and all its consequence *(seventh operative paragraph of the Judgment)*, as indicated in the ninth and thirteenth considering paragraphs of this Order.

AND DECIDES:

1.   To close the case of Kimel, because the Argentine Republic has complied fully with the provisions of the Judgment delivered by the Inter-American Court of Human Rights on May 2, 2008.

2.   To archive the file of this case.

Monitoring Compliance with Judgment in the Case of Las Dos Erres v. Guatemala

24-Nov-2009

Preliminary Objection, Merits, Reparations and Costs

THE COURT,

DECIDES:

unanimously,

1.   To partially dismiss the preliminary objection of *ratione temporis* filed by the State, in accordance with . . . of this Judgment.

AND DECLARES,

unanimously, that:

1.   It accepts the partial acknowledgement of international responsibility made by the State, pursuant to the terms . . . of this Judgment.

2.   The State violated the right to a fair trial and judicial protection enshrined in Articles 8(1) and 25(1) of the American Convention on Human Rights, in relation to Article 1(1) thereof, as well as the obligations established in Articles 1, 6 and 8 of the Inter-American Convention to Prevent and Punish Torture and Article 7(b) of the Inter-American Convention on the Prevention, Punishment, and Eradication of Violence against Women, to the detriment of the 155 victims of the instant case, in their corresponding circumstances, according to the terms . . . of this Judgment.

3.   The State violated the obligation to respect rights and the obligation to adopt domestic legal effects enshrined, respectively, in Articles 1(1) and 2 of the American Convention on Human Rights, pursuant to the terms . . . of this Judgment.

4.   The State violated the rights of the family and right to a name enshrined in Articles 17 and 18 of the American Convention on Human Rights, in relation to Articles 1(1) and 19 thereof, to the detriment of Ramiro Antonio Osorio Cristales . . .

5.   The State violated the right to humane treatment recognized in Article 5(1) of the American Convention on Human Rights, in relation to Article 1(1) thereof, to the detriment of the 153 victims, in accordance with . . . this Judgment. Furthermore, the State violated the right to humane treatment embodied in Article 5(1) of the American Convention on Human rights, in relation to Articles 1(1) and 19 thereof, to the detriment of Ramiro Antonio Osorio Cristales andSalomé Armando Gómez Hernández . . .

6.   It does not correspond to the Court to issue a determination regarding the alleged violation of the right to property embodied in Article 21 of the Convention . . .

6-Jul-2011

Order of the Inter-American Court of Human Rights
HAVING SEEN:

1. The judgment on preliminary objection, merits, reparations and costs (hereinafter "the judgment") delivered by the Inter-American Court of Human Rights (hereinafter "the Inter-American Court" or "the Court") on November 24, 2009, in which it ordered, *inter alia*, that:

> 8. The State must investigate, without delay, in a serious and effective manner, the facts that originated the violations declared in th[e] judgment in order to prosecute and, as appropriate, punish those responsible, in the terms of paragraphs 231 to 236 of th[e] judgment.

> 9. The State must file the necessary disciplinary, administrative or criminal actions, according to its domestic law, against

those State authorities who may have committed the facts and obstructed the investigation, in the terms of paragraph 233(d) of th[e] judgment.

10. The State must adopt the necessary measures to amend the Law on *Amparo, Habeas Corpus* y Constitutionality in Guatemala, in the terms of paragraphs 238 to 242 of [the] judgment.

11. The State must proceed with the exhumation, identification and return to the next of kin of the mortal remains of the people who died in the Dos Erres Massacre, in the terms of paragraphs 244 to 249 of [the] judgment.

12. The State must provide training courses on human rights for different State
 authorities, in the terms of paragraphs 251 to 254 of [the] judgment.

13. The State must publish, once, in the Official Gazette and in another national
newspaper, Chapters I, VIII; IX and X; paragraph 222 of Chapter XI, and paragraphs 225, 229 to 236, 238 to 242, 244 to 249, 251 to 254, 256, 259 to 264, 265, 268 to 270, 271 to 274 and 283 to 291 of Chapter XII of th[e] judgment, including the titles of each chapter and the corresponding section—without the corresponding footnotes—as well as the operative paragraphs. In addition, the entire judgment must be published, for at least one year, on an appropriate official website of the State, in the terms of paragraph 256 of th[e] judgment.

14. The State must organize the public acts ordered, in the terms of paragraphs 259 to 264 of th[e] judgment.

15. The State must erect a monument, in the terms of paragraph 265 of th[e] judgment.

16. The State must provide the medical and psychological treatment required by the 155 victims, in the terms of paragraphs 268 to 270 of th[e] judgment.

17. The State must create a website for the search for children abducted and illegally held, in the terms of paragraphs 271 to 274 of th[e] judgment.

18. The State must pay the amounts awarded in paragraphs 292 to 295 and 303 and 304 of th[e] judgment as compensation for non-pecuniary damage and reimbursement of costs and expenses, in the terms of paragraphs 278 to 295, 300 to 304 and 305 of th[e] judgment.

(A) Obligation to investigate the facts that originated the violations declared in the judgment, and obligation to file the appropriate disciplinary, administrative or criminal actions, according to its domestic legislation (eighth and ninth operative paragraphs of the judgment)

7. In its report of December 21, 2009, the State advised that "in order to comply with the decisions of the [...] Inter-American Court, and the decisions of the Criminal Chamber of the Supreme Court of Justice, the Human Rights Prosecutor of the Public Prosecution Service took the necessary steps to execute the arrest warrants ordered against the individuals declared responsible in the [...] criminal proceedings." As a result, "on February 10, 2010, [...] Manuel Pop Sun was arrested" and transferred to the Criminal, Drug Trafficking and Environmental Crimes Court of First Instance to give his first statement. A "commitment order and an indictment" were issued against him "on February 12, 2010, implicating him in proceedings for murder and human rights crimes." In addition, on February 9, 2010, "Reyes Collin Gualip was arrested" and a commitment order and an indictment were issued against him on February 17, 2010, by the Criminal, Drug Trafficking and Environmental Crimes Court of First Instance, implicating him in proceedings for the crime of murder." In addition, the State indicated that on "March 3, 2010, Carlos Antonio Carías López, who during the massacre held the rank of Second Lieutenant of the Guatemalan Army, came forward voluntarily and was implicated in the proceedings for murder and theft." The State also reported that the "Public Prosecution Service had requested the extradition of Gilberto Jordán, Jorge Vinicio Sosa Orantes and Pedro Pimentel Ríos, who had been captured in the United States." Regarding the other defendants implicated in the proceedings, the State advised that, to "date they have not yet been arrested, and it is presumed that they have left Guatemala; therefore, a red notice is being processed to locate them abroad." The State also underscored that, given its importance, the case had been transferred to the High Risk Court of the Supreme Court of Justice where the proceedings were currently being conducted.

8. In addition, the State reported that on "February 23, 2010, the defense counsel of one the defendants presented an application for *amparo* as a result of the Criminal Chamber's decision, claiming [...]: 'the rights to liberty and to defense, as well as the juridical principle of due process.' [The claim] was decided on January 18, 2011 by the Constitutional Court in favor of the defendants. The State also indicated that the *Asociación de Familiares de Detenidos y Desaparecidos de Guatemala* [Association of the Next of Kin of Detainees and Missing Persons of Guatemala] (hereinafter "FAMDEGUA") had filed an appeal for clarification and expansion against the decision of the Constitutional Court, considering that "the

decision violated an international obligation of the State." This appeal is pending a decision. The State reiterated, through the Presidential Coordination Commission for the Executive's Policies on Human Rights (hereinafter "COPREDEH"), its willingness to comply with all the measures ordered by the Inter-American Court, but that the "Executive is unable to interfere in the decisions of the Constitutional Court." Therefore, it was awaiting the ruling, which would be communicated to the Inter-American Court in due course.

9.   The representatives observed that, regarding the "reactivation of the arrest warrants and the arrests, [...] even though two of the defendants had been arreste —largely through the insistence and collaboration of the representatives at the domestic level—and another one turned himself in voluntarily, since then (around March 2010), no further sustained and serious efforts had been made to discover the whereabouts of the other individuals who had been found responsible and arrest them [...], either on or outside Guatemalan territory." They indicated that the "lack of diligence in the immediate and conscientious search for those responsible, especially those of higher rank in the army, only make the possibility of discovering the truth more distant and justice illusory." In addition, they observed that, although the State indicates that it has "requested the extradition of several of those responsible captured in the United States, [...] this request has not been made effective." They considered it important that "the State forward this Court updated information on the progress of the requests for extradition regarding the three defendants who are in the United States, and the other defendants who were abroad."

10.   The representatives also stressed that it is "essential that the State [...] coordinate opportunely with the international police intelligence organizations and those of other States in order to bring the individuals who have already been captured to justice for these grave acts, as well as those who are still fugitives from justice." In addition, they observed that it is especially important "to explore immediately lines of inquiry that take into consideration the pattern of systematic human rights violations at the time the facts occurred [...], and that they cover all the facts of the massacre." The representatives asked the Inter-American Court to "require the State to report on the measures it has adopted to guarantee the right to life and integrity of all those involved in the investigations, and to forward a report that includes a "timetable of the different steps taken in the investigation and those that are pending, as well as the resources assigned to conduct them." Similarly, the representatives observed "with concern that the State has failed to provide any information regarding the measures taken to analyze the possible irregularities and violations committed during the investigation." Therefore, they considered it important to reiterate "that the effective and diligent investigation of the facts must cover, among other factors, the intimidation and threats against the

victims' next of kin, witnesses and other procedural subjects." They also asked this Court to "urge the State to present information on the measures it has adopted and will adopt to remove the *de facto* and *de iure* obstacles that maintain impunity in this case [...].

11.   Regarding the appeal admitted by the Constitutional Court of Guatemala on January 18, 2011, in favor of nine of the defendants, against the decision issued on February 8, 2010, by the Criminal Chamber of the Supreme Court of Justice, the representatives indicated that, given the incongruity of the ruling, they had filed a request for clarification and expansion of the decision. They also observed that "the result of the decision of the [Constitutional Court of Guatemala] is to paralyze once again the process of investigating the grave acts that resulted in these international proceedings." Therefore, the representatives reiterated that this Court should summon the parties to a hearing on the impunity of several cases, including this one.

12.   The Commission took note of the information forwarded by the State and appreciated the efforts made to reactivate the domestic proceedings and to execute the pending arrest warrants. However, it "consider[ed] that the State should report on its follow-up on the corresponding extradition requests, notifications, and other procedures, on and outside Guatemalan territory to determine the identification and possible prosecution of those responsible. In addition, it indicated that "it is not possible to discern the actions taken [by the State to comply with the ninth operative paragraph]." Furthermore, from the information forwarded, it is not possible to infer "which of the crimes ascribed to them is specifically related to this aspect of the judgment," and there is no indication of the level of participation of those allegedly responsible with regard to the obstruction of justice in this case. Lastly, the Commission considered that "this aspect of the judgment represents an obligation, which although related to the [eighth operative] paragraph, must be assumed by the State independently, because the obligation to investigate and punish does not only cover the acts that occurred during the massacre, but also the irregularities and delays in the subsequent judicial proceedings, and the acts of harassment perpetrated and tolerated by the State agents, which have prolonged impunity in the case."

13.   Based on the information provided by the State and the observations presented by the representatives and the Commission, the Court assesses positively all the efforts made and measures taken by the State to conduct the investigation into the facts of the instant case, which, owing to its importance, was forwarded to the High Risk Court of the Supreme Court of Justice. The Inter-American Court stresses that, on February 9, 10 and 12, 2010, three of those allegedly responsible for the facts were arrested, and on March 3, 2010, an individual who, at that time of the massacre was a Second Lieutenant in the Guatemalan Army, came

forward voluntarily, and was implicated in the proceedings. In addition, the Court takes notes that the Public Prosecution Service requested the extradition of three of those who were possibly responsible for the facts, who were detained in the United States of America, but that, to date, other defendants have not been arrested because they appear to have left Guatemala.

14.   The Court recalls that, in paragraphs 233, subparagraphs (a) to (f), 234 and 235 of its judgment, it established the criteria to be followed during the investigation of the facts in this case. In addition, the Court finds that, even though the State has taken different measures to arrest those allegedly responsible, it must make every effort to investigate the facts that gave rise to the violations declared in the judgment, because, more than 28 years after the facts occurred, impunity still exists in this case. Based on the foregoing, the Court reiterates to the State its obligation to intensify its efforts and take all appropriate actions as soon as possible in order to make progress in the corresponding investigations. Thus, this Court considers it essential that the State present complete, detailed and updated information on the implementation of the investigation, the measures taken and their results in compliance with the judgment.

(B) Obligation to adopt the necessary measures to amend the Law on Amparo, Habeas Corpus and Constitutionality in Guatemala (tenth operative paragraph of the judgment)

15.   The State advised that "the amendments to the Law on *Amparo, Habeas Corpus*, and Constitutionality [...] must be approved [by] at least two-thirds of all the members of the Congress of the Republic and, following their approval on third reading, they must be submitted to the consideration of the Constitutional Court." In addition, it reported that, on March 28, 2008, it had forwarded the favorable opinion of the Special Justice Sector Reform Commission on bill No. 3319, which amends the said law, to the Constitutional Court. However, the State indicated that, "considering that bill No. 3319 did not include some important aspects to be amended, Congress, presented bill No. 3942 to complement it." This bill, which was filed before a plenary session of Congress, was not approved on third reading. The State noted that "it appears that the Supreme Court of Justice is drafting another bill to amend the law in question; further information on this matter will be provided in due course."

16.   In this regard, the representatives observed that "although [they are] aware that the amendment of laws, especially an [amendment] with the characteristics of the Law on *Amparo*, requires an open and participatory process of consultation and discussion, the State is obliged to adopt measures to ensure that the amendment is adopted within a reasonable period of time." They considered that the State's report was "omissive with regard to the measures aimed at guaranteeing the effective use of the remedy of *amparo*, while its amendments are discussed and approved."

17.   In its observations, the Commission indicated that "it appreciates the initiatives adopted by the State." However, it observed that "more than a year has gone by since the judgment was notified and there have been no specific results regarding compliance with this obligation." In addition, it indicated that "the information provided by the State with regard to bill No. 3319 was presented in the [merits] proceeding before the Court, and was assessed by the Court at the appropriate time"; thus, it considered that "the State must forward the information regarding:

(a) the timetable for discussion of the legislative initiatives that were not approved by Congress;

(b) the compatibility of the new legislative proposals under discussion, with the standards established by the Court regarding the regulation of the remedy of *amparo*, and,

(c) the measures being taken to guarantee the effective use of the remedy of *amparo* while the corresponding amendment procedures are being carried out." On this last point, the Commission indicated that the State "had not forwarded information."

18.   Based on the foregoing, the Court observes that the information forwarded by the State had already been provided during the merits proceeding of the present case, prior to issuing the judgment. Taking this into consideration and also the comments of the representatives and the Commission, this Court observes that the approval of an amendment to the Law on *Amparo, Habeas Corpus* and Constitutionality in Guatemala is currently dependent upon the drafting of amendments by the Constitutional Court, because the bill that was before the Congress of the Republic had not been promulgated. In this regard, the Court observes that, as mentioned by the State itself, on March 28, 2008, the favorable opinion on the bill was forwarded to the Constitutional Court for the drafting of the amendments to this law, without having produced any results to date, four years later. Therefore, the Court considers that the State must report on all the specific new initiatives, actions and measures, and their results, that have been implemented by the State in order to make progress towards amending the Law on *Amparo, Habeas Corpus*, and Constitutionality in Guatemala, and also on the measures it has adopted to guarantee the effective use of *amparo* while the corresponding law is being amended, in order to assess compliance with this measure of reparation.

(C) Obligation to proceed with the exhumation, identification and return of the remains of those who died during the massacre (eleventh operative paragraph of the judgment)

19.   The State indicated that "the Public Prosecution Service, in a communication of March 11, 2010, advised that the Forensic Anthropology

Foundation of Guatemala (hereinafter "FAFG" or "the Foundation") was appointed as the expert to perform the exhumations." In addition, it indicated that these exhumations were commenced on April 6, 2010, and that "the procedures for the extraction and classification of skeletal remains concluded on April 13, 2010, when they were transferred to the FAFG laboratory for the extraction of samples and subsequent DNA testing." In addition, the State reported that the extraction of samples from the exhumed remains is currently being carrying out in order to map the DNA profiles to compare them with the DNA samples taken from the surviving next of kin. In this regard, the State indicated that "the remains "had not been classified individually, which has delayed their classification [...]. Also, owing to the ground conditions, the remains are in poor condition; therefore, there is a risk that it may not be possible to extract the DNA samples, which will complicate the individualization and full identification of the victims."

20.   The representatives observed that the "participation of the FAFG in the implementation of this measure has been crucial in ensuring that it can be considered a true measure of reparation." They stated that said the Foundation's work has been "characterized at all times by the highest technical and professional quality, but also by the enormous compassion of its entire team, who have given special attention to providing accessible and detailed information to the victims' next of kin regarding the procedure and what they can expect." They also appreciated greatly the Foundation's commitment, and urged the State to "guarantee all the necessary conditions to allow the Foundation to continue its work."

21.   In this regard, the Commission appreciated the measures adopted to comply with the obligation to identify and return the remains to the next of kin of the victims. It indicated that "it awaits further information from the State on the actions aimed at overcoming the reported difficulties and on the progress made with the rest of the procedure," and that the State should continue "providing the necessary resources to allow the work to be performed so that the identification and return of the remains is carried out within the time frame granted by the Court."

22.   The Court assesses positively the efforts made by the State to comply with this measure. The representatives and the Commission both agree in appreciating the steps taken by the State and the technical and professional work performed by the Foundation in the exhumation of the bodies. At the same time, the Court takes into account the State's comments on the difficulties encountered to compare the DNA samples extracted from the victims' next of kin with the remains, because these were not classified individually and were in poor condition, and that, consequently, there is a risk that it may not be possible to extract DNA samples.

23.   In addition, the Court recalls the provisions of paragraph 249 of the

judgment, which stated that "to make the individualization of the those exhumed viable and effective, the State must advise the representatives of the victims in writing of the procedure for the identification and return of the remains of those killed during the massacre and, if necessary, request their collaboration for the pertinent effects." Therefore, the Court finds that, as indicated in the judgment, the State must continue reporting on the measures implemented to identify those exhumed and the results, in order to comply with the eleventh operative paragraph of the judgment.

(D) Obligation to implement training courses on human rights for different State authorities (twelfth operative paragraph of the judgment)

24.   In its report of December 21, 2010, the State indicated that "through the Training Unit of the Public Prosecution Service, and with the support of COPREDEH, it had prepared a project to offer the course 'Application of national and international human rights law in proceedings for grave violations in Guatemala,' which seeks to train public prosecutors and assistant prosecutors of the Public Prosecution Service." It specified that the course is intended to be offered in four modules "covering concepts, classification, human rights institutions, and specific cases of the Inter-Commission on Human Rights and the Inter-American Court of Human Rights." It also indicated that, owing to the lack of funds it has not been possible to open the course immediately; therefore, "the Public Prosecution Service is currently seeking the necessary financial resources to implement the course." Lastly, the State indicated that the Ministry of National Defense "has advised that human rights issues are included at all levels of academic training (mid-level, university, and specializations)."

25.   In their observations, the representatives indicated that "regarding training for the Armed Forces, the State merely indicated that, according to information from the Ministry of Defense, human rights topics are included at all levels of training, [...] without providing specific details that would allow the purpose, content and impact to be evaluated." Similarly, they added that "despite the State's obligation to 'enhance' existing courses, the information provided reveals that it has not even made a retrospective analysis of the training courses provided to the members of the Armed Forces [...]." They considered it important that these courses include "the obligation of all the authorities to collaborate in gathering evidence and guaranteeing access to information in cases of grave human rights violations." Regarding the projected course "Application of national and international human rights law in proceedings for grave violations in Guatemala," the representatives observed that it is "crucial that the training be addressed at influencing and improving the work of prosecutors and their assistants [, as well as providing them] with tools that allow them to conduct investigations effectively and within a reasonable time." Lastly, the representatives indicated that "the State

has never refer[red] to the measures it has adopted to train judges."

26.   The Commission appreciated the initiatives taken by the State; however, it observed that, based on "the information available, it cannot be concluded that the State is complying adequately with this aspect of the judgment." Thus, it noted that "the State had not forwarded information regarding the results of the measures taken to offer training on human rights to justice operators in Guatemala," and also that "despite the *pensum* on human rights included at the different training levels of the Armed Forces, the Court had specified in its judgment that the scope of this obligation included the creation of a permanent education program on human rights for members of the Armed Forces, judges and prosecutors, independently of, or to strengthen, those that already exist." Furthermore, it indicated that the State must remove "all the obstacles that prevent or delay compliance with its obligations, including the allocation of the necessary financial, human and any other resources to train and strengthen the system of justice in Guatemala comprehensively." Lastly, it indicated that the "six-month term granted for complying with this obligation has expired without effective compliance being achieved."

27.   According to the information presented by the parties, the Court observes that even though the State has taken some measures relating to the implementation of training courses, particularly measures regarding the elaboration of the project to offer the course "Application of national and international human rights law in proceedings for grave violations in Guatemala," it also considers that these measures have been insufficient to comply with this aspect. The Court finds that the State must take, as soon as possible, all necessary measures to implement the training courses on human rights for the different State authorities indicated in paragraphs 251, 252 and 253 of the judgment. Consequently, the Court awaits that, in its next report, the State refer in detail to the measures it has adopted to offer the training courses, indicating the scheduling of the respective actions and the content of the training courses, who they will be offered to, and, if appropriate, the results.

(E) Obligation to publish, once, in the Official Gazette and in another national newspaper all the relevant parts of the judgment, and also to publish the entire judgment, for at least one year, on an appropriate official website of the State (thirteenth operative paragraph of the judgment)

28.   In its brief of March 25, 2010, the State reported that, on February 5 and 14, 2010, it had published in the *Diario de Centroamérica* and *El Periódico*, respectively, the extracts of the judgment indicated by the Court in the thirteenth operative paragraph. The State acknowledged that "there had been an involuntary error in the omission of section C of Chapter XII, 'Measures of satisfaction,

rehabilitation, and guarantees of non-repetition,' and also in the publication in *El Periódico* in which section C of Chapter XII appeared incorrectly as C.1"; it also indicated that this "does not affect the substance or the purpose of the publications because no paragraphs have been omitted in the proven facts or in the operative paragraphs of the judgment." In addition, it indicated that it would publish an erratum in *El Periódico*[5][156] in this regard. The State also affirmed that the paragraphs had not been numbered in any other publication that the Court had ordered it to make, and argued that, in those cases, the Court had decided that "the State has complied" with the publication. Lastly, it indicated that, as of April 26, 2010, the entire judgment in this case has been available on the COPREDEH webpage (www.copredeh.gob.gt).

29.   The representatives indicated that, as they had stated in their communication of April 20, 2011, the publications of the relevant parts had some errors, because in the "publication in the *Diario de Centroamérica* section C of Chapter XII had been omitted, [...] as well as paragraph 255." Also, "in *El Periódico*," it "erroneously" referred "to section C of Chapter XII as C.1, and omitted sub-paragraph C.1, as well as paragraph 255." Regarding the State's obligation to comply with publishing the judgment on an official website, the representatives indicated that the "hyperlink available on the said webpage does not include the complete name of the judgment delivered by the Court. Similarly, a brief summary should be included on this website in which the State of Guatemala acknowledges its international responsibility for human rights violations." They also considered that "for this reparation to be adequate, it must at least include the complete name of the judgment, because a partial reference prevents the correct identification of the published document and therefore the proposed scope of this measure is not achieved." Lastly, in their observations of January 19, 2011, the representatives indicated that the "problems regarding the publication of the entire judgment on the [COPREDEH] webpage have been rectified."

30.   The Inter-American Commission took note of the information presented and reiterated that, "despite the omissions pointed out by the representatives, the publications that have been made [...] represent an important step towards compliance with this measure of reparation. The Commission is awaiting information from the State regarding the erratum to be published, so as to be able "to verify full compliance regarding the publications." In relation to the integral publication on the website, the Commission appreciated the measures taken by the State.

31.   Based on the information provided by the parties, the Court observes that the State has published the entire judgment on the website. Regarding the publication of the relevant parts of the judgment, the Court underlines that, on February 5 and 14, 2010, the State published the relevant parts of the judgment in the *Diario de Centroamérica* and *El Periódico*, respectively. In addition, it

notes that, according to the information provided by the parties, the State acknowledged that, owing to an involuntary error, it named section C of Chapter XII erroneously and omitted subsection "C.1) Satisfaction." In this regard, the State itself indicated that it would publish an erratum to rectify the said errors (*supra* considering paragraph 28). The Court considers that this omission and the error in the designation of the section do not affect the essence of the purpose of publishing the relevant parts of the judgment. Furthermore, the representatives indicated that, in the publication made by the State, it had also omitted paragraph 255 of the judgment. In this regard, the Court indicates that it did not order the publication of this paragraph in the judgment. Consequently, the Court finds that the State has complied with the thirteenth operative paragraph of the judgment regarding its publication on the website, as well as in relation to the publication in the Official Gazette and a major national newspaper.

(F) Obligation to organize the public acts (fourteenth operative paragraph of the judgment)

32.   The State indicated that "the legal representative of FAMDEGUA had advised that the beneficiaries would not accept any public act until the State has paid [the] financial compensation." Therefore, the State indicated that it "will coordinate the organization of the public acts with the petitioners after payment has been made of the financial compensation awarded in the judgment."

33.   In this regard, the representatives observed that "an integral part of our work is to follow-up on the victims' requests and concerns and present them to the authorities. Specifically, the assertion made in the State's report occurred during a telephone conversation to communicate the feelings of some of the victims [...] and in no way signified that the representatives considered it necessary to delay compliance [with this measure]. The representatives also indicated that "it is truly regrettable and incompatible with its international responsibilities that the State attempts to fail to comply with a judgment of the Court [...] based on the content of an informal conversation regarding the concerns of some of the victims regarding payment of the compensation."

34.   The Inter-American Commission recalled that "the provision of this measure of reparation by the Court responded, among other matters, to the Court's assessment of the opinions of the expert witnesses, psychologists, who confirmed the feeling of guilt and stigmatization to which the victims have been exposed due to the absence of justice [...]." Therefore, the Commission observed "that the State must coordinate with the representatives of the injured party to organize the required acts, in order to overcoming the stated obstacles and comply with this measure of reparation."

35.   Based on the information provided by the parties, the Court notes that the act of public acknowledgment of international responsibility and the projection

of the documentary on the facts of the massacre of the Dos Erres community have not yet been carried out. According to paragraph 264 of the judgment, these measures should have been implemented within one year of notification of the judgment. Consequently, the Court finds that the State must take all the necessary steps to carry out this public act as soon as possible, as decided in paragraphs 261, 262 and 263 of the judgment, and in coordination with the victims and their representatives, who should provide their collaboration. In order to monitor compliance with this obligation, in its next report, the State must indicate:

(a) the steps it has taken and will take in order to organize this measure of reparation, and

(b) the scheduling or provisional dates on which the act will be held.

(G) Obligation to erect a monument (fifteenth operative paragraph of the judgment)

36.　　The State advised that "due to the time that has elapsed since the massacre, the site of the Dos Erres community is now private property; consequently, access on foot or by car is restricted, and the owner's authorization is needed to construct the said monument." Therefore, the State indicated that "it is working on locating the owner of the property in order to arrange the respective authorization."

37.　　The representatives stated that, more than a year after notification of the judgment, "the explanations provided by the State to justify its delay are [...] unacceptable," and it is "incomprehensible that the State claims that it requires more than a year to identify the owner of the property in question, especially when most of the victims, and the residents of the neighboring areas, know who it is." They added that "the State itself had to obtain permission from this person in order to exhume the remains that were in a well on this property; hence it cannot claim that it does not know [...] his identity." They indicated that they believe that "the State's arguments reveal not only poor coordination between the State institutions, but also the reluctance to comply with this measure of reparation."

38.　　The Commission noted that the State had "indicated that it would forward information on this matter "opportunely." In this regard, the Commission considered that "under this procedure to monitor judgment, the presentation by the State of detailed and updated information is essential in order to define the progress made or compliance with the obligations ordered by the Court." It added that the time granted by the Court had already expired and that "the information available does not permit identifying the specific actions that the State has taken to construct the monument, or the proposals made to overcome the problems that have arisen."

39.　　Based on the information provided by the parties, the Court notes that, to date, the State has not taken any steps to build the monument in the place occupied by the Dos Erres community in order to comply with the provisions of paragraph 265 of the judgment, and specifically its fifteenth operative paragraph. The Court considers that the identification of the owners of the land should not represent a problem. Therefore, the Court reiterates to the State its obligation to increase its efforts and to take all the necessary steps, as soon as possible, to make progress in complying with this measure of reparation. Consequently, this Court considers it essential that the State present updated and detailed information on the steps taken to comply with this measure, and their results.

(H) Obligation to provide psychological and medical treatment to the victims (sixteenth operative paragraph of the judgment)

40.   In its report of December 21, 2010, the State indicated that "the Ministry of Public Health and Social Welfare is the State institution in charge of providing medical services and psychological care." In addition, it indicated that, on "May 12, 2010, it had requested the legal representatives in the case to present information on the age, identification number, and exact addresses of the beneficiaries" so as to locate them, because many of the victims no longer live in the department of Petén. It added that "the information requested has not been forwarded by the legal representatives," and that on "December 13 and 14, 2010, they sent some identification documents; however, the State does not have the home address of the beneficiaries."

41.   In this regard, the representatives indicated that "it was a matter of concern that the State authorities were arguing that they are unable to obtain the personal information of the victims more than one year after notification of the judgment, and attempting to hold one of the representative organizations responsible for its noncompliance." The representatives added that they are "very willing to collaborate and help" and that, consequently, "since the first half of 2010, FAMDEGUA has made lists available with the names and addresses of all the people who reside in different parts of the country about whom it had information. It was precisely these lists [...] that made it possible for the State to contact the victims to start payment of the financial compensation; however, the State has not taken the initiative to coordinate the implementation of this measure of reparation through these channels."

42.   The Commission took note of the information provided by the State and observed that Guatemala "has not forwarded information on the actions or work plans in place to implement an adequate program of medical and psychological care for the victims; nor has it forwarded information on any other measures it would be using to locate the beneficiaries." With regard to locating the victims, the Commission understood that the collaboration of the representatives was required, but indicated that "it is the State's obligation to provide adequate

reparation deriving from the attribution of international responsibility [...]. The State must use all available means to comply with this obligation."

43.   Based on the above, the Court observes that the State has not complied with the obligation to provide the medical and psychological treatment ordered in the sixteenth operative paragraph of the judgment. The Court takes into account the information provided by the parties and considers it important that the State coordinate with the representatives the necessary measures to locate the beneficiaries, and that the representatives cooperate in this regard. Consequently, this Court considers it essential that the State take all the necessary measures conducive to providing the victims immediately with adequate and free medical and psychological treatment, determined according to their health needs and by mutual agreement with the victims, including the provision of medication. In accordance with paragraph 270 of the judgment, this medical and psychological treatment may be provided by State specialized personnel and institutions or, if necessary, the State can have recourse to specialized private or civil society institutions. In order to monitor compliance with this obligation, the State must provide detailed and updated information on the measures adopted and the results.

(I) Creation of a webpage to search for children abducted and illegally held (seventeenth operative paragraph)

44.   The State advised that "several human rights institutions had been invited to working meetings during which it had expressed its commitment." Despite this, it indicated that "some of the institutions [had been unable] to assume this commitment, owing to their budget, competence or mandate." It added that the State was "studying other possibilities to comply with what was ordered."

45.   The representatives stated that the information provided by the State "again reveals the absence of resolve and a serious lack of coordination between the different State entities."

46.   The Commission observed that "the time frame for complying with this measure of reparation has already expired and the information presented by the State fails to show that it has taken even minimally effective measures to comply with it." It also stated that Guatemala "must fulfill the requirements established by the Court, specifically regarding:

(a) the allocation of the human, financial, logistic and any other resources required for its creation and operation, and

(b) the State must collaborate with the national and international institutions or associations responsible for locating children abducted during the domestic conflict."

47.   Based on the information provided by the parties, the Court concludes that the webpage to search for children abducted and illegally held has yet to be created and, the State specifically mentioned the difficulties it faced to comply

with this measure of reparation. According to paragraph 274 of the judgment, this measure should have been implemented within one year of notification of the judgment. In this regard, the Court considers it essential that the State adopt the necessary measures and allocate the human, financial, logistic and any other resources required to create the webpage, so that it functions satisfactorily and fulfills the purpose for which it was created, in keeping with paragraphs 271, 272 and 273 of the judgment. In order to monitor compliance with this obligation, in its next report, the State must indicate the measures it has taken and will take to create the webpage and, if appropriate, the results obtained.

(J) Payments for pecuniary and non-pecuniary damage and costs (eighteenth operative paragraph of the judgment)

48.   In its report of December 17, 2010, the State indicated that, after verifying the identification documents forwarded by the legal representatives on December 14 and 15, 2010, it "determined that several of the names on the identification documents submitted differed from the names indicated in the said judgment." It indicated that, in order to be able to make the payment and comply with all the requirements of the Guatemalan public administration auditing bodies, "the identity of the beneficiary" must be duly verified; therefore, it asked the Court to rule in this regard. In its following report, dated December 21, 2010, the State indicated that "after obtaining the funds from a deficit national budget, it had been able to allocate them and payment will be made before December 31, 2010."

49.   In its report of May 16, 2011, the State indicated that, on December 27, 2010, and January 13 and April 14, 2011, it had paid a total of 115 beneficiaries, as well as the costs and expenses of the legal representatives from [...] FAMDEGUA. It added that, at May 4, 2011, "13 people [were yet to be paid]; but their cheques have already been prepared, together with the payment certifications, and all that remains pending is that these beneficiaries contact COPREDEH to arrange the date of payment. Consequently, the State asks the Court, through the legal representatives, to locate these people and forward their requested identification documents." It also indicated that it had not been able to contact a group of seven people, so that it did not have their personal data and it had not been possible to prepare the cheque and the settlement agreement in order to make the payment. In addition, it indicated that, based on the documents forwarded by the representatives, it had taken note that 20 beneficiaries were deceased and, as it had informed the representatives of FAMDEGUA, in accordance with domestic provisions, "their next of kin must carry out the intestacy inheritance procedures established in Guatemalan law, [because this] is required for the heirs to receive the corresponding financial compensation."

50.   In response to the Secretariat's communication of May 30, 2011, the State submitted the following updated information on July 4, 2011: (a) regarding

the payment to Rodrigo Mayén Ramírez, it forwarded copies of the corresponding cheque and certification; (b) after May 9, 2011, it had paid six beneficiaries, and forwarded the corresponding cheques and certifications of payment; thus, according to the State, 121 beneficiaries have received the respective payment of compensation; (c) it had noted the death of two beneficiaries: Merigilda Marroquín Miranda and Rafael Barrientos Mazariegos, and reported that the cheque and the certification issued in favor of the latter would be canceled due to his decease, and (d) that six beneficiaries, for whom the cheques and certifications of payment have already been prepared, had not come forward to collect their compensation.

51.   Furthermore, in its report of May 9, 2011, the State indicated that it had been unable to contact seven people. However, in its latest report, it indicated that, on June 28, 2010, COPREDEH had received a special power of attorney granted by Dionicio Rodríguez Campos to his wife Elena López, and the State was taking the necessary administrative measures to pay her the compensation. In addition, according to new information provided by the representatives, three of the beneficiaries listed had already received their payment. Lastly, the State indicated that, since it did not have information on all the beneficiaries, it had arranged a meeting with representatives of FAMDEGUA on July 6, 2011, in order to compare information and seek support from the regional headquarters of COPREDEH to locate people who are still owed compensation.

52.   Regarding the costs and expenses of CEJIL, the State reported that, in order to comply with this commitment, it had issued the corresponding cheque, but it was not accepted by the representatives owing to banking difficulties. Subsequently, talks were resumed with CEJIL to coordinate the transaction and the signature of the certification of settlement. Therefore, it would duly inform the Court and forward the vouchers confirming payment of the corresponding costs and expenses.

53.   The representatives indicated that "last December 27, [2010, members] of FAMDEGUA accompanied the victims to receive the payments owed to them by the State, after submitting the required documentation." However, they also indicated that they did not have "detailed information for each victim," so they were awaiting the information from the State. On June 28, 2011, the representatives initially stated that "based on the information obtained by FAMDEGUA, 115 people—including Rodrigo Mayen-Ramirez—had received the payment corresponding to the compensation ordered by the Court." In their brief of July 4, 2011, the representatives stated that, according to the "information obtained by FAMDEGUA, [they could] confirm that from May 9, 2011, to date, [five beneficiaries] have received the amount [...] corresponding to compensation for non-pecuniary damage; but, at present, they did not have additional documentation to forward to the Court. Hence, according to the representatives, 120 beneficiaries have received payment of the corresponding compensation.

54.   The representatives added that, in addition to the 20 deceased victims indicated by the State, two other victims had died: Rafael Barrientos Mazariegos and Meregilda Marroquín Miranda. The corresponding inheritance procedure was pending with regard to all the deceased victims. Moreover, of the 13 people who, according to the State, have yet to claim their compensation, FAMDEGUA indicated that some of them have already received the payment, without specifying their names. Lastly, with regard to those who have not been contacted, the representatives stated that contact details were provided to the State. Nevertheless, there were willing to provide the data again.

55.   Regarding the reimbursement of costs and expenses, the representatives confirmed that, on December 27, 2010, the State had made the respective payment to FAMDEGUA. In the case of the reimbursement of costs and expenses to CEJIL, the representatives clarified that, in early 2011, they had informed "State officials that, receiving the cheque could compromise there safety during their working visit to Guatemala and, given the amount in question, they could have difficulty bringing the money into Costa Rica; therefore they proposed that the payment be made via bank transfer. To this end and in accordance with the State's requirements, on May 30, 2011, CEJIL sent a draft settlement agreement to COPREDEH and is waiting for the payment to be made."

56.   The Commission assessed positively the information submitted by the parties and awaited specific data regarding the beneficiaries of the reparations.

57.   Based on the above, the Court assesses positively the efforts made by the State to pay the compensation for non-pecuniary damage to 121 beneficiaries,[6] [157] regarding whom the State submitted the respective proof of payment.[7] [158] In addition, this Court notes that, from the information provided by the parties, seven people have not collected the payment of the compensation, five people have not contacted COPREDEH to receive the corresponding payment, and 22 beneficiaries are deceased; in other words, 34 beneficiaries have not received the compensation payment. In this regard, the Court considers that the State and the representatives should coordinate the necessary measures to locate the people who have not received payment yet and, in the case of the deceased victims, the representatives should provide advice or initiate the appropriate legal measures or procedures so that their next of kin can receive the corresponding compensation. Furthermore, the State submitted the required information on the payment made to each victim, and the respective documentation, which was forwarded to the representatives and the Commission. At the date of this order, the Court is awaiting the observations of the Commission in this regard.

58.   Notwithstanding the foregoing, this Court has verified that the State has made the payment of compensation for non-pecuniary damage to 121 beneficiaries, and the payment of costs and expenses to FAMDEGUA; hence,

it considers that the eighteenth operative paragraph has been complied with partially. Consequently, the Court finds it pertinent that the State continue to report on the measures taken and their results in relation to the 34 victims who have yet to receive payment, either because they have not contacted the State officials or because they are deceased.

59.   Furthermore, regarding payment of the reimbursement of costs and expenses to CEJIL, the Court takes into account the observations of the State and the representatives, and awaits pertinent information concerning the payment.

THEREFORE:

THE INTER-AMERICAN COURT OF HUMAN RIGHTS,

in exercise of its authority to monitor compliance with its decisions in accordance with Articles 33, 61(1), 62(3), 65, 67, and 68(1) of the American Convention on Human Rights, 25(1) and 30 of its Statue, and 31(2) and 69 of its Rules of Procedure,

DECLARES:

1.   As indicated in this order, the State has complied with the publication of the relevant parts of the judgment in the Official Gazette and in another national newspaper, as well as the publication of the whole judgment on an appropriate official website of the State *(thirteenth operative paragraph of the judgment)*.

2.   As indicated in this order, the State has complied partially with the payment of the compensation for non-pecuniary damages to 121 victims, while payment to 34 beneficiaries remains pending, either because they have not contacted the State or because they are deceased; in addition it has complied with the reimbursement of costs and expenses to FAMDEGUA *(eighteenth operative paragraph of the judgment)*.

3.   In order to monitor full compliance with the judgment issued in the instant case, and after analyzing the information provided by the State, the Commission, and the representatives, the Court will keep the procedure open to monitor compliance with those aspects that remain pending compliance in this case, namely:

(a) To investigate, without delay, in a serious and effective manner, the facts that gave rise to the violations declared in the judgment, in order to prosecute and, as appropriate, punish those responsible *(eighth operative paragraph of the judgment)*;

(b) To initiate the pertinent disciplinary, administrative or criminal actions under domestic law, against the State authorities who may have committed the facts and obstructed the investigation of them *(ninth operative paragraph of the judgment)*;

(c) To adopt the pertinent measures to amend the Law on *Amparo, Habeas Corpus* and Constitutionality in Guatemala *(tenth operative paragraph of the judgment)*;

(d) To proceed with the exhumation, identification and return to their next of kin of the remains of those who died during the Dos Erres massacre (*eleventh operative paragraph of the judgment*);

(e) To implement the training courses on human rights for different State authorities (*twelfth operative paragraph of the judgment*);

(f) To organize the public acts ordered (*fourteenth operative paragraph*);

(g) To erect a monument (*fifteenth operative paragraph*);

(h) To provide the psychological and medical treatment required by the 155 victims (*sixteenth operative paragraph*);

(i) To create a webpage to search for children abducted and illegally retained (*seventeenth operative paragraph*); and,

(j) To pay the amounts established as compensation for non-pecuniary damage to the 34 people who, to date, have not yet received it for the reasons indicated in considering paragraphs 57 and 58 of this order, and the reimbursement of costs and expenses to CEJIL (*eighteenth operative paragraph of the judgment*).

4-Sep-2012
Order of the Inter-American Court of Human Rights
Monitoring Compliance with Judgment

I. Duty to investigate the facts that gave rise to the violations declared in the judgment, and duty to initiate the relevant disciplinary, administrative or criminal actions under domestic law (*eighth and ninth operative paragraphs of the judgment*)

7.   In its report of May 4, 2012, the State pointed out that:

[o]n August 2, 2011, the Criminal Court of First Instance for Criminal Matters, Drug-Trafficking, and Environmental Crimes concluded that accused persons Reyes Colin Gualip, Manuel Pop Sun, Daniel Martínez Méndez and Carlos Antonio Carías López:

(a) were found to be the perpetrators of the crime of murder committed against the life and integrity of the inhabitants of *Las Dos Erres*; for which they were sentenced to [...] 6,030 years' incommutable imprisonment;

(b) were found to be the perpetrators of crimes against humanity, committed against the security of the State; for which they were sentenced to 30 years' incommutable imprisonment;

(c) that Carlos Antonio Carías Lopez is responsible as perpetrator of the crime of aggravated theft, committed against the property of the inhabitants of community of *Las Dos Erres,* for which he was sentenced to six years' incommutable imprisonment; and

(d) the Office of the Public Prosecutor was ordered to continue investigating the other persons that might have participated in those events. The State also informed that the appeals filed against the decision of August 2, 2011, were declared inadmissible.

8.   Moreover, the State indicated that "the Court of High-Risk First B [...] decided "to sentence Mr. Pedro Pimentel Rios "to a total of 6,060 years" in prison for the crime of "murder committed against the life of 201 inhabitants of Las Dos Erres community" and "[f]or crimes against humanity" committed against those same persons. Furthermore, it ordered, *inter alia*, "the Office of the Public Prosecutor to continue with the investigation into the chain of command and other persons of the Guatemalan Army that might be related to the events". In addition, the State pointed out that "[o]n September 10, 2010, the Court of First Instance Court on Criminal Matters, Drug-Trafficking and Environmental Crimes of Guatemala ordered the active extradition to the United States of the accused persons, whose arrest is still pending. In turn, it requested the active extradition in Canada of Jorge Vinicio Sosa Orantes, who was arrested on January 14, 2011, in Calgary, Canada".

9.   The representatives, in turn, "valu[ed] the great importance of these convictions" but noted that the State has still the obligation to adopt measures to make progress in the investigations "regarding all the perpetrators" and emphasized that, according to the press, Mr. Efraín Rios Montt, "former Head of State and Commander in Chief of the Armed Forces at the time of the facts of the massacre" was linked to the process, though for different crimes to those referred to in the convictions. In addition to this, they mentioned that "there are arrest warrants pending execution" and that the State "did not refer to the disciplinary, administrative or criminal actions that it has taken against the authorities [...] who might have [...] prevented the investigation of the facts". Finally, they sustained that the part related to the human and material resources of the judicial system "keeps [...] being an obstacle [...] for the progress in the investigation regarding grave human rights violations".

10.   The Inter-American Commission valued the progress made in the investigation into the facts and stated that it waits for updated information regarding the conduct of the proceeding. It also indicated that "[a]ccording to public information, by the end of June 2012, the Fourth Appeals Chamber of the Supreme Court of Justice would have admitted a provisional *amparo* filed by Mr. Rios Montt, which would suspend the criminal proceeding against him". It considered it necessary for the State "to present the decision admitting the *amparo* and to explain what is the judicial effect – as to the merits and the procedure- of prosecuting [Mr.] Rios Montt as a figure different to [the one applied] to the *kaibiles* already convicted".

11.   The Court values the actions implemented by the State to make progress in the investigation of the facts of the instant case, including the convictions obtained. Without detriment to the foregoing, the Tribunal deems that the State must continue adopting the pertinent measures to complete the investigation in order to investigate, prosecute and, if applicable, punish all those alleged responsible for the facts that gave rise to the violations declared in the Judgment. Hence, this Court continues considering that it is essential for the State to present updated, detailed and complete information regarding the implementation of the investigation, the actions taken and results obtained, to comply with the Judgment.

II. Duty to organize the public acts ordered (*fourteenth operative paragraph of the judgment*)

12.   In the report of May 4, 2012, the State pointed out that:

[...] on December 15, 201[1][5 159], at *Patio de la Paz* of Palacio Nacional de la Cultura, it organized the Act of International Acknowledgment, which was presided over by President Álvaro Colom Caballeros (2008-2012), for which it coordinated together with the representatives of the relatives, the transfer of those persons residing at different parts of the country to the city; moreover, the State provided them with meals and accommodation. Some State's authorities attended the event.

13.   It also informed regarding the duty to show the video on the facts of the Massacre of Las Dos Erres community during the ceremony and also "to show it at a public act in the capital of Petén and in a department of the western area in which grave human rights violations occurred during the internal armed conflict" [6 160]. It indicated that "together with the representatives of the relatives, it arranged for the presentation of the video on December 7, 2011, on the anniversary of the facts" and that this act took place in Santa Elena, Petén, with the presence of local authorities. It further alleged that "regarding the second act, it agreed with the victims' representatives to carry it out in the Department of Alta Verapáz [and that] the schedule is still pending".

14.   The representatives confirmed that the public acts took place in the city of Guatemala and in Santa Elena in December 2011, with the participation of "the victims and in coordination with their representatives of FAMDEGUA". They expressed that "[a]ccording to the victims themselves, [said] acts constituted an important measure of satisfaction". They stated that they are waiting to be notified in relation to "the public act that is still pending" and that they are not aware of the distribution of the copies of the video to universities and public libraries.

15.   The Inter-American Commission noted that "the parties agree about the public act of acknowledgement organized"; in addition, it "observ[ed] that the planning of the second act to show the video is still pending" and it considered that the State must present "detailed information regarding the distribution of the documentary video in several universities".

16.   The Court takes note of the two public acts organized, in the city of Guatemala and Santa Elena, and of the presentation of the documentary video at the act held in Santa Elena. In this respect, taking into account the arguments presented by the representatives and the Commission (*supra* fourteenth and fifteenth considering paragraphs), in view of the fact that the former expressed their agreement with the manner in which the public acts took place, this Court considers that the State has complied with what was ordered in the fourteenth operative paragraph of the judgment, as to the organization of the two public acts and the presentation of the respective documentary video on the facts of the Massacre of Las Dos Erres community in one of the acts.

17.   Moreover, the Court notes that it is still pending the obligation to show the video before mentioned "in a department of the western area in which grave human rights violations occurred during the internal armed conflict"[7][161]. In turn, the State has not presented information on the compliance with its duty, according to paragraph 263 of the judgment, to distribute the video as widely as possible. These measures must have been implemented within the term of one year, as of notice of the judgment. In view of the foregoing, the Court deems that the State must take, within a reasonable term, and in coordination with the victims and their representatives, all the necessary actions, as soon as possible, to implement the aforementioned measures pending compliance.

III. Duty to pay the amounts established as compensation for nonpecuniary damage and reimbursement of costs and legal expenses (*eighteenth operative paragraph of the judgment*)

18.   In the report received by the Court on February 28, 2012, the State expressed that in the months of November and December 2011, it made the corresponding payments of the amounts for compensation of non-pecuniary damage to 15 persons who were declared victims in the judgment.[8][162] It explained that, in some cases, it made some of the payments directly to the victims or their agents and, in other cases, to their heirs. Afterwards, in its report of May 4, 2012, it indicated that it made the payments corresponding to the compensatory amounts ordered in favor of three more victims.[9][163]

19.   Moreover, according to information forwarded on February 28 and May 4, 2012, the State indicated that it has been not possible to contact seven victims[10][164]; that, in relation to another victim, it is taking some actions[11][165], and that in relation to the 13 victims who died, "their relatives must initiate the probate proceeding".[12][166]

20.   Furthermore, in relation to the aforementioned 13 deceased victims, and in relation to those victims that the State indicated that it was not possible to contact, the representatives expressed that "it has been difficult to locate some of the heirs [...] and some of the beneficiaries" and, given that the representatives

"have very limited resources to make long trips through the interior of the country in order to locate these persons [...] they request the State to collaborate with them in order to, through its agencies and registries, be able to gather the missing information". They further alleged that some relatives of the deceased victims are facing various difficulties to take the pertinent actions, for instance, they "could not obtain the certificates from the National Registry of Individuals [RENAP] since the books had been destroyed or are badly preserved"; some of them cannot remedy the loss of such certificates since they lack "the documents and transcripts required" so that the Attorney General's Office [PGN] may order the "untimely entry" and, "for several months now, they have been waiting for the [Attorney General's Office] to deliver its decision within the framework of several probate proceedings conducted".

21.   The Inter-American Commission sustained that "in view of the difficulties faced in order to obtain official identity documents, the State must provide active support from its institutions".

22.   Based on the foregoing, the representatives and the Inter-American Commission did not contest the information presented by the State regarding the new payments of the compensatory amounts made. However, in view of said information, this Court notes that the payments corresponding to the compensations ordered in favor of five victims, indicated by the State in its report of February 28, 2012, had been already mentioned in previous State's communications; for which they were considered by the Court upon issuance of its Order of July 6, 2011. [13][167]

23.   This Court values the efforts made by the State to pay the compensatory amounts for non-pecuniary damage ordered in favor of 13 more victims[14][168] and considers said payments to be fulfilled. Moreover, the Court notes that of a total of 155 victims in respect of whom it ordered the payment of compensations, to date, the State has complied with the payment in favor of 134 of them.

24.   Moreover, from the information provided by the parties and the Commission (*supra* eighteenth to twenty-first considering paragraphs), this Court notes that the State has still not paid the amounts corresponding to the compensations established in favor of 21 victims, namely: Luciana Cabrera Galeano, María Menegilda Marroquín Miranda[15][169], María Vicenta Moral Solís, Enriqueta González G. de Martínez[16][170], Eugenia Jiménez Pineda, Felicita Lima Ayala, Sara Pérez López, Telma Guadalupe Aldana Canan, Tomasa Galicia González, Nicolasa Pérez Méndez, Ever Ismael Antonio Coto, Héctor Coto, Santos Osorio Lique, Jorge Granados Cardona, Rafael Barrientos Mazariegos, Ángel Cermeño Pineda, Augusto Mayen Ramírez,[17][171] Marcelino Deras Tejada, Olegario Rodríguez Tepec, Teodoro Jiménez Pernillo and Edwin Saúl Romero García.[18][172] In this respect, the Court deems it is appropriate to indicate that the

State as well as the representatives must coordinate the necessary actions to locate the persons who have still not received the payment and, in the case of the deceased victims, they must render assistance in order for their relatives to take the actions or carry out the judicial proceedings that are pertinent to be able to receive the corresponding compensations.

25. Lastly, in relation to the payment of the reimbursement of costs and legal expenses in favor of the Center for Justice and International Law (hereinafter, "CEJIL"), the State informed that "it paid [CEJIL] as reimbursement of legal costs and expenses [the amount of US$] 27,500.00 [(twenty-seven thousand five hundred] dollars of the United States of America])]". The representatives confirmed that "the State [...] effectively paid the amount ordered by the Inter-American Court to CEJIL". In consequence, the Court considers that the State has fully complied with the payment of the costs and legal expenses ordered in the judgment.

IV. Other measures of reparation pending compliance

26. The Court notes that the State has not presented fundamental and detailed information regarding the progress made in the observation of the other measures of reparation ordered that are pending compliance.[19][173]

27. In light of the foregoing, the Court considers it is necessary to reiterate the request made to the State in the Order of July 6, 2011. To this end, it requests the State to adopt, forthwith, all measures that are necessary to promptly and effectively comply with the measures of reparation ordered in the judgment on the preliminary objection, merits, reparations and costs of November 24, 2009, which are pending compliance. Moreover, it requests the State to submit updated, complete and detailed information on such actions.

THEREFORE:

THE INTER-AMERICAN COURT OF HUMAN RIGHTS,

by virtue of its authority to monitor compliance with its own decisions and pursuant to Articles 33, 62(1), 62(3), 65, 67 and 68(1) of the American Convention on Human Rights, and Articles 25(1) and 30 of its Statute and 31(2) and 69 of its Rules of Procedure,

DECLARES THAT:

1. In accordance with the terms of sixteenth, twenty-third and twenty-fifth considering paragraphs, respectively, of this Order, the State has complied with:

 (a) the duty to hold public acts, having organized a public act of acknowledgment of international responsibility in the city of Guatemala, as well as another one in Santa Elena, and to show, in the last act, the documentary video on the facts of the Massacre of Las Dos Erres (*fourteenth operative paragraph of the judgment*)

 (b) the duty to make the payments established as compensation for nonpecuniary damage in favor of 13 victims (*eighteenth operative paragraph of the judgment)*

(c) the duty to make the payment as reimbursement of costs and legal expenses (*eighteenth operative paragraph of the judgment)*

2.   In monitoring overall compliance with the Judgment delivered in the instant case and having analyzed the information provided by the parties and the Commission, the Court will maintain open the procedure for monitoring compliance with those aspects still pending compliance in the instant case, namely:

(a) To investigate, without delay, in a serious and effective manner, the facts that gave rise to the violations declared in the judgment, in order to prosecute and, as appropriate, punish those responsible (*eighth operative paragraph of the judgment)*;

(b) To initiate the pertinent disciplinary, administrative or criminal actions under domestic law, against the State authorities who may have committed the facts and obstructed the investigation of them (*ninth operative paragraph of the judgment)*;

(c) To adopt the pertinent measures to amend the Law on Amparo, Habeas Corpus and Constitutionality in Guatemala (*tenth operative paragraph of the judgment)*;

(d) To proceed with the exhumation, identification and return to their next of kin of the remains of those who died during the Dos Erres massacre (*eleventh operative paragraph of the judgment)*;

(e) To implement the training courses on human rights for different State authorities (*twelfth operative paragraph of the judgment)*;

(f) To show the documentary video on the facts of the Massacre of Las Dos Erres Community in a department of the western area in which grave human rights violations occurred during the internal armed conflict and to take whatever action is necessary, according to the terms of paragraph 263 of the Judgment, "so that the video [is] distributed as widely as possible among the victims, the representatives, and the universities in the country, for its promotion and subsequent showing" (*fourteenth operative paragraph of the judgment)*.

(g) To erect a monument (*fifteenth operative paragraph);*

(h) To provide the psychological and medical treatment required by the 155 victims (*sixteenth operative paragraph)*;

(i) To create a webpage to search for children abducted and illegally retained (*seventeenth operative paragraph)*; and

(j) To make the payments established as compensation for non-pecuniary damage in favor of the 21 victims named in twenty-fourth considering paragraph (*eighteenth operative paragraph of the Judgment)*.

2-Feb-2012
Order of the Inter-American Court of Human Rights
Monitoring Compliance with Judgment

HAVING SEEN:

1.   The Judgment on merits, reparations and costs (hereinafter "the Judgment") in this case delivered by the Inter-American Court of Human Rights (hereinafter "the Inter-American Court" or "the Court") on May 2, 2008, in which the Court accepted the acknowledgment of international responsibility made by the Argentine Republic (hereinafter "the State" or "Argentina") and declared that the latter had violated the principle of legality, the right to freedom of thought and expression, and the right to be heard within a reasonable time, to the detriment of Eduardo Kimel. The Inter-American Court considered that the criminal judgment handed down on March 17, 1999, in which Mr. Kimel was sentenced for the crime of libel, did not meet the requirements of legality, necessity and proportionality and, consequently, constituted a restriction incompatible with the American Convention and violated his freedom of expression. In this regard the Court emphasized that the critical opinion expressed by Mr. Kimel in his 1989 book entitled *"La Masacre de San Patricio"* [The St. Patrick's Church Massacre], related to issues of significant public interest, because it referred to the conduct of the judge in charge of the investigation into the 1976 murder of five members of the clergy during the military dictatorship.

2.   The Order of the Court of May 18, 2010, concerning monitoring compliance with the Judgment, in which it declared, *inter alia*, that the State had complied fully with the following obligations:

(a)   To pay the amounts established in th[e] judgment for pecuniary and non-pecuniary damage, and reimbursement of costs and expenses *(sixth operative paragraph of the Judgment);*

(b)   To eliminate the name of Mr. Kimel from the public records in which it appear[ed] with a criminal record in relation to the instant case (*operative paragraph octavo of the Judgment*);

(c)   To make the publications indicated in paragraph 125 of the Judgment *(ninth operative paragraph of the Judgment*), and

(d)   To adapt its domestic law to the American Convention, in order to correct the ambiguity acknowledged by the State, so as to meet the requirements of legal certainty and, consequently, not to impair the exercise of the right to freedom of expression *(eleventh operative paragraph of the Judgment).*

3.   The Order of the Court of November 15, 2010, concerning monitoring compliance with the Judgment, in which it declared that:

(a)   The State ha[d] complied fully with the obligation to organize a public act of acknowledgment of responsibility *(tenth operative paragraph of the Judgment)*; [...]

(b) It w[ould] keep the monitoring proceeding open until the pending obligation in this case ha[d] been complied with; namely, to annul the criminal sentence imposed on Mr. Kimel and all the ensuing consequences *(seventh operative paragraph of the Judgment).* [...]

4.   The notes of the Secretariat of the Court of June 27, 2011, and April 18, 2012, in which, on the instructions of the President of the Court, the State was requested to provide specific information on its position in relation to the request of the representatives that it assume the costs and expenses arising from the appeal for review they had filed in order to comply with the provisions of the seventh operative paragraph of the Judgment, and the representatives were asked to advise the possible amount of the corresponding expenditure.

5.   The briefs of May 2 and September 9, 2011, and February 24 and June 12, 2012, and their annexes, in which the State presented information on compliance with the Judgment, and also referred to the request of the representatives of the victim's family regarding the costs arising from the filing of an appeal for review.

6.   The briefs of June 3 and 21, October 12 and December 20, 2011, and April 4 and 27, 2012, and their annexes, in which the representatives presented their observations on the information provided by the State, as well as the information requested on the alleged costs they incurred by filing the appeal for review in order to ensure compliance with the provisions of the seventh operative paragraph of the Judgment.

7.   The briefs of June 23 and October 25, 2011, and of April 24, 2012, in which the Inter-American Commission on Human Rights (hereinafter "the Inter-American Commission" or "the Commission") presented its observations on the information forwarded by the State and on the briefs of the representatives.

CONSIDERING THAT:

1.   One of the inherent attributes of the jurisdictional functions of the Court is to monitor compliance with its decisions.

2.   Under the provisions of Article 67 of the American Convention on Human Rights (hereinafter "the American Convention" or "the Convention"), the State must comply with the judgments of the Court fully and promptly. Furthermore, Article 68(1) of the American Convention stipulates that "[t]he States Parties to the Convention undertake to comply with the judgment of the Court in any case to which they are parties." To this end, the States must ensure the implementation of the decisions of the Court in its rulings. This obligation to comply with the Court's decisions includes the State's obligation to provide information on the measures taken in that regard. The prompt fulfillment of the State's obligation to inform the

Court on how it is complying with each element ordered by the Court is essential for assessment of the status of compliance with the Judgment as a whole.

3.   The obligation to comply with the decisions in the Court's judgments corresponds to a basic principle of international law, supported by international case law, according to which, States must comply with their international treaty-based obligations in good faith (pacta sunt servanda) and, as this Court has already indicated and as established in Article 27 of the 1969 Vienna Convention on the Law of Treaties, a party may not invoke the provisions of its internal law as justification for its failure to perform a treaty. The treaty-based obligations of the States Parties are binding for all the powers and organs of the State.

4.   The States Parties to the Convention must guarantee compliance with its provisions and their inherent effects (effet utile) within their respective domestic legal systems. This principle is applicable not only with regard to the substantive norms of human rights treaties (that is, those which contain provisions concerning the protected rights), but also with regard to procedural norms, such as those referring to compliance with the decisions of the Court. These obligations must be interpreted and applied so that the protected guarantee is truly practical and effective, bearing in mind the special nature of human rights treaties.

5.   According to the provisions of the Order of the Court of November 15, 2010 (supra Having Seen paragraph 3), the only measure of reparation pending compliance by the State is the one relating to annulling the criminal sentence imposed on Mr. Kimel and any ensuing consequences (seventh operative paragraph the Judgment). This Order placed on record that the State had expressed its willingness to comply with the measure of reparation and informed the Court that it had consulted different State bodies in order to find out the appropriate way to achieve this. According to the State, its domestic organs concluded that an appeal for review of the criminal sentence should be filed, but that the State lacked procedural standing to file the appeal; however, it indicated "its firm intention to submit [...] an amicus curiae to the corresponding court," "in the event that the petitioners decided to file this appeal for review." In addition, in this Order, this Court took into account the intention expressed by the representatives to file the appeal for review in order to expedite compliance with the said reparation, but also recalled that the obligation established in the seventh operative paragraph of the Judgment was an obligation of the State, which may not, for domestic reasons, fail to assume the international responsibility that has been established. In this regard, the Court indicated that it was awaiting information from the representatives and the State concerning the execution and results of the said appeal for review, and asked the latter to provide complete and detailed information "on the measures and actions taken to ensure total and effective compliance with the said measure of reparation."

6.   The State provided a copy of the amicus curiae that the National Human

Rights Secretariat had submitted to the National Criminal Cassation Chamber, which heard the appeal for review filed by the representatives of Mr. Kimel's daughter. Subsequently, it presented a copy of the judgment deciding this appeal for review, which was delivered by the Third Chamber of the National Criminal Cassation Chamber on November 10, 2011, and asked the Court to "consider that the seventh operative paragraph of the Judgment had been complied with [...] and [... to] order the closure of the case because it [had been] complied with fully." Regarding the request of the representatives that the State assume the expenses and costs arising from the appeal for review they had filed, Argentina indicated that "it had no objections in this regard and [...] awaited the decision adopted by the Court [...]." When referring to the amount requested by the representatives for expenses arising from the processing of this appeal, Argentina asked the Court to "determine the [said expenses] based on equity and the criteria [...] set out [in its brief]." These criteria referred to the way in which the representatives calculated the costs and expenses, the laws regulating the way in which this calculation should have been made, the amount requested by the representatives during the processing of the case before the Court, and that the amount awarded by this Court in the Judgment for costs and expenses included "the future expenses that Mr. Kimel might incur at the domestic level or during monitoring compliance with [the] Judgment."

7.   The representatives affirmed that, "in view of the obstacles described by the Argentine State" to compliance with this pending obligation, "the conditions should have been established to make [the said] compliance possible, since a further appeal had to be filed." They provided a copy of the appeal for review filed on November 15, 2010, "against the judgment handed down in the case of 'Kimel, Eduardo Gabriel ref./libel'" before the National Criminal Cassation Chamber and, on June 3, 2011, before the Court, asked that Argentina pay the expenses and costs arising from this proceeding. After the State had indicated that it had no objections with regard to the representatives' request (supra considering paragraph 6), they asked the Court to "consider that the Argentine State had indicated its decision" and to "establish an amount" in equity. When the Third Chamber of the National Criminal Cassation Chamber had delivered judgment deciding the appeal for review, the representatives reiterated the said request to the Court and also expressed their "concern" because the Chamber had "refuted that the appeal for review was admissible based on the existence of the judgment of the [Inter-American] Court," and annulled the sentence convicting Mr. Kimel based on "a more favorable criminal law which determined that the conduct was not criminalized." Regarding the amount of the costs incurred by the representatives in processing the appeal for review (supra having seen paragraph 4), they mentioned that "the Chamber [...] did not [...] establish costs" and

explained the reasons why, in their opinion, these amounted to US$4,000 (four thousand United States dollars).

8.   The Commission indicated that the State should "pay the expenses incurred by [the representatives] in the judicial processing of the appeal for review." It indicated that "the State failed to take measures ex officio to comply with this aspect of the Judgment and that the mechanism used to try and eliminate the effects of the conviction [placed] an unwarranted burden on the representatives." In addition, it took note of "the State's willingness to cover the costs incurred by the representatives as a result of processing the appeal for review before the National Criminal Cassation Chamber" (supra considering paragraph 4). After it had been informed of the said judgment handed down by the Third Chamber of the National Criminal Cassation Chamber deciding the appeal for review, the Commission indicated that all the measures of reparation ordered by the Court had been fulfilled and stated that, once the representatives had forwarded the information on the costs they incurred, the State should reimburse them.

9.   The Court recalls that, in its Judgment, it ordered the State to annul "every aspect" of the criminal judgment delivered against Mr. Kimel, "including its implications for third parties, namely: (1) the accusation of Mr. Kimel as the author of the offense of libel; (2) the imposition of a suspended sentence to one year's imprisonment, and (3) the sentencing to pay $20,000.00 (twenty thousand Argentine pesos)," which had to be paid within six months of notification of that judgment.

10.   The Court has verified that, because the State considered that domestic law prevented it from taking measures ex officio to annul the judgment convicting Mr. Kimel, the representatives had to file an appeal for review before the National Criminal Cassation Chamber on November 15, 2010. In this appeal, they argued as grounds for its admissibility both "the obligation of the Argentine State to comply with the judgment delivered by the Inter-American Court in this case" and also the "principle of the most favorable law" ("paragraph 5 of article 479 of the National Code of Criminal Procedure"), because "a subsequent law [had been enacted] that decriminalized the act based on which the guilty verdict was handed down." The Court notes that, when filing the said appeal, the representatives asked that "[the court] order that the name of Eduardo Gabriel Kimel be eliminated immediately from any public record in which he appears with a criminal record in relation to this case." On this point, the Court recalls that, in its Order of May 18, 2010 (supra Having Seen paragraph 2), it declared that the State "had complied fully with the eighth operative paragraph of the Judgment"; in this regard, it took into account both the evidence provided and the fact that the representatives had confirmed that "Mr. Kimel's name had, indeed, been eliminated from the public records of individuals with criminal records."

11.   Furthermore, it has been proved that, on November 10, 2011, the Third Chamber of the National Criminal Cassation Chamber delivered judgment ruling on the said appeal for review. In this judgment, it decided:

[...]

(a) To annul the ruling [...] condemning [Mr.] Kimel to a suspended sentence of one year's imprisonment, with costs of both instances, considering him criminally responsible for the offense of libel [...] and, consequently, to acquit [Mr.] Kimel of the act attributed to him;

(b) To annul the ruling condemning [Mr.] Kimel to pay the complainant, Guillermo Federico Rivarola, the sum of twenty thousand pesos ($20.000), as compensation to repair the non-pecuniary damage caused.

12.   Taking into account that the said judicial decision of November 10, 2011, decided to annul the judgment against Mr. Kimel, with regard to both the attribution of criminal responsibility and the payment of civil compensation for non-pecuniary damage, and also taking into consideration the observations of the parties and of the Commission, the Court finds that the State has complied with the measure of reparation established in the seventh operative paragraph of the Judgment.

13.   Nevertheless, the Court notes that, although this was an obligation that the State should have fulfilled, the latter did not comply *ex officio* with the measures of reparation ordered in the seventh operative paragraph of the Judgment, but rather the representatives had to file an appeal for review at the domestic level in order to obtain the annulment of the criminal judgment against Mr. Kimel.

14.   Regarding the costs requested by the representatives because they had to file the said judicial remedy, the Court does not find it appropriate to establish an additional amount for this concept at the actual stage of monitoring compliance with judgment. The additional costs and expenses incurred by the representatives owing to the filing and processing of the said remedy can be claimed in the domestic sphere, in keeping with the pertinent national procedures under domestic law.

THEREFORE:

THE INTER-AMERICAN COURT OF HUMAN RIGHTS,

in exercise of its attributes for monitoring compliance with its decisions under Articles 33, 62(1), 62(3), 65, 67 and 68(1) of the American Convention on Human Rights, 24 and 30 of its Statute, and 31 and 69 of its Rules of Procedure,

DECLARES THAT:

1.   The State has complied fully with the obligation to annul the criminal conviction imposed on Mr. Kimel and all its consequence (seventh operative paragraph of the Judgment), as indicated in the ninth and thirteenth considering paragraphs of this Order.

AND DECIDES:

1.   To close the case of Kimel, because the Argentine Republic has complied fully with the provisions of the Judgment delivered by the Inter-American Court of Human Rights on May 2, 2008.

2.   To archive the file of this case.

3.   To communicate this Order to the General Assembly of the Organization of American States, by means of the 2013 Annual Report of the Inter-American Court of Human Rights.

4.   That the Secretariat of the Inter-American Court of Human Rights notify this Order to the Argentine Republic, the representatives of the victim's next of kin, and the Inter- American Commission on Human Rights.

Monitoring Compliance with Judgment in the Case of Cepeda Vargas v. Colombia
30-Nov-2011
Order of the Inter-American Court of Human Rights

HAVING SEEN:

1.   The Judgment on the preliminary objections, merits and reparations (hereinafter, the "Judgment") delivered by the Inter-American Court of Human Rights (hereinafter, the "Court", "the Inter-American Court" or the "Tribunal") on May 26, 2010, whereby it was decided, *inter alia*, that the State should:

> 8. [...] conduct the domestic investigations that are underway effectively and, if applicable, those opened in future to identify, prosecute and, when applicable, punish all those responsible for the extrajudicial execution of Senator Manuel Cepeda Vargas, in the terms of paragraphs 214 to 217 of [the] judgment.
>
> 9. [...] adopt all necessary measures to guarantee the safety of the next-of-kin of Senator Manuel Cepeda Vargas and to prevent them having to move or to leave the country again as a result of threats, or acts of harassment or persecution against them following notification of [the] judgment, in the terms of paragraph 218 of [the] judgment.
>
> 10. [...] publish, once, in the official gazette and in another national newspaper, paragraphs 1 to 5, 13 to 23, 71 to 73, 85 to 87, 88, 100 to 102, 103, 114, 115, 122 to 126, 167, 175 to 177, 179, 180, 181, 194 to 196, 201, 202, 204, 209, 210, 216 to 218, 220, 223, 228, 233 and 235 of [the] judgment, including the headings of each chapter and of the respective section – without

the corresponding footnotes – and the operative paragraphs hereof. In addition, this judgment must be published integrally, for at least one year, on an appropriate official web page of the State, in the terms of paragraph 220 of the judgment.

11. [...] organize a public act of acknowledgement of international responsibility for the facts of [the] case, in the terms of paragraphs 223 to 225 of [the] judgment.

12. [...] prepare a publication and make an audio-visual documentary on the political life, journalism career and political role of Senator Manuel Cepeda Vargas, in coordination with the next-of-kin, and disseminate it, in the terms of paragraphs 228 and 229 of [the] judgment.

13. [...] award a one-time grant bearing the name of Manuel Cepeda Vargas, in the terms of paragraph 233 of [the] judgment.

14. [...] provide the medical and psychological treatment that the victims require, in the terms of paragraph 234 of [the] judgment.

15. [...] pay the amounts established in paragraph 247 [t]hereof, as compensation
for pecuniary damage [...].

16. [...] pay the amounts established in paragraphs 251, 253 and 259 [t]hereof, as
compensation for non-pecuniary damage, and reimbursement of costs and expenses [...].

17. Within one year of notification of the judgment, and in order to monitor the
judgment, the State must submit a report to the Court on the measures it has adopted [...].

(A) On the duty to conduct the domestic investigations that are underway effectively and, if applicable, those opened in future to identify, prosecute and, when applicable, punish all those responsible for the extrajudicial execution of Senator Manuel Cepeda Vargas (*operative paragraph eight of the Judgment*)

7.   The State made reference to several investigation procedures: it reiterated that, by the time the Court delivered the Judgment, the State was already aware of the fact that on October 14, 2009, a former Director of the DAS (Security Administrative Department) was implicated in the proceeding by means of an inquiry and in addition, on May 17, 2011, he was sentenced to preventive detention without the benefit of being released on bail for his

alleged participation as instigator of the crime of murder. It also recalled what it informed before the delivery of the Judgment, as to the fact that on April 13, 2010, the investigation in favor of Edilson Jimenez Ramirez, a.k.a. "El Ñato", was precluded given that his death was proven. Moreover, the State informed that on May 3, 2010, the implication of another person in the proceeding was ordered, to whom one of the weapons used in the crime was allocated and on August 24, 2010, that person was sentenced to preventive detention. Likewise, the State informed that "[...] the Solicitor General's Office had ordered several proceedings in order to shed light on the existence of a "plan" intended to systematically murder the members of the UP, including Manuel Cepeda Vargas, as well as the alleged participation or conspiracy of civil and military authorities or state intelligence services."

8.   The representatives indicated that they positively valued the decision made by the Solicitor General by which a high-ranking civil authority was implicated in the proceeding as alleged perpetrator of the murder of Senator Cepeda Vargas. However, they considered "the progress made to be insufficient" and that the investigation procedures of the State are not guided by the criteria established by the Court in the Judgment. In this respect, they indicated that "the State has not adequately investigated the participation of all the perpetrators and instigators [;] that there are obstacles to question the commanders of paramilitary groups who were extradited to the United States of America; [that] no investigation was conducted to shed light on the existence of a "coup de grâce plan" and finally [that] the State officials, who are currently being investigated, enjoy benefits during their detention. They asserted, regarding the investigation into the "coup de grâce plan", that "the State has made no effort to shed light on the existence, the perpetrators, the purpose of the Plan [...] or the patterns of violence against the UP; it has neither identified the persons who are members of the so-called 'group of the six or the eight" [grupo de los seis o de los ocho]. They also sustained that there is "no body of evidence" related to other cases concerning the process of extermination of the Patriotic Union, or a more immediate manner regarding other crimes possibly concerning the execution of the Plan, like the murder of Miller Chacón, the attack against the President of the UP, Aida Abella and the threats against other UP leaders".

9.   Regarding the investigation into State officials, the representatives indicated that "there were no investigations underway to verify the chain of command of the two military officers who were convicted of the murder of Senator Cepeda". They also mentioned that it was "worrying that [one of the high-ranking civil authority, who was found responsible and accused] is not detained in a common prison, but in a special penitentiary attached to the Armed Forces, that is, the Escuela de Comunicaciones de Facatativá (Cundinarmarca)".

Following this line of thought, they stated that they did not intend to question the need to separate in the prison, for security reasons, public officials from the rest of inmates, but that "said detention must be served in special blocks of common prisons, as established by criminal law".

10.   Apart from the foregoing, as to the investigation into paramilitary officers, the representatives noted that "the perpetrators and instigators have not been fully identified and that, despite some of them were identified, their situations have not been defined in the specific case". They mentioned that the information gathered in the criminal proceeding contains valuable indicia about the responsibility of paramilitary officers who had not confessed to their participation in the facts and, especially, that the 26th Office of the Special Public Prosecutor for International Humanitarian Law had not included any paramilitary officer in the investigation. They also emphasized that "[…] in the instant case, there is a statement of the extradited paramilitary leader, Diego Fernando Murillo Bejarano, alias "*Don Berna*", rendered on September 17, 2009, in New York and that [...] his extradition objectively hinders the possibility of obtaining information from him, in order for him to elaborate upon the information related to the murder of Senator Cepeda." Regarding the extraditions, they alleged that "it is up to the Colombian State to adopt adequate mechanisms and enter into the necessary cooperation agreements in order to guarantee the participation of the victims in the proceedings followed against the paramilitary leaders; however, no progress was made in the cooperation agreements."

11.   The Commission considered the detention of the high-ranking civil authority, allegedly involved in the instant case, to be a positive step. Nevertheless, it noted that "most of the information gathered in relation to the investigations corresponds to proceedings before Judgment". It also argued that, therefore, it was waiting for updated information, "as well as the evidence on this respect." In addition, it requested the Court "to order the State to implement the necessary measures to conduct and finish the investigation promptly and effectively."

12.   In view of what was informed by the State and the observations submitted by the representatives and the Commission, the Court values the efforts made and actions taken by the State to conduct the investigation into the facts of the instant case, *inter alia*, by implicating a high-ranking civil authority and other alleged perpetrators of the facts in the criminal proceeding. However, from the information furnished by the State, it is not possible to determine further progress than what the Court already knew upon the delivery of the Judgment, especially in relation to the lines of investigation to determine the joint action of state agents and members of paramilitary groups; the functioning of mechanism to ensure the appearance or collaboration of extradited persons who could have relevant information and the duly coordination of domestic authorities to ensure the adequate handling of relevant information in all the investigations.

13.   The Court recalls that, in paragraph 216, subparagraph a) to g), 217 and 218 of the Judgment, the Tribunal established the criteria that must be applied in the investigations into the facts of the instant case. In addition, the Tribunal deems that even though the State has taken several actions to detain the alleged responsible, it must make every effort to effectively investigate into the facts that gave rise to the violations declared in the Judgment, since 17 years have elapsed from the occurrence of the facts and there is still partial impunity surrounding the case. In view of the above, the Court recalls the State's duty to make every effort and take all pertinent actions, as soon as possible, to make progress in the corresponding investigations. It is essential that the State present updated, detailed and complete information on the investigations, actions taken and the results thereof.

(B) On the duty to publish, once, in the official gazette and in another national newspaper, the pertinent parts of the judgment, and the duty to publish the entirety of the Judgment, for at least one year, on an appropriate official web page of the State (*operative paragraph ten of the Judgment*).

14.   The State informed that "on July 16, 2010, it published the entire judgment of the Court on the web page of the Ministry of Foreign Affairs and the Presidential Program on Human Rights. Moreover, on July 21, 2010, it published the judgment on the web page of the Public Prosecutor's Office and the Ministry of National Defense." In addition, it mentioned that "the publication of the chapters of the judgment in a national newspaper was made on an additional offspring in [...] El Espectador newspaper, on Sunday November 28, 2010 [...] Lastly, regarding the publication of the chapters of the Judgment of the [..] Court in the official gazette, it mentioned that said chapters were published in the Official Gazette No. 47931 of December 22, 2010, page No.67" and, consequently, it requested to declare full compliance with this measure.

15.   The representatives noted that "the publications made by the Colombian State in the official gazette, in 'El Espectador' newspaper and on four official web pages, comply with the requirements established by the Court in its judgment"; for which they considered that the Court must declare that this measure was complied with.

16.   The Commission valued the information presented by the State, but it noted that "the State has not submitted the annex containing the physical publication; moreover, regarding the electronic publication, it notes that it was not possible to locate it on the web page of the Ministry of Foreign Affairs".

17.   Considering that the State published the pertinent parts of the Judgment in the Official Gazette No. 47.931 of December 22, 2010, page 67; in the 'El

Espectador' national newspaper, on November 28, 2010 and that it published the entire judgment on the web page of the Presidential Program on Human Rights on July 16, 2010; and on the web page of the Ministry of National Defense on July 21, 2010; and given that the representatives expressed their satisfaction about this, the Court concludes that Colombia has fully complied with operative paragraph ten of the Judgment, with the understanding that it will guarantee the adequate publication of the Judgment on the Internet sites.

(C) On the duty to adopt all necessary measures to guarantee the safety of the next-of-kin of Senator Manuel Cepeda Vargas and to prevent them from having to move or leave the country again as a result of threats, or acts of harassment or persecution against them (*operative paragraph nine of the Judgment*).

18.   The State expressed that it agrees with providing the necessary protective measures to guarantee the safety of the next-of-kin of Senator Cepeda Vargas. Moreover, "regarding the situation of Mr. Ivan Cepeda Castro and Claudia Girón [...] it indicated that it [was] providing the necessary protective measures to guarantee their lives and personal integrity within the framework of the precautionary measures requested by the Commission".

19.   In this respect, the representatives informed that "during the last year, Ivan Cepeda has been receiving threats" and they considered that the information contained in the last report was insufficient in order to verify that the actions taken by the State are adequate to guarantee the safety of the next-of-kin. They indicated that "on February 5, 2011, a threat, issued by the paramilitary groups called "Rastrojos Urbanos – Comandos Urbanos and Aguilas Negras—Bloque capital D.C., was sent to the electronic mails of [...] human rights defenders' organizations [...] including that of Ivan Cepeda". The representatives alleged that the perpetrators of the threats had previously issued seven threatening "messages", and that the "authorities had not done a diligent work to individualize and identify the electronic accounts from which they were sent and their perpetrators"; moreover, they indicated that "such lack of investigation results has been acknowledged at different spheres of the National Government, without adopting remedial measures in that respect. Based on the foregoing, they requested the Court to order the State to report on the actions taken to investigate, within a reasonable time, the threats against the next-of-kin of the Senator.

20.   In its observations, the Commission indicated that it does not have updated information regarding the protection provided to Mr. Cepeda Castro, and to Claudia Girón and that, from the information furnished by the State, it does not spring that it is affording protection to all the next-of-kin of Senator Cepeda Vargas; therefore, it requested the Court to order the State to present detailed information in that respect.

21.   Based on the above, this Tribunal urges the State to continue adopting the necessary security measures to guarantee the safety of the next-of-kin of Senator Cepeda Vargas and requests the State to present, in its next report, detailed and complete information in that regard.

(D) On the duty to organize a public act of acknowledgement of international responsibility for the facts of this case (*operative paragraph eleven of the Judgment*)

22.   The State indicated that the public act of acknowledgement of international responsibility was carried out on August 9, 2011, and that the act was honored by the participation of the then Minister of Interior and Justice [...] at the request of the victim's next-of-kin and their representatives. It also informed that "the public act was organized by means of an informal session of the Two Chambers of the Congress [...], to which the [...] Senators of the Republic and [...] Representatives of the Chamber [....] were convened. In turn, the act was honored by the presence of several persons invited by the victims' representatives, such as non-governmental organizations, civil society and representatives of different State institutions, like the Attorney General's Office, the Ministry of Interior and Justice, the Ministry of National Defense, the Presidential Program on Human Rights, the Solicitor General's Office, the Ombudsman and the Judicial branch". The State also indicated that "afterwards, Mr. Iván Cepeda Castro, in his capacity as the victim's son, [had accepted], on behalf of the family, the public apology offered by the Colombian State". Lastly, the State indicated that the representatives pointed out that the "public act was broadcasted live by the national television channel '*Canal Institucional*' and the regional television channels, *Telemedellín* and *Telepacífico*".

23.   In its observations, the representatives and the Commission acknowledged that the public act was carried out on the date mentioned. The representatives agreed that this measure of reparation has been complied with by the Colombian State. The Commission assigned value to the public act and highlighted the public apology offered to the victims by the State's representatives as a fundamental gesture within the spirit of the reparations ordered.

24.   In the Judgment, the Tribunal determined that: a) the public act of acknowledgment of international responsibility must be organized in Colombia; b) during the act reference must be made to the facts relating to the execution of Senator Manuel Cepeda Vargas, committed in the context of generalized violence against members of the UP by act and omission of public officials, and the human rights violations declared in the Judgment; c) insofar as possible, the organization and characteristics of the public ceremony must be decided with the agreement and participation of the victims, if they so wish; d) to create awareness about the consequences of the facts of the instant case, the acknowledgement act or event

should be held in the Congress of the Republic of Colombia, or in a prominent public place, and e) in the presence of members of the two chambers, as well as the highest-ranking State authorities.

25.   In its statement before the Congress of the Republic, the Minister of Interior and Justice sustained that the murder of Senator Manuel Cepeda "[w] as committed by State officials, that is, the State itself together with members of paramilitary groups." It also sustained that "said reprehensible and disgraceful action frustrated the life plan of a public man like the Senator was: a political leader and active member of the Patriotic Union and the Colombian Communist Party," and that "[o]n behalf of the Colombian State, acting in the name of the National Government, and in [his] capacity as Minister of Interior and Justice, [he offered] a public apology for the crime committed against Senator Cepeda Vargas" and expressed "his most sincere condolences to his [next-of-kin]."

26.   Mr. Ivan Cepeda, in his capacity as victim and representative of the next-of[-]kin, mentioned, during the formal act of acknowledgment of responsibility of the State, that "by complying with the judgment of the Inter-American Court [...], the National Government is not only performing its duty to comply with and implement the measures of reparation ordered by the international tribunal in a particular case. It is, at the same time, doing a symbolic act which has, at least, four profound meanings for the Colombian society [...] In the first place, "by officially acknowledging its responsibility in the case of the murder of Senator Manuel Cepeda Vargas, it is doing justice in one of the thousands of facts of genocide committed against the UP" [...] In the second place, [said] act [...] it is defending the historical truth and, in this sense, the dignity [of the next-of-kin] and the dignity of Senator Manuel Cepeda Vargas". In the third place, "the acknowledgment made by the State [...] is an act with profound meaning for the democracy and the commencement of a procedure of political reparation in the case of the Patriotic Union". Lastly, it mentioned that the "official apology offered in the case of Manuel Cepeda Vargas is an act that builds up the hope that Colombia may put an end to the endless armed conflict that is destroying the country".

27.   The Tribunal recognizes and positively values the ceremony of the acknowledgment acts which are a series of actions that contribute to the preservation of the historic memory of the victims of the human rights violations committed in this case and promote the non-repetition of similar acts. The act was carried out in the Congress of the Republic and it was honored by the presence of the then Minister of Interior and Justice, the State authorities and civil society organizations and persons, as well as the next-of-kin. The statements made by the authorities, acting on behalf of the State, allowed the audience to identify, from the oral point of view and graphic as

well, the facts and some of the authorities implicated in the proceeding. Mr. Ivan Cepeda accepted the ceremony on behalf of the next-of-kin. The Court considers that said act for acknowledgment of responsibility adequately satisfies the formalities previously noted (*supra* Considering clause 27) and, therefore, the purpose of the reparation ordered, given that it was organized by a high-ranking State authority; it was broadly disseminated by the television and the press and it made express reference to the victims and facts of the instant case. The Court declares that the State has fully complied with this measure of reparation, in the terms of operative paragraph eleven of the Judgment.

(E) On the duty to prepare a publication and make an audio-visual documentary on the political life, journalism career and political role of Senator Manuel Cepeda Vargas, in coordination with the next-of-kin, and disseminate it (*operative paragraph twelve of the Judgment*)

28.   The State indicated that, in a meeting held with the representatives and Mr. Ivan Cepeda Castro on November 30, 2010, it was agreed that they would send a proposal for the compliance with the measure of reparation, "a commitment that [would have been] reminded by the State by means of electronic mails of February 2, 2011 and March 7, 2011 and official letter of April 5, 2011". The State further alleged that "once the State hears the proposal made by the victims and their representatives, it will proceed to analyze it in order to make progress in the compliance".

29.   The representatives expressed that the first meeting to follow up the compliance with the judgment was in fact held and that, in such meeting, they were informed about the fact that the documentary will be filmed by RTI Producciones and they agreed that the documentary's producers will be Lisandro Duque. They mentioned that "in the next months [they would inform] the [...] Court [on] the progress related to this measure of reparation". The Inter-American Commission valued the information submitted by the State regarding these obligations, as well as the State's will to make progress and comply with these measures.

30.   The Court values the will expressed by the State to comply with this measure of reparation. Based on the information presented by the State and the representatives, the Tribunal is looking forward to receive information on the effective compliance therewith.

(F) On the duty to award a grant bearing the name of Manuel Cepeda Vargas (*operative paragraph thirteen of the Judgment*)

31.   The State indicated that Mr. Ivan Cepeda Castro and his representatives were informed that this measure of reparation "would be implemented by means of an agreement entered into between the Ministry

of Education and ICETEX and that said measure could be enforced as from the second semester of 2011, as long as the representatives inform what may correspond by the end of April 2011 at the latest". It further alleged that this information was reiterated to the representatives by means of electronic mails of February 2, 2011 and March 7, 2011 and official letter of April 5, 2011. It indicated that, on May 25, 2011, the representatives responded and that, as soon as the State is familiar with "the terms of the call, it would take the necessary actions to disseminate it".

32.   The representatives indicated that "the Manuel Cepeda Foundation, together with the Voz newspaper, is defining the terms of the call, which, as agreed, will be broadly disseminated"; all of which was agreed with the State. To that end, they requested the State authorities to publish the terms of the call by means of institutional communications, like web pages, institutional radio and television stations, through which the call may be disseminated".

33.   The Inter-American Commission made no specific reference to this aspect.

34.   The Court values the actions taken by the State in consultation with the representatives to comply with this measure of reparation, according to the terms of paragraph 233 of the Judgment. The Tribunal is looking forward to information on the effective compliance with this measure of reparation.

(G) On the duty to pay the amounts established as compensation for pecuniary and non-pecuniary damage and reimbursement of legal costs and expenses (*operative paragraphs fifteen and sixteen of the Judgment*)

35.   In its report of August 30, 2011, the State pointed out that "compliance with the payment of compensatory amounts, costs and expenses [was] ordered by means of Resolution 6096 of 2010 of the Ministry of National Defense in favor of Claudia Giron Ortiz, Ivan Cepeda Castro, Maria Stella Cepeda Vargas and Maria Cepeda". It further alleged that, taking into account that the heirs of Mrs. Olga Navia Soto had not requested the payment of the compensation that was acknowledged to them, the State will proceed to "enforce paragraph 262 of the Judgment, by depositing the amount in their favor in an account or a deposit certificate in a solvent Colombian banking institute". The State requested the Court to declare that it partially complied with operative paragraphs 15 and 16 of the Judgment.

36.   On this regard, the representatives stated that, by means of Resolutions 6390 and 6096 of November 24 and November 9, 2010, respectively, the State made the payment corresponding to the compensation of pecuniary damage, non-pecuniary damage and reimbursement of legal costs and expenses, according to what was ordered by the Court in paragraphs 247, 251, 253, 259, 260 to 264 of

the Judgment, for which they considered that this measure must be declared to be complied with. The Commission valued the progress made in the payment made in favor of the victims and is waiting for the necessary evidentiary information to issue a ruling in that respect.

37.   According to the foregoing, the Tribunal values the actions taken by the State to comply in full with the terms of paragraphs 247, 251, 257 and 259 of the Judgment. Given that the representatives stated that they considered these measures of reparation to be complied with, the Court declares that Colombia has fully complied with operative paragraphs fifteen and sixteen of the Judgment.

THEREFORE:

THE INTER-AMERICAN COURT OF HUMAN RIGHTS,

by virtue of its authority to monitor compliance with its decisions, according to articles 33, 62.1, 62.3, 65, 67 and 68.1 of the American Convention, 25.1 and 30 of its Statute and 31.2 and 69 of its Rules of Procedure,

DECLARES:

1.   According to the terms of this Order, the State has complied with the following operative paragraphs of the Judgment:

(a) Duty to publish, once, in the official gazette and in another national newspaper, the pertinent parts of the Judgment, as well as the entire Judgment on an appropriate official web page of the State (*operative paragraph ten of the Judgment*);

(b) Duty to organize a public act of acknowledgement of international responsibility for the facts of the case, in the terms of paragraphs 223 to 225 of the judgment. (*operative paragraph eleven of the Judgment*)

(c) Duty to pay the amounts established as compensation for pecuniary and nonpecuniary damage and reimbursement of legal costs and expenses (*operative paragraphs fifteen and sixteen of the Judgment*).

2.   In monitoring overall compliance with the Judgment delivered in the instant case and having analyzed the information provided by the State, the Commission and the representatives, the Court will maintain open the procedure for monitoring compliance with those aspects still pending compliance in the instant case, namely:

(a) Duty to conduct the domestic investigations that are underway effectively and, if applicable, those opened in future to identify, prosecute and, when applicable, punish all those responsible for the extrajudicial execution of Senator Manuel Cepeda Vargas (*operative paragraph eight of the Judgment*);

(b) Duty to adopt all necessary measures to guarantee the safety of the next-of[-]kin of Senator Manuel Cepeda Vargas and to prevent them from having to move or to leave the country again as a result of threats, or acts of harassment or persecution against them following notification of the Judgment (*operative paragraph nine of the Judgment);*

(c) Duty to prepare a publication and make an audio-visual documentary on the political life, journalism career and political role of Senator Manuel Cepeda Vargas, in coordination with the next-of-kin, and disseminate it (*operative paragraph twelve of the Judgment*)

(d) Duty to award a grant bearing the name of Manuel Cepeda Vargas (*operative paragraph thirteen of the Judgment*) and

(e) Duty to provide the medical and psychological treatment that the victims require (*operative paragraph fourteen of the Judgment*).

Monitoring Compliance with Judgment in the Case of La Rochela v. Colombia
16-Aug-2010
Order of the Inter-American Court of Human Rights

THE INTER-AMERICAN COURT OF HUMAN RIGHTS,
in exercising its power to monitor compliance with its own decisions, pursuant to Articles 33, 62(1), 62(3), 65, 67 and 68(1) of the American Convention on Human Rights, 25(1) and 30 of its Statute and 31 and 69 of its Rules of Procedure,[37 174]
DECLARES THAT:
1. The State has fully complied with the obligations to:
    (a) Modify the text and relocate the commemorative plaque that was at the Office of the Prosecutor General (*operative paragraph eight and paragraph 277(I)(3) of the Judgment*),
    (b) Issue a publication on the facts of La Rochela Massacre (*operative paragraph eight and paragraph 277(I)7 of the Judgment),*
    (c) Request the Superior Council of the Judicature that the Courthouse of the municipality of San Gil be given a name that evokes the memory of the victims (*operative paragraph eight and paragraph 277(I)(8) of the Judgment*),
    (d) Publish in a widely circulated national newspaper, a "summary of the key elements in the instant case" (*operative paragraph eight and paragraph 277(II)(1) of the Judgment),*
    (e) Refer the Court's Judgment to the National Reparations and Reconciliation Commission (*operative paragraph eight and paragraph 277(II)(2) of the Judgment)*; and,
    (f) Implement training programs on human rights for the Colombian Armed Forces (*operative paragraph twelve of the Judgment).*
2. The State has partially complied with the obligations to:

(a) Install a commemorative plaque and a photographic gallery of the victims in a visible place at the Courthouse of San Gil Municipality, Santander department (*operative paragraph eight and paragraph 277(I) (1) of the Judgment);* and,

(b) To pay the compensation and reimburse the costs and expenses (*operative paragraph thirteen of the Judgment).*

3.   The State has been complying with and must continue implementing the following reparation measures:

(a) As a "best effort obligation", it "shall continue providing educational assistance (scholarships) for the victims' next of kin for state or private, secondary, technical and higher education institutions in Colombia" (*operative paragraph eight and paragraph 277(III)(1) of the Judgment)*; and,

(b) The Colombian Prosecutor's Office shall continue offering job vacancies for the victims and their next of kin, "insomuch as they meet the standards required to occupy the positions" (*operative paragraph eight and paragraph 277(III)(2) of the Judgment).*

4.   The State, the representatives and the Commission have reported on the measures adopted to comply with the obligation to provide the medical and psychological treatment needed by the next of kin of the deceased victims, as well as surviving victim Arturo Salgado Garzón and his next of kin (*operative paragraph eleven of the Judgment*), which shall be assessed by the Tribunal in a subsequent Order.

5.   It will keep the procedure to monitor compliance with the following outstanding obligations open, namely:

(a) To install a commemorative plaque and a photographic gallery of the victims in a visible place at the Courthouse of San Gil Municipality, Santander department (*operative paragraph eight and paragraph 277(I) (1) of the Judgment),*

(b) To place a commemorative plaque in Paloquemao judicial complex in the city of Bogotá (*operative paragraph eight and paragraph 277(I)(2) of the Judgment),*

(c) To report, in the television program of the judicial branch, on the events of The Rochela Massacre, the State's partial recognition of responsibility and the Judgment (*operative paragraph eight and paragraph 277(I)(4) of the Judgment),*

(d) To establish a diploma course on Human Rights, which will include the study of this case (*operative paragraph eight and paragraph 277(I)(5) of the* Judgment),

(e) To establish a scholarship for a specialization in human rights, which shall be named so as to evoke the memory of the victims (*operative paragraph eight and paragraph 277(I)(6) of the Judgment*),

(f) A "best efforts obligation" to "contin[ue] providing educational assistance (scholarships) for the victims' next-of-kin for state or private, secondary, technical and higher education institutions in Colombia" (*operative paragraph eight and paragraph 277(III)(1) of the Judgment*),

(g) The Office of the Prosecutor General shall continue offering job vacancies to the victims and their next of kin, "insofar as that they meet the standards required to occupy the positions" (*operative paragraph eight and paragraph 277(III)(2) of the Judgment*),

(h) To investigate the facts, identify, prosecute and, if applicable, punish the responsible (*operative paragraph nine of the Judgment*),

(i) To protect the justice officials, witnesses, victims and next-of-kin (*operative paragraph ten of the Judgment*),

(j) To provide the medical and psychological treatment needed by the next-of-kin of the deceased victims, as well as surviving victim Arturo Salgado Garzón and his next-of-kin (*operative paragraph eleven of the Judgment*); and,

(k) To pay the compensation and reimburse the costs and expenses (*operative paragraph thirteen of the Judgment*).

8-Feb-2012
Order of the Inter-American Court of Human Rights
Monitoring Compliance with the Measures of Reparation Concerning the Medical and Psychological Attention Ordered in Nine Colombian Cases[1][175]
Notice of a Private Hearing

HAVING SEEN:
1.   The order issued by the Inter-American Court of Human Rights (hereinafter "the Inter-American Court" or "the Court") on April 29, 2010, giving notice of a hearing in the context of monitoring compliance with the measures of reparation concerning the medical and psychological attention ordered in the cases of the 19 Tradesmen, the Mapiripán Massacre, Gutiérrez Soler, the Pueblo Bello Massacre, the La Rochela Massacre, the Ituango Massacres, Escué Zapata, and Valle Jaramillo, all with regard to the Republic of Colombia (hereinafter "the State" or "Colombia").

2.   The private hearing held by the Court on May 19, 2010, in the above-mentioned cases (*supra* Having Seen paragraph 1), during which the State, the representatives of the victims (hereinafter "the representatives") and the Inter-

American Commission on Human Rights (hereinafter "the Inter-American Commission" or "the Commission") referred to the status of compliance with the measures of reparation concerning medical and psychological attention ordered by the Court in each case.

3.   The briefs of June 28, and July 2 and 26, 2010, in which the representatives of the victims forwarded information on compliance with the measures of reparation in the said cases (*supra* Having Seen paragraph 1), and also on the proposed "Integral health care reparation program (medical and psychological treatment) from a psychosocial perspective, in the context of compliance with the judgments" delivered in these cases.

4.   The brief of July 2, 2010, in which the State forwarded a report with diverse observations and "proposals" designed "to advance the commencement of the medical and psychological attention for the beneficiaries" in the above-mentioned cases.

5.   The brief of April 26, 2011, in which the State provided information on compliance with the measure of reparation and forwarded a "memorandum of understanding" in which the parties "acknowledged and assumed compliance with the measure of reparation" and agreed on a "coordination mechanism."

6.   The brief of August 22, 2011, in which the State presented a report on compliance with the measure of reparation concerning medical and psychological treatment and submitted the document entitled "Proposed initial method of attention to the victims."

7.   The communications of May 6 and August 16, 2011, forwarded by Deycci Marcela Salgado Bolaños, daughter of Arturo Salgado Garzón, victim in the case of the *La Rochela Massacre v. Colombia*, in which she asked for the "support" of the Court in view of the "complex" health situation of her father and "the serious health conditions" of her aunt, María Sara Salgado.

8.   The briefs of July 8 and October 3, 2011, in which the representatives presented observations on the State's report on compliance with the measure of reparation on medical and psychological attention in the nine Colombian cases (*supra* having seen paragraphs 5 and 6).

9.   The briefs of August 16, 2010, June 22, 2011, and January 26, 2012, in which the Commission presented its observations on the State's report on medical and psychological attention in the nine Colombian cases.

CONSIDERING THAT:

I. Implementation of the measure of reparation in 2010

1.   The private hearing on monitoring compliance held in relation to this measure of reparation (*supra* having seen paragraph 2) concluded with the commitment of the parties to initiate a "process of *rapprochement*" and to present a "timetable for actions as well as substantive proposals" to settle the disputes that existed at that time.

2.   On July 2, 2010, the representatives referred to the "proposal for implementation of the measures of reparation concerning medical and psychological attention" that they had forwarded to the State, and advised the Court that, "although they had delivered [...] [this] proposed memorandum of understanding," they had not received "any observation or response."

3.   On July 2, 2010, the State submitted to the Court a brief with "considerations" and "proposals [...] aimed at initiating the provision of the service." In this document, the State indicated that:

(a) "Despite the State's willingness to comply fully with the measure of reparation," several obstacles to its implementation had arisen, above all:

   (i) "its innovative nature," and

   (ii) the institutional adjustments required to comply fully with the criteria established by the Court";

(b) The Ministries of Social Protection and of Foreign Affairs had been working to elaborate the "most appropriate methodological path" to implement the measure of reparation; however, various "concerns" had arisen following the final diagnostic reports presented by the non-governmental organizations. These concerns reflected aspects that made it difficult "to comply with the measure" and which, in the State's opinion, "go beyond" its obligation "in the context of complying with what the Court ordered";

(c) Regarding the comments made by the representatives during the private hearing held on May 19, 2010, it indicated that:

   (i) the signature of the contract with CAPRECOM cannot be interpreted as "a way of delaying the start of the treatment stage";

   (ii) regarding the "supposed limitation of the attention to the beneficiaries identified in the judgments," it indicated that, in compliance with the Court's rulings in the cases of the Mapiripán Massacre and the Pueblo Bello Massacre, it had included in the budget of the contract signed with CAPRECOM "resources that ensure the medical and psychological care of the beneficiaries to the extent that they are identified, and

   (iii) it has not disregarded the diagnoses made during the first stage of coordination," because "most" of the recommendations are reflected in the contract signed with CAPRECOM.

(d) It reiterated its "willingness and capacity" to initiate the treatment of the beneficiaries of the measure of reparation "by means of the interadministrative contract signed by the Ministry of Social Protection and the health care company, CAPRECOM." In addition, the State advised its intention of "reaching agreement on and coordinating" with the representatives a "mechanism to monitor the health care stage within the framework of [that] contract." To this end, it proposed "to request the support of the Pan-American Health Organization." Lastly, it urged the elaboration of a "simple informative manual" that included "the basic elements" that the beneficiaries, the authorities, and the health care providers should take into account, as well as the holding of "periodical evaluation meetings to identify problems" in the provision of the service.

5.   On July 26, 2010, the representatives forwarded their proposed "Integral health care reparation program (medical and psychological treatment) from a psychosocial perspective, in the context of compliance with the judgments of the Inter-American Court in eight Colombian cases" (*supra* Having Seen paragraph 3). In this regard, they indicated that:

(a) The State had "ignored the agreements and understandings on the way in which the required treatment should be provided [...] based on the assessments [...] that had been made," taking into account that the obligation to make reparation implies "ensuring a treatment that is able to act on the harm," and not merely providing "access to affiliation" in the health care system, which, far from being a reparation, constitutes a "State obligation";

(b) The State had not indicated how the reparation mechanism possesses "the integral dimensions required by the measure ordered" and maintained that the treatment must be implemented with a "psychosocial approach," which it explained "substantially and operationally" throughout its proposal;

(c) The State had disregarded "the consent of and coordination with the beneficiaries of the measure" and "the results of the initial assessment," and this had resulted in "a process of re-victimization that annuls the usefulness of the measure of reparation," and

(d) The State must provide attention that is: (i) preferential; (ii) free of charge; (iii) complete, and (iv) integral.

II. The coordination process during 2011

6.   The State indicated that, on December 9, 2010, the parties had agreed "to establish a committee in which, together, they [would] prepare a timetable of work following the signature of a memorandum of understanding [...] with the central objective of making progress towards complying with the measure." On that occasion, the victims were advised that the above-mentioned contract with CAPRECOM was no longer valid.

7.   On March 15, 2011, a "memorandum of understanding [was signed by the State and the representatives], by the representatives of the victims, the Director of the Human Rights and International Humanitarian Law Directorate of the Ministry of Foreign Affairs, and the Head of the International Relations and Cooperation Office of the Ministry of Social Protection" (*supra* Having Seen paragraph 5). Among other matters, the memorandum affirms that:

(a) The measure of reparation would be composed of two stages:
   (i) assessment and diagnosis, and
   (ii) treatment;
(b) "The implementation of the treatment stage would be defined by the parties [...] based on the framework of the General Social Security System for Health Care," in keeping with the criteria established by the Court, namely:
   "(i) priority;
   (ii) preferential;
   (iii) integral;
   (iv) cost-free;
   (v) prior informed consent;
   (vi) through specialized institutions;
   (vii) with the provisions of any medication required, and
   (viii) for the time necessary";
(c) Until the treatment stage is implemented, urgent cases would be attended as a priority;
(d) A "coordination committee" would be established in order to reach agreement on "the program to attend and treat the victims [of the eight cases], based on the proposal presented by the representatives." This committee would be composed of representatives of the State, [4][176] the victims, [5][177] and the representatives of the victims. [6][178] The committee's mandate "would be exercised for an initial period of two months," during which the parties would "define the program of attention and treatment of the victims and a timetable for its implementation," to be sent to the Court "within two months, at the most, of the date of signature of the memorandum."

8.   On April 26, 2011, the State submitted a document entitled "Memorandum of understanding concerning compliance with the judgments of the Inter-American Court of Human Rights. Measure of medical and psychological attention" and another document entitled "Road map for attention to victims," in which it indicated the proposals for the State's implementation of the measures (*supra* Having Seen paragraph 5).

9.   On June 22, 2011, the Commission indicated that the State had "failed to explain to what extent [...] the recommendations of the assessment reports prepared [by the non-governmental organizations] would be applied at the treatment stage." Similarly, the Commission stated that the State had not referred to "the differentiated impact on the beneficiaries of the measure compared to the other users of the social security" system, or the "path to follow for urgent cases." Lastly, the Commission recalled that "the principle that should guide implementation [...] of reparations

is effectiveness," and that the State should not confuse "the provision of social services that it provides to the individual, with the reparations to which the victims of human rights violations have a right."

10.　　On July 11, 2011, the representatives indicated that the State "had again failed to comply with the agreements" regarding the meetings established, as well as the substantive agreements signed by the parties during previous meetings. On this last point, they considered that "the document entitled 'Road map for attention' did not respond to the previously agreed criteria," because "it is not a special urgency mechanism for victims of human rights violations," and "its contents reproduce, [or] at most summarize, the same procedure of individual insurance coverage and access to health care services established for all Colombians under the General Social Security System." The representatives maintained that "the major obstacle [to the implementation of the measure of reparation] relates to the reluctance and inexperience of the officials responsible for preparing the proposal" and they called attention to the effect of re-victimization that "the State's numerous and unjustifiable delays over the course of [...] six years" have caused to the victims.

11.　　On August 22, 2011, the State described the progress made in the implementation of the coordination process following the declarations of "disagreement [...] [by] the representatives," owing to the "supposed non-compliance of the Ministry of Social Protection with what was agreed in [... the] memorandum [of understanding]." In this context, the State forwarded "a new proposal for the road map for attending priority cases, and also those that can be included in group with addictions." In the proposal, the State specified that:

(a) The road map for attention seeks "to ensure that the victims can access the Colombian General Social Security System for Health Care." In this regard, they will have access to the provisions of health services through "an insurance plan";

(b) The "general elements" of the proposal are:

(i) to provide "coverage to all the victims";

(ii) to ensure free choice of the Health Care Enterprise (hereinafter "EPS");

(iii) to equalize the benefit plans of the beneficiaries who have a subsidized regime [for those who are unable to pay] to those who are affiliated to the contributive regime. Regarding the services that are not included in the compulsory health plan of the contributive regime (hereinafter "POS-C"), "they will be covered by a process of insuring them with each EPS";

(iv) "the beneficiaries of the Court's judgments" will be exempt from payment of the financial contribution known as the "moderating quota" when they use the health care services they require, in accordance with domestic law. Likewise, they will be exempt from paying "co-payments," understood as the "financial contribution corresponding to part of the cost of the service required";

(v) the victims who are part of the contributive regime must continue "making their regular contributions to the health system";

(vi) "identification of each EPS that will be given a program of preferential attention for beneficiaries of the judgments of the Court";

(vii) creation of a working team by the Ministry of Social Protection "to train the beneficiaries in the use of the system," to supervise and evaluate the provision of the services, and "to design and measure attention, satisfaction and quality indicators";

(c) The "prior actions" will be:

(i) the precise identification of "the beneficiaries of the nine judgments," in order "to carry out a validation with the Affiliates' Database (hereinafter "BDUA") in order to detect the population that needs to be affiliated," to identify the beneficiaries as "users belonging to 'preferential groups'" and to train the EPS in attending to this type of groups;

(ii) insurance coverage according to the situation of "not affiliated," "affiliated to the subsidized regime," "affiliated to the contributive regime," or "affiliated to a special regime," as well as the "harmonization [with the] contributive benefits plan for those who are affiliated to the subsidized regime";

(d) In order to "use the health care services," the beneficiary must "request [...] an appointment" and come to the Health Care Institution (hereinafter "IPS") for "an initial general examination." If the beneficiary should require, "the provision of more complex health care services, he or she must be referred [...] to the institutions of second and/or third level of care";

(e) For the "provision of emergency health services," the beneficiary must "go immediately to the nearest IPS" and, following attention, the beneficiary's "affiliation to the system will be verified," and

(f) For treatment of addictions, the beneficiary must "go to the IPS [...] for an initial general examination" and, subsequently, the "EPS [...] will determine a treatment program through specialized institutions."

12.   On October 3, 2011, the representatives of the victims indicated that "it was not pertinent [...] to submit observations" on the State's proposal, because it "had not been approved by the parties and [continues to be] the subject of discussions." They indicated that the State's proposal "does not incorporate

progress in the attention to victims; still contains provisions that increase administrative procedures, [...] and reveals difficulties to ensure access to all the beneficiaries of the measure."

13.   On January 26, 2012, the Commission indicated "its concern" because "once again, the State fails to provide information [...] on the differentiated impact on the beneficiaries of the measure compared to the other users of the social security system," as well as the description "of the road map for urgent cases." The Commission observed that "it cannot be inferred from the information provided that rapid and immediate assistance is being provided to the beneficiaries." In addition, it maintained that "it appears that the prior diagnoses are not being taken into account," and that it is unclear whether "those responsible for the treatment have "the specialization required by each individual, or group of individuals, personally." Lastly, it considered that it would be "desirable" to hold a private hearing in which the "parties present a joint proposal that reflects the needs of the beneficiaries and responds to the concerns of the Court."

III. Notice of a private hearing

14.   At this stage of monitoring compliance with judgment, the President deems it pertinent to convene a private hearing for the Court to receive, as stipulated in Article 69 of its Rules of Procedure, complete and detailed information from the State on compliance with these measures of reparation and to hear the respective observations of the Inter-American Commission and the representatives.

THEREFORE:

THE PRESIDENT OF THE INTER-AMERICAN COURT OF HUMAN RIGHTS,

in exercise of the Court's authority to monitor compliance with its decisions, pursuant to Articles 62(3), 67 and 68(1) of the American Convention, 25(2) of its Statute, and 15(1), 31(2) and 69(3) of its Rules of Procedure, [7179]

DECIDES:

1.   To convene the State of Colombia, the Inter-American Commission on Human Rights and the representatives of the victims and their next of kin, to a private hearing to be held at the seat of the Court on February 23, 2012, from 9 a.m. to 10.30 a.m. during the Court's ninety-fourth regular session, in order to obtain information from the State on compliance with the measures of reparation concerning medical and psychological attention ordered in the nine cases that are the subject of this order, and to hear the respective observations of the Inter-American Commission and the representatives of the victims.

2.   To require the Secretariat to notify this order to the State, the Inter-American Commission, and the representatives.

Monitoring Compliance with Judgment in the Case of Velez Loor v. Panama
13-Feb-2013
Order of the Inter-American Court of Human Rights

HAVING SEEN:
1.   The Judgment on preliminary objections, merits, reparations and costs delivered on November 23, 2010 (hereinafter "the Judgment") by the Inter-American Court of Human Rights (hereinafter "the Inter-American Court" or "the Court"), in which it accepted the partial acknowledgement of responsibility made by the Republic of Panama (hereinafter "the State" or "Panama") and declared the internationally responsibility of the latter for the violation of the rights to personal liberty, judicial guarantees, the principle of legality, and personal integrity of Jesús Tranquilino Vélez Loor, an Ecuadorian national, as well as for failing to undertake an investigation into the alleged acts of torture that were denounced, and for failing to comply with the obligation to ensure, without discrimination, the right of access to justice. The Court determined, *inter alia*, that the detention of an individual for failing to comply with the migratory laws should never have a punitive purpose and that, if detention is necessary and proportionate in a specific case, migrants should be detained in establishments specifically designed to this end that accord with their legal situation, and not in ordinary prisons whose purpose of which is incompatible with the nature of the possible detention of an individual owing to his or her migratory situation, or other places where they may be detained together with persons accused or convicted of criminal offenses.[1] [180] In the Judgment, the Court established that:

> [...]
> 12. The State must pay the amount established in paragraph 264 of th[e] Judgment for specialized medical attention and psychological treatment, as well as for medicines and other future related expenses within six months.
> 13. The State must make the publications ordered, as established in paragraph 266 of th[e] Judgment.
> 14. The State must continue effectively, with the greatest diligence and within a reasonable time, the criminal investigation opened in relation to the facts denounced by Mr. Vélez Loor, in order to determine the corresponding criminal responsibilities and apply, as appropriate, the punishments and other consequences provided for by law, as established in paragraph 270 of th[e] Judgment.
> 15. The State must, within a reasonable time, take the necessary measures to ensure that there are establishments with sufficient

capacity to accommodate those individuals whose detention is necessary and proportionate in the specific case owing to migratory issues, which offer the physical conditions and a regime that is adapted to migrants, staffed by duly trained and qualified civilian personnel, as established in paragraph 272 of th[e] Judgment.

16. The State must implement, within a reasonable time, an education and training program on international standards relating to the human rights of migrants, guarantees of due process of law, and the right to consular assistance for the personnel of the National Immigration and Naturalization Service, as well as for other officials who, owing to their terms of reference, deal with migrants, as established in paragraph 278 of th[e] Judgment.

17. The State must implement, within a reasonable time, training programs on the obligation to open investigations, *ex officio*, whenever a report or a well-founded reason exists to believe that an act of torture has been committed under its jurisdiction, for members of the Public Prosecution Service, the Judiciary, the National Police, and health sector personnel with competence in this type of case and who, owing to their functions, are the first persons called on to attend victims of torture, as established in paragraph 280 of th[e] Judgment.

18. The State must pay the amounts established in paragraphs 304, 307, 314 and 319 of th[e] Judgment, as compensation for pecuniary and non-pecuniary damage and for reimbursement of costs and expenses, as appropriate, within one year of notification of th[e] Judgment, as established in paragraphs 321 to 326 of the Judgment.

[...]

(a) **Obligation to pay Mr. Vélez Loor the amount established for specialized medical attention and psychological treatment, as well as for medicines and other future related expenses (*twelfth operative paragraph of the Judgment*)**

5.   The State advised that it had paid the sum of US$7,500.00 (seven thousand five hundred United States dollars) to Mr. Vélez Loor through the Embassy of Panama in the Republic of Ecuador "for specialized medical attention and psychological treatment, as well as for medicines and other future related expenses."

6.   The representatives confirmed that, on June 10, 2011, the State had delivered a check for US$7,500.00 (seven thousand five hundred United States dollars) to Mr. Vélez Loor, thus complying with the provision established by the Court in its Judgment.

7.   The Commission considered that, based on the information submitted by the parties, this aspect of the Judgment had been fulfilled.

8.   Panama has provided the payment vouchers that prove that, on June 10, 2011, Mr. Vélez Loor received the payment ordered for specialized medical attention and psychological treatment, as well as for medicines and other future related expenses. Consequently, and also based on the conformity expressed by the parties, this Court finds that the twelfth operative paragraph of the Judgment has been complied with. In addition, it assesses positively the State's efforts to comply with the obligation ordered in this aspect of the Judgment within the six months established to this end.

(b) Obligation to make the publications established in the Judgment
(thirteenth operative paragraph of the Judgment)

9.   The State advised that on March 6 and May 16, 2012, respectively, it had published the official summary of the Judgment in the Panamanian national newspaper *"La Estrella,"* as well as in the newspaper *"El Universo"* of Ecuador. It also indicated that the publication of the entire judgment could be found following the link *Caso Vélez Loor vs. Panama. Sentencia de 23 de noviembre de 2010*, in the Human Rights section of the official web page: www.mire.gob.pa. Furthermore, it reported that, on April 17, 2012, the Judgment had been published in Official Gazette No. 27016, with the respective headings and sub-headings, without the footnotes, together with the operative paragraphs, and this can be found on the webpage: www. gacetaoficial.gob.pa.

10.   The representatives indicated that the information available revealed that the State had indeed published the summary of the Judgment in a newspaper with widespread circulation in Panama and another in Ecuador and that, currently, the Judgment delivered in this case was available on an official web page. In addition, the State had published the Judgment of the Court in the Official Gazette of the State of Panama with the respective headings and sub-headings, without the footnotes, together with the operative paragraphs. Therefore, the State had complied with this measure of reparation.

11.   The Commission considered that, based on the information submitted, the State had complied with this measure of reparation.

12.   The information available indicates that the State has complied with the publication of the Judgment in digital Official Gazette No. 27016 of April 17, 2012, [6 181] in the terms established by the Court. Furthermore, copies of the publication

of the official summary of the Judgment made in a newspaper with widespread circulation in Panama and another in Ecuador were provided. The State has also published the entire Judgment on an official web site. [7][182] In the understanding that this last publication will be available for one year as of its publication, the Court finds that the thirteenth operative paragraph of the Judgment has been complied with entirely. In this regard, it assesses positively the efforts made by the State to comply fully with this aspect of the Judgment.

 (c) **Obligation to continue effectively, with the greatest diligence and within a reasonable time, the criminal investigation opened in relation to the facts denounced by Mr. Vélez Loor, in order to determine the corresponding criminal responsibilities and to apply, as appropriate, the punishments and other consequences provided for by law (fourteenth operative paragraph of the Judgment)**

13. The State indicated that, in Hearing No. 272 of August 31, 2010, the Eleventh Circuit Criminal Prosecutor of the First Judicial Circuit of the province of Panama asked the judge of the case to issue an order relinquishing jurisdiction to the Darién Circuit. In response, the Fifth Circuit Criminal Court of the First Judicial Circuit of Panama, in Decision No. 52 of February 8, 2011, disqualified itself from hearing the criminal inquiry and decided to relinquish jurisdiction in favor of the Darien Criminal Judicial Circuit, on the grounds that the incident being heard was committed in the province of Darién, the place where it initiated, without disregarding the fact that the events also continued in the La Joyita Prison. In this regard, the State emphasized that this relinquishment "does not exclude the investigation and prosecution" of the events that occurred subsequently in the La Joyita-Joya Prison, located in the province of Panama, by the Preliminary Investigation Agency and the Combined Circuit Court of the province of Darién. Consequently, on January 24, 2012, the case file with the written proceedings relating to the inquiry for the supposed perpetration of the offense against the liberty of Mr. Vélez Loor was forwarded to the Criminal Circuit Judge of the province of Darién, and was received on February 10, 2012. In addition, the State presented information on the measures taken in the context of the criminal investigation, which included: (a) two site inspections on June 8, 2012, in the offices of the National Border Service; the first in the district of La Palma, and the second in the community of Piedra Candela, Metetí, as well as a third inspection carried out on June 21, 2012, in the former Police headquarters of the community of La Esperanza on June 22, 2012; (b) two sworn statements from residents of the community of La Esperanza of June 22, 2012; (c) request for judicial assistance No. 01/12 of June 2012 to the judicial authorities of the Plurinational State of Bolivia, under the provisions of the Inter-American Convention on Mutual Assistance in Criminal Matters, in order to obtain the

sworn statement of Mr. Vélez Loor. In this regard, it can be inferred that the said request was presented to the Attorney General on June 11, 2012, and that, on July 5, 2012, the International Affairs Secretariat of the Attorney General's office returned the said request for a correction to be made, and (d) on July 18, 2012, the National Directorate of Legal Advisory Services forwarded information relating to the identification of two police agents to the Prosecutor of the province of Darién.

14. The representatives observed that, following the Judgment handed down by the Court, the State "has taken very few actions to comply with the measures ordered." In this regard, they indicated that the disqualification to hear the case by the Fifth Criminal Circuit Judge of the First Judicial Circuit of Panama and the relinquishment in favor of the Darién Judicial Circuit was a matter of concern, because "this procedural measure seriously delayed the investigation," because the disqualification occurred on February 8, 2011, while the case file was only forwarded to the prosecutor of the Darién Judicial Circuit on January 24, 2012, and it was only on February 10, 2012, that it was decided to declare the investigation open. [8][183] Regarding the on-site inspection made in La Palma on June 8, 2012, they considered that it was a useless action that did not provide any relevant information because a previous inspection carried out on May 17, 2010, had the same purpose, and this had been recorded. As regards the on-site inspections made in Metetí and in La Esperanza, they indicated that the investigating authority had merely recorded a general description and taken some photographs. In relation to the two sworn statements obtained by this authority, they considered that, since the statements were made by two individuals chosen at random, they did not provide any substantive information to the investigation. Furthermore, they indicated that Mr. Vélez Loor had not been able to make his initial statement, "a procedural measure that was essential for determining the events denounced," "because the Panamanian authorities had not communicated with him, even though his contact information in Bolivia had been formally provided to the Head of International Affairs of the Panamanian Public Prosecution Service." According to the representatives, there is also no evidence in the case file that the State has taken any measure following the communication of the International Affairs Secretariat of the Attorney General's Office indicating that the request for assistance should be corrected. Regarding the identification of the two police agents, they indicated that the State had not specified where these individuals were, or what other measures it was taking to investigate their possible participation in the events denounced; also, that their statements had not been received and Mr. Vélez Loor had not been asked to identify them. They therefore asked the Court to require the State to provide an account of the measures that were pending and a timetable for implementing them.

15. The Commission indicated that the information provided by the State

was minimum and revealed that no measures had been taken. In addition, it was waiting for the State to "provide an explanation with regard to the representatives' observations on the transfer of jurisdiction to the province of Darién," and that it indicate "whether this transfer meant that the investigations do not include the events denounced by Mr. Vélez Loor during the time he was detained in the La Joya-Joyita prison."

16.   First, the case file provided reveals that, from February 8, 2011, the date on which the Fifth Criminal Circuit Judge relinquished jurisdiction to the Judicial Criminal Circuit of Darién, and June 6, 2012, no investigative measures were taken. However, the waiver of jurisdiction to the Judicial Criminal Circuit of Darién cannot become an obstacle or a mechanism to delay the criminal investigation into the facts denounced. Subsequently, according to the State, on-site inspections were carried out, sworn statements were received, an attempt was made to request judicial assistance from the judicial authorities of the Plurinational State of Bolivia in order to obtain Mr. Vélez Loor's sworn statement, notes were sent out requesting specific documentary evidence, and information was exchanged with regard to the identification of two police agents. In this regard, the Court considers that, although certain investigative activity by the authorities responsible for the investigation can be observed, the truth is that, more than nine years after the State was advised of the alleged acts of torture and ill-treatment, and more than three years after the investigations were initiated, [9][184] the information provided by the State does not reveal significant progress in the criminal investigation.

17.   The Court reiterates to the State that it has an obligation to continue effectively, with greater diligence and within a reasonable time, the criminal investigation initiated into the events reported by Mr. Vélez Loor, which refer to:

  (i)   those that occurred in the context of the detention of Mr. Vélez Loor in the Darién;

  (ii)   those that occurred in the Public Prison in La Palma, and

  (iii) those that occurred in the La Joya-Joyita Prison.

In order to monitor compliance with this obligation, the State must provide information on: (a) the measures taken in order to take the statement of Jesús Tranquilino Vélez Loor in the Plurinational State of Bolivia, and (b) other measures tending to identify the possible authors of the facts and, as appropriate, involve them in the proceedings. Also, it is essential that the State present updated information on any new measures that it has taken to comply with this aspect of the Judgment, as well as a copy of the respective documentation.

  (d) Obligation to adopt, within a reasonable time, the necessary measures to ensure that there are establishments with sufficient capacity to accommodate those individuals whose detention is necessary and proportionate in the particular case owing to migratory issues,

specifically adapted to these purposes, which offer the physical conditions and a regime that is adapted to migrants, staffed by duly trained and qualified civilian personnel (*fifteenth operative paragraph of the Judgment*)

18.   The State advised that there are two shelters on the premises of the National Immigration Service. The men's shelter – consisting of two buildings each one able to accommodate 50 people, and also a building that can lodge 10 people–located in Curundú, and the women's shelter–with the capacity to accommodate 30 people–located at Avenida Cuba/Calle 25 in front of the Fire Station of the Republic of Panama. According to the State, the women's shelter could contain 50 beds, and the men's shelter up to 150 beds. It also explained that, on average, seven people enter the shelters and they remain there for 10 days "if the deportation cycle is completed." Subsequently (*supra* Having Seen paragraph 5), the State advised that the women's shelter has the capacity to accommodate 33 people and that "at the present time, it houses 14 and the most it has lodged is 26 migrants." Meanwhile, regarding the men's shelter, it indicated that "currently, it houses 80 men." In this regard, it indicated that the capacity of the different shelters was sufficient, "because less people are retained that the number stipulated for each shelter." Regarding the length of time spent in the shelters, the State indicated that, if the documents of the person retained are in order, he or she is released immediately; to the contrary, an investigation is carried out and the person's consulate is called so that it may provide the necessary support. The length of stay in this case "was based on 18 days," which is the duration of the procedure from the first day of entry until the day on which the deportation is carried out; measures that are taken on working days. Nevertheless, if the person retained appeals the migratory situation, this period may be longer.

19.   The State also indicated that both shelters offer meals and medical services, and that all the inspectors who guard these shelters are civilians who receive training at the Immigration Academy (newly established) that places an emphasis general knowledge of immigration laws and human rights. This training is provided periodically to the personnel involved in this task, to ensure that the integrity of each foreigner who is retained is not violated. In the case of migrant families, the State indicated that they are not separated; rather a writ is issued so that they remain together. In addition, a Humanitarian Affairs Unit had been created within the National Immigration Service in order to deal with cases of pregnant women and children, so that they can receive immediate assistance and be sent back to their countries of origin. Regarding legal aid, the State explained that migrants who might need assistance can request this from non-profit organizations, the Ombudsman's Office, and the United Nations High

Commissioner for Refugees (UNHCR), among other agencies, and they "work in conjunction with the National Immigration Service." Lastly, the State indicated that the shelters contain telephone directories and posters with information on consulates, organizations, foundations and telephone numbers for each of them, and that this information is provided in Spanish and in English. Furthermore, in the shelters, access can be had to the webpage: http://www.panamatramita.gob.pa/. In addition, visits to the shelters are coordinated with the Consuls, who also provide the information required, and also non-governmental organizations specialized in providing advisory services, as well as agencies of the United Nations with which cooperation agreements have been signed to provide health care to those detained.

20.   The representatives presented the following observations on the State's reports (*supra* Having Seen paragraph 3): (a) it was not possible to infer the average daily occupation of each shelter referred to by the State from the information provided and this figure is essential in order to assess whether the installed capacity is sufficient to accommodate those who are detained, because the State has only provided the average number of entries and the length of the stays when "the deportation cycle is completed," without indicating the numbers for each shelter, or the actual length of stays or the percentage of cases in which the deportation cycle is completed in 10 days. In addition, there appeared to be inconsistencies in the information provided by the State as regards the capacity of the shelters; (b) the State had not provided any probative element that could allow verification of its data, or of the physical conditions that it asserts exist in the shelters; (c) they considered that it was necessary to have more elements than those provided in the State's report in order to assess whether or not an appropriate regime for migrants was observed including, especially, the possibility of not separating the family group based solely on the gender of its members, and the special measures for migrant children; (d) the State had merely indicated that the inspectors receive periodic training, without detailing what this training consists of, whether it is compulsory, how often it is offered, the specific content, the way in which the personnel are chosen and evaluated, and the way in which the State ensures that the training is effective and has an impact on the way in which the said officials perform their work; (e) the State's report refers only to the "inspectors who guard" the shelters, when the training should extend to all the personnel of detention centers for migrants and not only to the guards; (f) of all the information that the Court ordered to be available in the shelters, the State only referred to the consulates, omitting information on legal advisers and organizations that could provide support to the migrants, as well as data on the legal status of those detained. In addition, the State did not indicate how it ensured that this information was visible to those detained, or in which languages it was posted. Based on the foregoing, the representatives considered that the

information provided by the State was insufficient and did not allow a clear and objective assessment of the status of compliance with this measure of reparation. Consequently, they asked the Court to order the State to forward complete and detailed information on the measures adopted to comply with its obligation to ensure that the detention conditions of migrants were appropriate.

21.   The Commission agreed with the representatives that the information provided by the State was insufficient to determine whether these places met the conditions stipulated by the Court in the Judgment; thus, it awaited any supplementary information that the State might present on this aspect.

22.   First, the Court underscores that the information provided by the State refers to the existence of two shelters on the premises of the National Immigration Service in Panama City and their physical conditions, without attaching any documentary support that would allow the Court to assess this, especially in relation to the information that was provided during the proceedings on the merits and assessed in the Judgment (*supra* having seen paragraph 1). Indeed, during the proceedings on the merits, the Court noted that "Panama ha[s] two migratory shelters, which are located in the capital city, so that the persons retained in border areas, whether irregular migrants or individuals seeking international protection, [were] lodged in provincial prisons or police stations until it was possible to transfer them to the shelters of the National Immigration Service in Panama City."[10 185]

23.   The Court recalls that, according to paragraph 272 of the Judgment, this reparation was ordered as a measure to ensure non-repetition of events such as those of the instant case; hence, its purpose is to ensure that "persons deprived of liberty for migratory issues, under no circumstance be taken to prisons or other places where they may be detained together with individuals accused or convicted of criminal offenses." Thus, the Court notes that the information presented by the State indicates that: (i) there are still only two shelters, and (ii) these shelters are only located in Panama City. Consequently, the information provided reveals no difference in this regard from the situation when the Judgment was delivered. In addition, the State has not explained what happens to those who are retained in other areas of the country.

24.   Furthermore, according to the information provided, the Court notes that the men's shelter has been moved, without the State specifying whether the new establishment was built especially for this purpose or, if applicable, whether its facilities were adapted to offer physical conditions and a regime appropriate for migrants. In addition, regarding the State's other assertions concerning the civilian status of the personnel in charge and their training, as well as concerning the information apparently provided on the consulates, the Court reiterates that no proof was provided that would allow it to verify this information.

25.   Based on the above, the Court requests Panama to present the supporting

documentation, as well as information on the situation throughout the country, that substantiates the measures that have been adopted to ensure that there are establishments with sufficient capacity to accommodate those persons whose detention is necessary and proportionate in the specific case for migratory issues, so that no person may be detained because of his or her irregular migratory status together with individuals who are being prosecuted and/or have been convicted for committing criminal offenses.

   (e) Obligation to implement, within a reasonable time, an education and training program on international standards concerning the human rights of migrants, guarantees of due process of law, and the right to consular assistance for the personnel of the National Immigration and Naturalization Service, as well as for other officials who, owing to their terms of reference, deal with migrants (*sixteenth operative paragraph of the Judgment*)

26.   The State advised that the National Immigration Service has a Victims' Attention Unit headed by officials specialized in psychology, whose main functions are to attend "to migrants suspected of being victims of people smuggling and trafficking, humanitarian cases, and exceptional cases." According to the State, this Unit coordinates and directs the Psycho-educational Program, with the support of the Immigration Academy, whose main purpose is to provide on-going training to the officials of the National Immigration Service. Moreover, the main topics discussed in this program are: management of human relations, leadership, emotional intelligence, stress management, personality development, human rights, management of depression, work motivation, teamwork, ethical and moral values, self-esteem, dissemination of the institution's internal regulations, humanitarian cases and victims. The Unit also has a Psycho-diagnosis Program for regular or irregular migrants who are in the custody of the National Immigration Service, which provides free psychological treatment to any retained foreigner who expresses the need to receive this service. In its brief of February 5, 2013 (*supra* Having Seen paragraph 5), the State presented the following additional information: (a) starting in 2012, the National Immigration Service included in its training the "International diploma course on migratory matters"; the three-month course was attended by officials from the different departments of this institution. The State also referred in detail to the content of this diploma course; (b) in 2012, training sessions were offered by the Ombudsman's Office during the "Seminar on the obligations of the Panamanian State towards migrants and the obligation to investigate acts of torture: case of Vélez Loor" and "Human rights and vulnerable groups," and (c) the training diploma on migratory matters will continue to be offered in 2013, and the annual program will include a seminar on the international protection of refugees and human rights.

27.   The representatives indicated that the State had not provided details of the content of the psycho-educational program offered by the Victims' Unit of the National Immigration Service in coordination with the Immigration Academy, or of the training that the State's officials receive at this Academy. They also observed that, at no time had the State provided elements to explain how the information provided is related to compliance with the obligation to implement education and training programs for State officials and that, when it mentions training programs, the information is so succinct that it does not allow verification of whether it relates to the measures ordered by the Court. Consequently, they considered it pertinent that the Court ask the State to provide detailed information on the way in which it was complying with this measure of reparation.

28.   The Commission affirmed that the State had presented information on matters that were unrelated to the measures ordered by the Court. In this regard, it indicated that, for this measure of non-repetition to have the desired impact, the State must tackle the specific issues ordered by the Court and address the officials indicated in the Judgment; furthermore, the training program should have been implemented after the Judgment. Consequently, it was waiting for the State to present specific information on this point.

29.   First, the Court finds that, the information that the State has provided to date on the psycho-educational program does not reveal that it is related to the obligation established by the Court; particularly taking into account its curriculum (*supra* considering paragraph 26). In this regard, the Court reminds Panama that, according to paragraph 278 of the Judgment, the education and training program ordered by the Court must refer to the international standards on the human rights of migrants, the guarantees of due process of law, and the right to consular assistance, and must make special mention of the Judgment and the international human rights instruments to which Panama is a party. Second, the Court notes that, although the State provided information on the training offered to officials of the National Immigration Service, it failed to submit any supporting documentation or detailed information on how many officials had taken part in it, as well as with regard to other officials who, based on their terms of reference, deal with migrants. Consequently, the Court asks the State to present completed, detailed and recent information on the measures taken to comply with this aspect of the Judgment, as well as a copy of the respective supporting documentation.

(f) Obligation to implement, within a reasonable time, training programs on the obligation to open investigations, ex officio, whenever a report or a well-founded reasons exists to believe that an act of torture has been committed under its jurisdiction, for members of the Public Prosecution Service, the Judiciary, the National Police, and health

sector personnel with competence in this type of case and who, owing to their functions are the first persons called on to attend victims of torture (*seventeenth operative paragraph of the Judgment*)

30.   The State advised that the cases of torture would be channeled through the corresponding authorities, clarifying with regard to the Tourism Police responsible for the surveillance, security and orientation of both nationals and foreigners in tourist areas, that they received training on how visitors should be treated and that "most of the time, they only respond to cases related to tourists who have been victims of crime, without any record of acts of torture." In addition, it referred to the signature of "Agreements on inter-institutional arrangements" signed by the Ministry of Health and the Ministry of the Interior and Justice, "in order to take measures designed to ensure respect for human rights, as well as to improve the living conditions and health of those deprived of liberty."

31.   The representatives observed that the State had never provided elements that would allow it to be understood how the information submitted is related to compliance with the State's obligation to implement training and education programs for State officials. In this regard, they considered that, although some of the attachments presented by the State revealed that some official documents mention the existence of training programs for prison system personnel, the information was so concise that "it did not permit establishing whether it referred to the measures ordered by the [...] Court."

32.   The Commission indicated that the State had not presented any information concerning training programs on the specific issue ordered by the Court and, therefore, it awaited this information.

33.   The Court noted that the State has submitted two inter-institutional agreement dated January 24, 2006, and August 25, 2009, signed by the Ministry of the Interior and Justice and the Ministry of Health, which establish agreements to provide health services to persons deprived of liberty, but contain no reference to training programs relating to the obligation to open investigations *ex officio* whenever there is a report or a well-founded reason to believe that an act of torture has been committed under its jurisdiction, for members of the Public Prosecution Service, the Judiciary, the National Police, and personnel from the health sector with competence in this type of case and who, based on their functions, are the first to attend victims of torture. In addition, the Court underlines that these agreements were signed before the delivery of the Judgment (*supra* having seen paragraph 1), so that they do not form part of the measures taken by the State to comply with the reparation ordered in this aspect of the Judgment. It is also pertinent to note that the information provided by the State concerning the training provided to the Tourism Police does not include relevant aspects relating to compliance with this measure of reparation.

34.   Consequently, the Court finds it necessary that the State present complete, detailed and recent information on the measures that have been taken after the delivery of the Court's Judgment to comply with this operative paragraph, as well as a copy of the respective documentation.

(g) Obligation to pay the amounts established as (compensation for pecuniary and non-pecuniary damage and for reimbursement of costs and expenses (*eighteenth operative paragraph of the Judgment*)

35.   The State advised that it had delivered, in a single payment, the amounts established in the Judgment as compensation for pecuniary and non-pecuniary damage and for reimbursement of costs and expenses, as well as the accrued interest for the delay in complying with the payment ordered.

36.   The representatives indicated that it was only on April 3, 2012, that the State, through its Embassy in the Plurinational State of Bolivia, had delivered a check for the sum of US$27,500.00 to Mr. Vélez Loor. Subsequently, and also through its Embassy, on April 26, 2012, the State delivered another check to Mr. Vélez Loor for the sum of US$912.44 for the interest on arrears. Mr. Vélez Loor confirmed that he had received the said amounts. For their part, the representatives confirmed the receipt of the sum of US$24,000.00 for reimbursement of costs and expenses, as well as the interest on arrears amounting to 826.31 balboas.

37.   The Commission observed that the information presented by the parties indicated that the payments for pecuniary and non-pecuniary damage, costs and expenses had been complied with fully.

38.   The Court confirms that, according to the vouchers provided by the State, on March 29 and April 3, 2012, the State delivered to CEJIL and to Mr. Vélez Loor the sums ordered in the Judgment for reimbursement of costs and expenses and for pecuniary and non-pecuniary damage, respectively. In addition, based on the documentation presented by the State, the Court confirms that, on April 26, 2012, Mr. Vélez Loor received the sum owed to him for interest on arrears. Similarly, on April 19, 2012, CEJIL received a payment for interest on arrears.

39.   Based on the foregoing and the conformity expressed by the representatives, the Court finds that the eighteenth operative paragraph of the Judgment has been complied with fully. In addition, it assesses positively the efforts made by the State to comply with the obligation ordered in this aspect of the Judgment.

THEREFORE:

THE INTER-AMERICAN COURT OF HUMAN RIGHTS,

in exercise of its authority to monitor compliance with its decisions and pursuant to Articles 33, 62(1), 62(3) and 68(1) of the American Convention on Human Rights, 24 and 30 of its Statute, and 31(2) and 69 of its Rules of Procedure,

DECLARES THAT:

1.   As indicated in considering paragraphs 5 to 8, 9 to 12 and 35 to 39 of this Order, the State has complied fully with the following operative paragraphs of the Judgment:

   (a) Pay Mr. Vélez Loor the amount established for specialized medical attention and psychological treatment, as well as medicines and other future related expenses (*twelfth operative paragraph of the Judgment*);

   (b) Make the publications ordered in the Judgment (*thirteenth operative paragraph of the Judgment*), and

   (c) Pay the amounts established as compensation for pecuniary and non-pecuniary damage and for reimbursement of costs and expenses (*eighteenth operative paragraph of the Judgment*).

2.   In this proceeding of monitoring full compliance with the Judgment handed down in this case, and having analyzed the information provided by the State, the representatives and the Commission, the Court will keep open the proceeding of monitoring compliance with regard to the pending aspects of this case, namely:

   (a) Continue effectively, with the greatest diligence and within a reasonable time, the criminal investigation opened in relation to the facts denounced by Mr. Vélez Loor, in order to determine the corresponding criminal responsibilities and apply, as appropriate, the punishments and other consequences provided for by law (*fourteenth operative paragraph of the Judgment*);

   (b) Take, within a reasonable time, the necessary measures to ensure that there are establishments with sufficient capacity to accommodate those individuals whose detention is necessary and proportionate in the specific case owing to migratory issues, which offer physical conditions and a regime that is adapted to migrants, staffed by duly trained and qualified civilian personnel (*fifteenth operative paragraph of the Judgment*);

   (c) Implement, within a reasonable time, an education and training program on international standards relating to the human rights of migrants, guarantees of due process of law, and the right to consular assistance for the personnel of the National Immigration and Naturalization Service, as well as for other officials who, owing to their terms of reference, deal with migrants, (*sixteenth operative paragraph of the Judgment),* and

   (d) Implement, within a reasonable time, training programs on the obligation to open investigations, *ex officio,* whenever a report or a well-founded reason exists to believe that an act of torture has been committed under its jurisdiction, for members of the Public Prosecution Service, the Judiciary, the National Police, and health sector personnel with competence in this type of case and who, owing to their functions, are the first persons called on to attend victims of torture (*seventeenth operative paragraph of the Judgment*).

31-Aug-2015
Order of the Inter-American Court of Human Rights

THE INTER-AMERICAN COURT ON HUMAN RIGHTS
In exercising its supervisory attributions of complying with its decisions, in conformity with articles 33, 62.1, 62.3, 65, 67 and 68.1 of the American Convention on Human Rights, 25.1 and 30 of the Charter, and 31 and 69 of its Rules of Procedure,

DECLARES THAT:

1. The State has fully complied with the following methods of reparation:
   (a) posting a commemorative plaque in the Paloquemao judicial square in the City of Bogotá (resolution point 8 and paragrapgh 277.I.2 of the Sentence)
   (b) "obligation" to "continue providing educational help (scholarships) for the relatives of the victims, in secondary, technical, and superior institutions, either public or private, in Colombia" (resolution point * and paragrapgh 277.III.1 of the Sentence);
   (c) establish a certified program in human rights that includes a study of this case (resolution point 8 and paragrapgh 277.I.5 of the Sentence) and
   (d) pay the idemnization and the reimbursments of costs and expenses (resolution point 13 of the Sentence).

2. The State has partially complied with the following
   (a) mounting a commemorative plaque and a photographic gallery of the victims in the Palace of Justice in the Municipality of San Gil, pending the transmission of the act of mounting the plaque and the unveiling of the gallery in the [location] assigned to the Superior Council of the Judiciary, in conformity with the indications in Considering 7 to 9 and 15 to 17 in the present Resolution (resolution point 8 and paragraph 277.I.1 of the Sentence) and
   (b) creating a scholarship for specializing in human rights at the Superior School of Public Administration, pending the denomination of the scholarship with a name that evokes the memories of the victims, in conformity with the indication in Considering 25 of the present Resolution (resolution point 8 and paragraph 277.I.6 of the Sentence).

3. The State has began complying with, and must continue to implement the following reparations:
   (a) continue to deliver labor opportunities to the victims and their relative

in the State's Prosecutor's office, "so long as they meet the necessary requisites to qualify for the positions" (resolution point eight and paragraph 277.III.2 of the Sentence), and

(b) "guarantee that prosecutors, judicial and investigative public servants and other justice operators can count on an adequate system of safety and protection" and "ensure the effective protection of witnesses, victims and relatives of grave human rights violation, particularly and immediately with regards to the investigation of the facts in the current case" (resolution point 10 of the Sentence).

4.   The process of supervision of compliance with the following will remain open:

(a) Create a transmission in a television program in the corresponding jurisdiction about the facts of the case, the partial recognition of responsibility, and the Sentence (resolution point 8 and paragraph 277.I.4 of the Sentence);

(b) Transmit the act through which the commemorative plaque and the photographic gallery of the victims in the Palace of Justice in Municipality of San Gil, Santander, were created, in conformity with what is indicated in Consdering 7 to 9 and 15 to 17 of this present Resolution (resolution point 8 and paragraph 277.I.1 of the Sentence);

(c) Name the scholarship for specializing in human rights with a name that evokes the memories of the victims, in conformity with the indication in Considering 25 of the present Resolution (resolution point 8 and paragraph 277.I.6 of the Sentence).

(d) Continue to deliver labor opportunities to the victims and their relative in the State's Prosecutor's office, "so long as they meet the necessary requisites to qualify for the positions" (resolution point eight and paragraph 277.III.2 of the Sentence), and

(e) investigate the facts, identify and try and, in this case, sanction those responsible (resolution point 9 of the Sentence), and

(f) "guarantee that prosecutors, judicial and investigative public servants and other justice operators can count on an adequate system of safety and protection" and "ensure the effective protection of witnesses, victims and relatives of grave human rights violation, particularly and immediately with regards to the investigation of the facts in the current case" (resolution point 10 of the Sentence).

DECIDES:

1.   To require the State to adopt the necessary measures to effectively and immediately comply with the pending reparation measures that were ordered by the Tribunal in the Sentence, in conformity with the stipulated article 68.1 of the American Conventions.

2.   To ask the State to present, no later than February 1, 2016, a report that contains detailed, current, and precise information about the points that are still pending compliance, providing especially the information requested in detail in Considering 17, 25, 37, 51, and 60 of the present Resolution.

3.   To ask the representatives of the victims and their relatives and the Inter-American Comission on Human Rights to present observations to the State's report, mentioned in the previous paragraph, within four and six weeks, respectively, beginning once the said report is received.

4.   To continue supervising the pending compliance points of the Judgment regarding merits, reparations, and costs of May 11, 2007.

5.   Request that the Secretary of the Court notify the State of Colombia, the representatives of victims and their relatives, and the Inter-American Commission on Human Rights of the present Resolution.

Monitoring Compliance with Judgment in the Case of Rosendo Cantu et al v. Mexico
25-Nov-2010
Order of the Inter-American Court of Human Rights

HAVING SEEN:

1.   The Judgment on Preliminary Objections, Merits, Reparations and Costs, issued on August 31, 2010, (hereinafter "the Judgment") by the Inter-American Court of Human Rights (hereinafter "the Inter-American Court", "the Court" or "the Tribunal "), whereby, *inter alia*, it ordered that:

> 10. The State must conduct in the regular courts, effectively and within a reasonable time period, the investigation and, if appropriate, the criminal proceedings processed in connection with the rape of Mrs. Rosendo Cantú, in order to determine the corresponding criminal liability and, where appropriate, implement penalties and other consequences provided for by the law, in accordance with the provisions of paragraphs 211 to 213 of the [...] Judgment.
>
> [...]
>
> 14. The State must hold a public ceremony to acknowledge international responsibility in relation to the facts of the present case, in accordance with the provisions of paragraph 226 of the [...] Judgment.
>
> 15. The State must make the ordered publications, in accordance with the provisions of paragraph 229 of the [...] Judgment.
>
> [...]

20. The State must grant scholarships for Mexican public institutions to Mrs. Rosendo Cantú and her daughter, Yenys Bernardino Rosendo, as provided for in paragraph 257 of the [...] Judgment.

21. The State must continue to provide treatment to female victims of sexual violence at the Caxitepec health center, which should be strengthened by providing material and personnel resources in accordance with the provisions of paragraph 260 of the [...] Judgment.

[...]

24. The State must pay the amounts set out in paragraphs 274, 279 and 286 of the [...] Judgment, as compensation for pecuniary and non-pecuniary damages, and as reimbursement of costs and expenses, where and when appropriate, within one year following the notification of the [...] Judgment, in accordance with paragraphs 287 to 294 thereof.

2. The note of the Secretariat of the Court (hereinafter "the Secretariat") of October 1, 2010, whereby, following the President of the Court's instructions (hereinafter "the Secretariat"), requested the representatives to "sub[mit] express written consent from Mrs. Rosendo Cantú regarding the publication of specific reparation measures set forth in paragraphs 213, 226, and 229 of the Judgment."

3. The brief of November 1, 2010, of the Organization of the Indigenous People of Tlapaneco/Me'phaa, the Human Rights Center of Mount "Tlachinollan" and the Center for Justice and International Law (all hereinafter "the representatives"), whereby it responded to the Tribunal's request regarding the publication of specific reparation measures set forth in the Judgment.

CONSIDERING:

1.   The Court stated in the Judgment (paragraphs 213, 226 and 229) that if Mrs. Rosendo Cantú were to give consent:

   (a) "the results of the proceedings [internal criminal investigation] [would be] publicly disclosed so that the Mexican society know the true facts;"

   (b) "[the public ceremony to acknowledge international responsibility in relation to the facts of the case would be] broadcast over a radio station with coverage in Guerrero;" and,

   (c) "The State [must]: i) publish the official summary issued by the Court in a nationally circulated newspaper, in Spanish, and in a widely circulated newspaper in the state of Guerrero, in Spanish and Me'paa [...]; ii) publish the entire [...] Judgment [...], together with the Me'paa translation of the official summary, on an appropriate website of the federal state and the state of Guerrero, taking into account the characteristics of the ordered publication, which must be available for at least one year; and, iii) issue the official summary, in both languages —on just one occasion— on a radio station [...] with coverage in Barranca Bejuco."

2.   Regarding Mrs. Rosendo Cantú's consent for the effective implementation of the reparation measures referred to in heading a) and b) in the above paragraph, the representatives stated that the victim explicitly gave her consent for:

    (a) "the public disclosure of the results of the criminal investigations that the State must carry out pursuant to [the Judgment];"

    (b) "the transmission of the public ceremony to acknowledge international responsibility on a radio station with coverage in Guerrero [...] on the understanding that [...] "[t]he State must agree the means of compliance of the public recognition ceremony with [Rosendo Cantú] and/or her representatives, as well as any other details that are required."

3.   The Court takes note of the express consent manifested by Mrs. Rosendo Cantú, and thus the Court believes that Mexico must proceed to effectively comply with these measures, in accordance with the Judgment.

4.   Regarding the publication of the official summary of the Judgment in nationwide print media and in the state of Guerrero, the radio broadcast of the official summary on a radio station with coverage in Barranca Bejuco, and the publication of the Judgment and the official summary in Me'paa on a website belonging to the federal state and on a website belonging to the state of Guerrero, the representatives indicated that Mrs. Rosendo Cantú gives express consent for the implementation of these measures, provided that in such publications, and the radio broadcast, the following parts be excluded: i) the provision of scholarships for her and her children; ii) the provision of treatment for female victims at the Caxitepec health centre; and, iii) payment of the amounts awarded as pecuniary and nonpecuniary damages, and costs and expenses.

5.   Representatives substantiated this condition on the potential increase in risk and uncertainty that could affect Mrs. Rosendo Cantú, as well as her family members and community. Such an increase would occur if "notice were given of the granting of a direct, monetary or any other kind of benefit to the victims or [their] community [...]." They stated that "the collective or communal dimension of certain reparation measures makes it necessary to collectively communicate, evaluate, and discuss such measures within the communities. This process is being carried out [...] and it could be affected by the publication of certain aspects of [the Judgment] and certain reparation measures." Finally, they emphasized that if the Court were to consider that the request cannot be carried out as requested by Mrs. Rosendo Cantú, "the Court should consider that [she] does not [give] her consent for these publications."

6.   In this regard, the Court notes that the consent given by Mrs. Rosendo

Cantú to implement the measures provided for in paragraph 229 of the Judgment was depend[e]nt upon its partial publication, i.e., eliminating information that is unrelated to the aim of the Tribunal's question and not in accordance with the Judgment of the present case. Notwithstanding the foregoing, the Court notes the lack of consent given by Mrs. Rosendo Cantú for the aforementioned publications and, therefore, rules that this process to monitor compliance with the Judgment is considered closed with respect to these reparation measures.

THEREFORE:

THE INTER-AMERICAN COURT OF HUMAN RIGHTS,

in exercising its authority to monitor compliance with its decisions in accordance with Articles 67 and 68(1) of the American Convention on Human Rights, Article 30 of the Statue, and Article 31(1) of its Rules of Procedure,

DECIDES:

1.   In accordance with the provisions of Considering Clauses 2 and 3 of this Order, Mrs. Rosendo Cantú expressly gave consent to the State to carry out the following measures set forth in the Judgment:

(a) Public disclosure of the results of investigations and prosecutions conducted by the State as part of the present case; and,

(b) To broadcast, on a radio station with coverage in Guerrero, the public ceremony acknowledging international responsibility in relation to the facts of the case.

2.   In accordance with the provisions of Considering Clauses 4 and 6 of this Order, Mrs. Rosendo Cantú has not given consent to the State to carry out the following measures set forth in the Judgment:

(a) Publish the official summary—issued by the Court—in Spanish in a nationally circulated newspaper, as well as in a newspaper that is widely circulated in the state of Guerrero in Spanish and Me'paa,

(b) Publish this Sentence in its entirety, together with the Me'paa translation of the official summary, on an appropriate federal State website and an appropriate Guerrero State website, taking into account the characteristics of the ordered publication, which must be made available for at least one year; and,

(c) Issue the official summary, in both languages—on just one occasion—on a radio station with coverage in Barranca Bejuco.

Monitoring Compliance with Judgment in the Case of Radilla Pacheco v. United Mexican States
19-May-2011
Order of the Inter-American Court of Human Rights

HAVING SEEN:

1.   The Judgment on Preliminary Objections, Merits, Reparations and Costs (hereinafter "the Judgment") issued by the Inter-American Court of Human Rights (hereinafter "the Court," "the Inter-American Court" or "the Tribunal") on November 23, 2009, whereby it held that:

> [...]
>
> 8. The State shall effectively carry out, with due diligence and within a reasonable time, the investigation and, if applicable, criminal proceedings with regard to the arrest and subsequent forced disappearance of Mr. Rosendo Radilla Pacheco in order to determine the corresponding criminal responsibilities and effectively apply the punishments and consequences established by law, in accordance with paragraphs 329 through 334 of the [...] Judgment.
>
> 9. The State shall continue with the effective search for and the immediate location of Mr. Rosendo Radilla Pacheco or, if applicable, of his remains, in accordance with paragraphs 335 through 336 of the [...] Judgment.
>
> 10. The State shall adopt, within a reasonable time, appropriate legislative reforms in order to make Article 57 of the Code of Military Justice compatible with international standards on the subject and the American Convention on Human Rights, in accordance with paragraphs 337 through 342 of the [...] Judgment.
>
> 11. The State shall adopt, within a reasonable time, appropriate legislative reforms in order to make Article 215 of the Federal Criminal Code compatible with international standards on the subject and the Inter-American Convention on Forced Disappearance of Persons, in accordance with paragraphs 343 through 344 of the [...] Judgment.
>
> 12. The State shall implement, within a reasonable time and with the corresponding budgetary allocation, programs or permanent courses on the analysis of the jurisprudence of the Inter-American System of Human Rights Protection regarding the limits of military criminal jurisdiction, as well as a training program on the proper investigation and prosecution of acts that constitute forced disappearance of persons, in accordance with paragraphs 345 through 348 of the [...] Judgment.
>
> 13. The State shall publish once in the Official Gazette of the Federation and in another newspaper of ample national

circulation paragraphs 1 through 7, 52 through 66, 114 through 358 of the [...] Judgment and its operative paragraphs, without the footnotes. In addition, the State shall publish this Judgment in its totality on the official website of the Attorney General of the Republic in a six and two-month term, respectively, as of the notification of th[e] Judgment, in accordance with paragraphs 349 through 350 therein.

14. The State shall hold a public act of acknowledgment of responsibility with regard to the facts of the present case and to restore the memory of Mr. Rosendo Radilla Pacheco, in accordance with paragraphs 351 through 354 of the [...] Judgment.

15. The State shall prepare a bibliographical sketch of the life of Mr. Rosendo Radilla Pacheco, in accordance with paragraphs 355 through 356 of the [...] Judgment.

16. The State shall provide free psychological and/or psychiatric attention immediately, adequately, and effectively, through its specialized public health institutions, to the victims declared in the [...] Judgment that request it, in accordance with paragraphs 357 through 358 therein.

17. The State shall pay the amounts awarded in paragraphs 365, 370, 375, and 385 of the [...] Judgment as compensation for pecuniary and non-pecuniary damages, and the reimbursement of costs and expenses, as appropriate, within a one-year as of the date that notice of the [...] Judgment is served, in accordance with paragraphs 360 through 392 therein.

[...]

2.   The communications of April 27, May 12, and December 1, 15, and 29, 2010, as well as the communications of 28 January and 15 February 2011, in which the United Mexican States (hereinafter "the State" or "Mexico") submitted information on its compliance with the Judgment issued by the Court in the present case (*supra* Having Seen 1).

3.   The briefs of December 15, 2010 and March 3, 2011, through which the representatives of the victims (hereinafter "the representatives") submitted their observations on the information submitted by the State (*supra* Having Seen 2).

4.   The communications of February 8, and April 13, 2011, whereby the Inter-American Commission on Human Rights (hereinafter "the Inter-American Commission" or "the Commission") submitted its observations on the information submitted by the State and the representatives (*supra* Having Seen 3).

5.   The communication of December 16, 2010, in which the Human Rights

Committee of the Bar of England and Wales and the Solicitor's International Human Rights Group submitted an *amicus curiae* brief.

CONSIDERING:

A. Obligation to investigate the facts of the case (*Operative Paragraph 8 of the Judgment*)

7.   The State reported on various measures undertaken as of March 22, 2010 in preliminary inquiry SIEDF/CGI/454/2007, which is overseen by the Attorney General's Office and seeks information on what happened to Mr. Rosendo Radilla Pacheco. The State reported that "various meetings [...] were held in order to develop a work plan with the victims' next of kin [...] for the purpose of continuing with investigations[.]" Additionally, the State indicated that "Tita Radilla Martínez's legal representatives [...] have had full access to the investigation['s files] every time they have requested it."

8.   The representatives indicated that "to date, no military or civilian authority with power over the Armed Forces that were active at the time of [Mr.] Radilla [Pacheco]'s disappearance has been called to give a statement." They also affirmed that none of the actions that the Attorney General's Office has carried out "has been directed toward [military and civilian] officials who were employed at the time that [Mr.] Radilla [Pacheco] was detained/disappeared." According to the representatives, the only "relevant [measures] carried out that are vaguely linked to the Armed Forces [are] those related to the excavations at the ex-military barracks in Atoyac de Álvarez, Guerrero State." Additionally, the representatives stated that the Attorney General's Office "has not addressed the last proposals [they] made during the preliminary inquiry," and "the Public Ministry has not taken concrete actions demonstrating that investigations in the case are advancing effectively." Finally, the representatives indicated to the Tribunal that although they have had full access to the preliminary inquiry's files at the Attorney General's Office, they have been denied copies of those files, which "restricts [the] right to participate in the investigation and violates [...] the victims' right to access justice." Additionally, the representatives stated that "they were denied participation" in a ministerial inspection, "which consisted of a search for registries in cemeteries in the area of unknown persons that died in the 70's," since authorization had not been granted to them.

9.   The Inter-American Commission affirmed that it "value[d] the [State's] efforts to reactivate the investigations of the case." However, it observed that "no significant advances had been verified [in those investigations] since the date that the [J]udgment was issued." For that reason, it indicated that "the State should carry out all efforts necessary to act with due diligence and take relevant actions that will lead to effective compliance with these aspects of the Judgment." Finally, the Commission "showe[d] concern over the information submitted by the representatives with respect to the State's refusal to give them copies of the investigations, given that

this situation was evaluated by [the Court] in its [J]udgment, in which it indicated that this [was] incompatible with their right to access justice."

10.   The Court observes that the State undertook measures in the aforementioned preliminary inquiry, which is being carried out by civilian authorities, as ordered in the Judgment. However, from the information presented by the State, it is not possible for the Court to ascertain how the preliminary inquiry complies with the standards set out in the Judgment with respect to the elements that must be considered in the investigation of facts such as those that occurred in this case. [5 186] The Tribunal reminds the parties that in this case, the obligation to investigate entails not only the duty to search for Mr. Radilla Pacheco, but also to undertake effective investigations with due diligence and in a reasonable time that could lead to a determination of criminal responsibility and to the effective implementation of any possible criminal punishments and other consequences provided for by the law. The Court highlights that 37 years have passed since Mr. Radilla Pacheco disappeared at the hands of State agents. Due to the foregoing, it is necessary that the State submit updated, detailed, and complete information on all of the actions it is undertaking with respect to the investigation into the facts of this case, in such a way that the Court may verify that the investigations are being carried out in accordance with the purpose of this reparation measure.

11.   Additionally, as to the State's refusal to provide copies of the preliminary inquiry's files so indicated by the representatives (*supra* Considering Clause 8), this point was specifically addressed by the Court in its Judgment, indicating that this refusal was "incompatible with the right to participate in the preliminary inquiry[, which] translated into a violation of Tita Radilla Martinez's right to fully participate in the investigation." The Court held that "the victims in the present case must have the right to access the case file, as well as to request and obtain copies of it, given that the information contained therein is not subject to confidentiality" because it relates to grave human rights violations. Additionally, with respect to the alleged denial of the representatives' participation in an examination of cemetery registries, the Court reminds the parties that in its Judgment it repeated that "during the investigation and prosecution, the State shall guarantee the victims full access and the capacity to act at all stages." [6 187] Therefore, in its next report, the State must submit information regarding these statements made by the representatives.

B. The obligation to continue with the effective search for and the immediate location of Mr. Radilla Pacheco or, if applicable, of his remains (*Operative Paragraph 9 of the Judgment*)

12.   The State indicated that from October 19 to 28, 2010 new excavations aimed at locating Rosendo Radilla Pacheco were carried out at the place "where

he presumably disappeared." It indicated that "it has continued these efforts in full agreement with the victims and their representatives," and that the excavations have been carried out by experts proposed by Ms. Tita Radilla Martínez. The State affirmed that on October 28, 2010, the excavation concluded "without having found clues, evidence, or skeletal remains."[7][188] It also indicated that "the archeological expert [proposed by Ms. Radilla Pacheco] was asked to conclusively certify his experience [...], documenting cases [in which he has intervened as part of the Forensic Anthropology Foundation of Guatemala, the methodology used, and the results obtained." The State also indicated that the expert "was asked to state the similarities or analogies between those cases and [this one]. Once [this] requirement is fulfilled, [...] the agent of the Federal Public Ministry of the Federation shall proceed according to the law."

13.   The representatives affirmed that actions carried out by the Attorney General's Office "still do not reflect the seriousness necessary in this case, as the most important measure ordered in the investigation since the Judgment was handed down is the excavation ordered in the former military barracks of Atoyac de Álvarez [but] this excavation was ordered in places that had already been investigated in 2008." In that regard, they indicated that the experts proposed by Ms. Tita Radilla, who were accredited during the preliminary inquiry, issued a series of recommendations after excavations concluded on October 28, 2010. They stated that despite the fact that these experts "were authorized by the [Attorney General's Office], the [agent] of the Public Ministry has questioned their recommendations and[,] thus[,] measures aimed at searching for Mr. Rosendo Radilla Pacheco's skeletal remains have been delayed." This agent indicated to the representatives that "excavations could not continue until the expert of the Forensic Anthropology Foundation of Guatemala could prove the Foundation's experience." Finally, the representatives stated that the agent of the Public Ministry, in charge of executing the aforementioned preliminary inquiry, told them that the Ministry did not have the resources necessary to continue with excavations or to hire experts in forensic archeology, and thus "the cost of hiring experts would be charged to [the representatives if they] offere[d] them as collaborators in the measures carried out, even if the Attorney General's Office were to decide to consider them as official experts and not as independent experts."

14.   The Commission "recogniz[ed] the actions undertaken by the State in the search for and locating of Mr. Radilla Pacheco or his mortal remains." However, "it observe[d] that [the State had not] reported on any other follow-up action." Thus, it requested that the Court require the State to "report on other measures undertaken, as well as the follow-up and continuity it has given to those that have already been carried out." Finally, the Commission highlighted that it is necessary to prevent the occurrence of "undue delays in the State's compliance with this reparation measure."

15.   The Court observes that the State has reported on excavations aimed at locating Mr. Radilla Pacheco. However, these excavations took place ten months after notice of the Judgment was served. However, from the information presented by the State (*supra* Considering Clause 10), it is not possible for the Court to ascertain how the excavations comply with the standards set out in the Judgment with respect to the elements that must be considered in the investigation of facts such as those that occurred in this case, including locating Mr. Radilla Pacheco. The Tribunal has not been informed of other investigations that the State may have been carrying out to that end.

16.   Additionally, the Tribunal notes that the State has permitted Ms. Tita Radilla Martínez's participation, through her representatives and experts, in the aforementioned excavations. However, the Court notes that the representatives affirm that they were informed by a State agent that the excavations could not continue due to a lack of resources and that the continuation of the excavations depended on the accreditation that Ms. Radilla Martínez's expert could provide for his expertise and on the representatives' financing the cost of the expert's reports. The Court highlights that in the Judgment it indicated that "for an investigation into a forced disappearance [...] to be carried out effectively and with due diligence, all means necessary must be used to promptly implement all measures and inquiries that are timely and necessary to bring the victims' fate to light and identify those responsible for their disappearance, particularly the disappearance that occurred in this case." For this purpose, the State must provide the corresponding authorities with the logistic and scientific resources necessary to collect and process evidence and, in particular, the power to access relevant information and documents in order to investigate the alleged facts and obtain clues or evidence of the location of the victims."[8][189] Consequently, the State and the representatives are asked to submit updated and detailed information on this matter.

C. Regarding the obligation to adopt appropriate legislative reforms in order to make Article 57 of the Code of Military Justice compatible with both international standards on the subject and the American Convention on Human Rights (*Operative Paragraph 10 of the Judgment*)

17.   The State indicated that "the federal executive organ submitted a reform initiative to the Congress of the Union which includes the amendments ordered by the Inter-American Court to Article 57 of the Code of Military Justice." It affirmed that "the initiative proposes the exclusion of the crimes of forced disappearance of persons, torture, and rape from military jurisdiction so that they fall under [ordinary] jurisdiction." The initiative also "provides for the obligation of the Military Public Ministry to submit records of investigations, from which

it may be possible for the crimes to be inferred, to the Public Ministry of the Federation," and that "the measures that constitute the record shall not lose their validity, even when if they were carried under [the Code of Military Justice] and subsequently under the Code of Criminal Procedure." The reform initiative also includes modifications to the Organic Law of the Federal Judicial Branch in order to give "district court judges criminal jurisdiction so that they can try crimes committed by members of the military under the terms proposed." Last, the State indicated that "the discussion and, if applicable, the modification and approval of [the] legislative reform shall be [...] the task of the Federal Judicial Branch." [9] [190] Finally, it indicated that the State manifested that "although the operative paragraphs of the [Judgment] did not provide for the withdrawal of the reservation made by the [State] on Article IX of the [Inter-American Convention on the Forced Disappearance of People,] it did analyze the matter." Thus, the State has "*motu proprio* initiated the corresponding internal processes to eventually retract the reservation, and this process is linked to the initiatives for the reforms of the Code of Military Justice brought before the Congress of the Union."

18.   The representatives stated that "the reform proposed by the Federal Executive [...] does not conform with guidelines for independence and impartiality guarantees required under Article 8(1) of the American Convention." They also indicated that "the initiative only proposed the exclusion of the crimes of forced disappearance of persons, torture, and rape from the military criminal jurisdiction so that they fall under the [ordinary] jurisdiction, [but] the power to investigate and the power to analyze whether the facts fall under a normative category remains in the hands of the Office of the Prosecutor General of Military Justice." They stated that with this reform, "there is a risk that the crimes may be reclassified so as to prevent them from being tried in a civilian court" and that there is a risk that the facts may be manipulated. The representatives also indicated that there continues to be "a lack of domestic recourses for questioning the jurisdiction of military authorities to prosecute and/or adjudicate the facts."

19.   The Commission affirmed that it "value[d] the State's legislative initiative." However, it "observe[d] that pursuant to the proposed reform, Article 57 of the Code of Military Justice d[id] not fully adhere to the standards established [in the J]udgment." It indicated that, in particular, "it consider[ed] that the law should be written in such a way so that it is clear that the military jurisdiction should only intervene when crimes or wrongs are committed by military personnel and, by nature, affect juridical rights that are unique to the military." Additionally, it stated that it observed from the proposed reform that, "it would be possible for the military jurisdiction to intervene in the investigation of a crime that does not belong to it and that this intervention could limit proceedings in the ordinary jurisdiction inasmuch as its legal force is recognized over that

of the ordinary jurisdiction, which are two aspects that are not compatible with regional standards." Finally, it indicated that "the State should continue with its reform initiatives, taking into account the full application of the standards set out [in the J]udgment so that the scope of military criminal jurisdiction 'is restricted and exceptional and that it is directed only toward 'the protection of special military interests linked to functions that are unique to the armed forces'."

20.   The Tribunal observes that the State has carried out efforts to reform Article 57 of the Code of Military Criminal Justice. The Court considers it appropriate to recall that the Judgment established that, "taking into account the nature of the crime and the judicial right harmed, criminal military jurisdiction is not competent to investigate and, if applicable, try and punish the perpetrators of human rights violations. Instead, proceedings against those responsible should always be carried out in an ordinary jurisdiction." [10][191] Based on the foregoing, in its Judgment, the Court found the State of Mexico responsible because the cited provision is "vague and imprecise, [and] impedes a determination of the strict connection between the crime belonging to the ordinary jurisdiction and military service, objectively assessed," [11][192] and because "it extend[ed] military jurisdiction to crimes that do not have a strict connection to military discipline and to juridical rights that are unique to the military sphere." [12][193]

21.   With this in mind, the Court deems that although the State's efforts to amend Article 57 of the Code of Military Justice are a positive step, the proposed initiative is insufficient because it does not fully comply with the standards specified in the Judgment. This reform only sets forth that military jurisdiction shall have no jurisdiction in cases related only to forced disappearance, torture and rape committed by soldiers. However, in the Judgment, the Court reiterated its constant jurisprudence that, "the military justice system should only try military for the commission of crimes or offenses that by their very nature violate the legal rights of the military," [13][194] so that human rights violations committed by soldiers against civilians can not be subject to the jurisdiction of military courts. [14][195]

22.   At the same time, the Court observes that, according to the proposed reform, the measures carried out by the public ministry prior to its "release" to the ordinary jurisdiction would be valid. In the Judgment, the Court referred to the military jurisdiction's lack of competence not only to try and, if applicable, punish those responsible, but also to investigate all acts that violate the human rights of civilians. [15][196] From the foregoing, it is evident that the military prosecutor does not have competence to investigate such human rights violations either. Therefore, the Court urges the State to adopt measures directed toward amending Article 57 of the Code of Military Justice to make it compatible with the standards set out in the Judgment.

23.   As to the representatives' observation regarding the lack of domestic

recourses to dispute the military forum's jurisdiction, the Court considers that though it discussed the matter in its Judgment, the order that the State reform Article 57 of the Code of Military Justice was limited to adapting this article to the standards of exceptionality and restriction that characterize criminal military jurisdiction. Thus, the Tribunal shall not rule on the representatives' additional allegations.

> **D. Obligation to adopt legislative reforms appropriate for the purpose of making Article 215A of the Federal Criminal Code compatible with international standards on the subject and with the Inter-American Convention on the Forced Disappearance of Persons (*Operative Paragraph 11 of the Judgment*)**

24.   The State indicated that the same initiative mentioned in the section above "includes reforms to the Federal Criminal Code on the topic of forced disappearance that fully comply with the Judgment." The text of the proposed reform states that "the public servant who, on his own or through others, commits, permits, authorizes, or supports the deprivation of liberty of one or more persons and intentionally brings about or maintains that person or persons hidden in any way, or refuses to acknowledge that deprivation of liberty, or to inform on the whereabouts of the person, is considered to have committed the crime of forced disappearance of persons." Additionally, the State maintained that the crime "may also be committed by a private individual when he or she acts on the order, or with the acquiescence or support, of a public servant." The initiative also proposes that the crime prescribe after thirty-five years, a prohibition of amnesty, pardons and "pre-release benefits," or any other substitutes regarding this crime and that, pursuant to Article 215B of the Federal Criminal Code, the sentence for public servants who commit this crime should be 20 to 50 years in prison, and that the sentence for private individuals be set at 10 to 25 years in prison. [16][197]

25.   The representatives indicated that the period of prescription of 35 years for the crime of forced disappearance included in the proposed reform "does not meet standards set forth by the [Inter-American Convention on Forced Disappearance of Persons]." They affirmed that "if the reform is approved as the Federal Executive Branch proposes, the State of Mexico [will continue] infringing Article 2 of the American Convention."

26.   The Commission stated that it valued "the legislative initiative of the State and consider[ed] that it [was] a step forward in the process of achieving compliance." In particular, it considered that the inclusion of elements such the refusal to acknowledge the deprivation of liberty or to give information on the disappeared person that distinguish this crime from other crimes often related to the forced disappearance of persons, as well as the prohibition of privileges in its prosecution, to be "positive aspects" of the initiative. However, it indicated that the

proposed reform still fails to conform "integrally with the standards established [in the J]udgment and those established in the Inter-American Convention on Forced Disappearance of Persons." The Commission indicated that "the definition of the perpetrator of the crime should be broad so as to ensure the punishment of all "principals, accomplices, and accessories to the crime, regardless of whether they are State agents or persons or groups that act with the authorization, support, or acquiescence of the State." Additionally, it stated that "the standards of application of the quantum of the sentence are based on the perpetrator's status as a 'public servant' or a 'private individual,' which is incompatible with Article III of the Inter-American Convention on Forced Disappearance of Persons, which establishes the possible mitigating factors that could apply in cases of forced disappearance." Last, the Commission manifested its concern that "a period of prescription be provided for this crime despite the fact that the Inter-American Convention on Forced Disappearance of Persons establishes the imprescriptibility of that crime as a general rule." In any case, the State "did not specify whether the established period of prescription of 35 years is compatible with the exceptions established by the Inter-American Convention on Forced Disappearance of Persons in Article VII therein."

27.   The Court observes that the State has begun to adopt measures for the purpose of reforming Article 215A of the Federal Criminal Code that defines the crime of forced disappearance of persons. In order to analyze whether the proposed reform presented by the State adheres to the standards set out by the Court, it is necessary to specify that in its Judgment, the Tribunal only referred to two elements of that article that were incompatible with the Inter-American Convention on Forced Disappearance of Persons. First, the Court indicated that this law limited the possible perpetrator of the crime of forced disappearance of persons to "public servants," while Article II of the Inter-American Convention on Forced Disappearance of Persons establishes that States must ensure that all "those persons who commit or attempt to commit the crime of forced disappearance of persons and their accomplices and accessories" receive punishment, whether they are State agents or "persons or groups of persons acting with the authorization, support, or acquiescence of the State."[17][198] Furthermore, the Judgment established that the forced disappearance of persons "is characterized by a refusal to acknowledge the deprivation of liberty or to provide information on the fate or whereabouts of persons," and that this element should be present in the definition of the crime because it allows for a "distinction to be made between forced disappearance and other crimes that are usually associated with it, such as kidnapping and homicide, so that adequate evidentiary standards may be applied and sentences that consider the extreme gravity of this crime may be imposed on all those implicated."[18][199] Consequently, the Court will limit its analysis to these two issues.

28.   The Court affirms that in its proposed reform, the State has incorporated the elements indicated by the Tribunal for an adequate definition of the crime of forced disappearance in accordance with the Inter-American Convention on Forced Disappearance of Persons. It is evident from the information provided by the State that this crime can be committed by private individuals when acting "under the order, or with the acquiescence or support" of a public servant. Additionally, the proposed reform sets forth that the crime can be committed by any public servant or private individual who, among other things, "refuses to acknowledge the deprivation of liberty or to provide information as to his whereabouts." In this regard, the Court takes note of the reform initiative proposed by the State to amend section 215A of the Federal Criminal Code in accordance with the standards specified in the Judgment and the Inter-American Convention on Forced Disappearance, and it will continue to monitor the aforementioned legislative reform procedure until it is fully compatible with said standards.

E.   **Obligation to implement permanent programs or courses on the analysis of the jurisprudence of the inter-American System of Human Rights Protection regarding the limits of military criminal jurisdiction, as well as a training program on the proper investigation and prosecution of acts that constitute forced disappearance of persons (*Operative Paragraph 12 of the Judgment*)**

29.   The State indicated that the Attorney General's Office "is working on the creation, implementation and release of a training and/or specialization program for public servants who are part of the Office of the General Coordinator of Investigation that addresses the orders of the Court." It affirmed that "a training session led by the expert Santiago Corcuera, former member of the United Nations Working Group on Enforced or Involuntary Disappearances, has been scheduled for the first two months of 2011 for the personnel of the Office of the General Coordinator of Investigation." Additionally, it reported that "ministerial personnel of the Attorney General's Office attended the Central American Seminar on the Search for Disappeared Persons and Forensic Investigations: Implementation of the International Council of Minimum Principles and Norms regarding psycho-social work in cases of [F]orced Disappearance, Arbitrary Executions, and Forensic Investigation of Grave Human Rights Violations, held on September 16, 17, and 18, 2010, in the city of Antigua, Guatemala." This seminar "contributed to the reaffirmation of the knowledge of those public servants who attended for the purpose of carrying out excavations" in order to locate Mr. Radilla Pacheco. Moreover, the State referred to a series of activities carried out as part of the "permanent training in human rights" offered by the Attorney General's Office. Additionally, the State referred to activities carried out by the Supreme Court

of Justice of the Nation for the promotion, diffusion, and application of human rights, as well as "activities carried out by the Federal Council of the Judiciary."

30.   The representatives affirmed that although "the activities indicated by the State are positive under the framework of the general training in human rights that all public servants should receive, [...] they do not have anything to do with that ordered by the Inter-American Court [in the Judgment]." They stated that the activities "were not aimed at the Armed Forces," they "did not specifically discuss the analysis of the jurisprudence of the Inter-American System [...] in relation to the limits of the military criminal jurisdiction," and "they did not discuss the proper investigation and adjudication of facts that constitute forced disappearance of persons," and were not "aimed at Public Ministry agents from the Attorney General's Office or at judges of the Judicial Branch of the Federation." They also stated that the training scheduled for the first two months of 2011, to be led by the former member of the United Nations Working Group on Enforced or Involuntary Disappearances, still has not been carried out.

31.   The Commission stated that it "value[d] the activities carried out by the State regarding promotion and training on human rights aimed at officials of various State institutions." Additionally, it "considere[d] that the efforts to address the special requirements established by the Court in the [J]udgment should be incentivized."

32.   The Court observes that in its Judgment it specified the type of activities (as well as the subjects they should cover and the persons who should participate in them) that the State must impart in order to comply with this reparation measure. [19][200] The Court values that the State trains its officials on human rights issues. However, the Tribunal observes that the State has extensively referred to a series of activities that are not related to the reparation ordered in the Judgment. The only concrete information submitted by the State related to its compliance with the specific orders of the Court is that related to the planning of a training session to be imparted to personnel of the Attorney General's Office by the former member of the United Nations Working Group on Enforced or Involuntary Disappearances during the first two months of 2011, as well as the attendance of personnel of that body to a seminar carried out in Antigua, Guatemala. The Court was not informed of activities aimed at the training of judges of the Judicial Branch of the Federation on this subject, nor on the permanent courses or programs on "the limits of the military jurisdiction [and] the rights to due process and judicial protection." The Court highlights the importance of the activities ordered as guarantees of non-repetition, as they have a reach that goes beyond that of this specific case. Thus, the State must submit concrete information to the Court on the measures carried out to strictly comply with this aspect of the Judgment to fulfill the aims of the reparation measure.

F. **Obligation to publish the Judgment in the Official Gazette of the Federation and in another widely circulated national newspaper, as well as in the web page of the Attorney General's Office (*Operative Paragraph 13 of the Judgment*)**

33.   The State reported that on February 17, 2010, "paragraphs 1 to 7, 52 to 66, and 114 to 358, as well as the Operative Paragraphs of the Judgment, were published without footnotes" in the Official Gazette of the Federation and in the *El Universal* newspaper. It submitted these publications to the Tribunal. Additionally, it indicated that on "January 21, 2010, the Attorney General's Office published the [J]udgment issued on November 23, 2009 on its web page" and it specified the corresponding web address. [20][201] Finally, in response to statements made by the petitioners with respect to the visibility of the publication on the Attorney General's Office web page, the State indicated that it "took the measures necessary so that the [J]udgment could be accessed from the home page of the Attorney General's Office."

34.   The representatives affirmed that the State "unilaterally published the Judgment." They also indicated that they were informed of the publication the day after it was carried out, and that they were never contacted for the purpose of concerting "a date for the publication."

35.   The Commission stated that "the information available indicates that the State has complied with this order of the [J]udgment."

36.   The Court observes that the information provided by the parties indicates that the State fully complied with this reparation measure before the deadline established in the Judgment expired.

G. **Obligation to carry out a public act of acknowledgement of responsibility with regard to the facts of the present case and in order to restore the memory of Mr. Rosendo Radilla Pacheco and to place a plaque in the city of Atoyac de Álvarez (Guerrero) commemorating his forced disappearance (*Operative Paragraph 14 of the Judgment*)**

37.   With respect to the public act of acknowledgement, the State affirmed that "over the course of 2010, it [...] has reiterated to the representatives of the victims its willingness to carry out [that] ceremony as soon as possible and to arrive at a consensus on the way this reparation measure should be complied with." It indicated that it understood that this reparation measure should be carried out within one year, as the Judgment does not set out a deadline for compliance. With respect to the commemorative plaque, it affirmed that "the State submitted a proposal for its text and reiterated its willingness to comply with the [J]udgment, as well as its understanding that the unveiling of the plaque should also be carried out within one year," as the Judgment does not set out a specific deadline for compliance, and it should be carried out "in the context of the public act of

acknowledgement of responsibility." [21] [202] It indicated that the representatives considered that the plaque should also include "an acknowledgement of the context of the systematic human rights violations that occurred during the so-called 'Dirty War,'" but that the State considered that it had made an effort to include in its proposal practically all of the representatives' suggestions and that, in its opinion, "the text of the proposal fully complies with the orders of the [J] udgment." The State also indicated that the representatives had expressed that "the unveiling of the plaque does not have to be carried out within one year as of the publication of the [J]udgment, and that they had other reasons that they would have to carefully consider in order to come to an agreement on the fulfillment of this order." Thus, the State signaled its commitment to "maintaining channels of communication open with the representatives of the victims for the purpose of coming to an agreement on the public act of acknowledgment of responsibility and on the unveiling of the plaque, and its commitment to informing the Court on the results of these measures."

38.   The representatives stated that no agreement exists with respect to the "realization of the act and the unveiling of the commemorative plaque." They also expressed their willingness to "maintain the channel of communication with the State open in order to come to an agreement with respect to this point, considering the integrality of the [...] document's contents."

39.   The Commission did not submit observations regarding this point.

40.   The Tribunal reminds the parties that in its Judgment it ordered the way in which the public act of acknowledgement of responsibility should be carried out, including particularities such as that the place and date on which it is held should be agreed upon with Mr. Radilla Pacheco's next of kin or their representatives. [22] [203] The Court also indicated that the unveiling of the commemorative plaque could be carried out during the public act or at a later time. [23] [204] The State has submitted information on the efforts made in order to comply with this reparation measure. However, the Court does not have sufficient information on the part of the representatives as to the aspects of the text proposed by the State for the commemorative plaque text and the realization of the public act of acknowledgment of responsibility with which they disagree. The Tribunal highlights that it is necessary that all parties submit specific and detailed information so that the Court may adequately evaluate advances in compliance with the reparation measures ordered.

41.   With respect to the representatives' affirmation that the text of the plaque should refer to the context in which Mr. Radilla Pacheco's forced disappearance took place, the Court reminds the parties that the Judgment indicated that, "Mr. Radilla Pacheco's forced disappearance c[ould] not be isolated from the circumstances in which they [...] occurred, and the corresponding legal consequences c[ould] not be

determined in the vacuum created by decontextualization." [24] [205] Notwithstanding the agreements that the representatives and the State may come to, the Court considers it important that the text of the plaque mention that context. That said, with regard to the compliance periods of both reparation measures, the Court considers that although the Judgment did not establish deadlines both should be complied with as soon as possible, provided that the representatives and the State make the necessary agreements, so that the reparation measure fulfills its purpose. The Tribunal values that that the State initiated measures to carry out the act of acknowledgment of responsibility and the unveiling of the plaque before the one-year deadline for the submission of its report on compliance with the Judgment. Therefore, the Court urges the representatives and the State to maintain communications going with the purpose of complying with these reparation measures.

H. Obligation to prepare a biographical sketch of the life of Mr. Rosendo Radilla Pacheco (*Operative Paragraph 15 of the Judgment*)

42.   The State indicated that it had already received the representatives authorization for the publication of the biographical sketch ordered by the Court, with an edition of 1000 copies, which, considering the representatives' requests, will include "the full text of the book *Voces Acalladas* [Silenced Voices] written by Ms. Andrea Radilla," as well as additional information regarding the fact that the sketch was written pursuant to the Judgment delivered by the Court in this case.

43.   The representatives indicated that "compliance with the publication of the biographical sketch is in progress."

44.   The Commission indicated that "the implementation of this form of reparation is still in progress and that agreements [...] have been reached in order to implement it."

45.   The Court values the actions taken by the State to comply with the publication of the biographical sketch that is the object of this reparation measure. Based on the information provided by the State, the Tribunal awaits information on the publication of the work.

I. Obligation to provide psychological and/or psychiatric assistance through specialized public health institutions to the victims that request it (*Operative Paragraph 16 of the Judgment*)

46.   The State reported that the representatives rejected the Public Security Secretariat's offer of "psychological assistance, through the Comprehensive System of Assistance for Victims (SIAV, in Spanish), for all of Mr. Rosendo Radilla's next of kin, regardless of whether they had been designated as beneficiaries by the Court [...] in its [J]udgment." Therefore, "the Ministry of the Interior informed the victims and their representatives that it is negotiating so

that the psychological assistance be provided through the National Human Rights Commission, and the psychiatric assistance, if required, through a public health institution in the state of Guerrero."

47.   The representatives stated that the State continues to "negotiate with the National Human Rights Commission concerning the psychological assistance, and it is [unknown] which health institution of the state of Guerrero will provide the psychiatric assistance."

48.   The Commission indicated that it "considere[d] the fact that the parties have reached agreements on implementation of this reparation measure to be positive"; therefore, it requested that the Court require the State to submit "updated information on the measures carried out to comply with this order of the [J]udgment."

49.   The Court values the State's offer to provide psychological and/or psychiatric assistance not only to the victims declared in the Judgment, but also to other relatives of Mr. Rosendo Radilla Pacheco. However, it notes that, to date, the State has not provided psychological and/or psychiatric care for the victims in this case, as ordered in the Judgment, because it has not yet been determined which public institutions will be charged with that task. Therefore, the Court finds that the State must continue with appropriate steps so that the victims begin to receive the required attention as soon as possible.

J.   **Obligation to pay the compensation awarded as pecuniary and nonpecuniary damages and costs and expenses (*Operative Paragraph 17 of the Judgm*ent)**

50.   The State reported that it had "made the necessary resources available in order to pay [the compensations] as indicated in the [J]udgment." However, "the corresponding amounts have not been paid [...] due to circumstances beyond the control of the State." It indicated that it has proposed to the representatives diverse procedures for payment, such as "a procedure before a civil judge or public notary," the deposit of the appropriate amounts in "an account or deposit certificate in a solvent Mexican banking institution and in the most favorable financial conditions permitted under Mexican law and banking practice," and even the option requested by the petitioners that "the compensations be deposited at the Inter-American Court." However, it indicated that the representatives have only accepted "the compensation of one of the victims, Ms. Andrea Radilla Martínez, via voluntary jurisdiction before a notary public." According to the State, the other beneficiaries of indemnifications have expressed their desire not to receive the amounts ordered in the Judgment until progress is made in the ongoing criminal investigation into the forced disappearance of Mr. Rosendo Radilla. Thus, the State noted that "with the purpose of fulfilling this obligation, the funds

will remain available at the Ministry of Interior until the next of kin of the victims wish to receive it."

51.   With respect to the indemnification for Mr. Rosendo Radilla Pacheco, the representatives indicated that the forms of compliance offered by the State are "unacceptable," as they require the presentation of a "declaration of death" by a judge or a death certificate, including the "new method of payment consisting of a voluntary jurisdiction proceeding before a notary public in Mexico City." In that regard, they stated that "it is highly shameful to the family of Mr. Rosendo Radilla Pacheco to force them to initiate the procedure of declaration of death, as they have taken all necessary actions to achieve justice and learn of his whereabouts for over 35 years." Thus, Tita and Rosendo Radilla Martínez, Mr. Rosendo Radilla Pacheco's children, decided "not to accept, for the moment, the compensation corresponding to [their father]," nor the compensation "allocated directly to them." Finally, they requested, "as a preferred alternative to a deposit in a Mexican financial institution," that the amounts be deposited at the Inter-American Court of Human Rights, as "this alternative would give greater confidence to the victims and create less emotional distress."

52.   The Commission noted that "the implementation of this reparation measure cannot become a factor that re-victimizes Mr. Radilla Pacheco's relatives [...]." In this regard, it indicated that the State must "provide special attention to the needs and desires of the beneficiaries of reparations," and it noted that the indemnification payment for Ms. Andrea Radilla Martínez has been agreed upon. Finally, it emphasized that neither the State nor the representatives had submitted information on the payment of costs and expenses.

53.   From the submissions of the representatives and the State, the Court observes that there are two different controversies: one the one hand, that related to the payment of the indemnification corresponding to Mr. Rosendo Radilla Pacheco, and on the other hand, that related to the payment to other beneficiaries. The Court considers it appropriate to clarify that the Judgment, in a general manner, established that the State must pay the indemnifications directly to their beneficiaries within one year as of the date on which the Judgment was served.

54.   With respect to the indemnifications corresponding to Mr. Radilla Pacheco, the Court ordered in the Judgment that the compensation corresponding to Mr. Radilla Pacheco be distributed equally among his heirs. In this regard, the Court considers that it is acceptable that domestic procedures be used in order to achieve payment of the corresponding indemnifications. However, these procedures cannot generate a disproportionate burden to victims that unnecessarily impedes the implementation of this reparation measure in their favor. Additionally, the Court notes that, in its Judgment, it did not provide for receiving deposits for the payment of indemnification for Mr. Radilla Pacheco as a possibility. However,

the Court highlights that the State proposed a method of payment in a Mexican financial institution which conforms to the Judgment if it were necessary for the compensation to be paid in that manner.[25][206] Considering that the deadline established in the Judgment for compliance with this reparation measure in favor of Mr. Radilla Pacheco has elapsed, the Tribunal requests that the State submit specific and detailed information on the statements made by the representatives that payment may not be carried out through a voluntary jurisdiction proceeding before a notary public. Likewise, the Court requests that the representatives provide specific and detailed information as to the reasons why they do not want payments to be made through a deposit in a Mexican banking institution.

55.   The Court notes that the State manifested that the representatives authorized the compensation payment for Ms. Andrea Radilla Martínez, daughter of Rosendo Radilla Pacheco, through voluntary jurisdiction before a public notary. Additionally, both the State and the representatives indicated that Ms. Tita and Mr. Rosendo Radilla Martínez have not accepted payment of their indemnifications. According to the State, this is because they consider that there has been no progress in investigations. This statement was not denied by the representatives. In this regard, the Court reiterates, first, that the Judgment established a one-year deadline for the State's compliance with this reparation measure and, second, that the Judgment did not condition the payment of indemnifications on the progress of investigations into the facts of this case. The payment of indemnifications is an autonomous obligation which is independent of other forms of reparations ordered from the State. Therefore, given that the State indicated that it was able to make the payments corresponding to Ms. Rita and Mr. Rosendo Radilla Martínez, among others, and given that these beneficiaries do not wish to receive payment, the Court considers that the requirements set out in paragraph 390 of the Judgment for the State to proceed, following the criteria in that paragraph, with compliance with this reparation measure through a bank deposit in a Mexican financial institution have been satisfied.

56.   Furthermore, the Court notes that neither the representatives nor the State have submitted information concerning the payment of costs and expenses. The Court therefore requests both parties to present relevant information to it.

K. Request of the victims' representatives for a hearing to monitor compliance

57.   The representatives stated that in virtue of the "current contradictions between the State and the representatives of the victims with regard to full compliance with the Judgment," and "with the purpose of requesting the Court to urge the United Mexican States to effectively comply [therewith]," they requested that the Tribunal hold a "hearing to monitor compliance with the [J]udgment at the next Regular Period of Sessions."

58.   The Court considers that this Order clarifies those issues over which there

is controversy regarding compliance with the Judgment. Therefore, the Tribunal does not consider a hearing for monitoring compliance with this Judgment to be necessary at the moment.

THEREFORE:

THE INTER-AMERICAN COURT OF HUMAN RIGHTS,

in exercising its authority to monitor compliance with its decisions and in accordance with Articles 33, 61(1), 62(3), 65, 67, and 68(1) of the American Convention on Human Rights, Article 25(1) and 30 of the Statue, and Article 31(2) and 69 of its Rules of Procedure,

DECLARES:

1.   In accordance with Considering Clause 19 of the present Order, the State has complied with the following operative paragraph of the Judgment:

  (a) To publish once in the Official Gazette of the Federation and in another widely circulated newspaper paragraphs 1 through 7, 52 through 66, 114 through 358 of the Judgment and its operative paragraphs, without the footnotes. Also, the State shall publish this Judgment in its totality on the official *website* of the Attorney General of the Republic in a six and two-month term, respectively, as of the notification of the Judgment (*Operative Paragraph 13 and Considering Clause 36*).

2.   In accordance with the relevant Considering Clauses of this Order, the following Operative Paragraphs of the Judgment are still pending fulfillment:

  (a) To effectively carry out, with due diligence and within a reasonable time, the investigation and, if applicable, the criminal proceedings established with regard to the arrest and subsequent forced disappearance of Mr. Rosendo Radilla Pacheco in order to determine the corresponding criminal responsibilities and effectively apply the punishments and consequences established by law (*Operative Paragraph 8 and Considering Clause 10 and 11*);

  (b) To continue with the effective search for and the immediate location of Mr. Radilla Pacheco or, if applicable, of his remains (*Operative Paragraph 9 and Considering Clauses 15 and 16 of the Judgment*);

  (c) To adopt appropriate legislative reforms in order to make Article 57 of the Code of Military Justice compatible with both international standards on the subject and the American Convention on Human Rights (*Operative Paragraph 10 and Considering Clauses 20 to 22*);

  (d) To adopt legislative reforms appropriate for the purpose of making article 215A of the Federal Criminal Code compatible with international standards on the subject and with the Inter-American Convention on the Forced Disappearance of Persons (*Operative Paragraph 11 and Considering Clauses 27 and 28*);

(e) To implement, within a reasonable time and with the corresponding budgetary allocation, programs or permanent courses on the analysis of the jurisprudence of the Inter-American System of Human Rights Protection regarding the limits of military criminal jurisdiction, as well as a training program on the proper investigation and prosecution of acts that constitute forced disappearance of persons (*Operative Paragraph 12 and Considering Clause 32*);

(f) To hold a public act of acknowledgement of responsibility with regard to the facts of the present case and in order to restore the memory of Mr. Rosendo Radilla Pacheco and to place *a* commemorative plaque in the city of Atoyac de Álvarez (Guerrero) for his forced disappearance (*Operative Paragraph 14 and Considering Clauses 40 and 41*);

(g) To prepare a biographical sketch of the life of Mr. Rosendo Radilla Pacheco (*Operative Paragraph 15 and Considering Clause 45*);

(h) To provide free psychological and/or psychiatric attention immediately, adequately, and effectively, through its specialized public health institutions, to the victims declared in the Judgment that request it (*Operative Paragraph 16 and Considering Clause 49*), and

(i) To pay the compensation awarded in paragraphs 365, 370, 375 and 385 as pecuniary and non-pecuniary damages and costs and expenses (*Operative Paragraph 17 and Considering Clauses 53 to 56*).

1-Dec-2011
Order of the Inter-American Court of Human Rights

HAVING SEEN:

2.   The order on monitoring compliance with judgment issued by the Court on May 19, 2011, in which it declared, *inter alia*, that the following obligation remained pending:

[...]

f) To hold a public act of acknowledgement of responsibility with regard to the facts of the present case and in order to restore the memory of Rosendo Radilla Pacheco, and to place a plaque recalling the facts of his forced disappearance in Atoyac de Álvarez (Guerrero) (*fourteenth operative paragraph of the judgment* [...]);

[...]

3.   The communications of July 14 and August 29, 2011, in which the United Mexican States (hereinafter "the State" or "Mexico") presented information on compliance with the judgment delivered by the Court in this case (*supra* having

seen paragraph 1). Also, the communications of November 16, 18 and 29, 2011, in which the State presented information on the public act of acknowledgement of responsibility and the unveiling of a plaque recalling the forced disappearance of Rosendo Radilla Pacheco (*supra* having seen paragraphs 1 and 2).

4.   The brief of October 17, 2011, in which the representatives of the victims (hereinafter "the representatives") presented their observations on the State's communications of July 14 and August 29, 2011 (*supra* having seen paragraph 3). Also, the briefs of November 10, 18 and 29, 2011, in which the representatives referred to the public act of acknowledgement of responsibility and the unveiling of a memorial plaque in this case (*supra* having seen paragraph 3).

5.   The communication of November 8, 2011, in which the Inter-American Commission on Human Rights (hereinafter "the Inter-American Commission" or "the Commission") presented its observations on the State's report of August 29, 2011 (*supra* Having Seen paragraph 3). In addition, the communication of November 29, 2011, in which the Commission presented its observations on the information forwarded by the State and the representatives on the public act of acknowledgement of responsibility and the unveiling of a memorial plaque (*supra* having seen paragraphs 3 and 4).

CONSIDERING THAT:

4.   The Court has recently received from the parties a vast amount of information on the organization by the State of a public act of acknowledgement of responsibility during which a plaque was unveiled recalling the forced disappearance of Rosendo Radilla Pacheco. Based on the information submitted and the claims made, principally by the State and the representatives, in this order the Court will rule on this aspect.

Obligation to hold a public act of acknowledgement of responsibility with regard to the facts of the case and in order to restore the memory of Rosendo Radilla Pacheco, and to place a plaque recalling the facts of his forced disappearance in Atoyac de Álvarez, Guerrero (*fourteenth operative paragraph of the judgment*)

A. Arguments of the State

5.   The State advised that, in compliance with the judgment, on November 17, 2011, it had organized a public act of acknowledgement of responsibility in Atoyac de Álvarez, Guerrero, in the presence of the acting Minister of the Interior, and the Minister for Foreign Affairs, together with the following officials of the state of Guerrero: the Governor, the heads of the Legislature and the Judiciary, and the President of the Guerrero Human Rights Commission. In addition, during this act, a plaque was unveiled recalling the forced disappearance of Mr. Radilla Pacheco. The State forwarded various documents, videos and audios on the coordination and the logistics for the organization of this act, as well as on its implementation. Regarding this point, in the report it presented on August 29,

2011, the State indicated that, "as an act of good faith and full commitment to the promotion and respect for human rights, the Federal Executive, through the [then] Deputy Minister of Legal Affairs and Human Rights of the Interior Ministry [...] delivered a message of acknowledgement of responsibility with regard to what happened in the case of Rosendo Radilla Pacheco[; which] was televised during the hour of national transmissions on Sunday, August 14, [2011]." The State forwarded a copy of the video that was disseminated.

6.   Regarding the information presented by the representatives concerning the failure to comply with some aspects of this measure of reparation (*infra* eighth and ninth considering paragraphs), the State indicated that, in its opinion, the said public act "complied with all the requirements of the judgment." In this regard, the State mentioned that "not only had [it] held extensive discussions [with the victims and their representatives], but it had responded to all their requirements, including the program of the event, the place where it would be held, the level of representation of the State, the text of the plaque acknowledging responsibility, the speech of the Minister of the Interior, and even the paragraphs of the judgment which were read as part of the State's acknowledgement of responsibility." [2][207] In addition, it asserted that "the State has complied amply, and even excessively, with all the agreements reached with the petitioners during the five meetings held previously, even at a very complex institutional moment as a result of the tragic accident [...] resulting in the death of the [then] Interior Minister [...] and the Vice Minister for Legal Affairs and Human Rights of the Ministry [...] who was directly responsible for the organization of the act of acknowledgement of responsibility." The State mentioned that "the Court must be aware that the Government of Mexico is making indisputable efforts to respond to all the requests of the victims and their representatives, even on aspects that are not necessarily specified in the judgment."

7.   Furthermore, the State indicated that "the absence of the victims and their representatives [at the public act of acknowledgement of responsibility] was based on their exclusive decision and responsibility." In this regard, it mentioned that, in a meeting with the representatives on November 9, 2011, in response to the latter's request that the then Interior Minister should attend the act, the State undertook to take the necessary steps to ensure his presence. However, in the State's opinion, the assistance of other State officials, which the representatives were already aware of, complied with the ruling of the judgment concerning the "presence of senior national authorities." The State indicated that, the following day, the decision was taken that the Interior Minister would attend the public act of acknowledgement of responsibility that, initially, was to be held on November 14, 2011. Nevertheless, on November 11, the representatives issued a press communiqué and informed the Court that the said official had "cancelled

his participation" in the said public act. In this regard, the State indicated that, subsequently, the representatives claimed that there had been "confusion regarding the State's position." However, the State clarified that there was no confusion, because, during the meeting held on November 9, the State had undertaken to take the necessary steps with regard to the assistance of the Interior Minister. Hence on November 11, 2011, it confirmed to the representatives that this official would attend the public act of acknowledgement of responsibility but, to the State's surprise, the representatives indicated that they would not attend the event. Following the accident in which the then Interior Minister died, on November 15, 2011, the President of the Republic issued a series of instructions to "the competent State officials," among others, "to make every effort to ensure that the act of acknowledgement of responsibility is held as soon as possible," and "to ask for the comprehension of the victims and their representatives in this regard."[3] [208] Consequently, "for easily understandable scheduling reasons, it was decided that the date on which [the federal and state officials who had been designated to attend the even] could agree was November 17, 2011." The State indicated that it "considered that it would have the comprehension and the presence of the victims and their representatives" at the said act, because "they had been offered all the material and any other type of assistance to take part in it, given the very high level of representation of the State and that all the requests of the victims and their representatives, without exception, had been satisfied."

B. Arguments of the representatives

8.   The representatives indicated that "the State held the public act of acknowledgement ordered by the Court [complying] partially with the elements ordered in the judgment [...]," such as implementing it "in a public ceremony," "in the presence of senior national authorities," and "to make reparation to Rosendo Radilla Pacheco, in the agreed place, [with] speeches by the officials referring to the human rights violations declared in the judgment [...]." Nevertheless, they also indicated that Mexico had "not complied with [...] basic elements" required by the Court in this regard, because "it decided the date of the act unilaterally"; namely, November 17, 2011, and because it was not held in the presence of the next of kin of Mr. Radilla Pacheco. The representatives referred to several measures taken by the State previously, in order to hold the public act of acknowledgement of responsibility originally on November 14, 2011. In this regard, they stated that, owing to a discrepancy regarding the Interior Minister's assistance at the said act, which, according to the representatives had been agreed to by the State, they "assumed that it had been suspended on the day initially programmed," and this was confirmed by the State following the death, on November 11, 2011, of the officials who would have presided this event. The representatives indicated that "discussions were resumed by the parties, and the Government proposed,

initially, to hold the act on November 25 or 18." However, since "Tita Radilla had commitments abroad during the week of November 25, that she had made several months before and that, in addition, she would receive the Ponciano Arriaga Leija Award from the Human Rights Commission of the Federal District on November 18 in [Mexico City], the Government was asked to consider other dates." In a letter of November 14, 2011, addressed to the State by the representatives, they also mentioned that "following consultations with the Radilla family, they and their representatives, did not agree that the event [be] held on [November 18, 2011, …] owing to the emotional stress caused by the process [of preparation and cancellation of the public act of acknowledgement of responsibility]."

9.   In addition, the representatives asserted that, even though the State had undertaken to hold a meeting on November 18, 2011, to fix a new date for the public act by mutual agreement, the representatives were notified at 2 p.m. on November 16, 2011, that the said act would be held the following morning; and this is what happened, despite the objections of the representatives. In this regard, they indicated that the assistance of the next of kin of Rosendo Radilla Pacheco at the public act of acknowledgement of responsibility would be "materially" impossible, because: (i) the members of the family had scattered and faced "physical difficulty to regroup in less than 24 hours"; (ii) Tita Radilla had scheduled a doctor's appointment in Acapulco, […] which she could not cancel given her actual state of health," and (iii) there was a "real difficulty to ensure a timely invitation to attend the act to all the organizations of victims, national and international human rights, and civil society in general that had been invited by the Radilla family and their representatives for the original date […]."

C. Arguments of the Commission

10.   The Inter-American Commission assessed positively the information provided by the State "with regard to the implementation of the act on November 17, 2011." Nevertheless, it observed with concern the failure of the representatives to take part in this public act of acknowledgement of responsibility and, therefore, found that this "prevents considering that this aspect of the judgment has been complied with." Consequently, it asked the Court to request information from the parties on the measures that could be adopted in the near future to comply fully with this obligation.

D. Considerations of the Court

11.   The information in the case file indicates that the representatives and the State concur that they held several meetings in order to reach agreement on the details of the public act of acknowledgement of responsibility and the unveiling of the plaque recalling the forced disappearance of Rosendo Radilla Pacheco, both ordered in the judgment. Originally, this public act was going to be held on November 14, 2011. To this end, the details of the event had been approved by

the representatives; however, they insisted that the Minister of the Interior attend the said act. In this regard, in its judgment, the Court ordered that the public act of acknowledgement of responsibility should be held, *inter alia*, in the presence of senior national authorities and the next of kin of Mr. Radilla Pacheco." Therefore, even though the judgment did not specifically require the presence of the Mexican Minister of the Interior, the Court takes note that, nevertheless, the State made a major effort, to ensure that the said official could attend this public act. However, owing to his death, the act was postponed. Finally, the public act to acknowledge responsibility and to unveil the plaque took place on November 17, 2011, in Atoyac de Álvarez, Guerrero.

12.   The judgment also ordered that the "State and the next of kin of Mr. Radilla Pacheco and/or their representatives reach agreement on how [the public act of acknowledgement of responsibility] is held, as well as on its details, such as the place and date." In this regard, the information provided by the parties reveals that agreements already existed between the representatives and the State regarding the program of the public act of acknowledgement of responsibility, the place where it would be held, the text of the plaque to be unveiled, the speech that the Minister of the Interior would give, and the paragraphs of the judgment that would be read during the act. In this regard, the Court does not find that the information presented by the representatives includes satisfactory reasons to consider that Mr. Radilla Pacheco's next of kin were faced with insurmountable obstacles to attend the act held on November 17, 2011. Even though the representatives only received one day's notice of when it would be held, the level of the State officials whose presence was confirmed, which included two State Ministers, at least one of them at the request of the representatives themselves, and the fact that the essential aspects of the act had been agreed previously with the representatives, merited the next of kin of Rosendo Radilla Pacheco making an effort to attend the public act of acknowledgement of responsibility. In addition, it is on record that the State offered them any assistance they required to be able to attend.

13.   Based on the information submitted by the parties, together with the documentary support provided, the Court finds that the State has complied with the fourteenth operative paragraph of the judgment delivered in this case (*supra* Having Seen paragraph 1).

THEREFORE:

THE INTER-AMERICAN COURT OF HUMAN RIGHTS,

in exercise of its authority to monitor compliance with its decisions and in accordance with Articles 33, 62(1), 62(3) and 68(1) of the American Convention on Human Rights, 25(1) of its Statute, and 31(2) and 69 of its Rules of Procedure,

DECLARES THAT:

1.   As indicated in the eleventh to thirteenth considering paragraphs of

this order, the State has complied with the fourteenth operative paragraph of the judgment on preliminary objections, merits, reparations and costs delivered in this case.

AND DECIDES:

1.   To keep open the proceedings on monitoring compliance with regard to the other obligations of the judgment that remain pending in this case, in accordance with the order of May 19, 2011.

2.   To require the Secretariat of the Court to notify this Order to the United Mexican States, the Inter-American Commission on Human Rights and the representatives of the victims.

28-Jun-2012
Order of the Inter-American Court of Human Rights

HAVING SEEN:

2.   The Order for Monitoring Compliance with the Judgment issued by the Court on May 19, 2011, in which it declared, *inter alia*, that fulfillment of the following obligations is still pending:

> [...]

> g) To pay the compensation awarded in paragraphs 365, 370, 375 and 385 of the Judgment for pecuniary and non-pecuniary damages and costs and expenses, as appropriate (*Operative Paragraph 17 and Considering Paragraphs 53 to 56*).

> [...]

CONSIDERING THAT:

5.   In the briefs submitted by the State and the representatives, as well as during the private hearing held in the instant case (*supra* Having Seen 6), the parties referred in detail, *inter alia*, to the status of compliance with the obligation to pay the amounts awarded as compensation for pecuniary and non-pecuniary damages and the reimbursement of costs and expenses, where applicable, pursuant to Operative Paragraph 17 of the Judgment. Given that during the private hearing both the State and the representatives requested that the Court issue a decision on this point, this Order shall only address this measure of reparation. The Court shall also refer to the State's request concerning the obligation to investigate and determine the whereabouts of Mr. Rosendo Radilla Pacheco.

I. Obligation to pay the compensation awarded for pecuniary and nonpecuniary damages and the reimbursement of costs and expenses (*Operative paragraph 17 of the Judgment*)

> **A. *Information submitted by the State***

6.   The State reported that in compliance with the Judgment, and given the refusal by Mrs. Tita and Mr. Rosendo Radilla Martínez to accept the amounts

awarded to them as compensation, the State proceeded to deposit all the amounts ordered in the Judgment as compensation in favor of the four beneficiaries in the *Banco de Ahorro Nacional y Servicios Financieros*, S.N.C. (BANSEFI), through the purchase of certificates of deposit, and that it deposited the payment before the Tenth District Court for Civil Matters in the Federal District. Likewise, the State indicated that on September 22, 2011 the executor of the estate, Justino García Téllez, widower of Mrs. Andrea Radilla Martínez, went to the aforementioned court to collect two checks for the amounts allocated to Andrea Radilla Martínez, a victim in this case now deceased. Furthermore, the State mentioned that on September 25, 2011 Mrs. Tita and Mr. Rosendo Radilla Martínez presented a brief to the aforementioned court requesting that it issue the bills of deposit (checks) that were deposited by the State. Mrs. Tita and Mr. Rosendo Radilla Martínez submitted the brief, requesting payment of the amounts awarded in their favor by the Inter-American Court. Also, on their own behalf and in representation of Rosa, Romana, Evelina, Ana María, Agustina, Victoria, Judith, María del Pilar and María del Carmen, all with the surnames Radilla Martínez, and of Justino García Téllez, as heir and executor of the intestate succession of Andrea Radilla Martínez, they requested that the compensation awarded to Mr. Rosendo Radilla Pacheco for pecuniary and non-pecuniary damages be handed over to them. The District Court notified the State of this information, through the Ministry of the Interior, on May 3, 2012, which, in turn, informed said court that the persons requesting the handover of the checks deposited were authorized to receive and claim the payments.

7.   During the private hearing the State indicated that "since June 8 [2012] the judge before whom the checks were deposited determined that the payment in favor of Tita and Rosendo Radilla [Martínez] was in order [and that] in this regard [,] the checks are available to be cashed by [those persons] on the court's premises." Similarly, during the hearing, regarding the payment to the heirs of Mr. Rosendo Radilla Pacheco for pecuniary and non-pecuniary damages, the State indicated that it "[considered] that said amount[s] should be distributed in equal parts to the [heirs] of Mr. Radilla Pacheco," and therefore requested that the Court issue "a ruling so that the bill of deposit may be handed over to one of the representatives for payment and subsequent equitable distribution among Mr. Radilla Pacheco's heirs, namely, his children Rosendo, Tita, Rosa, Romana, Evelina, Ana María, Agustina, Victoria, Judith, María del Pilar and María del Carmen, all with the surnames Radilla Martínez, as well as Justino García Téllez, as heir and executor of the intestate succession of Andrea Radilla Martínez." The State considered that this would "avoid the need for the victims to initiate a procedure for the declaration of absence and presumption of death, which in the State's view is a disproportionate burden to the victims," for which reason

the Court's ruling was "of the utmost importance because without its approval the money could not be handed over to the persons mentioned." Accordingly, it requested that once the bills of deposit have been withdrawn, the Court declare that Operative Paragraph 17 of the Judgment has been fulfilled.

B. Observations of the representatives

8.   Initially, the representatives had informed the Court that Mr. Rosendo Radilla Pacheco's next of kin had accepted the payment ordered by the Court, and had asked the State to "withdraw" the deposit and hand over the checks directly to them, indicating that the deposit made before a judge is contrary to the Court's provisions since "for the beneficiary victims and heirs it implies the burden of undertaking disproportionate and unnecessary judicial procedures, which not only seriously complicate compliance with the Judgment, but also imply their re-victimization," specifically with regard to the [heirs] of Mr. Radilla Pacheco." The representatives emphasized that they had no objection to the amounts awarded in favor of Mr. Radilla Pacheco being deposited in a banking institution, but to their subsequent deposit before a judge, even though the heirs, through their representatives, had already informed the State of their decision to directly receive the amounts due. They pointed out that in order for Mr. Radilla Pacheco's heirs to receive the corresponding amounts they would need to initiate a voluntary jurisdiction proceeding, under domestic legislation, and also obtain a legal declaration of presumption of death of Mr. Rosendo Radilla Pacheco, all of which was burdensome. In that regard, they reported that on June 11, 2012 the aforementioned Tenth District Court for Civil Matters had ruled that in order to hand over the amounts corresponding to Mr. Radilla Pacheco's "claimants" further information is required for the "'purpose of having additional elements and so as not to incur in any liability on the part of [that] federal court.'" Briefly, the representatives indicated that it is now up to a judge to rule on the payment of this compensation. Therefore, they explained that they were "echoing the petition made by the State" in requesting a ruling from the Court so that the competent judicial authority may take this into account for the prompt payment of the bill of deposit for all the indemnities that are pending.

9.   Regarding Tita and Rosendo Radilla Martínez, victims in the instant case and direct beneficiaries of the indemnities ordered in the Judgment, the representatives stated that "there is no dispute whatsoever, since each one can directly approach the court to claim their respective checks." Likewise, regarding Mrs. Andrea Radilla Martínez, the representatives stated that her situation is based on the presumption of death of the beneficiary prior to payment of the compensation, and therefore her heirs are in a position to claim the respective funds in accordance with the civil law of the State of Guerrero.

10.   Finally, the representatives indicated, on the one hand, that on August 12 and 16, 2011, several national daily newspapers reported that the State had proceeded to deposit before a judge the amounts awarded as pecuniary and non-pecuniary damages in the Judgment. They stated that these reports "describe specific amounts, beneficiaries and the date of the deposit, as well as the court before which the funds were deposited." The representatives considered that this information puts the "Radilla family" at risk, since the State of Guerrero "is extremely violent and unsafe and the Radilla family is not exempt from that grave situation." For this reason, they requested that the Court urge the State to "abstain from issuing public reports on the process of compliance with the Judgment as regards the payment of the financial compensation and [,] in particular [,] the amounts and payment dates." On the other hand, the representatives petitioned the Court to "[,] request [that] the Mexican State reconsider the possibility of recognizing and extending the financial compensation to all of Mr. Radilla Pacheco's heirs in the adoption of the reparation measures, as the Court indicated in its Judgment in this case."

C. Observations of the Inter-American Commission on Human Rights

11.   The Commission noted that significant progress has been made and that the controversy regarding the mode of compliance with the compensation payments ordered in the Judgment had been settled. The Commission also acknowledged "the fluid dialogue which, according to the latest reports, has evidently taken place between the judicial authority in charge of authorizing the payments, and the Ministry of the Interior," and that according to said information, most of the indemnities can now be paid. Nevertheless, it noted that "the judge who would need to authorize this last compensation payment in favor of Rosendo Radilla, had asked for additional information." Furthermore, it endorsed the request made by the State, and reiterated by the representatives, that the Court issue a ruling on this point so that the payment of the compensation can be made effective.

D. Considerations of the Court

12.   In order for the Court to properly assess the degree of compliance with the instant reparation measure, it is necessary to recall that the Judgment ordered, on the one hand, the payment of certain amounts for the pecuniary and non-pecuniary damages suffered by Mr. Rosendo Radilla Pacheco. Pursuant to paragraph 387 of the Judgment, said amounts were to be distributed, in equal parts, among his heirs. On the other hand, the Court also ordered the payment of certain amounts for the non-pecuniary damage suffered by Tita, Andrea and Rosendo Radilla Martínez, which, according to paragraph 386 of the Judgment, were to be paid directly to these persons. Likewise, paragraph 388 of the Judgment indicates that in the event that the beneficiaries, namely, Tita, Andrea and Rosendo Radilla Martínez, should die before delivery of the corresponding compensations, these shall be

delivered directly to their successors, in accordance with the applicable domestic legislation. Finally, the Court also ordered an amount for costs and expenses to be paid to Mrs. Tita Radilla Martínez who, in turn, was required to pass this on to the relevant organizations, pursuant to paragraphs 385 and 386 of the Judgment.

13.   In the instant Order it is evident that several assumptions have arisen, regarding compliance with this measure of reparation, which should be addressed separately. In the first place, the Court recalls that in the Order of May 19, 2011 in this case it was decided that, given that the State had indicated that it was able to make the payments corresponding to Tita and Rosendo Radilla Martínez, and given that these persons did not wish to receive those payments, the Court considered that the requirements set out in paragraph 390 of the Judgment for the State proceed to comply with this measure of reparation through a bank deposit in a Mexican financial institution, following the criteria established in that paragraph, had been satisfied. Secondly, regarding the payment of the rest of the indemnities, the Court did not authorize the State to proceed with the bank deposit, but on the contrary, requested that the State provide further information on the matters reported by the representatives in the sense that that the payment could not be made through a voluntary jurisdiction proceeding before a notary public, as was asserted at that time. The Court also required the representatives to provide specific and detailed information on the reasons why they did not wish the payments to be made through a deposit in a Mexican banking institution.

14.   Regarding the foregoing, the Court notes that the State proceeded to deposit, without distinction, all the amounts ordered as compensation in a banking institution, something that was not ordered by the Court, and that, in addition, the State deposited the corresponding payments before a judge, which also was not authorized by the Court, under the terms specified in the preceding paragraph. In the aforementioned Order of May 19, 2011, the Court made it clear that while it is acceptable to use domestic procedures to ensure effective payment of the indemnities, such procedures cannot create a disproportionate burden for the victims, which unnecessarily hinders compliance with this measure of reparation in their favor.

15.   Nevertheless, regarding the compensation awarded directly to Tita, Rosendo and Andrea Radilla Martínez, victims in this case, the Court takes into account the representatives' statement that, despite the deposit of the payment before the judge, Mrs. Tita and Mr. Rosendo Radilla Martínez are in a position to petition the judge to request the handover of the amounts deposited in their favor. In view of the representatives' comments, the Court requests that these beneficiaries carry out the relevant procedures for this purpose since, if for reasons not attributable to the State said amounts were not received, the Court may consider this aspect of the reparation to have been fulfilled. In any case,

under the circumstances indicated, the Court cannot consider this point of the reparation to have been fulfilled until such time as Tita and Rosendo Radilla Martínez effectively receive the amounts awarded in their favor, under the terms indicated. Moreover, regarding the specific status of the compensation to be paid to Andrea Radilla Martínez, now deceased, this should follow the procedure ordered under domestic legislation so that her heirs may receive the amount due. This is also contemplated in paragraph 388 of the Judgment, as already noted. Once the heirs of Mrs. Andrea Radilla Martínez receive the amounts due to them, the Court shall consider this reparation measure to have been fulfilled.

16.   With regard to the deposit before a judge of the compensation awarded for the pecuniary and non-pecuniary damages suffered by Mr. Rosendo Radilla Pacheco in favor of his heirs, the Court considers, as was accepted by the State during the private hearing (*supra* Considering paragraph 7), that the manner in which the State chose to comply with this measure creates a disproportionate burden for the beneficiaries, which is unnecessarily hindering compliance with this reparation measure. As is evident from the information provided by the representatives, and from the documents contained in the case file, the beneficiaries would need to obtain, among other things, a declaration of absence and, after two years, a declaration of presumed death, and would also need to cover a number of expenses for the processing thereof. In particular, the Court considers it unacceptable that, in a case of a person's forced disappearance, a declaration of presumed death should be required so that the heirs may receive the compensation ordered by this Court. In accordance with the Inter-American Convention on Forced Disappearance of Persons, to which Mexico has been a Party since April 9, 2002 (*supra* Considering paragraph 2), and with the Judgment issued in this case, Mr. Rosendo Radilla Pacheco is forcibly disappeared, and his death cannot be presumed given that for this the State must, in turn, prove that situation, as established in the Judgment. "Forced disappearance" and "death" are two juridical situations distinct from each other which, in light of International Human Rights Law, cannot be treated on an equal footing or on the basis of the same assumptions and do not necessarily generate the same legal consequences.

17.   In its Judgment, the Inter-American Court ordered that the compensation corresponding to Mr. Rosendo Radilla Pacheco be distributed among his heirs. Therefore, the Mexican State must comply fully with this obligation. Article 68 of the American Convention establishes that States must comply with the rulings of the Inter-American Court in any case to which they are parties. Likewise, in the Judgment (*supra* Having Seen 1, paragraph 339) it was also established that the Judiciary must exercise a "control of conventionality" *ex officio* between domestic regulations and the American Convention, within the framework of its respective jurisdictions and of the relevant procedural regulations. In this regard,

the Judiciary must take into account not only the treaty, but also the interpretation of the Inter-American Court as the final interpreter of the American Convention. All this was also established by the Supreme Court of Justice of Mexico when it ruled on the Judgment of this Court in File 912/2010, a decision contained in the file on this case.

18.   Bearing in mind the foregoing, and given that the Judgment states that the amounts payable in compensation for the damage suffered by Mr. Radilla Pacheco must be distributed in equal parts among his heirs (*supra* Having Seen 1, paragraph 387), and given that there is no dispute between the State and the representatives as to who Mr. Radilla Pacheco's beneficiaries are, the State, through the competent authority, must immediately proceed to pay those amounts, either directly to the beneficiaries or through their chosen representative. This does not preclude continuing with the relevant domestic proceedings, provided that these do not impose a disproportionate burden on the beneficiaries.

19.   The Court further notes that neither the representatives nor the State submitted information concerning payment of the amount ordered for costs and expenses, as reiterated in the Order of May 19, 2011 (*supra* Having Seen 1, Considering paragraph 56). The Court once again requests the presentation of that information.

20.   In view of the foregoing considerations, the Court considers that compliance is pending with the obligation of pay the amounts set for compensation for pecuniary and nonpecuniary damages, and for reimbursement of costs and expenses (Operative paragraph 17 of the Judgment).

21.   Finally, regarding the representatives' request that the State abstain from making public the details of the compensation payment, from the information submitted, the Court cannot presume that the publication of the alleged payment of the compensation in national newspapers was made at the request of the State itself. Likewise, the Court considers it pertinent to recall that the Judgment issued in this case, together with the procedure to monitor its fulfillment, are public. As to the representatives' request that the Court urge the State to "reconsider the possibility of recognizing and extending the financial compensation to all of Mr. Radilla Pacheco's heirs in the adoption of the reparation measures," the Court recalls that although the Judgment, having regard to the State's acknowledgement of international responsibility in this case, urged the State to consider granting in good faith adequate compensation to the rest of Mr. Rosendo Radilla Pacheco's relatives who were not identified as victims by the Inter-American Commission (*supra* Having Seen 1, para. 328), the verification of whether or not the State has agreed to grant such reparations to these relatives of Mr. Radilla Pacheco is not the purpose of this procedure to monitor compliance with this Judgment. Given that this point was not included in the Judgment, the Court cannot rule on this matter.

Nevertheless, the Court notes that the State reported that the psychological and/or psychiatric care ordered in the Judgment for Tita, Rosendo and Andrea Radilla Martínez, was also offered to other relatives of Mr. Rosendo Radilla Pacheco who were not considered as victims in the Judgment. Regarding compliance with that measure of reparation, the Court shall issue a ruling at another time.

II. Petition by the State.

22.   Finally, regarding the obligations to investigate the facts and identify, bring to trial and, if applicable, sanction those responsible, and to determine the whereabouts of Mr. Rosendo Radilla Pacheco, the State requested that the Court allow it to submit information on compliance with these points every six months, and not every three months as required by the Court in its Order of May 19, 2011. Neither the representatives nor the Commission raised any objections in this regard. Therefore, the Court grants the petition of the State, which may submit the aforementioned information every six months.

THEREFORE:

THE INTER-AMERICAN COURT OF HUMAN RIGHTS,

In exercise of its authority to monitor compliance with its decisions, pursuant to Articles 33, 62(1), 62(3), 65, 67 and 68(1) of the American Convention on Human Rights, Articles 25(1) and 30 of its Statute, and Article 31(2) of its Rules of Procedure,

DECLARES THAT:

1.   In accordance with the relevant provisions of the Considering paragraphs of this Order, compliance is pending with the obligation set forth in Operative Paragraph 17 of the Judgment on Preliminary Objections, Merits, Reparations and Costs issued in this case.

AND DECIDES:

1.   To require the United Mexican States to adopt such measures as are necessary to effectively and promptly comply with the points that are pending fulfillment, in accordance with Declarative Paragraph 1 of this Order and with Declarative Paragraphs a) a e), and g) to i) of the Order of May 19, 2011 issued in this case.

2.   To request that the United Mexican States submit, by October 3, 2012 at the latest, a detailed report on the measures adopted to comply with the reparations ordered that are still pending fulfillment, under the terms of this Order and the Order of May 19, 2011. Subsequently, the Mexican State shall continue to submit a compliance report every three months. Regarding the investigation of the facts, and the identification, trial and, if applicable, sanction of those responsible, and the determination of the whereabouts of Mr. Rosendo Radilla Pacheco, the State may submit information every six months, after the report of October 3, 2012 has been submitted.

3.   To request the victims' representatives and the Inter-American Commission

on Human Rights to submit any observations deemed pertinent to the reports of the United Mexican States mentioned in Operative Paragraph 2 of this Order, within a period of four and six weeks, respectively, as from the date of their receipt.

4.   To continue monitoring compliance with the Judgment on Preliminary Objections, Merits, Reparations and Costs of November 23, 2009.

5. To require the Secretariat of the Inter-American Court of Human Rights to notify this Order to the United Mexican States, the victims' representatives and the Inter-American Commission on Human Rights.

14-May-2013
Order of the Inter-American Court of Human Rights

HAVING SEEN:

1.   The Judgment on preliminary objections, merits, reparations and costs (hereinafter "the Judgment") delivered by the Inter-American Court of Human Rights (hereinafter "the Inter-American Court" or "the Court") on November 23, 2009. In this Judgment, it was established that, on August 25, 1974, members of the Army of the United Mexican States (hereinafter "the State" or "Mexico") forcibly disappeared Rosendo Radilla Pacheco, in the systematic context of numerous forced disappearances of persons. Furthermore, the State itself acknowledged, on the one hand, that Mr. Radilla Pacheco had been illegally and arbitrarily deprived of his liberty by a public official and, on the other hand, that Mexico had delayed unjustifiably the investigations conducted into these facts. Consequently, the Court decided that the State was responsible for the violation, to the detriment of Mr. Radilla Pacheco, of Articles 3, 4(1), 5(1), 5(2) and 7(1) of the American Convention on Human Rights (hereinafter "the American Convention" or "the Convention"), in relation to Article 1(1) of this instrument, and to Articles I and XI of the Inter-American Convention on Forced Disappearance of Persons (hereinafter "the ICFDP"). In addition, it declared the State's responsibility for the violation, to the detriment of the next of kin of Mr. Radilla Pacheco, of Articles 5(1) and 5(2) of the Convention, in relation to Article 1(1) thereof, owing to the suffering they endured as a result of his forced disappearance, and of Articles 8(1) and 25(1) of the Convention, in relation to its Articles 1(1) and 2 and to Articles I(a), (b) and (d), IX and XIX of the ICFDP, owing to the absence of a judicial response to clarify the facts of the case, and because it extended the competence of the military jurisdiction to crimes that were not strictly related to military discipline or legal rights intrinsic to the military sphere. Lastly, the Court determined that the State had failed to comply with the obligation to adopt provisions of domestic law established in Article 2 of the Convention, in relation to Articles I and III of the ICFDP, owing to the incomplete definition of the crime of forced disappearance of persons in the Federal Criminal Code.

2.   The Orders on monitoring compliance with judgment issued by the Court on May 19, and December 1, 2011, and on June 28, 2012. In these Orders the Court declared that the following aspects of the Judgment remained pending:

   (a) To conduct effectively with due diligence and within a reasonable time, the investigation and, as applicable, the criminal proceedings that are underway in relation to the detention and subsequent disappearance of Rosendo Radilla Pacheco, in order to determine the corresponding criminal responsibilities and apply the punishments and consequences that the law establishes (*eighth operative paragraph*);

   (b) To continue the genuine search for, and the prompt discovery of, Mr. Radilla Pacheco or, if applicable, his mortal remains (*ninth operative paragraph*);

   (c) To adopt, within a reasonable time, the pertinent legislative reforms to make article 57 of the Code of Military Justice compatible with the relevant international standards and with the American Convention on Human Rights (*tenth operative paragraph*);

   (d) To adopt, within a reasonable time, the pertinent legislative reforms to make article 215A of the Federal Criminal Code compatible with the relevant international standards and with the Inter-American Convention on Forced Disappearance of Persons (*eleventh operative paragraph*);

   (e) To implement, within a reasonable time and with the respective budgetary allocation, permanent programs or courses to analyze the case law of the inter-American system for the protection of human rights concerning the limits of the military criminal justice system, as well as a training program on the proper investigation and prosecution of acts that constitute forced disappearance of persons (*twelfth operative paragraph*);

   (f) To prepare a profile of the life of Rosendo Radilla Pacheco (*fifteenth operative paragraph*);

   (g) To provide free psychological and/or psychiatric treatment immediately, adequately and effectively, through its specialized public health institutions, to those declared victims in the Judgment who request this (*sixteenth operative paragraph*), and

   (h) To pay the amounts established in paragraphs 365, 370, 375 and 385 of the Judgment as compensation for pecuniary and non-pecuniary damage and to reimburse costs and expenses, as applicable (*seventeenth operative paragraph*).

CONSIDERING THAT:

5.   First, the Court observes that, on July 14, 2011, the Supreme Court of Justice of the Nation (hereinafter "the Supreme Court" or "the SCJN") issued

a "Ruling of the Court in Plenary" in the case file "Various matters 912/2010," [7][209] in which it described the specific obligations of the Mexican State and, in particular, of the Judiciary of the Federation, as a result of the Judgment handed down in the case of *Radilla Pacheco* (*supra* Having Seen paragraph 1). In this ruling, the SCJN stated that the Judiciary was obliged to exercise, *ex officio,* control of conformity between domestic laws and the American Convention and that, to this end, it must take into account article 1 of the Mexican Constitution, which, following the reform of July 10, 2011, establishes that "[l]aws relating to human rights shall be interpreted in accordance with [the] Constitution and with the international treaties on this matter, at all times giving preference to the greatest protection for the individual." In addition, this ruling indicated that the decisions of the Inter-American Court with regard to Mexico and, in particular, the Judgment handed down in the case of *Radilla Pacheco* (*supra* Having Seen paragraph 1), "are obligatory for all the organs [of the State ...] within their respective terms of reference [...]. Therefore, not only the specific operative paragraphs of the Judgment, but also all the criteria contained in the Judgment deciding this litigation are binding for the Judiciary. Furthermore, it shall be considered that the rest of the case law of the Inter-American Court, arising from the judgments in which the Mexican State is not a party, provides guiding criteria for all the decisions of the Mexican judges, provided that these are the most favorable for the individual [...]." [8][210] In addition, in this Ruling, the SCJN also established that "the military justice system may not, under any circumstance, be used in situations that violate human rights of civilians," because the latter have the right to "be subject to the jurisdiction of an ordinary judge or court." [9][211]

6.   The Inter-American Court underlines that this Ruling of the Supreme Court of Justice of the Nation constitutes an important step forward as regards the protection of human rights, not only in the context of this case, but in all the domestic spheres of the Mexican State. Consequently, this Court assesses positively the considerations made by the highest court of the State, which are extremely significant for the enhancement of human rights in the region.

> **A. Obligation to conduct effectively with due diligence and within a reasonable time, the investigation and, if applicable, the criminal proceedings that are underway in relation to the detention and subsequent disappearance of Rosendo Radilla Pacheco, in order to determine the corresponding criminal responsibilities and apply the punishments and consequences that the law establishes (*eighth operative paragraph of the Judgment*)**

7.   The State indicated that "the investigation into the facts related to the forced disappearance of Mr. [...] Radilla Pacheco is being conducted under preliminary inquiry SIEDF/CGI/454/2007, for which the [Office of the Prosecutor General of the Republic (PGR)] is responsible." It also indicated that, despite the

death of one of the accused in the criminal proceedings, "the necessary measures continue to be taken in order to prove the probable responsibility of the other members of the military services who were denounced." In this regard, it advised that, "in order to identify the individuals who took part in the facts and to prove the crime of forced disappearance of persons, in June and August 2012, statements were taken from [four] individuals who, at the time of the events, worked in the 27th military zone in the state of Guerrero." The State also indicated that "the Public Prosecution Service took the statement of one witness [...] who, at the time of the events, [...] was able to interview a General from the Atoyac de Álvarez Barracks, Guerrero, and who indicated that during their meeting he noted that, on a shelf, there were files that apparently belonged to those detained."

8.   The State also indicated that "the Investigations Coordination Bureau of the [Prosecutor General's Office had] requested [the] service records of eight members of the Army [...] so as to be able to summon them to appear before the Social Agency of the Federation." According to the State, these soldiers were questioned regarding "the mass or clandestine graves and places where the deceased persons were buried." In addition, it advised that "plans are underway to continue taking statements from retired soldiers who had command functions in the 1970s and who were attached to the 27th Military Zone [...]."

9.   Lastly, regarding the victims' access to the case file of the proceedings underway for the facts of the case, Mexico advised that "the representatives of the victims [had] full access and legal standing in the investigation of the facts, participating with the Public Prosecution Service as additional parties" and, also, that it had complied with the "undertaking made to the victims [...] to provide them with copies of the public version of the preliminary inquiry on a monthly basis," delivering these in keeping with a timetable established with the representatives. Also, "in compliance [with the] commitment made during the hearing on monitoring compliance held on June 22, 2012," before the Inter-American Court, the State forwarded "the digitized public version of the volumes of the preliminary hearing [...] that have been handed over to the next of kin of Mr. Radilla Pacheco".

10.   The representatives appreciated "that the State [...] had taken the initiative to make [...] a more complete examination of the documentation and to receive testimony, mainly from individuals who were soldiers posted in the zone of conflict where [...] the facts occurred that resulted in the disappearance of [Mr.] Radilla Pacheco." However, they observed that "many of the people indicated as participants in the facts [...] are already deceased, [and that ...] it is regrettable that the Mexican authorities have taken so much time to further the investigations," because this has meant that "many lines of investigation have evaporated with the passage of time [...]." The representatives also indicated that

the lines of investigation followed by the State have not taken into account the systematic pattern surrounding the facts of the disappearance of Rosendo Radilla Pacheco, as ordered in the Judgment. Thus, they underscored that, the probable perpetrators of the facts have still not been identified, and asked the Court to require the State to present more detailed information on the preliminary inquiry. Nevertheless, the representatives indicated their agreement regarding "the way in which [the State ...] has been complying" with the regular delivery of the file of the preliminary inquiry.

11.   The Commission expressed its "concern [owing to] the State's failure to present complete and detailed information on the steps taken in the preliminary inquiry." It also indicated that, more than "three years after the Judgment was handed down [...] and almost forty years after the facts occurred, there is no evidence of any substantial progress in the investigation into the forced disappearance of Mr. Radilla Pacheco. In addition, it stated that "there is no evidence that those presumably responsible for the victim's disappearance have been identified, or that the context in which the facts occurred has been taken into account." Lastly, the Commission considered that this situation was growing worse with the passing of time, because, according to the information forwarded by the State, "one of the individuals allegedly involved in the facts that being investigated has apparently died." Thus, it asked "the Court to require the State to present detailed and updated information on compliance with this aspect, including: (i) the specific results of the measures taken; (ii) the timetable for the measures to be taken, and (iii) the information obtained from State archives, and the use to which it will be put."

12.   The Court appreciates the efforts made by the State under the preliminary inquiry being conducted by the authorities of the ordinary system of justice; in particular, the reception of the statements of 13 possible witnesses, who include members of the armed forces. However, from the information provided by the parties, the Court notes that statements remain pending that could lead to substantial progress in determining those responsible for the forced disappearance of Mr. Radilla Pacheco, and that individuals indicted in the proceedings have died as a result of the passage of time. In this regard, the Court recalls that the implementation of this measure of reparation not only involves the obligation to conduct investigations into the whereabouts of Mr. Radilla Pacheco, but also the efficient implementation, with due diligence and within a reasonable time, of investigations designed to determine the corresponding criminal responsibilities and the consequences that the law establishes, bearing in mind the systematic pattern that permitted the perpetration of grave human rights violations in this case. [10][212] The Court emphasizes that, around 39 years have passed since Mr. Radilla Pacheco was disappeared by State agents, and therefore urges the State to take, within a reasonable time, the measures that remain pending under the preliminary inquiry. In this regard, the Court recalls that

the passage of time has a directly proportional relationship to the limitation–and, in some cases, the impossibility–to obtain evidence and/or testimony, making the practice of probative measures to clarify the facts under investigation, to identify the possible authors and participants, and to determine the eventual criminal responsibilities difficult and even nugatory or ineffective. Despite this, the national authorities are not exempt from making every effort required to comply with their obligation to investigate. [11][213]

13.   Nevertheless, the Court appreciates the delivery of the public version of the preliminary investigation to the representatives, in keeping with the timetable agreed with the parties, and urges the State to continue complying with this undertaking. Lastly, based on the foregoing, the Court requests the State to provide recent information that is as complete as possible on the progress made in implementing this measure of reparation.

B. Obligation to continue the genuine search for, and the prompt discovery of, Mr. Radilla Pacheco or, if applicable, his mortal remains (*ninth operative paragraph of the Judgment*)

14.   The State indicated that "the search for the disappeared Rosendo Radilla [Pacheco] has not only been effective, but also founded and motivated by investigations carried out by the Social Agency of the Federations since 2008[, with the full agreement of the victims and, also, characterized [...] by a high degree of professionalism of the experts from different disciplines and institutions [...]." It also indicated that, "on October 31, 2011, excavation work was commenced in the area" of Atoyac, with the presence of a professional who provided psychosocial support to the victims' next of kin during the procedure. However, "no clandestine graves or evidence of skeletal remains were detected" on that occasion. The State also indicated that "the reports were received of the experts in social anthropology from the Prosecutor General's Office and from the National Institute of Anthropology and History (INAH)"; they had been requested by the latter institution, and "based on the recommendations made in the two reports, the Public Prosecution Service inspected the suggested areas on January 24, 2013," avoiding a repetition of certain places. In addition, the State indicated that, on February 12, 2013, following a working meeting in the offices of the PGR with INAH experts, "orders were given to scan the subsoil in three areas, [...] and this was done from March 11 to 16, 2013." Lastly, the State emphasized "that, during these procedures, access was provided to the next of kin of disappeared persons who were on the scene [...]."

15.   The representatives indicated repeatedly that this measure "is the most important one as regards integral reparation for the human rights violations caused by the State, [...] because the uncertainty about [the whereabouts of Mr. Radilla Pacheco] prevents the victim's next of kin [...] from concluding their mourning

process [...]." Furthermore, they welcomed the State's initiative "to undertake a thorough search for [Mr.] Radilla Pacheco, gathering relevant documentation and testimony that could reveal information on his whereabouts. However, once again, [they] regret[ted] that the Mexican State had delayed so long in undertaking this search, which seriously affects the possibilities of its success." In addition, they advised that, "even though the prosecution authorities [collected] information by recovering historical archives and testimony, this information has not yet been duly systematized." Lastly, they indicated that "from May 20 to June 1, 2013, the fourth stage of excavations in the former Atoyac Military Barracks will be carried out," and that they will be "monitoring the way in which the procedure is carried out," in order to provide the Court with information in this regard.

16.   The Commission assessed positively the efforts made by the State "owing to the reports [of the experts in social anthropology] that would eventually assist in the search for Mr. Radilla [Pacheco]." It also stressed "the meeting that the State had held with the victim's next of kin to provide them with specific information on the plans to continue the search." Furthermore, it stated that it was awaiting the results of the fourth stage of excavations at the former Atoyac Military Barracks.

17.   The Court underlines the efforts made by the State to find the remains of Mr. Radilla Pacheco, particularly the work of excavation and scanning that has been carried out in the area corresponding to the municipality of Atoyac, as well as the preparation of social anthropology reports in order to obtain new lines of investigation so as to locate them. The Court also appreciates the fact that the State has coordinated with the search measures taken by the victims, as ordered in the Judgment.[12][214] Consequently, the Court urges the State to continue the searches that are underway, within the framework of the communication that it has developed with the victims and their representatives. In this regard, the Court recalls that the effective search for and prompt finding of Mr. Radilla Pacheco or his mortal remains forms part of the next of kin's right to know the truth,[13][215] and will help alleviate the anguish and suffering caused to his family. Thus, the Court requires the State to provide updated information on the measures taken to find Mr. Radilla Pacheco or, if applicable, his mortal remains.

C. **Obligation to adopt, within a reasonable time, the pertinent legislative reforms in order to make article 57 of the Code of Military Justice compatible with the American Convention on Human Rights, article 215A of the Federal Criminal Code compatible with the Inter-American Convention on Forced Disappearance of Persons, and both articles compatible with the relevant international standards (*tenth and eleventh operative paragraphs of the Judgment*)**

18.   The State reiterated that, on October 19, 2010, the Federal Executive

had submitted to the Congress of the Union the initiative for the issue of a decree, which "would reform, partially annul, and add to, several provisions of the Code of Military Justice, [including its article 57, and …] of the Federal Criminal Code[, including its article 215A…]." In this regard, the State advised that the Joint Committees on Justice and on Legislative Studies of the Senate had approved the report on the proposed decree, so that it had been forwarded to the Plenary of the Senate. However, "the senators had not reached a consensus for [the bill] to be discussed formally during the Plenary session […]." Therefore, according to the State, "work was being done on a new bill that would permit compliance with the measure established by the Court […]."

19.   Furthermore, regarding the modification of the Code of Military Justice, the State reiterated that "the bill proposed to exclude from the military jurisdiction the crimes of forced disappearance of persons, torture and rape, so that these fall within the competence of the ordinary courts."[14 216] In addition, the State underlined that, under the above-mentioned ruling of July 14, 2011[15 217] (*supra* Considering paragraph 5), the Plenary of the Supreme Court of Justice of the Nation had determined that national judges at all levels were obliged to exercise, *ex officio*, control of conformity with the Convention in the terms established by the Inter-American Court, and that the judges of the ordinary justice system must hear all the cases of human rights violations presumably committed by members of the Armed Forces. The SCJN also established that ordinary justice would have competence to hear all the military cases that do not refer to military discipline alone.[16 218]

20.   Furthermore, regarding the amendment of the Federal Criminal Code ordered in the Judgment, the State affirmed that it had proposed the definition of the crime of forced disappearance appropriately and based on the relevant international standards. In addition, it recalled that in the Order on monitoring compliance with judgment of May 19, 2011, the Inter-American Court had noted that this proposed reform incorporated the elements established in the Judgment and in the Inter-American Convention on Forced Disappearance for an appropriate definition of the crime.

21.   For their part, regarding the amendment of the Code of Military Justice, the representatives indicated that "the [decree] that the Mexican State referred to […] is not compatible with what was ordered […] in the Judgment," because "it only proposes to exclude from the military criminal jurisdiction the crimes of forced disappearance of persons, torture and rape, so that these will fall within the competence of the ordinary courts, [reserving] the authority to investigate and to analyze whether the facts are in keeping with the legal assumptions [to] the Office of the Prosecutor General for Military Justice […]." They indicated, also, that, "since October 2010, 16 amendments have been presented to the Congress of the Union to limit the competence of the military jurisdiction and, at this

time, no report has been produced that results in a discussion in the chambers of the Congress of the Union." Consequently, they affirmed that "the only way in which the State can comply with [this measure of reparation is] by presenting and approving an initiative that is in accordance with the international standards for the protection of human rights established in the Judgment [...]."

22.   Regarding the said Ruling of the SCJN of July 14, 2011 (*supra* Considering paragraph 5), the representatives indicated that this "constitutes a progressive opinion, but it is not legally binding for other Mexican judges, because [the SCJN] has still not decided the contentious cases that it is hearing on this issue." They underscored that, "[f]or the said opinion to be obligatory for the authorities, the laws of Mexico establish that it is necessary to produce case law, which will not happen until the [SCJN] decides five cases in the sense indicated; that is, prohibiting the military jurisdiction from hearing cases of human rights violations." In addition, they indicated that this ruling "is far from constituting a guarantee that [all] cases of human rights violations will be heard promptly by ordinary courts," because, according to the representatives, "it is a rather fragile element that could change according to the composition of the highest court."

23.   Now, regarding the required amendment of the Federal Criminal Code, the representatives considered that this obligation "will not be complied with until amendments are made to the law, [... adapting] the definition of forced disappearance to the provisions of the international standards." In addition, they indicated that compliance with the Judgment of the Inter-American Court is an obligation "for the State, not only the Executive"; hence, according to the representatives, "the authorities involved have the obligation to expedite the reforms to ensure that this is implemented."

24.   Lastly, the representatives indicated that the document "Pact for Mexico" establishes that "the legal framework shall be updated to prevent and to punish effectively inhuman and degrading acts, as well as torture, cruelty and forced disappearance," and that "the framework for the justice system will be restructured so as to ensure that no one has privileges," and in order to restrict the competence of the military jurisdiction. However, they expressed their concern in view of the fact that compliance with this obligation was not a priority, because, according to this document, the State only planned to initiate the said process of legislative reform in the second half of 2013, despite the fact that more than three years have passed since the Judgment was handed down in this case.

25.   The Commission indicated that the ruling of the Supreme Court of Justice of the Nation of July 14, 2011, "constitutes a significant step forward as regards limiting the military jurisdiction in Mexico and reveals the impact of the inter-American System [on the] protection of human rights in order to overcome obstacles in compliance with the international obligations of the State in this

regard." However, it noted that this change in case law had to be incorporated into legislative reforms. In this regard, the Commission noted with concern that the State had "merely repeated information [... that] does not reveal specific progress in compliance with these measures of reparation," and "insists on promoting a legislative reform that would not be fully in line with the terms [of the Judgment]." In this regard the Commission asked the Inter-American Court to require the State to provide information on how the draft reform of article 57 of the Code of Military Justice was adapted to the standards established in the Judgment in relation to the intervention of the military jurisdiction in crimes committed by Army officials, and regarding the possible intervention of the military jurisdiction at the investigation stage "of a crime that is not an offense committed during the course of duties." In addition, it observed with concern that the legislative reform of article 57 of the Code of Military Justice "is in its initial stages, and no report has been approved," so that "the State continues to fail to comply with the order of the Inter-American Court." Lastly, it asked the Court to require further information on the reform of article 215A of the Federal Criminal Code and recalled that the Judgment maintains that the State "cannot merely present the bill with the aforementioned modifications, but must "ensure its prompt approval and entry into force.'"

26.   The Court reiterates that the ruling of the SCJN of July 14, 2011 (*supra* Considering paragraph 5), makes a positive contribution to the protection and promotion of human rights in the Mexican State, among others, by requiring that members of the Judiciary exercise, *ex officio*, control of conformity with the Convention in the terms of the Judgment delivered by the Inter-American Court in this case.[17 219] Specifically, this "Ruling of the Plenary" determined that:

> "Article 57, paragraph II, of the Code of Military Justice, is incompatible with the provisions of [...] article 13 [of the Federal Constitution ...] in light of Articles 2 and 8(1) of the American Convention [...] because establishing which crimes are against the military discipline does not guarantee to civilians or their next of kin who are victims of human rights violations [that] they can be subject to the jurisdiction of an ordinary judge or court. Consequently, since the second paragraph of article 1 of the Federal Constitution provides that the norms relating to human rights will be interpreted in the terms of the Constitution and in accordance with the relevant international treaties, always giving preference the greatest protect for the individual, it should be considered that, under no circumstance, can the military justice system operate in relation to situations that violate the human rights of civilians."[18 220]

27.   In addition, the case file before the Inter-American Court reveals that, from August 6 to September 13, 2012, "the Plenary of the SCJN took over the

hearing of [13] cases related to the restriction of the military jurisdiction, in all of them deciding to refer the case to the ordinary justice system."[19][221]

28.   In addition, the Court appreciates the efforts made by the State to amend article 57 of the Code of Military Justice. Despite this, the Court reiterates what it stated in the Order on compliance in this case issued on May 19, 2011, to the effect that the initiative presented to the Congress of the Union on October 19, 2010, "is insufficient because it does not comply fully with the standards indicated in the Judgment," since it would allow the Military Public Prosecution Service to investigate crimes perpetrated against civilians by military personnel, and because "the said reform only establishes that the military jurisdiction will not be competent [to deal with] forced disappearance of persons, torture and rape committed by military personnel."[20][222]

29.   Nevertheless, the Court underlines the efforts made by the State to make the definition of the crime of forced disappearance contained in article 215A of the Federal Criminal Code compatible with the relevant international standards. However, the Court reiterates that, in order to comply with this aspect of the Judgment, "the State should not merely 'present' the corresponding bill, but also ensure its prompt approval and entry into force, according to the respective procedures established in domestic law."[21][223] The Court also recalls that the said bill must respect the corresponding criteria described in the Judgment in this case.[22][224] Lastly, based on the foregoing, the Court asked the State to forward updated information on the effective implementation of the reforms that were ordered to the Code of Military Justice and to the Federal Criminal Code.

D. **Obligation to implement, within a reasonable time and with the respective budgetary allocation, permanent programs and courses relating to the analysis of the case law of the inter-American system for the protection of human rights in relation to the limits of the military criminal justice system, as well as a training program on the proper investigation and prosecution of acts that constitute forced disappearance of persons (*twelfth operative paragraph of the Judgment*)**

30.   The State advised that it had offered various training sessions, courses, seminars and conferences to the judges of the Judiciary of the Federation, the agents of the Public Prosecution Service of the Prosecutor General's Office (PGR), and the judges and members of the Defense Secretariat (SEDENA) and the Navy Secretariat (SEMAR).

31.   Regarding the implementation of the training sessions for officials of the Federation's Judiciary, the State advised that, under the ruling issued on July 14, 2011, in the case file "Various matters 912/2010" (*supra* Considering paragraph 5), the Plenary of the Supreme Court had outlined a series of actions designed to

implement training courses on the standards of the inter-American system for the protection of human rights "in relation to the limits of the military jurisdiction, judicial guarantees and judicial protection, and also the international standards applicable to the administration of justice and [...] the proper prosecution of the crime of forced disappearance." It also indicated that, on September 23 and 24, 2011, the SCJN had organized an introductory training seminar for approximately 1,800 of the country's federal judges and magistrates focused, among other matters, on examining the judgments of the Inter-American Court in cases relating to Mexico, including the Judgment handed down in the case of *Radilla Pacheco*.[23]
[225] In addition, it stressed, from 2010 to 2012, "jurisdictional and juridical" officials had taken part in different academic programs and seminars on topics such as the forced disappearance of persons and the military jurisdiction. Furthermore, the State advised that the Judiciary of the Federation had implemented "itinerant workshops [on] the impact of the constitutional reform of *amparo,* and of human rights, on jurisdictional activities," which were organized in three stages[24][226] and in conjunction with the Federal Council of the Judicature, the Ministry of Foreign Affairs, the National Commission of Superior Courts of Justice, the Mexican Association of Dispensers of Justice, and the Office in Mexico of the United Nations High Commissioner for Human Rights. According to the State, one of the objectives of these workshops was "to share with the heads of district and circuit courts different ways of applying extensive control of conformity with the Convention by examining a practical case on the issue of forced disappearance and the military jurisdiction."

32.   Regarding the training of agents of the Public Prosecution Service of the Prosecutor General's Office (PGR), the State indicated that, from July 9 to 30, 2011, it had imparted the course "Forced disappearance of persons and international criminal law on human rights," in the National Institute of Criminal Science. Moreover, among other training activities,[25][227] on May 19 and August 10, 2012, the Deputy Ombudsman for attention to victims and community services of the PGR imparted a 50-hour specialization course on "Human rights, and forced disappearance of persons" to 37 PGR officials.

33.   Furthermore, regarding the training for members of the military forces, the State advised that the Defense Secretariat (SEDENA) had imparted different courses addressed at this sector, particularly "as part of the module on 'Human rights and international humanitarian law' that is one of the Officers' Training Courses,[26][228] [...] and of the courses of the General and Air Force Chief of Staff of the War College, [in which] the rights to judicial guarantees and to judicial protection [are studied]." In addition, the State provided information on a course offered in the Center for Advanced Studies of the Army and the Air Force, and in the course of the Joint Chief of Staff of the War College on the analysis of the case

law of the inter-American system for the protection of human rights in relation to judicial guarantees and judicial protection, the limits to the military criminal jurisdiction, and the forced disappearance of persons. In this regard, the State indicated that "the Navy Secretariat (SEMAR) imparted courses on the analysis of the case law of the inter-American system to the personnel attached to the different naval commands [...] on the limits to the military criminal jurisdiction, and on the rights to judicial guarantees and to judicial protection." In addition, it indicated that, by February 27, 2013, 165,903 marines had been trained, so that "95% of the operational and non-operational personnel have received training on human rights, and the remaining 5% corresponds to personnel who have recently been incorporated or who have been appointed to other offices."

34.   Lastly, the State forwarded information on the approval of the 2008-2012 National Human Rights Program, in which the President of the Republic ordered the different entities with competence in this area to "incorporate into their preliminary budgets of expenses, resources to ensure compliance with the objectives and goals of [the said program] in the context of the programming of public expenditure and the applicable provisions."

35.   For their part, the representatives stated, in relation to the training of agents of the Public Prosecution Service of the Prosecutor General's Office, that the courses mentioned by the State had been imparted without consulting the victims or their representatives. In addition, they indicated that the State had not sent them any information about the implementation of other training courses on scientific and specialized investigation techniques for cases of forced disappearance, or information that revealed the State's intention to implement permanent training programs. Nevertheless, the representatives acknowledged the implementation of training sessions on human rights for officials of the Federation's Judiciary. However, they indicated that these sessions related to human rights in general or specific topics that had little or no relationship to the limits to the military jurisdiction or to the forced disappearance of persons. Lastly, regarding the training for officials of the Defense Secretariat (SEDENA) and the Navy Secretariat (SEMAR), the representatives acknowledged that these were imparted "structurally and permanently" in these institutions; however, they indicated that it would be desirable to have information on the specific content. In this regard, they considered that "while the Mexican State does not establish these training sessions on disappearances permanently, and using intensive programs outlined by the [Inter-American] Court, it cannot be considered that this operative paragraph of the Judgment has been fulfilled [...]."

36.   The Commission assessed positively the courses and workshops on human rights imparted in the different State agencies, especially programs focused on "the limits of the military criminal jurisdiction, [...] judicial guarantees and

judicial protection, and the proper investigation and prosecution of the forced disappearance of persons." However, it indicated that some of them were not adapted to the topics ordered by the Court in its Judgment. In addition, it indicated that these programs are not offered permanently, so that the obligation on this aspect has not been met. Consequently, the Commission asked the Court to require "the State to provide a detailed plan that describes the way in which [this type of program] has been incorporated, or will be incorporated" permanently into training for State agents, and with the topics established by the Court.

37.   The Court recalls that, in the Judgment, it ordered the implementation of "[p]ermanent programs or courses relating to the analysis of the case law of the inter-American system for the protection of human rights in relation to the limits of the military criminal justice system, as well as the rights to judicial guarantees and to judicial protection, [...] for the members of all the Armed Forces, including the agents of the Public Prosecution Service and judges, as well as for agents of the Public Prosecution Service of the Prosecutor General's Office and judges of the Federation's Judiciary [...]." Furthermore, it ordered the implementation of "[a] training program on the proper investigation and prosecution of acts that constitute forced disappearance of persons, for the agents of the Public Prosecution Service of the Prosecutor General's Office and judges of the Federation's Judiciary, with jurisdiction in the investigation and prosecution of acts such as those that occurred in this case [...]."[27][229]

38.   In this regard, the Court appreciates the numerous activities undertaken by the Mexican State designed to implement the permanent training programs and courses ordered in the Judgment. In this way, from the information provided by the State, the Court notes that different courses have been implemented on the case law of the inter-American system and the limits of the military criminal justice system, as well as on judicial guarantees and judicial protection, for members of the Armed Forces, through the Defense Secretariat and the Navy Secretariat.[28][230] In addition, the Court observes that training has been provided on the proper investigation and prosecution of acts that constitute forced disappearance of persons to agents of the Public Prosecution Service of the Prosecutor General's Office,[29][231] and on the inter-American system and the limits to the military criminal justice system, judicial guarantees and judicial protection, and the due investigation and prosecution of acts that constitute forced disappearance of persons to the judges of the Federation's Judiciary.[30][232]

39.   Taking into account all the actions described by the State, which reflects its commitment to continue developing and implementing these training courses within the different echelons of the State, the Court considers that Mexico has complied with this measure of reparation.

E. Obligation to produce a profile of the life of Rosendo Radilla Pacheco *(fifteenth operative paragraph of the Judgment)*

40.   The State advised that, based on the discrepancies with the victims

and their representatives concerning the publication of the profile of the life of Rosendo Radilla Pacheco, it had undertaken to make the publication again, but of an electronic version provided by the representatives. It indicated that the preliminary version of the text had been sent to the representatives on July 23, 2012, and, following its revision, it was returned on August 2, 2012, with some observations. According to the State, on September 7, 2012, the work of preparing the profile for publishing commenced and on October 8, 2012, the State, the victims and their representatives agreed on the content of the text and on the front page of a final version of the document. The State also indicated that, on December 21, 2012, the Secretariat of the Interior gave the victims' representative 1,945 copies of the book entitled "*Señores, soy campesino. Semblanza de Rosendo Radilla Pacheco, desaparecido.*" Lastly, it advised that on March 1, 2013, senior authorities of the Federal Government, together with Ana María Radilla Martínez and Rosendo Radilla Martínez, representing Rosendo Radilla Pacheco's 11 children, made a public presentation of the book.

41.   The representatives indicated their agreement with the publication of the profile published by the Mexican State.

42.   The Commission appreciated "the efforts made by the State and the representatives to complete the edition and publication" of the profile of the life of Mr. Radilla Pacheco, and considered that the State had complied with this aspect of the Judgment.

43.   The Court assesses the measures taken by the State to publish a new profile of the life of Mr. Radilla Pacheco, as well as the organization of an act to present it, with the participation of senior Government officials. Based on the information provided by the parties, the Court finds that the State has complied fully with this measure of reparation.

F.   Obligation to provide free psychological and/or psychiatric treatment immediately, adequately and effectively, through its specialized public health institutions, to those declared victims in the Judgment who request this (*sixteenth operative paragraph of the Judgment*)

44.   The State indicated that, as established in the working meeting held with the victims and their representatives on May 23, 2012, the Guerrero Victims' Center of Attention of the *Procuraduría Social de Atención a las Víctimas de Delitos* (hereinafter PROVÍCTIMA) would provide the psychological care ordered in the Judgment. It also reported that, during this meeting, "[t]his offer was formally accepted" by Tita Radilla Martínez, declared victim and injured party in the Judgment, and by another seven family members who are not considered injured parties in the Judgment. The State also indicated that the "Radilla sisters [also] requested psychological care" for María del Carmen, Victoria and Rosa, all with the surnames Radilla Martínez, since they did not attend the said meeting, as

well as "support for the children of the deceased [...] Andrea Radilla Martínez," declared victim and injured party in the Judgment. Thus, according to the State, on August 22, 2012, the representatives forwarded the data and requirements of each of the "114 persons who w[ould] be beneficiaries of the care" that, in good faith, it had undertaken to provide. In this way, according to the State, since June 2012, every month and continuously, PROVÍCTIMA provides the required psychological care.[31][233] In addition, the State indicated that, "in addition to the psychological care ordered by the Court [...], all the members of the family of Rosendo Radilla Pacheco were being offered comprehensive medical care." In this regard, it indicated that, on March 21, 2013, a meeting had been held in order "to hear the requirements of the [victims] with regard to the psychological and medical care [provided], based on which, several measures are currently being planned."

45.   The representatives indicated that they had reached agreement with the State that psychological care would be provided to the victims through PROVÍCTIMA, once a month, in the place whether they reside. In addition, they stated that, in an act of good faith, Mexico had accepted to provide these services to all the other daughters of Rosendo Radilla Pacheco who had not been declared victims en the Judgment, as well as to other family members. Thus, the victims and their representatives considered that the State's willingness was a positive factor. Nevertheless, in their observations of May 2, 2013, the representatives indicated that this "care was offered without any type of planning or agreement with the victims [...] about the profile of the professional who would be responsible for providing the psychological care. Owing to this lack of planning, towards the end of 2012, the psychological care was interrupted, because [...] the victims had no confidence in it." "In this regard, to ensure that the psychological care provided to the Radilla Martínez family complies with basic criteria that are appropriate for the problem [of forced disappearance of persons], both the victims and the representatives ask[ed] that the State certify before the victims and before [the Inter-American Court], the experience and level of specialization in this area of the professionals appointed to treat the victims [...]." They also asked the Court to require the State to present "the work plan that w[ould] be followed for this care (initial comprehensive diagnosis, therapeutic plan, informed consent, prognosis based on the diagnosis and the work plan, general follow-up, [...] etc.)," to ensure that "the care provided to the victims meets the highest professional standards and that its continuity is guaranteed." In this way, they indicated that, "currently, [they were] awaiting the offer of psychological care to be presented by the State, [which would] be consulted with the victims in order to obtain their consent to this care." Lastly, they asked the Court not to find that this measure of reparation had been complied with, "until an agreement is reached on the type of psychological care that will be provided to the victims and until these rehabilitation services have been provided for a reasonable time [...]."

46.   The Commission "appreciate[d] the meeting that had been held between the parties and recalled that, over the last year, disagreements had arisen regarding the type of services that the beneficiaries receive, the specialty of the institutions, and the failure to differentiate the service from that provided to the rest of the population." In addition, it stated that "the implementation of the health measures should be differentiated, individualized, preferential, comprehensive, and provided by specialized institutions and personnel." Thus, it indicated that it "awaited information on the agreements reached at the meeting of March 2013, as well as on the steps taken to comply with them."

47.   The Court recalls that, in the Judgment, the State was ordered to provide free psychological and/or psychiatric treatment immediately, adequately and effectively, through its specialized public health institutions to Tita, Andrea and Rosendo, all with the surnames Radilla Martínez, if they requested this, following a physical and psychological evaluation.[32][234] Furthermore, it urged the State "based on its acknowledgement of international responsibility in this case, [...] to consider granting, in good faith, adequate reparation to the other members of Rosendo Radilla Pacheco's family, [...] without them having to take legal action [...]."[33][235]

48.   In this regard, the Court observes that the State offered psychological care to those declared victims in the Judgment and to other members of Rosendo Radilla Pacheco's family, through an institution specialized in attending victims of crime, pursuant to the agreement reached with the representatives on May 23, 2012[34][236] (*supra* Considering paragraphs 44 and 45). The Court appreciates the initial agreement reached by the parties and, particularly, the undertaking made by the State, in good faith, to provide psychological and medical care and attention through the *Procuraduría Social de Atención a las Víctimas de Delitos* (PROVÍCTIMA), not only to those declared victims in the Judgment, but also to other next of kin who request this within the framework of this agreement.[35][237] Nevertheless, of those declared victims in the Judgment, only Tita Radilla Martínez "accepted" this attention, because the representatives did not request the implementation of this measure of reparation in favor of Rosendo Radilla Martínez under the said agreement, and Andrea Radilla Martínez is deceased. In addition, the information provided by the State[36][238] and the representatives reveals that, subsequently, Rita Martínez refused to receive the required treatment owing to her concerns about the aptness of the professionals of the said institution (PROVÍCTIMA) to provide psychological attention to the next of kin of a person forcibly disappeared. Consequently, the Court decides that the State must forward the Court, together with its next report on compliance with the Judgment (*infra* operative paragraph 3), the necessary documentation to prove the capacity of the said professionals to attend this type of victim.

In addition, the Court asks the representatives to advise whether Rosendo Radilla Martínez has asked that the State provide him with psychological and/or psychiatric attention.

G. Obligation to pay the amounts established in the Judgment, as compensation for pecuniary and non-pecuniary damage and to reimburse costs and expenses, as applicable, within one year of notification of the Judgment (*seventeenth operative paragraph of the Judgment*)

49.   The State indicated that it had deposited the amounts ordered in the Judgment in the *Banco del Ahorro Nacional y Servicios Financieros, S.N.C.* (BANSEFI), and had reported the payment before the Tenth District Civil Court in the Federal District. In this regard, it advised that, "on September 22, 2011, C. Justino García Téllez, widower of Andrea Radilla Martínez, and the executor of her will, went to the Court to collect two [cheques ...] for the amounts allocated" in the Judgment in favor of the latter, equivalent to US$40,000.00 and US$325.00. Also, "in a decision of June 8, 2012, the judge [of the case ...] decided the admissibility of handing over the deposit slips corresponding to Tita [Radilla Martínez], for pecuniary and non-pecuniary damage, and also costs and expenses, and to Rosendo Radilla Martínez, for pecuniary and non-pecuniary damage." In addition, "on July 19, 2012 [the said] judge [...] decided that the deposit slips in favor of Rosendo Radilla Pacheco should be delivered to his heirs, through the person holding his power of attorney, Rosendo Radilla Martínez." According to the State, the corresponding deposit slips have already been exchanged in BANSEFI. Consequently, it considered that this measure of reparation had been accomplished.

50.   The victims and their representatives expressed their satisfaction for the fulfillment of the payment of the compensation ordered by the Court. For its part, the Commission "appreciate[d] the information presented by the State with regard to the payment of the amounts established in the Judgment."

51.   The Court understands that the information provided by the parties reveals that the State has complied fully with this measure of reparation.

THEREFORE:

THE INTER-AMERICAN COURT OF HUMAN RIGHTS,

in exercise of its authority to monitor compliance with its decisions and pursuant to Articles 33, 621), 62(3) and 68(1) of the American Convention on Human Rights, 24 and 30 of the Statute, and 31(2) and 69 of its Rules of Procedure,

DECIDES THAT:

1.   As indicated in the pertinent considering paragraphs of this Order, the State has complied fully with its obligations:

    (a) To implement, within a reasonable time and with the respective budgetary allocation, permanent programs or courses analyzing the case law of the inter-American system for the protection of human rights in relation to the limits of the military criminal jurisdiction, as well as a training program on the proper investigation and prosecution of acts that constitute forced disappearance of persons, pursuant to the twelfth operative paragraph of the Judgment.

(b) To produce a profile of the life of Rosendo Radilla Pacheco, pursuant to the fifteenth operative paragraph of the Judgment.

(c) To pay the amounts established in paragraphs 365, 370, 375 and 385 of the Judgment as compensation for pecuniary and non-pecuniary damage and to reimburse costs and expenses, as applicable, pursuant to the seventeenth operative paragraph thereof.

2.   It will maintain open the proceeding of monitoring compliance in relation to operative paragraphs 8, 9, 10, 11 and 16 of the Judgment, regarding the obligations of the State:

(a) To conduct effectively, with due diligence and within a reasonable time, the investigation and, as appropriate, the criminal proceedings that are underway in relation to the detention and subsequent forced disappearance of Rosendo Radilla Pacheco, in order to determine the corresponding criminal responsibilities and to apply the punishments and consequences that the law establishes;

(b) To continue with the genuine search and prompt discovery of Mr. Radilla Pacheco or, if applicable, his mortal remains;

(c) To adopt, within a reasonable time, the pertinent legislative reforms to make article 57 of the Code of Military Justice compatible with the relevant international standards and with the American Convention on Human Rights;

(d) To adopt, within a reasonable time, the pertinent legislative reforms to make article 215A of the Federal Criminal Code compatible with the relevant international standards and with the Inter-American Convention on Forced Disappearance of Persons, and

(e) To provide free psychological and/or psychiatric treatment immediately, adequately and effectively, through its specialized public health institutions, to those declared victims in the Judgment who request this.

3.   The United Mexican States must adopt all necessary measures to comply truly and promptly with the aspects pending compliance indicated in the second operative paragraph *supra*, in accordance with the provisions of Article 68(1) of the American Convention on Human Rights.

4.   The United Mexican States must present to the Inter-American Court of Human Rights, by September 7, 2013, at the latest, a report indicating all the measures adopted to comply with the reparations ordered by this Court that remain pending, as indicated in considering paragraphs 7 to 29 and 44 to 48, as

well as in the second operative paragraph of this Order. Subsequently, the State must continue reporting to the Court in this regard every three months.

5.　　The representatives of the victims and the Inter-American Commission on Human Rights must present any observations they deem pertinent on the reports of the State mentioned in the preceding operative paragraph within four and six weeks, respectively, of receiving them.

6.　　The Secretariat of the Court shall notify this Order to the United Mexican States, the Inter-American Commission on Human Rights, and the representatives of the victims.

Monitoring Compliance with Judgment in the Case of Miguel Castro Castro Prison v. Peru
29-Jul-2013
Order of the Acting President of the Inter-American Court of Human Rights

HAVING SEEN:

1.　　The Judgment on merits, reparations and costs (hereinafter "the Judgment") issued by the Inter-American Court of Human Rights (hereinafter "the Inter-American Court" or "the Court") on November 25, 2006.

2.　　The Interpretation of said Judgment issued by the Inter-American Court on August 2, 2008.

3.　　The notes of the Secretariat of the Court (hereinafter "the Secretariat") of June 4 and July 9 and 23, 2013, in which the parties and the Inter-American Commission on Human Rights were informed that the Court had decided to reschedule the private hearing on monitoring compliance with the Judgment in this case, and to hold it on August 19, 2013, at the Court's seat, during its 100th Regular Period of Sessions.

4.　　The brief presented on July 13, 2013, in which Mrs. Monica Feria Tinta, a victim and the common intervener for the representatives of the victims and their relatives in this case (hereinafter "the common intervener" or "Mrs. Feria Tinta"), requested support from the Victims' Legal Assistance Fund of the Inter-American Court (hereinafter "the Victims' Assistance Fund" or "the Assistance Fund") for the appearance at the aforementioned private hearing on monitoring compliance.

5.　　The notes of the Secretariat of July 18, 2013, informing the common intervener Monica Feria Tinta, the other common intervener of the representatives of the victims, Mr. Douglas Cassel, the State of Peru and the Inter-American Commission that said request was brought to the attention of the acting President of the Court for this case.

CONSIDERING THAT:

1.   The Court issued the Judgment on merits, reparations and costs in the Case of the Miguel Castro Castro Prison v. Peru on November 25, 2006, and therefore this case is currently at the stage of monitoring compliance with judgment.

2.   The Court decided to summon the parties and the Inter-American Commission on Human Rights to a private hearing, to be held on August 19, 2013, at the seat of the Court, for the purpose of monitoring compliance with the Judgment. This hearing is being convened for the purpose of receiving up-to-date and detailed information from the State regarding compliance with the measures of reparation ordered in the Judgment and to hear the observations of the two common interveners for the representatives of the victims and the opinion of the Inter-American Commission (*supra* Having Seen 3).

3.   On July 13, 2013 Mrs. Monica Feria Tinta, a victim and the common intervener for the representatives, submitted a request for support from the Victims' Legal Assistance Fund "to be able to attend [the] private hearing" on monitoring compliance with judgment (supra Having Seen 4). With respect to the expenses requested, she specified that the assistance was to cover "air tickets, board and lodging expenses and the payment of exit taxes from Costa Rica, for 3 people, namely: the legal representative (who [would] travel from the United Kingdom), a relative who has been negotiating the implementation [of the Judgment] in Peru (who is part of the team submitting its report to the Court) and a survivor who [would] also travel from Peru and who would also form part of the team that [would] present its report to the Court, on behalf of the largest group of victims." She added that "[t]he presence of these last two [individuals] on the team that will present a report to the Court on behalf of the largest group of victims is of the utmost importance, given that this group has made many efforts to ensure the implementation of the Judgment in the case of Castro Castro Prison and its participation in the hearing is important to answer any questions that could arise during the examination of the case, on the actions by Peruvian State in the stage of implementation of the Judgment." The common intervener also stated that she represents the "largest group of victims [, which] includes the majority of the beneficiaries (over 100) of those who were murdered in the Castro Castro Prison (more than 20 families) and more than 200 survivors" and indicated that "[this] group [...] has been monitoring the implementation of this Judgment, without receiving funds or assistance of any type of six years."

4.   In 2008, the General Assembly of the Organization of American States (hereinafter the "OAS") created the Legal Assistance Fund of the Inter-American Human Rights System (hereinafter "the Assistance Fund of the Inter-American System"), in order to "facilitate access to the inter-American human rights system

by persons who currently lack the resources needed to bring their cases before the system." As established in the Rules of Procedure adopted by the Permanent Council of the OAS in November 20092, the Assistance Fund of the Inter-American System maintains two separate accounts: one for the Inter-American Commission and the other for the Inter-American Court. As to the financing of the Assistance Fund of the Inter-American System, this is currently comprised of "voluntary capital contributions from Member States of the OAS, the Permanent Observer States, and other States and donors that may wish to collaborate with the Fund."

5.   As stipulated in Article 3 of the Rules of the Inter-American Court on the Operation of the Victims' Legal Assistance Fund (hereinafter the "Rules of the Assistance Fund"), the request for assistance was submitted by the Secretariat of the Court to the consideration of the acting President of the Court who is to decide this matter.

6.   According to Article 2 of the Rules of the Fund, alleged victims wishing to have access to the Fund must follow three steps: 1) request assistance in the brief containing pleadings, motions and evidence; 2) demonstrate, by means of a sworn affidavit and other probative evidence that will satisfy the Court, that they lack the financial resources needed to cover the cost of litigation before the Inter-American Court, and 3) state precisely the aspects of their participation in the proceedings that require the use of resources of the Court's Legal Assistance Fund.

7.   Article 6 of the Rules of the Assistance Fund establishes that "The Court shall decide matters not governed by these Rules and questions regarding their interpretation" Accordingly, the Court issued a ruling on September 10, 2010 in relation to a request for support from the Assistance Fund submitted during the stage of monitoring compliance with judgment in this case. In that ruling, the Court defined the scope of its authority to consider, exceptionally, requests for support from the Assistance Fund outside the context of litigation on the merits of contentious cases.

8.   In the Order of September 10, 2010, the Court stated that, pursuant to Article 2 of the Rules of the Assistance Fund, the Fund's resources are used to cover the cost of litigation before the Court during the processing of a contentious case prior to delivery of the judgment. Accordingly, the Acting President reiterates that the rules and the funds available from the Victims' Assistance Fund are aimed at covering expenses that could arise during the litigation of the merits and possible reparations and costs in contentious cases before the Court pending a decision, with priority given to expenses related to an effective appearance and presentation of evidence at hearings before the Court. The Acting President further recalls that the Assistance Fund of the Court does not receive resources form the OAS' regular budget, but rather is comprised of voluntary contributions (*supra* Considering para. 4).

9.   Likewise, the Court established the possibility, as an exception, of considering the admissibility of a request for support from the Assistance Fund outside the framework of the litigation on the merits of contentious cases, in the following terms:

> the Court is aware that the amounts ordered for costs and expenses in the Judgment issued by the Court in [the] case [of the Miguel Castro Castro Prison] did not include future expenses that the victims or their representatives might incur during the stage of monitoring compliance with judgment, and that Article 69(3) of the Court's current Rules of Procedure allow the Court to summon hearings during that stage to evaluate the status of compliance with the judgment. Thus, the Court may consider requests for resources from the Assistance Fund outside the framework of the litigation of the merits of contentious cases, provided that the expenses are reasonable and necessary, and duly proven, so that the victims or their representatives who can demonstrate a lack of sufficient economic resources can attend a future hearing.

10.   It is important to emphasize that, as the Court pointed out, the possibility that the Court or its President might consider the admissibility of a request for support from the Assistance Fund outside the framework of the litigation on the merits of contentious cases "will depend on the resources available in the Assistance Fund at the time when the request is submitted." Therefore, the request "shall be assessed specifically, bearing in mind that the Fund is primarily intended to give preference to requests related to the litigation of contentious cases prior to the issuance of the Judgment."

11.   On this occasion, having regard to the resources currently available in the Assistance Fund, the Acting President deems it feasible to consider the request for assistance submitted by Mrs. Feria Tinta in the current stage of monitoring compliance with judgment, since this would not impair the attention given to requests for support from the Assistance Fund to cover costs related to an effective appearance and presentation of evidence at hearings before the Court in contentious cases currently at the stage of merits, and possible reparations and costs.

12.   During the stage of monitoring compliance in the case of the *Miguel Castro Castro Prison* two other factors arise which together influence the acting President's decision to consider the aforementioned request for support from the Assistance Fund. The first is that the sum ordered by the Court in the Judgment for reimbursement of costs and expenses did not include any future expenses that might be incurred by victims in the stage of monitoring compliance with judgment. This Presidency also takes into account the fact that, according to the

reports submitted by the State during the stage of monitoring compliance with judgment and the corresponding observations, more than six years have elapsed since the Judgment was issued, and Peru has not made any payment whatsoever to Mrs. Monica Feria Tinta as reimbursement for the costs and expenses ordered in paragraphs 456 and 464 of the Judgment. From that information it is also clear, *prima facie*, that Peru has not paid any of the compensation for pecuniary and non-pecuniary damages ordered in Operative Paragraphs 18 to 23 of the Judgment.

13.   In order to assess the admissibility of the request submitted by Mrs. Feria Tinta, this Presidency shall now determine whether the requirements established by the Court have been fulfilled (supra Considering para. 9).

14.   Regarding the requirement that any victim requesting support must "lack sufficient economic resources", Mrs. Feria Tinta did not submit, together with her request, any evidence of her own lack of resources or that of the other two people mentioned in her brief of July 13, 2013. However, the Acting President considers that Mrs. Feria Tinta's lack of resources was demonstrated in evidence provided for an order issued in October 2012 in another case regarding Peru.

15.   The Acting President considers that her application also complies with the requirement that any support requested must be used to cover reasonable and necessary expenses to appear at a hearing on monitoring compliance summoned by the Court. Mrs. Feria Tinta requested limited and specific financial assistance to appear at the private hearing to be held by the Court on August 19, 2013 at its seat (*supra* Having Seen 4 and Considering para. 3). Given that Mrs. Feria Tinta represents the majority of the victims and relatives in this case, the Acting President considers it reasonable to grant assistance, both for the appearance of Mrs. Feria Tinta, and for the appearance of one of the two persons specified by Mrs. Feria Tinta (*supra* Considering para. 3). The Acting President also takes into account the explanation provided by Mrs. Feria Tinta that, because she lives in England, she has been unable to participate in the domestic procedures in Peru at this stage of monitoring compliance with judgment and that these procedures have been carried out by the other victim and by a relative of a victim who live in Peru.

16.   Based on the foregoing, the Acting President considers admissible the request of Mrs. Feria Tinta and orders that financial resources from the Legal Assistance Fund be assigned to cover the travel and board and lodging expenses necessary to enable Mrs. Feria Tinta, and one of the two individuals mentioned in the request, to appear before the Court on August 19, 2013 at the private hearing on monitoring compliance with judgment in this case. Mrs. Feria Tinta shall provide the name of the victim or relative who shall receive assistance from the Fund, no later than August 2, 2013.

17.   The Court shall take the pertinent and necessary measures to cover the costs of travel, board and lodging of the persons summoned to appear with resources from the Assistance Fund.

18.   In accordance with Article 4 of the Rules of the Court on the Operation of the Assistance Fund, the Secretariat shall open a file of costs in order to record all expenditures made in relation to said Fund.

19.   Finally, the Acting President recalls that, pursuant to Article 5 of the Rules of the Assistance Fund, Peru shall be notified, in due course, of the expenditures made from said Fund, so that it may submit any observations, if it so wishes, within the term established for that purpose. The Court shall then decide whether it is appropriate to order the State to reimburse the Assistance Fund for the expenditures incurred.

THEREFORE:
THE ACTING PRESIDENT OF THE INTER-AMERICAN COURT OF HUMAN RIGHTS IN THIS CASE,
in the exercise of his authority in relation to the Victims' Legal Assistance Fund, and in accordance with Article 31 of the Court's Rules of Procedure and Articles 2 to 6 of the Rules of the Legal Assistance Fund,
DECIDES:
1.   To declare admissible the request submitted by Mrs. Monica Feria Tinta, a victim and common intervener for the representatives of the victims and their relatives in the case of the *Miguel Castro Castro Prison*, to receive support from the Victims' Legal Assistance Fund of the Inter-American Court of Human Rights, specifically to cover reasonable and necessary costs of travel, board and lodging so that Mrs. Feria Tinta and one of the two persons indicated in said request may appear before the Court on August 19, 2013 at the private hearing on monitoring compliance with judgment in this case, in accordance with Considering paragraphs 7 to 19 of this Order.

2.   Pursuant to Article 4 of the Rules of the Court on the Operation of the Victims' Legal Assistance Fund, to require the Secretariat of the Court to open a file on expenses, documenting each of the expenditures made in application of said Fund.

3.   To require the Secretariat of the Court to notify this Decision to the common intervener, Monica Feria Tinta, to the common intervener Douglas Cassel, to the State of Peru and to the Inter-American Commission on Human Rights.

Monitoring Compliance with Judgment in the Case of Miguel Castro Castro Prison v. Peru
7-Aug-2013
Order of the Acting President of the Inter-American Court of Human Rights

HAVING SEEN:

1.   The Judgment on merits, reparations and costs (hereinafter "the Judgment") delivered by the Inter-American Court of Human Rights (hereinafter "the Inter-American Court" or "the Court") on November 25, 2006.

2.   The interpretation judgment handed down by the Inter-American Court on August 2, 2008.

3.   The notes of the Secretariat of the Court (hereinafter "the Secretariat") of June 4, and July 9 and 23, 2013, in which it advised the parties and the Inter-American Commission on Human Rights that the Court had decided to reschedule the private hearing on monitoring compliance with the Judgment in this case in order to hold it at the seat of the Court on August 19, during its one hundredth regular session.

4.   The Order issued by the acting President of the Court for this case on July 28, 2013, in which he ruled on the request filed by Mónica Feria Tinta, victim and common intervener of the representatives of the victims and their next of kin, for access to the Victims' Legal Assistance Fund of the Inter-American Court of Human Rights (hereinafter "the Victims' Assistance Fund" or "the Assistance Fund").

5.   The brief of August 5, 2013, and its attachment, in which Douglass Cassel, common intervener of the representatives of the victims and their next of kin in this case, presented a request for support from the Victims' Legal Assistance Fund of the Inter-American Court in relation to the appearance of a victim at the said private hearing on monitoring compliance.

6.   The notes of the Secretariat of August 6, 2013, in which it advised the common intervener Douglass Cassel, the other common intervener of the representatives of the victims, Mónica Feria Tinta, the State of Peru and the Inter-American Commission that the acting President of the Court for this case had been informed of this request. Judge Diego García-Sayán did not take part in the deliberation and signature of the Judgment in this case. Pursuant to Articles 4(2) and 5 of the Court's Rules of Procedure, Judge Manuel E. Ventura Robles, Vice President of the Court, was the acting President for this case.

CONSIDERING THAT:

1.   On November 25, 2006, the Court delivered the Judgment on merits, reparations and costs in the case of the Miguel Castro Castro Prison v. Peru, which is therefore at the stage of monitoring compliance with judgment.

2.   The Court decided to convene the parties and the Inter-American Commission on Human Rights to a private hearing on monitoring compliance with the Judgment, which was held at the seat of the Court on August 19, 2013. The purpose of this hearing was to receive detailed and updated information from the State on compliance with the measures of reparation ordered in the Judgment and to hear the observations of the two common interveners of the representatives

of the victims and the opinion of the Inter-American Commission (*supra* Having Seen paragraph 3).

3.   On August 5, 2013, Douglass Cassel, common intervener of the representatives, presented a request for support from the Victims' Legal Assistance Fund to cover "the reasonable and necessary transportation, accommodation and subsistence expenses so [that the victim Sebastián Chávez Sifuentes may] attend the hearing on August 19" (*supra* Having Seen paragraph 3). Mr. Cassel also explained that he himself was "covering the expenses of [the] three lawyers who [would be travelling] from the United States to attend the hearing," but neither he nor the other two lawyers participate directly in the efforts made in the domestic sphere to achieve compliance with the Judgment. He stressed that Mr. Chávez Sifuentes was the main collaborator for the actions taken in Peru and for direct communication with the victims. Mr. Cassel stated that, for this reason, he considered that the "presence [of Mr. Chávez Sifuentes] at the hearing would be extremely useful to ensure that the Court has the most complete information as regards the purpose of the hearing."

4.   In 2008, the General Assembly of the Organization of American States (hereinafter "the OAS") created the Legal Assistance Fund of the Inter-American Human Rights System (hereinafter "Assistance Fund of the Inter-American System"), in order to "facilitate access to the inter-American human rights system by persons who currently lack the resources needed to bring their cases before the system." According to the provisions of the Rules of Procedure adopted by the OAS Permanent Council in November 2009, the Assistance Fund of the Inter-American System has two separate accounts: one corresponding to the Inter-American Commission and the other to the Inter-American Court. Regarding the financing of the Assistance Fund of the Inter-American System, currently this depends on "[v]oluntary capital contributions from the Member States of the OAS, the permanent observer States, and other States and donors that may wish to collaborate with the Fund."

5.   In accordance with Article 3 of the Rules of the Inter-American Court for the Operation of the Victims' Legal Assistance Fund (hereinafter "the Rules of the Assistance Fund"), the Secretariat of the Court submitted the request for assistance to the consideration of the acting President of the Court for this case, who was responsible for taking the respective decision.

6.   Pursuant to article 2 of the Rules of the Assistance Fund, in order to access this Fund, presumed victims must meet three requirements; they must: (1) request this in the brief with pleadings, motions and evidence; (2) indicate, by means of an affidavit or other probative means that satisfy the Court, that they lack the necessary financial resources to cover the cost of litigation before the Inter-American Court, and (3) state precisely the aspects of their participation in the

proceedings that require the use of the resources of the Court's Assistance Fund.

7.　　Article 6 of the Rules of the Assistance Fund establishes that "[t]he Court shall decide matters not governed by these Rules and questions regarding their interpretation." In this regard, the Court issued an Order on September 10, 2010, ruling on the request for support from the Assistance Fund presented during the stage of monitoring compliance with judgment in this case. In this Order, the Court ruled on the scope of its power to consider, exceptionally, requests for support from the Assistance Fund outside the framework of the litigation on the merits of contentious cases.

8.　　In the said Order of September 10, 2010, the Court indicated that, according to article 2 of the Rules of the Assistance Fund, the Fund's resources are intended to cover the costs of the litigation before the Court during the contentious case prior to the delivery of the judgment. The Court also established the exceptional possibility of assessing the admissibility of a petition for support from the Assistance Fund outside the framework of the litigation on the merits of contentious cases.

9.　　The acting President reiterates that the regulation of the Victims' Assistance Fund and the resources available are intended to cover expenses that could arise during the litigation on merits and eventual reparations and costs in contentious cases before the Court that are pending a decision and, among these expenses, priority is given to those relating to an adequate appearance and presentation of evidence in hearings before the Court. Furthermore, the acting President recalls that the Court's Assistance Fund does not receive resources from the regular budget of the OAS; rather it is composed of voluntary contributions (*supra* Considering paragraph 4). It should be stressed that, as the Court has noted previously, the possibility for the Court or its President to consider assessing the admissibility of a request for the support of the Assistance Fund outside the framework of the litigation on the merits of contentious cases "will depend on the resources available in the Assistance Fund when the request is submitted." Thus, the request "must be assessed specifically taking into account that the Fund is intended to give preference to requests relating to the litigation of contentious cases prior to the delivery of the judgment."

10.　　The acting President reiterates that the Fund's resources are intended to cover the costs of the litigation before the Court during the proceedings in the contentious case prior to the delivery of the judgment and that only exceptionally can they be destined to cover the costs of an appearance at a hearing on monitoring compliance convened by the Court, and this has already been accepted in this case. In an Order of July 29, 2013 (*supra* Having Seen paragraph 3), this President considered that the necessary factors were present to analyze the request for the support of the Assistance Fund made by Mónica Feria Tinta, victim and common intervener of the representatives of the victims and their next of kin, and also that the requirements for its admissibility had been met. Consequently, he decided to approve providing the support of the Assistance Fund to cover the reasonable and necessary expenses of the transportation, accommodation and subsistence for Ms. Feria Tinta and another victim to appear before the Court on August 19, 2013, at the said hearing on monitoring compliance with the Judgment. When granting the assistance to both Ms. Feria Tinta and to another victim, the acting President took into account that, since she lived in England, Ms. Feria Tinta has been unable to take any actions in Peru at this stage of compliance with judgment.

11.   On this occasion, the acting President does not find the request for the support of the Assistance Fund made on behalf of the victim, Sebastián Chávez Sifuentes, admissible (*supra* Considering paragraph 3), taking into account that, at this stage of monitoring compliance with judgment, the financial assistance of the said Fund has been approved to enable two victims in this case to appear at the private monitoring hearing to be held on August 19, 2013. One of these two victims, Ms. Feria Tinta, is also the representative of most of the victims. Even though Mr. Chávez Sifuentes is not represented by Ms. Feria Tinta, but rather by the other common intervener of the representatives, Mr. Cassel, the President takes into consideration that the latter is able to appear at the said hearing together with two other lawyers. In addition, the acting President underscores that the said representatives have a limited time in which to provide their observations during the hearing and that, with the support of the Fund, two victims will appear at the hearing. Consequently, the representative of Mr. Chávez Sifuentes should take the necessary steps to present information to the Court on the actions taken by this victim at the domestic level to ensure that the State complies with the reparations ordered by the Court.

THEREFORE:

THE ACTING PRESIDENT OF THE INTER-AMERICAN COURT OF HUMAN RIGHTS FOR THIS CASE,

in exercise of his authority in relation to the Victims' Legal Assistance Fund and pursuant to Article 31 of the Rules of Procedure of the Court and article 2 to 6 of the Rules of the Assistance Fund,

DECIDES:

1.   To reject the request submitted by Douglass Cassel, common intervener of the representatives of the victims and their next of kin in the case of the Miguel Castro Castro Prison, on behalf of the victim, Sebastián Chávez Sifuentes, to receive support from the Victims' Legal Assistance Fund of the Inter-American Court of Human Rights to appear at the private hearing on monitoring compliance with judgment to be held on August 19, 2013.

2.   To require the Secretariat of the Court to notify this Order to the common

intervener Douglas Cassel, the common intervener Mónica Feria Tinta, the State of Peru and the Inter-American Commission on Human Rights.

ANALYSIS AND QUESTIONS RAISED BY THE COURT'S JURISPRUDENCE

- In its monitoring of Peru's compliance with several contentious cases, including that of the *Constitutional Court*, the Inter-American Court of Human Rights stressed that Peru is under the duty to comply with its obligations under international conventions in good faith (pursuant to the principle of *pacta sunt servanda*) and that it could not disregard its obligations by arguing domestic reasons, thus clarifying that the State may not simply withdraw its consent to the contentious jurisdiction of the Court. Additionally, the Court noted Peru's partial compliance to-date with each of the cases at issue. In its subsequent monitoring of compliance with the *Constitutional Court* judgment, the Court systematically articulated the obligations of States to comply with the judgments in contentious cases and to give practical effect to human rights treaties (*effet utile*) in their respective domestic legal systems by complying with such judgments. In this circumstance the Court addressed these cases together because Peru's attempted withdrawal would have affected its compliance with judgments in all its outstanding contentious cases before the Court. Later, in the Court's monitoring of compliance with reparations measures concerning medical and psychological attention ordered in nine Colombian cases, the Court again addressed the issue of the State's compliance with similar orders in these nine cases together in a private hearing attended also by the Commission and representatives from each case. Based on these orders, what criteria does the Court utilize to issue joint orders for multiple cases? Is any pattern sufficient to trigger a unified response by the Court or are more specific criteria necessary?
- The Court typically provides timeframes and deadlines for the State's compliance and reporting back regarding implementation of the measures ordered by the Court. Should the timeframes associated with each of the ordered measures be determined on a case-by-case basis, or is it reasonable to have pre-determined timeframes for particular types of measures (e.g., reimbursement of costs and expenses) regardless of the circumstances of each case?
- In monitoring compliance with *La Cantuta v. Peru*, the Court ordered the State, amongst other measures, to conduct criminal investigations, locate and return the remains of victims, and implement human rights programs "within a reasonable time." How can the Court determine

whether the State is making good faith efforts to implement and comply with the judgment within a reasonable time? In cases, such as *Herrera Ulloa v. Costa Rica* and *Almonacid-Arellano et al. v. Chile*, where the respective States must make domestic legal reforms (to Costa Rica's criminal law and to Chile's amnesty laws), what timeframes might be considered reasonable, or should good faith efforts be judged on progressive steps periodically reported to the Court by the State and/or by the representatives in the case?

- Panama was relatively rapid in compliance with the Court's orders in *Velez Loor*. Clearly, a State's acceptance of the Court's judgment and willingness to comply with the Court's decisions are critical. What other conditions encourage a State, such as Panama in *Velez Loor*, to implement the Court's judgment relatively quickly?

Endnotes

1   Approved by the Court during its XLIX Ordinary Period of Sessions, held from November 16 to 25, 2000, and partially amended by the Court during its LXXXII Ordinary Period of Sessions, held from January 19 to 31, 2009.

2 9   Added by the Court during its LXXXII Ordinary Period of Sessions, in the session held on January 29, 2009.

3 10   Added by the Court during its LXXXII Ordinary Period of Sessions, in the session held on January 29, 2009.

4 11   Added by the Court during its LXXXII Ordinary Period of Sessions, in the session held on January 29, 2009.

5 12   Added by the Court during its LXXXII Ordinary Period of Sessions, in the session held on January 29, 2009.

6 35   Added by the Court during its LXXXII Ordinary Period of Sessions, in the session held on January 29, 2009.

7   Organization of American States (OAS), American Convention on Human Rights, "Pact of San Jose" (22 Nov. 1969).

8 1   *Cfr. Inter alia*, Order of the President of the Inter-American Court of Human Rights of October 28, 1996, Provisional Measures in the *Giraldo-Cardona Case*, Considering N° 7; Order of the President of the Inter-American Court of Human Rights of March 23, 1998, in the *Clemente Teherán et al. Case*, Considering N° 7; Order of the Inter-American Court of Human Rights of November 17, 1999, Provisional Measures in the *Digna Ochoa and Plácido et al. Case*, Considering N°7; and Order of the President of the Inter-American Court of Human Rights of April 7, 2000, Urgent Measures in the *Constitutional Court Case*, Considering N° 9, and *supra* Having Seen N° 9.

9 2   *Cfr. Inter alia*, Order of the Inter-American Court of Human Rights of June 19, 1998, in the *Carpio-Nicolle Case*; Order of the Inter-American Court of Human Rights of November 27, 1998 in the *Carpio-Nicolle Case*; Order of the Inter-American Court of Human Rights of November 27, 1998, in the *Giraldo-Cardona Case;* Order of the Inter-American Court of Human Rights of September 30, 1999, in the *Giraldo-Cardona Case*; and Order of the Inter-American Court of Human Rights of November 19, 1999, in the *Cesti-Hurtado Case*.

10 3   I-A Court H.R., *Ivcher-Bronstein Case*, Competence, Judgment of September 24, 1999, Se-

ries C N° 54, par. 37, and *Constitutional Court Case,* Competence, Judgment of September 24, 1999, Series C N° 55, par. 36.

11 4   *Cfr. inter alia,* I-A Court H.R. *Castillo-Petruzzi et al. Case.* Compliance with judgment. Order of November 17, 1999. Series C N° 59, Considering N° 4; and *Loayza-Tamayo Case.* Compliance with judgment. Order of November 17, 1999, Series C N° 60, Considering N° 7; Order of the Court of June 14, 1998, Provisional Measures in the *James, Briggs, Noel, García and Bethel Case,* Considering N° 6; Order of the Court of August 29, 1998, Provisional Measures in the *James et al. Case,* Considering N° 7; and Order of the Court of May 27, 1999, Provisional Measures in the *James et al. Case,* Considering N° 9.

12 1   This Court has followed the same practice at the reparations stage (*ICourtHR, Loayza Tamayo case. Reparations (Article 63.1 American Convention on Human Rights). Judgment of November 27, 1998. Series C No. 42; ICourtHR, Suárez Rosero case. Reparations (Article 63.1 American Convention on Human Rights). Judgment of January 20, 1999. Series C No. 44*).

13 1   In this respect, see the article signed by 119 journalists entitled: "*No nos dejan decir...*", published in the newspaper, *La Nación,* on May 6, 2001.

14 1   *Cfr. Compulsory membership in an association prescribed by law for the practice of journalism* (Arts. 13 and 29 American Convention on Human Rights). Advisory Opinion OC-5/85 of November 13, 1985. Series A No.5, paragraphs 70 and 71.

15 2   *Cfr. Compulsory membership in an association prescribed by law for the practice of journalism* (Arts. 13 and 29 American Convention on Human Rights). Advisory Opinion OC-5/85 of November 13, 1985. Series A No.5, para. 74.

16 1   *Cf., inter alia, Case of the Gómez-Paquiyauri Brothers.* Provisional Measures. Order of the Inter-American Court of Human Rights of May 7, 2004, '*Considering*' sixteen; *Case of Bámaca-Velásquez.* Provisional Measures. Order of the Inter-American Court of Human Rights of November 20, 2003, '*Considering*' twelve; and *Matter of Marta Colomina and Liliana Velásquez.* Provisional Measures. Order of the Inter-American Court of Human Rights of September 8, 2003, '*Considering*' five.

17 2   *Cf., inter alia, Matter of The Communities of Jiguamiandó and Curbaradó.* Provisional Measures. Order of the Inter-American Court of Human Rights of March 6, 2003, '*Considering*' nine; *Matter of the Peace Community of San José de Apartadó.* Provisional Measures. Order of the Inter-American Court of Human Rights of June 18, 2002, '*Considering*' eight; and *Matter of the Peace Community of San José de Apartadó.* Provisional Measures. Order of the Inter-American Court of Human Rights of November 24, 2000, '*Considering*' seven. See also, *Case of the Mayagna (Sumo) Awas Tingni Community.* Judgment of August 31, 2001, Series C No. 79, para. 149.

18 3   *Cf. Matter of The Communities Jiguamiandó and Curbaradó.* Provisional Measures. Order of the Inter-American Court of Human Rights of March 6, 2003, '*Considering*' eleven, and *Matter of the Peace Community of San José de Apartadó.* Provisional Measures. Order of the Inter-American Court of Human Rights of June 18, 2002, '*Considering*' eleven.

19 4   *Cf. Case of the "Street Children" (Villagrán-Morales et al.).* Judgment of November 19, 1999. Series C No. 63, para. 144.

20 5   *Cf., inter alia, Case of Lysias Fleury.* Provisional Measures. Order of the Inter-American Court of Human Rights of December 2, 2003, '*Considering*' eight; *Case of Lysias Fleury.* Provisional Measures. Order of the Inter-American Court of Human Rights of June 7, 2003, '*Considering*' ten; *Matter of The Communities Jiguamiandó and Curbaradó.* Provisional Measures. Order of the Inter-American Court of Human Rights of March 6, 2003, '*Considering*' twelve; and *Matter of the Urso Branco Prison.* Provisional Measures. Order of the Inter-American Court of Human Rights of June 18, 2002, '*Considering*' ten.

21 1   *Cfr. Matter of Monagas Judicial Confinement Center ("La Pica").* Provisional Measures. Order of the Inter-American Court of Human Rights of February 9, 2006, Considering Clause No. 7; *Matter of the Mendoza Prisons.* Provisional Measures. Order of the In-

ter-American Court of Human Rights of June 18, 2005, Considering Clause No. 5; and *Matter of* Peace *Community of San José de Apartadó*. Provisional Measures. Order of the Inter-American Court of Human Rights of March 15, 2005, Considering Clause No.5.

22 2   *Cfr.*, by virtue of its contentious function, *Case of the Pueblo Bello Massacre.* Judgment of January 31, 2006. Series C. No. 140, paras. 113 and 114; *Case of the Mapiripán Massacre.* Judgment of September 15, 2005. Series C. No. 134, paras. 111 and 112; *Case of the Moiwana Community.* Judgment of June 15, 2005, Series C. No. 124, para. 211; *Case of Tibi.* Judgment of September 7, 2004. Series C. No. 114, para. 108; *Case of the Gómez-Paquiyauri Brothers.* Judgment of July 8, 2004. Series C. No. 110, para. 91; *Case of 19 Tradesmen.* Judgment of July 5, 2004. Series C No. 109, para. 183; *Case of Maritza Urrutia.* Judgment of November 27, 2003. Series C No. 103, para. 71; *Case of Bulacio.* Judgment of September 18, 2003. Series C No. 100, para. 111; and *Case of Juan Humberto Sánchez.* Judgment of June 7, 2003. Series C No. 99, para. 81. See also, by virtue of its advisory powers, *cfr. Juridical Condition and Rights of the Undocumented Migrants.* Advisory Opinion OC-18/03, para. 140. Furthermore, upon ordering provisional measures, *cfr. Matter of Monagas Judicial Confinement Center ("La Pica"),* supra note 1, Considering Clause No. 16; *Matter of Children Deprived of Liberty in the "Complexo do Tatuapé" of FEBEM.* Provisional Measures. Order of the Inter-American Court of Human Rights of November 30, 2005, Considering Clause No. 14; *Matter of Mendoza Prisons.* Provisional Measures. Order of June 18, 2005; *Matter of Pueblo Indígena de Sarayaku.* Provisional Measures. Order of July 6, 2004; *Case of the Pueblo Indígena de Kankuamo.* Provisional Measures. Order of July 5, 2005; *Matter of the Communities of Jiguamiandó and Curbaradó.* Provisional Measures. Order of March 6, 2003, page 169; *Matter of* Peace *Community of San José de Apartadó* . Provisional Measures. Order of June 18, 2002, page 141, and *Matter of Urso Branco Prison.* Provisional Measures. Order of June 18, 2002, page 53.

23 3   *Cfr. Matter of Monagas Judicial Confinement Center ("La Pica"),* supra note 1, Considering Clause No. 11; *Matter of Children Deprived of Liberty in the "Complexo do Tatuapé" of FEBEM, supra* note 2, Considering Clause No. 17; and *Matter of Mendoza Prison.* Order of the Inter-American Court of Human Rights of June 18, 2005, considering No. 11.

24 4   *Cfr. Matter of Mendoza Prisons.* Provisional Measures. Order of the Inter-American Court of Human Rights of June 18, 2005, Considering Clause No. 7, and *Case of the "Juvenile Reeducation Institute".* Judgment of September 2, 2004. Series C No. 112, para. 159.

25 5   *Cfr. Case of the Pueblo Bello Massacre, supra* note 2, para. 111; *Case of Mapiripán Massacre, supra* note 2, para. 111; and *Juridical Condition and Rights of the Undocumented Migrants.* Advisory Opinion OC-18/03 of September 17, 2003. Series A No. 18, para. 140.

26 6   *Cfr.Case of the Pueblo Bello Massacre,* supra note 2, para. 111; *Case of Mapiripán Massacre, supra* note 2, para. 108; *Case of the Gómez-Paquiyauri Brothers, supra* note 2, para. 72.

27 7   *Cfr. Matter of the Communities of Jiguamiandó and Curbaradó.* Provisional Measures. Order of the Inter-American Court of Human Rights of February 7, 2006, considering No. 7; *Case of Hilaire, Constantine, Benjamin et. al.* Judgment of June 21, 2002. Series C No. 94, paras. 196-200. See also, *Matter of James et al.* Provisional Measures. Order of May 25, 1999. Series E No. 2, Operative Clause 2(b); Orders of June 14, 1998, of August 29, 1998, and of May 25, 1999; Order of August 16, 2000. Series E No. 3, Having Seen Clauses No. 1 and 4; and Order of November 24, 2000. Series E No. 3, Having Seen Clause No. 3.

28 8   *Cfr., inter alia, Matter of the Communities of Jiguamiandó and Curbaradó, supra* note 7, Considering Clause No. 16; *Matter of Luisiana Ríos et al. (Radio Caracas Televisión – RCTC).* Provisional Measures. Order of the Inter-American Court of Human Rights of September 12, 2005, Considering Clause No.17; and *Matter of Luis Uzcátegui.* Provisional Measures. Order of the Inter-American Court of Human Rights of December 2, 2003, Considering Clause No. 12.

29 9   Cfr., *inter alia, Matter of the Communities of Jiguamiandó and Curbaradó,* supra note 7,

Considering Clause No. 16; *Matter of Peace Community of San José de Apartadó*, supra note 1, Considering Clause 12; and *Matter of the Communities of Jiguamiandó and Curbaradó*. Provisional Measures. Order of the Inter-American Court of Human Rights of March 15, 2005, Considering Clause 11.

30 1   *Cf., inter alia, Matter of Urso Branco Prison. Provisional Measures.* Order of the Inter-American Court of Human Rights of June 18, 2002, Considering Clauses No. six and eight; *Matter of Children Deprived of Liberty in the "Complexo do Tatuapé" of FEBEM. Provisional Measures.* Order of the Inter-American Court of Human Rights of July 3, 2007, Considering Clause No. seven; *Matter of Yare I and Yare II Capital Region Penitenciary Center. Provisional Measures.* Order of the Inter-American Court of Human Rights of March 30, 2006, Considering Clause No. nine; and Matter of the Mendoza Prisons. Provisional Measures. Order of the Inter-American Court of Human Rights of November 22, 2004, Considering Clause No. six.

31 2   *Cf. Case of the "Juvenile Reeducation Institute".* Judgment of September 2, 2004. C Series No. 112, par. 159; *Matter of the Mendoza Prisons, supra* note 1, Considering Clause No. ten. See also *Matter of Urso Branco Prison. Provisional Measures.* Order of the Inter-American Court of Human Rights of September 21, 2005, Considering Clause no. six; *Matter of Children Deprived of Liberty in the "Complexo do Tatuapé" of FEBEM. Provisional Measures.* Order of the Inter-American Court of Human Rights of November 30, 2005, Considering Clause no. seven, and *Matter of Yare I and Yare II Capital Region Penitenciary Center, supra* note 1, Considering Clause no. nine.

32 11   *Cf. Case of James et al.* Provisional Measures regarding Trinidad and Tobago. Order of the Inter-American Court of August 29, 1998, Considering 6; *Matter of Eloisa Barrios et al.* Provisional Measures regarding Venezuela. Order of the Court of February 4, 2010, Considering 3, and *Matter of Belfort Istúriz et al.* Request for Provisional Measures presented by the Inter-American Commission on Human Rights with regard to Venezuela. Order of the Court of April 15, 2010, Considering 9.

33 12   The State made reference, *inter alia*, to the carrying out of "projects to disinfect the accommodations;" to provide the inmates on a monthly basis with basic products for personal cleaning and the cleaning of the facilities; in the Boulogne Sur Mer complex, medical care for the population is provided under a model that allows for efficient and organized medical, dental, and psychiatric supervision of the inmates; "permanent control of the population [has been established] for the control of the HIV virus;" "the opening of a 'Health Statistics and Planning' office [has been formalized] whose primary function focuses on all the possible information concerning the medical and sanitary system."

34 13   *Matter of the Mendoza Penitentiaries.* Order of the Court of June 18, 2005, *supra* footnote 4, operative paragraphs.

35 14   *Matter of the Mendoza Penitentiaries.* Order of the Court of June 18, 2005, *supra* footnote 4, Considering 12.

36 15   Thus the State indicated that in the Boulogne Sur Mer and San Felipe complexes, general basic adult education and higher education are offered for free through the execution of the program "Education in the context of imprisonment" in partnership with the Universidad Nacional de Cuyo. It specified that "total school enrollment at all levels of formal education is 325 students;" 18 inmates are seeking university degrees; a "'Movie Debate' program [was implemented], carried out jointly by the Education and Psychological Areas [where] 163 inmates currently participate," as was a "radio workshop" involving 18 inmates who do weekly broadcasts at the radio station of the Universidad Tecnológica Nacional; and in the "San Felipe" complex, there are different work training courses that benefit 44 inmates In addition, the library was inaugurated. Also, general repair, carpentry, plumbing, and electrical work are done constantly in the blocks.

37 16   *Cf. Case of Raxcacó Reyes et al.* Provisional Measures regarding Guatemala. Order of the Court of August 30, 2004, Considering 10; *Matter of Fernández Ortega et al.* Provisional

Measures regarding Mexico. Order of the Court of April 30, 2009, Considering 14, and [.
. .] *Matter of Centro Penitenciario de Aragua "Cárcel de Tocorón."* Provisional Measures
regarding Venezuela. Order of the Court of November 11, 2010, Considering 14.

38 17   *Cf. Matter of the Indígena Kankuamo Indigenous People.* Provisional Measures regarding
Colombia. Order of the Court of April 3, 2009, Considering 7; *Matter of A.J. et al.* Provisional Measures regarding Haiti. Order of the Court of September 21, 2009, Considering
18, and *Case of the Mapiripán Massacre.* Provisional Measures regarding Colombia. Order of the Court of September 2, 2010, Considering 26.

39 18   *Cf. Matter of Gallardo Rodríguez.* Provisional Measures regarding Mexico. Order of the
Court of July 11, 2007, Considering 11; *Matter of Pilar Noriega García et al.* Provisional
Measures regarding Mexico. Order of the Court of February 6, 2008, Considering 14; *Mat-
ter of Liliana Ortega et al.* Provisional Measures regarding Venezuela. Order of the Court
of July 9, 2009, Considering 40, and *Case of the Mapiripán Massacre, supra* footnote 18,
Considering 28.

40 19   *Cf. Matter of Luis Uzcátegui.* Provisional Measures regarding Venezuela. Order of the
Court of February 20, 2003, Considering 13; *Case of Raxcacó Reyes et al.* Provisional
Measures regarding Guatemala. Order of the Court of February 2, 2007, Considering 12,
and *Case of Carpio Nicolle et al.* Provisional Measures regarding Guatemala. Order of the
Court of July 6, 2009, Considering 21.

41 20   *Matter of the Mendoza Penitentiaries regarding Argentina.* Order of the Court of June 18,
2005. Considering 31.

42 21   Cf. *Matter of the Mendoza Penitentiaries.* Provisional Measures regarding Argentina. Order of the Court of August 22, 2007, Considering 14.

43 22   *Cf.* Second Oversight Court. Judicial Branch of Mendoza, *habeas corpus* dated June 18,
2008 (case file of the provisional measures, Volume XIX, pages 6362 to 6372).

44 23   *Cf. Matter of the Mendoza Penitentiaries.* Provisional Measures regarding Argentina. Order of the Court of August 22, 2007, Considering 14, and *Matter of Capital El Rodeo I & El
Rodeo II Judicial Confinement Center.* Provisional Measures regarding Venezuela. Order
of the Court of February 8, 2008, Considering 15.

45 24   *Cf.* with regard to "Convention related oversight" see, among others: *Case of Almonacid
Arellano et al. v. Chile, Preliminary Objections, Merits, Reparations and Costs.* Judgment
of September 26, 2006. Series C No. 154, paras. 124 and 125; *Case of the Dismissed
Congressional Employees (Aguado - Alfaro et al.) v. Peru, Preliminary Objections, Merits,
Reparations and Costs.* Judgment of November 24, 2006. Series C No. 158, para. 128,
and *Case of Cepeda Vargas v. Colombia. Preliminary Objections, Merits and Reparations.*
Judgment of May 26, 2010. Series C No. 213, paras. 206 to 208.

46 25   *Cf.* The referenced "friendly settlement agreement" in the proceeding before the Commission contains the following sections: I) recognition of the Argentine State's responsibility
for the facts; II) pecuniary measures of redress; III) nonpecuniary measures of reparation,
including legal measures and other measures of satisfaction; IV) action plan and budget;
and V) ratification and circulation. Friendly settlement agreement (case file provisional
measures, Volume XIV, pages 4172 to 4176).

47 26   With regard to the pecuniary measures, the State reported that in Article 2 of Decree
2.740/07, ratified by Provincial Law No. 7.930, it recognized the responsibility of the Government of the Province of Mendoza in "the cases of violent deaths and serious attacks on
personal integrity for having failed to guarantee the minimal conditions of security, protection, and physical integrity for the inmates," submitting the case to an *ad hoc* arbitration
tribunal to determine the corresponding indemnities. This arbitration tribunal was to meet
and rule in June of 2010 in Mendoza. The State also indicated that the friendly settlement
included several nonpecuniary reparatory measures, among them legal measures in which
the Province of Mendoza committed to submitting four bills to the legislature, namely: i)
a bill that would create an ombudsman's office for individuals deprived of liberty, while

another would create a local mechanism for prevention in the framework of the Optional Protocol to the Convention against Torture and other Cruel, Inhuman or Degrading Treatment or Punishment; these were combined into a single bill creating "an external body to oversee the detention conditions of those deprived of liberty," ii) a bill creating the Ombudsman's Office of the People of Mendoza, and iii) a bill creating an official provincial public defenders office for proceedings on sentence execution. All these projects were to be submitted before the provincial legislature. However, the State indicated that they have not been addressed yet by the plenary of that body. With regard to other measures of satisfaction, the State indicated that there is a commemorative plaque in Penitentiary Complex 1, Boulogne Sur Mer, making reference to the precautionary and provisional measures before the Inter-American System. Likewise, there is a measure to guarantee participation of the petitioners in the preparation of an "action plan on penitentiary policy to allow for the establishment of short, medium, and long term public policies." Toward doing so, the State had scheduled a meeting for this past May 29.

48 27   *Cf. Case of García Asto and Ramírez Rojas v. Peru. Preliminary Objections, Merits, Reparations and Costs.* Judgment of November 25, 2005. Series C No. 137, para. 221; *Case of Raxcacó Reyes v. Guatemala. Merits, Reparations and Costs.* Judgment of September 15, 2005. Series C No. 133, para. 95, and *Case of Durand and Ugarte v. Peru. Merits.* Judgment of August 16, 2000. Series C No. 68, para. 78.

49 28   *Cf. Case of Neira Alegría et al. v. Peru. Merits.* Judgment of January 19, 1995. Series C No. 20, para. 60, and *Matter of the Urso Branco Prison.* Provisional Measures regarding Brazil. Order of the Court of May 2, 2008, Considering 19, and *Matter of Capital El Rodeo I & El Rodeo II Judicial Confinement Center.* Provisional Measures regarding Venezuela. Order of the Court of February 8, 2008, Considering 11.

50 29   *Cf. Case of Velásquez Rodríguez.* Provisional Measures regarding Honduras. Order of the Court of January 15, 1988, Considering 3; *Matter of the Urso Branco Prison.* Provisional Measures regarding Brazil. Order of the Court of May 2, 2008, Considering 19, and *Matter of Carlos Nieto et al.* Provisional Measures regarding Colombia. Order of the Court of August 5, 2008, Considering 3.

51 30   *Cf. Matter of Natera Balboa* Provisional Measures regarding Venezuela. Order of the Inter-American Court of Human Rights of December 1, 2009, Considering 14, and *Matter of Guerrero Larez.* Provisional Measures regarding Venezuela. Order of the Court of November 17, 2009, Considering 13.

52 31   *Cf. Case of Montero Arangueren et al. (Catia Prison) v. Venezuela.* Preliminary Objections, Merits, Reparations and Costs. Judgment of July 5, 2006. Series C No. 150, para. 85 to 99.

53 32   *Cf. Case of Montero Arangueren et al. (Catia Prison) v. Venezuela. Preliminary Objections, Merits, Reparations and Costs.* Judgment of July 5, 2006. Series C No. 150, para. 67, 71, 77, and 78; *Case of Penal Miguel Castro Castro v. Peru. Merits, Reparations and Costs.* Judgment of November 25, 2006. Series C No. 160, paras. 239 and 240; *Matter of Yare I and Yare II Capital Region Penitentiary Center.* Provisional Measures regarding Venezuela. Order of the Court of March 30, 2006, Considering 15, and *Monagas Judicial Confinement Center ("La Pica").* Provisional Measures regarding Venezuela. Order of the Court of February 9, 2006, Considering 17.

54 6   The Commission indicated that "several photographs have been taken with the same device, which have been named "Me" and allow it to be inferred that this person is the owner of the mobile telephone in question and the person who made the said videos."

55 7   *Cf., inter alia, Matter of Case of Vogt.* Provisional measures with regard to Guatemala, Order of the President of the Inter-American Court of Human Rights of April 12, 1996, fifth Considering paragraph; *Matter of María Lourdes Afiuni.* Provisional measures with regard to Venezuela, Order of the Inter-American Court of Human Rights of December 10, 2010, ninth considering paragraph; *Matter of Gladys Lanza Ochoa.* Provisional measures with regard to Honduras, Order of the Inter-American Court of Human Rights of September 2,

2010, tenth considering paragraph.

[56 8] *Cf. Case of Loayza Tamayo,* Provisional measures with regard to Peru. Order of the Inter-American Court of Human Rights of December 13, 2000, the measures were lifted by the Order of the Inter-American Court of Human Rights of November 11, 1997; *Case of Carpio Nicolle et al.* Provisional measures with regard to Guatemala. Order of the Inter-American Court of Human Rights of July 8, 2004, fifteenth Considering paragraph.

[57 9] *Cf. Case of Raxcacó Reyes et al.* Provisional measures with regard to Guatemala. Order of the Inter-American Court of Human Rights of August 30, 2004, tenth Considering paragraph; *Matter of Guerrero Larez.* Provisional measures with regard to the Bolivarian Republic of Venezuela. Order of the Inter-American Court of Human Rights of November 17, 2009, fourteenth Considering paragraph, and *Matter of Alvarado Reyes et al.* Provisional measures with regard to the United Mexican States. Order of the Inter-American Court of Human Rights of May 26, 2010, fourteenth considering paragraph.

[58 10] *Cf. Matter of the Kankuamo Indigenous People.* Provisional measures with regard to Colombia. Order of the Inter-American Court of Human Rights of April 3, 2009, seventh Considering paragraph; *Matter of A. J. et al.* Provisional measures with regard to Haiti. Order of the Inter-American Court of Human Rights of September 21, 2009, eighteenth Considering paragraph, and *Matters of the Monagas Detention Center ("La Pica"); the Capital Region Penitentiary Center Yare I and Yare II (Yare Prison); the Occidental Region Penitentiary Center (Uribana Prison), and the Capital Detention Center El Rodeo I and El Rodeo II.* Provisional measures with regard to Venezuela. Order of the Inter-American Court of Human Rights of November 24, 2009, fourth considering paragraph.

[59 11] *Cf. Case of James et al.* Provisional measures with regard to Trinidad and Tobago. Order of the Inter-American Court of Human Rights of August 29, 1998, sixth Considering paragraph; *Matter of Eloisa Barrios et al.* Provisional measures with regard to Venezuela. Order of the Inter-American Court of Human Rights of February 4, 2010, third Considering paragraph, and *Matter of Belfort Istúriz et al.* Provisional measures with regard to Venezuela. Order of the Inter-American Court of Human Rights of April 15, 2010, ninth Considering paragraph.

[60 12] *Cf. Matter of the Capital Detention Center El Rodeo I and El Rodeo II.* Provisional measures with regard to Venezuela. Order of the Inter-American Court of Human Rights of February 8, 2008, seventh to ninth Considering paragraphs; *Matter of the Urso Branco Prison,* Provisional measures with regard to Brazil. Order of the Inter-American Court of Human Rights of May 2, 2008, fourth Considering paragraph.

[61 13] *Cf. Matter of Four Ngöbe Indigenous Communities and their Members.* Provisional measures with regard to Panama. Order of the Inter-American Court of Human Rights of May 28, 2010, eighth Considering paragraph.

[62 14] *Cf. Matter of Four Ngöbe Indigenous Communities and their Members, supra* note 15, ninth considering paragraph.

[63 15] *Cf. Matter of the Aragua Penitentiary Center "Tocorón Prison."* Provisional measures with regard to Venezuela. Order of the Inter-American Court of Human Rights of November 24, 2010, thirteenth Considering paragraph.

[64 16] *Cf., Matter of the Mendoza Prisons, supra* note 3, eighth Considering paragraph.

[65 17] *Cf.* Annual Report of Amnesty International published on May 25, 2005, on significant events between January and December 2004, folio 1114 of the case file.

[66 18] *Cf. Matter of the Mendoza Prisons, supra* note 3, Having Seen paragraph 51(d).

[67 19] *Cf.* Special report of November 16, 2008, on the situation of the Provisional Prison and the "Dr. Juan Bautista Vitale Nocera" Penal Farm in the Gustavo André district, Lavalle department, Mendoza, Argentina, and observations on the State's most recent reports on implementation of the provisional measures ordered by the Court on November 22, 2004, paragraph 17, folio 6912 of the case file.

[68 20] *Cf. Matter of the Mendoza Prisons. supra* note 4, and *Matter of the Capital Detention*

Center El Rodeo I and El Rodeo II. Provisional measures with regard to Venezuela, Order of the Inter-American Court of Human Rights of February 8, 2008, fifteenth considering paragraph.

69 21   *Cf.* Regarding "control of respect for the provisions of the Convention," see, *inter alia*: *Case of Almonacid Arellano et al. v. Chile. Preliminary objections, merits, reparations and costs.* Judgment of September 26, 2006. Series C No. 154, paras. 124 and 125; *Case of the Dismissed Congressional Employees (Aguado Alfaro et al.) v. Peru, Preliminary objections, merits, reparations and costs.* Judgment of November 24, 2006, Series C No. 158, para. 128, and *Case of Cepeda Vargas v. Colombia. Preliminary objections, merits and reparations.* Judgment of May 26, 2010. Series C No. 213, paras. 206 to 208.

70   [1] *Cf. Case of Velasquez Rodriguez. Provisional Measures respecting Honduras.* Order of the Court of January 15, 1988, Considering thirteenth. *Matter of Carlos Nieto Palma et al. Provisional Measures respecting Venezuela.* Order of the Court of January 26, 2009, Considering twenty-second, and Matter of *Fernandez Ortega. Provisional Measures respecting Mexico.* Order of the Court of April 30, 2009, Considering fourth.

71 2   *Cf.* Appendix to the report inserted by Paola Martinez Ortiz before the Office of Assignments of the Prosecutor General on October 5, 2009 (case file of provisional measures, volume I, page 13); Appendix to the reports inserted by Luz Nelly Carvajal Londoño before the Office of Assignments of the Prosecutor General of the Nation on October 5, 2009 (case file of provisional measures, volumen I, page 14), and appendix to the report inserted by Esperanza Uribe Mantilla before the Office of Assignments of the Prosecutor General of the Nation on October 7, 2009 (case file of provisional measures, volume I, page 15).

72 3   *Cf. Case of Caballero Delgado and Santana. Provisional Measures regarding Colombia.* Order of the Court of December 7, 1994, Considering thirteenth; Matter of *Kawas Gernandez. Provisional Measures respecting Honduras.* Order of the Court of December 12, 2008, Considering ninth, and Case of *Mack Chang et al. Provisional Measures regarding Guatemala.* Order of the Court of January 26, 2009, Considering thirty-second.

73 4   *Cf. Matter of Millacura Llaipén and other. Provisional Measures regarding Argentina.* Order of the Court of February 6, 2008, Considering twenty-second; Case of *Carlos Nieto Palma et al. Provisional Measures regarding Venezuela.* Order of the Court of August 5, 2008, Considering sixteenth, and Case of *Mack Chang et al., supra* note 3, Considering thirty-second.

74 5   Rules approved by the Court in the XLIX Period of Ordinary Sessions, held November 16-25 of 2000 and partially reformed during the LXXXII Period of Ordinary Session, held January 19-31, 2009, in conformity with Articles 71 and 72 of the same.

75 1   Rules of Procedure the Court approved in the LXXXV Ordinary Period of Sessions, held November 16-28, 2009.

76 2   *Cf. Case of Velásquez Rodríguez.* Provisional Measures regarding Honduras. Order of the Inter-American Court of Human Rights of January 15, 1988, Considering third; *Case of the Rochela Massacre.* Provisional Measures regarding Colombia. Order of the Inter-American Court of Human Rights of November 19, 2009, Considering fourth, and *Matter of Guerrero Larez.* Provisional Measures regarding Venezuela. Order of the Inter-American Court of Human Rights of November 17, 2009, Considering thirteenth.

77 3   *Cf. Case of Herrera Ulloa.* Provisional Measures regarding Costa Rica. Order of the Inter-American Court of Human Rights of September 7, 2001, Considering fourth; *Matters of Matter of Monagas Judicial Confinement Center ("La Pica"); Matter of Yare I and Yare II Capital Region Penitentiary Center; Matter of the Penitentiary Center of the Central Occidental Region (Uribana Prison), and Matter of Capital El Rodeo I & El Rodeo II Judicial Confinement Center.* Provisional Measures regarding Venezuela. Order of the Inter-American Court of Human Rights of November 24, 2009, Considering sixth and *Matter of Guerrero Larez, supra* note 2, Considering fourth.

78 4   *Cf. Matter of James et al.* Provisional Measures regarding Trinidad and Tobago. Order of the Inter-American Court on Human Rights of June 14, 1998, Considering sixth; *Matter of the Communities of Jiguamiandó and Curbaradó.* Provisional Measures regarding Colombia. Order of the Inter-American Court on Human Rights of November 17, 2009, Considering fourth, and Matter *Guerrero Larez, supra* note 2, Considering fifth.

79 5   *Cf. Matter of Fernández Ortega et al.* Provisional Measures regarding México. Order of the President of the Inter-American Court on Human Rights of December 23, 2009, Considering ninth.

80 6   *Cf. Case of Carpio Nicolle et al.* Provisional Measures regarding Guatemala. Order of the Inter-American Court of Human Rights of July 6, 2009, Considering fourteenth; *Case of the Rochela Massacre, supra* note 2, Considering fourteenth, and *Matter of Guerrero Larez, supra* note 2, Considering tenth.

81 7   *Cf. Matter of Pueblo Indígena Kankuamo.* Provisional Measures regarding Colombia. Order of the Inter-American Court of Human Rights of April 3, 2009 Considering seventh; *Matters of Monagas Judicial Confinement Center ("La Pica"); Matter of Yare I and Yare II Capital Region Penitentiary Center; Matter of the Penitentiary Center of the Central Occidental Region (Uribana Prison), and Matter of Capital El Rodeo I & El Rodeo II Judicial Confinement Center, supra* note 3, Considering fourth, and *Matter of A.J. et al.* Provisional Measures regarding Haiti. Order of the Inter-American Court of Human Rights of September 21, 2009, Considering eighteenth.

82 8   *Cf. Caso Carpio Nicolle et al., supra* note 6, Considering fifteenth; *Matters of Monagas Judicial Confinement Center ("La Pica"); Matter of Yare I and Yare II Capital Region Penitentiary Center; Matter of the Penitentiary Center of the Central Occidental Region (Uribana Prison), and Matter of Capital El Rodeo I & El Rodeo II Judicial Confinement, supra* note 3, Considering fourth, and *Matter of A.J. et al., supra* note 7, Considering eighteenth.

83 9   *Cf. Matter of James et al.* Provisional Measures regarding Trinidad and Tobago. Order of the Inter-American Court of Human Rights of August 29, 1998, Considering sixth; *Matters of the Monagas Judicial Confinement Center ("La Pica"); Matter of Yare I and Yare II Capital Region Penitentiary Center; Matter of the Penitentiary Center of the Central Occidental Region (Uribana Prison), and Matter of Capital El Rodeo I & El Rodeo II Judicial Confinement Center supra* note 3, Considering fifth, and *Matter of Guerrero Larez, supra* note 2, Considering sixteenth.

84 10   *Cf. Matter of James et al.* Provisional Measures regarding Trinidad and Tobago. Order of the Inter-American Court of Human Rights of July 13, 1998, Considering sixth; *Matter of the Urso Branco Prison.* Provisional Measures regarding Brazil. Order of the Inter-American Court of Human Rights of November 25, 2009, Considering fourth, and *Matter of Guerrero Larez, supra* note 2, Considering seventeenth.

85 11   *Cf. Matter of James et al., supra* note 9, Considering seventh; *Matter of Fernández Ortega et al.* Provisional Measures regarding México. Order of the Inter-American Court of Human Rights of April 30, 2009, Considering nineteenth, and *Case of Kawas Fernández.* Provisional Measures regarding Honduras. Order of the Inter-American Court of Human Rights of November 29, 2008, Considering fifth.

86 11   *Cf. Case of Velásquez Rodríguez.* Provisional Measures regarding Honduras. Order of the Inter-American Court of Human Rights of January 15, 1988, Considering Clause 3; *Matter of Caballero Delgado and Santana.* Provisional Measures regarding the Republic of Colombia. Order of the Inter-American Court of Human Rights of November 25, 2010, Considering Clause 21, and *Matter of the Mapiripán Massacre.* Provisional Measures regarding the Republic of Colombia. Order of the Inter-American Court of Human Rights of March 1, 2011, Considering Clause 32.

87 12   *Cf. Matter of Pilar Noriega García et al.* Provisional Measures regarding México. Order

of the Inter-American Court of Human Rights of February 6, 2008, Considering Clause 24; *Matter of Giraldo Cardona et al.* Provisional Measures regarding the Republic Colombia. Order of the Inter-American Court of Human Rights of February 22, 2011, Considering Clause 42, and *Matter of Caballero Delgado and Santana, supra* note 11, Considering Clause 24.

88 2   *Cf.* Vienna Convention on the Law of Treaties, Article 26. *The Right to Information on Consular Assistance in the Framework of the Guarantees of the Due Process of Law.* Advisory Opinion OC-16/99 of October 1, 1999. Series A No. 16, para. 128; and *International Responsibility for the Promulgation and Enforcement of Laws in violation of the Convention (Articles 1 and 2 of the American Convention on Human Rights),* Advisory Opinion OC-14/94 of December 9, 1994. Series A No. 14, para. 35.

89 1   See *Case of Baena-Ricardo et al.. Competence.* November 28, 2003 Judgment. *Series C* No. 104, *para.* 131.

90 2   See *Matters of: Liliana Ortega et al., Luisiana Ríos et al., Luis Uzcátegui, Marta Colomina and Liliana Velásquez.* Provisional Measures. May 4, 2004 Order of the Inter-American Court of Human Rights, Whereas seven; *Case of Baena-Ricardo et al., supra* note 1, *para.* 128; and *Case of Barrios Altos.* Compliance with Judgment. November 28, 2003 Order of the Inter-American Court of Human Rights, Whereas six.

91   ³ See *Matters of: Liliana Ortega et al., Luisiana Ríos et al., Luis Uzcátegui, Marta Colomina and Liliana Velásquez.* Provisional Measures. May 4, 2004 Order of the Inter-American Court of Human Rights, Whereas twelve; *Case of Baena-Ricardo et al.. Competence, supra* note 1, *para.* 66; *Case of Constantine et al.. Preliminary Objections.* September 1, 2001 Judgment. Series C No. 82, para. 74; *Case of Benjamin et al.. Preliminary Objections.* September 1, 2001 Judgment. Series C No. 81, para. 74; *Case of Hilaire. Preliminary Objections.* September 1, 2001 Judgment. Series C No. 80, para. 83; *Case of the Constitutional Court. Competence.* September 24, 1999 Judgment. *Series C* No. 55, *para.* 36; and *Case of Ivcher-Bronstein. Competence.* September 24, 1999 Judgment. *Series C* No. 54, *para.* 37. Also see, *inter alia, Case of the "Juvenile Reeducation Institute".* September 2, 2004 Judgment. *Series C* No. 112, *para.* 205; *Case of the Gómez-Paquiyauri Brothers.* July 8, 2004 Judgment. *Series C* No. 110, paras. 150 and 151; and *Case of Bulacio.* September 18, 2003 Judgment. *Series C* No. 100, *para.* 142. Likewise, see *Klass and others v. Germany, (Merits) Judgment of 6 September 1978, ECHR, Series A no. 28, para. 34;* and *Permanent Court of Arbitration, Dutch-Portuguese Boundaries on the Island of Timor, Arbitral Award of June 25,* 1914.

92 4   See *Case of Tibi.* September 7, 2004 Judgment. Series C No. 114, para. 278; *Case of the "Juvenile Reeducation Institute", supra* note 3, para. 338; and *Case of Ricardo Canese.* August 31, 2004 Judgment. Series C No. 111, para. 221.

93 5   See *Case of Baena-Ricardo et al.. Compliance with Judgment.* November 22, 2002 Order of the Court, Whereas 12; *Case of Velásquez-Rodríguez. Interpretation of the Judgment on Compensation* (Art. 67 American Convention on Human Rights). August 17, 1990 Judgment. Series C No. 9, para. 40, operative paragraph 4; and *Case of Godínez-Cruz. Interpretation of the Judgment on Compensation* (Art. 67 American Convention on Human Rights). August 17, 1990 Judgment. Series C No. 10, para. 40, operative paragraph 4.

94 1   *Cfr. Case of Cantos.* Compliance with Judgment. Ruling of the Inter-American Court of Human Rights of November 28, 2005, third whereas clause; *Case of Barrios Altos.* Compliance with Judgment. Ruling of the Inter-American Court of Human Rights of September 22, 2005, third Whereas clause, and *Case of Herrera Ulloa.* Compliance with Judgment. Ruling of the Inter-American Court of Human Rights of September 12, 2005, third Whereas clause.

95 2   *Cfr. Case of Cantos.* Compliance with Judgment. Ruling of the Inter-American Court of Human Rights of November 28, 2005, fifth Whereas clause; *Case of Barrios Altos.* Compliance with Judgment. Ruling of the Inter-American Court of Human Rights of September

22, 2005, fifth Whereas clause, and *Case of Herrera Ulloa.* Compliance with Judgment. Ruling of the Inter-American Court of Human Rights of September 12, 2005, fifth Whereas clause.

^{96 3} *Cfr. Case of Cantos.* Compliance with Judgment. Ruling of the Inter-American Court of Human Rights of November 28, 2005, sixth Whereas clause; *Case of Barrios Altos.* Compliance with Judgment. Ruling of the Inter-American Court of Human Rights of September 22, 2005, sixth Whereas clause, and *Case of Herrera Ulloa.* Compliance with Judgment. Ruling of the Inter-American Court of Human Rights of September 12, 2005, sixth Whereas clause. In this sense, *cfr. Klass and others v. Germany, (Merits) Judgment of 6 September 1978, ECHR, Series A no. 28, para. 34;* y *Permanent Court of Arbitration, Dutch-Portuguese Boundaries on the Island of Timor, Arbitral Award of June* 25, 1914.

^{97 4} *Cfr. Case of the Constitutional Court.* Compliance with Judgment. Ruling of the Inter-American Court of Human Rights of November 17, 2004, ninth Whereas clause; *Case of Tibi.* Judgment of September 7, 2004. Series C No. 114, para. 278, and *Case of the "Juvenile Reeducation Institute".* Judgment of September 2, 2004. Series C No. 112, para. 338.

^{98 5} *Cfr. Case of the Constitutional Court.* Compliance with Judgment. Ruling of the Inter-American Court of Human Rights of November 17, 2004, ninth whereas clause; *Case of Baena Ricardo et al.* Compliance with Judgment. Ruling of the Court of November 22, 2002, 12 Whereas clause, and *Case of Velásquez Rodríguez.* Interpretation of the Compensatory Damages Judgment (Art. 67 American Convention on Human Rights). Judgment of August 17, 1990. Series C No. 9, para. 40, operative paragraph 4.

^{99 4} *Cf.* Case of *Barrios Altos v. Peru.* Monitoring Compliance with Judgment. Order of the Inter-American Court of Human Rights of September 22, 2005; Considering Clause seven; *Case of Claude Reyes et al v. Chile.* Monitoring Compliance with Judgment. Order of the Inter-American Court of Human Rights of May 2, 2008; Considering Clause seven and *Case of Gómez- Paquiyauri Brothers v. Peru.* Monitoring Compliance with Judgment. Order of the Inter-American Court of Human Rights of May 3, 2008, Considering Clause seven.

^{100 5} General Assembly, Resolution AG/RES 2292 (XXXVII-O/07) adopted at the fourth plenary session, held on June 5, 2007, entitled "Observations and Recommendations on the Annual Report of the Inter-American Court of Human Rights".

^{101 6} *Cf. Case of Baena Ricardo et al v. Panamá.* Competence. Judgment of November 28, 2003. Series C No. 104, para. 60; *Case of the Sawhoyamaxa Indigenous Community v. Paraguay.* Monitoring Compliance with the Judgment. Order of the Inter-American Court of Human Rights of February 8, 2008; Considering Clause fifty-four and *Case of the Indigenous Community of Yakye Axa v. Paraguay.* Monitoring Compliance with Judgment. Order of the Inter-American Court of Human Rights of February 8, 2008, third Considering forty-nine.

^{102 4} The aforementioned paragraph 195 of the Judgment of the Inter-American Court stated that "[t]he effects of the [domestic] judgment [of November 12, 1999] are as follows: 1) Mr. Mauricio Herrera Ulloa was declared guilty on four counts of the crime of publishing offenses constituting defamation; 2) the penalty imposed on Mr. Herrera Ulloa consisted of 40 days' fine per count, at ¢2,500.00 (two thousand five hundred colones) a day, for a total of 160 days' fine. In application of the rule of *concurso material* (where a number of related crimes are combined to reduce the penalty that would have been required had each separate crime carried its own weight) "the fine [wa]s reduced to be three times the maximum imposed;" in other words, the fine was reduced from 160 to 120 days, for a total of ¢300,000.00 (three hundred thousand colones); 3) in the civil award, Mr. Mauricio Herrera Ulloa and the newspaper *"La Nación,"* represented by Mr. Fernán Vargas Rohrmoser, were held jointly and severally liable and ordered to pay ¢60,000,000.00 (sixty million colones) for the moral damages caused by the articles carried in *"La Nación"* on March 19, 20,

and 21, 1995, and then again on December 13, 1995; 4) Mr. Mauricio Herrera Ulloa was ordered to publish the "Now, Therefore" portion of the judgment in the newspaper *"La Nación,"* in the section called "El País," in the same print face used for the articles about which the criminal complaint was filed; 5) *"La Nación"* was ordered to take down the link at the *La Nación Digital* website on the internet, between the surname Przedborski and the articles about which the criminal complaint was filed; 6) *La Nación* was ordered to create a link at the *La Nación Digital* website on the internet between the articles about which the complaint was filed and the operative part of the judgment; 7) Mr. Mauricio Herrera Ulloa and the newspaper *"La Nación,"* represented by Mr. Fernán Vargas Rohrmoser, were ordered to pay court costs in the amount of ¢1,000.00 (one thousand colones) and personal damages totaling ¢3,810,000.00 (three million eight hundred ten thousand colones); and 8) Mr. Mauricio Herrera Ulloa's name was entered into the Judiciary's Record of Convicted Felons."

103 5 Aspects of the domestic judgment of November 12, 1999 referred to in paragraph 195(3) and (7) of the Judgment of the Inter-American Court. *Cf. supra* note 4.

104 6 *Cf. Case of Barrios Altos v. Peru.* Monitoring Compliance with Judgment. Order of the Inter-American Court of Human Rights of September 22, 2005, Considering clause No. 7; *Case of Cantoral-Huamaní and García Santa Cruz v. Peru, supra* note 2, Considering clause No. 7, and *Case of the Miguel Castro-Castro Prison v. Peru.* Monitoring Compliance with Judgment. Order of the Inter-American Court of Human Rights of April 28, 2009, considering clause No. 7.

105 7 Rules adopted by the Court in its XLIX Ordinary Session held from November 16 to 25, 2000, as partially amended during the LXXXII Ordinary Session, held from January 19 to 31, 2009, pursuant to Articles 71 and 72 thereof.

106 1 *Cf. Case of Baena Ricardo and others v. Panama. Competence* Judgment of November 28, 2003. Series C No. 104, paragraph 131; *Case of Ivcher Bronstein vs. Peru.* Monitoring Compliance with Judgment. Order of the Court of August 27, 2010, Considering Clause three, and Case of *Santander Tristán Donoso vs. Panama.* Monitoring Compliance with Judgment. Order of the Court of September 1, 2010, Considering Clause three.

107 2 *Cf. Case of De la Cruz Flores v. Peru.* Supervision of Compliance of Judgment. Order of the Court of September 1, 2010, Considering Clause four, and *Case of Santander Tristán Donoso, supra* note 1, Considering Clause four.

108 3 *Cf. International Responsibility for the Promulgation and Enforcement of Laws in Violation of the Convention (Arts. 1 and 2 of the American Convention on Human Rights). Advisory Opinion OC-14/94 of December 9, 1994.* Series A No. 14, par. 35; *Case of Baena Ricardo and others, supra* note 2, Considering Clause five, and Case of *Vargas Areco, supra* note 2, Considering Clause four.

109 4 *Cf. Case of Castillo Petruzzi et al. v. Peru.* Monitoring Compliance with Judgment. Order of the Inter-American Court of Human Rights of November 17, 1999, Considering Clause three; *Case of Ivcher Bronstein, supra* note 1, Considering Clause four, and Case of Santander Tristán Donoso, *supra* note 1, Considering Clause five.

110 5 *Cf. Case of Ivcher Bronstein v. Peru. Competence.* Judgment of September 24, 1999, Series C No. 54, paragraph. 37; *Case of De la Cruz Flores, supra* note 2, Considering Clause six, and *Case of Santander Tristán Donoso,* supra note 1, Considering Clause six.

111 6 *Cf.* Article 458.- Appealable Orders, Code of Criminal Procedure, reformed by Article 4 of the "Law of Creation of Creation of Recourses of Appeal of Judgments, other reforms to the regimen of challenges and implementation of new rules of orality in the criminal process"

112 7 *Cf.* Article 459.- Origin of the Recourse of Appeal, Code of Criminal Procedure, reformed by Article 4 of the "Law of Creation of Recourses of Appeal of Judgments, other reforms to the regimen of challenges and implementation of new rules of orality in the criminal process."

113 8   *Cf.* Article 462.- Processing, Code of Criminal Procedure, reformed by Article 4 of the "Law of Creation of Recourses of Appeal of Judgments, other reforms to the regimen of challenges and implementation of new rules of orality in the criminal process."

114 9   *Cf.* Article 464.- Evidence in Appeals of Judgment, Code of Criminal Procedure, reformed by Article 4 of the "Law of Creation of Recourses of Appeal of Judgments, other reforms to the regimen of challenges and implementation of new rules of orality in the criminal process."

115 10   *Cf.* Article 465.- Examination and resolution, Code of Criminal Procedure, reformed by Article 4 of the "Law of Creation of Recourses of Appeal of Judgments, other reforms to the regimen of challenges and implementation of new rules of orality in the criminal process."

116 11   *Cf.* Article 465. - Examination and Resolution, *supra* note 10, and Article 466.- Referring trial, Code of Criminal Procedure, reformed by Article 4 of the "Law of Creation of Recourses of Appeal of Judgments, other reforms to the regimen of challenges and implementation of new rules of orality in the criminal process."

117 12   *Cf.* Article 467.- Appealable Orders, Code of Criminal Procedure, reformed by Article 5 of the "Law of Creation of Recourses of Appeal of Judgments, other reforms to the regimen of challenges and implementation of new rules of orality in the criminal process."

118 13   *Cf.* Article 468.- Motives, Code of Criminal Procedure, reformed by Article 5 of the "Law of Creation of Recourses of Appeal of Judgments, other reforms to the regimen of challenges and implementation of new rules of orality in the criminal process."

119 14   *Cf.* Article 468.- Motives, Code of Criminal Procedure, *supra* note 13.

120 15   *Cf. Case of Herrera Ulloa v. Costa Rica,* Supervision of Compliance of Judgment. Order of the Court of July 9, 2009, Considering Clause twenty-eight.

121 5   The representative submitted a copy of the resolution issued by the Supreme Court of Justice of Chile, whereby it ordered to make the background facts available to the special visiting judge appointed by the Appeals Court for Rancagua as well as the order passed down by the first instance judge, which provided for the nullification of the enforcement of the amnesty law and the dismissal ordered in the case.

122 6   *Cf. Case of Almonacid Arellano v. Chile. Preliminary Objections, Merits, Reparations and Costs.* Judgment of September 26, 2006. Series C No. 154, para. 146.

123 7   *Cf. Case of Almonacid Arellano et al. v. Chile, supra* note 6, para. 145-147.

124 8   *Cf. Case of Almonacid Arellano et al. v. Chile, supra* note 6, para. 151-155.

125 9   *Cf. Case of Almonacid Arellano et al. v. Chile, supra* note 6, para. 156.

126 10   *Cf. Case of Almonacid Arellano et al. v. Chile, supra* note 6, para. 157.

127 11   In particular, in the case file concerning monitoring compliance with the Judgment there are copies of the Resolution issued on December 24, 2008, by the aforementioned special visiting judge (*supra* Considering Clauses 6(a) and 6(b)), as well as the ruling of December 3, 2008 of the Supreme Court of Justice for Chile (*supra* Considering Clause 6(a)).

128 12   *Cf. Case of the Pueblo Bello Massacre v. Colombia. Monitoring Compliance with Judgment.* Order of the Inter-American Court of Human Rights of July 9, 2009, Considering Clause ten.

129 13   *Cf. Case of Palamara Iribarne v. Chile. Merits, Reparations and Costs.* Judgment of November 22, 2005. Series C No. 135, dispositive point fourteen; *Case of Palamara Iribarne v. Chile.* Monitoring Compliance with Judgment. Order of the Court of November 30, 2007, Considering Clause twenty, and *Case of Palamara Iribarne v. Chile.* Monitoring Compliance with Judgment Order of the Court of September 21, 2009, Considering Clause fourteen and nineteen.

130 14   In the sole article of the aforementioned bill it envisages "establish[ing] the true meaning and scope of the grounds for the extinction of legal liability provided for in Article 93 of the Penal Code, such that it must be understood that the use of prescription periods, amnesty and pardon in criminal proceedings and punishments is not enforceable for crimes and

single offences that, in accordance with International Law, constitute genocide, war crimes and crimes against humanity. Furthermore, it must be understood that Art[icle] 103 of the Penal Code [that provides for the gradual, or semi, prescription of punishments] will not be enforceable for crimes and single offenses that, in accordance with International Law, constitute genocide, war crimes and crimes against humanity, committed by State agents or individuals acting on the State's behalf."

[131 15] Previously, by means of a brief of May 30, 2008, (*supra* Having Seen 2), the State had informed the Court that the Senate Committee on Constitution, Legislation, Justice and Regulations had "analy[zed] and report[ed] on the bill" and once it had been brought before the Senate and this process concluded, the State would present the text of the bill to the Court.

[132 16] The text of the second bill presented by the State proposes, in its sole article, "add[ing] two new grounds [for the recourse to review] to Article 657 of the Criminal Procedure Code: 5. When facts recognized in a judicial resolution showing that the judgment is based on statements made under torture. 6. When the judgment has been made in violation of obligations assumed by the State of Chile, under customary international law, conventional law, general principles of law and *jus cogens* norms, in matters concerning war crimes or crimes against humanity."

[133 17] *Cf. Case of Liliana Ortega et al.* Provisional Measures regarding Venezuela. Order of the Court of December 2, 2003. Considering Clause twelve; *Case of the Moiwana Community v. Surinam.* Monitoring Compliance with Judgment. Order of the President of the Court of December 18, 2009, Considering Clause ten, and *Case of El Amparo v. Venezuela.* Monitoring Compliance with Judgment. Order of the Court of February 4, 2010, Considering Clause twenty-one.

[134 18] *Cf. Case of Barrios Altos v. Peru.* Monitoring Compliance with Judgment. Order of the Court of September 22, 2005, Considering Clause seven; *Case of Baena Ricardo et al. v. Panama.* Monitoring Compliance with Judgment. Order of the Court of May 28, 2010, Considering Clause seven, and *Case of Cantos v. Argentina.* Monitoring Compliance with Judgment. Order of the Court of August 26, 2010, Considering Clause five.

[135 19] *Cf. Case of Ricardo Canese v. Paraguay.* Monitoring Compliance with Judgment. Order of the Court of February 2, 2006, Considering Clause ten.

[136 188] *Cf. Case of Goiburú et al. supra note 1*, para. 162; *Case of Ximenes-Lopes, supra note 6*, para. 240; and *Case of Baldeón-García, supra note 163*, para. 192.

[137 4] Superior Court of Justice of Lima, First Special Criminal Court, case file No. 03-2003, Judgment of April 8, 2008, para. 252.

[138 9] Rules of Procedure approved by the Court in its LXXXV Regular Period of Sessions, held from November, 16 to 28, 2009.

[139 3] *Cf. International Responsibility for the Promulgation and Enforcement of Laws in Violation of the Convention (Arts. 1 and 2 of the American Convention on Human Rights).* Advisory Opinion OC-14/94 of December 9, 1994. Series A No. 14, par. 35; *Ca[s]e of De la Cruz Flores v. Perú, supra* note 2, Considering fifth, and *Case Tristán Donoso v. Panama, supra* note 1, Considering Clause five.

[140 4] *Cf. Case of Tristán Donoso V. Panama, supra* note 1, Considering Clause twelve to nineteen.

[141 5] *Cf. Case* of *Castillo Petruzzi and others v. Peru. Compliance with the Judgment.* Order of November 17, 1999, Series C No. 59, Considering third; *Case De la Cruz Flores v. Peru, supra* note 2, Considering Clause three, and *Case of Tristán Donoso v. Panama, supra* note 1, Considering Clause five.

[142 6] *Cf. Case of Herrera Ulloa v. Costa Rica.* Monitoring of Compliance the Judgment. Order of the Court of September 22, 2006, Considering Clause sixteen.

[143 7] *Cf. Case of "Instituto de Reeducación del Menor" v. Paraguay.* Monitoring of Compliance with the Judgment. Order of the Court of November 19, 2009, Considering Clause for-

ty-six.

144 8   *Cf. Caso Kimel v. Argentina.* Monitoring of Compliance with Judgment. Order of the Court of May 18, 2010, Considering Clause twenty eight.

145 9   In their brief of July 8, 2010, (*supra* Having Seen 4), the representatives included several electronic links to press notes published in Argentina, regarding the aforementioned act of acknowledgement of responsibility on behalf of the State.

146 10   *Cf. Case of La Cantuta v. Peru.* Supervision of Compliance with Judgment. Order of the Court of November 20, 2009, Considering Clause eighteen.

147 11   Rules of Procedure approved by the Court during its LXXXV Ordinary Period of Sessions, celebrated between November 16 and 28, 2009.

148 6   *Case of Kimel v. Argentina. Monitoring compliance with judgment.* Order of the Court of November 15, 2010, seventh Considering paragraph.

149 7   *Cf. International Responsibility for the Promulgation and Enforcement of Laws in Violation of the Convention (Arts. 1 and 2 American Convention on Human Rights).* Advisory opinion OC-14/94 of December 9, 1994. Series A No. 14, para. 35, and *Case of Lori Berenson Mejía v. Peru. Monitoring compliance with judgment.* Order of the Court of June 20, 2012, fourth Considering paragraph.

150 8   *Cf. Case of Kimel v. Argentina. Monitoring compliance with judgment.* Order of the Court of November 15, 2010, eleventh and thirteenth Considering paragraphs and second operative paragraph.

151 9   *Cf. Case of Kimel v. Argentina. Monitoring compliance with judgment.* Order of the Court of November 15, 2010, seventh Considering paragraph.

152 10   The representatives stated that "[t]he figure that should be used as a basis for making the calculation, is the amount of the initial proceedings against [Mr.] Kimel. The civil and criminal action included a financial claim and, at the time, was filed for the sum of 20,000 pesos/dollars." They indicated that "the appeal for review that was filed, [...] is not understood as an appeal, but rather as a new proceeding." They also stated that "[a]ccording to the law on honoraria, based on the civil compensation requested, the costs amount to between US\$2,200 (minimum) and US\$4,000 (maximum)." In addition, they stated that "[s]ince this was a short trial in a single instance, without evidence and without adversarial proceedings, the minimum might have been considered, but it should also be taken into account that the action obtained the annulment of the criminal conviction; thus, it is in order to request the maximum."

153 11   Judgment handed down on March 17, 1999, by the Fourth Chamber of the National Criminal and Correctional Chamber of the Federal Capital in which Eduardo Gabriel Kimel was convicted of the offense of libel.

154 12   *Cf. Case of Kimel v. Argentina. Merits, reparations and costs.* Judgment of May 2, 2008. Series C No. 177. Para. 123.

155 13   Rules of Procedure approved by the Court at its eighty-fifth regular session held from November 16 to 28, 2009.

156 5   *Cf.* Erratum: "Clarification of the publication of February 14, 2010, of the Dos Erres Massacre. Section C of Chapter XII was incorrectly designated C.1 Measures of satisfaction, rehabilitation, and guarantees of non-repetition, whereas the correct designation is C) Measures of satisfaction, rehabilitation and guarantees of non-repetition. Since subsection 'C.1) Satisfaction' was omitted, it should be added."

157 6   In this regard, it is worth emphasizing that the representatives confirmed the payment of compensation to 120 beneficiaries, regarding whom the State presented the corresponding proofs of payment. However, in the communication of July 4, 2011, the State included another beneficiary who had received the payment, and forwarded a copy of the corresponding cheque and proof of payment, but the representatives did not include the name of this person in the communication of July 4, 2011. Given that the Court has verified payment of the corresponding compensation to this beneficiary from the respective proofs of payment,

the Court determines that the State has compensated 121 beneficiaries.

158 7   This Court notes that, with regard to the compensation payment for one of the victims, the stub of check No. 00000141 indicates a different amount to that indicated in proof of payment No. 28 and check No. 00000141. However, this Court understands that this person was paid the amount indicated in the last two documents mentioned.

159 5   The State indicated, literally, that the act was carried out "on December 15, 2012". However, the Court understands that it is a material error and the correct reference is December 15, 2011.

160 6   *Cf. Case of "Las Dos Erres" Massacre v. Guatemala. Preliminary Objection, Merits, Reparations and Costs.* Judgment of November 24, 2009. Series C N° 211, para. 263.

161 7   *Cf. Case of "Las Dos Erres" Massacre v. Guatemala. Preliminary Objection, Merits, Reparations and Costs,* para. 263.

162 8   Said persons are: Juan de Dios Cabrera Ruano, Oscar Adelso Antonio Jiménez, Rodrígo Mayen Ramírez, Dionicio Campos Rodríguez (in the judgment, his name was written as "Dionisio"), José Ramiro Gómez Hernández, Israel Portillo Pérez, Ladislao Jiménez Pernillo, Mirna Elizabeth Aldana Canan, Felipa de Jesús Medrano Pérez, Valeria Garcia, Luz Castillo Flores (in the judgment, her name was written as "Luz Flores"), Leonarda Falla Sazo (in the judgment, her last name was written as "Saso Hernández"), María Luisa Corado, Inés Otilio Jiménez Pernillo and Abelina Flores.

163 9   Said victims are: Toribia Ruano Castillo, María Dolores Romero Ramírez, and Andrés Rivas.

164 10   Namely: Ever Ismael Antonio Coto, Héctor Coto, Santos Osorio Lique, Jorge Granados Cardona, María Vicenta Moral Solís, Luciana Cabrera Galeano and María Menegilda Marroquín Miranda (indicated in the State's report of February 28, 2012, as "María Meregilda Marroquin Miranda") .

165 11   The victim is Edvin Saul Romero García (his name was indicated as such in the State's report of February 28, 2012; in the judgment, his name was indicated as "Edwin Saúl Romero Garcia"). The State mentioned that it is waiting for his attorneys to present "the power of attorney as required by the law".

166 12   According to the information presented by the State, said victims are the following persons: Rafael Barrientos Mazariegos, Ángel Cermeño Pineda, Agusto Mayen Ramírez (his name was indicated as such in the State's Report; in the judgment, his name was indicated as "Augusto Mayen Ramirez"), Marcelino Deras Tejada, Olegario Rodríguez Tepec, Teodoro Jiménez Pernillo, Enriqueta González Gómez (her name was indicated as such in the State's Report; in the judgment, her name was indicated as "Enriqueta Gonzalez G. de Martínez"), Eugenia Jiménez Pineda, Felicita Lima Ayala, Sara Pérez López, Telma Guadalupe Aldana Canan, Tomasa Galicia González and Nicolasa Pérez Méndez.

167 13   The Court has ver[]ified that, according to the corresponding entries, presented by Guatemala as documentation attached to its communication of July 4, 2011, Mrs. Valeria Garcia received the respective payment on December 27, 2010, as well as Mr. Juan de Dios Cabrera Ruano, Rodrigo Mayen Ramirez and Oscar Adelso Antonio Jimenez and that Mrs. Luz Castillo Flores, in turn, received it on April 7, 2011. Therefore, in the Order of the Court of July 6, 2011, it was concluded that the State has complied with the payment of the compensations in favor of said persons (*Cf. Case of "Las Dos Erres" Massacre v. Guatemala. Monitoring Compliance with Judgment.* Order of the Court of July 6, 2011, fiftieth Considering paragraph and second declarative paragraph).

168 14   Namely: Dionicio Campos Rodriguez (in the judgment, his name was indicated as "Dionisio"), José Ramiro Gomez Hernández, Israel Portillo Perez, Ladislao Jimenez Pernillo, Mira Elizabeth Aldana Canan, Felipa de Jesus Medrano Perez, Leonarda Falla Sazo (in the judgment, her last name was indicated as "Saso Hernandez"), Maria Luisa Corado, Inés Otilio Rodriguez Pernillo, Abelina Flores, Toribia Ruano Castillo, Maria Dolores Romero Ramirez and Andres Rivas.

169 15   The State referred to her as "María Meregilda Marroquin Miranda", *supra* note 11.

170 16   The State referred to her as "Enriqueta González Gomez", *supra* note 13.

171 17   The State referred to him as "Agusto Mayen Ramirez", *supra* note 13.

172 18   The State referred to this person as "Edvin Saul Romero García", *supra* note 12.

173 19   In this respect, it has only made reference, in its report of May 4, 2012, to the adoption of measures to amend the Law on Amparo, Habeas Corpus and Constitutionality, and it emphasized that there are two legislative bills (registered under numbers "3319" and "2942") which had obtained favorable votes but have been under deliberation since November 29, 2007 and April 28, 2010, respectively. In this regard, the State has presented information on such bills prior to the Order of the Court of July 6, 2011 and the Judgment (Cf. *Case of "Las Dos Erres" Massacre v. Guatemala. Monitoring Compliance with Judgment, supra* note 14, considering paragraphs fifteen to eighteen). In its report of December 20, 2010, the State referred to bill "3942" and in its report of May 4, 2012, to bill "2942". However, from the information presented, it does not spring that the State had made reference to a different legislative proposal. In this regard, the representatives "not[ed] with concern that the State did not refer to new bills, actions or specific measures to make progress in the compliance with the measure of reparation in question [and that] it has neither referred to measures adopted to guarantee the effective use of the remedy of amparo until the corresponding [amendment] is effective". In turn, the Commission "observ[ed] with concern the lack of progress in relation to the order of the Court".

174 37   Approved by the Court during its LXXXV Ordinary Period of Sessions, held from November 16 to 28, 2009.

175 1   *Case of the 19 Tradesmen v. Colombia. Merits, reparations and costs.* Judgment of July 5, 2004. Series C No. 109, *Case of Gutiérrez Soler v. Colombia. Merits, reparations and costs.* Judgment of September 12, 2005. Series C No. 132, *Case of the "Mapiripán Massacre" v. Colombia. Merits, reparations and costs.* Judgment of September 15, 2005. Series C No. 134, *Case of the Pueblo Bello Massacre v. Colombia. Merits, reparations and costs.* Judgment of January 31, 2006. Series C No. 140, *Case of the Ituango Massacres v. Colombia. Preliminary objection, merits, reparations and costs.* Judgment of July 1, 2006. Series C No. 148, *Case of the La Rochela Massacre v. Colombia. Merits, reparations and costs.* Judgment of May 11, 2007. Series C No. 163, *Case of Escué Zapata v. Colombia. Merits, reparations and costs.* Judgment of July 4, 2007. Series C No. 165, and *Case of Valle Jaramillo et al. v. Colombia. Merits, reparations and costs.* Judgment of November 27, 2008. Series C No. 192. In addition, on March 15, 2011, the parties agreed "to include the Case of Manuel Cepeda Vargas within the framework of the measure of reparation concerning health." *Case of Manuel Cepeda Vargas v. Colombia.* Preliminary objections, merits, reparations and costs. Judgment of May 26, 2010. Series C No. 213.

176 4   A representative of the Ministry of Social Protection, of the Ministry of Foreign Affairs, and of the National Health Superintendence will act on behalf of the State.

177 5   A victim from each case will be a member of the coordination committee.

178 6   A representative of each non-governmental organization accredited to the Court.

179 7   Rules of Procedure approved by the Court at its eighty-fifth regular session held from November 16 to 28, 2009, which entered into force on January 1, 2010.

180 1   The official summary of the Judgment delivered by the Court can be consulted [in Spanish] on the following webpage: http://www.corteidh.or.cr/docs/casos/articulos/resumen_218_esp.pdf.

181 6   A note of the Secretariat of the Court of July 24, 2012, confirmed that, in the State's report of May 21, 2012 (*supra* Having Seen paragraph 2), the State advised that "[t]he Judgment [...] delivered by the Court was published in Official Gazette No. 27016 of April 17, 2012, [...]" without the State having "forwarded the respective proof of this publication. However, a publication that refers to the judgment in the *Case of Vélez Loor v. Panama* appears on the webpage of the digital Official Gazette." Therefore, the Court proceeded to incorporate

the said publication *ex officio* into the body of evidence in this case and asked the parties, if they considered it pertinent, to submit their observations in this regard. In response, in a brief of August 30, 2012, the representatives indicated "that it is the State's obligation to demonstrate compliance with the reparations ordered in a judgment of the [...] Court," and that "this information is essential for the satisfactory evolution of the process of monitoring judgments." In addition, they expressed their "concern owing to the practice of the State of Panama of submitting incomplete reports to the [...] Court, without the attachments to substantiate its assertions." In a brief of September 20, 2012, the State advised that the said publication was available on the following webpage of the Official Gazette: http://www. gacetaoficial.gob.pa/pdfTemp/27016/37529.pdf (last visited February 13, 2013).

182 7 The link is as follows: http://www.mire.gob.pa/sites/default/files/documentos/dere-chos-humanos/Caso-Velez-Loor-vs-Panama-Sentencia-del-23-de-noviembre-de-2010.pdf (last visited February 13, 2013).

183 8 The representatives also indicated their concern owing to Order No. 52 issued by the Fifth Criminal Circuit Court of the First Judicial Circuit of Panama on February 8, 2011, be-cause they considered it essential that the investigation in this case include all the facts denounced by Mr. Vélez Loor, including those that occurred during his detention in the Public Prison in La Palma and in the La Joya-Joyita Prison in Panama City.

184 9 *Cf. Case of Vélez Loor v. Panama. Preliminary objections, merits, reparations and costs.* Judgment of November 23, 2010. Series C No. 218, paras. 235 and 242.

185 10 *Case of Vélez Loor v. Panama. Preliminary objections, merits, reparations and costs.* Judg-ment of November 23, 2010. Series C No. 218, para. 199.

186 5 *Cf. Case of Radilla Pacheco v. Mexico. Preliminary Objections, Merits, Reparations and Costs.* Judgment of November 23, 2009. Series C No. 209, para. 206, 215 and 222.

187 6 *Case of Radilla Pacheco v. Mexico, supra note 5, para. 334.*

188 7 It indicated that during the excavations, representatives of the National Commission on Human Rights, the Unit for the Promotion and Defense of Human Rights of the Ministry of the Interior, and the "Office of the High Commissioner of the United Nations [...] were present. Additionally, personnel of the Social Communications Department of the Attorney General's Office were also present. The latter "took on the task of ensuring that the media was given access to the place and of issuing various bulletins that were presented" through the web page of the Attorney General's Office. Other members of the organization that represents the victims that are not accredited in proceedings were allowed to be present "in order to strengthen the psycho-social support of Rosendo Radilla Pacheco's next of kin."

189 8 *Case of Radilla Pacheco v. Mexico, supra* note 5, para. 222.

190 9 The following is the text of the init[i]ative reform:
Article 57.- ...
I. ...
II. ...
a). ...
The crimes of Forced Disappearance of Persons, Rape, and Torture, provided for under Articles 215-A, 265, and 266 of the Federal Criminal Code, as well as Articles 3 and 5 of the Federal Law for the Prevention and Punishment of Torture, committed to the detriment of civilians, shall fall under the jurisdiction of the Federal Tribunals.
When investigations into the a crime evidence the probable commission of one of those crimes signaled in the preceding paragraph, the Military Prosecutor must immediately, through the corresponding agreement, detail proceedings carried out and records made in the preliminary inquiry and turn the information over to the Attorney General's Office. The proceedings detailed will not lose their validity, even when they were carried out under this Code and, later, under the Code of Criminal Procedure.
b). a e). ...
In cases under Section II where both members of the military and civilians are implicated,

the former shall be tried by military courts, except in cases falling under the second paragraph of subsection a) of Section II. In such cases, the corresponding federal tribunals shall have jurisdiction, notwithstanding the jurisdiction of the military tribunals over crimes committed against military discipline.

[191 10] *Case of Radilla Pacheco v. Mexico, supra* note 5, para. 273.

[192 11] *Case of Radilla Pacheco v. Mexico, supra* note 5, para. 286.

[193 12] *Case of Radilla Pacheco v. Mexico, supra* note 5, para. 289.

[194 13] *Case of Radilla Pacheco v. Mexico, supra* note 5, para. 277. *Cfr.* also *Case of Castillo Petruzzi et al. v. Peru. Merits, Reparations and Costs.* Judgment of May 30, 1999. Series C No. 52, para. 128; *Case of Durand and Ugarte v. Peru. Merits.* Judgment of August 16, 2000. Series C No. 68, para. 117; *Case of Caso Cantoral Benavides v. Peru. Merits.* Judgment of August 18, 2000. Series C No. 69, para. 112; *Case of Las Palmeras v. Colombia. Merits.* Judgment of December 6, 2001. Series C No. 90, para. 51; *Case of 19 Tradesmen v. Colombia. Merits, Reparations and Costs.* Judgment of July 5, 2004. Series C No. 109, para. 165; *Case of Lori Berenson Mejía v. Peru. Merits, Reparations and Costs.* Judgment of November 25, 2004. Series C No. 119, para. 142; *Case of the "Mapiripán Massacre" v. Colombia. Merits, Reparations and Costs.* Judgment of September 15, 2005. Series C No. 134, para. 202; *Case of Palamara Iribarne v. Chile. Merits, Reparations and Costs.* Judgment of November 22, 2005. Series C No. 134, para. 124 and 132; *Case of the Pueblo Bello Massacre v. Colombia. Merits, Reparations and Costs.* Judgment of January 31, 2006. Series C No. 140, para. 189; *Case of Almonacid Arellano et al. v. Chile. Preliminary Objections, Merits, Reparations and Costs.* Judgment of September 26, 2006. Series C No. 154, para. 131; *Case of La Cantuta v. Peru. Merits, Reparations and Costs.* Judgment of November 29, 2006. Series C No. 162, para. 142; *Case of La Rochela Massacre v. Colombia. Merits, Reparations and Costs.* Judgment of May 11, 2007. Series C No. 163, para. 200; *Case of Escué Zapata v. Colombia. Merits, Reparations and Costs.* Judgment of July 4, 2007. Series C No. 165, para. 105; *Case of Tiu Tojín v. Guatemala. Merits, Reparations and Costs.* Judgment of November 26, 2008. Series C No. 190, para. 118; *Case of Usón Ramírez v. Venezuela. Preliminary Objections, Merits, Reparations and Costs.* Judgment of November 20, 2009. Series C No. 207, paras. 108 and 110; *Case of Fernández Ortega et al. v. Mexico. Preliminary Objections, Merits, Reparations and Costs.* Judgement of August 30, 2010, Series. C. No. 215, para. 176; *Case of Rosendo Cantú et al. Mexico. Preliminary Objections, Merits, Reparations and Costs.* Judgement of August 31, 2010, Series. C. No. 216, para. 160, and *Case of Cabrera García and Montiel Flores v. Mexico. Preliminary Objections, Merits, Reparations and Costs.* Judgement of November 26, 2010, Series. C. No. 220, para. 206.

[195 14] *Cf. Case of Radilla Pacheco v. Mexico, supra* note 5, para. 274.

[196 15] *Cf. Case of Radilla Pacheco v. Mexico,* supra note 5, para. 273.

[197 16] The State manifests that the following is the text of the init[i]ative reform:

Article 215 A. The public servant who, on his own or through others, commits, permits, authorizes, or supports the deprivation of liberty of one or more persons and intentionally brings about or maintains that person or persons hidden in any way, or refuses to acknowledge that deprivation of liberty, or to inform on the whereabouts of the person commits the crime of forced disappearance of persons.

The crime defined in the preceding paragraph may also be committed by a private individual when he or she acts on the order, or with the acquiescence or support, of a public servant. This crime prescribes after a period of thirty-five years.

Amnesty, pardons, pre-release benefits, or other substitutes are not applicable to this crime.

[198 17] The Court affirmed that "[f]or [...] a correct definition of the crime, the condition of "State agent" must be set in the broadest possible way. *Case of Radilla Pacheco v. Mexico, supra* note 5, para. 320 and 321.

[199 18] *Case of Radilla Pacheco v. Mexico, supra* note 5, para. 323.

200 19   *Cf. Case of Radilla Pacheco v. Mexico, supra* note 5, para. 347.

201 20   http://www.pgr.gob.mx/prensa/2007/docs08/sentenciacoidh.pdf.

202 21   The State proposed the following text for the commemorative plaque:

The State of Mexico unveils this plaque in memory and as an acknowledgment of its international responsibility for the human rights violations derived from the forced disappearance of Mr. Rosendo Radilla Pacheco, social defender, on 25 August 1974.

This is done in compliance with the order of the Inter-American Court of Human Rights which handed down a Judgment in the Case of Rosendo Radilla Pacheco v. United Mexican States on 23 November 20[09].

This lamentable event has given invaluable lessons to the Mexican nation.

The State of Mexico recognizes the inexhaustible and continuous search of victims for justice, truth, and reparation.

203 22   *Cf. Case of Radilla Pacheco v. Mexico, supra* note 5, para. 353.

204 23   *Cf. Case of Radilla Pacheco v. Mexico, supra* note 5, para. 354.

205 24   *Case of Radilla Pacheco v. Mexico, supra* note 5, para. 116.

206 25   *Cf. Case of Radilla Pacheco v. Mexico, supra* note 5, para. 390. "If, for reasons attributable to the beneficiaries of the compensations or their heirs, respectively, it were not possible for them to receive the amounts within the indicated period, the State shall deposit those amounts in their favor in an account or a deposit certificate in a Mexican financial institution, in United States dollars, and in the most favorable financial conditions permitted by law and banking practices. If, after 10 years, the compensation has not been claimed, the amounts shall revert to the State with the accrued interest."

207 2   The State indicated that, *inter alia*, it agreed to the representatives' request that the public act of acknowledgement of responsibility would be held in Atoyac de Álvarez, Guerrero, even though the judgment did not specify this; that the program of the said act was agreed with the representatives, and also the text of the memorial plaque that was unveiled, as well as the paragraphs of the judgment that were read during the act; also, the speech given by the acting Interior Minister "was submitted to the consideration of the victims and their representatives."

208 3   In addition, the President of the Republic instructed these officials "to re-organize their agendas giving priority to the immediate satisfaction of the requests of the petitioners; to hold the event with the presence of even two State Ministers; to provide all the assistance that the victims and their representatives require for the event, and to request the support of senior authorities of the state de Guerrero to this end."

209 7   At the private session of the Prosecution Service held on September 20, 2011, the title of the case file "Various matters 912/2010 was approved by a unanimous 11 votes." Available at: http://fueromilitar.scjn.gob.mx/Resoluciones/Varios_912_2010.pdf.

210 8   *Cf.* Decision of the Plenary of the Supreme Court of Justice of the Nation of July 14, 2011, case file *Various matters 912/2010*. Published in the Official Gazette of the Federation on October 4, 2011. Annex to the State's brief of November 30, 2011 (file on monitoring compliance, tome III, folio 1497).

211 9   *Cf.* Decision of the Plenary of the Supreme Court of Justice of the Nation of July 14, 2011, case file *Various matters 912/2010*. Published in the Official Gazette of the Federation on October 4, 2011. Annex to the State's brief of November 30, 2011 (file on monitoring compliance, tome III, folio 1512).

212 10   *Cf. Case of Radilla Pacheco v. Mexico. Preliminary objections, merits reparations and costs.* Judgment of November 23, 2009. Series C No. 209, paras. 206, 215 and 222.

213 11   *Cf. Case of Radilla Pacheco v. Mexico. Preliminary objections, merits reparations and costs.* Judgment of November 23, 2009. Series C No. 209, para. 215.

214 12   *Cf. Case of Radilla Pacheco v. Mexico. Preliminary objections, merits reparations and costs.* Judgment of November 23, 2009. Series C No. 209, para. 336.

215 13   *Cf. Case of Radilla Pacheco v. Mexico. Preliminary objections, merits reparations and*

costs. Judgment of November 23, 2009. Series C No. 209, para. 336.

216 14   *Cf. Case of Radilla Pacheco v. Mexico. Monitoring compliance with judgment.* Order of the Inter-American Court of Human Rights de 19 de mayo de 2011, seventeenth Considering paragraph. In this Order, it was noted that, according to the State, the said initiative "establishes the obligation of the Military Public Prosecution Service to forward the summary of the findings of any inquiry it conducts and of those from which the possible perpetration of the crimes mentioned can be inferred to the Federation's Public Prosecution Service," and stipulated that "the measures taken that form part of the summary shall not lose their validity, even though [the Code of Military Justice] was applied when taking them and, subsequently, the Code of Criminal Procedure".

217 15   *Cf.* Ruling of the Plenary of the Supreme Court of Justice of the Nation of July 14, 2011, Case file *Various matters 912/2010.* Published in the Official Gazette of the Federation on October 4, 2011. Annex to the State's brief of November 30, 2011 (file on monitoring compliance, tome III, folio 1471).

218 16   The State also indicated that, on another occasion, the Supreme Court of Justice of the Nation had determined that "the Judiciary of the Federation must exercise, *ex officio,* a control of conformity with the Constitution and the Convention of article 57, paragraph II, of the Code of Military Justice. […] Thus, the interpretation of this principle of the Code of Military Justice must be interpreted that, in the face of situations that violation the human rights of civilians, under no circumstance may the military justice system have jurisdiction […]." *Cf.* Ruling No. LXXI/2011 (9). *"Restrictive interpretation of the military justice system. Incompatibility of the actual text of article 57, paragraph II, of the Code of Military Justice, with the provisions of article 13 of the Constitution, in light of Articles 2 and 8(1) of the American Convention on Human Rights"* of June 10, 2011. Annex to the State's brief of May 30, 2012 (file on monitoring compliance, tome IV, folios 2327 a 2328).

219 17   In the Judgment, the Inter-American Court established that "the Judiciary must exercise *ex officio* the control of conformity between domestic laws and the American Convention, pursuant to their respective terms of reference and the corresponding rules of procedure." *Cf. Case of Radilla Pacheco v. Mexico. Preliminary objections, merits reparations and costs.* Judgment of November 23, 2009. Series C No. 209, para. 339.

220 18   *Cf.* Ruling of the Plenary of the Supreme Court of Justice of the Nation of July 14, 2011, Case file *Various matters 912/2010.* Published in the Official Gazette of the Federation of October 4, 2011. Annex to the State's brief of November 30, 2011 (file on monitoring compliance, tome III, folio 1512).

221 19   *Cf.* Note of September 17, 2012, signed by Justice Juan N. Silva Meza, President of the SCJN. Annex 6 to the brief of October 3, 2012 (file on monitoring compliance, tome V, folio 2899).

222 20   *Cf. Case of Radilla Pacheco v. Mexico. Monitoring compliance with judgment.* Order of the Inter-American Court of Human Rights of May 19, 2011, twenty-first and twenty-second Considering paragraphs.

223 21   *Cf. Case of Radilla Pacheco v. Mexico. Preliminary objections, merits reparations and costs.* Judgment of November 23, 2009. Series C No. 209, para. 344.

224 22   In the Judgment, the Court referred to two element of this provision that were not compatible with the ICFDP. First, it indicated that "the said provision restricts the authorship of the crime of forced disappearance of persons to 'public servants,'" while Article II of the ICFDP indicates that States must "ensure the punishment of all the 'authors, accomplices and accessories to the crime of forced disappearance of persons', whether they are agents of the State or 'persons or groups of persons acting with the authorization, support or acquiescence of the State.'" The Judgment also establishes that "the forced disappearance of persons is characterized by the refusal to acknowledge the deprivation of liberty or to provide information on the fate or whereabouts of the individuals," and that "[t]his element must be present in the definition of the crime, because it allows forced disappearance to be

distinguished from other illegal acts with which it is usually related, such as kidnapping or abduction, and murder, so that appropriate probative criteria can be applied and punishments imposed on all those implicated in its perpetration that take into consideration the extreme gravity of this crime." *Cf. Case of Radilla Pacheco v. Mexico. Preliminary objections, merits reparations and costs.* Judgment of November 23, 2009. Series C No. 209, paras. 320 to 324.

225 23   This seminar was offered in the following places: Puebla, León, Saltillo, Mazatlán, Tuxtla Gutiérrez and the Federal District. According to the State, around 90 speakers took part, including the Justices of the Supreme Court of Justice of the Nation, members of the Federal Council of the Judicature, and representatives of the Inter-American Commission and the Inter-American Court of Human Rights, the Juridical Research Institute of the *Universidad Nacional Autónoma de México* (UNAM), the Institute of Public Policies of Mercosur, the Latin American School of Social Sciences (FLACSO), the Electoral Court of the Judiciary of the Federation, the Ministry of Foreign Affairs, and the Secretariat of the Interior.

226 24   The first stage was held during March and April 2012; the second stage, in May 2012, and the third stage on December 6, 2012, and it culminated on February 28, 2013. According to the State, the workshops included lectures in different cities attended by 820 heads of federal courts and tribunals. In addition, "36 discussion and analysis roundtables were organized with personnel from the Inter-American Commission and the Inter-American Court of Human Rights as the main speakers," and with the participation of 891 judges. Also, special material had been designed to study "precedents of forced disappearance of persons, the military jurisdiction, due process of law, and judicial protection," and this was distributed to participants.

227 25   For example, "on March 14, 2011, a conference was held in the PGR on 'The INAH: Tasks and responsibilities'" relating to the performance of functions relating to the prosecution of cases. In addition, a course on the "investigation and prosecution of acts that constitute forced disappearance of persons" was held in this entity from November 28 to 30, 2011.

228 26   According to the information provided by the State, these courses were held in the following entities: "*Heroico Colegio Militar, Colegio del Aire, Escuela Médico Militar, Escuela Militar de Odontología, Escuela Militar de Enfermeras, Escuela Militar de Oficiales de Sanidad, Escuela Militar de Transmisiones* and *Escuela Militar de Materiales de Guerra.*"

229 27   *Cf. Case of Radilla Pacheco v. Mexico. Preliminary objections, merits reparations and costs.* Judgment of November 23, 2009. Series C No. 209, para. 347.

230 28   The Secretariat of Defense provided information on training session on "Analysis of case law of the inter-American system for the protection of human rights in relation to the limits to the military criminal justice system, and the rights to judicial guarantees and to judicial protection." *Cf.* Note of the Secretariat of Defense to the Unit for the Promotion and Defense of Human Rights dated February 28, 2013. Annex 7 to the State's brief of April 5, 2013 (file on monitoring compliance, tome V, folio 3359). The Navy Secretariat advised that training sessions had been provided on the inter-American human rights system, among other topics. *Cf.* Note of the Navy Secretariat to the Unit for the Promotion and Defense of Human Rights dated February 27, 2013. Annex 8 to the State's brief of April 5, 2013 (file on monitoring compliance, tome V, folio 3363).

231 29   *Cf.* "Course of specialization in human rights and forced disappearance of persons." Annex 7 to the brief of October 3, 2012 (file on monitoring compliance, tome V, folio 2911).

232 30   *Cf.* "Legal framework and precedents concerning the forced disappearance of persons and the military jurisdiction," subject matter of the "Itinerant workshops: the impact of the constitutional reforms of *amparo* and human rights on jurisdictional tasks." Annex 16 to the brief of May 30, 2012 (file on monitoring compliance, tome IV, folio 2410). The State also forwarded the basic documents, timetable, and speakers responsible for the itinerant workshops. *Cf.* Annexes 13, 14 and 15 to the State's brief of May 30, 2012 (file on monitoring compliance, tome IV, folios 2393, 2403 and 2406). In addition, it sent the Court the

content of the "Diploma course on human rights imparted to the Federation's Judiciary." *Cf.* Annex 6 to the State's brief of April 5, 2013 (file on monitoring compliance, tome V, folio 3353).

233 31   The State advised that the following had received psychological care: Agustina, María del Pilar, Judith, Ana María, María del Carmen, Evelina, Romana and Victoria, all with the surnames Radilla Martínez. Furthermore, it indicated that it had not been possible to provide care to Tita Radilla Martínez, because she had repeatedly refused to receive it. *Cf.* Annex 9 to the State's brief of April 5, 2013 (file on monitoring compliance, tome V, folio 3366).

234 32   *Cf. Case of Radilla Pacheco v. Mexico. Preliminary objections, merits reparations and costs.* Judgment of November 23, 2009. Series C No. 209, para. 358.

235 33   *Cf. Case of Radilla Pacheco v. Mexico. Preliminary objections, merits reparations and costs.* Judgment of November 23, 2009. Series C No. 209, para. 328.

236 34   *Cf.* Agreement dated May 23, 2012, signed by the Unit for the Promotion and Defense of Human Rights of the Secretariat of the Interior and PROVÍCTIMA (file on monitoring compliance, tome IV, folios 2182 and 2183). The Court notes that, in the note of PROVÍCTIMA of June 11, 2012, addressed to the Unit for the Promotion and Defense of Human Rights of the Deputy Secretariat for Legal Affairs and Human Rights the State indicated that "the psychological care ordered will continue to be provided until a psychological report is issued determining that it is not necessary for them to continue receiving [the said] care […]." *Cf.* Annex 9 to the State's brief of April 5, 2013 (file on monitoring compliance, tome V, folio 3373).

237 35   The documentation provided by the State includes two notes from PROVÍCTIMA addressed to the Unit for the Promotion and Defense of Human Rights of the Deputy Secretariat for Legal Affairs and Human Rights, dated February 28 and June 11, 2013, advising that psychological care had been provided to some of Mr. Radilla Pacheco's next of kin who were not declared victims in the Judgment. *Cf.* Annex 9 to the State's brief of April 5, 2013 (file on monitoring compliance, tome V, folio 3366).

238 36   *Cf.* Annex 9 to the State's brief of April 5, 2013 (file on monitoring compliance, tome V, folio 3366).

INDEX

X

Y